abled. Plaintiffs primarily used the Rehabilitation Act of 1973 (29 U.S.C.A. § 701 et seq.), the earliest law of this type. But the Rehabilitation Act has a limited scope: it applies only to federally funded workplaces and institutions, and says nothing about those that do not receive government money.

With passage of the ADA in 1990, Congress gave broad protection to people with AIDS who work in the private sector. In general, the ADA is designed to increase access for disabled persons, and it also forbids discrimination in hiring or promotion in companies with fifteen or more employees. Specifically, employers may not discriminate if the person in question is otherwise qualified for the job. Moreover, they cannot use tests to screen out disabled persons, and they must provide reasonable accommodation for disabled workers. The ADA, which took effect in 1992, has quickly emerged as the primary means for bringing AIDS-related discrimination lawsuits.

AIDS and Health Care Closely related to work is the issue of health care. In some cases, the two overlap: health insurance, Social Security, and disability benefits for AIDS victims were often hard to obtain during the 1980s. Insurance was particularly difficult because employers feared rising costs and insurance companies did not want to pay claims. To avoid the costs of AIDS, insurance companies used two traditional industry techniques: they attempted to exclude AIDS coverage from general policies, and they placed caps (limits on benefits payments) on AIDS-related coverage.

In January 1995, the settlement in a lawsuit brought by a Philadelphia construction worker with AIDS illustrated that the ADA can be used to fight caps on coverage. In 1992, the joint union-management fund for the Laborers' District Council placed a $10,000 limit on AIDS benefits, in stark contrast to the $100,000 allowed for other catastrophic illnesses. At that time, the fund said the cap on AIDS benefits was designed to curb all health costs. In 1993, the EEOC ruled that it violated the ADA, and, backed by the AIDS Law Project of Philadelphia, the worker sued. Rather than fight an expensive lawsuit, the insurance fund settled.

AIDS and Education Issues in the field of education include the rights of HIV-positive students to attend class and of HIV-positive teachers to teach, the confidentiality of HIV records, and how best to teach young people about AIDS. A few areas have been settled in court: for instance, the right of students to attend classes was of greater concern in the early years of the epidemic, and no longer remains in dispute.

Certain students with AIDS may assert their right to public education under the Education for All Handicapped Children Act of 1975 (EAHCA), but the law is only relevant in cases involving special education programs. More commonly, students' rights are protected by the Rehabilitation Act.

Schools play a major role in the effort to educate the public on AIDS. Several states have mandated AIDS prevention instruction in their schools. But the subject is controversial: it evokes personal, political, and moral reactions to sexuality. During the 1980s, those who often criticized liberal approaches to sex education argued that AIDS materials should not be explicit, encourage sexuality, promote the use of contraceptives, or favorably portray gays and lesbians.

Civil Litigation TORT law has seen an explosion of AIDS-related suits. This area of law is used to discourage individuals from subjecting others to unreasonable risks, and to compensate those who have been injured by unreasonably risky behavior. The greatest number of AIDS-related LIABILITY lawsuits has involved the receipt of HIV-infected blood and blood products. A second group has concerned the sexual transmission of HIV. A third group involves AIDS-related psychic distress. In these cases, plaintiffs have successfully sued and recovered damages for their fear of having contracted HIV.

CROSS-REFERENCES
Disabled Persons; Discrimination; Food and Drug Administration; Gay and Lesbian Rights; Health Care; Patients' Rights; Physicians and Surgeons; Privacy.

BIOGRAPHY

Gloria Allred

ALLRED, GLORIA Gloria Allred, born July 3, 1941, in Philadelphia, is a flamboyant, widely recognized lawyer, feminist, activist, and radio talk show host. Though her critics dismiss her as a publicity monger and a dilettante, Allred has received praise from others who believe that she is a master at using the power of the news media to draw attention to the day-to-day struggles of ordinary people.

Born Gloria Rachel Bloom, Allred grew up in Philadelphia with her parents, Morris Bloom, a door-to-door salesman, and Stella Davidson Bloom, a homemaker. Her conventional middle-class childhood gave no hint of the outspoken activist to come. Allred graduated with honors from the University of Pennsylvania in 1963 with a bachelor's degree in English. She moved to New York to pursue a master's degree in teaching at New York University. W___ interested in the CIVIL RIGHT___ was beginning to gain mom___ her master's degree in 19___

Annotations:

Cross-references at end of article

Timeline for subject of biography, including general historical events and life events

Biography of contributor to American law

Internal cross references

Quotation from subject of biography

Full cite for case

Definition enclosed in book logos with Latin translation provided

---

GLORIA ALLRED 1941–

1941 Born, Philadelphia, Pa.

1955–68 Martin Luther King active in civil rights movement.

Graduated from Univ. Pennsylvania, with honors.

1965 Received master's in teaching from NYU; moved to Los Angeles to teach in Watts

1965 Watts riots in Los Angeles.

1973 U.S. Supreme Court upheld Roe v. Wade, legalizing abortion.

1974 Received J.D. from UCLA; formed law partnership with Nathan Goldberg and Michael Maroko.

1980 Sued L.A. County to stop shackling of pregnant inmates during labor and delivery. Larson v. Pacheco, 1980.

1986 Sued El Segundo, LA, for job discrimination.

Wrote "Prosecution of Prevention" for L.A. Times, advocating legalization of prostitution.

1925   1950   1975   2000

Philadelphia to teach at a high school with a predominantly black enrollment.

Allred says her interest in the struggle for equal rights arose from personal experiences. While she was in college, she married, gave birth to a daughter, and divorced. Unable to collect CHILD SUPPORT from her former husband, she was forced to return to her parents' home. She also recalls being paid less than a man for what she considered equal work. The reason given was that the man had a family to support, but at the time, Allred was the single mother of an infant.

After moving to California, Allred taught in the turbulent Watts section of Los Angeles and became the first full-time female staff member in United Teachers of Los Angeles, the union representing Los Angeles teachers. The experience stirred her interest in CIVIL RIGHTS and collective bargaining and prompted her to go to law school. She received her law degree, with honors, from Loyola Marymount University, Los Angeles, Law School in 1974. Soon after, she entered a law firm partnership with her classmates Nathan Goldberg and Michael Maroko.

Allred is probably the most flamboyant and well known member of her firm. She has achieved notoriety and name recognition through staged press conferences and demonstrations publicizing and dramatizing the cause she is championing at the time. She also accepts controversial cases that naturally attract media attention. During her years in practice, she has successfully sued Los Angeles County to stop the practice of shackling and chaining pregnant inmates during labor and delivery; put a halt on the city of El Segundo's quizzing job applicants about their sexual histories (*Thorne v. City of El Segundo*, 802 F.2d 1131 [9th Cir. 1986]); represented a client who was turned down for a job as a police officer after a six-hour lie detector exam that included questions about her sex life; and sued a dry cleaning establishment for discrimination because it charged more to launder women's shirts than men's.

Allred relishes confrontation, and her showy tactics have earned her both praise and criticism.

"THERE ARE ENOUGH HIGH HURDLES TO CLIMB, AS ONE TRAVELS THROUGH LIFE, WITHOUT HAVING TO SCALE ARTIFICIAL BARRIERS CREATED BY LAW OR SILLY REGULATIONS."

Defending what many have called self-promoting publicity stunts, Allred says she tries to use the few moments she is in the spotlight to make her point as forcefully as possible. Her detractors say that she wastes her time and energy on trivial issues that do not advance any worthwhile cause and deflect attention away from serious issues. Yet, she points out, she is often stopped on the street by people who recognize her and want to thank her for taking on the small fights that no one else wants.

Some critics say she is all show and no substance. But Allred has many supporters as well. Among them is Justice Joan Dempsey Klein, of the California Court of Appeal, who credits Allred with moving women's issues forward. Klein also points out that Allred saves her dramatics for outside the courtroom and always observes proper decorum when before the bench. According to Klein, Allred is always well-prepared and, for that reason, is quite successful.

Dressed in her trademark reds and electric blues, her striking black hair set off by deep red lipstick, Allred is a potent combination of scholarship and theatrics. Her keen intelligence and shrewd understanding of the power of the media have made her a contemporary success story in the world of law and politics.

ARBITER [*Latin, One who attends something to view it as a spectator or witness.*] Any person who is given an absolute power to judge and rule on a matter in a dispute.

WEST'S
ENCYCLOPEDIA
of
AMERICAN
LAW

WEST'S ENCYCLOPEDIA *of* AMERICAN LAW

Volume 6

WEST GROUP

This encyclopedia is the result of efforts by numerous individuals and entities from the Twin Cities and around the United States. West Group wishes to thank all who made this publication, its quality and content, a priority in their lives.

In addition to the individuals who worked on *West's Encyclopedia of American Law*, West Group recognizes Harold W. Chase (1922–1982) for his contributions to *The Guide to American Law: Everyone's Legal Encyclopedia*.

West's encyclopedia of American law.
     p.   cm.
   Includes bibliographical references and
     indexes.
    ISBN 0-314-20159-9 (hard :
     alk. paper)
    1. Law—United States—Encyclopedias.
    2. Law—United States—Popular works.
    I. West Publishing Company.
  KF154.W47 1997
  348.73′03—dc20
  [347.30803]   96-34350
                CIP

PRODUCTION CREDITS
Cover, interior design, and page layout:
  David J. Farr, ImageSmythe
Composition: Carlisle Communications
Proofreading: Maureen Meyer; Wiest
  International
Photo research: Elsa Peterson Ltd.
Art research: Nanette E. Bertaut
Editorial research: Pat Lewis
Artwork: Patricia Isaacs, Parrot Graphics
Indexing: Schroeder Indexing Services

WEST'S COMMITMENT TO THE ENVIRONMENT

In 1906, West Publishing Company began recycling materials left over from the production of books. This began a tradition of efficient and responsible use of resources. Today, 100 percent of our legal bound volumes are printed on acid-free, recycled paper consisting of 50 percent new paper pulp and 50 percent paper that has undergone a de-inking process. We also use vegetable-based inks to print all of our books. West recycles nearly 27,700,000 pounds of scrap paper annually—the equivalent of 229,300 trees. Since the 1960s, West has devised ways to capture and recycle waste inks, solvents, oils, and vapors created in the printing process. We also recycle plastics of all kinds, wood, glass, corrugated cardboard, and batteries, and have eliminated the use of polystyrene book packaging. We at West are proud of the longevity and the scope of our commitment to the environment.

West pocket parts and advance sheets are printed on recyclable paper and can be collected and recycled with newspapers. Staples do not have to be removed. Bound volumes can be recycled after removing the cover.

Production, printing, and binding by West Group.

PREFACE

The legal system of the United States is admired around the world for the freedoms it allows the individual and the fairness with which it attempts to treat all persons. On the surface, it may seem simple. Yet, those who have delved into it know that this system of federal and state constitutions, statutes, regulations, and common-law decisions is elaborate and complex. It derives from the English common law, but includes principles older than England, and from other lands. Many concepts are still phrased in Latin. The U.S. legal system, like many others, has a language all its own. Too often it is an unfamiliar language.

In 1983, West published *The Guide to American Law: Everyone's Legal Encyclopedia*, in response to a dearth of reference sources weaving the language of the law into the language of everyday life. *West's Encyclopedia of American Law (WEAL)*, developed with generous feedback from users of *The Guide*, replaces that set as an improved and updated legal encyclopedia. *WEAL* is a reference source devoted to the terms and concepts of U.S. law. It also covers a wide variety of persons, entities, and events that have shaped the U.S. legal system. *WEAL* contains thousands of entries, and a number of unique features and visual aids. It is the most complete reference source of its kind.

Main Features of This Set

Entries This encyclopedia contains over 4,000 entries devoted to terms, concepts, events, movements, cases, and persons significant to U.S. law. Entries on legal terms contain a definition of the term, followed by explanatory text if necessary. Entries are arranged al-phabetically in standard encyclopedia format for ease of use. A wide variety of additional features, listed later in this preface, provide interesting background and supplemental information.

Definitions Every entry on a legal term is followed by a definition, which begins and ends with the symbol of an open book (📖). The appendix volume includes a glossary containing all the definitions from the *WEAL*.

Cross-References To facilitate research, *WEAL* provides two types of cross-references, within and following entries. Within the entries, terms are set in small capital letters—for example, LIEN—to indicate that they have their own entry in the encyclopedia. At the end of the entries, related entries the reader may wish to explore are listed alphabetically by title.

In Focus Pieces In Focus pieces accompany related entries and provide additional facts, details, and arguments on particularly interesting, important, or controversial issues raised by those entries. The subjects covered include hotly contested issues, such as abortion, capital punishment, and gay rights; detailed processes, such as the Food and Drug Administration's approval process for new drugs; and important historical or social issues, such as debates over the formation of the U.S. Constitution. In Focus pieces are marked by the symbol that appears in the margin.

Sidebars Sidebars provide brief highlights of some interesting facet of accompanying entries. They complement regular entries and In Focus pieces by adding informative details. Sidebar topics include the Million Man March, in Washington, D.C., and the branches of the

IN FOCUS

U.S. armed services. Sidebars appear at the top of a text page and are set in a blue box.

Biographies WEAL profiles a wide variety of interesting and influential people—including lawyers, judges, government and civic leaders, and historical and modern figures—who have played a part in creating or shaping U.S. law. Each biography includes a time line, which shows important moments in the subject's life as well as important historical events of the period. Biographies appear alphabetically by the subject's last name.

Additional Features of This Set

Milestones in the Law A special section, Milestones in the Law, appearing at the end of selected volumes, allows readers to take a close look at landmark cases in U.S. law. Readers can explore the reasoning of the judges and the arguments of the attorneys that produced major decisions on important legal and social issues. Included in the Milestones section are the opinions of the lower courts; the briefs presented by the parties to the U.S. Supreme Court; and the decision of the Supreme Court, including the majority opinion and all concurring and dissenting opinions for each case.

Enhancements Throughout WEAL, readers will find a broad array of photographs, charts, graphs, manuscripts, legal forms, and other visual aids enhancing the ideas presented in the text.

Tables and Indexes WEAL features several detailed tables and indexes at the back of each volume, as well as a cumulative index contained in a separate volume.

Appendixes An appendix volume included with WEAL contains hundreds of pages of documents, laws, manuscripts, and forms fundamental to and characteristic of U.S. law.

Citations Wherever possible, WEAL entries include citations for cases and statutes mentioned in the text. These allow readers wishing to do additional research to find the opinions and statutes cited. Two sample citations, with explanations of common citation terms, can be seen below and opposite.

Bibliography A bibliography is included at the end of each book and in the index volume.

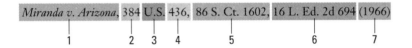

1. *Case title.* The title of the case is set in italics and indicates the names of the parties. The suit in this sample citation was between Ernesto A. Miranda and the state of Arizona.
2. *Reporter volume number.* The number preceding the reporter name indicates the reporter volume containing the case. (The volume number appears on the spine of the reporter, along with the reporter name.)
3. *Reporter name.* The reporter name is abbreviated. The suit in the sample citation is from the reporter, or series of books, called *U.S. Reports,* which contains cases from the U.S. Supreme Court. (Numerous reporters publish cases from the federal and state courts.)
4. *Reporter page.* The number following the reporter name indicates the reporter page on which the case begins.
5. *Additional reporter citation.* Many cases may be found in more than one reporter. The suit in the sample citation also appears in volume 86 of the *Supreme Court Reporter,* beginning on page 1602.
6. *Additional reporter citation.* The suit in the sample citation is also reported in volume 16 of the *Lawyer's Edition,* second series, beginning on page 694.
7. *Year of decision.* The year the court issued its decision in the case appears in parentheses at the end of the cite.

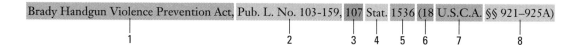

Brady Handgun Violence Prevention Act, Pub. L. No. 103-159, 107 Stat. 1536 (18 U.S.C.A. §§ 921–925A)

1. *Statute title.*
2. *Public law number.* In the sample citation, the number 103 indicates that this law was passed by the 103d Congress, and the number 159 indicates that it was the 159th law passed by that Congress.
3. *Reporter volume number.* The number preceding the reporter name indicates the reporter volume containing the statute.
4. *Reporter name.* The reporter name is abbreviated. The statute in the sample citation is from *Statutes at Large.*
5. *Reporter page.* The number following the reporter name indicates the reporter page on which the statute begins.

6. *Title number.* Federal laws are divided into major sections with specific titles. The number preceding a reference to the *U.S. Code Annotated* is the title number. Title 18 of the U.S. Code is Crimes and Criminal Procedure.
7. *Additional reporter.* The statute in the sample citation may also be found in the *U.S. Code Annotated.*
8. *Section numbers.* The section numbers following a reference to the *U.S. Code Annotated* indicate where the statute appears in that reporter.

continued

HATE CRIME 📖 A crime motivated by racial, religious, gender, sexual orientation, or other PREJUDICE. 📖

A hate crime is based, at least in part, on the defendant's belief regarding the status of the victim. Hate-crime statutes were first passed by legislatures in the late 1980s and early 1990s in response to studies that indicated an increase in crimes motivated by prejudice. Approximately thirty states and the federal government have some form of hate-crime statute. Many localities have also enacted their own hate-crime ordinances.

The precise definition of a hate crime varies from state to state. Some states define a hate crime as any crime based on a belief regarding the victim's race, religion, color, disability, sexual orientation, national origin, or ancestry. Some states exclude crimes based on a belief regarding the victim's sexual orientation. Others limit their definition to certain crimes such as harassment, ASSAULT, and damage to property. In all states the victim's actual status is irrelevant. For example, if a victim is attacked by someone who believes that the victim is gay, the attack is a hate crime whether or not the victim is actually gay.

Generally, there are three types of hate-crime statutes. Two provide for punishment; the third type mandates only the collection of hate-crime data.

One version defines a hate crime as a discrete offense and provides stiff punishment for the offense. Under Ohio's statute, for example, any person who commits aggravated menacing, menacing, criminal damage or criminal endangerment, criminal mischief, or telephone ha-rassment "by reason of the race, color, religion, or national origin of another person or group of persons" is guilty of the hate crime termed ethnic intimidation (Ohio Rev. Code Ann. § 2927.12 [Baldwin 1996]). Ethnic intimidation is always one degree higher than a base offense. For example, menacing is a MISDEMEANOR of the fourth degree, but menacing based on ethnicity is a more serious offense, classified in Ohio as a misdemeanor of the third degree.

Another type of hate-crime law enhances punishment for certain offenses that are motivated by hate. In Wisconsin, for example, defendants who intentionally select their victims based at least in part on the victims' race, religion, color, disability, sexual orientation, national origin, or ancestry are subject to more severe penalties than they would receive in the

The Reverend W. D. Lewis stood outside the remains of the Little Zion Church in Greene County, Alabama, in January 1996. Three churches had been burned in the previous month, and many believed the actions were a racial hate crime.

AP/WIDE WORLD PHOTOS

absence of such hate-based intent (Wis. Stat. § 939.645 [1995]). Thus in Wisconsin, for a class A misdemeanor based on hate, the maximum fine is $10,000 and the maximum period of imprisonment is two years in jail or prison (Wis. Stat. Ann. § 939.645(2)(a)), whereas an ordinary class A misdemeanor is punishable by a maximum fine of $10,000 or up to nine months in jail, or both (§ 939.51(3)(a)). For a class B misdemeanor, a less serious crime, the maximum fine is $1,000 and the maximum imprisonment is 90 days in jail. If the class B misdemeanor is a hate crime, the maximum fine is $10,000 and the maximum sentence is one year in jail.

A third type of hate-crime statute simply requires the collection of statistics. On the federal level, the Hate Crime Statistics Act of 1990 (Pub. L. No. 101-275, 104 Stat. 140 [28 U.S.C.A. § 534 (1990)]) requires the Department of Justice to collect statistics on crimes that manifest evidence of prejudice. Data must be acquired for crimes based on race, religion, disability, sexual orientation, or ethnicity. The purpose of the act is to provide the data necessary for Congress to develop effective policies against hate-motivated violence, to raise public awareness, and to track hate-crime trends.

Laws against hate crimes may conflict with rights under the FIRST AMENDMENT to the U.S. Constitution. Generally, the First Amendment protects a citizen's right to the free expression of thoughts. However, the courts have ruled that First Amendment rights may give way to the greater public good. For example, there is no First Amendment protection for someone who falsely yells "Fire" in a crowded theater because such speech endangers the safety of others. Such expression may give rise to a DISORDERLY CONDUCT charge or similar charge. In determining the constitutionality of hate-crime legislation, a primary question is whether the prohibited speech deserves First Amendment protection.

In 1992 the U.S. Supreme Court struck down a St. Paul, Minnesota, ordinance on the ground that it violated the First Amendment (*R.A.V. v. City of St. Paul*, 505 U.S. 377, 112 S. Ct. 2538, 120 L. Ed. 2d 305 [1992]). In *R.A.V.* several juvenile defendants were tried and convicted after they allegedly assembled a crude wooden cross and set it on fire in the yard of an African American family in St. Paul. The teenagers were arrested and charged under St. Paul's Bias-Motivated Crime Ordinance (Minn. Legis. Code § 292.02). Under the ordinance a person who placed "on public or private prop-

erty a symbol, object, appellation, characterization or graffiti, including, but not limited to, a burning cross or Nazi swastika" and who had reason to know that the display would arouse anger or alarm in others based on "race, color, creed, religion or gender" was guilty of a misdemeanor.

The trial court dismissed the charge on the grounds that it was overbroad and unconstitutionally content based. Specifically, the court ruled that the statute criminalized too much behavior and infringed on First Amendment rights of free speech. The city of St. Paul appealed to the Minnesota Supreme Court, which reversed the trial court. The teenagers then appealed to the U.S. Supreme Court.

The High Court was unanimous in striking down the St. Paul ordinance. However, it was divided in its legal reasoning. According to the majority opinion, the ordinance violated the First Amendment. Justice ANTONIN SCALIA, writing for the majority, declared the statute unconstitutional because it prohibited "otherwise permitted speech solely on the basis of the subjects the speech addresses." Scalia illustrated this point by noting that a government may proscribe libelous speech, but it may not proscribe only libelous speech that is critical of the government. The St. Paul ordinance violated this constitutional rule by proscribing only hate speech delivered through symbols.

In a separate opinion, the concurring justices argued that the majority opinion weakened previous First Amendment jurisprudence. Specifically, the majority opinion protected fighting words, a form of speech that provokes hostile encounters and is not protected by the First Amendment. By holding that "lawmakers may not regulate some fighting words more strictly than others because of their content," the majority had forced legislatures to criminalize all fighting words to legally prohibit the most dangerous fighting words.

According to the concurring justices, the statute was merely overbroad—that is, it legitimately regulated unprotected speech, but it also impermissibly prohibited speech that can cause only hurt feelings or resentment. With more careful wording, the concurring justices argued, hate-crime laws could pass constitutional muster. However, under the Court's majority opinion, this did not seem possible.

In 1993 the Supreme Court revisited hate-crime legislation and unanimously adopted a coherent approach. In *State v. Mitchell*, 508 U.S. 476, 113 S. Ct. 2194, 124 L. Ed. 2d 436 (1993), Todd Mitchell, a young black man from

DO HATE-CRIME LAWS RESTRICT FIRST AMENDMENT RIGHTS?

The U.S. Supreme Court's upholding of the state "hate-crime" law in *Wisconsin v. Mitchell*, 508 U.S. 476, 113 S. Ct. 2194, 124 L. Ed. 2d 436 (1993), has not stopped some legal commentators from arguing that such laws violate the First Amendment of the U.S. Constitution. Though these critics generally admit that hate crimes are on the rise, they believe that laws that increase the severity of punishment on the basis of the motives of the perpetrator create a dangerous precedent for government interference with freedom of expression and thought. Defenders of hate-crime laws reject these fears, claiming that the laws deal with criminal conduct and are meant to send a message that discrimination will not be tolerated.

Critics of the laws have articulated a number of reasons for their opposition, some constitutional, some practical. The foremost concern is that hate-crime laws violate a person's right to freedom of thought. These statutes enhance the penalties for conduct already punished under state law when the perpetrator is motivated by a type of bigotry the legislature finds offensive. Therefore, if a rich man assaults a homeless person because he hates the poor, the rich man can be charged only with assault, because the legislature has not specifically found bigotry against the poor to be offensive. However, if a man assaults an African American because he hates persons of that race, he can be charged with assault and intimidation, which carries a more severe penalty, or his sentence for assault can be increased, because the legislature has penalized a racially discriminatory motive. For the critics of hate-crime laws, this result reveals that the legislature is regulating the defendant's thoughts, in violation of the First Amendment.

Critics also charge that the focus on motive distorts the traditional rules of criminal law. In the past, criminal law was interested in a defendant's mental state only to the extent that it would reveal whether the defendant had engaged in deliberate conduct. As a general rule, the motive of a crime has never been considered an element that must be proved at trial. Whether a person robbed a bank to buy food for a family or to pay back a gambling debt is considered irrelevant. The key state-of-mind question is whether the person intended to rob the bank.

Some critics also ask what good the additional penalty will do for persons convicted of hate crimes. If a person is filled with prejudices, extra time spent in prison is not likely to help eradicate those beliefs; it may, in fact, reinforce them. These critics do not believe that hate-crime laws seek to deter criminal activity. They feel that instead such laws appear to seek retribution for acts of violence motivated by racism, sexism, anti-Semitism, and homophobia. The critics contend the retribution model is not compatible with the modern goals of the criminal and penal systems.

Another criticism is that hate-crime laws do not address deeper forces within society that create prejudice. Some social psychologists believe that prejudice and the behavior that may accompany it are caused by a combination of social, economic, and psychological conflicts. Adding more punishment for those who act on their prejudice may give the community the illusion it is dealing with the problem, but, in fact, hate-crime laws do little to help change thought and behavior.

Defenders of hate-crime laws reject the idea that they are taking away anyone's First Amendment rights. They note that in *Mitchell* the Supreme Court rejected as "too speculative a hypothesis" the "chilling effect" argument, which maintains that these laws chill, or inhibit, free thought and speech. The Court also cited precedent that permitted the "evidentiary use of speech to establish the elements of a crime or to prove motive or intent." This means that persons are free to express their ideas, no matter how repugnant, but when they engage in unlawful conduct based on these beliefs, they surrender their First Amendment rights.

Defenders also believe that hate-crime laws, like other criminal laws, are aimed at preventing harmful acts. The focus is not on stifling disagreeable and prejudicial beliefs or biases, but on preventing the particularly harmful effects of hate crimes. Even critics of the laws admit that hate-crime violence is often brutal and severe. Defenders argue that increasing the penalties for this type of behavior is therefore justified.

Supporters of hate-crime laws point out, as did the Supreme Court in *Mitchell*, that most of the statutes use the same language as title VII of the Civil Rights Act of 1964 (42 U.S.C.A. § 2000e et seq.). Why, they ask, is it acceptable to penalize employment discrimination that is based on racism and bigotry, but not criminal acts based on similar biases? The courts have long upheld federal and state discrimination laws as acceptable methods of penalizing conduct and promoting nondiscriminatory practices. Intentional employment discrimination requires a person to communicate his or her bias. Supporters conclude that once a person verbalizes a prejudice and acts on it, the state is free to regulate that conduct.

Hate Crime
Number of Bias-Motivated Crime Incidents
Reported in 1995

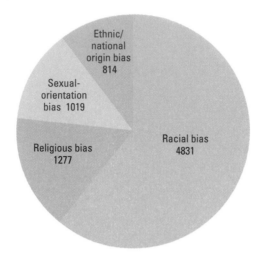

Ethnic/
national
origin bias
814

Sexual-
orientation
bias 1019

Religious bias
1277

Racial bias
4831

Types of Offenses Reported in
Hate Crime Incidents, 1995

Crimes against property, 2725
    Destruction/Damage/Vandalism, 2315
    Robbery or burglary, 290
    Arson, 62
    Larceny or motor vehicle theft, 58

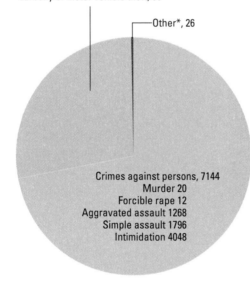

Other*, 26

Crimes against persons, 7144
Murder 20
Forcible rape 12
Aggravated assault 1268
Simple assault 1796
Intimidation 4048

*Includes offenses other than those listed that are collected in the National Incident-Based Reporting System

Source: Federal Bureau of Investigation, Uniform Crime Reports.

Kenosha, Wisconsin, was convicted of aggravated BATTERY and received an increased sentence under the Wisconsin hate-crime statute. The incident at issue began with Mitchell asking some friends, "Do you all feel hyped up to move on some white people?" Shortly thereafter Mitchell spotted Gregory Reddick, a fourteen-year-old white male, walking on the other side of the street. Mitchell then said to the group, "You all want to fuck somebody up? There goes a white boy; go get him." The group attacked Reddick. Reddick suffered extensive injuries, including brain damage, and was comatose for four days.

Mitchell appealed his conviction to the Wisconsin Supreme Court, which held that the hate-crime statute violated the First Amendment. The state of Wisconsin appealed to the U.S. Supreme Court, which reversed the Wisconsin Supreme Court. The High Court ruled that the Wisconsin statute was constitutional because it was directed at conduct, not expression. The Court distinguished the *R.A.V.* case by explaining that the St. Paul ordinance was impermissibly aimed at expression. The primary purpose of the St. Paul ordinance was to punish specifically the placement of certain symbols on property. This violated the rule against content-based speech legislation. The Wisconsin law, by contrast, merely allowed increased sentences based on motivation, always a legitimate consideration in determining a criminal sentence.

Hate-crime laws complicate the work of police officers by requiring them not only to capture criminals and investigate their criminal acts, but also to conduct a broad investigation of their personal life to determine whether a crime was motivated by prejudice. This determination may be difficult to make, and most laws offer little assistance in defining motivation.

The extra investigative work required by hate-crime laws also touches on PRIVACY issues and the boundaries of police investigations. Defendants who have been accused of a hate crime may have their home and workplace searched for information on group memberships, personal and public writings, and reading lists, and for other personal information that may have been inadmissible at trial before the advent of the hate-crime statute.

Advocates of hate-crime laws concede that those laws do not root out all hate crimes, but note that no criminal law is completely effective. They also contend that the difficulty in determining prejudiced motivation is no different from the difficulty that judges and juries face every day in determining whether the evidence presented in a case supports the charge. Supporters dismiss free speech and privacy concerns by reminding detractors that protections for both regularly give way when public safety requires their restriction. According to advocates of hate-crime laws, fighting hatred and prejudice is an important government function, especially when hatred and prejudice motivate victimization.

See also CRIMINAL LAW; FREEDOM OF SPEECH; MOTIVE.

HAVE AND HOLD 📖 The opening words, or HABENDUM CLAUSE, found in a DEED to REAL PROPERTY, which describes the ownership rights of the individual to whom such property is being conveyed. 📖

HAWKERS AND PEDDLERS 📖 A *hawker* is an individual who sells wares by carrying them through the streets. The person's ordinary methods of attracting attention include addressing the public, using placards, labels, and signs, or displaying merchandise in a public place. A *peddler* is defined as a retail dealer who brings goods from place to place, exhibiting them for sale. The terms are frequently defined in state statutes or city ordinances and are often used interchangeably. 📖

An individual is ordinarily considered to be a peddler in the legal sense if he or she does not have a fixed place of conducting business, but regularly carries the goods for sale with himself or herself. The wares must be offered for immediate sale and delivery and must be sold to customers as opposed to dealers who sell such wares. The goods may be BARTERED rather than sold for cash.

A single act of selling is generally insufficient to make the salesperson a peddler. Such individual must be engaged in this type of selling as a regular occupation or business, although it need not be the person's sole or main business. In addition, the individual, in order to be considered a hawker or peddler, need not earn sufficient funds for support from the business, nor does the business need to gain a profit in order for the individual to be considered a hawker or peddler.

The business of peddling has traditionally been distinguished from the service delivery of perishable goods, such as eggs, milk, or bakery products. An individual who delivers this type of perishable goods to regular customers is not considered a peddler. When, however, an individual travels from house to house, and sells goods to different persons in small quantities, the person is a peddler, even though he or she might make daily sales to somewhat regular customers. For example, a person who sharpens knives or an ice cream truck driver might fall into this category.

The individual who actually engages in the solicitation, makes the sale, and delivers the goods is the peddler, irrespective of whether the person owns the goods or is an AGENT or employee of the owner. An agent who sells his or her principal's merchandise can be considered a peddler; however, a principal who does not make sales calls or deliver merchandise is not. Ordinarily, an individual who merely solicits orders or sells by sample but does not deliver the goods sold is not considered a peddler.

Municipalities are permitted to set forth reasonable regulations concerning hawking and peddling within their borders. It may be required for such salespeople to obtain LICENSES; however, municipalities cannot prohibit the business through the requirement of an excessive fee.

In situations where a license is required, a peddler or hawker must obtain it prior to the time when he or she begins to sell wares and it must be issued to the individual who is actually engaged in the peddling. It is not transferrable. In order for an applicant to obtain a license, the person must establish certain facts, such as acceptable moral character. Some statutes and ordinances require a person seeking a license to take a prescribed oath, give a BOND, or deposit a particular amount of money.

Licensing statutes and ordinances often exempt certain individuals from their requirements; persons within the exempt classes need not obtain licenses. Such exemptions include persons selling goods or articles they have made themselves, honorably discharged or disabled veterans, poor or generally disabled persons, and clergy. The exemption is personal and cannot be extended to agents or employees of the licensed person.

HAYES, GEORGE E. C. George E. C. Hayes was an attorney and CIVIL RIGHTS activist, and a member of the team of lawyers who argued the landmark SCHOOL DESEGREGATION cases before the U.S. Supreme Court in 1954.

Hayes was born July 1, 1894, in Richmond, and lived most of his life in Washington, D.C., where he attended public schools. He graduated from Brown University, in Providence, in 1915 and received his law degree from Howard University in 1918. While at Howard, he attained one of the highest academic averages on record there.

Hayes's involvement in the burgeoning CIVIL RIGHTS MOVEMENT began in the 1940s. As a member of the District of Columbia Board of Education from 1945 to 1949, he worked to desegregate the schools in the nation's capital. Through his efforts, he met the NATIONAL ASSOCIATION FOR THE ADVANCEMENT OF COLORED PEOPLE (NAACP) lawyers who were mounting desegregation battles in other states. Their work culminated in the U.S. Supreme Court's landmark decision in *Brown v. Board of Educa-*

BIOGRAPHY

© WASHINGTON POST. REPRINTED COURTESY OF D.C. PUBLIC LIBRARY.

George E. C. Hayes

"[THE COUNTENANCING OF SCHOOL SEGREGATION] BY FEDERAL LAWMAKERS . . . WAS A MATTER OF POLITICS . . . IT WAS DONE AS AN EXPEDIENT."

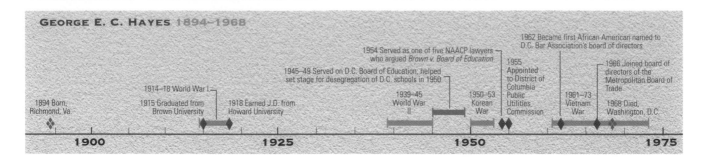

1962 Became first African American named to
D.C. Bar Association's board of directors

1954 Served as one of five NAACP lawyers
who argued *Brown v. Board of Education*

1945–49 Served on D.C. Board of Education; helped
set stage for desegregation of D.C. schools in 1950

1966 Joined board of
directors of the
Metropolitan Board of
Trade

1955
Appointed
to District of
Columbia
Public
Utilities
Commission

1894 Born,
Richmond, Va.

1914–18 World War I
1915 Graduated from
Brown University

1918 Earned J.D. from
Howard University

1939–45
World War
II

1950–53
Korean
War

1961–73
Vietnam
War

1968 Died,
Washington, D.C.

1900   1925   1950   1975

tion, 347 U.S. 483, 74 S. Ct. 686, 98 L. Ed. 873 (1954). Hayes was one of five NAACP lawyers, including THURGOOD MARSHALL and James Nabrit, Jr., who convinced the High Court that segregation in public schools was unconstitutional. The *Brown* decision, repudiating the long-established "SEPARATE-BUT-EQUAL" doctrine, marked the beginning of the end of segregation in all public accommodations. After the decision was handed down, Hayes and the other NAACP lawyers continued to press for immediate desegregation and urged the Court not to grant the states' appeals for a delay in implementation of the changes.

In 1954, Hayes clashed with Senator JOSEPH R. MCCARTHY, a Wisconsin Republican who headed the Senate Subcommittee on Investigations. McCarthy, looking into possible Communist infiltration of the armed services, accused Annie Lee Moss, a civilian employee of the Army Signal Corps, of Communist affiliation. Hayes defended Moss, who repeatedly denied the allegations against her. He sharply criticized McCarthy's investigative methods and presumption that Moss was guilty. Ultimately, Moss was cleared of the charges, and the secretary of defense restored her to a position with the Army.

Hayes has been described as independent and a "quiet pioneer." He was a lifelong Republican, choosing an unusual affiliation for an African American civil rights activist. In 1955, President DWIGHT D. EISENHOWER appointed him to a post on the District of Columbia Public Utilities Commission, and Hayes thus became the first African American in nearly one hundred years to serve in a municipal agency in the District of Columbia. In 1962, the District of Columbia Bar Association named him to its board of directors, making him the first African American to hold office in that group.

Hayes had open and sometimes bitter differences with the younger, more militant activists who assumed leadership of the civil rights movement in the early 1960s. In 1966, they criticized him for accepting membership on the previously segregated board of directors of the

BIOGRAPHY

LIBRARY OF CONGRESS

Rutherford Birchard Hayes

Metropolitan Washington Board of Trade, one of the District of Columbia's most conservative groups. As Howard University counsel, he advised and assisted his friend Nabrit, then president of Howard, in his handling of the black power student uprising on the campus in 1967.

Hayes was highly respected among his colleagues, who knew him to be calm, diligent, modest, and unassuming. He was noted for his elegance in language, manner, and dress, and he projected an image of intelligence and confidence. In addition to holding a long tenure as counsel to Howard University, Hayes acted as counsel to the NAACP for many years. He died December 20, 1968, in Washington, D.C.

HAYES, RUTHERFORD BIRCHARD Rutherford Birchard Hayes was a respected and successful lawyer in his home state of Ohio. He achieved further success while serving in the Union Army during the U.S. Civil War, and he went on to gain prominence as a politician from Ohio. His service as governor of Ohio and as a member of the U.S. House of Representatives led to his election as the nineteenth president of the United States.

Hayes was born October 4, 1822, in Delaware, Ohio. His father, Rutherford Hayes, died before Hayes was born and Hayes was raised by his mother, Sophia Birchard Hayes, with the help of his uncle, Sardis Birchard, a bachelor. Hayes was enrolled at Norwalk Academy, a Methodist school in Ohio, in the spring of 1836. The next year he joined Isaac Webb's Preparatory School, in Middletown, Connecticut, where Sardis aided with his tuition. In 1838 Hayes enrolled at Kenyon College, in Gambier, Ohio. He graduated first in his class in August 1842 and delivered the valedictory address. After graduating he studied French and German on his own.

He went on to Harvard Law School in 1843 and was later admitted to the Ohio bar. He began practicing law in Lower Sandusky (now Fremont), Ohio, as a partner of Ralph P. Buckland, a leading legal figure in the town. He assumed an active role in politics in 1848 when he worked to elect ZACHARY TAYLOR, the Whig

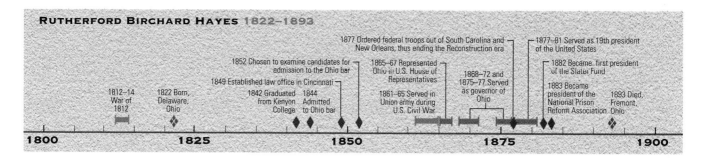

RUTHERFORD BIRCHARD HAYES 1822–1893

1877 Ordered federal troops out of South Carolina and
New Orleans, thus ending the Reconstruction era

1877–81 Served as 19th president
of the United States

1852 Chosen to examine candidates for
admission to the Ohio bar

1865–67 Represented
Ohio in U.S. House of
Representatives

1882 Became first president
of the Slater Fund

1849 Established law office in Cincinnati

1883 Became
president of the
National Prison
Reform Association

1812–14
War of
1812

1822 Born,
Delaware,
Ohio

1842 Graduated
from Kenyon
College

1844
Admitted
to Ohio bar

1861–65 Served in
Union army during
U.S. Civil War

1868–72 and
1875–77 Served
as governor of
Ohio

1893 Died,
Fremont,
Ohio

1800   1825   1850   1875   1900

candidate for president. In 1849 he established a law office in Cincinnati, and eventually he became a prominent attorney in the city. In 1852 he was chosen to examine candidates for admission to the Ohio bar. Later that year he married Lucy Webb, whom he had known for nearly eight years.

Hayes developed into a leading and somewhat radical figure in Ohio politics. Like many Republicans he opposed SLAVERY but saw no need to punish the South. He chose other avenues in the fight to end slavery, offering his services to the Underground Railroad, which helped Southern slaves escape to freedom in the North. In 1853 he defended a number of escaped slaves in court. He went on to form a well-known Cincinnati law firm, Corwine, Hayes, and Rogers.

In the 1860 presidential campaign, he worked for the election of ABRAHAM LINCOLN, but with no great enthusiasm. After Lincoln's election at the beginning of the Civil War, Hayes wrote in his diary, "Six states have 'seceded.' Let them go." Nevertheless, when the war broke out, Hayes became active in the Union's military effort to unify the nation. In 1862 he was promoted to full colonel and given command of the Twenty-third Ohio Regiment. Hayes was wounded four times, once seriously, during the war. His composure in battle gained him the respect of those who served under him.

Hayes's popularity helped his political career. On October 19, 1864, he was elected to the U.S. House of Representatives for the Second Congressional District of Ohio. He was reelected in 1866. In 1867 the Ohio Republican party nominated Hayes as its candidate for governor. He gained considerable support from Radical Republicans who, like Hayes, opposed President ANDREW JOHNSON's vetoes of legislation calling for military government in the South. On January 13, 1868, Hayes was inaugurated as governor of Ohio. He was reelected governor in 1870 and again in 1875.

Hayes favored a sound fiscal policy with regard to the use of public money, and he opposed public funds for Catholic schools.

"POLITICS AND LAW ARE MERELY RESULTS, MERELY THE EXPRESSION OF WHAT THE PEOPLE WISH."

These issues struck a chord with Republicans throughout the United States, who sought to extend his fiscal policies to the federal level. He received the Republican nomination for president in 1876, to run against SAMUEL J. TILDEN of New York.

Even before election results were in, Hayes wrote in his diary that he feared a contested election and perhaps even an armed conflict because of it. He apparently anticipated the most complicated election in the nation's history. On November 7, 1880, election results showed that Tilden had won 4.300 million popular votes to Hayes's 4.036 million, giving Tilden 184 electoral votes (one short of the needed majority) and Hayes 166.

A congressional election committee was designated to determine the winner of the election. After months of deliberation, Republicans managed to sway the committee by filling it with Republican loyalists. On March 2, 1877, Congress declared Hayes and his vice presidential candidate, William Almon Wheeler, of New York, the winners of the 1876 election.

In his inaugural address, Hayes stressed the importance of settling the problems left by Union occupation of Southern states. In April 1877 he ordered federal troops out of South Carolina and New Orleans. The era of the Reconstruction of the South initiated by former president ULYSSES S. GRANT was over.

During Hayes's administration he renewed the economic policy of satisfying the public debt with government currency, and he opposed measures passed by Congress to freely coin silver. Hayes reformed the process for appointing civil servants. He also signed legislation permitting women to practice law before the Supreme Court.

Hayes refused to run for reelection in 1880, and retired from politics. However, he continued to contribute to the landscape of American life. In 1882 he became the first president of the Slater Fund, founded to aid African American education programs in the South. He later gave a scholarship to a promising young man, W. E. B. DU BOIS, who went on to attend Fisk and Harvard Universities and ultimately became a leading figure in the NATIONAL ASSOCIATION FOR THE ADVANCEMENT OF COLORED PEOPLE. In 1883 Hayes became the first president of the National Prison Reform Association, a post he held for nearly ten years. Hayes was also a trustee of Ohio Wesleyan and Ohio State Universities.

On January 14, 1893, Hayes suffered severe chest pain while in Cleveland on business for Western Reserve and Ohio State Universities. His son Webb C. Hayes accompanied him to Speigel Grove, in Fremont, Ohio, where his wife had been buried three years earlier. On January 17 Hayes died, at the age of seventy.

HAYMARKET RIOT In the Haymarket Riot of May 4, 1886, the police clashed violently with militant anarchists and labor movement protesters in Chicago. Seven policemen and several protesters were killed, leading to murder convictions for seven radicals, four of whom were executed. The strong public and state reaction against the Haymarket protesters has been called the first RED SCARE in U.S. history, and their trial has been widely critized for improper procedure and prosecutorial excess.

The Haymarket Riot grew out of labor unrest that had been brewing since the 1870s. Unhappy with difficult working conditions and feeling the pressure of economic depression, workers had engaged in periodic strikes. Strong, sometimes violent police opposition to these strikes led to greater labor militancy. Radicals became increasingly convinced that the struggle between labor and capital had come to a head and that the time for revolution was near. Many anarchists publicly advocated the use of explosives to bring down the capitalist system.

In 1886, a broad coalition of labor organizations joined to campaign for an eight-hour workday. On May 1, 1886, this coalition initiated a general strike throughout the United States, the effects of which were particularly strong in Chicago. On May 3, fighting broke out at the McCormick Reaper Works in Chicago, and at least two workers were killed by the police.

Outraged at these killings, anarchists, members of the labor movement, and other radicals met for a rally in Chicago's Haymarket Square on May 4. The rally was peaceable until the police attempted to disperse the crowd. Then a bomb was thrown into the police ranks, killing seven officers and wounding sixty more. The police fired in response, killing and wounding like numbers of participants.

In an ensuing crackdown against the labor movement, the police arrested hundreds of anarchists and other radicals. Two leading anarchist newspapers were put out of business, and their staffs were imprisoned. Finally, eight noted Chicago radicals and anarchists, including nationally known radical leaders August Spies and Albert Parsons, were indicted for the murder of one of the policemen at Haymarket Square. Public opinion turned swiftly against the protesters, in part because seven of the eight defendants in the case were foreign-born.

The trial in the criminal court of Cook County began on June 21, 1886. Despite a lack of evidence linking them directly to the bombing, seven of the eight were convicted of murder and sentenced to death, and the eighth was sentenced to fifteen years in prison. The defendants were held liable for the murder on the ground that they had incited the bombing through inflammatory public speech.

The defendants appealed their case to the Illinois Supreme Court which upheld the lower court's decision on September 14, 1887 (*Spies v. People*, 122 Ill. 1, 12 N.E. 865). Supporters of the defendants undertook a CLEMENCY campaign that gathered forty thousand petition signatures. Under pressure from all sides, Governor Richard Oglesby, of Illinois, pardoned two of the seven sentenced to death but sustained the sentences of the other five. One of the seven committed suicide shortly before the date of execution by detonating a small dynamite bomb smuggled to him by a friend. The other four, including Spies and Parsons, were hanged on November 11, 1887.

The three remaining Haymarket defendants were pardoned in 1893 by Governor John Peter Altgeld, of Illinois, who also issued a report condemning the trial as unfair. He noted that the presiding judge was clearly biased against the defendants, that the defendants were not proved to be guilty of the crime with which they were charged, and that the jury was "packed" by state prosecutors with members who were prejudiced against the defendants. Later legal scholars have supported Altgeld's conclusions.

The questionable jury selection practices in the Haymarket trial, which allowed the seating of jurors who were clearly prejudiced against the defendants, were struck down by a later decision of the Illinois Supreme Court (*Coughlin v. People*, 144 Ill. 140, 33 N.E. 1 [1893]).

CROSS-REFERENCES

Anarchism; Darrow, Clarence; Goldman, Emma; Labor Law; Labor Union.

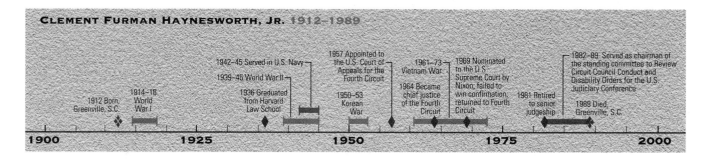

HAYNESWORTH, CLEMENT FURMAN, JR.

Clement Furman Haynesworth, Jr., was a controversial judge on a federal appellate court who was nominated to the U.S. Supreme Court but failed to win confirmation.

Born October 30, 1912, in Greenville, South Carolina, and raised in South Carolina, Haynesworth graduated from Furman University in 1933 and from Harvard Law School in 1936. He then returned to his home state and practiced law there for nearly twenty years. In 1957 President DWIGHT D. EISENHOWER appointed Haynesworth to the U.S. Court of Appeals for the Fourth Circuit. Haynesworth became chief judge of the court in 1964.

In May 1969 Associate Justice ABE FORTAS, whose earlier nomination to become chief justice was withdrawn amid charges of financial impropriety and conflict of interest, resigned his seat on the U.S. Supreme Court after new charges of unethical conduct were raised. Later that summer President RICHARD M. NIXON nominated Haynesworth to succeed Fortas.

Reaction to Haynesworth's nomination was mixed. Some commentators thought him to be a competent nominee, if not particularly distinguished, whereas others expressed disappointment at his conservative judicial views. But no Supreme Court nominee had been denied confirmation since 1930 and it initially appeared that Haynesworth would be confirmed with little debate.

However, in the confirmation hearings that followed Haynesworth faced serious CONFLICT-OF-INTEREST allegations. It was disclosed that he

Clement Furman Haynesworth, Jr.

William Harrison Hays

had participated in two cases involving subsidiaries of companies in which he held stock. Senators opposing his nomination also revealed that Haynesworth had purchased stock in a corporation after he voted in its favor in a decision but before the decision was announced by the court. In addition, labor and CIVIL RIGHTS groups voiced opposition to Haynesworth's nomination, contending that he did not support their causes. Nevertheless, the Senate Judiciary Committee narrowly approved Haynesworth's appointment in a 10–7 vote.

In November 1969, the full Senate, mindful of the controversy that had surrounded Fortas's ethical improprieties, rejected Haynesworth's nomination by a vote of 55–45. This was the widest margin of defeat ever for a Supreme Court nominee.

Haynesworth's failure to win confirmation was widely viewed as a major political setback for President Nixon. A second Nixon nominee for the Fortas seat, Judge G. HARROLD CARSWELL, another southern conservative, was widely viewed as unqualified for the Court and was also defeated. The vacancy was finally filled, in May 1970, by Judge HARRY A. BLACKMUN, of the Eighth Circuit Court of Appeals, who was confirmed unanimously.

Following his defeat, Haynesworth returned to the court of appeals. He became a senior judge in 1981, and he remained with the court until his death November 22, 1989, at the age of seventy-seven.

HAYS, WILLIAM HARRISON

William Harrison Hays is mainly known for his estab-

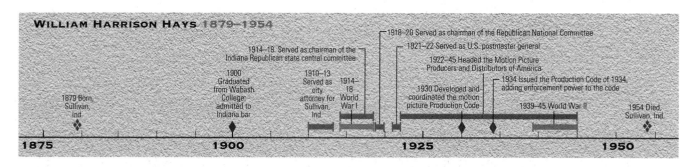

lishment of the code through which motion picture producers regulated themselves, thereby avoiding outside CENSORSHIP.

Hays was born in Sullivan, Indiana, on November 5, 1879, to John T. Hays and Mary Cain Hays. He first gained attention through a series of increasingly important positions within the Indiana Republican party. In February 1918 his party career culminated in his appointment as chairman of the Republican National Committee. From that position he aided in the 1920 election of WARREN G. HARDING as president of the United States. As reward for his service, Harding appointed Hays U.S. postmaster general in March 1921, after which Hays relinquished his position as Republican chairman.

At this time a widely reported series of sex scandals contributed to a growing perception that the movie industry was out of control and out of step with U.S. society. With over thirty state legislatures considering bills to censor movies, producers intervened to repair their image. In March 1922 they hired Hays, known as a teetotaler and an elder in the Presbyterian Church, to head the Motion Picture Producers and Distributors of America (MPPDA) at $100,000 a year. With his high political profile, his personal moral characteristics, and his connections with businesspeople, including Hollywood executives, Hays was seen as an outsider who could restore public confidence in the morality of the movie industry.

The effort to head off federal or local censorship through hiring Hays was successful. In 1930 the Hays Office, as it became commonly known, coordinated the Production Code among the producers of movies to provide rules for the film industry's self-regulation. The 1930 code had no enforcement mechanism. Still, the hiring of Hays, the goodwill implied in the code, and a lack of cooperation and agreement among reformers, mainly Protestant, dissipated any danger of censorship in the early 1930s.

In 1934, with box office receipts down as the Great Depression widened, Hays responded to a renewed call for morality in the movies spearheaded by the Catholic Church's Legion of Decency. Operating with support from parish priests, from the church hierarchy, and from Protestant and Jewish reform groups, the Legion avoided efforts at government legislated censorship. Rather, it threatened to call for boycotts of films that failed to satisfy its requirements for moral behavior. Hays issued the Production Code of 1934, which added enforcement power to his earlier code. Though the 1934 code provided for fines and suggested that scripts should be preapproved by the Hays Office, its real strength lay in requiring that a film receive the Hays Code Purity Seal of Approval in order to be shown in any movie theater owned by the studios. With the movie industry vertically integrated, so that studios controlled both a large segment of film production and the most successful and profitable movie theaters nationwide, even foreign and nonstudio films were submitted for code approval.

The Hays code went through refinements and shifts in emphasis, both before and after the addition of enforcement in 1934. In general, it was designed to protect impressionable moviegoers by clamping down on sex, language, and violence on screen, with rules relating to sex being particularly stringent. One overarching rule was that sympathetic portrayals of sinners or criminals were prohibited; transgressors had to be punished appropriately for their sins by the end of each film.

Hays maintained his partnership in Hays and Hays, a law firm begun by his father, throughout his tenure with the MPPDA. In 1945 he left his position as head of the MPPDA. He died in Indiana on March 7, 1954.

See also MOVIE RATING.

HAYWOOD, MARGARET A.

Margaret A. Haywood is a senior judge for the Superior Court of the District of Columbia. She also was the first black woman to attain a top leadership position in a biracial U.S. church, the United Church of Christ.

Haywood was born October 8, 1912, in Knoxville, Tennessee. When she was eight, she and her parents moved to Washington, D.C. Although she was aware of segregation, her loving home life helped her to grow up feeling

BIOGRAPHY

Margaret A. Haywood

COURTESY JUDGE MARGARET A. HAYWOOD

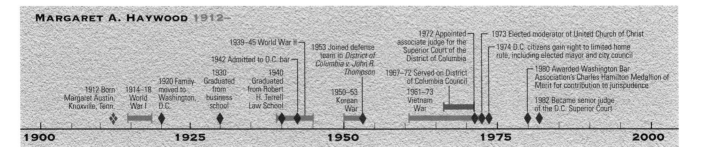

MARGARET A. HAYWOOD 1912–

1912 Born Margaret Austin, Knoxville, Tenn.

1914–18 World War I

1920 Family moved to Washington, D.C.

1930 Graduated from business school

1939–45 World War II

1940 Graduated from Robert H. Terrell Law School

1942 Admitted to D.C. bar

1950–53 Korean War

1953 Joined defense team in *District of Columbia v. John R. Thompson*

1961–73 Vietnam War

1967–72 Served on District of Columbia Council

1972 Appointed associate judge for the Superior Court of the District of Columbia

1973 Elected moderator of United Church of Christ

1974 D.C. citizens gain right to limited home rule, including elected mayor and city council

1980 Awarded Washington Bar Association's Charles Hamilton Medallion of Merit for contribution to jurisprudence

1982 Became senior judge of the D.C. Superior Court

1900   1925   1950   1975   2000

secure and self-confident. Haywood's parents, Mayme F. Austin and J. W. M. Austin, were able to provide her with a relatively comfortable childhood, although her father lost his job in 1929. After two years, he found another job with the Works Progress Administration, helping people obtain public assistance. Reading the letters people wrote to her father detailing their plights, Haywood learned that to help people, you had to listen to them.

Haywood was always an independent decision maker. While she was in high school, her teachers encouraged her to become a teacher, the best career option for black women in the 1930s. However, Haywood's interests were elsewhere, for reasons that were both practical and compelling. At the height of the Great Depression, in 1930, she came out of business school with no job and no money for college. She married and had a daughter, but the marriage, as she described it, "was disastrous." Before long, she found herself divorced and raising a child alone. "I wanted my daughter to have a good education, but I was earning only $15 a week as a secretary," she said. "That's when I began to think about going into law."

Determined to provide her daughter and herself with economic security, Haywood enrolled in Robert H. Terrell Law School, an institution for African American students where she could attend classes at night and work during the day. During her first two years at Terrell, she was the only woman student; during the last two years, she was one of two woman students. This did not deter her, and she graduated from Terrell with her bachelor of laws degree in 1940.

After her admission to the District of Columbia bar in 1942, Haywood joined a well-known black law firm. She quickly realized that the firm expected her to specialize in domestic relations cases, whereas she was interested in practicing in other fields. Unwilling to compromise, she left the security of the firm and opened her own general practice, where she handled the full range of legal cases. In the early 1950s, she participated in the landmark CIVIL RIGHTS case *District of Columbia v. John R. Thomp-*

son Co. (345 U.S. 921, 73 S. Ct. 784, 97 L. Ed. 1353 [1953]), which confirmed the validity of post–Civil War laws that prohibited segregation. For her efforts, Haywood received threats from the KU KLUX KLAN and was labeled a Communist.

Haywood had practiced law for more than twenty-five years before President LYNDON B. JOHNSON appointed her to a part-time post on the District of Columbia Council. She served in that capacity from 1967 to 1972, during a time when the governance of the district was being reevaluated and reorganized. The revamped system of government, including an elected mayor and the council on which Haywood served, was approved in 1974.

In 1972, President RICHARD M. NIXON appointed Haywood as associate judge for the Superior Court of the District of Columbia, the district's highest trial court. The following year, the United Church of Christ elected her its moderator, making her the first black woman to hold such a high position in a biracial U.S. church. As moderator, she presided over 728 delegates to the church's ninth biennial general synod, or governing council. Her position with the church was a two-year unsalaried post, which she combined with her duties on the court.

During her career, Haywood has received many honors and awards. These include a NATIONAL ASSOCIATION FOR THE ADVANCEMENT OF COLORED PEOPLE trophy in 1950, the Women's Bar Association's Woman Lawyer of the Year award in 1972, induction into the District of Columbia Women's Commission Hall of Fame, and the Washington Bar Association's Charles Hamilton Medallion of Merit for contribution to jurisprudence in 1980. Haywood has received honorary degrees from Elmhurst College (1974), Carleton College (1975), Catawba College (1976), and Doane College (1979).

In 1982, Haywood achieved the rank of senior judge of the District of Columbia Superior Court.

HAYWOOD, WILLIAM DUDLEY Labor leader Bill Haywood was regarded as a radical in the growing labor movement in the United

BIOGRAPHY

LIBRARY OF CONGRESS

William Dudley Haywood

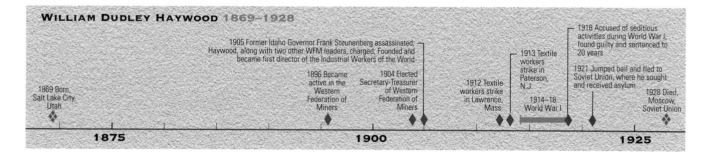

WILLIAM DUDLEY HAYWOOD 1869–1928

1869 Born, Salt Lake City, Utah

1896 Became active in the Western Federation of Miners

1904 Elected Secretary-Treasurer of Western Federation of Miners

1905 Former Idaho Governor Frank Steunenberg assassinated; Haywood, along with two other WFM leaders, charged; Founded and became first director of the Industrial Workers of the World

1912 Textile workers strike in Lawrence, Mass

1913 Textile workers strike in Paterson, N.J.

1914–18 World War I

1918 Accused of seditious activities during World War I; found guilty and sentenced to 20 years

1921 Jumped bail and fled to Soviet Union, where he sought and received asylum

1928 Died, Moscow, Soviet Union

1875   1900   1925

States. A public figure throughout most of his life, Haywood was the central figure in two famous court cases.

Haywood was born in 1869 in Salt Lake City, Utah. In 1896, Haywood, a coal miner, became an active participant in the Western Federation of Miners. He rapidly rose to prominence in the federation, securing offices of leadership by 1904. His tactics were militant in nature, as was evidenced by the violence of the Cripple Creek strike that occurred in Colorado in 1904.

In 1905, former Idaho Governor Frank Steunenberg was killed by an explosion caused by a bomb hidden in his home by Harry Orchard. Orchard admitted his guilt and implicated three leaders of the Western Federation of Miners: President Charles H. Moyer, Secretary-Treasurer Haywood, and retired leader George A. Pettibone. These men were abducted from Denver and taken to Boise, Idaho, to stand trial. The Haywood-Moyer-Pettibone case took on national significance for two reasons: (1) it involved a radical labor organization, and (2) eminent attorney CLARENCE DARROW acted as defense attorney. The three men were subsequently acquitted (*Pettibone v. Nichols*, 203 U.S. 192, 27 S. Ct. 111, 51 L. Ed. 148 [1906]).

The INDUSTRIAL WORKERS OF THE WORLD (IWW) was established in 1905, and Haywood was the founder and director of this labor organization. He was a proponent of group action and class struggle, and he abhorred compromise. He continued to use violence in his fight for labor, and led two infamous textile workers' strikes in Lawrence, Massachusetts (1912), and in Paterson, New Jersey (1913).

Haywood and other members of his IWW organization attempted to become members of the Socialist party but were rejected for their theories of violent action.

In 1918, Haywood was again on trial. One hundred sixty-five IWW leaders, including Haywood, were accused of seditious activities during World War I. Haywood was found guilty and sentenced to spend the next twenty years in prison.

Haywood was free on bail in 1921, pending the date of a new trial, when he escaped and sought asylum in the Soviet Union. He died in Moscow seven years later.

See also LABOR UNION; SOCIALISM.

H.B. An abbreviation for a *house bill*, a proposed law brought before the House of Representatives, as opposed to the Senate.

House bills are usually designated by the initials H.R. plus a number—for example, H.R. 40637.

See also CONGRESS OF THE UNITED STATES.

"IT IS THE HISTORIC MISSION OF THE WORKING CLASS TO DO AWAY WITH CAPITALISM."

HEADNOTE A brief summary of a legal rule or a significant fact in a case that, among other headnotes that apply to the case, precedes the full text opinion printed in the REPORTS or REPORTERS. A SYLLABUS to a reported case that summarizes the points decided in the case and is placed before the text of the opinion.

Each JURISDICTION usually determines whether headnotes are part of the law or only an editorial device to facilitate research. There are, however, exceptions to this rule. For example, the headnotes to the UNIFORM COMMERCIAL CODE (UCC), adopted in whole or in part by every state, were written as part of the law. In states that treat headnotes as merely an editorial device, the UCC headnotes are considered as part of the law.

HEAD OF HOUSEHOLD An individual in one family setting who provides actual support and maintenance to one or more individuals who are related to him or her through ADOPTION, blood, or MARRIAGE.

The designation *head of household*, also termed *head of family*, is applied to one whose authority to exercise family control and to support the dependent members is founded upon a moral or legal obligation or duty.

Head of household is also a filing status for federal income taxpayers. There are five basic categories of tax statuses: (1) single persons; (2) heads of households; (3) married taxpayers filing joint returns; (4) married taxpayers filing separate returns; and (5) surviving spouses. Each of these persons pays at different rates. The tax rates for single persons are ordinarily higher than rates for heads of household, while rates for a husband and wife filing a joint return are lower.

In order for an individual to qualify as head of household for INCOME TAX purposes, the person need not be unmarried all year as long as the person is unmarried on the final day of the tax year. In addition, the person must support and maintain a household to the extent that his or her monetary contribution exceeds one-half of the total cost of maintenance. The person's home must be the main place of residence of one relative, with the exception of a mother and father, for the whole year. Relatives include children, grandchildren, stepchildren, brothers and sisters, half brothers or half sisters, and stepbrothers and stepsisters. The individual's parents need not reside in the same home as the taxpayer for him or her to claim this status, provided the person meets the support requirements specified.

HOMESTEAD exemption statutes, which have been passed in a majority of JURISDICTIONS, permit a head of household to designate a house and land as a homestead and exempt it from EXECUTION for general debts in the event of BANKRUPTCY. In addition, some states make available property tax exemptions for homestead property. Such statutes often require the formal recording of a declaration of homestead.

HEALTH AND HUMAN SERVICES DEPARTMENT

The Department of Health and Human Services (HHS) is the cabinet-level department of the federal EXECUTIVE BRANCH of the government most involved with the United States' human concerns. It administers a wide variety of agencies and programs that provide financial assistance to needy persons, as well as health care and advocacy; conduct medical and scientific research; and enforce laws and regulations related to human services.

The HHS originated in the Department of Health, Education, and Welfare (HEW), which was created in 1953. In 1980, the Department of Education Organization Act (20 U.S.C.A. § 3508) redesignated HEW the Department of Health and Human Services.

The secretary of HHS advises the president of the United States on the federal government's health, WELFARE, and income security plans, policies, and programs. The secretary directs HHS staff in carrying out department programs and activities and promotes public understanding of HHS goals, programs, and objectives. The secretary administers these functions through the Office of the Secretary and the five operating divisions of the HHS: the Administration on Aging, Administration for Children and Families, Public Health Service, Substance Abuse and Mental Health Services Administration, and Health Care Financing Administration.

Office of the Secretary The Office of the Secretary of the HHS includes the Offices of the Deputy Secretary, the Assistant Secretaries, the Inspector General, and the General Counsel. Individuals in these offices, along with other senior officials at HHS, assist the secretary with the overall management responsibilities of the HHS and aid in the day-to-day operations of the department. In addition, the Office for Civil Rights administers and enforces laws that prohibit DISCRIMINATION in federally assisted health and human services programs. These laws include title VI of the CIVIL RIGHTS ACT of 1964 (42 U.S.C.A. § 2000d et seq.), which prohibits discrimination with regard to race, color, or national origin in programs and activities receiving federal financial assistance; the Age Discrimination Act of 1975 (42 U.S.C.A. § 6101 et seq.); and the Americans with Disabilities Act of 1990 (42 U.S.C.A. § 12101 et seq.).

The U.S. Office of Consumer Affairs, also part of the HHS, advises the secretary on consumer-related policy and programs and handles consumer matters. The office coordinates the implementation of all federal activities in the area of CONSUMER PROTECTION, with an emphasis on finding and recommending ways to make government consumer programs more effective. The director of the office also chairs the U.S. Consumer Affairs Council, which comprises representatives of all federal agencies that provide consumer-related programs.

The secretary is accountable to Congress and to the public for departmental expenditures of taxpayers' money. Thus, the secretary and other members of the HHS staff spend a great deal of time testifying before congressional committees, making speeches before national organizations interested in and affected by HHS policy, and meeting with the press and the public to explain HHS actions. The secretary and the HHS staff also prepare special reports, sometimes at the request of the president, on national problems related to health and human services. In addition, the secretary is required by law to submit to the president and to Congress periodic reports that explain how tax money was spent to address and solve a particular problem and whether progress on the problem was achieved.

The headquarters of the HHS Department is located in Washington, D.C., and ten regional HHS offices are located throughout the United States. The regional directors of these offices represent the secretary in any official HHS dealings with state and local government organizations. They promote a general understanding of HHS programs, policies, and objectives; advise the secretary on the potential local effects of HHS policies and decisions; and pro-

The Centers for Disease Control and Prevention, an agency of the Public Health Service, may recommend inoculations for young people in its effort to control disease and respond to public health emergencies.

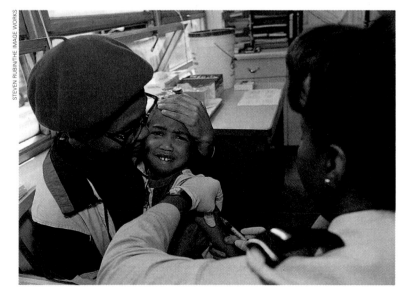

STEVEN RUBIN/THE IMAGE WORKS

Health and Human Services Department

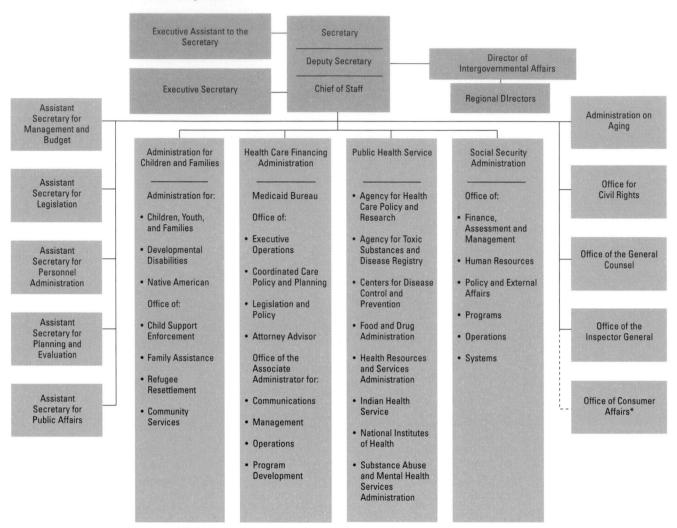

*Located administratively in HHS, but reports to the President.

vide administrative services and support to HHS programs and activities in the regions.

Administration on Aging The Administration on Aging (AOA) is the principal agency of the HHS designated to carry out the provisions of the Older Americans Act of 1965, as amended (42 U.S.C.A. § 3001 et seq.). The Older Americans Act was enacted to promote the well-being of older U.S. citizens by providing services and programs designed to help them live independently in their home and community. The act also empowers the federal government to distribute funds to the states for supportive services for older people. The AOA advises the secretary and other federal departments and agencies on the characteristics, circumstances, and needs of older citizens; develops policies and programs to promote the welfare of older citizens and advocates for their needs in HHS policy development and plan-

ning; and administers to the states grants that establish at the state and local levels programs providing services to older citizens, such as group meals and nutrition education. The AOA also administers programs providing legal and protective services for older people.

Administration for Children and Families The Administration for Children and Families (ACF) was created in 1991 and is headed by the assistant secretary for children and families, who reports to the secretary of the HHS. The ACF consists of several component administrations, including the Administration on Children, Youth, and Families (ACYF), which advises the secretary, through the assistant secretary, on matters relating to the sound development of children, youth, and families and administers grant programs to help the states provide child welfare services as well as foster care and adoption assistance. The ACYF also administers state grant programs for the prevention of CHILD ABUSE; the Head Start Program, which appropriates funds for health, education, nutrition, social, and other services to economically disadvantaged children and their families; and programs providing services to prevent drug abuse among youth. In addition, the ACYF supports and encourages in the private and voluntary sectors programs for children, youth, and families.

Other components of the ACF include the Administration on Developmental Disabilities (ADD) and the Administration for Native Americans (ANA). ADD advises the secretary of the HHS on matters relating to persons with developmental disabilities and their families, and helps provide services to such individuals. ADD also helps the states provide services at the local level through grants and other programs. ANA represents the concerns of Native Americans and serves as the focal point within the HHS for providing developmental, social, and economic strategies to support Native American self-determination and self-sufficiency. ANA administers grant programs to Indian tribes and other Native American organizations in both urban and rural areas and acts as a liaison with other federal agencies on Native American affairs.

Yet another component of the ACF is the Office of Child Support Enforcement (OCSE), which advises the secretary on matters relating to CHILD SUPPORT enforcement and provides direction and guidance to state offices for child enforcement programs. The OCSE helps states develop programs establishing and enforcing support obligations by locating absent parents, establishing paternity, and collecting child support payments.

Public Health Service The Public Health Service was first established in 1798 to create hospitals to care for U.S. merchant seamen. Subsequent legislation substantially broadened the scope of its activities. Today, its mission is to protect and advance the nation's physical and mental health.

The Public Health Service accomplishes its goals through a number of agencies, including the Agency for Health Care Policy and Research, which produces and disseminates information about the quality, medical effectiveness, and cost of health care, and the Centers for Disease Control and Prevention (CDC), which provides leadership in the prevention and control of diseases and responds to public health emergencies. Other agencies within the Public Health Service include the Agency for Toxic Substances and Disease Registry, which carries

out the health-related responsibilities of the Comprehensive Environmental Response, Compensation, and Liability Act of 1980 (CERCLA) (42 U.S.C.A. § 9601 et seq.), as well as the FOOD AND DRUG ADMINISTRATION, which is charged with protecting the health of the nation against unsafe foods, DRUGS, cosmetics, and other hazards.

The health status of American Indians and Alaska Natives is the concern of the Indian Health Service. The Indian Health Service administers a comprehensive health care delivery system for these groups, developing and managing programs to meet their health needs.

The National Institutes of Health (NIH) is the principal biomedical research agency of the federal government. Included within the NIH are the National Cancer Institute; National Heart, Lung, and Blood Institute; National Institute of Child Health and Human Development; and other institutes conducting research in the areas of ALCOHOL and drug abuse, mental health, communication and neurological disorders, and aging.

The Substance Abuse and Mental Health Services Administration (SAMHSA) provides national leadership in the prevention and treatment of addictive and mental disorders, through programs and services for individuals who suffer from these disorders. Within SAMHSA are several component centers designated to carry out its purposes, including the Center for Substance Abuse Prevention, Center for Substance Abuse Treatment, and Center for Mental Health Services. SAMHSA is also served by the Office of Management, Planning, and Communications, which is responsible for the financial and administrative management of SAMHSA components, monitors and analyzes legislation affecting these components, and oversees SAMHSA public affairs activities.

Health Care Financing Administration The Health Care Financing Administration (HCFA) was created in the late 1970s to oversee the Medicare Program and the federal portion of the Medicaid Program. Medicare provides health insurance for U.S. citizens age sixty-five or older, for younger people receiving SOCIAL SECURITY benefits, and for persons needing dialysis or kidney transplants. Medicaid covers health care expenses for recipients of Aid to Families with Dependent Children, as well as for low-income pregnant women and other individuals whose medical bills qualify them as medically needy. Through these programs, the HCFA serves 68 million older, disabled, and poor U.S. citizens. In addition, a quality assurance program administered by the HCFA develops health and safety standards for providers of health care services authorized by Medicare and Medicaid legislation.

HEALTH CARE FINANCING ADMINIS-TRATION The Health Care Financing Administration (HCFA), an operating division of the Department of Health and Human Services, was established in 1977 to combine under one administration the oversight of the Medicare Program and the federal portion of the Medicaid Program (Reorg. Order of Mar. 9, 1977, 42 Fed. Reg. 13262).

Medicare provides health INSURANCE coverage for U.S. citizens age sixty-five or older, for younger people receiving SOCIAL SECURITY benefits, and for persons needing dialysis or kidney transplants for the treatment of end-stage renal disease (42 U.S.C.A. § 1395 et seq.). Medicare beneficiaries may receive medical care through physicians of their own choosing or through health maintenance organizations and other medical plans that have contracts with Medicare.

Medicaid is a medical assistance program jointly financed by state and federal governments for low-income individuals (42 U.S.C.A. § 1396 et seq.). Medicaid covers health care expenses for recipients of Aid to Families with Dependent Children, as well as for low-income pregnant women and other individuals whose medical bills qualify them as medically needy. Most states also cover medical expenses for older U.S. citizens who are needy, as well as for individuals who are blind and disabled who receive assistance under the Supplemental Security Income Program. Coverage is further extended to some infants and low-income pregnant women and, depending on the state, to other low-income individuals with medical bills that qualify them as medically needy.

The mission of the HCFA is to promote the timely delivery of quality health care to Medicare and Medicaid beneficiaries and to ensure that the Medicare and Medicaid Programs are administered in an efficient manner. The agency must also ensure that program beneficiaries are aware of the services for which they are eligible, that those services are accessible and of high quality, and that agency policies and actions promote efficiency and quality within the total health care delivery system. A quality assurance program administered by the HCFA is responsible for developing health and safety standards for providers of health care services authorized by Medicare and Medicaid legislation. This program helps to ensure that Medicare and Medicaid beneficiaries receive quality health care services at a reasonable cost. Through Medicare and Medicaid, the HCFA serves 68 million older, disabled, and poor U.S. citizens, nearly a quarter of all U.S. citizens.

HEALTH CARE LAW Health care law involves many facets of U.S. law, including TORTS, CONTRACTS, antitrust, and insurance. In 1990 it was estimated that the United States spent over $500 billion on health care, which was more than 11 percent of the gross national product. The total annual expenditure on health care could double or even triple by the twenty-first century.

Medical Malpractice One major area within health care law is MEDICAL MALPRACTICE, which is professional misconduct or lack of skill in providing medical treatment or services. The victims of medical malpractice seek compensation for their physical or emotional injuries, or both, through a NEGLIGENCE action.

A defendant physician may be found liable for medical malpractice if the plaintiff patient can establish that there was in fact a patient-physician relationship; that the physician breached (violated or departed from) the accepted standard of medical care in the treatment of the patient; that the patient suffered an injury for which she should be compensated; and that the physician's violation of the standard of care was the cause of the injury.

To protect themselves against the huge costs of such claims, physicians commonly purchase malpractice INSURANCE. Physicians' malpractice PREMIUMS total billions of dollars each year and add substantially to the cost of health care in the United States. In some specialties, such as obstetrics, 50 percent of the cost for medical services goes for the provider's malpractice premiums. Many physicians, faced with the rising tide of malpractice premiums, practice "defensive medicine" by ordering tests and procedures that may not be necessary, so that the records will show that they did all they could. Several studies have estimated the cost of defensive tests and procedures at tens of billions of dollars.

Most states have enacted legislation modifying the COMMON-LAW action of medical malpractice, in an attempt to stem the rising tide of lawsuits. Restrictions on plaintiff patients include shorter STATUTES OF LIMITATIONS (times within which a lawsuit must be filed after injury) than provided for in common-law ACTIONS, and a required AFFIDAVIT from a physician expert witness, certifying that the applicable standard of care in the particular case was violated by the defendant physician and that the violation caused the plaintiff patient's injuries.

Medical malpractice liability can extend to hospitals and even to health maintenance organizations (HMOs). In the case of severe injuries, this can provide a plaintiff patient with an additional source of compensation. A complicating element is a historical doctrine disallowing the corporate practice of medicine—which in effect, and sometimes in actuality through statutes, prohibits the employment of physicians. In states that disallow the corporate practice of medicine, plaintiffs cannot bring medical malpractice claims against HMOs or hospitals based on a physician's treatment because the doctors are not considered employees.

Because every state prohibits the practice of medicine without a LICENSE, and because a corporate or business entity cannot get a license to practice medicine, the historical model provided that all physicians were independent contractors (separate economic entities), even in their role on the medical staff of a hospital. Without an explicit employer-employee relationship, the LIABILITY of a physician for malpractice most likely could not be imputed (passed along to) a hospital.

The legal theory of *respondeat superior* holds an employer liable for the negligent acts of an employee acting within the SCOPE OF EMPLOYMENT. Historically, since most physicians were not employees, this theory of liability was often defeated in medical malpractice suits. Today, however, most courts look beyond the title given to the relationship, to the control that the hospital or health care organization exerts over the physician in question, to determine whether the relationship is more like that of an employer and employee (e.g., where the processes and treatment decisions are tightly prescribed by the organization, and liability may be imputed) or is truly that of an INDEPENDENT CONTRACTOR and a client (e.g., where the physician acts alone to accomplish a particular end result, and liability may not be imputed).

The legal theory of ostensible AGENCY can also attach liability to a hospital or health care organization for an individual physician's malpractice. No employer-employee relationship needs to be shown here. OSTENSIBLE agency liability is created where the PRINCIPAL (the hospital or health care organization) represents or creates the appearance to third persons that the physician is an AGENT of the principal, subject to the principal's control. This theory focuses on the reasonable expectations and beliefs of the patient based on the conduct of the hospital or health care organization. The actual relationship of the physician and the hospital or organization is immaterial.

Physician Malpractice Records In the past it was very difficult for patients to discover malpractice information about their physicians. The federal government maintains the National Practitioners Data Bank, which lists doctors and malpractice claims in excess of $20,000, along with state disciplinary records. Its list is not made available to the public, but is provided to state medical boards, hospitals, and other organizations that grant credentials. Because of the great demand by patients for this information, many states are enacting legislation that makes it readily available. For example, Washington state provides access to physician information through several sources: insurance company claims records, which are required by law to be reported to the state; the National Practitioners Data Bank; and the state board of medicine, which administers physician licensing and discipline. Massachusetts created a similar system, called the Physician's Profiles Project, and other states, including Florida, California, and New York, are considering the same kind of initiative.

A Physician's Duty to Provide Medical Treatment Medical malpractice dominates the headlines, but a more basic legal question involving medical care is the affirmative duty, if any, to provide medical treatment. The historical rule is that a physician has no duty to accept a patient, regardless of the severity of the illness. A physician's relationship with a patient was understood to be a voluntary, contracted one. Once the relationship was established, the physician was under a legal obligation to provide medical treatment, and was a FIDUCIARY in this respect. (A fiduciary is a person having a duty to act primarily for the benefit of another.)

Once the physician-patient relationship exists, the physician can be held liable for an intentional refusal of care or treatment, under the theory of ABANDONMENT. (Abandonment is an intentional act; negligent lack of care or treatment is medical malpractice.) When a treatment relationship exists, the physician must provide all necessary treatment to a patient unless the relationship is ended by the patient, or by the physician provided that the physician gives the patient sufficient notice to seek another source of medical care. Most doctors and hospitals routinely ensure that alternative sources of treatment—other doctors or hospitals—are made available for patients whose care is being discontinued.

The discontinuation of care involves significant economic issues. Reimbursement procedures often limit or cut off the funding for a particular patient's care. Under the diagnosis-related group (DRG) system of MEDICARE, part A, 42 USC § 1395c, a hospital is paid a preset amount for the treatment of a particular diagnosis, regardless of the actual cost of treatment.

Health Care Coverage for Persons Under 65, 1994

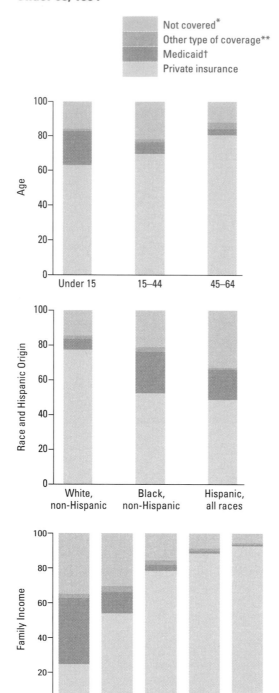

- Not covered*
- Other type of coverage**
- Medicaid†
- Private insurance

*Includes persons not covered by private insurance, Medicaid, Medicare, or military plans.

**For example, Medicare and military coverage

†Includes persons receiving AFDC and SSI or those with current Medicaid cards.

Source: U.S. Department of Health and Human Services, National Center for Health Statistics, *Health United States 1995.*

Patients covered by private insurance or HMOs may lose their coverage if they fail to pay premiums. Physicians and hospitals must act carefully when this happens, because the fiduciary nature of the relationship between provider and patient is not changed by a patient's unexpected inability to pay. Health care providers must notify a patient and even help secure alternative care when funds are not reimbursed as expected.

A Hospital's Duty to Provide Medical Treatment The historical rule for hospitals is that they must act reasonably in their decisions to treat patients. Hospitals must acknowledge that a common practice of providing treatment to all emergency patients creates among members of a community an expectation that care will be provided any time a person seeks care in an "unmistakable emergency." Seeking alternative care in a time-sensitive emergency situation could result in avoidable permanent injury or death, so it is not surprising that hospitals are held to a more flexible "reasonable duty" standard in their admission of patients for treatment.

Owing to the high cost of emergency room care, many private hospitals in the early 1980s began refusing to admit indigent patients and instead had them transferred to emergency rooms at municipal or county hospitals. This practice, called patient dumping, has since been prohibited by various state statutes, and also by Congress as part of the Consolidated Omnibus Budget Reconciliation Act of 1985 (Public Law No. 99-272), in a section titled Emergency Medical Treatment and Active Labor Act (EMTALA) (§ 9121(b), codified at 42 U.S.C.A. § 1395dd). Under EMTALA hospitals that receive federal assistance, maintain charitable nonprofit tax status, or participate in Medicare are prevented from denying emergency treatment based solely on an individual's inability to pay. EMTALA created private enforcement actions (lawsuits by individuals) and civil penalties (fines) for hospitals that violate its provisions. Patients who must receive medical treatment include people whose health is in "serious jeopardy" and pregnant women in active labor. The EMTALA duty to provide treatment can be relieved only if a patient is stabilized to the point where a transfer to another hospital will result in "no material deterioration of [his or her] condition."

Similar federal statutes require that hospitals treat all patients who do have the ability to pay. Federal law prohibits discrimination on the basis of race, color, or national origin, by any program that receives federal financial assistance (42 U.S.C.A. § 2000d). Almost all hospitals receive this kind of funding, and many derive half or more of their revenue from Medicare or MEDICAID. Section 504 of the Rehabilitation Act of 1973 (29 U.S.C.A. § 794) prohibits federally funded programs and activities (including hospitals that receive federal funds) from excluding any "otherwise handicapped individual . . . solely by reason of his handicap."

The broad definition of handicap is "physical or mental impairment that substantially limits one or more of a person's major life activities." This has been construed to include AIDS and asymptomatic HIV. Thus, hospitals receiving federal aid may not deny treatment to patients who are HIV-positive or who have AIDS. At the state level, similar legislation protects access to all state-licensed health care facilities and to the services of treating physicians.

Antitrust and Monopoly The same antitrust and monopoly laws that govern businesses and corporations apply to physicians, hospitals, and health care organizations.

Sherman Act The SHERMAN ANTI-TRUST ACT of 1890 (15 U.S.C.A. § 1) prohibits conspiracies in RESTRAINT OF TRADE that affect interstate commerce. Often physicians who are denied admittance to or are expelled from the medical staff of a hospital file a lawsuit in federal court, against the medical staff and the hospital, claiming violation of the Sherman Act.

To understand why this kind of federal action applies in this situation, one must first understand the unique relation of doctors to hospitals. Doctors generally do not work for a particular hospital, but instead enjoy staff, or "admitting," privileges at several hospitals. They are accepted for membership on a medical staff by the staff itself pursuant to its bylaws. The process of selecting and periodically reevaluating medical staff members (called credentialing or peer review) can result in a denial of admittance to or expulsion from the medical staff.

Physicians who are denied admittance to or expelled from a hospital's medical staff and file a claim of Sherman Act violation in FEDERAL COURT are essentially claiming that they are being illegally restrained from their trade (practicing medicine). It is the unique relation between doctors and hospitals, described earlier, that satisfies the first element of a Sherman Act violation, which is that a CONSPIRACY must exist. Normally, a single business cannot conspire with itself to restrain trade—a conspiracy requires a concerted, or joint, effort between two or more entities. Because physicians, as independent contractors, constitute individual economic entities, when they vote as a medical staff to admit or expel a physician, they are acting in the concerted, or joint, fashion described by the statute.

The second element of a Sherman Act violation is that a restraint of trade must occur. One rule states that any restraint of trade, especially in the commercial arena, can be viewed as PER SE (inherently) illegal. However, courts have often resorted to comparative analysis to balance the pro-competitive versus anticompetitive effects of a medical staff's decision. For example, if a physician has a history of incompetent or unethical behavior, then a denial of medical staff privileges can be independently justified. On the other hand, if there is only one hospital in a small town, and the physician in question meets all qualifications for ETHICS and competence, a denial of medical staff privileges may well constitute illegal restraint of trade.

The final element of a Sherman Act violation, that the action must substantially affect interstate commerce, is a jurisdictional requirement, which means that if it is not satisfied, the federal court has no JURISDICTION to hear the dispute and the Sherman Act does not apply. Courts are split as to whether a medical staff's decision to admit or deny medical staff privileges satisfies this element. Some courts view the practice of a single physician to have a minimal, as opposed to the required substantial, effect on interstate commerce, and hold that the jurisdictional element is not met. Other courts focus on the activity of the entire hospital (receipt of federal funds, purchase of equipment from other states, reimbursement from national insurance companies, and so on), and find that the jurisdictional element is met.

Challenged medical staffs and hospitals often raise the "state-action" exemption, which exempts from federal ANTITRUST LAW activities required by state law or regulations. Many states mandate the peer review process even at private hospitals, but for an exemption based on this mandate to negate a finding of a Sherman Act violation, the state must closely supervise the process.

Clayton Act Section 7 of the Clayton Anti-Trust Act of 1914 (15 U.S.C.A. § 18) prohibits mergers if they "lessen competition or tend to create a monopoly." To be valid a merger must not give a few large firms total control of a particular market, because of the risks of PRICE-FIXING and other forms of illegal COLLUSION.

Market share statistics control merger analysis, and these statistics are based on a "relevant market." The CLAYTON ACT can prohibit a national hospital management company from purchasing several hospitals in one town, and sometimes even joint ventures between hospitals and physicians or even between formerly competing groups of practicing physicians.

Several exceptions apply to these prohibitions. If a hospital is on the verge of BANKRUPTCY and certain closure, but for the merger, then the merger will be allowed. Nonprofit hospitals long enjoyed complete exemption from section 7 of the Clayton Act, but now federal district courts are split on whether the act applies to nonprofit hospitals. In any case a careful market analysis that shows that particular relevant markets do not overlap—and hence do not lessen competition or create a monopoly—can be used as evidence to uphold a merger decision between two or more health care entities.

Health Care Insurance A trend toward "managed care" and away from "fee-for-service" medicine has been sparked by significant changes in the HEALTH INSURANCE industry. Health care insurance originated in the 1930s with Blue Cross (hospitalization coverage) and Blue Shield (physician services coverage). It has traditionally stayed out of the provision of health care services and has served as a third party indemnitor for health care expenses. That is, in exchange for the payment of a monthly premium, a health care insurance company agrees to INDEMNIFY, or be responsible for, its insured's health care costs pursuant to the specific provisions in the health insurance policy purchased.

Skyrocketing costs in health care spurred public and private reform. The federal Medicare Program introduced diagnosis-related-groups (DRGs) in 1983, which for the first time set predetermined limits on the amounts Medicare would pay to hospitals for patients with a particular diagnosis. Employers seeking lower health care costs for employees have increasingly chosen managed care options like HMOs and preferred provider organizations (PPOs), both of which use cooperation and joint efforts between patients, care providers, and payers to manage health care delivery so as to reduce costs by eliminating administrative inefficiency as well as unnecessary medical treatment.

Health care law will continue to be affected by the country's move toward managed care as the predominant health care delivery model. For example, HMOs' potential liability for medical malpractice could increase because many HMOs operate on a "staff model" whereby physicians are explicitly hired as "employees," making it easier to demonstrate *respondeat superior* liability for the negligent acts of their physicians. In addition, many HMOs exercise greater control over the discretion of individual physicians with regard not only to primary care but also to specialist referrals and the prescribing of certain drugs. The historical bright line forbidding the corporate practice of medicine is thus blurred even further by managed care.

HMOs operate on a prepaid basis, making monthly capitation (per patient) payments to participating physicians and physician groups. PPOs operate on a reduced-fee schedule, offering lower fees for patients who seek care from a "preferred provider," who functions both as a primary care doctor and as a gatekeeper for specialist referrals and so forth. Both use "networks" of physicians and care providers. The standard duty to provide medical care applies to physicians in these networks, but new issues arise regarding the payment or reimbursement of expenses. Some managed care plans offer limited "out-of-network" benefits, some offer none at all. Should an employer change health plans, an employee with an established physician-patient relationship may find that the treating physician is not part of the new provider's network. If the patient cannot or will not cover subsequent medical costs independently, who has the responsibility to secure alternative treatment for the patient? Who should pay for that treatment? These questions have not yet

U.S. Health Expenditures, 1960 to1994

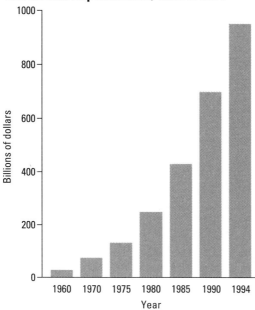

Source: Office of National Health Statistics.

been resolved. Many patients in this situation start over again with a new physician out of economic necessity, and many are not happy about that involuntary termination of the physician-patient relationship.

Another potential issue for physician networks and "integrated delivery systems" (which include primary care physicians, specialists, and hospitals) is price-fixing, which has traditionally been held to be per se illegal under the Sherman Act. PPOs are under particular scrutiny in this regard, since a PPO is a group of health care providers who agree to discounted fees in exchange for bulk business (e.g., medical care for all of a particular company's employees). These providers are individual economic entities and as such must exercise great care in the concerted, joint effort of setting prices and fees, to avoid accusations of conspiracy to restrain trade through illegal price-fixing. Likewise, integrated delivery systems must be ever mindful of Clayton Act prohibitions against monopolies, and must carefully tailor their joint ventures and other agreements to minimize their anti-competitive effects on relevant markets.

CROSS-REFERENCES

Abortion; Acquired Immune Deficiency Syndrome; Animal Rights; Death and Dying; Drugs and Narcotics; Fetal Rights; Fetal Tissue Research; Food and Drug Administration; Physicians and Surgeons.

HEALTH INSURANCE Health insurance originated in the Blue Cross system developed between hospitals and schoolteachers in Dallas in 1929. Blue Cross covered a preset amount of hospitalization costs for a flat monthly premium, and set its rates according to a "community rating" system: single people paid one flat rate, families another flat rate, and the economic risk of high hospitalization bills was spread throughout the whole employee group. The only requirement for participation by an employer was that all employees, whether sick or healthy, had to join, again spreading the risk over the whole group. Blue Shield was developed following the same plan to cover ambulatory (nonhospital) medical care.

The Blue Cross/Blue Shield plans were developed to complement the traditional method of paying for health care, often called fee for service. Under this method a physician charges a patient directly for services rendered, and the patient is legally responsible for payment. The Blue Cross/Blue Shield plans are called INDEMNITY plans, meaning they reimburse the patient for medical expenses incurred. Indemnity insurers are not responsible directly to physicians for payment, although physicians typically submit

claims information to the insurers as a convenience for their patients. For insured patients in the fee-for-service system, two CONTRACTS are created, one between the doctor and the patient and one between the patient and the INSURANCE company.

Traditional property and casualty insurance companies had not offered health insurance because with traditional rate structures, the risks were great and the return uncertain. After the Blue Cross/Blue Shield plans were developed, however, the traditional insurers noted the community rating practices and realized that they could enter the market and attract the healthier community members with lower rates than the community rates. By introducing health screening to identify the healthier individuals, and offering lower rates to younger individuals, these companies were able to lure lower-risk populations to their health plans. This left the Blue Cross/Blue Shield plans with the highest-risk and costliest population to insure. Eventually the Blue Cross/Blue Shield plans also began using risk-segregation policies, and charged higher-risk groups more expensive PREMIUMS.

In the 1960s Congress enacted the MEDICARE program to cover health care costs of older patients and MEDICAID to cover health care costs of indigent patients (Pub. L. No. 81-97). The federal government administers the Medicare Program and its components: part A, which covers hospitalization, and part B, which covers physician and outpatient services. The federal government helps the states fund the Medicaid Program, and the states administer it. Medicare, part A, initially covered 100 percent of hospitalization costs, and Medicare, part B, covered 80 percent of the usual, customary, and reasonable costs of physician and outpatient care.

Under both the fee-for-service system of health care delivery where private indemnity insurers charge premiums and pay the bills, and the Medicare-Medicaid system where taxes fund the programs and the government pays the bills, the relationship between the patient and the doctor remains distinct. Neither the doctor nor the patient is concerned about the cost of various medical procedures involved, and fees for services are paid without significant oversight by the payers. In fact, if more services are performed by a physician under a fee-for-service system, the result is greater total fees.

From 1960 to 1990, per capita medical costs in the United States rose 1,000 percent, which was four times the rate of inflation. As a consequence a different way of paying for health care rose to prominence. "Managed care," which had been in existence as long as indemnity health insurance plans, became the health plan of choice among U.S. employers seeking to reduce the premiums paid for their employees' health care.

Managed care essentially creates a triangular relationship between the physician, patient (or member), and payer. Managed care refers primarily to a prepaid health services plan where physicians (or physician groups or other entities) are paid a flat per-member per-month (PMPM) fee for basic health care services, regardless of whether the patient seeks those services. The risk that a patient is going to require significant treatment shifts from the insurance company to the physicians under this model.

Managed care is a highly regulated industry. It is regulated on the federal level by the Health Maintenance Organization Act of 1973 (Pub. L. No. 93-222) and by the states in which it operates. The health maintenance organization (HMO) is the primary provider of managed care, and it does so in four basic models:

- The staff model HMO employs physicians and providers directly, and they provide services in facilities owned or controlled by the HMO. Physicians under this model are paid a salary (not fees for service) and share equipment and facilities with other physician-employees.
- The group model HMO contracts with an organized group of physicians who are not direct employees of the HMO, but who agree to provide basic health care services to the HMO's members in exchange for capitation (that is, PMPM) payments. The capitation payments must be spread among the physicians under a predetermined arrangement, and medical records and equipment must be shared.
- The individual practice association (IPA) model HMO is based around an association of individual practitioners who organize to contract with an HMO, and as a result treat the HMO's patients on a discounted fee-for-service basis. Although there is no periodic limit on the amount of payments from the HMO, the physicians in an IPA must have an explicit agreement that determines the distribution of HMO receipts and also sets forth the services to be performed.
- The direct-service contract/network HMO model is the most basic model. Under it an HMO contracts directly with individual providers to provide service to the HMO's patients, on either a capitated or discounted fee-for-service basis.

All four of these models share one very important feature of HMOs: the health care providers may not bill patients directly for services rendered, and must seek any and all reimbursement from the HMO.

Another form of managed care is the preferred provider organization (PPO). A PPO does not take the place of the traditional fee-for-service provider (as does a staff model HMO), and does not rely on capitated payments to providers. Instead a PPO contracts with individual providers and groups to create a network of providers. Members of a PPO can choose any physician they wish for medical care, but if they choose a provider in the PPO network, their co-payments—predetermined fixed amounts paid per visit, regardless of treatment received—are significantly reduced, providing the incentive to stay in the network. No federal statutes govern PPOs, but many states do regulate their operations. There are three basic PPO models:

- In the gatekeeper plan, a patient must choose a primary care provider from the PPO network. This primary care provider handles most of the patient's health care needs, and must authorize any referrals to specialists or other providers. If the patient "self-refers" without authorization, the cost savings of the PPO will not apply.
- The open panel plan, on the other hand, allows a patient to see different primary care physicians and to self-refer within the PPO network. The financial penalties for seeking medical care out of the PPO network are much greater in this less-structured model than in the gatekeeper model.
- The exclusive provider plan shifts onto the patient all the costs of seeking medical care from a nonnetwork provider, and in this respect is very similar to an HMO plan.

Other forms of health care delivery that encompass features of managed care include point-of-service (POS) plans and physician-hospital organizations (PHOs). A POS plan is a combination of an HMO and an indemnity insurance plan, allowing full coverage within the network of providers and partial coverage outside the network. A patient must choose one primary care physician, and may pay a higher monthly rate to the POS if the physician is not in the HMO network. Another version of the POS plan creates "tiers" of providers, which are rated by cost-effectiveness and quality of patient outcomes. A patient may choose a provider from any tier, and then will owe a monthly premium payment set to the level of that tier.

A PHO is very similar to an IPA, in that it is an organization between various physicians (or physician groups) and a hospital, set up to contract as a unit with an HMO. Physician-hospital networks, within HMOs or through PHO contracts, further the managed care mission of "vertical integration," which is the co-ordination of health care (and payment for that care) from primary care through specialists to acute care and hospitalization.

Managed care has affected Medicare as well as private health care. In 1983 Congress changed the payment system for Medicare, part A, from a fee-for-service-paid-retroactively system to a prospective payment system, which fixes the amount that the federal government will pay based on a patient's initial diagnosis, not on the costs actually expended (Pub. L. No. 98-369). Medical diagnoses are grouped according to the medical resources usually consumed to treat them, and from that grouping is determined a fixed amount that will be paid by Medicare for each diagnosis. Although this system is applicable only to the acute-care hospital setting, it is clearly an example of shifting the risk of the cost of health care from the payer (in this case Medicare) to the provider, which is an important element of managed care. In addition, many HMOs are now offering Medicare managed care plans, and many older citizens are opting for these plans because of their paperless claims and preset co-payments for physician visits and pharmaceuticals.

The most recent development in the area of health insurance is the medical savings account (MSA), a pilot program that was created by the Health Insurance Portability and Accountability Act of 1996 (Pub. L. No. 104-191). The premise behind the MSA is to take the bulk of the financial risk, and premium payments, away from the managed care and indemnity insurers, and allow individuals to save money, tax free, in a savings account for use for medical expenses. Individuals or their employers purchase major-medical policies, medical insurance policies with no coverage for medical expenses until the amount paid by the patient exceeds a predeter-mined maximum amount, such as $2500 per year. These policies have extremely high de-ductibles and correspondingly low monthly premiums, and the participants take the money that they would have spent on higher premiums and deposit it in an MSA. This money accrues through monthly deposits and also earns inter-est, and can be spent only to pay for medical care. The major-medical policy kicks in if a certain amount equal to the high deductible is expended or if the account is depleted. MSAs do not incorporate any of the cost-controlling aspects of managed care organizations, and in-stead depend on competition between providers for patients (who are generally more cost-conscious about spending their own money) to encourage efficient health care delivery and discourage unnecessary expense.

See also HEALTH CARE LAW; PHYSICIANS AND SURGEONS.

HEARING 📖 A legal proceeding where an is-sue of law or fact is tried and EVIDENCE is presented to help determine the issue. 📖

Hearings resemble TRIALS in that they ordi-narily are held publicly and involve opposing PARTIES. They differ from trials in that they feature more relaxed standards of evidence and procedure, and take place in a variety of settings before a broader range of authorities (judges, examiners, and lawmakers). Hearings fall into three broad categories: judicial, administrative, and legislative. Judicial hearings are tailored to suit the issue at hand and the appropriate stage at which a legal proceeding stands. Administra-tive hearings cover matters of rule making and the adjudication of individual cases. Legislative hearings occur at both the federal and state levels and are generally conducted to find facts and survey public opinion. They encompass a wide range of issues relevant to law, govern-ment, society, and public policy.

Judicial hearings take place prior to a trial in both civil and criminal cases. EX PARTE hearings provide a forum for only one side of a dispute, as in the case of a TEMPORARY RESTRAINING ORDER, whereas adversary hearings involve both par-ties. PRELIMINARY HEARINGS, also called prelimi-nary examinations, are conducted when a per-son has been charged with a crime. Held before a MAGISTRATE or judge, a preliminary hearing is used to determine whether the evidence is suf-ficient to justify detaining the ACCUSED or dis-charging the accused on BAIL. Closely related are detention hearings, which can also deter-mine whether to detain a juvenile. Suppression hearings take place before trial at the request of an attorney seeking to have illegally obtained or irrelevant evidence kept out of trial.

Administrative hearings are conducted by state and federal AGENCIES. Rule-making hear-ings evaluate and determine appropriate regu-lations, and adjudicatory hearings try matters of fact in individual cases. The former are com-monly used to garner opinion on matters that affect the public—as, for example, when the Environmental Protection Agency (EPA) con-siders changing its rules. The latter commonly take place when an individual is charged with violating rules that come under the agency's

The U.S. Senate Armed Services Committee held hearings on gays in the military in order to gather information and let both sides air their views before the committee recommended new legislation.

jurisdiction—for example, violating a pollution regulation of the EPA, or, if incarcerated, violating behavior standards set for prisoners by the Department of Corrections.

Some blurring of this distinction occurs, which is important given the generally more relaxed standards that apply to some administrative hearings. The degree of formality required of an administrative hearing is determined by the liberty interest at stake: the greater that interest, the more formal the hearing. Notably, rules limiting the admissibility of evidence are looser in administrative hearings than in trials. Adjudicatory hearings can admit, for example, HEARSAY that generally would not be permitted at trial. (Hearsay is a statement by a witness who does not appear in person, offered by a third party who does appear.) The Administrative Procedure Act (APA) (5 U.S.C.A. § 551 et seq.) governs administrative hearings by federal agencies, and state laws largely modeled upon the APA govern state agencies. These hearings are conducted by a civil servant called a HEARING EXAMINER at the state level and known as an administrative law judge at the federal level.

Legislative hearings occur in state legislatures and in the U.S. Congress, and are a function of legislative committees. They are commonly public events, held whenever a lawmaking body is contemplating a change in law, during which advocates and opponents air their views. Because of their controversial nature, they often are covered extensively by the media.

Not all legislative hearings consider changes in legislation; some examine allegations of wrongdoing. Although lawmaking bodies do not have a judicial function, they retain the power to discipline their members, a key function of state and federal ethics committees. Fact finding is ostensibly the reason for congressional hearings into public scandals. Often, however, critics will argue that these hearings are staged for attacking political opponents. Throughout the twentieth century, legislative hearings have been used to investigate such things as allegations of Communist infiltration of government and industry (the House Un-American Activities Committee hearings) and abuses of power by the EXECUTIVE BRANCH (the Watergate and Whitewater hearings).

See also ADMINISTRATIVE LAW AND PROCEDURE.

HEARING EXAMINER ◫ An employee of an ADMINISTRATIVE AGENCY who is charged with conducting adjudicative proceedings on matters within the scope of the JURISDICTION of the agency. ◫

Hearing examiners are employees of federal, state, and local administrative agencies who act as judges to resolve conflicts that are within the jurisdiction of their particular agency. Hearing examiners have also been called hearing officers, and since the 1980s, they are commonly referred to as administrative law judges (ALJs).

The growth of administrative law started with the creation of the federal INTERSTATE COMMERCE COMMISSION and the Federal Trade Commission in the late nineteenth century.

Administrative law burgeoned in the 1930s, as President FRANKLIN D. ROOSEVELT's New Deal policies led to the establishment of executive branch agencies that were charged with regulating the economy and overseeing social welfare policies. Since the 1930s, all levels of government have established administrative agencies.

ALJs are governed by the Administrative Procedure Act (5 U.S.C.A. § 551 et seq. [1966]). They are appointed through a professional merit selection system that requires high test scores and, in many instances, experience in the particular regulatory program in which they wish to serve. Once appointed, ALJs may not be removed or disciplined, except for GOOD CAUSE. These parameters are meant to shield administrative law from political appointments and political pressure.

Hearing examiners serve in different adjudicative areas and are involved in all types of government activity, from the administration of environmental regulations to the review of unemployment compensation claims. For example, when an agency is charged with issuing permits, appropriate procedures are set out in administrative regulations. If there are objections to the granting of a permit, a HEARING may be held to determine the merits of the application. A hearing examiner conducts the hearing, enforces appropriate rules of EVIDENCE and procedure, and issues a decision. This decision may be appealed to a higher level of authority in the agency, and if that does not resolve the issue, to a court proceeding in the judicial branch.

Even though they are not as insulated from political pressures as judicial branch judges, hearing examiners seek to maintain their independence. During the Reagan administration, in the 1980s, this independence was challenged in the Social Security Administration's (SSA's) disability review section. SSA officials, concerned with perceived inconsistencies and inaccuracies in disability rulings, singled out for review federal ALJs who rendered the highest percentage of decisions favorable to claimants. The review program received much criticism for allegedly putting subtle pressure on the ALJs to rule against claimants more often. Though the most intrusive features of the program were abandoned, the program itself served as a reminder that ALJs were part of an administrative agency and not independent, judicial branch decision makers.

HEARSAY 📖 A statement made out of court that is offered in court as EVIDENCE to prove the truth of the matter asserted. 📖

It is the job of the judge or JURY in a court proceeding to determine whether evidence offered as proof is credible. Three evidentiary rules help the judge or jury make this determination: (1) Before being allowed to TESTIFY, a WITNESS generally must swear or affirm that his or her TESTIMONY will be truthful. (2) The witness must be personally present at the trial or proceeding in order to allow the judge or jury to observe the testimony firsthand. (3) The witness is subject to CROSS-EXAMINATION at the option of any party who did not call the witness to testify.

Hearsay involves a statement that is oral or written or consists of gestures. Essentially anything intended to assert a fact is considered a statement for the purposes of the hearsay rule. A nodding of the head may be a silent assertion of the word *yes*. A witness pointing to a gun may be asserting, "That is the murder weapon." Even silence has been accepted as a statement, as when the passengers' failure to complain was offered to prove that a train car was not too cold (*Silver v. New York Central Railroad*, 329 Mass. 14, 105 N.E.2d 923 [1952]).

In keeping with its three evidentiary requirements, the rule against hearsay prohibits most statements made outside a courtroom from being used as evidence in court. This is because statements made out of court normally are not made under OATH, a judge or jury cannot personally observe the demeanor of someone who makes a statement outside the courtroom, and an opposing party cannot cross-examine such a declarant. Out-of-court statements hinder the ability of the judge or jury to probe testimony for inaccuracies caused by ambiguity, insincerity, faulty perception, or erroneous memory.

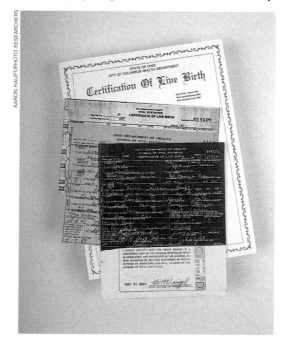

AARON HAUPT/PHOTO RESEARCHERS

Records of vital statistics, such as birth certificates, are considered admissible hearsay in a court proceeding.

Thus, statements made out of court are perceived as untrustworthy.

But not all out-of-court statements or assertions are impermissible hearsay. If an attorney wishes the judge or jury to consider the fact that a certain statement was made, but not the truthfulness of that statement, the statement is not hearsay and may be admitted as evidence. Suppose a hearing is held to determine a woman's mental competence. Out of court, when asked to identify herself, the woman said, "I am the pope." There is little question that the purpose of introducing that statement as evidence is not to convince the judge or jury that the woman actually is the pope; the truthfulness of the statement is irrelevant. Rather, the statement is introduced to show the woman's mental state; her belief that she is the pope may prove that she is not mentally competent. On the other hand, a defendant's out-of-court statement "I am the murderer," offered in a murder trial to prove that the defendant is the murderer, is hearsay.

Federal and state rules of evidence generally prohibit the admissibility of hearsay but make exceptions for certain categories of statements that inherently contain sufficient guarantees of trustworthiness. Some hearsay exceptions are not based on whether the declarant of the statement is available to testify; others apply only if it can be shown that the declarant is unavailable to testify. A witness who has died is unavailable. A witness who claims some sort of testimonial privilege, such as the ATTORNEY-CLIENT PRIVILEGE, is also unavailable to testify for purposes of these exceptions, as is the witness who refuses to testify despite a judge's order, testifies to lack of memory regarding the subject matter, or is too physically or mentally ill to testify.

Hearsay Exceptions When the Declarant's Availability Is Immaterial

1. **Present Sense Impressions.** "A statement describing or explaining an event or condition made while the declarant was perceiving the event or condition, or immediately thereafter," is ADMISSIBLE hearsay (Fed. R. Evid. 803(1)). An example is the statement "That green pickup truck is going to run that red light."

2. **Excited Utterance.** "A statement relating to a startling event or condition made while the declarant was under the stress of excitement caused by the event or condition" is admissible hearsay (Fed. R. Evid. 803(2)). For example, "The robber is pointing a gun at the cop!" is admissible.

3. **A Statement Describing a Then Existing Mental, Emotional, or Physical Condition.** A statement of the declarant's then existing intent, plan, motive, design, mental feeling, pain, or bodily health is admissible, but generally a statement of memory or belief to prove the fact remembered or believed is not. For example, "After eating at that restaurant, I'm feeling rather ill" could be admitted under this exception. But the out-of-court statement "I believe Julie to be the murderer" would not be admitted under this exception.

4. **A Statement Made for Purposes of Medical Diagnosis or Treatment.** A statement describing medical history, or past or present symptoms, pain, or sensations, or the general character of the cause or external source of those symptoms, is admissible. For example, this statement made to a physician following an accident is admissible: "I slipped and fell on the ice, and then my left leg became numb."

5. **A Recorded Recollection.** "A memorandum or record concerning a matter about which a witness once had knowledge but now has insufficient recollection to enable the witness to testify fully and accurately" is admissible (Fed. R. Evid. 803(5)). The record must have been made when the matter was fresh in the witness's memory and must reflect that knowledge correctly. One example is a detailed phone message.

6. **A Record of Regularly Conducted Activity.** A record, report, or memo of regularly conducted business activities is exempt from the hearsay prohibition under this rule. Written minutes of a business meeting are a common example. The absence of information normally contained in these types of records may also be excluded from the hearsay prohibition (Fed. R. Evid. 803(6)).

7. **A Public Record or Report.** A record, report, statement, or data compilation, in any form, of a public office or agency, setting forth the activities of the office or agency or matters for which there is a legal duty to report, is admissible. Voting records of a city council are an example. Matters observed by law enforcement personnel in criminal cases are excluded under this rule (Fed. R. Evid. 803(6)).

8. **A Record of a Vital Statistic.** A data compilation, in any form, of births, fetal deaths, other deaths, or marriages, if the report is made to a public office pursuant to

Nicole Brown Simpson's Journals: Inadmissible as Hearsay

During the 1995 criminal trial of O. J. Simpson, the prosecution argued that Simpson killed his former wife Nicole Brown Simpson, and that the murder was the culmination of a long pattern of domestic violence. The prosecution discovered in a safe-deposit box journals that Brown Simpson had written concerning her problems with Simpson. The journals contained graphic language and described episodes of physical violence and threats committed by Simpson. They appeared to be a powerful demonstration of the couple's relationship, yet they were never entered into evidence at the criminal trial, and Simpson was acquitted in the killings of his former wife and her friend Ronald Lyle Goldman.

The journals were inadmissible because they constituted hearsay evidence. The rules of evidence are generally the same in every state and federal jurisdiction. In California, where Simpson's criminal trial was held, hearsay evidence cannot be admitted unless it meets the requirements of a well-defined exception.

Oral hearsay (what one person tells another about a third person) is the same as written hearsay. In her journal Brown Simpson told readers what Simpson did to her. With her death, there was no way for the defense to challenge her memory, perception, and sincerity about what she had written. The rules of evidence view such nonchallengeable out-of-court statements as unreliable when they are intended to prove the truth of the matter they assert—here, that Simpson had beaten Brown Simpson, stalked her, and made her fear for her life.

For the same reasons, the journals were not admitted at Simpson's civil trial in 1997, in which he was found liable for the wrongful deaths of Brown Simpson and Goldman.

See also Simpson, O. J.

---

requirements of the law, is a hearsay exception (Fed. R. Evid. 803(9)).

9. **A Record of a Religious Organization.** A statement contained in a regularly kept record of a religious organization may be exempt from the prohibition against hearsay. Some examples are statements of birth, marriage, divorce, death, legitimacy, ancestry, relationship by blood or marriage, or similar facts of personal or family history (Fed. R. Evid. 803(11)).

10. **A Marriage, Baptismal, or Similar Certificate.** "Statements of fact contained in a certificate that the maker performed a marriage or other ceremony or administered a sacrament, made by a clergyman, public official, or other person authorized by the rules or practices of a religious organization or by law to perform the act certified, and purporting to have been issued at the time of the act or within a reasonable time thereafter," are admissible (Fed. R. Evid. 803(12)).

11. **A Family Record.** "Statements of fact concerning personal or family history contained in family Bibles, genealogies, charts, engravings on rings, inscriptions on family portraits, engravings on urns, crypts, or tombstones" are hearsay exceptions (Fed. R. Evid. 803(13)).

12. **A Record of Documents Affecting an Interest in Property.** A record purporting to establish or affect an interest in property, such as a notice of a tax LIEN placed on a house, is admissible hearsay if the record is a record of a public office and an applicable statute authorizes the recording of documents of that kind in that office.

13. **A Statement in an Ancient Document.** A statement in a document in existence twenty years or more, the authenticity of which is established, is admissible hearsay. One example is a statement in a letter written thirty years ago, provided the letter's authenticity can be proved.

14. **A Market Report or Other Commercial Publication.** "Market quotations, tabulations, lists, directories, or other published compilations, generally used and relied upon by the public or by persons in particular occupations," are exceptions to the rule against hearsay (Fed. R. Evid. 803(17)).

15. **A Learned Treatise.** Statements contained in a published treatise, periodical, or pamphlet on a subject of history, medicine, or other science or art, established as a reliable authority by the testimony or admission of an expert witness, are admissible (Fed. R. Evid. 803(18)).

16. **Reputation Concerning Personal or Family History.** A reputation among members of a person's family by blood, adoption, or marriage, or among a person's associates, or in the community, concerning the person's birth, adoption, marriage, divorce, death, ancestry, or legitimacy is an exception to the rule against hearsay. For example, the out-of-court statement "My sister was adopted," although hearsay, is admissible (Fed. R. Evid. 803 (19)).

17. **Reputation Concerning Boundaries or General History.** "Reputation in a community, arising before the controversy, as to boundaries of or customs affecting lands in the community, and reputation as to events of general history important to the community or state or nation in which located," are admissible (Fed. R. Evid. 803(20)). For example, "Stein's land extends south to the river" involves the reputation of a land's boundary and falls within this exception.

18. **Reputation as to Character.** The "reputation of a person's character among associates or in the community" is admissible hearsay (Fed. R. Evid. 803(21)). One example is the statement "Sergei has never said a dishonest word."

19. **A Judgment of a Previous Conviction.** A plea or judgment of guilt for a crime punishable by death or imprisonment of more than one year is admissible hearsay (Fed. R. Evid. 803(22)).

Hearsay Exceptions When the Declarant Is Unavailable to Testify

1. **Former Testimony.** Testimony given as a witness at another hearing in the same or a different proceeding, or in a DEPOSITION, is admissible when the declarant is unavailable, provided the party against whom the testimony is now being offered had the opportunity to question or cross-examine the witness (Fed. R. Evid. 804(1)).

2. **A Statement Made Under the Belief of Impending Death.** A statement made by a declarant who, when making the statement, believed death to be imminent, is admissible to show the cause or circumstances of the death. For example, the statement "Horace shot me," made moments before the declarant died, is admissible for the purpose of proving that Horace committed murder (Fed. R. Evid. 804(2)).

3. **A Statement Against the Declarant's Interest.** A statement that, at the time of its making, was contrary to the declarant's pecuniary or proprietary interest, or that subjected the declarant to civil or criminal liability, is admissible if the declarant is unavailable to testify. For example, the statement "I never declare all my income on my tax returns" could subject the declarant to criminal tax fraud liability, and is thus an admissible statement against interest (Fed. R. Evid. 804(3)).

4. **A Statement of Personal or Family History.** A statement concerning the declarant's own birth, adoption, marriage, divorce, legitimacy, or similar fact of personal family history is admissible hearsay when the declarant is unavailable to testify (Fed. R. Evid. 804(4)).

HEARST, PATTY In the 1990s, she could be seen in John Waters's motion picture *Crybaby*, and heard as an offscreen caller to a radio talk show on the TV series *Frasier*. She had appeared on the runways of Paris as a fashion model, wearing a sequined evening gown designed by friend Thierry Mugler. Her story had been told as a movie, *Patty Hearst*, in which she was played by Natasha Richardson, and even as an opera, Anthony Davis's *Tania*. Ever since the 1970s, Patricia Campbell Hearst has been very much in the public eye.

On February 4, 1974, Hearst, the nineteen-year-old daughter of Randolph A. Hearst and Catherine C. Hearst, of the Hearst newspaper chain, was kidnapped by a tiny group of political extremists who called themselves the Symbionese Liberation Army (SLA). They locked Hearst in a closet for many weeks, where she was taunted, sexually assaulted, and raped repeatedly. The SLA held her for an unusual form of ransom: they demanded that the Hearst family distribute millions of dollars of food to poor and needy people of the San Francisco Bay area. Although the Hearsts complied with this and other SLA demands, the young woman did not return to her parents. Instead, she sent them a tape recording in which she announced that she had decided to become a revolutionary, join the SLA, and go underground.

On April 15, 1974, the members of the SLA, accompanied by Hearst, robbed the Hibernia Bank in San Francisco. A month later, a botched shoplifting attempt at a sporting goods store by SLA members Bill Harris and Emily Harris led the police to the SLA hideout. A gunfight ensued, and all six SLA members inside at the time were killed. Only Hearst, the Harrises, and Wendy Yoshimura survived.

Sixteen months later, and eighteen months after her abduction, Hearst was arrested by the FEDERAL BUREAU OF INVESTIGATION after an investigation that had covered the entire United

Patty Hearst assisted the Symbionese Liberation Army (SLA) in a bank robbery in 1974. When the SLA was later captured and Hearst was freed from her kidnappers, she claimed she had been brainwashed and had not participated in the robbery voluntarily.

States. She was tried by jury for armed bank robbery, convicted, and sentenced to seven years in prison. On February 1, 1979, after Hearst had served approximately two years of the original sentence, President JIMMY CARTER, stopping short of a full PARDON, commuted her sentence.

Hearst claimed at her 1976 federal trial for armed bank robbery that she had, in fact, undergone no political conversion. She claimed that even as she stood in the Hibernia Bank cradling a rifle in her arms, she remained the same person who, only a few months earlier, had chosen the china and crystal patterns for her upcoming marriage. Her defense, orchestrated by her attorneys, F. LEE BAILEY and Albert Johnson, was that she had been brainwashed. This defense did not exist in law and had only been attempted in "collaboration-with-the-enemy" charges against U.S. prisoners of war during the Korean War. As in the Korean War cases, the Hearst attorneys were forced to add a defense that was allowed by law: DURESS. The crux of the defense's case was that Hearst, owing to brainwashing or COERCION, had not had criminal intent when she participated in the bank robbery.

Three defense psychiatrists testified that the defendant had not been responsible for her actions; two prosecution psychiatrists testified that she had been responsible. The young woman testified that she had been in fear of her life as she stood inside the Hibernia Bank. The judge instructed the jurors,

> You are free to accept or reject the defendant's own account of her experience with her captors. . . . Duress or coercion may provide a legal excuse for the crime charged against her. But a compulsion must be present and immediate . . . a well-founded fear of death or bodily injury with no possible escape from the compulsion.

The jury found her guilty BEYOND A REASONABLE DOUBT, thereby implicitly stating its belief that she had acted intentionally and voluntarily in robbing the Hibernia Bank; she had been neither brainwashed nor forced to participate.

In August 1987 Hearst filed a PETITION for a pardon before President RONALD REAGAN. Her attorney, George Martinez, stated that "she wants to put it all behind her. And she wants to get some indication that there is now complete understanding by the government of the extraordinary circumstances under which she participated" in the Hibernia Bank robbery. In 1977, as governor of California, Reagan had called for executive CLEMENCY for Hearst; he was thus considered Hearst's best chance for a pardon. But Reagan left office in 1988 without granting the pardon. Hearst's petition then fell to GEORGE BUSH, who also failed to grant the pardon.

In 1996, Hearst, now forty-one, was a member of the Screen Actors Guild and lived just fifty miles outside of Manhattan with her husband and former bodyguard, Bernard Shaw, and her two children. Her petition for pardon is still pending and is now before the Clinton administration.

HEART BALM ACTS Statutes that abrogate or restrict lawsuits brought by individuals who seek pecuniary DAMAGES to salve their broken hearts.

Heart balm actions are founded on the precept that the law disfavors any intrusion with the marital relationship or family ties. Such suits include actions for BREACH OF MARRIAGE PROMISE, ALIENATION OF AFFECTION, CRIMINAL CONVERSATION, and SEDUCTION.

Breach of Marriage Promise Breach of promise actions are based on the theory that a promise made should be kept. A subscription to this principle, however, defeats the purpose of the engagement period prior to marriage that is designed to determine whether or not the couple is sufficiently compatible to get married. In certain situations, however, one party might take advantage of the other, as where a woman becomes engaged to a man merely for the purpose of gaining access to substantial wealth. In such cases, breach of promise actions can be utilized to compensate the individual who has been injured from such a relationship.

A number of states, however, have eliminated breach of marriage promise suits.

Alienation of Affection and Criminal Conversation A legal action may be brought against an individual who intrudes upon a marital relationship. Alienation of affection means interfering in such manner as to win away the love of a husband or wife from his or her spouse.

Criminal conversation is ADULTERY. Conversation is used to mean sexual relations in this context. These actions were designed to protect the sanctity of MARRIAGE and the family relationship. Today, suits for alienation of affection and criminal conversation have been abolished in most states.

Seduction The right to sue for seduction belonged to a father who could bring an action against a man who had sexual relations with his daughter.

At COMMON LAW, the daughter did not ordinarily have the right to sue on her own behalf. A woman who was seduced by a marriage promise could sue for breach of promise if the marriage did not take place. If she became sexually involved with a man due to force or duress, she might be able to bring action for RAPE or ASSAULT. The general rule was, however, that regardless of whether the woman was an adult or a MINOR, her seduction was regarded as an injury to her father.

In early cases, a father was permitted to be awarded pecuniary damages only as compensation for services that he lost as a result of the seduction. Subsequently, fathers were also allowed to recover COMPENSATORY DAMAGES for medical expenses, as well as damages for distress or sorrow.

Seduction suits are very seldom brought in modern times and have been abolished by some states. One of the primary reasons for this is that they publicize the individual's humiliation.

Limitations on Heart Balm Actions
A majority of judges and legal scholars are in agreement that all heart balm suits should be eliminated. Most states have enacted heart balm statutes that place limitations upon the amount of recovery. The abolition of heart balm suits does not, however, prevent either individual from recovering GIFTS made in contemplation of marriage. Many states have ruled that gifts, such as engagement rings, must be recovered if the promise to marry is revoked.

HEAT OF PASSION 📖 A phrase used in criminal law to describe an intensely emotional state of mind induced by a type of PROVOCATION that would cause a reasonable person to act on impulse or without reflection. 📖

A finding that a person who killed another acted in the heat of passion will reduce MURDER to MANSLAUGHTER under certain circumstances. The essential prerequisites for such a reduction are that the ACCUSED must be provoked to a point of great anger or rage, such that the person loses his or her normal capacity for self-control; the circumstances must be such that a reasonable person, faced with the same degree of provocation, would react in a similar manner; and finally, there must not have been an opportunity for the accused to have "cooled off" or regained self-control during the period between the provocation and the killing.

The RULE OF LAW that adequate provocation may reduce murder to manslaughter was developed by the English courts. It was a means of avoiding the severity of the death penalty, a fixed punishment for murder under the COMMON LAW, when the act of killing was caused by natural human weakness.

The type of provocation considered serious enough to induce a heat of passion offense varies slightly from one jurisdiction to another, although the usual test is reasonableness. Depending upon the circumstances, ASSAULT, BATTERY, ADULTERY, and illegal arrest are illustrative of what may be held to be sufficient provocation.

In almost all cases, the reasonableness of a provocation is a decision made by a jury.

HEGEL, GEORG WILHELM FRIEDRICH Philosopher Georg Wilhelm Friedrich Hegel had a profound effect on modern thought. Hegel wrote his earliest work in 1807 and his groundbreaking *Philosophy of Right* in 1827. An idealist, he explored the nature of rationality in an attempt to create a single system of thought that would comprehend all knowledge. Among his chief contributions was developing the hegelian dialectic, a three-part process for revealing reason that ultimately influenced nineteenth- and twentieth-century theories of law, political science, economics, and literature. Especially in the late twentieth century, scholars debated the ideas of Hegel for their relevance to contemporary legal issues.

Born August 27, 1770, in Stuttgart, Germany, Hegel achieved fame in his lifetime as a teacher and writer. The son of a German government official, he was originally a divinity student who later turned to philosophy. He worked as a tutor in his twenties, and later as a

BIOGRAPHY

Georg Wilhelm Friedrich Hegel

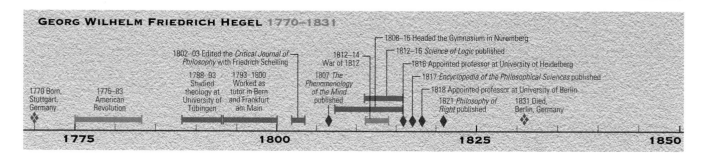

GEORG WILHELM FRIEDRICH HEGEL 1770–1831

1808–16 Headed the Gymnasium in Nuremberg

1802–03 Edited the *Critical Journal of Philosophy* with Friedrich Schelling

1812–16 *Science of Logic* published

1812–14 War of 1812

1816 Appointed professor at University of Heidelberg

1788–93 Studied theology at University of Tübingen

1793–1800 Worked as tutor in Bern and Frankfurt am Main

1807 *The Phenomenology of the Mind* published

1817 *Encyclopedia of the Philosophical Sciences* published

1818 Appointed professor at University of Berlin

1770 Born, Stuttgart, Germany

1775–83 American Revolution

1821 *Philosophy of Right* published

1831 Died, Berlin, Germany

1775   1800   1825   1850

school principal and a professor at German universities in Heidelberg and Berlin. At the same time, he wrote far-ranging and lengthy books, including *Science of Logic* (1812–16) and *Encyclopedia of the Philosophical Sciences* (1817), which contains every element of his system of philosophy. He died November 14, 1831, in Berlin.

Hegel's theories arose partly in response to those of his predecessor, the Prussian philosopher IMMANUEL KANT. Believing that perception alone could determine what is real, Kant had provided a concept of reason that Hegel was able to use in building a complete theoretical system. In doing so Hegel created his own form of the dialectic (a method of critical reasoning), which he divided into three parts. Essentially, it held: (1) A thesis (idea) encourages the development of its reverse, or antithesis. (2) If these two combine, they form an entirely new thesis, or synthesis. (3) This synthesis is the beginning of a new series of developments. Hegel believed that life eternally forms itself by setting up oppositions.

Hegel's system has special implications for the progress of history, particularly the evolution of people and government. He believed that the ideal universal soul can be created through logic that is based on his dialectic. This, he argued, was the foundation of all development. Using his three-part dialectic, he laid out the development of society. Hegel's thesis was that the primary goal of persons is to acquire property, and the pursuit of property by all persons necessitates the antithesis of this goal, laws. The association of persons and laws produces a synthesis, called ethos, that combines the freedom and interdependence of the people and creates a state. According to Hegel, the state is above the individual. Allowed to reach its highest form of development, Hegel believed, the state evolves into a monarchy (a government ruled by a single person, often called a king or queen).

Hegel's view of government is at odds with the historical course pursued by the United States. In fact, he was a critic of the individual-

"THE HISTORY OF THE WORLD IS NONE OTHER THAN THE PROGRESS OF THE CONSCIOUSNESS OF FREEDOM."

ism at the heart of the American Revolution. But his ideas have nonetheless had an immeasurable effect on modern thought in the United States as well as Europe. He saw human history as the progression from bondage to freedom, attainable only if the will of the individual is made secondary to the will of the majority. This view shaped the development of the philosophy of idealism in the United States and Europe. Hegel's dialectic was also adapted by KARL MARX as the basis for Marx's economic theory of the struggle of the working class to achieve REVOLUTION over the owners of the means of production. In the twentieth century, Hegel inspired the academic methodology called deconstructionism, used in fields ranging from literature to law as a means to interpret texts.

Although Hegel was largely ignored or attacked by U.S. legal scholars for two centuries, the 1950s brought a new interest in his ideas that has grown in the ensuing decades. Generally speaking, scholars have examined his work for its views on liberalism and the concepts of freedom and responsibility. Hegelian thought has been used to address everything from historical problems such as SLAVERY to contemporary issues in CONTRACTS, PROPERTY, TORTS, and CRIMINAL LAW. It has also influenced the CRITICAL LEGAL STUDIES movement.

See also JURISPRUDENCE.

HEIR ⬚ An individual who receives an interest in, or ownership of, land, TENEMENTS, or HEREDITAMENTS from an ancestor who has died INTESTATE, through the laws of DESCENT AND DISTRIBUTION. At COMMON LAW, an heir was the individual appointed by law to succeed to the ESTATE of an ancestor who died without a WILL. It is commonly used today in reference to any individual who succeeds to PROPERTY, either by will or law. ⬚

An *heir of the body* is an heir who was either conceived or born of the individual who has died, or a child of such heir. This type of heir is anyone who descends lineally from the decedent, excluding a surviving spouse, adopted children, and collateral relatives. Ordinarily, property can be given by will to anyone named or can be shared by all heirs, but historically, the owner of an ENTAIL could only pass his or her property on to heirs of the body. This type of inheritance is largely abolished by statute today.

HELD 📖 In relation to the opinion of a court, decided. 📖

The HOLDING in a particular case is the ultimate decision of a court of a JUSTICIABLE controversy.

HELMS, JESSE ALEXANDER, JR. The career of Senator Jesse Alexander Helms, Jr., is unique in post–World War II U.S. politics. Few legislators have fought as relentlessly, caused as much uproar, or finally had as much influence as the ultraconservative Republican from North Carolina. As a fiery radio editorialist in the 1960s, Helms waged a one-man war on liberalism. His notoriety helped him win a historic 1972 Senate race, a breakthrough in a state that had not elected a Republican in the twentieth century, and three reelections followed. He has emerged not only as a party leader but as an independent legislator with his own tough agenda on social issues and foreign policy.

Born October 18, 1921, in the small segregated town of Monroe, North Carolina, Helms was named for his formidable father. Jesse Helms, Sr., was the town's police and fire chief, and he exacted obedience from Monroe and his two sons alike. "My father was a six-foot, two-hundred pound gorilla," Helms affectionately said. "When he said, 'Smile,' I smiled." His mother, Ethel Mae Helms, marshaled her family off to the First Baptist Church twice a week. In Helms's childhood, Monroe still romantically celebrated Confederate Memorial Day, and patriotism, regional pride, religion, and racial separation were formative influences on the boy. He showed early promise in writing, by high school already reporting for the local newspaper.

Journalism held such interest for Helms that he quit Wake Forest College in 1939 to work on the *Raleigh News and Observer.* The twenty-year-old moved up rapidly. By 1941, he was assistant city editor of the *Raleigh Times,* the

Jesse Alexander Helms, Jr.

city's smaller, more conservative paper. Then Pearl Harbor intervened. Accepted by the Navy for limited duty in recruitment and public speaking, Helms made a crucial discovery: he was good at broadcasting. Starting in 1948, he began a new career as a radio news director at station WRAL in Raleigh. Helms soon moved from the role of political observer to that of political insider. His reporting in the vicious, racially divided 1950 Democratic primary race for the Senate led to accusations that he had doctored a photo of the wife of the loser, Frank Graham, so that she appeared to be dancing with a black man—a fatal blow to the candidate's chances in the segregated state. Helms denied it. The winner, Senator Willis Smith, took him to Washington as his administrative assistant in 1951.

Working in the Senate propelled Helms closer to a political career. From 1953 to 1960, he was a lobbyist and editorialist for the North Carolina Bankers Association. He had an opportunity to exercise his politics in a weekly column and at the same time held his first elective office, on the Raleigh City Council, where, although nominally a Democrat, he opposed virtually all taxes.

The great turning point in Helms's life came in 1960. As the executive vice president of the Capital Broadcasting Company, he began broadcasting fierce radio editorials on radio station WRAL. Here, for the next twelve years, he developed views that would last the rest of his life. These broadcasts were fire and brimstone. In much the same way that radio host Rush Limbaugh criticized liberals in the 1990s, Helms attacked liberal trends in the 1960s. He referred to the 1960s as "this time of the fast buck and the 'New Morality'—the age of apathy and indifference, the season of disdain for simple virtues and common honesty." What riled him most was the CIVIL RIGHTS MOVEMENT. Carried across the state of North Carolina, Helms's attacks on desegregation were reprinted in newspapers under titles such as "Nation Needs to Know of Red Involvement in Race Agitation!" The liberal media were to

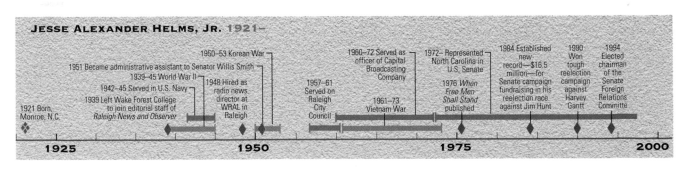

JESSE ALEXANDER HELMS, JR. 1921–

1921 Born, Monroe, N.C.

1939 Left Wake Forest College to join editorial staff of *Raleigh News and Observer*

1939–45 World War II

1942–45 Served in U.S. Navy

1948 Hired as radio news director at WRAL in Raleigh

1950–53 Korean War

1951 Became administrative assistant to Senator Willis Smith

1957–61 Served on Raleigh City Council

1960–72 Served as officer of Capital Broadcasting Company

1961–73 Vietnam War

1972– Represented North Carolina in U.S. Senate

1976 *When Free Men Shall Stand* published

1984 Established new record—$16.5 million—for Senate campaign fundraising in his reelection race against Jim Hunt

1990 Won tough reelection campaign against Harvey Gantt

1994 Elected chairman of the Senate Foreign Relations Committee

1925   1950   1975   2000

blame, Helms reasoned, and if they would stop distorting the truth, then "there would be millions around the world who would change their minds about race relations in the South." Despite his own biases, Helms and WRAL survived repeated complaints to the FEDERAL COMMUNICATIONS COMMISSION.

It was only a matter of time before the conservative Helms gave up on the Democratic party. In 1972, he switched parties and ran for the U.S. Senate as a Republican. Helms liked to tell his radio listeners that he had never voted for a Democrat for president, and now, with the decidedly liberal George S. McGovern as the Democratic nominee, he had even more reason to sever his symbolic ties to the party. McGovern stood for everything that Helms detested: support for welfare and ABORTION, and opposition to the war in Vietnam. To Helms, such views were typical of the way liberalism betrayed traditional values, and why he could not remain a Democrat.

When Helms jumped ship, he took an extreme gamble. North Carolina—indeed, the South as a whole—had been the Democratic party's stronghold for generations. In fact, not since the late nineteenth century had the state elected a Republican senator. Helms changed everything. One key to his beating the favorite, Democrat Nick Galifianakis (by only 120,000 votes) was Helms's use of national politics. The presidential election offered excellent coattails to ride on. Helms allied himself with Republican candidate RICHARD M. NIXON, linking Galifianakis with the highly unpopular McGovern. Galifianakis saw a much different, and worse, kind of tarring at work. He accused the Helms campaign of using his Greek American ethnicity to imply that he was not a loyal U.S. citizen.

Not surprisingly, Helms's first term in Washington, D.C., established the same hardline politics of his broadcasting career. He was soon nicknamed Senator No for voting against federal spending—with the exception of support for the military and farmers. He opposed federal aid to education, food stamps for striking workers, government-subsidized abortion, and the creation of the Consumer Protection Agency.

Returning politics to traditional values would be the hallmark of his career, a philosophy outlined in his 1976 book, *When Free Men Shall Stand.* During his first term in the U.S. Senate, he introduced an amendment designed to circumvent the Supreme Court's decisions banning prayer in public schools. Although the effort failed, it paid personal dividends: Helms came to the attention of conservative organizations and contributors who would be increasingly supportive of him over the next two decades. He saw no conflict with his faith in opposing government aid to the needy. He believed it was the role of the private individual to help others, as he and his wife, Dorothy Helms, had done by adopting a nine-year-old orphan with cerebral palsy. In Congress he voted against federal aid to disabled people and against school lunch programs.

Unlike some social conservatives, Helms had an equal passion for foreign policy. His anti-Communism was a lifelong belief, forming the basis for his opposition to any cooperation between the United States and left-wing governments. He opposed President Nixon's historic opening of ties to China. Supporting right-wing governments—even those associated with abuses of human rights, such as Turkey, or with all-white rule, such as Rhodesia and South Africa—made more sense to him.

Helms gained influence as his career progressed. By the late 1970s, he was already shaping the Republican presidential platform behind the scenes. In Senate votes, he could openly defy the party on nominations and policy decisions. Helms had little fear of the party leadership because he was building a national base of support. He did this with the help of a powerful insider in national politics, Richard A. Viguerie, publisher of the *Conservative Digest.* Viguerie was an early advocate of using direct-mail techniques, a marketing tool borrowed from business. As campaign manager for Helms in 1978, he blanketed the United States with letters asking for support. It worked, fantastically. Helms raised $6.2 million for his successful 1978 reelection, two-thirds of it from outside of North Carolina. Politicians of all kinds soon followed his lead in using this powerful technology.

In the 1980s, the importance of direct mail to Helms grew in proportion to the rise of conservative Christian politics. Analysts called this emerging constituency the New Right. It favored mandating SCHOOL PRAYER, outlawing abortion, and preventing gays and lesbians from acquiring equal rights. Helms tapped its members with dramatic fund-raising letters. By 1982, Helms could count on great support for brash, independent actions in the Senate: FILIBUSTERING against the renewal of the Voting Rights Act, for example, or attaching a school prayer amendment to the annual extension of the national debt.

The 1980s were a period of great activity for Helms in domestic policy. He railed against the National Endowment for the Arts (NEA) for

"WE ARE LIVING IN AN AGE WHERE ANYTHING GOES."

funding art that he found offensive, chiefly that of the homosexual photographer Robert Mapplethorpe and of the artist Andres Serrano, whose work *Piss Christ* depicted a crucifix submerged in urine. The national controversy he engendered continued to divide liberals and conservatives well into the 1990s. He also led a highly publicized attempt to take over CBS, exhorting conservatives to buy up stock in order to end liberal bias in news reporting. He introduced antiabortion legislation that made him the leading enemy of pro-abortion forces, which began demonizing Helms in their own direct-mail campaigns. He was most successful in agriculture policy. Helms won continued backing for tobacco price supports, an issue key to one of his most active advocates, the tobacco industry.

In a combative 1990 reelection campaign, Helms nearly lost to African American Harvey Gantt. The former Democratic mayor of Charlotte was ahead of Helms until the last weeks of the campaign, when Helms' forces mailed 125,000 postcards to voters warning them that they could be prosecuted for FRAUD if they voted improperly. At least 44,000 cards were sent to black voters, according to the U.S. Department of Justice, which sent observers to the state to ensure fair elections. Helms edged out Gantt by just over 100,000 votes. In 1992, the Justice Department ruled that the Helms campaign had violated federal CIVIL RIGHTS and voting laws by intimidating, threatening, and discouraging blacks from voting. Helms's office denied that he was involved in the mailings.

Helms was an outspoken critic of President BILL CLINTON. The Republican takeover of Congress in November 1994 gave him chairmanship of the Foreign Relations Committee, a powerful post from which he could authorize money for foreign aid, make recommendations on ambassadors and foreign treaties, and control the budget of the State Department. Almost immediately, he blasted the president as unfit to conduct foreign policy and warned that Clinton "better have a bodyguard" if he planned to visit North Carolina military bases.

Politicians from both parties denounced the remark, which came on the anniversary of the assassination of President JOHN F. KENNEDY. Helms called his statement a "mistake" but refused to apologize.

Despite surgery for serious health problems, Helms seemed eager to enter more battles. He was reelected to another term in 1996, again defeating Harvey Gantt.

See also ELECTION CAMPAIGN FINANCING; REPUBLICAN PARTY.

HENCEFORTH 📖 From this time forward. 📖

The term *henceforth*, when used in a legal document, statute, or other legal instrument, indicates that something will commence from the present time to the future, to the exclusion of the past.

HENRY, PATRICK Patrick Henry was a leading statesman and orator at the time of the American Revolutionary War. Several of Henry's speeches have remained vivid documents of the revolutionary period, with "Give me liberty or give me death" his most remembered statement.

Henry was born May 29, 1736, in Hanover County, Virginia. Though Henry attended public school for a short time, he was largely taught by his father, who had a good education. From 1751 to 1760, Henry was a storekeeper and farmer. When his business and farming ventures failed, he turned to the study of law, and received his license to practice in 1760.

Within three years, Henry had become a prominent attorney, owing in great measure to his oratorical skills. He was drawn to politics, and was elected to the Virginia House of Burgesses in 1765. In this colonial legislature, Henry became an outspoken critic of British policies toward the thirteen colonies. He introduced seven resolutions against the STAMP ACT, which levied a tax by requiring that stamps be affixed to documents and other papers. In one speech opposing the act, he stated, "If this be treason, make the most of it."

Henry's efforts led the Virginia House of Burgesses to pass five of the seven resolutions he introduced. All seven resolutions were re-

BIOGRAPHY

LIBRARY OF CONGRESS

Patrick Henry

"THE BATTLE, SIR, IS NOT TO THE STRONG ALONE; IT IS TO THE VIGILANT, THE ACTIVE, THE BRAVE."

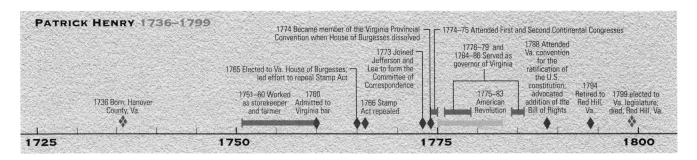

PATRICK HENRY 1736–1799

1736 Born, Hanover County, Va.

1751–60 Worked as storekeeper and farmer

1760 Admitted to Virginia bar

1765 Elected to Va. House of Burgesses; led effort to repeal Stamp Act

1766 Stamp Act repealed

1773 Joined Jefferson and Lee to form the Committee of Correspondence

1774 Became member of the Virginia Provincial Convention when House of Burgesses dissolved

1774–75 Attended First and Second Continental Congresses

1775–83 American Revolution

1776–79 and 1784–86 Served as governor of Virginia

1788 Attended Va. convention for the ratification of the U.S constitution; advocated addition of the Bill of Rights

1794 Retired to Red Hill, Va.

1799 elected to Va. legislature; died, Red Hill, Va.

1725   1750   1775   1800

printed in newspapers as the Virginia Resolves. Colonial businesspeople, in support of the resolves, agreed not to import British goods until the Stamp Act was repealed. Trade diminished, and business owners refused to use the stamps on business documents. Faced with organized resistance in the colonies, and the displeasure of British businesses that had lost trade, the British Parliament repealed the Stamp Act on March 4, 1766.

Henry grew more radical after the repeal of the act, arguing that the colonies should break away from Great Britain. In 1773, he joined with THOMAS JEFFERSON and Richard Henry Lee to form the Committee of Correspondence to transmit messages throughout the colonies. When the House of Burgesses was dissolved in 1774, he became a member of the Virginia Provincial Convention, which advocated revolution. Before this convention, he made his most famous remarks, words that became the clarion call that led the colonies into revolution: "I know not what course others may take, but as for me, give me liberty or give me death."

During 1774 and 1775, Henry attended the First CONTINENTAL CONGRESS as a member of the Virginia delegation, advocating military mobilization. When the Second Continental Congress convened in 1775, he helped draft the legislation that organized the Continental Army. In 1776 he also helped draft the Virginia Constitution.

In 1776 Henry was elected governor of the newly independent commonwealth of Virginia. A tireless administrator, Henry worked vigorously to meet the demands of the Revolutionary War. As commander in chief, he recruited the state's quota of six thousand men for the Continental Army, plus the state militia's allotment of five thousand soldiers.

After the war, Henry continued as governor, eventually serving five terms. During his second term, Henry provided supplies to George Rogers Clark for his expedition to the Northwest Territory. Clark rid the territory of British control.

In 1788, Henry attended the Virginia convention for the ratification of the U.S. Constitution. Henry opposed ratification, fearing that it imperiled the rights of states and individuals, but Virginia ratified it. Henry successfully advocated the addition of the BILL OF RIGHTS to the document. This first ten amendments to the Constitution protect the rights of states and individuals, allowing Henry to support the Constitution.

Following ratification, Henry was offered many government posts, but was forced to resume his Virginia law practice to rescue himself from personal debt. He quickly became a wealthy man, since his fame attracted many clients. In 1794, he retired to his estate at Red Hill, near Appomattox, Virginia. Despite his new wealth, Henry refused pleas to resume public service, turning down President GEORGE WASHINGTON's request to serve as chief justice of the U.S. Supreme Court.

Washington finally persuaded Henry to seek election to the Virginia legislature. Henry won election in 1799. He died June 6, 1799, before he could take office.

HENRY II OF ENGLAND King Henry II was born March 5, 1133, in Le Mans, France. He reigned from 1154 to 1189 and founded the Plantagenet dynasty of English rulers. Henry's many innovations in civil and criminal procedure had a lasting effect upon English law and his expansion of the royal court system made royal justice available throughout England.

Building upon the earlier tradition of the INQUEST, Henry issued several ASSIZES, or ordinances, that introduced the procedures that eventually developed into the GRAND JURY. He also developed a number of writs to bring cases from the feudal courts of the barons into the royal courts. In addition, Henry sent itinerant justices on regular circuits through the kingdom to make royal justice more easily obtainable.

Henry's expansion of royal justice did, however, bring him into conflict with THOMAS BECKET, the archbishop of Canterbury, who opposed the king's efforts to punish members of the clergy who had been convicted of crimes in

BIOGRAPHY

Henry II of England

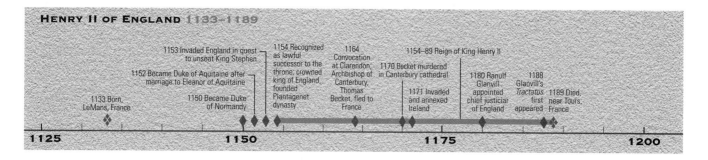

HENRY II OF ENGLAND 1133–1189

1133 Born, LeMans, France

1150 Became Duke of Normandy

1152 Became Duke of Aquitaine after marriage to Eleanor of Aquitaine

1153 Invaded England in quest to unseat King Stephen

1154 Recognized as lawful successor to the throne; crowned king of England, founded Plantagenet dynasty

1164 Convocation at Clarendon; Archbishop of Canterbury, Thomas Becket, fled to France

1154–89 Reign of King Henry II

1170 Becket murdered in Canterbury cathedral

1171 Invaded and annexed Ireland

1180 Ranulf Glanvill appointed chief justiciar of England

1188 Glanvill's *Tractatus* first appeared

1189 Died, near Tours, France

1125   1150   1175   1200

ECCLESIASTICAL COURTS and removed from their clerical status. Becket was murdered in 1170 by some of the king's men, though apparently not at his command, and Henry thereafter gave up his efforts to punish members of the clergy. Henry died July 6, 1189, near Tours, France.

HEREAFTER In the future.

The term *hereafter* is always used to indicate a future time—to the exclusion of both the past and present—in legal documents, statutes, and other similar papers.

HEREDITAMENT Anything that can be passed by an individual to HEIRS.

There are two types of hereditaments: CORPOREAL and INCORPOREAL.

A *corporeal hereditament* is a permanent tangible object that can be seen and handled and is confined to the land. Materials, such as coal, timber, stone, or a house are common examples of this type of hereditament.

An *incorporeal hereditament* is an intangible right, which is not visible but is derived from real or personal property. An EASEMENT is a classic example of this type of hereditament, since it is the right of one individual to use another's property and can be inherited.

HIERARCHY A group of people who form an ascending chain of power or authority.

Officers in a government, for example, form an escalating series of ranks or degrees of power, with each rank subject to the authority of the one on the next level above. In a majority of hierarchical arrangements, there are a larger number of people at the bottom than at the top.

Originally, the term was used to mean government by a body of priests. Currently, a hierarchy is used to denote any body of individuals arranged or classified according to capacity, authority, position, or rank.

HIGGINBOTHAM, A. LEON, JR. A. Leon Higginbotham, Jr., is an attorney and a retired federal judge. His distinguished judicial career culminated in his attaining the rank of chief judge of the U.S. Court of Appeals for the Third Circuit.

Higginbotham was born February 25, 1928, in Trenton, New Jersey. Although he attended segregated public schools, his mother was determined that he would receive the same opportunities available to white students. "She knew that education was the sole passport to a better life," he said. No black student had been admitted to the academic high school program in Trenton because Latin, a requirement for the program, was not offered at the black elementary schools. But Higginbotham's mother fought for her son's right to enroll and finally convinced the principal to allow him into the program. Higginbotham has no doubt that his mother's advocacy made a difference in the outcome of his life. "When I see students who went to [elementary school] with me now working as elevator operators or on street maintenance," he said, "I often wonder what their future would have been if the school had offered Latin."

After finishing high school, Higginbotham decided to become an engineer and enrolled at Purdue University, in West Lafayette, Indiana. A winter spent sleeping in an unheated attic with eleven other black students caused him to rethink his career goals. "One night, as the temperature was close to zero, I felt that I could suffer the personal indignities and denigration no longer," he wrote in the preface to his book, *In the Matter of Color: Race and the American Legal Process; The Colonial Period* (1978). He spoke to the university president, who told him the law did not require the university to "let colored students in the dorm." Higginbotham was advised to accept the situation or leave. "How could it be that the law would not permit twelve good kids to sleep in a warm dormitory?" he wondered. He decided then and there to abandon engineering and pursue a career in law.

Higginbotham left Purdue to attend Antioch College, in Ohio, where he studied sociology, earning his bachelor of arts degree in 1949. He went on to Yale Law School, and received his bachelor of laws degree in 1952. Another incident that helped galvanize his commitment to racial equality occurred shortly after his graduation from Yale. He was a job candidate for a

BIOGRAPHY

© LEANDRE JACKSON

A. Leon Higginbotham, Jr.

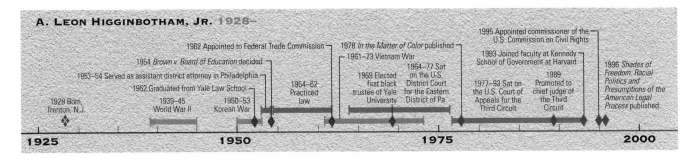

A. LEON HIGGINBOTHAM, JR. 1928–

1928 Born, Trenton, N.J.

1939–45 World War II

1950–53 Korean War

1952 Graduated from Yale Law School

1953–54 Served as assistant district attorney in Philadelphia

1954 *Brown v. Board of Education* decided

1954–62 Practiced law

1962 Appointed to Federal Trade Commission

1961–73 Vietnam War

1964–77 Sat on the U.S. District Court for the Eastern District of Pa.

1969 Elected first black trustee of Yale University

1978 *In the Matter of Color* published

1977–93 Sat on the U.S. Court of Appeals for the Third Circuit

1993 Joined faculty at Kennedy School of Government at Harvard

1989 Promoted to chief judge of the Third Circuit

1995 Appointed commissioner of the U.S. Commission on Civil Rights

1996 *Shades of Freedom: Racial Politics and Presumptions of the American Legal Process* published

1925   1950   1975   2000

prominent Philadelphia law firm that did not know he was black until he arrived for the interview. Although the partner who spoke with him praised his qualifications, he told Higginbotham he could not do anything for him except direct him to local black law firms who might hire him.

Discouraged but not daunted, Higginbotham began his legal career as an assistant district attorney in Philadelphia and then became a partner in a law firm that handled business, church, and CIVIL RIGHTS cases. President JOHN F. KENNEDY made him a commissioner with the Federal Trade Commission in 1962; he was the youngest person ever appointed to the post and the first African American. The same year, the U.S. Junior Chamber of Commerce named him one of its ten outstanding young men. In 1964, President LYNDON B. JOHNSON named him a U.S. district judge for the Eastern District of Pennsylvania; at age thirty-six, he was the youngest federal judge to be appointed in three decades. In 1977, President JIMMY CARTER elevated him to the U.S. Court of Appeals for the Third Circuit, which encompasses Pennsylvania, New Jersey, Delaware, and the Virgin Islands.

Higginbotham's distinguished judicial career was capped in 1989 when he was promoted to chief judge for the Third Circuit Court of Appeals. At the time, he was the only black judge directing one of the federal judiciary's twelve circuits. His ascendancy was hailed by many who saw it as proof that the U.S. judicial system was becoming more inclusive. Guido Calabresi, dean of Yale Law School, praised him as "a first-rate judge, a sensitive judge, who is powerful in style and analytically strong." But some black lawyers felt that too much emphasis was placed on Higginbotham's skin color and on the racial import of his promotion. "There is no more significance to it than anybody else becoming Chief Judge," said THURGOOD MARSHALL, associate justice of the U.S. Supreme Court. "I think he is a great lawyer and a very great judge. Period."

Higginbotham is an outspoken proponent of civil rights and racial equality. In 1990, he declined to officiate at a moot court competition at the University of Chicago Law School because, he said, Chicago was the only one of the United States' top ten schools that "for two decades has not had even one black professor in either a tenured position or a tenure-track position." Higginbotham speaks often of his early life, but not for the purpose of highlighting his own hardships. Rather, he seeks to demonstrate the importance of ensuring that all

children be given the opportunity to develop their potential. "Today," he said, "on the streets of New Haven, Chicago, Philadelphia and New York, there are thousands of kids who would do the same thing I did, the same thing [former head of the Joint Chiefs of Staff] Colin Powell has done, if they didn't get pushed out of the system."

Higginbotham's devotion to civil rights was evident in his criticism of Justice CLARENCE THOMAS, a conservative African American whose nomination to the U.S. Supreme Court in 1991 provoked criticism and controversy. In an article titled "An Open Letter to Justice Clarence Thomas from a Federal Judicial Colleague" (*U. Pa. L. Rev.*, Jan. 1992), Higginbotham called upon Thomas to remain cognizant of his responsibilities as a black on the Supreme Court. He reminded Thomas of the discrimination both men's grandfathers had faced and of Thomas's debt to the CIVIL RIGHTS MOVEMENT, commenting that without the movement, "probably neither you nor I would be Federal judges today." He was also sharply critical of Thomas's record. He noted that after studying nearly all of Thomas's speeches and writings, "I could not find one shred of evidence suggesting an insightful understanding on your part of how the evolutionary movement of the Constitution and the work of the civil rights organizations have benefited you."

Higginbotham is well-known for his prolific writings, including more than one hundred articles and the book *In the Matter of Color*. During his career, he has been awarded over forty honorary degrees, and in 1969, he was elected the first black trustee of Yale University.

In 1993, Higginbotham retired from the circuit court and formed an association with the law firm of Paul, Weiss, and Rifkin, in New York City.

HIGH CRIMES AND MISDEMEANORS

The offenses for which presidents, vice presidents, and all civil officers, including federal judges, can be removed from office through a process called IMPEACHMENT.

The phrase *high crimes and misdemeanors* is found in the U.S. Constitution. It also appears in state laws and constitutions as a basis for disqualification from holding office. Originating in English COMMON LAW, these words have acquired a broad meaning in U.S. law. They refer to criminal actions as well as any serious misuse or abuse of office, ranging from tax evasion to obstruction of justice. The ultimate authority for determining whether an offense constitutes a ground for impeachment rests with Congress.

"*BROWN* CHANGED THE MORAL TONE OF AMERICA; BY ELIMINATING THE LEGITIMIZATION OF STATE-IMPOSED RACISM IT IMPLICITLY QUESTIONED RACISM WHEREVER IT WAS USED."

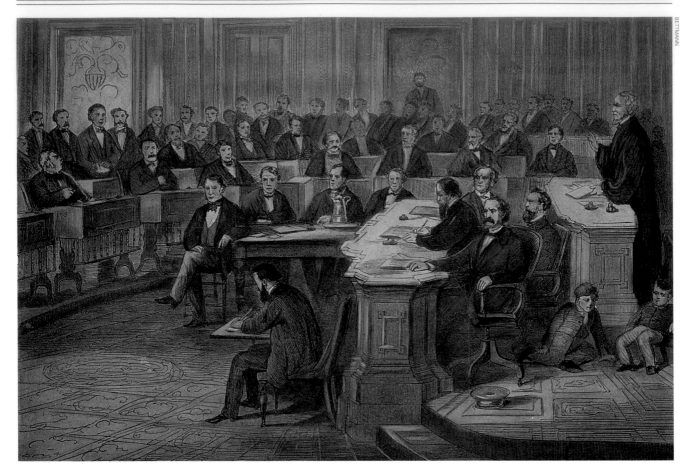

In 1868 President Andrew Johnson underwent impeachment proceedings. The U.S. Constitution says that a president may be removed from office for treason, bribery, or "other High Crimes and Misdemeanors," but it does not clearly define high crimes and misdemeanors. The vote to impeach Johnson failed in the Senate.

The exact meaning of the phrase cannot be found in the Constitution itself. Article II, Section 4, establishes, "The President, Vice President and all civil Officers of the United States, shall be removed from Office on Impeachment for, and Conviction of, Treason, Bribery, or other High Crimes and Misdemeanors." *Treason* and *bribery* are specific, but *high crimes and misdemeanors* is not. In fact, considerable debate occupied the Framers of the Constitution over the issue of impeachment, and the wording of the grounds for impeachment was itself controversial. A proposed offense of maladministration was rejected as being too vague and susceptible to political abuse. Finally, they chose to use a phrase from English common law that had no precisely settled meaning at the time yet at least connoted serious offenses.

The reason for the choice lies in the Framers' approach to the larger question of impeachment. Although borrowing language from the law they knew best, they explicitly chose not to imitate the English model of impeachment. Traditionally, this approach had allowed the British Parliament to conduct a simple review of charges and then remove officials by a majority vote. Instead, the Framers intended for removal from office to be the final step in a two-part process that began in the House of Representatives and, if charges should result, ended in a trial-like hearing before the U.S. Senate. Thus, two goals would be achieved: a full public inquiry into allegations, and, if necessary, the adjudication of those charges requiring a two-thirds majority for removal.

Generally, debate over the phrase *high crimes and misdemeanors* has split into two camps. The minority view is held by critics who undertake a literal reading of the Constitution. They maintain that *high crimes* means what it says—criminal activity—and argue that the Framers wanted only criminal activities to be the basis for impeachment. The generally accepted viewpoint is much broader. It defines high crimes and misdemeanors as any serious abuse of power—including both legal and illegal activities. Supporters of this reading believe that because impeachment is a public inquiry, first and foremost, it is appropriate to read the phrase broadly in order to provide the most thorough inquiry possible. Thus, a civil officer may face impeachment for misconduct, violations of oath of office, serious incompetence, or, in the case of judges, activities that undermine public confidence in or damage the integrity of the judiciary.

The vagueness of the standard has left much interpretive power to Congress. In 1868, President ANDREW JOHNSON underwent impeachment proceedings when he ordered the firing of his secretary of war. His opponents charged that this order violated the TENURE OF OFFICE ACT, which set the tenure of certain officials. Johnson escaped conviction in the Senate by only one vote, but the attempt to impeach him quickly came to be seen as a politically motivated mistake. In 1974, the House Judiciary Committee recommended that the full House of Representatives approve articles of impeachment against President RICHARD M. NIXON. It did not cite any single impeachable offense, but instead found a broad pattern of wrongdoing: Nixon had conspired with his advisers to obstruct federal and congressional investigations of the WATERGATE break-in, the burglarizing of the Democratic National Committee headquarters in Washington, D.C., which was eventually linked to the Nixon administration. Nixon resigned from office before the process could continue.

HIGHWAY 📖 A main road or thoroughfare, such as a street, boulevard, or parkway, available to the public for use for travel or transportation. 📖

The nature of a public way is determinable from its origin, as well as the intention and plans of the appropriate authorities and the use to which it has been put. If a particular road or highway is designated as private, its character will not be altered if it is actually a public road or highway. PRIVATE ROADS are intended for use by a few private individuals, as distinguished from highways that are for public use.

It is essential that a highway be established in a manner recognized by the particular JURISDICTION, whether it be by long use—PRESCRIPTION—or by DEDICATION to the public by the owner of the property subject to the consent of public authorities. Prior to the time that any statutory procedure for the establishment of highways was devised, prescription and dedication were the methods used in COMMON LAW. Currently, most highways are created by statute.

Extended Use or Prescription One method of establishing a highway or public road is through prescription—the extended use of a piece of land for a certain length of time by the public, absent the owner's consent.

The actual number of persons using the road or the frequency or extent of such use is immaterial provided the property is openly and continuously used as a road with no restrictions. In addition, such public use must not be interrupted by acts of the owner that are designed to stop the use of his or her property as a public highway. For example, the posting of several "no trespassing" signs around the land and the erection of a fence would most likely prevent a highway from being recognized. Verbal objections alone, or unsuccessful attempts to curtail use as a highway, are ordinarily insufficient.

Any property subject to the right of the state to lay out a public way over it can become a highway by extended use if the conditions prescribed by statute are met. The public is given an EASEMENT in the land as a highway, and the width and extent of a highway are determined by the extent of its actual use for such purposes.

Statute The creation of highways is a function of the government that stems from its power of EMINENT DOMAIN—the authority to take private property for public use. The legislature makes the determination needed for public use and convenience and provides for establishment of highways by local boards or courts. In deciding whether the need for a highway exists, factors for consideration include topography, soil character, population, location, condition, convenience of highways already established or proposed, and the probable extent of use.

In the absence of statutory authorization, a highway cannot be constructed through lands of the state, or property that has already been designated for public use, such as a park. Additionally, some state laws proscribe the creation of highways through residences, buildings used for trade, gardens, or orchards.

Public Authorities Public officials, such as state highway commissioners, act on behalf of the particular COUNTY or MUNICIPAL CORPORATION upon which the state has conferred power to establish highways.

A highway and road district is a subdivision of the state, which the legislature creates to facilitate the administration of highways. The legislature defines and sets the territorial extent, limits, and boundaries of the road or highway district, and, generally, only lands that will be benefited are included. Highway boards and commissions are ordinarily responsible for the construction, improvement, and maintenance of highways.

Abandonment, Alteration, and Vacation The right of the public to use a highway may be forfeited by *abandonment*. Nonuse might be considered ABANDONMENT under statutory provisions. The evidence that a highway is in such a dangerous state of disrepair for a number of years that the public stops using it and a county fails to repair it constitutes abandonment in some jurisdictions. Where provided by statute, delay in opening a highway might be regarded as abandonment if it extends over an unreasonable length of time.

An *alteration* of a highway ordinarily refers to a change in its course that the state may effect in exercise of its POLICE POWER. A proceeding for a change or alteration in a public road generally will not be brought unless the change will further safety, convenience, or other public interests.

Vacation of a highway occurs when its existence is terminated by the direct action of public officials. The authority to vacate is generally delegated to the appropriate authorities or local agencies. Certain statutes make the provision that highways may be vacated by a vote of the town in a town meeting. Ordinarily, highways cannot be vacated unless they are useless, inconvenient, or burdensome, and the grounds are usually regulated by statutes. A highway that has been laid out but not constructed may be discontinued due to a change of circumstances, such as where a variation in traffic patterns makes the proposed highway unnecessary.

Title The public only acquires the right to use a highway, whereas TITLE to the land remains in the owner, subject to the public's rights. When a highway is constructed, the public has the right of way as well as privileges incident thereto, including the right to construct, improve, and repair the highway. When a highway is abandoned or discontinued, however, total and unlimited ownership reverts to the true owner.

An individual whose land abuts a public highway might have special rights, including the right to a reasonable passageway to the highway from his or her land.

Construction and Maintenance The construction and maintenance of highways are assumed by either the state, local communities, or a specifically designated agency. The actual plan of work in constructing, maintaining, or repairing highways is in the discretion of the highway authorities, whereas the state legislature determines their routes. The designation and location of a federally-aided state highway must be in accordance with federal and state law. A state, in its construction of a highway under the federal-aid primary system might be required to obtain the approval of federal agencies if the highway has a marked affect on the environment. The authorities may make provisions for the drainage of surface waters and for the building of ditches and culverts.

The construction and repair of public roads may be funded by general taxation, since the public roads are for a public purpose. The power to impose highway taxes vests in the legislature, and funds may be raised from vehicle taxes, gasoline taxes, property taxes, the sale of bonds, or by special assessments on the property benefited only for the amount necessary to cover the costs of construction or improvement.

The U.S. Department of Transportation, established by Congress, works with the states to

The construction and maintenance of highways are the responsibility of states, local communities, or designated agencies.

establish and maintain a national highway system (23 U.S.C.A. § 101 et seq.). Federal revenues pay for most of the national highway system. Congress may withhold portions of these funds if states do not enact certain laws related to highways or highway use and affecting interstate commerce. For example, Congress may withhold funding if a state does not set the minimum age for ALCOHOL consumption at twenty-one years; suspend, for at least six months, the driver's license of persons convicted of drug offenses; or prohibit driving under the influence of alcohol.

See also AUTOMOBILES.

Obstruction   Any unauthorized obstruction that hinders the use of a public highway, such as a fence, gate, or ditch, is illegal and constitutes a NUISANCE. Officials may, however, lawfully obstruct highways temporarily under their jurisdictions for a reasonable period to make necessary repairs or improvements. Anyone who causes or allows an obstruction to be placed on a public highway is liable and may be enjoined to compel its removal.

In addition, the authorities or private individuals who have sustained special damages—financial or other losses that differ from those incurred by the public—may sue for DAMAGES against one who obstructs a highway. What constitutes special damages is dependent upon the facts of each case. Special injury might exist where the obstruction blocks access to the plaintiff's property. In a number of jurisdictions the obstruction of highways is a criminal offense.

Use   The state has the power to control and regulate the use of public highways, provided its regulations do not constitute an unreasonable interference with the right of travel or impede interstate commerce. The state may determine the character of motor vehicles that use its highways and may properly exclude vehicles weighing in excess of a maximum set by statute. A reasonable tax may be imposed on vehicles based on their excess weight in order to compensate the state for the additional costs of maintaining the highway as a result of the severe wear and tear placed on the road by such vehicles. To protect the public health, the state may prohibit trucks that transport chemicals or EXPLOSIVES from driving through populated or residential areas. The secretary of transportation regulates the safety performance of all commercial motor CARRIERS transporting explosives or dangerous articles, such as flammable or radioactive materials, in interstate or foreign commerce. The state may restrict the speed of

Highway Mileage in U.S. in 1993
Functional Systems of U.S. Highways
Number of miles of road surface

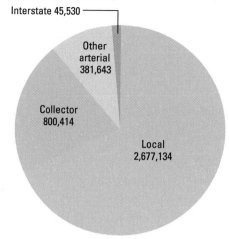

Interstate 45,530

Other arterial 381,643

Collector 800,414

Local 2,677,134

Urban vs. Rural Location of Highway
Number of miles of road surface

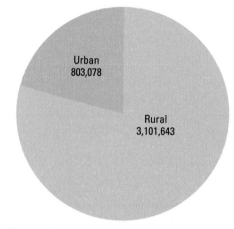

Urban 803,078

Rural 3,101,643

Source: U.S. Federal Highway Administration, *Highway Statistics*.

vehicles, or proscribe parking alongside the highway except in emergencies. Bicycles used on highways may be subject to reasonable restrictions, such as the requirement that they be equipped with lights at night.

The *law of the road* is comprised of a system of rules and regulations based upon the traditional practices and customs that govern safe travel on highways. The law is often embodied in statutes or government regulations and is regarded as being so well-known that there is a legal presumption that everyone knows it. Highway travelers, therefore, may properly make the assumption that other travelers will observe the law and comply with rules and regulations. When an individual fails to observe the law of the road without justification, he or she will be held liable for injuries precipitated by the NEGLIGENCE. A violation of a particular rule of the road may be justified by special circumstance.

HIJACKING ▥ The seizure of a commercial vehicle—airplane, ship, or truck—by force or threat of force. ▥

Hijacking is the modern term for "piracy." It is derived from the phrase "High, Jack!" which is a command to raise one's hands before being robbed. The word gained popular currency during Prohibition (1920–33), when bootleggers commandeered truckloads of liquor from each other, and reappeared when political activists began to seize commercial airplanes in the 1960s.

Airplane Hijacking The first U.S. airplane hijacking occurred in 1961. The number of such incidents, also known as skyjackings or air piracies, grew during the 1960s, with forty attempts made in 1969. Many of these incidents involved persons seeking to divert airplanes to Cuba, where they could gain asylum. Hijackings became so numerous that the phrase "Take me to Havana" entered popular culture.

In 1973 the United States and Cuba were able to reach an agreement that allows either country to request the EXTRADITION of a hijacker. The agreement came about through an exchange of diplomatic notes. It was in Cuba's interest to make the agreement because many Cubans had hijacked planes from Cuba and forced them to fly to the United States. The agreement allows either country to take into account extenuating circumstances when the hijackers acted "for strictly political reasons and were in real and imminent danger of death without a viable alternative, provided there was no financial extortion or physical injury" to crew, passengers, or other persons (12 *I.L.M.* 370–76, No. 2 [March 1973]).

In addition to this agreement, the United States in 1961 made the hijacking of an airplane a federal crime. Under the Aircraft Piracy Act (18 U.S.C.A. § 32), the attempted or successful execution of the following actions is considered hijacking: damaging an aircraft; placing or bringing a destructive device or substance on an aircraft; damaging or interfering with an air navigation facility, or equipment and property used in connection with the operation of an aircraft; committing an act of violence against or otherwise injuring an individual on an aircraft; or making threats or statements that they know are false against or about the safety of an aircraft that is already in flight.

Hijacking has not been confined to the United States and Cuba. In 1970 hijackers seized more than ninety planes around the world. The growth of international TERRORISM, specifically in the Middle East, led to widely publicized hijackings. In these situations hijackers sought the satisfaction of political demands and a platform to air their views. In 1970 members of the Popular Front for the Liberation of Palestine hijacked three airliners to the desert near Amman, Jordan. The hijackers demanded the release of Palestinian prisoners in European prisons and in Israeli jails. When their demands were not met, they removed the passengers from the airliners and destroyed the planes one by one.

Faced with increased numbers of air hijackings, the international community sought to negotiate agreements that would prevent hijackers from finding safe haven. The 1970 Hague Convention for the Suppression of Unlawful Seizure of Aircraft (22 U.S.T. 1641, T.I.A.S. 7192 [effective in the United States in 1971]) deals specifically with the hijacking of aircraft in flight. The 1971 Montreal Convention for the Suppression of Unlawful Acts against the Safety of Civil Aviation (24 U.S.T. 564, T.I.A.S. 7570 [effective in the United States in 1973]) addresses attacks on or sabotage of civil aircraft either in flight or on the ground, or destruction of or damage to air navigation facilities when this is likely to endanger the safety of aircraft in flight. Either the state of registration or the state in which the aircraft lands can exercise JURISDICTION. The state having the hijackers in custody must prosecute or extradite them. A state may decline to extradite if it considers the offense political, or may prefer not to extradite to a state that imposes the death penalty, but in either of these cases, it is obligated to prosecute the offenders.

The United States passed the Antihijacking Act of 1974 (49 U.S.C.A. § 1301 et seq.) to implement these international conventions. This act seeks to prevent nations from adopting a permissive posture toward illegal activities such as the commandeering of aircraft, by providing penalties for hijackers and for nations that shield or fail to take adequate precautions against hijackers. The act gives the president the power to terminate air service between an offending nation and the United States if the president determines that the offending nation has acted inconsistently with its obligations under the antihijacking conventions. Since the signing of these international conventions in the 1970s, airplane hijacking has fallen sharply, especially in the United States.

Ship Hijacking Ship hijacking is rare, but the seizure of the *Achille Lauro* made clear that it can happen. The Italian cruise ship was commandeered on October 7, 1985, by four members of a faction of the Palestine Liberation Organization. The hijackers boarded the ship posing as tourists, and waited until the ship was off the Egyptian coast before taking its crew and passengers hostage. They threatened to kill the HOSTAGES if Israel did not meet their demand to release fifty Palestinian prisoners. They also threatened to blow up the ship if anyone attempted a rescue mission. When the hijackers' demands were not met the next day, they shot and killed Leon Klinghoffer, a U.S. citizen who was partially paralyzed and used a wheelchair. They dumped Klinghoffer's body in the sea.

Denied access to a Syrian port, the hijackers sailed to Alexandria, where they surrendered to Egyptian authorities. The hijackers were allowed to leave Egypt for Italy to stand trial, where they were convicted for violating an Italian statute that made terrorist kidnapping illegal. The hijacker who confessed to killing Klinghoffer was sentenced to thirty years in prison.

HILL, ANITA FAYE A little-known law professor testifying before a U.S. Senate committee in 1991 became a cause célèbre when she accused a respected U.S. Supreme Court nominee of SEXUAL HARASSMENT. Anita Faye Hill became a household name during the televised confirmation hearings of U.S. Supreme Court candidate CLARENCE THOMAS, the second African American in U.S. history to be tapped for the High Court. Hill, who is also African American, was calm and articulate as she withstood an intense grilling by the all-male, all-white Senate Judiciary Committee. Despite skepticism and open hostility from some of the senators, Hill stood firm on her account of sexually explicit remarks and behavior by Thomas, her former boss. Conservatives reviled Hill, feminists revered her—and by the end of the hearings, U.S. citizens of all political persuasions had a keener awareness of the problem of sexual harassment in the workplace.

Nothing in Hill's background prepared her for the unremitting media attention she received during and after the Thomas confirma-

"WE NEED TO TURN THE QUESTION AROUND TO LOOK AT THE HARASSER, NOT THE TARGET. WE NEED TO BE SURE THAT WE CAN GO OUT AND LOOK AT ANYONE WHO IS A VICTIM OF HARASSMENT . . . AND SAY, 'YOU DO NOT HAVE TO REMAIN SILENT ANYMORE.' "

BIOGRAPHY

APWIDE WORLD PHOTOS

Anita Faye Hill

tion hearings. The youngest of Albert Hill and Erma Hill's thirteen children, she was an extremely private person. Hill was born July 30, 1956, and raised on a struggling family farm near Morris, Oklahoma. Her religious parents emphasized the importance of hard work, strong moral values, and education. Intelligent and disciplined, Hill was valedictorian of her high school class and an honor student at Oklahoma State University, in Stillwater, where she graduated in 1977 with a degree in psychology. After college, Hill attended Yale University Law School on a scholarship from the NATIONAL ASSOCIATION FOR THE ADVANCEMENT OF COLORED PEOPLE.

Hill graduated from law school with honors in 1980, and worked briefly for the Washington, D.C., law firm of Wald, Harkrader, and Ross. In 1981, she left private practice to become special counsel to the assistant secretary in the U.S. Department of Education's Office of Civil Rights. The assistant secretary was Thomas. It was during this time that Thomas asked her out and, according to Hill, sexually harassed her. In 1982, Thomas was appointed chair of the EQUAL EMPLOYMENT OPPORTUNITY COMMISSION (EEOC), and Hill moved to the EEOC with her boss in what she felt was a necessary career step.

In 1983, Hill decided to leave Washington, D.C., to became a law professor at Oral Roberts University. In 1986, she accepted a teaching position at the University of Oklahoma. Although full professorship and tenure are normally granted at Oklahoma after six years, Hill achieved both in just four years.

Hill's transformation from legal scholar to feminist icon came about after Thomas was offered the career opportunity of a lifetime. President GEORGE BUSH nominated Thomas, then a federal appeals court judge, to fill an opening on the U.S. Supreme Court. During the mandatory Senate investigation of Thomas, Hill disclosed in private sessions the alleged incidents of sexual harassment by Thomas. Reports of Hill's private testimony were leaked to a National Public Radio reporter. When Hill's

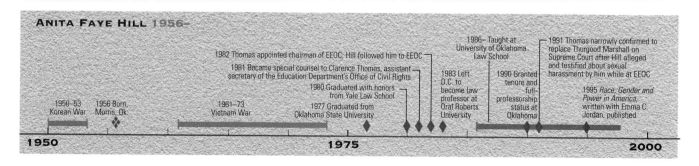

ANITA FAYE HILL 1956–

1950–53 Korean War

1956 Born, Morris, Ok.

1961–73 Vietnam War

1977 Graduated from Oklahoma State University

1980 Graduated with honors from Yale Law School

1981 Became special counsel to Clarence Thomas, assistant secretary of the Education Department's Office of Civil Rights

1982 Thomas appointed chairman of EEOC; Hill followed him to EEOC

1983 Left D.C. to become law professor at Oral Roberts University

1986– Taught at University of Oklahoma Law School

1990 Granted tenure and full-professorship status at Oklahoma

1991 Thomas narrowly confirmed to replace Thurgood Marshall on Supreme Court after Hill alleged and testified about sexual harassment by him while at EEOC

1995 *Race, Gender and Power in America,* written with Emma C. Jordan, published

1950

1975

2000

allegations became public, they stood as a potential roadblock to Thomas's confirmation.

During a live broadcast of the Senate hearings, Hill's personal motives, character, and politics were scrutinized relentlessly. Both Hill and Thomas brought in witnesses to support their separate versions of events. Thomas angrily denied Hill's charges and accused the Senators of conducting a media circus and a "high tech lynching." Hill stood by her story, despite the accusations of some senators who suggested that she was delusional. Her testimony was detailed and graphic. In a clear, dispassionate manner, she described Thomas's alleged interest in pornographic films and bragging comments about his sexual performance. She steadfastly denied that she was lying or prone to fantasies.

Despite Hill's damaging testimony, Thomas weathered the hearings and received Senate confirmation by a narrow margin on October 15, 1991. Hill returned to the University of Oklahoma Law School and tried to resume her quiet private life.

Immediately after the Hill-Thomas hearings, only 24 percent of the registered voters who responded to a *Wall Street Journal*–NBC News poll indicated that they believed Hill. Forty percent thought Thomas was telling the truth. Just one year after Thomas's confirmation, public opinion had changed. In a 1992 *Wall Street Journal*–NBC News poll, 44 percent of the people interviewed sided with Hill and 34 percent believed Thomas. One possible explanation for this shift in loyalties is the nation's year-long posthearings examination of the nature and effects of sexual harassment. Perhaps as more people became aware of the problem and more women revealed their own encounters with sexual harassment, Hill's credibility increased.

To some, the Hill-Thomas hearings illustrated the almost insurmountable difficulty in bringing a sexual harassment claim; to others, they showed how vulnerable men are to false accusations by women with ulterior motives.

Oliver W. Hill

"I DECIDED TO GO TO LAW SCHOOL TO SEE WHAT I COULD DO ABOUT TRYING TO GET THE SUPREME COURT TO CHANGE ITS MIND."

Although some women were discouraged after witnessing Hill's treatment by the Senate panel, others found the courage to file their own sexual harassment complaints after watching Hill's example.

HILL, OLIVER W. Oliver W. Hill is an African American attorney who was instrumental in the CIVIL RIGHTS struggles of the 1950s and 1960s.

Hill was born May 1, 1907, in Richmond. He received his bachelor of arts degree from Howard University in 1931, then continued at Howard and received his doctor of jurisprudence degree in 1933. The following year, he opened a law practice in Roanoke, Virginia, which he later moved to Richmond. He became active in such organizations as the NATIONAL ASSOCIATION FOR THE ADVANCEMENT OF COLORED PEOPLE (NAACP) and the Urban League as well as the local faction of the Democratic party. Hill served a two-year stint in the military from 1943 to 1945, then returned to private practice.

In August 1947, Hill ran for the Virginia House of Delegates. He lost that election by a mere 190 votes, missing an opportunity to become the first black to occupy a seat in Virginia's general assembly since 1890. He returned to politics the following year, and on June 10, 1948, he was elected to a seat on Richmond's city council. With that victory, he became the first black elected to office in Richmond since Reconstruction.

Hill's election was significant because at least two thousand of the nine thousand voters who backed him were white. Such racial crossover voting was unprecedented at the time, but Hill had made an effort to appeal to voters from both races. He shrewdly realized that many whites, some motivated by moral conviction and others by simple pragmatism, understood that change was imminent in the South. The treatment of black soldiers during World War II had forced harsh scrutiny on a system that was coming to an end. "There is rising in the South a large body of white citizens who recognize the importance of extending constitutional

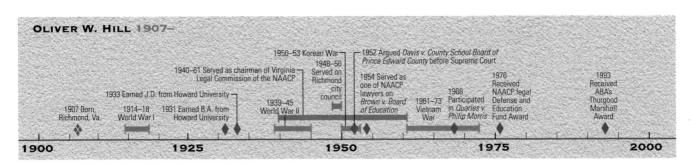

OLIVER W. HILL 1907–

1907 Born, Richmond, Va.

1914–18 World War I

1931 Earned B.A. from Howard University

1933 Earned J.D. from Howard University

1939–45 World War II

1940–61 Served as chairman of Virginia Legal Commission of the NAACP

1948–50 Served on Richmond city council

1950–53 Korean War

1952 Argued *Davis v. County School Board of Prince Edward County* before Supreme Court

1954 Served as one of NAACP lawyers on *Brown v. Board of Education*

1961–73 Vietnam War

1968 Participated in *Quarles v. Philip Morris*

1976 Received NAACP legal Defense and Education Fund Award

1993 Received ABA's Thurgood Marshall Award

1900   1925   1950   1975   2000

guarantees to Negroes in order to strengthen their own economic and political security," he said.

During his stint on the Richmond council, Hill was voted the second-most-effective member of the nine-member body. But his triumph was short-lived: in 1950, he lost his bid for reelection. Later, he was a popular contender for appointment to a vacancy on the council, but because of his uncompromising position on civil rights, he was denied the appointment. African American leaders in Richmond were angered by the rejection, and much of the racial tension that had characterized Richmond before Hill's 1948 victory was rekindled.

Hill returned to his law practice and joined the ranks of the pioneers in the fight for civil rights. During a career that has spanned six decades, he has been involved in many of the landmark cases that secured constitutional rights for minorities in housing, education, and employment. As a member of the Richmond Democratic Committee, he worked diligently to secure minority VOTING rights and to encourage involvement in political activity. From 1940 to 1961, Hill served as chairman of the Virginia Legal Commission of the NAACP and participated in such celebrated legal battles as *Brown v. Board of Education*, 347 U.S. 483, 74 S. Ct. 686, 98 L. Ed. 873 (1954), abolishing segregated public schools, and *Quarles v. Philip Morris*, 279 F. Supp. 505 (ED. Va.), a 1968 case establishing the right of minorities to equal employment opportunities. In August 1955, because of his participation in *Brown*, a fiery cross, the symbol of the KU KLUX KLAN, was burned on the front lawn of his home.

In 1952, President HARRY S. TRUMAN named Hill to the Committee on Government Contract Compliance. This organization was charged with policing the enforcement of federal contract clauses barring racial or religious discrimination in employment. Hill also served, under President JOHN F. KENNEDY, as assistant to the commissioner of the Federal Housing Administration. He returned to his law practice after Kennedy's death.

Hill has received numerous awards and recognitions during his long and distinguished career, including the Howard University Alumni Award (1950), National Bar Association Lawyer of the Year Award (1959), Washington Bar Association Charles H. Houston Medallion of Merit (1976), NAACP Legal Defense and Education Fund Award (1976), NAACP William Ming Advocacy Award (1980), National Council of Christians and Jews Brotherhood Citation (1982), American Bar Association's Thurgood Marshall Award (1993), and Urban League of Richmond Lifetime Achievement Award (1994).

Hill continues to be active in the general practice of law in Richmond and is a partner in the firm of Hill, Tucker, and Marsh. He and his late wife, Beresenia A. Walker Hill, had one son, Oliver W. Hill, Jr., and three grandchildren.

See also BROWN V. BOARD OF EDUCATION OF TOPEKA, KANSAS.

HIROHITO Hirohito was the emperor of Japan from 1926 to 1989. His reign encompassed a period of Japanese militarism that resulted in Japan's participation in World War II, the United States' dropping of atomic bombs on Hiroshima and Nagasaki, and the United States' military occupation of Japan following Japan's defeat. After World War II, Hirohito's authority changed, and he was reduced to a ceremonial figure.

Hirohito was born in Tokyo on April 29, 1901, and was educated in Japan. He became emperor on December 25, 1926, at a time when Japanese parliamentary government suggested that democracy and international cooperation would continue to grow. However, forces within the military sought to dominate the government and embark on a course of expansionism within Asia. Though he had private misgivings about the rise of militarism, Hirohito took no action to stop the generals. His advisers were concerned that imperial opposition would lead to the military overthrow of the monarchy.

As the 124th direct descendant of Japan's first emperor, Jimmu, Hirohito was considered sacred and was referred to as Tenno Heika, meaning "son of heaven." Because Hirohito was unwilling to exercise his divine authority against the military, the Japanese army invaded China in 1937 and in 1940 joined in a military alliance with the Axis powers. The alliance led to Japan's participation in World War II and its attack on Pearl Harbor and the United States on December 7, 1941.

The attack on the United States led to severe consequences for Japanese Americans. On February 19, 1942, President FRANKLIN D. ROOSEVELT issued Executive Order No. 9066, forcing the relocation of all 112,000 Japanese Americans living on the West Coast (including 70,000 U.S. citizens) to detention camps in places such as Jerome, Arkansas, and Heart Mountain, Wyoming. Roosevelt issued the order after U.S. military leaders, worried about a

Emperor Hirohito ruled Japan for most of the twentieth century. After World War II he renounced his divine authority and put the government in the hands of elected officials.

Japanese invasion, argued that national security required such drastic action.

The U.S. Supreme Court upheld the forced relocation in *Korematsu v. United States*, 323 U.S. 214, 65 S. Ct. 193, 89 L. Ed. 194 (1944). Justice HUGO L. BLACK noted that curtailing the rights of a single racial group is constitutionally suspect, but in this case military necessity justified the exclusion of Japanese Americans from the West Coast. In retrospect historians have characterized the removal and detention as the most drastic invasion of individual CIVIL RIGHTS by the government in U.S. history.

Hirohito gradually became more open, within the inner circles of government, about his desire to end the war, especially after the United States inflicted numerous military defeats on Japan. But many members of the military wished to fight until the very end. With the United States' dropping of atomic bombs on Hiroshima and Nagasaki in August 1945, Hirohito pushed for the surrender of Japan. On August 15 he broadcast Japan's surrender to the Allied forces. He broadcast to the Japanese people additional messages that were credited for the smooth transfer of power from Japan to the U.S. military occupation force, under the leadership of General Douglas MacArthur.

Although Hirohito was implicated in Japanese war plans, he was exonerated in the war crimes trials of 1946–48. He had changed the importance of the monarchy in 1946, when he publicly renounced his divine authority. The 1947 constitution that was written for Japan by MacArthur and his advisers had transformed Hirohito from a sovereign with supreme authority into a "symbol of the state," and placed control of the government in the hands of elected officials. Hirohito had endorsed the change, which reduced the emperor to a ceremonial figure.

Hirohito embraced the ceremonial role. He traveled widely and became more accessible. He also pursued his interest in marine biology. He died on January 7, 1989.

CROSS-REFERENCES

Japanese American Evacuation Cases; *Korematsu v. United States.*

HISS, ALGER   For the United States, the prosecution of Alger Hiss was a pivotal domestic event of the cold war. A former high-ranking federal official with a seemingly impeccable reputation, Hiss was accused in 1948 of having spied for the Soviet Union. The charges shocked the nation. Not only had Hiss held government positions of extreme importance, but he was also one of the architects of postwar international relations, having helped establish the UNITED NATIONS. He steadfastly maintained his innocence in hearings before the House Un-American Activities Committee (HUAC). But a relentless probe by the committee's lead investigator, Representative RICHARD M. NIXON, of California, led to a GRAND JURY investigation. In 1950, Hiss was convicted of two counts of PERJURY, for which he served forty-four months in prison. His case became a cause célèbre for liberals, who regarded him as a victim of the era's anti-Communist hysteria. It also fueled a passion for anti-Communist investigations and legislation that preoccupied Congress for the next several years.

Before coming under suspicion, Hiss had a meteoric rise in public service. A Harvard graduate in 1929, the international law specialist served in the Departments of Agriculture and Justice from 1933 to 1936. He then moved to the State Department, where he assumed the post of counselor at global conferences during World War II. In 1945, Hiss advised President FRANKLIN D. ROOSEVELT at the Yalta Conference, at which the Allied powers planned the end of the war. He was forty-one years old. Next came a leading role in the establishment of the United Nations, appointment to the administration of the U.S. Office of Special Political Affairs, and, in 1946, election to the presidency of the Carnegie Endowment for International Peace. As a statesman, Hiss had proved himself in no small way; his career had earned him the highest confidence of his government in times of crisis.

But soon Hiss was swept up in a round of damaging public accusations. By the late 1940s, the U.S. House of Representatives had spent several years investigating Communist influence in business and government. This was the work of HUAC, first established in 1938 and increasingly busy in the years of suspicion that followed World War II. In August 1948, HUAC heard testimony from Whittaker Chambers, an editor at *Time* magazine, who had previously admitted to spying for the Soviet Union. Now Chambers fingered Hiss. He charged that Hiss had secretly been a Communist party member in the 1930s, and most dramatically, he accused Hiss of giving him confidential State Department documents to deliver to the Soviets in 1938.

Accusations of Communist affiliation were common at HUAC hearings—in a sense, they were its chief business. The process of naming names was triggered by the committee's threat of legal action against witnesses who did not cooperate. But even by HUAC's standards, the accusations against Hiss were spectacular. Furthermore, Chambers had evidence. He offered the committee microfilm of the confidential documents, which he claimed had been prepared on Hiss's own typewriter. The charges particularly excited committee member Nixon, a California freshman, who used them to establish his credentials as a tough anti-Communist. In a highly publicized event, Chambers took Nixon to his Maryland farm, where the microfilm was hidden in a hollow pumpkin. Hiss was soon called before HUAC to be grilled by Nixon. He denied Chambers's accusations and dramatically questioned Chambers himself in a vain attempt to clear his name.

A grand jury was impaneled and held hearings in December 1948. Because of the STATUTE OF LIMITATIONS, Hiss could not be tried on charges of ESPIONAGE in 1948 for allegedly passing documents to the Soviets in 1938. But the grand jury returned a two-count INDICTMENT of perjury: it charged that he had lied about giving Chambers the official documents in 1938, and when claiming that he had not even seen Chambers after January 1, 1937.

After his first trial in 1948 ended in a hung jury, Hiss was retried in 1950 (*United States v. Hiss*, 88 F. Supp. 559 [S.D.N.Y. 1950]). Hiss's defense hinged on portraying Chambers, the government's primary witness, as unreliable. He claimed that Chambers was a psychopathic

The trial and conviction of Alger Hiss gave momentum to the anti-Communist sentiment in Washington, D.C., in the early 1950s.

personality prone to chronic lying. In what became the seminal ruling of its kind, the court admitted psychiatric evidence for the reason of discrediting the witness. But despite challenging Chambers's credibility, the validity of Chambers's testimony, and the accuracy of other evidence, Hiss was convicted. Sentenced to five years in prison, he served nearly four years. His career in law and public service was ruined. He spent the next two decades working as a salesman while writing books and giving lectures.

The question of Hiss's guilt has divided intellectuals for decades. Hiss always maintained his innocence—in 1957, when he published a memoir, *In the Court of Public Opinion*, and even more in 1975, when, with prominent help, he successfully sued for reinstatement to the bar of Massachusetts (*In re Hiss*, 368 Mass. 447, 333 N.E.2d 429). Since 1975, some wordsmiths have used Federal Bureau of Investigation files to argue in favor of or against Hiss's guilt: notably, author Allan Weinstein in *Perjury* (1978) and editor Edith Tiger in *In Re Alger Hiss* (1979).

The *Hiss* case profoundly affected the politics of its era. It gave impetus to anti-Communist sentiment in Washington, D.C., which led to more hearings before HUAC as well as legislation such as the McCarran Act (50 U.S.C.A. § 781 et seq.), intended as a crackdown on the American Communist party. The case also helped launch the careers of Nixon and of Senator JOSEPH R. McCARTHY, of Wisconsin, providing the latter with ammunition for an infamous crusade against alleged Communist infiltration of the federal government.

Hiss died November 15, 1996, in New York City.

CROSS-REFERENCES

Cold War; Communism; Communism *In Focus*: House Un-American Activities Committee; Rosenberg, Julius and Ethel.

HITLER, ADOLF   Adolf Hitler ruled Germany as a dictator from 1933 to 1945. Hitler's National Socialist (Nazi) German Workers' party was based on the idea of German racial supremacy and a virulent anti-Semitism. Hitler's regime murdered more than 6 million Jews and others in concentration camps and started World War II.

Hitler was born in Braunauam Inn, Austria, on April 20, 1889, the son of a minor government official and a peasant woman. A poor student, Hitler never completed high school. In 1907 he moved to Vienna and tried to make a living as an artist. He was unsuccessful and had to work as a day laborer to support himself. During this period Hitler immersed himself in anti-Jewish and antidemocratic literature. He was also a passionate German nationalist who believed that Austria should be merged with Germany so as to unite the German people.

In 1913 he moved to Munich. He gave up his Austrian citizenship and enlisted in the German army when World War I began in 1914. He rose to lance corporal in his infantry regiment, won the Iron Cross, and was wounded in 1917. When Germany admitted defeat and signed the armistice terminating World War I in November 1918, Hitler was in a hospital, temporarily blinded by a mustard gas attack and suffering from shock. Outraged at the defeat, Hitler blamed Jews and Communists for stabbing the German army in the back.

Other members of the German army felt the same way. After his discharge from the hospital, Hitler was assigned to spy on politically subversive activities in Munich. In 1919 he joined a small nationalist party. The German Workers' party was transformed in 1920 by Hitler into the National Socialist German Workers' party. The Nazis advocated the uniting of all German people into one nation and the repudiation of the Versailles treaty, which the Allies had forced Germany to sign. This treaty imposed large REPARATIONS on Germany and restricted the size of its armed forces.

In 1923 the Nazis tried to capitalize on political and economic turmoil in Germany. On November 8 Hitler called for a Nazi revolution. The beer hall *putsch* (revolution), named for its place of origin, failed because Hitler had no

Adolf Hitler ruled Germany from 1933 to 1945. He capitalized on Germans' anger at the harsh reparations imposed on them after World War I and built his Nazi party on theories of racial supremacy and anti-Semitism. He led Europe into World War II when he started annexing other nations to Germany.

military support. When he led two thousand storm troopers in revolt, the police opened fire and killed sixteen people. Hitler was arrested and sentenced to five years in prison for TREASON.

While in prison Hitler wrote *Mein Kampf* (My Struggle), a rambling book that was both an autobiography and a declaration of his political beliefs. He made his intentions plain: If he was to assume control of Germany, he would seek to conquer much of Europe and he would destroy the Jewish race. He rejected democracy and called for a dictatorship that would be able to withstand an assault by COMMUNISM.

Hitler served only nine months in prison, as political pressure forced the Bavarian government to commute his sentence. He was set free in December 1924.

From 1924 to 1928, Hitler and the Nazis had little political success. The Great Depression, which started in late 1929, was the catalyst for Hitler's rise to power. As the economy declined, Hitler railed against the Versailles treaty and a conspiracy of Jews and Communists who were destroying Germany. By 1932 the Nazis had become the strongest party in Germany. On January 30, 1933, Hitler was named chancellor, or prime minister, of Germany.

Many German leaders believed that Hitler could be controlled by industrialists and the German army. Instead, Hitler quickly moved to make Germany a one-party state and himself the führer (leader). He abolished labor unions, imposed government CENSORSHIP, and directed that Nazi propaganda dominate the press and the radio. The gestapo, Hitler's secret police, waged a war of terror on Nazi opponents. Jews were fired from jobs, placed in concentration camps, and driven from Germany. By 1934 Hitler was securely in charge.

The majority of Germans supported Hitler enthusiastically. He restored full employment, rebuilt the German economy, and allowed Germans to escape the feelings of inferiority instilled after World War I.

Hitler broke the Versailles treaty and proceeded with a massive buildup of the German armed forces. In 1936 he reclaimed the Rhineland from French control, and in 1938 he annexed Austria to Germany. Also in 1938 he took over the German areas of Czechoslovakia, and in 1939 he annexed all of that country. When he invaded Poland on September 1, 1939, Great Britain and France declared war on Germany. World War II had begun.

During the early years of Hitler's regime, some prominent U.S. citizens had believed he was a positive force for Germany. As Hitler became more aggressive and war clouds appeared, U.S. isolationists argued against involvement. People such as aviator Charles A. Lindbergh argued for an America First policy.

Concerns about Nazism led in part to the SMITH ACT (54 Stat. 670) in 1940. Nazi sympathizers organized groups such as the Silvershirts and the German-American Bund, raising the specter of subversion. The Smith Act required ALIENS to register with and be fingerprinted by the federal government. More important, it made it illegal not only to conspire to overthrow the government, but to advocate or conspire to advocate to do so. The U.S. Supreme Court upheld the constitutionality of the act in *Dennis v. United States*, 341 U.S. 494, 71 S. Ct. 857, 95 L. Ed. 1137 (1951).

Hitler's quick and easy conquest of western Europe in 1940 left Great Britain alone. With the Japanese attack on Pearl Harbor on December 7, 1941, the United States and Great Britain became allies in World War II. They were joined by the Soviet Union, which Hitler had invaded in June 1941. In 1942 the war turned against Hitler. North Africa and then Italy were lost to the Allies. In June 1944, the Allies invaded France and were soon nearing Germany. On the eastern front, the Soviet army moved toward Berlin. During these last years of the war, Hitler directed the extermination of Jews and other "undesirables" in concentration camps.

On July 20, 1944, Hitler escaped an ASSASSINATION attempt. As the military situation crumbled, Hitler realized that defeat was inevitable. While Soviet troops entered Berlin in April 1945, Hitler married his longtime mistress, Eva Braun. On April 30 the two committed suicide. Their bodies were burned by Hitler's aides.

CROSS-REFERENCES

Dennis v. United States; Hirohito; Mussolini, Benito; Nuremberg Trials.

BIOGRAPHY

Ebenezer Rockwood Hoar

HOAR, EBENEZER ROCKWOOD

Ebenezer Rockwood Hoar served as attorney general of the United States from 1869 to 1870 under President ULYSSES S. GRANT.

Hoar was born February 21, 1816, in Concord, Massachusetts. His grandfather, Captain Samuel Hoar, was a Revolutionary War hero. His father, Samuel Hoar, Jr., was a Harvard graduate, a Massachusetts state senator, a U.S. representative—and a lifelong activist in partisan politics. Hoar's father was affiliated with the Federalist party until it disappeared after the

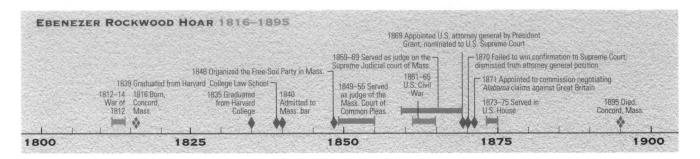

EBENEZER ROCKWOOD HOAR 1816–1895

1869 Appointed U.S. attorney general by President Grant; nominated to U.S. Supreme Court

1848 Organized the Free-Soil Party in Mass.

1859–69 Served as judge on the Supreme Judicial court of Mass.

1870 Failed to win confirmation to Supreme Court; dismissed from attorney general position

1839 Graduated from Harvard College Law School

1861–65 U.S. Civil War

1871 Appointed to commission negotiating *Alabama* claims against Great Britain

1812–14 War of 1812

1816 Born, Concord, Mass.

1835 Graduated from Harvard College

1840 Admitted to Mass. bar

1849–55 Served as judge of the Mass. Court of Common Pleas

1873–75 Served in U.S. House

1895 Died, Concord, Mass.

1800   1825   1850   1875   1900

War of 1812, was associated with the Whig party in the 1830s, was an organizer of the Massachusetts Free-Soil party in the 1840s, and joined the Republican party toward the end of his life.

Hoar's educational path, professional career, and political interests closely mirrored those of his father. Hoar graduated from Harvard College in 1835 and from Harvard Law School in 1839. He was admitted to the bar in 1840 and he practiced law in Concord and Boston. His father's legal and political connections allowed him to try cases with leading attorneys of his day, including RUFUS CHOATE and DANIEL WEBSTER.

Like his father, Hoar began his political career at the state level. In the early 1840s, he was elected to the Massachusetts state senate. His chance remark that he would rather be a Conscience Whig than a Cotton Whig gave the former name to the antislavery arm of the Whig party. By 1848, he was working with his father to organize the Free-Soil party in Massachusetts. This party emerged in the late 1840s to oppose the extension of SLAVERY in newly acquired western territories and to curb the resulting legislative and electoral power that expansion would bring to southern cotton and tobacco interests.

From 1849 to 1855 Hoar served as a judge of the Massachusetts Court of Common Pleas. In 1859 he was named to the Supreme Judicial Court of Massachusetts. During his early years on the bench, Hoar took a special interest in the skills of the young lawyers who appeared before him. He was known to write to them— or their mentors—critiquing their courtroom appearances. After hearing OLIVER WENDELL HOLMES, JR., for the first time, Hoar wrote to Holmes's father, telling him that Holmes "made a very creditable appearance." Hoar also noted that the young Holmes's argument in the case at hand had been "a little savoring of experimental philosophy."

In March 1869, Hoar was named attorney general of the United States by President Grant. Hoar was popular with the public and

thoroughly qualified to serve but he was also independent and outspoken. As attorney general, he severely alienated patronage-seeking senators when he insisted on filling nine new circuit judgeships with competent judges rather than using the positions as opportunities for political paybacks.

When a vacancy on the U.S. Supreme Court occurred shortly after Hoar became attorney general, President Grant offered him the seat. Hoar's formal nomination in December 1869 drew expected opposition from the Senate. Citing Hoar's effort to eliminate government PATRONAGE, as well as his opposition to the IMPEACHMENT of President ANDREW JOHNSON, conservative Republican senators were especially vocal in their disapproval.

When a second vacancy on the High Court opened while Hoar's nomination was pending, the Senate moved quickly to see that President Grant named a candidate for that vacancy who was more to their liking. Their choice was the late president ABRAHAM LINCOLN's secretary of war, EDWIN M. STANTON. In exchange for Grant's nomination and support of Stanton, the Senate agreed to confirm Hoar.

The Senate pushed ahead on Stanton's nomination, confirming him in less than four hours, but Stanton never took his seat on the Court. Just four days after his confirmation, he suffered a fatal heart attack. Meanwhile, the Senate continued to debate Hoar's suitability for the position. "[R]egarding a dead Justice of its choosing to be an insufficient half of a bargain," it rejected Hoar by a vote of 33–24 on February 3, 1870.

The battle between President Grant and the Senate over Hoar's Supreme Court nomination remained a source of antagonism even after the vote. To end the fight and to cultivate Senate support for his other programs, Grant dismissed Hoar as attorney general in July 1870.

Hoar understood the political reasons for Grant's decision and he maintained a cordial relationship with the president. For his part, Grant remembered both Hoar's legal skills and his allegiance. Grant called on Hoar again in

1871 to serve on a joint commission to negotiate the treaty of arbitration that eventually settled the United States' *Alabama* claims against Great Britain.

Following the Civil War, relations between the United States and Great Britain were jeopardized by U.S. claims that England should pay for damages done during the war by the *Alabama* and other Confederate ships—which had been accorded belligerency status by Great Britain. (In international law, belligerency refers to the status of de facto statehood attributed to a body of insurgents, by which their hostilities are legalized). Hoar served as the Grant administration's liaison with senators who urged a hard-line approach to settling the claims. He was influential in convincing Grant to deny belligerency status to insurgents in Cuba (as Britain had done to the Confederacy), because the action would weaken the U.S. bargaining position with England during the treaty negotiations.

Following his work on the treaty, Hoar returned to his home in Massachusetts. As a Republican candidate, he sought and won a seat in the U.S. House, which he subsequently held from December 1, 1873, to March 3, 1875. His brother, George Frisbie Hoar, was serving as a representative from Massachusetts at the same time, having been elected in 1868.

After leaving office, Hoar continued to be active in local and national Republican politics until his death, on January 31, 1895, in Concord.

HOBBES, THOMAS
Sixteenth-century political theorist, philosopher, and scientist Thomas Hobbes left a stark warning to succeeding generations: strong central authority is the necessary basis for government. In several influential works of legal, political, psychological, and philosophical theory, Hobbes's view of society and its leaders was founded on pessimism. He saw people as weak and selfish, and thus in constant need of the governance that could save them from destruction. These ideas profoundly affected the Federalists during the early formation of U.S. law. The Federalists turned to

BIOGRAPHY

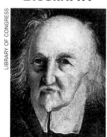

Thomas Hobbes

Hobbes's work for justification for passage of the U.S. Constitution as well as for intellectual support for their own movement in the years following that passage. Today, Hobbes is read not only for his lasting contributions to political-legal theory in general but for the ideas that helped shape U.S. history.

Born on April 5, 1588, in Westport, Wiltshire, England, the son of an Anglican clergyman, Hobbes was a prodigy. By the age of fifteen, he had entered Oxford University; by twenty, he was appointed tutor to a prominent family, a post he would later hold with the Prince of Wales. His considerable output of work began with English translations of Francis Bacon and Thucydides while he was in his late thirties. Soon, mathematics interested him, and his travels brought him into contact with some of the greatest minds of his age: Galileo and René Descartes. His writing canvassed many subjects, such as language and science, to arrive at a general theory of people and their leaders. The most influential works of this polymath came in the 1650s: *Leviathan, or the Matter, Form, and Power of a Commonwealth, Ecclesiastical and Civil* (1651), *De Corpore* (1655), and *Questions Concerning Liberty, Necessity, and Chance* (1656). Hobbes died December 4, 1679, at age 91.

Hobbes was a supreme pessimist. To him, people were inherently selfish; they struggled constantly against one another for survival. "[T]he life of a man," he wrote in his masterwork, *Leviathan*, "is solitary, poor, nasty, brutish and short." Thus, people could not survive on their own in the state of nature. This foundation led him to a theory of the law: only by submitting to the protection of a sovereign power could individuals avoid constant anarchy and war. The sovereign's authority would have to be absolute. Law derived from this authority rather than from objective truth, which he argued did not exist. All citizens of the state were morally bound to follow the sovereign's authority; otherwise, law could not function. Hobbes chose the leviathan (a large sea animal) to represent the state, and he maintained that

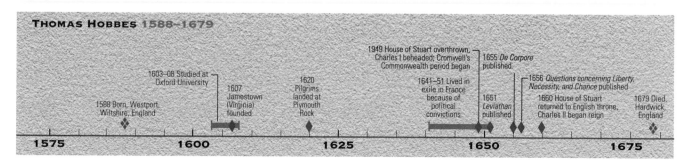

THOMAS HOBBES 1588–1679

1588 Born, Westport, Wiltshire, England

1603–08 Studied at Oxford University

1607 Jamestown (Virginia) founded

1620 Pilgrims landed at Plymouth Rock

1949 House of Stuart overthrown, Charles I beheaded; Cromwell's Commonwealth period began

1641–51 Lived in exile in France because of political convictions

1651 *Leviathan* published

1655 *De Corpore* published

1656 *Questions concerning Liberty, Necessity, and Chance* published

1660 House of Stuart returned to English throne, Charles II began reign

1679 Died, Hardwick, England

1575   1600   1625   1650   1675

like a whale, the state could only be guided by one intelligence: its sovereign's.

The influence of Hobbes's ideas varied dramatically over the seventeenth and eighteenth centuries. English politicians and clerics derided him as a heretic. But his theories eventually lent support to loyalists who wanted to preserve the Crown's control over the American colonies: Thomas Hutchinson, the last royal governor of Massachusetts, viewed the upstart challengers to royal authority in a Hobbesian light. Later, Hobbes proved useful to the other side: after the American Revolution, his ideas influenced the Federalists in their arguments for adoption of the federal Constitution in 1787. Embracing Hobbes's pessimism, the Federalists saw the American people as unable to survive as a nation without a strong central government that would protect them from foreign powers.

Hobbes is still taught, and scholars continue to discuss contemporary legal issues in the light of his critique. Particularly relevant are his insights into the form of law and the interrelationship of law and politics, and his subtle explorations of language and meaning.

HOFFA, JAMES RIDDLE One of the most powerful labor leaders in U.S. history, James Riddle Hoffa ruled with brawn and charisma for fourteen years as president of the International Brotherhood of Teamsters, Chauffeurs, Warehousemen, and Helpers of America. From 1957 to 1971, Hoffa bound the loose-knit Teamsters into a cohesive organization that won higher wages and tremendous bargaining power for its members. Loved by his union rank and file, he was thought ruthless, cunning, and corrupt by his enemies, among them law enforcement leaders such as ROBERT F. KENNEDY. Federal investigators pursued Hoffa for several years because of his reputed ties to ORGANIZED CRIME. He dodged conviction until being found guilty in 1964 on unrelated charges of jury tampering and MALFEASANCE in a real estate deal. He began serving a thirteen-year prison sentence in 1967, which President RICHARD M. NIXON commuted in late 1971. He disappeared mysteriously in 1975.

"THE CONDITION OF MAN . . . IS A CONDITION OF WAR OF EVERYONE AGAINST EVERYONE."

BIOGRAPHY

APWIDE WORLD PHOTOS

James Riddle Hoffa

Hoffa rose from obscure origins to stand in the national spotlight. He was born February 14, 1913, in Brazil, Indiana, and his family lived in Indiana by modest means. His father, a coal driller, died of an occupational respiratory disease when Hoffa was seven. The second of four children, Hoffa, an athletic, shy B-student, quit school after the ninth grade to work full-time as a stock boy in a department store.

In 1930, still a teenager, Hoffa became a freight handler in a warehouse of the Kroger Grocery and Baking Company in Clinton, Indiana. Here came a turning point in his life, brought on by what he called a need for self-preservation in the face of meager pay and poor working conditions. The young man soon led the other warehousemen in a successful STRIKE that would become a part of the Hoffa legend: by refusing to unload a shipment of perishable strawberries, they forced the company to accede to their demands. With his prowess as an organizer quickly recognized, Hoffa left the warehouse in 1932 to become a full-time Teamster organizer in Detroit. The four coworkers who had helped him carry off the strike at Kroger left with him and remained his staff members throughout his career.

Hoffa found his new work difficult in the beginning. During the 1930s, opposition to labor organizers was fierce and often violent. Clashes with management strikebreakers and police officers would turn bloody—Hoffa himself was beaten up twenty-four times, by his count, during his first year alone. Describing this "war" in his 1970 autobiography, *The Trials of Jimmy Hoffa*, he recalled, "Managements didn't want us around . . . and the police, recognizing who the big taxpayers were and responding to orders of politicians who knew quite well where the big contributions came from, seemed not only willing but anxious to shove us around." Tenacity, bullish strength, and a persuasive personal style were traits that helped him not only survive opposition but win new recruits to his side.

In the Depression era, the Teamsters were loosely organized in isolated areas. In 1937, Hoffa joined forces with the Trotskyite leader

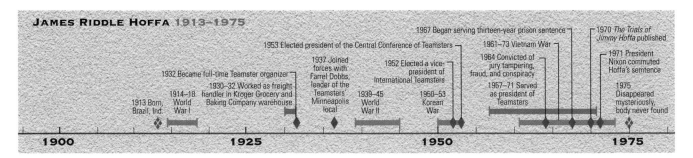

JAMES RIDDLE HOFFA 1913–1975

1913 Born, Brazil, Ind.
1914–18 World War I
1930–32 Worked as freight handler in Kroger Grocery and Baking Company warehouse
1932 Became full-time Teamster organizer
1937 Joined forces with Farrel Dobbs, leader of the Teamsters' Minneapolis local
1939–45 World War II
1950–53 Korean War
1952 Elected a vice-president of International Teamsters
1953 Elected president of the Central Conference of Teamsters
1957–71 Served as president of Teamsters
1961–73 Vietnam War
1964 Convicted of jury tampering, fraud, and conspiracy
1967 Began serving thirteen-year prison sentence
1970 *The Trials of Jimmy Hoffa* published
1971 President Nixon commuted Hoffa's sentence
1975 Disappeared mysteriously, body never found

1900   1925   1950   1975

of the Minneapolis local Teamsters, Farrel Dobbs, a socialist who was successfully unionizing drivers in the Midwest. Hoffa helped Dobbs organize long-haul highway truck drivers under the Central States Drivers Council. However, Hoffa was never above using strong-arm tactics, and later, when it served him, he would help the federal government suppress the Trotskyites.

Whether with management or with rival unions, his policy was toughness. By 1941, he was making his first contacts with organized crime figures, as his biographer, Arthur A. Sloane, documented: that year, he enlisted the help of Detroit mobsters—the so-called East Side Crowd—to drive a rival union out of town. Thereafter, dealings with mobsters became regular. Never admitting any illegality, Hoffa nonetheless did not hide these connections. In later years, he claimed, "I'm no different than the banks, no different than the insurance companies, no different than the politicians."

Hoffa ascended to power during the 1940s. He became vice president of the Central States Drivers Council, then president of the Michigan Conference of Teamsters, later an examiner of the Teamster's books, and eventually president of the Teamsters Joint Council 43 in Detroit. In 1952, he was elected an International Teamsters vice president. By 1953, as president of the Central Conference of Teamsters, he was the chief negotiator for truck drivers in twenty states. Over the next decade, Hoffa set about centralizing the Teamsters. As his power grew, local union leaders were encouraged to call Hoffa for authorization to hold strikes. The national bargaining unit that he created amassed such clout that it forged the trucking industry's first national contract in January 1964.

Although his gains were resisted by industry leaders, Hoffa won a reputation for being faithful to contracts. Within the Teamsters, the rank and file respected the gains he won for them and regarded him with open affection. At rallies and in interviews, he employed a speaking style more polished than his ninth-grade education might have suggested, gravelly yet authoritative. Frequently referring to himself in the third person, he would often boast, "Hoffa can take care of Hoffa."

But Hoffa was also running into trouble. Prompted by allegations of labor racketeering, the U.S. Senate began investigating several unions in January 1957. Nationally televised hearings were conducted by the Senate Select Committee on Improper Activities in the Labor or Management Field—popularly known as the McClellan Committee, after its presiding of-

ficer, Senator JOHN LITTLE MCCLELLAN. Over two years, the committee uncovered widespread corruption in the Teamsters. Teamster president Dave Beck resigned; he was later convicted of LARCENY, EMBEZZLEMENT, and income TAX EVASION. Hoffa, succeeding Beck as president, faced months of intense questioning by Senator JOHN F. KENNEDY and the committee's chief counsel, ROBERT KENNEDY.

The committee alleged that Hoffa had used union funds for his own profit, accepted payoffs from trucking companies, and associated with convicted labor racketeer John Dioguardi. Pressed by the Kennedys during hearings that had an air of open animosity, Hoffa admitted nothing. Just before one of his scheduled appearances, FEDERAL BUREAU OF INVESTIGATION (FBI) agents arrested him on charges of trying to bribe a lawyer to leak confidential committee memos to him. Robert Kennedy announced he would jump off the dome of the Capitol building if the union leader was not convicted. When Hoffa was acquitted after a four-month trial, his attorney offered to send Kennedy a parachute.

The McClellan Committee report condemned Hoffa and the Teamsters. One result was the passage of more stringent legislation concerning unions; another was the expulsion of the Teamsters from the American Federation of Labor and Congress of Industrial Organizations (AFL-CIO). For Hoffa, the hearings marked the beginning of a feud between himself and Robert Kennedy that would deepen upon the latter's appointment in 1960 as attorney general. Kennedy devoted considerable resources within the U.S. Justice Department to prosecuting Hoffa, whom he described as heading a conspiracy of evil. Despite several indictments, Hoffa escaped conviction until 1964. First, he was convicted of jury tampering and sentenced to eight years in prison. The manner in which the conviction was obtained later brought a rebuke from U.S. Supreme Court chief justice EARL WARREN: the U.S. Justice Department used a jailed Teamster member to trap Hoffa. At a second 1964 trial, Hoffa received an additional five years for FRAUD and CONSPIRACY in the handling of a Teamster benefit fund.

In March 1967, with his appeals exhausted, Hoffa began serving his thirteen-year sentence in Lewisburg Federal Penitentiary, in Pennsylvania. Hoffa refused to relinquish control of the Teamsters. He was denied PAROLE three times. Then, in December 1971, President Nixon commuted his sentence on the condition that he refrain from union activities until the year 1980. His attorneys worked to reverse the limi-

"IN THE OLD DAYS ALL YOU NEEDED WAS A HANDSHAKE. NOWADAYS YOU NEED FORTY LAWYERS."

tation, while he campaigned on behalf of prison reform. But he never regained power.

In 1975, Hoffa drove to a suburban Detroit restaurant to meet reputed crime figure Anthony ("Tony Pro") Provenzano. Hoffa's car was found later, but he was never seen again. For several years, the FBI maintained an open file on Hoffa, yet it never solved the mystery. Theories about his disappearance abound, including the belief that Hoffa was buried underneath the goalposts at the Meadowlands football stadium, in New Jersey. In 1989, the retiring FBI chief in Detroit, Kenneth P. Walton, told the press that he knew the identity of Hoffa's killer. But Walton said the case would never be prosecuted because doing so would compromise the security of FBI sources and informants.

Hoffa's legacy is still controversial. Critics charged that the script for the 1993 film dramatization of his life, by screenwriter David Mamet, celebrated Hoffa while purposely ignoring the extent of his involvement with crime figures. Also in 1993, the longtime suspicion that Hoffa had been involved in a plot to assassinate President Kennedy generated renewed interest. Frank Ragano, a former mob lawyer, claimed that he personally delivered a message from Hoffa to two mobsters, which read "kill the president." Such speculation has never been substantiated, but another aspect of Hoffa's legacy is beyond doubt. Although he was enormously successful in building the Teamsters, his association with mobsters left a stain on the union that would linger for decades to come. Not until the late 1980s, when the federal government took control of the union's national elections, did the Teamsters begin to emerge from the shadow of organized crime.

See also LABOR LAW; LABOR UNION.

HOFFMAN, WALTER EDWARD Federal district judge Walter Edward Hoffman "single-handedly cleared a legendary backlog" of cases in the late 1950s by "working around the clock and seven days a week." A firm believer that justice delayed is often justice denied, Hoffman created the "rocket docket" system to move cases through his courtroom more efficiently.

Hoffman's workaholic spirit came to characterize his court—and years after his retirement, the Eastern District of Virginia was still one of the fastest and most efficient courts in the United States. (Studies conducted in the 1980s by the Administrative Office of the U.S. Courts showed that the Eastern District of Virginia consistently beat all other federal JURISDICTIONS in elapsed time between the filing of litigants' papers and the start of a civil trial.) Owing in large part to the timesaving tactics developed by Hoffman, the Eastern District of Virginia, which stretches from Northern Virginia to the North Carolina line and includes Alexandria, Norfolk, and Richmond courts, in 1987 averaged only five months (compared with a national average of fourteen months) from the filing of a case to the start of its trial. The court also maintained one of the lowest reversal rates in the country.

Speed, efficiency, and the ability to juggle a wide variety of tasks simultaneously were lifelong character traits of the man who developed the rocket docket. He was born July 18, 1907, in Jersey City, New Jersey. After completing a bachelor of science degree in economics at the University of Pennsylvania in 1928, Hoffman attended the Marshall-Wythe School of Law, at the College of William and Mary. He later transferred to Washington and Lee University School of Law, where he received a bachelor of laws degree in 1931.

In 1931, he joined the Norfolk law firm of Rumble and Rumble and also began teaching law on a part-time basis at the College of William and Mary. In 1935, he and a colleague established the law firm of Breeden and Hoffman; their partnership thrived until Hoffman was appointed to the federal bench in 1954. While practicing law, Hoffman continued to teach—and he took an active role in the Norfolk and Portsmouth Bar Association, serving as president in 1948. He also maintained memberships in the Virginia Bar Association and the American Bar Association, serving on numerous committees and taking leadership roles when called upon to do so. His committee work brought Hoffman to the attention of the na-

BIOGRAPHY

COURTESY OF W. E. HOFFMAN

Walter Edward Hoffman

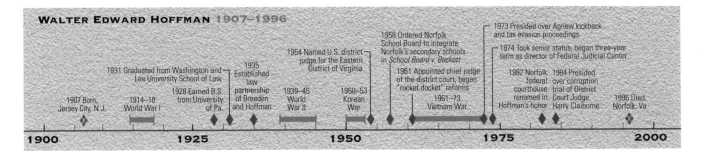

WALTER EDWARD HOFFMAN 1907–1996

1907 Born, Jersey City, N.J.

1914–18 World War I

1928 Earned B.S. from University of Pa.

1931 Graduated from Washington and Lee University School of Law

1935 Established law partnership of Breeden and Hoffman

1939–45 World War II

1950–53 Korean War

1954 Named U.S. district judge for the Eastern District of Virginia

1958 Ordered Norfolk School Board to integrate Norfolk's secondary schools in *School Board v. Beckett*

1961 Appointed chief judge of the district court; began "rocket docket" reforms

1961–73 Vietnam War

1973 Presided over Agnew kickback and tax evasion proceedings

1974 Took senior status; began three-year term as director of Federal Judicial Center

1982 Norfolk federal courthouse renamed in Hoffman's honor

1984 Presided over corruption trial of District Court Judge Harry Claiborne

1996 Died, Norfolk, Va.

1900   1925   1950   1975   2000

tional legal community, and before long, he was considered for a federal judgeship.

Hoffman was named U.S. district judge for the Eastern District of Virginia on September 3, 1954. Soon after his appointment, the issue of SCHOOL DESEGREGATION came to his court. In 1958, he ordered the Norfolk School Board to admit seventeen black students to white secondary schools (*School Board v. Beckett*, 260 F.2d 18 [1958]). The schools were immediately closed under state laws intended to thwart integration, and Hoffman became the target of segregationist attacks from around the country. Despite public and private pressure to do otherwise, Hoffman held firm in his order and in his denial of a request by the school to delay admitting the seventeen students until the following year.

In the late 1950s, both the volume of cases on his DOCKET and their volatile nature prompted Hoffman to explore ways of delivering more timely justice in his jurisdiction. He made a personal commitment to clear his own backlog of cases and to put future trials on a tighter schedule. His marathon court sessions to achieve this goal are now judicial legend. As he worked to clear his backlog, Hoffman began to develop courtroom procedures and a philosophy for speeding justice. He also began to seek out professional colleagues with similar concerns. To that end, he volunteered to serve on the U.S. Judicial Conference Advisory Committee on Criminal Rules in 1960.

When Hoffman became chief judge in 1961, he put his theories into practice. On July 31 of that year, he wrote an open letter to attorneys in his jurisdiction: "[W]ith an excess of 750 civil and admiralty cases pending on the dockets . . . it is apparent that there must be a drastic change in procedure relating to the preparation of cases for trial." The next day, he issued a lengthy order that became the basis for the rocket docket system—an order that has sped up justice in Virginia ever since.

The foundation of Hoffman's system was setting firm trial dates and keeping them. Hearings and trials were scheduled early; and pretrial investigation was limited, as were the number of character and expert WITNESSES at trial. STIPULATIONS were encouraged so that time would not be wasted proving facts that all parties agreed to accept. And Hoffman made it clear to all parties that delaying tactics would not be tolerated in his court. "We decided we didn't want to miss a single trial date," he recalled in 1987, "and we still don't."

Hoffman felt that delays are costly because "lawyers are less keen, witnesses are harder to locate, and every type of confusion and slip-up is more likely." Critics of Hoffman's approach said that the pace of litigation in his court favored large law firms and businesses with access to vast legal resources, and that too often his system allowed little time to negotiate a settlement before trial. But the vast majority of litigators in Hoffman's jurisdiction praised his methods. In 1968, the Virginia Trial Lawyers Association presented him with its annual award, for his contributions to the advancement of justice in Virginia.

Although speedy justice was important to Hoffman, he also recognized that the quality of justice ultimately rested on the quality of judges and of judicial education. Perhaps for this reason, he joined the Board of Directors of the FEDERAL JUDICIAL CENTER in 1972, and served as director of the center from 1974 to 1977. As director, he was responsible for the development and delivery of seminars instructing new judges on both law and administrative issues. Hoffman took a central role in many of the seminars, drawing on his experience to lead discussions and alert attendees to the difficulties encountered, and errors made, by inexperienced judges.

Hoffman took senior (or semiretired) status in 1974. As a senior judge, he accepted assignments to district and circuit courts throughout the federal system. In his capacity as senior judge, he was involved in a number of high-profile cases, including the criminal prosecutions of former vice president Spiro T. Agnew for tax evasion, former U.S. district judge Harry E. Claiborne for tax evasion, former Charleston mayor Mike Roark for cocaine possession and obstruction of justice, and former West Virginia governor Arch A. Moore, Jr., for extortion, mail fraud, tax fraud, and obstruction of justice.

Even at senior status, Hoffman often heard more cases than many of his younger colleagues. "He's regarded as one of the premier federal trial judges in the United States," said U.S. district judge John T. Copenhaver, Jr., at one of the many award ceremonies acknowledging Hoffman's lifelong contributions to the bench. In 1976, the American Judicature Society presented Hoffman with the Herbert Harley Award for aiding the effective administration of justice throughout the United States.

In 1977, the U.S. Judicial Conference passed a resolution commending Hoffman's past services to the judiciary, with special emphasis on his services as director of the Federal Judicial Center. Also in 1977, Hoffman began a fifteen-year tenure on the Temporary Emergency Court of Appeals, and he returned to the College of William and Mary as a visiting professor. In 1982, the U.S. Senate voted to rename the federal courthouse in Norfolk in his honor.

"FOR MANY, DEFENDANTS AS WELL AS PLAINTIFFS, JUSTICE DELAYED MAY BE JUSTICE DENIED OR JUSTICE MITIGATED IN QUALITY."

Hoffman responded by saying he doubted "that a single United States senator knew what he was voting for" that day.

In 1984, Hoffman became the second recipient of the Devitt Distinguished Service to Justice Award, which is administered by the American Judicature Society. This award—named for Edward J. Devitt, former chief U.S. district judge for Minnesota—acknowledges the dedication and contributions to justice made by all federal judges, by recognizing the specific achievements of one judge who has contributed significantly to the profession. Hoffman was acknowledged for improving the quality of justice through efficient judicial administration.

In his late eighties, Hoffman had slowed his pace, but he continued to hear some cases in the nation's federal courts. Hoffman died November 21, 1996, in Norfolk, Virginia. He was married to Helen Caulfield Hoffman and was the father of two children.

HOLDER 📖 An individual who has lawfully received possession of a COMMERCIAL PAPER, such as a CHECK, and who is entitled to payment on such instrument. 📖

A holder is distinguishable from a HOLDER IN DUE COURSE since, in addition to possession of the instrument, the latter takes it for value, in good faith, and in the absence of any NOTICE that there is any claim against it or that it is overdue or has been dishonored, which means that payment of it has been refused.

HOLDER IN DUE COURSE 📖 An individual who takes a COMMERCIAL PAPER for value, in good faith, with the belief that it is valid, with no knowledge of any defects. 📖

The UNIFORM COMMERCIAL CODE (UCC) defines a holder in due course as one who takes an instrument for value in good faith absent any NOTICE that it is overdue, has been dishonored, or is subject to any defense against it or claim to it by any other person.

HOLD HARMLESS AGREEMENT 📖 An agreement or CONTRACT in which one party agrees to hold the other free from the responsibility for any LIABILITY or damage that might arise out of the transaction involved. 📖

For example, a company might agree in an employee's contract to pay the judgment if the person is successfully sued for injuries sustained by a plaintiff if the employee is acting within the scope of his or her authority on company time.

In certain cases, particular parties may not, however, be exempted from liability. For example, a provision exempting a COMMON CARRIER from all liability for loss would ordinarily be void, as against PUBLIC POLICY.

Hold harmless agreements are ordinarily contained in LEASES and EASEMENTS.

HOLDING 📖 A comprehensive term applied to the property, whether real, personal, or both, owned by an individual or a business. The legal principle derived from a judicial decision. That part of the written opinion of a court in which the law is specifically applied to the facts of the instant controversy. It is relied upon when courts use the case as an established PRECEDENT in a subsequent case. 📖

A holding is distinguishable from DICTA, which is language in the opinion relating some observation or example that may be illustrative, but which is not part of the court's judgment in the case.

HOLDING COMPANY 📖 A CORPORATION that limits its business to the ownership of STOCK in and the supervision of management of other corporations. 📖

A holding company is organized specifically to hold the stock of other companies and ordinarily owns such a dominant interest in the other company or companies that it can dictate policy. Holding companies must comply with the federal ANTITRUST laws that proscribe the secret and total acquisition of the stock of one corporation by another, since this would lessen competition and create a MONOPOLY.

HOLD OVER 📖 To continue in possession of an office and exercise the functions associated therewith following the expiration of the term thereof. To retain possession as a TENANT of REAL PROPERTY following the termination of the LEASE or tenancy at will. 📖

A *hold over tenant* is also known as a *tenant at sufferance*, since the tenant has no ESTATE or TITLE to the property but only possession thereof.

HOLIDAY 📖 A day of recreation; a consecrated day; a day set apart for the suspension of business. 📖

A *legal holiday* is a day set aside by statute for recreation, the cessation of work, or religious observance. It is a day that is legally designated as exempt from the conduct of all judicial proceedings, SERVICE OF PROCESS, and the demand and protest of COMMERCIAL PAPER. A prohibition against conducting public business transactions on holidays does not, however, have an effect upon private business. Private transactions will not, therefore, be invalidated solely because they are conducted on a holiday.

HOLMES, OLIVER WENDELL, JR. Oliver Wendell Holmes, Jr., was a justice of the U.S. Supreme Court and legal philosopher who has become a celebrated legal figure. His writings on JURISPRUDENCE have shaped discussions on

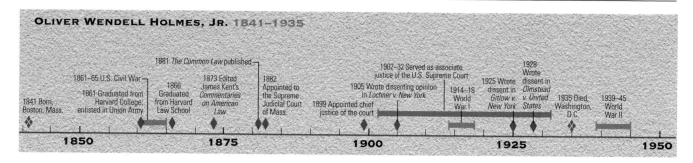

OLIVER WENDELL HOLMES, JR. 1841–1935

1841 Born, Boston, Mass.

1861 Graduated from Harvard College; enlisted in Union Army

1861–65 U.S. Civil War

1866 Graduated from Harvard Law School

1873 Edited James Kent's *Commentaries on American Law*

1881 *The Common Law* published

1882 Appointed to the Supreme Judicial Court of Mass.

1899 Appointed chief justice of the court

1902–32 Served as associate justice of the U.S. Supreme Court

1905 Wrote dissenting opinion in *Lochner v. New York*

1914–18 World War I

1925 Wrote dissent in *Gitlow v. New York*

1928 Wrote dissent in *Olmstead v. United States*

1935 Died, Washington, D.C.

1939–45 World War II

1850   1875   1900   1925   1950

the nature of law, and his court opinions have been studied as much for their style as for their intellectual content. Though Holmes has been widely praised, he does have critics who contend that he paid too much deference to the power of the state to control individual freedom.

Holmes was born March 8, 1841, in Boston. His father, Oliver Wendell Holmes, Sr., was a well-known physician, a lecturer at Harvard Medical School, an author who was widely read in England and the United States, and a founder of the *Atlantic Monthly*. Holmes attended private school and then Harvard College, graduating in 1861. With the outbreak of the Civil War in 1861, Holmes enlisted as an officer in the Twentieth Massachusetts Volunteer Infantry.

His military service was difficult. Holmes was wounded three times, twice almost fatally, and suffered from dysentery. In 1863 he accepted a position as an aide to a Union general, and he served in that capacity until 1864. He resigned his commission before the end of the war and returned, exhausted, to Boston, where he began preparations for a legal career.

He attended Harvard Law School and graduated in 1866. He was admitted to the Massachusetts bar in 1867. Because of inherited wealth Holmes had the financial luxury of pursuing his intellectual interests. He edited the twelfth edition of jurist JAMES KENT's *Commentaries on American Law* (1873) and wrote many articles for the *American Law Review*. Following his marriage to Fanny Dixwell in 1873, Holmes joined a prominent Boston law firm, where he practiced commercial law.

Holmes did not abandon his inquiries into the nature of law. He was invited to Boston to present a series of lectures on the law, which were published in 1881 as *The Common Law*. This volume is the most renowned work of legal philosophy in U.S. history. It allowed Holmes systematically to analyze, classify, and explain various aspects of U.S. COMMON LAW, ranging from TORTS to CONTRACTS to crime and punishment.

BIOGRAPHY

ARTIST CHARLES SYDNEY HOPKINSON. COLLECTION OF THE SUPREME COURT OF THE UNITED STATES.

Oliver Wendell Holmes, Jr.

In *The Common Law*, Holmes traced the origins of the common law to ancient societies where LIABILITY was based on feelings of revenge and the subjective intentions of a morally blameworthy wrongdoer. For example, Holmes observed that in such societies creditors were permitted to cut up and divide the body of a debtor who had breached the terms of a contract. Advanced societies, Holmes noticed, no longer settle contractual disputes in such a barbaric fashion. These societies have evolved to the point where liability is now premised on objective and external standards that separate moral responsibility from legal obligation, and wholly eliminate concerns regarding the actual guilt of the wrongdoer. Holmes noted that common-law principles require judges and juries to interpret contractual relations from the perspective of an average person with ordinary intelligence, regardless of how a particular agreement may have actually been understood or performed by the parties themselves.

The importance of *The Common Law* rests in its rejection of the idea that law is a logical system and that legal systems obey the rules of logic. In his most famous quotation, Holmes concluded,

> The life of the law has not been logic: it has been experience. The felt necessities of the time, the prevalent moral and political theories, intuitions of public policy, avowed or unconscious, even the prejudices which judges share with their fellow-men, have had a good deal more to do than the syllogism in determining the rules by which men should be governed.

Holmes's jurisprudence led to the conclusion that judges first make decisions and then come up with reasons to explain them. His approach, which has been characterized as cynical, touched a nerve with succeeding generations of legal scholars. He had a profound effect on the development of sociological jurisprudence and LEGAL REALISM. Sociological jurisprudence and legal realism were twentieth-century schools of thought that emphasized the need to examine social, economic, and political forces rather than confine the study of law to logic and abstract thought.

Holmes joined the faculty of the Harvard Law School in 1882, then left after one semester to accept an appointment as justice on the Supreme Judicial Court of Massachusetts, the highest tribunal in the state. In 1899 he was appointed chief justice of that court, and he served in that position until 1902, when President THEODORE ROOSEVELT named him to the U.S. Supreme Court.

His service on the Supreme Court gave Holmes the opportunity to apply his philosophy. He believed that judges should not impose their private beliefs on law, especially law created by a legislature. When reviewing the constitutionality of legislation, Holmes said a legislature can do whatever it sees fit unless a law it enacts is not justified by any rational interpretation of, or violates an express prohibition of, the Constitution (*Tyson & Brothers United Theatre Ticket Offices v. Banton*, 273 U.S. 418, 47 S. Ct. 426, 71 L. Ed. 718 [1927]). Holmes was skeptical about his ability to determine the "goodness or badness of laws" passed by the legislature, and felt that in most situations he had no choice but to practice judicial restraint and defer to the desires of the popular will.

Holmes's dissenting opinion in *Lochner v. New York*, 198 U.S. 45, 25 S. Ct. 539, 49 L. Ed. 937 (1905), is recognized as his most famous opinion. It is based on the idea of judicial restraint. In *Lochner* Holmes disagreed with the majority, which struck down a New York law that limited the number of hours a baker could work during a week. The majority held that the law violated the "liberty of contract" guaranteed by the FOURTEENTH AMENDMENT, which provides that no state is to "deprive any person of life, liberty, or property, without due process of law" (§ 1). In his dissent Holmes suggested that the majority had based its decision on its members' personal ideological preference for freedom of contract, and not on the Constitution. He said it was improper to overturn a legislative act simply because the Court embraced an economic theory antagonistic to government work regulations.

But Holmes rarely deferred to the popular will in cases raising free speech questions under the FIRST AMENDMENT. If the law must correspond to powerful interests in society, Holmes reasoned, then all facets of society must be given a fair opportunity to compete for influence through the medium of public speech. In *Gitlow v. New York*, 268 U.S. 652, 45 S. Ct. 625, 69 L. Ed. 1138 (1925), Holmes dissented from a decision upholding the conviction of a man

who had been arrested for violating the New York Criminal Anarchy Law (N.Y. Penal Law §§ 160, 161 [ch. 88, McKinney 1909; ch. 40, Consol. 1909]) by advocating the establishment of a socialist government. In his dissent he argued for "the free trade in ideas" as the best way of testing the truth of particular beliefs. He stated that FREEDOM OF SPEECH must be permitted unless it is intended "to produce a clear and imminent danger." This "clear-and-imminent-danger" test for subversive advocacy was first labeled by Holmes as the "clear-and-present-danger" test in *Schenck v. United States*, 249 U.S. 47, 39 S. Ct. 247, 63 L. Ed. 470 (1919). It remains influential as a way of protecting what Holmes termed the marketplace of ideas.

Holmes also contributed to modern FOURTH AMENDMENT jurisprudence. In *Olmstead v. United States*, 277 U.S. 438, 48 S. Ct. 564, 72 L. Ed. 944 (1928), the Supreme Court ruled that incriminating evidence illegally obtained by the police was ADMISSIBLE against a defendant during prosecution. Foreshadowing the Court's later recognition of an EXCLUSIONARY RULE that prohibits prosecutors from using illegally obtained evidence during trial, Holmes wrote that the "government ought not to use evidence" that is "only obtainable by a criminal act" of the police. While acknowledging the legitimate objectives of law enforcement, Holmes concluded that it was "a less[er] evil that some criminals should escape than that the government should play an ignoble part."

Despite Holmes's substantial reputation, he is not without critics. *Buck v. Bell*, 274 U.S. 200, 47 S. Ct. 584, 71 L. Ed. 1000 (1927), is the case most frequently cited to point out faults in his jurisprudence. In his majority opinion in *Buck*, Holmes upheld the constitutionality of a state statute (Va. Law of March 20, 1924, ch. 394) authorizing the sterilization of "feeble-minded" (mentally retarded) persons. Reviewing the family history of Carrie Buck, her mother, and her daughter, Holmes stated, "Three generations of imbeciles are enough." He believed that sterilization was the best way to end the procreation of mentally retarded persons, and in looking at these three generations of women he believed they were all mentally retarded. Later evidence suggested that none of the three were in fact mentally retarded. The case also suggested that deference to legislative acts, such as forced sterilization, was not an unfettered good and that questions of morality and justice have a place in the law, despite Holmes's protests to the contrary.

Holmes's jurisprudence also suggested that the law is what the government says it is. This approach, called legal positivism, was called

"IF THERE IS ANY PRINCIPLE OF OUR CONSTITUTION THAT MORE IMPERATIVELY CALLS FOR ATTACHMENT THAN ANY OTHER IT IS THE PRINCIPLE OF FREE THOUGHT—NOT FREE THOUGHT FOR THOSE WHO AGREE WITH US BUT FOR THE THOUGHT THAT WE HATE."

into question in the 1930s and 1940s with the rise of totalitarian regimes in Germany and Italy and the rule of Stalin in the Soviet Union. Many legal scholars criticized POSITIVISM as lacking a basis in morality and fundamental societal values.

Holmes retired from the Supreme Court in 1932. He died in Washington, D.C., on March 6, 1935, two days before his ninety-fourth birthday.

CROSS-REFERENCES

Clear and Present Danger; *Gitlow v. New York*; Judicial Review; Labor Law; *Lochner v. New York*; *Olmstead v. United States*; *Schenck v. United States*.

HOLOGRAPH 📖 A WILL or DEED written entirely by the TESTATOR or GRANTOR with his or her own hand and not witnessed. 📖

State laws vary widely in regard to the status of a holographic will. Some states absolutely refuse to recognize any will not in compliance with the formal statutory requirements pertaining to the execution of the will. Many states that do not recognize holographic wills executed by their own citizens within their borders will nevertheless admit a holographic will to PROBATE if it was validly executed in accordance with the statutory requirements of another JURISDICTION that recognizes such wills.

HOMELESS PERSON 📖 An individual who lacks housing, including an individual whose primary residence during the night is a supervised public or private facility that provides temporary living accommodations, an individual who is a resident in transitional housing, or an individual who has as a primary residence a public or private place not designed for, or ordinarily used as, a regular sleeping accommodation for human beings. 📖

The number of homeless people in the United States is estimated to be between 250,000 and 3 million. Unemployment, cutbacks in social service programs, a lack of affordable housing, and the deinstitutionalization of mentally ill patients are some of the circumstances that have led to people living in shelters or on the streets. By the mid-1990s, the homeless population included men, women, and children, individuals and families. The rights of these people have become important societal and legal issues.

Shelter Although federal law provides for emergency shelter for homeless families in most states, there is no federal or constitutional right to shelter. In 1987, the Stewart B. McKinney Homeless Assistance Act (42 U.S.C.A. § 11301) was passed to provide public resources and programs to assist the homeless population. Under the act the federal government was to provide underutilized public buildings for use by people who are homeless. In *National Law Center v. United States Department of Veterans Affairs*, 964 F.2d 1210 (D.C. Cir. 1992), a homeless rights group sought to enforce compliance with the McKinney Act. The court agreed with the plaintiffs and held that the government must comply with the McKinney Act by allowing people who are homeless access to underused federal property.

Because the federal courts have refused to recognize a federal constitutional right to shelter, several states have enacted local laws to recognize this right. Many of these statutes require that cities provide shelter for people who are homeless but do not outline enforcement procedures. Although statutes require state agencies to provide shelter, the agencies often cannot keep up with the demand, citing expense and overcrowding. In *Atchison v. District of Columbia*, 585 A.2d 150 (D.C. App. 1991), the court imposed daily fines on a shelter for failure to provide services. The level of fines combined with the cost of litigation stimulated the adoption of an emergency act that allowed the agency to provide a shelter program based on the availability of funds.

Economic Assistance By the late 1990s, public assistance was a prominent political issue. As the government began cutting WELFARE programs, people who were homeless found it increasingly difficult to rise above the poverty level. In addition, substantial cuts to welfare programs created the possibility that more people would be forced into homelessness.

Existing public assistance programs often fail to help those who are homeless. Some programs require that recipients have temporary or permanent addresses, effectively eliminating otherwise eligible recipients. In some instances,

Families make up an increasing proportion of the homeless population. Young people are especially vulnerable to the lack of education, housing, and health care available to homeless people.

MARK LUDAK/IMPACT VISUALS

Federal Homeless Assistance Programs, Funding for Fiscal Year 1997

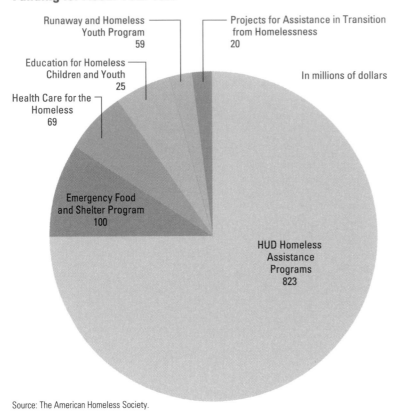

Runaway and Homeless Youth Program
59

Education for Homeless Children and Youth
25

Health Care for the Homeless
69

Emergency Food and Shelter Program
100

Projects for Assistance in Transition from Homelessness
20

In millions of dollars

HUD Homeless Assistance Programs
823

Source: The American Homeless Society.

money that could be spent providing permanent, affordable housing for people who are homeless is used to provide temporary housing in "welfare hotels." A welfare hotel is inexpensive housing that is used for temporary shelter for low-income or homeless persons. In 1995, legislation was introduced to control welfare spending and reduce welfare dependence. (H.R. 1157, 104th Cong., 1st Sess.). The features of this legislation included discontinuing welfare benefits to certain groups and creating state demonstration projects to reduce the number of homeless families in welfare hotels.

Education One alarming aspect of the growth of the homeless population is the increasing numbers of families and children without a place to live. Children are more strongly affected by homelessness than are adults because they are less able to overcome a lack of food, shelter, health care, and education. Many children in homeless families lack the transportation, documentation, and even clothing needed to attend public schools.

State residency guidelines typically require children to attend school within the district in which their parent or guardian lives. Homeless children cannot meet these residency requirements. Because education is often critical to

overcoming poverty and homelessness, the McKinney Act specifically addresses the issue of education for children who are homeless. The act ensures that these children have every opportunity for a public school education. It requires states to revise their residency requirements in order to give such children a free education.

Another barrier to the education rights of children without a home is the inability to track education and medical records. Students can be refused enrollment if they have no documentation of previous schooling. The McKinney Act requires local education agencies to maintain records so that those records can be readily available when a student moves to a new school district. Under the act, children must also have equal access to special education programs in the public school system.

Voting The right to vote is expressly stated in the U.S. Constitution. Because most states require that a citizen have a permanent residence in order to vote, the right to vote is often denied people who are homeless. The right to vote provides a way for a person who is homeless to be heard—by electing public officials sympathetic to the concerns of people who are without a home—and thus is an important right to protect.

New Jersey was one of the first states to allow people who are homeless the right to vote. The only requirement was that they meet the age and residency requirement of the state's constitution. They could satisfy the residency requirement by specifying a place they regarded as home and providing the name of at least one contact who could verify their residence in that place.

By 1994, thirteen states had legislation protecting the VOTING rights of people who are homeless. In *Collier v. Menzel*, 176 Cal. App. 3d 24, 221 Cal. Rptr. 110 (1985), three persons who were homeless listed a local park as their address on a voter registration card. The court held that they had satisfied the residency requirement because they had indicated a fixed habitation in which they intended to remain for an extended period. In addition, even though a city ordinance prohibited camping and sleeping overnight in the park, the court held that denying the voter registration would violate EQUAL PROTECTION.

Antihomeless Legislation With an increased homeless population comes increased concern on the part of members of the general public when they find members of that population loitering on the streets. VAGRANCY ordinances were passed to keep people who are homeless from staying too long in any one location. Many of these statutes have been labeled antihomeless legislation because they particularly target behavior some homeless people have no control over.

In *Papachristou v. Jacksonville*, 405 U.S. 156, 92 S. Ct. 839, 31 L. Ed. 2d 110 (1972), eight homeless people challenged their conviction for violating a vagrancy ordinance. The Supreme Court held that the ordinance was too vague and criminalized otherwise innocent conduct. In this and similar cases, the Court has stated that these "crimes" do not cause any harm to others that outweighs the violation of the rights of the individuals arrested.

Protections against an illegal SEARCH AND SEIZURE also apply to people who are homeless and to their belongings, even though their belongings may not be located in a traditional home setting. In *State v. Mooney*, 218 Conn. 85, 588 A.2d 145 (1991), police officers searched belongings of a homeless man that were found under a bridge embankment. As a result of the search, the man was arrested and charged with robbery and felony murder. The man appealed his conviction, claiming it was an illegal search because the police did not have a WARRANT to search his home, a cardboard box. The court agreed with the man that he had a reasonable expectation of PRIVACY in the contents of his belongings. It disagreed, however, with his contention that he had an expectation of privacy in the bridge abutment area.

When people without a home are arrested and jailed, their property is often destroyed or stolen while they are incarcerated. Laws that target people who are homeless are thus viewed as unreasonable searches and seizures of property. In *Pottinger v. City of Miami*, 810 F. Supp. 1551 (S.D. Fla. 1992), a CLASS ACTION suit was brought on behalf of thousands of homeless people. The court agreed that certain city ordinances unfairly targeted those people and that resulting arrests and seizures of property were in violation of their constitutional rights.

HOMEOWNER'S WARRANTY

An INSURANCE protection program offered by a number of builders of residential dwellings in the United States.

Homeowner's warranty, commonly known as HOW, was developed by the Home Owner's Warranty Corporation and protects the original homeowner of a new home for a period of ten years against major structural defects. If such defects occur, the builder, and not the original buyer, is financially responsible for their repair. In a number of states, similar warranty protection is afforded by statute.

HOME RULE

Home rule involves the authority of a local government to prevent state government intervention with its operations. The extent of its power, however, is subject to limitations prescribed by state constitutions and statutes.

When a municipality or other political subdivision has the power to decide for itself whether to follow a particular course of action without receiving specific approval from state officials, it acts pursuant to such powers. For example, a town exercises its home rule powers when it puts the issue of allowing the sale of alcoholic beverages within its borders on the ballot.

HOMESTEAD

The dwelling house and its adjoining land where a family resides. Technically, and pursuant to the modern homestead exemption laws, an artificial ESTATE in land, created to protect the possession and enjoyment of the owner against the claims of CREDITORS by preventing the sale of the property for payment of the owner's DEBTS so long as the land is occupied as a home.

Laws exempting the homestead from liability for debts of the owner are strictly of U.S. origin. Under the English COMMON LAW, a homestead right, a personal right to the peaceful, beneficial, and uninterrupted use of the home property free from the claims of creditors, did not exist. Homestead rights exist only through the constitutional and statutory provisions that create them. Nearly every state has enacted such provisions. The earliest ones were enacted in 1839 in the Republic of Texas.

Homestead exemption statutes have been passed to achieve the PUBLIC POLICY objective of providing lodgings where the family can peacefully reside irrespective of financial adversities.

Homestead right—a personal right to enjoy the use of one's property without interference from creditors—is a theory that originated in the United States. Many families like this one in Custer County, Nebraska, obtained their land through the Homestead Act of 1862.

These laws are predicated on the theory that preservation of the homestead is of greater significance than the payment of debts.

Property tax exemptions, for all or part of the tax, are also available in some states for homesteaded property. Statutory requirements prescribe what must be done to establish a homestead.

A PROBATE *homestead* is one that the court sets apart out of the estate property for the use of a surviving spouse and the MINOR children or out of the real estate belonging to the deceased.

A *homestead corporation* is an enterprise organized for the purpose of acquiring lands in large tracts; paying off ENCUMBRANCES, charges attached to and binding REAL PROPERTY; improving and subdividing tracts into homestead lots or parcels; and distributing them among the shareholders and for the accumulation of a fund for such purposes.

HOMESTEAD ACT OF 1862
The Homestead Act of 1862 was a landmark in the evolution of federal agriculture law. Passed by Congress during the Civil War, it had an idealistic goal: it sought to shape the U.S. West by populating it with farmers. The law's Northern supporters had pursued a vision of taming the rough frontier for several decades, as a means both to create an agrarian base there and to break the institution of SLAVERY that was entrenched in the South. To achieve this end, they engineered a vast giveaway of PUBLIC LANDS. The Homestead Act provided 160 acres of land for a small filing fee and a modest investment of time and effort. The overly optimistic law failed in several ways. Most important, it was exploited by railroads and other powerful interests for profit. After making basic changes to it Congress finally repealed the law in 1977.

The Homestead Act arose from the struggle between the North and the South that culminated in the Civil War (1861–65). During this struggle, the nation followed two competing paths of agricultural development: the industrialized North favored giving public lands to individual settlers, while the South clung to its tradition of slave labor. From the early 1830s, Northern proponents of the free distribution of public land, organized around the Free-Soil party and later in the Republican party, had their ideas blocked by Southern opponents. The secession of Southern states in 1861 cleared the way for passage of the Homestead Act in 1862, against a backdrop of other important legislation that would define national agriculture policy for the next century: the Morrill Land-Grant College Act, the PACIFIC RAILROAD ACT, and the creation of the Department of Agriculture. The Homestead Act went into effect on January 1, 1863, just as President ABRAHAM LINCOLN signed the EMANCIPATION PROCLAMATION freeing slaves.

In this context of controversy and war, the Homestead Act offered a simple plan to achieve the goals of the North. As yet not fully settled, western states would be populated with a flood of homesteaders—individual farmers whose hard work would create a new agricultural industry. On its face, the law was generous. Anyone who was at least twenty-one years of age, the head of a family, or a military veteran was qualified to claim land; moreover, citizens and immigrants alike were entitled to participate. They paid a small filing fee in return for the temporary right to occupy and farm 160 acres. The land did not become theirs immediately; the law stipulated that it had to be improved, and only after living on and maintaining it for five years would the homesteader gain ownership. Proponents viewed the law with an almost utopian fondness: through the federal government's largesse, a new West would be created.

In actual application, the act did not achieve this happy outcome. Although the East offered sufficient rainfall, the West was unforgiving. There, harsh land and arid conditions made farming 160 acres a dismal prospect for the settlers, who lived in houses usually made of sod. Often, they simply needed more acreage in order to succeed. In addition, homesteaders seldom had the best land. By bribing residents who bought the land for them, or simply by filing fraudulent claims, speculators managed to reap the lion's share of land at public expense. It is estimated that only a quarter of the trillion acres made available through the Homestead Act ever served their intended purpose. The bulk of this land went to corporate interests, particularly in the railroad and timber industries, rather than individual settlers.

The Homestead Act left a complicated legacy to U.S. law. Its passage was a triumph for Northern states in their decades-long battle to control the destiny of national agricultural policy. But its limitations and its exploitation meant that the vision of those states could scarcely be realized. Congress made changes to the law during its 105-year history—chiefly, modifying the limits on acreage that it made available—but these amendments did little to alter the act's net effect on the course of national agricultural policy. The law was finally repealed in 1977. Popularly romanticized during the nineteenth century and even into the twentieth, the Homestead Act is now widely viewed by scholars as a failed experiment and a lesson in the contrasts between the intentions and outcomes of law.

See also AGRICULTURAL LAW; RAILROADS.

HOMICIDE 📖 The killing of one human being by another human being. 📖

Although the term *homicide* is sometimes used synonymously with *murder*, homicide is broader in scope than murder. MURDER is a form of criminal homicide; other forms of homicide may not constitute criminal acts. These homicides are regarded as justified or excusable. For example, individuals may, in a necessary act of SELF-DEFENSE, kill a person who threatens them with death or serious injury, or may be commanded or authorized by law to kill a person who is a member of an enemy force or who has committed a serious crime. Typically, the circumstances surrounding a killing determine whether it is criminal or noncriminal. The intent of the killer usually determines whether a criminal homicide is classified as murder or MANSLAUGHTER and at what degree.

English courts developed the body of COMMON LAW on which U.S. JURISDICTIONS initially relied in developing their homicide statutes. Early English common law divided homicide into two broad categories: felonious and nonfelonious. Historically, the deliberate and premeditated killing of a person by another person was a felonious homicide and was classified as murder. Nonfelonious homicide included justifiable homicide and excusable homicide. Although justifiable homicide was considered a crime, the offender often received a pardon. Excusable homicide was not considered a crime.

In the early common law, murder was a felony punishable by death. It was defined as the unlawful killing of a person with "malice aforethought," which was generally defined as a premeditated intent to kill. As U.S. courts and jurisdictions adopted the English common law and modified the various circumstances that constituted criminal homicide, various degrees of criminal homicide developed. Modern statutes generally divide criminal homicide into two broad categories: murder and manslaughter. Murder is usually further divided into first degree, which typically involves a premeditated intent to kill, and second degree, which typically does not involve a premeditated intent to kill. Manslaughter typically involves an unintentional killing that resulted from a person's CRIMINAL NEGLIGENCE or reckless disregard for human life.

All homicides require the killing of a living person. In most states, the killing of a viable fetus is generally not considered a homicide unless the fetus is first born alive. In some states, however, this distinction is disregarded and the killing of an unborn viable fetus is classified as homicide. In other states, statutes separately classify the killing of a fetus as the crime of feticide.

Generally, the law requires that the death of the person occur within a year and a day of the fatal injury. This requirement initially reflected a difficulty in determining whether an initial injury led to a person's death, or whether other events or circumstances intervened to cause the person's death. As forensic science has developed and the difficulty in determining cause of death has diminished, many states have modified or abrogated the year-and-a-day rule.

Justifiable or Excusable Homicide A homicide may be justifiable or excusable by the surrounding circumstances. In such cases, the homicide will not be considered a criminal act. A justifiable homicide is a homicide that is commanded or authorized by law. For instance, soldiers in a time of war may be commanded to kill enemy soldiers. Generally, such killings are considered justifiable homicide unless other circumstances suggest that they were not necessary or were not within the scope of the soldiers' duty. In addition, a public official is

Homicide Rate

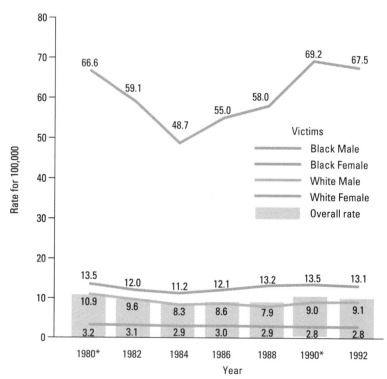

*Rate based on enumerated population figures as of April 1 for 1980 and 1990; July 1 estimates for other years.

Source: U.S. National Center for Health Statistics, *Vital Statistics of the United States.*

justified in carrying out a death sentence because the execution is commanded by state or federal law.

A person is authorized to kill another person in self-defense or in the defense of others, but only if the person reasonably believes the killing is absolutely necessary in order to prevent serious harm or death to herself or himself or to others. If the threatened harm can be avoided with reasonable safety, some states require the person to first retreat before using DEADLY FORCE. Most states do not require retreat if the individual is attacked or threatened in her or his home, place of employment, or business. In addition, some states do not require a person to retreat unless that person in some way provoked the threat of harm. Finally, police officers may use deadly force to stop or apprehend a fleeing felon, but only if the suspect is armed or has committed a crime that involved the infliction or threatened infliction of serious injury or death. A police officer may not use deadly force to apprehend or stop an individual who has committed or is committing a MISDEMEANOR offense. Only certain FELONIES are considered in determining whether deadly force may be used to apprehend or stop a suspect. For instance, a police officer may not use deadly force to prevent the commission of LARCENY unless other circumstances threaten the officer or other persons with imminent serious injury or death.

Excusable homicide is sometimes distinguished from justifiable homicide on the basis that excusable homicide involves some fault on the part of the person who ultimately uses deadly force. For instance, if a person provokes a fight and subsequently withdraws from the fight but, out of necessity and in self-defense, ultimately kills the other person, the homicide is sometimes classified as excusable, rather than justifiable. Generally, however, the distinction between justifiable homicide and excusable homicide has largely disappeared, and only the term *justifiable homicide* is widely used.

Other Defenses Other legal defenses to a charge of criminal homicide include insanity, NECESSITY, ACCIDENT, and intoxication. Some of these defenses may provide an absolute defense to a charge of criminal homicide; some will not. For instance, a successful defense of voluntary intoxication will generally allow an individual to avoid prosecution for a premeditated murder, but it will typically not allow an individual to escape liability for any lesser charges, such as second-degree murder or manslaughter. As with any defense to a criminal charge, the accused's mental state will be a critical determinant of whether the individual had the requisite intent or mental capacity to commit a criminal homicide.

Euthanasia and Physician-Assisted Suicide The killing of oneself is a SUICIDE, not a homicide. If a person kills another person in order to end the other person's pain or suffering, the killing is considered a homicide. It does not matter if the other person is about to die or is terminally ill just prior to being killed; the law generally views such a killing as criminal. Thus, a "mercy killing," or act of euthanasia, is generally considered a criminal homicide.

As medical technology advances and the medical profession is able to prolong life for many terminally ill patients, a person's right to die by committing suicide with the help of a physician or others has become a hotly contested issue. In the 1990s, the issue of physician-assisted suicide came to the forefront of U.S. law. Dr. JACK KEVORKIAN, a Michigan physician, helped many terminally ill patients commit suicide. Michigan authorities prosecuted Kevorkian for murder on a number of occasions, but because aiding, assisting, or causing a suicide is generally considered a separate crime from homicide, Kevorkian has not been convicted. Michigan authorities also prosecuted Kevorkian under a common-law doctrine that prohibited helping another commit suicide, but Kevorkian was acquitted of the charges each time they were brought against him.

See also DEATH AND DYING; INSANITY DEFENSE; PREMEDITATION.

HONOR 📖 As a verb, to accept a BILL OF EXCHANGE, or to pay a NOTE, CHECK, or accepted bill, at maturity. To pay or to accept and pay, or, where a credit so engages, to purchase or discount a DRAFT complying with the terms of the draft.

As a noun, in old English law, a seigniory of several MANORS held under one baron or lord paramount. Also those dignities or privileges, degrees of nobility, knighthood, and other titles that flow from the crown.

In the United States, the customary title of courtesy given to judges, and occasionally to some other officers, as, "his honor," "your honor," "honorable." 📖

HONORARY TRUST 📖 An arrangement whereby property is placed in the hands of another to be used for specific noncharitable purposes where there is no definite ascertainable BENEFICIARY—one who profits by the act of another—and that is unenforceable in the absence of statute. 📖

TRUSTS for the erection of monuments, the care of graves, the saying of Masses, or the care of specific animals, such as a cat, dog, or horse,

are examples of honorary trusts. Honorary trusts for the benefit of specific animals differ from CHARITABLE TRUSTS that have as a trust purpose the benefit of animals in general. In many JURISDICTIONS, legislation validates special provisions for the upkeep of graves and monuments. Similarly, trusts for the saying of Masses are upheld as charitable trusts.

As a general rule, the designated TRUSTEE, one appointed or required by law to execute a trust, can effectuate the intent of the SETTLOR—one who creates a trust—if he or she chooses to do so. Since there is no beneficiary who can enforce the trust, the implementation of the purposes of the trust depends upon the honor of the trustee. If the person does not execute the trust duties, he or she holds the property for the settlor or the settlor's HEIRS on the theory of a RESULTING TRUST.

Jurisdictions differ as to the extent to which honorary trusts will be recognized, if at all. Honorary trusts are usually limited by considerations of PUBLIC POLICY. For instance, they cannot exist beyond the period of the RULE AGAINST PERPETUITIES, and their amounts cannot be unreasonably large for the purpose to be accomplished. The purpose must also be that of a reasonably normal TESTATOR and cannot be capricious.

A settlor bequeaths $1,000 to a trustee to care for the settlor's cat and dog, and $1,000 for the purpose of maintaining the settlor's home in the same condition as of the instant of his death for twenty years thereafter, with all win-

An honorary trust may be created for the care of a grave.

dows and doors blocked shut. Upon the settlor's death, the residuary LEGATEE inherits any money that remains in the ESTATE after all other claims are paid and makes claims to both sums of money under these testamentary provisions. A court will find that the residuary legatee has no right to the $1,000 left for the cat and dog unless the trustee refuses to fulfill the obligations of caring for the dog and cat. The residuary legatee is, however, entitled to the other $1,000. Neither of these provisions of the settlor's will created a private trust.

As a general rule, the beneficiary of a private trust must be competent to come into court either in person or by GUARDIAN and enforce the trust duties against the trustee. Neither the cat nor the dog can appear in court. Some states permit provisions for reasonable sums to specific animals to be valid honorary trusts as long as public policy is not violated. If the trustee fails to properly execute his or her duties, he or she holds the property in resulting trust for the heirs or next of kin of the DECEDENT. In this example, if the trustee spends the $1,000 in caring for the dog and cat, he or she is not liable, but if he or she does not, a court will order the trustee to turn the money over to the residuary legatee as the beneficiary of a resulting trust. If the purpose of an intended honorary trust is capricious, the trust will fail. In this case, there is no legitimate end to be served by keeping the settlor's home boarded up for twenty years. The purpose is capricious and the trust fails. Therefore, the $1,000 set aside for this purpose is held by the trustee in resulting trust for the residuary legatee who must receive it.

HOOKS, BENJAMIN LAWSON   Civil rights advocate Benjamin Lawson Hooks is best known as the forceful executive director of the NATIONAL ASSOCIATION FOR THE ADVANCEMENT OF COLORED PEOPLE (NAACP) from 1977 to 1993. Before he led the NAACP, Hooks made a virtual career out of shattering the United States' racial barriers. He was the first African American ever appointed to a Tennessee criminal court and the first African American named to the FEDERAL COMMUNICATIONS COMMISSION

BIOGRAPHY

Benjamin Lawson Hooks

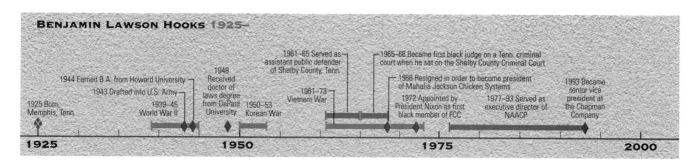

BENJAMIN LAWSON HOOKS 1925–

1925 Born, Memphis, Tenn.

1943 Drafted into U.S. Army

1944 Earned B.A. from Howard University

1939–45 World War II

1948 Received doctor of laws degree from DePaul University

1950–53 Korean War

1961–65 Served as assistant public defender of Shelby County, Tenn.

1961–73 Vietnam War

1965–68 Became first black judge on a Tenn. criminal court when he sat on the Shelby County Criminal Court

1968 Resigned in order to become president of Mahalia Jackson Chicken Systems

1972 Appointed by President Nixon as first black member of FCC

1977–93 Served as executive director of NAACP

1993 Became senior vice president at the Chapman Company

1925   1950   1975   2000

(FCC). Hooks has also achieved personal and professional success as an ordained minister, a television host and producer, a savings and loan administrator, a public speaker, and a fast-food executive.

Hooks was born January 31, 1925, in Memphis. As an African American living under Jim Crow laws, he experienced the daily indignities of southern segregation. His parents, Bessie Hooks and Robert B. Hooks, Sr., raised their seven children with high moral and academic standards. After high school, Hooks enrolled at LeMoyne College, in Memphis. His college career was interrupted by World War II. Hooks was drafted into the U.S. Army in 1943 and rose to the rank of staff sergeant.

After his military service, Hooks attended Howard University, in Washington, D.C., and graduated with a bachelor of arts degree in 1944. Hooks then traveled to Chicago to study law at DePaul University. Although Hooks wanted to enroll in a Tennessee law school, he could not do so because law schools in Tennessee refused to admit African Americans. Hooks graduated with a doctor of laws degree from DePaul in 1948. In 1949, he moved back to Memphis and started his own law practice. In 1952, he married Frances Dancy, and later, they had one child, Patricia.

During the 1950s, Hooks became active in the growing national CIVIL RIGHTS MOVEMENT. Along with MARTIN LUTHER KING, JR., Hooks served on the Board of Directors for the SOUTHERN CHRISTIAN LEADERSHIP CONFERENCE. During this time, Hooks also became an ordained Baptist minister and accepted a call as pastor of the Middle Baptist Church, in Memphis. Adding to an already busy life, Hooks became vice president of a savings and loan association he helped found in Memphis in 1955.

In 1961, Hooks took over as assistant public defender of Shelby County. His role led to an appointment by Governor Frank G. Clement, of Tennessee, in 1965, to the Shelby County Criminal Court. With this appointment, Hooks became the first African American to serve as judge on the Tennessee criminal bench. In 1966, he was elected on his own to a full eight-year term. In the meantime, Hooks became minister of the Greater New Mount Moriah Baptist Church, in Detroit. He flew to Detroit twice a month to lead his congregation.

In 1968, Hooks resigned his criminal court judgeship to become president of Mahalia Jackson Chicken Systems, a fast-food franchise. In 1972, he was appointed by President RICHARD M. NIXON to become a member of the previously all-white FCC, the federal agency that

licenses and regulates radio, television, satellite communications, telephones, and telegraph transmissions. This position allowed him to focus public attention on the image of African Americans in radio and television and to increase minority jobs in BROADCASTING.

In 1977, Hooks assumed the position with which he is most commonly identified: executive director of the NAACP. Following in the footsteps of the retiring ROY WILKINS, Hooks accepted the job because he deeply respected the NAACP and because he wanted to complete some of the unfinished business of the equal rights movement. A tireless worker, Hooks spent long days in the NAACP Baltimore headquarters performing what he called the "killing job."

During Hooks's tenure, the NAACP expressed concern over homelessness, drug abuse, inadequate education, and neighborhood safety. Hooks lamented the rise of an intractable urban underclass and warned that the promise of jobs and economic independence for African Americans must be met soon.

Some of Hooks's proudest accomplishments with the NAACP include his work on sanctions against South Africa, fair housing legislation, VOTING rights, and the Martin Luther King, Jr., federal holiday.

Hooks's achievements with the NAACP take on a special significance in view of the political conservatism that prevailed during his fifteen-year tenure as its head—a period when RONALD REAGAN and GEORGE BUSH were in the White House. Hooks vowed to keep the NAACP true to its progressive mission. In fact, under his leadership, the NAACP refused to endorse the nomination of African American CLARENCE THOMAS to the U.S. Supreme Court because Thomas's views were too conservative.

By the time Hooks retired from the NAACP in 1993, its membership had grown to over five hundred thousand people in over twenty-two hundred chapters across the United States. Hooks was gratified by the results of a 1992 survey in which the NAACP earned an 86 percent approval rating among those polled. The organization has worked hard to counter criticism that it is mired in the past and out of touch with African American youths.

When Hooks retired from the NAACP post in April 1993, the sixty-four members of the NAACP Board of Directors elected Benjamin F. Chavis, Jr., as his successor. Hooks left the NAACP to embark on yet another career challenge—as a senior vice president at the Chapman Company, a minority controlled brokerage and investment banking firm with offices in seven cities.

"THERE WILL ALWAYS BE A NEED FOR THE NAACP. ONCE WE THOUGHT THERE WOULD COME A TIME WHEN OUR WORK WOULD BE FINISHED. BUT RACISM STILL EXISTS AND INEQUALITY IS STILL BUILT INTO THIS SOCIETY."

HOOVER, HERBERT CLARK   Herbert Clark Hoover was the thirty-first president of the United States, serving from 1929 to 1932. A wealthy mining engineer, Hoover directed humanitarian relief efforts during and after World Wars I and II. His presidency was devastated by the stock market crash of 1929 and the ensuing Great Depression.

Hoover was born August 10, 1874, in West Branch, Iowa. His father and mother died when he was young, and he was raised by an uncle in Oregon. He entered the first first-year class at Stanford University and graduated in 1895 with a degree in mining engineering. He became an expert on managing and reorganizing mines throughout the world. He spent time in Australia and China before setting up his own engineering firm in London in 1908. By 1914 Hoover had become a millionaire.

Hoover became involved in relief work during World War I. In 1914 he served as director of the American Relief Commission in England, which helped one hundred twenty thousand U.S. citizens return home after being stranded at the outbreak of the war. The British government then asked him to lead the Commission for Relief in Belgium. His main achievement during this period was the distribution of supplies to civilian victims of the war in Belgium and France.

After the United States entered the war in 1917, President WOODROW WILSON named Hoover U.S. food administrator. In this capacity Hoover coordinated the production and conservation of food supplies that could be used for the war effort. Hoover also chaired the European Relief and Reconstruction Commission, directing activities of numerous relief departments and organizing the distribution of provisions. After the war Hoover coordinated the American Relief Administration. This agency provided food to millions during the famine of 1921 in the Soviet Union.

Hoover's humanitarian efforts made him an international figure. Democrats and Republicans sought to make him a presidential candidate in 1920, but Hoover rejected their offers.

Herbert Clark Hoover

"FREE SPEECH DOES NOT LIVE MANY HOURS AFTER FREE INDUSTRY AND FREE COMMERCE DIE."

Instead, in 1921 he accepted the position of secretary of commerce in the administration of President WARREN G. HARDING, a Republican. Hoover was an energetic administrator, reorganizing the department and expanding its oversight into commercial aviation, highway safety, and radio broadcasting. He chaired commissions that established the Hoover Dam and the St. Lawrence Seaway.

In 1928 Hoover won the Republican presidential nomination. He easily defeated Democrat Alfred E. Smith, on a platform of continued economic prosperity and support for Prohibition.

Hoover devoted the early days of his presidency to improving the economic conditions of farmers. He advocated foreign TARIFFS on imported farm products as a way to protect domestic farm prices. Congress went beyond Hoover's recommendation and in 1930 enacted the Hawley-Smoot Tariff Act (19 U.S.C.A. § 1303 et seq.), which placed tariffs on nonfarm products as well. The act severely damaged U.S. foreign trade.

The control of Prohibition pursuant to the EIGHTEENTH AMENDMENT and the VOLSTEAD ACT (41 Stat. 305 [1919]) had become a serious problem by 1929. Organized crime had seized the opportunity to sell illegal ALCOHOL. The only way large-scale liquor and speakeasy traffic could flourish was with the cooperation of law enforcement, so state and local law enforcement agencies were tainted with corruption. In 1929 Hoover established the National Commission on Law Observance and Law Enforcement, appointing GEORGE W. WICKERSHAM to direct an investigation of the effectiveness of law enforcement practices in the United States. The Wickersham Commission report was an important inquiry into the practices of the U.S. criminal justice system. The report examined all facets of police work and, for the first time, discussed police brutality and the "third degree" method of interrogating suspects. The report called for the professionalization of police.

The U.S. economy appeared to be robust in 1929, but a rising stock market had been built

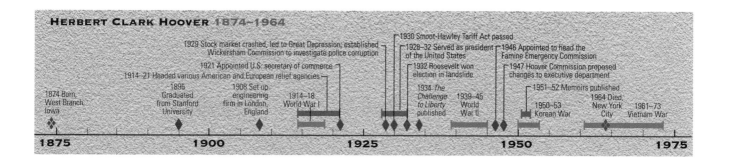

HERBERT CLARK HOOVER 1874–1964

1874 Born, West Branch, Iowa

1895 Graduated from Stanford University

1908 Set up engineering firm in London, England

1914–21 Headed various American and European relief agencies

1914–18 World War I

1921 Appointed U.S. secretary of commerce

1929 Stock market crashed, led to Great Depression; established Wickersham Commission to investigate police corruption

1928–32 Served as president of the United States

1930 Smoot-Hawley Tariff Act passed

1932 Roosevelt won election in landslide

1934 *The Challenge to Liberty* published

1939–45 World War II

1946 Appointed to head the Famine Emergency Commission

1947 Hoover Commission proposed changes to executive department

1950–53 Korean War

1951–52 Memoirs published

1964 Died, New York City

1961–73 Vietnam War

1875   1900   1925   1950   1975

on stock purchases financed by widespread borrowing. When the stock market crashed on October 29, individuals, banks, and other economic institutions were devastated. Hoover sought to inspire public confidence by meeting with business leaders and by proclaiming that the economic downturn would be brief.

Hoover's prediction was wrong. The United States slid into the worst economic depression in its history. Hoover resisted massive federal intervention because he believed that the economy would correct itself. He did approve some federal public works projects that provided jobs, but he opposed federal aid to the unemployed. In his view private charity should help those who had fallen on hard times.

In 1932, with 12 million people out of work and hundreds of banks failing, Hoover created the Reconstruction Finance Corporation (RFC) to extend loans to revitalize industry and to keep banks from going into bankruptcy. Congress authorized the RFC to loan up to $300 million to states for relief. Many persons viewed these actions as too little and too late.

The troubles of the Hoover administration culminated in the Bonus Army March on Washington, D.C. In 1932 World War I veterans demanded monetary bonuses that had been promised them in 1924, even though the bonuses were not scheduled to be paid until 1945. The House of Representatives had passed a bill authorizing early payment, and the veterans sought to pressure the Senate to follow suit. Over fifteen thousand veterans, in desperate need of funds, organized a march on Washington, D.C., to secure immediate payment from the government. The "bonus army" constructed a makeshift city and declared that its members were ready to stay until their goal was achieved. Hoover dispatched federal troops to destroy the encampment and drive the veterans out of the nation's capital. For doing so he received nationwide criticism.

The Republican party nominated Hoover for a second term in 1932, but his candidacy attracted little enthusiasm. The Democratic party nominee, Governor FRANKLIN D. ROOSEVELT of New York, mounted a vigorous campaign against Hoover's economic policies, calling for a "new deal" for U.S. citizens. Roosevelt promised to balance the budget, provide relief to the unemployed, help the farmer, and repeal Prohibition. He carried forty-two of the forty-eight states.

Hoover was angered by Roosevelt's New Deal, which made the federal government the dominant player in the national economy. In 1934 he published *The Challenge to Liberty*, which attacked Roosevelt and his policies. He then withdrew from public life until 1946, when President HARRY S. TRUMAN asked him to return to relief work. Hoover subsequently directed the Famine Emergency Commission, which distributed food supplies to war-torn nations. In 1947 Truman authorized him to investigate the executive department of the U.S. government. The resulting Hoover Commission proposed changes in the EXECUTIVE BRANCH that saved money and streamlined government.

Hoover had a continuing interest in the Hoover Institution on War, Revolution, and Peace, which he founded at Stanford in 1919 and which remains an important research center. He published his memoirs in three volumes (1951–52) and *The Ordeal of Woodrow Wilson* (1958).

Hoover lived longer after leaving the presidency than did any other president. He died at age ninety on October 20, 1964, in New York City.

BIOGRAPHY

John Edgar Hoover

HOOVER, JOHN EDGAR John Edgar Hoover served from 1924 to 1972 as the director of the FEDERAL BUREAU OF INVESTIGATION (FBI). During his long tenure, Hoover built the FBI into a formidable law enforcement organization, establishing standards for the collection and evaluation of information that made the FBI an effective crime fighting agency. However, Hoover's reputation was tarnished by his collection of damaging information on prominent politicians and public figures for his personal use, and by his aggressive investigation of civil rights leaders and left-wing radicals.

Hoover was born January 1, 1895, in Washington, D.C. Following graduation from high school, he turned down a scholarship from the

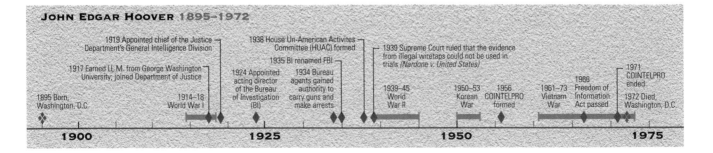

JOHN EDGAR HOOVER 1895–1972

1919 Appointed chief of the Justice Department's General Intelligence Division

1917 Earned LL.M. from George Washington University; joined Department of Justice

1895 Born, Washington, D.C.

1914–18 World War I

1924 Appointed acting director of the Bureau of Investigation (BI)

1938 House Un-American Activites Committee (HUAC) formed

1935 BI renamed FBI

1934 Bureau agents gained authority to carry guns and make arrests

1939 Supreme Court ruled that the evidence from illegal wiretaps could not be used in trials (*Nardone v. United States*)

1939–45 World War II

1950–53 Korean War

1956 COINTELPRO formed

1961–73 Vietnam War

1966 Freedom of Information Act passed

1971 COINTELPRO ended

1972 Died, Washington, D.C.

1900   1925   1950   1975

University of Virginia, electing to stay home and study law at night at George Washington University. In 1916 he received a bachelor of laws degree. In 1917 he added a master of laws degree. Upon graduation from college, Hoover joined the U.S. Department of Justice.

Hoover started in a minor position, but his intelligence, energy, and mastery of detail were quickly noticed by his superiors. By 1919 he had risen to the rank of special assistant attorney general. During these early years, Hoover first became involved with the suppression of political radicals, assisting Attorney General A. MITCHELL PALMER in the arrest and deportation of left-wing ALIENS. In 1919 he was appointed chief of the department's General Intelligence Division (GID), a unit designated by Palmer to hunt down radicals. Within three months Hoover collected the names of 150,000 alleged subversives. Armed with this information, federal agents conducted nationwide dragnets, arresting over ten thousand people. Critics argued that these Palmer Raids violated civil liberties. Nevertheless, thousands of persons were deported. By 1921 the GID had nearly half a million names of persons suspected of subversive activities.

In 1924 Hoover was appointed acting director of the Bureau of Investigation (BI), the forerunner of the FBI. The BI was a weak agency, hampered by limited investigatory powers, the inability of its agents to carry weapons, and the swelling of its rank with political appointments. After several scandals revealed the extent of the BI's problems, Attorney General HARLAN F. STONE appointed Hoover to clean up the agency.

Though only twenty-nine, Hoover met the challenge head-on. He began a thorough reorganization of the bureau, imposing strict discipline on his employees. Hoover's goal was to establish a professional law enforcement agency of unquestioned integrity. Between 1924 and 1935, he introduced a series of innovations that changed national law enforcement. Hoover established a national fingerprint collection, the first systematic database that federal, state, and local agencies could use to match FINGERPRINTS at crime scenes with those on file at the bureau. He also created a crime laboratory, which developed scientific procedures for obtaining forensic evidence. Finally, Hoover made a point of changing the character of his agents. He established a training academy for new agents, who were selected on the basis of their qualifications, not on their political connections. Agents were required to be college educated and to maintain the highest standard of personal and professional ethics.

As the agency became more professional, its jurisdiction increased. In 1935 President FRANKLIN D. ROOSEVELT signed crime bills giving agents the authority to carry guns and make arrests, and in the same year, the bureau officially became the FBI. During the 1930s Hoover moved from internal reorganization to external promotion of himself and his agency. The gangster era, from 1920 to 1935, ended in the arrest or killing of well-publicized hoodlums such as John Dillinger, Pretty Boy Floyd, and Bonnie and Clyde. Hoover and his G-men were celebrated for these exploits in newspapers, radio, newsreels, and Hollywood movies, establishing Hoover as the nation's leading crime fighter.

Hoover's focus shifted to political subversion and foreign ESPIONAGE during World War II. Again, the FBI was celebrated in the news media and popular culture, this time for tracking down Nazi saboteurs and spies. With the end of World War II and the beginning of the cold war with the Soviet Union, Hoover directed his efforts at rooting out Communist subversives. Harkening back to his early work with Palmer, Hoover's zealousness for this task led him to make alliances with the House Un-American Activities Committee; anti-Communist politicians such as Representative RICHARD M. NIXON, of California, and Senator JOSEPH R. MCCARTHY, of Wisconsin; and members of the news media who were eager to print Hoover's inside information.

During the 1950s Hoover concentrated on anti-Communist initiatives, ignoring calls to investigate the growth of organized crime. He published *Masters of Deceit* (1958), a book that articulated his views on what he perceived to be the Communist CONSPIRACY to overthrow the U.S. government. He established the FBI's Counterintelligence Program (COINTELPRO) to disrupt the U.S. Communist party and to discredit its members through informants, disinformation, and anonymous letters and telephone calls. He also enlisted the cooperation of the Internal Revenue Service to conduct selective tax audits of people he suspected of being Communists. Critics of Hoover argued—and continue to argue—that he went beyond law enforcement in these efforts, using so-called dirty tricks to undermine the reputation of persons he believed to be subversive.

Despite these charges Hoover remained a powerful federal official. His use of wiretaps on phones, and of other forms of ELECTRONIC SURVEILLANCE, provided him with a wealth of information on the private affairs of many prominent political figures. Hoover shared some of this information with his political allies, but

"WE ARE A FACT-GATHERING ORGANIZATION ONLY. WE DON'T CLEAR ANYBODY. WE DON'T CONDEMN ANYBODY."

much of it remained in his private files. Over time many politicians came to fear Hoover, who they believed might have incriminating information about them that could destroy their political careers. Armed with these files, Hoover enjoyed immense power in the 1950s and 1960s.

With the birth of the modern CIVIL RIGHTS MOVEMENT, Hoover discovered what he considered another subversive group. He became convinced that MARTIN LUTHER KING, JR., was a pawn of the Communist conspiracy. He had agents follow King and record sexual encounters in various hotel rooms. King's Southern Christian Leadership Conference offices were wiretapped and burglarized by the FBI many times, all in the hope of finding information that would discredit King. Though Hoover's efforts proved futile, they demonstrated his ability to use the FBI as his personal tool.

During the 1960s Hoover also had the FBI investigate the KU KLUX KLAN and other white supremacist groups. The same techniques used against King and other alleged subversives were also employed against right-wing radicals who threatened physical violence. And with the growth of opposition to the VIETNAM WAR in the 1960s, Hoover targeted war protesters.

Presidents LYNDON B. JOHNSON and Richard M. Nixon allowed Hoover to serve past the mandatory retirement age. During his last years, Hoover was criticized for his authoritarian administration of the FBI. Agents who displeased him could be banished to an obscure FBI field office or discharged. Perhaps most troubling was his refusal to investigate organized crime with the same resources expended on politically subversive organizations.

Hoover died May 2, 1972, in Washington, D.C.

See also COMMUNISM; FORENSIC SCIENCE.

HORNBLOWER, WILLIAM BUTLER

William Butler Hornblower was a noted corporate and trial lawyer who was nominated to the U.S. Supreme Court but failed to win confirmation.

Hornblower was born May 13, 1851, in Paterson, New Jersey, with an unusually distin-

"[T]HE INDEPENDENCE OF THE JUDICIARY IS THE KEYSTONE OF OUR FORM OF GOVERNMENT, THAT IF THE KEYSTONE IS REMOVED THE WHOLE STRUCTURE IS IN DANGER OF DISINTEGRATION AND DESTRUCTION."

BIOGRAPHY

William Butler Hornblower

LIBRARY OF CONGRESS

guished family background. His great-grandfather was a member of the Congress of the Confederation and a judge, his grandfather was a chief justice of the Supreme Court of New Jersey, his father was a noted theologian and pastor, and his mother was a descendant of Revolutionary leaders and colonial judges. In addition, one of his uncles was JOSEPH P. BRADLEY, an associate justice of the U.S. Supreme Court, and another was Lewis B. Woodruff, a highly respected federal circuit court judge.

Hornblower was first educated at prestigious preparatory schools and in 1871 graduated with honors from the College of New Jersey (later known as Princeton University). At the encouragement of Bradley and Woodruff, he then entered Columbia University to study law. In 1875, he graduated with distinction, was admitted to the bar, and became a trial lawyer with the New York City firm of Caton and Eaton, where he had been a clerk while a law student. In 1888, he founded the firm of Hornblower and Byrne. Throughout his legal career, Hornblower represented a number of major corporate clients, including the New York Life Insurance Company; the Chicago, Milwaukee, and St. Paul Railway Company; the New York Security and Trust Company; and several tobacco companies. He also served on many public commissions, held office in state and national bar associations, and was active in the Democratic party.

In 1893, President GROVER CLEVELAND nominated Hornblower to succeed SAMUEL BLATCHFORD, who had died, as an associate justice of the U.S. Supreme Court. Given his long and distinguished career, Hornblower appeared headed for easy confirmation, but a bitter political battle intervened to prevent Hornblower from taking the seat.

A year before his nomination to the Court, Hornblower had been appointed to a New York City Bar Association committee convened to investigate Judge Isaac H. Maynard. Maynard was accused of improper conduct in a contested election while he was deputy attorney general. The investigation ultimately led to Maynard's

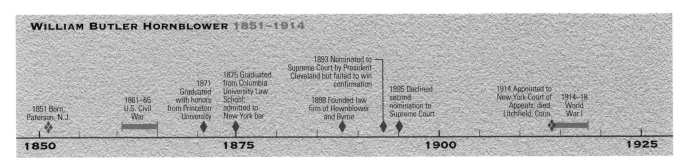

WILLIAM BUTLER HORNBLOWER 1851–1914

1851 Born, Paterson, N.J.

1861–65 U.S. Civil War

1871 Graduated with honors from Princeton University

1875 Graduated from Columbia University Law School; admitted to New York bar

1888 Founded law firm of Hornblower and Byrne

1893 Nominated to Supreme Court by President Cleveland but failed to win confirmation

1895 Declined second nomination to Supreme Court

1914 Appointed to New York Court of Appeals; died, Litchfield, Conn.

1914–18 World War I

1850   1875   1900   1925

defeat for a seat on the New York Court of Appeals. David B. Hill, a powerful New York senator and a close friend of Maynard's, retaliated against Hornblower for his role in the investigation by vigorously campaigning against Hornblower's nomination. Hill's efforts were successful: the Senate rejected Hornblower's nomination by a vote of 30–24.

In 1895, President Cleveland nominated Hornblower for another vacancy on the Court. This time, Hornblower declined the nomination, citing the financial sacrifice he would incur if he left his very lucrative law practice.

In 1914, Hornblower was nominated to the New York Court of Appeals and was confirmed unanimously by the New York state senate. He took his seat on the court in March, but left after only one week owing to illness. He died two months later, on June 16, 1914, in Litchfield, Connecticut.

HORNBOOK   A primer; a book explaining the basics, fundamentals, or rudiments of any science or branch of knowledge. The phrase *hornbook law* is a colloquial designation of the rudiments or general principles of law.

A colloquial reference to a series of textbooks that review various fields of law in summary, narrative form, as opposed to casebooks, which are designed as primary teaching tools and include many reprints of court opinions.

HOSTAGES   Persons taken by an individual or organized group in order to force a state, government unit, or community to meet certain conditions: payment of ransom, release of prisoners, or some other act.

The taking of hostages, whether during wartime or periods of peace, is generally condemned under INTERNATIONAL LAW.

HOSTILE FIRE   In INSURANCE law, a combustion that cannot be controlled, that escapes from where it was initially set and confined, or one that was not intended to exist.

A hostile fire differs from a FRIENDLY FIRE, which burns in a place where it was intended to burn, such as one confined to a fireplace or furnace.

HOSTILE WITNESS   A witness at a trial who is so adverse to the party that called him or her that he or she can be cross-examined as though called to testify by the opposing party.

The Federal Rules of Evidence provide that WITNESSES who are hostile, or adverse, can be interrogated through the use of LEADING QUESTIONS.

HOTCHPOT   The process of combining and assimilating property belonging to different individuals so that the property can be equally divided; the taking into consideration of funds or property that have already been given to children when dividing up the property of a decedent so that the respective shares of the children can be equalized.

HOT LINE AGREEMENT, 1971   The original "hot line" agreement was a memorandum of understanding between the United States and the Soviet Union reached in 1963 to establish a direct communications link between the governments of the two nations.

The need for such a communications channel was evident in the CUBAN MISSILE CRISIS of 1962 and its establishment was viewed as a means of forestalling an unnecessary resort to force. The 1971 hot line agreement updated the 1963 accord by increasing the communications capability between the two governments. It called for the addition of two separate circuits of communications employing a U.S. and a Russian satellite system.

See also COLD WAR.

HOT PURSUIT   A doctrine that provides that the police may enter the premises where they suspect a crime has been committed without a WARRANT when delay would endanger their lives or the lives of others and lead to the escape of the alleged perpetrator; also sometimes called fresh pursuit.

Countless crime dramas have portrayed police officers in a high-speed chase barking into their radio that they are "in hot pursuit" of a suspect. This popular image says little about the legal rule of hot pursuit. As established by the U.S. Supreme Court, the rule is an important exception to the freedoms guaranteed by the FOURTH AMENDMENT. That constitutional provision safeguards citizens against excessive police intrusion into their life and property. Its foremost protection is the SEARCH WARRANT, which must be obtained from a judge or MAGISTRATE before the police can conduct most searches. Under special circumstances, the rule of hot pursuit gives the police extra powers to enter private property and conduct a search without a warrant. The rule recognizes practical limitations on Fourth Amendment rights in light of the realities of police work, especially in emergencies, but it stops far short of giving the police complete freedom to conduct warrantless searches.

As a powerful deterrent to the abuse of power, the Fourth Amendment is designed to prevent the rise of a police state. The requirement that police officers obtain search warrants prevents arbitrary violations of freedom, applying equally to federal and state authority. Yet this freedom is not absolute. In the twentieth century, the Supreme Court has carved out a

The doctrine of hot pursuit provides that police officers may enter the premises where they suspect a crime has been committed without a warrant in certain cases. It is an exception to the freedoms granted by the Fourth Amendment.

few exceptions to its protections. These exceptions exist under "exigent circumstances": the emergencylike demands of specifically defined situations that call for immediate response by the police, who must have PROBABLE CAUSE to conduct a search. Generally, these are circumstances under which obtaining a search warrant would be impractical—ranging from those requiring officers to frisk suspects for weapons to those requiring officers to stop and search AUTOMOBILES—as well as when suspects explicitly consent or imply consent to a search.

Hot pursuit is one such exigent circumstance. It usually applies when the police are pursuing a suspected felon into private premises or have probable cause to believe that a crime has been committed on private premises. The Supreme Court stated that " 'hot pursuit' means some sort of a chase, but it need not be an extended hue and cry 'in and about the public streets' " (*United States v. Santana*, 427 U.S. 38, 96 S. Ct. 2406, 49 L. Ed. 2d 300 [1976]). Hot pursuit also applies when the lives of police officers or others are in danger. Thus, the Court has recognized two specific conditions that justify warrantless searches under the rule of hot pursuit: the need to circumvent the destruction of EVIDENCE, and the need to prevent the loss of life or serious injury.

The Supreme Court enunciated the rule of hot pursuit in 1967, in *Warden v. Hayden*, 387 U.S. 294, 87 S. Ct. 1642, 18 L. Ed. 2d 782. It

had used the term before, but in *Warden*, it explicitly condoned a certain form of this warrantless search. In this case, police officers pursuing a suspected armed robber were told that he had entered a dwelling moments before their arrival. They entered the dwelling, searched it and seized evidence, and then apprehended the suspect in bed. The man alleged in court that the warrantless search of the premises had violated his Fourth Amendment rights. When the case reached the Supreme Court, it disagreed, justifying the search under exigent circumstances.

Since *Warden*, lower courts have applied the rule to determine whether police officers acted reasonably or unreasonably when conducting a search without obtaining a search warrant. Other cases have permitted warrantless entry and arrest in hot pursuit under different circumstances: when the police saw a suspect standing in her doorway who retreated inside carrying a package that contained marked money from a drug sting (*United States v. Santana*, 427 U.S. 38, 96 S. Ct. 2406, 49 L. Ed. 2d 300 [1976]); when the police had probable cause to arrest a suspect because he fit the description of an assailant who had threatened others and fled arrest (*United States v. Lopez*, 989 F.2d 24 (1st Cir. 1993), *cert. denied*, 510 U.S. 872, 114 S. Ct. 201, 126 L. Ed. 2d 158 [1993]); and when a police officer at the threshold of an apartment viewed a narcotics deal taking place inside (*United States v. Sewell*, 942 F.2d 1209 [7th Cir. 1991]).

Although hot pursuit expands the powers of the police to conduct warrantless searches, it does so under strict circumstances. Its purpose is grounded in practical necessity; it does not give law officers license to ignore constitutional safeguards. Courts make the final determination of whether a warrantless search is permissible, and they will reject misuses of the rule. One improper use of hot pursuit occurred in *O'Brien v. City of Grand Rapids*, 23 F.3d 990 (6th Cir. 1994). In this case, police officers pursued a suspect to his house, called for backup, surrounded the residence, and ultimately spent six hours in a standoff without seeking a search warrant. The court held that the suspect could not have fled the scene and that the officers had no fear of destruction of evidence or of a threat to safety. Thus, no exigent circumstances authorized their warrantless search.

See also SEARCHES AND SEIZURES.

HOUSEBREAKING 📖 The act of using physical force to gain access to, and entering, a house with an intent to commit a FELONY inside. 📖

In most states, housebreaking that occurs at night constitutes the crime of BURGLARY. Some statutes expand the definition of housebreaking to include breaking out of a house after entry has been achieved without the use of physical force, such as when access was gained under FALSE PRETENSES.

HOUSEHOLD Individuals who comprise a family unit and who live together under the same roof; individuals who dwell in the same place and comprise a family, sometimes encompassing domestic help; all those who are under the control of one domestic head.

For the purposes of INSURANCE, the terms *family* and *household* are frequently used interchangeably.

See also HEAD OF HOUSEHOLD.

HOUSE OF REPRESENTATIVES The lower chamber, or larger branch, of the U.S. Congress, or a similar body in the LEGISLATURE of many of the states.

The U.S. House of Representatives forms one of the two branches of the U.S. Congress. The House comprises 435 members who are elected to two-year terms. The U.S. Constitu-

tion vests the House with the sole power of introducing bills for raising revenue, making it one of the most influential components of the U.S. government.

Members According to Article I, Section 2, of the U.S. Constitution, a member of the House must be at least twenty-five years of age and a U.S. citizen for seven years before his or her election. In addition, representatives must reside in the state that they represent. Members of the House are generally called congressmen, congresswomen, or representatives.

During the First Congress (1789–91), the House had sixty-five members, each representing approximately 30,000 people. Until 1929 the law required the number of members in the House to increase in proportion to the national population. That year Congress passed the Permanent Apportionment Act (46 Stat. 21, 26, 27), which limited the size of the House to 435 representatives. During the 1990s each House member represented an average of 572,000 people.

House of Representatives

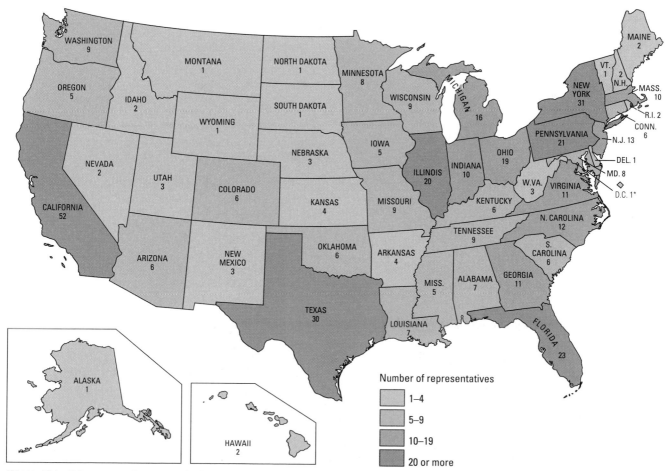

Number of representatives
- 1–4
- 5–9
- 10–19
- 20 or more

*District of Columbia has one non-voting representative. Puerto Rico, Guam, American Samoa and the U.S. Virgin Islands also have one non-voting representative each.

Source: Voter News Service

The First U.S. House of Representatives, 1789–1791: Setting Precedent for Future Lawmakers

Today the U.S. House of Representatives is known as an institution with established traditions and procedures. It has 435 members, standing committees, rules for evaluating legislation, and well-defined relations with the Senate, the president, and the executive agencies of the federal government. However, the structure and operations of the House have not always been well established. In 1789, as it began the task of creating laws for a new nation, the House had no precedent to guide it.

The House of Representatives first convened April 1, 1789, in New York City. Representatives slowly made the long journey to New York, and the First House eventually reached a total of sixty-five members. Fifty-five representatives belonged to the Federalist party, and ten allied themselves with the Anti-Federalist party.

The new House members were not without experience in legislative matters. Fifty-two had served in a state legislature, the Continental Congress, or the Constitutional Convention. Their legislative experience proved invaluable during this First Congress, because the Constitution gave them only limited guidance on how to establish the House. It was up to the representatives to work out the details of an effective lawmaking body.

On its first day in session, the House elected its officers, choosing Frederick A. C. Muhlenberg, of Pennsylvania, as its first Speaker. On succeeding days it established rules relating to debate, legislation, committees, and cooperation with the Senate. It also defined the duties of the Speaker, modeling that position after the Speaker of the English House of Commons. The Speaker was to preside over House sessions, preserve order, resolve disputed points, and appoint certain committees.

The lack of precedent made operations difficult for the First House. James Madison, of Virginia, a principal Framer of the Constitution and a leading member of the First House, complained, "In every step the difficulties arising from novelty are severely experienced. . . . Scarcely a day passes without some striking evidence of the delays and perplexities springing merely from the want of precedents." Madison was confident that the House would resolve its problems, however, concluding, "Time will be a full remedy for this evil."

The House gradually found ways to improve the problems cited by Madison and others. One important solution was the development of committees. The first legislation passed by the House was created by the Committee of the Whole—that is, the entire House acting as one large committee. Representatives soon found that this was a cumbersome way to pass legislation. When meeting as the Committee of the Whole, they could consider only one piece of legislation at a time. Moreover, the chamber often became bogged down by seemingly endless debate as each member sought to join the argument.

The House responded to this predicament by creating temporary committees to research and draft legislation, forming a separate committee for each bill. This relieved the entire chamber of the necessity of debating every detail of each piece of legislation. The contemporary House, by contrast, has permanent, or standing, committees, each of which handles many bills. The sole standing committee to come out of the first House was the Committee on Elections.

With these and other changes, the First House of Representatives was able to accomplish many tasks of vital importance to the young nation. Together with the Senate, it passed sixty statutes, including laws that founded the Departments of War, Treasury, and Foreign Affairs. The House also established its power to give limited orders to executive agencies, such as when it requested Secretary of the Treasury Alexander Hamilton to report on issues such as the federal debt, plans to promote manufacturing, and the establishment of a national mint. No less important, under the leadership of James Madison, it drafted the first ten amendments to the Constitution, known as the Bill of Rights.

The House has changed greatly in more than two centuries, but the foundation built by the first representatives remains. Their innovations have become flexible traditions that allow the House to maintain order even as it evolves and adapts to new situations.

Reapportionment or redistribution of House seats—a process whereby some states lose House representatives while others gain them—occurs after CENSUS figures have been collected. The Constitution requires that a census be conducted every ten years (art. 1, § 2). Each state must have at least one representative.

Puerto Rico elects a nonvoting resident commissioner to the House for a four-year term. Nonvoting delegates from American Samoa, the District of Columbia, Guam, and the Virgin Islands are elected to a two-year term. These special representatives are allowed to participate in debates and vote in committees.

Committees House committees are responsible for most of the work involved in the creation of new laws. After a bill is introduced in the House, it is referred to a committee. The committee studies the bill and may hold public hearings on it or suggest amendments. If the bill has the support of a majority of committee members, it is reported to the House, which then debates it and votes on it. The Committee on Rules determines how long a bill may be debated and the procedure by which it is amended.

The number of standing, or permanent, House committees has varied over time. In 1800 five standing committees existed. By 1910 the number of standing committees had increased to sixty-one. Between 1950 and the 1990s, the total stabilized at nineteen to twenty-two. During the 104th Congress (1995–97), there were nineteen standing committees in the House: Agriculture; Appropriations; Banking and Financial Services; Budget; Commerce; Economic and Educational Opportunities; Government Reform and Oversight; House Oversight; International Relations; Judiciary; National Security; Resources; Rules; Science; Small Business; Standards of Official Conduct; Transportation and Infrastructure; Veterans' Affairs; and Ways and Means.

Each committee has an average of eight to ten subcommittees. Committee membership is determined by a vote of the entire House, and committee chairs are elected by the majority party. The House may also create special committees, including investigative committees.

Officers The Speaker of the House has the most powerful position in the House and is traditionally the leader of the majority party. The Speaker interprets and applies House rules and refers bills to committees. Party leadership positions in the House include the majority and minority leaders, or floor leaders, and the majority and minority whips.

The elected officers of the House include the clerk, the sergeant at arms, and the doorkeeper. The clerk oversees the major legislative duties of the House. He or she takes all votes and certifies the passage of bills, calls the House to order at the commencement of each Congress, administers legislative information and reference services, and supervises television coverage of House floor proceedings. The sergeant at arms, a member of the U.S. Capitol Police Board, is the chief law enforcement officer for the House. The sergeant maintains order in the House and arranges formal ceremonies such as presidential inaugurations and joint sessions of Congress. The doorkeeper monitors admission to the House and its galleries and organizes the distribution of House documents.

CROSS-REFERENCES

Apportionment; Congress of the United States; Constitution of the United States.

HOUSING AND URBAN DEVELOPMENT DEPARTMENT

The Department of Housing and Urban Development (HUD) is the principal federal agency responsible for programs concerned with housing needs, fair housing opportunities, and improving and developing the United States' communities.

HUD was established in 1965 by the Department of Housing and Urban Development Act (42 U.S.C.A. § 3532–3537). Its major functions include insuring MORTGAGES for single-family and multifamily dwellings and extending loans for home improvements and for the purchase of mobile homes; channeling funds from investors into the mortgage industry through the Government National Mortgage Association; and making loans for the construction or rehabilitation of housing projects for older and handicapped persons. HUD also provides federal housing subsidies for low- and moderate-income families, makes grants to states and local communities for development activities related to housing, and promotes and enforces laws, policies, and regulations supporting fair housing and equal housing opportunities.

HUD is administered under the supervision and direction of a cabinet-level secretary appointed by the president. The secretary of HUD formulates recommendations for housing and community development policy, and works with the Executive Office of the President and other federal agencies to ensure that housing policies are consistent with other economic and fiscal policies of the government. In addition, the secretary encourages private enterprise to serve the housing and community development needs of the nation whenever possible, and promotes the use of initiatives within the state, local, and private sectors to spur the growth of housing and community development resources. Equally important, the secretary ensures equal access to housing and promotes nondiscrimination. The secretary also oversees the FEDERAL NATIONAL MORTGAGE ASSOCIATION (FNMA). The FNMA, also known as Fannie Mae, was chartered by Congress in the late 1960s as a stockholder-owned, privately managed corporation to provide a secondary market

Housing and Urban Development Department

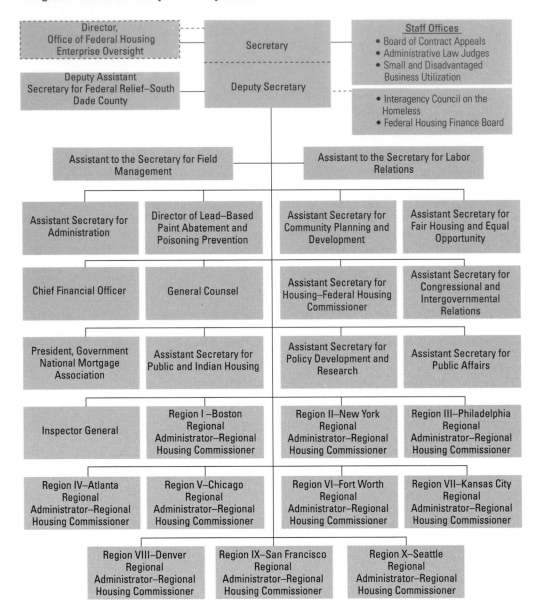

for home mortgages. Fannie Mae purchases home mortgages and then issues securities funded by the monthly principal and interest payments of homeowners.

A number of program areas within HUD carry out the department's goals and functions. The assistant secretary for housing, who also acts as the federal housing commissioner, underwrites property improvement loans and loans for manufactured homes, and administers programs that help provide housing for special groups, including the elderly, the disabled, and the chronically mentally ill. The assistant secretary also administers housing programs to assist low-income families having difficulties affording housing and to protect consumers against

fraudulent practices of land developers and promoters.

The assistant secretary for community planning and development implements a number of programs, including the Community Development Block Grant (CDBG) Program for local communities. The CDBG Program was established in 1974 to meet a wide variety of community development needs, including the need to expand economic opportunities for persons of low and moderate income by helping to provide them with decent and affordable housing. Block grants can be used to revitalize neighborhoods in blighted areas as well as to meet other community development needs.

The assistant secretary for community planning and development also implements Hope for Ownership of Single Family Homes, which helps low-income persons become homeowners by providing federal assistance to help finance the purchase and rehabilitation of single-family homes at affordable prices. Another similar program administered by the Community Planning and Development area of HUD is Home Investment in Affordable Housing, which also provides federal assistance to localities and Indian tribes for housing rehabilitation, assistance to first-time home buyers, and funding for the new construction of rental housing in areas where such housing is needed. Other programs provide assistance for procuring both transitional and permanent housing for homeless people and for relocating property owners displaced by federal projects under the Uniform Relocation Assistance and Real Property Acquisition Policies Act of 1970 (42 U.S.C.A. § 4601 et seq.).

The assistant secretary for community planning and development is also responsible for implementing the Neighborhood Development Demonstration Program, which was designed to determine the ability of neighborhood organizations to fund and implement neighborhood development activities. The program uses cooperative efforts and monetary support from individuals, businesses, and nonprofit organizations in conjunction with federal matching funds to encourage neighborhood organizations to become more self-sufficient in their development activities.

The assistant secretary for policy development and research evaluates and analyzes existing and proposed HUD programs and policies. The office of this secretary conducts field studies to determine the effectiveness of HUD programs through cost-benefit research and provides the secretary of HUD with economic, legal, and policy analyses of issues related to the department's oversight responsibilities.

The Office of Lead-Based Paint Abatement develops policy, conducts research, and drafts regulations to increase awareness of the dangers associated with lead-based paint poisoning and to develop safe and effective methods for the detection and abatement of lead-based paint poisoning. It also encourages state and local governments to develop programs for public education and hazard reduction surrounding such poisoning.

The assistant secretary for fair housing and equal opportunity administers fair housing laws and regulations prohibiting discrimination in public and private housing on the basis of race, color, religion, sex, national origin, handicap, or

familial status. This assistant secretary thus acts as the principal adviser to the secretary of HUD on all matters relating to CIVIL RIGHTS and equal opportunity in housing. The assistant secretary also administers equal employment opportunity laws and regulations that prohibit discrimination on the basis of race, color, religion, sex, national origin, handicap, or age.

The assistant secretary for public and Indian housing administers a number of programs to help meet the housing needs of Native Americans. These programs include the Comprehensive Improvement Assistance Grant Program, which helps modernize and upgrade low-income housing projects; the Resident Initiatives Program, which supports resident participation in the management of properties, economic development, and other services, including programs to help ensure drug-free neighborhoods; and other programs that determine eligibility for public housing.

The Government National Mortgage Association (GNMA), another component of HUD, is a government corporation that guarantees mortgages issued by private lenders. In addition, through its mortgage-backed securities programs, Ginnie Mae, as it is known, works to promote and expand the housing market by increasing the supply of credit available for housing by channeling funds from the securities market into the mortgage market.

The headquarters of the HUD Department is located in Washington, D.C., and ten HUD field offices are located throughout the United States. Each field office is headed by a secretary's representative, who is responsible for the management of the office and reports directly to the secretary. The representatives carry out the objectives of HUD as they relate to state and local governments, and monitor the potential local effects of HUD policies and decisions.

HOUSTON, CHARLES HAMILTON

Charles Hamilton Houston was a law professor and CIVIL RIGHTS lawyer who argued many landmark cases on behalf of the NATIONAL ASSOCIATION FOR THE ADVANCEMENT OF COLORED PEOPLE (NAACP).

Houston was born September 3, 1895, in Washington, D.C. His father, William Houston, was trained as a lawyer and worked for a while as a records clerk to supplement the family's income; his mother, Mary Ethel Houston, worked as a hairdresser. Houston's father eventually began practicing law full-time and later became a law professor at Howard University, a predominantly black institution located in Washington, D.C. An only child, Houston received his primary and secondary

BIOGRAPHY

ARTIST: BETSY GRAVES, SCHOMBURG CENTER FOR RESEARCH IN BLACK CULTURE.

Charles Hamilton Houston

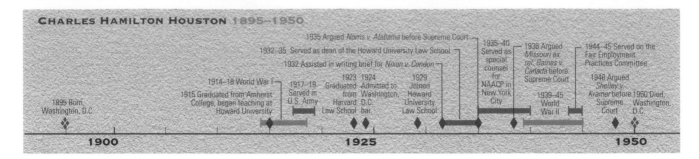

CHARLES HAMILTON HOUSTON 1895–1950

1895 Born, Washington, D.C.

1914–18 World War I

1915 Graduated from Amherst College, began teaching at Howard University

1917–19 Served in U.S. Army

1922 Graduated from Harvard Law School

1924 Admitted to Washington, D.C., bar

1929 Joined Howard University Law School

1932 Assisted in writing brief for *Nixon v. Condon*

1932–35 Served as dean of the Howard University Law School

1935 Argued *Norris v. Alabama* before Supreme Court

1935–40 Served as special counsel for NAACP in New York City

1938 Argued *Missouri ex rel. Gaines v. Canada* before Supreme Court

1939–45 World War II

1944–45 Served on the Fair Employment Practices Committee

1948 Argued *Shelley v. Kraemer* before Supreme Court

1950 Died, Washington, D.C.

1900   1925   1950

education in segregated Washington, D.C., schools. After graduating from high school, he received a full scholarship to the University of Pittsburgh. At the urging of his parents, he instead entered Amherst College, where he was the only black student enrolled. An outstanding student, he was elected Phi Beta Kappa, and graduated magna cum laude in 1915.

After Amherst, Houston taught English composition and literature at Howard for two years. In 1917, shortly after the United States entered World War I, Houston left teaching for military service. He enrolled in an officer candidate school for blacks, established at Des Moines. After four months of training, Houston became a first lieutenant in the infantry and was assigned to duty at Camp Meade, Maryland. He later entered field artillery school, despite the widely held belief that blacks could not serve effectively as field artillery officers.

Houston served in France until 1919, then returned to the United States to enroll at Harvard Law School. He was one of the few black students admitted at that time. His outstanding academic record earned him a place on the editorial board of the *Harvard Law Review*, making him the first black student to be so honored. In 1922, he received a bachelor of laws degree cum laude. He remained at Harvard for an additional year of graduate study, and earned a doctor of juridical science degree in 1923. He then won a fellowship to study for a year at the University of Madrid, where he earned a doctor of civil law degree.

In 1924, his studies completed, Houston was admitted to the bar of the District of Columbia and became his father's partner in the law firm of Houston and Houston. He quickly developed a successful practice, specializing in trusts and estates, probate, and landlord-tenant matters. He also taught law part-time at Howard University. In 1929, he left law practice to become an associate professor and vice dean of the School of Law at Howard. In 1932, he became dean, a post he held until 1935.

While at Howard, Houston worked to upgrade the law school's facilities, reputation, and

"WHETHER ELECTED OR APPOINTED, PUBLIC OFFICIALS SERVE THOSE WHO PUT AND KEEP THEM IN OFFICE. WE CANNOT DEPEND UPON THEM TO FIGHT OUR BATTLES."

academic standards and was instrumental in securing full accreditation for the school. He also found time to participate in important civil rights cases. He helped write the brief for *Nixon v. Condon*, 286 U.S. 73, 52 S. Ct. 484, 76 L. Ed. 984 (1932), in which the U.S. Supreme Court held that a "whites-only" primary election was unconstitutional. He also helped argue *Norris v. Alabama*, 294 U.S. 587, 55 S. Ct. 579, 79 L. Ed. 1074 (1935), where the Court overturned the convictions of nine black men charged with rape, because Alabama's systematic exclusion of blacks from juries violated the FOURTEENTH AMENDMENT of the Constitution. See also POW-ELL V. ALABAMA.

In 1935, Houston left Washington, D.C., to become the first special counsel for the NAACP, headquartered in New York City. As special counsel, Houston initiated legal challenges in support of civil rights and argued landmark cases before the U.S. Supreme Court, including *Missouri ex rel. Gaines v. Canada*, 305 U.S. 337, 59 S. Ct. 232, 83 L. Ed. 208 (1938). In *Gaines*, the Supreme Court ruled that a state could not exclude a black applicant from a state-supported all-white law school. Houston also argued *Shelley v. Kraemer*, 334 U.S. 1, 68 S. Ct. 836, 92 L. Ed. 1161 (1948). In the *Shelley* decision, the Court held that a clause in a real estate contract prohibiting the sale of property to nonwhites could not be enforced by state courts. Houston was widely praised for the thorough and sometimes painstaking preparation of his legal briefs and his impassioned oral arguments before the Court.

In 1940, Houston left the NAACP to return to private practice in Washington, D.C., though he remained a member of the NAACP's national legal committee. He was succeeded as special counsel by THURGOOD MARSHALL, a colleague at the NAACP whom he had taught at Howard and who later became the first African American justice on the U.S. Supreme Court. Houston remained active in civil rights work, winning before the U.S. Supreme Court two cases that struck down racially discriminatory practices by the railroads: *Steele v. Louisville and*

Nashville Railroad Company, 323 U.S. 192, 65 S. Ct. 226, 89 L. Ed. 173 (1944), and *Tunstall v. Brotherhood of Locomotive Firemen*, 323 U.S. 210, 65 S. Ct. 235, 89 L. Ed. 187 (1944).

In 1944, Houston was appointed by President FRANKLIN D. ROOSEVELT to the Fair Employment Practices Committee (FEPC). He resigned the following year after a dispute with President HARRY S. TRUMAN over alleged discriminatory hiring practices on the part of the Capital Transit Company, of Washington, D.C. Capital Transit Company was the transportation system in Washington, D.C. Houston alleged that it engaged in discriminatory policies by not hiring black workers or promoting current black workers to positions as bus operators or streetcar conductors. The FEPC wanted to issue a directive ending discrimination. Truman did not respond to Houston's efforts to have the directive issued, so Houston resigned from the FEPC. Truman finally did respond, maintaining that, because Capital Transit had earlier been seized under the War Labor Dispute Act because of a labor dispute, enforcement of the order ending discrimination should be postponed.

After battling heart disease for several years, Houston died in Washington, D.C., on April 22, 1950, at the age of fifty-four.

HOWARD, BENJAMIN CHEW Benjamin Chew Howard was a lawyer who served as the Supreme Court REPORTER of decisions from 1843 to 1861.

Howard, born November 5, 1791, in Baltimore, was the son of a distinguished Revolutionary War officer and the grandson of the president of the Pennsylvania Court of Errors and Appeals before the Revolution. Howard earned bachelor's and master's degrees from the College of New Jersey (later known as Princeton University). In 1812, he began the study of law, which was interrupted by military service during the War of 1812. Howard was a captain in the war and played a prominent role in the defense of Baltimore during the Battle of North Point, fought in September 1814.

Following the war, Howard resumed his legal studies. He was admitted to the Maryland

BIOGRAPHY

bar in 1816. Active in the Maryland Democratic party, in 1820, he was elected to the Baltimore City Council, and in 1824, he won a seat in the Maryland House of Delegates. In 1829, he was elected to the U.S. Congress, where he served four terms. During his time in Congress, he was chairman of the House Foreign Relations Committee for several years. In 1840, he left Congress to return to Maryland state politics, serving as a senator in the Maryland General Assembly. In January 1843, he resigned before the expiration of his term, to become reporter of the U.S. Supreme Court, a position created by Congress in 1816.

As reporter, Howard was primarily responsible for editing, publishing, and distributing the Court's opinions. He replaced Richard Peters, who was fired after he disagreed with several of the justices about whether their opinions should be published in the reports. Howard, though highly praised for publishing thorough and well-edited reports, did create a controversy of his own when he refused to include the complete arguments raised by both sides in a fugitive slave case decided by the Court, thus calling his impartiality into question.

In Howard's day, the reporter was paid a modest yearly salary and usually earned additional income selling copies of the bound volume in which an important case appeared or printing the opinion separately in a pamphlet for sale to the public. When the *Dred Scott* decision outlawing SLAVERY was issued by the U.S. Supreme Court in 1857, the U.S. Senate sought to publicize it as broadly as possible and printed twenty thousand copies for free distribution to the public (*Dred Scott v. Sandford*, 60 U.S. [19 How.] 393, 15 L. Ed. 691 [1856]). Howard protested strongly that his income from the sale of the opinion would suffer from the competition. As a result, the Senate voted to pay him $1,500 in compensation and agreed not to distribute its version until Howard's bound volume and pamphlet version were made available.

Howard, who edited twenty-four volumes of reports, remained active in politics while Su-

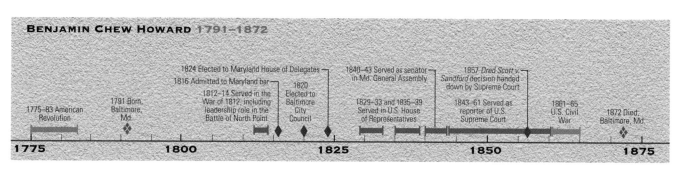

BENJAMIN CHEW HOWARD 1791–1872

1775–83 American Revolution

1791 Born, Baltimore, Md.

1812–14 Served in the War of 1812; including leadership role in the Battle of North Point

1816 Admitted to Maryland bar

1820 Elected to Baltimore City Council

1824 Elected to Maryland House of Delegates

1829–33 and 1835–39 Served in U.S. House of Representatives

1840–43 Served as senator in Md. General Assembly

1843–61 Served as reporter of U.S. Supreme Court

1857 *Dred Scott v. Sandford* decision handed down by Supreme Court

1861–65 U.S. Civil War

1872 Died, Baltimore, Md.

1775   1800   1825   1850   1875

preme Court reporter. He resigned from the Court in 1861 to run as the Democratic candidate for governor of Maryland. Following his defeat, Howard retired from public life. He died March 6, 1872, in Baltimore.

H.R. An abbreviation for the House of Representatives.

HUD An abbreviation for the HOUSING AND URBAN DEVELOPMENT DEPARTMENT.

HUGHES, CHARLES EVANS The long public career of Charles Evans Hughes prepared him to be a powerful chief justice of the U.S. Supreme Court. Hughes was a legal and political dynamo. Beginning as a lawyer and law professor in New York in the 1880s, he became known nationally for his role in investigating power utilities and the insurance industry. He went on to a career in national and international affairs—first as a two-term governor of New York, second as a Republican nominee for president, and third as secretary of state. He was twice appointed to the U.S. Supreme Court, serving as an associate justice from 1910 to 1916 and as chief justice from 1930 to 1941. His intellectual vigor and strong hand guided the Court through the critical period of the New Deal era when it made significant changes in its views on the constitutional limits on government power.

Hughes was born April 11, 1862, in Glen Falls, New York. Educated at Columbia University Law School, he spent his twenties and thirties in private practice and teaching law at Columbia and Cornell Universities. His expertise was in commercial law and by the time he was in his forties he had built a considerable reputation in that area. The New York state legislature chose him in 1905 to lead public investigations of the gas and electrical utilities in New York City and to probe the state's insurance industry. His work not only resulted in groundbreaking regulatory plans, later highly influential across the United States, but also catapulted Hughes into a political career. He immediately ran for governor of New York and twice won election to that office as a politician

BIOGRAPHY

ARTIST: GEORGE BURROUGHS TORREY. COLLECTION OF THE SUPREME COURT OF THE UNITED STATES

Charles Evans Hughes

"WHEN WE LOSE THE RIGHT TO BE DIFFERENT, WE LOSE THE PRIVILEGE TO BE FREE."

known for independence of mind and commitment to administrative reform. In 1910, his second term as governor had not yet expired when he stepped down and accepted President WILLIAM HOWARD TAFT'S appointment to the Supreme Court.

This move characterized the lifelong tension between Hughes's attractions to the legal and political spheres. He left public office to join the Court; later he would leave the Court to run for office again, then return to the Court as chief justice. In his nearly seven years on the Court as an associate justice, he displayed a flexibility of thought that led him to side at times with liberals and at times with the conservative majority. His most significant opinions turned on the issue of federal power. In particular, these opinions weighed the extent to which the COMMERCE CLAUSE of the Constitution gave the federal government authority to regulate the national economy. The opinions were delivered in the *Minnesota* and *Shreveport Rate* cases, in which the Court's decisions laid the groundwork for the expansion of federal REGULATION in the years to come (*Simpson v. Shepard*, 230 U.S. 352, 33 S. Ct. 729, 57 L. Ed. 1511 [1913]; *Houston, East & West Texas Railway Co. v. United States*, 234 U.S. 342, 34 S. Ct. 833, 58 L. Ed. 1341 [1914]).

The middle years of Hughes's career saw tumultuous change. In 1916 he stepped down from the Court to return to politics. Although he had not actively sought the Republican party's nomination for president, the party drafted him, and he reluctantly agreed to run against WOODROW WILSON. Despite a hard-fought campaign, Hughes lost the close election and returned to private practice. His respite from public service was brief. In 1921 President WARREN G. HARDING appointed Hughes secretary of state, a difficult position because of the challenges facing the United States in the aftermath of World War I: the war debt, REPARATIONS, the newly established Soviet Union, and especially relations with East Asia. Naval disarmament ranked high among Hughes's con-

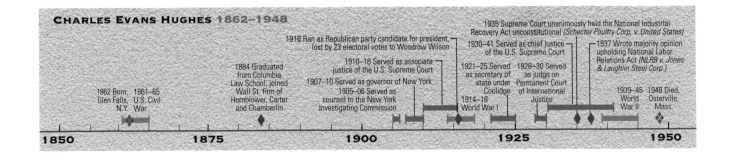

CHARLES EVANS HUGHES 1862–1948

1862 Born, Glen Falls, N.Y.
1861–65 U.S. Civil War
1884 Graduated from Columbia Law School, joined Wall St. firm of Hornblower, Carter and Chamberlin
1905–06 Served as counsel to the New York Investigating Commission
1907–10 Served as governor of New York
1910–16 Served as associate justice of the U.S. Supreme Court
1916 Ran as Republican party candidate for president, lost by 23 electoral votes to Woodrow Wilson
1914–18 World War I
1921–25 Served as secretary of state under Coolidge
1928–30 Served as judge on Permanent Court of International Justice
1930–41 Served as chief justice of the U.S. Supreme Court
1935 Supreme Court unanimously held the National Industrial Recovery Act unconstitutional (*Schecter Poultry Corp. v. United States*)
1937 Wrote majority opinion upholding National Labor Relations Act (*NLRB v. Jones & Laughlin Steel Corp.*)
1939–45 World War II
1948 Died, Osterville, Mass.

1850   1875   1900   1925   1950

cerns. In 1921 and 1922, he organized the Washington Conference, which for nearly a decade curbed naval growth and brought stability to the western Pacific.

The final chapter in Hughes's career returned him to the Supreme Court. Hughes served as secretary of state to Harding's successor, CALVIN COOLIDGE, then resigned in 1925 to work in private practice. In 1930 President HERBERT HOOVER nominated him for chief justice. Bitter opponents, critical of Hughes's political career and his earlier resignation from the Court, failed to block his appointment in a confirmation vote of 52–26. At age sixty-eight, Hughes became the oldest man ever to be chosen chief justice.

The Hughes Court sat during a controversial period in U.S. legal history. The Depression years had brought misery and a radical federal response. President FRANKLIN D. ROOSEVELT's economic recovery plans, known collectively as the New Deal, met opposition in Congress and from the justices of the Court. Several pieces of New Deal legislation faced constitutional tests and failed. After unanimously holding unconstitutional the NATIONAL INDUSTRIAL RECOVERY ACT (48 Stat. 195 [1933]) in *Schecter Poultry Corp. v. United States*, 295 U.S. 495, 55 S. Ct. 837, 79 L. Ed. 1570 (1935), the Court provoked a battle with the frustrated president. Roosevelt proposed an increase to the number of seats on the Court, hoping to then pack the Court with justices favorable to his views. Hughes wrote to the Senate Judiciary Committee in a move to help thwart Roosevelt's plan.

By taking a largely dim view of both federal and state regulatory power, the Hughes Court differed little from its conservative predecessors. In 1937 this changed dramatically. In upholding the National Labor Relations Act, 29 U.S.C.A. § 151 et seq., Hughes wrote a landmark opinion that greatly strengthened the labor movement (*NLRB v. Jones & Laughlin Steel Corp.*, 301 U.S. 1, 57 S. Ct. 615, 81 L. Ed. 893 [1937]). Also that year the Court upheld a state MINIMUM WAGE law, in *West Coast Hotel v. Parrish*, 300 U.S. 379, 57 S. Ct. 578, 81 L. Ed. 703. The *Parrish* decision was a striking departure from rulings of previous decades. Only fifteen years earlier, for example, the Court had refused to force employers of adult women to pay a minimum wage, viewing such a requirement as an unconstitutional infringement of the liberty of contract. The 1937 decisions together have been called a constitutional revolution because they marked a great change in JURISPRUDENCE that liberalized the Court's view of government power.

When Hughes retired at last in 1941, at age eighty, he had made a powerful impression on the law and on the Court. During his tenure as chief justice, he had shown the same flexibility of mind that marked his period as an associate justice: siding alternately with liberal and conservative colleagues, he often cast the swing vote. He had clearly run the Court with a strong hand, not only in leading the discussion but frequently in persuading justices to vote with him. Justice FELIX FRANKFURTER, who served under Hughes, likened him to the conductor of an orchestra: "He took his seat at the center of the Court with a mastery, I suspect, unparalleled in the history of the Court."

Hughes died August 27, 1948, in Osterville, Massachusetts. Succeeding generations have compared his bold leadership to that of Chief Justice EARL WARREN, who headed the Court two decades later.

CROSS-REFERENCES

Labor Law; Labor Union; *Schecter Poultry Corp. v. United States;* Supreme Court of the United States; *West Coast Hotel v. Parrish.*

HUMAN RIGHTS 📖 Personal liberties that protect individuals and groups against individual or state conduct prohibited by INTERNATIONAL LAW or custom. 📖

Human rights are freedoms established by custom or international agreement that impose standards of conduct on all nations. Human rights are distinct from civil liberties, which are freedoms established by the law of a particular state and applied by that state in its own JURISDICTION.

Specific human rights include the right to personal LIBERTY and DUE PROCESS OF LAW; to freedom of thought, expression, religion, organization, and movement; to freedom from DISCRIMINATION on the basis of race, religion, age, language, and sex; to basic education; to employment; and to property. Human rights laws have been defined by international conventions, by treaties, and by organizations, particularly the UNITED NATIONS. These laws prohibit practices such as torture, SLAVERY, summary execution without trial, and arbitrary detention or exile.

History Modern human rights law developed out of customs and theories that established the rights of the individual in relation to the state. These rights were expressed in legal terms in documents such as the English Bill of Rights of 1688, the U.S. DECLARATION OF INDEPENDENCE of 1776, the U.S. BILL OF RIGHTS added to the U.S. Constitution in 1789, and the French Declaration of the Rights of Man and the Citizen added to the French Constitution in 1791.

Human rights law also grew out of earlier systems of international law. These systems, developed largely during the eighteenth and nineteenth centuries, were predicated on the doctrine of national SOVEREIGNTY, according to which each nation retains sole power over its internal affairs without interference from other nations. As a result, early international law involved only relations between nation-states and was not concerned with the ways in which states treated their own citizens.

During the late nineteenth and early twentieth centuries, the notion of national sovereignty came under increasing challenge, and reformers began to press for international humanitarian standards. In special conferences such as the Hague Conference of 1899 and 1907, nations created laws governing the conduct of wars and handling of prisoners.

Not until after World War II (1939–45) did the international community create international treaties establishing human rights standards. The United Nations, created in 1945, took the lead in this effort. In its charter, or founding document, the United Nations developed objectives for worldwide human rights standards. It called for equal rights and self-determination for all peoples, as well as "universal respect for, and observance of, human rights and fundamental freedoms for all without distinction as to race, sex, language, or religion" (art. 55). The Universal Declaration of Human Rights, adopted by the U.N. General Assembly in 1948, also became an important human rights document.

To develop the U.N. Charter into an international code of human rights law, the international community created a number of multilateral human rights treaties. The two most significant of these are the International Covenant on Civil and Political Rights and the International Covenant on Economic, Social, and Cultural Rights, both put into effect in 1976. These treaties forbid discrimination on the basis of race, color, sex, language, religion, political or other opinion, national or social origin, property, birth, or other status. The two covenants, along with the U.N. Charter, the Universal Declaration of Human Rights, and an accord called the Optional Protocol to the Covenant on Civil and Political Rights (1976), constitute a body of law that has been called the International Bill of Human Rights.

The Covenant on Civil and Political Rights includes protections for the right to life, except after conviction for serious crime (art. 6); freedom from torture and other cruel and inhumane punishment (art. 7); freedom from slavery and prohibition from slave trade (art. 8); freedom from arbitrary arrest or detention (art. 9); humane treatment of prisoners (art. 10); freedom of movement and choice of residence (art. 12); legal standards, including equality before the law, fair hearings before an impartial tribunal, presumption of innocence, a prompt and fair trial, the right to counsel, and the right to review by a higher court; freedom of thought, conscience, and religion (art. 18); and freedom of association, including association in TRADE UNIONS (art. 22).

The Covenant on Economic, Social, and Cultural Rights protects additional rights, many of which have yet to be realized in poorer countries. These include the right to work (art. 6); to just wages and safe working conditions (art. 7); to social security and social insurance (art. 9); to a decent standard of living and freedom from hunger (art. 11); to universal basic education (art. 13); and to an enjoyment of the cultural life and scientific progress of the country.

The international community has also adopted many other human rights treaties. These include the Convention on the Prevention and Punishment of the Crime of Genocide (1948); the Convention on the Political Rights of Women (1953); the Convention to Suppress the Slave Trade and Slavery (revised 1953); the Convention against Torture and Other Cruel, Inhuman, or Degrading Treatment (1987); and the Convention on the Rights of the Child (1990).

In addition to worldwide human rights agreements, countries have also established regional conventions. These include the European Convention for the Protection of Human Rights and Fundamental Freedoms, the American Convention on Human Rights, and the African Charter on Human and Peoples' Rights.

The United States and Human Rights Although the United States was an active participant in the formation and implementation of international human rights organizations and treaties following World War II, and although it ratified selected treaties such as the Convention to Suppress the Slave Trade and Slavery in 1967 and the Convention on the Political Rights of Women in 1976, it did not ratify any of the major rights treaties until 1988, when it approved the Convention on the Prevention and Punishment of the Crime of Genocide. Four years later it ratified the International Covenant on Civil and Political Rights.

The U.S. Senate, which has authority to ratify all treaties, has been slow to review and approve human rights provisions, for a number of reasons. Senators have expressed concern about the effect of international treaties on U.S. domestic law. Article VI of the U.S. Constitution provides, "This Constitution, and the Laws of the United States which shall be made in Pursuance thereof; and all Treaties made, or which shall be made, under the Authority of the United States, shall be the supreme Law of the Land." Treaties therefore stand as federal law, though they are not considered to be law if they conflict with the Constitution (*Reid v. Covert*, 354 U.S. 1, 77 S. Ct. 1222, 1 L. Ed. 2d 1148 [1957]). In some cases a TREATY federalizes an issue that was previously governed by state law.

Conservative senators blocked early ratification of human rights treaties largely out of concern that the treaties would invalidate racial segregation laws that existed in the United States until the 1960s. Many human rights advocates claimed that these laws violated existing international treaties. Some senators argued that human rights should fall under domestic authority only and should not be subject to international negotiations. Others contended that ratification of human rights treaties would federalize areas of law better left to the states.

Since the late 1960s, such objections in the Senate have been overcome by attaching to treaties modifying terms called reservations, understandings, and declarations (RUDs). RUDs modify the treaties so that their effect on U.S. law will be acceptable to the two-thirds majority required for treaty ratification in the Senate. A reservation, for example, may state that the United States will not accept any element of a treaty found to be in conflict with the U.S. Constitution or existing laws, or that ratification will not federalize areas of law currently controlled by the states.

The U.S. Congress has also enacted its own human rights legislation. Under the leadership of Representative Donald M. Fraser (D-Minn.) during the 1970s, the House Committee on Foreign Affairs added language to the Foreign Assistance Act of 1973 (22 U.S.C.A. § 2151 et seq.) that required the president to cancel military and economic assistance to any government that "engages in a consistent pattern of gross violations of internationally recognized human rights," including torture and arbitrary detention without charges (§§ 2151n, 2304). This new legislation authorized the State De-

partment to collect and analyze data on human rights violations. Congress has also passed laws that require cutting off or limiting aid to countries with significant human rights violations.

In 1977 Congress gave human rights greater priority within the EXECUTIVE BRANCH by creating a new State Department office, the Bureau on Human Rights and Humanitarian Affairs, headed by an assistant secretary of state (Pub. L. No. 95-105, 91 Stat. 846). In 1994 the administration of President BILL CLINTON renamed the office the Bureau for Democracy, Human Rights, and Labor. The bureau is charged with administering programs and policies to promote democratic institutions and respect for human rights and workers' rights around the world. It also presents to Congress an annual report on the status of human rights all over the globe.

Nongovernment Organizations Amnesty International, the Center for Constitutional Rights, Human Rights Watch, the International Commission of Jurists, and other international human rights organizations closely monitor states' compliance with human rights standards. These groups also publicize rights violations and coordinate world public opinion against offending states. In many cases they induce governments to modify their policies to meet rights standards.

Domestic human rights organizations such as the Vicaria de Solidaridad, in Chile, and the Free Legal Assistance Group of the Philippines also play a significant role as human rights watchdogs, often at great personal risk to their members.

CROSS-REFERENCES

Civil Rights; Genocide; Nuremberg Trials; Tokyo Trials.

BIOGRAPHY

LIBRARY OF CONGRESS

David Hume

HUME, DAVID David Hume was an eighteenth-century Scottish philosopher, historian, and social theorist who influenced the development of skepticism and empiricism, two schools of philosophical thought. Hume's economic and political ideas influenced Adam Smith, the Scottish economist and theorist of modern capitalism, and JAMES MADISON, the American statesman who helped shape the republican form of government through his work on the U.S. Constitution.

Hume was born August 25, 1711, in Chirnside, near Edinburgh, Scotland. He entered Edinburgh University when he was twelve. He left the university after several years of study and attempted to study law. He did not like the subject, and instead read widely in philosophy.

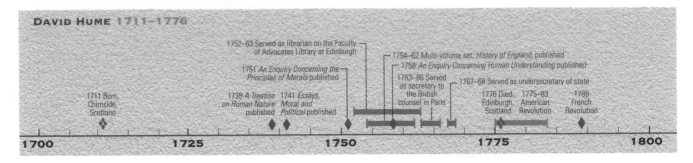

DAVID HUME 1711-1776

1752–63 Served as librarian on the Faculty
of Advocates Library at Edinburgh

1751 An Enquiry Concerning the
Principles of Morals published

1754–62 Multi-volume set, History of England, published

1758 An Enquiry Concerning Human Understanding published

1763–66 Served
as secretary to
the British
counsel in Paris

1767–68 Served as undersecretary of state

1711 Born,
Chirnside,
Scotland

1739 A Treatise
on Human Nature
published

1741 Essays,
Moral and
Political published

1776 Died,
Edinburgh,
Scotland

1775–83
American
Revolution

1789
French
Revolution

1700   1725   1750   1775   1800

In 1729 he suffered a nervous breakdown. After a prolonged recovery, he moved to France in 1734, where he wrote his first work, *A Treatise on Human Nature*. The book was not published until 1739 and was largely ignored. His next work, *Essays, Moral and Political* (1741), attracted favorable notice. Throughout the 1740s Hume's religious skepticism doomed his chances for a professorship at Edinburgh University. He spent the decade as a tutor and then as secretary to a Scottish general. During this period he wrote several more works of philosophy, including *An Enquiry Concerning the Principles of Morals* (1751).

In 1752 he was made librarian of the Faculty of Advocates Library at Edinburgh. From 1754 to 1762, he published his monumental *History of England*, which for many years was considered the basic text of English history. This work brought him international fame. He later served as secretary to the British counsel in Paris. He died August 25, 1776, in Edinburgh.

As a philosopher, Hume espoused a skeptical viewpoint, distrusting speculation. He believed that all knowledge comes from experience and that the mind contains nothing but a collection of perceptions, that all events are viewed and interpreted through the sensations of the mind. He attacked the principle of causality, which states that nothing can happen or exist without a cause. Hume was willing to admit that one event, or set of sense impressions, always precedes another, but he argued that this did not prove that the first event causes the second. A person can conclude that causality exists, but

"THE HEART OF MAN IS MADE TO RECONCILE CONTRADICTIONS."

BIOGRAPHY

LIBRARY OF CONGRESS

Hubert Horatio Humphrey

that conclusion is based on belief, not proof. Therefore, a person cannot expect the future to be similar to the past, because there is no rational basis for that expectation.

Like his philosophical beliefs, Hume's essays on politics and economics were influential in his time. Historians have concluded that James Madison read Hume's *Essays, Moral and Political* and applied some of the ideas from this work while helping write the Constitution and *The Federalist Papers*. Hume was concerned about the formation of factions based on religion, politics, and other common interests. He concluded that a democratic society needs to prevent factions, which ultimately undermine the government and lead to violence. Madison agreed that factions can divide government but came to the opposite conclusion: the more factions the better. In Madison's view more factions made it less likely that any one party or coalition of parties would be able to gain control of government and invade the rights of other citizens. The system of checks and balances contained in the Constitution was part of Madison's plan for placing some limits on factions.

See also HOBBES, THOMAS; JURISPRUDENCE; LOCKE, JOHN.

HUMPHREY, HUBERT HORATIO Hubert Horatio Humphrey served as a U.S. senator from Minnesota and as the thirty-eighth vice president of the United States. From his election to the U.S. Senate in 1948 to his death in 1978, Humphrey was the quintessential COLD WAR liberal. His unsuccessful presidential cam-

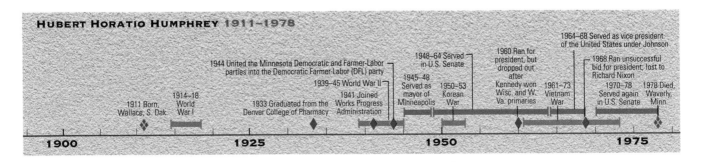

HUBERT HORATIO HUMPHREY 1911-1978

1964–68 Served as vice president
of the United States under Johnson

1944 United the Minnesota Democratic and Farmer-Labor
parties into the Democratic Farmer-Labor (DFL) party

1948–64 Served
in U.S. Senate

1960 Ran for
president, but
dropped out
after
Kennedy won
Wisc. and W.
Va. primaries

1968 Ran unsuccessful
bid for president; lost to
Richard Nixon

1939–45 World War II

1945–48
Served as
mayor of
Minneapolis

1950–53
Korean
War

1961–73
Vietnam
War

1970–78
Served again
in U.S. Senate

1978 Died,
Waverly,
Minn.

1911 Born,
Wallace, S. Dak.

1914–18
World
War I

1933 Graduated from the
Denver College of Pharmacy

1941 Joined
Works Progress
Administration

1900   1925   1950   1975

paign in 1968 was weakened by his support of President LYNDON B. JOHNSON's VIETNAM WAR policies.

Humphrey was born in Wallace, South Dakota, on May 27, 1911. He grew up in Doland, South Dakota, where his father ran the local drugstore. He received a degree from the Denver College of Pharmacy in 1933 and helped run the family drugstore before entering the University of Minnesota. After graduating from the University of Minnesota in 1939, he earned a master's degree from Louisiana State University. He taught at the University of Minnesota, Louisiana State University, and Macalester College, in St. Paul, Minnesota, before joining the federal Works Progress Administration in Minnesota in 1941.

Humphrey became a leader in Minnesota DEMOCRATIC PARTY politics during World War II. After narrowly losing the Minneapolis mayoral election in 1943, he cemented his position in 1944 when he united the Minnesota Democratic and Farmer-Labor parties into the Democratic Farmer-Labor (DFL) party. The Farmer-Labor party had advocated more radical political policies in the 1930s and 1940s, and had gained national attention through Governor Floyd B. Olson, of Minnesota. In the 1930s Olson and the Farmer-Labor party had advocated more aggressive governmental intervention to deal with the Great Depression. Olson criticized President FRANKLIN D. ROOSEVELT for not doing enough to help the nation's unemployed. By the mid-1940s, the party had attracted many Communist-influenced members. In 1947 Humphrey and his allies forced the more radical Farmer-Labor members out of leadership positions and ultimately out of the DFL. On a national level, Humphrey helped form Americans for Democratic Action, a liberal organization that trumpeted its anti-Communist credentials.

His political leadership paid quick dividends. In 1945 he was elected mayor of Minneapolis by more than thirty thousand votes. He increased his margin of victory to fifty thousand in his 1947 reelection campaign. As mayor he rooted out political graft and corruption and began to implement pieces of his liberal agenda. He secured the passage of the first municipal fair employment act in the United States and gained additional funds for public housing and WELFARE.

Humphrey galvanized liberal Democrats in 1948 at the Democratic National Convention. Southern Democrats on the platform committee had rejected President HARRY S. TRUMAN's CIVIL RIGHTS proposals. Humphrey, a delegate to the convention and a candidate for the U.S. Senate, led a fight from the convention floor to restore the civil rights plank. His passionate oratory helped bring back the proposals and fixed in the public mind the image of Humphrey as a fiery liberal, an image he would evoke the rest of his public career.

He was elected to the Senate in 1948, and found that his aggressive style clashed with the gentleman's-club atmosphere of that institution. A quick learner, he sought the mentorship of Lyndon Johnson, soon to be Senate majority leader. Humphrey was reelected to the Senate in 1954 and 1960. In 1960, along with Senator JOHN F. KENNEDY and Johnson, he sought the Democratic presidential nomination. Following victories by Kennedy in the Wisconsin and West Virginia primaries, Humphrey dropped out of the race and stood for reelection to the Senate.

During the Kennedy administration, Humphrey displayed his command of parliamentary procedure and political persuasion. He became assistant majority leader and helped pass the LIMITED TEST BAN TREATY of 1963. Following Kennedy's ASSASSINATION in November 1963, Humphrey worked closely with President Johnson to pass the many pieces of social welfare legislation that Johnson dubbed his Great Society program. Humphrey's plan for providing federal medical insurance to older people, called MEDICARE, was enacted. Most important, Humphrey played a critical role in securing the passage of the CIVIL RIGHTS ACT of 1964 (42 U.S.C.A. § 2000a et seq.).

In 1964 Johnson selected Humphrey as his vice presidential running mate. Johnson's landslide victory over conservative Republican BARRY M. GOLDWATER promised more liberal legislation. Humphrey worked to enhance civil rights for minorities and increase economic opportunities. But the political climate turned sour with rising protests over Johnson's escalation of U.S. involvement in Vietnam. Humphrey, who initially doubted the wisdom of U.S. military intervention, became an energetic and unrepentant advocate of Johnson's policies.

Humphrey had always dreamed of becoming president. When President Johnson announced in March 1968 that he would not seek reelection, Humphrey entered the race against Senator Eugene McCarthy, of Minnesota, and Senator ROBERT F. KENNEDY, of New York. McCarthy, a longtime friend and ally of Humphrey's, opposed the Vietnam War, as did Kennedy. Humphrey continued to support it.

"THERE ARE NOT ENOUGH JAILS, NOT ENOUGH POLICEMEN, NOT ENOUGH COURTS TO ENFORCE A LAW NOT SUPPORTED BY THE PEOPLE."

By May Humphrey had secured enough delegates to win the nomination. In June Kennedy was assassinated.

The Democratic National Convention, in Chicago, was a debacle. Confrontations between antiwar demonstrators and Chicago police officers led to a series of violent outbursts by the police. Though Humphrey won the nomination, he remained staunchly loyal to Johnson and refused to make a clean break on Vietnam policy, which would have won votes from disaffected Democrats. In November Republican RICHARD M. NIXON won the election with 301 electoral votes to Humphrey's 191. Humphrey lost the popular vote by less than one percent.

Following his defeat Humphrey returned to Minnesota and taught again at Macalester College. In 1970 he was reelected to the Senate. In 1972 he campaigned unsuccessfully for the Democratic presidential nomination. Reelected to the Senate again in 1976, Humphrey soon was engaged in a personal battle with cancer. He died at his home in Waverly, Minnesota, on January 13, 1978.

HUNDRED 📖 A political subdivision in old England. 📖

Under the Saxons, each shire or county in England was divided into a number of hundreds, which were made up of ten TITHINGS each. The tithings were groups of ten families of freeholders. The hundred was governed by a high constable and had its own local court called the Hundred Court. The most remarkable feature of the hundred was the collective responsibility of all the inhabitants for the crimes or defaults of any individual member.

HUNG JURY 📖 A trial jury duly selected to make a decision in a criminal case regarding a defendant's guilt or innocence, but who are unable to reach a VERDICT due to a complete division in opinion. 📖

When a JURY has been given an adequate opportunity to deliberate and is unable to reach a verdict, a retrial takes place at the discretion of the prosecution. The subsequent trial does

"THE CITIZEN OF THIS COUNTRY WHERE NEARLY EVERYTHING IS SUBMITTED TO THE POPULAR TEST AND WHERE OFFICE IS EAGERLY SOUGHT, WHO POSSESSES THE RIGHT TO VOTE, HOLDS A POWERFUL INSTRUMENT FOR HIS OWN ADVANTAGE."

not constitute a violation of the constitutional prohibition of DOUBLE JEOPARDY.

HUNT, WARD   The legal career of Ward Hunt peaked when he was appointed to the U.S. Supreme Court by President ULYSSES S. GRANT in 1873. Hunt held a seat on the High Court for nine years, until January 1882. Although he was well liked and respected as a diligent lawyer and jurist, Ward's tenure on the Court was unspectacular and marked by a forced retirement.

Hunt was born June 14, 1810, in Utica, New York, to Montgomery Hunt and Elizabeth Stringham Hunt. He studied at the Oxford Academy, in England and the Geneva Academy, in Switzerland. In 1828 he graduated with honors from Union College, in Schenectady, New York. He attended law school in Litchfield, Connecticut. He returned to Utica to work in a local law office, and was admitted to the bar in 1831.

Hunt married Mary Ann Savage in 1837, and they raised three children until her death in 1845. Eight years later he married Maria Taylor. With his partner, Hiram Denio, Hunt ran a successful law practice in Utica for thirty-one years. While practicing law Hunt became active in politics. He supported the policies of ANDREW JACKSON, who defended the interests of the middle class and served two terms as president. In 1838 Hunt was elected to the New York legislature, where he served one term, and in 1844 he was elected mayor of Utica.

In the 1840s Hunt came to differ with the Democratic party when he opposed the expansion of slavery and the annexation of Texas. In 1848 Hunt supported the Free-Soil presidential candidacy of ex-Democrat and ex-president MARTIN VAN BUREN, who was defeated. Hunt ran for a spot on the New York Supreme Court in 1853, but he lost the election, a result that observers attributed to his defection from the Democratic party. In 1855 Hunt helped to form the Republican party in the state of New York. As a Republican he was elected to the New York Court of Appeals in 1865.

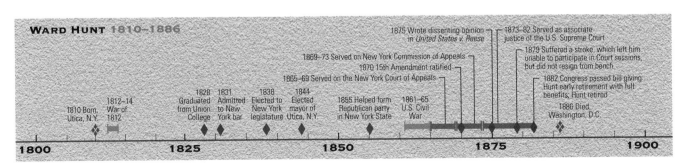

WARD HUNT 1810–1886

1810 Born, Utica, N.Y. | 1812–14 War of 1812 | 1828 Graduated from Union College | 1831 Admitted to New York bar | 1838 Elected to New York legislature | 1844 Elected mayor of Utica, N.Y. | 1855 Helped form Republican party in New York State | 1861–65 U.S. Civil War | | |

1865–69 Served on the New York Court of Appeals
1869–73 Served on New York Commission of Appeals
1870 15th Amendment ratified
1875 Wrote dissenting opinion in *United States v. Reese*
1873–82 Served as associate justice of the U.S. Supreme Court
1879 Suffered a stroke, which left him unable to participate in Court sessions, but did not resign from bench
1882 Congress passed bill giving Hunt early retirement with full benefits; Hunt retired
1886 Died, Washington, D.C.

1800   1825   1850   1875   1900

After three years on the New York Court of Appeals, Hunt was promoted to chief justice. A year later, in 1869, the New York court system was reorganized by an amendment to the state constitution, and Hunt was named commissioner of appeals. He held that position for three years, until January 1873, when he replaced fellow New Yorker SAMUEL NELSON as an associate justice on the U.S. Supreme Court.

Hunt had strong ties to the Republican party, and he had risen in the judicial ranks along with the party. At that time the Republican party promoted expansive federal powers. These powers were critical to the abolition of SLAVERY and the defeat of the Confederate forces in the Civil War. However, by the mid-1870s, the nation's appreciation of federal power had waned, and the judiciary began to emphasize the rights of the states. Perhaps as a result of this shift, Hunt, with his Republican views, authored few major opinions.

Hunt delivered his most memorable opinion in *United States v. Reese*, 92 U.S. (2 Otto) 214, 23 L. Ed. 563 (1875). In *Reese* the High Court struck down parts of the Enforcement Act of 1870, a federal act passed to ensure that African Americans would be allowed to vote. The act had been passed by Congress pursuant to the FIFTEENTH AMENDMENT, which provides, "The right of citizens of the United States to vote shall not be denied or abridged by the United States or by any State on account of race, color, or previous condition of servitude." *Reese* was brought by the U.S. government against two inspectors at a municipal election in Kentucky, alleging that they had refused to receive and count the vote of William Garner, an African American.

According to the majority in *Reese*, the Fifteenth Amendment did not confer on all adult citizens the right to vote. Rather, it merely prevented the state and federal governments from denying the right to vote based on race, color, or previous condition of servitude. Therefore, it was not within the power of the federal government to require that states give the vote to all adult citizens. Because parts of the Enforcement Act did not limit the application of criminal penalties to wrongful refusals based on race, the Court ruled that those parts unconstitutionally infringed on the powers of the states.

Hunt was the only dissenting justice. He argued that the Fifteenth Amendment was intended to confer on all persons the same political rights given to white persons. The guarantee of the right to vote, according to Hunt, was

one of those rights. He declared that the persons affected in the case "were citizens of the United States" and that the subject of the case "was the right of these persons to vote, not at specified elections or for specified officers, not for federal officers or for state officers, but the right to vote in its broadest terms." Hunt mournfully concluded that the majority's holding brought "to an impotent conclusion the vigorous amendments on the subject of slavery."

Hunt's defense of African American rights appeared to be short-lived. In another case dealing with the Enforcement Act and decided the same month as *Reese*, he sided with the majority in refusing to enforce the rights of African Americans. In *United States v. Cruikshank*, 92 U.S. (2 Otto) 542, 23 L. Ed. 588 (1875), approximately one hundred defendants were alleged to have assaulted two African American men in an attempt to keep the men from voting in a Louisiana state election. This assault violated provisions of the Enforcement Act that made it a federal offense for persons to band together to prevent a person from exercising any right guaranteed by the Constitution or federal law.

The defendants were charged with violations of the Enforcement Act and convicted at trial, but their convictions were overturned by a U.S. circuit court. On appeal by the United States, the Supreme Court held that legislation concerning the right to free assembly under the FIRST AMENDMENT was a matter reserved to the states, not to the federal government, and that Congress did not have the right to pass legislation on the matter. In response to the federal government's argument that in this case the mob had intended to prevent the two men from voting on account of their race, the Court declared, "[W]e may suspect that race was the cause of the hostility; but it is not so averred." Hunt could have dissented based on the same reasoning he used in his dissent in *Reese*, but he did not.

Hunt's failure to dissent in the *Cruikshank* case can be explained, in part, by his devotion to PRECEDENT. Hunt firmly believed that cases should be decided in accordance with the reasoning employed in previous cases. Because the Court in *Reese* had already struck down portions of the Enforcement Act, further attempts to prosecute under the act would meet a similar fate.

Hunt fell ill with gout in 1877 and missed many Court sessions. In January 1879 he suffered a paralytic stroke that left him temporarily speechless and permanently disabled on one side of his body. Hunt became too sick to function as a justice, but he refused to resign because he had not served long enough to qualify for a pension. In addition, Hunt's sponsor, Senator ROSCOE CONKLING, of New York, was quarreling with President RUTHERFORD B. HAYES, and Hunt did not want to let Hayes appoint Hunt's successor to the Court. Finally, three years after his stroke, Congress passed a special retirement bill that gave Hunt a pension if he agreed to resign within thirty days. Hunt resigned in January 1882, on the day the bill became law. He died March 24, 1886, in Washington, D.C.

HUNTER, ELMO BOLTON

Elmo Bolton Hunter, a federal judge, has been a leader in national efforts to take party politics out of the state courts through the adoption of judicial merit selection programs. (Under most merit selection systems, a nonpartisan commission of lawyers and nonlawyers evaluates candidates for judicial vacancies and sends recommendations to, usually, a governor, who makes appointments.) In 1990, the American Judicature Society (AJS) funded the first national clearinghouse for information on merit selection; located at AJS headquarters in Chicago, it is known as the Elmo B. Hunter Center for Judicial Selection. The AJS also gives the Elmo B. Hunter Award annually to a person who has made significant improvement in the judicial selection process. By 1995, owing in large part to Hunter's life-long efforts, thirty-four states had adopted merit selection programs.

Hunter was born in St. Louis on October 23, 1915. He attended the University of Missouri—Columbia, receiving a bachelor of arts degree in 1936 and a bachelor of laws degree in 1938. Named Phi Beta Kappa as an undergraduate, he continued his academic excellence in law school. Hunter graduated first in his class and was elected to the Order of the Coif. He was also a member of the law review and author of numerous articles.

In his final year of law school, Hunter was chosen by the Board of Curators of the University of Missouri to receive the Judge Shepard

BIOGRAPHY

Elmo Bolton Hunter

Barclay Award for "the greatest contribution in moral leadership to the school." Also in 1938, Hunter was selected by the board to represent the University of Missouri—and the state of Missouri—in the Rhodes Scholarship selection competition.

Hunter was admitted to the Missouri bar in 1938 and to the federal bar in 1939. He served as a law clerk to Judge Kimbrough Stone, Sr., from 1938 to 1939. Following his admission to the bar and clerkship, he accepted a position as senior assistant city counselor for Kansas City, Missouri. He left the position in 1940 to pursue graduate work in law, under a Cook Fellowship, at the University of Michigan.

In 1941, Hunter took a job as special assistant to the U.S. district attorney for the Western District of Missouri and Kansas, where he prosecuted war fraud cases. After a year, he joined the U.S. Army, and he served in military intelligence at the rank of first lieutenant from 1942 to 1945.

After World War II, he joined the firm of Sebree, Shook, Hardy, and Hunter, and began the practice of law. He also married Shirley Arnold during these years and fathered his only child, Nancy A. Hunter.

Hunter gave up the practice of law when he was appointed to the state circuit court by Governor Forrest Smith on December 12, 1951. Along with his new judicial duties, Hunter began a ten-year stint as a law instructor at the University of Missouri in 1952. For his work, he received the university's Outstanding Alumni Service Award in 1955.

In 1957, he was appointed to the Kansas City Court of Appeals. Following his appointment, Hunter served, by special order, as special judge to the Missouri Supreme Court, and he often sat with the Springfield Court of Appeals and the St. Louis Court of Appeals—and therefore has served on every court in the state of Missouri. He also has seen every type and variation of political influence brought to bear on the judges and courts in Missouri. During his years of service in the Missouri courts, he developed an interest in both the judicial selection process and the improved administration of justice.

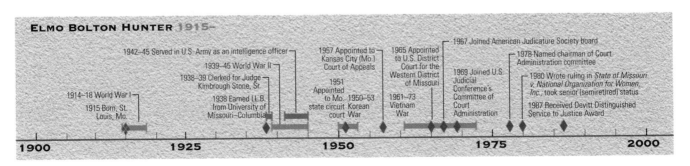

ELMO BOLTON HUNTER 1915–

1914–18 World War I
1915 Born, St. Louis, Mo.
1938 Earned LL.B. from University of Missouri–Columbia
1938–39 Clerked for Judge Kimbrough Stone, Sr.
1939–45 World War II
1942–45 Served in U.S. Army as an intelligence officer
1951 Appointed to Mo. state circuit court
1950–53 Korean War
1957 Appointed to Kansas City (Mo.) Court of Appeals
1961–73 Vietnam War
1965 Appointed to U.S. District Court for the Western District of Missouri
1967 Joined American Judicature Society board
1969 Joined U.S. Judicial Conference's Committee of Court Administration
1978 Named chairman of Court Administration committee
1980 Wrote ruling in *State of Missouri v. National Organization for Women, Inc.*; took senior (semiretired) status
1987 Received Devitt Distinguished Service to Justice Award

1900   1925   1950   1975   2000

In August 1965, President LYNDON B. JOHNSON appointed Hunter U.S. district judge for the Western District of Missouri. It was as a federal judge that Hunter began his distinguished commitment to the AJS. He served on the board of the AJS in 1966 and was elected vice president in 1967. He went on to serve as president, and he is the only person in the history of the AJS to have served as both president and chairman of the board, which he did simultaneously in 1969–70. As an AJS leader, Hunter spearheaded the organization's national efforts to promote merit selection systems for judges. He traveled across the United States to promote the concept and practice of merit selection, and he participated in hundreds of citizen conferences to discuss the issue. In conjunction with his efforts to promote merit selection, he was largely responsible for the E. G. Marshall–narrated movie titled *Who Shall Judge* (1974). In recognition of the role he played in citizen education on this important issue, Hunter received the AJS's Herbert Harley Award in 1975.

As a federal judge, Hunter has also made his presence felt within the U.S. Judicial Conference, which establishes the standards and shapes the policies governing the federal judiciary. Hunter became a member of the Judicial Conference's Committee on Court Administration in 1969 and was named committee chairman in 1978. His appointment as chairman followed his term as chairman of the Subcommittee on Judicial Improvements from 1976 to 1978. Former chief justice WARREN E. BURGER said Hunter was "a credit to all judges who recognize that the delivery of our product is at least as important as the quality of it."

Hunter took senior (or semiretired) status in 1980, shortly after handing down his noteworthy ruling that the National Organization for Women was within its rights in promoting an economic BOYCOTT of Missouri because the state had not approved the proposed EQUAL RIGHTS AMENDMENT (*State of Missouri v. National Organization of Women, Inc.*, 620 F.2d 1301 [8th Cir. 1980]). As a senior judge, Hunter heard the case of a Los Angeles drug dealer caught with PCP at the Kansas City Airport. He sentenced the defendant to life in prison without PAROLE, marking the first time a federal judge applied the mandatory penalty under the United States' three-strikes drug law (Anti–Drug Abuse Act of 1988, Pub. L. No. 104-126). Though many said the law violated constitutional protection against CRUEL AND UNUSUAL PUNISHMENT, Hunter disagreed. "I thought about the constitutional aspects," said Hunter. "I am satisfied that the statute is lawful."

In 1987, Hunter received the Devitt Distinguished Service to Justice Award. This award—named for Edward J. Devitt, former chief U.S. district judge for Minnesota—acknowledges the dedication and contributions to justice made by all federal judges, by recognizing the specific achievements of one judge who has contributed significantly to the profession. Hunter was acknowledged for his devotion to public education and to the administration of justice. Devitt said, "[Hunter] has been the mainstay in the judiciary's self-improvement efforts for more than 20 years."

Hunter continues to serve the U.S. District Court for the Western District of Missouri, keeping a full criminal and civil DOCKET. He also sits regularly on the Eighth Circuit Court of Appeals and accepts special sittings outside the circuit.

See also JUDICIAL CONFERENCE OF THE UNITED STATES.

HUNTING The regulation of hunting is a matter reserved to the states as part of their POLICE POWER under the TENTH AMENDMENT to the U.S. Constitution (*Totemoff v. Alaska*, 905 P.2d 954 [Alaska 1995]). Congress maintains statutes that regulate hunting on federal land. States may further regulate the federal lands located within their boundaries so long as their laws do not conflict with federal laws.

South Dakota and Georgia illustrate the sort of hunting laws typically maintained by a state. In South Dakota hunting is regulated by title 41 of the South Dakota Codified Laws Annotated, section 41-1-1 et seq. Under title 41 hunters must obtain from the game, fish, and parks commission a LICENSE for the privilege of hunting in South Dakota. Other states maintain similar commissions or boards to implement licensing procedures and policies.

Licensing parameters vary from state to state. Most states have minimum age requirements. In South Dakota, for example, no person under the age of twelve may obtain a license, but an eleven-year-old may obtain a license to hunt between September 1 and December 31 if she or he will turn twelve in that period. A child under the age of sixteen may obtain a basic game and fish license without cost, but only if she or he has completed a firearms safety course. A parent of the child must apply for the license, and the child may hunt only with a parent, GUARDIAN, or responsible adult (§ 41-6-13).

In Georgia any person over the age of twelve may hunt on his or her own land. If a person between the ages of twelve and fifteen seeks to hunt, he or she must complete a hunter education course, and then may hunt only with a parent or guardian. This is true even for children between the ages of twelve and fifteen who are hunting on the land of their parents or guardians. A person between the ages of sixteen and twenty-five must also complete a hunter education course before obtaining a hunting license.

States may make licensing exceptions for certain persons. In Georgia, for example, persons over the age of sixty-five may receive a hunting license without paying a fee. Furthermore, persons who are permanently and totally disabled may obtain a hunting or fishing license for free (Ga. Code Ann. § 27-2-4 [1996]).

In some states an additional license must be obtained to hunt certain animals whose populations are of concern to the state. In South Dakota these animals are small game, big game, fur-bearing animals, and migratory waterfowl. An additional license is required for these animals so that the commission can keep track of the number of persons hunting them and conserve their populations.

To control animal populations, state licensing commissions also allow the hunting of certain animals only at certain times of the year. These time periods are called open seasons, and they are set each year by the state regulatory commission. Open seasons limitations sometimes come with special exceptions. In South Dakota, for example, residents do not need a license to hunt game birds on their own land during an open season.

Most states place separate restrictions on resident versus nonresident licensing and hunting for certain animals. In South Dakota, for example, nonresidents may hunt only if they have obtained a special nonresident license. A nonresident may hunt small and big game, waterfowl, and wild turkey. A nonresident must obtain a nonresident predator license to hunt predators, but if the nonresident has a nonresident small-game, big-game, waterfowl, or wild turkey license, the nonresident may hunt predators in the animal group authorized by that license without a separate nonresident predator license (S.D. Codified Laws Ann. § 41-6-30). Predators include jackrabbits, prairie dogs, gophers, ground squirrels, coyotes, red foxes, gray foxes, skunks, crows, and porcupines.

States may place additional restrictions on the hunting of certain animals. In Georgia, for example, feral hogs may be hunted only in certain situations. For instance, a hunter may not shoot a feral hog during deer season unless the hunter and all persons accompanying the hunter are each wearing a total of at least five hundred square inches of daylight florescent orange material as an outer garment above the waistline. In South Dakota fur-bearing animals are completely off-limits to nonresidents. No person may apply for a license to take protected fur-bearing animals unless she or he has lived in the state for ninety days prior to the application date (§ 41-6-24).

State hunting statutes also specify standards for firearm power. In South Dakota, for example, no one may hunt big game with a muzzle loading rifle that discharges a projectile less than forty-four hundredths of an inch in diameter. No one may hunt big game with buckshot, or with a single ball or rifled slug weighing less than one-half ounce. No self-loading or autoloading firearm that holds more than six cartridges may be used to hunt big game, and no fully automatic weapons may be used to hunt big or small game (§ 41-8-10, -13).

States may enact a variety of other restrictions on hunting. In Georgia, at night no person may hunt any game bird or game animal except for raccoon, opossums, foxes, and bobcats. Those animals may be hunted at night, but only with a lantern or a light that does not exceed six volts (Ga. Code Ann. § 27-3-24). In South Dakota no dogs may be used in the hunting of big game, no person may use salt to entice big game, and no person may use artificial light in hunting (S.D. Codified Laws Ann. § 41-8-15, -16). However, an animal damage control officer may use an artificial light to take a nuisance animal from land, with the landowner's written permission (§ 41-8-17(3)).

Most states consider hunting a right of residents and a valuable promotional tool for tourism. Many states even have hunter harassment statutes, which punish persons for intentionally distracting hunters. Under such statutes a person may be arrested and prosecuted for attempting to discourage hunters or drive away game.

See also FISH AND FISHING.

HUNTLEY HEARING In New York state, a separate proceeding in a criminal action conducted solely for the purpose of determining the admissibility of the EXTRAJUDICIAL statements made by the defendant.

The name *Huntley hearing* is derived from the case of *People v. Huntley*, 15 N.Y. 2d 72, 255 N.Y.S. 2d 838, 204 N.E. 2d 179 (1965), which set forth the HEARING requirement.

HURTADO v. CALIFORNIA An 1884 decision of the Supreme Court, *Hurtado v. California*, 110 U.S. 516, 4 S. Ct. 111, 28 L. Ed. 232, that held that states are not required to comply with the FIFTH AMENDMENT provision that a criminal prosecution be initiated by an INDICTMENT by a GRAND JURY. 📖

The constitution of California and various penal statutes provided for the prosecution of a person charged with an offense by INFORMATION after a PRELIMINARY HEARING before a magistrate with RIGHTS TO COUNSEL and to cross-examine WITNESSES, or by indictment with or without a preliminary hearing. In February 1882, the district attorney of Sacramento County filed an information against Joseph Hurtado, charging him with the murder of Jose Stuardo. Hurtado was arraigned, tried, convicted of the crime, and sentenced to death. He unsuccessfully appealed his conviction throughout state appellate courts and brought a WRIT of error before the Supreme Court of the United States.

Hurtado alleged that his conviction and sentence were void because they were obtained in violation of his rights to DUE PROCESS OF LAW as guaranteed by the FOURTEENTH AMENDMENT. He was convicted and sentenced on the basis of an information, not an indictment or PRESENTMENT by a grand jury as required by the Fifth Amendment and, therefore, was deprived by the state of his liberty without due process.

After reviewing English treatises and numerous cases construing the term *due process of law*, the Court affirmed Hurtado's conviction. Only persons accused of federal crimes are entitled to a presentment or indictment of a grand jury. The Court refused to declare the proceedings that led to Hurtado's conviction under state law as violative of due process of law. Like an indictment, the information was "merely a preliminary proceeding," which would bring about a final judgment only as a consequence of a regular trial. Since it served the substantial interest of the prisoner and protected the principles of liberty and justice in a manner comparable to an indictment or presentment by a grand jury, an information satisfied the requirements of due process as guaranteed by the Constitution.

The effect of this decision—that the Fourteenth Amendment guarantee of due process of law does not mandate that an indictment or presentment to a grand jury is necessary for a conviction under state CRIMINAL LAWS to be upheld as legally valid—is still the law after more than one hundred years.

HUSBAND AND WIFE 📖

A man and woman who are legally married to one another and are thereby given by law specific rights and duties resulting from that relationship. 📖

The U.S. legal concept of MARRIAGE is founded in English COMMON LAW. Under common law, when a man and woman married, they became a single person in the eyes of the law—that person being the husband. The duties and benefits afforded a married woman, as well as the restrictions on her freedom, reflected this view. Even today, although the Equal Protection Clause provides that no state shall "deny to any person within its jurisdiction the equal protection of the laws" (U.S. Const. amend. 14, § 1), the U.S. Supreme Court has never interpreted this to mean that states must treat husbands and wives the same.

There is a strong public policy in favor of marriage. Because of this, a husband and wife are not always able to determine their duties and privileges toward one another; instead, these rights and responsibilities are set forth by special legal principles that define the parameters within which husbands and wives must act.

Support Under common law, because it was unusual for a wife to have a job and earn her own money, a husband was obliged to provide his wife with "NECESSARIES"—which included food, clothing, and shelter—but only the necessities he deemed appropriate. Today, judges have taken the support obligation further and construed the term *necessary* to include any item in furtherance of an established standard of living.

Most JURISDICTIONS make it a criminal offense for a spouse to fail to meet a support obligation. Criminal nonsupport statutes are created to prevent men and women from becoming public charges and are most frequently applied upon the dissolution of a marriage when a spouse does not meet ALIMONY and CHILD SUPPORT obligations. ACTIONS for support are rarely initiated by men although today an equal obligation of support applies.

Property Historically, wives were at a disadvantage as PROPERTY owners. At common law, when a woman married, her personal possessions were considered to be the property of her husband. In addition, the husband was entitled to use the land she owned or subsequently inherited, and to retain rents and profits obtained from it. A married woman's right to own property was not incorporated into U.S. law until the mid–nineteenth century, with the Married Women's Property Acts. These laws allowed husbands to permit their spouses to own separate property. Women were also granted the right to enter CONTRACTS, sell land, write WILLS, sue and be sued, work without their husband's permission and keep their earnings,

Tom and Kate Chappell own a business called Tom's of Maine. If one of them were to die or if they divorced, the structure of their ownership of the business and Maine law would affect how the company was distributed.

each community property state defines precisely what is considered separate property. In general, separate property includes whatever each party brought to the marriage and anything either spouse individually inherits during the marriage.

Equitable distribution is a method of property distribution that considers both the economic and noneconomic contributions of each spouse to the marital relationship, as well as each spouse's needs. It is based on the theory that a marriage should be regarded as a partnership of equal individuals.

Disputes over property ownership may arise when one spouse dies. A majority of jurisdictions have eliminated the common-law rights of DOWER and CURTESY, which require that a spouse receive a specific portion of an ESTATE. As an alternative, when one party leaves a will that disinherits her or his spouse, the survivor ordinarily has the right to acquire an ELECTIVE SHARE of the estate, which typically amounts to approximately one-third of its value. In some jurisdictions, this right is given only to a surviving wife. Elective shares do not prevent the dissipation of an estate prior to death. An individual can leave only a small amount in her or his estate in order to minimize the size of the spouse's elective share.

In separate-property states, if a husband or wife dies INTESTATE (without leaving a will), statutes provide for the surviving spouse to acquire a specified portion of the decedent's property. A statute might, for example, prescribe that the surviving spouse can acquire a one-half interest in the estate. The size of the portion depends on whether there are surviving children.

The distribution of property between a husband and wife might also be affected by a PREMARITAL AGREEMENT, also called an antenuptial or prenuptial agreement. Premarital agreements are typically entered into by a man and woman before they are married, to arrange for the distribution or preservation of property owned by each spouse in the event of divorce or death.

Sexual Relationship   The most unique aspects of the relationship between a husband and wife are the legal sanctions attached to their sexual relationship. A number of states will grant a divorce based on the ground that a husband or wife was denied sex by his or her spouse. Similarly, an individual is ordinarily able to obtain an ANNULMENT if his or her spouse is unable to engage in sexual relations. The right of the state to interfere with the marital

and in certain jurisdictions sue for injuries caused by their husbands.

Ordinarily, questions of who owns what property are brought to court only when a couple is obtaining a DIVORCE. Courts are otherwise reluctant to become involved in property disputes between a husband and wife. Various systems exist in the United States to determine who owns property in a marriage: a majority of states recognize separate property, whereas some adhere to COMMUNITY PROPERTY or equitable distribution doctrines.

The rule in separate-property states is that each person owns whatever items are in his or her name. In these states, various types of joint spousal ownership are recognized. A TENANCY BY THE ENTIRETY is a form of joint ownership whereby the husband and wife own all the property together. This type of arrangement ordinarily applies to REAL ESTATE. In a tenancy by the entirety, neither spouse can sell the property or his or her interest in it independently. If the husband or wife dies, the remaining spouse has full SURVIVORSHIP rights.

In states that adhere to community property laws, the husband and wife are each given an equal interest in everything they own with the exception of the separate property of either individual. A majority of the property obtained by a husband and wife during a marriage is considered community property. State law for sexual relationship is limited by the U.S. Constitution as interpreted by the Supreme Court.

In the landmark case of *Griswold v. Connecticut*, 381 U.S. 479, 85 S. Ct. 1678, 14 L. Ed. 2d 510 (1965), the Court held that state statutes cannot unreasonably intrude into the marital sexual relationship. In this case, Connecticut was not allowed to enforce a statute that made it a crime for a physician to counsel married people on birth control. This was viewed as an unreasonable intrusion into the marital sexual relationship, since the sanctity of the marital relationship would be invaded if the statute were enforced. The Court emphasized the significance and constitutional considerations of PRIVACY in marriage.

It was once thought that the degree of privacy to which a married couple is entitled could be restricted. Although some state statutes have used this reasoning to attempt to prohibit certain sex acts between a husband and wife, such as anal and oral sex, most courts have maintained that married couples have a constitutional privacy right over their marital sexual activities (*Lovisi v. Zahradnick*, 429 U.S. 977, 97 S. Ct. 485, 50 L. Ed. 2d 585 (mem)).

A husband and wife have the right to purchase and use birth control devices—although when an individual uses contraceptives or becomes sterilized contrary to his or her spouse's wishes, this might provide grounds for annulment or divorce.

ABORTION has been viewed as an additional restriction on the sexual rights of a husband and wife. A wife's right to choose abortion takes precedence over the husband-and-wife relationship. A husband may not preclude his wife from having a legal abortion, nor may he compel her to have one. The Supreme Court struck down statutory requirements that a husband must be notified of his wife's abortion, in *Planned Parenthood v. Casey*, 505 U.S. 833, 112 S. Ct. 2791, 120 L. Ed. 2d 674 (1992).

At one time, a husband was allowed to have sexual relations with his wife with or without her consent, and for many years, courts supported a marital exception to laws against RAPE. Under current law, the fact that the accused party and the victim were husband and wife can no longer be used as a defense to criminal charges. Violent assaults on a spouse are illegal in all states. A savage rape attack by a husband on his wife might be subject to prosecution as an ASSAULT or, in some cases, as an attempted MURDER.

Crimes   Common law put many restrictions on a husband and wife when crimes occurred between them or against the marriage relationship itself. At one time, the courts recognized lawsuits based on HEART BALM ACTS. In such an action, a husband asserted that a monetary recovery would salve the "broken heart" caused by a third party's intrusion into his marriage. The basis for many of these CAUSES OF ACTION was that a husband was being denied his rights to the affections and services of his wife; these lawsuits did not extend to a wife. A husband once had an ACTIONABLE injury if anyone induced his wife to leave him, under the theory that he was entitled to sue for damages any person who divested him of a servant. Similarly, a husband was able to bring an action for CRIMINAL CONVERSATION if his wife voluntarily engaged in ADULTERY. The theory was that criminal conversation interferes with a husband's exclusive privilege to obtain sexual services from his wife. The basis of recovery is the PUBLIC POLICY in favor of preserving marriage and the family. ALIENATION OF AFFECTION is another seldom prosecuted action. In this type of action, a husband must prove that another man won his wife away from him, thereby depriving him of love, comfort, and companionship.

Because of the theories that gave rise to such causes of action, very few jurisdictions recognize lawsuits based on heart balm acts. Yet, even today, TORT law retains some special rules for husbands and wives when an outsider causes injury to the marital or family relationship. CONSORTIUM is the marital relationship between two people that encompasses their mutual right to support, cooperation, and companionship. An action for LOSS OF CONSORTIUM is based on the inconvenience of having a debilitated spouse. Husbands and wives have won suits for DAMAGES for injuries to their spouse precipitated by such things as medical MALPRACTICE, automobile accidents, FALSE IMPRISONMENT, and WRONGFUL DEATH.

Under common law, a husband was held responsible for any crimes committed by his wife against a third party. Although a wife had responsibility for crimes she committed, there was a legal presumption that her husband compelled her to perform any act she undertook when he was present. Today, husbands and wives are equally liable for their own criminal actions.

Privileged Communication   The law of EVIDENCE includes a privilege extended to a married couple so that neither a husband nor a wife can be compelled to TESTIFY against a spouse. This rule was designed to protect intrafamily relations and privacy. In addition, it

TONY FREEMAN/PHOTOEDIT

Today a husband and wife are viewed as equal partners with the rights and duties of a marriage.

was meant to promote communication between husbands and wives by making revelations between them strictly confidential.

In 1980, the U.S. Supreme Court, in *Trammel v. United States*, 445 U.S. 40, 100 S. Ct. 906, 63 L. Ed. 2d 186, held that husbands and wives were permitted to testify against one another voluntarily in a federal criminal prosecution. Many states now allow a spouse to testify against a husband or wife, but with the caveat that the TESTIMONY is subject to the accused spouse's consent. Other states view the spouse of an accused person as an ordinary witness who can be forced to testify against the accused person.

Domestic Abuse It was once presumed that a husband should have the right to exert physical control over his wife, if only to protect himself from liability for his wife's actions. Therefore, common law permitted a husband to discipline his wife physically. Interspousal tort IMMUNITY made it impossible for a wife to succeed in an action against her husband. It was rare for a wife to accuse her husband of a crime, and a wife was forbidden to testify against her husband. Today, a wife is almost always permitted to testify against a husband who has been accused of causing intentional injury to her or their child. With interspousal tort immunity all but abrogated in most jurisdictions, husbands and wives can now recover in suits against one another under the theories of fraudulent mis-

representation, BATTERY, intentional infliction of emotional distress, and NEGLIGENCE.

The common-law right of a husband to discipline his wife combined with interspousal tort immunity prevented incidents of domestic abuse from becoming public. In addition, victims of domestic abuse often did not reveal the extent of their injuries for fear of reprisals. Little legal relief was available, as courts were hesitant to interfere in the husband-and-wife relationship. With the abrogation of interspousal tort immunity, the U.S. public has become aware of domestic abuse as a nationwide issue.

In some cases, victims of domestic abuse who have injured or killed their spouse as a means of SELF-DEFENSE against violence and abuse have been acquitted of criminal charges. The battered spouse syndrome is a defense these men and women have asserted. The syndrome, a subcategory of post-traumatic stress disorder, seeks to explain why some spouses remain in abusive relationships and others finally use violence to break out of such relationships. Because battered women are typically economically dependent on their husband, they hesitate to seek help until the violence escalates to the point where they believe the only way to free themselves is to kill their abuser.

Same-Sex Marriage Today's judicial intolerance for domestic abuse is one indication of how the legal implications of the husband-and-wife relationship have significantly changed over the years. Common law once defined the marriage relationship to be the merging of two individuals into one legal entity—the husband. Today, a husband and wife are viewed more as equal partners, as individuals with the benefit of additional rights and duties associated with a legal marriage. As society changes, the benefits of a legal marriage relationship may be expanded to include those who cohabitate without marriage and those who wish to marry someone of their own sex.

In the 1980s and early 1990s, lawsuits were initiated to expand the traditional husband-and-wife relationship, and the rights and privileges that relationship conveys, to partners of the same sex. In *Baehr v. Lewin*, 74 Haw. 645, 852 P.2d 44 (1993), although rejecting the idea that the Hawaii Constitution gives same-sex couples a fundamental right to marriage, the Hawaii Supreme Court held that Hawaii's marriage statute, Haw. Rev. Stat. § 572-1, discriminates on the basis of sex by barring people of the same sex from marrying and that such statutes are subject to STRICT SCRUTINY. Largely in response to the *Baehr* case, in 1996 Congress passed the Defense of Marriage Act (110 Stat. § 2419), which defines "marriage" and "spouse" to apply only to heterosexual relationships for the purposes of federal law and expressly allows states to ignore a same-sex marriage formed under the laws of another state.

Same-sex partners seek to overturn prejudices similar to those that barred interracial marriage in the 1960s. If gay and lesbian marriages were accepted, same-sex partners would be allowed state recognition and protection of the same economic benefits bestowed on heterosexual partners involving inheritance, property rights, and tax benefits.

CROSS-REFERENCES

Domestic Violence; Family Law; Gay and Lesbian Rights; *Griswold v. Connecticut.*

HYPOTHECATE
To pledge property as security or COLLATERAL for a DEBT. Generally, there is no physical transfer of the pledged property to the lender, nor is the lender given TITLE to the property, though he or she has the right to sell the pledged property in the case of DEFAULT.

HYPOTHESIS
An assumption or theory.

During a criminal trial, a hypothesis is a theory set forth by either the prosecution or the defense for the purpose of explaining the facts in EVIDENCE. It also serves to set up a ground for an INFERENCE of guilt or innocence, or a showing of the most probable motive for a criminal offense.

HYPOTHETICAL QUESTION
A mixture of assumed or established facts and circumstances, developed in the form of a coherent and specific situation, which is presented to an expert WITNESS at a trial to elicit his or her opinion.

When a hypothetical question is posed, it includes all the facts in EVIDENCE needed to form an opinion and, based on the assumption that the facts are true, the witness is asked whether he or she can arrive at an opinion, and if so, to state it.

IBID. An abbreviation of the Latin *ibidem*, meaning "in the same place; in the same book; on the same page."

I.C.C. An abbreviation for the INTERSTATE COMMERCE COMMISSION.

IDEM [*Latin, The same.*]

The term *idem* is used to indicate a reference that has previously been made.

I.E. An abbreviation for the Latin *id est*, "that is to say, meaning."

ILLEGAL ALIENS AND IMMIGRATION

See ALIENS; JUSTICE DEPARTMENT (IMMIGRATION AND NATURALIZATION SERVICE).

ILLEGITIMACY The condition before the law, or the social status, of a child whose parents were not married to each other at the time of his or her birth.

The term *nonmarital child* is also used interchangeably with *illegitimate child*.

English COMMON LAW placed harsh penalties on an illegitimate child, denying the child INHERITANCE and PROPERTY RIGHTS. Modern law has given the nonmarital child more rights but still differentiates between the marital and nonmarital status. In addition, a rising level of out-of-wedlock births in the United States has engaged the attention of politicians and policy makers.

Common Law and Illegitimacy A child was considered to be illegitimate at common law if the parents were not married to each other at the time of the child's birth even though the parents were married later.

There was a common-law presumption that a child born of a married woman was legitimate. This presumption was rebuttable, however, upon proof that her husband either was physically incapable of impregnating her or was

absent at the time of conception. In addition, a child born of a MARRIAGE for which an ANNULMENT was granted was considered illegitimate, since an annulled marriage is void retroactively from its beginning. Furthermore, if a man married a second time while still legally married to his first wife, a child born of the bigamous marriage was illegitimate.

At common law an illegitimate child was a FILLIUS NULLIUS (child of no one) and had no parental inheritance rights. This deprivation was based in part on societal and religious beliefs concerning the sanctity of the marital relationship, as well as the legal principles that

Illegitimacy

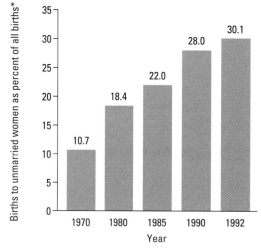

*Excludes births to nonresidents of the United States. Data for 1970 include estimates for states in which marital status data were not reported. Beginning in 1980, marital status is inferred from a comparison of the child's parents' surnames on the birth certificate for those states that do not report on marital status.

Source: U.S. National Center for Health Statistics, *Vital Statistics on the United States*, annual.

Robert L. Johnson's Son? The Rights of Illegitimate Heirs

Robert L. Johnson is an important figure in blues music. Though he recorded only twenty-nine songs before his death in 1938, at age twenty-seven, Johnson's songs, voice, and guitar playing have influenced many great musicians, including Muddy Waters, Keith Richards, and Eric Clapton. The Mississippi bluesman's recordings became a commercial success in the late 1960s, and by 1990 his collected works were released on compact discs.

Johnson married twice. Both wives died before he did and left no children. In 1974 Johnson's half-sister, Carrie Thompson, sold the copyrights of his songs and photographs, asserting that she was entitled to his estate. Upon her death in 1983, her half-sister Annye Anderson inherited her purported rights to Johnson's work.

When Anderson finally probated Johnson's estate in 1991, Claud L. Johnson filed a claim stating that he was the illegitimate son of Johnson and the sole heir of the bluesman. Claud Johnson produced a Mississippi birth certificate from 1931 that lists R. L. Johnson as his father.

But for the U.S. Supreme Court's ruling in *Trimble v. Gordon*, 430 U.S. 762, 97 S. Ct. 1459, 52 L. Ed. 2d 31 (1977), Claud Johnson could not have made his claim. Until *Trimble* Mississippi prohibited illegitimate children from inheriting from their father.

Anderson argued that Claud Johnson's claim should be dismissed because he had waited too long to file it. A county court agreed with Anderson, but the Mississippi Supreme Court reversed the lower court's decision, ruling that the intent of state law was to give the same rights to illegitimate as to legitimate children (*In re Estate of Johnson*, 1996 WL 138615 [Miss.]). The supreme court sent the case back to the county court, which is to determine whether Claud Johnson is the son of Robert Johnson. If so, he is entitled to Robert Johnson's estate.

property rights were determined by blood relationships. The legal rights and duties of a person born of married parents could be ascertained more accurately than those of a child with an unknown or disputed father. PUBLIC POLICY in favor of maintaining solid family relationships contributed significantly to the preference for a legitimate child.

Modern Law The harsher aspects of the common law dealing with an illegitimate child have been eliminated, primarily through the application of the Equal Protection Clause of the FOURTEENTH AMENDMENT to the U.S. Constitution. In *Levy v. Louisiana*, 391 U.S. 68, 88 S. Ct. 1509, 20 L. Ed. 436 (1968), the Supreme Court ruled that a state statute (La. Civ. Code Ann. Art. 2315) that barred illegitimate children from recovering DAMAGES for the WRONGFUL DEATH of their mother, but allowed legitimate children to recover in similar circumstances, was invalid because it denied illegitimate children EQUAL PROTECTION of the law.

The Supreme Court also enhanced the right of an illegitimate child to inherit property. Whereas most states had given legitimate and illegitimate children the same right to inherit property from the mother and her family, a number of states did not allow an illegitimate child to inherit property from the father in the absence of a specific provision in the father's WILL. In *Trimble v. Gordon*, 430 U.S. 762, 97 S.

Ct. 1459, 52 L. Ed. 2d 31 (1977), the Supreme Court ruled such provisions in an Illinois statute invalid.

A majority of states now subscribe to the theory that a child born of any union that has the characteristics of a formal marriage relationship is entitled to legitimate status. This theory includes children born of marriages that fail owing to legal technicalities as well as children of VOID or VOIDABLE marriages.

Some states still recognize the validity of COMMON-LAW MARRIAGE, which takes place when a man and woman cohabit for an extensive period, and hold themselves out to the public as being HUSBAND AND WIFE even though they were never formally married. In such states children born of such arrangements are considered legitimate. Common-law marriages were a convenient mechanism in the nineteenth century for establishing property rights and legitimating children. Frontier society accepted the economic necessity for permitting such marriages because it was difficult for people on the frontier to obtain a formal marriage license; without common-law marriages, many children would have been declared illegitimate.

Legal Presumption of Legitimacy The presumption of legitimacy is a strong legal presumption because public policy favors legitimacy to preserve stable family groupings. This presumption can be rebutted only if it can be clearly established that the child in question is illegitimate. A child born to a married couple is presumed to be their legitimate offspring in the absence of a clear demonstration that the husband could not possibly be the father.

Legitimation is the process whereby the status of a child is changed from illegitimate to legitimate. Some statutes provide that a child becomes legitimated upon an open acknowledgment of paternity by the alleged father. In some states an oral admission is sufficient, but in other states a written statement is required. A majority of states prescribe that an acknowledgment must be coupled with an act in order for the child to be declared legitimate. An adequate act in some states is the marriage of the child's natural parents. Once a child has been determined to be legitimate, she or he is entitled to the same rights and protections as any individual whose legitimacy has never been questioned.

Paternity Actions A PATERNITY SUIT, or AFFILIATION PROCEEDING, may be brought against a father by an unmarried mother. This CIVIL ACTION is intended not to legitimate the child but to obtain support for the child and often to obtain the payment of bills incident to the pregnancy. Ordinarily, the mother starts the civil lawsuit, but some states allow public authorities to bring a paternity action for the mother if she refuses to do so. If the mother is on WELFARE, a paternity action is a vehicle for the local government agency to obtain financial assistance from the father.

A paternity action must start within the time prescribed by the STATUTE OF LIMITATIONS, or the mother's right to establish the PUTATIVE father's paternity and corresponding support obligation will be lost. The evidence needed to establish paternity includes the testimony of the mother, blood and DNA tests, and in some states photographs from which to determine similar facial characteristics of the alleged father and the child.

Legal Rights of Fathers Whether a father acknowledges paternity or is adjudged to be the father in a paternity action, he has more custody rights today than at common law. At common law fathers were assumed to have little concern for the well-being of their illegitimate offspring. Historically, in most JURISDICTIONS, if a child was illegitimate, the child could be adopted with only the consent of his or her natural mother.

This assumption, as embodied in a New York statute (N.Y. Domestic Relations Law § 111), was challenged in *Caban v. Mohammed*, 441 U.S. 380, 99 S. Ct. 1760, 60 L. Ed. 2d 297 (1979). The key issue was whether the consent of an unwed biological father had to be obtained before an ADOPTION could be finalized. The Supreme Court ruled that a law depriving all unwed fathers of the right to decide against adoption, whether or not they actually took care of the children in question, was unconstitutional and a form of sex DISCRIMINATION.

Artificial Insemination Legitimacy issues have arisen when a child is conceived by ARTIFICIAL INSEMINATION. This process involves impregnating a woman, without sexual intercourse, with the semen of a donor who might be her husband or another party. Some states adhere to traditional views and consider any child conceived in this manner to be illegitimate, regardless of whether the husband gave his consent to the procedure. Other courts declare that a child is legitimate if the husband consented. A child is most likely considered illegitimate when the mother was unmarried and was artificially inseminated by an unknown donor, and remains unmarried. In most cases of artificial insemination, the father has donated semen anonymously, and his identity is not known.

Current Trends The rate of illegitimate births in the United States has risen sharply since the early 1970s. In the 1940s fewer than five percent of the total births were out of wedlock. By the 1990s, according to statistics compiled by the Center for Health Statistics at the U.S. Department of Health and Human Services, births to unmarried mothers accounted for nearly one-third of all U.S. births.

CROSS-REFERENCES

Child Custody; Child Support; DNA Evidence; Family Law; Parent and Child.

ILLICIT 📖 Not permitted or allowed; prohibited; unlawful; as an illicit trade; illicit intercourse. 📖

ILLUSORY PROMISE 📖 A statement that appears to assure a PERFORMANCE and form a CONTRACT but, when scrutinized, leaves to the speaker the choice of performance or nonperformance, which means that the speaker does not legally bind himself or herself to act. 📖

When the provisions of the purported promise render the performance of the person who makes the promise optional or completely within his or her discretion, pleasure, and control, nothing absolute is promised; and the promise is said to be illusory. For example, a court decided that a promise contained in an agreement between a railroad and an iron producer whereby the railroad promised to purchase as much iron as its board of directors might order was illusory and did not form a contract.

IMMATERIAL Not essential or necessary; not important or pertinent; not decisive; of no substantial consequence; without weight; of no material significance.

IMMEDIATE CAUSE The final act in a series of provocations leading to a particular result or event, directly producing such result without the intervention of any further PROVOCATION.

For example, if an individual who was driving while intoxicated crashed his or her car and was killed, the immediate cause of death was the crash. The PROXIMATE CAUSE, however, was the individual's state of intoxication.

IMMIGRATION The entrance into a country of foreigners for purposes of permanent residence. The correlative term *emigration* denotes the act of such persons in leaving their former country.

See also ALIENS.

IMMIGRATION AND NATURALIZATION See ALIENS; JUSTICE DEPARTMENT (IMMIGRATION AND NATURALIZATION SERVICE).

IMMINENT Impending; menacingly close at hand; threatening.

Imminent peril, for example, is danger that is certain, immediate, and impending, such as the type an individual might be in as a result of a serious illness or accident. The chance of the individual dying would be highly probable in such situation, as opposed to remote or contingent. For a GIFT *causa mortis* (Latin for "in anticipation of death") to be effective, the donor must be in imminent peril and must die as a result of it.

IMMUNITY Exemption from performing duties that the law generally requires other citizens to perform, or from a penalty or burden that the law generally places on other citizens.

Sovereign Immunity SOVEREIGN IMMUNITY prevents a sovereign state or person from being subjected to suit without its consent.

The doctrine of sovereign immunity stands for the principle that a nation is immune from suit in the courts of another country, and was first recognized by U.S. courts in the case of *The Schooner Exchange v. M'Faddon*, 11 U.S. (7 Cranch) 116, 3 L. Ed. 287 (1812). Courts at first espoused a theory providing absolute immunity from the JURISDICTION of a U.S. court for any act by a foreign state. But beginning in the early 1900s, courts relied on the political branches of government to define the breadth and limits of sovereign immunity.

In 1952, the U.S. State Department reacted to an increasing number of commercial transactions between the United States and foreign nations by recognizing foreign immunity only in noncommercial or public acts, and not in commercial or private acts. However, the STATE DEPARTMENT was easily influenced by foreign diplomats requesting absolute sovereign immunity, and the application of sovereign immunity became inconsistent, uncertain, and often unfair.

Complaints about inconsistencies led to the passage of the Foreign Sovereign Immunities Act of 1976 (28 U.S.C.A. §§ 1 note, 1330, 1332, 1391, 1441, 1602–1611). By this act, Congress codified the theory of sovereign immunity, listing exceptions for certain types of acts such as commercial acts, and granted the exclusive power to decide sovereign immunity issues to the courts, rather than the State Department.

Native American tribes have been granted sovereign immunity status by the United States, and therefore generally cannot be sued without the consent of either Congress or the tribe. This immunity is justified by two considerations: First, historically, with more limited resources and tax bases than other governments, Indian tribes have generally been more vulnerable to lawsuits than are other governments. Second, granting sovereign nation status to tribes is in keeping with the federal policy of self-determination for Native Americans.

Indian tribes are immune from suit whether they are acting in a governmental or a proprietary capacity, and immunity is not limited to acts conducted within a reservation. However, individual members of a tribe do not receive immunity for their acts; only the tribe itself is immune as a sovereign nation.

Governmental Tort Immunity Sovereign immunity may also apply to federal, state, and local governments within the United States, protecting these governments from being sued without their consent. The idea behind domestic sovereign immunity—also called governmental tort immunity—is to prevent money JUDGMENTS against the government, since such judgments would have to be paid with taxpayers' dollars. As an example, a private citizen injured by another private citizen who runs a red light generally may sue the other driver for NEGLIGENCE. But under a strict sovereign immunity doctrine, a private citizen injured by a city employee driving a city bus has no CAUSE OF ACTION against the city unless the city, by ordinance, specifically allows such a suit.

Governmental tort immunity is codified at the federal level by the FEDERAL TORT CLAIMS ACT (28 U.S.C.A. § 1291 [1946]), and most states and local governments have similar statutes. Courts and legislatures in many states have greatly restricted, and in some cases abolished, the doctrine of governmental tort immunity.

Official Immunity The doctrine of sovereign immunity has its roots in the law of feudal England and is based on the tenet that the ruler can do no wrong. PUBLIC POLICY grounds for granting immunity from civil lawsuits to judges and officials in the EXECUTIVE BRANCH of government survive even today. Sometimes known as official immunity, the doctrine was first supported by the U.S. Supreme Court in the 1871 case *Bradley v. Fisher*, 80 U.S. 335, 20 L. Ed. 646. In *Bradley*, an attorney attempted to sue a judge because the judge had disbarred him. The Supreme Court held that the judge was absolutely immune from the civil suit because the suit arose from his judicial acts. The Court recognized the need to protect judicial independence and noted that malicious or improper actions by a judge could be remedied by IMPEACHMENT rather than litigation.

The Court expanded the doctrine to include officers of the federal executive branch twenty-five years later in *Spalding v. Vilas*, 161 U.S. 483, 16 S. Ct. 631, 40 L. Ed. 780 (1896). In *Spalding*, an attorney brought a DEFAMATION suit against the U.S. postmaster general, who had circulated a letter that criticized the attorney's motives in representing local postmasters in a salary dispute. At that time the postmaster general was a member of the president's cabinet. The Court determined that the proper administration of public affairs by the executive branch of government would be seriously crippled by a threat of civil LIABILITY and granted the postmaster general absolute immunity from civil suit for discretionary acts within the scope of the postmaster's authority. Federal courts since *Spalding* have continued to grant absolute immunity—a complete bar to lawsuits regardless of the official's motive in acting—to federal executive officials, so long as their actions are discretionary and within the scope of their official duties.

In some cases, courts have granted only qualified, rather than absolute, immunity to executive officials. This occurs most often when a statute provides a cause of action for a violation of CIVIL RIGHTS by a member of the executive branch of government—for example, when students of a state-run college seek DAMAGES from the governor for a violation of their civil rights pursuant to the CIVIL RIGHTS ACT of 1964 (42 U.S.C.A. § 1983). To get qualified immu-

nity, officials must show that they acted without MALICE and that they reasonably believed that their conduct was legal. Courts employ a two-step analysis to make this determination: first, they analyze whether the statutory or constitutional right asserted by the plaintiff was clear when the wrongful act occurred; second, they decide whether the official should reasonably have known that the action was illegal. An affirmative answer to either of these questions generally results in a denial of immunity to the accused executive official.

In the 1982 case *Nixon v. Fitzgerald*, 457 U.S. 731, 102 S. Ct. 2690, 73 L. Ed. 2d 349, the Supreme Court held that former U.S. president RICHARD M. NIXON was entitled to absolute immunity from liability predicated on his official acts as president. In *Nixon*, a weapons analyst, A. Ernest Fitzgerald, had been fired by the U.S. Air Force after he disclosed to Congress certain cost overruns within the Defense Department. Fitzgerald sued Nixon and two former presidential aides for wrongful retaliatory termination.

The Supreme Court emphasized the singular importance of the duties of the president, and noted that the diversion of the president's energies over concern for private lawsuits "would raise unique risks to the effective functioning of government." The Court also observed that the president, in view of the visibility of the office, would be an easy target for civil lawsuits. A president distracted by this personal vulnerability would prove harmful to the nation.

Immunity from Prosecution State and federal statutes may grant WITNESSES immunity from prosecution for the use of their TESTIMONY in court or before a GRAND JURY. Sometimes, the

Air Force analyst A. Ernest Fitzgerald sued President Richard Nixon for firing him after Fitzgerald disclosed to Congress huge cost overruns in the Defense Department. The Supreme Court held that the president is immune from civil lawsuits arising from the president's official acts. (Presidential immunity does not apply to unofficial acts.)

testimony of one witness is so valuable to the goals of crime prevention and justice that the promise of allowing that witness to go unpunished is a fair trade. For example, the testimony of a drug dealer that could help law enforcers destroy an entire illegal drug manufacturing network is more beneficial to society than is the prosecution of that lone drug dealer. Although the FIFTH AMENDMENT to the U.S. Constitution grants witnesses a privilege against SELF-INCRIMINATION, the U.S. Supreme Court has permitted prosecutors to overcome this privilege by granting witnesses immunity. PROSECUTORS have the sole discretion to grant immunity to witnesses who appear before a grand jury or at trial.

States employ one of two approaches to prosecutorial immunity: Use immunity prohibits only the witness's compelled testimony, and evidence stemming from that testimony, from being used to prosecute the witness. The witness may still be prosecuted so long as the prosecutor can obtain other physical, testimonial, or CIRCUMSTANTIAL EVIDENCE apart from the witness's testimony. Transactional immunity completely immunizes the witness from prosecution for any offense to which the testimony relates.

Congressional committees have the power to grant testimonial immunity to witnesses who testify before members of Congress. Congressional investigations into allegations of misconduct—such as the WATERGATE investigations in the 1970s and the Iran-Contra investigations in the 1980s—rely heavily on witness testimony. Whereas prosecutors simply decide whether to grant immunity to a witness, congressional committees must follow more formal procedures. Immunity may be granted only after a two-thirds majority vote by members of the committee, and ten days before the immunized testimony, the committee must advise the Department of Justice or the independent counsel of its intention to grant immunity.

Family Immunity At common law, a child could sue a parent for breach of CONTRACT and for TORTS related to property. An adult could sue her or his parent for any tort, whether personal or related to property. In 1891, the Mississippi Supreme Court, in *Hewllette v. George*, 9 So. 885 (1891), held that a child could not seek compensation for personal injury caused by a parent's wrongdoing, so long as the parent and child were obligated by their family duties to one another. The decision was based not on PRECEDENT but rather on public policy: the court found that such a lawsuit would undermine the "peace of society and of the families composing society." Criminal laws, the court found, were adequate to protect children.

Other states fell in step with Mississippi, adopting parental immunity of varying degrees. Some parental immunity laws prohibited only claims of negligence, whereas others prohibited lawsuits for intentional torts such as rapes and beatings. The rationale supporting parental immunity laws includes the need to preserve family harmony and, with the availability of liability insurance, the need to prevent parents and the children from colluding to DEFRAUD insurance companies.

Unjust results have led courts in many states that espouse parental immunity to carve out exceptions to the rule. For example, a child can usually sue a parent for negligence when the parent has failed to provide food or medical care, but not when the parent has merely exercised parental authority. Most courts have abolished the parental immunity defense for car accident claims, and many allow children to sue their parents for negligent business or employment actions. Courts normally permit WRONGFUL DEATH suits to be brought by a child against a parent or by a parent against a child, because death terminates the parent-child relationship. And most states allow a child to sue a parent for injuries suffered in utero owing to the negligence of the mother.

CROSS-REFERENCES

Ambassadors and Consuls; Diplomatic Immunity; Feres Doctrine; Husband and Wife; Judicial Immunity.

IMMUNIZATION PROGRAMS In the 1950s, medical breakthroughs resulted in new vaccines to combat such diseases as polio and measles. States responded by requiring mandatory immunization for schoolchildren. One result was the near eradication of diseases that had previously been crippling or fatal. A second, unforeseen result was adverse side effects of the vaccines, which led to lawsuits against drug companies. Between the 1960s and late 1980s, millions of dollars in litigation forced drug manufacturers to retreat from the market, and prompted government action to help protect companies and ensure their presence in the vaccine market. Concern has also been raised over this problem's effect on the development of a vaccine against AIDS.

The 1950s saw great successes in the battle against childhood diseases. For example, pioneering researchers Drs. Jonas E. Salk and Albert B. Sabin developed vaccines that brought the dreaded virus poliomyelitis under control. This revolutionary work meant that a once rampant disease now could be stopped with a simple inoculation. In 1952 alone, more than fifty-seven thousand cases of polio in the United States left approximately twenty-one thousand people crippled; in 1985, only four cases of polio were reported in the nation. Measles was also effectively halted: it killed over two thousand people in 1941 but only two in 1985. And by the end of the 1970s, smallpox was virtually eliminated around the world.

Not only the vaccines accomplished this success. Government action helped, by enabling the widespread inoculation of children. By the 1960s, states had begun administering vaccines to school-age children, and their programs ultimately became mandatory. Today, each state requires parents to submit a proof of immunization before enrolling their child in school; thus, the majority of young children in the United States are inoculated against such diseases as tetanus, measles, polio, mumps, meningitis, and diphtheria, pertussis, tetanus, and whooping cough.

Vaccines are never entirely safe. Side effects range from mild to serious—from swelling and

Children Immunized Against Specific Diseases, 1993

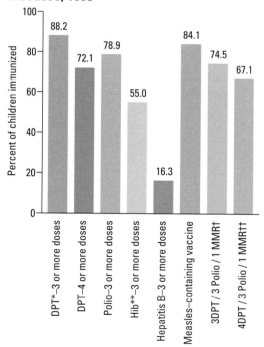

*Diphtheria-tetanus-pertussis
**Haemophilus Influenzae B
†Measles, measles/rubella, measles/mumps, and measles/mumps/rubella vaccine.
††Up-to-date for age.

Source: U.S. Centers for Disease Control and Prevention, Atlanta, GA, *The National Health Interview Study.*

fever to brain damage and death. These dangers were recognized early on. Between 1961 and 1963, federal agencies noted occasional serious side effects from polio vaccines. By 1964, the Surgeon General's Special Advisory Committee on Oral Poliomyelitis Vaccine found that fifty-three cases of polio could apparently be linked to the three types of the vaccine.

Public health authorities have nevertheless consistently urged the continuation of vaccine programs, arguing that the extremely minor incidence of adverse side effects is far outweighed by the health and lives they preserve. The Centers for Disease Control estimates, for example, that 1 in 310,000 children is adversely affected by the diphtheria, pertussis, and tetanus (DPT) vaccine. According to the American Medical Association, one in 3.2 million doses of polio vaccine will cause paralysis, and one in 1 million doses of measles vaccine will cause brain damage.

Beginning in the 1960s, vaccine-related injuries produced expensive litigation. Aggrieved families brought suit against drug manufacturers, sometimes winning large damages awards. These suits proceeded on a number of theories: NEGLIGENCE, failure to warn, design defect, production defect, breach of WARRANTY, and STRICT LIABILITY. In 1970, for instance, Epifanio Reyes, the father of eight-month-old Anita Reyes, filed suit against Wyeth Laboratories, charging that the company's vaccine had transmitted paralytic polio to his daughter. He claimed strict PRODUCT LIABILITY, breach of warranty, and negligence. The jury returned an award of $200,000, and the verdict was upheld on appeal in *Reyes v. Wyeth Laboratories,* 498 F.2d 1264 (5th Cir., 1974), *cert. denied,* 419 U.S. 1096, 95 S. Ct. 687, 42 L. Ed. 2d 688 (1974).

The lawsuits increased costs for drug companies, which, even when successful in court, faced increased expenses in LIABILITY insurance. Fearing greater losses in court, manufacturers fled the vaccine market. Between the mid-1960s and early 1990s, the number of vaccine makers shrank by half. The companies that remained drastically raised the price of vaccines: the DPT vaccine, for instance, sold for $1 a dose in the early 1980s, $11 a dose by the end of the decade. The exodus of companies from the market left measles, mumps, and rubella vaccines each with only one manufacturer. This raised worries about the possibility of a critical shortage if one of these manufacturers left the market.

Companies were not the only target of lawsuits. In the late 1970s, the federal government established a vaccine program called the National Swine Flu Immunization Program of 1976 (42 U.S.C.A. § 247 b(j)-(1), *amended by* Pub. L. No. 95-626, 92 Stat. 3574 [1978]), in anticipation of an onslaught of swine flu. To induce manufacturers to produce the drug, the act absolved them of all liability, and the federal government assumed all risk. The epidemic never materialized, but legal problems did. Plaintiffs alleging harmful side effects from the vaccine sued, and the government ended up paying out millions of dollars in settlements. In *Petty v. United States*, 740 F.2d 1428 (1984), for example, the Eighth Circuit upheld a damages award of some $200,000. The Court held that the warnings on the vaccine were inadequate.

Since the time of the swine flu immunization suits, courts and lawmakers have taken actions that have lessened the risks of liability facing drug manufacturers. Courts have restricted the grounds under which litigants can succeed in civil TORT actions. Where products are found to be unavoidably unsafe—having obvious benefits yet carrying certain risks—the courts have erected barriers to strict liability claims. The courts have presumed that certain vaccines are unavoidably unsafe and, in some JURISDICTIONS, that warnings provided by drug companies are adequate as long as they meet FOOD AND DRUG ADMINISTRATION (FDA) standards. The Restatement (Second) of Torts mentions the rabies vaccine as one of the products that, "in the present state of human knowledge, are quite incapable of being made safe for their intended and ordinary use," noting,

> Since the disease itself invariably leads to a dreadful death, both the marketing and the use of the vaccine are fully justified, notwithstanding the unavoidable high degree of risk which they involve. Such a product, properly prepared, and accompanied by proper directions and warning, is not defective, nor is it unreasonably dangerous. (§ 402A comment k [1965])

Courts in most jurisdictions now follow this standard in determining liability in vaccine cases.

The finding that a vaccine is unavoidably unsafe does not mean that manufacturers are completely absolved of liability. Plaintiffs may still overcome the two barriers of unavoidable danger and compliance with FDA standards. To prevail, they must show that vaccine-related injuries or deaths could have been prevented. Two chief means exist: they must show that the drugmaker engaged in illegal activity, or that the drugmaker failed to exercise due care in preparing or marketing the vaccine. Although both are difficult matters to prove, they can be established, as in *Petty*, where inadequate warnings on the swine flu vaccine were found to be more significant than the fact that the vaccine was unavoidably unsafe.

Congress used a similar liability standard in groundbreaking federal legislation passed in 1986, the National Childhood Vaccine Injury Act (42 U.S.C.A. § 300aa-1 et seq. [1990 Supp.]). The act established a federal no-fault compensation program for victims. It sought to stem civil litigation by providing an alternative: rather than sue drug companies, families alleging injury or death due to a child's compulsory inoculation could file suit in the federal Claims Court. This alternative reflected not only legal but commercial realities: Congress hoped to maintain an adequate national supply of vaccines by relieving drug companies of risk. The law set the maximum DAMAGES award at $250,000, and required plaintiffs to first file suit in the Claims Court. If successful, plaintiffs could accept the award, or reject it in favor of filing a separate CIVIL ACTION. Like the evolving standard in courts, this law protected defendant drug companies: their compliance with federal production and labeling standards is an acceptable defense against civil lawsuits, and no strict liability claims are allowed.

Judicial and legislative solutions have thus partially ameliorated the liability risks of drug manufacturers. But by the mid-1990s, concerns remained about the potential for marketing an AIDS vaccine if one was discovered. Some observers called for federal legislation to protect potential manufacturers of an AIDS vaccine, and two states—California (Cal. Health & Safety Code § 199.50 [West Supp. 1995]) and Connecticut (Conn. Gen. Stat. Ann. § 19a-591b [West Supp. 1994])—extended liability protection to them.

See also ACQUIRED IMMUNE DEFICIENCY SYNDROME; DRUGS AND NARCOTICS.

IMPANEL   The act of the CLERK of the court in making up a list of the jurors who have been selected for the trial of a particular cause. All the steps of ascertaining who shall be the proper jurors to sit in the trial of a particular case up to the final formation.

IMPARTIAL   Favoring neither; disinterested; treating all alike; unbiased; equitable, fair, and just.

IMPEACH   To accuse; to charge a liability upon; to sue. To dispute, disparage, deny, or contradict; as in to impeach a judgment or decree, or impeach a WITNESS; or as used in the rule that a jury cannot *impeach its verdict*. To proceed against a public officer for crime or misfeasance, before a proper court, by the presentation of a written accusation called ARTICLES OF IMPEACHMENT. 📖

In the law of EVIDENCE, the TESTIMONY of a witness is impeached by earlier statements that the witness has made if they are inconsistent with the statements to which the witness testifies.

IMPEACHMENT 📖 A process used to charge, try, and remove public officials for misconduct while in office. 📖

Impeachment is a fundamental constitutional power belonging to Congress. This safeguard against corruption can be initiated against federal officeholders from the lowest cabinet member all the way up to the president and the chief justice of the Supreme Court. Besides providing the authority for impeachment, the U.S. Constitution details the methods to be used. The two-stage process begins in the House of Representatives with a public inquiry into allegations, and culminates, if necessary, with a trial in the Senate. State constitutions model impeachment processes for state officials on this approach. At both the federal and state levels, impeachment is rare: from the passage of the Constitution to the mid-1990s, only fifty impeachment proceedings were initiated, and only a third of these went as far as a trial in the Senate. The reluctance of lawmakers to use this power is a measure of its gravity; it is generally only invoked by evidence of criminality or substantial ABUSE OF POWER.

The roots of impeachment date to ancient Athens. Its place in the U.S. Constitution was secured by the influence of English COMMON LAW on the Framers of the Constitution. Originally, any English subject, politician, or ruler could institute impeachment charges in Parliament. By the fourteenth century, this power became the exclusive domain of the House of Commons and the House of Lords. In 1776, the American colonies included much of the English tradition in state constitutions, but the delegates of the Constitutional Convention hotly debated how best to embody it in the federal Constitution. Their most contentious question was over which offenses should be considered impeachable.

The result of the Framers' debate was a compromise: they borrowed language from English common law, but adapted the grounds of impeachment. These grounds are specified in Article II, Section 4: "The President, Vice President and all civil Officers of the United States, shall be removed from Office on Impeachment for, and Conviction of, Treason,

Bribery, or other High Crimes and Misdemeanors." The choice of the phrase "High Crimes and Misdemeanors" left the exact definition of impeachable offenses open to interpretation by Congress. It has invited considerable debate, but it is generally read to mean both indictable offenses and other serious noncriminal misconduct. The latter has included corruption, dereliction of constitutional duty, and violation of limitations on the power of an office. Under the Constitution, federal judges are held to the most exacting standard: they may remain on the bench only "during good Behaviour" (art. III, sec. 1).

Impeachment is conducted in two stages. Impeachment proceedings begin in the House of Representatives (art. I, sec. 2). This stage satisfies the Framers' belief that impeachment should be a public inquiry into charges against an official, and it involves fact-finding at hearings. After accumulating all the evidence, the House votes on whether or not to impeach. A vote against impeachment ends the process. A vote to impeach formally advances the process to its second stage through what is called adoption of the ARTICLES OF IMPEACHMENT. Each article is a formal charge with conviction on any one article being sufficient for removal. The case is then sent to the Senate, which organizes the matter for trial (art. I, sec. 3).

During the trial, the Senate follows unique rules. There is no jury (art. III, sec. 2). Instead, the Senate is transformed into a quasi-judicial body that hears the case, and the impeached official can attend or be represented by counsel. The vice president presides over the trial of any official except the president, and the chief justice of the Supreme Court presides over the trial of the president. To convict, a two-thirds majority is needed. The punishments for conviction are removal from office and disqualification from holding office again. No presidential PARDON is possible (art. II, sec. 2). Additional criminal charges can be brought against convicted officials, but these are pursued in court and are separate from the impeachment process.

Impeachment is not often pursued. President ANDREW JOHNSON was nearly impeached as a result of a bitter struggle in 1868 between his exercise of executive power and congressional will. He escaped an impeachment conviction in the Senate by a single vote. In 1974, President RICHARD M. NIXON, embroiled in the WATERGATE scandal, resigned rather than face almost certain impeachment. The House Judiciary Committee had recommended that the full House take up three articles of impeachment

A Challenge to Impeachment

In 1989, federal judge Alcee Hastings was removed from the bench by a Senate vote, becoming the first judge in U.S. history to be impeached after being acquitted in a criminal trial. Hastings vigorously proclaimed his innocence, challenged the proceedings in court, and alleged that racism drove the proceedings.

An appointee of President Jimmy Carter, Hastings joined the U.S. District Court for the Southern District of Florida as its first African American judge in 1979. In 1981, federal prosecutors indicted him on conspiracy to accept a bribe from a Federal Bureau of Investigation agent posing as a defendant in a case before him. They charged Attorney William A. Borders, president of the National Bar Association, with offering the agent a lenient sentence from Hastings in exchange for $150,000. Borders was convicted in 1982. Hastings was acquitted in February 1983.

Hastings's troubles soon deepened. In April 1983, the U.S. Court of Appeals for the Eleventh Circuit set in motion a three-year investigation into charges that Hastings had manufactured evidence for his defense. The probe concluded that he was guilty, and in March 1987, the Judicial Conference of the United States recommended impeachment. The House of Representatives agreed. On August 3, 1988, the full House voted 413–3 to send the case to the Senate with seventeen articles of impeachment, including false testimony, fabrication of false records, and improper disclosure of confidential law enforcement information.

Hastings brought suit, seeking a preliminary injunction from the U.S. District Court for the District of Columbia (*Hastings v. United States Senate,* 716 F. Supp. 38 [1989]). In his three-part complaint, Hastings claimed that (1) the impeachment hearing was procedurally flawed because his trial would be conducted by committee and not by the full body of the Senate; (2) the impeachment hearings violated his Fifth Amendment double jeopardy rights against a second prosecution for the same crime; and (3) he was being denied effective counsel and was entitled to attorneys' fees.

The suit failed. U.S. district judge Gerhard Gesell held that (1) rule XI of the governing Rules of Procedure and Practice in the Senate When Sitting on Impeachment authorizes a committee format but does not prevent the full participation of the Senate; (2) double jeopardy principles did not apply in this case because impeachment is not a criminal proceeding and because Hastings faced separate impeachment charges; and (3) no statute provides for attorneys' fees.

In August 1989, the Senate panel heard twenty-four days of testimony. On October 20, it convicted Hastings on eight of the impeachment articles and removed him from office. Hastings left the bench continuing to profess his innocence, attacking the Senate's handling of evidence, and maintaining that he was the victim of racism.

See also Double Jeopardy.

---

against Nixon: obstruction of justice, abuse of constitutional authority, and refusal to answer the committee's SUBPOENAS.

Congress has adopted the articles of impeachment against one senator, William Blount; one cabinet member, William W. Belknap; and one Supreme Court justice, SAMUEL CHASE. It has also voted to impeach a small number of federal appeals and district court judges. In 1989, U.S. district court judge Alcee Hastings, of Miami, became only the twelfth federal judge in U.S. history to be impeached. His case was unique: he was the first African American to be appointed to the Florida federal bench, and also the only judge to be impeached after an ACQUITTAL in a criminal trial. The House voted to adopt seventeen articles of impeachment against him in 1988. After Hastings unsuccessfully challenged his impeachment in court in 1989, the Senate convicted him on eight of the articles and removed him from office.

Impeachment remains the ultimate check on the abuse of power. By providing this power to Congress, the Framers drew on a long tradition of democratic skepticism about leaders, ensuring that they will serve the people only so long as they respect the law and their office. In this sense, the power of impeachment also stands ready to thwart tyranny. Calls are occasionally made for reform that would streamline the impeachment process, but its rare invocation and tradition of service make such reform unlikely.

See also HIGH CRIMES AND MISDEMEANORS.

IMPEDIMENT 　A disability or obstruction that prevents an individual from entering into a CONTRACT.

INFANCY, for example, is an impediment in making certain contracts. Impediments to MAR-

RIAGE include such factors as CONSANGUINITY between the parties or an earlier marriage that is still valid.

IMPERSONATION The crime of pretending to be another individual in order to deceive others and gain some advantage.

The crime of false impersonation is defined by federal statutes and by state statutes that differ from JURISDICTION to jurisdiction. In some states, pretending to be someone who does not actually exist can constitute false impersonation. For example, suppose Bill attempts to evade prosecution for a crime by giving the arresting officer a fictitious name and address. In Colorado, where "[a] person who knowingly assumes a false or fictitious identity and, under that identity, does any other act intending unlawfully to gain a benefit for himself is guilty of criminal impersonation," Bill could be charged with a crime (Colo. Rev. Stat. Ann. § 18-5-113(1) [West 1996]). In this situation, the benefit Bill hopes to realize is avoiding prosecution, so that element of the offense has been satisfied. To be charged, the defendant does not need to seek a monetary benefit from the impersonation.

In New York, giving only a fictitious name does not constitute false impersonation. Under New York law, criminal impersonation is committed when an individual "[i]mpersonates another and does an act in such assumed character with intent to obtain a benefit or to injure or defraud another" (N.Y. Penal Law § 190.25 [McKinney 1996]). In other words, it is illegal to impersonate a real person, but not a fictitious one. Thus, if Carol forges Ann's name on checks made out to Ann so that Carol can cash the checks, Carol could be guilty of false impersonation—but only if Ann is a real person. Such laws are designed to protect innocent people from the losses they may incur owing to the wrongful acts of others and to restore any loss of dignity and reputation they may have suffered as a result of impersonation.

Most state laws also provide that the impersonation of a public official is a criminal act. In Texas, impersonating "a public servant with intent to induce another to submit to his pretended official authority or to rely on his pretended official acts" is a crime (Tex. Penal Code Ann. § 37.11 [West 1996]). Depending on the jurisdiction, the public servant being impersonated does not always have to actually exist. For example, suppose Carl pulls over a driver, shows her a fake police badge, and reprimands her for speeding but tells her that he will not arrest her if she pays him $50. Carl's actions constitute the crime of false impersonation, in addition to any other crimes, including EXTORTION, that may apply to the situation. Thousands of criminal reports are filed every year by individuals victimized in various ways by persons impersonating police officers.

Under federal law, pretending to be "an officer or employee acting under the authority of the United States" in order to demand or obtain "any money, paper, document, or thing of value" can result in a fine as well as imprisonment for up to three years (18 U.S.C.A. § 912). Like state false impersonation statutes, the federal law also seeks to protect interests such as the dignity and prestige of individuals, especially those who hold federal office. Federal statutes also prohibit other types of impersonation, including pretending to be a U.S. citizen; pretending to be a U.S. officer or employee attempting to arrest or search a person or search a building; pretending to be a creditor of the United States or a foreign official; and pretending to be an agent or member of 4-H or of the Red Cross.

IMPERTINENCE Irrelevancy; the flaw of bearing no reasonable relationship to the issues or proceeding at hand.

An *impertinent question* is one that is immaterial or has no logical relation to the issue or controversy before the court.

IMPLEADER A procedural device used in a CIVIL ACTION whereby a defendant brings into the lawsuit a third party who is not already a party to the action but may ultimately be liable for the plaintiff's claim against the defendant.

Impleader is most commonly used where the third party, often an INSURANCE company, has a duty to INDEMNIFY, or contribute to the payment of, the plaintiff's DAMAGES. An insurance policy usually provides that if the insured is sued, the insurance company will defend him or her in court and pay any damages owed if he or she is found liable in the action. For example, suppose a person slips and falls on a homeowner's property, suffers an injury, and sues the homeowner. If the homeowner has a homeowner's policy, he may implead his insurance company by filing a third-party COMPLAINT for approval by the court. If the court permits the complaint, the insurer is brought into the action. The homeowner is now both the defendant in the action and a third-party plaintiff. If he is found liable and ordered to pay damages, the insurance company will be expected to pay all or part of those damages.

Impleader, which was known as VOUCHING-IN at common law, is now governed by procedural rules on both the state and federal levels. "Vouching in" has its origins in the English

COMMON-LAW practice of "vouching to warranty." A defendant, sued by a plaintiff for the recovery of a certain piece of property, could "vouch in" another party who may have given a WARRANTY of TITLE when the property was sold to the defendant. Similar types of third-party actions began to appear in this country and eventually, in the interests of uniformity, a federal rule of CIVIL PROCEDURE providing for impleader was adopted. Rule 14 of the Federal Rules of Civil Procedure provides that "a defending party, as a third-party plaintiff, may cause a summons and complaint to be served upon a person not a party to the action who is or may be liable to the third-party plaintiff for all or part of the plaintiff's claim against the third-party plaintiff." State rules of civil procedure regulate the use of impleader in actions commenced in state courts. In Connecticut, for instance, "a defendant in any civil action may move the court for permission to serve a WRIT, SUMMONS and complaint upon a person not a party to the action who is or may be liable to him for all or part of the plaintiff's claim against him" (Conn. R. Super. Ct. 117). Both federal and state court impleader rules are designed to promote judicial economy by disposing of two or more trials in one action, thus eliminating the need for the defendant to sue the third party at a later time.

A third party who is brought into an action through impleader is entitled to defend herself or himself against the claims of both the plaintiff and the defendant, raising whatever defenses may be applicable. An insurance company may allege that the policy issued to the defendant does not cover the acts that gave rise to the lawsuit and thus led the defendant to implead the company. For example, suppose Ann has been sued for allegedly assaulting Susan and has filed an impleader to have her insurance company defend her and pay any damages against her. The insurance company may refuse to defend her on the ground that the policy does not cover intentional acts, such as assaulting another person. If the court agrees, the insurance company will not have to defend Susan or pay any damages that Ann is awarded by the court or a jury.

The court has a great deal of discretion in deciding whether a defendant may implead a third party. The court considers a number of factors, including whether joining the third party will unduly complicate the action, cause delay in deciding the main action (the original suit brought by the plaintiff against the defendant), adversely affect the plaintiff, or confuse the jury. If any of these factors is present, the court may refuse to permit the impleader. The court's decision to grant or deny the impleader will be overturned by an APPELLATE COURT only if it appears that the lower court abused its discretion.

IMPLIED 📖 Inferred from circumstances; known indirectly. 📖

In its legal application, the term *implied* is used in contrast with EXPRESS, where the intention regarding the subject matter is explicitly and directly indicated. When something is implied, its meaning is derived from the words or actions of the individuals involved. For example, when one individual gives another a gift, the recipient's acceptance is implied if he or she performs acts indicating ownership, such as using the gifts.

IMPLIED CONSENT 📖 CONSENT that is inferred from signs, actions, or facts, or by inaction or silence. 📖

Implied consent differs from EXPRESS consent, which is communicated by the spoken or written word.

Implied consent is a broadly based legal concept. Whether it is as valid as express consent depends on the situation and the applicable law. For example, the owner of a car generally is liable for an accident caused by someone who drove that car with his or her consent. In many states, that consent can be express or implied, and implied consent may arise from seemingly innocuous actions. For instance, a habit of leaving the keys in the car's ignition may under law imply that the owner consents to anyone else's—even a car thief's—driving the car.

CORPORATIONS that conduct business in a foreign state—that is, any state other than the state of incorporation—impliedly consent to be bound by the laws of the foreign state and to be subject to the foreign state's JURISDICTION. The rationale supporting this application of the implied consent rule is basic: a corporation that reaps the benefits of conducting business in a state also should be subject to the laws and the courts of that state. The fact that the corporation has business in the foreign state is all that is needed for a finding of implied consent.

Implied consent as the result of inaction is most commonly found in litigation procedures. For instance, a party to a lawsuit may have the legal right to object to a court HEARING that is scheduled to occur before the party has obtained certain crucial documents. But if the party appears at the hearing and allows it to proceed without objecting, the party has waived the right to later object or appeal. By failing to take action to cancel or reschedule the hearing, the party is said to have implied its consent to the hearing.

Perhaps the best known—and most often litigated—application of implied consent involves laws prohibiting driving while intoxicated. Most states have legislation that subjects motorists suspected of driving while under the influence of ALCOHOL or illicit drugs to blood, breath, or urine tests. These chemical tests can confirm the existence and the level of drugs or alcohol in a driver's body, and can be used as evidence against the driver. Pursuant to these state statutes, known as implied consent laws, anyone who drives on public roads or highways has, by that action, impliedly consented to such tests. Once stopped or arrested for suspicion of driving while impaired, a person must submit to a test or face revocation or suspension of his or her driver's LICENSE.

Implied consent statutes have been attacked for a variety of constitutional reasons, usually unsuccessfully. Courts have held that the statutes do not violate a driver's FOURTH AMENDMENT protection from unreasonable SEARCH AND SEIZURE, or FIFTH AMENDMENT right against SELF-INCRIMINATION. The statutes usually are upheld on DUE PROCESS grounds, although courts have struck down statutes that permit the revocation of a license without a hearing. Arguments that implied consent laws are an invasion of PRIVACY or an undue burden on interstate commerce have also been rejected by the courts.

Courts generally look to one of two theories supporting the validity of implied consent laws. According to the first theory, driving on public roads and highways is a PRIVILEGE, not a right. Only those who adhere to state laws, including laws prohibiting driving while intoxicated, are entitled to the driving privilege. Under the second theory, courts consider implied consent laws to be a reasonable regulation of driving pursuant to the state's POLICE POWER, so long as the laws do not violate due process. Courts have weighed the interests of society against the interests of individuals, and have determined that drunk or drug-impaired drivers are enough of a danger to society that a slight infringement on the liberty of individuals is justifiable.

The liberty of individuals is protected somewhat by the requirement that before a law officer can request a blood, urine, or breath test, the officer must have reasonable grounds to believe that the driver is intoxicated. What constitutes reasonable grounds is determined on a case-by-case basis. If a driver loses her or his license after refusing to comply with a

The most common application of implied consent is to laws prohibiting drunk driving. By using a public road, this motorist has impliedly consented to submitting to tests that measure the existence of alcohol or drugs in his body.

chemical test and a court later finds that reasonable grounds for the test did not exist, the court can invalidate the revocation or suspension of the license.

Courts generally hold that a revocation or suspension of a license caused by a driver's refusal to test for drugs or alcohol is separate and distinct from a prosecution for driving while intoxicated. Therefore, in most states, it makes no difference whether a driver pleads guilty to, is convicted of, or is acquitted of the crime: refusing to take a test for chemical impairment may result in a revoked or suspended license, and this punishment must be paid despite a subsequent ACQUITTAL of driving while intoxicated or in addition to any punishment that comes as a result of a conviction.

Many states require that a law officer warn a driver of the consequences of refusing to take a chemical test, and if that warning is not given, the license cannot be revoked or suspended. Some states offer drivers a limited right to consult an attorney before deciding whether to take a sobriety test. This right is not absolute, since a significant delay would render ineffective a blood, urine, or alcohol test. Several states offer drivers the opportunity for a second opinion—the right to have an additional test performed by the driver's choice of physicians.

States differ in their approach to implied consent laws, but their goal is the same: keeping dangerously impaired drivers off the roads. Courts and legislatures are reluctant to frustrate this goal.

See also AUTOMOBILES.

IMPLIED WARRANTY 📖 A PROMISE, arising by OPERATION OF LAW, that something that is sold will be MERCHANTABLE and fit for the purpose for which it is sold. 📖

Every time GOODS are bought and sold, a SALES contract is created: the buyer agrees to pay, and the seller agrees to accept, a certain price in exchange for a certain item or number of items. Sales CONTRACTS are frequently oral, unwritten agreements. The purchase of items like a candy bar hardly seems worth the trouble of drafting an agreement spelling out the buyer's expectation that the candy bar will be fresh and edible. Implied warranties protect the buyer whether or not a written sales contract exists.

Implied Warranty of Merchantability

Implied warranties come in two general types: merchantability and fitness. An implied warranty of merchantability is an unwritten and unspoken guarantee to the buyer that goods purchased conform to ordinary standards of care and that they are of the same average grade, quality, and value as similar goods sold under similar circumstances. In other words, merchantable goods are goods fit for the ordinary purposes for which they are to be used. The UNIFORM COMMERCIAL CODE (UCC), adopted by most states, provides that courts may imply a WARRANTY of merchantability when (1) the seller is the merchant of such goods, and (2) the buyer uses the goods for the ordinary purposes for which such goods are sold (§ 2-314). Thus, a buyer can sue a seller for breaching the implied warranty by selling goods unfit for their ordinary purpose.

There is rarely any question as to whether the seller is the merchant of the goods sold. Nevertheless, in *Huprich v. Bitto*, 667 So.2d 685 (Ala. 1995), a farmer who sold defective horse feed was found not to be a merchant of horse feed. The court stated that the farmer did not hold himself out as having knowledge or skill peculiar to the sale of corn as horse feed, and therefore was not a merchant of horse feed for purposes of determining a breach of implied warranty of merchantability.

The question of whether goods are fit for their ordinary purpose is much more frequently litigated. Thomas Coffer sued the manufacturer of a jar of mixed nuts after he bit down on an unshelled filbert, believing it to have been shelled, and damaged a tooth. Coffer argued in part that the presence of the unshelled nut among shelled nuts was a breach of the implied warranty of merchantability. Unquestionably, Coffer was using the nuts for their ordinary purpose when he ate them, and unquestionably, he suffered a dental injury when he bit the filbert's hard shell. But the North Carolina appellate court held that the jar of mixed nuts was nonetheless fit for the ordinary purpose for which jars of mixed nuts are used (*Coffer v. Standard Brands*, 30 N.C. App. 134, 226 S.E.2d 534 [1976]). The court consulted the state agriculture board's regulations and noted that the peanut industry allows a small amount of unshelled nuts to be included with shelled nuts without rendering the shelled nuts inedible or adulterated. The court also noted that shells are a natural incident to nuts.

The policy behind the implied warranty of merchantability is basic: sellers are generally better suited than buyers to determine whether a product will perform properly. Holding the seller liable for a product that is not fit for its ordinary purpose shifts the costs of nonperformance from the buyer to the seller. This motivates the seller to ensure the product's proper performance before placing it on the market. The seller is better able to absorb the costs of a product's nonperformance, usually by spreading the risk to consumers in the form of increased prices.

The policy behind limiting the implied warranty of merchantability to the goods' ordinary use is also straightforward: a seller may not have sufficient expertise or control over a product to ensure that it will perform properly when used for nonstandard purposes.

Implied Warranty of Fitness

When a buyer wishes to use goods for a particular, nonordinary purpose, the UCC provides a distinct implied warranty of fitness (§ 2-315). Unlike the implied warranty of merchantability, the implied warranty of fitness does not contain a requirement that the seller be a merchant with respect to the goods sold. It merely requires that the seller possess knowledge and expertise on which the buyer may rely.

For example, one court found that horse buyers who indicated to the sellers their intention to use the horse for breeding were using the horse for a particular, nonordinary purpose (*Whitehouse v. Lange*, 128 Idaho 129, 910 P.2d 801 [1996]). The buyers soon discovered that the horse they purchased was incapable of reproducing. Because the court found this use of the horse to be nonordinary, the buyers were entitled to an implied warranty of fitness.

Before a court will imply a warranty of fitness, three requirements must be met: (1) the seller must have reason to know of the buyer's particular purpose for the goods; (2) the seller must have reason to know of the buyer's reliance on the seller's skill and knowledge in furnishing the appropriate goods; and (3) the buyer must, in fact, rely on the seller's skill and knowledge. Even when these requirements are met, courts will not imply a warranty of fitness under certain circumstances. A buyer who specifies a particular brand of goods is not entitled to an implied warranty of fitness. Also, a buyer who has greater expertise than the seller regarding the goods generally is precluded from asserting an implied warranty of fitness, as is a buyer who provides the seller with specifications, such as a blueprint or design plan, detailing the types of material to be used in the goods.

IMPORT QUOTAS Import quotas are a form of protectionism. An import quota fixes the quantity of a particular good that foreign producers may bring into a country over a specific period, usually a year. The U.S. government imposes quotas to protect domestic industries from foreign competition. Import quotas are usually justified as a means of protecting workers who otherwise might be laid off. They also can raise prices for the consumer by reducing the amount of cheaper, foreign-made goods imported and thus reducing competition for domestic industries of the same goods.

The GENERAL AGREEMENT ON TARIFFS AND TRADE (GATT) (61 Stat. A3, T.I.A.S. No. 1700, 55 U.N.T.S. 187), which was opened for signatures on October 30, 1947, is the principal international multilateral agreement regulating world trade. GATT members were required to sign the Protocol of Provisions Application of the General Agreement on Tariffs and Trades (61 Stat. A2051, T.I.A.S. No. 1700, 55 U.N.T.S. 308). The Protocol of Provisions set forth the rules governing GATT and it also governs import quotas. This agreement became effective January 1, 1948, and the United States is still bound by it. GATT has been renegotiated seven times since its inception; the most recent version became effective July 1, 1995, with 123 signatories.

Import quotas once played a much greater role in global trade, but the 1995 renegotiation of GATT has made it increasingly difficult for a country to introduce them. Nations can no longer impose temporary quotas to offset surges in imports from foreign markets. Furthermore, an import quota that is introduced to protect a domestic industry from foreign imports is limited to at least the average import of the same goods over the last three years. In addition, the 1995 GATT agreement identifies the country of an import's origin in order to prevent countries from exporting goods to another nation through a third nation that does not have the same import quotas. GATT also requires that all import quota trade barriers be converted into TARIFF equivalents. Therefore, although a nation cannot seek to deter trade by imposing arbitrary import quotas, it may increase the tariffs associated with a particular import.

In the United States, the decade from the mid-1980s to the mid-1990s saw import quotas placed on textiles, agricultural products, automobiles, sugar, beef, bananas, and even underwear—among other things. In a single session of Congress in 1985, more than three hundred protectionist bills were introduced as U.S. industries began voicing concern over foreign competition.

Many U.S. companies headquartered in the United States rely on manufacturing facilities outside of the country to produce their goods. Because of import quotas, some of these companies cannot get their own products back into the United States. While such companies lobby Congress to change what they consider to be an unfair practice, their opposition argues that this is the price to be paid for giving away U.S. jobs to foreign countries.

Nearly every country restricts imports of foreign goods. For example, in 1996—even after the new version of GATT went into effect—

U.S. Imports and Exports of Merchandise, 1971 to 1994

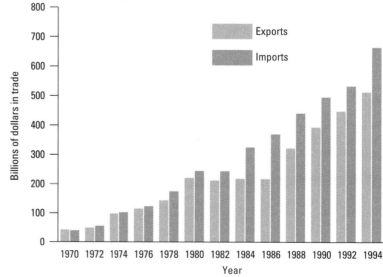

Includes silver ore and bullion; beginning in 1974, nonmonetary gold. Trade between Virgin Islands and foreign countries included since 1974.

Source: U.S. Bureau of the Census, 1970–88, *Highlights of U.S. Export and Import Trade*, FT 990, monthly; beginning 1989, *U.S. Merchandise Trade: Export, General Imports, and Imports for Consumption*, series FT 925, monthly.

Vietnam restricted the amount of cement, fertilizer, and fuel and the number of automobiles and motorcycles it would import. The import quotas of foreign countries can adversely affect U.S. industries that try to sell their goods abroad. The U.S. economy has suffered because of foreign import quotas on canned fruit, cigarettes, leather, insurance, and computers. In a market that has become overcrowded with U.S. entertainment, the European Communities have chosen to enforce import quotas on U.S.-made films and television in an effort to encourage Europe's own industries to become more competitive.

IMPOSSIBILITY 📖 A legal excuse or defense to an ACTION for the breach of a CONTRACT; less frequently, a defense to a criminal charge of an attempted crime, such as attempted robbery or murder. 📖

Historically, a person who entered a contract was bound to perform according to his or her promised duties, regardless of whether it became impossible to do so. Thus, early U.S. courts did not recognize the defense of impossibility of PERFORMANCE. Courts noted that if the parties to a contract had desired to take into account any events that may develop after they reached an agreement, then they should have accounted for such contingencies in the contract.

As contract law developed over the twentieth century—and in response to increasing commercial activities—courts began to recognize impossibility as a valid defense to an action for breach of a contract. This defense did not normally apply if one party found it unexpectedly difficult or expensive to perform according to the contract; rather, it applied only when the basis or subject matter of the contract was destroyed or no longer existed. In addition, the defense of impossibility became available only if objective impossibility existed. Objective impossibility occurred when the contractual obligation could not actually be performed. Objective impossibility is often referred to by the statement "The thing cannot be done." For example, if a musician promised to play a concert at a specific concert hall but the concert hall subsequently burned down, it would be impossible to perform according to the contractual agreement and the musician would be excused from performing at that particular venue. Subjective impossibility exists when only one of the parties to a contract subjectively believes that she or he cannot complete the required performance. For example, if a musician believed that he had not practiced sufficiently to perform a successful concert, this

belief would not excuse the musician from performing the concert. The statement "I cannot do it" frequently refers to the state of mind present in a case involving subjective impossibility.

Modern U.S. law uses the term *impracticability* synonymously with the term *impossibility*, primarily because some things may not be absolutely impossible to perform but are nevertheless impracticable to complete. Thus, the general rule is that a thing may be impossible to perform when it would not be practicable to perform. A contractual obligation is impracticable "when it can only be done at an excessive and unreasonable cost" (*Transatlantic Financing Corp. v. United States*, 363 F.2d 312 [D.C. Cir. 1966]).

When a party raises the defense of IMPRACTICABILITY, courts generally determine three things: first, whether something unexpected occurred after the parties entered the contract; second, whether the parties had assumed that this thing would not occur; and third, that the unexpected occurrence made performance of the contract impracticable. Some widely recognized occurrences that would normally provide a defense of impracticability are the death or illness of one of the necessary parties, the unforeseeable destruction of the subject matter of the contract (perhaps by an "act of God"), or a supervening illegality.

Impossibility has been used as a defense to charges of attempted crimes. Historically, courts recognized that a party could not be convicted of criminal attempt if the actual crime was legally impossible to accomplish. For example, if a person was accused of attempting to receive stolen property but the property was not actually stolen, the defense of legal impossibility could arise. Legal impossibility is distinguished from factual impossibility, where facts unknown to the person attempting to commit a crime render the crime factually impossible to complete. For example, if a pickpocket attempts to steal a wallet but no wallet is present, factual impossibility may exist. Courts generally have recognized legal impossibility as a defense to a criminal attempt, but not factual impossibility. They reasoned that since a person attempting to commit a crime had formed the required intent to commit the crime, it was irrelevant that the crime was factually impossible to complete.

Impossibility as a defense to a criminal attempt has largely been rejected by modern U.S. statutes and courts. The Model Penal Code—which many states have adopted since its introduction in 1962—expressly rejects impossibility as a defense to the charge of criminal attempt (§ 5.01 [1995]).

IMPOSTS ▥ Taxes or duties; taxes levied by the government on imported goods. ▥

Although *impost* is a generic term, which can be used in reference to all taxes, it is most frequently used interchangeably with CUSTOMS DUTIES.

IMPOUNDMENT ▥ An action taken by the president in which he or she proposes not to spend all or part of a sum of money appropriated by Congress. ▥

The current rules and procedures for impoundment were created by the Congressional Budget and Impoundment Control Act of 1974 (2 U.S.C.A. § 601 et seq.), which was passed to reform the congressional budget process and to resolve conflicts between Congress and President RICHARD M. NIXON concerning the power of the EXECUTIVE BRANCH to impound funds appropriated by Congress. Past presidents, beginning with THOMAS JEFFERSON, had impounded funds at various times for various reasons, without instigating any significant conflict between the executive and the legislative branches. At times, such as when the original purpose for the money no longer existed or when money could be saved through more efficient operations, Congress simply acquiesced to the president's wishes. At other times, Congress or the designated recipient of the impounded funds challenged the president's action, and the parties negotiated until a political settlement was reached.

Changes During the Nixon Administration The history of accepting or resolving impoundments broke down during the Nixon administration for several reasons. First, President Nixon impounded much greater sums than had previous presidents, proposing to hold back between 17 and 20 percent of controllable expenditures between 1969 and 1972. Second, Nixon used impoundments to try to fight policy initiatives that he disagreed with, attempting to terminate entire programs by impounding their appropriations. Third, Nixon claimed that as president, he had the constitutional right to impound funds appropriated by Congress, thus threatening Congress's greatest political strength: its power over the purse. Nixon claimed, "The Constitutional right of the President of the United States to impound funds, and that is not to spend money, when the spending of money would mean either increasing prices or increasing taxes for all the people—that right is absolutely clear."

In the face of Nixon's claim to impoundment authority and his refusal to release appropriated

DIANA WALKER/THE GAMMA LIAISON NETWORK

funds, Congress in 1974 passed the Congressional Budget and Impoundment Control Act, which reformed the congressional budget process and established rules and procedures for presidential impoundment. In general, the provisions of the act were designed to curtail the power of the president in the budget process, which had been steadily growing throughout the twentieth century.

The Impoundment Control Act divides impoundments into two categories: deferrals and rescissions. In a deferral, the president asks Congress to delay the release of appropriated funds; in a rescission, the president asks Congress to cancel the appropriation of funds altogether. Congress and the president must follow specific rules and procedures for each type of impoundment.

Deferrals To propose a deferral, the president must send Congress a request identifying the amount of money to be deferred, the program that will be affected, the reasons for the deferral, the estimated fiscal and program effects of the deferral, and the length of time for which the funds are to be deferred. Funds cannot be deferred beyond the end of the fiscal year, or for so long that the affected agency could no longer spend the funds prudently.

In the original Impoundment Control Act, the president was allowed to defer funds for any reason, including opposition to a specific program or for general policy goals, such as curtailing federal spending. Congress retained the right to review deferrals, and a deferral could be rejected if either the House or the Senate voted to disapprove it. In 1986, several members of Congress and a number of cities successfully challenged the constitutionality of these deferral procedures in *City of New Haven v. United*

In April 1996 President Bill Clinton signed the Legislative Line Item Veto Act, changing the way impoundments are handled and granting more budget authority to the president.

States, 809 F.2d 900 (D.C. Cir. 1987). *New Haven* was based on a 1981 case, *INS v. Chadha,* 454 U.S. 812, 102 S. Ct. 87, 70 L. Ed. 2d 80, in which the Supreme Court ruled that one-house vetoes of proposed presidential actions are unconstitutional. The *Chadha* ruling invalidated Congress's right to review and disapprove deferrals. In response, Congress took away most of the president's deferral power through provisions in the Balanced Budget and Emergency Deficit Control Reaffirmation Act of 1987 (2 U.S.C.A. § 901 et seq.) (otherwise known as Gramm-Rudman-Hollings II). These provisions allow presidential impoundment for only three reasons: to provide for special contingencies, to achieve savings through more efficient operations, and when such deferrals are specifically provided for by law. The president can no longer defer funds for policy reasons.

Once the president sends a message to Congress requesting a deferral, the comptroller general must submit a report on the proposed deferral to Congress. A proposed deferral is automatically considered to be approved unless the House or the Senate passes legislation specifically disapproving it. If the president still refuses to spend appropriated funds after Congress has formally disapproved of a deferral, the comptroller general has the power to sue the president in FEDERAL COURT.

Rescissions The rules and procedures for rescissions are very similar to those for deferrals. As with a deferral, the president must send Congress a message proposing a rescission. In this message, the president must detail how much money is to be rescinded, the department or agency that was targeted to receive the money, the specific project or projects that will be affected by the rescission, and the reasons for the rescission. The comptroller general handles a rescission as she or he would a deferral, preparing a report on the rescission for Congress. Unlike a deferral, a rescission must be specifically approved by both houses of Congress within forty-five legislative days after the message requesting the rescission is received. Congress can approve all, part, or none of the proposed rescission. If either house disapproves the rescission or takes no action on it, the president must spend the appropriated funds as originally intended. If the president refuses to do so, the comptroller general can sue the president in federal court.

Legislative Line Item Veto Act of 1995 The Legislative Line Item Veto Act of 1995 (Pub. L. No. 104-130, 110 Stat. 1200), signed by President BILL CLINTON on April 9, 1996, and made effective January 1, 1997, affects the way impoundments are handled. The Line Item Veto Act does not actually give the president the authority to VETO individual line items, which would require a constitutional amendment. It does, however, give the president the functional equivalent, allowing the president to veto, or rescind, specific items in appropriations bills, as well as targeted tax breaks affecting one hundred or fewer people and new entitlement programs. The president proposes these rescissions to Congress and they become effective in thirty days unless Congress passes a bill rejecting them. The president can in turn veto any congressional bill of disapproval, and Congress can override that veto with a two-thirds vote in both houses. Under the Line Item Veto Act, therefore, Congress still retains the ultimate power to override the president's rescission requests, but the president enjoys significantly enhanced rescission authority.

CROSS-REFERENCES

Congress of the United States; Federal Budget; Separation of Powers.

IMPRACTICABILITY 📖 Substantial difficulty or inconvenience in following a particular course of action, but not such insurmountability or hopelessness as to make performance impossible. 📖

Rule 23 of the Federal Rules of Civil Procedure establishes impracticability as one of the grounds for permitting a CLASS ACTION in FEDERAL COURTS. "[T]he class is so numerous that JOINDER of all members is impracticable." In such a situation, the court will permit a few individuals who have made a MOTION to it to represent in one lawsuit a large number of persons who will be similarly affected by the legal outcome of the particular action. The group to be represented must be so large that there would be significant problems or impracticability in bringing each member before the court to appear as a party to the action. For purposes of certification as a class, the prospective representatives must show that joinder can be accomplished only with substantial difficulty, expense, and hardship, but not that such joinder cannot be done at all. State procedural rules also require that joinder of all prospective class members be impracticable before permitting the commencement of a class action in state courts.

In the law governing SALES, the UNIFORM COMMERCIAL CODE allows either party to a CONTRACT to be excused from the legal obligations created by it where PERFORMANCE becomes impracticable because an unexpected event has occurred, such as a severe shortage of supplies due to unexpected and continual flooding.

See also IMPOSSIBILITY.

IMPRIMATUR [*Latin, Let it be printed.*] A license or allowance, granted by the constituted authorities, giving permission to print and publish a book. This allowance was formerly necessary in England before any book could lawfully be printed, and in some other countries is still required.

IMPRISONMENT Incarceration; the act of restraining the personal liberty of an individual; confinement in a PRISON.

Imprisonment can be effected without the application of physical restraint by verbal compulsion coupled with the display of available force. The TORT of FALSE IMPRISONMENT involves the illegal arrest or detention of an individual without a WARRANT, by an illegal warrant, or by an illegally executed warrant, either in a prison or any place used temporarily for such purpose, or by force and constraint without actual confinement.

IMPROVEMENTS Additions or alterations to REAL PROPERTY that increase the value thereof.

Improvements to land, for example, might include the planting of CROPS, the construction of fences, and the digging of wells.

IMPUTED Attributed vicariously.

In the legal sense, the term *imputed* is used to describe an action, fact, or quality, the knowledge of which is charged to an individual based upon the actions of another for whom the individual is responsible rather than on the individual's own acts or omissions. For example, in the law of AGENCY, the actions of an AGENT performed during the course of employment will be attributed to the agent's PRINCIPAL. The doctrine of imputed NEGLIGENCE makes one person legally responsible for the negligent conduct of another.

IMPUTED KNOWLEDGE The comprehension attributed or charged to a person because the facts in issue were open to discovery and it was that person's DUTY to apprise himself or herself of them; more accurately described as knowledge.

For example, if the stairway leading to a retail store is defective and a patron is injured on the stairway, the store owner cannot evade LIABILITY for the patron's injury by denying knowledge of the defect. Since the store owner is subject to a duty to discover and rectify the defect in an area known to be used by the public, knowledge of the defect is imputed to the store owner.

In the law of AGENCY, notice of facts brought to the attention of an AGENT (a person authorized by another, known as a PRINCIPAL, to act for him or her), within the scope of the agent's authority or employment, is usually imputed to his or her principal.

IMPUTED NOTICE Information regarding particular facts or circumstances that the law permits to affect the legal rights of a person who has no firsthand knowledge of them but who should have learned of them because his or her AGENT or representative had direct knowledge of that information and a DUTY to report it to him or her.

INADMISSIBLE That which, according to established legal principles, cannot be received into EVIDENCE at a trial for consideration by the JURY or judge in reaching a determination of the ACTION.

Evidence, for example, that is obtained as a result of an unlawful SEARCH AND SEIZURE is inadmissible, as is HEARSAY.

INADVERTENCE The absence of attention or care; the failure of an individual to carefully and prudently observe the progress of a court proceeding that might have an effect upon his or her rights.

The term *inadvertence* is generally used in reference to a ground upon which a JUDGMENT may be set aside or vacated under the Rules of Federal Civil Procedure or state rules of CIVIL PROCEDURE.

INALIENABLE Not subject to sale or transfer; inseparable.

That which is inalienable cannot be bought, sold, or transferred from one individual to another. The personal rights to life and liberty guaranteed by the Constitution of the United States are inalienable. Similarly, various types of PROPERTY are inalienable, such as rivers, streams, and HIGHWAYS.

IN BLANK Absent limitation or restriction.

The term *in blank* is used in reference to NEGOTIABLE INSTRUMENTS, such as CHECKS or PROMISSORY NOTES. When such COMMERCIAL PAPER is endorsed in blank, the designated payee signs his or her name only. The paper is not made payable to any one individual in particular, but anyone who presents it for payment is entitled to be paid.

INC. An abbreviation for incorporated; having been formed as a legal or political entity with the advantages of perpetual existence and succession.

See also CORPORATIONS.

IN CAMERA 📖 In CHAMBERS; in private. A judicial proceeding is said to be heard *in camera* either when the hearing is had before the judge in his or her private chambers or when all spectators are excluded from the courtroom. 📖

INCAPACITY 📖 The absence of legal ability, competence, or qualifications. 📖

An individual incapacitated by INFANCY, for example, does not have the legal ability to enter into certain types of agreements, such as MARRIAGE or CONTRACTS.

Under provisions of WORKERS' COMPENSATION laws, the term *incapacity* refers to the inability to find and retain employment due to a disease or injury that prevents the performance of the customary duties of a worker.

INCARCERATION 📖 Confinement in a JAIL or PRISON; imprisonment. 📖

Police officers and other law enforcement officers are authorized by federal, state, and local lawmakers to arrest and confine persons suspected of crimes. The judicial system is authorized to confine persons convicted of crimes. This confinement, whether before or after a criminal conviction, is called incarceration. Juveniles and adults alike are subject to incarceration.

A jail is a facility designed to confine persons after arrest and before trial, or for a short period upon conviction for a lesser offense. A prison is built to house persons for longer periods of time following conviction for a more serious offense. Jails also may be called detention centers, and prisons may be called correctional facilities or penitentiaries. Regardless of their name, their function is generally the same: to lock up accused and convicted criminals.

The pretrial detention of accused criminals is an ancient practice. From the fifth century to the tenth century, persons accused of crimes in England were confined in jail through the end of trial unless they had property to PLEDGE. If they pledged property, it was held by the court to ensure their appearance at trial, and they were released from jail. After the conquest of England by William the Conqueror in 1066, local SHERIFFS determined who deserved pretrial release. This practice continued until the thirteenth century, when widespread favoritism and abuse by the sheriffs led to the enactment of uniform procedures concerning pretrial release.

The custom of jailing criminal defendants was continued in the American colonies. The payment of BAIL as a condition of pretrial release was also adopted. In 1791 the EIGHTH AMENDMENT to the U.S. Constitution was ratified, stating, in part, that "[e]xcessive bail shall not be required . . . nor cruel and unusual punishments inflicted." This constituted the only provision in the Constitution directly addressing jails and incarceration.

There were no prisons in the United States before the Constitution was written in 1789. Convicted criminals were sentenced to more colorful punishments than incarceration. Punishment for serious crimes included banishment from the community; public pillory, which was detention in a wood device that held the head and hands by closing around the neck and wrists; and CORPORAL PUNISHMENT, which was designed to disfigure the offender using measures such as whipping, branding, or slicing off the body part thought to be responsible for the crime. The most serious crimes were punishable by death.

The first prison in the United States was built in Philadelphia in 1790, when the Walnut Street Jail added a new cell house to its existing jail and devoted the new cells to the confinement of convicted criminals. Established by the nonviolent Quakers as an alternative to capital punishment, prison was originally intended to be a progressive setting for hard work, reflection, self-examination, and spiritual guidance. However, by the 1820s prison had become the punishment most feared by criminal defendants. Federal, state, and local governments were free to confine convicts and accused criminals in the most inhumane conditions. A convict was considered a slave of the state, with no rights beyond the right to be kept alive.

Until the 1960s courts were reluctant to review the procedures, conditions, and treatment of persons held in jails and prisons. At that time, perhaps inspired by progressive social discourse and a growing emphasis on rehabilitation over punishment, courts began to scrutinize the actions of jailers and prison officials. They found numerous constitutional violations, including violations of DUE PROCESS, of the FIRST AMENDMENT guarantee of FREEDOM OF SPEECH, and of the Eighth Amendment.

Violence against prisoners was commonplace. Prisoners were beaten with leather straps; forced to consume milk of magnesia; handcuffed to fences or cells for long periods in uncomfortable positions; made to stand, sit, or lie on crates or stumps for long periods; and shot at to force them to keep moving or remain standing. In one prison officials made inmates strip naked, hosed them down with water, and then turned a fan on them while they were naked and wet (*Gates v. Collier*, 501 F.2d 1291 [5th Cir. 1974]).

Jail and prison inmates also had to endure brutal living conditions. The Charles Street

Jail, in Boston, represented incarceration at its worst. Originally erected in 1848, Charles Street contained both pretrial detainees and convicts serving sentences of less than one year. The building was constructed of several tiers comprised of long rows of cells. The cells were made of four walls of stone: three of them solid, and one with two small openings. Both wall openings were barred, and in some cases also had screens covering them. There were no heat vents in the cells; the only heat came from a blower at either end of the tier. One inmate commented that in winter, rain puddles that formed on the floor turned to ice.

The cells were eight feet wide, eleven feet long, and ten feet high. Each contained two beds, a sliver of open floor space between the beds, approximately one foot of open floor space at the end of one bed, and a sink and a toilet at the end of the other bed. The beds consisted of two iron slats covered by an old, soiled mattress with no protective cover. The sinks had no hot water. Many of the toilets had no seats, and many either leaked or did not flush. These conditions attracted cockroaches, water bugs, and rats. The electrical system was antiquated and lacked a backup generator, so power outages were common.

In 1971 inmates of the jail, then known as the Suffolk County Jail, sued the Suffolk County sheriff, the Massachusetts commissioner of correction, the mayor of Boston, and nine city councillors. The inmates claimed that the conditions in the jail amounted to punishment, and, because the detainees were presumed innocent, the punishment violated the Due Process Clause of the FOURTEENTH AMENDMENT. The inmates further argued that the conditions constituted CRUEL AND UNUSUAL PUNISHMENT in violation of the Eighth Amendment. The federal district court in Massachusetts agreed, ruling that the conditions unnecessarily and unreasonably infringed on the most basic liberties of presumptively innocent citizens (*Inmates of Suffolk County Jail v. Eisenstadt*, 360 F. Supp. 676 [1973]).

The *Suffolk County* decision was followed by several rounds of litigation. More than twenty-five years after the original COMPLAINT was filed, the matter of the Charles Street Jail was not finished. The major obstacle to improving the conditions was double-bunking, or the practice of placing two prisoners in a cell originally intended for one. Ultimately, the court allowed double-bunking in some cells, in an order that is to become final on June 14, 1999.

The procedures leading to incarceration in jail or prison vary, but certain procedural fea-

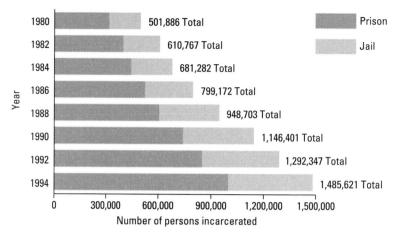

Incarcerated Population in the United States, 1980 to 1994

Year	Total
1980	501,886 Total
1982	610,767 Total
1984	681,282 Total
1986	799,172 Total
1988	948,703 Total
1990	1,146,401 Total
1992	1,292,347 Total
1994	1,485,621 Total

Prison / Jail

Number of persons incarcerated

Source: U.S. Bureau of Justice Statistics, *Correctional Populations in the United States.*

tures are common to all JURISDICTIONS. Many criminal defendants are released mere hours after being jailed if they agree to return for future proceedings. Other defendants are released after the first hearing before a judge, who orders them to return for future court dates. Still other defendants may be ordered by a judge to be held in jail until they pay a sum of money to secure their appearance at future proceedings. This sum of money is called bail. A defendant held on bail may obtain a release from jail by paying the full bail amount, or by paying a percentage of the bail amount to a licensed bail agent, who then pays the full amount to the court. If the defendant is unable to post bail, he or she is held in jail until the case is resolved.

A person confined to jail while awaiting trial is called a pretrial detainee. Where the crime alleged is particularly heinous, the judge may deny bail and order the defendant held until the case is resolved. Depending on the size and complexity of the case, a pretrial detainee may be confined in jail for several months, or sometimes even years.

Juveniles are usually held in separate facilities, called juvenile detention centers. However, not all states provide special facilities to keep minors separate from adults. Furthermore, if a juvenile is certified to stand trial as an adult, she or he may be transferred from the juvenile detention center to an adult detention facility. Also, if found guilty, a certified juvenile may be sentenced to adult prison.

If a criminal defendant is convicted, he or she may be sentenced to additional incarceration. Persons convicted of serious crimes are usually sentenced to at least one year in prison. For serious offenses an inmate may receive a prison sentence of several years to life (usually twenty years), or a life term without the possibility of PAROLE. For less serious offenses, the sentence may consist of continued confinement in jail or in a similar secure facility for up to one year. In most states a jail sentence does not exceed one year; other states allow jail sentences to last more than two years.

There are different levels of security within the jail and prison systems. Inmates in jail and prison are screened and then classified according to security concerns. For example, persons who present a danger to themselves or others may be placed in isolation under twenty-four-hour surveillance, and persons with infectious diseases may be quarantined in a separate cell block.

Most jurisdictions operate minimum-, medium-, and maximum-security prisons: security in these facilities ranges from relaxed to strict. The placement of a convict will depend on many factors, including the nature of the offense; perceived gang activity; and the defendant's personal and criminal history, sexual orientation, and physical and mental health. In some cases a judge may order a defendant to serve time at a specific prison.

The security measures in jail and prison vary. They include inspection of mail, searches of body cavities, searches of the inmate's cell, short-term placement in restraints, administration of psychotropic drugs if no alternative methods for security are available, limitations on the possession of personal effects, and placement in solitary confinement.

Daily life in jail and prison is strictly regulated. Physical contact visits are usually reserved for well-behaved inmates in minimum- and medium-security facilities. In most facilities inmates are not allowed to have physical contact with visitors. Visits are conducted through wire mesh, or through heavy glass by means of a telephone. Inmates are usually shackled at the hands and feet when they are moved from one part of the facility to another.

Federal and state laws address a minimum of issues concerning the operation of jails and prisons. Most legislatures and courts prefer to leave the matter of confinement to jail and prison administrators. Some prison administrators, or wardens, try to share political power with inmates to avoid prison violence and uprising. The general trend, however, is to limit PRISONERS' RIGHTS and freedoms. Sometimes lawmakers regulate the warden-inmate relationship with a law or ordinance. For example, some municipalities have overruled prison officials by passing laws that grant gay pretrial detainees the right to visit with their same-sex partners.

In most jurisdictions judges have a wide range of incarceration options. As an alternative to jail or prison, many states have created boot camps. These facilities emphasize hard work and physical conditioning. They are generally reserved for first-time offenders. The theory advanced for boot camps is REHABILITATION: they attempt to instill in inmates a sense of pride and capability. They also attempt to avoid turning youthful transgressors into experienced, hardened criminals by keeping them out of jail and prison, and therefore away from the influence of more serious offenders or career criminals.

Many states use home confinement as an alternative to institutional confinement. Home confinement allows a defendant to live at home and go to work while being monitored through an electronic bracelet. The bracelet is usually worn around the ankle, and detects the defendant's whereabouts at all times. If the defendant fails to comply with the conditions of the home confinement, the court may resentence the defendant to jail or prison.

Some states have halfway houses to help inmates reenter society after incarceration. These facilities are situated in communities. Their doors are not locked, but if an inmate fails to comply with the rules, she or he may be returned to jail or prison for the remainder of her or his sentence.

If a defendant needs drug or alcohol treatment, a judge may sentence the defendant to stay at a treatment center specializing in drug and ALCOHOL dependency. This is another alternative to incarceration in a correctional facility. If the defendant fails to comply with the rules of the treatment center or fails to remain sober, the judge may resentence the defendant to jail or prison.

Jail and prison can be more difficult for some inmates than others. Persons who are accused or convicted of sexual assault on a minor are often targets of violence. Youthful inmates are commonly raped. Short of requiring solitary confinement for all detainees and convicts, officials have found few solutions to the violence that occurs when accused and convicted criminals are grouped together in small spaces.

Incarceration may severely disrupt the equilibrium of mentally or physically ill persons. Jail and prison officials are not liable for the death or injury of an inmate because of lack of health care unless the staff exhibited deliberate indifference to the needs of the inmate. An inmate may be forced to take psychotropic drugs if the drugs are the least intrusive means available to control violent behavior.

Hunger strikes are common in jail and prison. Some inmates who participate in these strikes want to die, whereas others wish to call attention to a particular issue. The chief issue in these situations is whether officials may force-feed an inmate. In most cases courts uphold the right of the government to keep prisoners alive as being necessary to the effective administration of the criminal justice system. In other cases courts have not upheld that right. In Georgia, for example, a prisoner's right to PRIVACY includes the right to starve to death (*Zant v. Prevatte*, 248 Ga. 832, 286 S.E.2d 715 [1982]).

The United States imprisons more people per capita than any other country. In 1994 the number of persons incarcerated in U.S. prisons exceeded 1 million, and U.S. jails contained over 300,000 inmates. This was an incarceration rate of 373 out of every 100,000 U.S. citizens, up from 139 out of 100,000 in 1980. Over 60 percent of those incarcerated in federal facilities in 1994 were charged with drug-related offenses.

Many critics of the increase in incarceration argue that confinement serves only to "dehabilitate" convicts and breed more crime. According to these critics, incarceration too often turns individuals capable of rehabilitation into angry, vindictive persons. By the time many inmates are released from incarceration, they have been deprived of a means of self-support. Stripped of self-respect and resources, many ex-convicts find it nearly impossible to lead anything other than a life of crime and despair.

Other critics of wholesale incarceration point out that jail and prison inmates are disproportionately African American. In 1993 African American men between the ages of twenty and twenty-nine, who constitute four percent of the U.S. population, made up 50 percent of the total prison population.

Still other critics emphasize the unfairness reflected in the disparity between the tremendous number of drug offenders in jail and prison compared with the small number of white-collar criminals incarcerated. For example, in 1991 the FEDERAL COURTS sentenced more than fourteen thousand defendants to prison terms for drug offenses, compared with fewer than fifty-five hundred persons for FRAUD, EMBEZZLEMENT, and racketeering crimes.

Despite a growing number of critics, the majority of the general public in the United States is content to combat crime with incarceration. Although crime rates continue to rise with incarceration rates, the legislative trend is to build more jails and prisons and to increase the length of jail and prison terms.

See also JUVENILE LAW; SENTENCING.

INCEST 📖 The crime of sexual relations or MARRIAGE taking place between a male and female who are so closely linked by blood or AFFINITY that such activity is prohibited by law. 📖

Incest is a statutory crime, often classified as a FELONY. The purpose of incest statutes is to prevent sexual intercourse between individuals related within the degrees set forth, for the furtherance of the PUBLIC POLICY in favor of domestic peace. The prohibition of intermarriage is also based upon genetic considerations, since when excessive inbreeding takes place, undesirable recessive genes become expressed and genetic defects and disease are more readily perpetuated. In addition, the incest taboo is universal in human culture.

RAPE and incest are separate offenses and are distinguished by the fact that mutual consent is required for incest but not for rape. When the female is below the AGE OF CONSENT recognized by law, however, the same act can be both rape and incest.

The proscribed degrees of incest vary among the different statutes. Some include PARENT AND CHILD, brother and sister, uncle and niece, or aunt and nephew, and first cousins. In addition, intermarriage and sexual relations are also frequently prohibited among individuals who are related by half-blood, including brothers and sisters and uncles and nieces of the half-blood.

CORBIS-BETTMANN

The Roman emperor Domition (81–96), reportedly kept his niece as his mistress. Such a relationship was not considered incest under Roman law but came to be regarded as incestuous under the canon law of the Catholic church.

In a number of JURISDICTIONS, incest statutes extend to relationships among individuals related by affinity. Such statutes proscribe sexual relations between stepfathers and stepdaughters, stepmothers and stepsons, or brothers- and sisters-in-law, and such relations are punishable as incest. It is necessary for the relationship of affinity to exist at the time the intermarriage or sexual intercourse occurs in order for the act to constitute incest. In the event that the relationship has terminated prior to the time that the act takes place, the intermarriage or sexual intercourse is not regarded as incest.

Affinity ordinarily terminates upon the DIVORCE or death of the blood relation through whom the relationship was formed. Following the divorce or death of his spouse, it is not a violation of incest statutes for a man to marry or have sexual relations with his stepdaughter or his spouse's sister.

Certain statutes require that the individual accused of incest have knowledge of the relationship. In such cases, both parties need not be aware that their actions are incestuous in order for the party who does know to be convicted.

When intermarriage is prohibited by law, it need not be proved that sexual intercourse took place in order for a conviction to be sustained, since the offense is complete on intermarriage. In statutes that define incest as the intermarriage or CARNAL KNOWLEDGE of individuals within the prohibited degrees, incest can be committed either by intermarriage or sexual relations.

Some state laws provide that the crime of incest is not committed unless both parties consent to it. When the sexual relations at issue were accomplished by force, the act constitutes rape, and the individual accused cannot be convicted of incest.

It is no defense to incest that the woman had prior sexual relations or has a reputation for unchastity. Similarly, voluntary drunkenness, moral insanity, or an uncontrollable impulse are insufficient defenses.

Punishment for a conviction pursuant to an incest statute is determined by statute.

INCHOATE ▣ Imperfect; partial; unfinished; begun, but not completed; as in a contract not executed by all the parties. ▣

INCIDENTAL ▣ CONTINGENT upon or pertaining to something that is more important; that which is necessary, appertaining to, or depending upon another known as the principal. ▣

Under WORKERS' COMPENSATION statutes, a risk is deemed incidental to employment when it is related to whatever a worker must do in order to fulfill the employment CONTRACT, but is not the primary function that the worker was hired to do.

INCIDENT OF OWNERSHIP ▣ Some aspect of the exclusive possession or control over the disposition or use of property that demonstrates that the person with such exclusive rights has not relinquished them. ▣

A person who has kept the right to change the BENEFICIARIES on his or her life INSURANCE policy has retained an incident of ownership and is, therefore, considered the owner of the policy.

INCITE ▣ To arouse; urge; provoke; encourage; spur on; goad; stir up; instigate; set in motion; as in to *incite* a riot. Also, generally, in criminal law to instigate, persuade, or move another to commit a crime; in this sense nearly synonymous with *abet.* ▣

INCOME ▣ The return in money from one's business, labor, or capital invested; gains, profits, salary, wages, etc.

The gain derived from capital, from labor or effort, or both combined, including profit or gain through sale or conversion of capital. Income is not a gain accruing to capital or a growth in the value of the INVESTMENT, but is a profit, something of exchangeable value, proceeding from the property and being received or drawn by the recipient for separate use, benefit, and disposal. That which comes in or is received from any business, or investment of capital, without reference to outgoing expenditures. ▣

INCOME SPLITTING ▣ The right, created by provisions of federal tax laws, given to married couples who file joint returns to have their combined incomes subject to an INCOME TAX at a rate equal to that which would be imposed if each had filed a separate return for one-half the amount of their combined income. ▣

Income splitting was devised as a result of legislation enacted by Congress in 1948 to equalize the federal taxation of married couples who lived in common-law states and who paid higher taxes than couples who lived in COMMUNITY PROPERTY states and, as a result, have the tax benefits of income splitting.

INCOME TAX ▣ A charge imposed by government on the annual gains of a person, corporation, or other taxable unit derived through work, business pursuits, investments, property dealings, and other sources determined in accordance with the Internal Revenue Code or state law. ▣

Taxes have been called the building block of civilization. In fact, taxes existed in Sumer, the first organized society of record, where their payment carried great religious meaning. Taxes were also a fundamental part of ancient Greece and the Roman Empire. The religious aspect of taxation in Renaissance Italy is depicted in the Brancacci Chapel, in Florence. The fresco *Rendering of the Tribute Money* depicts the gods approving the Florentine income tax. In the United States, the federal tax laws are set forth in the INTERNAL REVENUE CODE and enforced by the INTERNAL REVENUE SERVICE (IRS).

History The origin of TAXATION in the United States can be traced to the time when the colonists were heavily taxed by Great Britain on everything from tea to legal and business documents that were required by the Stamp Tax. The colonists' disdain for this taxation without representation (so-called because the colonies had no voice in the establishment of the taxes) gave rise to revolts such as the Boston Tea Party. However, even after the Revolutionary War and the adoption of the U.S. Constitution, the main source of revenue for the newly created states was money received from customs and excise taxes on items such as carriages, sugar, whiskey, and snuff. Income tax first appeared in the United States in 1862, during the Civil War. At that time only about one percent of the population was required to pay the tax. A flat-rate income tax was imposed in 1867. The income tax was repealed in its entirety in 1872.

Income tax was a rallying point for the Populist party in 1892, and had enough support two years later that Congress passed the Income Tax Act of 1894. The tax at that time was two percent on individual incomes in excess of $4,000, which meant that it reached only the wealthiest members of the population. The Supreme Court struck down the tax, holding that it violated the constitutional requirement that DIRECT TAXES be apportioned among the states by population (*Pollock v. Farmers' Loan & Trust*, 158 U.S. 601, 15 S. Ct. 912, 39 L. Ed. 1108 [1895]). After many years of debate and compromise, the SIXTEENTH AMENDMENT to the Constitution was ratified in 1913, providing Congress with the power to lay and collect taxes on income without apportionment among the states. The objectives of the income tax were the equitable distribution of the tax burden and the raising of revenue.

Since 1913 the U.S. income tax system has become very complex. In 1913 the income tax laws were contained in eighteen pages of legislation; the explanation of the Tax Reform Act of 1986 was more than thirteen hundred pages long (Pub. L. 99-514, Oct. 22, 1986, 100 Stat. 2085). Commerce Clearing House, a publisher

of tax information, released a version of the Internal Revenue Code in the early 1990s that was four times thicker than its version in 1953.

Changes to the tax laws often reflect the times. The flat tax of 1913 was later replaced with a graduated tax. After the United States entered World War I, the War Revenue Act of 1917 imposed a maximum TAX RATE for individuals of 67 percent, compared with a rate of 13 percent in 1916. In 1924 Secretary of the Treasury Andrew W. Mellon, speaking to Congress about the high level of taxation, stated,

> The present system is a failure. It was an emergency measure, adopted under the pressure of war necessity and not to be counted upon as a permanent part of our revenue structure. . . . The high rates put pressure on taxpayers to reduce their taxable income, tend to destroy individual initiative and enterprise, and seriously impede the development of productive business. . . . Ways will always be found to avoid taxes so destructive in their nature, and the only way to save the situation is to put the taxes on a reasonable basis that will permit business to go on and industry to develop.

Consequently, the Revenue Act of 1924 reduced the maximum individual tax rate to 43 percent (Revenue Acts, June 2, 1924, ch. 234, 43 Stat. 253). In 1926 the rate was further reduced to 25 percent.

The Revenue Act of 1932 was the first tax law passed during the Great Depression (Revenue Acts, June 6, 1932, ch. 209, 47 Stat. 169). It increased the individual maximum rate from 25 to 63 percent, and reduced personal exemptions from $1,500 to $1,000 for single persons, and from $3,500 to $2,500 for married couples. The National Industrial Recovery Act of 1933 (NIRA), part of President FRANKLIN D. ROOSEVELT'S NEW DEAL, imposed a five percent excise tax on DIVIDEND receipts, imposed a CAPITAL STOCK tax and an excess profits tax, and suspended all DEDUCTIONS for losses (June 16, 1933, ch. 90, 48 Stat. 195). The repeal in 1933 of the EIGHTEENTH AMENDMENT, which had prohibited the manufacture and sale of ALCOHOL, brought in an estimated $90 million in new liquor taxes in 1934. The Social Security Act of 1935 provided for a wage tax, half to be paid by the employee and half by the employer, to establish a federal retirement fund (Old Age Pension Act, Aug. 14, 1935, ch. 531, 49 Stat. 620).

The Wealth Tax Act, also known as the Revenue Act of 1935, increased the maximum tax rate to 79 percent, the Revenue Acts of 1940 and 1941 increased it to 81 percent, the Revenue Act of 1942 raised it to 88 percent, and the Individual Income Tax Act of 1944 raised the individual maximum rate to 94 percent.

The post–World War II Revenue Act of 1945 reduced the individual maximum tax from 94 percent to 91 percent. The Revenue Act of 1950, during the Korean War, reduced it to 84.4 percent, but it was raised the next year to 92 percent (Revenue Act of 1950, Sept. 23, 1950, ch. 994, Stat. 906). It remained at this level until 1964, when it was reduced to 70 percent.

The Revenue Act of 1954 revised the Internal Revenue Code of 1939, making major changes that were beneficial to the taxpayer, including providing for child care deductions (later changed to credits), an increase in the charitable contribution limit, a tax credit against taxable retirement income, employee deductions for business expenses, and liberalized DEPRECIATION deductions. From 1954 to 1962, the Internal Revenue Code was amended by 183 separate acts.

In 1974 the EMPLOYEE RETIREMENT INCOME SECURITY ACT (ERISA) created protections for employees whose employers promised specified PENSIONS or other retirement contributions (Pub. L. No. 93-406, Sept. 2, 1974, 88 Stat. 829). ERISA required that to be tax deductible, the employer's plan contribution must meet certain minimum standards as to employee participation and vesting and employer funding. ERISA also approved the use of INDIVIDUAL RETIREMENT ACCOUNTS (IRAs) to encourage tax-deferred retirement savings by individuals.

The Economic Recovery Tax Act of 1981 (ERTA) provided the largest tax cut up to that time, reducing the maximum individual rate from 70 percent to 50 percent (Pub. L. No. 97-34, Aug. 13, 1981, 95 Stat. 172). The most sweeping tax changes since World War II were enacted in the TAX REFORM ACT OF 1986. This bill was signed into law by President RONALD REAGAN and was designed to equalize the tax treatment of various assets, eliminate tax shelters, and lower marginal rates. Conservatives wanted the act to provide a single, low tax rate that could be applied to everyone. Although this single, flat rate was not included in the final bill, tax rates were reduced to 15 percent on the first $17,850 of income for singles and $29,750 for married couples, and set at 28 to 33 percent on remaining income. Many deductions were repealed, such as a deduction available to two-income married couples that had been used to avoid the "marriage penalty" (a greater tax liability incurred when two persons filed their income tax return as a married couple rather than as individuals). Although the personal exemption exclusion was increased, an exemption for elderly and blind persons who itemize deductions was repealed. In addition, a special capital gains rate was repealed, as was an investment tax credit that had been introduced in 1962 by President JOHN F. KENNEDY.

The Omnibus Budget Reconciliation Act of 1993, the first budget and tax act enacted during the Clinton administration, was vigorously debated, and passed with only the minimum number of necessary votes (Pub. L. No. 103-66, Aug. 10, 1993, 107 Stat. 312). This law provides for income tax rates of 15, 28, 31, 36, and 39.6 percent on varying levels of income and for the taxation of SOCIAL SECURITY income if the taxpayer receives other income over a certain level.

Since the early 1980s, a flat-rate tax system rather than the graduated bracketed method has been proposed. (The graduated bracketed method is the one that has been used since GRADUATED TAXES were introduced: the percentage of tax differs based on the amount of taxable income.) The flat-rate system would impose one rate, such as 20 percent, on all income and would eliminate special deductions, credits, and exclusions. Despite firm support by some, the flat-rate tax has not been adopted in the United States.

Computation of Income Tax Regardless of the changes made by legislators since 1913, the basic formula for computing the amount of tax owed has remained basically the same. To determine the amount of income tax owed, certain deductions are taken from an individual's GROSS INCOME to arrive at an ADJUSTED GROSS INCOME, from which additional deductions are taken to arrive at the taxable income. Once the amount of taxable income has been determined, tax rate charts determine the exact amount of tax owed. If the amount of tax owed is less than the amount already paid through tax prepayment or the withholding of taxes from paychecks, the taxpayer is entitled to a refund from the IRS. If the amount of tax owed is more than what has already been paid, the taxpayer must pay the difference to the IRS.

Gross Income The first step in computing the amount of tax liability is the determination of gross income. Gross income is defined as "all income from whatever source derived," whether from personal services, business activities, or CAPITAL ASSETS (property owned for personal or business purposes). Compensation for services in the form of money, wages, tips, salaries, bonuses, fees, and commissions constitutes income. Problems in defining income of-

Individual Income Taxes Collected, 1980 to 1993

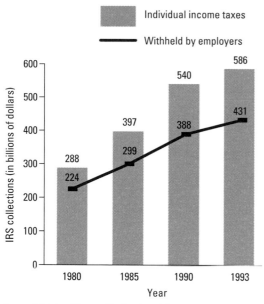

Source: U.S. Internal Revenue Service, *Annual Report.*

ten arise when a taxpayer realizes a benefit or compensation that is not in the form of money.

An example of such compensation is the fringe benefits an employee receives from an employer. The Internal Revenue Code defines these benefits as income and places the burden on the employee to demonstrate why they should be excluded from gross income. Discounts on the employer's products and other items of minimal value to the employer are usually not considered income to the employee. These benefits (which include airline tickets at nominal cost for airline employees and merchandise discounts for department store employees) are usually of great value to the employee but do not cost much for the employer to provide, and build good relationships between the employee and the employer. As long as the value to the employer is small and the benefit generates goodwill, it usually is not deemed to be taxable to the employee.

The value of meals and lodging provided to an employee and paid for by an employer is not considered income to the employee if the meals and lodging are furnished on the business premises of the employer for the employer's convenience (as when an apartment building owner provides a rent-free apartment for a caretaker who is required to live on the premises). However, a cash allowance for meals or lodging that is given to an employee as part of a compensation package is considered compensation, and is counted as gross income. An employer's pay-

ment for a health club membership is also included in gross income, as are payments to an employee in the form of stock. An amount contributed by an employer to a pension, qualified stock bonus, profit-sharing, ANNUITY, or bond purchase plan in which the employee participates is not considered income to the employee at the time the contribution is made, but will be taxed when the employee receives payment from the plan. Medical insurance premiums paid by an employer are generally not considered income to the employee. Although military pay is taxable income, veterans' benefits for education, disability and pension payments, and veterans' insurance proceeds and dividends are not included in gross income.

Other sources of income directly increase the wealth of the taxpayer and are taxable. These sources commonly include interest earned on bank accounts; dividends; rents; ROYALTIES from COPYRIGHTS, TRADEMARKS, and PATENTS; proceeds from life insurance if paid for a reason other than the death of the insured; annuities; discharge from the obligation to pay a DEBT owed (the amount discharged is considered income to the debtor); recovery of a previously deductible item, which gives rise to income only to the extent the previous deduction produced a tax benefit (this is commonly referred to as the tax benefit rule and is most often used when a taxpayer has recovered a previously deducted bad debt or previously deducted taxes); gambling winnings; lottery winnings; found property; and income from illegal sources. Income from prizes and awards is taxable unless the prize or award is made primarily in recognition of religious, charitable, scientific, educational, artistic, literary, or civic achievement; the recipient was chosen, without any action on his or her part, to enter the selection process; and the recipient is not required to render substantial future services as a condition to receiving the prize or award. For example, recipients of Nobel Prizes meet these criteria and are not taxed on the prize money they receive.

In some situations a taxpayer's wealth directly increases through income that is not included in the determination of income tax. For example, gifts and inheritances are excluded from income in order to encourage the transfer of assets within families. However, any income realized from a GIFT or INHERITANCE is considered income to the beneficiary—most notably rents, interest, and dividends. In addition, most scholarships, fellowships, student loans, and other forms of financial aid for education are not included in gross income, perhaps to equalize the status of students whose education is funded by a gift or inheritance and of students who do not have the benefit of such assistance. Cash REBATES to consumers from product manufacturers and most state UNEMPLOYMENT COMPENSATION benefits are also not included in gross income.

Capital gains and losses pose special considerations in the determination of income tax liability. Capital gains are the profits realized as a result of the sale or exchange of a capital asset. Capital losses are the deficits realized in such transactions. Capital gains and losses are determined by establishing a taxpayer's BASIS in the property. Basis is generally defined as the taxpayer's cost of acquiring the property. In the case of property received as a gift, the donee basically steps into the shoes of the donor and is deemed to have the same basis in the property as did the donor.

The basis is subtracted from the amount realized by the sale or other disposition of the property, and the difference is either a gain or a loss to the taxpayer.

Capital gains are usually included in gross income, with certain narrow exclusions, and capital losses are generally excluded from gross income. An important exception to this favorable treatment of capital losses occurs when the loss arises from the sale or other disposition of property held by the taxpayer for personal use, such as a personal residence or jewelry. When a capital gain is realized from the disposition of property held for personal use, it is included as income even though a capital loss involving the same property cannot be excluded from income. This apparent discrepancy is further magnified by the fact that capital losses on business or investment property can be excluded from income. Consequently, there have been many lawsuits over the issue of whether a personal residence, used at some point as rental property or for some other income producing use, is deemed personal or business property for income tax purposes.

Taxpayers age fifty-five or older who sell a personal residence in which they have resided for a specific amount of time can exclude their capital gains. This is a one-time exclusion, with specific dollar limits. Consequently, if future, greater gains are anticipated, a taxpayer age fifty-five or older may choose to pay the capital gains tax on a transaction that qualifies for the exclusion but produces smaller capital gains.

Even though a capital gain on a personal residence is realized, it may be temporarily deferred from inclusion in gross income if the taxpayer buys and occupies another home two years before or after the sale, and the new home costs the same as or more than the old home. The gain is merely postponed. This type of transaction is called a rollover. The gain that is not taxed in the year of sale will be deducted from the cost of the new home, thereby establishing a basis in the property that is less than the price paid for the home. When the new home is later sold, the amount of gain recognized at that time will include the gain that was not recognized when the home was purchased by the taxpayer.

Deductions and Adjusted Gross Income
Once the amount of gross income is determined, the taxpayer may take deductions from the income in order to determine adjusted gross income. Two categories of deductions are allowed. Above-the-line deductions are taken in full from gross income to arrive at adjusted gross income. Below-the-line, or itemized, deductions are taken from adjusted gross income and are allowed only to the extent that their combined amount exceeds a certain threshold amount. If the total amount of ITEMIZED DEDUCTIONS does not meet the threshold amount, those deductions are not allowed. Generally, above-the-line deductions are business expenditures, and below-the-line deductions are personal, or nonbusiness, expenditures.

The favorable tax treatment afforded business and investment property is also evident in the treatment of business and investment expenses. Ordinary and necessary expenses are those incurred in connection with a trade or business. Ordinary and necessary business expenses are those that others engaged in the same type of business incur in similar circumstances. With regard to deductions for expenses incurred for investment property, courts follow the same type of "ordinary-and-necessary" analysis used for business expense deductions, and disallow the deductions if they are personal in nature or are capital expenses. Allowable business expenses include insurance, rent, supplies, travel, transportation, salary payments to employees, certain losses, and most state and local taxes.

Personal, or nonbusiness, expenses are generally not deductible. Exceptions to this rule include CASUALTY and THEFT losses that are not covered by insurance. Certain expenses are allowed as itemized deductions. These below-the-line deductions include expenses for medical treatment, interest on home MORTGAGES, state income taxes, and charitable contributions. Expenses incurred for tax advice are deductible from federal income tax, as are a wide array of state and local taxes. In addition, an employee who incurs business expenses may deduct those expenses to the extent they are not reimbursed by the employer. Typical unreimbursed expenses that are deductible by employees include union dues and payments for mandatory uniforms. ALIMONY payments may be taken as a deduction by the payer and are deemed to be income to the recipient; however, CHILD SUPPORT payments are not deemed income to the parent who has custody of the child and are not deductible by the paying parent.

Contributions made by employees to an individual retirement account (IRA) or by self-employed persons to KEOGH PLANS are deductible from gross income. Allowable annual deductions for contributions to an IRA are lower than allowable contributions to a Keogh account. Contributions beyond the allowable deduction are permitted; however, amounts in excess are included in gross income. Both IRAs and Keogh plans create tax-sheltered retirement funds that are not taxed as gross income during the taxpayer's working years. The contributions and the interest earned on them become taxable when they are distributed to the taxpayer. Distribution may take place when the taxpayer is fifty-nine and one-half years old, or earlier if the taxpayer becomes disabled, at which time the taxpayer will most likely be in a lower tax bracket. Distribution may take place before either of these occurrences, but if so, the funds are taxable immediately and the taxpayer may also incur a substantial penalty for early withdrawal of the money.

Additional Deductions and Taxable Income Once adjusted gross income is determined, a taxpayer must determine whether to use the STANDARD DEDUCTION or to itemize deductions. In most cases the standard deduction is used because it is the most convenient option. However, if the amount of itemized deductions is substantially more than the standard deduction and exceeds the threshold amount, a taxpayer will receive a greater tax benefit by itemizing.

After the standard deduction or itemized deductions are subtracted from adjusted gross income, the income amount is further reduced by personal and dependency exemptions. Each taxpayer is allowed one personal exemption. A taxpayer may also claim a dependency exemption for each person who meets five specific criteria: the dependent must have a familial relationship with the taxpayer; have a gross income that is less than the amount of the deduction, unless she or he is under nineteen years old or a full-time student; receive more than one-half of her or his support from the taxpayer; be a citizen or resident of the United States, Mexico, or Canada; and, if married, be unable to file a joint return with her or his spouse. Each exemption is valued at a certain dollar amount, by which the taxpayer's taxable income is reduced.

Tax Tables and Tax Owed Once the final deductions and exemptions are taken, the resulting figure is the taxpayer's taxable income. The tax owed on this income is determined by looking at applicable tax tables. This figure may be reduced by tax prepayments or by an applicable tax credit. Credits are available for contributions made to candidates for public office; child and dependent care; EARNED INCOME; taxes paid in another country; and residential energy. For each dollar of available credit, a taxpayer's liability is reduced by one dollar.

Refund or Tax Owed Finally, after tax prepayments and credits are subtracted, the amount of tax owed the IRS or the amount of refund owed the taxpayer is determined. The taxpayer's TAX RETURN and payment of tax owed must be mailed to the IRS by April 15 unless an extension is sought. Taxpayers who make late payments without seeking an extension will be charged interest on the amount due and may be charged a penalty. A tax refund may be requested for up to several years after the tax return is filed. A refund is owed usually because the taxpayer had more tax than necessary withheld from his or her paychecks.

Tax Audits The IRS may AUDIT a taxpayer to verify that the taxpayer correctly reported income, exemptions, or deductions on the return. The majority of returns that are audited are chosen by computer, which selects those that have the highest probability of error. Returns may also be randomly selected for audit or may be chosen because of previous investigations of a taxpayer for TAX EVASION or for involvement in an activity that is under investigation by the IRS. Taxpayers may represent themselves at an audit, or may have an attorney, certified public accountant, or the person who prepared the return accompany them. The taxpayer will be told what items to bring to the audit in order to answer the questions raised. If additional tax is found to be owed and the taxpayer disagrees, she or he may request an immediate meeting with a supervisor. If the supervisor supports the audit findings, the taxpayer may appeal the decision to a higher level within the IRS or may take the case directly to court.

CROSS-REFERENCES

Pollock v. Farmers' Loan and Trust Co.; Tax Avoidance; Tax Court; Taxpayer Bill of Rights.

IN COMMON 📖 Shared in respect to title, use, or enjoyment; without apportionment or division into individual parts. Held by several for the equal advantage, use, or enjoyment of all. 📖

A TENANCY IN COMMON is ownership of REAL PROPERTY by two or more persons, each of whom holds an undivided interest in such property.

INCOMPATIBILITY 📖 The inability of a HUSBAND AND WIFE to cohabit in a marital relationship. 📖

INCOMPETENCY 📖 The lack of ability, knowledge, legal qualification, or fitness to discharge a required duty or professional obligation. 📖

The term *incompetency* has several meanings in the law. When it is used to describe the mental condition of a person subject to LEGAL PROCEEDINGS, it means the person is neither able to comprehend the nature and consequences of the proceedings nor able adequately to help an attorney with his defense. When it is used to describe the legal qualification of a person, it means the person does not have the legal CAPACITY to enter a contract. When it is employed to describe a professional duty or obligation, it means that the person has demonstrated a lack of ability to perform professional functions.

Mental Incompetency A person who is diagnosed as being mentally ill, mentally retarded, senile, or suffering from some other debility that prevents him from managing his own affairs may be declared mentally incompetent by a court of law. When a person is adjudged incompetent, a GUARDIAN is appointed to handle the person's property and personal affairs.

The legal procedure for declaring a person incompetent consists of three steps: (1) a motion for a competency HEARING, (2) a psychiatric or psychological evaluation, and (3) a competency hearing. Probate courts usually handle competency proceedings, which guarantee the allegedly incompetent person DUE PROCESS OF LAW.

In CRIMINAL LAW a defendant's mental competency may be questioned out of concern for the defendant's welfare or for strategic legal reasons. The prosecution may raise the issue as a preventive measure or to detain the defendant so that a weak case can be built into a stronger one. The defense may also request a competency hearing so that it can gather information to use in PLEA BARGAINING, to mitigate a sentence, or to prepare for a potential INSANITY DEFENSE.

A motion for a competency hearing must be made before SENTENCING takes place. In FEDERAL COURT a MOTION for a hearing will be granted "if there is a reasonable cause to believe that the defendant may be suffering from a mental disease or defect rendering him mentally incompetent" (18 U.S.C.A. § 4241 (a)). A psychiatric or psychological evaluation is then conducted, and a hearing is held on the matter. If the court finds that the defendant is incompetent, the defendant will be hospitalized for a reasonable period of time, usually no more than four months. The goal is to determine whether the defendant's competence can be restored.

This type of mental commitment is authorized by the U.S. Supreme Court only for defendants who "probably soon will be able to stand trial" (*Jackson v. Indiana*, 406 U.S. 715, 92 S. Ct. 1845, 32 L. Ed. 2d 435 [1972]). The possibility that a defendant committed a serious crime does not warrant an extended commitment period, because that would violate the defendant's due process rights.

At the end of a four-month commitment, if it appears that the defendant's competence can be restored but more time is needed to do so, the defendant may be hospitalized for an additional thirty days to eighteen months. If a hospital director certifies that the defendant's competence has been restored, the court holds another hearing. If the court agrees the defendant is COMPETENT, he is released and a criminal trial date is set. Such a competency ruling cannot be used as evidence against the defendant if he later pleads insanity as a defense in the criminal trial. (An insanity defense refers to the defendant's inability to know or appreciate right from wrong at the time of the alleged crime.)

State criminal competency proceedings have been shaped by the *Jackson* decision. Generally, under eighteen months is an acceptable period of time for a state to attempt to treat an incompetent person accused of a crime. Of the fifty states, Maine has the shortest limitation, at thirty days, and California has the longest, at eighteen months.

The *Jackson* ruling also specified that "treatment must stop if there is no substantial probability that the defendant will regain trial competence in the near future." If that decision is reached, the defendant can continue to be detained only if he is declared permanently incompetent in a civil commitment proceeding.

Legal Incapacity CIVIL LAW requires a person to be legally competent in order to enter a CONTRACT, sign a WILL, or make some other type of binding legal commitment. A person may be adjudged incompetent by virtue of age or mental condition.

In contract law a person who agrees to a transaction possesses complete legal capacity to become liable for duties under the contract unless she is legally incompetent. A person under the age of eighteen or twenty-one (depending on the JURISDICTION) can avoid the legal duty to perform the terms of a contract she signed without any LIABILITY for breach of contract. PUBLIC POLICY deems it desirable to protect an immature person from liability for unfair contracts that she is too inexperienced to negotiate on equal terms with the other party.

If a party does not comprehend the nature and consequences of the contract when it is formed, she is regarded as having mental incapacity. A distinction must be made between persons who have been adjudicated incompetent by a court and had a guardian appointed, and persons who are mentally incompetent but have not been so adjudicated. A person who has been declared incompetent in a court proceeding lacks the legal capacity to enter into a contract with another. Such a person is unable to consent to a contract, since the court has determined that she does not understand the obligations and effects of a contract. A contract made by such a person is VOID and without any legal effect. If there has been no adjudication of mental incompetency, a contract made by a mentally incapacitated individual is VOIDABLE by her. This means that the person can legally declare the contract void, making it unenforceable. However, a voidable contract can be ratified by the incompetent person if the person recovers the capacity to contract.

Contract law also holds that a contract made by an intoxicated person is voidable, as the person was incompetent at the time the contract was formed.

A marriage contract may be annulled if one of the parties was legally incompetent. Grounds for incompetency include age (under the AGE OF MAJORITY), mental incompetence such as insanity, and a preexisting marriage.

A person who executes a will must be legally competent. The traditional recital in a will states that the testator is of "sound mind." This language attempts to establish the competency of the testator, but the issue may be challenged when the will is probated.

Professional Obligation Lawyers, doctors, teachers, and other persons who belong to a profession are bound either by professional codes of conduct or by contracts that contain standards of conduct. A professional person who fails to meet the duties required of that profession may be adjudged incompetent. Such a ruling by a court, a professional disciplinary board, or an employer may result in professional discipline, including loss of a LICENSE to practice, demotion, or termination of employment.

INCOMPETENT EVIDENCE Probative matter that is not ADMISSIBLE in a legal proceeding; EVIDENCE that is not admissible under the Federal Rules of Evidence. That which the law does not allow to be presented at all, or in connection with a particular matter, due to lack of originality, a defect in the witness or the document, or due to the nature of the evidence in and of itself.

INCONSISTENT Reciprocally contradictory or repugnant.

Things are said to be inconsistent when they are contrary to each other to the extent that one implies the negation of the other. For example, a city ordinance might be inconsistent with a state statute; or two defenses to a crime, such as the defenses of alibi and SELF-DEFENSE, are inconsistent.

INCONTESTABILITY CLAUSE A provision in a life or health INSURANCE policy that precludes the insurer from alleging that the POLICY, after it has been in effect for a stated period (typically two or three years), is VOID because of MISREPRESENTATIONS made by the insured in the application for it.

An incontestability clause prevents an insurer from denying benefits on the ground of misrepresentation in the application. The clause applies only when the policy has been in effect for a specified period of time. This time period, the contestability period, is usually two or three years.

Most states maintain statutes that require an incontestability clause in life and health insurance CONTRACTS. The incontestability clause strikes a balance between providing predictable coverage and protecting the right of insurers to select the precise risks they seek to insure.

Most incontestability clauses are limited by a provision stating that the contestability period must be completed within the lifetime of the insured. With this nuance the insurer is able to contest a claim for benefits after the contestability period has lapsed if the insured dies before the end of that period. This protects insurers from providing benefits to someone who was already so ill at the inception of the policy that he or she died less than two years later. It means that the insurer may contest the flow of insurance benefits to the insured's HEIRS.

Another common caveat to incontestability clauses limits the period of DISABILITY. Under this provision any disability that begins prior to the expiration of the contestability period will toll the period. In other words, if an insured becomes physically disabled before the end of the contestability period, the clock stops ticking and the insurer may challenge claims during the illness and beyond. Without such language, an insured could always avoid contestability by waiting until the contestability period has expired before filing a claim.

Finally, some incontestability clauses contain a FRAUD exception. Such a clause might read, "After two years from the date of issue of this policy, only fraudulent misstatements made by the applicant may be used to void the policy or deny a claim that commences after the expiration of the two-year period." Generally, fraud is a false representation calculated to deceive another into acting against her or his legal interest. Statements that are inaccurate but made without the intent to deceive are not fraudulent.

The difference between fraud and simple misstatement can only be found in the facts of a particular case. In *Paul Revere Life Insurance Co. v. Haas*, 137 N.J. 190, 644 A.2d 1098 (1994), the Paul Revere Company brought an ACTION against Gilbert K. Haas, when it discovered that Haas had made false statements in his insurance application. Haas had received a policy on March 5, 1987, and on December 1, 1990, started a claim for disability payments related to a progressive eye disease. The company sought to RESCIND the policy or to secure a DECLARATORY JUDGMENT from the court that the policy did not cover Haas's disease.

The New Jersey law on incontestability clauses gave insurers two options: one reserving contestability in case of fraud, the other reserving contestability if the insured became disabled within the contestability period (N.J. Stat. Ann. § 17B:26-5 [West]). The Paul Revere Company chose to bring action under the disability provision.

The facts indicated that Haas had made false statements on his policy application. He had declared that he had not had "any surgical operation, treatment, special diet, or any illness, ailment, abnormality, or injury . . . within the past five years." Investigations by the insurance company revealed that Haas had been diagnosed and treated for retinitis pigmentosa as much as four years prior to applying for the policy. According to the New Jersey Supreme Court, neither incontestability option mandated in section 17:B-26-5 of the New Jersey Statutes Annotated could be construed to allow coverage for disabilities that an insured knew existed but concealed on the policy application.

The court held that Haas's policy continued in effect because the insurer had not proved its case under the disability provision, but that the incontestability clause did not prevent the insurer from contesting Haas's claims under the fraud provision.

INCORPORATE To formally create a CORPORATION pursuant to the requirements prescribed by state statute; to confer a corporate FRANCHISE upon certain individuals.

INCORPORATION BY REFERENCE The method of making one DOCUMENT of any kind become a part of another separate document by alluding to the former in the latter and declaring that the former shall be taken and considered as a part of the latter the same as if it were completely set out therein.

It is common drafting practice to incorporate by reference an existing writing into a PLEADING, contract, or other legal document in order to save space. The incorporating document, rather than copying the exact words of the existing document, describes it, and a photocopy is often attached to the incorporating document. This standard practice, however, encounters difficulty with the requirements prescribed by law for a WILL. If the will is a HOLOGRAPH—a document disposing of property that is written with one's own hand and not witnessed—the attachment might not be in the handwriting of the deceased and, therefore, invalid. If the will is formal, an attachment might violate the requirement that the TESTATOR (one who makes a will) or the witnesses SUBSCRIBE (sign at the end of the will) the attachment. If subscription is not required, the incorporated document raises the question whether the testator has declared it to be a part of the will if it was not present at the time the will was signed.

The document that is incorporated is usually not treated as a part of the will itself but as an external source from which the meaning of the will can be determined. This maintains the distinction between actual incorporation, an integration achieved by extensive copying of a document into the pages that constitute the will, and incorporation by reference, which is a figurative rather than literal integration. Incorporation by reference is treated as if it were actually integrated.

Fear of FRAUDULENT substitutions is probably the basis for the legal insistence upon compliance with certain conditions in order to incorporate a document into a will by reference. Certain requirements exist for incorporation by reference into a will. The document to be incorporated must exist at the time the will is executed. The will must manifest the intention of the testator to incorporate the provisions of the incorporated document. The incorporated document must be sufficiently described to permit its identification. Some courts emphasize that the incorporated document comply with the description. Some, but not all, statutes require that the incorporating document refer to the incorporated document as being in existence in addition to the requirement mentioned earlier that it actually be in existence.

Most states presently allow incorporation by reference into wills upon compliance with the foregoing conditions. In the states that permit holographic wills, most allow the incorporation by reference of nonholographic material, even if actual incorporation would otherwise invalidate the will because it is not entirely in the handwriting of the deceased.

INCORPORATION DOCTRINE 📖 A constitutional doctrine whereby selected provisions of the BILL OF RIGHTS are made applicable to the states through the Due Process Clause of the FOURTEENTH AMENDMENT. 📖

The doctrine of selective incorporation, or simply the incorporation doctrine, makes the first ten amendments to the Constitution—known as the Bill of Rights—binding on the states. Through incorporation, state governments are held to largely the same standards as the federal government with regard to many constitutional rights, including the FIRST AMENDMENT freedoms of speech, religion, and assembly, and the separation of church and state; the FOURTH AMENDMENT freedoms from unwarranted arrest and unreasonable SEARCHES AND SEIZURES; the FIFTH AMENDMENT privilege against SELF-INCRIMINATION; and the SIXTH AMENDMENT right to a speedy, fair, and public trial. Some provisions of the Bill of Rights—including the requirement of INDICTMENT by a GRAND JURY (SIXTH AMENDMENT) and the right to a JURY trial in civil cases (SEVENTH AMENDMENT)—have not been applied to the states through the incorporation doctrine.

Until the early twentieth century, the Bill of Rights was interpreted as applying only to the federal government. In the 1833 case *Barron ex rel. Tiernon v. Mayor of Baltimore*, 32 U.S. (7 Pet.) 243, 8 L. Ed. 672, the Supreme Court expressly limited application of the Bill of Rights to the federal government. By the mid–nineteenth century, this view was being challenged. For example, Republicans who were opposed to southern state laws that made it a crime to speak and publish against SLAVERY

alleged that such laws violated First Amendment rights regarding FREEDOM OF SPEECH and FREEDOM OF THE PRESS.

For a brief time following the ratification of the Fourteenth Amendment in 1868, it appeared that the Supreme Court might use the Privileges and Immunities Clause of the Fourteenth Amendment to apply the Bill of Rights to the states. However, in the *Slaughter-House* cases, 83 U.S. (16 Wall.) 36, 21 L. Ed. 394 (1873), the first significant Supreme Court ruling on the Fourteenth Amendment, the Court handed down an extremely limiting interpretation of that clause. The Court held that the clause created a distinction between rights associated with state citizenship and rights associated with U.S., or federal, citizenship. It concluded that the Fourteenth Amendment prohibited states from passing laws abridging the rights of U.S. citizenship (which, it implied, were few in number) but had no authority over laws abridging the rights of state citizenship. The effect of this ruling was to put much state legislation beyond the review of the Supreme Court.

Instead of applying the Bill of Rights as a whole to the states, as it might have done through the Privileges and Immunities Clause, the Supreme Court has gradually applied selected elements of the first ten amendments to the states through the Due Process Clause of the Fourteenth Amendment. This process, known as selective incorporation, began in earnest in the 1920s. In *Gitlow v. New York*, 268 U.S. 652, 45 S. Ct. 625, 69 L. Ed. 1138 (1925), one of the earliest examples of the use of the incorporation doctrine, the Court held that the First Amendment protection of freedom of speech applied to the states through the Due Process Clause. By the late 1940s, many civil freedoms, including freedom of the press (*Near v. Minnesota*, 283 U.S. 697, 51 S. Ct. 625, 75 L. Ed. 1357 [1931]), had been incorporated into the Fourteenth Amendment, as had many of the rights that applied to defendants in criminal cases, including the right to representation by counsel in capital cases (*Powell v. Alabama*, 287 U.S. 45, 53 S. Ct. 55, 77 L. Ed. 158 [1931]). In 1937 the Court decided that some of the PRIVILEGES AND IMMUNITIES of the Bill of Rights were so fundamental that states were required to abide by them through the Due Process Clause (*Palko v. Connecticut*, 302 U.S. 319, 58 S. Ct. 149, 82 L. Ed. 288).

In a 1947 dissent, Justice HUGO L. BLACK argued that the Fourteenth Amendment incorporated all aspects of the Bill of Rights and applied them to the states, but this view did not prevail (*Adamson v. People of the State of California*, 332 U.S. 46, 67 S. Ct. 1672, 91 L. Ed. 1903). The Court has continued to incorporate elements of the Bill of Rights selectively.

CROSS-REFERENCES

Due Process of Law; *Gitlow v. New York*; *Powell v. Alabama*; *Slaughter-House* Cases.

INCORPOREAL   Lacking a physical or material nature but relating to or affecting a body.

Under COMMON LAW, incorporeal property were rights that affected a TANGIBLE item, such as a CHOSE IN ACTION (a right to enforce a debt).

Incorporeal is the opposite of CORPOREAL, a description of the existence of a tangible item.

INCREMENTAL   Additional or increased growth, bulk, quantity, number, or value; enlarged.

Incremental cost is additional or increased cost of an item or service apart from its actual cost. When applied to the price of GAS, the incremental cost includes the actual cost of gas to the distributors plus the expenses incurred in its transportation as well as any taxes imposed upon it.

INCRIMINATE   To charge with a crime; to expose to an accusation or a charge of crime; to involve oneself or another in a criminal prosecution or the danger thereof; as in the rule that a WITNESS is not bound to give TESTIMONY that would tend to incriminate him or her.

INCULPATE   To accuse; to involve in blame or guilt.

When an individual who has committed a crime imputes guilt upon another individual, he or she is thereby inculpating such individual.

INCUMBENT   An individual who is in current possession of a particular office and who is legally authorized to discharge the duties of that office.

INCUR   To become subject to and liable for; to have liabilities imposed by act or OPERATION OF LAW.

Expenses are incurred, for example, when the legal obligation to pay them arises. An individual incurs a LIABILITY when a money JUDGMENT is rendered against him or her by a court.

INDEFEASIBLE   That which cannot be defeated, revoked, or made void. This term is usually applied to an ESTATE or right that cannot be defeated.

INDEFINITE TERM   A prison SENTENCE for a specifically designated length of time up to a certain prescribed maximum, such as one to ten years or twenty-five years to life.

INDEMNIFY   To compensate for loss or damage; to provide SECURITY for financial reimbursement to an individual in case of a specified loss incurred by the person.

INSURANCE companies indemnify their policyholders against damage caused by such things as fire, theft, and flooding, which are specified by the terms of the contract between the company and the insured.

INDEMNITY   Recompense for loss, damage, or injuries; RESTITUTION or reimbursement.

An *indemnity* CONTRACT arises when one individual takes on the obligation to pay for any loss or damage that has been or might be incurred by another individual. The *right to indemnity* and the *duty to indemnify* ordinarily stem from a contractual agreement, which generally protects against liability, loss, or damage. See also DAMAGES.

INDENTURE   The term *indenture*, which primarily describes financial contracts, has several applications in U.S. law. At its simplest, an indenture is an agreement that declares benefits and obligations between two or more parties. In BANKRUPTCY law, for example, it is a MORTGAGE or DEED OF TRUST that constitutes a claim against a DEBTOR. The most common usage of indenture appears in the bond market. Before a BOND is issued, the issuer executes a legally binding indenture governing all the bond's terms. Finally, the concept of indenture has an ignominious place in the history of U.S. labor. Indentured servants of the seventeenth and eighteenth centuries were commonly European workers who contracted to provide labor for a number of years and in return received passage to the American colonies as well as room and board.

An INVESTMENT product that is used to raise capital, a bond is simply a written document by which a government, CORPORATION, or individual promises to pay a definite sum of money on a certain date. The issuer of a bond, in cooperation with an underwriter (a financial organization that sells the bond to the public), prepares in advance an indenture outlining the terms of the bond. The issuer and the underwriter negotiate provisions such as the interest rate, the maturity date, and any restrictions on the issuer's actions. The last detail is especially important to corporate bonds, because corporations accrue liability upon becoming bond issuers and therefore seek to have the fewest possible restrictions placed on their business behavior by the terms of the indenture. As a consequence, potential buyers of corporate bonds should know what the indenture specifies before buying.

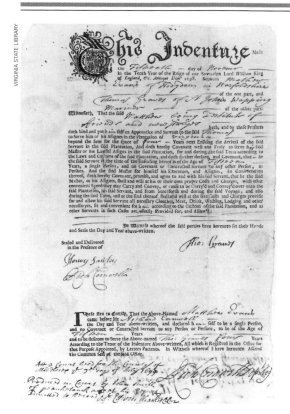

In the seventeenth and eighteenth centuries thousands of people emigrated to the American colonies to serve out contracts of indenture. This contract is for a fifteen-year-old named Matthew Evans from Harfordshire, England.

Federal law governs these indentures. For fifty years, the Trust Indenture Act of 1939 (TIA) (15 U.S.C.A. § 77aaa) was the relevant law. Significant changes in financial markets prompted Congress to amend the TIA through the Securities Act Amendments of 1990 (Pub. L. No. 101-550, 1990; 104 Stat. 2713), which included the Trust Indenture Reform Act (Pub. L. No. 101-550, 104 Stat. 2713). The reforms simplified the writing of indentures, recognized the increasing internationalization of corporations by creating opportunities for foreign institutions to serve as trustees, and revised standards for CONFLICTS OF INTEREST. The reforms also broadened the authority of the SECURITIES AND EXCHANGE COMMISSION.

In early American history indenture was a form of labor CONTRACT. Beginning in the colonial period, employers in the largely agricultural economy faced a labor shortage. They addressed it in two ways: by buying slaves and by hiring indentured servants. The former were Africans brought to the colonies against their will to serve for life; the latter were generally Europeans from England and Germany who had entered multiyear employment contracts. From the late sixteenth century to the late eighteenth century approximately half of the 350,000 European immigrants to the colonies were indentured servants. During the seventeenth century these servants outnumbered slaves.

An indentured servant agreed to a four- to seven-year contract, and in return received passage from Europe and guarantees of work, food, and lodging. Colonial courts enforced the contracts of indentured servants, which were often harsh. Employers were seen as masters, and the servants had not only to work for them but to obey their orders in all matters. For some, indentured servitude was not a voluntary act. Impoverished women and children were pressed into servitude, as were convicts. Nevertheless, this servitude was not equivalent to SLAVERY. Slaves remained slaves for life, whereas indentured servants were released at the end of their contract. Moreover, as parties to a contract, indentured servants had rights never enjoyed by slaves. The practice of indentured servitude persisted into the early nineteenth century.

INDEPENDENCE One of the essential attributes of a state under INTERNATIONAL LAW is external SOVEREIGNTY—that is, the right to exercise freely the full range of power a state possesses under international law. Recognition of a state as independent necessarily implies that the recognizing states have no legal authority over the independent state. The status of a fully independent state should be contrasted with that of dependent or vassal states, where a superior state has the legal authority to impose its will over the subject, or inferior, state.

INDEPENDENT AUDIT 📖 A systematic review of the accuracy and truthfulness of the ACCOUNTING records of a particular individual, business, or organization by a person or firm skilled in the necessary accounting methods and not related in any way to the person or firm undergoing the audit. 📖

INDEPENDENT CONTRACTOR 📖 A person who contracts to do a piece of work according to her or his own methods and is subject to another's control only as to the end product or the final result of the work. 📖

An independent contractor contracts with an employer to do a particular piece of work. This working relationship is a flexible one that provides benefits to both the worker and the employer. However, there are drawbacks to the relationship as well. The decision to hire or work as an independent contractor should be weighed carefully. Properly distinguishing between employees and independent contractors has important consequences, and the failure to maintain the distinction can be costly.

Taxes The status of independent contractor carries with it many tax ramifications. For example, an employee shares the costs of SOCIAL SECURITY and Medicare taxes with his or her employer; whereas an independent contractor is responsible for the entire amounts. Yet independent contractors generally qualify for more business deductions on their federal INCOME TAXES than do employees. Also, independent contractors must pay ESTIMATED TAXES each quarter, whereas employees generally have taxes withheld from their paychecks by their employer.

One important disadvantage of working as an independent contractor is that standard employment benefits—such as health, life, dental, and disability insurance; funded retirement plans; paid vacation time; and paid maternity or paternity leave—are not available. Independent contractors may fund their own benefits, but not on a tax-free basis—whereas many benefits provided by employers to employees are, by law, tax free.

Labor Relations Congress and the states have enacted numerous laws geared toward protecting employees. The National Labor Relations Act (29 U.S.C.A. § 152(3)) protects employees and union members from unfair bargaining practices; title VII of the CIVIL RIGHTS ACT of 1964 (42 U.S.C.A. § 2000 et seq.) protects employees from DISCRIMINATION on the basis of race, sex, religion, and national origin; the Age Discrimination in Employment Act (20 U.S.C.A. § 623) protects employees from AGE DISCRIMINATION; the FAIR LABOR STANDARDS ACT (29 U.S.C.A. § 203) establishes MINIMUM WAGE and overtime standards; the EMPLOYEE RETIREMENT INCOME SECURITY ACT of 1974 (29 U.S.C.A. § 1002) ensures the security of employee retirement funds; and the OCCUPATIONAL SAFETY AND HEALTH ACT (29 U.S.C.A. § 652) protects employees from environmental work hazards. Most states also have unemployment and WORKERS' COMPENSATION laws, which obligate employers to pay, directly or indirectly, for medical treatment or lost wages, or both, for employees who are injured while at work or who lose their job. None of these laws protect independent contractors. And because compliance often comes at great expense, employers can significantly reduce their liability and increase their profit margin by hiring independent contractors rather than employees.

Economics and Social Policy Although not protected by law to the extent of an employee, an independent contractor has far greater control over elements such as work hours and work methods. Unlike most employees, an independent contractor may opt to work at night or on weekends, leaving weekdays free. An independent contractor may choose to wear blue jeans or a business suit, take one week of vacation or thirty weeks, or interrupt work to attend a child's school play or to go to the beach. Moreover, although the other contracting party retains control over the finished work product, an independent contractor has exclusive control over the actual work process. Decisions such as whether to work for one person or several, whether to work a little or a lot, whether to accept or reject an undesirable work project, and how much money to charge are made by the independent contractor.

The other party, in turn, enjoys mainly profit-related advantages by hiring an independent contractor instead of an employee. For one thing, a person who hires need not provide an independent contractor vacation time, pension, insurance, or other costly benefits. Also, when business is bad and labor is plentiful, the other party to the contract transfers the problems of lack of work and low wages to the independent contractor. Management costs that ordinarily go toward training and overseeing large numbers of employees decrease when independent contractors do the work. Independent contractors benefit directly from their hard work, whereas employees usually do not and thus might be less motivated to work efficiently and effectively. And by hiring independent contractors, the other party enjoys the greater ease and flexibility to expand and contract the workforce as demand rises and falls.

Tort Liability The common-law doctrine of RESPONDEAT SUPERIOR holds an employer liable for the negligent acts of its employee. Generally, under COMMON LAW, the hiring party is not responsible for the NEGLIGENCE of an independent contractor. The Restatement (Second) of Torts identifies a few exceptions to this rule. The hiring party may be liable when, owing to its failure to exercise reasonable care to retain a competent and careful contractor, a third party is physically harmed. Also, when an independent contractor acts pursuant to orders or directions negligently given by the hiring party, the latter may be held liable. Notwithstanding the exceptions, the hiring party's risk of LIABILITY is greatly reduced by hiring independent contractors rather than employees.

Defining the Independent Contractor No consistent, uniform definition distinguishes an employee from an independent contractor. Some statutes contain their own definitions. The U.S. Supreme Court has held that when a statute contains the term *employee* but fails to define it adequately, there is a presumption that traditional agency-law criteria for identifying master-servant relationships apply (*National Mutual Insurance Co. v. Darden*, 503 U.S. 318, 112 S. Ct. 1344, 111 L. Ed. 2d 581 [1992]).

One comprehensive test that takes into account agency-law criteria and numerous other factors courts have created to define independent contractor status was developed by the Internal Revenue Service. Known collectively as the twenty-factor test, the enumerated criteria generally fall within three categories: control (whether the employer or the worker has control over the work performed), organization (whether the worker is integrated into the business), and economic realities (whether the worker directly benefits from his or her labor). The twenty factors serve only as a guideline. Each factor's degree of importance varies depending on the occupation and the facts involved in a particular case.

Twenty-factor test

1. A worker who is required to comply with *instructions* about when, where, and how he or she must work is usually an employee.
2. If an employer *trains* a worker—requires an experienced employee to work with the worker, educates the worker through correspondence, requires the worker to attend meetings, or uses other methods—this normally indicates that the worker is an employee.
3. If a worker's services are *integrated* into business operations, this tends to show that the worker is subject to direction and control and is thus an employee. This is the case particularly when a business's success or continuation depends to a large extent on the performance of certain services.
4. If a worker's services must be *rendered personally*, there is a presumption that the employer is interested in the methods by which the services are accomplished as well as in the result, making the worker an employee.
5. If an employer *hires, supervises, and pays assistants* for a worker, this indicates control over the worker on the job, making the worker an employee.
6. A *continuing relationship* between a worker and an employer, even at irregular intervals, tends to show an employer-employee relationship.
7. An employer who sets *specific hours of work* for a worker exhibits control over the worker, indicating that the worker is an employee.

B. BACHMANN/THE IMAGE WORKS

Construction work is often performed by independent contractors rather than employees of a single company. This affords the general contractor more flexibility in hiring.

8. If a worker is working *substantially full-time* for an employer, the worker is presumably not free to do work for other employers and is therefore an employee.
9. Work performed on an *employer's premises* suggests the employer's control over a worker, making the worker an employee. This is especially true when work could be done elsewhere. However, the mere fact that work is done off the employer's premises does not necessarily make the worker an independent contractor.
10. If a worker is required to perform services in an *order or sequence* set by an employer, the employer has control over the worker that demonstrates an employer-employee relationship.
11. A worker who is required to submit regular *oral or written reports* to an employer is likely an employee.

12. *Payment by the hour, week, or month* tends to indicate that a worker is an employee; payment made by the job or on a straight commission points to an independent contractor.

13. A worker is ordinarily an employee if an employer pays for the worker's *business or travel expenses.*

14. An employer who furnishes a worker with significant *tools, materials, or other equipment* tends to show that the worker is an employee.

15. A worker who *significantly invests* in facilities used to perform services and not typically maintained by employees (such as office space) is generally an independent contractor.

16. A worker who can *realize a profit or loss* resulting from her or his services is generally an independent contractor.

17. A worker who performs *for more than one firm at a time* is generally an independent contractor.

18. If a worker makes his or her *services available to the general public* on a regular and consistent basis, that worker is generally an independent contractor.

19. An employer's *right to discharge* a worker tends to show that the worker is an employee. An employee must obey an employer's instructions in order to stay employed; an independent contractor can be fired only if the work result fails to meet the agreed-upon specifications.

20. If a worker has the *right to terminate* her or his relationship with an employer at any time without incurring liability, such as breach of contract, that worker is likely an employee.

CROSS-REFERENCES

Employment Law; Labor Law; Master and Servant.

INDEPENDENT COUNSEL 📖 An attorney appointed by the federal government to investigate and prosecute federal government officials. 📖

Before 1988 independent counsel were referred to as special prosecutors. In 1988 Congress amended the Ethics in Government Act of 1978 (Ethics Act) (92 Stat. 1824 [2 U.S.C.A. § 701 et seq.]) to change the title to *independent counsel.* This change was made because lawmakers considered the term *special prosecutor* too inflammatory.

Independent counsel are attorneys who investigate and prosecute criminal activity in government. They hold people who make and implement laws accountable for their own criminal activity.

The need for independent counsel arises from the CONFLICT OF INTEREST posed by having the established criminal justice system investigate government misconduct. PROSECUTORS and law enforcement agencies work under the authority of government leaders. When government leaders are accused of wrongdoing, these entities face conflicting duties: the duty to uphold the laws on the one hand, versus the duty of loyalty to superiors on the other. Independent counsel do not answer to the government officials they are assigned to investigate, and therefore avoid much of this conflict of interest. One potential element for BIAS remains: the political affiliations of the accused government official and the independent counsel. The people rely on independent counsel's duty as members of the bar to uphold the laws and the U.S. Constitution, to overcome any similarities or differences in political beliefs. Independent counsel who appear to be motivated by political or other bias may be dismissed.

President ULYSSES S. GRANT was the first to appoint independent counsel to investigate high-level federal government officials. In 1875 Grant's personal secretary, Orville E. Babcock, was indicted in federal district court on charges of accepting bribes. Babcock had allegedly arranged favorable tax treatment for a group of moonshiners known as the Whiskey Ring. Grant removed the federal district attorney and replaced him with an independent counsel, who finished the investigation and the trial.

In the early 1920s, another BRIBERY scandal, known as TEAPOT DOME, led to the appointment of an independent counsel. President WARREN G. HARDING appointed independent counsel to investigate the sale of oil-rich federal lands. The independent counsel's investigation led to the prosecution of Harding's secretary of the interior Albert B. Fall.

In its later days, President HARRY S. TRUMAN's administration labored under allegations of corruption. Specifically, officials in the Internal Revenue Service and the Tax Division of the Department of Justice were accused of giving favorable treatment to tax evaders. Attorney General J. Howard McGrath appointed a special assistant attorney to investigate. When the special prosecutor sought to investigate McGrath, McGrath fired him. Truman then fired McGrath and refused to pursue the matter.

The WATERGATE scandals of the 1970s gave Congress the incentive to create the first statutory framework for investigating government officials. In 1973 newspaper reports concerning a burglary at the Democratic National Committee headquarters in the Watergate Hotel in Washington, D.C., implicated officials in the administration of President RICHARD M. NIXON. Attorney General Elliot L. Richardson appointed Archibald Cox, a Harvard law professor, independent counsel to investigate the situation.

Cox endeavored to uncover the facts surrounding Watergate. As it became apparent that White House officials were involved in the episode, Cox was forced to investigate the president himself. When Cox asked Nixon for White House tape recordings, Nixon sought to have Cox fired. One weekend in October 1973, in a turn of events later known as the Saturday Night Massacre, Richardson and Deputy Attorney General William D. Ruckelshaus resigned rather than carry out Nixon's order to fire Cox. That same night Solicitor General ROBERT H. BORK, who had just become acting head of the Department of Justice, carried out Nixon's request and fired Cox.

Nixon then appointed LEON JAWORSKI the second independent counsel to investigate Watergate. Like Cox, Jaworski sought Nixon's White House tapes. After a court battle that reached the U.S. Supreme Court in *United States v. Nixon*, 418 U.S. 683, 94 S. Ct. 3090, 41 L. Ed. 2d 1039 (1974), Jaworski successfully subpoenaed the tapes. Nixon resigned the office of president shortly thereafter.

After the Saturday Night Massacre and the Watergate matter, it became obvious that independent counsel were necessary to check government misconduct. In 1978 Congress passed the Ethics Act to establish on the federal level a statutory scheme for policing the EXECUTIVE BRANCH.

Ethics in Government Act Under the Ethics Act, the process of appointing independent counsel begins when the ATTORNEY GENERAL receives information on criminal activity. The attorney general may investigate all violations of criminal law other than minor MISDEMEANORS and minor violations. This permission includes special ethics laws that apply to executive branch officials, such as laws that make it illegal for an executive branch official to receive money from a person if the official has arranged for that person to be employed by the federal government.

There must be sufficient credible information of criminal activity to constitute grounds for an investigation, and the information must be in regard to the PRESIDENT, the VICE PRESIDENT, a member of the president's CABINET, a high-level executive officer, a high-level JUSTICE DEPARTMENT official, the director or deputy director of the CENTRAL INTELLIGENCE AGENCY, the commissioner of the INTERNAL REVENUE SERVICE, any person with a personal or financial relationship with the attorney general or any other officer in the Justice Department, or the president's campaign chairperson or treasurer.

Once the attorney general receives credible inculpatory information, the attorney general must decide within thirty days whether to investigate the matter. If the attorney general determines that the matter warrants an investigation, the attorney general must begin an investigation. The attorney general may not conduct this initial investigation for more than 150 days. At the close of the investigation, the attorney general must submit a report to the Independent Counsel Division of the U.S. Court of Appeals for the District of Columbia Circuit. The members of this three-judge panel are appointed by the chief justice of the U.S. Supreme Court.

In the report the attorney general must request or decline the appointment of independent counsel on the matter. This decision cannot be reviewed by a court. If the attorney general requests independent counsel, the panel must appoint one and define the scope of the investigation. Generally, the panel limits the counsel's investigation to certain persons or certain issues.

The appointment of independent counsel is unusual because the Department of Justice already is required to police the executive branch. In theory, the attorney general is an independent official. In practice, however, the attorney general usually is a political ally of the president. Like other executive branch officials, the attorney general is appointed by the president and reports to the president. Because the attorney general decides whether independent counsel should be appointed by the panel, an investigation can be influenced by the executive branch. An attorney general may be reluctant to recommend the prosecution of a political ally. However, if enough sources exert sufficient pressure, the attorney general may be forced to avoid the appearance of favoritism by requesting the appointment of independent counsel.

The appointment of independent counsel also is often politically charged in large part because independent counsel investigate executive branch officials and their political operatives. When politicians are investigated, an in-

LIBRARY OF CONGRESS

Orville Babcock was the first high-ranking government official investigated by independent counsel. President Ulysses S. Grant appointed independent counsel to investigate Babcock, Grant's personal secretary, who was indicted for accepting bribes.

variable response is that the investigation is politically motivated. Nevertheless, most politicians consider independent counsel crucial to conveying at least the appearance of propriety in the executive branch of government. The danger of independent counsel is that they may be called for on a regular basis by politicians opposed to the president, for the sole purpose of demoralizing the executive branch and gaining an electoral advantage.

Once appointed independent counsel may proceed as any other prosecutor. Counsel may file criminal charges in the U.S. District Court for the District of Columbia. Counsel has the power to SUBPOENA witnesses, and to grant IMMUNITY to WITNESSES.

Under the Ethics Act, only the attorney general may fire independent counsel. Independent counsel may be dismissed only for good cause or because a physical or mental condition prevents counsel from performing the position's duties. Dismissed independent counsel may appeal to the U.S. District Court for the District of Columbia.

The first government officials investigated under the new Ethics Act were two officials in the administration of President JIMMY CARTER. After investigating allegations of drug use and conflict of interest, the independent counsel declined to file criminal charges.

In May 1986 an official in the administration of President RONALD REAGAN mounted a challenge to the Ethics Act. Theodore B. Olson, a former assistant attorney general in the administration, argued that the executive branch had the power to conduct all criminal investigations, and that it was unconstitutional for Congress to give the judiciary the power to appoint independent prosecutors. The Supreme Court disagreed, ruling that the Ethics Act was constitutional because the attorney general, an officer within the executive branch, had the power to remove independent counsel and therefore retained ultimate control (*Morrison v. Olson*, 487 U.S. 654, 108 S. Ct. 2597, 101 L. Ed. 2d 569 [1988]).

The list of federal government officials investigated or prosecuted by independent counsel under the Ethics Act is long and ever growing. In December 1987 Michael Deaver, former aide to President Reagan, was convicted of PERJURY after prosecution by independent counsel. In February 1988 Lyn Nofziger, another presidential aide, was convicted of ethical violations. Nofziger's conviction was later overturned on appeal. President Reagan's attorney general EDWIN MEESE III resigned in July 1988 after an investigation by independent counsel James McKay. Although Meese was not prosecuted, McKay stated in his report to the panel that he believed that Meese had broken the law by helping a company in which Meese owned stock, Wedtech Corporation, solicit contracts with the U.S. military.

In December 1986, before he resigned, Meese appointed Lawrence E. Walsh independent counsel to investigate and prosecute wrongdoing in the burgeoning IRAN-CONTRA scandal. The Iran-Contra Affair involved trading arms to Iranians and diverting the proceeds to fund a covert war in Nicaragua. Walsh was able to obtain several convictions of high-level Reagan administration officials, but some of those were overturned on appeal.

The administration of President BILL CLINTON has also been investigated by independent counsel. Donald C. Smalz was appointed independent counsel to investigate Clinton's secretary of agriculture Mike Espy for receiving illegal gifts from companies regulated by the Department of Agriculture. In October 1994 Espy resigned his office.

In January 1994 Robert Fiske, Jr., was appointed independent counsel to investigate the death of White House counsel Vincent Foster and alleged financial misconduct by Clinton and the first lady, HILLARY RODHAM CLINTON.

Because the Ethics Act had lapsed, Attorney General JANET RENO chose Fiske herself. When Congress reauthorized the Ethics Act, Reno submitted the matter to the panel, and the panel appointed a new independent counsel, Kenneth W. Starr. Starr obtained several convictions.

Congress and Independent Counsel

When Congress is in session, independent counsel do not investigate and prosecute the criminal activities of members of Congress. Instead, Congress polices its members through ethics committees, and can expel a member with a two-thirds vote of the member's house (U.S. Const. art. I, § 5, cl. 2). Members of Congress cannot be arrested while Congress is in session, except for TREASON, FELONY, or BREACH OF THE PEACE (§ 6, cl. 1). When Congress is not in session, members of Congress are not exempt, and they may be prosecuted in the JURISDICTION where an offense occurred.

Congress may also investigate official wrongdoing in the executive branch. When Congress and independent counsel are investigating the same persons or events, the matter can become a political tug-of-war, and one investigation can run afoul of the other. For example, if Congress grants immunity to a witness who is under investigation by independent counsel, it becomes difficult for independent counsel to prosecute the witness. See also CONGRESS OF THE UNITED STATES.

State or Local Independent Counsel

Independent counsel also may be appointed at the state or local level. In Alaska, for example, executive branch officials may be investigated by independent counsel appointed by a special personnel board (Alaska Stat. § 39.52.310 [1995]).

In its broadest sense, the term *independent counsel* can describe any attorney who is appointed by one party to represent, prosecute, or bring suit against someone connected with that party. For example, in Alaska, a municipal school board is represented by a municipal attorney. If the municipal attorney has a conflict of interest in a particular matter, the school board may hire independent counsel for that matter (§ 29.20.370). Thus, if the municipal attorney owns stock in a construction company hired by the school board, the school board might seek a different attorney to handle legal issues associated with that company, in order to avoid the appearance of collusion between government and private business. The new attorney would be called an independent counsel to describe her or his independence in the matter.

INDEPENDENT PARTIES Although the United States has a firmly established two-party system, independent parties play an important role in U.S. politics. Democrats and Republicans win the vast majority of federal, state, and local ELECTIONS, but independent candidates often reflect popular attitudes and concerns. Most independent parties—also known as third parties—begin in response to a specific issue, candidate, or political philosophy.

The current two-party system of Democrats and Republicans evolved during the mid–nineteenth century. Before that, the Democrats squared off against the Whigs, led by HENRY CLAY and DANIEL WEBSTER. The Whig party was founded around 1834 to oppose the populist policies of Democratic president ANDREW JACKSON. Its members objected to Jackson's views on banking and the designation of federal funds, among other things.

Although Whig presidential candidates were successful in 1840 (WILLIAM HENRY HARRISON) and 1848 (ZACHARY TAYLOR), the party survived less than forty years. In the 1850s the Republicans entered the political scene as independents. After Republican ABRAHAM LINCOLN's victory in the 1860 U.S. presidential race, the REPUBLICAN PARTY replaced the Whig party as the main party opposing the Democrats. Many northern Whigs joined the Republicans, whereas southern Whigs became aligned with the Democrats.

The platforms and purposes of independent parties, both past and present, vary tremendously. Some independent parties, such as the Socialist party, the Communist party, and the Libertarian party, were formed to promote their political worldview rather than a single issue or a charismatic leader. The Socialist party, founded in 1901, has been relatively successful and long lasting. Its heyday was around 1912, when its candidate Eugene V. Debs received about six percent of the popular vote in the presidential election. That same year more than one thousand Socialists held elected positions throughout the United States.

Other independent parties were founded by dissident progressives from one or both of the major parties. In 1912 progressives in the Republican party broke off and formed the Progressive party, also known as the Bull Moose party, naming former U.S. president THEODORE ROOSEVELT as its presidential candidate. Roosevelt lost to Democratic nominee WOODROW WILSON in the general election.

In 1924 another progressive party, called the League for Progressive Political Action, was

Eugene Debs and Ben Hanford ran as the Socialist party candidates for president and vice president in 1904.

launched. This party backed Senator ROBERT M. LA FOLLETTE, from Wisconsin, who received 16 percent of the popular vote while losing to Republican incumbent CALVIN COOLIDGE.

In 1948 progressives in the DEMOCRATIC PARTY formed still another Progressive party. It supported Henry A. Wallace in an unsuccessful bid to unseat incumbent Democratic president HARRY S. TRUMAN.

Other offshoots of the two major parties include the Locofocos, or Equal Rights party, and the Mugwumps. The Locofocos emerged from the Democratic party in the early nineteenth century. They supported stricter bank regulation and antitrust laws. The Mugwumps broke from the Republican party in the 1884 presidential campaign and supported the Democratic nominee GROVER CLEVELAND. Their name was derived from the Algonquian word for *chief*. The Mugwumps' defection contributed to the Democrats' victory.

Some independent candidates transcend their party affiliation. Billionaire H. Ross Perot caught the public's imagination during the 1992 presidential campaign, which was won by Democrat BILL CLINTON. Of the 19 million U.S. citizens who voted for Perot, few if any cast their ballot in support of his independent party. People voted for Perot, the person, as an alternative to Clinton and the Republican candidate (for reelection) GEORGE BUSH. Perot ran again as an independent in 1996.

An independent candidate and a specific issue are often linked inextricably. This was the case in 1968 with Alabama governor GEORGE WALLACE and his American Independent party. Wallace was a vocal opponent of CIVIL RIGHTS. His position on segregation and STATES' RIGHTS and his bold personality were the sum total of the party.

Other important social issues have spawned independent parties. The Prohibition party was formed in 1869 by temperance activists who wanted to ban the sale and consumption of ALCOHOL. Before the Civil War, the Liberty party was created by abolitionists to outlaw SLAVERY. Similarly, the Free-Soil party—which later became part of the Republican party—was started in 1848 to prevent the extension of slavery into new U.S. territories and states.

On the other end of the ideological spectrum were the Dixiecrats. Led by STROM THURMOND, these were a group of southern Democrats opposed to President Truman's civil rights policies. The Dixiecrats splintered from the main party in 1948.

Bigotry was the driving force behind the Know-Nothing party—also called the American party—formed in 1849 to pursue discrimination against immigrants and Roman Catholics. The name referred to the secrecy surrounding the group: members were instructed to say, "I don't know," if asked about the party.

The effect of an independent party on a presidential race varies. In 1912 independent candidate Theodore Roosevelt, of the Bull Moose party, earned more votes than Republican nominee Taft, and in effect delivered the election to Democratic challenger Wilson. In other presidential elections, independents made barely a ripple. For example, in 1872 the Prohibition party candidate received a mere fifty-six hundred votes.

Some citizens are reluctant to vote for an independent candidate, feeling the gesture is futile. The odds for winning either the popular or electoral vote are slim. Still, the political dialogue generated by independent candidates is a meaningful contribution to the democratic process. Even when independent candidates lose the election, the public becomes more aware of their message.

See also ELECTION CAMPAIGN FINANCING.

INDETERMINATE 📖 That which is uncertain or not particularly designated. 📖

INDEX 📖 A book containing references, alphabetically arranged, to the contents of a series or collection of documents or volumes; or a section (normally at the end) of a single volume or set of volumes containing such references to its contents.

Statistical indexes are also used to track or measure changes in the economy (for example, the CONSUMER PRICE INDEX) and movement in stock markets (for example, Standard & Poor's Index). Such indexes are usually keyed to a base year, month, or other period of comparison.

In MORTGAGE financing, the term is used to determine adjustable-rate mortgage (ARM) interest rates after the discount period ends. Common indexes for ARMs are one-year Treasury securities and the national average cost of funds to savings and loan associations. 📖

INDEX TO LEGAL PERIODICALS 📖 The set of volumes that lists what has appeared in print from 1926 to the present in the major LAW REVIEWS and law-oriented magazines in various countries—usually organized according to author, title, and subject, and containing a table of cases. 📖

The *Index to Legal Periodicals* aids individuals who are conducting legal research by enabling them to search the contents of past and currently published periodicals, thereby providing access to secondary source materials. The *Index* is bound every three years, with annual supplements and ADVANCE SHEETS for every month except September.

INDIAN CHILD WELFARE ACT The Indian Child Welfare Act (ICWA), passed by Congress in 1978, intended to limit the historical practice of removing Native American children from their tribe and family and placing them in a non-Indian family or institution (25 U.S.C.A. §§ 1901–1963). The stated purpose of the act is to "[p]rotect the best interests of Indian children and to promote the stability and security of Indian tribes." The act seeks to achieve these goals through three principal methods: by establishing minimum federal standards for when Indian children can be removed from their family; by placing children who are removed in a foster or adoptive home that reflects the unique values of Indian culture; and by providing assistance to family services programs operated by Indian tribes.

The impetus behind the passage of the ICWA was a widespread recognition of the failure of the federal government's historical policy of removing Indian children from their family and tribe and attempting to assimilate them into white culture by placing them in a white family or institution. Since the late 1800s, a large percentage of Indian children had been taken from their home and placed in a boarding school off their tribal reservation in order to teach them white culture and practices. In many cases government authorities removed Indian children from their family because of vague allegations of neglect, when in fact the children's treatment reflected cultural differences in child rearing practices, and not neglect or abuse. In addition, the practice of removing Indian children from their tribe placed the very existence of the tribes in jeopardy.

The ICWA was written with the belief that it was in the best interests of Indian children for them to remain with their tribe and maintain their Indian heritage. To foster this goal, the ICWA enacts minimal federal standards for when Indian children can be removed from their family and seeks to ensure that children who are removed are placed in a foster or adoptive home that reflects the unique values of Indian culture. Examples of these standards include giving custodial preference to a child's extended family or tribal members, requiring remedial programs to prevent the breakup of Indian families, and requiring proof "BEYOND A REASONABLE DOUBT" that continued custody of a child will result in serious emotional or physical harm to the child.

To prevent a resumption of the practice of removing Indian children from their home, Congress, in the ICWA, gave tribal courts exclusive JURISDICTION over the ADOPTION and custody of Indian children who reside or are domiciled within their tribe's reservation, unless some federal law provides to the contrary (*domiciled* refers to a permanent residence while *residing* may be in a temporary residence). One such contrary law is Public Law 280 (28 U.S.C.A. § 1360). This law made certain tribes in Alaska, California, Minnesota, Nebraska, Oregon, and Wisconsin subject to state jurisdiction. ICWA allows these tribes to reassume jurisdiction over child custody proceedings by petitioning the secretary of the interior.

Tribes also have exclusive jurisdiction over such proceedings when they involve an Indian child who is a WARD of the tribal court, regardless of where the child resides. Custody proceedings covered by the act include foster care placement, the termination of parental rights, and pre-adoptive and adoptive placement; the act does not govern custody proceedings in DIVORCE settlements. The ICWA applies both to children who are tribal members and to children who are eligible for tribal membership; eligibility for tribal membership is determined by individual tribes.

In cases involving Indian children who neither reside nor are domiciled within a tribal reservation, tribal courts and state courts possess CONCURRENT JURISDICTION. This question of jurisdiction has resulted in several important judicial interpretations of the ICWA. One significant interpretation was the 1989 U.S. Supreme Court decision *Mississippi Band of Choctaw Indians v. Holyfield*, 490 U.S. 30, 109 S. Ct. 1597, 104 L. Ed. 2d 29, which declared that because Congress had clearly enacted the law to protect Native American families and tribes, tribal jurisdiction preempted both state authority and the wishes of the parents of the children at issue. The case involved twins born off the reservation to unmarried parents, who voluntarily consented to having the children adopted by a non-Indian family. The Supreme Court ruled that children born to unmarried parents are considered to share the domicile of the mother, and since the mother in this case was domiciled on the reservation, the tribal court had jurisdiction over the placement of the children, even if it opposed the parents' wishes.

In a significant state case, the Minnesota Supreme Court in August 1994 followed the reasoning in *Holyfield*, rejecting a white couple's petition to adopt three Ojibwa (also called Chippewa or Anishinabe) sisters (*In re S. E. G.*, 521 N.W.2d 357). The court ruled in favor of the Leech Lake band of Chippewa, which had contested the adoption, holding that the ICWA dictated that adopted Indian children should be raised within their own culture. Although non-Indian families may adopt Indian children in very limited circumstances if they prove there is "good cause," the court held that such good cause cannot be based on the European value of family permanence.

In some cases, however, courts have given less weight to the provisions of the ICWA, instead ruling in favor of state jurisdiction over Indian children. In 1995, for example, the Illinois Supreme Court ruled that the ICWA does not mandate exclusive jurisdiction for tribal courts in custody hearings when the location of the children's domicile is in question. *In re Adoption of S. S. & R. S.*, 167 Ill. 2d 250, 212 Ill. Dec. 590, 657 N.E.2d 935, involved two children of an unmarried Indian mother and non-Indian father, who had been living with their father. When the father died, his sister and brother-in-law sought to adopt the children. The mother's tribe, the Fort Peck tribe in Montana, objected and claimed jurisdiction over the proceeding. The Illinois Supreme Court ruled against the tribe, holding that because the children had never been domiciled on the mother's reservation and because the mother had "abandoned" the children, state law preceded tribal court jurisdiction. The court thus limited the scope of the ICWA in Illinois.

See also CHILD CUSTODY; NATIVE AMERICAN RIGHTS.

INDICIA 📖 Signs; indications. Circumstances that point to the existence of a given fact as probable, but not certain. For example, *indicia of partnership* are any circumstances which would induce the belief that a given person was in reality, though not technically, a member of a given firm. 📖

The term is much used in CIVIL LAW in a sense nearly or entirely synonymous with CIRCUMSTANTIAL EVIDENCE. It denotes facts that give rise to inferences, rather than the inferences themselves.

INDICTMENT 📖 A written accusation charging that an individual named therein has committed an act or omitted to do something that is punishable by law. 📖

An indictment is found and presented by a GRAND JURY legally convened and sworn. It originates with a prosecutor and is issued by the grand jury against an individual who is charged with a CRIME. Before such individual may be convicted, the charge must be proved at trial BEYOND A REASONABLE DOUBT.

The purpose of an indictment is to inform an accused individual of the charge against him or

_____ Court: Criminal Term

_____ County

THE PEOPLE OF THE STATE OF NEW YORK
                    against

_____,
                                    Defendant(s)

_____

THE GRAND JURY OF THE COUNTY OF _____, by this indictment, accuse the defendant(s) of the crime of _____ committed as follows:
    The defendant(s) _____, on or about _____, 19_____, in the County of _____ [*assert facts supporting every element of the offense(s) charged*] _____.

_____
Foreman, Grand Jury

_____
District Attorney
_____ County

A sample indictment

---

her so that the person will be able to prepare a defense.

INDIRECT EVIDENCE 📖 Probative matter that does not proximately relate to an issue but that establishes a hypothesis by showing various consistent facts. 📖

See also EVIDENCE.

INDISPENSABLE PARTY 📖 An individual who has an interest in the substantive issue of a legal action of such a nature that a final decree cannot be handed down without that interest being affected or without leaving the controversy in a condition whereby its final determination would be totally unconscionable. 📖

For example, a husband and wife seeking to dissolve a marriage are indispensable parties to their own DIVORCE action.

INDIVIDUAL RETIREMENT ACCOUNT 📖 A means by which an individual can receive certain federal tax advantages while investing for retirement. 📖

The federal government has several reasons for encouraging individuals to save money for their retirement. For one, the average life span of a U.S. citizen continues to increase. Assuming the average age of retirement does not change, workers who retire face more years of retirement and more years to live without a wage or salary.

Uncertainty over the future of the federal SOCIAL SECURITY system is another reason. U.S. workers generally contribute deductions from their paychecks to the Social Security fund. In theory, this money comes back to them, usually upon their retirement. But a substantial number of politicians, economists, and scholars contend that the Social Security fund is being drained faster than it is being filled, and will go broke in a number of years, leaving retirees to survive without government assistance.

Regardless of its future, many people consider the retirement benefits of Social Security to be inadequate, and look for other methods of funding their retirement years. Many employers offer retirement plans. These plans vary in form, but generally offer an employee retirement funds that grow with continued employment. Yet this benefit is not always available to workers. A changing economy has caused some employers to cut back retirement plans or cut them out completely. Often, part-time, new, or temporary workers do not qualify for an employer's retirement plan. And individuals who are self-employed cannot choose this job benefit.

To help people prepare for their retirement, Congress in 1974 established individual retirement accounts (IRAs) (EMPLOYEE RETIREMENT

Individual Retirement Account Plans–Value by Type of Holder, 1985 to 1994

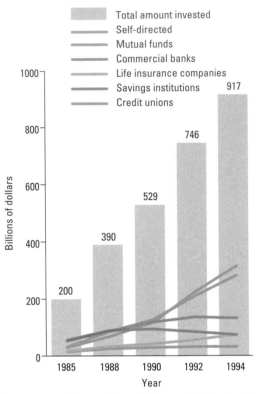

Source: Investment Company Institute, Washington, D.C., *Mutual Fund Fact Book*, annual.

INCOME SECURITY ACT [ERISA] [codified in scattered sections of 5, 18, 26, and 29 U.S.C.A.]). These accounts may take a variety of forms, such as savings accounts at a bank, CERTIFICATES OF DEPOSIT, or MUTUAL FUNDS of stocks. Initially, IRAs were available only to people who were not participating in an employer-provided retirement plan. This changed in 1981, when Congress expanded the IRA provisions to include anyone, regardless of participation in an employer's retirement plan (Economic Recovery Tax Act [ERTA] [codified in scattered sections of 26, 42, and 45 U.S.C.A.]). The goal of ERTA was to promote an increased level of personal retirement savings through uniform discretionary savings arrangements.

A movement to bolster the FEDERAL BUDGET by eliminating many existing tax shelters prompted portions of the Tax Reform Act of 1986 (codified in scattered sections of 19, 25, 26, 28, 29, 42, 46, and 49 U.S.C.A.) and another change in IRA laws. This time, Congress limited some of the IRA's tax advantages, making them unavailable to workers who participate in an employer's retirement plan or whose earnings meet or exceed a certain threshold. Yet, other tax advantages remain, and the laws

still allow anyone to contribute to an IRA, making it a popular investment tool.

It is difficult to understand the advantages an IRA offers without understanding a few basics about federal INCOME TAX law. Generally, a person calculating the amount of tax she or he owes to the government first determines the amount of income received in the year. This is normally employment income. Tax laws allow the individual to deduct from this figure amounts paid for certain items, such as charitable contributions or interest on a MORTGAGE. Some taxpayers choose to take a single STANDARD DEDUCTION rather than numerous ITEMIZED DEDUCTIONS. In either case the taxpayer subtracts any allowable DEDUCTIONS from yearly income, and then calculates the tax owed on the remainder.

Taking deductions is only one of the ways a taxpayer can reduce taxes by investing in an IRA. Under current laws, those who do not participate in a retirement plan through work or who earn less than $25,000 a year may receive the greatest tax advantages by contributing to an IRA.

Various plans may constitute employer-maintained retirement plans, such as standard

Percent Distribution of IRA Holdings

1985

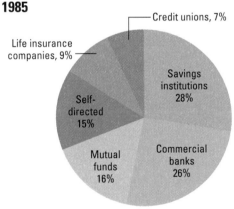

1994

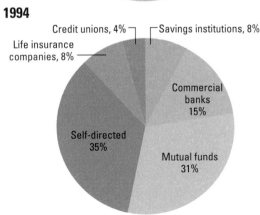

Source: Investment Company Institute, Washington, D.C., *Mutual Fund Fact Book*, annual.

PENSION plans, profit sharing or stock bonus plans, ANNUITIES, and government retirement plans. Someone who does not participate in such a plan—whether by choice or not—is entitled to contribute to an IRA up to $2,000 a year or 100 percent of her or his annual income, whichever is less. The amount contributed during the taxable year may then be taken as a deduction. Married couples may contribute $4,000 to IRAs each year and deduct the full $4,000, if neither spouse participates in an employer-provided retirement plan.

A married taxpayer who files a joint tax return with a spouse who does not work may deduct contributions toward what is called a spousal IRA, or an IRA established for the spouse's benefit. If neither spouse is a participant in an employer-provided retirement plan, up to $4,000 may be deductible.

An individual who participates in an employer's retirement plan may still be entitled to all the tax benefits of an IRA. If a person filing an individual tax return makes less than $25,000 a year, that person may contribute to an IRA and take a full deduction for the amount contributed during the tax year. A taxpayer filing an individual tax return who makes between $25,000 and $35,000 a year may take a partial deduction, the amount of which decreases as income increases. The same rules apply for married taxpayers filing a joint tax return with an income of less than $40,000 in the former instance and between $40,000 and $50,000 in the latter.

Taxpayers who contribute to IRAs usually realize tax benefits even when the law does not permit them to take deductions. That is because income earned on IRA contributions is not taxed until the funds are distributed, which usually occurs at retirement. Income that is allowed to grow, untaxed, for several years, grows faster than income that is taxed each year.

To avoid abuses and excessive tax shelters, Congress has placed limits on the extent to which IRAs can be used as a financial tool. Individuals with IRAs are permitted to make contributions of no more than $2,000 a year, and contributions exceeding that amount are subject to strict financial penalties by the INTERNAL REVENUE SERVICE each year until the excess is corrected. The owner of an IRA generally may not withdraw funds from that account until age 59½. Premature distributions are subject to a 10 percent penalty in addition to regular income tax. Taxpayers may be able to avoid this premature distribution penalty by "rolling over," or transferring, the distribution amount to another IRA within sixty days.

An individual may elect not to withdraw IRA funds at age 59½. However, the law requires IRA owners to withdraw IRA money at age 70½, either in a lump sum or in periodic (at least annual) payments based on a life expectancy calculation. Failure to comply with this rule can result in a 50 percent penalty on the amount of the required minimum distribution. Contributions to an IRA must stop at age 70½.

INDORSE 📖 To sign a paper or document, thereby making it possible for the rights represented therein to pass to another individual. 📖

The term *indorse* is also spelled *endorse*.

INDORSEMENT 📖 A SIGNATURE on a COMMERCIAL PAPER or document. 📖

An indorsement on a NEGOTIABLE INSTRUMENT, such as a CHECK or a PROMISSORY NOTE, has

Sample indorsements

In Blank

John Doe

or

Pay to bearer
    John Doe

Special

Pay to Richard Roe or order
    John Doe

or

Pay to the order of Richard Roe
    John Doe

or

Pay to Richard Roe
    John Doe

Restrictive

Pay Richard Roe only
    John Doe

or

For deposit only
    John Doe

Qualified

Pay to Richard Roe without recourse
    John Doe

Conditional

Pay to Acme Company on completion of building contract
    John Doe

Indorsement Without Recourse

Without recourse in any event and without representation or warranty whatsoever.

or

John Doe
Without Recourse
7/20/85

the effect of transferring all the rights represented by the instrument to another individual. The ordinary manner in which an individual indorses a check is by placing his or her signature on the back of it; however, it is valid even if the signature is placed somewhere else, such as on a separate paper, known as an ALLONGE, which provides a space for a signature.

The term *indorsement* is also spelled *endorsement*.

INDUCEMENT 📖 An advantage or benefit that precipitates a particular action on the part of an individual. 📖

In the law of CONTRACTS, the inducement is a pledge or promise that causes an individual to enter into a particular agreement. An *inducement to purchase* is something that encourages an individual to buy a particular item, such as the promise of a price reduction. CONSIDERATION is the inducement to a contract.

In CRIMINAL LAW, the term *inducement* is the motive, or that which leads an individual to engage in criminal conduct.

INDUSTRIAL UNION 📖 A labor organization composed of members employed in a particular field, such as textiles, but who perform different individual jobs within their general type of work. 📖

See also LABOR UNION.

INDUSTRIAL WORKERS OF THE WORLD The Industrial Workers of the World—also known as the IWW, or the Wobblies—is a radical LABOR UNION that had its beginnings in Chicago in 1905.

An outgrowth of the Western Federation of Mines, the IWW was created by WILLIAM D. HAYWOOD, Eugene V. Debs, and Daniel De-Leon. Its membership was open to all workers, skilled or unskilled, with no restrictions as to race, occupation, ethnic background, or sex. The Wobblies opposed the principles of capitalism and advocated SOCIALISM. They followed the tenets of syndicalism, a labor movement that evolved in Europe before World War I. The syndicalists sought to control industry through labor organizations. In their view the state represented oppression, which had to be replaced by the union as the essential element of society. To achieve their goals, the syndicalists advocated practices such as STRIKES and slowdowns.

The Wobblies adopted many of the ideologies of syndicalism and employed direct-action methods, such as propaganda, strikes, and BOYCOTTS. They rejected more peaceful means of achieving labor's goals, such as ARBITRATION and COLLECTIVE BARGAINING.

From 1906 to 1928, the IWW was responsible for 150 strikes, including a miners' strike in Goldfield, Nevada, from 1906 to 1907; a textile workers' strike in Lawrence, Massachusetts, in 1912; a 1913 silk workers' strike in Paterson, New Jersey; and a miners' strike in Colorado from 1927 to 1928.

During World War I, the IWW began to lose much of its strength. Its members were against the military, and many were convicted of draft evasion, seditious activities, and ESPIONAGE. In addition, many members left the organization to join the Communist party. By 1930, the IWW was no longer regarded as an influential labor force. Nevertheless, it still exists today.

Despite its radicalism, the IWW was responsible for several gains for organized labor. It brought together skilled and unskilled workers into one union; it achieved better working conditions and a shorter work week in many areas of labor, particularly in the lumber field; and it set a structural example that would be followed by future labor unions.

IN EVIDENCE 📖 Facts, documents, or exhibits that have been introduced before and accepted by the court for consideration as PROBATIVE matter. 📖

IN EXTREMIS 📖 [*Latin, In extremity.*] A term used in reference to the last illness prior to death. 📖

A CAUSA MORTIS gift is made by an individual who is in extremis.

INFAMY 📖 Notoriety; condition of being known as possessing a shameful or disgraceful reputation; loss of character or good reputation. 📖

At COMMON LAW, infamy was an individual's legal status that resulted from having been convicted of a particularly reprehensible crime, rendering him or her incompetent as a WITNESS at a trial. Infamy, by statute in certain JURISDICTIONS, produces other legal disabilities and is sometimes described as CIVIL DEATH.

INFANCY 📖 Minority; the status of an individual who is below the legal AGE OF MAJORITY. 📖

At COMMON LAW, the age of legal majority was twenty-one, but it has been lowered to eighteen in most states of the United States. Infancy indicates the condition of an individual who is legally unable to do certain acts. For example, an infant might not have the legal CAPACITY to enter into certain CONTRACTS. Similarly, infancy is a ground for ANNULMENT of a marriage in certain JURISDICTIONS.

Although many states have lowered the age of majority for most purposes to eighteen, they frequently retain the right to mandate support of a child by a parent beyond that age in the aftermath of DIVORCE.

INFANTS 📖 Persons who are under the age of legal majority—at COMMON LAW, twenty-one years, now generally 18 years. According to the sense in which this term is used, it may denote the age of the person, the contractual disabilities that nonage entails, or his or her status with regard to other powers or relations. 📖

Modern laws respecting the rights, obligations, and incapacities of children are rooted in ancient customs and practices. In 1765, SIR WILLIAM BLACKSTONE, in his *Commentaries on the Laws of England*, wrote that parents owe their children three duties: maintenance, protection, and education. Today, these three duties continue, and have been expanded by judicial and legislative advancements. The notion of children's rights has evolved into a highly controversial and dynamic area of law.

Common law held an infant, also called a MINOR or child, to be a person less than twenty-one years old. Currently, most state statutes define the AGE OF MAJORITY to be eighteen. Although a person must attain the age of majority to vote, make a WILL, or hold public office, children are increasingly being recognized by society, legislatures, and the courts as requiring greater protections and deserving greater rights than they were afforded under common law. The law is caught in a tug-of-war between two equally compelling and worthy societal interests: the desire to protect children from harmful situations and from their own immaturity and lack of experience, and the desire to give children as much autonomy as they can bear as soon as they can bear it.

Children do have the right to own and acquire property by SALE, GIFT, or INHERITANCE. Often property is given to a child as a BENEFICIARY of a TRUST. In the trust situation, a TRUSTEE manages the trust ASSETS for the child until the child reaches majority or otherwise meets the requirements specified in the trust for managing the property for herself or himself.

Children also have the right to enter into CONTRACTS. Because the law seeks to protect children from adverse consequences due to their lack of knowledge, experience, and maturity, an adult who enters into a contract with a child may be unable to enforce the contract against the child, whereas the child can enforce the contract against the adult if the adult breaches it. However, when a child enters into a contract for necessities (i.e., food, shelter, clothing, and medical attention) or with a bank, the child is legally bound and cannot later disaffirm or negate the contract. In addition, some state statutes provide that all contracts relating to a child's business are enforceable. This allows a child the opportunity to begin a business. Aside from these limited exceptions, a child may negate a contract before, and even sometimes soon after, reaching the age of majority.

Children have the right to bring lawsuits seeking legal redress for injuries they have suffered or for rights that have been violated. Most JURISDICTIONS require a child to have a representative during the litigation process. This representative, called a GUARDIAN AD LITEM, or next friend, advises and guides the child.

The right of a child to sue for PERSONAL INJURIES has been extended to cover prenatal injuries. A child may maintain an action for injuries that occurred during the early weeks in utero, before the child, then an embryo, was viable, or able to sustain life outside the womb. If an injured fetus is born alive and then dies as a result of her or his prenatal injuries, the child's parents may sue for the WRONGFUL DEATH of the child.

Although all states recognize a child's right to sue for prenatal injuries, the vast majority of states do not allow "wrongful life" actions. In a WRONGFUL LIFE lawsuit, the child sues a doctor for NEGLIGENCE or MALPRACTICE for failing to diagnose the child's mother with a disease that injured the child before birth or for failing to diagnose a severe, disabling condition of the child before birth. The argument continues that if the doctor had informed the child's parents of the child's condition, the mother would have had an ABORTION rather than delivering a child with such a debilitating condition. The child's theory in a wrongful life lawsuit is that life with the injury or debilitating condition is worse than no life at all and that he or she would have been better off having not been born.

The New Jersey Supreme Court has denied wrongful life claims, stating that "there is no precedent in appellate judicial pronouncements that holds a child has a fundamental right to be born as a whole, functional human being," and that it is almost impossible to calculate the damages in such a case (*Gleitman v. Cosgrove*, 49 N.J. 22, 227 A.2d 689 [1967]). In contrast, in *Curlender v. Bio-Science Laboratory*, 106 Cal. App. 3d 811, 165 Cal. Rptr. 477 (1980), a California court allowed a child with Tay-Sachs disease to recover for wrongful life, stating that to deny such a claim "permits a wrong with serious consequential injury to go wholly unaddressed." This court would not accept the "im-

J. KOONTZ/THE PICTURE CUBE

Under common law a young person was considered an infant until the age of twenty-one. Today in many states people reach the age of majority at eighteen.

possibility of measuring damages" as the sole reason to deny the child's claim.

A child may bring a lawsuit seeking EMANCIPATION from his or her parents. Emancipation is an ancient doctrine based on ROMAN LAW. An emancipated minor is a child who is entirely self-supporting and who has the legal right and duty to oversee his or her own behavior. An emancipated minor's parents surrender the right to the care, custody, and earnings of the child. Once emancipated, the child is precluded from demanding that his or her parents continue to support him or her. Historically, an express agreement between the parent and child, the marriage of the child, the entry of the child into the armed forces, or responsible conduct on the part of the child were all sufficient factors in seeking emancipation. Today, the doctrine is seen as a mechanism for ending troubled parent-child relationships and a way to alleviate the difficult task of finding foster families for older teenagers who have been taking care of themselves.

A child is permitted to TESTIFY in court if the judge believes that the child comprehends the meaning and importance of telling the truth, is sufficiently mature, and is able to recall and communicate her or his thoughts effectively. Most states do not have a specific age at which children are allowed to testify; consequently, even very young children are allowed to be placed under OATH and testify in court if the judge determines that these requirements have been met.

Although children do not have a constitutional right to a safe home, a permanent, stable family, or quality care, significant strides have been made to better the lives of children. The right of a state to ensure the welfare of the children within its boundaries stems from the ancient concept of *parens patriae*, which means

"the father of his country" and was used to describe the relationship between a king and his subjects. Today, this right is limited by the parents' legal right to be free from government intrusion in the raising and rearing of their children. The state's intervention is justified, however, if a parent is not living up to his or her responsibilities or when a child is endangered, neglected, or abused. The courts may then place the child in temporary foster care and require the parent to get assistance to remedy the problem, or may terminate the parent's rights to the child if that is found to be in the best interests of the child.

In 1960, the federal government spent only a few million dollars on child protective services. By 1980, this expenditure had risen to over $325 million. This dramatic increase probably does not reflect an actual increase in the incidence of child abuse but rather the effects of laws requiring health care and social workers to report any suspicions of CHILD ABUSE, an increase in public awareness of the problem, and a broadening of the definition of child abuse. Given this increase in reported cases and the fiscal limitations of child welfare agencies, children are increasingly "falling through the cracks" and not receiving timely or effective protection from the state. For example, in 1989, the U.S. Supreme Court held that the Due Process Clause did not impose an affirmative duty on the state to protect a four-year-old boy from his father's violence (*DeShaney v. Winnebago County Department of Social Services*, 489 U.S. 189, 103 L. Ed. 2d 249, 109 S. Ct. 998). In that case, a young boy named Joshua was beaten so severely that half of his brain was destroyed and he now is permanently brain-damaged and profoundly retarded. A social worker assigned to the family had noted signs of past abuse and several trips to the emergency room, but had taken no action to remove Joshua from his family home. Chief Justice WILLIAM H. REHNQUIST stated that the Due Process Clause "is phrased as a limitation on the State's power to act, not as a guarantee of certain minimal levels of safety and security."

State and federal funds are allotted for children whose parents are financially unable to provide for their basic needs, such as food, shelter, and medical attention. Aid to Families with Dependent Children (AFDC) is federal money given to financially needy parents to provide these basics for their children. Legislation has also been enacted to go after "deadbeat parents"—parents who are financially able to provide for their children but do not. These laws enable the government to garnish a parent's paycheck for past support owed and allow for the suspension of professional licenses until money owing is paid.

Although the Constitution does not in any way mention the right of children to an education, every state has adopted compulsory education laws. Traditionally, it was assumed that students would behave and express themselves in acceptable ways, and thus their rights did not need to be recognized or protected in any official manner. Since the 1960s, this notion has gone by the wayside. The Supreme Court has recognized that students do not shed their constitutional rights upon crossing the schoolhouse threshold. The Court has recognized that schools function as a "market-place of ideas" and that FIRST AMENDMENT rights must receive "scrupulous protection if we are not to strangle the free mind at its source and teach youth to discount important principles of our government as mere platitudes" (*Tinker v. Des Moines Independent Community School District*, 393 U.S. 503, 21 L. Ed. 2d 731, 89 S. Ct. 733 [1969]). The rights of students to wear black armbands in protest of the Vietnam War, to dance, and to use obscene and vulgar language on campus are but a few of the many First Amendment issues that have been litigated. In addition, debates over SCHOOL PRAYER, RELIGION in a public school curriculum, and government aid to parochial schools all affect the education children receive. Many court decisions limit the FOURTH AMENDMENT rights of students with regard to searches for DRUGS, to drug testing, and to searches of their lockers.

The strides in securing education for children occurred at the same time that CHILD LABOR LAWS were beginning to eradicate the exploitation of children in sweatshops. By the mid-1800s, several states had passed laws restricting the number of hours children could work and requiring children who worked to also attend school for a minimum number of months each year. However, because each state had different laws and competition was fierce among states eager to attract industry, many of the laws regarding child labor went unenforced. After several unsuccessful attempts at passing effective child labor laws, Congress passed the FAIR LABOR STANDARDS ACT (FLSA), 29 U.S.C.A. § 201 et seq., which places restrictions on the hours children may work and age limitations for children performing particular jobs and employed in certain hazardous occupations. Today, every state has child labor laws—most of which are patterned after the FLSA, although some differences do exist.

The same concern for children that brought about these protections was responsible for the creation of the juvenile justice system. From the founding of the United States until the end of the nineteenth century, children who were charged with a crime were treated the same as adults. The juvenile justice system arose from an emerging conviction that rehabilitation, not punishment, would better serve the child and the state. Today, juvenile court systems have been adopted by every state. These courts hear cases involving STATUS OFFENSES, abuse, dependency, neglect, and termination of parental rights. Status offenses are legal infractions based solely on the age of the person, such as truancy and curfew violations. Children in the juvenile justice system have the constitutional rights of notice, COUNSEL, privilege against SELF-INCRIMINATION, determination of guilt BEYOND A REASONABLE DOUBT, and protection against DOUBLE JEOPARDY. However, juveniles still do not have a federal constitutional right to a JURY trial and are not generally afforded BAIL.

All state juvenile codes provide for a juvenile to be removed from the juvenile justice system and transferred to the adult criminal courts, depending on the offense the juvenile allegedly committed or the juvenile's prior history of delinquent behavior. Once this move is made, the juvenile is entitled to all the constitutional protections afforded adults accused of crimes, such as bail and the right to a trial by jury,

What It Costs to Raise a Child to Age 18	
A Two-Parent Family	
Earning	**Will Spend**
Under $33,700 a year	$106,890
$33,700 to $56,700 a year	$145,320
Over $56,700 a year	$211,830
A Single-Parent Family	
Earning	**Will Spend**
Under $33,700 a year	$101,580
$33,700 or more a year	$213,240

Based on data available as of April 1996.

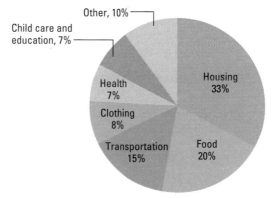

Source: *Expenditures on Children by Families*, annual, U.S. Department of Agriculture Center for Nutrition Policy and Promotion, Misc. Publication No. 1528.

Chart percentages are rounded and do not include the cost of inflation or college.

which may be more sympathetic and less likely to convict than would a juvenile court judge.

Traditionally, children have been deemed legally incapable of consenting to their own medical care or treatment. In general, parents have the authority to decide whether their minor children will receive medical treatment. Common law recognized an exception to the need for parental consent in cases of emergency. Statutory law has created more exceptions to this requirement, namely in cases where a child is emancipated, married, pregnant, or a parent. In addition, several states have enacted "minor treatment statutes," which typically provide that from fourteen to seventeen years old, a minor may consent to ordinary medical treatment. Owing to a high incidence of venereal diseases among teenagers, all states have adopted statutes authorizing minors to consent to the treatment of sexually transmitted diseases. Similarly, most states have laws allowing a child to seek treatment for ALCOHOL or drug abuse without parental consent. Constitutional guarantees of the right to abortion extend to minors, as does the right to PRIVACY. The Supreme Court has upheld state statutes that require the consent of only one parent if the statutes also offer an expeditious judicial bypass procedure (a hearing before a judge in which the minor requests that parental consent be waived). States can no longer absolutely require two-parent notification or consent before a minor may undergo an abortion. When a parent refuses to consent to medical attention for a seriously ill or dying child, even if on religious grounds, the states may act according to their PARENS PATRIAE power and obtain a court order to secure the necessary medical treatment.

CROSS-REFERENCES

Adoption; Child Custody; Children's Rights; Child Support; Family Law; Fetal Rights; In Loco Parentis; Juvenile Law; Parent and Child; Schools and School Districts; Welfare; Wrongful Birth; Wrongful Pregnancy.

INFERENCE ▥ In the law of EVIDENCE, a truth or proposition drawn from another that is supposed or admitted to be true. A process of reasoning by which a fact or proposition sought to be established is deduced as a logical consequence from other facts, or a state of facts, already proved or admitted. A logical and reasonable conclusion of a fact not presented by DIRECT EVIDENCE but which, by process of logic and reason, a trier of fact may conclude exists from the established facts. Inferences are deductions or conclusions that with reason and common sense lead the jury to draw from facts which have been established by the evidence in the case. ▥

INFERIOR COURT ▥ This term may denote any court subordinate to the chief APPELLATE tribunal in the particular judicial system (e.g., trial court); but it is also commonly used as the designation of a court of special, limited, or statutory JURISDICTION, whose record must show the existence and attaching of jurisdiction in any given case. ▥

INFIRMITY ▥ Flaw, DEFECT, or weakness. ▥

In a legal sense, the term *infirmity* is used to mean any imperfection that renders a particular transaction void or incomplete. For example, if a DEED drawn up to transfer ownership of land contains an erroneous description of it, an infirmity exists in the transaction.

IN FORMA PAUPERIS ▥ [Latin, *In the character or manner of a pauper.*] A phrase that indicates the permission given by a court to an indigent to initiate a legal action without having to pay for court fees or COSTS due to his or her lack of financial resources. ▥

INFORMATION ▥ The formal accusation of a criminal offense made by a public official; the sworn, written accusation of a CRIME. ▥

An information is tantamount to an INDICTMENT in that it is a sworn written statement which charges that a particular individual has done some criminal act or is guilty of some criminal omission. The distinguishing characteristic between an information and an indictment is that an indictment is presented by a GRAND JURY, whereas an information is presented by a duly authorized public official.

The purpose of an information is to inform the ACCUSED of the charge against him, so that the accused will have an opportunity to prepare a defense.

INFORMATION AND BELIEF ▥ A standard phrase added to qualify a statement made under OATH; a phrase indicating that a statement is made, not from firsthand knowledge but, nevertheless, in the firm belief that it is true. ▥

For example, an AFFIDAVIT may be needed at some point in a lawsuit even though the individual (whether a party to or a witness in the lawsuit) who has firsthand information is out of the country on business. In many such circumstances that individual's attorney may make an affidavit for him or her. The attorney must indicate that the individual is swearing only to facts that he or she has been told and believes to be true; in other words, on information and belief.

INFORMED CONSENT ▥ Assent to permit an occurrence, such as surgery, that is based on a complete disclosure of facts needed to make the decision intelligently, such as knowledge of the risks entailed or alternatives.

A sample
informed-consent
form

CONSENT TO MEDICAL/SURGICAL TREATMENT UPON
ADMISSION TO HOSPITAL

DATE: _____

1. I (or _____),
knowing that I (or _____) am (is) suffer-
ing from a condition requiring diagnosis and medical or surgical treatment do hereby voluntarily consent to such diagnostic procedures and hospital care and to such medical, surgical
or x-ray treatment by my attending physician, his assistants or his designees as is necessary
in their judgement. I further consent to the administration of anesthesia and to the use of
such anesthesia as may be deemed advisable.

2. I am aware that the practice of medicine and surgery is not an exact science and I
acknowledge that no guarantees have been made to me as to the result of treatments or examination in the hospital.

3. I hereby authorize _____ General Hospital to retain, preserve and use for scientific or teaching purposes, or dispose of at their convenience, any specimens or tissues taken
from my body during my hospitalization.

4. I hereby authorize _____ General Hospital to furnish such information from
Medical Records pertaining to the hospitalization as requested by either GROUP HOSPI-
TAL INSURANCE PLANS OR COMPANIES, or WORKER'S COMPENSATION IN-
SURANCE COMPANIES if applicable to this case.

5. This form has been fully explained to me and I certify that I understand its contents.

READ BEFORE SIGNING

_____
SIGNATURE OF PATIENT

Witness: _____   _____
SIGNATURE OF RELATIVE, LEGAL GUARDIAN
OR AUTHORIZED PERSON

_____

PATIENT VALUABLES RECORD AND STATEMENT

DEPOSITED IN SAFE	RETAINED BY PATIENT	RETURNED TO PATIENT'S HOME
ENVELOPE # _____ KEY # _____	BILLS $ _____ COINS $ _____	BILLS $ _____ WEDDING BAND _____
BILLS $ _____ COINS $ _____	WEDDING BAND _____ RINGS _____	RINGS _____ JEWELRY _____
WEDDING BAND _____ RINGS _____	WATCH _____ JEWELRY _____	OTHER _____
WATCH _____ JEWELRY _____	RADIO _____ SHAVER _____	_____
OTHER _____	HEARING AID _____ GLASSES _____	_____
_____	LUGGAGE _____ OTHER _____	SIGNATURE OF RESP. PERSON
_____	_____	(RELATIONSHIP) (DATE)

ADMISSION ACKNOWLEDGMENT AND STATEMENT

I, the undersigned, acknowledge that the above indicated items are correct and complete.
I also acknowledge that money and valuables (articles deemed valuable by the patient or his
family), unless deposited for safekeeping, are kept at the OWNER'S RISK: and the hospital
management **IS NOT LIABLE** in the event of loss.

This is to state that I have either read or had the foregoing information explained and
that I thoroughly understand its meaning:

Witness:

_____   _____   _____
(DATE)   (SIGNATURE OF PATIENT OR RESP. PERSON)

The name for a fundamental principle of law that a PHYSICIAN has a DUTY to reveal what a reasonably prudent physician in the medical community employing reasonable CARE would reveal to a patient as to whatever reasonably foreseeable risks of harm might result from a proposed course of treatment. This disclosure must be afforded so that a patient—exercising ordinary care for his or her own welfare and confronted with a choice of undergoing the proposed treatment, alternative treatment, or none at all—can intelligently exercise judgment by reasonably balancing the probable risks against the probable benefits. ▥

INFRA ▥ [*Latin, Below, under, beneath, underneath.*] A term employed in legal writing to indicate that the matter designated will appear beneath or in the pages following the reference. ▥

INFRACTION ▥ Violation or INFRINGEMENT; breach of a statute, CONTRACT, or obligation. ▥

The term *infraction* is frequently used in reference to the violation of a particular statute for which the penalty is minor, such as a parking infraction.

INFRINGEMENT ▥ The encroachment, breach, or violation of a right, law, regulation, or CONTRACT. ▥

The term is most frequently used in reference to the invasion of rights secured by COPYRIGHT, PATENT, or TRADEMARK. The unauthorized manufacture, sale, or distribution of an item protected by a copyright, patent, or trademark constitutes an infringement.

INGROSSING ▥ The act of making a perfect copy of a particular instrument, such as a DEED, LEASE, or WILL, from a rough draft so that it may be properly executed to achieve its purpose. ▥

INHERENT ▥ Derived from the essential nature of, and inseparable from, the object itself. ▥

An object which is *inherently dangerous* is one that possesses potential hazard by its mere existence, such as EXPLOSIVES. By contrast, other objects are dangerous only when used in a negligent manner, such as a pipe wrench or baseball bat. The rule of STRICT LIABILITY is applied when accidents arise from objects that are inherently dangerous.

INHERIT ▥ To receive property according to the state laws of INTESTATE SUCCESSION from a decedent who has failed to execute a valid WILL, or, where the term is applied in a more general sense, to receive the property of a decedent by will. ▥

INHERITANCE ▥ Property received from a DECEDENT, either by WILL or through state laws of INTESTATE SUCCESSION, where the decedent has failed to execute a valid will. ▥

INITIATIVE ▥ A process of a participatory democracy that empowers the people to propose legislation and to enact or reject the laws at the polls independent of the lawmaking power of the governing body. ▥

The purpose of an initiative, which is a type of ELECTION commenced and carried out by the people, is to permit the electorate to resolve questions where their elected representatives fail to do so or refuse to proceed with a change that the public desires.

INJUNCTION ▥ A court order by which an individual is required to perform or is restrained from performing a particular act. A WRIT framed according to the circumstances of the individual case. ▥

An injunction commands an act that the court regards as essential to justice, or it prohibits an act that is deemed contrary to good conscience. It is an EXTRAORDINARY REMEDY, reserved for special circumstances in which the temporary preservation of the status quo is necessary.

An injunction is ordinarily and properly elicited from other proceedings. For example, a landlord might bring an action for WASTE against a tenant in which the right to protect the landlord's interest in the ownership of the premises is at issue. The landlord might apply to the court for an injunction against the tenant's continuing harmful use of the property. The injunction is an ancillary remedy in the action against the tenant.

Injunctive relief is not a matter of right, but its denial is within the discretion of the court. Whether or not an injunction will be granted varies with the facts of each case.

The courts exercise their power to issue injunctions judiciously, and only when necessity exists. An injunction is usually issued only in cases where IRREPARABLE INJURY to the rights of an individual would otherwise result. It must be readily apparent to the court that some act has been performed or is threatened that will produce irreparable injury to the party seeking the injunction. An injury is considered irreparable when it cannot be adequately compensated by an award of DAMAGES. The pecuniary damage that would be incurred from the threatened action need not, however, be great. If a loss can be calculated in terms of money, there is no irreparable injury. The consequent refusal by a court to grant an injunction is, therefore, proper. Loss of profits alone is insufficient to establish irreparable injury. The potential destruction of property is, however, sufficient.

Injunctive relief is not a remedy that is liberally granted, and, therefore, the court will

A sample motion
for preliminary
injunction

[Title of Court and Cause]

Plaintiffs, _____ and _____, move the Court for a preliminary injunction in the above entitled cause enjoining the defendants, and _____ and _____, their agents, servants, employees and attorneys, [and those persons in active concert or participation with them] from _____

_____

_____

The grounds in support of this motion are as follows:

1. _____
2. _____

Unless restrained _____ and _____ will immediately [*state action defendants will take unless restrained*].

Immediate and irreparable injury, loss and damage will result to the plaintiffs by reason of the threatened action of the defendants, as more particularly appears in the verified complaint filed herein and the attached affidavit of _____. The plaintiffs have no adequate remedy at law.

If this preliminary injunction be granted, the injury, if any, to defendants herein, if final judgment be in their favor, will be inconsiderable and will be adequately indemnified by bond.

[Add if appropriate: Plaintiffs further move the Court that the trial of this action on the merits be advanced and consolidated with the hearing of this motion for preliminary injunction. The grounds in support of consolidation are as follows: . . .]

_____,
Attorney for Plaintiffs.

Address: _____.

always consider any hardship that the parties will sustain by the granting or refusal of an injunction. The court that issues an injunction may, in exercise of its discretion, modify or dissolve it at a later date if the circumstances warrant it.

Types of Injunction

Preliminary A *preliminary* or *temporary injunction* is a provisional remedy invoked to preserve the subject matter in its existing condition. Its purpose is to prevent dissolution of the plaintiff's rights. The main reason for use of a PRELIMINARY INJUNCTION is the need for immediate relief.

Preliminary or temporary injunctions are not conclusive as to the rights of the parties, and they do not determine the MERITS of a case or decide issues in controversy. They seek to prevent threatened wrong, further injury, and irreparable harm or injustice until such time as the rights of the parties can be ultimately settled. Preliminary injunctive relief ensures the ability of the court to render a meaningful decision and serves to prevent a change of circumstances that would hamper or block the granting of proper relief following a trial on the merits of the case.

A motion for a preliminary injunction is never granted automatically. The discretion of the court should be exercised in favor of a temporary injunction, which maintains the status quo until the final trial. Such discretion should be exercised against a temporary injunction when its issuance would alter the status quo.

Preventive An injunction directing an individual to refrain from doing an act is *preventive*, *prohibitive*, *prohibitory*, or *negative*. This type of injunction prevents a threatened injury, preserves the status quo, or restrains the continued commission of an ongoing wrong but cannot be used to redress a consummated wrong or to undo that which has already been done.

Mandatory The court is vested with wide discretion to fashion injunctive relief and is, therefore, restricted to restraint of a contemplated or threatened action. It might also compel affirmative performance of an act. In such a case, it issues a mandatory injunction, commanding the performance of a positive act. Since mandatory injunctions are harsh, they are not favored by the courts and are rarely granted. Such injunctions have been issued to compel the removal of buildings or other structures wrongfully placed upon the land of another.

Permanent   A *permanent* or *perpetual* injunction is one that is granted by the judgment that ultimately disposes of the injunction suit, ordered at the time of final judgment. This type of injunction must always be final relief. Permanent injunctions are perpetual, provided the conditions that produced them remain permanent. They have been granted to prevent blasting upon neighboring premises, to enjoin the dumping of earth or other material upon land, and to prevent pollution of a water supply.

An individual who has been licensed by the state to practice a profession may properly demand that others in the same profession subscribe to the ethical standards and laws that govern it. An injunction is a proper remedy to prevent the illegal practice of a profession, and the relief may be sought by either licensed practitioners or a professional association. The illegal practice of law, medicine, dentistry, and architecture has been stopped by the issuance of injunctions.

Acts that are injurious to the public health or safety may also be enjoined. For example, injunctions have been issued to enforce laws providing for the eradication of diseases in animals raised for food.

The government has the authority to protect citizens from damage by violence and from fear through threats and intimidation. In some states, an injunction is the proper remedy to bar the use of violence against those asserting their rights under the law.

Acts committed without just cause that interfere with the carrying on of a business may be enjoined if no other adequate remedy exists. A TRADE SECRET, for example, may be protected by injunction. An individual's right of personal PRIVACY may be protected by an injunction if there is no other adequate remedy or where a specific statutory provision for injunctive relief exists. An individual whose name or picture is used for advertising purposes without the individual's consent may restrain its use. The theory is that injunctive relief is proper because of a celebrity's unique property interest in the commercial use of his or her name and likeness.

Restraining Order   A restraining order is granted to preserve the status quo of the subject of the controversy until the hearing on an application for a temporary injunction. A TEMPORARY RESTRAINING ORDER is an extraordinary remedy of short duration issued to prevent unnecessary and irreparable injury. Essentially, such an order suspends proceedings until an opportunity arises to inquire whether an injunction should be granted. Unless extended by the court, a temporary restraining order ceases to operate upon the expiration of the time set by its terms.

Contempt   An individual who violates an injunction may be punished for CONTEMPT of court. A person is not guilty of contempt, however, unless he or she can be charged with knowledge of the injunction. Generally an individual charged with contempt is entitled to a trial or a hearing. The penalty imposed is within the discretion of the court. Ordinarily punishment is by fine, imprisonment, or both.

See also EQUITY.

INJURE 📖 To interfere with the legally protected interest of another or to inflict harm on someone, for which an ACTION may be brought. To damage or impair. 📖

The term *injure* is comprehensive and can apply to an INJURY to a person or property. See also TORTS.

INJURIOUS FALSEHOOD 📖 A fallacious statement that causes intentional damage to an individual's commercial or economic relations.

Any type of defamatory remark, either written or spoken, that causes pecuniary loss to an individual through DISPARAGEMENT of a particular business dealing. 📖

For example, the early cases on injurious falsehood involved oral aspersions cast upon an individual's ownership of land, which prevented the individual from leasing or selling it. This TORT has also been called *disparagement of property*, *slander of goods*, and *trade libel*.

Injurious falsehood is distinguishable from the more general harm to reputation in LIBEL AND SLANDER.

INJURY 📖 A comprehensive term for any wrong or harm done by one individual to another individual's body, rights, reputation, or PROPERTY. Any interference with an individual's legally protected interest. 📖

A civil injury is any damage done to person or property that is precipitated by a breach of CONTRACT, NEGLIGENCE, or breach of duty. The law of TORTS provides remedies for injury caused by negligent or intentional acts.

An *accidental injury* is an injury to the body caused unintentionally. Within the meaning of

WORKERS' COMPENSATION acts, it is an injury occurring in the COURSE OF EMPLOYMENT.

One who is injured might be able to recover DAMAGES against the individual who caused him or her harm, since the law seeks to provide a remedy for every injury.

IN KIND 📖 Of the same class, category, or species. 📖

A loan is repaid *in kind* when a substantially similar article is returned by the borrower to the lender.

INLAND WATERS 📖 CANALS, lakes, rivers, water courses, inlets, and bays that are nearest to the shores of a nation and subject to its complete SOVEREIGNTY. 📖

Inland waters, also known as internal waters, are subject to the total sovereignty of the country as much as if they were an actual part of its land territory. A coastal nation has the right to exclude foreign vessels, subject to the right of entry in times of distress.

Whether or not particular waters are to be regarded as inland waters has traditionally been dependent upon historical and geographical factors. Certain types of shoreline configurations have been regarded as confining bodies of water, such as bays. In addition, there has been a recognition that other areas of water that are closely connected to the shore may be regarded as inland waters based upon the manner in which they have been treated by the coastal nation, although they do not meet any exact geographical test. Historic TITLE to inland waters can be claimed only in situations when the coastal nation has asserted and maintained dominion and control over those waters.

See also NAVIGABLE RIVERS; WATER RIGHTS.

IN LIEU OF 📖 Instead of; in place of; in substitution of. It does not mean *in addition to.* 📖

IN LOCO PARENTIS 📖 [*Latin, In the place of a parent.*] The legal doctrine under which an individual assumes parental rights, duties, and obligations without going through the formalities of legal ADOPTION. 📖

In loco parentis is a legal doctrine describing a relationship similar to that of a parent to a child. It refers to an individual who assumes parental status and responsibilities for another individual, usually a young person, without formally adopting that person. For example, legal GUARDIANS are said to stand in loco parentis with respect to their WARDS, creating a relationship that has special implications for INSURANCE and WORKERS' COMPENSATION law. By far the most common usage of in loco parentis relates to teachers and students. For hundreds of years, the English common-law concept shaped the rights and responsibilities of public school teachers: until the late nineteenth century, their legal authority over students was as broad as that of parents. Changes in U.S. education, concurrent with a broader reading by courts of the rights of students, began bringing the concept into disrepute by the 1960s.

Taking root in colonial American schools, in loco parentis was an idea derived from English COMMON LAW. The colonists borrowed it from the English ideal of schools having not only educational but also moral responsibility for students. With this duty went the equivalent of parental authority. The idea especially suited the puritanical values of the colonists, and after the American Revolution, it persisted in elementary and high schools, colleges, and universities. The judiciary respected it: like their English counterparts, U.S. courts in the nineteenth century were unwilling to interfere when students brought grievances, particularly in the area of rules, discipline, and expulsion.

In 1866, for instance, one court stated, "A discretionary power has been given, . . . [and] we have no more authority to interfere than we have to control the domestic discipline of a father in his family" (*People ex rel. Pratt v. Wheaton College*, 40 Ill. 186). Well into the twentieth century, courts permitted broad authority to schools and showed hostility to the claims of student plaintiffs. In dismissing a claim by a restaurant owner against a college,

James Acton sued the school district of Veronia, Oregon, challenging its right to conduct random urinalysis tests on student athletes. The Supreme Court held that the school district's athlete drug policy did not violate a student's right to be free from unreasonable searches. (Acton is at center with his brother, mother, and father.)

AP/WIDE WORLD PHOTOS

the Kentucky Supreme Court found that a college's duties under in loco parentis gave it the power to forbid students to patronize the restaurant (*Gott v. Berea College*, 156 Ky. 376, 161 S.W. 204 [1913]).

Two important shifts in society and law diminished the effect of the doctrine. One was the evolution of educational standards. Beginning in the late 1800s and advancing rapidly during the mid-1900s, the increasing secularization of schools brought an emphasis on practical education over moral instruction. At a slower rate, courts adapted to this change, according greater rights to students than were previously recognized. This trend began during the turbulent era of social change in the 1960s.

The first to benefit were students in higher education, through rulings such as the landmark *Dixon v. Alabama State Board of Education*, 294 F.2d 150 (5th Cir. 1961). In *Dixon*, the U.S. Court of Appeals for the Fifth Circuit extended DUE PROCESS rights to students at tax-supported colleges, ruling that the Constitution "requires notice and some opportunity for hearing" before students can be expelled for misconduct. After *Dixon*, courts largely abandoned in loco parentis in favor of CONTRACT law for adjudicating disputes between students and their institutions. Partly in reaction to free speech movements, other changes came as courts recognized that students at public colleges and universities were entitled to full enjoyment of their FIRST and FOURTH AMENDMENT rights.

Over the next decade, public school students received greater recognition of their rights, too. In ruling that high school students could not be expelled for wearing black armbands to protest the Vietnam War, the U.S. Supreme Court held in 1969 that students do not "shed their constitutional rights ... at the schoolhouse gate" (*Tinker v. Des Moines Independent Community School District*, 393 U.S. 503, 89 S. Ct. 733, 21 L. Ed. 2d 731). In 1975, it held in *Goss v. Lopez*, 419 U.S. 565, 95 S. Ct. 729, 42 L. Ed. 2d 725, that the suspension of high school students for alleged disruptive or disobedient conduct required some sort of NOTICE of charges and a prior HEARING.

But the underlying premise of in loco parentis did not disappear completely from public schools. Instead, the Supreme Court limited students' rights based on what it found appropriate for children in school. In 1977, it held that the disciplinary paddling of public school students was not a CRUEL AND UNUSUAL PUNISHMENT prohibited by the Eighth Amendment (*Ingraham v. Wright*, 430 U.S. 651, 97 S. Ct. 1401, 51 L. Ed. 2d 711). Public school students have also traditionally enjoyed less protection of their First and Fourth Amendment rights. Recognizing the duty of schools to safeguard students, the Court in 1995 permitted high schools to conduct random urinalysis of student athletes even without prior suspicion (*Vernonia School District v. Acton*, 515 U.S. 646, 115 S. Ct. 2386, 132 L. Ed. 2d 564).

The progression from the courts' early acceptance of in loco parentis to a broader recognition of students' rights transformed U.S. education. Students in public universities gained the most from this shift in philosophy and law, but students in high school also earned recognition of their due process rights. The judicial revolution that began with *Dixon* did not give constitutional protection to the rights of private school students, who are distinct under the law from public school students.

In the 1980s, new issues involving the in loco parentis doctrine arose for colleges and universities. Victims of campus crime insisted that these institutions owed a duty to provide safe campuses to students. The schools, noting that the doctrine of in loco parentis was no longer upheld, resisted the idea because of the increased LIABILITY that would accrue to them. At the same time, many institutions enacted controversial rules governing so-called hate speech, and these codes returned them in some measure to the days when they tightly regulated student behavior.

CROSS-REFERENCES

Children's Rights; Colleges and Universities; Guardian and Ward; Infants; Juvenile Law; Schools and School Districts.

IN MEDIAS RES 📖 [*Latin, Into the heart of the subject, without preface or introduction.*] 📖

INNKEEPER 📖 An individual who, as a regular business, provides accommodations for guests in exchange for reasonable compensation. 📖

An inn is defined as a place where lodgings are made available to the public for a charge, such as a hotel, motel, hostel, or guest house. A *guest* is a transient who receives accommodations at an inn, transiency being the major characteristic distinguishing him or her from a boarder. In order for the relationship of innkeeper and guest to be established, the parties must intend to have such a relationship. The individual accommodated must be received as a guest and must obtain accommodations in such capacity. The individual need not, however, register.

An innkeeper must accept all unobjectionable individuals offering themselves as guests, provided the innkeeper has available accommodations and the guests are willing to pay the reasonable charges. Proper grounds for a refusal to receive a proposed guest are ordinarily restricted to either lack of accommodations or the unsuitability of the guest.

It is improper and a violation of an individual's CIVIL RIGHTS for an innkeeper to refuse accommodations on the basis of race, creed, or color. Upon assignment to a room, a guest is entitled to its exclusive occupancy for all lawful purposes, subject to the right of the innkeeper to enter the room for proper purposes, such as to assist the police in their investigation of a CRIME.

Compensation An innkeeper is permitted to charge a reasonable compensation only, and must ordinarily fulfill his or her entire obligation prior to being entitled to the compensation. In the event that a guest does not pay, the innkeeper has a LIEN on the guest's property. Such a lien ordinarily extends to all property brought by the guest to the inn and generally continues until the DEBT is satisfied unless the innkeeper voluntarily surrenders the goods. The innkeeper may remove a guest upon refusal to pay his or her bill but cannot, however, use excessive force.

Liability An innkeeper has an obligation to reasonably protect guests from injury while at the inn. This DUTY of reasonable care mandates vigilance in protection of the guests from foreseeable risks. The innkeeper must protect guests from injury at the hands of other guests and from ASSAULTS and negligent acts of his or her own employees. The obligation to protect guests is not met merely by warning them, but must be coupled with a policing of the premises.

An innkeeper must take reasonable care regarding the safety of the guests' property and must warn guests of any hidden dangers that can be reasonably foreseen. This duty includes making inspections to ascertain that the premises are safe. The innkeeper is liable for any injuries arising from his or her failure to comply with fire regulations. Reasonably safe means of ingress and egress must be provided.

An innkeeper is required to use reasonable care to keep the hallways, passageways, and stairways well lighted and free from obstructions or hazards. An innkeeper who furnishes appliances or furniture for the convenience of guests must maintain them in a reasonably safe condition. Similar duties are required in connection with plumbing apparatus and swimming pools.

Reasonable care must be exercised by an innkeeper in the operation and maintenance of an elevator, which means that the elevator must be inspected and repaired to keep it in safe condition. The obligation to maintain the premises in a reasonably safe condition applies to windows and screens that are defective or insecurely fastened. Failure to have protective window grills or to guard air shafts located on a roof does not, however, necessarily constitute negligence.

The prevalent COMMON LAW view makes an innkeeper liable as an INSURER for all PERSONAL PROPERTY brought by the guest to the inn that is lost through the innkeeper's fault. There is no LIABILITY, however, if the guest assumes the entire and exclusive care, control, and possession of his or her property. State laws have been enacted with respect to the liability of innkeepers for the property of their guests. Generally the statutes modify the common law by limiting the innkeeper's liability to a specified amount and by requiring deposit of valuables. Guests must have notice of any limitations of the innkeeper's liability.

INNOCENT 📖 Absent guilt; acting in GOOD FAITH with no knowledge of DEFECTS, objections, or inculpative circumstances. 📖

A person accused of and prosecuted for the commission of a crime is presumed innocent until proved guilty BEYOND A REASONABLE DOUBT.

INNOCENT PURCHASER 📖 An individual who, in GOOD FAITH and by an honest agreement, buys property in the absence of sufficient knowledge to charge him or her with NOTICE of any DEFECT in the transaction. 📖

An individual is an innocent or good-faith purchaser when he or she buys something, paying VALUABLE CONSIDERATION, without actual or CONSTRUCTIVE notice of any legal infirmity in the sale. The purchaser of a gold bracelet for $500 from a jewelry store cannot be charged with notice that the bracelet was stolen.

INNS OF CHANCERY 📖 Ancient preparatory colleges where qualified clerks studied the drafting of WRITS, which was a function of the officers of the Court of CHANCERY. 📖

Students attended Inns of Chancery to learn the basics of law and to qualify for admission after two years of instruction to the INNS OF COURT to which the Inn of Chancery was attached. The role of the Inns of Chancery in the English legal education process significantly declined in the eighteenth and nineteenth centuries.

INNS OF COURT 📖 Organizations that provide preparatory education for ENGLISH LAW students in order to teach them to practice in court. 📖

Inns of Court were founded in the beginning of the fourteenth century. Membership in an

Lincoln's Inn is one of four organizations that provide preparatory education for English law. It has existed since at least 1420.

inn is tantamount to membership in an INTEGRATED BAR association in the United States. Inns of Court have a common council of legal education, which gives lectures and holds examinations. Currently, inns have the exclusive authority to confer the degree of *barrister-at-law*, a prerequisite to practice as an advocate or counsel in the superior courts in England.

INOPERATIVE VOID; not active; ineffectual.

The term *inoperative* is commonly used to indicate that some force, such as a statute or CONTRACT, is no longer in effect and legally binding upon the persons who were to be, or had been, affected by it.

IN PARI DELICTO [*Latin, In equal fault.*] A descriptive phrase that indicates that parties involved in an ACTION are equally CULPABLE for a wrong.

When the parties to a legal controversy are *in pari delicto*, neither can obtain affirmative relief from the court, since both are at equal fault or of equal guilt. They will remain in the same situation they were in prior to the commencement of the action.

IN PARI MATERIA [*Latin, Upon the same subject.*] A designation applied to statutes or general laws that were enacted at different times but pertain to the same subject or object.

Statutes *in pari materia* must be interpreted in light of each other since they have a common purpose for comparable events or items.

IN PERPETUITY Of endless duration; not subject to termination.

The phrase *in perpetuity* is often used in the grant of an EASEMENT to a utility company.

IN PERSONAM [*Latin, Against the person.*] A lawsuit seeking a JUDGMENT to be enforceable specifically against an individual person.

An *in personam* action can affect the defendant's personal rights and interests and substantially all of his or her PROPERTY. It is based on the authority of the court, or JURISDICTION, over the person as an individual rather than jurisdiction over specific property owned by the person. This contrasts with IN REM jurisdiction, or actions that are limited to property of the defendant that is within the control of the court. A court with *in personam* jurisdiction in a particular case has enough power over the defendant and his or her property to grant a judgment affecting the defendant in almost any way.

INQUEST An inquiry by a CORONER or medical examiner, sometimes with the aid of a JURY, into the cause of a violent death or a death occurring under suspicious circumstances. Generally an inquest may result in a finding of natural death, accidental death, suicide, or murder. Criminal prosecution may follow when CULPABLE conduct has contributed to the death.

The body of jurors called to inquire into the circumstances of a death that occurred suddenly, by violence, or while imprisoned. Any body of jurors called to inquire into certain matters. (A GRAND JURY is sometimes called a grand inquest, for example.)

The determination or findings of a body of persons called to make a legal inquiry or the report issued after their investigation.

The foundation of the modern jury system can be traced back to the Carolingian empire of medieval Europe during the eighth to the tenth centuries. The monarchs used a procedure called inquest, or inquisition, to help them consolidate their authority in the realm. They called together the people of the countryside and required them to recite what they considered to be the immemorial rights of the king. Once these rights were ascertained, they were adopted by the government and considered established. There was no ACCUSATION, VERDICT, or JUDGMENT in these proceedings, but the inquest fixed the right of the government to obtain information from its citizens.

The Norman invaders were not long on English soil when they used the inquest to compile the DOMESDAY BOOK, a census compiled between 1085 and 1086 to record the ownership of land throughout the kingdom.

For this inquiry, citizens were called and required to give testimony under OATH about their land and PERSONAL PROPERTY.

The inquest was also used in local courts in England during the Middle Ages. Since a person could not be tried for a crime until accused,

a panel of four men from each VILL and twelve from each HUNDRED appeared before the court and charged certain individuals with crimes. The panel members appeared voluntarily, however, and were not summoned by a public officer as is done for an inquest today. Then in 1166 a law called the Assize of Clarendon made the inquest procedure mandatory. The panel of men was required to appear before local SHERIFFS and make regular accusations on their oaths. These cases then were tried in the royal courts because of the king's special interest in keeping the peace. This procedure was the origin of the modern grand jury.

A further step in consolidating the king's powers came with creation of the office of the coroner, so named for its service to the crown. In the Middle Ages the coroner was a powerful local official who kept records of appeals from lower courts, accusations, hangings, and public financial matters. He held inquests to investigate royal rights concerning fish, shipwrecks, treasure trove, and unexplained deaths. The purpose of such inquests was always to determine the extent of the king's financial interests. Anytime there was a death, the crown took whatever object had caused the death and all of the personal property of anyone who committed suicide or was convicted of a FELONY. From this early function of fiscal administration, the coroner today has become primarily responsible for managing dead bodies, but the inquest is still the procedure the coroner uses for investigation.

See also CLARENDON, CONSTITUTIONS OF.

INQUIRY, COMMISSIONS OF 📖 Individuals employed, during CONCILIATION, to investigate the facts of a particular dispute and to submit a report stating the facts and proposing terms for the resolution of the differences. 📖

A coroner or medical examiner may proceed with an inquest in the case of a death occurring under suspicious circumstances.

INQUISITORIAL SYSTEM 📖 A method of legal practice in which the judge endeavors to discover facts while simultaneously representing the interests of the state in a trial. 📖

The inquisitorial system can be defined by comparison with the adversarial, or accusatorial, system used in the United States and Great Britain. In the ADVERSARY SYSTEM, two or more opposing parties gather EVIDENCE and present the evidence, and their arguments, to a judge or JURY. The judge or jury knows nothing of the litigation until the parties present their cases to the decision maker. The DEFENDANT in a criminal trial is not required to TESTIFY.

In the inquisitorial system, the presiding judge is not a passive recipient of information. Rather, the presiding judge is primarily responsible for supervising the gathering of the evidence necessary to resolve the case. He or she actively steers the search for evidence and questions the WITNESSES, including the respondent or defendant. Attorneys play a more passive role, suggesting routes of inquiry for the presiding judge and following the judge's questioning with questioning of their own. Attorney questioning is often brief because the judge tries to ask all relevant questions.

The goal of both the adversarial system and the inquisitorial system is to find the truth. But the adversarial system seeks the truth by pitting the parties against each other in the hope that competition will reveal it, whereas the inquisitorial system seeks the truth by questioning those most familiar with the events in dispute. The adversarial system places a premium on the individual rights of the accused, whereas the inquisitorial system places the rights of the accused secondary to the search for truth.

The inquisitorial system was first developed by the Catholic Church during the medieval period. The ECCLESIASTICAL COURTS in thirteenth-century England adopted the method of adjudication by requiring witnesses and defendants to take an inquisitorial oath administered by the judge, who then questioned the witnesses. In an inquisitorial oath, the witness swore to truthfully answer all questions asked of him or her. The system flourished in England into the sixteenth century, when it became infamous for its use in the Court of the STAR CHAMBER, a court reserved for complex, contested cases. Under the reign of King Henry VIII, the power of the Star Chamber was expanded, and the court used torture to compel the taking of the inquisitorial oath. The Star Chamber was eventually eliminated as repugnant to basic liberty, and England gradually moved toward an adversarial system.

After the French Revolution, a more refined version of the inquisitorial system developed in France and Germany. From there it spread to the rest of continental Europe and to many African, South American, and Asian countries. The inquisitorial system is now more widely used than the adversarial system. Some countries, such as Italy, use a blend of adversarial and inquisitorial elements in their court system.

The court procedures in an inquisitorial system vary from country to country. Most inquisitorial systems provide a full review of a case by an appeals court. In civil trials under either system of justice, the defendant, or respondent, may be required to testify. The most striking differences between the two systems can be found in criminal trials.

In most inquisitorial systems, a criminal defendant does not have to answer questions about the crime itself but may be required to answer all other questions at TRIAL. Many of these other questions concern the defendant's history and would be considered irrelevant and INADMISSIBLE in an adversarial system.

A criminal defendant in an inquisitorial system is the first to testify. The defendant is allowed to see the government's case before testifying, and is usually eager to give her or his side of the story. In an adversarial system, the defendant is not required to testify and is not entitled to a complete examination of the government's case.

A criminal defendant is not presumed guilty in an inquisitorial system. Nevertheless, since a case would not be brought against a defendant unless there is evidence indicating guilt, the system does not require the PRESUMPTION OF INNOCENCE that is fundamental to the adversarial system.

A trial in an inquisitorial system may last for months as the presiding judge gathers evidence in a series of hearings.

The decision in an inquisitorial criminal trial is made by the collective vote of a certain number of professional judges and a small group of lay assessors (persons selected at random from the population). Neither the prosecution nor the defendant has an opportunity to question the lay assessors for BIAS. Generally, the judges vote after the lay assessors vote, so that they do not influence the conclusions of the lay assessors. A two-thirds majority is usually required to convict a criminal defendant, whereas a unanimous VERDICT is the norm in an adversarial system.

The inquisitorial system does not protect criminal defendants as much as the adversarial system. On the other hand, PROSECUTORS in the inquisitorial system do not have a personal incentive to win convictions for political gain, which can motivate prosecutors in an adversarial system. Most scholars agree that the two systems generally reach the same results by different means.

See also CRIMINAL PROCEDURE; DUE PROCESS OF LAW.

IN RE [*Latin, In the matter of.*] Concerning or regarding. The usual style for the name of a judicial proceeding having some item of property at the center of the dispute rather than adverse parties.

For example, proceedings to determine various claims to the assets of a bankrupt company could be called *In re Klein Company*, or *In the matter of Klein Company*.

Sometimes *in re* is used for a proceeding where one party makes an application to the court without necessarily charging an adversary. This may be done, for example, where a couple seeks to adopt a child or an adult wants to change his or her name.

Such actions may instead use the English translation "in the matter of" or the Latin words EX PARTE. The final decision on the style to be used for a particular lawsuit is usually made by the clerk of the court.

IN REM [*Latin, In the thing itself.*] A lawsuit against an item of PROPERTY, not against a person (IN PERSONAM).

An action *in rem* is a proceeding that takes no notice of the owner of the property but determines rights in the property that are conclusive against all the world. For example, an action to determine whether certain property illegally imported into the United States ought to be forfeited can be captioned *United States v. Thirty-nine Thousand One Hundred and Fifty Cigars*. The object of the lawsuit is to determine the disposition of the property, regardless of who the owner is or who else might have an interest in it. Interested parties might appear and make out a case one way or another, but the action is *in rem*, against the things.

In rem lawsuits can be brought against the property of DEBTORS in order to collect what is owed, and they are begun for the PARTITION of REAL PROPERTY, FORECLOSURE of MORTGAGES, and the enforcement of LIENS. They may be directed against real or personal property. *In rem* actions are permitted only when the court has control of the property or where its authority extends to cover it. For example, the courts in Kansas may determine rights to a farm in Kansas, but not the ownership of a cannery in Texas. The *in rem* jurisdiction of a court may be exercised only after parties who are known to have an interest in the property are notified of the proceedings and have been given a chance to present their claim to the court.

INSANITY DEFENSE 📖 A defense asserted by an ACCUSED in a criminal prosecution to avoid LIABILITY for the commission of a CRIME because, at the time of the crime, the person did not appreciate the nature or quality or wrongfulness of the acts. 📖

The insanity defense is used by criminal defendants. The most common variation is cognitive insanity. Under the test for cognitive insanity, a defendant must have been so impaired by a mental disease or defect at the time of the act that he or she did not know the nature or quality of the act, or, if the defendant did know the nature or quality of the act, he or she did not know that the act was wrong. The vast majority of states allow criminal defendants to invoke the cognitive insanity defense.

Another form of the insanity defense is volitional insanity, or IRRESISTIBLE IMPULSE. Irresistible impulse asserts that the defendant, though able to distinguish right from wrong at the time of the act, suffered from a mental disease or defect that made the defendant incapable of controlling her or his actions. This defense is common in crimes of vengeance. For example, assume that a child has been brutally assaulted. If an otherwise conscientious and law-abiding mother shoots the perpetrator, the mother may argue that she was so enraged that she became mentally ill and incapable of exerting self-control. Approximately five states allow the volitional insanity defense.

The insanity defense should not be confused with incompetency. Persons who are incompetent to stand trial are held in a mental institution until they are considered capable of participating in the proceedings.

The insanity defense should also be kept separate from issues concerning mental retardation. Mentally retarded persons, or persons with an IQ of seventy or lower, may be convicted and even sentenced to death if they are found COMPETENT to stand trial.

The insanity defense reflects the generally accepted notion that persons who cannot appreciate the consequences of their actions should not be punished for criminal acts. Most states regulate the defense with statutes, but a few states allow the courts to craft the rules for its proper use. Generally, the defense is available to a criminal defendant if the judge instructs the JURY that it may consider whether the defendant was insane when the crime was committed. The judge may issue this instruction if the defendant has produced sufficient EVIDENCE at trial to justify the theory. Sufficient evidence invariably includes expert TESTIMONY by psychologists and psychiatrists.

When invoking insanity as a defense, a defendant is required to notify the prosecution. In some states, sanity is determined by the judge or jury in a separate proceeding following the determination of guilt or innocence at trial. In other states, the defense is either accepted or rejected in the VERDICT of the judge or jury. Even if evidence of insanity does not win a verdict of not guilty, the sentencing court may consider it as a mitigating factor.

History "Complete madness" was first established as a defense to criminal charges by the common-law courts in late-thirteenth-century England. By the eighteenth century, the complete madness definition had evolved into the "wild beast" test. Under this test, the insanity defense was available to a person who was "totally deprived of his understanding and memory so as not to know what he [was] doing, no more than an infant, a brute, or a wild beast" (Feigl 1995, 161).

By 1840, most JURISDICTIONS had refined the wild beast test to cognitive insanity and supplemented that with irresistible impulse insanity. However, in 1843, a well-publicized ASSASSINATION attempt in England caused Parliament to eliminate the irresistible impulse defense. Daniel M'Naghten, operating under the delusion that Prime Minister Robert Peel wanted to kill him, endeavored to shoot Peel but shot and killed Peel's secretary instead. Medical testimony indicated that M'Naghten was psychotic, and the court acquitted him by reason of insanity (*M'Naghten's Case*, 8 Eng. Rep. 718 [1843]). In response to a public furor that followed the decision, the House of Lords ordered the Lords of Justice of the Queen's Bench to craft a new rule for insanity in the CRIMINAL LAW.

What emerged became known as the M'NAGHTEN RULE. This rule migrated to the United States within a decade of its conception, and it stood for the better part of the next century. The intent of the *M'Naghten* rule was to abolish the irresistible impulse defense and limit the insanity defense to cognitive insanity. Under the *M'Naghten* rule, insanity was a defense if

at the time of the committing of the act, the party accused was labouring under such a defect of reason, from a disease of the mind, as not to know the nature and quality of the act he was doing; or, if he did know it, that he did not know he was doing what was wrong.

Through the first half of the twentieth century, the insanity defense was expanded again.

IS THERE A NEED FOR THE INSANITY DEFENSE?

Though the insanity defense is rarely invoked in criminal trials, it remains a controversial issue. Legislators and the public generally question the need for the defense after a defendant in a highly publicized murder case is found not guilty by reason of insanity. For example, when John Hinckley successfully used the defense after shooting President Ronald Reagan to impress the actress Jodie Foster, there was a public outcry. Legal and medical commentators have divided opinions about the need for the insanity defense.

Those who wish to retain it note that forty-eight of the fifty states have some type of insanity defense. This, they claim, is evidence of the need for such a defense. The public is given a distorted view of who uses the defense and how it is employed. In fact about one percent of criminal defendants invoke the defense. More important, criminals rarely "beat the rap" by pleading insanity. When an insanity defense is employed, it means the defendant admits committing the criminal behavior and is now seeking a not guilty verdict on the basis of his state of mind. If the jury does not agree, the defendant will be convicted, and generally will serve a longer sentence than will someone convicted of the same crime who has not pleaded insanity.

Juries find for only about 20 percent of the defendants who plead insanity. Even this figure does not reflect the reality that many insanity pleas are the result of plea bargains, which indicates that prosecutors agree that such pleas are sometimes appropriate.

Finally, the fact that most highly publicized cases involve murder disguises the true demographics: 60 to 70 percent of insanity pleas are for crimes other than murder. They range from assault to shoplifting.

All these myths have led to the belief that criminals can avoid punishment by claiming insanity. The truth is that the insanity defense is a risky one at best.

Apart from combating these myths, advocates of the insanity defense contend that a fundamental principle of criminal law is at stake. The insanity defense is rooted in the belief that conviction and punishment are justified only if the defendant deserves them. The basic precondition for punishment is that the person who committed the criminal behavior must have responsibility as a moral agent. When a person is so mentally disturbed that her irrationality or compulsion is impossible to control, that person lacks responsibility as a moral agent. It would be unfair to punish a person in such an extreme condition.

Based on this argument, proponents of the insanity defense do not support its application to a person who willingly consumes a powerful hallucinogen and then commits a criminal act. Nor would they allow its application to a person who is able to control a mental disorder through medication but fails to do so. But they do support the defense for a person who unwittingly consumes hallucinogens and then commits a crime.

Some opponents attack the insanity defense for confusing psychiatric and legal concepts, in the process undermining the moral integrity of the law. Both sides agree that the word *insane* is a legal, not medical, term. It is too simplistic to describe a severely mentally ill person merely as insane, and the vast majority of people with a mental illness would be judged sane if current legal tests for insanity were applied. The legal tests for insanity, moreover, require that a defendant's mental condition become so impaired that the fact finder

may conclude the person has lost his or her free will. Because free will is not a concept that can be explained in medical terms, it may be impossible for a psychiatrist to determine if the mental impairment affected the defendant's capacity for voluntary choice. Without a way to measure insanity, it makes no sense to let prosecution and defense psychiatrists spar over the issue. A jury's decision based on psychiatrists' opinions may be grounded on unreliable evidence.

Another major argument against the insanity defense challenges its supposed moral basis. Critics contend that modern criminal law is concerned more with the consequences of crime and less with moral imperatives. If a person commits a criminal act, that person should be convicted. Mental illness can be taken into consideration at the time of sentencing. This line of reasoning supports laws that several states have adopted, which abolish the insanity defense and replace it with a new verdict of guilty but insane. This verdict carries a criminal penalty. It allows the judge to determine the length of imprisonment, which occurs in a hospital prison, and shifts the burden to the defendant to prove he is no longer dangerous or mentally ill in order to be released.

Finally, critics argue that the insanity plea is a rich person's defense. Only wealthy defendants can retain high-priced psychiatric experts. Persons represented by public defenders are usually afforded a psychiatric examination for the defense, but they may not get the same quality of exam, nor are they typically able to hire more than one examiner. Because a two-tiered criminal justice system is morally repugnant, critics contend that the insanity defense must be abolished.

Courts began to accept the theories of psycho-analysts, many of whom encouraged recognition of the irresistible impulse defense. Many states enacted a combination of the *M'Naghten* rule supplemented with an irresistible impulse defense, thereby covering both cognitive and volitional insanity.

The insanity defense reached its most permissive standard in *Durham v. United States*, 214 F.2d 862 (D.C. Cir. 1954). The *Durham* rule excused a defendant "if his unlawful act was the product of mental disease or mental defect." The *Durham* rule was lauded by the mental health community as progressive because it allowed psychologists and psychiatrists to contribute to the judicial understanding of insanity. But it was also criticized for placing too much trust in the opinions of mental health professionals. Within seven years of its creation, the rule had been explicitly rejected in twenty-two states. It is used only in New Hampshire.

In 1964, the American Law Institute (ALI) began to reassess the insanity defense in the course of promoting a new Model Penal Code. What emerged from the Model Penal Code Commission was a compromise between the narrow *M'Naghten* test and the generous *Durham* rule. The ALI test provided that a person was not responsible for criminal conduct if, at the time of the act, the person lacked "substantial capacity" to appreciate the conduct or to conform the conduct to the rule of law. The ALI test provided for both cognitive and volitional insanity. It also required only a lack of substantial capacity, less than complete impairment. The ALI version of the insanity defense was adopted by more than half the states and all but one federal circuit.

Several years later, another dramatic event led to another round of restrictions on the insanity defense. In 1981, John Hinckley, Jr., attempted to assassinate President RONALD REAGAN. Hinckley was prosecuted and acquitted of all charges by reason of insanity, and a resulting public outcry prompted Congress to enact legislation on the issue. In 1984, Congress passed the Insanity Defense Reform Act (Insanity Act) (18 U.S.C.A. § 17 [1988]) to abolish the irresistible impulse test from FEDERAL COURTS. Initially, Reagan had called for a total abolition of mental illness as a defense to criminal charges, but the Reagan administration backed down from this position after intense lobbying by various professional organizations and trade associations.

The Insanity Act also placed the burden on the defendant to prove insanity. Before the Insanity Act, federal prosecutors bore the burden of proving the defendant's sanity BEYOND A REASONABLE DOUBT.

Most states joined Congress in reevaluating the insanity defense after Hinckley's acquittal. The legislatures of these states modified and limited the insanity defense in many and varied ways. Some states shifted the burden of proof, and some limited the applicability of the defense in the same manner as Congress did. A few states abolished the defense entirely. Chief Justice WILLIAM H. REHNQUIST, of the Supreme Court, opined in a dissent that it is "highly doubtful that due process requires a State to make available an insanity defense to a criminal defendant" (*Ake v. Oklahoma*, 470 U.S. 68, 105 S. Ct. 1087, 84 L. Ed. 2d 53 [1985]).

Consequences   When a party successfully defends criminal charges on a ground of insanity, the consequences vary from jurisdiction to jurisdiction. Usually, the defendant is committed to a mental institution. On the average, a defendant found not guilty by reason of insanity and committed to a mental institution is confined twice as long as a defendant found guilty and sent to prison. Very few acquitted insanity defendants are given supervised release, and even fewer are released directly following their verdict.

The detention of an insanity acquittee is limited by law. The acquittee must be allowed periodic review in the mental institution to determine whether continued treatment is necessary. In addition, a hospital facility may not hold an insanity acquittee indefinitely merely because the acquittee has an antisocial personality (*Foucha v. Louisiana*, 504 U.S. 71, 112 S. Ct. 1780, 118 L. Ed. 2d 437 [1992]).

The procedural framework in Massachusetts illustrates the consequences that come with the insanity defense. Under chapter 123, section 16, of the Massachusetts General Laws Annotated, the court may order a person found not guilty by reason of insanity (an insanity acquittee) to be hospitalized for forty days for observation and examination. During this period, the district attorney or the superintendent of the mental hospital may petition the court to have the insanity acquittee committed to the hospital. If the judge orders the commitment, the acquittee is placed in the hospital for six months.

After the first six months have expired, the commitment is reviewed again, and then once a year thereafter. If the superintendent of the mental health facility moves to discharge the acquittee, the district attorney must respond with any objections within thirty days of notice from the superintendent. The mental health facility is authorized to restrict the movement

Colin Ferguson

Colin Ferguson was convicted in March 1995 for crimes associated with a massacre in Long Island, New York, on December 7, 1993. Ferguson killed six persons and injured nineteen after opening fire with an automatic pistol on a crowded commuter train.

Ferguson's trial was marked with controversy. He discharged his court-appointed attorneys, who believed him mentally incompetent to stand trial, and was allowed by the judge to act as his own attorney. He dropped the insanity defense prepared by his attorneys and argued that a mysterious gunman had committed the shootings.

His bizarre courtroom behavior appeared to contradict the judge's conclusion that Ferguson was competent to stand trial. Though many witnesses identified Ferguson as the gunman, he insisted a white man had taken the gun from his bag while he slept, shot the passengers, and then escaped, leaving Ferguson, who is black, to take the blame. During the trial he asserted that he had been charged with ninety-three counts only because the crime occurred in 1993.

Attorneys Ronald L. Kuby and William M. Kunstler, whom Ferguson had discharged, had asked the judge before trial to find that Ferguson's paranoia and delusional state made him mentally incompetent to stand trial. Yet Ferguson refused to be examined by either prosecution or defense psychiatrists, believing he was not insane. The judge allowed Ferguson to stand trial, believing he could understand the nature of the charges against him and could assist in his own defense.

of criminal defendants and insanity acquittees, so a commitment is tantamount to incarceration.

Defendants' Rights When pleading insanity, a defendant may not want to present the best possible image at trial. In *Riggins v. Nevada*, 504 U.S. 127, 112 S. Ct. 1810, 118 L. Ed. 2d 479 (1992), defendant David Riggins was charged with robbing and murdering Las Vegas resident Paul Wade. After being taken into custody, Riggins complained that he was hearing voices in his head and was having trouble sleeping. A psychiatrist at the jail prescribed 100 milligrams a day of Mellaril, an antipsychotic drug. By the time of trial, the psychiatrist was prescribing 800 milligrams a day of Mellaril.

Just before trial, Riggins's attorney moved the court to suspend administration of the Mellaril. Riggins was pleading not guilty by reason of insanity, and Riggins's attorney wanted the jury to see Riggins in his natural state. According to one psychiatrist, Dr. Jack Jurasky, Riggins "would most likely regress to a manifest psychosis and become extremely difficult to manage" if he were taken off Mellaril.

The court denied the motion, and Riggins was convicted and sentenced to death. The Nevada Supreme Court affirmed Riggins's convictions and death sentence. On appeal to the U.S. Supreme Court, the convictions were reversed. According to the High Court, Nevada had violated Riggins's DUE PROCESS rights under the Sixth and Fourteenth Amendments. In the absence of evidence that the treatment was medically appropriate and essential for Rig-

gins's own safety or the safety of others, and without an exploration of less intrusive alternatives, the trial court had erred by denying Riggins's liberty interest in freedom from antipsychotic drugs.

According to the High Court, the administration of the Mellaril jeopardized a number of Riggins's trial rights. Not only was it possible that the Mellaril had affected Riggins's outward appearance, and thus his defense, but the high daily dosage of Mellaril may also have affected Riggins's testimony, his ability to communicate with his attorney, and his ability to follow the proceedings. Although the defense had been allowed to present expert testimony on the nature of Riggins's mental condition, the Court concluded that the compromise of Riggins's trial rights was unacceptable.

Uses and Abuses Victims of abuse often allege temporary insanity in defending their own violent behavior. For example, in 1994, Virginia resident Lorena Bobbitt, charged with severing her husband's penis with a knife, was acquitted of ASSAULT charges on the ground of temporary insanity. At trial, Bobbitt testified that her husband had abused her physically and emotionally.

Critics complain that the insanity defense is abused by defense attorneys, who use it to free the perpetrators of deliberate criminal acts. However, 95 percent of all persons found not guilty by reason of insanity are detained in hospitals, and in practice, the insanity defense is rarely invoked and rarely successful. The insanity defense is used by defendants in only one percent of all FELONY cases, and it results in ACQUITTAL in only one-quarter of those cases.

INSECURITY CLAUSE 📖 Provision in a CONTRACT that allows a CREDITOR to make an entire DEBT come due if there is good reason to believe that the DEBTOR cannot or will not pay. 📖

INSIDER 📖 In the context of federal regulation of the purchase and sale of SECURITIES, anyone who has knowledge of facts not available to the general public. 📖

Insider information refers to knowledge about the financial status of a company that is obtained before the public obtains it, and which is usually known only by corporate officials or other insiders. The use of insider information in the purchase and sale of stock violates federal securities law.

Insider trading entails the purchase and sale of corporate SHARES by OFFICERS, DIRECTORS, and stockholders who own more than 10 percent of the stock of a CORPORATION listed on a national EXCHANGE (any association that provides facilities for the purchase and sale of securities, such as the New York Stock Exchange). *Insider reports* detailing such transactions must be submitted monthly to the SECURITIES AND EXCHANGE COMMISSION.

INSOLVENCY 📖 An incapacity to pay DEBTS upon the date when they become due in the ordinary course of business; the condition of an individual whose property and ASSETS are inadequate to discharge the person's debts. 📖

IN SPECIE 📖 Specific; specifically. Thus, to decree performance *in specie* is to decree SPECIFIC PERFORMANCE. In kind; in the same or like form. A thing is said to exist *in specie* when it retains its existence as a distinct individual of a particular class. 📖

INSPECTION 📖 An examination or investigation; the right to see and duplicate documents, enter land, or make other such examinations for the purpose of gathering EVIDENCE. 📖

The inspection of documents relevant to issues in a lawsuit is an important element of DISCOVERY.

INSTALLMENT 📖 Regular, partial portion of the same DEBT, paid at successive periods as agreed by a DEBTOR and CREDITOR. 📖

A sample installment loan agreement

Creditor:

Consumer Installment Note, Security Agreement and Disclosure

Borrower's name

Co-borrower's name

Date   Note no.
_____ , 19____

In this agreement, I, me and my refer to the borrower named. You and your refer to the Bank. This agreement contains my promise to repay my loan, and the conditions of my loan.

My Promise. I promise to pay to your order

_____ Dollars
($_____) plus interest on the unpaid balance at an annual rate of _____%. Interest starts on _____, 19____, and continues until my loan has been paid in full.
To repay you, I will make:
• a first payment of $_____ on _____, 19____;
• _____ payments of $_____ each on the _____ day of each _____ starting on _____, 19____; and
• a final payment on _____, 19____. If all my payments are made on schedule, the final payment will be $_____.
☐ If checked, Chapter 53 of Minnesota Statutes authorizes you to charge the interest that I am promising to pay.
Renewal. ☐ This agreement renews note no. _____
          dated _____, 19____, and is not in
          payment of that note.

Security.
☐ No security is required.
☐ To protect you if I default under this agreement (or for any extension or renewal of it) I give you a security interest in:
  ☐ Motor Vehicle year/make   Serial number
    1. _____   1. _____
    2. _____   2. _____
☐ All my property in your possession at any time.
☐ The following property _____
_____
_____
_____
_____
_____
_____
_____
_____
_____
_____
_____
_____

☐ This agreement (including extensions or renewals) is secured by a separate agreement ☐ written agreement ☐ mortgage.
Prepaying my loan: I MAY PREPAY MY LOAN AT ANY TIME WITHOUT PENALTY.

Federal Truth in Lending Disclosure

The Creditor in this agreement is the Bank named above.

ANNUAL PERCENTAGE RATE The cost of my credit as a yearly rate.	FINANCE CHARGE The amount the credit will cost me.	Amount Financed The amount of credit provided to me or on my behalf.	Total of Payments The amount I will have paid after making all payments as scheduled.
%	$	$	$

Payment Schedule. My schedule for paying my loan will be:

Number of payments	Amount of payment	When payments are due

Security. I am giving a security interest in:
☐ the goods or property being purchased.
☐ Brief description of other property: _____

_____

Itemization of the Amount Financed

Amount of money I receive	$ _____
Amount used to pay off a prior loan from you	$ _____
Amounts paid to others on my behalf:	
• to public officials	$ _____
• to insurance companies	$ _____
• to _____	$ _____
Prepaid finance charge	($ _____)
Total Amount Financed	$ _____

Insurance for My Loan

Property Insurance. Insurance on property I give as security ☐ is ☐ is not required. If insurance is required, I may buy it through any insurance agent or company of my choice. If I buy it through you, the term of the policy will be _____ and the premium will be $ _____

Credit Insurance. Credit insurance is not required for this loan. If I choose to buy it through you:
☐ Credit life insurance covering me alone for a term of _____
    costs $ _____
☐ Joint credit life insurance covering me and my co-borrower for a term of
    _____ costs $ _____ .
☐ Credit accident and health insurance covering me alone for a term of
    _____ costs $ _____
    ☐ I want the insurance checked above. ☐ I do not want credit insurance.

_____

My initials _____ Age _____ Date _____

Property securing other loans with you may also secure this loan.
Filing Fees paid to public officials are $ _____ .
Prepayment. I will not have to pay a penalty if I pay off my loan early.
Assumption. (Mobile home loans only). Anyone buying my mobile home may not be allowed to assume the remainder of my debt on the original terms.
Late Charge. If a payment is late by more than 10 days, I will be charged 5% of the unpaid installment.
Other Terms. I understand the rest of this agreement contains additional information about nonpayment, default, any required repayment in full before the scheduled date, and any prepayment penalties.

Borrower's Signature
I received and read a filled-in copy of this agreement before signing it. I agree to all its terms.
Borrower's signature
X _____
Address

Owner of the Security
The person signing here owns an interest in the property described above. By signing, he or she joins in granting the bank a security interest in that property. The owner is not personally responsible for payment of the loan.
Owner's signature
X _____
Address

Guarantor's Signature
The person signing here is the guarantor. The bank may require the guarantor to pay the loan at any time after it becomes due, whether or not the bank has then made any effort to collect the loan from the borrower or co-borrower. The guarantor will continue to be responsible even if the bank releases its security interest in property described above, consents to changes in this agreement, or releases any other person from responsibility. The guarantor must also pay any attorneys' fees and other costs of enforcing this guaranty. By signing, the guarantor takes on serious responsibilities. These responsibilities are summarized in the "Notice to Guarantor" on the back of this form. By signing here, the guarantor confirms that he or she has read that notice.
Guarantor's signature
X _____
Address

Additional Terms

Simple Interest
Interest on my loan will be calculated using the "simple interest" method. This means that the actual interest I pay will depend on my unpaid balance at the end of each day.

If I pay ahead of schedule, the finance charge may be less than estimated. If my payments are late, my finance charge may be higher. You will adjust my last payment accordingly, but you may excuse any additional finance charge due to late payments.

I understand that the simple interest method of calculating interest may not always give the same results as the method used in making the Truth in Lending disclosures. So, the actual amount I pay may not be exactly as disclosed.

Prepaying My Loan in Part
I may prepay part of my loan at any time without a prepayment penalty. However, partial prepayment will not excuse me from making the full amount of each payment on schedule until my loan is paid in full.

Your Rights if I Default
I will be in default if:

• I do not make a payment when due or in the full amount;
• I made misstatements on my loan application;
• someone tries by legal proceedings to get money or property I have on deposit with you;

• I do not make a payment when due on any other loans I may already have with you or on any other loans I may have with you in the future;
• a case under the U.S. Bankruptcy Code is started by me or against me or any guarantor of this loan;
• I do not keep required insurance on the security for this agreement, or I use the security for an unlawful purpose;
• an event of default occurs under any security agreement covering my loan;
• I die; or
• you believe in good faith that I may not be able or willing to pay you as promised.

If I am in default, you may require immediate payment of the unpaid balance of my loan, including the interest I owe. You do not have to give me notice.

You may also repossess and sell the property of mine you hold as security and use the proceeds to pay my loan. "Proceeds" means money from the sale of the property. You will notify me at least 10 days before the sale (unless notice is not required by law). You may also exercise any other legal rights you may have.

However, even if I am in default, you do not have to require immediate payment. You may delay enforcing any of your rights without losing them.

Legal and Collection Costs
I must pay any reasonable attorneys' fees, legal expenses, and costs of collection that result from my default (unless prohibited by law).

A sample installment loan agreement (continued)

Setoff

If I am in default, you may take the money from any of my accounts with you to pay this agreement. For this purpose, my accounts include all accounts to which I am a party. This may be done without notifying me.

Terms of Your Security Interest

I will make every effort to maintain the security interest I have given you.

Your security interest covers not only the property, but also all occasions. "Accessions" are goods installed in or attached to the property.

You may act on my behalf to buy or settle any property insurance required under this agreement. If you pay any premiums for this insurance, I will repay

you on demand with interest. Interest will be at the same rate as the interest on my loan. Interest will start on the date you pay the premium and will continue until the date I repay you.

You may sign my name to any check or other instrument issued under the required property insurance, and use the money or any unearned premium to pay my loan.

Late Charge

If I do not pay any installment of principal or interest within 10 days after it is due,. I will pay you a late charge equal to 5% of the late installment (unless prohibited by law).

Returned Checks

If I give you a check for a principal or interest payment and the check is returned to you unpaid, I will pay you an additional fee of $15 for the returned check (unless prohibited by law).

Governing Law

The law of Minnesota governs this agreement.

If FTC Notice is to be inserted, rubber stamp that Notice in the space below.

NOTICE TO GUARANTOR

You are being asked to guarantee this debt. Think carefully before you do. If the borrower doesn't pay the debt, you will have to. Be sure you can afford to pay if you have to, and that you want to accept this responsibility.

You may have to pay up to the full amount of the debt if the borrower does not pay. You may also have to pay late fees or collection costs, which increase this amount.

The Bank can collect this debt from you without first trying to collect from the borrower. The Bank can use the same collection methods against you that can be used against the borrower, such as suing you, garnisheeing your wages, etc. If this debt is ever in default, that fact may become a part of your credit record.

This notice is not the contract that makes you liable for the debt.

An *installment loan* is designed to be repaid in certain specified, ordinarily equal amounts over a designated period, such as a year or a number of months.

INSTANT Current or present.

When composing a legal BRIEF, an attorney might use the phrase *the instant case* in reference to the case currently before the court to distinguish it from other cases discussed.

INSTIGATE To incite, stimulate, or induce into action; goad into an unlawful or bad action, such as a CRIME.

The term *instigate* is used synonymously with ABET, which is the intentional encouragement or aid of another individual in committing a crime.

INSTITUTE To inaugurate, originate, or establish. In CIVIL LAW, to direct an individual who was named as HEIR in a WILL to pass over the ESTATE to another designated person, known as the substitute.

For example, to institute an ACTION is to commence it by the filing of a COMPLAINT.

INSTITUTION The commencement or initiation of anything, such as an ACTION. An establishment, particularly one that is eleemosynary or public by nature.

An institution can be any type of organized CORPORATION or society. It may be private and designed for the profit of the individuals composing it, or public and nonprofit.

INSTRUCTIONS Directives given by a judge to a JURY during a TRIAL prescribing the manner in which the jurors should proceed in deciding the case at bar.

Jury instructions ordinarily include a statement of the QUESTIONS OF FACT for determination by the jury, as well as a statement of the laws applicable to the facts of the case.

INSTRUMENT A formal or legal written document; a document in writing, such as a DEED, LEASE, BOND, CONTRACT, or WILL. A writing that serves as EVIDENCE of an individual's right to collect money, such as a CHECK.

INSTRUMENTALITY RULE A principle of corporate law that permits a court to disregard the corporate existence of a subsidiary CORPORATION when it is operated solely for the benefit of the parent corporation, which controls and directs the activities of the SUBSIDIARY while asserting the shield of limited LIABILITY.

The instrumentality rule, also called the ALTER EGO doctrine, destroys the corporate immunity from liability when the corporate nature of an organization is a sham that brings about injustice. When the rule is applied, the court is considered to pierce the corporate veil.

INSURABLE INTEREST A right, benefit, or advantage arising out of PROPERTY that is of such nature that it may properly be indemnified.

A sample installment loan agreement (continued)

In the law of INSURANCE, the INSURED must have an interest in the subject matter of his or her policy, or such policy will be void and unenforceable since it will be regarded as a form of gambling. An individual ordinarily has an insurable interest when he or she will obtain some type of financial benefit from the preservation of the subject matter, or will sustain pecuniary loss from its destruction or impairment when the risk insured against occurs.

In certain JURISDICTIONS, the innocent purchaser of a stolen car, who has a right of possession superior to all with the exception of the true owner, has an insurable interest in the automobile. This is not the case, however, where an individual knowingly purchases a stolen automobile.

Insurable interest is not dependent upon who pays the premiums of the policy. In addition, different people can have separate insurable interests in the same subject matter or property.

INSURANCE 📖 A CONTRACT whereby, for a specified CONSIDERATION, one party undertakes to compensate the other for a loss relating to a particular subject as a result of the occurrence of designated hazards. 📖

The normal activities of daily life carry the RISK of enormous financial loss. Many persons are willing to pay a small amount for protection against certain risks because that protection provides valuable peace of mind. The term *insurance* describes any measure taken for protection against risks. When insurance takes the form of a contract in an insurance policy, it is subject to requirements in statutes, ADMINISTRATIVE AGENCY regulations, and court decisions.

In an insurance contract, one party, the INSURED, pays a specified amount of money, called a PREMIUM, to another party, the INSURER. The insurer in turn agrees to compensate the insured for specific future losses. The losses covered are listed in the contract, and the contract is called a POLICY.

When an insured suffers a loss or damage that is covered in the policy, the insured can collect on the proceeds of the policy by filing a CLAIM, or request for coverage, with the insurance company. The company then decides whether to pay the claim. The recipient of any proceeds from the policy is called the BENEFICIARY. The beneficiary can be the insured person, or other persons designated by the insured.

A contract is considered to be insurance if it distributes risk among a large number of persons through an enterprise engaged primarily in the business of insurance. Warranties or service contracts for merchandise, for example, do not constitute insurance. Warranties and service contracts are not issued by insurance companies, and the risk distribution in the transaction is incidental to the purchase of the merchandise. Warranties and service contracts are thus exempt from strict insurance laws and regulations.

The business of insurance is sustained by a complex system of risk analysis. Generally, this analysis involves anticipating the likelihood of a particular loss and charging enough in premiums to guarantee that insured losses can be paid. Insurance companies collect the premiums for a certain type of insurance policy and use them to pay the few individuals who suffer losses that are insured by that type of policy.

Most insurance is provided by private corporations, but some is provided by the government. For example, the FEDERAL DEPOSIT INSURANCE CORPORATION was established by Congress to insure bank deposits. The federal government provides life insurance to military service personnel. Congress and the states jointly fund MEDICAID and MEDICARE, which are HEALTH INSURANCE programs for persons who are disabled or elderly. Most states offer health insurance to qualified persons who are indigent.

Government-issued insurance is regulated like private insurance, but the two are very different. Most recipients of government insurance do not have to pay premiums, but they also do not receive the same level of coverage available under private insurance policies. Government-issued insurance is granted by the legislature, not bargained for with a private insurance company, and it can be taken away by an act of the legislature. However, if a legislature issues insurance, it cannot refuse it to a person who qualifies for it.

History The first examples of insurance related to marine activities. In many ancient societies, merchants and traders pledged their ships or cargo as security for loans. In Babylon CREDITORS charged higher interest rates to merchants and traders in exchange for a promise to forgive the loan if the ship was robbed by pirates or was captured and held for ransom.

In postmedieval England local groups of working people banded together to create "friendly societies," forerunners of the modern insurance companies. Members of the friendly societies made regular contributions to a common fund, which was used to pay for losses suffered by members. The contributions were determined without reference to a member's age, and without precise identification of what claims would be covered. Without a system to anticipate risks and potential LIABILITY, many of the first friendly societies were unable to pay claims, and many eventually disbanded. Insurance gradually came to be seen as a matter best handled by a company in the business of providing insurance.

Insurance companies began to operate for profit in England in the seventeenth century. They devised tables to mathematically predict losses based on various data, including the characteristics of the insured and the probability of loss related to particular risks. These calculations made it possible for insurance companies to anticipate the likelihood of claims, and this made the business of insurance reliable and profitable.

The British Parliament granted a monopoly over the business of insurance in colonial America to two English corporations, London Assurance and Royal Exchange. In the 1760s colonial legislatures gave a few American insurance companies permission to operate. Since the Revolutionary War, U.S. insurance companies have grown in number and size, with most offering to insure against a wide range of risks.

Regulation and Control Until the middle of the twentieth century, insurance companies in the United States were relatively free from federal regulation. According to the U.S. Supreme Court in *Paul v. Virginia*, 75 U.S. (8 Wall.) 168, 19 L. Ed. 357 (1868), the issuing of an insurance policy did not constitute a commercial transaction. This meant that states had the power to regulate the business of insurance. In 1944 the High Court held in *United States v. South-Eastern Underwriters Ass'n*, 322 U.S. 533, 64 S. Ct. 1162, 88 L. Ed. 1440, that insurance did, in some cases, constitute a commercial transaction. This meant that Congress had the power to regulate it. The *South-Eastern* holding made the business of insurance subject to federal laws on rate fixing and monopolies.

In the late twentieth century, insurance is governed by a blend of statutes, administrative agency regulations, and court decisions. State statutes often control premium rates, prevent unfair practices by insurers, and guard against the financial INSOLVENCY of insurers to protect insureds. On the federal level, the McCARRAN-FERGUSON ACT (Pub. L. No. 79-15, 59 Stat. 33 [1945] [codified at 15 U.S.C.A. §§ 1011–1015 (1988)]) permits states to retain regulatory control over insurance, as long as their laws and regulations do not conflict with federal ANTITRUST LAWS on rate fixing, rate discrimination, and monopolies.

In most states an administrative agency created by the state legislature devises rules to cover procedural details missing from the statutory framework. To do business in a state, an insurer must obtain a LICENSE through a registration process. This process is usually managed by the state administrative agency. The same state agency may also be charged with the enforcement of insurance regulations and statutes.

Administrative agency regulations are many and varied. Insurance companies must submit to the governing agency yearly financial reports regarding their economic stability. This requirement allows the agency to anticipate potential insolvency, and to protect the interests of insureds. Agency regulations may specify the types of insurance policies that are acceptable in the state, though many states make these declarations in statutes. The administrative agency is also responsible for reviewing the competence and ethics of insurance company employees.

The judicial branch of government also shapes insurance law. Courts are often asked to resolve disputes between the parties to an insurance contract, and disputes with third parties. Court decisions interpret the statutes and regulations based on the facts of the case, creating many rules that must be followed by insurers and insureds.

Insurance companies may be penalized for violating statutes or regulations. Penalties for misconduct include FINES and the loss or suspension of the company's business license. In some states, if a court finds that an insurer's denial of coverage or refusal to defend an insured in a lawsuit was unreasonable, the insurance company may be required to pay court costs, attorneys' fees, and a percentage beyond the insured's recovery.

Types of Insurance Insurance companies create insurance policies by grouping risks according to their focus. This provides a measure of uniformity in the risks that are covered by a type of policy, which in turn allows insurers to anticipate their potential losses and set premiums accordingly. The most common forms of insurance policies include life, health, automobile, homeowners' and renters', personal property, fire and casualty, marine, and inland marine policies.

Life insurance provides financial benefits to a designated person upon the death of the insured. Many different forms of life insurance are issued. Some provide for payment only upon the death of the insured; others allow an insured to collect proceeds before death.

A person may purchase life insurance on her or his own life for the benefit of a third person or persons. Individuals may even purchase life insurance on the life of another person. For

Gene Testing

When a person applies for medical, life, or disability insurance, the insurance company typically requires the disclosure of preexisting medical conditions and a family medical history. In some cases the applicant must undergo a physical examination. Based on this information, the insurance company decides whether to offer coverage and, if so, at what price.

Breakthroughs in genetics now allow persons to be tested for rare medical conditions such as cystic fibrosis and Huntington's disease. In addition, genetic testing can reveal an increased risk of more common conditions, including breast, colon, and prostate cancer; lymphoma; and leukemia. Concerns have been raised that once these tests become affordable, insurance companies will use the results to deny coverage.

Research studies published in the 1990s indicate that persons already have been denied insurance coverage because of the risk of genetic disease. The prospect of widespread genetic discrimination troubles many professionals in the medical and legal communities. It is unfair, they charge, to deny a person coverage or to charge higher premiums, based on a potential risk of genetic disease that the person is powerless to modify.

The insurance industry, which currently collects medical information on genetic disease through the inspection of medical records and family histories, responds that a fundamental principle in writing insurance is charging people rates that reflect their risks. This means that each applicant pays the fairest possible price, based on her individual characteristics. The industry also notes that the concerns about genetic testing do not come into play with large-group health plans, where rates are based on methods other than individual assessments.

See also Genetic Screening.

example, a wife may purchase life insurance that will provide benefits to her upon the death of her husband. This kind of policy is commonly obtained by spouses and by parents insuring themselves against the death of a child. However, individuals may only purchase life insurance on the life of another person and name themselves beneficiary when there are reasonable grounds to believe that they can expect some benefit from the continued life of the insured. This means that some familial or financial relationship must unite the beneficiary and the insured. For example, a person cannot purchase life insurance on the life of a stranger in the hope that the stranger will suffer a fatal accident.

Health insurance policies cover only specified risks. Generally, they pay for the expenses incurred from bodily injury, disability, sickness, and accidental death. Health insurance can be purchased for one's self, and for others.

All AUTOMOBILE insurance policies contain liability insurance, which is insurance against injury to another person or against damage to another person's vehicle caused by the insured's vehicle. Auto insurance may also pay for the loss of, or damage to, the insured's motor vehicle. Most states require that all drivers carry, at a minimum, liability insurance under a no-fault scheme. In states recognizing no-fault insurance, damages resulting from an accident are paid for by the insurers, and the drivers do not have to go to court to settle the issue of

damages. Drivers in these states may bring suit over an accident only in cases of egregious conduct, or where medical or repair costs exceed an amount defined by statute.

Homeowners' insurance protects homeowners from losses related to their dwelling, including damage to the dwelling; personal liability for injury to visitors; and loss of, or damage to, property in and around the dwelling. Renters' insurance covers many of the same risks for persons who live in rented dwellings.

Personal property insurance protects against the loss of, or damage to, certain items of PERSONAL PROPERTY. It is useful when the liability limit on a homeowner's policy does not cover the value of a particular item or items. For example, the owner of an original painting by Pablo Picasso may wish to obtain, in addition to a homeowner's policy, a separate personal property policy to insure against loss of, or damage to, the painting.

Businesses can insure against damage and liability to others with FIRE and CASUALTY insurance policies. Fire insurance policies cover damage caused by fire, explosion, earthquake, lightning, water, wind, rain, collision, and riot. Casualty insurance protects the insured against a variety of losses, including those related to legal liability, BURGLARY and THEFT, accident, property damage, injury to workers, and insurance on CREDIT extended to others. Fidelity and surety bonds are temporary, specialized forms of casualty insurance. A FIDELITY BOND insures against losses related to the dishonesty of employees, and a SURETY bond provides protection to a business if it fails to fulfill its contractual obligations.

Marine insurance policies insure transporters and owners of cargo shipped on an ocean, a sea, or a navigable waterway. Marine risks include damage to cargo, damage to the vessel, and injuries to passengers.

Inland marine insurance is used for the transportation of goods on land and on land-locked lakes.

Many other types of insurance are also issued. Group health insurance plans are usually offered by employers to their employees. A person may purchase additional insurance to cover losses in excess of a stated amount or in excess of coverage provided by a particular insurance policy. Air travel insurance provides life insurance benefits to a named beneficiary if the insured dies as a result of the specified airplane flight. Flood insurance is not included in most homeowners' policies, but it can be purchased separately. MORTGAGE insurance requires the insurer to make mortgage payments when the insured is unable to do so because of death or disability.

Contract and Policy An insurance contract cannot cover all conceivable risks. An insurance contract that violates a statute, is contrary to PUBLIC POLICY, or plays a part in some prohibited activity will be held unenforceable in court. A contract that protects against the loss of burglary tools, for example, is contrary to public policy and unenforceable.

Insurable Interest To qualify for an insurance policy, the insured must have an insurable interest, meaning that the insured must derive some benefit from the continued preservation of the article insured, or stand to suffer some loss as a result of that article's loss or destruction. Life insurance requires some familial and pecuniary relationship between the insured and the beneficiary. Property insurance requires that the insured must simply have a lawful interest in the safety or preservation of the property.

Premiums Different types of policies require different premiums based on the degree of risk that the situation presents. For example, a policy insuring a homeowner for all risks associated with a home valued at $200,000 requires a higher premium than one insuring a boat valued at $20,000. Though liability for injuries to others may be similar under both policies, the cost of replacing or repairing the boat would be less than the cost of repairing or replacing the home, and this difference is reflected in the premium paid by the insured.

Premium rates also depend on characteristics of the insured. For example, a person with a poor driving record generally has to pay more for auto insurance than a person with a good driving record. Furthermore, insurers are free to deny policies to persons who present an unacceptable risk. For example, most insurance companies do not offer life or health insurance to persons who have been diagnosed with a terminal illness.

Claims The most common issue in insurance disputes is whether the insurer is obligated to pay a claim. The determination of the insurer's obligation depends on many factors, such as the circumstances surrounding the loss and the precise coverage of the insurance policy. If a dispute arises over the language of the policy, the general rule is that a court should choose the interpretation most favorable to the insured. Many insurance contracts contain an INCONTESTABILITY CLAUSE to protect the insured. This clause provides that the insurer loses the right to contest the validity of the contract after a specified period of time.

An insurance company may deny or cancel coverage if the insured party concealed or misrepresented a material fact in the policy application. If an applicant presents an unacceptably high risk of loss for an insurance company, the company may deny the application or offer prohibitively high premiums. A company may cancel a policy if the insured fails to make payments. A company may refuse to pay a claim if the insured intentionally caused the loss or damage. However, if the insurer knows it has the right to RESCIND a policy or deny a claim, but conveys to the insured that it has voluntarily surrendered such right, the insured may claim that the insurer waived its right to contest a claim.

An insurer may have a duty to defend an insured in a lawsuit filed against the insured by a third party. This duty usually arises if the claims in the suit against the insured fall within the coverage of a liability policy.

If a third party caused a loss covered by a policy, the insurance company may have the right to sue the third party in place of the insured. This right is called SUBROGATION, and it is designed to make the party that is responsible for a loss bear the burden of the loss. It also prevents an insured from recovering twice: once from the insurance company, and once from the responsible party.

An insurance company can subrogate claims only on certain types of policies. Property and liability insurance policies allow subrogation because the basis for the payment of claims is indemnification, or reimbursement, of the in-

HOMEOWNERS 1
BASIC FORM

AGREEMENT

We will provide the insurance described in this policy in return for the premium and compliance with all applicable provisions of this policy.

DEFINITIONS

In this policy, "you" and "your" refer to the "named insured" shown in the Declarations and the spouse if a resident of the same household. "We," "us" and "our" refer to the Company providing this insurance. In addition, certain words and phrases are defined as follows:

1. "Bodily injury" means bodily harm, sickness or disease, including required care, loss of services and death that results.
2. "Business" includes trade, profession or occupation.
3. "Insured" means you and residents of your household who are:
   a. Your relatives; or
   b. Other persons under the age of 21 and in the care of any person named above.

* * *

4. "Insured location" means:
   a. The "residence premises";

* * *

   e. Vacant land, other than farm land, owned by or rented to an "insured";
   f. Land owned by or rented to an "insured" on which a one or two family dwelling is being built as a residence for an "insured";
   g. Individual or family cemetery plots or burial vaults of an "insured"; or
   h. Any part of a premises occasionally rented to an "insured" for other than "business" use.

5. "Occurrence" means an accident, including continuous or repeated exposure to substantially the same general harmful conditions, which results, during the policy period, in:
   a. "Bodily injury"; or
   b. "Property damage."
6. "Property damage" means physical injury to, destruction of, or loss of use of tangible property.
7. "Residence employee" means:
   a. An employee of an "insured" whose duties are related to the maintenance or use of the "residence premises," including household or domestic services; or
   b. One who performs similar duties elsewhere not related to the "business" of an "insured."
8. "Residence premises" means:
   a. The one family dwelling, other structures, and grounds; or
   b. That part of any other building where you reside and which is shown as the "residence premises" in the Declarations.
   "Residence premises" also means a two family dwelling where you reside in at least one of the family units and which is shown as the "residence premises" in the Declarations.

SECTION I - PROPERTY COVERAGES

COVERAGE A - Dwelling

We cover:

1. The dwelling on the "residence premises" shown in the Declarations, including structures attached to the dwelling; and
2. Materials and supplies located on or next to the "residence premises" used to construct, alter or repair the dwelling or other structures on the "residence premises."

This coverage does not apply to land, including land on which the dwelling is located.

COVERAGE B - Other Structures

We cover other structures on the "residence premises" set apart from the dwelling by clear space. This includes structures connected to the dwelling by only a fence, utility line, or similar connection. This coverage

does not apply to land, including land on which the other structures are located.

We do not cover other structures:

1. Used in whole or in part for "business"; or
2. Rented or held for rental to any person not a tenant of the dwelling, unless used solely as a private garage.

The limit of liability for this coverage will not be more than 10% of the limit of liability that applies to Coverage A. Use of this coverage does not reduce the Coverage A limit of liability.

COVERAGE C - Personal Property

We cover personal property owned or used by an "insured" while it is anywhere in the world. At your request, we will cover personal property owned by:

Sample homeowners insurance policy—some portions omitted

1. Others while the property is on the part of the "residence premises" occupied by an "insured";
2. A guest or a "residence employee," while the property is in any residence occupied by an "insured."

Our limit of liability for personal property usually located at an "insured's" residence, other than the "residence premises," is 10% of the limit of liability for Coverage C, or $1000, whichever is greater. Personal property in a newly acquired principal residence is not subject to this limitation for the 30 days from the time you begin to move the property there.

* * *

1. $200 on money, bank notes, bullion, gold other than goldware, silver other than silverware, platinum, coins and medals.
2. $1000 on securities, accounts, deeds, evidences of debt, letters of credit, notes other than bank notes, manuscripts, personal records, passports, tickets and stamps. This dollar limit applies to these categories regardless of the medium (such as paper or computer software) on which the material exists.

This limit includes the cost to research, replace or restore the information from the lost or damaged material.

3. $1000 on watercraft, including their trailers, furnishings, equipment and outboard engines or motors.
4. $1000 on trailers not used with watercraft.
5. $1000 for loss by theft of jewelry, watches, furs, precious and semi-precious stones.
6. $2000 for loss by theft of firearms.
7. $2500 for loss by theft of silverware, silver-plated ware, goldware, gold-plated ware and pewterware. This includes flatware, hollowware, tea sets, trays and trophies made of or including silver, gold or pewter.
8. $2500 on property, on the "residence premises," used at any time or in any manner for any "business" purpose.
9. $250 on property, away from the "residence premises," used at any time or in any manner for any "business" purpose. However, this limit does not apply to loss to adaptable electronic apparatus as described in Special Limits **10.** and **11.** below.
10. $1000 for loss to electronic apparatus, while in or upon a motor vehicle or other motorized land conveyance, if the electronic apparatus is equipped to be operated by power from the electrical system of the vehicle or conveyance while retaining its capability of being operated by other sources of power. Electronic apparatus includes:
    a. Accessories or antennas; or
    b. Tapes, wires, records, discs or other media for use with any electronic apparatus.
11. $1000 for loss to electronic apparatus, while not in or upon a motor vehicle or other motorized land conveyance, if the electronic apparatus:

a. Is equipped to be operated by power from the electrical system of the vehicle or conveyance while retaining its capability of being operated by other sources of power;
b. Is away from the "residence premises"; and
c. Is used at any time or in any manner for any "business" purpose.

Electronic apparatus includes:
a. Accessories or antennas; or
b. Tapes, wires, records, discs or other media for use with any electronic apparatus.

Property Not Covered. We do not cover:
1. Articles separately described and specifically insured in this or other insurance;
2. Animals, birds or fish;
3. Motor vehicles or all other motorized land conveyances. This includes:
    a. Their equipment and accessories; or
    b. Electronic apparatus that is designed to be operated solely by use of the power from the electrical system of motor vehicles or all other motorized land conveyances. Electronic apparatus includes:
        (1) Accessories or antennas; or
        (2) Tapes, wires, records, discs or other media for use with any electronic apparatus.

    The exclusion of property described in 3.a. and 3.b. above applies only while the property is in or upon the vehicle or conveyance.

We do cover vehicles or conveyances not subject to motor vehicle registration which are:
a. Used to service an "insured's" residence; or
b. Designed for assisting the handicapped;

4. Aircraft and parts. Aircraft means any contrivance used or designed for flight, except model or hobby aircraft not used or designed to carry people or cargo;
5. Property of roomers, boarders and other tenants, except property of roomers and boarders related to an "insured";
6. Property in an apartment regularly rented or held for rental to others by an "insured," except as provided in Additional Coverages 9;
7. Property rented or held for rental to others off the "residence premises";
8. "Business" data, including such data stored in:
    a. Books of account, drawings or other paper records; or
    b. Electronic data processing tapes, wires, records, discs or other software media.

    However, we do cover the cost of blank recording or storage media, and of prerecorded computer programs available on the retail market; or
9. Credit cards or fund transfer cards except as provided in Additional Coverages **6.**

Sample homeowners insurance policy—some portions omitted (continued)

COVERAGE D - Loss of Use

The limit of liability for Coverage D is the total limit for all the coverages that follow.

1. If a loss covered under this Section makes that part of the "residence premises" where you reside not fit to live in, we cover, at your choice, either of the following. However, if the "residence premises" is not your principal place of residence, we will not provide the option under paragraph b. below.

    a. **Additional Living Expense,** meaning any necessary increase in living expenses incurred by you so that your household can maintain its normal standard of living; or

    b. **Fair Rental Value,** meaning the fair rental value of that part of the "residence premises" where you reside less any expenses that do not continue while the premises is not fit to live in.

    Payment under a. or b. will be for the shortest time required to repair or replace the damage or, if you permanently relocate, the shortest time required for your household to settle elsewhere.

2. If a loss covered under this Section makes that part of the "residence premises" rented to others or held for rental by you not fit to live in, we cover the:

    Fair Rental Value, meaning the fair rental value of that part of the "residence premises" rented to others or held for rental by you less any expenses that do not continue while the premises is not fit to live in.

    Payment will be for the shortest time required to repair or replace that part of the premises rented or held for rental.

3. If a civil authority prohibits you from use of the "residence premises" as a result of direct damage to neighboring premises by a Peril Insured Against in this policy, we cover the Additional Living Expense and Fair Rental Value loss as provided under 1. and 2. above for no more than two weeks.

The periods of time under 1., 2. and 3. above are not limited by expiration of this policy. We do not cover loss or expense due to cancellation of a lease or agreement.

* * *

SECTION I - PERILS INSURED AGAINST

We insure for direct physical loss to the property described in Coverages A, B and C caused by a peril listed below unless the loss is excluded in SECTION I - EXCLUSIONS.

1. **Fire or lightning.**

2. **Windstorm or hail.**

    This peril does not include loss to the inside of a building or the property contained in a building caused by rain, snow, sleet, sand or dust unless the direct force of wind or hail damages the building causing an opening in a roof or wall and the rain, snow, sleet, sand or dust enters through this opening. This peril includes loss to watercraft and their trailers, furnishings, equipment, and outboard engines or motors, only while inside a fully enclosed building.

3. **Explosion.**

4. **Riot or civil commotion.**

5. **Aircraft,** including self-propelled missiles and spacecraft.

6. **Vehicles.**

    This peril does not include loss caused by a vehicle owned or operated by a resident of the "residence premises."

7. **Smoke,** meaning sudden and accidental damage from smoke. This peril does not include loss caused by smoke from fireplaces or from agricultural smudging or industrial operations.

8. **Vandalism or malicious mischief.**

    This peril does not include loss to property on the "residence premises" if the dwelling has been vacant for more than 30 consecutive days immediately before the loss. A dwelling being constructed is not considered vacant.

9. **Theft,** including attempted theft and loss of property from a known place when it is likely that the property has been stolen.

    This peril does not include loss caused by theft:

    a. Committed by an "insured";

    b. In or to a dwelling under construction, or of materials and supplies for use in the construction until the dwelling is finished and occupied; or

    c. From that part of a "residence premises" rented by an "insured" to other than an "insured."

    This peril does not include loss caused by theft that occurs off the "residence premises" of:

    a. Property while at any other residence owned by, rented to, or occupied by an "insured," except while an "insured" is temporarily living there. Property of a student who is an "insured" is covered while at a residence away from home if the student has been there at any time during the 45 days immediately before the loss;

    b. Watercraft, and their furnishings, equipment and outboard engines or motors; or

    c. Trailers and campers.

10. **Volcanic eruption** other than loss caused by earthquake, land shock waves or tremors.

Sample homeowners insurance policy—some portions omitted (continued)

SECTION I - EXCLUSIONS

We do not insure for loss caused directly or indirectly by any of the following. Such loss is excluded regardless of any other cause or event contributing concurrently or in any sequence to the loss.

1. **Ordinance or Law,** meaning enforcement of any ordinance or law regulating the construction, repair, or demolition of a building or other structure, unless specifically provided under this policy.
2. **Earth Movement,** meaning earthquake including land shock waves or tremors before, during or after a volcanic eruption; landslide; mine subsidence; mudflow; earth sinking, rising or shifting; unless direct loss by:
   a. Fire;
   b. Explosion; or
   c. Breakage of glass or safety glazing material which is part of a building, storm door or storm window;

   ensues and then we will pay only for the ensuing loss. This exclusion does not apply to loss by theft.
3. **Water Damage,** meaning:
   a. Flood, surface water, waves, tidal water, overflow of a body of water, or spray from any of these, whether or not driven by wind;
   b. Water which backs up through sewers or drains or which overflows from a sump; or
   c. Water below the surface of the ground, including water which exerts pressure on or seeps or leaks through a building, sidewalk, driveway, foundation, swimming pool or other structure.

Direct loss by fire, explosion or theft resulting from water damage is covered.
4. **Power Failure,** meaning the failure of power or other utility service if the failure takes place off the "residence premises." But, if a Peril Insured Against ensues on the "residence premises," we will pay only for that ensuing loss.
5. **Neglect,** meaning neglect of the "insured" to use all reasonable means to save and preserve property at and after the time of a loss.
6. **War,** including the following and any consequence of any of the following:
   a. Undeclared war, civil war, insurrection, rebellion or revolution;
   b. Warlike act by a military force or military personnel; or
   c. Destruction, seizure or use for a military purpose.

   Discharge of a nuclear weapon will be deemed a warlike act even if accidental.
7. **Nuclear Hazard,** to the extent set forth in the Nuclear Hazard Clause of SECTION I - CONDITIONS.
8. **Intentional Loss,** meaning any loss arising out of any act committed:
   a. By or at the direction of an "insured"; and
   b. With the intent to cause a loss.

SECTION I - CONDITIONS

1. **Insurable Interest and Limit of Liability.** Even if more than one person has an insurable interest in the property covered, we will not be liable in any one loss:
   a. To the "insured" for more than the amount of the "insured's" interest at the time of loss; or
   b. For more than the applicable limit of liability.
2. **Your Duties After Loss.** In case of a loss to covered property, you must see that the following are done:
   a. Give prompt notice to us or our agent;
   b. Notify the police in case of loss by theft;
   c. Notify the credit card or fund transfer card company in case of loss under Credit Card or Fund Transfer Card coverage;
   d. Protect the property from further damage. If repairs to the property are required, you must:
      (1) Make reasonable and necessary repairs to protect the property; and
      (2) Keep an accurate record of repair expenses;
   e. Prepare an inventory of damaged personal property showing the quantity, description, actual

cash value and amount of loss. Attach all bills, receipts and related documents that justify the figures in the inventory;
   f. As often as we reasonably require:
      (1) Show the damaged property;
      (2) Provide us with records and documents we request and permit us to make copies; and
      (3) Submit to examination under oath, while not in the presence of any other "insured," and sign the same;
   g. Send to us, within 60 days after our request, your signed, sworn proof of loss which sets forth, to the best of your knowledge and belief:
      (1) The time and cause of loss;
      (2) The interest of the "insured" and all others in the property involved and all liens on the property;
      (3) Other insurance which may cover the loss;
      (4) Changes in title or occupancy of the property during the term of the policy;

Sample homeowners insurance policy—some portions omitted (continued)

(5) Specifications of damaged buildings and detailed repair estimates;

(6) The inventory of damaged personal property described in 2.e. above;

(7) Receipts for additional living expenses incurred and records that support the fair rental value loss; and

(8) Evidence or affidavit that supports a claim under the Credit Card, Fund Transfer Card, Forgery and Counterfeit Money coverage, stating the amount and cause of loss.

3. **Loss Settlement.** Covered property losses are settled as follows:

a. Property of the following type:

(1) Personal property;

(2) Awnings, carpeting, household appliances, outdoor antennas and outdoor equipment, whether or not attached to buildings; and

(3) Structures that are not buildings

at actual cash value at the time of loss but not more than the amount required to repair or replace.

b. Buildings under Coverage A or B at replacement cost without deduction for depreciation, subject to the following:

(1) If, at the time of loss, the amount of insurance in this policy on the damaged building is 80% or more of the full replacement cost of the building immediately before the loss, we will pay the cost to repair or replace, after application of deductible and without deduction for depreciation, but not more than the least of the following amounts:

(a) The limit of liability under this policy that applies to the building;

(b) The replacement cost of that part of the building damaged for like construction and use on the same premises; or

(c) The necessary amount actually spent to repair or replace the damaged building.

(2) If, at the time of loss, the amount of insurance in this policy on the damaged building is less than 80% of the full replacement cost of the building immediately before the loss, we will pay the greater of the following amounts, but not more than the limit of liability under this policy that applies to the building:

(a) The actual cash value of that part of the building damaged; or

(b) That proportion of the cost to repair or replace, after application of deductible and without deduction for depreciation, that part of the building damaged, which the total amount of insurance in this

policy on the damaged building bears to 80% of the replacement cost of the building.

(3) To determine the amount of insurance required to equal 80% of the full replacement cost of the building immediately before the loss, do not include the value of:

(a) Excavations, foundations, piers or any supports which are below the undersurface of the lowest basement floor;

(b) Those supports in (a) above which are below the surface of the ground inside the foundation walls, if there is no basement; and

(c) Underground flues, pipes, wiring and drains.

(4) We will pay no more than the actual cash value of the damage until actual repair or replacement is complete. Once actual repair or replacement is complete, we will settle the loss according to the provisions of b.(1) and b.(2) above.

However, if the cost to repair or replace the damage is both:

(a) Less than 5% of the amount of insurance in this policy on the building; and

(b) Less than $2500;

we will settle the loss according to the provisions of b.(1) and b.(2) above whether or not actual repair or replacement is complete.

(5) You may disregard the replacement cost loss settlement provisions and make claim under this policy for loss or damage to buildings on an actual cash value basis. You may then make claim within 180 days after loss for any additional liability according to the provisions of this Condition 3. Loss Settlement.

4. **Loss to a Pair or Set.** In case of loss to a pair or set we may elect to:

a. Repair or replace any part to restore the pair or set to its value before the loss; or

b. Pay the difference between actual cash value of the property before and after the loss.

5. **Glass Replacement.** Loss for damage to glass caused by a Peril Insured Against will be settled on the basis of replacement with safety glazing materials when required by ordinance or law.

6. **Appraisal.** If you and we fail to agree on the amount of loss, either may demand an appraisal of the loss. In this event, each party will choose a competent appraiser within 20 days after receiving a written request from the other. The two appraisers will choose an umpire. If they cannot agree upon an umpire within 15 days, you or we may request that the choice be made by a judge of a court of record

Sample homeowners insurance policy—some portions omitted (continued)

in the state where the "residence premises" is located. The appraisers will separately set the amount of loss. If the appraisers submit a written report of an agreement to us, the amount agreed upon will be the amount of loss. If they fail to agree, they will submit their differences to the umpire. A decision agreed to by any two will set the amount of loss. Each party will:

a. Pay its own appraiser; and

b. Bear the other expenses of the appraisal and umpire equally.

7. **Other Insurance.** If a loss covered by this policy is also covered by other insurance, we will pay only the proportion of the loss that the limit of liability that applies under this policy bears to the total amount of insurance covering the loss.

* * *

14. **Nuclear Hazard Clause.**

a. "Nuclear Hazard" means any nuclear reaction, radiation, or radioactive contamination, all whether controlled or uncontrolled or however caused, or any consequence of any of these.

b. Loss caused by the nuclear hazard will not be considered loss caused by fire, explosion, or smoke, whether these perils are specifically named in or otherwise included within the Perils Insured Against in Section I.

c. This policy does not apply under Section I to loss caused directly or indirectly by nuclear hazard, except that direct loss by fire resulting from the nuclear hazard is covered.

15. **Recovered Property.** If you or we recover any property for which we have made payment under this policy, you or we will notify the other of the recovery. At your option, the property will be returned to or retained by you or it will become our property. If the recovered property is returned to or retained by you, the loss payment will be adjusted based on the amount you received for the recovered property.

16. **Volcanic Eruption Period.** One or more volcanic eruptions that occur within a 72-hour period will be considered as one volcanic eruption.

SECTION II - LIABILITY COVERAGES

COVERAGE E - Personal Liability
If a claim is made or a suit is brought against an "insured" for damages because of "bodily injury" or "property damage" caused by an "occurrence" to which this coverage applies, we will:

1. Pay up to our limit of liability for the damages for which the "insured" is legally liable. Damages include prejudgment interest awarded against the "insured"; and

2. Provide a defense at our expense by counsel of our choice, even if the suit is groundless, false or fraudulent. We may investigate and settle any claim or suit that we decide is appropriate. Our duty to settle or defend ends when the amount we pay for damages resulting from the "occurrence" equals our limit of liability.

COVERAGE F - Medical Payments To Others
We will pay the necessary medical expenses that are incurred or medically ascertained within three years

from the date of an accident causing "bodily injury." Medical expenses means reasonable charges for medical, surgical, x-ray, dental, ambulance, hospital, professional nursing, prosthetic devices and funeral services. This coverage does not apply to you or regular residents of your household except "residence employees." As to others, this coverage applies only:

1. To a person on the "insured location" with the permission of an "insured"; or

2. To a person off the "insured location," if the "bodily injury":

a. Arises out of a condition on the "insured location" or the ways immediately adjoining;

b. Is caused by the activities of an "insured";

c. Is caused by a "residence employee" in the course of the "residence employee's" employment by an "insured"; or

d. Is caused by an animal owned by or in the care of an "insured."

SECTION II - EXCLUSIONS

1. **Coverage E - Personal Liability** and **Coverage F - Medical Payments to Others** do not apply to "bodily injury" or "property damage":

a. Which is expected or intended by the "insured";

b. Arising out of or in connection with a "business" engaged in by an "insured." This exclusion applies but is not limited to an act or omission, regardless of its nature or circumstance, involv-

ing a service or duty rendered, promised, owed, or implied to be provided because of the nature of the "business";

c. Arising out of the rental or holding for rental of any part of any premises by an "insured." This exclusion does not apply to the rental or holding for rental of an "insured location":

Sample homeowners insurance policy—some portions omitted (continued)

(1) On an occasional basis if used only as a residence;

(2) In part for use only as a residence, unless a single family unit is intended for use by the occupying family to lodge more than two roomers or boarders; or

(3) In part, as an office, school, studio or private garage;

d. Arising out of the rendering of or failure to render professional services;

e. Arising out of a premises:

(1) Owned by an "insured";

(2) Rented to an "insured"; or

(3) Rented to others by an "insured"; that is not an "insured location";

f. Arising out of:

(1) The ownership, maintenance, use, loading or unloading of motor vehicles or all other motorized land conveyances, including trailers, owned or operated by or rented or loaned to an "insured";

(2) The entrustment by an "insured" of a motor vehicle or any other motorized land conveyance to any person; or

(3) Vicarious liability, whether or not statutorily imposed, for the actions of a child or minor using a conveyance excluded in paragraph (1) or (2) above.

This exclusion does not apply to:

(1) A trailer not towed by or carried on a motorized land conveyance.

(2) A motorized land conveyance designed for recreational use off public roads, not subject to motor vehicle registration and:

(a) Not owned by an "insured"; or

(b) Owned by an "insured" and on an "insured location";

(3) A motorized golf cart when used to play golf on a golf course;

(4) A vehicle or conveyance not subject to motor vehicle registration which is:

(a) Used to service an "insured's" residence;

(b) Designed for assisting the handicapped; or

(c) In dead storage on an "insured location";

g. Arising out of:

(1) The ownership, maintenance, use, loading or unloading of an excluded watercraft described below;

(2) The entrustment by an "insured" of an excluded watercraft described below to any person; or

(3) Vicarious liability, whether or not statutorily imposed, for the actions of a child or minor using an excluded watercraft described below.

Excluded watercraft are those that are principally designed to be propelled by engine power or electric motor, or are sailing vessels, whether owned by or rented to an "insured."

* * *

h. Arising out of:

(1) The ownership, maintenance, use, loading or unloading of an aircraft;

(2) The entrustment by an "insured" of an aircraft to any person; or

(3) Vicarious liability, whether or not statutorily imposed, for the actions of a child or minor using an aircraft.

An aircraft means any contrivance used or designed for flight, except model or hobby aircraft not used or designed to carry people or cargo;

i. Caused directly or indirectly by war, including the following and any consequence of any of the following:

(1) Undeclared war, civil war, insurrection, rebellion or revolution;

(2) Warlike act by a military force or military personnel; or

(3) Destruction, seizure or use for a military purpose.

Discharge of a nuclear weapon will be deemed a warlike act even if accidental;

j. Which arises out of the transmission of a communicable disease by an "insured";

k. Arising out of sexual molestation, corporal punishment or physical or mental abuse; or

l. Arising out of the use, sale, manufacture, delivery, transfer or possession by any person of a Controlled Substance(s) as defined by the Federal Food and Drug Law at 21 U.S.C.A. Sections 811 and 812. Controlled Substances include but are not limited to cocaine, LSD, marijuana and allnarcotic drugs. However, this exclusion does not apply to the legitimate use of prescription drugs by a person following the orders of a licensed physician.

Exclusions e., f., g., and h. do not apply to "bodily injury" to a "residence employee" arising out of and in the course of the "residence employee's" employment by an "insured."

2. **Coverage E - Personal Liability,** does not apply to:

a. Liability:

(1) For any loss assessment charged against you as a member of an association, corporation or community of property owners;

(2) Under any contract or agreement. However, this exclusion does not apply to written contracts:

Sample homeowners insurance policy—some portions omitted (continued)

(a) That directly relate to the ownership, maintenance or use of an "insured location"; or

(b) Where the liability of others is assumed by the "insured" prior to an "occurrence"; unless excluded in **(1)** above or elsewhere in this policy;

b. "Property damage" to property owned by the "insured";

c. "Property damage" to property rented to, occupied or used by or in the care of the "insured." This exclusion does not apply to "property damage" caused by fire, smoke or explosion;

d. "Bodily injury" to any person eligible to receive any benefits:

(1) Voluntarily provided; or

(2) Required to be provided; by the "insured" under any:

(1) Workers' compensation law;

(2) Non-occupational disability law; or

(3) Occupational disease law;

e. "Bodily injury" or "property damage" for which an "insured" under this policy:

(1) Is also an insured under a nuclear energy liability policy; or

(2) Would be an insured under that policy but for the exhaustion of its limit of liability.

A nuclear energy liability policy is one issued by:

(1) American Nuclear Insurers;

(2) Mutual Atomic Energy Liability Underwriters;

(3) Nuclear Insurance Association of Canada;

or any of their successors; or

f. "Bodily injury" to you or an "insured" within the meaning of part a. or b. of "insured" as defined.

3. **Coverage F - Medical Payments to Others,** does not apply to "bodily injury":

a. To a "residence employee" if the "bodily injury":

(1) Occurs off the "insured location"; and

(2) Does not arise out of or in the course of the "residence employee's" employment by an "insured";

b. To any person eligible to receive benefits:

(1) Voluntarily provided; or

(2) Required to be provided; under any:

(1) Workers' compensation law;

(2) Non-occupational disability law; or

(3) Occupational disease law;

c. From any:

(1) Nuclear reaction;

(2) Nuclear radiation; or

(3) Radioactive contamination;

all whether controlled or uncontrolled or however caused; or

(4) Any consequence of any of these; or

d. To any person, other than a "residence employee" of an "insured," regularly residing on any part of the "insured location."

* * *

SECTION II - CONDITIONS

1. **Limit of Liability.** Our total liability under Coverage E for all damages resulting from any one "occurrence" will not be more than the limit of liability for Coverage E as shown in the Declarations. This limit is the same regardless of the number of "insureds," claims made or persons injured. All "bodily injury" and "property damage" resulting from any one accident or from continuous or repeated exposure to substantially the same general harmful conditions shall be considered to be the result of one "occurrence."

Our total liability under Coverage F for all medical expense payable for "bodily injury" to one person as the result of one accident will not be more than the limit of liability for Coverage F as shown in the Declarations.

2. **Severability of Insurance.** This insurance applies separately to each "insured." This condition will not increase our limit of liability for any one "occurrence."

3. **Duties After Loss.** In case of an accident or "occurrence," the "insured" will perform the following duties that apply. You will help us by seeing that these duties are performed:

a. Give written notice to us or our agent as soon as is practical, which sets forth:

(1) The identity of the policy and "insured";

(2) Reasonably available information on the time, place and circumstances of the accident or "occurrence"; and

(3) Names and addresses of any claimants and witnesses;

b. Promptly forward to us every notice, demand, summons or other process relating to the accident or "occurrence";

c. At our request, help us:

(1) To make settlement;

(2) To enforce any right of contribution or indemnity against any person or organization who may be liable to an "insured";

Sample homeowners insurance policy—some portions omitted (continued)

(3) With the conduct of suits and attend hearings and trials; and

(4) To secure and give evidence and obtain the attendance of witnesses;

d. Under the coverage - Damage to Property of Others - submit to us within 60 days after the loss, a sworn statement of loss and show the damaged property, if in the "insured's" control;

e. The "insured" will not, except at the "insured's" own cost, voluntarily make payment, assume obligation or incur expense other than for first aid to others at the time of the "bodily injury."

4. **Duties of an Injured Person - Coverage F - Medical Payments to Others.**

The injured person or someone acting for the injured person will:

a. Give us written proof of claim, under oath if required, as soon as is practical; and

b. Authorize us to obtain copies of medical reports and records.

The injured person will submit to a physical exam by a doctor of our choice when and as often as we reasonably require.

5. **Payment of Claim - Coverage F - Medical Payments to Others.** Payment under this coverage is not an admission of liability by an "insured" or us.

6. **Suit Against Us.** No action can be brought against us unless there has been compliance with the policy provisions. No one will have the right to join us as a party to any action against an "insured." Also, no action with respect to Coverage E can be brought against us until the obligation of the "insured" has been determined by final judgment or agreement signed by us.

7. **Bankruptcy of an Insured.** Bankruptcy or insolvency of an "insured" will not relieve us of our obligations under this policy.

8. **Other Insurance - Coverage E - Personal Liability.** This insurance is excess over other valid and collectible insurance except insurance written specifically to cover as excess over the limits of liability that apply in this policy.

SECTIONS I AND II - CONDITIONS

1. **Policy Period.** This policy applies only to loss in Section I or "bodily injury" or "property damage" in Section II, which occurs during the policy period.

2. **Concealment or Fraud.** The entire policy will be void if, whether before or after a loss, an "insured" has:

a. Intentionally concealed or misrepresented any material fact or circumstance;

b. Engaged in fraudulent conduct; or

c. Made false statements; relating to this insurance.

3. **Liberalization Clause.** If we make a change which broadens coverage under this edition of our policy without additional premium charge, that change will automatically apply to your insurance as of the date we implement the change in your state, provided that this implementation date falls within 60 days prior to or during the policy period stated in the Declarations. This Liberalization Clause does not apply to changes implemented through introduction of a subsequent edition of our policy.

4. **Waiver or Change of Policy Provisions.** A waiver or change of a provision of this policy must be in writing by us to be valid. Our request for an appraisal or examination will not waive any of our rights.

5. **Cancellation.**

a. You may cancel this policy at any time by returning it to us or by letting us know in writing of the date cancellation is to take effect.

b. We may cancel this policy only for the reasons stated below by letting you know in writing of the date cancellation takes effect. This cancellation notice may be delivered to you, or mailed to you at your mailing address shown in the Declarations.

Proof of mailing will be sufficient proof of notice.

(1) When you have not paid the premium, we may cancel at any time by letting you know at least 10 days before the date cancellation takes effect.

(2) When this policy has been in effect for less than 60 days and is not a renewal with us, we may cancel for any reason by letting you know at least 10 days before the date cancellation takes effect.

(3) When this policy has been in effect for 60 days or more, or at any time if it is a renewal with us, we may cancel:

(a) If there has been a material misrepresentation of fact which if known to us would have caused us not to issue the policy; or

(b) If the risk has changed substantially since the policy was issued.

This can be done by letting you know at least 30 days before the date cancellation takes effect.

(4) When this policy is written for a period of more than one year, we may cancel for any

Sample homeowners insurance policy—some portions omitted (continued)

reason at anniversary by letting you know at least 30 days before the date cancellation takes effect.

   c. When this policy is cancelled, the premium for the period from the date of cancellation to the expiration date will be refunded pro rata.

   d. If the return premium is not refunded with the notice of cancellation or when this policy is returned to us, we will refund it within a reasonable time after the date cancellation takes effect.

6. **Nonrenewal.** We may elect not to renew this policy. We may do so by delivering to you, or mailing to you at your mailing address shown in the Declarations, written notice at least 30 days before the expiration date of this policy. Proof of mailing will be sufficient proof of notice.

7. **Assignment.** Assignment of this policy will not be valid unless we give our written consent.

8. **Subrogation.** An "insured" may waive in writing before a loss all rights of recovery against any person. If not waived, we may require an assignment of rights of recovery for a loss to the extent that pay-

ment is made by us. If an assignment is sought, an "insured" must sign and deliver all related papers and cooperate with us. Subrogation does not apply under Section II to Medical Payments to Others or Damage to Property of Others.

9. **Death.** If any person named in the Declarations or the spouse, if a resident of the same household, dies:

   a. We insure the legal representative of the deceased but only with respect to the premises and property of the deceased covered under the policy at the time of death;

   b. "Insured" includes:

     (1) Any member of your household who is an "insured" at the time of your death, but only while a resident of the "residence premises"; and

     (2) With respect to your property, the person having proper temporary custody of the property until appointment and qualification of a legal representative.

Sample homeowners insurance policy—some portions omitted (continued)

sured for losses. Conversely, life insurance policies do not allow subrogation. Life insurance does not INDEMNIFY an insured for a loss that can be measured in dollars. Rather, it is a form of investment for the insured and the insured's beneficiaries. A life insurance policy pays only a fixed sum of money to the beneficiary and does not cover any liability to a third party. Under such a policy, the insured stands no chance of double recovery, and the insurance company has no need to sue a third party if it has to pay a claim.

INSURED 📖 The person who obtains or is otherwise covered by INSURANCE on his or her health, life, or property. The *insured* in a policy is not limited to the insured named in the policy but applies to anyone who is insured under the policy. 📖

INSURER 📖 An individual or company who, through a contractual agreement, undertakes to compensate specified losses, liability, or damages incurred by another individual. 📖

An insurer is frequently an INSURANCE company and is also known as an underwriter.

INSURRECTION 📖 A rising or rebellion of citizens against their government, usually manifested by acts of violence. 📖

Under federal law, it is a crime to incite,

assist, or engage in such conduct against the United States.

INTANGIBLES 📖 Property that is a "right" such as a PATENT, COPYRIGHT, or TRADEMARK, or one that is lacking physical existence, such as GOOD WILL. A nonphysical, noncurrent asset that exists only in connection with something else, such as the good will of a business. 📖

INTEGRATED 📖 Completed; made whole or entire. Desegregated; converted into a nonracial, nondiscriminatory system. 📖

A CONTRACT that has been adopted as a final and complete expression of an agreement between two parties is an integrated agreement.

A school that has been integrated has been made into one in which students, faculty, staff, facilities, programs, and activities combine individuals of different races. See also SCHOOL DESEGREGATION.

INTEGRATED AGREEMENT 📖 A CONTRACT that contains within its FOUR CORNERS the entire understanding of the parties and is subject to the PAROL EVIDENCE rule, which seeks to preserve the integrity of written agreements by refusing to allow the parties to modify their contract through the introduction of prior or contemporaneous oral declarations. 📖

An agreement is integrated when the parties

adopt the writing or writings as the final and complete expression of the agreement.

INTEGRATED BAR 📖 The process of organizing the ATTORNEYS of a state into an association, membership in which is a condition precedent to the right to practice law. 📖

Integration is usually attained by enactment of a statute that grants authority to the highest court of the state to integrate the bar, or by rule of court in the exercise of its inherent power. When the bar is integrated, all attorneys within an area, which can include a state, a county, or a city, are members.

INTEGRATION 📖 The bringing together of separate elements to create a whole unit. The bringing together of people from the different demographic and racial groups that make up U.S. society. 📖

In most cases, the term *integration* is used to describe the process of bringing together people of different races, especially blacks and whites, in schools and other settings. But it is also used to describe the process of bringing together people of different backgrounds. A primary purpose of the Americans with Disabilities Act of 1990 (ADA) (42 U.S.C.A. § 12101 et seq.), for example, was to more fully integrate disabled individuals into U.S. society. The House Judiciary Committee's report on the ADA described it as "a comprehensive piece of civil rights legislation which promises a new future: a future of inclusion and integration, and the end of exclusion and segregation" (H.R. Rep. No. 485, 101st Cong., 2d Sess., pt. 3, at 26 [1990], *reprinted in* 1990 U.S.C.C.A.N. 445, 449.7). See also DISABLED PERSONS.

The term *integration* is most commonly used in association with the efforts of African Americans in the United States to eliminate racial segregation and achieve equal opportunity and inclusion in U.S. society. Often, it has been used synonymously with *desegregation* to mean the elimination of discriminatory practices based on race. However, though similar, the terms have been used in significantly different ways by the courts, by legal theorists, and in the context of the CIVIL RIGHTS MOVEMENT. In general, *desegregation* refers to the elimination of policies and practices that segregate people of different races into separate institutions and facilities. *Integration* refers not just to the elimination of such policies but also to the active incorporation of different races into institutions for the purpose of achieving racial balance, which many believe will lead to equal rights, protections, and opportunities.

Throughout the CIVIL RIGHTS movement in the United States, black leaders have held different opinions about the meaning and value of integration, with some advocating integration as the ultimate goal for black citizens, and others resisting integration out of concern that it would lead to the assimilation of black citizens into white culture and society. In 1934, a disagreement over the value of integration versus segregation led W. E. B. DU BOIS—a cofounder of the NATIONAL ASSOCIATION FOR THE ADVANCEMENT OF COLORED PEOPLE (NAACP) and a leading scholar, writer, and civil rights activist—to resign from the NAACP. Du Bois rejected the NAACP's heavy emphasis on integration, calling instead for black citizens to maintain their own churches, schools, and social organizations, and especially to develop their own economic base separate from the mainstream white economy.

After Du Bois's resignation, the NAACP adopted a full-fledged campaign to eliminate segregation and promote integration. In 1940, NAACP leaders sent to President FRANKLIN D. ROOSEVELT, the secretary of the Navy, and the assistant secretary of war a memorandum outlining provisions for the "integration of the Negro into military aspects of the national defense program." This was the first instance where the NAACP had specifically used the term *integration* in a civil rights policy pronouncement. After World War II, the term *racial integration* became commonly used to describe civil rights issues pertaining to race.

On the legal front, the NAACP focused its efforts on eliminating segregation in the public schools. This campaign was led by THURGOOD MARSHALL, the first director-counsel of the NAACP Legal Defense and Educational Fund and later a Supreme Court justice. In 1954, Marshall successfully argued the landmark case *Brown v. Board of Education*, 347 U.S. 483, 74 S. Ct. 686, 98 L. Ed. 873, before the Supreme Court, which declared that racially segregated schools are inherently unequal and thus unconstitutional. Like other NAACP leaders, Marshall was strongly committed to the principle of racial integration. His arguments in *Brown* were heavily based on the work of Kenneth B. Clark, a black social psychologist whose research suggested that black children were stigmatized by being educated in racially segregated schools, causing them to suffer psychological and intellectual harm. Marshall used this theory of "stigmatic injury" to persuade the Supreme Court that racially segregated schools were inherently unequal. Although the *Brown* decision called for an end to formal segregation, it did not explicitly call for positive steps to ensure the integration of public schools.

UPI/CORBIS-BETTMANN

In September 1954, just months after the Brown *decision, two schools at military bases in Virginia were open to black children for the first time. Although integration was not yet required of public schools, the Defense Department had ordered all schools on military posts to be integrated.*

The desegregation momentum begun by *Brown* was enacted into law by the 1964 CIVIL RIGHTS ACT (Pub. L. No. 88-352, 78 Stat. 246), which denied federal funds to any program that discriminated illegally on the basis of race, sex, color, religion, or national origin, outlawing such DISCRIMINATION not only in public schools but also in areas of public accommodation and employment. To ensure the support necessary for passage of the act, its writers worded the act specifically to emphasize that its purpose was to desegregate, not to integrate. "Desegregation," the act said, was "the assignment of students to public schools . . . without regard to their race," but "not . . . the assignment of students to public schools in order to overcome racial imbalance."

Nevertheless, after the Civil Rights Act was passed, judges and other federal officials enforcing it required schools to go beyond racially neutral desegregation policies to try to remedy past segregation by enforcing a greater degree of racial integration. This policy was established by the Supreme Court in 1968 in *Green v. County School Board*, 391 U.S. 430, 88 S. Ct. 1689, 20 L. Ed. 2d 716, in which the Court ruled that a school district's desegregation plan was unacceptable under the *Brown* ruling. The *Green* case involved a school district that had two high schools that had previously been seg-

regated by race. When the district changed its rules to allow students to attend the school of their choice, few black students chose to attend the traditionally white school, and no whites chose the black school, thus leaving the schools segregated. In its ruling on *Green*, the Court called the "freedom-of-choice" plan a "deliberate perpetuation of the unconstitutional dual system" and said that school boards had an "affirmative duty to take whatever steps might be necessary to convert to a unitary system in which racial discrimination would be eliminated root and branch." Although a freedom-of-choice plan could theoretically be a viable method for converting to a "unitary, nonracial school system," the Court said, it would have to "prove itself in operation," adding that such methods as rezoning might prove speedier, and thus more acceptable. Although the Court did not explicitly require active integration, it suggested that the validity of desegregation plans would be measured by the amount of integration they actually produced.

This emphasis on achieving specific levels of integration as proof of desegregation was reinforced by the 1971 Supreme Court ruling in *Swann v. Charlotte-Mecklenburg Board of Education*, 402 U.S. 1, 91 S. Ct. 1267, 28 L. Ed. 2d 554. In *Swann*, the Court ruled that schools could use methods such as involuntary busing and the altering of attendance zones to achieve specific ratios of racial mixing, as long as those ratios were established as "starting point[s] in the process of shaping a remedy" for past discrimination.

In a 1974 case, *Milliken v. Bradley*, 418 U.S. 717, 94 S. Ct. 3112, 41 L. Ed. 2d 1069, the Supreme Court made it more difficult for city school districts to achieve racial integration. In *Milliken*, the Court ruled that a federally ordered desegregation remedy could not include suburban schools when a city's school district was officially segregated for reasons other than past illegal discrimination, such as the simple demographics of its residents. In other words, if the surrounding suburban districts had not contributed to past illegal segregation, they could not be held responsible for remedying it. A cross-district remedy, the Court ruled, would be permissible only to correct a cross-district wrong. The effect of *Milliken* has been to allow an increasing amount of resegregation in public schools as housing patterns divide black and white residents between cities and their surrounding suburbs. More recent cases, such as *Missouri v. Jenkins*, 515 U.S. 70, 115 S. Ct. 2038, 132 L. Ed. 2d 63, 63 U.S.L.W. 4486 (1995), have continued to impose strict judicial limits on the power of the courts to impose and enforce desegregation plans in the public schools.

Despite significant legal victories mandating greater integration, therefore, the actual amount of racial integration in the United States—in the schools and elsewhere—remains limited. This has led many black leaders to question whether integration is indeed possible in the United States and whether it would actually benefit African Americans. Those in favor of integration follow in the tradition of Marshall and MARTIN LUTHER KING, JR., who insisted that integration would lead to increased freedom, power, and opportunities for African Americans. "In our society," King insisted, "liberation cannot come without integration and integration cannot come without liberation." More recently, Andrew Young, civil rights activist, former U.N. ambassador, and former mayor of Atlanta, has emphasized that integration does not lead to assimilation. "Those who reject integration," he said, "do so because they see the black community as one way assimilation." In contrast, he said, "integration is a two way street, each side contributing their own values, virtues, and traditions."

Other black scholars and political leaders have followed the lead of Du Bois, questioning the value of integration for African Americans and recommending instead separate black schools, churches, and economic networks. In the 1960s, members of the black power and black nationalist movements, including MALCOLM X, argued that integration was an inappropriate strategy for blacks, who they believed could free themselves from racism and repression only by separating themselves from the mainstream white culture. Integration, they asserted, would result in African Americans being assimilated into the white community. In 1967, for example, STOKELY CARMICHAEL, a leader of the black power movement, said, "The fact is that integration, as traditionally articulated, would abolish the black community." More recently, some legal theorists of race relations have criticized the theory of stigmatic injury that Marshall presented in *Brown*, contending that it rests on a notion of African American inferiority by asserting that black children can receive an adequate education only in the presence of white children. DERRICK A. BELL, JR., a leading legal theorist on race relations, has been a particularly vocal critic of integrated schools,

The Most Segregated States for Black Students: 1991–1992		The Most Segregated States for Hispanic Students: 1991–1992	
State	**Mostly minority***	**State**	**Mostly minority***
1) Illinois	59.3%	1) New York	58.1%
2) Michigan	58.5%	2) New Jersey	44.4%
3) New York	57.5%	3) Texas	41.7%
4) New Jersey	54.6%	4) California	35.4%
5) Pennsylvania	45.7%	5) Illinois	33.7%
6) Tennessee	37.3%	6) Connecticut	33.7%
7) Alabama	36.8%	7) Florida	28.0%
8) Maryland	36.7%	8) Indiana	19.6%
9) Mississippi	36.6%	9) New Mexico	18.3%
10) Connecticut	36.2%	10) Arizona	16.2%

*"Mostly minority" is defined as a school whose enrollment of black and/or Hispanic students is at least 90 percent of the total enrollment. In the case of New York state, 57.5 percent of black students and 58.1 percent of Hispanic students attend schools in which the minority enrollment exceeds 90 percent of the total enrollment of their school.

SOURCE: William Celis 3d, "Study Finds Rising Concentration of Black and Hispanic Students," *New York Times*, December 14, 1993, pp. 1+.

insisting that they do not meet the needs of African American children, who, he says, would be better served by increased funding for schools in black neighborhoods, more black teachers and administrators, increased parental involvement, and higher expectations for academic achievement. Many educational experts concur, suggesting that many young black males would receive a higher-quality education by attending black male academies where the approach and curriculum were specifically designed to counter the social and cultural challenges faced by those young men in today's world.

Many of the black leaders who today advocate integration have refined the notion, insisting that it means more than simply mixing black and white students in the same school. Legal scholar john a. powell (who spells his name with only lowercase letters) said that true integration "transforms racial hierarchy" by "creat[ing] a more inclusive society where individuals and groups have opportunities to participate equally in their communities." Similarly, Ellis Cashmore, a leading scholar of race relations, said integration "describes a condition in which different ethnic groups are able to maintain group boundaries and uniqueness, while participating equally in the essential processes of production, distribution and government." Cashmore conceded, however, that in the United States, this type of integration "remains more of an ideal than a reality."

Cashmore and other current race relations scholars suggest that integration no longer means simply desegregation but rather now includes pluralism. Pluralism, in this context, refers to a condition in which no ethnic hierarchies exist, so there are no ethnic minorities per se; instead, the various groups in society participate equally in the social system, therefore experiencing balance and cohesion rather than contention and resentment. In this sense, said scholar Harold Cruse, "the separate-but-equal doctrine that *Brown* ruled unconstitutional *should* have been supplanted by the truly democratic doctrine of '*plural but equal.*'"

CROSS-REFERENCES

Brown v. Board of Education of Topeka, Kansas; School Desegregation; Separate but Equal.

INTELLECTUAL PROPERTY Intellectual property describes a wide variety of property created by musicians, authors, artists, and inventors. The law of intellectual property typically encompasses the areas of COPYRIGHT, patent, and TRADEMARK law. It is designed to encourage the development of art, science, and

information by granting certain PROPERTY RIGHTS to all artists, which include inventors in both the arts and the sciences. These rights allow artists to protect themselves from INFRINGEMENT, or the unauthorized use and misuse of their creations.

Copyright laws have roots in eighteenth-century English law. Comprehensive patent laws can be traced to seventeenth-century England, and they have been a part of U.S. law since the colonial period. The copyright and patent concepts were both included in the U.S. Constitution. Under Article I, Section 8, Clause 8, of the Constitution, "The Congress shall have Power ... To promote the Progress of Science and useful Arts, by securing for limited Times to Authors and Inventors the exclusive Right to their respective Writings and Discoveries." The first trademark laws were passed by Congress in the late nineteenth century.

The bulk of intellectual property law is contained in federal statutes. Copyrights are protected by the Copyright Act (17 U.S.C.A. § 101 et seq. [1994]), patents are covered in the Patent Act (35 U.S.C.A. § 101 et seq. [1994]), and trademark protection is provided by the LANHAM ACT (also known as the Trademark Act) (15 U.S.C.A. § 1501 et seq. [1994]).

Intellectual property laws give artists the exclusive right to profit from their work for a particular limited period. For copyrighted material, the exclusive right lasts for fifty years beyond the death of the author. The length of the right can vary for PATENTS, but in most cases it lasts for twenty years. Trademark rights are exclusive for ten years, and can be continually renewed for subsequent ten-year periods.

Intellectual property laws do not fall in the category of CRIMINAL LAW. Some copyright laws authorize criminal penalties, but by and large, the body of intellectual property law is concerned with prevention and compensation, both of which are civil matters. This means that the artist, not the government, is responsible for enforcement.

Intellectual property laws provide artists with the power to enforce their property rights in civil court. They provide for DAMAGES when unauthorized use or misuse has occurred. They also provide for INJUNCTIONS, or court orders, to prevent unauthorized use or misuse.

The property protected by intellectual property laws must be in a TANGIBLE form. For example, a musician cannot claim copyright protection for a melody unless it has been written down or somehow actualized and affixed with a recognizable abbreviation. A formula or device cannot receive patent protection unless it has been presented in whole to the Patent and Trademark Office. A symbol cannot receive trademark protection unless it has been placed on goods or used in connection with services.

Copyright Copyright laws grant to authors, artists, composers, and publishers the exclusive right to produce and distribute expressive and original work. Only expressive pieces, or writings, may receive copyright protection. A writing need not be words on paper: in copyright law, it can be a painting, sculpture, or other work of art. The writing element merely requires that a work of art, before receiving copyright protection, must be reduced to some tangible form. This may be on paper, on film, on audiotape, or on any other tangible instrument that can be reproduced.

The writing requirement ensures that copyrighted material is capable of being reproduced. Without this requirement artists could not be expected to know whether they were infringing on the original work of another person. The writing requirement also enforces the copyright rule that ideas cannot be copyrighted: only the expression of ideas can be protected.

Copyrighted material also must be original. This means that there must be something new about the work that sets it apart from previous similar works. If the variation is more than trivial, the work will receive copyright protection.

Functionality can be a factor in copyright law. The copyrights to architectural design, for example, are generally reserved for architectural works that are not functional. If the only purpose or function of a particular design is utilitarian, the work cannot be copyrighted. For instance, a person may not copyright a simple design for a water spigot. If, however, a person creates a fancy water spigot, the design is copyrightable.

Copyrighted material can receive varying degrees of protection. The scope of protection is generally limited to the original work that is in the writing. For example, assume that an artist has created a sculpture of the moon. The sculptor may not prevent others from making sculptures of the moon. However, the sculptor may prevent others from making sculptures of the moon that are exact replicas of his own sculpture.

Copyright protection gives the copyright holder the exclusive right to (1) reproduce the copyrighted work, (2) create derivative works from the work, (3) distribute the work, (4) perform the work, and (5) display the work. The first two rights are infringed whether they are violated in public or in private. The last three rights may be infringed only if they are violated in public. *Public* is defined under the Copyright Act as a performance or display to a "substantial number of persons" outside of friends and family (17 U.S.C.A. § 101).

Infringement of copyright occurs whenever someone exercises the exclusive rights of the copyright owner without the owner's permission. The infringement need not be intentional. Copyright owners usually prove infringement in court by showing that copying occurred, and that the copying amounted to impermissible appropriation. These showings require an analysis and comparison of the copyrighted work and the disputed work. Many general rules also relate to infringement of certain works. For example, a character created in a copyrighted work may not receive copyright protection unless the character is developed in great detail and a character in the disputed work closely resembles that character.

The most important exception to the exclusive rights of the copyright holder is the "fair use" doctrine. This doctrine allows the general public to use copyrighted material without permission in certain situations. These situations include educational activities, literary and social criticism, parody, and news reporting. Whether a particular use is fair depends on a number of factors, including whether the use is for profit, what proportion of the copyrighted material is used, and what economic effect the use has on the copyright owner.

Patent Patent laws encourage private investment in new technologies by granting to artists the right to forbid all others to produce and distribute technological information that is new, useful, and nonobvious. The statutory requirements for patent protection are more stringent than those for copyright protection. Furthermore, because patent protection for commercial products or processes can give a tremendous market advantage to businesses, those seeking patents often find opposition to their applications. Patent protection can be obtained only through the U.S. Patent Office. Generally, only new, useful, and nonobvious processes or products will be approved for patent protection.

The novelty requirement focuses on events that occur prior to the invention. Under section 102 of the Patent Act, an invention is not novel if it is publicly used, sold, or patented by another inventor within twelve months of the patent application. This definition implements the PUBLIC POLICY that favors quick disclosure of technological progress.

Often, two inventors apply for a patent for the same product or process within the same twelve-month period. Three factors determine who wins the patent: the date and time that the product or process was conceived, the date and time that the product or process was reduced to practice, and the diligence used to pursue patent protection and perfect the discovery. Generally, the first inventor to conceive the product or process has priority in the application process. However, if the second inventor is the first to reduce the product or process to practice, and the first inventor does not use diligence to obtain patent protection, the second inventor is given priority in the application process.

The utility requirement ensures that the product or process receiving patent protection will have some beneficial use. The inventor must specify in the application a specific utility for the invention. If the application is for a process, the process must be useful with respect to a product. A process that is new and nonobvious but useless does not increase knowledge or confer any benefit on society.

Nonobviousness is not the same as novelty. Not everything novel is nonobvious. However, anything that is nonobvious is novel, unless it has already been patented. The nonobvious requirement focuses on existing technology, or prior art. In determining whether an invention is nonobvious, the Patent Office analyzes the prior art, examines the differences between the invention and the prior art, and determines the level of ordinary skill in the art. Generally, if an invention is obvious to a person of ordinary skill in the relevant art, it is not patentable.

When an inventor claims that his or her patent has been infringed, the court generally engages in a two-step process. First, the court analyzes all the relevant patent documents. Then, the court reads the patent documents and compares them with the device or process that is accused of infringement. If each element of the accused device or process substantially duplicates an element in the patented device or process, the court may declare that the patent has been infringed. Infringement can occur only if another person uses, makes, or sells the patented device or process without the permission of the person who has received the patent, or the patentee.

When a patented device or process is infringed, the patent holder may recover in damages an amount equal to a reasonable royalty. If the infringement was willful, the infringing party may be forced to pay three times the reasonable royalty. If successful in court, the patent holder may also recover court costs and attorneys' fees. If the patent holder anticipates infringement, she or he may apply for an injunction, or court order. An injunction in such a case would prohibit a certain party from infringing the patent. An injunction may also issue after a finding of infringement, to prevent repeat infringement.

Trademark Trademark laws allow businesses to protect the symbolic information that relates to their goods and services, by preventing the use of such information by competitors. To receive trademark protection, a mark must be distinctive. *Distinctive* generally applies to any coined or fanciful word or term that does not closely resemble an existing mark. No mark will receive trademark protection if it is a common or descriptive term used in the marketplace.

To receive trademark protection, a mark must be used in the marketplace. If two or more marketers claim ownership of a certain mark, the first user of the mark will usually receive the protection. However, if the mark is known only in a limited geographic area, it may not receive protection in areas where it is unknown to consumers.

Infringement occurs if a mark is likely to cause confusion among consumers. In determining whether confusion is likely, the court examines a number of factors, including the similarity between the two marks in appearance, sound, connotation, and impression; the similarity of the goods or services that the respective marks represent; the similarity of the markets; whether the sale of the goods or services is inspired by impulse or only after careful consideration by the buyer; the level of public awareness of the mark; whether shoppers are actually confused; the number and nature of similar marks on similar goods or services; the length of time of concurrent use without actual confusion on the part of shoppers; and the variety of goods or services that the mark represents (*In re E. I. duPont de Nemours & Co.*, 476 F.2d 1357, 177 U.S.P.Q. 563 [1973]).

Defenses to infringement include fair use and collateral use. Fair use occurs when the second user, or repossessor, uses a protected mark in a nonconspicuous way to identify a component of a good or service. For example, a restaurant can use a protected mark to advertise that it serves a particular brand of soft drink without infringing the mark. The restaurant cannot, however, identify itself by the mark without infringing the mark.

Collateral use is use of the same mark in a different market. For example, assume that a tree surgeon has received trademark protection for the mark Tree Huggers. This protection may not prevent a business that sells logging boots from obtaining the same mark. However, if the mark for the boots is written or otherwise appears with the same defining characteristics as the mark for the tree surgeon, it risks being denied trademark protection, depending on whether it can be confused by consumers.

Remedies for infringement of a protected trademark consist of damages for the profits lost owing to the infringement, recovery of the profits realized by the infringer owing to the infringement, and attorneys' fees. A trademark holder may also obtain injunctive relief to prevent infringement.

Other Forms of Intellectual Property

The body of intellectual property law also includes laws relating to TRADE SECRETS, UNFAIR COMPETITION, and the right of publicity. Trade secret laws protect any formula, pattern, device, or compilation of information that provides a business advantage over competitors who do not use or know of the formula, pattern, device, or compilation of information. A strategy to increase worker productivity, for example, is a trade secret. Trade secrets do not receive patent protection because they are not inventive. Trade secret laws are included in intellectual property laws because, like other intellectual property laws, they prevent the unauthorized use of certain information.

Unfair competition laws cover the misuse and misappropriation of a product for financial gain, by protecting valuable information of a business that does not qualify for copyright or trademark protection. For example, assume that a business has developed a popular cologne with distinctive packaging. Now assume that another business has begun to manufacture the same product with virtually identical packaging in an attempt to capitalize on the success of the original cologne. Even though the knockoff is not an exact copy of the original and does not infringe trademark protection, the first business may protect itself through unfair competition laws. The test to determine whether a business is liable for unfair competition is whether the two products could be confused by a reasonable shopper.

The right of publicity is the right of a person to control the commercial value and exploitation of his or her name and likeness. Because right-of-publicity laws promote artistic pursuits, they are included in intellectual property law. These laws are usually reserved for celebrities and other public figures whose name and image are important to their career. By allowing celebrities the right to control the commercial use of their name and image, right-of-publicity laws protect the commercial potential of entertainers.

Recent Developments

One big problem that artists face is protecting their property in other countries. Not all countries subscribe to international agreements regarding intellectual property, and this has led to widespread unauthorized copying. In the 1990s China and Mexico were identified as serious offenders. In both countries music and films were copied and sold openly without compensation to the creators. The United States threatened to impose trade sanctions against China if it did not observe international copyright treaties. Such threats illustrate that the United States places a high priority on protecting the right of artists to profit from their work.

CROSS-REFERENCES

Art Law; Copyright, International; Entertainment Law; Literary Property; Music Publishing; Trade Names.

INTEMPERANCE ◫ A lack of moderation. Habitual intemperance is that degree of intemperance in the use of intoxicating liquor which disqualifies the person a great portion of the time from properly attending to business. Habitual or excessive use of liquor. ◫

See also ALCOHOL.

INTENT ◫ A determination to perform a particular act or to act in a particular manner for a specific reason; an aim or design; a resolution to use a certain means to reach an end. ◫

Intent is a mental attitude with which an individual acts, and therefore it cannot ordinarily be directly proved but must be inferred from surrounding facts and circumstances. Intent refers only to the state of mind with which the act is done or omitted. It differs from MOTIVE, which is what prompts a person to act or to fail to act. For example, suppose Billy calls Amy names and Amy throws a snowball at him. Amy's intent is to hit Billy with a snowball. Her motive may be to stop Billy's taunts.

The legal importance of what an individual intended depends on the particular area of law. In CONTRACT law, for example, the intention of the parties to a written contract is fixed by the language of the contract document.

In TORT law, intent plays a key role in determining the civil LIABILITY of persons who commit harm. An intentional tort is any deliberate invasion of, or interference with, the PROPERTY, PROPERTY RIGHTS, personal rights, or personal liberties of another that causes injuries without just cause or excuse. In tort an individual is considered to intend the consequences of an act—whether or not she or he actually intends those consequences—if the individual is substantially certain that those consequences will result.

Basic intentional torts include ASSAULT AND BATTERY, CONVERSION of property, FALSE ARREST, FALSE IMPRISONMENT, FRAUD, intentional infliction of emotional distress, invasion of PRIVACY, and TRESPASS. It is ordinarily not necessary that any wrongful or illegal means be used to accomplish the negative result, provided the wrongful conduct was intentional and was not accompanied by excuse or justification.

In CRIMINAL LAW the concept of criminal intent has been called MENS REA, which refers to a criminal or wrongful purpose. If a person innocently causes harm, then she or he lacks mens rea and, under this concept, should not be criminally prosecuted.

Although the concept of mens rea is generally accepted, problems arise in applying it to particular cases. Some crimes require a very high degree of intent, whereas others require substantially less. LARCENY, for example, requires that the defendant intentionally take property to which the person knows he or she is not entitled, intending to deprive the rightful owner of possession permanently. On the other hand, negligent HOMICIDE requires only that the defendant negligently cause another's death.

Criminal law has attempted to clarify the intent requirement by creating the concepts of "specific intent" and "general intent." SPECIFIC INTENT refers to a particular state of mind that seeks to accomplish the precise act that the law prohibits—for example, a specific intent to commit RAPE. Sometimes it means an intent to do something beyond that which is done, such as ASSAULT with intent to commit rape. The prosecution must show that the defendant purposely or knowingly committed the crime at issue.

GENERAL INTENT refers to the intent to do that which the law prohibits. It is not necessary for the prosecution to prove that the defendant intended the precise harm or the precise result that occurred. Thus, in most states, a defendant who kills a person with a gun while intoxicated, to the extent that the defendant is not aware of having a gun, will be guilty of second-degree MURDER. The law will infer that the defendant had a general intent to kill.

Criminal law dispenses with the intent requirement in many property-related crimes. Under common law the prosecution had to establish that the defendant intended to steal or destroy property. By 1900 many statutes eliminated the "intent-to-defraud" requirement for property crimes. Passing a bad check, obtaining property under false pretenses, selling mortgaged property, and embezzling while holding public office no longer required criminal intent.

Criminal law and tort law share the concept of transferred intent. For example, if A shoots a gun at B, intending to strike B, but the bullet hits C, the intent to strike is transferred to the act of shooting C and supplies the necessary intent for either a criminal conviction or a civil tort action. Under the criminal doctrine of transferred intent, the intent is considered to follow the criminal act regardless of who turns out to be the victim. Under the tort doctrine of transferred intent, the defendant is liable for monetary damages to the unintended victim.

INTER ALIA 📖 [*Latin, Among other things.*] A phrase used in PLEADING to designate that a particular statute set out therein is only a part of the statute that is relevant to the facts of the lawsuit and not the entire statute. 📖

Inter alia is also used when reporting court decisions to indicate that there were other rulings made by the court but only a particular holding of the case is cited.

INTEREST 📖 A comprehensive term to describe any right, claim, or privilege that an individual has toward real or personal property. Compensation for the use of borrowed money. 📖

There are two basic types of interest: legal and conventional. *Legal interest* is prescribed by the applicable state statute as the highest that may be legally contracted for, or charged. *Conventional interest* is interest at a rate that has been set and agreed upon by the parties themselves without outside intervention. It must be within the legally prescribed interest rate to avoid the criminal prosecution of the lender for violation of USURY laws.

INTERFERENCE 📖 In the law of PATENTS, the presence of two pending applications, or an existing patent and a pending application that encompass an identical invention or discovery. 📖

When interference exists, the PATENT AND TRADEMARK OFFICE conducts an investigation to ascertain the priority of invention between the conflicting applications, or the application and the patent. A patent is customarily granted to the earlier invention.

INTERIM 📖 [*Latin, In the meantime: temporary; between.*] 📖

An *interim dean* of a law school, for example, is an individual who is appointed to fill the office of dean during a temporary vacancy or a period during which the regular dean is absent due to an illness or disability.

INTERIOR DEPARTMENT The Interior Department is a federal department responsible for the United States' natural resources and for land owned by the federal government. The department fulfills this responsibility by promulgating and enforcing numerous regulations concerning natural resources and PUBLIC LANDS. The head of the Interior Department is the secretary of the interior, who sits on the president's CABINET and reports directly to the president.

The Department of the Interior was created by Congress in 1849 (9 Stat. 395 [43 U.S.C.A. § 1451]). The original duties of the Interior Department included supervision of all mining in the United States, the General Land Office, the Office of Indian Affairs, the Pension Office, the Patent Office, the District of Columbia penitentiary, the U.S. CENSUS, and accounts for federal court officers. These agencies and duties had little in common except that their focus was within U.S. borders, and they were out of place in other departments.

As a result of the continuing search for streamlined organization in government, the Interior Department eventually dropped a number of its original duties and developed an emphasis on natural resources. The department has retained responsibility for mining, federal lands, and American Indian issues. Over the years, it has added several offices and bureaus to help fulfill its responsibilities.

The chief functions of the Interior Department include efforts to conserve and develop mineral and water resources; conserve, develop, and utilize fish and wildlife resources; coordinate federal and state recreation programs; preserve and administer scenic and historic areas; operate the Job Corps Conservation Centers and Youth and Young Adult Conservation Corps Camps, and other youth training programs; irrigate arid lands; manage hydroelectric systems; provide social and economic services to U.S. territories; and provide programs and services to Native Americans and native Alaskans.

The Interior Department contains several different offices, departments, and bureaus. The Office of the Secretary includes the Offices of the Deputy Secretary, Assistant Secretaries, and Inspector General. The inspector general is charged with coordinating and supervising interior audits and with performing inspections to detect FRAUD and abuse. In addition, the inspector general is responsible for supervising the financial activities of U.S. territories such as Guam, American Samoa, and the Virgin Islands. The Office of Hearings and Appeals is also contained within the Office of the Secretary. Persons involved in disputes with the Interior Department may have their case heard at this office.

The hands-on work of the department is performed by several bureaus and services. The Bureau of Reclamation is devoted to the management of water resources. The Bureau of Land Management is in charge of public lands and resources. The U.S. Geological Survey exists to draw a wide variety of maps and to examine and classify public land structures and mineral resources. The Minerals Management

Interior Department

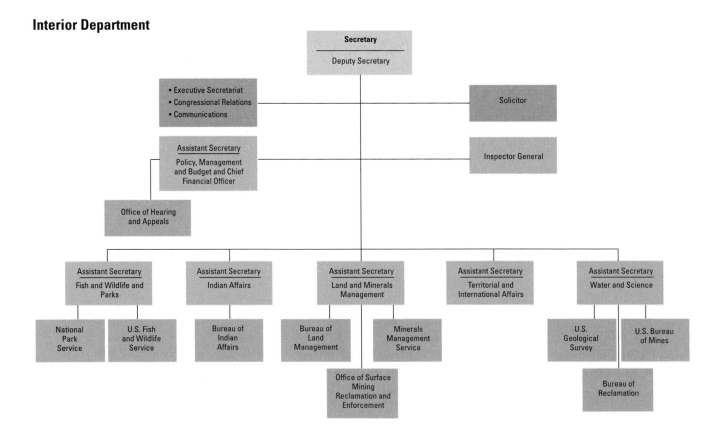

Service assesses the value of minerals and supervises mineral recovery. The Office of Surface Mining Reclamation and Enforcement is charged mainly with the operation of a nationwide program on coal mining. The U.S. Bureau of Mines researches mining issues to find the best technology for extracting, processing, using, and recycling nonfuel mineral resources. The National Biological Survey conducts research to promote the sound management of plant and animal life. The National Park Service is dedicated to the preservation of national parks, monuments, scenic parkways, preserves, trails, riverways, seashores, lakeshores, and recreation areas. The U.S. Fish and Wildlife Service is devoted primarily to the conservation and enhancement of the nation's fish and wildlife resources.

One controversial function of the Interior Department is the oversight of Native American affairs. The Bureau of Indian Affairs performs a number of functions having to do with Native American issues. The Interior Department played a dominant role in the drafting of tribal constitutions during the nineteenth century. In the twentieth century, the Bureau of Indian Affairs continued its control over Native American tribes by insisting on review and approval powers over amendments to tribal constitutions.

Like most other federal administrative agencies, the Interior Department is controlled by both Congress and the president. Congress created the Interior Department, and Congress could decide to reduce or eliminate it. However, also like most other administrative agencies, the Interior Department is a political necessity. Lawmakers are generally well versed in a broad range of topics, but few have the knowledge required to craft the best rules and regulations on, for example, mining or land management. The Interior Department possesses such expertise.

On the executive level, the Interior Department reports directly to the president, so the president also exerts control over it. The president has the power to remove and replace department personnel, to propose increases or reductions in responsibilities, and to redirect the department's goals. All these changes must be approved by Congress.

This dual control over the Interior Department makes it subject to political influence. For example, when a new president takes office, he or she will likely make personnel changes in the Interior Department to initiate new programs and directions promised in the campaign. Any high-level appointments to administrative

agencies will be reviewed by Congress. If a nominee holds views contrary to the majority in Congress, Congress may reject the nominee, and the president may have to choose one more acceptable to Congress. On the other hand, senators and representatives may be reluctant to resist the actions of a newly elected president for fear of alienating the voting public.

The Interior Department has historically been less concerned with conservation than with development. Interior Secretary Roy O. West commented in 1928 that the Interior Department should have been named the Department of Western Development. In the early twentieth century, U.S. citizens became aware that the resources needed for modern life were not inexhaustible, and the Interior Department gradually recognized the need for conservation. However, the Interior Department's original mission of managing development was at odds with conservation, and the department was incapable of concentrating exclusively on conservation. To fill the void created by this situation, Congress created the ENVIRONMENTAL PROTECTION AGENCY (EPA) in 1970.

Although the EPA has taken over the goals of conservation and pollution control, the Interior Department is still concerned with environmental matters. In 1987, the department reorganized the Bureau of Reclamation to reflect the bureau's new emphasis on management and conservation instead of construction. In the 1990s, Bruce Babbitt, the secretary of the interior under President BILL CLINTON, made several changes in the Interior Department to strengthen its environmental protection efforts. For example, in 1993, Babbitt arranged for several hundred scientists from agencies within the department to conduct the National Biological Survey. The purpose of the survey was

The U.S. Fish and Wildlife Service, a division of the Interior Department, is concerned with the conservation of wildlife, especially those species that are threatened by loss of habitat. Eagles and other birds of prey are sometimes tagged and then released back into the wild as part of these efforts.

STEVE FARRELL/U.S. FISH AND WILDLIFE SERVICE

to study ways to protect the natural habitats of endangered species.

CROSS-REFERENCES

Environmental Law; Fish and Fishing; Game; Mine and Mineral Law; Native American Rights.

INTERLINEATION 📖 The process of writing between the lines of an instrument; that which is written between the lines of a document. 📖

An interlineation frequently appears in a CONTRACT that has been typed and signed. If the parties agree that a sentence is to be inserted between the lines to clarify a particular provision, the new sentence is known as an interlineation. The new line should be initialed and dated to indicate that both parties are aware of and agree to its insertion. An interlineation results in the alteration of an instrument. See also ALTERATION OF INSTRUMENTS.

INTERLOCKING DIRECTORATE 📖 The relationship that exists between the BOARD OF DIRECTORS of one CORPORATION with that of another due to the fact that a number of members sit on both boards and, therefore, there is a substantial likelihood that neither corporation acts independently of the other. 📖

Because the same persons occupy seats on the boards of companies that are supposed to compete in the marketplace, there is a potential for violations of federal ANTITRUST acts, particularly the CLAYTON Act (15 U.S.C.A. §§ 12-27 [1914]) which prohibits the existence of interlocking directorates that substantially reduce commercial competition.

INTERLOCUTORY 📖 Provisional; INTERIM; temporary; not final; that which intervenes between the beginning and the end of a lawsuit or proceeding to either decide a particular point or matter that is not the final issue of the entire controversy or prevent irreparable harm during the pendency of the lawsuit. 📖

Interlocutory actions are taken by courts when a QUESTION OF LAW must be answered by an APPELLATE COURT before a TRIAL may proceed or to prevent irreparable harm from occurring to a person or property during the pendency of a lawsuit or proceeding. Generally, courts are reluctant to make interlocutory orders unless the circumstances surrounding the case are serious and require timely action.

Interlocutory appeals are restricted by state and federal appellate courts because courts do not want piecemeal litigation. Appeals courts generally review only cases that have reached final JUDGMENT in the trial courts. When a court administrator enters final judgment, this certifies that the trial court has ended its review of the case and JURISDICTION shifts to the appellate court.

Interlocutory appeals are typically permitted when the trial judge certifies to the appellate court in an interlocutory order that an important question of law is in doubt and that it will substantially affect the final result of the case. Judicial economy then dictates that the court resolve the issue rather than subject the parties to a trial that may be reversed on an APPEAL from a final judgment.

Appellate courts have the discretion to review interlocutory orders. The federal courts of appeal are governed by the Interlocutory Appeals Act (28 U.S.C.A. § 1292). This act grants discretion to the courts of appeal to review interlocutory orders in civil cases where the district judge states in the order that a controlling question of law is in doubt and that the immediate resolution of the issue will materially advance the ultimate termination of litigation. State appellate courts are governed by statutes and court rules of appellate procedure regarding the review of interlocutory orders.

When an appellate court reviews an interlocutory order, its decision on the matters contained in the order is final. The court enters an interlocutory judgment, which makes that part of the case final. Therefore, if a case proceeds to trial after an interlocutory judgment is entered, and an appeal from the trial court judgment follows, the matters decided by the interlocutory judgment cannot be reviewed by the court again.

Interlocutory orders may be issued in a DIVORCE proceeding to prevent injury or irreparable harm during the pendency of the lawsuit. For example, an interlocutory order may require one spouse to pay the other spouse a designated weekly sum for support, pending a decision on ALIMONY and CHILD SUPPORT. This prevents the spouse and children from being without income during the action.

Courts may also issue interlocutory orders where property is about to be sold or forfeited and a lawsuit has been filed seeking to stop the action. In this type of case, a court will enter an interlocutory INJUNCTION, preventing the transfer of property until it has made a final decision. To do otherwise would cause irreparable harm and would complicate LEGAL TITLE to the property if the person contesting the transfer ultimately prevailed.

Thus, though the courts value finality in most proceedings, interlocutory orders and appeals are available to protect important rights and to enhance judicial economy.

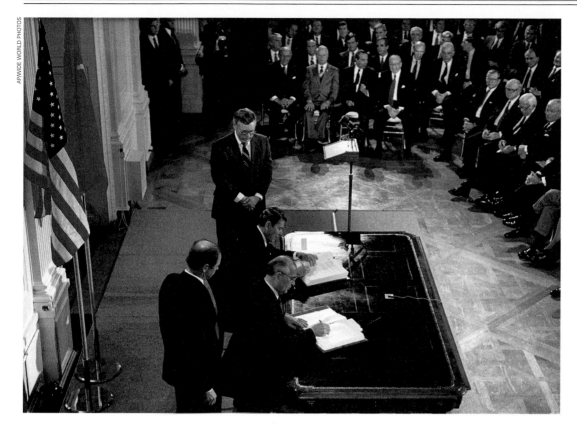

On December 8, 1987, U.S. President Ronald Reagan and Soviet leader Mikhail Gorbachev signed the Intermediate-Range Nuclear Forces Treaty, reducing the number of nuclear weapons held by each nation.

INTERMEDIATE-RANGE NUCLEAR FORCES TREATY

The Intermediate-Range Nuclear Forces Treaty of 1987 (INF) was the first nuclear weapons agreement requiring the United States and the Union of Soviet Socialist Republics (U.S.S.R.) to reduce, rather than merely limit, their arsenals of nuclear weapons. Signed by President RONALD REAGAN, of the United States, and General Secretary Mikhail Gorbachev, of the U.S.S.R., on December 8, 1987, the INF Treaty eliminated all land-based nuclear missiles with ranges of between three hundred and thirty-four hundred miles. The U.S. Senate quickly ratified the treaty in 1988 by a vote of 93–5.

The INF Treaty marked a historic shift in superpower relations and was the first superpower ARMS CONTROL treaty since 1979. It required the removal of 1,752 Soviet and 859 U.S. short- and intermediate-range missiles, most of which were located in Europe. It was the second superpower agreement to ban an entire class of weapons, the first being the 1972 Biological Weapons Convention. The INF Treaty also contained unprecedented verification procedures, including mandatory exchanges of relevant missile data, on-site inspections, and satellite surveillance.

Soviet concessions in the INF negotiations grew out of Gorbachev's efforts to limit military competition between the United States and the U.S.S.R. The new Soviet willingness to make arms control concessions was first evident in the 1986 Stockholm Accord, which established various confidence- and security-building measures between the superpowers and their allied countries, including on-site inspections and advance warning of military movements. In 1988, a year after signing the INF, Gorbachev continued his ambitious program of military cuts by announcing a unilateral reduction of half a million troops, including the removal of fifty thousand troops and five thousand tanks from eastern Europe. These developments met with a positive response from the United States and its NORTH ATLANTIC TREATY ORGANIZATION allies, and created an atmosphere conducive to future arms accords, including the Conventional Forces in Europe Treaty of 1990 and the Strategic Arms Reduction Treaties of 1991 and 1993.

CROSS-REFERENCES

Cold War; Conventional Armed Forces in Europe Treaty; Strategic Arms Reduction Talks.

INTERNAL AUDIT

An inspection and verification of the financial records of a company or firm by a member of its own staff to determine the accuracy and acceptability of its accounting practices.

INTERNAL REVENUE CODE The Internal Revenue Code is the body of law that codifies all federal tax laws, including income, estate, gift, excise, alcohol, tobacco, and employment taxes. These laws constitute title 26 of the U.S. Code (26 U.S.C.A. § 1 et seq. [1986]) and are implemented by the INTERNAL REVENUE SERVICE through its Treasury Regulations and Revenue Rulings.

Congress made major statutory changes to title 26 in 1939, 1954, and 1986. Because of the extensive revisions made in the Tax Reform Act of 1986, title 26 is now known as the Internal Revenue Code of 1986 (Pub. L. No. 99-514, § 2, 100 Stat. 2095 [Oct. 22, 1986]).

Subtitle A of the Code contains five chapters on INCOME TAXES. The chapters cover normal income taxes and surtaxes, taxes on self-employment income, withholding of taxes on nonresident aliens and foreign corporations, taxes on transfers to avoid income tax, and consolidated returns.

Subtitle B deals with ESTATE AND GIFT TAXES. The rules and regulations concerning the TAXATION of PROBATE estates and GIFTS are very complicated. This subtitle contains chapters on taxing generation-skipping transfers and rules on special valuation of property.

Subtitle C contains the law of employment taxes. It consists of chapters on general provisions relating to employment taxes and other sections dealing with federal insurance contributions, railroad retirement taxes, and federal unemployment taxes.

Subtitle D covers miscellaneous excise taxes. Its fifteen chapters cover a variety of issues, including retail excise taxes, manufacturers' excise taxes, taxes on wagering, environmental taxes, public charities, private foundations, pension plans, and certain group health plans.

Subtitle E covers alcohol, tobacco, and other excise taxes. Chapter 53 deals with machine guns, destructive devices, and certain other firearms.

Subtitle F contains provisions on procedure and administration. Under this subtitle are twenty chapters that deal with every step of the taxation process, from the setting of filing dates and the collection of penalties for late filing, to criminal offenses and judicial proceedings. The rules for administrative proceedings under the Code are addressed in the appendix to title 26.

Subtitle G addresses the organization of the Congressional Joint Committee on Taxation. Subtitle H contains the rules for the financing of presidential election campaigns. Subtitle I contains the Trust Fund Code. See also ELECTION CAMPAIGN FINANCING.

The Internal Revenue Code has grown steadily since the 1930s. The complexity of its provisions, most of which are written in technical language, has required law and accounting firms to develop specialists in the various areas of taxation.

INTERNAL REVENUE SERVICE The federal agency responsible for administering and enforcing all internal revenue laws in the United States, except those relating to alcohol, tobacco, firearms, and explosives, which are the responsibility of the Bureau of Alcohol, Tobacco and Firearms.

The Internal Revenue Service (IRS) is the largest agency in the TREASURY DEPARTMENT. By the mid-1990s it had approximately 110,000 employees, 650 office locations in the United States, and twelve offices abroad. The agency processes approximately 205 million tax returns and collects more than $1.2 trillion each year.

The U.S. tax system, which the IRS oversees and administers, is based on the principle of voluntary compliance. According to the IRS, this means "that taxpayers are expected to comply with the law without being compelled to do so by action of a federal agent; it does not mean that the taxpayer is free to decide whether or not to comply with the law."

Duties and Powers The IRS is responsible for enforcing the INTERNAL REVENUE CODE (U.S.C.A. tit. 26), which codifies all U.S. tax laws. Basic IRS activities include serving and educating taxpayers; determining, assessing, and collecting taxes; investigating individuals and organizations that violate tax laws; determining PENSION plan qualifications and exempt organization status; and issuing rulings and regulations to supplement the Internal Revenue Code.

Historically, Congress has given the IRS unique and wide-ranging powers for administering the U.S. tax system and enforcing its laws. For example, while in a criminal proceeding the government has the burden to prove that the defendant is guilty BEYOND A REASONABLE DOUBT, in a tax proceeding the burden is on the taxpayer to prove that he or she does not owe the amount claimed by the IRS. The IRS also has the power to impose civil penalties for any of a number of violations of tax law. These penalties are seldom employed, however, and with respect to penalties, the IRS bears the burden of proving that the penalty is justified.

The IRS has the power to collect large amounts of information on U.S. citizens, companies, and other institutions. The most obvious example of this power is that each year all taxpayers must file tax returns containing detailed financial and personal information. Many organizations are also required to notify the IRS of any payments they make to individuals; the IRS receives approximately 1 billion of these third-party reports annually. The IRS also has the legal authority to order banks, employers, and other institutions to provide information about a taxpayer without having to obtain a WARRANT from a judge; other law enforcement agencies, such as the Federal Bureau of Investigation and local police forces, must obtain a warrant in such situations.

Another crucial power of the IRS is the ability to withhold taxes automatically from employee paychecks. The IRS was given this authority in 1943, when Congress passed legislation requiring employers to withhold from employees' paychecks the income taxes owed to the government. This withholding requirement was one of several actions taken by the government to increase revenue so that it could meet the huge financial requirements for fighting World War II. Today, automatic withholding accounts for the majority of tax dollars paid to the government, with only a small portion sent in with tax returns by April 15, the IRS's annual tax deadline. Automatic withholding is important to the government because it enables it to receive a steady stream of tax revenue. It is also useful for enforcing voluntary compliance from taxpayers, because the individual's tax burden seems less onerous when taxes owed are subtracted from a paycheck before the check is received.

Organization The IRS is led by a commissioner, who works in the IRS National Office located in Washington, D.C. The commissioner and his or her chief counsel are appointed by the president and must be approved by the Senate. The chief counsel serves as the chief legal adviser to the IRS. At the next level are regional commissioners, who oversee IRS operations in the four regions into which the country is divided: the Northeast, Southeast, Midstates, and Western Regions. Within the four regions are thirty-three district offices, which are responsible for collecting revenue, examining returns, and pursuing criminal investigations within their geographic area. Also located across the country are ten service centers, five submission processing centers, two computing centers, and twenty-three customer service centers.

In addition to its geographic divisions, the IRS is organized into programs focusing on specific administrative tasks. Several of these, including the Taxpayer Services and Problem Resolution programs, focus on taxpayer assis-

tance and education. Others, including the Examination, Collection, and Criminal Investigation divisions, focus on ensuring taxpayer compliance. Additional IRS programs include Appeals, which attempts to resolve tax controversies without litigation; Statistics of Income, which compiles and publishes data relating to the operation of the Internal Revenue Code; and Tax Practitioner Conduct, which enforces tax laws applying to attorneys, accountants, and taxpayer agents.

History The IRS was created in 1952, though it was preceded by various other U.S. tax-collecting offices. The IRS's earliest incarnation, the Office of the Commissioner of Revenue, was established by Congress in 1792 in response to Secretary of the Treasury ALEXANDER HAMILTON's request that various TARIFFS and taxes be created to raise money to pay off the United States' Revolutionary War debt. Trench Coxe, of Pennsylvania, was the first person to hold the office. By creating the Office of the Commissioner of Revenue, Congress delegated its constitutional power to "lay and collect taxes, duties, imposts, and excises" to the Treasury Department, which has retained the power ever since (art. 1, § 8, U.S. Constitution).

By the time THOMAS JEFFERSON became president in 1801, the internal revenue program had grown to employ four hundred revenue officials, who enforced a wide variety of tax regulations, including taxes on distilled spirits, land, houses, and slaves. Jefferson, a Democrat who fiercely opposed Hamilton and his Federalist party programs, abolished the entire system and relied instead on taxes assessed on imported items for government revenue. When the War

Internal Revenue Gross Collection, by Source: 1993

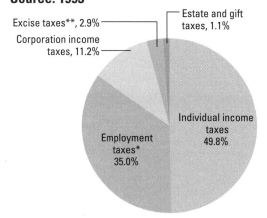

Excise taxes**, 2.9%
Corporation income taxes, 11.2%
Estate and gift taxes, 1.1%
Individual income taxes 49.8%
Employment taxes* 35.0%

*Includes OASDI, railroad retirement and unemployment insurance.
**Includes alcohol, tobacco and manufactures taxes, windfall profits tax and other excise taxes.

Source: U.S. Internal Revenue Service, *Annual Report.*

of 1812 increased the government's needs for funds, taxes were reimposed on items such as sugar, carriages, liquor, furniture, and luxury items. At the war's end, all internal taxes and collection offices were abolished, and CUSTOMS DUTIES again became the primary source for government revenue.

When the Civil War broke out in 1861, President ABRAHAM LINCOLN faced a financial crisis because the government needed much more money to finance the war effort than could be raised through customs duties. To address this problem, Congress passed sweeping new tax measures, including the Civil War Revenue Act of August 5, 1861, which authorized the country's first INCOME TAX and imposed a DIRECT TAX of $20 million apportioned among the states. The Revenue Act of July 1, 1862, created a wide variety of new taxes. To oversee their collection, Congress created the Bureau of Internal Revenue under the secretary of the treasury. This office, which represents the first form of the modern internal revenue collection system, administered the tax system by dividing the country into 185 collection districts. The commissioner was given the power to enforce tax laws through both seizure and prosecution. George S. Boutwell, of Massachusetts, was the first commissioner of internal revenue. Boutwell was initially assisted by three clerks. By January 1863 the office had grown to employ nearly four thousand people, most of whom worked in the field as revenue collectors or property assessors.

When the Civil War ended in 1865, the government's need for revenue was greatly reduced. Taxes were scaled back, the income tax was eliminated, and customs duties again became a sufficient source for federal funds. With the subsequent rise of industrialism and growth of populist political ideas, however, many citizens wanted the government to take a more active role and therefore lobbied for a reestablishment of the income tax to provide greater revenue. Most of the support for an income tax came from southern and western states. Most of the opposition came from the wealthier states whose citizens would be most affected by an income tax—Massachusetts, New Jersey, New York, and Pennsylvania.

After many attempts Congress finally passed a modest income tax in 1894. The Supreme Court quickly ruled it unconstitutional on the ground that it violated the constitutional provision requiring that federal taxes be apportioned equally among the various states. Supporters of the income tax overcame this hurdle in 1913, when Wyoming became the thirty-sixth state to pass the SIXTEENTH AMENDMENT to the Consti-

tution, giving Congress the power to collect taxes without regard to state apportionment. That same year Congress enacted the first income tax act under the amendment, and the income tax became a permanent feature of the U.S. tax system.

The passage of the Sixteenth Amendment marked the beginning of an era of significant expansion for the Bureau of Internal Revenue. The establishment of the Personal Income Tax Division greatly increased bureau staff, and many new taxes were imposed to finance World War I, thus requiring new bureau divisions and programs. As the bureau's responsibilities continued to multiply, operations became more inefficient and disorganized. In the 1920s, for example, the national office of the bureau was housed in a dozen different buildings located all around the metropolitan Washington, D.C., area. Tax returns became backlogged, tax fraud and evasion were rampant, and an extensive patronage system enabled politically appointed collectors to operate unchecked, outraging their CIVIL SERVICE staffs. Beginning in 1945 Congress and the Treasury Department began efforts to overhaul the whole tax collection system. In 1952 the Bureau of Internal Revenue was reorganized and given a new name: the Internal Revenue Service. This new moniker was intended to emphasize the agency's focus on providing service to taxpayers. Patronage was eliminated, and power was decentralized, with the states being divided into seven regional districts through which all return processing, auditing, billing, and refunding would be administered.

Since 1952 the IRS has continued to undergo major changes and reorganizations. Advancements in technology have had a tremendous effect on IRS operations, beginning with the opening of the automatic data processing system in Martinsburg, West Virginia, in 1962. This system revolutionized the collection and audit process by enabling the IRS to maintain a master file of every taxpayer's account. More recent technological applications have changed the way taxpayers interact with the IRS. In 1995, for example, more than 14 million individuals and businesses used the IRS's electronic filing program to submit their tax returns. Another approximately 685,000 taxpayers in ten states filed their tax return using their touch-tone telephone. Taxes were also paid electronically, with more than forty-one thousand businesses making more than $232 billion in federal tax deposits by electronic funds transfer.

Over the years the IRS has faced continuing pressure from Congress and the public to adopt more reasonable enforcement policies, to provide better service to taxpayers, and to protect private information more carefully. In an attempt to protect taxpayers' rights, Congress in 1988 passed the TAXPAYER BILL OF RIGHTS (Pub. L. No. 100-647, tit. VI, §§ 6226–6247, 102 Stat. 3730–3752 [Nov. 10, 1988]), which outlines the rights and protections a taxpayer has when dealing with the IRS. Included are the right to waive penalties if the taxpayer follows incorrect advice given by the IRS, the right to request relief when tax laws result in significant hardship, and the right to attorneys' fees in cases where IRS employees violate the Internal Revenue Code to the detriment of the taxpayer.

In 1995 the IRS's administrative structure underwent a major reorganization. The seven regions that had been established in 1952 were reduced to four, and management was consolidated, decreasing the number of districts within those regions from sixty-three to thirty-three.

CROSS-REFERENCES

Estate and Gift Taxes; *Pollock v. Farmers' Loan and Trust Co.*; Taxation; Tax Court; Tax Evasion.

INTERNAL WATERS See INLAND WATERS.
INTERNATIONAL COURT OF JUSTICE

📖 The main judicial tribunal of the UNITED NATIONS, to which all member states are parties. 📖

The International Court of Justice (ICJ) was established in 1946 by the United Nations (Statute of the International Court of Justice [ICJ Statute], June 26, 1945, 59 Stat. 1055, 3 Bevans 1179). The headquarters of the ICJ is located in the Peace Palace at The Hague.

When a country has a dispute with another country, it may submit the dispute to the ICJ for resolution. The decisions of the ICJ are only advisory: no mechanism for their enforcement is in place. The enforcement of an ICJ decision ultimately depends on the will of the countries involved in the dispute.

Membership in the United Nations does not automatically subject a country to the JURISDICTION of the ICJ. The ICJ will hear a case only if all the countries involved in the case consent to its jurisdiction. Some countries automatically accept the jurisdiction of the court. Other countries automatically accept the court's compulsory jurisdiction but reserve the right to opt out of ICJ proceedings on matters that are of vital national interest. (Although the word *compulsory* is used, a country may choose not to recognize the ICJ's jurisdiction. Participation is voluntary.)

Under the ICJ Statute, the ICJ must decide cases in accordance with INTERNATIONAL LAW. This means that the ICJ must apply (1) any international conventions and treaties; (2) international custom; (3) general principles recognized as law by civilized nations; and (4) judicial decisions and the teachings of highly qualified publicists of the various nations.

The ICJ can hear any case upon application by a U.N. member country. One common type of conflict presented to the ICJ is TREATY interpretation. In these cases the ICJ is asked to resolve disagreements over the meaning and application of terms in treaties formed between two or more countries. Other cases range from nuclear testing and water boundary disputes to conflicts over the military presence of a foreign country.

The ICJ is made up of fifteen jurists from different countries. No two judges at any given time may be from the same country. The court's composition is static but generally includes jurists from a variety of cultures.

Despite this diversity in structure, the ICJ has been criticized for favoring established powers. Under articles 3 and 9 of the ICJ Statute, the judges on the ICJ should represent "the main forms of civilization and . . . principal legal systems of the world." This definition suggests that the ICJ does not represent the interests of developing countries. Indeed, few Latin American countries have acquiesced to the jurisdiction of the ICJ. Conversely, most developed countries accept the compulsory jurisdiction of the ICJ.

The United States has not always agreed to submit to the jurisdiction of the ICJ. On April 6, 1984, the United States informed the United Nations that it would not accept the compulsory jurisdiction of the ICJ in disputes involving Central America. On April 9, 1984, Nicaragua asked the ICJ to hear a case it had against the United States. According to Nicaragua the

U.S. judge Gabrielle Kirk McDonald was sworn in as a member of the International War Crimes Tribunal for the Former Yugoslavia at the Peace Palace in The Hague in November 1993. The tribunal was the first since World War II to prosecute those charged with war crimes.

APWIDE WORLD PHOTOS

United States had violated customary and conventional international law by engaging in and supporting insurgent military and paramilitary activities against the Nicaraguan government.

The United States argued that its notification of April 6, 1984, deprived the ICJ of jurisdiction over the case. The ICJ disagreed and accepted the case. Though the United States had withdrawn from the case, the ICJ heard Nicaragua's arguments. On June 27, 1986, the ICJ issued an opinion in which it held for Nicaragua on most issues. Since this dispute the U.S. State Department has not accepted the compulsory jurisdiction of the court.

The ICJ has been maligned for the inconsistency of its decisions and its lack of enforcement power. But its ambitious mission—to resolve disputes between sovereign nations—makes it a valuable source of support for many countries in their political interaction with other countries.

See also WORLD COURT.

INTERNATIONAL LAW 🔖 The body of law governing the legal relations between states or nations. 🔖

To qualify as a subject under the traditional definition of international law, a state had to be sovereign: it needed a territory, a population, a government, and the ability to engage in diplomatic or foreign relations. States within the United States, provinces, and cantons were not considered subjects of international law, because they lacked the legal authority to engage in foreign relations. In addition, individuals did not fall within the definition of subjects possessing rights and obligations under international law.

A more contemporary definition expands the traditional notions of international law to confer rights and obligations on intergovernmental international organizations and even individuals. The UNITED NATIONS, for example, is an international organization that has the capacity to engage in TREATY relations governed by and binding under international law with states and other international organizations. Individual responsibility under international law is particularly significant in the context of prosecuting war criminals and the development of international HUMAN RIGHTS.

International Court of Justice The INTERNATIONAL COURT OF JUSTICE (ICJ) was established in 1945 as the successor to the Permanent International Court of Justice (PICJ), which was created in 1920 under the supervision of the LEAGUE OF NATIONS (the precursor to the United Nations). The PICJ ceased to function during the Second World War and was officially dissolved in 1946. The ICJ is a permanent international court located in The Hague, Netherlands, and it is the principal judicial organ of the United Nations. It consists of fifteen judges, each from a different state. The judges are elected by the U.N. General Assembly and the U.N. Security Council, and must receive an absolute majority from both in order to take office.

The ICJ has JURISDICTION only over states that have consented to it. It follows that the court cannot hear a dispute between two or more state parties when one of the parties has not accepted its jurisdiction. This can happen even where the nonconsenting party adheres to the court's statute, since mere adherence to the statute does not imply consent to its tribunals. In addition, the court does not have jurisdiction over disputes between individuals or entities that are not states (I.C.J. Stat. art. 34(1)). It also lacks jurisdiction over matters that are governed by domestic law instead of international law (art. 38(1)).

States can accept the court's jurisdiction in several different ways. First, they can consent to jurisdiction on an AD HOC basis, which means that they negotiate a special agreement to let the ICJ decide a particular case at hand. Second, they can adhere to a treaty in which the court's jurisdiction is automatically accepted as one of its conditions (art. 36(1)). This form of acceptance is mainly exercised in disputes that arise out of the interpretation or application of a treaty. Third, states can accept the court's jurisdiction under article 36(2) of the court's statute, known as the Optional Clause. This clause allows states to make a unilateral declaration recognizing "as compulsory *ipso facto* and without special agreement, in relation to any other state accepting the same obligation, the jurisdiction of the Court in all legal disputes."

Many states have accepted the court's jurisdiction under the Optional Clause. A few states have done so with certain restrictions. The United States, for instance, has invoked the so-called self-judging reservation, or Connally Reservation. This reservation allows states a way out of the court's jurisdiction previously accepted under the Optional Clause if they decide not to respond to a particular suit. It is commonly exercised when a state determines that a particular dispute is of domestic rather than international character and thus domestic jurisdiction applies. If a state invokes the self-judging reservation, another state may also invoke this reservation against that state and thus a suit against the second state would be dismissed. This is called the rule of reciprocity and stands for the principle that a state has to respond to a suit brought against it before the ICJ only if the state bringing the suit has also accepted the court's jurisdiction. In 1986, the United States terminated its acceptance of the court's jurisdiction under the Optional Clause after the U.S. government became dissatisfied with U.S.–Nicaragua litigation. Nonetheless, the United States is still a party to many treaties and has consented to the court's jurisdiction with regard to certain treaties automatically because it is a party to these treaties, under article 36(1).

The judgment of the ICJ is binding and cannot be appealed (arts. 59, 60) once the parties have consented to its jurisdiction and the court has rendered a decision. The ICJ statute does not explain how the court's judgment will be enforced. Instead, it relies on the parties to comply with the judgment, and a state's failure to do so violates the U.N. Charter, article 94(2).

Noncompliance can be appealed to the U.N. Security Council, which may either make recommendations or authorize other measures by which the judgment shall be enforced. Recommendations made by the Security Council are not binding on a noncomplying party. Decisions are binding, and can lead to enforcement measures should a party fail to comply. A decision by the Security Council to enforce compliance with a judgment rendered by the court is subject to the veto power of permanent members and thus depends on the members' willing-

ness not only to resort to enforcement measures but also to support the original judgment.

Sources of International Law Article 38(1) of the ICJ Statute enumerates the sources of international law and states that international law has its basis in international custom, international conventions or treaties, and general principles of law. A rule must derive from one of these three sources in order to be considered international law.

Custom Customary international law is defined as a general practice of law under article 38(1)(b). States follow such a practice out of a sense of legal obligation. Rules or principles must be accepted by the states as legally binding in order to be considered rules of international law. Thus, the mere fact that a custom is widely followed does not make it a rule of international law. States must also view it as obligatory to follow the custom, and not believe that they are free to depart from it whenever they choose or to observe it only as a matter of courtesy or moral obligation. This requirement is referred to as *opinio juris*.

Some criticism against customary international law is directed at its subjective character and its inconsistency. States vary greatly in their opinions and interpretations of issues regarding international law. Thus, it is almost impossible to find enough consistency among states to draw a customary international rule from general practice. In addition, even if one state or judge finds that a practice is a rule of customary international law, another decision maker might

VANESSA VICK/PHOTO RESEARCHERS

The United Nations is an international organization with the capacity to engage in treaty relations governed by and binding under international law.

reach a different conclusion. Altogether, the process of establishing rules of customary international law is lengthy and impeded by today's fast-changing world.

Conventions and Treaties Conventional international law includes international agreements and legislative treaties that establish rules expressly recognized by consenting states. Only states that are parties to a treaty are bound by it. However, a very large number of states voluntarily adhere to treaties and accept their provisions as law even without becoming parties to them. The most important treaties in this regard are the Genocide Convention, the Vienna conventions, and the provisions of the U.N. Charter.

U.N. Charter and United Nations

The U.N. Charter and the United Nations as an organization were established on October 26, 1945. The U.N. Charter is a multilateral treaty that serves as the organization's constitution. The U.N. Charter contains a supremacy clause that makes it the highest authority of law on the international plane. The clause states that the U.N. Charter shall prevail in the event of a conflict between the obligations of the members of the United Nations under the present charter and their obligations under any other international agreement (art. 103).

At its formation, the United Nations had 51 member states. Its membership had increased to 180 states in 1996, including almost all the world's independent nations. The United Nations is designed to serve a multitude of purposes and is charged with a variety of responsibilities. Among these are peacekeeping; developing friendly relations among nations; achieving international cooperation in solving international problems of an economic, social, cultural, and humanitarian character; and promoting human rights and fundamental freedoms for all human beings without discrimination (U.N. Charter art. 1).

The United Nations comprises the Trusteeship Council, the General Assembly, the Security Council, the Economic and Social Council, and the ICJ. The Trusteeship Council had its role in supervising the administration of non-self-governing territories. Since all these territories have now gained independence, the last one being Palau in 1993, the Trusteeship Council is no longer functional within the United Nations.

The General Assembly and the Security Council are the organs of the organization that are most involved in lawmaking and legislative activities. Their respective authority varies

greatly. Although the General Assembly lacks formal legislative authority to adopt resolutions that are binding on its members, it is highly active in the making and development of international law. This organ of the United Nations is required to initiate studies and make recommendations that encourage the progressive development of international law and its codification (U.N. Charter art. 13(1)(a)). Within this context, the General Assembly has originated much of the existing international legislation, and some of its resolutions are now accepted as customary international law, such as the Universal Declaration of Human Rights. Thus, resolutions adopted by the General Assembly, albeit formally considered nonbinding, do have legal character and contribute significantly to the development of international law.

The Security Council, on the other hand, does have the authority to adopt binding decisions, and noncompliance with these decisions constitutes a violation of the U.N. Charter. However, this does not give the Security Council a general lawmaking authority, as its subject matter jurisdiction is limited to concerns of international peace and security. According to the U.N. Charter, article 2(3), all nations are required to settle their disputes by peaceful means in such a manner that international peace, security, and justice are not endangered. Nations are advised to resort to peaceful dispute settlement mechanisms (art. 33(1)) such as negotiation, mediation, and conciliation. Where these measures fail, the parties must refer to the U.N. Security Council if their proposed measure would be a threat to peace and security. The Security Council then makes recommendations on further peaceful measures, and resorts to the powers conferred on it under the U.N. Charter for its peacekeeping operations. The General Assembly's role in peacekeeping focuses mainly on providing a forum for public discussion of the issues. The assembly does have the power, however, to bring issues potentially endangering the peace before the Security Council.

In a case where the Security Council fails to exercise its responsibility for maintaining international peace and security and there is a threat to peace or an act of aggression, the General Assembly may make appropriate recommendations and authorize the use of armed forces to maintain or restore international peace and security. However, the United Nations has not in general been very effective in preventing hostilities that involve the world's principal powers either directly or indirectly. It has been more effective in dealing with conflicts through the use of its multilateral peacekeeping force.

In addition to its provisions that apply to the peaceful interaction between nations, the U.N. Charter includes a general provision dealing with the human rights of the individual. On December 10, 1948, the United Nations adopted the Universal Declaration of Human Rights, which defines and enumerates specifically the human rights that the United Nations seeks to protect. Among those are freedom from systematic governmental acts and policies involving torture, SLAVERY, MURDER, prolonged arbitrary detention, disappearance, and racial discrimination. The declaration guarantees the right to life; to EQUAL PROTECTION of the law; to free speech, assembly, and movement; to PRIVACY; to work; to education; to health care; and to participation in the cultural life of the community. Although the Universal Declaration is not a binding instrument of international law, some of its provisions have nonetheless reached the status of customary international law. Under articles 55 and 56 of the U.N. Charter, member states have an obligation to promote these rights. At the same time, the declaration acknowledges that states can limit these rights as they deem necessary to ensure respect for the rights and freedoms of others.

In 1966, the U.N. General Assembly adopted three covenants that involve human rights: the International Covenant on Civil and Political Rights; the International Covenant on Economic, Social, and Cultural Rights; and the Optional Protocol to the Civil and Political Covenant. Unlike the Universal Declaration, these covenants are treaties that require ratification by member states. The United States is not a party to the covenants.

The human rights provisions of the U.N. Charter, the Universal Declaration of Human Rights, and the covenants constitute the International Bill of Human Rights. Other U.N. human rights instruments supplement this bill. The most important ones are the Genocide Convention (1948), the International Convention on the Elimination of All Forms of Racial Discrimination (1965), the Convention on the Political Rights of Women (1953), and the International Convention on the Suppression and Punishment of the Crime of Apartheid (1973). These conventions are legally binding on the parties that have ratified them. Most of the U.N. member states have ratified at least two: the Genocide Convention and the Racial Convention. The United States has ratified

only the Women's Rights Convention and the Genocide Convention.

CROSS-REFERENCES
Ambassadors and Consuls; Arms Control and Disarmament; General Agreement on Tariffs and Trade; Genocide; Law of Nations; North American Free Trade Agreement; War.

INTERNATIONAL MONETARY FUND
The International Monetary Fund (IMF) is a specialized agency of the UNITED NATIONS that seeks to promote international monetary cooperation and to stimulate international trade. The IMF has worked to stabilize world currencies and to develop programs of economic adjustment for nations that require economic reform.

The IMF was created in 1944 at the United Nations Monetary and Financial Conference, held at Bretton Woods, New Hampshire. It first began operation in 1947, from its headquarters in Washington, D.C., with a fund of $9 billion in bills and currency, of which the United States contributed almost a third. The creation of the IMF was seen as a way to prevent retaliatory currency devaluations and trade restrictions, which were seen as a major cause of the worldwide depression prior to World War II.

Membership is open to countries willing to abide by terms established by the board of governors, which is composed of a representative from each member nation. General terms include obligations to avoid manipulating exchange rates, abstain from discriminatory currency practices, and refrain from imposing restrictions on the making of payments and currency transfers necessary to foreign trade.

Largest IMF Members, by Quota, 1996

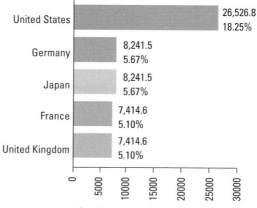

United States	26,526.8 — 18.25%
Germany	8,241.5 — 5.67%
Japan	8,241.5 — 5.67%
France	7,414.6 — 5.10%
United Kingdom	7,414.6 — 5.10%

Special Drawing Rights (in millions)

Source: International Monetary Fund.

The voting power of the governors is allocated according to the size of the quota of each member. The term *quota* refers to the IMF's unit of account, which is based on each member's relative position in the world economy. This position is measured by the size of the country's economy, foreign trade, and relative importance in the international monetary system. Once a quota is set by the IMF, the country must deposit with the organization, as a subscription, an amount equal to the size of the quota. Up to three-fourths of a subscription may consist of the currency of the subscribing nation. Each subscription forms part of the reserve available to countries suffering from balance-of-payment problems.

When a member has a balance-of-payment problem, it may apply to the IMF for needed foreign currency from the reserve derived from its quota. The member may use this foreign exchange for up to five years to help solve its problems, and then return the currency to the IMF's pool of resources. The IMF offers below-market rates of interest for using these funds. The member country whose currency is used receives most of the interest. A small amount goes to the IMF for operating expenses.

In its early years the IMF directed its major programs toward maintaining fixed exchange rates linked to the U.S. dollar, which in turn could be converted at a standard rate into gold. Present IMF policy emphasizes an orderly adjustment of currency exchange rates to reflect underlying economic forces. Special attention has been given to the needs of developing countries, in the form of programs to provide long-term assistance to cover foreign exchange demands necessitated by high import prices, declining export earnings, or development programs. In appropriate circumstances the IMF may impose conditions on the use of IMF resources to encourage recipient countries to make needed economic reforms.

Since 1982 the IMF has concentrated on the problems of developing nations. It has gone beyond its own resources, encouraging additional lending from commercial banks. The IMF has also established new programs, using funds from its richer members, to provide money in larger amounts and for longer periods than those granted under the quota-driven lending procedures. It works closely with the WORLD BANK on these and other international monetary issues.

INTERNATIONAL TRADE ORGANIZATION

The problems caused by the "beggar thy neighbor" trade policies employed by nations before World War II led the United States to propose that a new international trade organization be established to regulate trade policies and settle disputes between trading partners. Under the proposal by the United States the International Trade Organization (ITO) was to be a specialized agency of the UNITED NATIONS and was to have several broad functions: promoting the growth of trade by eliminating or reducing TARIFFS or other barriers to trade; regulating restrictive business practices hampering trade; regulating international commodity agreements; assisting economic development and reconstruction; and settling disputes among member nations regarding harmful trade policies. Negotiations to establish the ITO began in Geneva in 1947, with a more complete charter being drafted later in Havana, Cuba. Opposition to the charter of the ITO soon emerged, especially in the U.S. Congress. Subsequently, the Truman administration withdrew its support for the ITO, and interest in the ITO faded. The void left by the collapse of the ITO has been filled by other institutions, like the GENERAL AGREEMENT ON TARIFFS AND TRADE (GATT), the World Bank, and the United Nations Conference on Trade and Development (UNCTAD).

INTERNATIONAL WATERWAYS

Narrow channels of marginal sea or INLAND WATERS through which international shipping has a right of passage.

In INTERNATIONAL LAW, international waterways are straits, CANALS, and rivers that connect two areas of the high seas or enable ocean shipping to reach interior ports on international seas, gulfs, or lakes that otherwise would be landlocked. International waterways also may be rivers that serve as international BOUNDARIES or traverse successively two or more states. Ships have a right of passage through international waterways. This right is based on customary international law and TREATY arrangements.

Straits Some straits are more important than others because they are the sole connecting links between oceans and interior waters—for example, the Strait of Gibraltar gives access from the Atlantic Ocean to the Mediterranean and Aegean Seas. Other straits are not as important. The availability of alternate routes does not in itself deprive a strait of its character as an international waterway. In the *Corfu Channel* case, 1949 I.C.J. 4, 1949 WL 1 (I.C.J.), the International Court of Justice rejected the test of essentiality as the only route, ruling that "the decisive criterion is rather [the strait's] geographic situation as connecting two parts of the high seas and the fact of its being used for international navigation."

The 1958 Geneva Convention on the Territorial Sea and Contiguous Zone (516 U.N.T.S. 205, 15 U.S.T. 1606, T.I.A.S. No. 5639) does not deal comprehensively with international waterways, but does provide that "[t]here shall be no suspension of innocent passage of foreign ships through straits which are used for international navigation between one part of the high seas and another part of the high seas or the territorial sea of a foreign state" (art. 16, § 4). A territorial sea is the water that comes under the sovereign control of a state. See also TERRITORIAL WATERS.

A coastal state has somewhat greater control of innocent passage through its territorial seas than of innocent passage through a strait joining two areas of high seas. Passage may be suspended through territorial waters when essential for security. This means that warships are free to pass through straits but may be denied access to territorial seas.

Since the 1960s a great majority of coastal states have extended their claims on territorial seas from three miles to twelve miles from the low-water mark, some even farther. This change has been a matter of concern to the U.S. government, as a twelve-mile limit converts 121 straits to territorial seas, some of which have strategic military importance.

Canals With respect to international marine traffic, canals joining areas of the high seas or waters leading to them are geographically in the same position as straits. However, the significant canals have been constructed in accordance with international treaties or later placed under conventional legal regimes. The Suez Canal, located in Egypt, and the Panama Canal are the two most important canals in international commerce.

The United States played the major role in the construction of the Panama Canal, which joins the Atlantic and Pacific Oceans across the Isthmus of Panama. The canal is over forty miles long and has a minimum width of three hundred feet.

In 1903, after several European-financed efforts to build a canal across the isthmus had failed, the U.S. government negotiated the Hay-Bunau-Varilla Treaty (T.S. No. 431, 33 Stat. 2234, 10 Bevans 663). Under this treaty the United States guaranteed the independence of Panama (which had just broken away from Colombia) and secured a perpetual lease on a ten-mile strip for the canal. Panama was to receive an initial payment of $10 million and an annuity of $250,000, beginning in 1913.

Shipping Traffic through the Panama Canal, 1985 to 1995

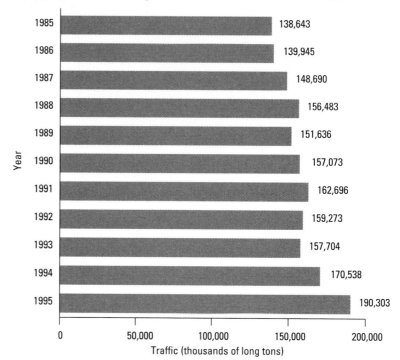

Year	Traffic (thousands of long tons)
1985	138,643
1986	139,945
1987	148,690
1988	156,483
1989	151,636
1990	157,073
1991	162,696
1992	159,273
1993	157,704
1994	170,538
1995	190,303

Source: Office of Executive Planning, Panama Canal Commission.

In 1906 President THEODORE ROOSEVELT directed construction of the canal to begin under the supervision of the U.S. Army Corps of Engineers. The Panama Canal was completed in 1914 and officially opened by President WOODROW WILSON on July 12, 1920.

The Hay-Bunau-Varilla Treaty stated that the canal was to be neutralized and to be free and open to vessels of commerce and war on terms of equality and without discrimination as to tolls or conditions of passage. However, it did not mandate open access in times of war. The United States decided in 1917 to close the canal and the territorial waters of the canal zone (the ten-mile-wide strip of land that contained the canal) to vessels of enemy states and their allies whenever the United States is a belligerent. This was done in World Wars I and II.

From the 1920s to the 1970s, the United States and Panama had many disputes concerning control of the Panama Canal Zone. Panamanians came to regard the zone as part of their country and believed that the 1903 treaty was unfairly favorable to the United States.

In 1971 the two countries began negotiations for a new treaty to replace the 1903 agreement. In 1977 Panama and the United States concluded the Treaty Governing the Permanent Neutrality and Operation of the Panama Canal, and the Panama Canal Treaty (both Washington, D.C., 1977, in force 1979;

Digest of United States Practice in International Law, 1978, at 1028–560).

The treaties provided that the United States would relinquish control and administration of the canal to Panama by December 31, 1999, and stipulated an interim period for the training of, and progressive transfer of functions to, Panamanian personnel under the supervision of a mixed Panama Canal Commission.

The first treaty declared that the canal would be permanently neutralized (as would any other international waterway later constructed wholly or partly in Panamanian territory), with the object of securing it for peaceful transit in time of peace or of war for vessels of all nations on equal terms (arts. 1, 2). The right of passage extends not only to merchant ships but to vessels of war and auxiliary vessels in noncommercial service of all nations "at all times," irrespective of their internal operations, means of propulsion, origin, destination, or armament (art. 3, § 1[e]).

Rivers Customary international law has never granted equal access and rights to countries that share NAVIGABLE RIVERS either as boundaries between them or as waterways that traverse them successively. Freer use of international rivers has occurred in the nineteenth and twentieth centuries through the negotiation of treaties.

The St. Lawrence Seaway, opened for navigation by large ships in 1959, is an example of a legal and an administrative regime wholly devised and controlled by the two states (the United States and Canada) that share it. Based on a river in part, the seaway was developed with the construction of bypass canals, locks, and channel improvements, sometimes wholly within the territory of one state. In 1909 Canada and the United States consolidated and extended a number of earlier piecemeal arrangements in the Boundary Waters Treaty (36 Stat. 2448, 12 Bevans 359), to give both nations equal liberty of navigation in the St. Lawrence River, the Great Lakes, and the canals and waterways connecting the lakes. An international boundary line was drawn generally along the median line of the lakes (with some variation in Lake Michigan), but both nations were to exercise concurrent admiralty and criminal JURISDICTION over the whole of the lakes and their connecting waterways. The admiralty jurisdiction reflected a disposition to treat the lakes as the high seas. This view was supported by the U.S. Supreme Court in *United States v. Rodgers*, 150 U.S. 249, 14 S. Ct. 109, 37 L. Ed. 1071 (1893), when it referred to the "high seas of the lakes."

The building of the St. Lawrence Seaway was complicated by the failure of Canada and the United States to negotiate an agreement for the creation of a joint international authority to supervise the project. Instead, each country established its own national agency to construct the canals, locks, and other works required for the twenty-seven-foot channel, making each agency responsible for work on its own side of the river. The agencies coordinated their work in a series of international agreements and informal arrangements. Where works extended over the international boundary, the two commissions allocated responsibility through the coordination of work at the technical level. They agreed on uniform rules of navigation, coordination of pilotage services, uniform tolls, and arrangements for collection.

Seagoing merchant vessels from other countries use the seaway regularly. Their right to do so rests not on any general principle of free navigation, but on national agreements and article V of the GENERAL AGREEMENT ON TARIFFS AND TRADE, which mandates freedom of transit for merchant ships through the territories of signatories for traffic to or from the territory of other signatories. As the Great Lakes are inland waters and have been demilitarized since the Rush-Bagot Agreement of 1817 (T.S. No. 110½, 2 Miller 645, 12 Bevans 54), it is unlikely that foreign warships will request or receive permission to visit their ports. See also ADMIRALTY AND MARITIME LAW.

INTERNET A worldwide telecommunications network of business, government, and personal computers.

The Internet is a network of computers linking the United States with the rest of the world. Originally developed as a way for U.S. research scientists to communicate with each other, by the mid-1990s the Internet had become a popular form of telecommunication for personal computer users. The dramatic growth in the number of persons using the network heralded the most important change in telecommunications since the introduction of TELEVISION in the late 1940s. However, the sudden popularity of a new, unregulated communications technology raised many issues for U.S. law.

The Internet, popularly called the Net, was created in 1969 for the U.S. Department of Defense. Funding from the Advanced Research Projects Agency (ARPA) allowed researchers to experiment with methods for computers to communicate with each other. Their creation, the Advanced Research Projects Agency Network (ARPANET), originally linked only four

SHOULD THE INTERNET BE POLICED?

Few observers could have predicted the fuss that the Internet began to generate in political and legal circles in the mid-1990s. After all, the global computer network linking 160 countries was hyped relentlessly in the media in the early 1990s. It spawned a multimillion-dollar industry in Net services and a publishing empire devoted to the on-line experience—not to mention Hollywood movies, newspaper columns, and new jargon. But the honeymoon did not last. Like other communications media before it, the Net provoked controversy about what was actually sent across it. Federal and state lawmakers proposed crackdowns on its content. Prosecutors took aim at its users. Civil liberties groups fought back. As the various factions engaged in a tug-of-war over the future of this sprawling medium, the debate became a question of freedom or control: should the Net be left alone as a marketplace of ideas, or should it be regulated, policed, and ultimately "cleaned up"?

More than two decades after Defense Department contractors put it up, the network remains free from official control. This system has no central governing authority for a very good reason: the general public was never intended to use it. Its designers in the late 1960s were scientists. Several years later, academics and students around the world got access to it. In the 1990s, millions of people in U.S. businesses and homes signed on. Before the public signed on its predecessors had long since developed a kind of Net culture—essentially, a freewheeling, anything-goes setting. The opening of the Net to everyone from citizens to corporations necessarily ruptured this formerly closed society, and conflicts appeared.

Speech rights quickly became a hot topic of debate. The Net is a communications medium, and people raise objections to speech on-line just as they do to speech in the real world. The Net

allows for a variety of media—text, pictures, movies, and sound—and pornography is abundantly accessible on-line in all these forms. It is commonly "posted" as coded information to a part of the Net called Usenet, a public issues forum that is used primarily for discussions. With over ten thousand topic areas, called news groups, Usenet literally caters to the world's panoply of interests and tastes. Certain news groups are devoted entirely to pornography.

IN FOCUS

Several signs in 1994 predicted a legal crackdown on the Net. Early on, U.S. attorney general Janet Reno said criminal investigators were exploring the originators of on-line child pornography. In July 1994, federal prosecutors won an obscenity conviction in Tennessee against the operators of a computer bulletin board system (BBS) called the Amateur Action BBS, a private porn subscription service. Quickly becoming a cause célèbre in the on-line world, the case raised the question of how far off a general Net crackdown could be.

In December 1994, a college student's fiction raised a furor. Jake Baker, a sophomore in linguistics at the University of Michigan, published a story about sexual torture in the alt.sex.stories news group on Usenet. Its lurid detail was not unique in the news group, but something else was: Baker used the name of a female classmate for one of his fictional victims. Once the name was recognized, campus critics of pornography lashed out at Baker.

Baker's case demonstrated how seriously objections to Net material would be taken. In January 1995, the University of Michigan opened an investigation, and soon, Federal Bureau of Investigation agents began reviewing Baker's E-mail. Baker insisted he meant no harm; he wanted to be a creative writer. He even submitted to a psychological profile, which determined that he posed no danger to the student

named in his story, or to anyone else. But on February 9, 1995, federal authorities arrested him. He was charged with five counts of using interstate communications to make threats to injure—and kidnap—another person. Lacking any specific target for Baker's alleged threats, yet armed with allegedly incriminating E-mail, prosecutors charged that he was dangerous to other university students. The American Civil Liberties Union (ACLU) came to his aid, arguing in a friend-of-the-court brief that the accusations were baseless and moreover violated Baker's First Amendment rights. A U.S. district court judge threw out the case.

The U.S. Senate had its own ideas about on-line speech. In February 1995, Senator J. James Exon (D-Neb.) introduced the Communications Decency Act (S. 314, 104th Cong., 1st Sess. [1995]). Targeting "obscene, lewd, lascivious, filthy, or indecent" electronic communications, the bill called for two-year prison sentences and fines of up to $100,000 for anyone who makes such material available to anyone under the age of eighteen. In its original form, the bill would have established broad criminal liability: users, on-line services, and the hundreds of small businesses providing Internet accounts would all be required to keep their messages, stories, postings, and E-mail decent. After vigorous protest from access providers, the bill was watered down to protect them: they would not be held liable unless they knowingly provided indecent material.

Several groups lined up to stop the Decency Act. Opposition came from civil liberties groups including the ACLU, the Electronic Frontier Foundation (EFF), and Computer Professionals for Social Responsibility, as well as from on-line services and Internet access providers. They argued that the bill sought to criminalize speech that is constitutionally protected under the First Amendment.

(continued on next page)

SHOULD THE INTERNET BE POLICED?
(CONTINUED)

Beyond the bill's philosophical problems, opponents said it was impractical. In Senate debate, Senator Patrick J. Leahy (D-Vt.) said, "A typical Internet provider carries more than 10,000 groups. As many as 100 million new words go through them every day. Are we going to have a whole new group in the Justice Department checking these 100 million new words to find out if they are wrong?" (141 Cong. Rec. S8310-03, S8332). Others deplored the bill's burden to businesses and the courts. The EFF illustrated how difficult it would be to enforce the Decency Act: Usenet, the Internet's most popular feature, can be censored only partly by an Internet access provider. Providers could seek legal immunity by limiting what their own customers see. But because Usenet is networked through computers worldwide—with each computer doing its share to propagate the entire contents—it would still be help-ing to transmit pornography, and thus run afoul of the law. Moreover, opponents raised doubts about jurisdiction. Under the U.S. Supreme Court's "community standards" definition, each community decides what is obscene. Since the Internet is a web of thousands of communities, critics asked, how would that standard be applied?

On June 14, 1995, the Senate approved S. 314 by a vote of 84–16 as an amendment to its omnibus telecommunications deregulation bill. That amendment died in the House of Representatives. However, other lawmakers were eager to fill the void. Essentially similar to the defunct Exon bill, the Electronic Anti-Stalking Act of 1995 (H.R. 5015, 103d Cong., 2nd Sess. [1994]) took aim at "harassing communications"— including under its definition of stalking any stories depicting acts of violence against women. By mid-1995, at least eleven states were considering pieces of legislation designed to protect minors on-line. Proposed in state legislatures from New York to Florida, these bills targeted on-line pornography, sexual harassment, and the solicitation of sex from minors.

The Net has ceased to belong only to specialists and students. As the larger public capitalizes on this resource, it brings along traditional expectations about civility, manners, and morality. The Internet probably will not be able to resist all efforts to regulate it, any more than print, radio, television, or cable could. Nonetheless, the tradition of freedom also has deep roots in U.S. law, and the First Amendment was designed to protect a broad range of speech activity. It will take some time for lawmakers and the courts to determine just bounds for this vast, young medium.

---

separate computer sites at U.S. universities and research institutes, where it was used primarily by scientists.

In the early 1970s, other countries began to join ARPANET, and within a decade it was widely accessible to researchers, administrators, and students throughout the world. The National Science Foundation (NSF) assumed responsibility for linking these users of ARPA-NET, which was dismantled in 1990. The NSF Network (NSFNET) now serves as the technical backbone for all Internet communications in the United States.

The Internet grew at a fast pace in the 1990s as the general population discovered the power of the new medium. A significant portion of the Net's content is written text, in the form of both electronic mail (E-MAIL) and articles posted in an electronic discussion forum known as the Usenet news groups. In the mid-1990s the appearance of the World Wide Web made the Internet even more popular. The Web is a multimedia interface that allows for the transmission of text, pictures, audio, and video together, known as Web pages, which commonly resemble pages in a magazine. Together these various elements have made the Internet a medium for communication and for the retrieval of information on virtually any topic.

The sudden growth of the Internet caught the legal system unprepared. Before 1996 there was little federal legislation on this form of telecommunication. In 1986 Congress passed the Electronic Communications Privacy Act (ECPA) (18 U.S.C.A. § 2701 et seq. [1996]), which made it illegal to read private E-mail. The ECPA extended most of the protection already granted to conventional mail to electronic mail. Just as the post office may not read private letters, neither can the providers of private bulletin boards, on-line services, or Internet access. However, law enforcement agencies can subpoena E-mail in a criminal investigation. The ECPA also permits employers to read their workers' E-mail. This provision was intended to protect companies against industrial spying but has generated lawsuits from employees who objected to the invasion of their PRIVACY. FEDERAL COURTS, however, have allowed employers to secretly monitor an employee's E-mail on a company-owned computer system, concluding that employees have no reasonable expectation of privacy when they use company E-mail.

Criminal activity on the Internet generally falls into the category of COMPUTER CRIME. It includes so-called hacking, or sneaking into computer systems, stealing account passwords and credit-card numbers, and illegally copying INTELLECTUAL PROPERTY. Because personal computers can easily copy information—including everything from software to photographs and books—and the information can be sent anywhere in the world quickly, it has become much more difficult for COPYRIGHT owners to protect their work.

Public and legislative attention has focused on Internet content, specifically sexually explicit material. The distribution of PORNOGRAPHY became a major concern in the 1990s, as private individuals and businesses found an unregulated means of giving away or selling pornographic images. As hard-core and child pornography proliferated, Congress sought to impose restrictions on OBSCENE and indecent content on the Internet.

In 1996 Congress passed the Communications Decency Act (CDA) as part of the Telecommunications Competition and Deregulation Act of 1996 (47 U.S.C.A. § 223(a)(h)). The CDA forbade the dissemination of obscene or indecent material to children through computer networks or other telecommunications media. The act included penalties for knowing violations of up to five years imprisonment and fines of up to $250,000. First Amendment advocates and on-line services immediately brought suit to challenge the act as an unconstitutional restriction on free speech. A special three-judge federal panel in Pennsylvania agreed with these groups, concluding that the law was overly broad because, in attempting to protect children, it would also limit the speech of adults (*American Civil Liberties Union v. Reno*, 929 F.Supp. 824 [1996]). On June 26, 1997, the Supreme Court affirmed, finding the challenged provisions overbroad (1997 WL 348012).

Another area of legal concern is the issue of libel. In TORT law LIBEL AND SLANDER occur when the communication of false information about a person injures the person's good name or reputation. Where the traditional media are concerned, it is well settled that libel suits provide both a means of REDRESS for injury and a punitive corrective against sloppiness and MALICE. Regarding communication on the Internet, however, there is little CASE LAW, especially on the key issue of LIABILITY.

In suits against newspapers, courts traditionally held publishers liable, along with their reporters, because publishers were presumed to have reviewed the libelous material prior to publication. Because of this legal standard, publishers and editors are generally careful to review anything they publish. However, the Internet is not a body of material carefully reviewed by a publisher, but an unrestricted flood of information. If a libelous or defamatory statement is posted on the Internet, which is essentially owned by no one, the law is uncertain about whether anyone other than the author can be held liable.

Some courts have held that on-line service providers, companies that connect their subscribers to the Internet, should be held liable if they allow their users to post libelous statements on their sites. An on-line provider is thus viewed like a traditional publisher.

Other courts have rejected the publisher analogy and have instead compared Internet service providers to bookstores. Like bookstores, providers are distributors of information and cannot reasonably be expected to review everything they sell. U.S. libel law gives greater protection to bookstores because of this theory (*Smith v. California*, 361 U.S. 147, 80 S. Ct. 215, 4 L. Ed. 2d 205 [1959]), and some courts have applied it to on-line service providers.

The continued growth of the Internet (twenty-four million subscribers in 1995) has placed enormous burdens on telephone networks. Telephone systems were not designed to handle thousands of Internet connections that may last several hours at a time. Telephone companies, concerned about their capacity to handle the volume of both voice and electronic communication, have proposed changing rate structures and raising rates for Internet users that reflect the higher demands placed on the telephone systems.

See also TELECOMMUNICATIONS.

INTERPLEADER ◐ An equitable proceeding brought by a third person to have a court determine the ownership rights of rival claimants to the same money or property that is held by that third person. ◐

Interpleader is a form of equitable relief. Equitable remedies are ways for courts to enforce rights other than by issuing a judgment for money damages. Interpleader is employed when two or more parties seek ownership of money or property that is held by a third party. The property in question is called the stake, and the third party who has custody of it is called the stakeholder. The stakeholder is faced with a legal dilemma: giving the property to either one of the parties will likely lead to a lawsuit by the other party against the stakeholder and the new property owner.

Interpleader enables the stakeholder to turn the controversy over to a court and to be dismissed from the legal action. It is designed to eliminate multiple lawsuits over the same stake and to protect the stakeholder from actual or potential multiple liability. Typically, interpleader will involve corporate securities or proceeds from insurance policies.

The stakeholder initiates an interpleader by filing an ACTION that states that he or she has no claim to the money or property in controversy, and does not know to which claimant it should be lawfully delivered. The stakeholder must also establish the possibility of multiple lawsuits. The stakeholder then may be required to deposit the stake with the court, and notifies possible claimants that they can present their claims of ownership in court for determination.

The court must decide whether the interpleader is proper. It has discretion to allow the interpleader, and may deny the relief if the stakeholder is guilty of LACHES (unreasonable delay) or was responsible for the creation of the adverse claim. If the court grants the interpleader, the stakeholder is dismissed from the action. The rival claimants are given the right to litigate their claims, and they will be bound by the decision of the court.

Interpleader is primarily a device of federal CIVIL PROCEDURE. Two types of interpleader are available in FEDERAL COURTS: one under the Federal Rules of Civil Procedure and one under federal statute. When interpleader is sought through rule 22 of the Federal Rules of Civil Procedure, more than $10,000 must be at issue in the action, and the claimants must reside in the same state and must be citizens of a state other than the one in which the stakeholder is a citizen. The action can be tried where the stakeholder resides, where the CAUSE OF ACTION arose, or where the claimants reside. The stakeholder is not obligated to deposit the stake with the court, an important advantage when the property is used for purposes of investment and to generate income.

Interpleader authorized under 28 U.S.C.A. § 1335 differs in several respects from rule 22 interpleader. The dispute may involve as little as $500, at least two of the claimants must be from different states, and the citizenship of the stakeholder is immaterial. The VENUE, or place of trial, is anywhere that a claimant resides. At the time the suit is filed, the stakeholder must deposit the stake or post a BOND in an amount equivalent to its value.

Claimants in an interpleader proceeding may be permitted to assert additional claims against each other or the stakeholder if they satisfy jurisdictional requirements and do not unreasonably complicate or delay the action. Courts must decide, on the particular facts of each case, whether such claims will be considered.

See also EQUITY.

INTERPOL 📖 The acronym for the International Criminal Police Organization, which is a group designed to coordinate international law enforcement. 📖

Interpol is an international organization of police forces from 176 countries. The purpose of Interpol is to further mutual aid and cooperation among the police forces of its national members and to prevent and inhibit crime.

Interpol was established in 1923, with the General Secretariat—the international headquarters—located in Lyons, France. Delegates from member countries meet once a year to discuss police problems and admit new members. Each member nation maintains and staffs its own national central bureau. In the United States, the bureau is located in Washington, D.C. The U.S. bureau is under the direction and control of the Departments of Justice and of the Treasury, and is staffed by personnel from those departments.

The General Secretariat is supported by membership dues. Its budget is based on the Swiss franc, since that is a stable currency. Approximately five percent of the total budget is paid by the United States.

Interpol is forbidden by its constitution to undertake any intervention or activities of a political, military, religious, or racial character. Each national central bureau coordinates and responds to inquiries received from local and foreign law enforcement agencies. Each bureau also arranges for resolutions adopted by Interpol to be applied at the national level, and works to ensure that the basic principles laid down by Interpol's constitution are followed. National central bureaus are linked electronically to the Interpol General Secretariat's main database in Lyons.

The organization uses a system of international notices (circulars) to inform peace officers in the national bureaus of cases where known criminals abandon their usual residence and travel abroad surreptitiously. The color coded circulars are distributed by Interpol Headquarters to member countries within twenty days of their issue, or, in urgent cases, the same day. In the case of a fugitive whose arrest is requested and whose EXTRADITION is likely, a wanted notice containing details of the ARREST WARRANT and the offense committed is circulated.

In addition, Interpol conducts investigations of criminal activities, including drug trafficking, terrorism, COUNTERFEITING, SMUGGLING, organized crime, and new forms of economic crime.

It conducts criminal history checks for VISA and import permits and traces vehicle registration and ownership. Interpol also performs humanitarian services such as locating missing persons and providing notification of serious illness or death.

INTERPOLATION ◫ The process of inserting additional words in a complete document or instrument in such manner as to alter its intended meaning; the addition of words to a complete document or instrument. ◫

Interpolation is synonymous with INTERLINEATION.

INTERPRETATION ◫ The art or process of determining the intended meaning of a written document, such as a CONSTITUTION, STATUTE, CONTRACT, DEED, or WILL. ◫

The interpretation of written documents is fundamental to the process and practice of law. Interpretation takes place whenever the meaning of a legal document must be determined. Lawyers and judges search for meaning using various interpretive approaches and rules of construction. In constitutional and statutory law, legal interpretation can be a contentious issue.

Legal interpretation may be based on a literal reading of a document. For example, when John Doe signs a will that names his wife, Jane Doe, as his personal representative, his intent to name her the administrator of his estate can be determined solely from the specific language used in the will. There is no need to consider the surrounding facts and circumstances that went into his choice.

When the intended meaning of the words in a document is obscure and conjecture is needed to determine the sense in which they have been used, mixed interpretation occurs. In such a case, the words express an individual's intent only when they are correctly comprehended. If John Doe refers only to "my wife" in his will, a probate court will have to determine who his wife was at the time of his death. How a lawyer or judge ascertains intent when words are unclear is typically governed by rules of construction. For example, the general definition of a word will govern interpretation, unless through custom, usage, or legal precedent a special meaning has been attached to the term.

When a court interprets a statute, it is guided by rules of statutory CONSTRUCTION. Judges are to first attempt to find the "plain meaning" of a law, based solely on the words of the statute. If the statute itself is not clear, a court then may look to EXTRINSIC EVIDENCE, in this case LEGISLATIVE HISTORY, to help interpret what the legislature meant when it enacted the statute. It is now common practice for statutes to contain "interpretation clauses," which include definitions of key words that occur frequently in the laws. These clauses are intended to promote the plain meaning of the law and to restrict courts from finding their own meaning.

Concern over whether courts apply strict or liberal methods of interpretation has generated the most controversy at the constitutional level. How the U.S. Supreme Court interprets the Constitution has been widely debated since the 1960s. Critics of the WARREN COURT, of the 1950s and 1960s, charged that the Court had usurped the lawmaking function by liberally interpreting constitutional provisions.

This criticism led to JURISPRUDENCE of "original intent," a philosophy that calls on the Supreme Court and other judges to seek the plain meaning of the Constitution. If plain textual meaning is lacking, the justices should attempt to determine the original intentions of the Framers. Those who advocate an ORIGINAL INTENT method of interpretation also emphasize the need for the justices to respect history, tradition, and legal precedent.

Opponents of original intent jurisprudence argue that discerning the intent of the Framers is impossible on many issues. Even if the original intent is knowable, some opponents believe that this intent should not govern contemporary decision making on constitutional issues. In their view the Constitution is a living document that should be interpreted according to the times. This interpretive philosophy would permit justices to read the Constitution as a dynamic document, with contemporary values assisting in the search for meaning.

See also JUDICIAL REVIEW; PLAIN-MEANING RULE.

INTERROGATION, POLICE See CUSTODIAL INTERROGATION; MIRANDA V. ARIZONA.

INTERROGATORIES ◫ Written questions submitted to a party from his or her adversary to ascertain answers that are prepared in writing and signed under oath and that have relevance to the issues in a lawsuit. ◫

Interrogatories are a DISCOVERY device used by a PARTY, usually a defendant, to enable the individual to learn the facts that are the basis for, or support, a PLEADING with which he or she has been served by the opposing party. They are used primarily to determine what issues are present in a case and how to frame a responsive pleading or a DEPOSITION. Only parties to an ACTION must respond to interrogatories, unlike depositions that question both parties and witnesses.

Interrogatories are used to obtain relevant information that a party has regarding a case,

A sample of
interrogatories by
plaintiff, directed
to a corporation

[Title of Court and Cause]

To _____ Company, Defendant:

The plaintiff requests that the following interrogatories be answered under oath by any of your officers competent to testify in your behalf who know the facts about which inquiry is made and that the answers be served on plaintiff within 30 days [*or _____ days, the number of days to be computed on the basis that Rule 33(a) now provides that a defendant may serve answers or objections within 45 days after service of the summons and complaint upon that defendant*] from the time these interrogatories are served on you:

Interrogatory No. 1: What officer of your company passed upon the insurability of the plaintiff, N _____, at the time he applied for a policy of life insurance with your company in 19_____?

Interrogatory No. 2: Detail completely the investigation made by your company as to his physical condition and insurability at that time and the information that you received as to such.

Interrogatory No. 3: Did you or any of your officers, employees, or agents, receive any information in 19_____ as to his physical condition and insurability at that time other than detailed in your answer to Interrogatory No. 2?

Interrogatory No. 4: If so, what was it?

Interrogatory No. 5: For what reason did you decline to insure his life in 19_____?

Interrogatory No. 6: What information had you received which supported your reason for declining to insure plaintiff's life?

Interrogatory No. 7: Did you learn in 19_____ that plaintiff had suffered with or was suffering with any kind of heart trouble or any other disease?

Dated: _____, 19_____.

_____,
Attorney for Plaintiff.

Address: _____.

---

but they cannot be used to elicit PRIVILEGED COMMUNICATIONS. The question must be stated precisely to evoke an answer relevant to the litigated issues. A party can seek information that is within the personal knowledge of the other or that might necessitate a review of his or her records in order to answer. The federal rules of CIVIL PROCEDURE and the rules governing state court proceedings provide that when interrogatories seek disclosure of information contained in corporate records, the party upon whom the request is served can designate the records that contain the answers, thereby making the requesting party find the answer for himself or herself. No party can be compelled to answer interrogatories that involve matters beyond the party's control. Objections to questions submitted can be raised and a party need

not answer them until a court determines their validity.

Interrogatories are one of the most commonly used methods of discovery. They can be employed at any time and there is no limit on the number that can be served. Although they are not generally used for purposes of EVIDENCE in a trial, they might be ADMISSIBLE if they satisfy the rules of evidence, such as the BEST EVIDENCE rule or are an exception to the HEARSAY rule.

IN TERROREM ◫ [*Latin, In fright or terror; by way of a threat.*] A description of a LEGACY or GIFT given by WILL with the condition that the DONEE must not challenge the validity of the will or other testament. ◫

Conditions of such nature, labeled in terrorem clauses, are ordinarily regarded as threats, since the potential loss of the gift is thought to provoke fear or dread of litigation over the will in the recipient.

INTERSTATE COMMERCE ACT The Interstate Commerce Act of 1887 (24 Stat. 379 [49 U.S.C.A. § 1 et seq.]) stands as a watershed law in the history of the federal regulation of business. Originally designed to prevent unfair business practices in the railroad industry, the act shifted responsibility for the regulation of economic affairs from the states to the national government. Among its many provisions, the act established the INTERSTATE COMMERCE COMMISSION (ICC). The act has been amended over the years to embrace new and different forms of interstate transportation, including pipelines, water transportation, and motor vehicle transportation.

The Interstate Commerce Act was passed as a result of public concern with the growing power and wealth of CORPORATIONS, particularly railroads, during the late nineteenth century. Railroads had become the principal form of transportation for both people and goods, and the prices they charged and the practices they adopted greatly influenced individuals and businesses. In some cases, the railroads abused their power as a result of too little competition, as when they charged scandalously high fares in places where they exerted monopoly control. Railroads also grouped together to form TRUSTS that fixed rates at artificially high levels.

Too much competition also caused problems, as when railroads granted REBATES to large businesses in order to secure exclusive access to their patronage. Such a rebate prevented other railroads from serving those businesses. Larger railroads sometimes lowered prices so much that they drove other carriers out of business, after which they raised prices dramatically. Also, railroads often charged more for short hauls than for long hauls, a scheme that effectively discriminated against smaller businesses. These schemes resulted in BANKRUPTCY for many rail carriers and their customers.

Responding to a widespread public outcry, states passed laws designed to curb railroad abuses. However, in an 1886 decision, *Wabash, St. Louis, & Pacific Railway Co. v. Illinois*, 118 U.S. 557, 7 S. Ct. 4, 30 L. Ed. 244, the U.S. Supreme Court ruled that state laws regulating interstate railroads were unconstitutional because they violated the COMMERCE CLAUSE, which gives Congress the exclusive power "to regulate Commerce with foreign nations, and among the several States, and with the Indian Tribes" (art. I, § 8). *Wabash* left a regulatory void that was soon filled by Congress. The following year, it passed the Interstate Commerce Act, which was signed into law by President GROVER CLEVELAND on February 4, 1887.

The act required that railroad rates be "reasonable and just," but did not empower the government to fix specific rates. It prohibited trusts, rebates, and discriminatory fares. It required railroads to publish their fares, and allowed them to change fares only after giving the public ten days' notice.

The act also created the ICC, the first independent regulatory agency of the U.S. government. As part of its mission, the ICC heard complaints against the railroads and issued CEASE AND DESIST ORDERS to combat unfair practices. It later regulated many other forms of surface transportation, including motor vehicle and water transportation. The ICC was abolished in 1995, and many of its remaining functions were transferred to the Department of Transportation.

CROSS-REFERENCES

Carriers; Common Carriers; Railroads; Shipping Law.

INTERSTATE COMMERCE COMMISSION The first independent regulatory agency created by the federal government, the Interstate Commerce Commission (ICC) regulated interstate surface transportation between 1887 and 1995. Over its 108-year history, the agency regulated and certified trains, trucks, buses, water CARRIERS, freight forwarders, pipelines, and many other elements of interstate transportation.

The ICC was created by the INTERSTATE COMMERCE ACT of 1887 (24 Stat. 379 [49 U.S.C.A. § 1 et seq.]). The act created a five-person commission—later expanded to seven and then to eleven—to be appointed by the president and confirmed by the Senate. Among the commission's first actions was the election of its first president, THOMAS MCINTYRE COOLEY, a noted legal scholar who had been nominated by President GROVER CLEVELAND.

Congress established the ICC to control the powerful railroad industry, then plagued by monopolistic and unfair pricing practices that often discriminated against smaller railroads and businesses as well as individual consumers. In its early years, the agency's regulatory effectiveness was severely limited by the courts, which in many cases retained the ability to review ICC rate rulings. The agency lost fifteen of its first sixteen lawsuits against the railroads, and the Supreme Court issued several decisions that hampered its regulatory powers.

Later laws gave the agency's rulings more teeth. The Elkins Act of 1903 (32 Stat. 847) allowed the ICC to punish shippers who prac-

Interstate Commerce Commission

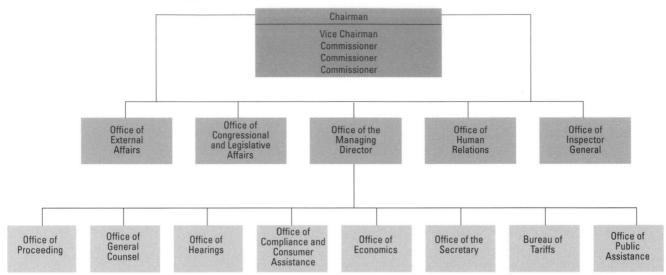

ticed unfair competitive methods. The Hepburn Act of 1906 (34 Stat. 584) gave the agency wider powers to regulate railroad rates, making its rulings binding without a court order. The act also assigned to the ICC the oversight of all pipelines other than gas and water.

Over the years, Congress changed the focus and tasks of the ICC, gradually expanding its regulatory powers. In 1893, it entrusted the agency with the regulation of railroad safety. Later, the Motor Carrier Act of 1935 (49 Stat. 543) gave the ICC authority to regulate interstate trucking and other HIGHWAY transportation. The agency even regulated telephone and telegraph communication from 1888 until 1934, when this task was transferred to the FEDERAL COMMUNICATIONS COMMISSION.

Other tasks performed by the ICC included conducting hearings to examine alleged abuses; authorizing mergers in the transportation industry; overseeing the movement of railroad traffic in certain areas; granting the right to operate railroads, trucking companies, bus lines, and water carriers; and maintaining consumer protection programs that ensured fair, nondiscriminatory rates and services. At times, the agency participated in important social and political changes, as when it desegregated interstate buses and trains in the 1960s.

By the 1960s, the ICC had reached a peak size of twenty-four hundred employees, with field offices in forty-eight states. Its growth made it a target for those who sought to reduce the power and size of federal regulatory agencies. Critics claimed that ICC regulation created artificially high rates for many forms of transportation. Some charged the agency with corruption.

In 1976, the Railroad Revitalization and Regulatory Reform Act (90 Stat. 31 [45 U.S.C.A. § 801]) reduced the commission's powers to regulate carrier rates and practices except in a few areas where a single railroad or trucking firm monopolized a transportation route. This trend toward the deregulation of interstate commerce caused the ICC to shrink gradually in size until December 29, 1995, when President BILL CLINTON signed Public Law No. 104-88, Title 1, § 102(a), 109 Stat. 807 (1995), dissolving the ICC.

In its final year, the ICC employed three hundred people and had a budget of $40 million. The legislation ending its existence moved two hundred former ICC employees to the Transportation Department, which assumed authority over former ICC functions deemed essential by Congress. These essential functions included approving railroad and bus mergers and handling railroad disputes. The new three-person Intermodal Surface Transportation Board within the Department of Transportation oversees many of the functions formerly conducted by the ICC.

See also COMMON CARRIERS; RAILROADS; SHIPPING LAW.

INTERSTATE COMPACT 📖 A voluntary arrangement between two or more states that is designed to solve their common problems and that becomes part of the laws of each state. 📖

Interstate compacts in the United States were first used by the American colonies to settle boundary disputes. After the American

Revolution, states continued to use interstate compacts to meet their various needs. Although these compacts were necessary for peaceful interaction between the states, they posed a threat to the future of the United States: if states were allowed to form powerful coalitions, they might be tempted to break away from the rest of the country and fracture the Union.

Under Article I, Section 10, Clause 3, of the U.S. Constitution, "No State shall, without the Consent of Congress . . . enter into any Agreement or Compact with another State." This clause, the Interstate Compact Clause, was adopted with no debate. Moreover, it received only cursory discussion in subsequent papers written by the Constitution's Framers, so its purpose and scope were not developed.

Most courts followed the lead of Justice JOSEPH STORY (1779–1845), of the Supreme Court, an influential legal commentator of the nineteenth century. According to Story, the clause was meant to protect the supremacy of the federal government. With this general principle as guidance, courts interpreted the clause to give Congress the power to nullify an interstate compact if it frustrated federal aims.

Over the years, four steps have evolved to guide courts in their review of interstate compact cases. First, there must be an agreement between two or more states. If no concerted effort is actually undertaken by two or more states, Congress has no power to review the state actions under the Interstate Compact Clause. In determining whether there is an agreement, the court may ask whether the states have officially formed a joint organization, whether a state's action is conditioned on action by another state, and whether any state is free to modify its position without consulting other states.

If the court finds that there is an agreement, the court will examine the agreement to determine whether it infringes on federal SOVEREIGNTY. Not all interstate compacts infringe on federal supremacy. The question the court asks is whether the agreement between the states interferes with federal statutes or initiatives. For example, consider the federal legislation that outlaws certain automatic and semiautomatic assault weapons: title XI of the Public Safety and Recreational Firearms Use Protection Act (Pub. L. No. 103-322, 108 Stat. 1807 [codified as amended in scattered sections of 42 U.S.C.A.]). The purpose of the legislation is to limit firearm ownership. An interstate compact that legalized the banned assault weapons, and thus expanded firearm ownership, would in-

fringe on the federal statute, whereas an interstate compact that outlawed additional assault weapons, and thus further limited firearm ownership, would not infringe on the federal statute.

If an interstate compact is found to infringe on federal initiatives, the court will then determine whether Congress has given its approval for the compact. Congress may grant approval before or after a compact is formed. Congress may also give indirect approval to a compact. For example, Congress may give its tacit approval to a compact on state BOUNDARIES if it subsequently approves the federal elections, appointments, and tax schemes of the states.

Finally, Congress may seek to amend or change an interstate compact after it has been approved. Congress may amend a compact or completely revoke its approval of a compact. Congress may also grant its approval with conditions attached.

The most common interstate compacts concern agreements to share natural resources, such as water; build regional electric power sources; share parks and parkways; conserve fish and wildlife; protect air quality; manage radioactive and other hazardous wastes; control natural disasters, such as floods; share educational resources and facilities; share police and fire departments; and grant reciprocity for driver's licenses. Congress has passed statutes that require prior congressional approval for many such compacts.

If Congress has not asserted its authority over an interstate compact prior to its formation, the compact probably does not violate the Interstate Compact Clause. In *Northeast Bancorp v. Board of Governors*, 472 U.S. 159, 105 S. Ct. 2545, 86 L. Ed. 2d 112 (1985), Massachusetts

An interstate compact is a voluntary arrangement between states. The White Mountain range of the eastern United States extends across New Hampshire and into Maine. Its management is shared by the two states.

ALAN BRIERE/LIAISON INTERNATIONAL

and Connecticut passed statutes that allowed out-of-state HOLDING COMPANIES in the New England region to acquire in-state BANKS. These statutes applied only if the state in which the out-of-state company was based also allowed out-of-state holding companies to acquire in-state banks. When the FEDERAL RESERVE BOARD (FRB) approved the interstate acquisition of banks in Massachusetts and Connecticut, three banking companies brought suit against the board.

The plaintiffs argued, in part, that the statutes constituted an interstate compact, and that the compact required congressional approval that had not been received. The U.S. Supreme Court disagreed. Assuming the statutes did create an interstate compact, they did not require congressional approval because they did not encroach on any asserted power of the federal government. In fact, Congress had authorized interstate bank acquisitions in an amendment to the Bank Holding Company Act of 1956 (70 Stat. 133 [as amended, 12 U.S.C.A. § 1841, 1842(d)). The amendment prevented the FRB from approving interstate bank acquisitions unless the states had reciprocating statutes. Massachusetts and Connecticut had merely accomplished what was implicitly authorized by the amendment, and the High Court cleared the way for final approval of the acquisitions.

In practice, few interstate compacts are held to violate federal imperatives. Despite the freedom of states to form interstate compacts, the trend is toward increased federal participation and control. Congress has inserted itself into the negotiations over, administration of, and participation in interstate compacts. This level of control may decrease as the United States seeks to trim its budget. However, Congress will remain constitutionally required to prevent states from forming coalitions that wield powers challenging those of the federal government.

See also FEDERALISM; SUPREMACY CLAUSE.

INTERVENING CAUSE 📖 A separate act or omission that breaks the direct connection between the defendant's actions and an injury or loss to another person, and may relieve the defendant of LIABILITY for the injury or loss. 📖

Civil and criminal defendants alike may invoke the intervening cause doctrine to escape liability for their actions.

A defendant is held liable for an injury or loss to another person if the defendant's negligent or reckless conduct was the PROXIMATE CAUSE of the resulting injury or loss. This means that the defendant's conduct must have played a substantial part in bringing about or directly causing the injury or loss. However, the defen-

dant may escape liability by showing that a subsequent act or event, or intervening cause, was the real cause of the injury.

Not all intervening causes relieve a defendant of liability. An intervening cause relieves a defendant of liability only if it would not have been foreseeable to a REASONABLE PERSON, and only if damage resulting from the defendant's own actions would not have been foreseeable to a reasonable person.

For example, assume that a farmer agrees to store a large, heavy sculpture for an artist. The sculpture is designed for outdoor display, so the farmer leaves it in her backyard. A tornado throws the sculpture several thousand feet, ruining it.

If the artist sues the farmer for damage to the sculpture, the farmer may argue that the tornado intervened between her negligent storage and the damage, relieving her from any liability. The farmer may claim that she could not have anticipated any detrimental effects of outdoor storage on the sculpture, because the sculpture was made for outdoor display.

At trial the issue of the farmer's liability is a QUESTION OF FACT to be determined by the judge or jury. The judge or jury asks whether a reasonable person would have anticipated a tornado. Generally, extraordinary weather conditions are deemed an unforeseeable intervening cause. However, if the farmer lives in Kansas, where tornadoes may be expected, and stored the sculpture outside without tethers during tornado season, the judge or jury may find that she should have anticipated the tornado and its damaging effects, and thus is liable for the damage.

Next, the fact-finder considers whether the farmer could have foreseen damage resulting from outdoor storage. Since the artist made the sculpture for outdoor display, damage to the sculpture from outdoor storage may be considered unforeseeable. Under these facts the tornado may be deemed an unforeseeable intervening cause of the damage to the sculpture, and the farmer may avoid liability.

Two types of intervening causes are considered: dependent and independent. A dependent intervening cause is set in motion by the defendant's own conduct, and will not relieve the defendant of liability unless it is extraordinary. For example, suppose the defendant poked an associate in the chest during a friendly discussion around a watercooler, and the associate subsequently jumped out a window. This unusual reaction may be deemed an extraordinary intervening cause that relieves the defendant of liability.

An independent intervening cause arises

through no fault of the defendant. It relieves a defendant of liability unless it was foreseeable by the defendant.

The most common intervening causes cited by defendants are natural forces and negligent human conduct. Natural forces include extraordinary weather, earthquakes, volcanic eruptions, and the conduct of animals. Negligent human conduct is conduct that exposes a person to abnormal risks. Criminal human conduct by a third party will not be considered an intervening cause relieving the defendant of liability if the defendant's NEGLIGENCE has contributed to the victim's loss. For example, assume that Martin borrows Tasha's vehicle, drives it to a neighborhood notorious for its high crime rate, and leaves it unlocked with the keys in the ignition. If the vehicle is stolen, Martin may be held liable to Tasha for her loss because a reasonable person would have anticipated the theft.

Cohen v. Petty, 62 App. D.C. 187, 65 F.2d 820 (D.C. Cir. 1933), illustrates how the doctrine of intervening cause works. In *Cohen*, Jeanette Cohen sued Joseph Petty for permanent injuries she suffered as a passenger in a vehicle when Petty drove it into an embankment.

At trial Petty argued that he had become sick without warning and had fainted while driving. The sudden sickness and fainting spell were, Petty claimed, an intervening cause that relieved him of liability. Petty testified that he had never fainted before and that he was feeling fine up to the point of the sudden illness. Petty's wife, Theresa Petty, who was sitting in the front passenger's seat, testified that just before the accident, Petty said, "Oh, Tree, I feel sick." Cohen herself testified that shortly before the accident, she heard Petty exclaim to his wife that he felt sick.

The trial court agreed with Petty and entered judgment in his favor. On appeal the Court of Appeals of the District of Columbia affirmed. According to the appeals court, the sudden illness was an intervening cause. Petty had had no reason to anticipate the illness, and because he had not been negligent in any way prior to the accident, the illness relieved him of all liability for Cohen's injuries.

Some JURISDICTIONS use two terms to define the intervening cause doctrine: *intervening cause* and *superseding cause*. In these jurisdictions *intervening cause* describes any cause that comes between a defendant's conduct and the resulting injury, and an intervening cause that relieves a defendant of liability is called a superseding cause. Other jurisdictions do not use the term *superseding cause*. These jurisdictions simply ask whether the intervening cause is sufficient to relieve a defendant of liability. All jurisdictions differentiate between an intervening cause that relieves a defendant of liability and one that does not: the only difference is in the terminology.

INTERVENOR 📖 An individual who is not already a PARTY to an existing lawsuit but who makes himself or herself a party either by joining with the plaintiff or uniting with the defendant in resistance of the plaintiff's claims. 📖

INTERVENTION 📖 A procedure used in a lawsuit by which the court allows a third person who was not originally a PARTY to the suit to become a party, by joining with either the plaintiff or the defendant. 📖

The federal rules of CIVIL PROCEDURE recognizes two types of intervention: *intervention of right* and *permissive intervention*.

Intervention of right arises when the INTERVENOR, the person who seeks to become a party to an existing lawsuit, can satisfactorily show that his or her interest is not adequately represented by the present parties, that the interest relates to the subject of the ACTION, and that the disposition of the action might in some way impair his or her ability to protect such interest.

Permissive intervention is up to the discretion of the court. It arises when the intervenor's claim or defense and the instant suit have a QUESTION OF LAW or fact in common.

In deciding whether or not to permit intervention, the court ordinarily balances the needs and interest of the intervenor against the potential hardship on the existing parties if such intervention is allowed. The court will determine whether the intervenor and the parties to the suit share common issues. If the intervenor attempts to inject new CAUSES OF ACTIONS into the pending suit, his or her request will be denied, since to permit intervention would increase the potential for prejudice and delay in the original action. An intervenor need not argue that he or she will be prejudiced by the judgment if not joined, provided the intervenor is able to show that his or her interest will be impaired by the action if he or she is not involved.

INTER VIVOS 📖 [*Latin, Between the living.*] A phrase used to describe a GIFT that is made during the DONOR's lifetime. 📖

In order for an *inter vivos* gift to be complete, there must be a clear manifestation of the giver's intent to release to the DONEE the object of the gift, and actual delivery and acceptance by the donee.

An *inter vivos* gift is distinguishable from a gift CAUSA MORTIS, which is made in expectation of impending death.

INTESTACY 📖 The state or condition of dying without having made a valid WILL or without having disposed by will of a segment of the property of the DECEDENT. 📖

INTESTATE 📖 The description of a person who dies without making a valid WILL or the reference made to this condition. 📖

INTESTATE SUCCESSION 📖 The inheritance of an ancestor's property according to the laws of DESCENT AND DISTRIBUTION that are applied when the deceased has not executed a valid WILL. 📖

INTOXICATION 📖 A state in which a person's normal capacity to act or reason is inhibited by ALCOHOL or DRUGS. 📖

Generally, an intoxicated person is incapable of acting as an ordinary prudent and cautious person would act under similar conditions. In recognition of this factor, the law may allow intoxication to be used as a defense to certain crimes. In many JURISDICTIONS, intoxication is a defense to SPECIFIC-INTENT crimes. The underlying rationale is that the intoxicated individual cannot possess the requisite mental state necessary to establish the offense.

Other jurisdictions recognize it as a defense to GENERAL-INTENT crimes as well. For example, although RAPE is commonly considered a general-intent crime, there are states in which extreme intoxication may be alleged as a defense. It is unlikely, however, that the defense will be successful in such cases absent proof that the defendant was so intoxicated that he or she could not form the intent to have intercourse.

In HOMICIDE cases, intoxication is relevant to negate PREMEDITATION and deliberation neces-

sary for first-degree MURDER. When the defense is successfully interposed, it will reduce a charge of first-degree murder to second-degree murder.

When a person is forced to consume an intoxicant against his or her will, the person is involuntarily intoxicated. In most jurisdictions, the defense of involuntary intoxication is treated similarly to the INSANITY DEFENSE. For example, an intoxicated person who cannot distinguish right from wrong at the time of committing the wrongful act would have a valid defense.

INTRINSIC EVIDENCE 📖 Information necessary for the determination of an issue in a lawsuit that is gleaned from the provisions of a document itself, as opposed to TESTIMONY from a WITNESS or the terms of other writings that have not been admitted by the court for consideration by the trier of fact. 📖

INURE 📖 To result; to take effect; to be of use, benefit, or advantage to an individual. 📖

For example, when a WILL makes the provision that all PERSONAL PROPERTY is to inure to the benefit of a certain individual, such an individual is given the right to receive all the personal property owned by the TESTATOR upon his or her death.

INVALID 📖 Null; void; without force or effect; lacking in authority. 📖

For example, a WILL that has not been properly witnessed is invalid and unenforceable.

INVENTORY 📖 An itemized list of PROPERTY that contains a description of each specific article. 📖

An employee of a large pharmaceutical manufacturing company takes inventory in order to determine the value of the stock on hand.

Inventory of a company, for example, is the annual account of stock taken in the business, or the quantity of goods or materials in stock. The term is also used to describe a list made by the EXECUTOR or administrator of the estate of a deceased individual.

INVESTITURE 📖 In ecclesiastical law, one of the formalities by which an archbishop confirms the election of a bishop. During the feudal ages, the rite by which an overlord granted a portion of his lands to his vassal. 📖

The investiture ceremony, which took place in the presence of other vassals, consisted of the vassal taking an oath of fealty to the overlord who, in turn, gave him a clod of dirt or a twig, symbolic of the open and notorious transfer of possession of the land. The ritual, used at a time when writing and record keeping were not widely practiced, fixed the date of the vassal's acquisition of the land and, in cases of disputes over the land, provided a source of evidence in the form of testimony of the vassals who witnessed the proceedings.

See also FEUDALISM.

INVESTMENT 📖 The placement of a particular sum of money in business ventures, real estate, or securities of a permanent nature so that it will produce an income. 📖

INVITATION 📖 The act by which an owner or occupier of particular land or premises encourages or attracts others to enter, remain in, or otherwise make use of his or her PROPERTY. 📖

Common examples of those who extend invitations are the proprietors of stores, theaters, or banks, since they invite the general public to enter and utilize their facilities.

An individual who enters property as a result of an invitation is owed a higher duty of care than one who is a TRESPASSER or licensee, one who enters another's property for his or her own purposes. The owner of property must exercise reasonable care toward an invitee to ascertain that the property is safe for his or her use.

INVITEE 📖 An individual who enters another's premises as a result of an express or implied invitation of the owner or occupant for their mutual gain or benefit. 📖

For example, a customer in a restaurant or a depositor entering a bank to cash a check are both invitees. The owner or occupier of the premises onto which an invitee goes has a duty to exercise reasonable care for such invitee's protection.

An invitee is distinguishable from a licensee, who enters another's premises with the occupier's consent, but for his or her own purpose or benefit alone. A further distinction exists between an invitee and a TRESPASSER, or one who intentionally enters another's property without consent or permission.

INVOICE 📖 An itemized statement or written account of goods sent to a purchaser or consignee by a VENDOR that indicates the quantity and price of each piece of merchandise shipped. 📖

A *consular invoice* is one used in foreign trade. It is signed by the consul of the nation to which the merchandise is shipped. Such an invoice facilitates the entry through the destination country, since the quality and value of the shipment are verified prior to its arrival.

INVOLUNTARY CONFESSION 📖 An admission, especially by an individual who has been accused of a crime, that is not freely offered but rather is precipitated by a threat, fear, torture, or a promise. 📖

The criminal justice system relies on CONFESSIONS by defendants to help prove guilt at trial or to induce a guilty plea. Police interrogation of suspects has long been a controversial area of U.S. criminal procedure, as critics charge that coercion and trickery have unfairly and unconstitutionally led to involuntary confessions. The FIFTH AMENDMENT grants a suspect the privilege against SELF-INCRIMINATION, yet many suspects confess anyway. Because questioning of suspects takes place behind station house doors, little empirical evidence is available to document what usually occurs in a police interrogation.

The 1931 federal Wickersham Commission looked at police practices throughout the United States. This commission raised the issue of coercive interrogations, coining the term *the third degree* to describe physical and mental abuse inflicted on suspects during questioning. From 1936 to the early 1960s, the U.S. Supreme Court dealt with confessions admitted in state criminal proceedings in terms of the fundamental fairness required by the FOURTEENTH AMENDMENT's Due Process Clause. The Court used a "voluntariness" test, which depended on the "totality of the circumstances," to determine whether a confession must be excluded from EVIDENCE. This approach became difficult to administer, as it called on courts to find and appraise all relevant facts for each case.

Legal debate over the validity of confessions gained momentum in the 1960s, as the U.S. Supreme Court took a hard look at the constitutionality of CRIMINAL PROCEDURE. In *Escobedo v. Illinois*, 378 U.S. 478, 84 S. Ct. 1758, 12 L. Ed. 2d 977 (1964), Justice ARTHUR J. GOLDBERG stated that "a system of criminal law enforcement which comes to depend on the 'confession' will, in the long run, be less reliable and more subject to abuses than a system which depends on extrinsic evidence independently secured through skillful investigation." In *Escobedo* the defendant's confession was suppressed because it was obtained in violation of his RIGHT TO COUNSEL at the time of interrogation.

In 1966 the Supreme Court set out the *Miranda* warnings (*Miranda v. Arizona*, 384 U.S. 436, 86 S. Ct. 1602, 16 L. Ed. 2d 1694), which the police must communicate to a person who is placed in their custody. The warnings cover the right to remain silent, the fact that anything said can and will be used against the individual in court, the right to have a lawyer during interrogation, the right to have an attorney appointed if the individual cannot afford one, and the right to exercise the privilege against self-incrimination at any time during interrogation. These warnings provide basic avenues of inquiry for a court evaluating the "voluntariness" of a confession.

Miranda has been criticized by those who see it as an unfair restriction on law enforcement. Nevertheless, empirical studies conducted in the 1970s and 1980s have concluded that the *Miranda* warnings have not appreciably reduced the amount of talking by suspects, and police officers obtain about as many confessions now as they did before *Miranda*.

Yet the protection afforded to suspects by *Miranda* can be illusory. Police officers may sometimes give the required warnings but then engage in tactics that could make the confession involuntary. It is clear, however, that if police officers use interrogation practices that in the view of a court violate basic notions of human dignity, a confession produced from these practices will be judged involuntary. Physical violence, threats of violence, prolonged isolation, deceit, and trickery are some tactics that may render a confession involuntary, even when no danger exists that the confession is untrue. A defendant's age, state of health, mental condition, and intelligence are also relevant factors. The more vulnerable a defendant is, the more likely a court is to find certain interrogation practices abusive, leading to the conclusion that the confession was involuntary.

Each possibly relevant factor must be evaluated in the context of each specific case. For example, no absolute rule exists that police trickery of a defendant will render a confession involuntary. However, if a defendant is particularly youthful and ignorant, such trickery may be an important factor inducing a court to find a confession involuntary.

CROSS-REFERENCES

Custodial Interrogation; Due Process of Law; *Miranda v. Arizona*.

INVOLUNTARY MANSLAUGHTER

The act of unlawfully killing another human being unintentionally.

Most unintentional killings are not MURDER but involuntary manslaughter. The absence of the element of intent is the key distinguishing factor between voluntary and involuntary man-

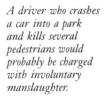

A driver who crashes a car into a park and kills several pedestrians would probably be charged with involuntary manslaughter.

JON LEVY/THE GAMMA LIAISON NETWORK

slaughter. In most states involuntary manslaughter results from an improper use of reasonable care or skill while performing a legal act, or while committing an act that is unlawful but not felonious.

Many states do not define involuntary manslaughter, or define it vaguely in COMMON-LAW terms. Some JURISDICTIONS describe the amount of NEGLIGENCE necessary to constitute MANSLAUGHTER with terms such as *criminal negligence, gross negligence,* and *culpable negligence.* The only certainty that can be attached to these terms is that they require more than the ordinary negligence standard in a civil case. With this approach the state does not have to prove that the defendant was aware of the risk.

Other jurisdictions apply more subjective tests, such as "reckless" or "wanton," to describe the amount of negligence needed to constitute involuntary manslaughter. In this approach the defendant must have personally appreciated a risk and then chosen to take it anyway.

There are two types of involuntary manslaughter statutes: criminally negligent manslaughter and unlawful act manslaughter. Criminally negligent manslaughter occurs when death results from a high degree of negligence or RECKLESSNESS. Modern criminal codes generally require a consciousness of risk and under some codes the absence of this element makes the offense a less serious HOMICIDE.

An omission to act or a failure to perform a DUTY constitutes criminally negligent manslaughter. The existence of the duty is essential. Since the law does not recognize that an ordinary person has a duty to aid or rescue another in distress, a death resulting from an ordinary person's failure to act is not manslaughter. On the other hand, an omission by someone who has a duty, such as a failure to attempt to save a drowning person by a lifeguard, might constitute involuntary manslaughter.

In many jurisdictions death that results from the operation of a vehicle in a criminally negligent manner is punishable as a separate offense. Usually it is considered a less severe offense than involuntary manslaughter. These jurisdictions usually call the offense reckless homicide, negligent homicide, or vehicular homicide. One reason for this lesser offense is the reluctance of juries to convict AUTOMOBILE drivers of manslaughter.

Unlawful act manslaughter occurs when someone causes a death while committing or attempting to commit an unlawful act, usually a MISDEMEANOR. Some states distinguish between conduct that is *malum in se* (bad in itself) and conduct that is *malum prohibitum* (bad because it is prohibited by law). Conduct that is *malum in se* is based on common-law definitions of crime; for example, an ASSAULT AND BATTERY could be classified as *malum in se.* Acts that are made illegal by legislation—for example, reckless driving—are *malum prohibitum.* In states that use this distinction, an act must be *malum in se* to constitute manslaughter. If an act is *malum prohibitum,* it is not manslaughter unless the person who committed it could have foreseen that death would be a direct result of the act.

In other states this distinction is not made. If death results from an unlawful act, the person who committed the act may be prosecuted for involuntary manslaughter even if the act was *malum prohibitum.* Courts will uphold unlawful act manslaughter where the statute was intended to prevent injury to another person.

See also CRIMINAL NEGLIGENCE; GROSS NEGLIGENCE.

INVOLUNTARY SERVITUDE 📖 SLAVERY; the condition of an individual who works for another individual against his or her will as a result of force, coercion, or imprisonment, regardless of whether the individual is paid for the labor. 📖

The term *involuntary servitude* is used in reference to any type of slavery, PEONAGE, or compulsory labor for the satisfaction of debts. Two essential elements of involuntary servitude are involuntariness, which is compulsion to act against one's will, and SERVITUDE, which is some form of labor for another. Imprisonment without forced labor is not involuntary servitude, nor is unpleasant labor when the only direct penalty for not performing it is the withholding of money or the loss of a job.

The importation of African slaves to the American colonies began in the seventeenth century. By the time of the American Revolution, the slave population had grown to over five hundred thousand people, most concentrated in the southern colonies. The Framers of the U.S. Constitution did not specifically refer to slavery in the document they drafted in 1787, but they did afford protection to southern slaveholding states. They included provisions prohibiting Congress from outlawing the slave trade until 1808 and requiring the return of fugitive slaves.

Between 1820 and 1860, political and legal tensions over slavery steadily escalated. The U.S. Supreme Court attempted to resolve the legal status of African Americans in *Dred Scott v. Sandford,* 60 U.S. (19 How.) 393, 15 L. Ed. 691 (1857). The Court concluded that Congress was powerless to extend the rights of U.S. citizenship to African Americans.

With the secession of southern states and the beginning of the Civil War in 1860 and 1861, the Union government was under almost complete control of free states. In 1865 Congress enacted the THIRTEENTH AMENDMENT, which the Union states ratified. Section 1 of the amendment provides that "[n]either slavery nor involuntary servitude, except as a punishment for crime whereof the party shall have been duly convicted, shall exist within the United States, or any place subject to their jurisdiction." Section 2 gives Congress the authority to enforce the provisions of section 1.

The Thirteenth Amendment makes involuntary servitude unlawful whether the compulsion is by a government or by a private person. The penalty for violation of the amendment must be prescribed by law. Although the principal purpose of the amendment was to abolish African slavery, it also abolished other forms of compulsory labor similar to slavery, no matter what they are called. For example, it abolished bond service and peonage, forms of compulsory service based on a servant's indebtedness to a master.

An individual has a right to refuse or discontinue employment. No state can make the quitting of work a crime, or establish criminal sanctions that hold unwilling persons to a particular labor. A state may, however, withhold unemployment or other benefits from those who, without just cause, refuse to perform available gainful work.

A court has the authority to require a person to perform affirmative acts that the person has a legal duty to perform. It has generally been held, however, that this power does not extend to compelling the performance of labor or personal services, even in cases where the obligated party has been paid in advance. The remedy for failure to perform obligated labor is generally limited to monetary damages. A court may, without violating the Thirteenth Amendment, use its EQUITY authority to ENJOIN, or prevent, a person from working at a particular task. Equity authority is the power of a court to issue INJUNCTIONS that direct parties to do or refrain from doing something. A court also may prevent an artist or performer who has contracted to perform unique services for one person on a given date from performing such services for a competitor.

The Thirteenth Amendment does not interfere with the enforcement of duties a citizen owes to the state under the COMMON LAW. Government may require a person to serve on a petit or GRAND JURY, to work on public roads or instead pay taxes on those roads, or to serve in the MILITIA. Compulsory military service (the draft) is not a violation of the Thirteenth Amendment, nor is compulsory labor on work of national importance in lieu of military service, assigned to CONSCIENTIOUS OBJECTORS.

Forced labor, with or without imprisonment, as a punishment upon conviction of a crime is a form of involuntary servitude allowed by the Thirteenth Amendment under its "punishment-for-crime" exception.

CROSS-REFERENCES

Celia, a Slave; *Dred Scott v. Sandford*; Emancipation Proclamation; Fugitive Slave Act of 1850; Selective Service System.

IPSE DIXIT [*Latin, He himself said it.*] An unsupported statement that rests solely on the authority of the individual who makes it.

A court decision, for example, that is in conflict with a particular statute might be said to have no legal support with the exception of the *ipse dixit* of the court.

IPSO FACTO [*Latin, By the fact itself; by the mere fact.*]

IRAN-CONTRA The Iran-Contra Affair involved a secret foreign policy operation directed by White House officials in the National Security Council (NSC) under President RONALD REAGAN. The operation had two goals: first, to sell arms to Iran in the hope of winning the release of U.S. HOSTAGES in Lebanon, and second, to illegally divert profits from these sales to the Contra rebels fighting to overthrow the Sandinista government of Nicaragua. Discovery of the secret operation in 1986 triggered a legal and political uproar that rocked the Reagan administration. The numerous related investigations and INDICTMENTS did not end until 1993 and even then questions remained about the roles of senior White House officials in this arms-for-hostages deal.

The affair came to public attention on November 3, 1986, when a Lebanese publication, *Al-Shiraa*, first reported that the United States had sold arms to Iran. The news was shocking because the Reagan administration had previously denounced Iran as a supporter of international terrorism. Shortly after the *Al-Shiraa* report Nicaraguan forces downed a U.S. plane and captured its pilot. The pilot's confession led to a second startling revelation: a private U.S. enterprise was supplying arms to Contra rebels.

The enterprise seemed designed to circumvent the will of Congress. In the early 1980s, after bitter debate, Congress had passed legislation barring the use of federal monies to overthrow the Nicaraguan government. Through a series of amendments to appropriations bills enacted between 1982 and 1986, known as the Boland amendments, this legislation blocked the Reagan administration's wish to go on supporting the Contras. Now it had been revealed that private citizens and private monies were being used to this end. Moreover, the operation was being directed from within the White House by the NSC—the president's advisory cabinet on security affairs and covert operations. Directing the Iran-Contra enterprise were Vice Admiral John Poindexter, national security assistant, and his subordinate, Lieutenant Colonel Oliver North, deputy director for political-military affairs.

Each branch of government quickly began a separate investigation into the affair. In December 1986 President Reagan issued an EXECUTIVE ORDER creating the Tower Commission, named after its chair, John Tower. The purpose of this three-member review board was to recommend changes in executive policy regarding the future roles and procedures of the NSC staff. Reagan's creation of the commission was a tacit disavowal of presidential knowledge or responsibility for the actions of Iran-Contra participants. Although admitting that his administration had negotiated secretly with Iran in order to free the hostages in Lebanon, he publicly denied knowing about the arms-supplying enterprise directed by his own NSC staff.

ARTHUR GRACE/STOCK BOSTON

Vice Admiral John Poindexter, security assistant to President Ronald Reagan, directed the Iran-Contra operation and was charged with providing false information and making false statements to Congress.

Simultaneously the Senate and the House of Representatives each created a select Iran-Contra committee. These committees were charged with holding hearings to uncover facts and to recommend legislative action to prevent future illegal foreign policy operations. In their zeal to fully expose the affair, the committees granted limited forms of IMMUNITY to several key WITNESSES. This decision proved to be a mixed blessing. On the one hand, it provided Congress and the U.S. public with a wider understanding of the affair through televised hearings (which also made a public favorite out of Lieutenant Colonel North). But it ultimately proved harmful to efforts to prosecute North and Vice Admiral Poindexter.

The attorney general requested that an INDEPENDENT COUNSEL be appointed to investigate wrongdoing. An independent counsel is a special appointee who is given the authority to bring indictments and pursue convictions. For this important role, the U.S. Court of Appeals for the District of Columbia Circuit, Independent Counsel Division, selected Lawrence E. Walsh, a former AMERICAN BAR ASSOCIATION president and former federal judge. Legal authority for Walsh's appointment existed in provisions of the Ethics in Government Act (Pub. L. No. 95-521 [Oct. 26, 1978], 92 Stat. 1824 [28 U.S.C.A. § 592(c) (1) (1982)]).

The various Iran-Contra investigations soon found a plethora of legal violations. The covert arms sales to Iran violated numerous statutes that restricted the transfer of arms to nations that support international terrorism, principally the Arms Export Control Act of 1976 (Pub. L. No. 90-629, 89 Stat. 1320 [22 U.S.C.A. §§ 2751–2796c (1989 Supp.)]). By failing to report the Iranian sales to Congress, the Reagan administration had ignored reporting provisions in the 1980 Intelligence Oversight Act (Pub. L. No. 96-450, tit. IV, 407(b) (1), 94 Stat. 1981 [50 U.S.C.A. § 413 (1982)]). That law required the president to notify Congress in a timely fashion of any "significant anticipated intelligence activity, and to make a formal written "finding" (declaration) that each covert operation was important to national security. Three findings were at issue in the Iran-Contra affair: (1) Not only had President Reagan failed to report the first arms sales, but he had also authorized them through Israeli intermediaries by "oral" findings that were not authorized by intelligence oversight statutes. (2) The CENTRAL INTELLIGENCE AGENCY (CIA) justified a second shipment of arms to the Iranians through a "retroactive" finding issued by the CIA's general counsel; Poindexter admitted destroying this finding. (3) President Reagan admitted signing a third written finding, in January 1986, but later claimed he had never read it.

The investigations took two turns. Congress and the Tower Commission completed their hearings and issued reports and independent counsel Walsh pursued wide-ranging indictments against several Reagan administration officials and others. In 1987, Congress issued the 690-page *Report of the Congressional Committees Investigating the Iran-Contra Affair* (S. Rep. No. 216, H.R. Rep. No. 433, 100th Cong., 1st Sess. 423). The report charged the president with failing to execute his constitutional duty to uphold the law. However, its conclusion did not support changes in legislation to prevent a future breakdown of legality in foreign policy affairs. Iran-Contra, the report said, reflected a failure of people rather than of laws. This assertion pointed to a central political disagreement about the affair: although Democrats were harsh in their condemnation, Republican members of Congress tended to view the investigation itself as an effort by Democrats to interfere with a Republican president's foreign policy. In like fashion, the 1987 Tower Commission report downplayed any need for legislation to revise national security decision making. Instead, it criticized Reagan's lax management style.

After the reports, attention shifted to the independent counsel's investigation. In March 1988, GRAND JURY indictments were brought against North, Poindexter, Richard V. Secord, and Albert Hakim. The indictments included four distinct charges: conspiring to obstruct the U.S. government; diverting public funds from arms sales to Iran to aid the Contras in Nicaragua; stealing public funds for private ends; and lying to Congress and other government officials. With the exception of the routine criminal charge of theft, the most serious points in the indictments essentially accused the defendants of conducting a private foreign policy in violation of constitutional norms.

Before independent counsel Walsh could begin his prosecutions, several pretrial delays took place. First, the law providing for an independent counsel was challenged. The Reagan administration, joining a number of its former officials who were subject to other independent counsel investigations, argued that the law unconstitutionally denied the president important executive power. In June 1988, the U.S. Supreme Court rejected this argument and upheld the law's constitutionality in *Morrison v. Olson*, 487 U.S. 654, 108 S. Ct. 2597, 101 L. Ed. 2d

569. Next, the first four Iran-Contra defendants—Poindexter, North, Secord, and Hakim—moved for dismissal of the charges brought by Walsh. They argued that their compelled testimony before the joint congressional committees had violated their FIFTH AMENDMENT rights against SELF-INCRIMINATION. In *United States v. Poindexter*, 698 F. Supp. 300 (D.D.C. 1988), U.S. district judge Gerhard Gesell denied the motion, clearing the way for the trials to begin. But the defendants' argument was later to have serious repercussions.

Soon, a more serious obstacle hampered Walsh's prosecution: the Justice Department and the White House refused to release classified information crucial to the case on the grounds that it was vital to national security. Without this information, much of Walsh's case collapsed. He was forced to dismiss the broader charges of CONSPIRACY and diversion—the crux of the Iran-Contra Affair's illegality—and to pursue instead the less serious charges remaining in the indictments.

Walsh won a conviction against Lieutenant Colonel North on May 4, 1989, for obstructing Congress, destroying documents, and accepting an illegal gratuity (*United States v. North*, 713 F. Supp. 1448 [D.D.C.]). The trial disclosed evidence that suggested that both presidents Reagan and Bush had greater roles in the Iran-Contra Affair than either the Tower Commission or the congressional committees had concluded. During the trial, North's attorneys

Lieutenant Colonel Oliver North was convicted of obstructing Congress, destroying documents, and accepting an illegal gratuity, but the decision was reversed by a higher court.

failed in an attempt to SUBPOENA Reagan, whom North would later squarely blame for complete knowledge of the affair, in his memoir *Under Fire: An American Story.* Subsequent to the conviction, Judge Gesell denied two motions for an acquittal and a mistrial. Gesell sentenced North to two years' probation, twelve hundred hours of community service, and a $150,000 fine.

North appealed. On July 20, 1990, the U.S. Court of Appeals for the District of Columbia suspended all three of North's FELONY convictions and completely overturned his conviction for destroying classified documents. At issue was North's earlier testimony before Congress. The appellate ruling was based on the same reasoning as the contention made by North, Poindexter, Secord, and Hakim before their trials: Congress's decision to grant immunity to North had clashed with the Fifth Amendment protection of witnesses against self-incrimination. The appeals court directed the trial court to reexamine North's earlier testimony. Some critics argued that the appellate ruling, written by Judge Laurence Silberman, smacked of partisanship; Silberman had been, in 1980, cochair of the Reagan-Bush foreign policy advisory group. Walsh pressed on, but on September 16, 1991, Judge Gesell dropped all charges against North (*North,* 920 F. 2d 940 [D.C. Cir. 1990], *cert. denied,* 500 U.S. 941, 111 S. Ct. 2235, 114 L. Ed. 2d 477 [1991]).

Vice Admiral Poindexter's trial was similar to North's. After failing to win release of classified subpoenaed materials, Walsh narrowed his case to charges that Poindexter had provided false information and made false statements to Congress. Unlike North's attorneys, however, Poindexter's successfully subpoenaed former president Reagan, who became the first former president ordered to testify in a criminal trial regarding the conduct of affairs during his administration. Reagan provided an eight-hour videotaped DEPOSITION. However, Poindexter failed to win access to the former president's diaries, which his attorneys argued were crucial to Poindexter's defense.

Walsh's prosecution of Poindexter succeeded through a PREPONDERANCE OF EVIDENCE. In testimony for the prosecution, Lieutenant Colonel North said that he had seen Poindexter destroy a high-level secret document, signed by the president, that described the Iran arms sales as an exchange-for-hostages deal. North also described lying to members of Congress at Poindexter's direction. Other testimony revealed that Poindexter had erased some five thousand computer files after the Iran-Contra story broke in the media in November 1986.

On April 7, 1990, jurors convicted Poindexter on all five of the counts in the indictment. Sentenced on June 11, 1990, to six months in prison, he became the first Iran-Contra defendant to receive a prison term, but remained free pending his appeal. Here, as in *North,* the conviction was overturned. The Court of Appeals for the District of Columbia ruled that Poindexter's testimony before Congress had been unfairly used against him in his trial (*Poindexter,* 951 F. 2d 369 [D.C. Cir. 1991]).

If the reversal of convictions against Poindexter and North represented a defeat to Walsh, so did several PLEA BARGAINS that his office secured in the late 1980s. Critics had expected more serious convictions to result from his intense investigation. In March 1988, former national security adviser Robert McFarlane pleaded guilty to four MISDEMEANOR counts of withholding information from Congress and was fined a modest amount. Two private fundraisers, Carl Channell and Richard Miller, pleaded guilty to using a tax-exempt organization to raise money to purchase arms for the Contras. Channell was sentenced to probation only; Miller was ordered to do minimal public service. In November 1989, Secord, Hakim, and a corporation owned by Hakim all pleaded guilty to relatively minor counts. As Walsh's office persevered, it could show little in terms of prosecutions, and Republicans in Congress

Retired Air Force Major General Richard Secord pled guilty to lying to Congress. He is alleged to have helped divert money from Iranian arms sales to the Contra rebels in Nicaragua.

TERRY ASHE/GAMMA LIAISON

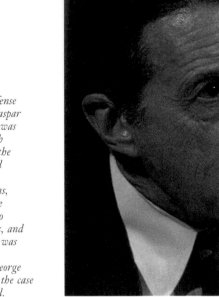

ARTHUR GRACE/STOCK BOSTON

Former Defense Secretary Caspar Weinberger was charged with obstructing the congressional committees' investigations, making false statements to investigators, and perjury. He was pardoned by President George Bush before the case went to trial.

derided the multimillion-dollar investigation as a vindictive exercise in partisan politics.

Then, in 1992, Walsh brought an indictment against the highest-ranking Reagan administration official to be charged in the Iran-Contra Affair: Caspar W. Weinberger, former defense secretary. Weinberger was indicted on June 16, 1992, on five felony counts: one count of obstructing the congressional committees' investigations; two counts of making false statements to investigators working for Walsh and Congress; and two counts of PERJURY related to his congressional testimony. Penalties for each count were a maximum of five years in prison and up to $250,000 in fines.

Walsh based the case on evidence gathered from notes that Weinberger had written while serving for six years in the Reagan administration. These nearly illegible notes, scrawled on seventeen hundred small scraps of paper, formed a personal diary. Weinberger had given them to the Library of Congress, with the requirement that no one could read them without his personal consent. Throughout Iran-Contra investigations, Weinberger had repeatedly testified to Congress and the Tower Commission that he had argued against the arms-for-hostages scheme when it was discussed by White House officials. Walsh did not make Weinberger's involvement an issue in the 1992 indictment. Instead, he zeroed in on Weinberger's testimony under oath that he had

not kept notes or a personal diary during the arms sale period. The discovery of the notes in the Library of Congress suggested that Weinberger had presented false testimony.

On June 19, 1992, Weinberger pleaded not guilty to all five felony charges. Judge Thomas F. Hogan set a tentative trial date of November 2, 1992, one day before the presidential election. This timing raised the question of whether Weinberger's trial would cause political embarrassment for President GEORGE BUSH, who was campaigning against BILL CLINTON. Four days before the election, Walsh announced a new indictment against Weinberger. It centered on a note that had been written by Weinberger about a 1986 White House meeting and that seemed to contradict Bush's claim that as vice president he had not been involved in the arms-for-hostages decision making. Senate Republicans, angered by the indictment, asked the Justice Department to name an independent counsel to investigate whether the Clinton campaign had been behind the indictment. Attorney General WILLIAM P. BARR denied the request.

The case progressed no further. In a surprise reprieve on Christmas Eve, 1992, President Bush pardoned Weinberger and five others implicated in the Iran-Contra Affair. The PARDON cited Weinberger's record of public and military service, his recent ill health, and a desire to put Iran-Contra to rest. Bush also pardoned former assistant secretary of state Elliot Abrams; former CIA officials Clair George, Duane Clarridge, and Alan Fiers; and former national security adviser McFarlane. Bush deemed all six men patriots and said their prosecution represented not law enforcement but the "criminalization of policy differences," essentially repeating his long-standing argument that Iran-Contra was really a case where Democrats had pursued a political witch-hunt to punish Republican officials over disagreements on foreign policy (Grant of Exec. Clemency, Proclamation No. 6518, 57 Fed. Reg. 62,145).

Reaction to the pardons divided along party lines, with Republicans hailing Bush and Democrats criticizing him. Walsh accused Bush of furthering a cover-up and thwarting judicial process. He had long maintained that top Reagan administration officials had engaged in a cover-up to protect their president. Now, he promised, Bush would become the subject of his remaining investigation.

Bush's only testimony had taken place in a January 1988 videotaped deposition. An unsettled question was why Bush's personal diaries were withheld from prosecutors for six years; their existence was only disclosed to the independent counsel's office following the 1992 presidential election. Throughout 1993, Walsh sought to interview the former president but was blocked by Bush's attorneys. Bush consistently insisted on placing limits on any interview. Walsh refused those limits, complained that Bush was stalling the investigation, and ultimately abandoned the attempt to question Bush.

Walsh also chose in 1993 not to indict another high-ranking Reagan administration official, former attorney general EDWIN MEESE III. In 1986, Meese said that Reagan did not know about the arms sales to Iran. Walsh contended that the statement was false, but admitted that building a criminal case against Meese would have been difficult: too much time had passed and could therefore have bolstered memory loss as a defense.

On August 6, 1992, after six-and-a-half years and $35.7 million, Walsh concluded the Iran-Contra investigation and submitted his final report to the special court that had appointed him. The court may decide to make the report's contents public but is not required to do so. Portions of the report leaked to the press have indicated that it accused aides to former president Bush of concealing evidence, but its overall conclusions remain secret.

By 1993, the Iran-Contra Affair seemed over, in one sense. The STATUTE OF LIMITATIONS on crimes that may have been committed during it had expired, and no further prosecution would be forthcoming. However, additional revelations followed as historians sifted through emerging evidence, notably in the memoirs of key participants. The lessons of the affair continued to be debated. Some said that Iran-Contra exposed a pattern of zealous disregard, by the EXECUTIVE BRANCH, of legislative constraint on foreign policy, that dated back to the Vietnam War. Others took the view held by the Reagan and Bush administrations: namely, that nothing terrible had happened.

James Iredell

"A WRITTEN OPINION MUST FOR EVER AFTERWARDS SPEAK FOR ITSELF, AND COMMIT THE CHARACTER OF THE WRITER, IN LASTING COLORS, EITHER OF FAME OR INFAMY, OR NEUTRAL INSIGNIFICANCE, TO FUTURE AGES, AS WELL AS TO THE PRESENT."

IREDELL, JAMES James Iredell was one of the original U.S. Supreme Court justices appointed by GEORGE WASHINGTON.

Iredell was born October 5, 1751, in Lewes, England. At age seventeen he began working in his family's mercantile business in North Carolina and also undertook the study of law. He was licensed to practice law in 1771. In the next few years, he became active in the Revolutionary cause, arguing that the colonies not separate from England and advocating in his writings that the conflict be resolved through reconciliation rather than war. In 1776 he was appointed to a commission to draft and revise the laws for the governance of North Carolina. A year later he served as a judge on the state superior court, and from 1779 to 1781 he was state attorney general. In 1787 he codified and revised the statutes of North Carolina, a process that resulted in the publication of *Iredell's Revisal* four years later.

A staunch supporter of the Constitutional Convention, Iredell led North Carolina in the movement for ratification through a series of acclaimed and well-publicized floor debates and speeches. In 1790 he drew the attention of President Washington, who appointed him to the newly formed U.S. Supreme Court. At age thirty-eight, Iredell was the youngest of the original justices.

In addition to hearing cases before the entire Supreme Court, the justices at that time presided over CIRCUIT COURT sessions throughout the United States, which required them to travel extensively to hear arguments. Iredell was assigned to the Southern Circuit and quickly developed a reputation as an exceptional jurist with respect to constitutional law matters. He wrote a number of notable opinions, including a dissent in *Chisholm v. Georgia,* 2 U.S. (Dall.) 419, 1 L. Ed. 440 (1793), in which he argued that only a constitutional provision could supersede the COMMON-LAW principle that a state cannot be sued by a citizen from another state. Iredell maintained that the states were sovereign and did not owe their origins to the federal government. Iredell's view of STATES' RIGHTS

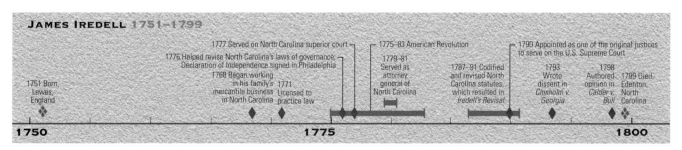

would prevail in Congress's subsequent adoption of the ELEVENTH AMENDMENT.

Iredell also authored *Calder v. Bull*, 3 U.S. (Dall.) 386, 1 L. Ed. 648 (1798), in which he argued that a legislative act unauthorized by or in violation of the Constitution was void and that the courts were responsible for determining an act's status in that regard. This principle of JUDICIAL REVIEW would be amplified five years later in the landmark decision *Marbury v. Madison*, 5 U.S. (1 Cranch) 137, 2 L. Ed. 60 (1803), which held that the courts were indeed ultimately responsible for deciding the validity of laws passed by the legislative branch of government.

The strain of the travel required to cover his circuit, in addition to the heavy caseload of the Supreme Court, eventually took its toll on Iredell's health. He died at his home in North Carolina in 1799, less than ten years after ascending to the High Court.

IRELAND, PATRICIA Patricia Ireland is an attorney and social activist who became the ninth president of the National Organization for Women (NOW) on December 15, 1991.

Ireland was born October 19, 1945, in Oak Park, Illinois. She grew up on a farm in Valparaiso, Indiana, where her family raised honeybees. She is the younger of two daughters of James Ireland and Joan Filipek. Ireland's father, a metallurgical engineer, taught her to be passionate about her profession. Her mother was a volunteer counselor with Planned Parenthood who became the first director of the local chapter. She was Ireland's social activist role model.

Ireland was educated in a two-room schoolhouse and attended the local Presbyterian church. In high school she was an honor roll student and also participated in the pep squad and the spring beauty court. Her childhood was punctuated by a traumatic experience that may have been a cause behind her drive and commitment. Her older sister, Kathy, died at the age of seven after an accident.

Ireland seems to have been destined to be a standard-bearer for the women's movement. During her first year as a math major at DePauw University, she was humiliated by a cal-

BIOGRAPHY

JACK KUNTZ/IMPACT VISUALS

Patricia Ireland

culus teacher who ridiculed her questions and complained about having to teach math to girls. As a result, she never raised her hand in class again, and later changed her field of study to education. Also while at DePauw, Ireland became pregnant and was forced to travel to Japan to obtain a legal ABORTION. She then married and transferred to the University of Tennessee, where she obtained a degree in German in 1966. Her first marriage lasted only a short time. In 1968, she married her second husband, James Humble, an artist.

Ireland began work as a graduate student and German teacher but she quickly became bored with teaching. She and her husband moved to Miami, where she became a flight attendant for Pan American World Airways. Working as a flight attendant was a pivotal experience for Ireland. She discovered that her employee health insurance plan would not cover her husband's dental expenses, even though it did pay such expenses for the wives of male employees. Ireland consulted Dade County NOW for advice. It referred her to the Labor Department, the EQUAL EMPLOYMENT OPPORTUNITY COMMISSION, and the flight attendants' union. As a result of Ireland's challenge, the insurance policy was amended. Her characteristic good humor is evident in her comments on the experience: "The vice-president of the labor task force at Dade County NOW is now the dean of women lawmakers in the Florida legislature. I am the president of NOW. And Pan Am is bankrupt."

Taking on Pan Am's discriminatory insurance plan whet Ireland's appetite for more knowledge of the law. She enrolled in the law school at Florida State University while continuing to work as a flight attendant. Ireland began to notice that if she introduced herself as a flight attendant, people had little to say to her, but if she introduced herself as a law student, they were eager to discuss complex legal issues and current events. The denigration of work traditionally done by women offended her growing feminist sensibilities. "My brain was the same, my ideas were just as worthy or unworthy, but there was a tremendous differ-

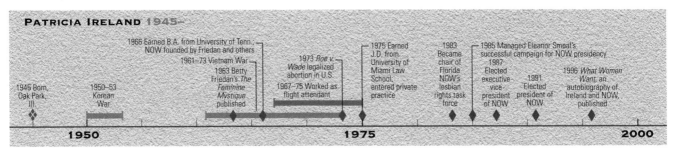

PATRICIA IRELAND 1945–

1945 Born, Oak Park, Ill.

1950–53 Korean War

1961–73 Vietnam War

1963 Betty Friedan's *The Feminine Mystique* published

1966 Earned B.A. from University of Tenn.; NOW founded by Friedan and others

1967–75 Worked as flight attendant

1973 *Roe v. Wade* legalized abortion in U.S.

1975 Earned J.D. from University of Miami Law School; entered private practice

1983 Became chair of Florida NOW's lesbian rights task force

1985 Managed Eleanor Smeal's successful campaign for NOW presidency

1987 Elected executive vice president of NOW

1991 Elected president of NOW

1996 *What Women Want*, an autobiography of Ireland and NOW, published

1950   1975   2000

ence in the way that people perceived and treated me," she said. "... I think traditional women's work is undervalued—teaching, health care, social work. That was part of the experience that made me want to be an activist."

Ireland earned her law degree from the University of Miami, where she had transferred from Florida State, in 1975. She served on both the Law Review and the Lawyer of the Americas and did pro bono work for Dade County NOW. After graduation, she practiced corporate law for twelve years, continued working for Dade County NOW, and helped corporate clients formulate AFFIRMATIVE ACTION programs.

Ireland's work in the WOMEN'S RIGHTS movement expanded during her years as an attorney. In 1983, she became the chair of Florida NOW's lesbian rights task force. In 1985, she managed Eleanor C. Smeal's successful campaign for the presidency of NOW, and in 1987, she was elected NOW's executive vice president, a post she held until May 1991, when she became acting president following the illness of Molly Yard. On December 15, 1991, Ireland was officially named NOW's ninth president.

As NOW's top officer, Ireland is charged with pursuing the group's four priority issues: reviving the EQUAL RIGHTS AMENDMENT, protecting abortion rights, expanding lesbian rights, and improving women's economic status. She says that she wants to stir things up. She admires the tactics used by former governor GEORGE WALLACE, of Alabama, in his drive to mobilize political conservatives in the South to form a third national political party. Ireland hopes to use some of the same tactics to garner support for an alternative to what she calls the Republicrats. She is disdainful of politics as usual. She is also committed to continuing the practice of "shadow lobbying," whereby lawmakers' wives and daughters lobby their husbands and fathers about women's issues. In a departure from her usual soft-spoken, concensus-building style, Ireland has indicated that, under her leadership, NOW may call for acts of civil disobedience in order to ensure women's access to legal abortion services.

NOW has been a controversial organization since its inception. With Ireland at its helm, questions have arisen as to whether it represents the majority of U.S. women. About the time the group announced that lesbian rights would be one of its top priorities, the *Advocate*, a gay and lesbian newspaper, revealed that Ireland, while maintaining her long-standing marriage to Humble, who lives in Florida, also has a female companion with whom she lives in Washington, D.C. At the same time, she steadfastly refuses to discuss her sexuality, insisting that she be evaluated for her positions on issues and not for her lifestyle.

Some of NOW's allies are concerned that a perception of NOW as a fringe group that does not address the concerns of the majority will erode support for their causes. NOW has also been criticized by insiders such as BETTY N. FRIEDAN, the group's founding president, who says the organization has assumed a focus that is too narrow and that it is failing to address women's current concerns, such as juggling families and jobs. Friedan feels that NOW is stuck in an outdated mode and is no longer in touch with the majority of U.S. women. Ireland, however, is convinced that NOW is on the right track for carrying on the fight for women's rights. "Someone has to raise the issues that make people uncomfortable, the issues that other people don't want to talk about. ... it's healthy to be angry at the situation women face. So, yes, we may be militant and angry but we're also thoughtful and intelligent."

CROSS-REFERENCES

Gay and Lesbian Rights; Sex Discrimination; Steinem, Gloria.

IRRECONCILABLE DIFFERENCES

The existence of significant differences between a married couple that are so great and beyond resolution as to make the marriage unworkable, and for which the law permits a DIVORCE.

A divorce premised on the ground of irreconcilable differences is considered a no-fault divorce since there is no need to establish that one party is more responsible or at fault for the end of the marriage than the other.

IRREGULARITY A defect, failure, or mistake in a legal proceeding or lawsuit; a departure from a prescribed rule or regulation.

An irregularity is not an unlawful act, however, in certain instances, it is sufficiently serious to render a lawsuit invalid. For example, a number of states have statutes that require the appointment of a GUARDIAN to represent the interests of a child who is being sued. The failure to do so is an irregularity that can be used as a ground for invalidating and setting aside a judgment entered against the child.

In other cases, however, the flaw might be a simple HARMLESS ERROR that can be easily rectified, and, therefore, does not render the proceeding invalid.

IRRELEVANT Unrelated or inapplicable to the matter in issue.

Irrelevant EVIDENCE has no tendency to prove or disprove any contested fact in a lawsuit.

"FOR MOST WOMEN, EQUALITY IS A BREAD-AND-BUTTER ISSUE. WOMEN ARE STILL PAID LESS ON THE JOB AND CHARGED MORE FOR EVERYTHING FROM DRY CLEANING TO INSURANCE."

IRREPARABLE INJURY 📖 Any harm or loss that is not easily repaired, restored, or compensated by monetary DAMAGES. A serious wrong, generally of a repeated and continuing nature, that has an equitable remedy of injunctive relief. 📖

IRRESISTIBLE IMPULSE 📖 A test applied in a criminal prosecution to determine whether a person accused of a crime was compelled by a mental disease to commit it and therefore cannot be held criminally responsible for her or his actions; in a WRONGFUL DEATH case, a compulsion to commit SUICIDE created by the defendant. 📖

In most JURISDICTIONS, a person may defend criminal charges on a ground of insanity. The INSANITY DEFENSE comes in two main forms. First, a defendant may argue that because of mental disease or defect, he or she lacked the capacity to distinguish right from wrong. This is cognitive insanity.

Second, a defendant may argue that because of mental disease or defect, she or he was unable to act in conformance with the law. This is volitional insanity, and it is known as the irresistible impulse defense. Under this defense, a defendant may be found not guilty by reason of insanity even though she or he was capable of distinguishing right from wrong at the time of the offense.

The success of an irresistible impulse defense depends on the facts of the case. For example, assume that a child has been molested. If the child's mother shoots and kills the suspected molester, the mother could argue that she was so enraged by the violation of her child that she was unable to control her actions. The mother need not have been diagnosed as mentally ill. Rather, she would need to show that she was mentally ill at the time of the shooting, and that the illness impaired her self-control.

Irresistible impulse emerged as a defense in the nineteenth century, when psychoanalysts formulated the concept of moral insanity to describe the temporary inability of otherwise sane persons to resist criminal behavior. Courts began to recognize the condition as one that rendered conduct involuntary and therefore not suitable for punishment. For the better part of a century, many states allowed both cognitive insanity and irresistible impulse insanity as defenses.

Congress and most states abolished the irresistible impulse defense after John Hinckley was acquitted on grounds of insanity for the attempted ASSASSINATION of President RONALD REAGAN in 1981. Only a handful of states currently allow irresistible impulse as a defense to criminal charges. These states permit it as a supplement to the cognitive insanity defense, which is the only insanity defense recognized in most jurisdictions. On the federal level, Congress abolished the irresistible impulse defense in the Insanity Defense Reform Act of 1984 (18 U.S.C.A. §§ 1 note, 17).

In some states, the irresistible impulse defense has never been adopted. In others, it has been adopted and subsequently withdrawn. Where it has been rejected, the reasons are generally the same: to prevent sane persons from escaping LIABILITY simply because they were unable to control their actions. In the words of one court, "There are many appetites and passions which by long indulgence acquire a mastery over men . . . but the law is far from excusing criminal acts committed under the impulse of such passions" (*State v. Brandon*, 53 N.C. 463 [1862]).

Under the Model Penal Code definition of irresistible impulse, a person may be found not guilty by reason of insanity if, at the time of the offense, he or she lacked "substantial capacity either to appreciate the criminality of [the] conduct or to conform [the] conduct to the requirements of law" (§ 4.01(1) [1962]). The "lacked substantial capacity" language creates a low threshold for the defendant: in some states, the defendant must allege complete impairment in order to invoke the defense.

Irresistible impulse is also a factor in CIVIL ACTIONS. When a person commits suicide, survivors may sue for damages with a wrongful death claim or similar action if they can show that the suicide was caused by the actions of another person. In such a case, the plaintiffs must prove that the defendant caused a mental condition that caused the decedent to experience an irresistible impulse to commit suicide.

IRRETRIEVABLE BREAKDOWN OF MARRIAGE 📖 The situation that exists when either or both spouses no longer are able or willing to live with each other, thereby destroying their HUSBAND AND WIFE relationship with no hope of resumption of spousal duties. 📖

The irretrievable breakdown of a marriage provides the ground for a no-fault DIVORCE in many JURISDICTIONS.

IRREVOCABLE 📖 Unable to cancel or recall; that which is unalterable or irreversible. 📖

IRS 📖 An abbreviation for the INTERNAL REVENUE SERVICE, a federal agency charged with the responsibility of administering and enforcing internal revenue laws. 📖

ISLAND 📖 A land area surrounded by water and remaining above sea level during high tide. 📖

The Statue of Liberty is on an island that is part of New York State.

Land areas exposed only during low tide are called low-tide elevations or drying rocks, reefs, or shoals. The existence of islands has generated numerous disputes, centering primarily on the size of the territorial sea surrounding an island and the determination of what state has SOVEREIGNTY over a particular island. The size of the territorial sea has become an important question affecting fishing rights and the right of unrestricted passage for foreign vessels. Although the territorial sea of an island is usually determined by reference to its coastal baseline, some adjustments have been recognized in the cases of archipelagoes and islands located close to the mainland.

Determination of what state has title to an island has traditionally depended upon an open and continuous assertion of sovereignty over the island, which is usually, but not always, accompanied by physical presence of some representative of the state.

See also TERRITORIAL WATERS.

ISSUE 📖 To promulgate or send out. In a lawsuit, a disputed point of law or QUESTION OF FACT, set forth in the PLEADINGS, that is alleged by one party and denied by the other.

In the law governing the transfer or distribution of property, a child, children, and all individuals who descend from a common ancestor or descendents of any degree. 📖

As applied to NOTES or BONDS of a series, date of issue means the day fixed as the start of the period for which they run, with no reference to a specific date when the bonds or notes are to be sold and delivered. With regard to bonds only, bonds are issued to the purchaser when they are delivered.

When an issue of fact arises, the court or jury must consider and evaluate the weight of the evidence in order to reach a decision. An issue of law exists thereby providing a ground for a SUMMARY JUDGMENT sought by a party to the action when only one conclusion can be drawn by the court from the undisputed evidence, obviating the need for deliberation by a jury.

The term *issue* is frequently found in provisions of a DEED. In TESTAMENTARY matters, the meaning of issue is derived from the intent of the TESTATOR, a maker of a WILL. The intent is determined from the provisions of the will.

ISSUE PRECLUSION 📖 A concept that refers to the fact that a particular QUESTION OF FACT or law, one that has already been fully litigated by the parties in an ACTION for which there has been a JUDGMENT on the MERITS, cannot be relitigated in any future action involving the same parties or their PRIVIES (persons who would be bound by the judgment rendered for the party). 📖

The term *issue preclusion* is synonymous with COLLATERAL ESTOPPEL, a doctrine which bars the relitigation of the same issue that was the basis of a finding or verdict in an action by the same parties or their privies in subsequent lawsuits involving the same or different causes of action. It is not, however, the same as the doctrine of RES JUDICATA which bars the relitigation of an entire CAUSE OF ACTION, claim or demand, as opposed to an issue that makes up a cause of action, claim, or demand.

ITEMIZE 📖 To individually state each item or article. 📖

Frequently used in tax ACCOUNTING, an itemized account or claim separately lists amounts that add up to the final sum of the total account on claim.

ITEMIZED DEDUCTION See INCOME TAX.

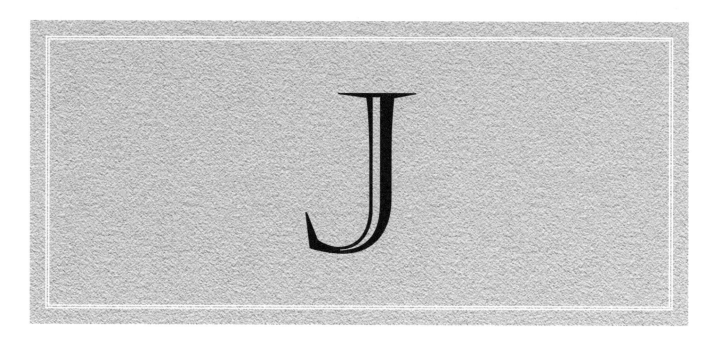

JACKSON, ANDREW

JACKSON, ANDREW Andrew Jackson achieved prominence as a frontiersman, jurist, and military hero, and as seventh president of the United States. His two administrations, famous for ideologies labeled Jacksonian Democracy, encouraged participation in government by the people, particularly the middle class.

Jackson was born March 15, 1767, in Waxhaw, South Carolina. In 1781, Jackson entered the military, fought in the Revolutionary War, and was subsequently taken prisoner and incarcerated at Camden, South Carolina. After his release, he pursued legal studies in North Carolina and was admitted to the bar of that state in 1787.

Jackson relocated to Nashville in 1788 and established a successful law practice. Three years later, he married Rachel Donelson. When it was subsequently discovered that Mrs. Jackson was not legally divorced from her previous husband, Jackson remarried her in 1794 after her divorce became final. His enemies, however, used the scandal to their advantage.

Jackson began his public service career in 1791 and performed the duties of prosecuting attorney for the Southwest Territory. He at-

BIOGRAPHY

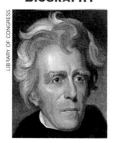

Andrew Jackson

tended the Tennessee constitutional convention in 1796 and entered the federal government system in that same year.

As a member of the U.S. House of Representatives, Jackson represented Tennessee for a year before filling the vacant position of senator from Tennessee in the U.S. Senate during 1797 and 1798.

Jackson embarked on the judicial phase of his career in 1798, presiding as judge of the Tennessee Superior Court until 1804.

During the War of 1812, Jackson returned to the military and was victorious at the Horseshoe Bend battle in 1814. He conquered the British at New Orleans at the close of the war, which resulted in national recognition as a war hero.

In 1818, Jackson was involved in a military incident that almost catapulted the United States into another war with Great Britain and Spain. Dispatched to the Florida border to quell Seminole Indian uprisings, Jackson misunderstood his orders, took control of the Spanish possession of Pensacola, and killed two British subjects responsible for inciting the Indians. Spain and Great Britain were in an uproar over the incident, but Secretary of State

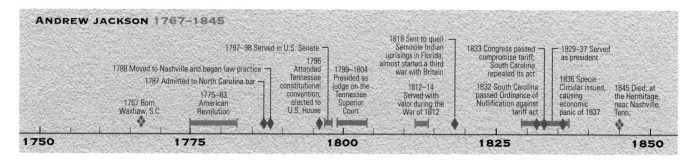

ANDREW JACKSON 1767–1845

1797–98 Served in U.S. Senate

1796 Attended Tennessee constitutional convention; elected to U.S. House

1788 Moved to Nashville and began law practice

1787 Admitted to North Carolina bar

1767 Born, Waxhaw, S.C.

1775–83 American Revolution

1799–1804 Presided as judge on the Tennessee Superior Court

1818 Sent to quell Seminole Indian uprisings in Florida, almost started a third war with Britain

1812–14 Served with valor during the War of 1812

1833 Congress passed compromise tariff; South Carolina repealed its act

1832 South Carolina passed Ordinance of Nullification against tariff act

1929–37 Served as president

1836 Specie Circular issued, causing economic panic of 1837

1845 Died; at the Hermitage, near Nashville, Tenn.

1750   1775   1800   1825   1850

John Quincy Adams supported Jackson. The incident added to Jackson's popularity as a rugged hero.

Jackson sought the office of president of the United States in 1824 against Henry Clay, John Quincy Adams, and William Crawford. No single candidate received a majority of electoral votes, and the House of Representatives decided the election in favor of Adams. Four years later, Jackson defeated the incumbent Adams and began the first of two terms as chief executive.

During his first administration, Jackson relied on a group of informal advisers known as the Kitchen Cabinet. The unofficial members included journalists and politicians, as opposed to the formal CABINET members traditionally involved in policymaking. He also initiated the spoils system, rewarding dutiful and faithful party members with government appointments, regardless of their qualifications for the positions. Many of Jackson's intimate associations did not include members from the traditional families associated with politics, and public dissatisfaction came to a head with the marriage of his Secretary of War John Eaton to the provincial Margaret O'Neill. The social politics employed by cabinet members and their wives, particularly Vice President and Mrs. John C. Calhoun, caused much upheaval in the Jackson cabinet, and the eventual resignation of Eaton.

Calhoun and Jackson disagreed again in 1832 over a protective TARIFF, which Calhoun believed was not beneficial to the South. Calhoun initiated the policy of nullification, by which a state could judge a federal regulation null and void and, therefore, refuse to comply with it if the state believed the regulation to be adverse to the tenets of the Constitution. Calhoun resigned from the office of vice president after South Carolina adopted the nullification policy against the tariff act, and Jackson requested the enactment of the Force Bill from Congress to authorize his use of MILITIA, if necessary, to enforce federal law. The Force Bill proved to be solely a strong threat, because Jackson sympathized with the South and advocated the drafting of a tariff compromise. Henry Clay was instrumental in the creation of

"EVERY MAN WHO HAS BEEN IN OFFICE A FEW YEARS BELIEVES HE HAS A LIFE ESTATE IN IT, A VESTED RIGHT. THIS IS NOT THE PRINCIPLE OF OUR GOVERNMENT. IT IS ROTATION OF OFFICE THAT WILL PERPETUATE OUR LIBERTY."

BIOGRAPHY

Howell Edmunds Jackson

ARTIST: TEMPELMAN, COLLECTION OF THE SUPREME COURT OF THE UNITED STATES

this agreement, which appeased South Carolina.

The most significant issue during Jackson's term was the controversy over the BANK OF THE UNITED STATES. The bank became a topic in the 1832 presidential campaign and continued into the second administration of the victorious Jackson.

The charter of the bank expired in 1836, but Henry Clay encouraged the passage of a bill to secure its recharter in 1832. Jackson was against the powerful bank and overruled the recharter. He proceeded to transfer federal funds from the bank to selected state banks, called "pet banks," which significantly diminished the power of the bank. Secretary of Treasury Louis McLane refused to remove the funds and was dismissed; similarly, the new treasury secretary, W. J. Duane, also refused. Jackson replaced him with Roger B. Taney, who supported Jackson's views and complied with his wishes. In response to this loyalty, Jackson subsequently nominated Taney as a U.S. Supreme Court justice in 1836.

In 1836, Jackson faced another financial crisis. He issued the Specie Circular of 1836, which declared that all payments for public property must be made in gold or silver, as opposed to the previous use of paper currency. This proclamation precipitated the economic panic of 1837, which ended Jackson's second term and extended into the new presidential administration of Martin Van Buren.

Jackson spent his remaining years in retirement at his estate in Tennessee, "The Hermitage," where he died on June 8, 1845.

JACKSON, HOWELL EDMUNDS Howell Edmunds Jackson was a U.S. senator, federal judge on the U.S. Sixth Circuit Court of Appeals, and U.S. Supreme Court justice. Jackson toiled diligently without fanfare for many years before garnering widespread attention for the last case he heard while sitting on the Supreme Court, *Pollock v. Farmers' Loan & Trust Co.*, 158 U.S. 601, 15 S. Ct. 912, 39 L. Ed. 1108 (1895).

Jackson was born April 8, 1832, in Paris, Tennessee. He graduated from West Tennessee College in 1849, then studied for a time at the University of Virginia. He read the law with a Tennessee Supreme Court judge for a year, and

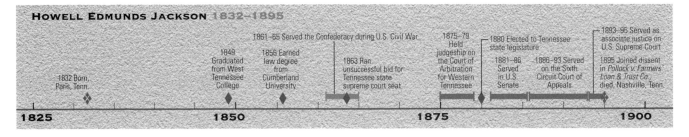

HOWELL EDMUNDS JACKSON 1832–1895

1832 Born, Paris, Tenn.

1849 Graduated from West Tennessee College

1856 Earned law degree from Cumberland University

1861–65 Served the Confederacy during U.S. Civil War

1863 Ran unsuccessful bid for Tennessee state supreme court seat

1875–79 Held judgeship on the Court of Arbitration for Western Tennessee

1880 Elected to Tennessee state legislature

1881–86 Served in U.S. Senate

1886–93 Served on the Sixth Circuit Court of Appeals

1893–95 Served as associate justice on U.S. Supreme Court

1895 Joined dissent in *Pollock v. Farmers' Loan & Trust Co.*, died, Nashville, Tenn.

1825   1850   1875   1900

obtained his law degree from Cumberland University in Lebanon, Tennessee, in 1856. Thereafter, he practiced law in Jackson and Memphis. Although Jackson opposed Tennessee's secession in the Civil War, he served the Confederacy as a receiver of confiscated property. Following the Civil War, he served for a short time on the Court of Arbitration for West Tennessee, a provisional court helping the regular Tennessee Supreme Court dispose of a backlog of cases caused by the war. He also made an unsuccessful bid for a seat on the state supreme court.

A Whig before the war, Jackson was elected to the Tennessee state legislature as a Democrat in 1880. The following year the legislature assembled to choose a U.S. senator on a joint ballot. No candidate, including the incumbent, could muster enough votes in the divided assembly. After a number of deadlocked days, a Republican legislator cast his vote for Jackson, who had not been a candidate, and Jackson was quickly elected. In the Senate he gained a reputation as a tireless worker. He was nonpartisan in his friendships, becoming close with Democrat president GROVER CLEVELAND and Republican Senate colleague BENJAMIN HARRISON.

Jackson resigned from the Senate in 1886 when President Cleveland appointed him to the Sixth Circuit Court of Appeals, and eventually became that court's presiding judge. In 1893 lame-duck president Harrison appointed Jackson to fill a vacancy on the U.S. Supreme Court. Harrison appointed Jackson in part because Cleveland was about to become president, and Harrison doubted that any Republican could garner confirmation by the Democratic Senate. Harrison, a former Union general, saw in Jackson, a former member of the Confederate government, not another secessionist southern Democrat but a man committed to serving his entire nation.

In August 1894, Congress imposed a nationwide two percent INCOME TAX on all annual incomes in excess of $4,000. The new law, popular in the South and West but despised in the North and East, was quickly challenged as being unconstitutional. Soon, the Supreme Court agreed to hear the case.

Tuberculosis struck Jackson, and shortly after the October 1894 session began, his deteriorating health kept him off the bench. He was absent in April 1895 when the Court held in *Pollock* that part of the new tax law was unconstitutional. The Court was evenly divided on whether the entire law must be declared unconstitutional, and therefore did not express an

"[THE POLLOCK] DECISION DISREGARDS THE WELL-ESTABLISHED CANON . . . THAT AN ACT PASSED BY A CO-ORDINATE BRANCH OF THE GOVERNMENT HAS EVERY PRESUMPTION IN ITS FAVOR, AND SHOULD NEVER BE DECLARED INVALID BY THE COURTS UNLESS ITS REPUGNANCY TO THE CONSTITUTION IS CLEAR BEYOND ALL REASONABLE DOUBT."

BIOGRAPHY

Jesse Louis Jackson

opinion on the matter. The absence of a firm decision by the justices meant that the courts could expect a flood of litigation from unwilling taxpayers. The Supreme Court quickly granted a rehearing to reexamine the issue.

To break the deadlock, it appeared essential that Justice Jackson either resign so that a new justice could be appointed, or agree to hear the case. Jackson decided to hear the case. At Chief Justice MELVILLE W. FULLER's insistence, he obtained his doctor's permission to travel from Tennessee, where he had been recuperating, to Washington, D.C., to return to the bench.

The case was argued for three days in early May, 1895. Strong passions about the income tax law, widespread speculation about how Jackson would vote, and the drama of the obviously ailing justice made the case one of keen public interest. Reporters speculated that the effort of participating in the hearing might well shorten Jackson's life.

The decision was rendered less than two weeks after oral arguments. Ironically, Jackson's vote was not crucial, because one of his colleagues changed his opinion. Jackson and three other justices voted to uphold the constitutionality of the tax; five justices, including the colleague who had changed his opinion, voted to declare the entire law void. Jackson, too weak to prepare a formal, written opinion, spoke from notes as he announced his dissent in the Supreme Court chamber. Jackson declared that the decision was "the most disastrous blow ever struck at the constitutional power of Congress." An income tax was not resurrected until passage of the SIXTEENTH AMENDMENT in 1913.

After the rehearing in *Pollock*, Jackson returned to his home outside Nashville. He died less than three months later, on August 8, 1895.

See also POLLOCK v. FARMERS' LOAN AND TRUST CO.

JACKSON, JESSE LOUIS Reverend Jesse Louis Jackson is a CIVIL RIGHTS activist, clergyman, and prominent African American leader in the United States.

Jackson was born October 8, 1941, in Greenville, South Carolina. His mother, Helen Burns, was only sixteen when Jackson was born. His father, Noah Louis Robinson, acknowledged Jackson as his son, but because he was married to another woman and had several other children, he was not involved in Jackson's life. When he was three, his mother married Charles Jackson. The family eventually moved out of the poor section of town to a new housing project, where, for the first time, they enjoyed hot and cold running water and an indoor bathroom. Jackson was legally adopted

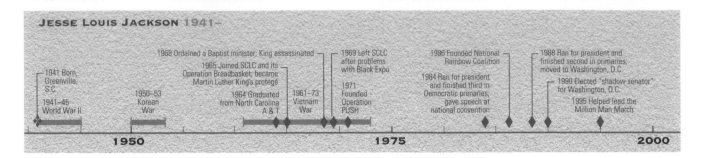

JESSE LOUIS JACKSON 1941–

1968 Ordained a Baptist minister; King assassinated
1969 Left SCLC after problems with Black Expo
1986 Founded National Rainbow Coalition
1988 Ran for president and finished second in primaries; moved to Washington, D.C.

1941 Born, Greenville, S.C.
1965 Joined SCLC and its Operation Breadbasket; became Martin Luther King's protégé
1971 Founded Operation PUSH
1984 Ran for president and finished third in Democratic primaries; gave speech at national convention
1990 Elected "shadow senator" for Washington, D.C.

1941–45 World War II
1950–53 Korean War
1964 Graduated from North Carolina A & T
1961–73 Vietnam War
1995 Helped lead the Million Man March

1950   1975   2000

by his stepfather when he was twelve. He has one brother, Charles Jackson, Jr.

Jackson attended the all-black Sterling High School, in Greenville, where he was a star football player. After graduation in 1959, he went north to the University of Illinois on a football scholarship. The following year he transferred to North Carolina Agricultural and Technical College (North Carolina A&T), a mostly black school in Greensboro. There he met his wife, Jacqueline Lavinia Brown, a fellow student who had also grown up in poverty. The couple married December 31, 1962, and have five children: Santita, Jesse Louis, Jr., Jonathan Luther, Yusef DuBois, and Jacqueline Lavinia.

While at North Carolina A&T, Jackson began the work that would make him a widely recognized civil rights leader. He led a series of protest demonstrations and sit-ins throughout the South and joined one of the first organized groups in the CIVIL RIGHTS MOVEMENT, the Congress of Racial Equality (CORE).

After graduating from college in the fall of 1964, Jackson left the fledgling civil rights movement and moved north again, to attend Chicago Theological Seminary. He immersed himself in his studies, determined to learn how he could bring about change through the ministry. Then, in 1965, the civil rights movement began to gain momentum, and Jackson wanted to be a part of it. He joined the SOUTHERN CHRISTIAN LEADERSHIP CONFERENCE (SCLC) of MARTIN LUTHER KING, JR., and expanded its Operation Breadbasket, an economic campaign that used BOYCOTTS and negotiations to secure jobs for minorities. Six months before he was to graduate from the seminary, he left to work full-time for the SCLC. Nevertheless, he was ordained a Baptist minister in 1968.

Jackson saw King as his mentor and role model, and he became King's protégé. He worked closely with King and the other SCLC leaders and was with King when King was assassinated on April 4, 1968.

In 1969 Jackson organized the first Black Expo, a promotional festival for the companies involved in Operation Breadbasket. The expo

"AMERICA IS . . . LIKE A QUILT—MANY PATCHES, MANY PIECES, MANY COLORS, MANY SIZES, ALL WOVEN AND HELD TOGETHER BY A COMMON THREAD."

was intended to be an annual fund-raiser for the SCLC, but Jackson had quietly incorporated the event independently. SCLC officials were enraged, and Jackson finally left the organization.

In the early 1970s, Jackson formed Operation People United to Serve Humanity (Operation PUSH). He negotiated with large corporations such as the Coca-Cola Company, Heublein, and Ford Motor Company to increase minority employment and minority-owned dealerships and franchises. He also began holding rallies at high schools to raise the self-image of African American students. He stressed the importance of education, personal responsibility, and hard work to achieve one's goals. Jackson's work with teenagers attracted the attention of President JIMMY CARTER, whose administration rewarded Jackson with grants and contracts to continue his outreach. He named his school ministry PUSH for Excellence, or PUSH-Excel.

During the late 1970s and early 1980s, Jackson emerged as a preeminent African American leader in the United States. He decided to make a bid for the presidency. He mounted an ambitious voter registration drive throughout the South, and barnstormed through Western Europe enlisting support among U.S. service personnel. In an effort to enhance his image and prove that his expertise extended beyond domestic matters, he traveled to trouble spots such as the Middle East, Latin America, and Cuba to meet with leaders there. In 1983, he negotiated the release of Lieutenant Robert O. Goodman, Jr., a U.S. citizen whose jet had been shot down over Syrian-held territory in Lebanon.

Critics dismissed these activities as opportunistic grandstanding. Particularly troubling to some was Jackson's perceived anti-Semitic bias. During a private conversation in 1984, Jackson referred to Jews as Hymies and to New York as Hymietown. He later apologized. A short time later, Louis Farrakhan, head of the controversial NATION OF ISLAM and a Jackson supporter, threatened the reporter who had written about

Jackson's remarks. Jackson later distanced himself from Farrakhan and his organization because of their perceived militant anti-white and anti-Semitic stance.

Jackson placed third in the 1984 presidential primaries, behind former vice president Walter F. Mondale and Colorado senator Gary W. Hart. His delegate votes did not give him the clout he needed to compel the Democrats to accept his controversial platform proposals. Jackson gracefully conceded the nomination to Mondale and gave a rousing speech at the Democratic National Convention in San Francisco, which was in part a response to his critics:

> If in my low moments, in word, deed, or attitude, through some error of temper, taste, or tone, I have caused anyone discomfort, created pain, or revived someone's fears, that was not my truest self. . . . I am not a perfect servant. I am a public servant doing my best against the odds. As I develop and serve, be patient. God is not finished with me yet.

After the convention, Jackson resumed his duties as head of Operation PUSH. He continued to be active in progressive causes, leading what he called a counterinaugural march and prayer vigil in January 1985, and participating in a reenactment of the civil rights march from Selma, Alabama, to Montgomery, Alabama, in March 1985. He also began building toward his second campaign for the presidency. He formed the National Rainbow Coalition, his vision of a modern populist movement comprising blacks, working families, liberal urbanites, Hispanics, women's rights groups, college faculty and students, environmentalists, farmers, and labor unions—a cultural as well as racial alliance searching for alternatives within the Democratic party.

Jackson made another run for president in 1988 and finished second behind Michael Dukakis in the primaries. However, much to his disappointment, he was not chosen as the vice presidential nominee.

BIOGRAPHY

NATIONAL ARCHIVES

Robert Houghwout Jackson

"IT IS NOT THE FUNCTION OF OUR GOVERNMENT TO KEEP THE CITIZEN FROM FALLING INTO ERROR; IT IS THE FUNCTION OF THE CITIZEN TO KEEP THE GOVERNMENT FROM FALLING INTO ERROR."

After the 1988 election, Jackson moved from Chicago to Washington, D.C., and was elected one of the city's "shadow senators." In this unpaid, nonvoting position, which was created by the Washington City Council, Jackson represents the district's interests on Capitol Hill. His main responsibility is to lobby Congress for statehood for the nation's capital.

In the mid-1990s Jackson saw the need to change the focus of the civil rights movement. He called for the black community to take action against the violence that was claiming so many of its young people.

JACKSON, ROBERT HOUGHWOUT

Robert Houghwout Jackson served as general counsel for the Federal Bureau of Internal Revenue, attorney general of the United States, and justice of the U.S. Supreme Court. During his service on the Court from 1941 to 1954 Jackson delivered unconventional opinions that did not always coincide with those of the president who had appointed him, FRANKLIN D. ROOSEVELT. Jackson was nonetheless chosen to be chief counsel at the NUREMBERG TRIALS following World War II.

Jackson's straightforward style as a lawyer and a justice stemmed from his rural upbringing. The first Jacksons immigrated to the United States from England in 1819. They settled in Spring Creek, Pennsylvania, where Jackson was born on February 13, 1892. His father, William Eldred Jackson, provided for the family through farming and lumbering.

In September 1911 Jackson entered Albany Law School, passing the bar in 1913. He then began a lengthy career with the establishment of a law practice at Jamestown, New York, and formed a friendship with fellow New Yorker Roosevelt.

In 1934 Jackson was selected by the recently elected president Roosevelt to serve as general counsel for the Federal Bureau of Internal Revenue. In 1936 he became assistant attorney general of the United States, a position he held until 1938. Between 1938 and 1939, he performed the duties of U.S. solicitor general. He

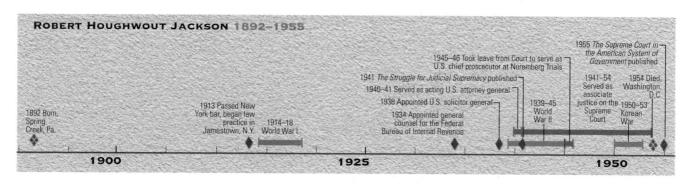

ROBERT HOUGHWOUT JACKSON 1892–1955

1892 Born, Spring Creek, Pa.

1913 Passed New York bar, began law practice in Jamestown, N.Y.

1914–18 World War I

1934 Appointed general counsel for the Federal Bureau of Internal Revenue

1938 Appointed U.S. solicitor general

1940–41 Served as acting U.S. attorney general

1941 *The Struggle for Judicial Supremacy* published

1945–46 Took leave from Court to serve as U.S. chief prosecutor at Nuremberg Trials

1939–45 World War II

1941–54 Served as associate justice on the Supreme Court

1950–53 Korean War

1954 Died, Washington, D.C.

1955 *The Supreme Court in the American System of Government* published

1900   1925   1950

acted as the U.S. attorney general from 1940 until his appointment in July 1941 as justice of the U.S. Supreme Court.

Jackson earned the trust and admiration of his associates through his wit and wisdom. Many of his philosophies on essential constitutional issues came to be known as Jacksonisms. Throughout his career he withheld blind praise of the U.S. system of government. He stated, "A free man must be a reasoning man, and he must dare to doubt what a legislative or electoral majority may most passionately assert" (*American Communications Ass'n v. Douds*, 339 U.S. 382 70 S. Ct. 674, 94 L. Ed. 925 [1950]).

Jackson voted against government actions that imposed upon free speech and religion, and voiced mistrust of LABOR UNIONS. Many of his opinions were dissents from a majority that tended to uphold union interests and to support New Deal legislation.

Following the end of the second world war, Jackson was chosen as chief counsel for the United States at the Nuremberg trials, where Nazi leaders were tried for war crimes. Included among the defendants was Hermann Goring, second in command of the Nazi regime, and ADOLF HITLER's designated successor.

In his opening remarks before Goring's trial began, Jackson noted the place of the proceedings in history when he said:

> We must never forget that the record on which we judge these defendants today is the record on which history will judge us tomorrow. To pass these defendants a poisoned chalice is to put it to our own lips as well. We must summon such detachment and intellectual integrity to our task that this trial will commend itself to posterity as fulfilling humanity's aspirations to do justice.

On September 30 and October 1, 1946, the Nuremberg tribunal found nineteen of the twenty-two defendants guilty on one or more counts. Twelve defendants, including Goring, were sentenced to death by hanging.

For his success at Nuremberg, Jackson received a number of honors in the United States, including honorary doctoral degrees from Dartmouth College and Syracuse University. Recognition also came from other nations, including honorary degrees in law from the University of Brussels and the University of Warsaw.

After the trials, Jackson continued his service on the Court. He died on October 9, 1954.

JACTITATION ⬛ Deceitful boasting, a deceptive claim, or a continuing assertion prejudicial to the right of another. ⬛

One form of jactitation at COMMON LAW is slander of title—defaming another person's TITLE TO REAL PROPERTY. Some jurisdictions provide a remedy when the injured party brings an ACTION for jactitation.

JAIL ⬛ A building designated or regularly used for the confinement of individuals who are sentenced for minor crimes or who are unable to gain release on BAIL and are in CUSTODY awaiting trial. ⬛

Jail is usually the first place a person is taken after being arrested by police officers. Most cities have at least one jail, and persons are taken directly there after they are arrested; in less populated areas, arrestees may be taken first to a police station and later to the nearest jail. Many jails are also used for the short-term INCARCERATION of persons convicted of minor crimes.

For homeless and destitute persons, temporary incarceration in jail may, at times, seem a relief from living on the streets. Once people are inside the criminal justice system, officers, prosecutors, and judges can sometimes identify those who need help from social services more than they deserve criminal prosecution. More often than not, persons confined in jail do not wish to be there and seek prompt release.

A person in jail has little choice in being there. Those awaiting trial (pretrial detainees) have been forcibly confined by law enforcement officers, and those serving a sentence (convicts) have been ordered there by the court. A sentence of confinement to jail is backed by the power of law enforcement personnel. Flight from prosecution or confinement is a FELONY that usually results in a prison sentence.

Though they are similar, jails are not the same as PRISONS. Prisons are large facilities that hold large numbers of people for long terms; jails are usually smaller and hold smaller numbers of people for short terms. Prisons confine only convicted criminals; jails can hold convicted criminals, but usually only for short periods. Many jails are used for the sole purpose of detaining DEFENDANTS awaiting trial. In JURISDICTIONS with these jails, a subsequent sentence of short-term incarceration is served at a different facility, such as a work farm or workhouse.

Persons sentenced to a workhouse may be forced to work, but pretrial detainees are not. Convicts in prison are usually required to work if they are able. Some convicts sentenced to jail are able to come and go, serving their term on weekends or other designated days. Pretrial detainees in jail may leave if they can make bail. Inmates in prison are rarely allowed to leave until their prison sentence has been completed or they are granted early release on PAROLE.

Conviction Status for Inmates in Local Jails, 1993

Inmates awaiting court disposition 50.3%

Convicted Inmates 49.7%

Local jails are those operated by counties and municipalities and administered by local government agencies. They do not include state and federal prisons.

Source: *Jails and Jail Inmates 1993–94: Census of Jails and Survey of Jails,* Bureau of Justice Statistics.

Jails and prisons are both dangerous. Both house persons accused or convicted of crimes, making anger, humiliation, and violence regular features of life on the inside. Violent gangs are not as prevalent in jail as in prison, because the incarceration periods are shorter and inmates are less able to organize. However, jail inmates do not have the incentive from "good-time" credits that prison inmates have. A good-time credit reduces the sentence of a prison inmate for good behavior. Transgressions in prison can result in the loss of these credits.

Though jail terms are usually shorter than prison terms, they are not always. Many states limit jail terms to one year, but some allow jail sentences to reach more than two years. In Massachusetts, for example, a person can be sentenced to confinement in a jail or house of correction for as long as two-and-a-half years (Mass. Gen. Laws Ann. ch. 279, § 23 [West]). In large, complex cases and in cases of retrial, pretrial detention can last months, sometimes years.

Though they are presumed innocent in a court of law, pretrial detainees can claim few rights beyond those of convicted defendants. The U.S. Supreme Court does not find a reason for distinguishing between pretrial detainees and convicted defendants in jail. In fact, the High Court has stated that security measures in the federal system should be no different than those for convicted criminals because only the most dangerous defendants are held before trial (*Bell v. Wolfish,* 441 U.S. 520, 99 S. Ct. 1861, 60 L. Ed. 2d 447 [1979]).

Nevertheless, pretrial detainees do possess the same rights as convicted criminals. These include the rights to FREEDOM OF SPEECH and RELIGION, to freedom from DISCRIMINATION based on race, and to DUE PROCESS OF LAW before additional deprivation of life, liberty, or property. Detainees and inmates also have the rights to sanitary conditions; to freedom from constant, loud noise; to nutritious food; to reading materials; and to freedom from constant physical restraint. All these rights may, however, be infringed by jail and prison officials to the extent that they threaten security in the facility.

Jails exist on the federal, state, and local levels. The authority of states to build, operate, and fill jails can be found in the TENTH AMENDMENT, which has been construed to grant to states the power to pass their own laws to preserve the safety, health, and welfare of their communities. On the federal level, the authority to build and fill jails is inherent in the GENERAL WELFARE Clause, the Necessary and Proper Clause, and various clauses authorizing federal punishment in Article I, Section 8, of the U.S. Constitution.

The money to build, maintain, and operate jails is usually provided by taxpayers. In the 1980s, private business leaders began to push for the opportunity to construct and operate jails and prisons. These entrepreneurs claimed that their companies could do the job more efficiently than the government, and make a profit at the same time. Critics argued that the private operation of jails and prisons violates the THIRTEENTH AMENDMENT'S prohibition of SLAVERY and is an abrogation of governmental responsibility, but many state and local lawmakers have approved these endeavors.

In 1984, Congress took action to curb the release of pretrial detainees in the federal system, with the Bail Reform Act of 1984 (18 U.S.C.A. § 3141 et seq.). This act required the judge to find that the defendant is not a danger to the community before determining a bail amount or granting bail at all. The act identified a wide range of criminal activities by defendants as dangerous to the community, and created a presumption in favor of preventive detention for certain alleged acts. In general, the act made it more difficult for many accused criminals to remain free pending trial.

Generally, the matter of assigning bail and determining the conditions of pretrial release is left to the discretion of the judge presiding over the case. However, many states have followed the lead of Congress by passing laws that restrict the conditions under which a judge may grant pretrial release from jail. These laws, combined with an increase in arrest and incarceration rates, have created cramped conditions in jails.

To alleviate overcrowding, many states have turned to alternative forms of sentencing. When defendants are sentenced to a form of imprisonment outside the traditional jail and prison settings, questions have arisen regarding whether their sentences constitute incarceration or official detention. This is significant because if a defendant violates the terms of the incarceration or subsequent PROBATION and is resentenced to prison or jail, the defendant may want credit for the time served in the alternative setting.

In *Michigan v. Hite*, 200 Mich. App. 1, 503 N.W.2d 692 (1993), Marvin Hite was convicted of receiving and concealing stolen property and was sentenced to a boot camp program at Camp Sauble, in Freesoil, Michigan. The boot camp imposed intensive regimentation, strict discipline, strenuous physical labor, and grueling physical activities. The four separate buildings of the camp were enclosed by an eighteen-foot-high fence topped with barbed wire. Hite was also sentenced to a term of probation.

Hite successfully completed the boot camp, but violated the terms of his probation. For that violation, the court resentenced him to serve two to five years' imprisonment. The court also denied credit for the time Hite served in the boot camp. Hite appealed the denial of credit, arguing that it violated the DOUBLE JEOPARDY Clause of the FIFTH AMENDMENT to the U.S. Constitution.

The Court of Appeals of Michigan agreed with Hite and reversed the decision. According to the court, although the boot camp did not have cells with bars, "the discipline, regimentation, and deprivation of liberties" at the camp were greater than those at any minimum-security prison in Michigan. The court ruled that the boot camp constituted incarceration, and Hite's sentence was decreased by the amount of time he had already served at the camp.

The landmark case of *Wolfish* describes the conditions and treatment that pretrial detainees can expect in jail. In *Wolfish*, pretrial detainees at the federal Metropolitan Correctional Center (MCC), in New York City, challenged an array of prison practices, including double-bunking (housing two inmates in the space intended for one inmate); the prohibition of hardcover books not mailed directly from publishers, book clubs, or bookstores; the prohibition of food and personal items from outside the jail; body cavity searches of pretrial detainees following visits with persons from outside the jail; and the requirement that pretrial detainees remain outside their cell while MCC officials conduct routine searches.

The primary issue in *Wolfish* was whether any of the practices amounted to punishment of the detainee. The standard for determining this was whether the measures were reasonably related to a legitimate, nonpunitive government objective, such as security. The Supreme Court determined that because the practices were related to security, none constituted a violation of the constitutional rights of the pretrial detain-

In Mighigan v. Hite, *Marvin Hite successfully argued that the boot camp program he had completed should count as credit against a term of imprisonment.*

ees. According to the Court, "There must be a 'mutual accommodation between institutional needs and objectives and the provisions of the Constitution that are of general application' " (quoting *Wolff v. McDonnell*, 418 U.S. 539, 94 S. Ct. 2963, 41 L. Ed. 2d 935 [1974]).

In 1984, the High Court revisited *Wolfish*. In *Block v. Rutherford*, 468 U.S. 576, 104 S. Ct. 3227, 82 L. Ed. 2d 438 (1984), the Court held that random searches of cells in the absence of the detainee, random double-bunking, and the prohibition of physical contact between detainees and outside visitors were all constitutionally permissible.

Not all the risks facing incarcerated persons are physical. Fellow inmates may give prosecutors information on crimes in exchange for leniency in SENTENCING or an early release and prosecutors often place undercover agents in jail or prison to obtain information from inmates. Unwitting inmates often regret cultivating new friendships with these persons.

In *Illinois v. Perkins*, 496 U.S. 292, 110 S. Ct. 2394, 110 L. Ed. 2d 243 (1990), Lloyd Perkins, while detained on murder charges, told a fellow inmate of his involvement in a different murder. The fellow inmate was undercover agent John Parisi. Perkins was prosecuted and found guilty of the other murder. He appealed, arguing that he was entitled to *Miranda* warnings before being questioned by law enforcement personnel, and that his statements to Parisi should have been excluded from trial. The U.S. Supreme Court rejected the argument, ruling in part that employing an undercover agent in an incarceration setting does not make a CONFESSION involuntary.

JAILHOUSE LAWYER

Jailhouse lawyers are PRISON inmates with some knowledge of law who give legal advice and assistance to their fellow inmates. The important role that jailhouse lawyers play in the criminal justice system has been recognized by the U.S. Supreme Court, which has held that jailhouse lawyers must be permitted to assist illiterate inmates in filing petitions for postconviction relief unless the state provides some reasonable alternative (*Johnson v. Avery*, 393 U.S. 483, 89 S. Ct. 747, 21 L. Ed. 2d 718 [1969]).

A notable example of a jailhouse lawyer is Jerry Rosenberg, a school dropout who completed the eighth grade. He has been serving a life sentence since 1963 at the Auburn Correctional Facility in upstate New York for the murder of two New York City police officers during a holdup in 1962.

While in prison, Rosenberg has received two separate law degrees from Illinois correspon-

Jerry Rosenberg is one of the country's shrewdest jailhouse lawyers.

dence schools. As a convicted felon, Rosenberg is unable to get a law license, but he can still make use of his legal education. In 1978 the U.S. Supreme Court ordered the release of Rosenberg's fellow inmate, Carmine Galante, upon reviewing a brief filed by Rosenberg on Galante's behalf.

In June 1988, Rosenberg made news as he attempted to secure his own release with an imaginative legal argument. In 1986, Rosenberg had suffered a heart attack during open-heart surgery, and his heart had stopped beating for a short time. A patient's heart frequently stops beating during such surgery, but Rosenberg seized on the fact to argue that since his heart had stopped, he "died" while on the operating table. Therefore, he argued, he had met the requirements of his New York life sentence, and should, perhaps as a new man, be freed immediately.

Acting New York State Supreme Court Justice Peter Corning denied Rosenberg's petition. The justice agreed with New York Assistant Attorney General Kenneth Goldman's argument for the state that death is an irrevocable condition, and therefore Rosenberg has not yet died.

BIOGRAPHY

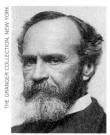

William James

JAMES, WILLIAM

William James was a popular and influential philosopher whose writings and theories influenced various areas of U.S. life, including the movement known as LEGAL REALISM.

James was born in New York City on January 11, 1842, to Henry James, Sr., and Mary Walsh James. Comfortably supported by an inheritance, his parents stressed their children's abilities to make independent choices. James's formal schooling was irregular, and he studied frequently in England, France, Switzerland, and

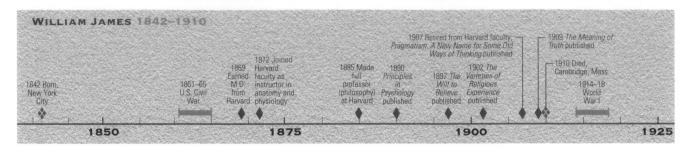

Germany. James pursued an enduring interest in the natural sciences, earning a medical degree from Harvard University in 1869, though he never intended to practice medicine. He joined Harvard's faculty in 1872, teaching anatomy and physiology. He was also interested in psychology and philosophy, seeing these as related fields through his grounding in scientific studies. He began teaching those disciplines at Harvard in 1875 and 1879, respectively. He retired from the Harvard faculty in 1907.

In his first major work, *Principles in Psychology* (1890), James began to articulate a philosophy based on free will and personal experience. In a theory popularized as stream of consciousness, James argued that each person's thought is independent and personal, with the mind free to choose between any number of options. The subjective choices each individual makes are determined by the interconnected string of prior experiences in that person's life. In James's thought, choice and belief are always contingent, with no possibility for some permanent, definitive structure based outside of personal experience.

James's *Pragmatism: A New Name for Some Old Ways of Thinking* (1907) developed further his idea that knowledge, meaning, and truth are essentially the result of each person's understanding of the experiences in her or his life. Mere formalism has no absolute authority; personal experience forms the framework of belief and action for each individual.

These important elements provided the basis for the movement known as legal realism. James's rejection of immutable truths in favor of experience as the mode to interpret reality was picked up by ROSCOE POUND, OLIVER WENDELL HOLMES, JR., and others in the 1920s and 1930s as a challenge to the prevailing belief that legal principles are based on an absolute structure of truth. Legal realists connected law with social and economic realities, both as legislated and as ruled on by courts. They argued that law is a tool for achieving social and policy goals, rather than the implementation of absolute truth, whether or not it is consciously treated

"ALL THE HIGHER, MORE PENETRATING IDEALS ARE REVOLUTIONARY. THEY PRESENT THEMSELVES FAR LESS IN THE GUISE OF EFFECTS OF PAST EXPERIENCE THAN IN THAT OF PROBABLE CAUSES OF FUTURE EXPERIENCE."

that way. James's empiricism, based on experience as the root of human action, had a corollary within legal realism's use of social science as an analytical tool within law.

Though legal realism as a movement was considered to be played out by the 1940s, the belief that varied forces influence the actors and changes within the legal system has become more standard than the view that legal principles are immutable truths. James provided the philosophical underpinning for this shift in thinking.

See also JURISPRUDENCE.

JAPANESE AMERICAN EVACUATION CASES

From 1942 to 1944, the U.S. Army evacuated Japanese Americans living on the West Coast from their homes and transferred them to makeshift detention camps. The Army insisted that it was a "military necessity" to evacuate both CITIZENS and noncitizens of Japanese ancestry, and its actions were supported by President FRANKLIN D. ROOSEVELT and the U.S. Congress. Those who were evacuated suffered tremendous losses, being forced to sell their homes and belongings on very short notice and to live in crowded and unsanitary conditions. A few Japanese Americans challenged the constitutionality of the evacuation orders, but the Supreme Court eventually ruled against them. In the years since the end of World War II, the U.S. government has acknowledged the injustice suffered by the Japanese American evacuees, and it has made several efforts to redress their losses.

History After Japan bombed Pearl Harbor on December 7, 1941, persons of Japanese descent living in the western United States became a target for widespread suspicion, fear, and hostility. Several forces contributed to this sense of anger and paranoia. First, the devastating success of the Pearl Harbor attack led many to question how the U.S. military could have been caught so unprepared. A report commissioned by President Roosevelt directly blamed the Army and Navy commanders in Hawaii for their lack of preparedness, but it also claimed that a Japanese ESPIONAGE network in Hawaii had sent "information to the Japanese Empire respecting the military and naval establishments" on the island. This espionage ring, the report asserted, included both Japanese consular officials and "persons having no open relations with the Japanese foreign service" (88 *Cong. Rec.* pt. 8, at A261). This accusation against Japanese Hawaiians, though never proved, inflamed the mainland press and contributed to what quickly became an intense campaign to evacuate Japanese Americans from the West Coast.

A second cause for the hostility directed at Japanese Americans was the widespread belief after Pearl Harbor that Japan would soon try to invade the West Coast of the United States. Much of the Pacific fleet had been destroyed by the Pearl Harbor attack, and the Japanese had gone on to achieve a series of military victories in the Pacific. A West Coast invasion seemed imminent to many, and statements by government officials and newspaper editors stoked fears about the loyalty of Japanese Americans and their possible involvement in espionage activities. On January 28, 1942, for example, an editorial in the *Los Angeles Times* argued that "the rigors of war demand proper detention of Japanese and their immediate removal from the most acute danger spots" on the West Coast. Syndicated columnist Henry McLemore was less restrained in his assessment, which appeared in the *San Francisco Examiner* on January 29: "I am for immediate removal of every Japanese . . . to a point deep in the interior. I don't mean a nice part of the interior either . . . Let 'em be pinched, hurt, hungry and dead up against it. . . . Personally I hate the Japanese."

On February 14, 1942, Lieutenant General John L. De Witt, commanding general of the Western Defense Command, issued a final recommendation to the secretary of war arguing that it was a military necessity to evacuate "Japanese and other subversive persons from the Pacific Coast." The recommendation contained a brief analysis of the situation, which read, in part, as follows:

> In the war which we are now engaged, racial affinities are not severed by migration. The Japanese race is an enemy race and while many second and third generation Japanese born on United States soil, possessed of United States citizenship, have become "Americanized," the racial strains are undiluted. . . . It, therefore, follows that along the vital Pacific Coast over 112,000 potential enemies of Japanese extraction are at large today. There are indications that the very fact that no sabotage has taken place to date is a disturbing and confirming indication that such action will be taken. (War Department 1942, 34)

Many other leading politicians and government officials shared De Witt's views. The California congressional delegation, for example, wrote to

In February 1942 President Franklin Roosevelt signed an executive order that authorized the designation of military zones from which people could be excluded. More than one hundred thousand Japanese Americans were evacuated to detention camps.

President Roosevelt urging the removal of the entire Japanese population from the coastal states. California state attorney general EARL WARREN, who would later become governor of California and chief justice of the Supreme Court, strongly advocated the evacuation of the Japanese, arguing before a congressional committee that to believe that the lack of SABOTAGE activity among Japanese Americans proved their loyalty was foolish.

De Witt's report, combined with pressure from other military leaders and political groups, led President Roosevelt on February 19, 1942, to sign Executive Order No. 9066, which gave the War Department the authority to designate military zones "from which any or all persons may be excluded." Despite warnings from the U.S. attorney general, FRANCIS BIDDLE, that the forced removal of U.S. citizens was unconstitutional, Roosevelt signed 9066 with the clear intent of removing both citizens and noncitizens of Japanese descent. The order theoreti-

cally also affected German and Italian nationals, who greatly outnumbered Japanese people living in the designated areas. However, Germans and Italians who were considered suspect were given individual hearings and very few were interned. The Japanese, on the other hand, were treated not as individuals but as the "enemy race" that De Witt had labeled them in his evacuation recommendation. Congress hurriedly sanctioned the president's order when, with little debate and a unanimous voice vote, it passed Public Law No. 503, which incorporated the procedures of 9066, criminalizing the violations of military orders, such as the curfews and evacuation directives outlined in the order.

The signing of 9066 and its passage into law immediately set in motion the steps leading to the removal of Japanese Americans on the West Coast from their homes and communities. On February 25 General De Witt ordered the eviction of the two thousand Japanese living on Terminal Island, in Los Angeles, giving them twenty-four hours to sell their homes and businesses. On March 2 De Witt issued Military Proclamation No. 1, which declared the western half of California, Oregon, and Washington to be military zones with specific zones of exclusion. This order allowed Japanese living there to "voluntarily evacuate" the area. Because the Japanese knew they were not welcome in other parts of the country and because those who had tried to resettle had frequently been the targets of violence, the majority remained where they were.

On March 24 De Witt issued Military Order No. 3, which established a nighttime curfew and a five-mile travel restriction to be imposed only on persons of Japanese ancestry. On the same day, the first civilian exclusion order was issued on Bainbridge Island, in Washington, ordering the Japanese Americans there to leave the island within twenty-four hours. The Japanese began to sense that they would all soon be evicted from the entire West Coast, but because they were subject to the five-mile travel restriction, they were unable to leave the military zones and attempt to resettle elsewhere.

By early April 1942, orders began to be posted in Japanese communities directing all persons of Japanese ancestry, both citizens and resident ALIENS, to report to assembly points. With only a matter of days to prepare for removal, the Japanese were forced to sell their homes, cars, and other possessions, at tremendous losses, to neighbors and others who were eager to take advantage of the situation.

By the beginning of June 1942, all Japanese Americans living in California, Oregon, and

This 1942 map shows the prohibited and restricted zones for Japanese Americans and one of the detention camps, Manzaner, to which Japanese Americans were sent.

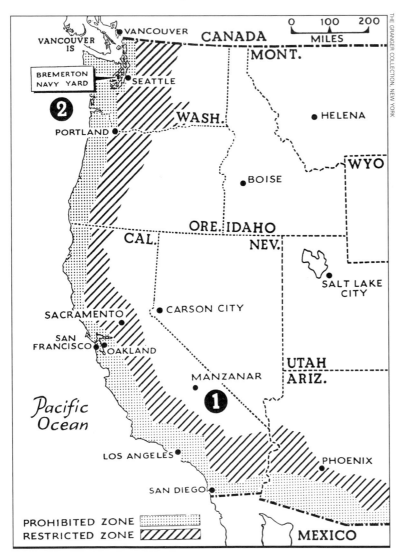

Washington had been evacuated and transported by train or bus to detention camps, which were officially labeled assembly centers. Over 112,000 Japanese Americans were evacuated and detained, approximately 70,000 of them U.S. citizens. Because the detention camps had been hastily arranged, they were largely made up of crude shacks and converted livestock stables located in hot and dry desert areas. Privacy was nonexistent; families were separated by only thin partitions, and toilets had no partitions at all. These bleak, crowded, and unsanitary conditions, combined with inadequate food, led to widespread sickness and a disintegration of family order and unity.

Internees were forced to remain in the detention camps until December 1944, when the War Department finally announced the revocation of the exclusion policy and declared that the camps would be closed. This was two-and-a-half years after the June 2, 1942, Battle of Midway, which had left the Japanese naval fleet virtually destroyed, leading U.S. Naval Intelligence to send reports to Washington dismissing any further threat of a West Coast invasion.

Supreme Court Challenges Though the majority of the Japanese Americans on the West Coast obeyed the harsh curfews, evacuations, and detentions imposed on them in a surprisingly quiet and orderly fashion, over one hundred individuals attempted to challenge the government's orders. Most of these people were convicted in court and lacked the financial resources to appeal. But a few cases reached the Supreme Court, including *Yasui v. United States*, 320 U.S. 115, 63 S. Ct. 1392, 87 L. Ed. 1793 (1943), *Hirabayashi v. United States*, 320 U.S. 81, 63 S. Ct. 1375, 87 L. Ed. 1774 (1943), and *Korematsu v. United States*, 323 U.S. 214, 65 S. Ct. 193, 89 L. Ed. 194 (1944).

Minoru Yasui, an attorney from Portland, Oregon, raised the first legal test of De Witt's curfew orders. A well-educated and very patriotic U.S. citizen of Japanese ancestry, Yasui did not object to the general principle of the curfew order or to a curfew applied only to aliens. His objection was that De Witt's orders applied to all persons of Japanese ancestry, both citizens and noncitizens alike. "That order," Yasui declared, "infringed on my rights as a citizen" (Irons 1983, 84). Determined to become a test case for the constitutionality of De Witt's curfews, Yasui walked into a Portland police station on the evening of March 28, 1942, hours after the curfew was first imposed, and demanded to be arrested for curfew violation.

Yasui was arrested. His case went to trial in June 1942, where he argued that Executive Order No. 9066 was unconstitutional. The judge in the case, James Alger Fee, did not return a verdict until November, when he found Yasui guilty. Fee asserted that Yasui's previous employment as a Japanese consular agent had constituted a FORFEITURE of his U.S. citizenship, and thus he was subject to the curfew order as an enemy alien (*Yasui*, 48 F. Supp. 40 [D. Or. 1942]). Fee sentenced Yasui to the maximum penalty, one year in prison and a fine of $5,000. The Supreme Court unanimously upheld his conviction for curfew violation, though it found that Fee had been incorrect in holding that Yasui had forfeited his U.S. citizenship.

The second test case involved Gordon Kiyoshi Hirabayashi, a twenty-four-year-old student at the University of Washington. A committed Christian and a pacifist, Hirabayashi also decided to make himself a test case for the constitutionality of De Witt's orders, particularly the evacuation order scheduled to take effect on May 16, 1942. He therefore chose to break the curfew three times between May 4 and May 10, and recorded these instances in his diary. On May 16 Hirabayashi went to the Federal Bureau of Investigation office in Seattle, accompanied by his lawyer, and told a special agent there that he had no choice but to reject the evacuation order.

Hirabayashi was convicted of intentionally violating De Witt's evacuation and curfew orders. The Supreme Court ruled on Hirabayashi's case on June 21, 1943, upholding his conviction for violating curfew. The Court avoided ruling on the issue of whether evacuation was constitutional by arguing that since Hirabayashi's sentences on the two counts were to run concurrently, his conviction on the curfew violation was sufficient to sustain the sentence.

The Court did, however, rule on one important constitutional issue in *Hirabayashi*: the question of whether De Witt's curfew orders could be applied selectively on the basis of race. Writing for the majority, Chief Justice HARLAN F. STONE emphasized that it was necessary for the Court to defer to the military in security matters, and thus the Court was bound to accept the assertion that "military necessity" required Japanese Americans to be selectively subject to the curfew order. Stone argued that the government needed only a minimum rational basis for applying laws on a racial basis, declaring that "the nature and extent of the racial attachments of our Japanese inhabitants to the Japanese enemy were . . . matters of grave concern." Citing undocumented allegations

Japanese American Internment Camps

■ Internment camp locations

about the involvement of Japanese Americans in espionage activities, Stone concluded that the "facts and circumstances" showed "that one racial group more than another" constituted "a greater source of danger" to the Army's wartime efforts and thus the military was justified in applying its orders solely on the basis of race.

The third test case involved Fred Toyosaburo Korematsu, a twenty-three-year-old welder living in San Leandro, California. Korematsu had no intention of becoming a test case for the constitutionality of De Witt's orders. He simply neglected to report for evacuation because he wanted to remain with his Caucasian fiancée and because he believed that he would not be recognized as a Japanese American. He was soon arrested by the local police, and was convicted of remaining in a military area contrary to De Witt's exclusion orders.

When Korematsu's case reached the Supreme Court in December 1944, the Court was forced to rule on the constitutionality of evacuation and internment, something it had avoided doing in *Hirabayashi* by focusing only on the curfew conviction. In a 6–3 decision, the Court upheld Korematsu's conviction, arguing that the "Hirabayashi conviction and this one thus rest on the . . . same basic executive and military orders, all of which orders were aimed at the twin dangers of espionage and sabotage." Noting that being excluded from one's home was a "far greater deprivation" than being subjected to a curfew, Justice Hugo L. Black wrote in the majority opinion that "we are unable to conclude that it was beyond the war power of Congress and the Executive to exclude those of Japanese ancestry from the West Coast area at the time they did." Black based his argument on the minimum rationality test established in *Hirabayashi* and on the military's assertion that Japanese Americans had to be evacuated en masse because it "was impossible to bring about an immediate segregation of the disloyal from the loyal."

The Movement to Redress Victims

Though the move to evacuate and detain Japanese Americans on the West Coast enjoyed substantial support from most U.S. citizens, it incited significant protests as well. Some critics, such as Eugene V. Rostow, professor and later dean of the Yale Law School, contended that the evacuation program was a drastic blow to civil liberties and that it was in direct contradiction to the constitutional principle that punishment should be inflicted only for individual behavior, not for membership in a particular demographic group. Others, such as Lieutenant Commander Kenneth D. Ringle, of the Office of Naval Intelligence, questioned the validity of De Witt's assertions concerning the disloyalty of Japanese Americans.

In a memorandum written in February 1942 that became known as the Ringle Report, Ringle estimated that the highest number of Japanese Americans "who would act as saboteurs or agents" of Japan was less than three percent of the total, or about 3500 in the United States; the most dangerous of these, he said, were already in custodial detention or were well known to the Naval Intelligence service or the FBI. In his summary Ringle concluded that the "Japanese Problem" had been distorted largely because of the physical characteristics of the people and should be handled based on the individual, regardless of citizenship, and not on race.

The Ringle Report was known to De Witt, who thus knew that Naval Intelligence estimated that at least 90 percent of the Army's evacuation of Japanese Americans was unnecessary. In addition, the Department of Justice knew of the Ringle Report's conclusions when it filed its briefs in the *Hirabayashi* and *Korematsu* cases. A senior Justice Department official, Edward Ennis, had sent a memo to Solicitor General Charles Fahy warning, "I think we should consider very carefully whether we do not have a [legal] duty to advise the Court of the existence of the Ringle memorandum . . . It occurs to me that any other course of conduct might approximate the suppression of evidence." But Fahy chose not to mention the Ringle Report in the government's brief, instead asserting that Japanese Americans as an entire class had to be evacuated because "the identities of the potentially disloyal were not readily discoverable," and it would be "virtually impossible" to determine loyalty on the basis of individualized hearings (205).

After the end of the war, some Japanese Americans began to seek financial redress for the losses they had suffered as a result of the government's evacuation program. In 1948 Congress passed the American Japanese Evacuation Claims Act (Pub. L. No. 80-886, ch. 814, 62 Stat. 1231 [codified as amended at 50 U.S.C.A. app. § 1981 (1982)]) to compensate evacuees for property damage. The Justice Department received more than 26,500 claims, and the federal government ultimately paid out approximately $37 million. Because the act required elaborate proof of property losses, the amount paid out was much less than full compensation for losses sustained.

By the 1970s and 1980s, the movement to achieve redress had won additional victories. In 1976 President GERALD R. FORD formally revoked Executive Order No. 9066 and proclaimed, "We know now what we should have known then—not only was [the] evacuation wrong, but Japanese Americans were and are loyal Americans" (Proclamation No. 4417, 3 C.F.R. 8, 9 [1977]). In 1980 Congress established the Commission on Wartime Relocation and Internment of Civilians, whose report, released in 1983, concluded that 9066 was not justified by military necessity and that the policies of detention and exclusion were the result of racial prejudice, war hysteria, and a failure of political leadership. The commission recommended several types of redress. In 1988 Congress passed the Civil Liberties Act of 1988 (50 U.S.C.A. app. § 1989 [1988]), which provided for a national apology and $20,000 to each victim to compensate for losses suffered as a result of the evacuation program.

A final major development in the redress movement has been the use of CORAM NOBIS, the common-law WRIT of error, to reopen the *Korematsu*, *Yasui*, and *Hirabayashi* convictions. A writ of *coram nobis* allows one who has served time for a criminal conviction to petition the court for a vacation of that conviction. Vacations are granted if there is evidence of prosecutorial impropriety or if there are special circumstances or errors that resulted in a miscarriage of justice. In 1983 U.S. district court judge Marilyn Hall Patel granted a vacation in the *Korematsu* case. Patel based her decision on the newly discovered evidence that "the Government knowingly withheld information from the Courts when they were considering the critical question of military necessity in this case" (*Korematsu*, 584 F. Supp. 1406 [N.D. Cal. 1984]). Yasui's and Hirabayashi's convictions were also vacated on this basis (*Yasui*, No. 83-151 [D. Or. Jan. 26, 1984]; *Hirabayashi*, 828 F.2d 591 [9th Cir. 1987]).

See also KOREMATSU V. UNITED STATES.

JAWORSKI, LEON Leon Jaworski, like RICHARD M. NIXON, came from a poor, deeply religious background. In the WATERGATE scandal, Jaworski's rise to national prominence almost seemed to parallel Nixon's descent. Watergate is the name given to the scandal that began with the bungled burglary in June 1972 of the Democratic National Committee's headquarters in the Watergate apartment complex in Washington, D.C., by seven employees of the Committee to Re-Elect the President (CREEP). A lifelong Democrat who twice voted for the Republican Nixon, Jaworski was responsible for bringing to light many damaging facts of the Watergate break-in and subse-

BIOGRAPHY

APWIDE WORLD PHOTOS

Leon Jaworski

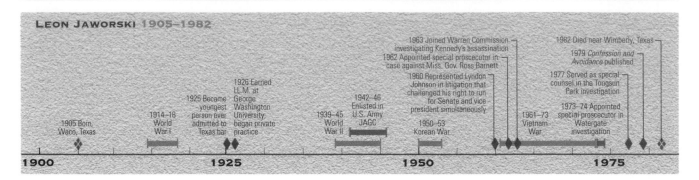

LEON JAWORSKI 1905–1982

1963 Joined Warren Commission investigating Kennedy's assassination
1962 Appointed special prosecutor in case against Miss. Gov. Ross Barnett
1960 Represented Lyndon Johnson in litigation that challenged his right to run for Senate and vice president simultaneously

1982 Died near Wimberly, Texas
1979 *Confession and Avoidance* published
1977 Served as special counsel in the Tongsun Park investigation
1973–74 Appointed special prosecutor in Watergate investigation

1926 Earned LL.M. at George Washington University; began private practice
1925 Became youngest person ever admitted to Texas bar
1914–18 World War I
1905 Born, Waco, Texas

1942–46 Enlisted in U.S. Army JAGC
1939–45 World War II
1950–53 Korean War

1961–73 Vietnam War

1900   1925   1950   1975

quent cover-up, ultimately leading to the only resignation ever by a U.S. president. When Nixon appointed him to the post of SPECIAL PROSECUTOR on the case November 1, 1973, Jaworski expected to find wrongdoing and possible criminal activity by Nixon's aides, but the possibility that the president was involved never occurred to him.

Jaworski was born in Waco, Texas, on September 19, 1905, to an Austrian mother and a Polish father. He was christened Leonidas, after a king of ancient Sparta who courageously gave his life for his beliefs. Jaworski's father, an evangelical minister, instilled in him from an early age a deep and abiding Christian faith and sense of duty. By the time he was fourteen, he was the champion debater at Waco High School. He graduated at age sixteen and enrolled in Baylor University. After one year of undergraduate work, he was admitted to the law school. He graduated at the top of his class in 1925, and became the youngest person ever admitted to the Texas bar.

In 1926 Jaworski obtained a master of laws degree from George Washington University, in Washington, D.C., and then returned to Waco to practice. Prohibition was at its height, and Jaworski began his career defending moonshiners and bootleggers. His flair in the courtroom developed early. In one capital murder case, he concealed a stiletto in his pocket. During the trial he whipped it out and tried to hand it to a juror, exhorting the jury to kill the defendant immediately instead of sending him to the electric chair later. In 1931 he joined the Houston firm of Fulbright, Crooker, Freeman, and Bates. The firm, eventually known as Fulbright and Jaworski, grew to be one of the largest in the United States. It was the first in Houston to hire black and Jewish staff.

Jaworski enlisted in the Army in 1942, and was commissioned as a captain in the Judge Advocate General's Corps, the legal branch of the Army. One of the first prosecutors of war crimes in Europe, Jaworski successfully brought action against a German civilian mob that

"ONE OF THE THINGS THAT THE NEXT GENERATION WILL LEARN FROM WATERGATE IS THAT THE PRESIDENT IS SUBJECT TO THE LAWS HE IS SWORN TO ADMINISTER. HIS POWERS ARE NOT ABSOLUTE."

stoned to death six U.S. airmen, and employees of a German sanatorium who participated in the "mercy killing" of over four hundred Poles and Russians. He was also in charge of the war crimes investigation of the Dachau concentration camp, which led to proceedings in which all forty defendants were convicted and thirty-six were sentenced to death.

The Colonel, as he became known after his Army stint, returned to Houston and quickly became enmeshed in representing bankers and big business. LYNDON B. JOHNSON became a client and friend. In 1960 Jaworski handled litigation that challenged Johnson's right to run simultaneously for the Senate and the vice presidency. The case was resolved in Johnson's favor a few days before his inauguration as vice president. In 1962 U.S. attorney general ROBERT F. KENNEDY appointed Jaworski special prosecutor in a CONTEMPT case against Mississippi governor Ross Barnett. The segregationist Barnett had defied a federal order to admit the first black student, JAMES MEREDITH, to the University of Mississippi. It was a volatile time of highly unpopular, court-ordered desegregation in the South, and Jaworski endured some vicious criticism by colleagues, clients, and southerners for prosecuting the case. Following President JOHN F. KENNEDY's assassination in Dallas in 1963, Jaworski worked with the Warren Commission, as the Commission investigated Kennedy's assassination, acting as liaison between Texas agencies and the federal government.

In October 1973 Watergate special prosecutor Archibald Cox was fired in the so-called Saturday Night Massacre when he tried to force Nixon into supplying tapes pursuant to a subpoena. In response to pressure from Cox, Nixon ordered Attorney General Elliot Richardson to fire Cox; Richardson refused because Cox and Congress had received assurances that the special prosecutor would not be fired except for gross improprieties. Richardson resigned rather than fire Cox. Deputy Attorney General William Ruckelshaus also resigned after refusing to fire Cox. Nixon's order was finally carried out by Solicitor General ROBERT BORK. Jaworski accepted Cox's vacated position, on the condition that he would not be dismissed except for extraordinary impropriety and that he would have the right to take the president to court if necessary. His new office was in charge of collecting evidence, presenting it to the Watergate grand juries, and directing the prosecution in any trials resulting from grand jury INDICTMENTS. His job was separate from, although in many respects parallel to, that of the House Judiciary Committee, which was conducting its own investigation.

Jaworski's integrity was never questioned, but his appointment was greeted with suspicion. Some felt he was too much in awe of the presidency to execute the job whatever the consequences. Almost immediately, however, he began showing his mettle. He soon learned of an eighteen-minute gap on a crucial tape that had been subpoenaed but had not yet been turned over to the special prosecutor's office. The White House wangled for a delay in informing federal judge John J. Sirica of the apparent erasure. Jaworski pushed forward, and Sirica ordered that all subpoenaed tapes be turned over within days. Shortly thereafter the tapes were submitted, and Jaworski and his staff listened in disbelief to one from March 21, 1973, in which the president and White House counsel John W. Dean III discussed BLACKMAIL, payment of hush money, and PERJURY in connection with the cover-up of Watergate.

As Jaworski and his staff sifted through evidence and presented it to the GRAND JURY, Jaworski was forced to decide whether a sitting president could be indicted for offenses for which the grand jury had heard evidence. He concluded that the Supreme Court might well find such an action to be unconstitutional, that the nation would suffer great trauma in the interim, and that the IMPEACHMENT inquiry by the House of Representatives was the appropriate forum for determining whether Nixon should be removed from office. Carefully wielding a prosecutor's influence with the grand jury, he convinced the jurors to name Nixon as an unindicted coconspirator. This information was not to be made public until the trial of the grand jury's other indictees. At Jaworski's prompting, and with Judge Sirica's approval, evidence heard by the grand jury regarding Nixon's involvement was forwarded to the House Judiciary Committee and was kept from the public until later.

In the spring of 1974, Jaworski subpoenaed sixty-four more tapes. The White House sought to QUASH the SUBPOENA, and made a desperate attempt to curry public support by releasing edited transcripts of some tapes. The White House claimed that as unsettling as the transcripts were, they contained no evidence of crime, and that they represented all the relevant tapes possessed by the White House. The prosecutors found many important omissions from the transcripts. Moreover, the White House claimed that a key tape from June 23, 1972 (six days after the Watergate break-in) was unaccountably missing. When Judge Sirica ordered the White House to turn over the subpoenaed tapes, it immediately appealed to the District of Columbia Court of Appeals. Jaworski then had to decide whether to attempt to bypass the court of appeals and ask the Supreme Court to review Sirica's order. A special rule permitted such a bypass in cases that required immediate settlement in matters of "imperative public importance." Jaworski's decision would be crucial because it was unclear whether the Supreme Court would bypass the court of appeals, something it had done only twice since the end of World War II. If the Supreme Court refused to accept the case, trials against defendants already indicted would be delayed and momentum in the investigation would be lost. Jaworski decided to seek review in the Supreme Court.

Jaworski's gambit paid off. The Supreme Court agreed to hear the case. On July 24, 1974, it ruled 8–0, with Justice WILLIAM H. REHNQUIST abstaining, that the special prosecutor had the right and the power to sue the president, and that the president must comply with the subpoena. Within days of the ruling, the tapes started trickling in to the special prosecutor's office, including one of a conversation between President Nixon and H. R. Haldeman on June 23, 1972. This tape became known as the smoking gun, because it proved decisively that the president not only knew of the Watergate cover-up but also participated in it, only six days after the break-in. This was contrary to earlier assertions that President Nixon first learned of the cover-up in March 1973.

On July 27, 1974, the House Judiciary Committee passed a first article of impeachment, charging that President Nixon had obstructed justice in attempting to cover up Watergate. Within days the Judiciary Committee passed two more articles of impeachment, charging abuse of presidential powers and defiance of subpoenas. The committee's action, in conjunction with Jaworski's win in the Supreme Court and a concomitant public release of the tapes, finally left Nixon facing almost certain impeachment. On August 9, 1974, he resigned from the presidency.

Nixon's resignation did not end the matter for the special prosecutor. Most of Jaworski's staff pushed hard for an indictment of the former president. Public sentiment seemed to favor indictment. Jaworski studied the issue, but he considered the problem of getting the president a fair trial to be paramount and almost insurmountable.

On September 9, 1974, President GERALD R. FORD pardoned Nixon of all possible federal crimes he may have committed while serving as president. The special prosecutor's office then examined whether the PARDON could be attacked in court, on the ground that it preceded any indictment or conviction. Jaworski concluded that Ford was acting within his constitutional powers in granting the pardon. He declined to precipitate a court challenge by indicting Nixon after the pardon, as some called for him to do.

Jaworski resigned as special prosecutor on October 25, 1974. Watergate prosecutions continued for some time thereafter under a new special prosecutor.

In 1977 Jaworski reluctantly agreed to serve as special counsel to the House Ethics Committee's investigation to determine whether members of the House had indirectly or directly accepted anything of value from the government of the Republic of Korea. The investigation, known as Koreagate or the Tongsun Park investigation, potentially involved hundreds of members of Congress and their families and associates, and charges of BRIBERY and influence peddling sought by way of envelopes stuffed with $100 bills. Tongsun Park was a central figure in the Korean LOBBYING scandal, but exactly who he was remains unclear. U.S.-educated, at times he may have posed as a South Korean ambassador and may have been employed by the Korean CIA or been an agent of the Korean government. He was found trying to enter the United States with a list containing the names of dozens of members of Congress including information regarding contributions.

Jaworski's work was thwarted by difficulties getting key Korean figures to testify under oath, as well as the difficulties inherent when a body investigates itself. Jaworski was disappointed with the fruits of his labor. Only two former members of Congress faced criminal charges, two private citizens were indicted and convicted, and three members of Congress were reprimanded.

Jaworski died of a heart attack at his beloved Circle J Ranch, near Wimberly, Texas, on December 9, 1982, while chopping wood, a favorite pastime. Married for fifty-one years, he had three children and five grandsons.

See also UNITED STATES V. NIXON.

JAY, JOHN John Jay was a politician, statesman, and the first chief justice of the Supreme Court. He was one of the authors of *The Federalist*, a collection of influential papers written with JAMES MADISON and ALEXANDER HAMILTON prior to the ratification of the Constitution.

Jay was born in New York City on December 12, 1745. Unlike most of the colonists in the New World, who were English, Jay traced his ancestry to the French Huguenots, His grandfather, August Jay, immigrated to New York in the late seventeenth century to escape the persecution of non-Catholics under Louis XIV. Jay graduated from King's College, now known as Columbia University, in 1764. He was admitted to the bar in New York City in 1768.

One of Jay's earliest achievements was his participation in the settlement of the boundary line between New York and New Jersey in 1773. During the time preceding the Revolutionary War, Jay actively protested against British treatment of the colonies but did not fully advocate independence until 1776, when the DECLARATION OF INDEPENDENCE was created. Jay then supported independence wholeheartedly. He was a member of the Continental Congress from 1774 to 1779, acting as its president from 1778 to 1779.

In 1776, Jay was a member of the Provincial Congress of New York and was instrumental in the formation of the constitution of that state.

John Jay

ARTIST, C. GREGORY STAPKO, COLLECTION OF THE SUPREME COURT OF THE UNITED STATES.

"A DISTINCTIVE CHARACTER OF THE NATIONAL GOVERNMENT, THE MARK OF ITS LEGITIMACY, IS THAT IT OWES ITS EXISTENCE TO THE ACT OF THE WHOLE PEOPLE WHO CREATED IT."

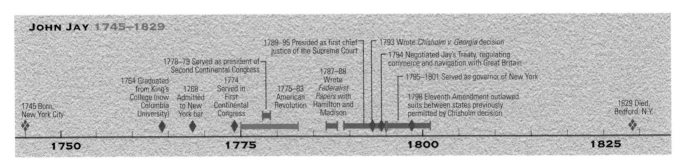

JOHN JAY 1745–1829

1745 Born, New York City

1764 Graduated from King's College (now Columbia University)

1768 Admitted to New York bar

1774 Served in First Continental Congress

1775–83 American Revolution

1778–79 Served as president of Second Continental Congress

1787–88 Wrote *Federalist Papers* with Hamilton and Madison

1789–95 Presided as first chief justice of the Supreme Court

1793 Wrote *Chisholm v. Georgia* decision

1794 Negotiated Jay's Treaty, regulating commerce and navigation with Great Britain

1795–1801 Served as governor of New York

1798 Eleventh Amendment outlawed suits between states previously permitted by Chisholm decision

1829 Died, Bedford, N.Y.

1750   1775   1800   1825

From 1776 to 1778, he performed the duties of New York chief justice.

Jay next embarked on a foreign service career. His first appointment was to the post of minister plenipotentiary to Spain in 1779, where he succeeded in gaining financial assistance for the colonies.

In 1782, Jay joined BENJAMIN FRANKLIN in Paris for a series of peace negotiations with Great Britain. In 1784, Jay became secretary of foreign affairs and performed these duties until 1789. During his term, Jay participated in the arbitration of various international disputes.

Jay recognized the limitations of his powers in foreign service under the existing government of the Articles of Confederation, and this made him a strong supporter of the Constitution. He publicly displayed his views in the five papers he composed for *The Federalist* in 1787 and 1788. Jay argued for ratification of the Constitution and the creation of a strong federal government.

In 1789, Jay earned the distinction of becoming the first chief justice of the United States. During his term, which lasted until 1795, Jay rendered a decision in *Chisholm v. Georgia*, 2 U.S. (2 Dall.) 419, 1 L.Ed. 440 (1793), which subsequently led to the enactment of the ELEVENTH AMENDMENT to the Constitution. This 1793 case involved the ability of inhabitants of one state to sue another state. The Supreme Court recognized this right but, in response, Congress passed the ELEVENTH AMENDMENT denying the right of a state to be prosecuted or sued by a resident of another state in FEDERAL COURT.

During Jay's tenure on the Supreme Court, he was again called upon to act in foreign service. In 1794 he negotiated a treaty with Great Britain known as Jay's Treaty. This agreement regulated commerce and navigation and settled many outstanding disputes between the United States and Great Britain. The treaty, under which disputes were resolved before an international commission, was the origin of modern international arbitration.

In 1795 Jay was elected governor of New York. He served two terms, until 1801, at which time he retired.

He died May 17, 1829.

CROSS-REFERENCES

Constitution of the United States; *Federalist Papers*; New York Constitution of 1777.

J.D. An abbreviation for JURIS DOCTOR, the degree awarded to an individual upon the successful completion of law school.

JEFFERSON, THOMAS Thomas Jefferson served as an American Revolutionary and political theorist and as the third president of the United States. Jefferson, who was a talented architect, writer, and diplomat, played a profound role in shaping U.S. government and politics.

Jefferson was born April 13, 1743, at Shadwell, in Albemarle County, Virginia. His father was a plantation owner and his mother belonged to the Randolph family, whose members were leaders of colonial Virginia society. Jefferson graduated from the College of William and Mary in 1762, and worked as a surveyor before studying law with GEORGE WYTHE. He was admitted to the Virginia bar in 1767.

His interest in colonial politics led to his election to the Virginia House of Burgesses in 1769. In the legislature he became closely aligned with PATRICK HENRY, Richard Henry Lee, and Francis Lightfoot Lee, all of whom espoused the belief that the British Parliament had no control over the American colonies. He helped form the Virginia Committee of Correspondence, which protested legislation imposed on the colonies by Great Britain.

In 1774 Jefferson wrote *A Summary View of the Rights of British America*, a pamphlet that denied the power of Parliament in the colonies and stated that any loyalty to England and the king was to be given by choice. He attended the Second Continental Congress in 1775 and drafted the *Reply to Lord North*, in which Congress rejected the British prime minister's proposal that Parliament would not

BIOGRAPHY

LIBRARY OF CONGRESS

Thomas Jefferson

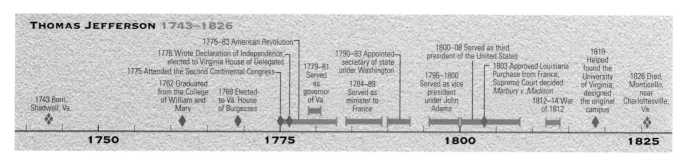

THOMAS JEFFERSON 1743–1826

1775–83 American Revolution
1776 Wrote Declaration of Independence; elected to Virginia House of Delegates
1775 Attended the Second Continental Congress
1762 Graduated from the College of William and Mary
1769 Elected to Va. House of Burgesses
1779–81 Served as governor of Va.
1790–93 Appointed secretary of state under Washington
1784–89 Served as minister to France
1800–08 Served as third president of the United States
1803 Approved Louisiana Purchase from France; Supreme Court decided *Marbury v. Madison*
1796–1800 Served as vice president under John Adams
1812–14 War of 1812
1819 Helped found the University of Virginia; designed the original campus
1826 Died, Monticello, near Charlottesville, Va.
1743 Born, Shadwell, Va.

1750   1775   1800   1825

tax the colonists if they agreed to tax themselves.

After the Revolutionary War began, Jefferson and four others were asked to draft a declaration of independence. Jefferson actually wrote the DECLARATION OF INDEPENDENCE in 1776, which stated the arguments justifying the position of the American Revolutionaries. It also affirmed the natural rights of all people and affirmed the right of the colonists to "dissolve the political bands" with the British government.

Jefferson served in the Virginia House of Delegates from 1776 to 1779 and became governor of Virginia in 1779. He was responsible for many changes in Virginia law, including the abolition of religious persecution and the end to ENTAIL (inheritance of land through a particular line of descent) and PRIMOGENITURE (inheritance only by the eldest son). Jefferson also disestablished the Anglican Church as the state-endorsed religion. Jefferson's term as governor expired in 1781, the same year the British invaded Virginia. He was at first blamed for the state's lack of resistance but later cleared after an official investigation.

From 1783 to 1784, he was a member of the Continental Congress, where he contributed a monetary program, and secured approval of the Treaty of Paris, which ended the Revolutionary War. As a member of that congress he also drafted a decree for a system of government for the Northwest Territory, which lay west of the Appalachian Mountains. This decree was later incorporated into the NORTHWEST ORDINANCE of 1787.

Jefferson served as minister to France from 1784 to 1789. In 1790 he reentered politics as secretary of state in the cabinet of President GEORGE WASHINGTON. Jefferson soon became embroiled in conflict with ALEXANDER HAMILTON, the secretary of the treasury. Jefferson did not share Hamilton's Federalist views, which he believed favored the interests of business and the upper class. Jefferson, a proponent of agricultural interests, disliked the Federalist's desire to expand the power of the federal government.

The chief dispute between them was over the BANK OF THE UNITED STATES, which Hamilton approved of and Jefferson attacked as unconstitutional. Hamilton won the issue, and Jefferson and his supporters began to form a group known as Republicans, which evolved into the current Democratic party. In 1791 editor Philip M. Freneau published Republican views in the *National Gazette*, which increased the agitation between Jefferson and Hamilton. Jefferson resigned his position in 1793.

"THAT GOVERNMENT IS THE STRONGEST OF WHICH EVERY MAN HIMSELF FEELS A PART."

After JOHN ADAMS was elected president in 1796, Jefferson served as his vice president and presiding officer in the Senate. In 1798 he opposed Congress's adoption of the Alien and Sedition Acts (1 Stat. 570, 596), which provided for the DEPORTATION or imprisonment of any citizen or ALIEN judged dangerous to the U.S. government. As a result Jefferson and JAMES MADISON drafted the KENTUCKY RESOLUTIONS, which denounced the constitutionality of these acts. These resolutions, which were adopted by the Kentucky and Virginia legislatures, declared that the federal government could not extend its powers over the states unless the Constitution expressly granted authority. The resolutions were the first affirmation of STATES' RIGHTS and were central to Jefferson's belief that state and local governments were the most democratic political institutions.

The presidential election in 1800 ended in a tie between Jefferson and AARON BURR. The House of Representatives decided the election. Hamilton, who despised Burr even more than Jefferson, lobbied the Federalists in the House to elect Jefferson. Jefferson won the election and became the first president to be sworn into office in Washington, D.C.

As president, Jefferson reduced spending and appointed Republicans to assume former Federalist positions. He made a lasting contribution to legislative procedure when he composed in 1801 *A Manual of Parliamentary Practice*, which is still used today. He approved the Louisiana Purchase from France in 1803, and supported the Lewis and Clark Expedition to explore the West from 1803 to 1806. He supported the repeal of the JUDICIARY ACT OF 1801, which would have created federal courts of appeals and would have encouraged appeals from state courts.

Jefferson also expressed concern about the decision in *Marbury v. Madison*, 5 U.S. 137, 2 L. Ed. 60 (1803), which declared that the Supreme Court could review the constitutionality of acts of Congress. The concept of JUDICIAL REVIEW, which is not described in the Constitution, expanded the power of the judiciary. Jefferson and the Republicans worried that Federalist-appointed judges would use judicial review to strike down Republican legislation.

After he was reelected in 1805, Jefferson encountered the problem of attacks on independent U.S. ships by England and France, which were engaged in war. To discourage these attacks, Congress passed the Nonimportation Act of 1806 (2 Stat. 315), forbidding the importation of British goods, and the EMBARGO ACT of 1807 (2 Stat. 451), prohibiting the exportation of U.S. goods to England and France. These measures proved to be detrimental to U.S. commerce.

After the end of his second presidential term, Jefferson retired to his estate, Monticello. He served as president of the American Philosophical Society from 1797 to 1815 and helped found the University of Virginia in 1819.

Jefferson's *Notes on the State of Virginia*, published in 1784 and 1785, remain an important historical resource. Written to a French correspondent, the book contains social, political, and economic reflections that show Jefferson to be a person committed to rational thought. The book also reveals that Jefferson, a slaveholder, believed that African Americans were inferior to whites. Throughout his life Jefferson defended the institution of SLAVERY, casting a cloud over his professed belief in human dignity.

Jefferson died July 4, 1826, at Monticello, near Charlottesville, Virginia.

See also MARBURY V. MADISON; MARSHALL, JOHN.

JEOPARDY 📖 Danger; hazard; peril. In a criminal action, the danger of conviction and punishment confronting the defendant. 📖

A person is in jeopardy when he or she is placed on trial before a court of competent jurisdiction upon an INDICTMENT or INFORMATION sufficient in form and substance to uphold a conviction, and a jury is charged or sworn. Jeopardy attaches after a valid indictment is found and a PETIT JURY is sworn to try the case. See also DOUBLE JEOPARDY.

JETSAM 📖 The casting overboard of goods from a vessel, by its owner, under exigent circumstances in order to provide for the safety of the ship by lightening its cargo load. 📖

JIM CROW LAWS The Jim Crow Laws emerged in southern states after the Civil War. First enacted in the 1880s by lawmakers bitter about their loss to the North and the end of SLAVERY, the statutes separated the races in all walks of life. The resulting legislative barrier to equal rights created a racial caste system that favored whites and repressed blacks, an institutionalized form of inequality that grew in subsequent decades with help from the U.S. Supreme Court. Although the laws came under attack over the next half century, real progress against them did not begin until the Court began dismantling segregation in the 1950s. The remnants of the Jim Crow system were finally abolished in the 1960s through the efforts of the CIVIL RIGHTS MOVEMENT.

The origins of Jim Crow lie in the battered South of the midnineteenth century. The Civil War had ended, but its antagonisms had not; the war of values and political identity continued. Many whites refused to welcome blacks into civic life, believing them inferior and resenting northern demands in the era of Reconstruction, especially the requirement that southern states ratify the THIRTEENTH AMENDMENT, which would abolish slavery. Southern states initially resisted by passing so-called Black Codes, which prohibited former slaves from carrying firearms or joining MILITIAS. More hostility followed when Congress enacted the CIVIL RIGHTS ACT of 1875 (18 Stat. 335), which guaranteed blacks access to public facilities. As the federal government pressed the South to enfranchise blacks, a backlash developed in the form of state regulations that separated whites from blacks in public facilities. The laws were named for a minstrel show character, Jim Crow.

In the late nineteenth century, southern states took comfort from two U.S. Supreme Court decisions. First, in 1883, the Court struck down the Civil Rights Act of 1875 as unconstitutional, in the so-called *Civil Rights* cases, 109 U.S. 3, 3 S. Ct. 18, 27 L. Ed. 835. It ruled that Congress had exceeded its powers under the Reconstruction amendments. This decision encouraged southern states to extend Jim Crow restrictions, as in an 1890 Louisiana statute requiring white and "colored" persons to be furnished "separate but equal" accommodations on railway passenger cars. In fact, that law came under attack in the Court's next significant decision, the 1896 case of *Plessy v. Ferguson*, 163 U.S. 537, 16 S. Ct. 1138, 41 L. Ed. 256. In *Plessy*, the Court upheld the Louisiana law, ruling that establishing separate-but-equal public accommodations and facilities was a reasonable exercise of the POLICE POWER of a state to promote the public good. *Plessy* kept the

Jim Crow Laws separated blacks and whites in public facilities such as cafes and restaurants.

principle of SEPARATE BUT EQUAL alive for the next sixty years.

By the start of World War I, every southern state had passed Jim Crow laws. Becoming entrenched over the next few decades, the laws permeated nearly every part of public life, including railroads, hotels, hospitals, restaurants, neighborhoods, and even cemeteries. Whites had their facilities; blacks had theirs. The white facilities were better built and equipped. In particular, white schools were almost uniformly better in every respect, from buildings to educational materials. States saw to it that their black citizens were essentially powerless to overturn these laws, using POLL TAXES and literacy tests to deny them the right to vote. Jim Crow even extended to the federal government: early in the twentieth century, discriminatory policies were rife throughout federal departments, and not until the Korean War (1950–53) did the armed forces stop segregating black and white units.

Opposition to the policy of Jim Crow came chiefly from African Americans. Early leadership was provided by the Afro-American National League in the 1890s and, after the turn of the century, the influential author and activist W. E. B. DU BOIS. The NATIONAL ASSOCIATION FOR THE ADVANCEMENT OF COLORED PEOPLE (NAACP), established in 1909, became the most powerful force for the repeal of Jim Crow laws during the next half century. The NAACP fought numerous battles in two important arenas: the court of public opinion and the courts of law.

At first, legal progress came slowly. In a series of decisions in the 1940s, the U.S. Supreme Court began dismantling individual Jim Crow laws and practices. The Court ruled that political parties could not exclude voters from primary ELECTIONS on the basis of race (*Smith v. Allwright*, 321 U.S. 649, 64 S. Ct. 757, 88 L. Ed. 987 [1944]). It ruled that black passengers on interstate buses need not follow the segregation laws of the states through which those buses passed (*Morgan v. Virginia*, 328 U.S. 373, 66 S. Ct. 1050, 90 L. Ed. 1317 [1946]). It also held that the judiciary could no longer enforce private agreements—called RESTRICTIVE COVENANTS—that excluded ownership or occupancy of property based on race (*Shelley v. Kraemer*, 334 U.S. 1, 68 S. Ct. 836, 92 L. Ed. 1161 [1948]).

By 1950, legal changes were coming in leaps. The Court decided in favor of black student Heman Marion Sweatt concerning his appeal for entrance to the University of Texas Law School. In *Sweatt v. Painter*, 339 U.S. 629, 70 S. Ct. 848, 94 L. Ed. 1114 (1950), the Court ruled that the educational opportunities offered to white and black law students by the state of Texas were not substantially equal, and that the Equal Protection Clause of the FOURTEENTH AMENDMENT required that Sweatt be admitted to classes with white students at the University of Texas law school. Four years later came the Court's most significant decision affecting Jim Crow: *Brown v. Board of Education*, 347 U.S. 483, 74 S. Ct. 686, 98 L. Ed. 873 (1954). Overturning the precedent that had existed since *Plessy* in 1896, the Court in *Brown* decreed unconstitutional the policy of separate-but-equal educational facilities for blacks and whites.

Brown marked a turning point in the battle against the institution of segregation that Jim Crow laws had created. It was not the death knell, however. Much remained to be done not only to topple legal restrictions but to remove the barriers of prejudice and violence that stood in the way of full integration. The final blows were administered by the civil rights movement, whose BOYCOTTS, sit-ins, and lawsuits continued over the next two decades. By the mid-1960s, the last vestiges of legal segregation were ended by a series of federal laws including the Civil Rights Act of 1964 (42 U.S.C.A. § 2000a et seq.), the Voting Rights Act of 1965 (42 U.S.C.A. § 1971 et seq.), and the Fair Housing Act of 1968 (42 U.S.C.A. § 3601 et seq.).

CROSS-REFERENCES

Brown v. Board of Education of Topeka, Kansas; Civil Rights; *Civil Rights* Cases; Equal Protection; Ku Klux Klan; Ku Klux Klan Act; *Plessy v. Ferguson*; School Desegregation.

J.N.O.V. See JUDGMENT NOTWITHSTANDING THE VERDICT.

JOBBER 📖 A merchant, middle person, or wholesaler who purchases goods from a manufacturer in lots or bulk and resells the goods to a consumer, or to a retailer, who then sells them to a consumer. One who buys and sells on the stock exchange or who deals in stocks, shares, and securities. 📖

In the law of TRADEMARKS and TRADE NAMES, the term *jobber* refers to an intermediary who receives goods from manufacturers and sells them to retailers or consumers. In this context a jobber may acquire a trademark and affix it to the goods, even though the jobber did not manufacture the products.

In the law governing monopolies, jobbers are referred to as wholesalers. This body of law involves price-fixing scenarios, in which, for example, a manufacturer enters into contracts with numerous wholesalers, wherein the latter agree to resell the manufacturer's product at prices set by the manufacturer. ANTITRUST LAWS also concern scenarios where, for example, a PATENT owner who deals through wholesalers restricts the resale of the patented article to a specified territory, thereby limiting rightful competition between wholesalers.

JOHN DOE A fictitious name used for centuries in the law when a specific person is not known by name.

The name *John Doe* can be used in a hypothetical situation for the purpose of argument or illustration. For example, the ACTION of EJECTMENT may be used in some states by a person who has possession of a parcel of land but wishes to clear up some doubt concerning his or her right to hold it. Rather than wait until someone else sues to challenge his or her right to the land, that person may bring an action of ejectment against a fictitious defendant, sometimes called a CASUAL EJECTOR. John Doe has traditionally been used for the name of this nonexistent party, but he has also been named *Goodtitle*.

John Doe may be used for a specific person who is known but cannot be identified by name. The form *Jane Doe* is often used for anonymous females, and Richard ROE is often used when more than one unknown or fictitious person is named in a lawsuit.

The tradition of fictitious names comes from the Romans, who also had names that they commonly used for fictitious parties in lawsuits. The two names most commonly used were Titius and Seius.

JOHNSON, ANDREW Andrew Johnson ascended to the U.S. presidency after the ASSASSINATION of ABRAHAM LINCOLN. He was the seventeenth president and the first to undergo an IMPEACHMENT trial.

Johnson was born December 29, 1808, in Raleigh, North Carolina. Little is known of his early life. His ancestry is usually traced only to the family of his father, Jacob Johnson, who raised his family in Raleigh and served as the

"AMENDMENTS TO THE CONSTITUTION OUGHT NOT BE TOO FREQUENTLY MADE; . . . [IF] CONTINUALLY TINKERED WITH IT WOULD LOSE ALL ITS PRESTIGE AND DIGNITY, AND THE OLD INSTRUMENT WOULD BE LOST SIGHT OF ALTOGETHER IN A SHORT TIME."

BIOGRAPHY

Andrew Johnson

city's constable and sexton, was a porter to the state bank, and was a respected captain in the militia of North Carolina. He was viewed as a hero after saving two men from drowning in a pond outside Raleigh. He died of health complications only a year later, leaving the Johnson family in poverty.

From the age of ten to the age of seventeen, Johnson worked as an apprentice to a Raleigh tailor, J. J. Selby. Shortly after, he settled in Greeneville, Tennessee, where he opened his own tailor shop. Before he reached the age of nineteen, he had met Eliza McCardle, a respected teacher in Greeneville, whom he married on May 17, 1827.

Johnson's wife encouraged his aspirations to become politically active, and Johnson turned his tailor shop into a center for men throughout Greeneville to debate and practice their oratory. In 1828 Johnson was overwhelmingly elected city alderman. Two years later his supporters elected him mayor. From 1835 to 1843, he served in the Tennessee legislature. For the next ten years, he served in the U.S. House of Representatives. He returned to Tennessee in 1853 and was elected governor of the state. When his term expired in 1857, he became a member of the U.S. Senate, where he served until 1862. He was the only southern senator who refused to resign during the Civil War.

Johnson attracted the attention of Union president Lincoln. In 1862 Lincoln appointed the Tennessee congressman to serve as military governor of the state. After Johnson effectively managed the state throughout the Civil War, Lincoln selected him to run for vice president in the 1864 election. The pro-Union ticket of Lincoln and Johnson was victorious.

Lincoln was assassinated on April 14, 1865, and Johnson assumed the duties of president on April 15. He had been left with the daunting task of assimilating the former confederacy of southern states back into the United States. Johnson sought to overlook the secession of the South. He granted many pardons and allowed southern politicians to restore oppressive practices toward former slaves, such as forcing them

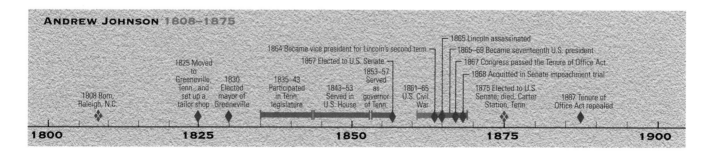

ANDREW JOHNSON 1808–1875

1808 Born, Raleigh, N.C.

1825 Moved to Greeneville, Tenn., and set up a tailor shop

1830 Elected mayor of Greeneville

1835–43 Participated in Tenn. legislature

1843–53 Served in U.S. House

1853–57 Served as governor of Tenn.

1857 Elected to U.S. Senate

1861–65 U.S. Civil War

1864 Became vice president for Lincoln's second term

1865 Lincoln assassinated

1865–69 Became seventeenth U.S. president

1867 Congress passed the Tenure of Office Act

1868 Acquitted in Senate impeachment trial

1875 Elected to U.S. Senate; died, Carter Station, Tenn.

1887 Tenure of Office Act repealed

1800   1825   1850   1875   1900

to give land back to their old masters, and depriving them of the right to vote. A group of congressional Republicans, led by Thaddeus Stevens, a representative from Pennsylvania, opposed Johnson's practices. Against Johnson's wishes, the South was put under military rule. The CIVIL RIGHTS ACT of 1866, passed in spite of Johnson's VETO, granted blacks the right to vote.

In 1867 Congress passed the TENURE OF OFFICE ACT (14 Stat. 430), also over Johnson's veto. This act declared that the president could not, without the Senate's permission, remove from federal office any official whose appointment had been approved by the Senate. In August 1867, Johnson refused to follow the Tenure Act when he requested the removal of Secretary of War EDWIN M. STANTON. He did so on the ground that Stanton had conspired with radical Republicans against the president.

In removing Stanton from his position, Johnson aroused the wrath of even moderate Republicans in Congress. On February 24, 1868, the House passed resolutions to impeach Johnson for high crimes and misdemeanors. By early March, the House had drawn up twelve articles of impeachment against Johnson. Eight of these concerned his alleged violations of the Tenure of Office Act. The ninth alleged a lesser charge, that he had overstepped his boundaries in suborning a U.S. general. The tenth and eleventh articles accused Johnson of defaming Congress in public speeches. A twelfth and final article, dubbed the omnibus article, was intended to induce senators who might have qualms about specific charges against Johnson to find him guilty on general grounds.

Under the Constitution at least two-thirds of the Senate must vote to impeach the president. In Johnson's case this meant that thirty-six senators would have to vote for impeachment. The defense knew that vote would have to come from the Senate's forty-two Republican members—the Senate's ten Democrats and two Johnsonites were bound to support his acquittal. Johnson's lawyers were confident that if

they could appeal to the senses of moderate Republicans—whom the defense presumed were loyal to the restoration of the Union—the impeachment effort would fail.

On May 16 and May 26, 1868, the Senate voted 35–19 against Johnson on three of the articles of impeachment. By only one vote less than the two-thirds majority necessary to remove him, Johnson was acquitted of the most serious charges. The Senate subsequently adjourned its court, and Johnson was allowed to finish his term. His presidency ended in 1869, and he returned to Tennessee.

The people of Tennessee welcomed Johnson home, and elected him to the U.S. Senate in 1875. He died soon after the election, on July 31, 1875, near Carter Station, Tennessee.

Ultimately, the consensus of scholars, historians, and even the Supreme Court was that removing Johnson on the specified charges would have set a dangerous precedent. In 1887 the Tenure of Office Act was repealed. In 1926 the Supreme Court rendered an ex post facto (retroactive) judgment declaring it unconstitutional (272 U.S. 52, 47 S. Ct. 21).

JOHNSON, FRANK MINIS, JR. As a federal judge in Alabama during the tumultuous CIVIL RIGHTS era, Frank Minis Johnson, Jr., earned an outstanding reputation. Serving on the U.S. District Court for the Middle District of Alabama (1955–79) and the U.S. Courts of Appeals for the Fifth and Eleventh Circuits (1979–91), Johnson was a strong, if sometimes cautious, defender of constitutional liberties for all U.S. citizens, regardless of race or social status.

Johnson was one of only a few judges to apply vigorously the U.S. Supreme Court's SCHOOL DESEGREGATION decision in *Brown v. Board of Education*, 347 U.S. 483, 74 S. Ct. 686, 98 L. Ed. 873 (1954). He made history in 1956 when he and another judge overturned a Montgomery, Alabama, ordinance requiring segregation on city buses (*Browder v. Gayle*, 142 F. Supp. 707 [M.D. Ala.]). That decision gave the nascent CIVIL RIGHTS MOVEMENT an encouraging

BIOGRAPHY

AP/WIDE WORLD PHOTOS

Frank Minis Johnson, Jr.

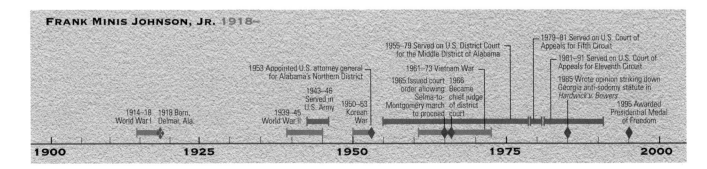

FRANK MINIS JOHNSON, JR. 1918–

1914–18 World War I

1918 Born, Delmar, Ala.

1939–45 World War II

1943–46 Served in U.S. Army

1950–53 Korean War

1953 Appointed U.S. attorney general for Alabama's Northern District

1955–79 Served on U.S. District Court for the Middle District of Alabama

1961–73 Vietnam War

1965 Issued court order allowing Selma-to-Montgomery march to proceed

1966 Became chief judge of district court

1979–81 Served on U.S. Court of Appeals for Fifth Circuit

1981–91 Served on U.S. Court of Appeals for Eleventh Circuit

1985 Wrote opinion striking down Georgia anti-sodomy statute in *Hardwick v. Bowers*

1995 Awarded Presidential Medal of Freedom

1900   1925   1950   1975   2000

victory and helped catapult MARTIN LUTHER KING, JR., who had led a BOYCOTT of Montgomery buses, to the forefront as a civil rights leader. During the 1970s Johnson issued court orders requiring sweeping changes in Alabama's mental health institutions and prisons. Although his judicial decisions brought death threats to himself and his family from whites who opposed INTEGRATION, Johnson remained faithful to his convictions regarding individual rights.

Johnson was born October 30, 1918, in Delmar, a town in northern Alabama's Winston County. The county, in which Johnson spent his youth, was a Republican stronghold in an overwhelmingly Democratic state; in fact, it had attempted to remain neutral during the Civil War. Johnson's father, Frank Minis Johnson, Sr., served as one of the few Republicans in the Alabama state legislature. Johnson studied law at the University of Alabama and graduated in the top of his class in 1943 with a bachelor of laws degree. He gained admission to the Alabama bar the following year.

Johnson distinguished himself during World War II while serving as an officer in the U.S. Army. Wounded in the Normandy Invasion, he received numerous decorations, including the Purple Heart with Oak Leaf Cluster and the Bronze Star. He left the military in 1946 and returned to Alabama. Settling in Jasper, he cofounded a law firm and quickly earned a reputation as an outstanding defense lawyer.

In 1952 Johnson worked as a state manager for the presidential campaign of Republican DWIGHT D. EISENHOWER. After Eisenhower became president the following year, he rewarded Johnson with the post of U.S. attorney for Alabama's Northern District. In 1955 Eisenhower named Johnson to the U.S. District Court for Alabama's Middle District. At age thirty-seven, Johnson was the country's youngest federal judge. He became the court's chief judge in 1966.

In 1956, shortly after taking his seat on the bench, Johnson became involved in a formative event of the civil rights movement. A year earlier an African American woman named ROSA L. PARKS had been arrested for violating a Montgomery ordinance requiring racial segregation on the city's buses. In response the African American community organized a boycott of the Montgomery bus system and nominated King as its leader. In addition, the NATIONAL ASSOCIATION FOR THE ADVANCEMENT OF COLORED PEOPLE challenged the city ordinance in court and eventually appealed the case to the federal district court (*Browder*). Citing the U.S.

Supreme Court's reasoning in *Brown*, Johnson and Judge Richard T. Rives, members of a three-judge panel, ruled that the Montgomery ordinance violated the Due Process and Equal Protection Clauses of the FOURTEENTH AMENDMENT.

The ruling was the first of many by Johnson, either alone or as part of a three-judge panel, that eliminated racial segregation in public accommodations such as parks, libraries, bus stations, and airports during the 1950s and 1960s. In many instances Johnson's decisions were the first of their kind, earning him a national reputation as a staunch defender of civil rights.

Johnson's rulings in support of integration often put him at odds with GEORGE WALLACE, a former law school classmate who served four terms as Alabama's governor (1963–67, 1971–75, 1975–79, and 1983–87). Wallace and the state of Alabama actively opposed the desegregation decrees issued by the FEDERAL COURTS. In response Johnson pioneered the use of INJUNCTIONS (court orders) to force the desegregation of public schools and to monitor compliance with court orders. Wallace and Johnson also clashed in 1965 over King's Selma-to-Montgomery march for civil rights. After Wallace stopped the march, Johnson issued a court order allowing it to proceed. The march was later credited with sparking passage of the Voting Rights Act of 1965 (42 U.S.C.A. § 1971). Because of the sweeping effect of his judicial decisions on Alabama society, Johnson was sometimes called the "real" governor of Alabama.

Soon after the Selma march, Johnson tried a celebrated case involving the murder of VIOLA LIUZZO, a white civil rights worker who had been shot to death while riding in her car with an African American. After an all-white jury acquitted three KU KLUX KLAN members of the murder in state court, a federal case against the men was brought in Johnson's court. Johnson skillfully maneuvered to avoid a deadlocked jury, and the trial resulted in the conviction of the Klan members for violation of the woman's civil rights.

Johnson's rulings on voting rights cleared the way for African Americans to vote on an equal basis with whites. In several decisions during the 1960s, Johnson developed the "freeze" doctrine, by which African Americans were allowed to vote as long as their qualifications matched those of the least qualified white. The doctrine was later incorporated into the Voting Rights Act. In addition, Johnson outlawed the POLL TAX and issued the first court order requiring equitable APPORTIONMENT of leg-

"THE SELMA-TO-MONTGOMERY MARCH . . . DEMONSTRATED SOMETHING ABOUT DEMOCRACY: THAT IT CAN NEVER BE TAKEN FOR GRANTED; [IT] ALSO SHOWED THAT THERE IS A WAY IN THIS SYSTEM TO GAIN HUMAN RIGHTS."

islative seats. Johnson also struck down a state law barring blacks and women from juries, required that court-appointed lawyers be paid, ordered significant changes in Alabama's property tax system, and desegregated the state trooper force.

Johnson's pro–civil rights decisions made him many enemies. Opponents burned crosses on the lawn of his Montgomery home, fire-bombed his mother's house, and sent hate mail by the bagful. Many leading Montgomery residents ostracized Johnson and his family.

After the civil rights era came to an end in the late 1960s, Johnson continued to issue decisions that had a broad and reforming effect on Alabama society. Just as he had done with school desegregation, Johnson used the judicial injunction as an instrument of social reform. He issued injunctions to remedy inhumane conditions in mental hospitals (*Wyatt v. Stickney*, 334 F. Supp. 1341 [M.D. Ala. 1971]) and prisons (*Newman v. Alabama*, 349 F. Supp. 278 [M.D. Ala. 1972]; *Pugh v. Locke*, 406 F. Supp. 318 [M.D. Ala. 1976]). In both of these instances, Johnson established a human rights committee to implement and monitor his orders.

In 1977 President JIMMY CARTER named Johnson director of the Federal Bureau of Investigation, but a heart condition prevented Johnson from taking the job. Surgery improved Johnson's health, and he remained on the federal bench. In 1979 Carter appointed Johnson to the U.S. Court of Appeals for the Fifth Judicial Circuit; in 1981 redistricting made him part of the Eleventh Circuit. In one notable case from his tenure on the Eleventh Circuit court, *Hardwick v. Bowers*, 760 F.2d 1202 (11th Cir. 1985), Johnson wrote an opinion declaring that a Georgia SODOMY statute (Georgia Code. Ann. § 16-6-2 [1984]) violated constitutional rights. The U.S. Supreme Court reversed the decision (*Hardwick*, 478 U.S. 186, 106 S. Ct. 2841, 92 L. Ed. 2d 140 [1986]).

Johnson retired to senior status on the Eleventh Circuit in 1991. He has received many honors and awards, including honorary doctorates of law from Notre Dame, Princeton, Ala-bama, Boston, Yale, Mercer, and the Tuskegee Institute. He has also received the Thurgood Marshall Award. In 1992 the government renamed the federal courthouse in Montgomery the Frank M. Johnson, Jr., Federal Building and U.S. Courthouse. And in 1995 President BILL CLINTON awarded Johnson the Presidential Medal of Freedom, the nation's highest civilian honor. In presenting the award, Clinton noted Johnson's "landmark decisions in the areas of desegregation, voting rights, and civil liberties."

In 1984, Johnson was awarded the Devitt Distinguished Service to Justice Award, which is administered by the American Judicature Society. This award is named for Edward J. Devitt, a former chief U.S. district judge for Minnesota. It acknowledges the dedication and contributions to justice made by all federal judges, by recognizing the specific achievements of one judge who has contributed significantly to the profession.

CROSS-REFERENCES

Brown v. Board of Education of Topeka, Kansas; Gay and Lesbian Rights; Separate but Equal.

BIOGRAPHY

THE GRANGER COLLECTION, NEW YORK

James Weldon Johnson

JOHNSON, JAMES WELDON James Weldon Johnson was a key figure in the NATIONAL ASSOCIATION FOR THE ADVANCEMENT OF COLORED PEOPLE (NAACP) between 1916 and 1930, and helped transform that organization into the leading African American CIVIL RIGHTS advocacy group in the United States. Johnson's efforts as NAACP field secretary greatly increased the number of NAACP branches and members, and his work as executive secretary during the 1920s expanded the association's lobbying, litigation, fund-raising, and publicity campaigns. Johnson was also a highly accomplished writer and played a vital role in the African American literary movement known as the Harlem Renaissance.

Johnson was born June 17, 1871, in Jacksonville, Florida. His parents, James Johnson and Helen Louise Dillette Johnson, encouraged his pursuit of education, and he graduated from Atlanta University in 1894. He then took a job as principal at the Stanton School in Jackson-

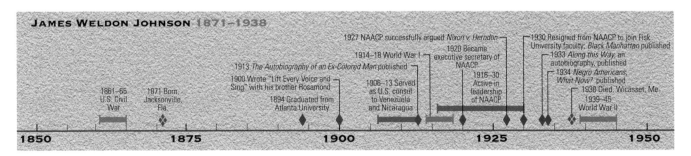

JAMES WELDON JOHNSON 1871–1938

1861–65 U.S. Civil War

1871 Born, Jacksonville, Fla

1894 Graduated from Atlanta University

1900 Wrote "Lift Every Voice and Sing" with his brother Rosamond

1913 *The Autobiography of an Ex-Colored Man* published

1906–13 Served as U.S. consul to Venezuela and Nicaragua

1914–18 World War I

1916–30 Active in leadership of NAACP

1920 Became executive secretary of NAACP

1927 NAACP successfully argued *Nixon v. Herndon*

1930 Resigned from NAACP to join Fisk University faculty; *Black Manhattan* published

1933 *Along this Way*, an autobiography, published

1934 *Negro Americans, What Now?* published

1938 Died, Wiscasset, Me.

1939–45 World War II

1850   1875   1900   1925   1950

ville, where he established a high school program.

He studied law with a white lawyer in his spare time, and in 1898 was admitted to the Florida bar. He also wrote lyrics for songs composed by his brother, J. Rosamond Johnson. In 1900 the two wrote the song "Lift Every Voice and Sing," which later became known as the "Negro National Anthem." The two brothers moved to New York in 1902 and went on to become a highly successful songwriting team.

Johnson became involved in New York politics. In 1904 he became treasurer of the city's Colored Republican Club, helping with the campaign to reelect THEODORE ROOSEVELT to the presidency. On the recommendation of W. E. B. DU BOIS, an African American scholar and civil rights leader, Johnson was named U.S. consul to Puerto Cabello, Venezuela, in 1906. Two years later he was appointed consul to Corinto, Nicaragua. He remained in that position until 1913, when he resigned. Johnson believed that the election of WOODROW WILSON, a Democrat, to the presidency, as well as significant racial prejudice, would interfere with his advancement in the consular service. In 1910 he married Grace Nail. The couple had no children.

Johnson returned to New York and in 1914 became an editorialist and columnist at the *New York Age* newspaper. Two years later he was offered a position as field secretary for the NAACP, which was founded in 1909 to improve the situation of African Americans. In that office Johnson traveled widely and did much to help the NAACP grow from nine thousand members in 1916 to ninety thousand in 1920. Under Johnson's direction the number of branches multiplied rapidly as well. In the South, where NAACP activity had been weak, the number of branches increased from 3 to 131. Johnson also spoke widely on the subject of racial discrimination, and he organized NAACP protests. In 1917 he coordinated a silent march in New York to protest lynching of African Americans and other forms of racial oppression. Throughout his tenure at the NAACP, he remained committed to keeping it an interracial organization, seeking the membership and aid of whites as well as blacks.

By 1920 Johnson had risen to executive secretary of the NAACP, the organization's highest leadership position. Under his guidance the NAACP publicized the continued lynching of African Americans, which the organization estimated had caused the death of three thousand people between 1889 and 1919. Johnson

"THE DWARFING, WARPING, DISTORTING INFLUENCE WHICH OPERATES UPON EACH AND EVERY COLOURED MAN IN THE UNITED STATES . . . FORCES [HIM] TO TAKE HIS OUTLOOK ON ALL THINGS, NOT FROM THE VIEW-POINT OF A CITIZEN, OR MAN, OR EVEN A HUMAN BEING, BUT FROM THE VIEW-POINT OF A COLOURED MAN."

BIOGRAPHY

LIBRARY OF CONGRESS

Lyndon Baines Johnson

directed the NAACP's support of the 1921 Dyer antilynching bill (which did not become law), LABOR UNION movements, and policies to improve living and working conditions for African Americans. In addition, Johnson issued an influential report on the U.S. occupation of Haiti occurring at that time. Furthermore, Johnson was a highly successful fund-raiser.

Johnson's leadership greatly increased the NAACP's influence on U.S. law. He helped expand the organization's campaigns to end laws and practices that segregated African Americans and denied them basic freedoms such as the right to vote. Under Johnson's leadership the NAACP successfully argued *Nixon v. Herndon*, 273 U.S. 536, 47 S. Ct. 446, 71 L. Ed. 759 (1927), before the Supreme Court. The decision held that a whites-only Democratic party primary in Texas was unconstitutional, and marked a significant step toward establishing equal VOTING rights for African Americans.

In 1930 Johnson resigned from the NAACP to become a professor of creative literature and writing at Fisk University, in Nashville. Johnson's writings include *The Autobiography of an Ex-Colored Man* (1913), a novel; three volumes of poetry; *Black Manhattan* (1930), a history of African Americans in New York; *Along This Way* (1933), an autobiography; and *Negro Americans, What Now?* (1934), a treatise on the situation of African Americans. He edited three influential anthologies: *The Book of American Negro Poetry* (1922), *The Book of American Negro Spirituals* (1925), and *The Second Book of American Negro Spirituals* (1926), the last two with his brother.

Johnson received much recognition during his lifetime, including honorary degrees from Atlanta University and Howard University and the NAACP's Spingarn Medal (1925). He was killed in a car accident in Wiscasset, Maine, on June 26, 1938.

JOHNSON, LYNDON BAINES Lyndon Baines Johnson was the thirty-sixth president of the United States, serving from 1963 to 1969. Like three other vice presidents in U.S. history, he assumed the office following the ASSASSINATION of the president. He took office November 22, 1963, after JOHN F. KENNEDY was killed in Dallas. Johnson's administration was marked by landmark changes in CIVIL RIGHTS laws and social WELFARE programs, yet political support for him collapsed because of his escalation of the Vietnam War.

Johnson was born August 27, 1908, near Stonewall, Texas. He was raised in Johnson City, Texas, which was named for his grandfa-

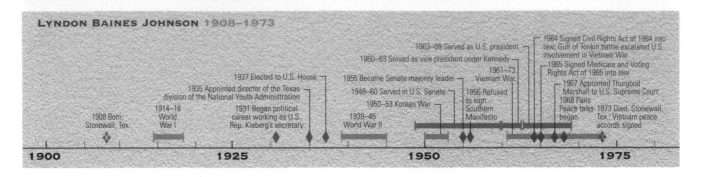

LYNDON BAINES JOHNSON 1908–1973

1964 Signed Civil Rights Act of 1964 into law; Gulf of Tonkin battle escalated U.S. involvement in Vietnam War

1963–69 Served as U.S. president

1960–63 Served as vice president under Kennedy

1965 Signed Medicare and Voting Rights Act of 1965 into law

1937 Elected to U.S. House

1955 Became Senate majority leader

1961–73 Vietnam War

1967 Appointed Thurgood Marshall to U.S. Supreme Court

1935 Appointed director of the Texas division of the National Youth Administration

1948–60 Served in U.S. Senate

1956 Refused to sign Southern Manifesto

1968 Paris Peace talks began

1973 Died, Stonewall, Tex.; Vietnam peace accords signed

1950–53 Korean War

1908 Born, Stonewall, Tex.

1914–18 World War I

1931 Began political career working as U.S. Rep. Kleberg's secretary

1939–45 World War II

1900   1925   1950   1975

ther, who had served in the Texas Legislature. Johnson's father, Sam Ealy Johnson, also served in the Texas Legislature. Johnson graduated from Southwest Texas State Teachers College in 1930 with a teaching degree. He taught high school in Houston, until 1931, when he became involved with Democrat Richard M. Kleberg's campaign for the U.S. House of Representatives. Johnson gave speeches and spoke to voters on Kleberg's behalf. When Kleberg was elected, he asked Johnson to accompany him to Washington, D.C., as his secretary. Johnson agreed, and his political career in Washington, D.C., was launched.

Johnson was not satisfied to be a secretary to a congressman. He began making friends with powerful Democrats, most notably Representative Sam Rayburn, of Texas. Rayburn, who would soon become Speaker of the House, had enormous influence. In 1935, after President FRANKLIN D. ROOSEVELT named him director of the Texas division of the National Youth Administration, Johnson used his connections to put twelve thousand young people to work in public service jobs and to help another eighteen thousand go to college.

He quit this position in 1937 to run in a special election for the U.S. House of Representatives in Texas's Tenth Congressional District. In his campaign he supported Roosevelt's policies, which came under heavy attack by Johnson's opponents. After Johnson was elected, Roosevelt made a point of getting to know him. Soon the two developed a long and lasting friendship.

Johnson remained in the House of Representatives until 1948, though he did spend a brief period in the Navy during World War II. He ran for the U.S. Senate in 1941, and lost to Governor W. Lee O'Daniel by fewer than fourteen hundred votes. He ran again in 1948, this time against Coke R. Stevenson, a former Texas governor. Johnson won the 1948 Democratic primary election by eighty-seven votes, but Stevenson claimed that election fraud had al-

"POVERTY HAS MANY ROOTS, BUT THE TAP ROOT IS IGNORANCE."

lowed Johnson supporters to stuff the ballot box with votes from dead or fictitious persons. A federal district court judge ordered Johnson's name removed from the final election ballot pending an investigation of the fraud charges. Johnson enlisted a group of prominent Washington, D.C., attorneys, led by ABE FORTAS, to overturn the order. The attorneys convinced Justice HUGO L. BLACK, of the U.S. Supreme Court, to reverse the order. With his name back on the ballot, Johnson went on to an easy victory.

Johnson moved quickly to gain power and influence in the Senate. Senator Richard B. Russell, of Georgia, became his mentor in the same way Sam Rayburn had been in the 1930s. In 1951 Johnson became the Democratic whip, which required that he maintain party discipline and encourage the attendance of Democratic senators. Two years later he was elected minority leader, at age forty-four the youngest member ever elected to that position. In 1955, after the Democrats took control of the Senate, he assumed the position of majority leader, the most powerful position in that body.

As majority leader Johnson worked at developing consensus with members from both parties. During this period he became famous for the "LBJ treatment," where he would use clever stratagems and steady persuasion to win reluctant colleagues over to his side. He developed a bipartisan approach with the administration of Republican president DWIGHT D. EISENHOWER and sought common ground. He sustained a setback in 1955 when he suffered a heart attack, but returned to government service later that year.

Johnson wanted to be president, and he knew that opposing civil rights would destroy his chances on a national level. He was one of three Southern senators who refused to sign the Southern Manifesto, a 1956 document that urged the South to resist with all legal methods the Supreme Court's decision outlawing racially segregated schools in *Brown v. Board of Educa-*

tion, 347 U.S. 483, 74 S. Ct. 686, 98 L. Ed. 873 (1954). In 1957 he put through the Senate the first civil rights bill in more than eighty years.

Senator John F. Kennedy, of Massachusetts, won the Democratic presidential nomination in 1960 and named Johnson his vice presidential running mate. Johnson helped Kennedy in the southern states, and Kennedy won a narrow victory over Vice President RICHARD M. NIXON.

As vice president under Kennedy, Johnson performed numerous diplomatic missions and presided over the National Aeronautics and Space Council and the President's Committee on Equal Employment Opportunities. When Kennedy was assassinated in 1963, Johnson took the oath of office in Dallas. In the months that followed, he concentrated on passing the slain president's legislative agenda. He proposed a war-on-poverty program, helped pass a tax cut, and oversaw the enactment of the landmark CIVIL RIGHTS ACT of 1964 (42 U.S.C.A. § 2000a et seq.). This act outlawed racial and other types of discrimination in employment, education, and public accommodations. Civil rights for all persons was one part of Johnson's vision of what he called the Great Society.

Johnson easily defeated conservative Republican senator BARRY M. GOLDWATER in the 1964 presidential election. Under his administration Congress in 1965 enacted the MEDICARE bill (42 U.S.C.A. § 1395 et seq.), which provided free supplementary health care for older persons as part of their SOCIAL SECURITY benefits. Johnson also obtained large increases in federal aid to education; established the Departments of Transportation and of Housing and Urban Development; and proposed the Voting Rights Act of 1965 (42 U.S.C.A. § 1971 et seq.), which ensured protection against racially discriminatory voting practices that had disenfranchised nonwhites. This act changed the South, as it allowed African Americans to register to vote for the first time since Reconstruction. Finally, Johnson appointed to the U.S. Supreme Court THURGOOD MARSHALL, the first African American to sit on the High Court.

International affairs did not go as smoothly for Johnson, especially regarding Vietnam. Kennedy had sent U.S. advisers to help South Vietnam repel what the government characterized as a Communist insurgency that was supported by North Vietnam. Johnson did not wish to abandon the South Vietnamese government, and soon his administration began escalating U.S. involvement. In August 1964 Johnson announced that North Vietnamese

ships had attacked U.S. naval vessels in the Gulf of Tonkin. Johnson asked Congress for the authority to employ any necessary course of action to safeguard U.S. troops. Based on what turned out to be inaccurate information supplied by the Johnson administration, Congress gave the president this authority in its Gulf of Tonkin Resolution (78 Stat. 384).

Following his reelection in 1964, Johnson used this resolution to justify military escalation. In February 1965 he authorized the bombing of North Vietnam. To continue the protection of the South Vietnamese government, Johnson increased the number of U.S. soldiers fighting in South Vietnam from twenty thousand to five hundred thousand during the next three years.

As the war escalated, so did antiwar sentiments, especially among college students, many of whom were subject to military CONSCRIPTION. As casualties mounted, antiwar demonstrations increased and support in Congress decreased. The strategy of escalation did not produce the victory military leaders predicted.

The cost of funding a war ended Johnson's Great Society initiatives. More important, the VIETNAM WAR became the focal point for the nation. Johnson's popularity plummeted, and the nation was torn by conflict over the unpopular war. On March 31, 1968, Johnson announced he would not seek reelection. He spent the remainder of his term attempting to convince the South and North Vietnamese to begin a peace process. By the end of his administration, the Paris peace talks were started, which began a long negotiating process between North and South Vietnam.

Johnson left office in January 1969 and returned to his ranch near Johnson City. There he wrote an account of his years in office, *The Vantage Point: Perspectives of the Presidency* (1971). His health deteriorated. Johnson died of a heart attack at his ranch, on January 22, 1973, less than one week before the signing of the accords that ended the Vietnam War.

JOHNSON, REVERDY　Reverdy Johnson served as U.S. attorney general from 1849 to 1850. Johnson also served in the U.S. Senate and was an influential constitutional lawyer. He represented the defense in *Dred Scott v. Sandford,* 60 (19 How.) U.S. 393, 15 L. Ed. 691 (1857).

Johnson was born May 21, 1796, in Annapolis, Maryland. He graduated from St. John's College, in Annapolis, in 1811 and was admitted to the Maryland bar in 1815. After establishing a law practice in Upper Marlboro,

BIOGRAPHY

LIBRARY OF CONGRESS

Reverdy Johnson

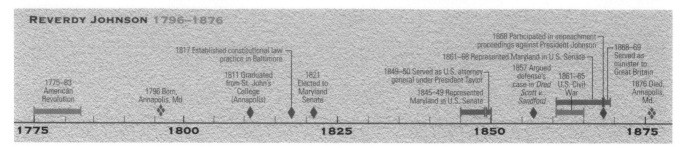

REVERDY JOHNSON 1796–1876

1868 Participated in impeachment proceedings against President Johnson

1868–69 Served as minister to Great Britain

1817 Established constitutional law practice in Baltimore

1861–68 Represented Maryland in U.S. Senate

1811 Graduated from St. John's College (Annapolis)

1821 Elected to Maryland Senate

1849–50 Served as U.S. attorney general under President Taylor

1857 Argued defense's case in *Dred Scott v. Sandford*

1861–65 U.S. Civil War

1775–83 American Revolution

1796 Born, Annapolis, Md.

1845–49 Represented Maryland in U.S. Senate

1876 Died, Annapolis, Md.

1775   1800   1825   1850   1875

Maryland, Johnson relocated to Baltimore in 1817 and opened a new firm that specialized in constitutional law.

After his relocation Johnson became interested in politics and government service. He was deputy attorney general of Maryland before being elected to the Maryland Senate in 1821. In 1845 he was elected to the U.S. Senate, then resigned in 1849 to serve as U.S. attorney general in the administration of President ZACHARY TAYLOR.

Johnson's talents in constitutional law were demonstrated in the *Dred Scott* case. Dred Scott was an African American slave from Missouri who had been transported to Minnesota, then a "free" (non-slaveholding) territory. Scott sued for his freedom, arguing that he was no longer a slave because he had resided in a free territory. Missouri law had established the principle "once free, always free." John F. A. Sandford, who controlled Scott, objected to the trial court's declaration that Scott was free. The Missouri Supreme Court agreed with Sandford and overturned the once-free, always-free doctrine. Scott appealed to the U.S. Supreme Court.

When the case reached the U.S. Supreme Court, Scott's lawyer framed it as a suit for Scott's freedom. Johnson, one of several lawyers representing Sandford, injected into the proceeding several new issues that transformed the case into a debate over the constitutionality of SLAVERY. Johnson argued that Scott had no right to sue in FEDERAL COURT, raising the issue of a black person's claim to be a U.S. CITIZEN. Johnson also attacked the constitutionality of the 1820 MISSOURI COMPROMISE, which gave Congress the power to forbid slavery in the territories. Johnson claimed that slaves were private property protected by the Constitution, and therefore Congress could not abolish slavery in the territories. These arguments transformed the issue from whether Scott could be returned to slavery to whether Scott had ever been free at all.

The Supreme Court adopted most of Johnson's arguments. Chief Justice ROGER B. TANEY's majority opinion concluded that at the

"THE CONSTITUTION . . . ANNOUNCES A GREAT PRINCIPLE OF AMERICAN LIBERTY, . . . THAT AS BETWEEN A MAN AND HIS CONSCIENCE, AS RELATES TO HIS OBLIGATIONS TO GOD, IT IS NOT ONLY TYRANNICAL BUT UNCHRISTIAN TO INTERFERE."

BIOGRAPHY

Thomas Johnson

time of the ratification of the Constitution, there were no African American citizens in the United States. Therefore, the Framers never contemplated that African Americans could be federal citizens. In practical terms Scott's lack of citizenship meant he could not sue in federal court. In addition, the Court ruled that the Missouri Compromise was unconstitutional.

The *Dred Scott* case helped precipitate the secession of southern states and the Civil War, yet Johnson supported the Union during the war. He waged a successful campaign to prevent Maryland from seceding, before returning to the U.S. Senate in 1861.

After the Civil War, Johnson was the lone Democratic member of the U.S. Senate to support the ideas of the Radical Republicans' Reconstruction policy. He was a member of the Reconstruction committee and of a joint congressional committee that looked into these issues.

In 1868, as a member of the Senate Rules Committee, Johnson participated in IMPEACHMENT proceedings against President ANDREW JOHNSON. He was strongly in favor of a verdict of acquittal, which occurred by the slimmest of margins.

Johnson entered the foreign service in 1868 as a minister to Great Britain. In 1869 he returned to his law practice. He spent much of his later years defending southerners charged with disloyalty to the federal government. He successfully argued that the FOURTEENTH AMENDMENT applied only to illegal acts committed by the government, not to acts committed by private citizens, including vigilantes.

Johnson died February 10, 1876, in Annapolis, Maryland.

See also DRED SCOTT V. SANFORD.

JOHNSON, THOMAS Thomas Johnson was the first governor of Maryland. He served in the Maryland House of Delegates in the early 1780s and was chief judge of the Maryland General Court from 1790 to 1791. Johnson was appointed to the U.S. Supreme Court in 1791, where he served a brief and uneventful term before resigning because of poor health.

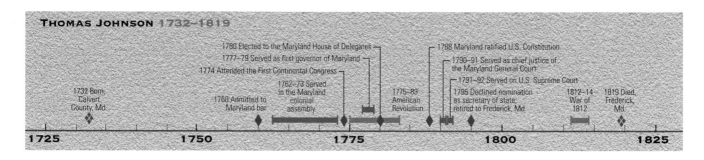

THOMAS JOHNSON 1732–1819

1732 Born, Calvert County, Md.

1760 Admitted to Maryland bar

1762–73 Served in the Maryland colonial assembly

1774 Attended the First Continental Congress

1777–79 Served as first governor of Maryland

1780 Elected to the Maryland House of Delegates

1775–83 American Revolution

1788 Maryland ratified U.S. Constitution

1790–91 Served as chief justice of the Maryland General Court

1791–92 Served on U.S. Supreme Court

1795 Declined nomination as secretary of state; retired to Frederick, Md.

1812–14 War of 1812

1819 Died, Frederick, Md.

1725   1750   1775   1800   1825

Johnson was born November 4, 1732, to Thomas Johnson and Dorcas Sedgwick Johnson, in Calvert County, Maryland. Johnson was one of twelve children, and he received no formal education as a child. His parents sent him to Annapolis, Maryland, to work as a registry clerk at the land office under Thomas Jennings. Following his apprenticeship, Johnson began to study law in the office of Stephen Bordley, an Annapolis attorney. He was admitted to the bar in 1760, and practiced law before entering politics.

In 1766 Johnson married Ann Jennings, the daughter of his former instructor at the Annapolis land office. They were married for twenty-eight years, until Ann died. They had eight children.

From 1762 to 1773, Johnson was a member of the Maryland colonial assembly. In 1765 he became famous for his strong opposition to the STAMP ACT, which was the first tax imposed on the colonists by Great Britain. Johnson was named a delegate to the Maryland convention in 1774, and a Maryland representative to the First Continental Congress, in Philadelphia. He also served on a committee that drafted a petition of grievances to King George III. Johnson formally nominated GEORGE WASHINGTON before the Continental Congress in 1775 for the position of commander in chief of the Continental Army.

Johnson supported the DECLARATION OF INDEPENDENCE, although he was not present in Philadelphia on the day it was signed. He voted for Maryland's independence on July 6, 1776, and contributed to the new state constitution that year. During the American Revolution, he served in the Maryland militia as first brigadier general. In 1777 Johnson led nearly two thousand men from Frederick, Maryland, to General Washington's headquarters in New Jersey. Also in 1777 Johnson was elected the first governor of Maryland, from which position he was able to provide crucial assistance in keeping Washington's army peopled and equipped. Johnson continued to serve as Maryland's governor until 1779, when he declined a fourth

"AMERICA[NS] WISH . . . TO PRESERVE THE CONSTITUTIONAL LIBERTY . . . HANDED DOWN TO US BY OUR ANCESTORS. IF OUR PETITION IS REJECTED BY . . . OUR FRIENDS IN ENGLAND, WILL NOT OUR VERY MODERATE MEN ON THIS SIDE OF THE WATER BE COMPELLED TO OWN THE NECESSITY OF OPPOSING FORCE BY FORCE?"

term. He entered the Maryland House of Delegates in 1780.

Johnson also pursued interests outside of politics. In 1785 he helped organize the state-chartered Potomac Company. This company grew from Johnson's idea to improve navigation along the Potomac River and open a passageway to the West Coast. Johnson began the company with the help of his good friend Washington, who served as president of the company. In the end the enterprise proved unprofitable.

In 1788 Johnson supported ratification of the U.S. Constitution at the Maryland Constitutional Convention. From 1790 to 1791, he served as chief judge of the Maryland General Court. In 1791 President Washington nominated him to the U.S. Supreme Court.

Johnson was hesitant to serve on the Supreme Court because at that time each justice was responsible for riding circuit court duties. Chief Justice JOHN JAY assured Johnson that every effort would be made to relieve the rigors of the CIRCUIT COURT duty, but Johnson was assigned to the Southern Circuit, which included all the territory south of the Potomac. Johnson sought a reassignment. When Jay refused to accommodate that request, Johnson resigned, citing poor health. He had served as an associate justice for just over one year. During his brief and uneventful Supreme Court tenure, he had authored only one opinion.

Johnson continued his public service, becoming a member of the board of commissioners of the federal city, appointed by President Washington to plan a new national capital on the Potomac. That commission voted to name the new city Washington and selected a design submitted by Pierre L'Enfant. Johnson was present in September 1793 when the cornerstone for the new Capitol was laid.

President Washington nominated Johnson to serve as secretary of state in 1795, but Johnson declined. Instead, Johnson retired to Frederick, Maryland, where he died October 26, 1819.

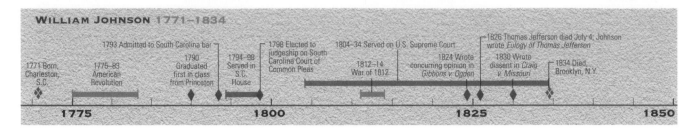

WILLIAM JOHNSON 1771–1834

1771 Born, Charleston, S.C.

1775–83 American Revolution

1790 Graduated first in class from Princeton

1793 Admitted to South Carolina bar

1794–98 Served in S.C. House

1798 Elected to judgeship on South Carolina Court of Common Pleas

1804–34 Served on U.S. Supreme Court

1812–14 War of 1812

1824 Wrote concurring opinion in *Gibbons v. Ogden*

1826 Thomas Jefferson died July 4; Johnson wrote *Eulogy of Thomas Jefferson*

1830 Wrote dissent in *Craig v. Missouri*

1834 Died, Brooklyn, N.Y.

1775   1800   1825   1850

JOHNSON, WILLIAM William Johnson served in the South Carolina House of Representatives from 1794 to 1798 and as speaker of the house in 1798. He was then elected judge of the South Carolina Court of Common Pleas. In 1804 he was appointed to the U.S. Supreme Court. He served on the U.S. Supreme Court until his death in 1834, earning a reputation as a critic of Chief Justice JOHN MARSHALL, a writer of dissenting opinions, and a nationalist with regard to federal-state relations.

Johnson was born December 27, 1771, in Charleston, South Carolina. He was the son of Sarah Nightingale Johnson and of William Johnson, a blacksmith, legislator, and well-known Revolutionary patriot. During the Revolutionary War, when the British captured Charleston, Johnson's father was sent to detention in Florida, and the family was exiled from its home. The Johnsons returned to South Carolina after being reunited months later.

Johnson graduated first in his class from Princeton in 1790. He then returned to Charleston to study law under Charles C. Pinckney, a prominent adviser to President GEORGE WASHINGTON. Johnson was admitted to the bar in 1793.

In 1794 Johnson married Sarah Bennett, sister of Thomas Bennett, a future governor of South Carolina. The couple had eight children, six of whom died in childhood. They also later adopted two refugee children from Santo Domingo.

From 1794 to 1798, Johnson served in South Carolina's house of representatives as a member of THOMAS JEFFERSON's new Republican party. Johnson was speaker of the house in 1798. He was then elected judge of the court of common pleas, the state's highest court.

In 1804 President Jefferson appointed Johnson to the U.S. Supreme Court. During his thirty years of service on the Court, Johnson became known as a critic of Chief Justice John Marshall. Johnson has been called the first great Court dissenter because he established a tradition of dissenting opinions. Among his most noteworthy opinions was his dissent in *Craig v. Missouri*, 29 U.S. (4 Pet.) 410, 7 L. Ed. 903 (1830). In *Craig v. Missouri*, Johnson argued in

BIOGRAPHY

LIBRARY OF CONGRESS

William Johnson

"IN A COUNTRY WHERE LAWS GOVERN, COURTS OF JUSTICE NECESSARILY ARE THE MEDIUM OF ACTION AND REACTION BETWEEN THE GOVERNMENT AND THE GOVERNED."

his dissent that states should be able to issue temporary bills of credit or loans.

In general, Johnson leaned toward the nationalist position in judicial issues involving federal-state relations, as illustrated by his concurring opinion in *Gibbons v. Ogden*, 22 U.S. (9 Wheat.) 1, 6 L. Ed. 23 (1824). *Gibbons* was a landmark decision that held that the COMMERCE CLAUSE gave to Congress, to the exclusion of the states, the power to regulate interstate commerce, which included navigation between the states. In his CIRCUIT COURT duties as well, Johnson steadfastly held that the federal government had the right to control interstate commerce, including the commerce of slaves. This position proved so unpopular in his native state that he was forced to move to Pennsylvania in 1833.

In the first part of his career as a Supreme Court justice, Johnson sought a different appointment. He wrote to President Jefferson that he found the Court to be no "bed of roses." Nevertheless, he remained on the Court until his death.

Johnson's other accomplishments included the publication of *Sketches of the Life and Correspondence of Nathaniel Greene*, in 1822, and *Eulogy of Thomas Jefferson*, in 1826. Johnson also was a founder of the University of South Carolina. He died following surgery in 1834.

See also GIBBONS V. OGDEN.

JOINDER The union in one lawsuit of multiple PARTIES who have the same rights or against whom rights are claimed as coplaintiffs or codefendants. The combination in one lawsuit of two or more CAUSES OF ACTION, or grounds for RELIEF. At COMMON LAW the acceptance by opposing parties that a particular issue is in dispute.

Joinder of Parties For two or more persons to join together as coplaintiffs or codefendants in a lawsuit, they generally must share similar rights or liabilities. At common law a person could not be added as a PLAINTIFF unless that person, jointly with the other plaintiffs, was entitled to the whole recovery. A person could not be added as a DEFENDANT unless that person, jointly with the other defendants, was liable for the entire demand. To be more efficient, reduce costs, and reduce litigation, the modern practice of law does not proceed on the same principles.

Permissive Joinder According to modern law, a person who has no material interest in the subject of the litigation or in the relief demanded is not a proper party and may not be part of the legal ACTION. A proper party is one who may be joined in the action but whose failure to do so does not prevent the court from hearing the case and settling the controversy. A proper party may be added to a lawsuit through a process called permissive joinder.

The statutes that govern permissive joinder generally provide that plaintiffs may unite in one action if they claim a right to relief for injuries arising from the same occurrence or transaction. Likewise, persons may join as defendants in an action if assertions made against them claim a right to relief for DAMAGES emerging from the same transaction or occurrence.

Compulsory Joinder If a court is being asked to decide the rights of a person who is not named as a party to the lawsuit, that party must be joined in the lawsuit or else the court may not hear the case. Such persons are deemed indispensable or necessary parties, and they may be added as parties to the lawsuit through a process termed compulsory joinder. For reasons of EQUITY and convenience, it is often best for the court not to proceed if an INDISPENSABLE PARTY is absent and cannot be joined. In some circumstances, however, a court may still hear a matter if an indispensable party is absent, but its judgment can affect only the interests of the parties before it.

To determine whether a person is an indispensable party, the court must carefully examine the facts of the case, the relief sought, and the nature and extent of the absent person's interest in the controversy raised in the lawsuit. The Federal Rules of Civil Procedure and many state rules give courts flexible guidelines for this determination. These rules provide that the court should look to various pragmatic factors and determine whether it is better to dismiss the action owing to the absence of a party, or to proceed without that party. Specifically, the court should consider whether complete relief could still be accorded the parties who are present, whether the absence of the particular party impairs that party's ability to protect an interest, or whether the absence will leave a party that is present subject to a substantial risk of incurring multiple obligations. If the court decides, based on principles of equity and good conscience, that it is best to dismiss the action rather than hear it without the absent party

joining the lawsuit, then the absent party is an indispensable party and the case is said to be dismissed for nonjoinder. For example, if one party to a CONTRACT asks the court to determine his rights under the contract, and the other party to the contract is absent and cannot be joined, then the court will refuse to hear the case because the other party is indispensable to determining rights under the contract.

Joinder of Action Under certain circumstances a plaintiff may join several causes of action, or claims for relief, in one COMPLAINT, declaration, or petition, even though each could have been the basis for a separate lawsuit. This procedure is not the same as the common one in which a plaintiff relies on more than one theory of RECOVERY or mode of REDRESS to correct a single wrong.

To determine if the plaintiff is joining separate causes of action, as opposed to merely pursuing more than one means of redress, some courts look to whether the plaintiff is seeking to enforce more than one distinct primary right or whether the complaint addresses more than one subject of controversy. Other courts look to whether the claims emanate from a single occurrence or transaction. If the court's inquiry shows that a plaintiff is attempting to join several causes of action into one lawsuit, the court must look to the applicable court rules and statutes to determine if such a joining is permissible.

Modern statutes and rules of practice governing joinder of causes of action vary by JURISDICTION. In general, however, they are liberal and encourage joinder when it promotes efficiency in the justice system. For example, the Federal Rules of Civil Procedure provide that a plaintiff may join in one suit as many claims as she or he has against an opposing party. Some state rules are similarly broad. Many states provide that the court, on its own MOTION or on the motion of a party, may consolidate similarly related cases.

Joinder is not always favored by modern rules of court and statutes. Some statutes will not permit the joinder of causes of action that require different places of trial. Also, the various joinder statutes generally provide that inconsistent causes of action—that is, ones that disprove or defeat each other—cannot be joined in the same lawsuit. For example, a plaintiff may not in a single suit rely on a contract as valid and also treat the same contract as RESCINDED. However, contract and TORT actions may be combined in one suit when they arise out of the same occurrence or transaction and are not inconsistent.

Misjoinder Misjoinder is an objection that may be made when a plaintiff joins separate causes of action that cannot be joined according to the applicable law. Some states require the plaintiff to decide which of the misjoined claims he or she wants to pursue. Other states allow the court to sever the misjoined claims into separate actions.

Joinder of Issue At COMMON LAW joinder of issue occurs when one party pleads that an allegation is true and the opposing party denies it, such that both parties are accepting that the particular issue is in dispute.

See also CIVIL PROCEDURE.

JOINT 📖 United; coupled together in interest; shared between two or more persons; not solitary in interest or action but acting together or in unison. A combined, undivided effort or undertaking involving two or more individuals. Produced by or involving the concurring action of two or more; united in or possessing a common relation, action, or interest. To share common rights, duties, and liabilities. 📖

JOINT AND SEVERAL LIABILITY 📖 A designation of LIABILITY by which members of a group are either individually or mutually responsible to a PARTY in whose favor a JUDGMENT has been awarded. 📖

Joint and several liability is a form of liability that is used in civil cases where two or more people are found liable for DAMAGES. The winning plaintiff in such a case may collect the entire judgment from any one of the parties, or from any and all of the parties in various amounts until the judgment is paid in full. In other words, if any of the defendants do not have enough money or assets to pay an equal share of the award, the other defendants must make up the difference.

Defendants in a civil suit can be held jointly and severally liable only if their concurrent acts brought about the harm to the plaintiff. The acts of the defendants do not have to be simultaneous: they must simply contribute to the same event. For example, assume that an electrician negligently installs an electrical line. Years later, another electrician inspects the line and approves it. When the plaintiff is subsequently injured by a short circuit in the line, the plaintiff may sue both electricians and hold them jointly and severally liable.

Joint and several liability can also arise where a HUSBAND AND WIFE or members of an organization owe the government INCOME TAXES. In such cases, the revenue agency may collect on the debt from any and all of the debtors. In a contractual situation, where two or more persons are responsible for the same PERFORMANCE and DEFAULT on their obligations, a nondefaulting party may hold any and all parties liable for damages resulting from the breach of performance.

A small number of states do not strictly follow the doctrine of joint and several liability. In such JURISDICTIONS, called comparative NEGLIGENCE jurisdictions, liability is prorated according to the percentage of the total damages attributable to each defendant's conduct.

JOINT ESTATE 📖 PROPERTY owned by two or more people at the same time, under the same TITLE, with the same interest, and with the same right of POSSESSION. 📖

Although *joint estate* is sometimes used interchangeably with *joint tenancy*, the two terms are not synonymous. *Joint estate* denotes a broad category of ownership that includes JOINT TENANCY, TENANCY IN COMMON, and TENANCY BY THE ENTIRETY. A more apt synonym for *joint estate* is *concurrent estate*, which depicts the simultaneous ownership of property by more than one person.

Joint Tenancy Joint tenants acquire the same interest in the same property through the same CONVEYANCE, commencing at the same time, and each holds the property under the same individual possession. Each owner possesses the entire property by the appropriate designated fraction as well as by the whole, and has the right to enjoy both the fraction and the whole, but shares that right with all other joint tenants. A joint tenancy is created through a simple and straightforward process—for example, through a DEED or WILL.

The principal difference between joint tenancy and other forms of co-ownership is that upon the death of a joint tenant, the surviving tenants have the right to the sole ownership of the property. This right, known as the RIGHT OF SURVIVORSHIP, exists without regard to the relationship between the tenants. In other words, two people who are not related in any way can be joint tenants, and either will, upon the death of the other, possess all of the deceased's rights of ownership in that parcel of property. The property does not become part of the decedent's ESTATE, and the disposition of the property cannot be changed by will. When one joint tenant dies, the remaining tenants take an increased share of the property, and this process continues until the last survivor owns the entire parcel. That survivor then ceases to be a joint tenant and may do with the property what she wishes, as its sole owner.

Joint tenancy has enjoyed great popularity because it provides a simple mechanism for holding title to property without that title having to pass through PROBATE. The cumbersome nature of certain probate proceedings and the cost and time that they entail provide ample motivation for many people to seek a joint tenancy arrangement. Joint tenancy is often used by a HUSBAND AND WIFE who wish, for example, to have their homestead remain under the sole ownership of the surviving spouse when one dies. The property becomes part of a probated estate only when the second spouse dies.

Four unities are necessary for the establishment of a joint tenancy: time, title, interest, and possession. This means that the interests of the joint owners must come into existence at the same time and by the same conveying document, the interests of all tenants must be identical, and each tenant must have an equal right to enjoy the property. Formerly, if any of these unities did not exist or ceased to exist, a joint tenancy was disallowed or extinguished, and a tenancy in common was created. Today, courts tend not to examine the technical existence of the four unities in considering a joint tenancy case. Where it was the clear intention of the parties to create a joint tenancy and where the requirements have generally been met, most courts will find that a joint tenancy exists.

It is still a well-accepted principle of the unities that if a joint tenant conveys his interest in a property to a third party, the third party becomes a tenant in common, while the remaining tenant continues as a joint tenant but no longer enjoys the right of survivorship. The right of survivorship is lost whether or not the conveyor seeks its loss. Thus, since any joint tenant has the INALIENABLE right to sever the joint tenancy by conveying her property to another party, the existence of a joint tenancy is not a complete protection of the right of survivorship. Other problems may arise owing to the joint tenants' inability to control the distribution of the property through a will. In addition, a federal gift tax may be imposed if the joint tenancy was created primarily from the funds of only one joint tenant.

Many states have tended to favor tenancies in common over joint tenancies because a joint tenant may not clearly understand that the property goes to the surviving tenants. Courts differ on the language required to create a joint tenancy. Where a desire to create a joint tenancy is not clearly expressed, courts will often find in favor of a tenancy in common rather than a joint tenancy.

Tenancy in Common Tenancy in common provides ownership of an undivided interest of the whole but not of the whole itself. It bestows no right of survivorship, and the interest of the tenant in common is freely alienable and will pass to the HEIRS of the tenant upon the tenant's death. When a sole owner dies without having specified the disposition of the property, the heirs will inherit as tenants in common.

Tenancy by the Entirety Tenancy by the entirety is similar to joint tenancy in providing the right of survivorship and requiring the four unities. But it is a more restricted type of joint estate that may exist only between a husband and a wife. Each spouse owns the undivided whole of the property so that upon the death of one spouse, the surviving spouse is entitled to the decedent's full share. Neither spouse can voluntarily dispose of his interest in the property, and the tenancy can be created only by will or by deed.

If a conveyance specified a tenancy by the entirety but the GRANTEES were other than husband and wife, some courts have declared that a joint tenancy resulted, whereas others have found a tenancy in common.

JOINT OPERATING AGREEMENT

Any CONTRACT, AGREEMENT, JOINT VENTURE, or other arrangement entered into by two or more businesses in which the operations and the physical facilities of a failing business are merged, although each business retains its status as a separate entity in terms of profits and individual mission.

The purpose of a joint operating agreement (JOA) is to protect a business from failure, yet prevent monopolization within an industry by allowing each party to retain some form of separate operation. JOAs are used in the newspaper, health care, GAS and oil, and other industries.

JOAs have been questioned as providing a means of avoiding antitrust problems. With *International Shoe Co. v. FTC*, 280 U.S. 291, 50 S. Ct. 89, 74 L. Ed. 431 (1930), the Supreme Court created the "failing-company" defense, by which mergers that would ordinarily violate ANTITRUST LAWS are permitted where one of the businesses faces certain failure if no other action is taken. It was argued that a merger between two competitors, one of which is failing, cannot adversely affect competition because, either way, the failing company will disappear as a competitive entity.

In the newspaper business, JOAs are used so that a failing newspaper can be paired with a parent newspaper and still retain separate editorial and reporting functions. In 1965 the Justice Department questioned the legality of JOAs by issuing charges of antitrust violations to two publishers of daily newspapers operated under a JOA in Tucson, Arizona. In *Citizens Publishing Co. v. United States*, 394 U.S. 131, 89 S. Ct. 927, 22 L. Ed. 2d 148 (1969), even though the newspapers used the failing-company defense, the Supreme Court upheld findings of antitrust violations. Its decision narrowed the scope of the failing-company defense. The Court set three strict conditions for claiming failing-company immunity: (1) the failing company must be about to LIQUIDATE, and the JOA must be its last chance to survive; (2) the acquiring company must be the only available purchaser; and (3) REORGANIZATION prospects in BANKRUPTCY must be dim or nonexistent.

Congress responded to *Citizens Publishing* by passing the Newspaper Preservation Act (NPA) (15 U.S.C.A. § 1802 et seq.) in 1970. The NPA lets newspapers form a JOA if they pass a less strict test. Under the NPA the attorney general may grant limited exemption from antitrust laws by approving a JOA.

In the health care industry, hospitals may form a JOA to provide a stronger financial structure. The JOA, also known in this industry as a virtual merger, allows the hospitals to retain separate BOARDS OF DIRECTORS but turns over management to a separate company. The hospitals coordinate services, construction needs, and the purchase of major equipment, yet maintain some of their own policies. Religious hospitals gain the benefits of a hospital network and still retain their religious affiliation. For example, a Catholic hospital entering into a JOA can maintain its stand against ABORTION and continue its individual programs for treating people who are poor.

Two or more gas and oil operators can enter into a JOA to share the risk and expense of gas and oil exploration. One party is given responsibility for day-to-day operations, often charging back expenses to the other participants in the JOA. The operator is able to keep costs down, and the other participants still retain rights to their share of the gas and oil, which they can use at their own discretion. The parties are seldom considered to be in a PARTNERSHIP unless the agreement specifically states that they are.

In all JOAs the parties retain some aspect of their original organization, whether it is editorial voice, religious affiliation, mission statement, or the ability to use the resources of the business as they choose. All the parties share in the financial risks of the joint operation and gain the potential for an increased market presence and thus increased profits.

See also MERGERS AND ACQUISITIONS; MONOPOLY.

JOINT RESOLUTION   A type of measure that Congress may consider and act upon, the other types being bills, CONCURRENT RESOLUTIONS, and simple resolutions, in addition to treaties in the Senate.

Like a BILL, a joint resolution must be approved, in identical form, by both the House and the Senate, and signed by the president. Like a bill, it has the force of law if approved.

A joint resolution is distinguished from a bill by the circumstances in which it is generally used. Although no rules stipulate whether a proposed law must be drafted as a bill or a joint resolution, certain traditions are generally followed. A joint resolution is often used when Congress needs to pass legislation to solve a limited or temporary problem. For example, it is used as a temporary measure to provide continuing appropriations for government programs when annual appropriations bills have not yet been enacted. This type of joint resolution is called a continuing resolution.

Joint resolutions are also often used to address a single important issue. For example, between 1955 and January 1991, on six occasions Congress passed joint resolutions authorizing or approving presidential requests to use armed forces to defend specific foreign countries, such as Taiwan, or to protect U.S. interests in specific regions, such as the Middle East. Two of these resolutions—the TONKIN GULF RESOLUTION of 1964 (78 Stat. 384) and the Persian Gulf Resolution of 1991 (105 Stat. 3)—were used, in part, to justify U.S. participation in a full-scale war.

Another use of joint resolutions is to propose amendments to the U.S. Constitution. Resolutions proposing CONSTITUTIONAL AMENDMENTS must be approved by two-thirds of both houses. They do not require the president's signature, but instead become law when they are ratified by three-fourths of the states.

Finally, joint resolutions are commonly used to establish commemorative days. Of the ninety-nine joint resolutions that became law in the 103d Congress, for example, eighty-three were items of commemorative legislation.

See also CONGRESS OF THE UNITED STATES.

JOINT STOCK COMPANY   An association engaged in a business for profit with ownership interests represented by shares of STOCK.

A joint stock company is financed with capital invested by the members or stockholders who receive transferable shares, or stock. It is under the control of certain selected managers called DIRECTORS.

A joint stock company is a form of PARTNERSHIP, possessing the element of personal liability where each member remains financially responsible for the acts of the company. It is not a legal entity separate from its stockholders.

Anxious investors look for news about the South Sea Company, a joint stock company that was formed in London, England, in 1711. The company assumed the national debt in exchange for a trading monopoly in the South Seas and Spanish America. South Sea stock was a popular investment until 1720 when fraud caused the company's collapse.

A joint stock company differs from a partnership in that the latter is composed of a few persons brought together by shared confidence. Partners are not free to retire from the firm or to substitute other persons in their place without prior assent of all the partners. A partner's death causes the DISSOLUTION of the firm.

In contrast, a joint stock company consists of a large number of stockholders who are unacquainted with each other. A change in membership or a transfer of stock has no effect on the continued existence of the company and the death of a stockholder does not result in its dissolution. Unlike partners in a partnership, a stockholder in a joint stock company has no AGENCY relationship to the company or any of its members.

A joint stock company is similar to a CORPORATION in that both are characterized by perpetual succession where a member is allowed to freely transfer stock and introduce a stranger in the membership. The transfer has no effect on the continuation of the organization since both a joint stock company and a corporation act through a central management, BOARD OF DIRECTORS, trustees, or governors. Individual stockholders have no authority to act on behalf of the company or its members.

A joint stock company differs from a corporation in certain respects. A corporation exists under a state CHARTER, while a joint stock company is formed by an agreement among the members. The existence of a joint stock company is based upon the right of individuals to contract with each other and, unlike a corporation, does not require a grant of authority from the state before it can organize.

While members of a corporation are generally not held liable for debts of a corporation, the members of a joint stock company are held liable as partners.

In a legal action, a corporation sues and is sued in its corporate name, but a joint stock company sues and defends in the name of a designated officer.

JOINT TENANCY A type of ownership of real or PERSONAL PROPERTY by two or more persons in which each owns an undivided interest in the whole.

In ESTATE law, joint tenancy is a special form of ownership by two or more persons of the same PROPERTY. The individuals, who are called joint tenants, share equal ownership of the property and have the equal, undivided right to keep or dispose of the property. Joint tenancy creates a right of SURVIVORSHIP. This right provides that if any one of the joint tenants dies, the remainder of the property is transferred to the survivors. Descended from COMMON-LAW tradition, joint tenancy is closely related to two other forms of CONCURRENT property ownership: TENANCY IN COMMON, a less restrictive form of ownership that sometimes results when joint tenancies cease to exist, and TENANCY BY THE ENTIRETY, a special form of joint tenancy for married couples.

Joint tenants usually share ownership of land, but the property may instead be money or other items. Four main features mark this type of ownership: (1) The joint tenants own an undivided interest in the property as a whole; each share is equal, and no one joint tenant can ever have a larger share. (2) The estates of the joint tenants are vested (meaning fixed and unalterable by any condition) for exactly the same period of time—in this case, the tenants' lifetime. (3) The joint tenants hold their property under the same TITLE. (4) The joint tenants all enjoy the same rights until one of them dies. Under the right of survivorship, the death of one joint tenant automatically transfers the remainder of the property in equal parts to the survivors. When only one joint tenant is left alive, he or she receives the entire estate.

If the joint tenants mutually agree to sell the property, they must equally divide the proceeds of the sale. Because disagreement over the disposition of property is common, courts sometimes intervene to divide the property equally among the owners. If one joint tenant decides to convey her or his interest in the property to a new owner, the joint tenancy is broken and the new owner has a tenancy in common.

Tenancy in common is a form of concurrent ownership that can be created by DEED, WILL, or OPERATION OF LAW. Several features distinguish it from joint tenancy: A tenant in common may have a larger share of property than the other tenants. The tenant is also free to dispose of his or her share without the restrictive conditions placed on a joint tenancy. Unlike joint tenancy, tenancy in common has no right of survivorship. Thus, no other tenant in common is entitled to receive a share of the property upon a tenant in common's death; instead, the property goes to the deceased's HEIRS.

Tenancy by the entirety is a form of joint tenancy that is available only to a HUSBAND AND WIFE. It can be created only by will or by deed. As a form of joint tenancy that also creates a right of survivorship, it allows the property to pass automatically to the surviving spouse when a spouse dies. In addition, tenancy by the entirety protects a spouse's interest in the property from the other spouse's CREDITORS. It differs from joint tenancy in one major respect: neither party can voluntarily dispose of her or his interest in the property. In the event of DIVORCE, the tenancy by the entirety becomes a tenancy in common, and the right of survivorship is lost.

See also REAL PROPERTY.

JOINT TORTFEASOR 📖 Two or more individuals with JOINT AND SEVERAL LIABILITY in a TORT action for the same injury to the same person or property. 📖

Enova Corporation president and CEO Stephen Baum demonstrates the new Philips Screen Phone, which was developed by Enova Corporation and Philips Home Services in a joint venture.

To be considered joint tortfeasors, the parties must act together in committing the wrong, or their acts, if independent of each other, must unite in causing a single injury. All who actively participate in the commission of a civil wrong are joint tortfeasors. Persons responsible for separate acts of NEGLIGENCE that combine in causing an injury are joint tortfeasors. The plaintiff has the option of suing one or more of the tortfeasors, either individually or as a group.

If the plaintiff is awarded DAMAGES, each joint tortfeasor is responsible for paying a portion of the damages, based on the percentage of the injury caused by his or her negligent act. The defendant who pays more than his or her share of the damages, or who pays more than he or she is at fault for, may bring an action to recover from the other culpable defendants under the principle of CONTRIBUTION.

JOINT VENTURE 📖 An association of two or more individuals or companies engaged in a solitary business enterprise for profit without actual PARTNERSHIP or incorporation; also called a joint adventure. 📖

A joint venture is a contractual business undertaking between two or more parties. It is similar to a business partnership, with one key difference: a partnership generally involves an ongoing, long-term business relationship, whereas a joint venture is based on a single business transaction. Individuals or companies choose to enter joint ventures in order to share strengths, minimize risks, and increase competitive advantages in the marketplace. Joint ventures can be distinct business units (a new business entity may be created for the joint venture) or collaborations between businesses. In a collaboration, for example, a high-technology firm may contract with a manufacturer to bring its idea for a product to market;

the former provides the know-how, the latter the means.

All joint ventures are initiated by the parties' entering a CONTRACT or an agreement that specifies their mutual responsibilities and goals. The contract is crucial for avoiding trouble later; the parties must be specific about the intent of their joint venture as well as aware of its limitations. All joint ventures also involve certain rights and duties. The parties have a mutual right to control the enterprise, a right to share in the profits, and a DUTY to share in any losses incurred. Each joint venturer has a FIDU-CIARY responsibility, owes a standard of care to the other members, and has the duty to act in GOOD FAITH in matters that concern the common interest or the enterprise. A *fiduciary responsibility* is a duty to act for someone else's benefit while subordinating one's personal interests to those of the other person. A joint venture can terminate at a time specified in the contract, upon the accomplishment of its purpose, upon the death of an active member, or if a court decides that serious disagreements between the members make its continuation impractical.

Joint ventures have existed for centuries. In the United States, their use began with the railroads in the late 1800s. Throughout the middle part of the twentieth century they were common in the manufacturing sector. By the late 1980s, joint ventures increasingly appeared in the service industries as businesses looked for new, competitive strategies. This expansion of joint ventures was particularly interesting to regulators and lawmakers.

The chief concern with joint ventures is that they can restrict competition, especially when they are formed by businesses that are otherwise competitors or potential competitors. Another concern is that joint ventures can reduce the entry of others into a given market. Regulators in the Department of Justice and the Federal Trade Commission routinely evaluate joint ventures for violations of ANTITRUST LAW; in addition, injured private parties may bring antitrust suits.

In 1982 Congress amended the SHERMAN ANTI-TRUST ACT of 1890 (15 U.S.C.A. § 6a)—the statutory basis of antitrust law—to ease restrictions on joint ventures that involve exports. At the same time, it passed the Export Trading Company Act (U.S.C.A. § 4013) to grant exporters limited IMMUNITY to antitrust prosecution. Two years later the National Co-operative Research Act of 1984 (Pub. L. No. 98-462) permitted venturers involved in joint research and development to notify the government of their joint venture and thus limit their LIABILITY in the event of prosecution for antitrust violations. This protection against liability was expanded in 1993 to include some joint ventures involving production (Pub. L. No. 103-42).

JONES, ELAINE RUTH A leading African American attorney, Elaine Ruth Jones has devoted her career to the cause of CIVIL RIGHTS. Since 1993 she has served as director-counsel of the Legal Defense and Educational Fund (LDF) of the NATIONAL ASSOCIATION FOR THE ADVANCEMENT OF COLORED PEOPLE (NAACP). Known for her eloquence and tenacity as well as for her creative approach to the cause of civil rights, Jones heads the LDF's eighty-member staff while frequently speaking out on legal, social, and political issues.

When Jones was born on March 2, 1944, in Norfolk, Virginia, opportunities for blacks in her birthplace were limited. Her father was a Pullman porter who had been taught to read by her college-educated mother. Jones, her brother, and her parents felt the sting of being turned away from whites-only facilities. Yet the family believed in success through hard work and especially in education. Jones graduated third in her class from Booker T. Washington High School, in Norfolk, in 1961, and then attended Howard University, from which she graduated cum laude with a political science degree in 1965.

Jones served in the Peace Corps in Turkey between 1965 and 1967. She returned to the United States determined to pursue social change through the law. Particularly inspiring to her was the career of THURGOOD MARSHALL, founder of the LDF and later a Supreme Court justice. In 1970, she became the first black woman to graduate from the University of Virginia Law School. Jones's distinction in law

BIOGRAPHY

Elaine Ruth Jones

NAACP LEGAL DEFENSE AND EDUCATIONAL FUND, INC.

"WE FIND IT EMOTIONAL, WE FIND IT UNCOMFORTABLE, WE FIND IT HARD AS A NATION TO HAVE A CALM, RATIONAL DISCUSSION ABOUT THE IMPACT OF RACE ON INSTITUTIONS IN OUR SOCIETY."

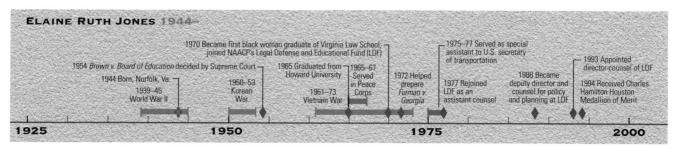

ELAINE RUTH JONES 1944–

1925 ・ 1950 ・ 1975 ・ 2000

1939–45 World War II

1944 Born, Norfolk, Va.

1954 *Brown v. Board of Education* decided by Supreme Court

1950–53 Korean War

1961–73 Vietnam War

1965 Graduated from Howard University

1965–67 Served in Peace Corps

1970 Became first black woman graduate of Virginia Law School; joined NAACP's Legal Defense and Educational Fund (LDF)

1972 Helped prepare *Furman v. Georgia*

1975–77 Served as special assistant to U.S. secretary of transportation

1977 Rejoined LDF as an assistant counsel

1988 Became deputy director and counsel for policy and planning at LDF

1993 Appointed director-counsel of LDF

1994 Received Charles Hamilton Houston Medallion of Merit

school earned her a lucrative offer from the New York–based law firm of Nixon, Mudge, Rose, Guthrie, and Alexander, at that time the firm of President RICHARD M. NIXON. At the last minute, she chose not to accept the offer; she wanted to pursue Marshall's work.

Jones joined the LDF as an attorney. As the NAACP's litigation and public education arm, the LDF provides legal assistance to African Americans, and has brought more cases before the U.S. Supreme Court than any other legal body except the solicitor general's office. Assigned death penalty cases, Jones represented numerous black defendants in state and federal court. Only two years into her career, she worked on the landmark Supreme Court case *Furman v. Georgia*, 408 U.S. 238, 92 S. Ct. 2726, 33 L. Ed. 2d 346 (1972), in which the Court struck down death penalty statutes in thirty-nine states after finding that the death penalty violated the Cruel and Unusual Punishments Clause of the EIGHTH AMENDMENT. The ruling held up hundreds of executions until states could rewrite their laws.

Starting in 1975, Jones spent two years working for the federal government. As a special assistant to the U.S. secretary of transportation, she helped to formulate official policies on a broad range of transportation issues. Among other accomplishments, she helped open the doors of the U.S. Coast Guard to women. But she longed to return to her former job at the LDF. "Once you get started doing civil rights work, it is hard to put it aside and move on to something else," she said. "I believe that is because there is still so much injustice. You see it everywhere and you want to do everything possible to stop it" (Jones 1994).

Jones returned to the LDF in 1977, to work in its Washington, D.C., office as an assistant counsel. She again litigated civil rights cases, but the new position also required her to review government actions and policies and she monitored civil rights enforcement activities of EXECUTIVE BRANCH agencies and legislative initiatives of Congress. In 1988, she became deputy director and counsel for policy and planning, devoting herself to determining new areas in which the LDF could pursue its civil rights agenda.

Both positions gave Jones a political education that broadened her public visibility and her view of the LDF's mission. When an opening for the organization's highest position, director-counsel, appeared in 1993, she was the board of director's obvious choice. "[She] was precisely the kind of person whom Justice Marshall no doubt envisioned to take up the lead-

ership position," commented LDF president Robert H. Preiskel. "Elaine shared a good many of the characteristics that made him such a powerful leader" (Preiskel 1994).

Jones soon began pursuing a broader agenda for the LDF. She identified new civil rights issues such as the dumping of toxic waste in minority communities and the presence of dangerous lead-based paint in buildings in which black families lived. She also used the LDF's public education function to address traditional issues, advocating continued support for AFFIRMATIVE ACTION programs and opposing racial inequity in death penalty cases. She has continued to support the Racial Justice Act (H.R. 3315, 103d Cong., 2d Sess. [1994] §§ 601–611), legislation ultimately dumped from President BILL CLINTON's 1994 crime bill that would prohibit executions that fit a racially discriminatory pattern. In 1994, she received the Washington Bar Association's prestigious Charles Hamilton Houston Medallion of Merit, an award given to leaders who use the law for social change.

See also CAPITAL PUNISHMENT; CRUEL AND UNUSUAL PUNISHMENT.

JONES ACT 📖 Federal legislation enacted in 1920 (46 U.S.C.A. § 688) to provide a remedy to sailors for injuries or death resulting from the NEGLIGENCE of an owner, a master, or a fellow sailor of a vessel. 📖

The federal Jones Act defines the legal rights of seamen who are injured or killed in the course of maritime service. It entitles them, or their survivors, to sue their employer in the event that their fellow workers or shipmasters are negligent (unreasonably careless), and to receive a trial by jury. Prior to the law's passage in 1920, sailors did not enjoy these rights, largely because of antiquated legal concepts and court opinions that tended to protect employers. A milestone in LIABILITY law, the Jones Act was intended to demolish such barriers in recognition of the special risks taken by sailors. Interpreting the law has been a long and difficult challenge for the FEDERAL COURTS, which have exclusive JURISDICTION over Jones Act claims. The crux of the problem is the Jones Act's failure to define the term *seaman*, which courts have generally, but not always, construed to mean "a shipmaster or crew member."

Until the early twentieth century, the rights of sailors were limited. If a sailor was injured through the negligence of another sailor or the master of the ship, the injured party could not hope to win a suit against the employer. Nor could survivors of a sailor who died in the line of service win such a suit. Under general maritime law, sailors were entitled to "maintenance and cure"—a form of contractual compensation that provided a living allowance for food, lodging, and medical expenses. Only when a ship was proved to be unseaworthy could sailors recover damages from their employer.

The U.S. Supreme Court emphasized these limitations in 1903 in *The Osceola*, 189 U.S. 158, 23 S. Ct. 483, 47 L. Ed. 760. In that case the Court ruled that the owner of a ship was not responsible for a sailor's injuries simply because those injuries were caused by the negligent order of the ship's master. The decision had its roots in a COMMON-LAW doctrine known as the FELLOW-SERVANT RULE. This now outdated concept shifted blame partly, and sometimes entirely, from employers to fellow workers. If sued because a worker was injured on the job, employers could avert liability by blaming the accident on the negligence of fellow employees. In *Osceola* the Court based its reasoning on a so-called fellow-seaman doctrine, thus curtailing the legal remedies available to an injured sailor.

Several historical developments motivated Congress to give sailors greater legal rights. The sinking of the *Titanic* in 1912 heightened public awareness of the perils of service at sea, and it was soon followed by concerns about merchant marines at the onset of World War I. In 1915 Congress enacted safety requirements for vessels through the Act to Promote the Welfare of American Seamen in the Merchant Marine of the United States (Act of March 4, 1915, ch. 153, 38 Stat. 1164). This act overruled the Supreme Court's decision in *Osceola*, explicitly stating that the fellow-seaman doctrine could not be used as a defense. But the law had little force. In 1918 the Court ruled that Congress had failed to provide a remedy for negligent acts, and therefore allowed a lower court's dismissal of a sailor's negligence suit to stand (*Chelentis v. Luckenbach Steamship Co.*, 247 U.S. 372, 38 S. Ct. 501, 62 L. Ed. 1171). Federal lawmakers viewed the decision as undermining their will.

Two years later Congress responded by passing the Merchant Marine Act of 1920 (46 App. U.S.C.A. § 861 et seq.), section 33 of which has come to be known as the Jones Act. Lawmakers defined the rights of sailors to sue in explicit language:

Any seaman who shall suffer personal injury in the course of his employment may, at his election, maintain an action for damages at law, with the right of trial by jury. . . . and in case of the death of any seaman as a result of any such personal injury the personal representative of such seaman may maintain an action for damages at law with the right of trial by jury.

Though Congress had eliminated the barriers that the Supreme Court had erected, a key question remained: who qualified as a seaman? In 1927 Congress provided a partial answer through the passage of the Longshoremen's and Harbor Workers Compensation Act (LHCA) (33 U.S.C.A. § 901 et seq.). The LHCA provided workers' compensation benefits to dockhands, who by that time had replaced sailors in the tasks of loading and unloading ships. But the LHCA specifically excluded any crew member of a vessel from its coverage; thus, by extension, sailors were not eligible for the benefits afforded dockworkers.

Because Congress did not see a need in 1920 to define *seaman*, it remained ambiguous who qualified to bring a suit under the Jones Act. Nevertheless, the courts had little trouble deciding until 1940, when the Supreme Court ruled that a crew member was not a seaman if his duties did not pertain to navigation (*South Chicago Coal & Dock Co. v. Bassett*, 309 U.S. 251, 60 S. Ct. 544, 84 L. Ed. 732). Yet, over the next several decades, some courts liberally construed both who constituted a sailor and what constituted a vessel. More confusion followed as a result of the Supreme Court's 1955 decision in *Gianfala v. Texas Co.*, 350 U.S. 879, 76 S. Ct. 141, 100 L. Ed. 775, which reinstated the district court's ruling that the determination of a sailor's status belonged to the jury. The definition of *seaman* came to include workers on dredges and floating oil drilling platforms. Still, no precise test existed, and the result was an explosion of Jones Act litigation. Between 1975 and 1985, nearly one hundred thousand Jones Act suits were filed in southern states.

During the 1980s critics of the Jones Act called for reform. They asked Congress to limit the act's scope, and the Supreme Court to define whom the act covered. Although Congress did not act, the Court returned a partial answer in 1995 in *Chandris, Inc. v. Latsis*, 515 U.S. 347, 115 S. Ct. 2172, 132 L. Ed. 2d 314. The decision established two elements that must be met by a plaintiff in order for the plaintiff to qualify as a sailor: the worker's duties "must contribute to the function of the vessel or to the accomplishment of its mission," and the worker "must have a connection to a vessel in navigation (or an identifiable group of vessels) that is substantial in both its duration and its nature." One key result of the decision was that sailors could now sue under the Jones Act even if their work required going ashore. But scholars did not believe *Chandris* was a conclusive ruling on all matters of interpretation in the law.

See also ADMIRALTY AND MARITIME LAW.

JORDAN, BARBARA C.

Barbara C. Jordan, attorney, legislator, and educator, was the first African American woman from a southern state to win election to the U.S. Congress.

Jordan was born February 21, 1936, in Houston, Texas, the third and youngest daughter of the Reverend Benjamin Jordan and Arlyne Jordan. In 1952 she graduated at the top of her class from Phyllis Wheatley High School and enrolled in Texas Southern University (TSU), an all-black college, where she joined the debate team and traveled to competitions throughout the United States. The team was restricted to blacks-only motels and restaurants in many of the states bordering Texas.

In 1956 Jordan graduated magna cum laude from TSU with a bachelor's degree in history and political science. She enrolled in Boston University, in Massachusetts—one of six women, including two black women, in the law school's first-year class. During her first year of law school, Jordan realized how inadequate her education had been in the all-black schools of Houston. But Jordan was successful at Boston, and upon her graduation in 1959, she returned to Houston and opened a law practice.

Jordan was also drawn to politics. She became involved in the 1960 presidential campaign and went to work for JOHN F. KENNEDY and for fellow Texan LYNDON B. JOHNSON, both Democratic party nominees. In 1962 she made her first unsuccessful bid for a seat in the Texas House of Representatives, running from Harris County. She ran again in 1964, and again was defeated. Jordan decided to make a third attempt at winning public office and in 1966 she was elected to the Texas Senate. She was the first black state senator elected in Texas since 1883.

Shortly after her election, Jordan was invited to the White House by President Johnson to discuss his upcoming CIVIL RIGHTS legislation. In

Barbara C. Jordan

"WHAT PEOPLE WANT IS VERY SIMPLE. THEY WANT AN AMERICA AS GOOD AS ITS PROMISE."

1972 Jordan was elected to the U.S. House of Representatives, becoming the first black woman from a southern state to serve in Congress. She immediately enlisted former president Johnson's assistance in winning an appointment to the House Judiciary Committee, where she gained national recognition for her remarks at the IMPEACHMENT proceedings against President RICHARD NIXON.

Jordan gained additional prominence in July 1976 when she gave a keynote address at the Democratic National Convention. Her speech about the Democratic party and the meaning of democracy in the United States brought her a standing ovation. A movement to put Jordan on the ticket as vice president gained tremendous support but, Jordan held a press conference to announce that she did not wish the position.

Jordan served three terms in the House of Representatives and sponsored landmark legislation to expand the Voting Rights Act, 42 U.S.C.A. § 1973 et seq., to require printing of bilingual ballots, and to toughen enforcement of civil rights laws. She resigned from Congress in 1972 and became a professor at the Lyndon Baines Johnson School of Public Affairs, at the University of Texas at Austin. In 1982 she was appointed to the university's Lyndon B. Johnson Centennial Chair in National Policy, where she taught courses on ethics and national policy issues.

In December 1990, Governor Ann W. Richards, of Texas, appointed Jordan as a special adviser to her administration on ETHICS in government. Richards had made ethics a primary focus of her campaign, and she asked Jordan to author ethics legislation and work with gubernatorial appointees on guidelines for ethical behavior in their public service.

Jordan died in Austin, Texas on January 17, 1996.

CROSS-REFERENCES

Apportionment; *Brown v. Board of Education of Topeka, Kansas*; School Desegregation.

JOURNAL A book or log in which entries are made to record events on a daily basis. A

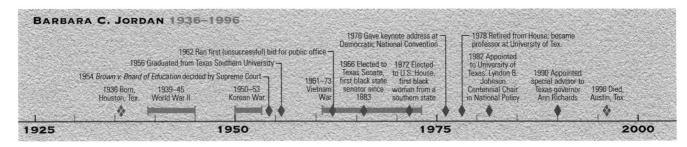

BARBARA C. JORDAN 1936–1996

1954 *Brown v. Board of Education* decided by Supreme Court

1936 Born, Houston, Tex.

1939–45 World War II

1950–53 Korean War

1956 Graduated from Texas Southern University

1961–73 Vietnam War

1962 Ran first (unsuccessful) bid for public office

1966 Elected to Texas Senate, first black state senator since 1883

1972 Elected to U.S. House, first black woman from a southern state

1976 Gave keynote address at Democratic National Convention

1978 Retired from House, became professor at University of Tex.

1982 Appointed to University of Texas' Lyndon B. Johnson Centennial Chair in National Policy

1990 Appointed special advisor to Texas governor Ann Richards

1996 Died, Austin, Tex.

1925   1950   1975   2000

book where transactions or events are recorded as they occur.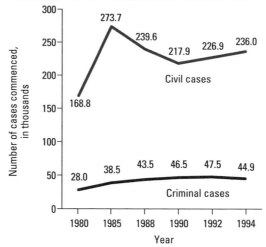

A legislative journal is kept by the clerk and is a daily record of the legislative proceedings. Typical entries include actions taken by various committees and a chronological accounting of bills introduced on the floor.

J.P. ◫ An abbreviation for JUSTICE OF THE PEACE, a minor ranking judicial officer with limited statutory JURISDICTION over preservation of the peace, civil cases, and lesser criminal offenses. ◫

J.S.D. ◫ An abbreviation for Doctor of Juridical Science, a degree awarded to highly qualified individuals who have successfully completed a prescribed course of advanced study in law after having earned J.D. and LL.M. degrees. ◫

The standards for admission to J.S.D. programs are stringent. Although specific academic requirements for acceptance into a J.S.D. program vary from one law school to another, ordinarily applicants must hold J.D. and LL.M. degrees. They must have completed their courses of study with a certain minimum grade average in order to qualify for this advanced program.

Once accepted, each student generally has a full-time faculty member who acts as research advisor concerning the preparation of the student's thesis, which is a requirement for obtaining the J.S.D. degree. It is often mandatory that all work required for a J.S.D. degree must be completed within five years of the commencement of the student's program of study.

J.S.D. is also commonly abbreviated as S.J.D.

JUDGE ◫ To make a decision or reach a conclusion after examining all the factual evidence presented. To form an opinion after evaluating the facts and applying the law.

A public officer chosen or elected to preside over and to administer the law in a COURT of justice; one who controls the proceedings in a courtroom and decides questions of law or discretion. ◫

As a verb the term *judge* generally describes a process of evaluation and decision. In a legal case this process may be conducted by either a judge or a JURY. Decisions in any case must be based on applicable law. Where the case calls for a jury VERDICT, the judge tells the jury what law applies to the case.

As a noun *judge* refers to a person authorized to make decisions. A judge is a court officer authorized to decide legal cases. A judge presiding over a case may initiate investigations on related matters, but generally judges do not

U.S. District Courts – Number of Civil and Criminal Cases Commenced: 1980 to 1994

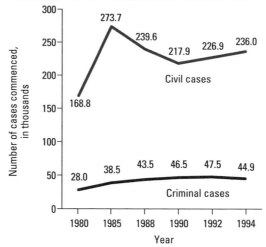

Source: Administrative Office of the U.S. Courts, *Annual Report of the Director.*

have the power to conduct investigations for other branches or agencies of government.

Judges must decide cases based on the applicable law. In some cases a judge may be asked to declare that a certain law is unconstitutional. Judges have the power to rule that a law is unconstitutional and therefore void, but they must give proper deference to the legislative body that enacted the law.

There are two types of judges: trial court and APPELLATE. Trial court judges preside over trials, usually from beginning to end. They decide pretrial MOTIONS, define the scope of DISCOVERY, set the trial schedule, rule on oral motions during trial, control the behavior of participants and the pace of the trial, advise the jury of the law in a jury trial, and sentence a guilty defendant in a criminal case.

Appellate judges hear appeals from decisions of the trial COURTS. They review trial court records, read briefs submitted by the parties, and listen to oral arguments by attorneys, and then decide whether error or injustice occurred in the trial.

Judges can also be distinguished according to their JURISDICTION. For example, FEDERAL COURT judges differ from state court judges. They operate in different courtrooms, and they hear different types of cases. A federal court judge hears cases that fall within federal jurisdiction. Generally, this means cases that involve a question of federal law or the U.S. Constitution, involve parties from different states, or name the United States as a party. State court judges hear cases involving state law, and they also have jurisdiction over many federal cases.

Some judges can hear only certain cases in special courts with limited SUBJECT MATTER JURISDICTION. For example, a federal BANKRUPTCY court judge may preside over only bankruptcy cases. Other special courts with limited subject matter jurisdiction include tax, PROBATE, juvenile, and traffic courts.

Justices make up the upper echelon of appellate judges. The term *justice* generally describes judges serving on the highest court in a jurisdiction. In some jurisdictions a justice may be any appellate judge.

Judges are either appointed or elected. On the federal level, district court judges, appellate court judges, and justices of the Supreme Court are appointed by the president subject to the approval of Congress. On the state level, judges may be appointed by the governor, selected by a joint ballot of the two houses of the state legislature, or elected by the voters of the state.

On the federal level, judges have lifetime tenure. Most state court judges hold their office for a specified number of years. If a state court judge is appointed by the governor, the judge's term may be established by the governor. In some states a judge's term is fixed by statute. All state jurisdictions have a mandatory retirement age. In New Hampshire, for example, a judge must retire by age 70 (N.H. Const. pt. 2, art. 78). There is no mandatory retirement age for justices and judges on the federal level.

Judges' retirement benefits are provided for by statute. On the federal level, a retiring judge may receive for the remainder of the judge's life the salary that she or he was receiving at the time of retirement. To qualify for retirement benefits, a judge must meet minimum service requirements. For example, a judge who retires at age 65 must have served 15 years as a judge in the federal court system; at age 66, 14 years; and so on until age 70 (§ 371). If a judge is forced to retire because of disability and has not qualified for benefits under § 371, the judge may still receive a full salary for life if she or he served 10 years. If the judge served less than 10 years, she or he may receive half of her or his salary for life (28 U.S.C.A. § 372).

Judges must follow ethical rules. In all jurisdictions statutes specify that a judge may hold office only during a time of GOOD BEHAVIOR. If a judge violates the law or an ethical rule, the judge may be removed from office. In jurisdictions in which judges are elected, they may be removed from office by popular vote or impeached by act of the legislature. In states where judges are appointed, the legislature or the governor is authorized to remove them from office, but only for ethical or legal viola-

tions. This is because the power of the JUDICIARY is separate from and equal to the power of the legislative and executive branches, and unfettered control of the judiciary by the other two branches would upset the balance of power.

Judges are distinct from MAGISTRATES. Magistrates are court officers who are empowered by statute to decide pretrial issues and preside over minor cases. Their judicial powers are limited. In the federal court system, for example, magistrates may not preside over FELONY criminal trials. They may preside over civil trials and MISDEMEANOR criminal trials, but only with the consent of all the parties (28 U.S.C.A. §§ 631–639).

CROSS-REFERENCES

Canons of Judicial Ethics; Code of Judicial Conduct; Court Opinion; Discretion in Decision Making; Judicial Action; Judicial Conduct; Judicial Review.

JUDGE ADVOCATE 📖 A legal adviser on the staff of a military commander. A designated officer of the Judge Advocate General's Corps of the Army, Navy, Air Force, or Marine Corps. 📖

Judge advocates are attorneys who perform legal duties while serving in the U.S. Armed Forces. They provide legal services to their branch of the armed forces and legal representation to members of the ARMED SERVICES. They serve as prosecutors and defense attorneys for courts-martial (military criminal trials) under the Uniform Code of Military Justice. In addition, judge advocates practice international, labor, contract, environmental, tort, and administrative law. They practice in military, state, and federal courts. A judge advocate attorney does not need to be licensed to practice law in the state in which he or she practices because they are part of a separate, military system of justice.

The Judge Advocate General's Corp (JAGC) was created by GEORGE WASHINGTON on July 29, 1775, only forty-four days after he took command of the Continental Army. Since that time the Army's JAGC has grown into the largest government "law firm," numbering fifteen hundred judge advocates on active duty.

Judge advocates are the central participants in a military COURT-MARTIAL. A judge advocate administers the oath to other members of the court, advises the court, and acts either as a prosecutor or as a defense counsel for the accused. A judge advocate acting as defense counsel advises the military prisoner on legal matters, protects the accused from making incriminating statements, and objects to irrelevant or improper questions asked at the military proceeding. All sentences with a penalty of dismissal, punitive discharge, confinement for a year or more, or death are subject to review by a court of military review in the office of the judge advocate general of the Army, Navy, or Air Force, depending on the branch of service to which the defendant belongs. A sentence imposed on a member of the Marine Corps would be reviewed by the office of the judge advocate general of the Navy.

A judge advocate is admitted to the armed services as an officer. Because the Uniform Code of Military Justice is different from civilian law in many respects, a judge advocate undergoes an orientation and then education in MILITARY LAW. The Army's JAGC School, for example, at Charlottesville, Virginia, provides a ten-week academic course for new JAGC officers to learn about the mission of the corps and to receive an overview of military law.

Each branch of the armed forces has a judge advocate general, an officer in charge of all judge advocates and responsible for all legal matters affecting that branch of the service. In the Army and Air Force, the judge advocate general holds the rank of major general. In the Navy this officer is a rear admiral. The judge advocate general serves as a legal adviser to the chief of staff of their service and, in some cases, to the secretary of the department.

JUDGMENT 📖 A decision by a court or other tribunal that resolves a controversy and determines the rights and obligations of the parties. 📖

A judgment is the final part of a court case. It states who wins the case and what remedies the winner is awarded. Remedies may include money DAMAGES, injunctive relief, or both. A judgment also signifies the end of the court's JURISDICTION in the case. The Federal Rules of Civil Procedure and most state rules of CIVIL PROCEDURE allow APPEALS only from final judgments. Finally, a judgment gives the winner the ability to collect damages from the losing party, to place a judgment lien on the losing party's REAL PROPERTY, to garnish (collect from an employer) the losing party's salary, or to attach the losing party's PERSONAL PROPERTY. A judgment lien is a claim against the real estate of a party; the real estate cannot be sold until the judgment holder is paid. ATTACHMENT is the physical seizure of property owned by the losing party by a law officer, usually a SHERIFF, who gives the property to the person holding the judgment.

A valid judgment resolves all the contested issues and terminates the lawsuit, since it is regarded as the court's official pronouncement of the law on the ACTION that was pending

before it. It must be rendered for or against an actual litigant; individuals who are not named parties to a lawsuit cannot have their rights and liabilities adjudicated.

A judgment must be in writing and must clearly show that all the issues have been adjudicated. It must specifically indicate the parties for and against whom it is given. Monetary judgments must be definite, specified with certainty, and expressed in words rather than figures. Judgments affecting real property must contain an explicit description of the realty so that the land can easily be identified.

Once a court makes a judgment, it must be dated and docketed with the court administrator's office. Prior to modern computer databases, judgments were entered in a DOCKET book, in alphabetical order, so that interested outsiders could have official notice of them. An index of judgments was prepared by the court administrator for record keeping and notification purposes. Most courts now record their judgments electronically and maintain computer docketing and index information. Though the means of storing the information are different, the basic process remains the same.

A court may amend its judgment to correct inaccuracies or ambiguities that might cause its actual intent to be misconstrued. Omissions, erroneous inclusions, and descriptions are correctable. However, persons who were not parties to the action cannot be brought into the lawsuit by an amended judgment. The Federal Rules of Civil Procedure allow a judgment to be amended by a motion served within ten days after the judgment is entered. State rules of civil procedure also permit amendment of a judgment.

Different types of judgments are made, based on the process the court uses to make the

The attorney (center) and the family of Nicole Brown Simpson were happy with the judgment in O. J. Simpson's wrongful death civil suit.

Enforcement of Foreign Judgments

The principle of territoriality generally limits the power of a state of judicial enforcement of actions to be taken within its territory. Consequently, when a judgment is to be enforced out of property in another state, or requires some act to be done in that other state, the judgment must be brought to the judicial tribunals of the second state for implementation. This allows the judicial tribunal of the enforcing state to examine the judgment to determine whether it should be recognized and enforced.

Conditions for recognizing and enforcing a judgment of a court of another country may be established by treaty or follow general principles of international law. Under those principles, a court of one state will enforce a foreign judgment if (1) the judgment is final between the parties; (2) the court that granted the judgment was competent to do so and had jurisdiction over the parties; (3) regular proceedings were followed that allowed the losing party a chance to be heard; (4) no fraud was worked upon the first court; and (5) enforcement will not violate the public policy of the enforcing state.

FINAL DECISION. A judgment on the MERITS is a decision arrived at after the facts have been presented and the court has reached a final determination of which party is correct. For example, in a negligence lawsuit that is tried to a jury, the final decision will result in a judgment on the merits.

A judgment based solely on a procedural error is a DISMISSAL without prejudice and generally will not be considered a judgment on the merits. A party whose case is dismissed WITHOUT PREJUDICE can bring the suit again as long as the procedural errors are corrected. A party that receives a judgment on the merits is barred from relitigating the same issue by the doctrine of RES JUDICATA. This doctrine establishes the principle that an issue that is judicially decided is decided once and for all.

A SUMMARY JUDGMENT may occur very early in the process of a lawsuit. Under rule 56 of the Federal Rules of Civil Procedure and analogous state rules, any party may make a MOTION for a summary judgment on a CLAIM, COUNTERCLAIM, or CROSS-CLAIM when he or she believes that there is no genuine issue of material fact and that he or she is entitled to prevail as a MATTER OF LAW. A motion for summary judgment can be directed toward the entire claim or defense or toward any portion of the claim or defense. A court determines whether to grant summary judgment.

A JUDGMENT NOTWITHSTANDING THE VERDICT is a judgment in favor of one party despite a VERDICT in favor of the opposing litigant. A court may enter a judgment notwithstanding the verdict, thereby overruling the jury verdict, if the court believes there was insufficient evidence to justify the jury's decision.

A consent judgment, or agreed judgment, is a final decision that is entered on agreement of the litigants; is examined and evaluated by the court; and, if sanctioned by the court, is ordered to be recorded as a binding judgment. Consent judgments are generally rendered in domestic relations cases after the husband and wife agree to a property and support settlement in a DIVORCE.

A DEFAULT JUDGMENT results from the named defendant's failure to appear in court or from one party's failure to take appropriate procedural steps. It is entered upon the failure of the party to appear or to plead at an appropriate time. Before a default judgment is entered, the defendant must be properly served notice of the pending action. The failure to appear or answer is considered an admission of the truth of the opposing party's PLEADING, which forms the basis for a default judgment.

A DEFICIENCY JUDGMENT involves a CREDITOR and a DEBTOR. Upon a debtor's failure to pay his or her obligations, a deficiency judgment is rendered in favor of the creditor for the difference between the amount of the indebtedness and the sum derived from a JUDICIAL SALE of the debtor's property held in order to repay the debt.

Once a judgment is entered, the prevailing party may use it to collect damages. Under the FULL FAITH and CREDIT CLAUSE of the Constitution, a judgment by a state court must be fully recognized and respected by every other state. For example, suppose the prevailing party in a California case knows that the defendant has assets in Arizona that could be used to pay the judgment. The prevailing party may docket the California judgment in the Arizona county

[*Title of Court and Cause*]

This action came on for trial before the Court and a jury, Honorable _____ , District Judge, presiding and the issues having been duly tried and verdict having been directed for defendants,

It is Ordered and Adjudged that the plaintiff take nothing, that the action be dismissed on the merits, and that defendants _____ and _____ recover of the plaintiff, _____ , their costs of action.

Dated at _____ , this _____ day of _____ , 19 _____ .

_____ ,
Clerk of Court.

A sample judgment on directed verdict, for the defendant

court where the defendant's property is located. With the judgment now in effect in Arizona, the prevailing party may obtain a WRIT of execution that will authorize the sheriff in that Arizona county to seize the property to satisfy the judgment.

Once a judgment has been paid by the losing party in a lawsuit, that party is entitled to a formal discharge of the obligation, known as a SATISFACTION of judgment. This satisfaction is acknowledged or certified on the judgment docket.

JUDGMENT CREDITOR

A party to which a DEBT is owed that has proved the debt in a LEGAL PROCEEDING and that is entitled to use judicial process to collect the debt; the owner of an unsatisfied court decision.

A party that wins a monetary award in a lawsuit is known as a judgment creditor until the award is paid, or satisfied. The losing party, which must pay the award, is known as a JUDGMENT DEBTOR. A judgment creditor is legally entitled to enforce the debt with the assistance of the court.

State laws provide remedies to a judgment creditor in collecting the amount of the JUDGMENT. These measures bring the debtor's property into the CUSTODY of the court in order to satisfy the debtor's obligation: they involve the seizure of property and money. The process of enforcing the judgment debt in this way is called EXECUTION. The process commences with a HEARING called a SUPPLEMENTARY PROCEEDING. The judgment debtor is summoned to appear before the court for a hearing to determine the nature and value of the debtor's property. If the property is subject to execution, the court orders the debtor to relinquish it.

Because debtors sometimes fail to surrender property to the court, other means of satisfying the debt may be necessary. In these cases the law refers to an unsatisfied execution—an outstanding and unfulfilled order by the court for property to be given up. Usually this will lead the judgment creditor to seek a WRIT of ATTACHMENT, the legal means by which property is seized. To secure a writ of attachment, the judgment creditor must first place a judgment lien on the property. Also called an ENCUMBRANCE, a LIEN is a legal claim on the debtor's property that gives the CREDITOR a qualified right to it. Creditors holding liens are called SECURED CREDITORS. The writ of attachment sets in motion the process of a LEVY, by which a SHERIFF or other state official actually seizes the property and takes it into the physical possession of the court. The property can then be sold to satisfy the debt.

Occasionally the judgment creditor is frustrated in the course of enforcing a judgment debt. Debtors may transfer property to another owner, which makes collection through attachment more difficult. Liens on property usually prevent the transfer of ownership. Where a transfer of ownership has occurred, state laws usually allow the judgment creditor to sue the third party who now possesses the property. Some states provide additional statutory relief to creditors in cases where debtors fraudulently transfer ASSETS in order to escape a judgment debt. Florida's Uniform Fraudulent Transfer Act (Fla. Stat. § 726.101 et seq.), for instance, allows creditors more time to pursue enforcement of the debt.

Another process for recovery is GARNISHMENT, which targets the judgment debtor's salary or income. Through garnishment a portion of the judgment debtor's income is regularly deducted and paid to the judgment creditor. The creditor is known as a garnishor, and the debtor as a garnishee.

JUDGMENT DEBTOR 📖 A party against which an unsatisfied court decision is awarded; a person who is obligated to satisfy a court decision. 📖

The term *judgment debtor* describes a party against which a court has made a monetary award. If a court renders a JUDGMENT involving money DAMAGES, the losing party must satisfy the amount of the award, which is called the judgment debt. Such a decision gives the winner of the suit, or JUDGMENT CREDITOR, the right to recover the DEBT, or award, through extraordinary means, and the court may help the CREDITOR do so. State law governs how the debt may be recovered. Although the recovery process can be harsh, the law provides the DEBTOR with certain rights and protection.

Following the VERDICT, other legal steps are usually taken against the judgment debtor. The court can order the debtor to appear for an oral hearing to assess the debtor's ASSETS. If it is determined that the debtor has assets sufficient to satisfy the judgment debt, the court may order the debtor to surrender certain property to it. Commonly the judgment creditor must take additional legal action. This involves seeking the court's assistance in seizing the debtor's property, by the process known as ATTACHMENT, or a portion of the debtor's salary, by the process called GARNISHMENT.

For centuries, attachment of property was allowed EX PARTE—without first allowing the defendant debtor to argue against it. However, contemporary law affords the debtor some protection. The debtor has the right to minimal DUE PROCESS. States generally require that the judgment creditor first secure a WRIT of attachment, that the debtor be given NOTICE before seizure occurs, and that the debtor have the right to a prompt HEARING afterward to challenge the seizure.

Other protections apply to both property and wages. First, not every kind of property is subject to attachment. States provide exemptions for certain household items, clothing, tools, and other essentials. Additional provisions may protect individuals in cases of extreme hardship. Where the creditor seeks garnishment in order to seize the judgment debtor's wages, laws generally exempt a certain amount of the salary that is necessary for personal or family support.

Courts can exercise their discretion to go beyond the statutory protections for judgment debtors. They can exempt more property from attachment than that specified in a statute. In some cases they can also deny the attachment or garnishment altogether. This can occur when the creditor seeks more in property than the value of the judgment debt, or where the property sought is an ongoing business that would be destroyed by an attachment.

JUDGMENT DOCKET 📖 A list under which judicial orders of a particular court are recorded by a clerk or other designated officer to be available for inspection by the public. 📖

A judgment docket serves an important function by providing parties interested in learning of the existence of a JUDGMENT or a LIEN on property to enforce a judgment with access to such information. The recording of a judgment in a judgment docket is considered official notice to all parties of its existence. The rules of procedure of the particular court govern the maintenance of the judgment docket.

JUDGMENT NOTE 📖 A PROMISSORY NOTE authorizing an attorney, holder, or clerk of court to appear for the maker of the note and confess, or assent to, a JUDGMENT to be entered against the maker due to DEFAULT in the payment of the amount owed. 📖

A judgment note is also called a COGNOVIT NOTE and is invalid in many states.

JUDGMENT NOTWITHSTANDING THE VERDICT 📖 A JUDGMENT entered by the court in favor of one party even though the JURY returned a VERDICT for the opposing party. 📖

The phrase "judgment notwithstanding the verdict" is abbreviated JNOV, which stands for its Latin equivalent, judgment *"non obstante veredicto."* The remedy of JNOV applies only in cases decided by a jury. Originally this remedy could be entered only in favor of the PLAINTIFF, and the similar remedy of ARREST OF JUDGMENT could be entered only in favor of the DEFENDANT. Under modern law a JNOV is generally available to both plaintiffs and defendants, and an arrest of judgment is primarily used with judgments in criminal cases. A JNOV is proper when the court finds that the party bearing the burden of proof fails to make out a prima facie case (a case that on first appearance will prevail unless contradicted by evidence).

To be granted RELIEF by a JNOV, a party must make a MOTION seeking that relief. The motion generally must be made in writing and must set forth the specific reasons entitling the party to relief. Many statutes and rules require that the moving party must have previously sought a DIRECTED VERDICT, and that the grounds for the JNOV motion be the same or nearly the same as those for the directed verdict. A directed verdict is a request by a party that the judge enter a verdict in that party's behalf

In a case heard by a jury, the judge may rule in favor of the party against whom the jury ruled. A judgment notwithstanding the verdict is a reversal of the jury's verdict.

before the case is submitted to the jury.

Although a jury generally must return a verdict before a motion for JNOV can be made, if the jury does not agree on a verdict, as in a jury deadlocked, some courts will hear a motion for JNOV. However, some statutes do not permit a court to hear a motion for JNOV under such circumstances.

In deciding a motion for JNOV, the court is facing questions only of law, not fact. The court must consider only the EVIDENCE and any inferences therefrom, and must do so in the light most advantageous to the nonmoving party. The court must resolve any conflicts in favor of the party resisting the motion. If there is enough evidence to make out a prima facie case against the moving party, or evidence tending to support the verdict, then the court must deny the motion for JNOV. Some courts maintain that if there is a conflict of evidence, such that the jury could decide either way based on factors such as the credibility of witnesses, the court should deny the motion. Courts approach motions for JNOV with extreme caution and generally will grant them only in clear cases in which the evidence overwhelmingly supports the moving party.

In entering a JNOV, the court is simply reversing the jury's verdict; the motion cannot be the basis for increasing or decreasing the verdict. When granting a JNOV, the court

needs to independently assess the damages or order a new trial on the issue of damages.

Under the Federal Rules of Civil Procedure, both a JNOV and a motion for directed verdict are now encompassed within a motion for judgment as a MATTER OF LAW. The change is one of terminology only and not of substance. Many state statutes or rules of court provide for the remedy of a JNOV, although they may call it something different. The applicable state statutes or rules are substantially similar to the federal rules.

A motion for JNOV is made at the close of all the evidence, after the jury returns a verdict, within a period of time specified by statute. An order granting a motion for a JNOV is often considered a delayed-action directed verdict because it presents the same issues. In fact, in some JURISDICTIONS the denial of a motion for a directed verdict is a prerequisite to the entry of a JNOV. If the particular case involves several plaintiffs or defendants, each of them must separately make a proper motion for a directed verdict in order to move properly for a JNOV later. Current procedure holds a motion for JNOV proper when a prior motion for a directed verdict has been denied. If the court denies a motion for a directed verdict after all the evidence has been presented, then the court is deemed to have submitted the case to the jury subject to a later determination of the legal issues raised by the motion, and the court may grant a motion for JNOV after the jury returns a verdict.

To promote judicial economy, some statutes, including the federal rules, permit a party to make alternative motions for a JNOV and for a new trial. Those motions can also be made separately. The statutes that permit the alternative motions generally provide that the motions should be decided together, such that the trial court's rulings can be reviewed together on appeal. If the court denies the motion for a new trial, then the alternative motion for JNOV is also assumed to be denied. If the court grants the motion for a new trial, then the motion for JNOV is deemed to be effectively disposed of or denied. The court does not have to rule on the motion for JNOV if the motion presents the same issues on which the court ruled in considering motions for a directed verdict and for a new trial. Some court rules and statutes, including the federal rules, provide that a court may grant both of the alternative motions, even though they are inconsistent. Courts may avoid the inconsistency by providing that the ruling granting a new trial is effective only if the ruling granting a JNOV is overturned on APPEAL. In fact, FEDERAL COURTS have held that it is the duty of the trial court to so condition an order granting these alternative motions.

JUDGMENT PROOF 📖 A term used to describe an individual who is financially unable to pay an adverse court decision awarding a sum of money to the opposing party. 📖

A judgment-proof individual has no money or property within the JURISDICTION of the court to satisfy the JUDGMENT or is protected by wage laws that exempt salaries and property from formal judicial process.

JUDICARE 📖 To decide or determine in a JUDICIAL manner. 📖

In civil and old English law, judicare means to judge, to pass judgment or sentence, or to decide an issue in an impartial fashion. It refers to the interpretation and application of the laws to the facts and the administration of justice.

JUDICATURE 📖 A term used to describe the judicial branch of government; the JUDICIARY; or those connected with the court system. 📖

Judicature refers to those officers who administer justice and keep the peace. It signifies a tribunal or court of justice.

The JUDICATURE ACTS of England are the laws that established the present court system in England.

JUDICATURE ACTS 📖 English statutes that govern and revise the organization of the JUDICIARY. 📖

Parliament enacted a series of statutes in 1873 during the reign of Queen Victoria that changed and restructured the court system of England. Consolidated and called the Judicature Act of 1873, these enactments became effective on November 1, 1875, but were later amended in 1877. As a result, superior courts were consolidated to form one supreme court of judicature with two divisions, the High Court of Justice, primarily endowed with ORIGINAL JURISDICTION, and the Court of Appeal, which possessed APPELLATE jurisdiction.

The present court system of England is organized according to the Judicature Acts, which were redrafted in 1925 as the Supreme Court of Judicature (Consolidation) Act and which made the Court of Appeals, consisting of a civil division and criminal division, the center of the English judiciary.

JUDICIAL 📖 Relating to the courts or belonging to the office of a judge; a term pertaining to the administration of justice, the courts, or a judge, as in judicial power. 📖

A judicial act involves an exercise of discretion or an unbiased decision by a court or judge, as opposed to a ministerial, clerical, or routine procedure. A judicial act affects the rights of the parties or property brought before the court. It is the interpretation and application of the law to a particular set of facts contested by litigants in a court of law, resulting from discretion and based upon an evaluation of the evidence presented at a hearing.

Judicial connotes the power to punish, sentence, and resolve conflicts.

JUDICIAL ACTION 📖 The ADJUDICATION by the court of a controversy by hearing the cause and determining the respective rights of the parties. 📖

A JUDGMENT, decree, or decision rendered by a court, which concerns a contested issue brought before the tribunal by parties who voluntarily appear or who have been notified to appear by SERVICE OF PROCESS. It is the interpretation, application, and enforcement of existing law relating to a particular set of facts in a particular case. Judicial action is the determination of the rights and interests of adverse parties.

Judicial action is taken only when a JUSTICIABLE controversy arises or where a claim of right is asserted against a party who has an interest in contesting that claim. A court does not make a decision when a hypothetical difference exists but only when there is an actual controversy affecting the rights and interests of the parties.

JUDICIAL ADMINISTRATION 📖 The practices, procedures, and offices that deal with the management of the administrative systems of the COURTS. 📖

Judicial administration, also referred to as court administration, is concerned with the day-to-day and long-range activities of the court system. Every court in the United States has some form of administrative structure that seeks to enhance the work of judges and to provide services to attorneys and citizens who use the judicial system. Since the 1970s the administration of the courts has played a central role in the judiciary's response to increased court filings and shrinking budgets.

The administration of the courts has traditionally been concerned with overseeing budgets, selecting juror pools, assigning judges to cases, creating court calendars of activities, and supervising nonjudicial personnel. Often administrative decisions are made by judges, either individually or as a group. CLERKS of court, now more commonly known as COURT ADMINISTRATORS, and their staff are called on to accept the filing of court documents, to maintain a file system of cases and a record of all final JUDGMENTS, and to process paperwork generated by judges.

Early in the twentieth century, ROSCOE POUND, a noted jurist and scholar, called for the reform of court administration to ensure efficiency, accuracy, and consistency in the judicial system. Nevertheless, few systematic attempts to modernize and rationalize courts were made until the early 1970s. In 1971 the creation of the National Center for State Courts (NCSC)—an independent, nonprofit organization dedicated to the improvement of justice—provided local and state courts with technical assistance on how to modernize. The NCSC, located in Williamsburg, Virginia, was started at the urging of Chief Justice WARREN E. BURGER, who saw a need for leadership in this field.

The staffing of administrative personnel in the courts has changed since the 1970s. The Institute for Court Management (ICM), a division of the NCSC, develops court leaders through education, training, and a court executive development program. The ICM has provided valuable assistance to thousands of court administrators in the United States, disseminating information on new methods and techniques of court administration. More court administrators now have college and advanced degrees, and many have attended law school.

Judicial administration has largely been taken over by court managers. State courts are organized at the state level, under the direction of a state court administrator. State court administration oversees legislative budgets, personnel administration, and court research and planning. Planning for the future is an integral part of the administrative agenda. The FEDERAL COURTS are organized somewhat differently. There is at least one U.S. district court in each state, but states with larger populations have two or more. There is a clerk of court in each federal district who has duties similar to that of a state court administrator.

Court administrators explore alternative ways of managing court cases, often by statistical research. Various systems of case management are employed in the United States, but the trend has been to seek methods that reduce the amount of time a case remains active in the courts. Consequently, judges often have less control over their time as court managers set out the work that must be accomplished.

Computers have also reshaped the administration of the courts. Before the 1980s courts recorded everything on paper. With the integration of computers and database software, case information is now recorded and retrieved electronically. The use of new technology has improved the efficiency of court administration. APPELLATE COURTS distribute court opinions and court rules through computer bulletin boards and the Internet. Some courts allow access to their database information through computer modems.

Another function of judicial administration is to eliminate BIAS. Many state court systems have appointed committees and task forces to investigate racial and gender bias in the courts. Court administrators have been charged with developing ways of eliminating bias, ensuring diversity in the court system, and providing easier access to the courts for PRO SE litigants, also called pro per litigants in some jurisdictions, (persons representing themselves without

Judicial administration is the management of daily and long-term activities of the court system. Effective judicial administration provides assistance to judges, attorneys, and people who use the judicial system so that cases are handled consistently and efficiently.

A. RAMEY/PHOTOEDIT

an attorney). The certification of court interpreters for testimony given in languages other than English has emerged as a leading issue in court administration.

New divisions of administrative oversight have developed since the 1970s. Offices of professional responsibility, which administer and investigate ethical complaints against lawyers, are commonplace. Many states require that lawyers take CONTINUING LEGAL EDUCATION (CLE) courses so as to maintain professional competence. Offices have been created in state court administration to accredit CLE programs and to monitor compliance by lawyers.

JUDICIAL ASSISTANCE ◫ Aid offered by the judicial tribunals of one state to the judicial tribunals of a second state. ◫

Judicial assistance may consist of the enforcement of a JUDGMENT rendered by a court of another state or other actions to assist current judicial proceedings taking place in the state requesting the cooperation of the foreign court. A *letter rogatory*, the formal term for such a request, asks a foreign court to take some judicial action, such as issue a SUMMONS, compel production of documents, or take evidence. Treaties may be concluded between countries to establish regular methods of transmitting these requests and to assure reciprocal treatment in furnishing assistance. See also LETTERS ROGATORY.

JUDICIAL CONDUCT   See CODE OF JUDICIAL CONDUCT.

JUDICIAL CONFERENCE OF THE UNITED STATES   The Judicial Conference of the United States formulates the administrative policies for the FEDERAL COURTS. The Judicial Conference also makes recommendations on a wide range of topics that relate to the federal courts. The conference is chaired by the chief justice of the U.S. Supreme Court. Other members include the chief judge of each federal judicial circuit, one district judge from each federal judicial circuit, and the chief judge of the U.S. Court of International Trade.

The Judicial Conference was created in response to a need for uniformity in rules and procedures in the federal court system. In the early 1920s, Chief Justice WILLIAM H. TAFT, of the Supreme Court, led a reform effort that urged centralized review of federal DISTRICT COURTS. Until that time the procedures and practices in federal trial courts varied widely from circuit to circuit, causing confusion among attorneys and judges. The result of the reform effort was the passage in 1922 of a federal statute that created the Conference of Senior Circuit Judges (Pub. L. No. 67-297, 423 Stat. 837, 838). The conference of Senior Circuit Judges was renamed the Judicial Conference of the United States in 1948 (Act of June 25, 1948, ch. 646, 62 Stat. 902, § 331 [codified as amended at 28 U.S.C.A. § 331 (1988)]).

The Judicial Conference is a creation of Congress, and it has only the powers that Congress gives it. Its membership and duties have been expanded by Congress, but its primary missions have remained the same.

The Judicial Conference performs two major functions. The first is to study and offer improvements on federal court rules and procedures. These rules and procedures cover matters ranging from the SENTENCING of a criminal defendant to the service of a COMPLAINT and court SUMMONS on a civil defendant. The second major function of the Judicial Conference is to supervise the administration of the federal courts.

In its administrative capacity, the Judicial Conference oversees the ADMINISTRATIVE OFFICE OF THE U.S. COURTS. This is the administrative nerve center of the federal courts. The Judicial Conference formulates the fiscal and personnel policies for the federal courts, and the Administrative Office implements those policies.

The Judicial Conference also reviews orders that judicial councils for the federal circuits issue on complaints of judicial misconduct or judicial disability, and it may reassign federal judges to different federal courts. The final decision on administrative matters that are not covered by existing statutes, rules, and regulations is made by the judicial council of the appropriate federal circuit.

The Judicial Conference recommends ways to improve rules and procedures in the federal courts. Its recommendations do not carry the force of law, but the conference is widely recognized as the authority on federal court rules and procedures.

The Judicial Conference makes yearly suggestions on legislation to Congress, and recommendations on federal court rules to the U.S. Supreme Court. The Supreme Court fashions the rules for federal courts and submits them to Congress for final approval. The attorney general of the United States, by request of the chief justice of the Supreme Court, is required to report to the Judicial Conference on the business of the federal courts. Under the Judicial Conference statute, 28 U.S.C.A. 331, the attorney general's reports must discuss with particularity the progress of cases in which the U.S. government is a party.

The Judicial Conference may offer its opinion on legislation passed by Congress that affects the rules and procedures of the federal courts. For example, in 1990 the Federal Courts

Study Commission of the Judicial Conference released a study that was critical of federal legislation on mandatory minimum sentences for criminal defendants. Also in the 1990s, the Judicial Conference publicly opposed federal legislation that limited the right of a criminal defendant to file HABEAS CORPUS petitions in federal court. For persons in prison, habeas corpus petitions are generally the last chance for court review of their criminal conviction.

The Judicial Conference has established committees that specialize in certain topics, including court schedules (known as DOCKETS), court budgets, judicial conduct, and the disclosure of finances by judges and the federal courts. Other committees supervise the support of specialized federal court features, such as the offices of PUBLIC DEFENDERS, probation officers, and MAGISTRATES (judicial officers who make decisions on pretrial matters).

Although the power of the Judicial Conference is limited to administrative matters, these matters can be controversial and far reaching. For example, the Judicial Conference has authority over the presence of cameras in federal courtrooms. In 1994 it voted to discontinue a three-year experiment allowing cameras to film civil trials in some federal courts. A majority of the Judicial Conference members expressed a fear that cameras could affect the outcome of a trial. The decision drew criticism from many legal circles, and in March 1995 the Judicial Conference said that it would reconsider its position on the issue. In March 1996 the Conference decided to ban cameras in all federal courts except for federal appeals courts. The Conference allowed each individual circuit to decide whether it would allow cameras in its appeals courts.

See also CAMERAS IN COURT; JUDICIAL ADMINISTRATION.

JUDICIAL IMMUNITY 📖 A judge's complete protection from personal LIABILITY for exercising judicial functions. 📖

Judicial immunity protects judges from liability for monetary DAMAGES in civil court, for acts they perform pursuant to their judicial function. Generally a judge has IMMUNITY from civil DAMAGES if the judge had JURISDICTION over the subject matter in issue. This means that a judge has immunity for acts relating to cases before the court, but a judge does not have immunity for acts relating to cases beyond the court's reach. For example, a criminal court judge would not have immunity if she tried to influence proceedings in a juvenile court.

Some states codify the judicial immunity doctrine in statutes. Most legislatures, including Congress, let court decisions govern the issue.

Judicial immunity is a COMMON-LAW concept, derived from judicial decisions. It originated in the courts of medieval Europe to discourage

Stump v. Sparkman

The U.S. Supreme Court has consistently upheld absolute immunity for judges performing judicial acts, even when those acts violate clearly established judicial procedures. In *Stump v. Sparkman*, 435 U.S. 349, 98 S. Ct. 1099, 55 L. Ed. 2d 331 (1978), the Court held that an Indiana state judge, who ordered the sterilization of a female minor without observing due process, could not be sued for damages under the federal civil rights statute (42 U.S.C.A. § 1983).

In 1971 Judge Harold D. Sparkman, of the Circuit Court of DeKalb County, Indiana, acted on a petition filed by Ora McFarlin, the mother of fifteen-year-old Linda Spitler. McFarlin sought to have her daughter sterilized on the ground she was a "somewhat retarded" minor who had been staying out overnight with older men.

Judge Sparkman approved and signed the petition, but the petition had not been filed with the court clerk and the judge had not opened a formal case file. The judge failed to appoint a guardian ad litem for Spitler, and he did not hold a hearing on the matter before authorizing a tubal ligation. Spitler, who did not know what the operation was for, discovered she had been sterilized only after she was married. Spitler, whose married name was Stump, then sued Sparkman.

The Supreme Court ruled that Sparkman was absolutely immune because what he did was "a function normally performed by a judge," and he performed the act in his "judicial capacity." Although he may have violated state laws and procedures, he performed judicial functions that have historically been absolutely immune to civil lawsuits.

In a dissenting opinion, Justice Potter Stewart argued that Sparkman's actions were not absolutely immune simply because he sat in a courtroom, wore a robe, and signed an unlawful order. In Stewart's view the conduct of a judge "surely does not become a judicial act merely on his say so. A judge is not free, like a loose cannon, to inflict indiscriminate damage whenever he announces that he is acting in his judicial capacity."

SHOULD JUDGES HAVE ABSOLUTE OR QUALIFIED IMMUNITY?

The U.S. Supreme Court has made clear that when judges perform judicial acts within their jurisdiction, they are absolutely immune from money damages lawsuits. When judges act outside their judicial function, such as in supervising their employees, they do not have absolute immunity. The Court's upholding of absolute immunity has troubled some legal commentators, who believe that in appropriate circumstances judges should be held personally accountable for judicial actions that are unlawful.

IN FOCUS

Defenders of absolute immunity claim that it is required for the benefit of the public, not for the protection of malicious or corrupt judges. The legitimacy of U.S. courts rests on the public's belief that judges have the freedom to act independently, without fear of the consequences. Absolute immunity provides the buffer needed for a judge to act.

In the adversarial process, one party wins, and the other party loses. Losing parties are inevitably disappointed, and some seek ways of venting their frustration at the legal system. Some file complaints with lawyer discipline boards, alleging ethical misconduct by the opposing party's attorney or their own attorney. Some file complaints with a judicial conduct board, claiming that the trial judge violated a canon of judicial conduct. Though these types of complaints do not result in the relitigation of a lawsuit, they do illustrate the vexatious litigation that faces attorneys and judges. Allowing parties to sue a judge for a judicial act would invite a torrent of meritless suits that would impede the judicial system.

Defenders of absolute immunity note that a flood of litigation would not be the only consequence of relaxing the immunity standard. They say that once judges became liable for damages suits, self-interest would lead them to avoid making decisions likely to provoke such suits. The resulting overcautiousness and timidity might be hard to detect,

but it would impair independent and impartial adjudication.

Judges do make honest mistakes during the course of trial. The law is complex, and judges cannot call a recess of court to research every motion before making a decision. If a judge could be sued for damages, another judge might have to rule that the defendant judge was liable for injuries due to an erroneous decision or procedural flaw. Having judges judge one another could erode the integrity of the courts and undermine public confidence.

Defenders of absolute immunity also point out that appellate review is a viable remedy for correcting judicial conduct. In addition, if a judge has violated the canons of judicial conduct, judicial conduct boards may issue sanctions, including a recommendation of removal from the bench. A judge can be prosecuted for criminal acts. In some states judges may be impeached, and most state court judges must stand for election periodically. All these options serve as checks on judicial behavior and provide protection to the public.

Those who criticize absolute immunity recognize that judicial independence must be preserved. Nevertheless, they claim that in certain situations the only way to protect the public is to allow personal lawsuits against judges. By totally insulating judges from personal responsibility for their actions, the judicial system allows a small number of judges to escape the consequences of unlawful and outrageous behavior. The public loses respect when it sees a judge "beat the system," while the victim loses the chance to be made whole for the injuries flowing from the judicial act.

These critics believe that a qualified immunity standard would protect judges from meritless lawsuits and guarantee victims of unlawful judicial conduct their opportunity to seek damages. Qualified immunity is a lesser form of immunity that may be granted by a court if the judge demonstrates that the

law was not clear on the subject in which the judge's actions occurred. They point out that the executive branch is governed by qualified immunity. There is no indication that the administration of government has ground to a halt, or that the executive branch cannot attract high-quality individuals to government service. A well-articulated qualified immunity standard would allow a lawsuit against a judge to be dismissed if it could be established that the judge was operating within accepted judicial authority.

The critics note that the alternative remedies offered by the defenders of absolute immunity do not address the type of conduct that would be the focus of a personal injury lawsuit against a judge. For example, in *Stump v. Sparkman*, 435 U.S. 349, 98 S. Ct. 1099, 55 L. Ed. 2d 331 (1978), the judge issued an order to sterilize a teenage girl without the order's ever having been filed with the clerk of court. Because there was no record of a case filing or decision, the order could not be reviewed by an appellate court. The judge could be sanctioned by the judicial conduct board, but that would not compensate the victim of the illegal sterilization. Absolute immunity allowed the court to dismiss the girl's claim because the "judicial act" was one normally performed by a judge and was within the judge's judicial capacity.

Supporters of qualified immunity discount the assumption that it would precipitate a flood of litigation. They maintain that decisions that judges typically make will seldom be litigated, as appellate review will satisfy most litigants. However, in the rare circumstances where a judge abuses her authority and someone is injured, these supporters contend, it is only fair to qualify a judge's personal immunity. They argue that the removal of absolute immunity would, over time, deter judicial abuse: judges would not be intimidated, but they would be more careful to safeguard the rights of all parties.

persons from attacking a court decision by suing the judge. Losing parties were required instead to take their complaints to an APPELLATE COURT. The idea of protecting judges from civil damages was derived from this basic tenet and served to solidify the independence of the judiciary. It became widely accepted in the English courts, and in the courts of the United States.

Judicial immunity was first recognized by the U.S. Supreme Court in *Randall v. Brigham*, 74 U.S. (7 Wall.) 523, 19 L. Ed. 285 (1868). In *Randall* the Court held that an attorney who had been banned from the practice of law by a judge could not sue the judge over the disbarment. In its opinion the Court stated that a judge was not liable for judicial acts unless they were done "maliciously or corruptly."

In *Bradley v. Fisher*, 80 U.S. (13 Wall.) 335, 20 L. Ed. 646 (1871), the High Court clarified judicial immunity. Joseph H. Bradley had brought suit seeking civil damages against George P. Fisher, a former justice of the Supreme Court of the District of Columbia. Bradley had been the attorney for John H. Suratt, who was tried in connection with the ASSASSINATION of President ABRAHAM LINCOLN. In Suratt's trial, after Fisher had called a recess, Bradley accosted Fisher "in a rude and insulting manner" and accused Fisher of making insulting comments from the bench. Suratt's trial continued, and the jury was unable to reach a VERDICT.

Immediately after discharging the jury, Fisher ordered from the bench that Bradley's name be stricken from the rolls of attorneys authorized to practice before the Supreme Court of the District of Columbia. Bradley sued Fisher for damages relating to lost work as a result of the order. At trial Bradley attempted to introduce evidence in his favor, but Fisher's attorney objected to each item, and the judge excluded each item. After three failed attempts to present evidence, the trial court directed the jury to deliver a verdict in favor of Fisher.

On appeal by Bradley, the U.S. Supreme Court affirmed the trial court's decision. Judges could be reached for their malicious acts, but only through IMPEACHMENT, or removal from office. Thus, the facts of the case were irrelevant. Even if Fisher had exceeded his jurisdiction in single-handedly banning Bradley from the court, Fisher was justified in his actions. According to the Court, "A judge who should pass over in silence an offence of such gravity would soon find himself a subject of pity rather than respect."

Since *Bradley* the Supreme Court has identified some exceptions to judicial immunity. Judges do not receive immunity for their ad-

ministrative decisions, such as in hiring and firing court employees (*Forrester v. White*, 484 U.S. 219, 108 S. Ct. 538, 98 L. Ed. 2d 555 [1988]). Judges also are not immune from declaratory and injunctive relief. These forms of relief differ from monetary relief. Generally they require parties to do or refrain from doing a certain thing. If a judge loses a suit for DECLARATORY JUDGMENT or injunctive relief, the judge may not be forced to pay money damages, but may be forced to pay the court costs and attorneys' fees of the winning party.

For example, assume that a judge requires the posting of BAIL by persons charged in criminal court with offenses for which they cannot be jailed. If a person subjected to this unconstitutional practice files suit against the judge, the judge will not be given judicial immunity and, upon losing the case, will be forced to pay the plaintiff's attorneys' fees and court costs (*Pulliam v. Allen*, 466 U.S. 522, 104 S. Ct. 1970, 80 L. Ed. 2d 565 [1984]).

Filing a civil COMPLAINT against a judge can be risky for attorneys because the doctrine of judicial immunity is well established. In *Marley v. Wright*, 137 F.R.D. 359 (W.D. Oklahoma 1991), Attorney Frank E. Marley sued two Oklahoma state court judges, Thornton Wright, Jr., and David M. Harbour, their court reporter, and others. Marley alleged in his complaint that Wright and Harbour had violated his constitutional rights in connection with a custody case concerning Marley's children. The court not only dismissed the case, it ordered Marley to pay the attorneys' fees that Wright and Harbour incurred in defending the suit. According to the court, Marley's complaint "was not warranted by existing law," and Marley had used the suit "not to define the outer boundaries of judicial immunity but to harass judges and judicial personnel who rendered a decision he did not like."

JUDICIAL NOTICE 📖 A doctrine of EVIDENCE applied by a court that allows the court to recognize and accept the existence of a particular fact commonly known by persons of average intelligence without establishing its existence by admitting evidence in a civil or criminal ACTION. 📖

When a court takes judicial notice of a certain fact, it obviates the need for parties to prove the fact in court. Ordinarily, facts that relate to a case must be presented to the judge or jury through TESTIMONY or TANGIBLE evidence. However, if each fact in a case had to be proved through such presentation, the simplest case would take weeks to complete. To avoid burdening the judicial system, all legislatures have approved court rules that allow a court to recognize facts that constitute common knowledge without requiring proof from the parties.

On the federal trial court level, judicial notice is recognized in rule 201 of the Federal Rules of Evidence for U.S. District Courts and Magistrates. Rule 201 provides, in part, that "[a] judicially noticed fact must be one not subject to reasonable dispute in that it is either (1) generally known within the territorial jurisdiction of the trial court or (2) capable of accurate and ready determination by resort to sources whose accuracy cannot reasonably be questioned."

Under rule 201 a trial court must take judicial notice of a well-known fact at the request of one of the parties, if the court is provided with information supporting the fact. A court also has the option to take judicial notice at its discretion, without a request from a party.

Rule 201 further provides that a court may take judicial notice at any time during a proceeding. If a party objects to the taking of judicial notice, the court must give that party an opportunity to be heard on the issue. In a civil JURY trial, the court must inform the jury that it must accept the judicially noticed facts in the case as conclusively proved. In a criminal trial by jury, the court must instruct the jury "that it may, but is not required to, accept as conclusive any fact judicially noticed." All states have statutes that are virtually identical to rule 201.

The most common judicially noticed facts include the location of streets, buildings, and geographic areas; periods of time; business customs; historical events; and federal, state, and international law. Legislatures also maintain statutes that give courts the power to recognize certain facts in specific situations. For example, in Idaho any document affixed with the official SEAL of the state public utilities commission must be judicially noticed by all courts (Idaho Code § 61-209 [1996]). In Hawaii, when a commercial vehicle is cited for violating vehicle equipment regulations, a trial court must take judicial notice of the driver's subordinate position if the driver works for a company that owns the vehicle (Haw. Rev. Stat. § 291-37 [1995]).

The danger of judicial notice is that, if abused, it can deprive the fact finder of the opportunity to decide a contestable fact in a case. In *Walker v. Halliburton Services*, 654 So. 2d 365 (La. App. 1995), Johnny Walker fell from a tank truck approximately ten feet to a concrete floor. Walker sought WORKERS' COMPENSATION benefits for his injuries, and his claim was denied by the Office of Workers' Compensation.

At the application hearing, the hearing officer stated that it was her experience that a soft-tissue injury heals in six weeks. She then took judicial notice of the fact that a soft-tissue injury heals in six weeks—preventing Walker from contesting that proposition—and disallowed Walker's claim. On appeal the Louisiana Court of Appeal, Third Circuit, reversed the decision and ordered the payment of workers' compensation benefits. According to the court, it was a clear error of law for the hearing officer to take judicial notice of such intricate medical knowledge.

JUDICIAL REVIEW A court's authority to examine an executive or legislative act and to invalidate that act if it is contrary to constitutional principles.

The power of courts of law to review the actions of the executive and legislative branches is called judicial review. Though judicial review is usually associated with the U.S. Supreme Court, it is a power possessed by most courts of law in the United States. State courts exercise this power in ruling on the validity of state executive acts or state statutes, in terms of their interpretation of the state constitution. They base such rulings on the principle that a state law that violates the state constitution is invalid. Normally the U.S. Supreme Court cannot review such decisions unless the case clearly involves a federal constitutional issue.

Judicial review is an invention of U.S. law, based on the existence of a written constitution that can be changed only by CONSTITUTIONAL AMENDMENT. Though legislation is accorded a general PRESUMPTION of validity, a court has the power to strike down a law if it violates constitutional or statutory principles.

Though a few state courts exercised judicial review prior to the adoption of the U.S. Constitution, the Framers did not resolve the question of whether the newly created FEDERAL COURTS should have this power. Article III, which established the judicial branch, is silent on the subject. During the early years of the Republic, the Supreme Court upheld congressional acts, which implied the power of judicial review. But the key question was whether the Court had the power to strike down an act of Congress.

The issue was settled by the Supreme Court in 1803, in *Marbury v. Madison*, 5 U.S. (1 Cranch) 137, 2 L. Ed. 60, which ruled an act of Congress unconstitutional. In *Marbury* Chief Justice JOHN MARSHALL reasoned that since it is the duty of a court in a lawsuit to declare the law, and since the Constitution is the supreme law of the land, where a rule of statutory law conflicts with a rule of the Constitution, then the law of the Constitution must prevail. Marshall asserted that it is "emphatically the province and duty of the judicial department, to say what the law is."

Having established the power of judicial review, the Supreme Court applied it only once prior to the Civil War, in 1857, ruling the MISSOURI COMPROMISE OF 1820 unconstitutional in *Dred Scott v. Sandford*, 60 U.S. (19 How.) 393, 15 L. Ed. 691. In the same period, the Court invalidated several state laws that came in conflict with the Constitution. In *M'Culloch v. Maryland*, 17 U.S. 316, 4 L. Ed. 579 (1819), the Court invalidated a state's attempt to tax a branch of the BANK OF THE UNITED STATES. In *Gibbons v. Ogden*, 22 U.S. 1, 6 L. Ed. 23 (1824), the Court struck down a New York law granting a MONOPOLY to a steamboat company, saying that the state law conflicted with a federal law granting a LICENSE to another company.

In addition to asserting the power to invalidate state laws, the Marshall Court established the authority to overrule decisions of the highest state APPELLATE COURTS on questions of federal constitutional and statutory law. Article VI of the U.S. Constitution provides that the Constitution, laws, and treaties of the United States "shall be the Supreme Law of the Land; and the Judges in every State shall be bound thereby, any Thing in the Constitution or Laws of any State to the Contrary notwithstanding." The Supreme Court affirmed its power to review state court decisions in *Martin v. Hunter's Lessee*, 14 U.S. 304, 4 L. Ed. 97 (1816).

Following the Civil War, the Supreme Court began to invalidate acts of Congress, yet avoided the great issues of public debate and thus avoided conflict like that which engulfed it following its *Dred Scott* decision. Beginning in 1890, however, the Court again became the source of political controversy when it exercised its power of judicial review to limit government regulation of business. In *Chicago, Milwaukee, & St. Paul Railroad Co. v. Minnesota*, 134 U.S. 418, 10 S. Ct. 462, 33 L. Ed. 970 (1890), the Court struck down a state law establishing a commission to set railroad rates. This case was the first of many where the Court applied the doctrine of "substantive due process" to invalidate state and federal legislation that regulated business. Substantive due process was a vague concept that required legislation to be fair, reasonable, and just in its content.

Through the early 1900s, the Court came under attack from Populists and Progressives for its desire to insulate capitalism from government intervention. Unmoved by its critics, the Court proceeded to invalidate a federal INCOME TAX (*Pollock v. Farmers' Loan & Trust Co.*, 157 U.S. 429, 15 S. Ct. 673, 39 L. Ed. 759 [1895]), limit the scope of the SHERMAN ANTI-TRUST ACT (*United States v. E. C. Knight Co.*, 156 U.S. 1, 15 S. Ct. 249, 39 L. Ed. 325 [1895]), and forbid states to regulate working hours (*Lochner v. New York*, 198 U.S. 45, 25 S. Ct. 539, 49 L. Ed. 937 [1905]).

The Supreme Court's use of substantive due process brought charges of "judicial activism," which asserted that in determining whether laws would meet constitutional muster, the Court was acting more as a legislative body than as a judicial body. Justice OLIVER WENDELL HOLMES, JR., in his famous dissenting opinion in *Lochner*, argued for "judicial restraint," cautioning the Court that it was usurping the function of the legislature.

Despite Holmes's warning the Court continued to strike down laws dealing with economic regulation into the 1930s. In 1932 the United States, in the midst of the Great Depression, elected FRANKLIN D. ROOSEVELT president. Roosevelt immediately began to implement his NEW DEAL program, which was based on the federal government's aggressive regulation of the national economy. The Supreme Court used its power of judicial review to invalidate eight major pieces of New Deal legislation.

Roosevelt, angry at the conservative justices for blocking his reforms, proposed legislation that would add new appointees to the Court, so as to create a liberal majority. This "court-packing" plan aroused bipartisan opposition and ultimately failed. But the Court may have gotten Roosevelt's message, for in 1937 it made an abrupt turnabout: a majority of the Court abandoned the substantive due process doctrine and voted to uphold the Wagner Act, which guaranteed to industrial workers the right to unionize and bargain collectively (*National Labor Relations Board v. Jones & Laughlin Steel Corp.*, 301 U.S. 1, 57 S. Ct. 615, 81 L. Ed. 893 [1937]).

With this decision the Court ceased to interpret the Constitution as a barrier to social and economic legislation. The Court subsequently upheld congressional legislation that affected labor relations, agricultural production, and social welfare. It also exercised judicial restraint with respect to state laws regulating economic activity.

Beginning in the 1950s, the Supreme Court exercised its judicial review power in cases involving CIVIL RIGHTS and civil liberties. During the tenure of Chief Justice EARL WARREN, from 1953 to 1969, the Court declared federal statutes unconstitutional in whole or in part in twenty-five cases, most of the decisions involving civil liberties. The Warren Court's decision in *Brown v. Board of Education*, 347 U.S. 483, 74 S. Ct. 686, 98 L. Ed. 873 (1954), however, invalidated state laws that mandated racially segregated public schools.

The Supreme Court became increasingly conservative in the 1970s. Yet, in 1973, under Chief Justice WARREN E. BURGER, it invalidated state laws prohibiting ABORTION in *Roe v. Wade*, 410 U.S. 113, 93 S. Ct. 705, 35 L. Ed. 2d 147. Since the elevation of WILLIAM H. REHNQUIST to chief justice in 1986, the Court has continued its movement to the right, although it has not retreated from most of the protections it recognized under Warren in the realm of civil rights and civil liberties.

The exercise of judicial review is subject to important rules of judicial self-restraint, which restrict the Supreme Court, and state courts as well, from extending its power. The Supreme Court will hear only cases or controversies, actual live disputes between adversary parties who are asserting valuable legal rights. This means the Court cannot issue advisory opinions on legislation. In addition, a party bringing suit must have STANDING (a direct stake in the outcome) in order to challenge a statute.

The most important rule of judicial restraint is that statutes are presumptively valid, which means that judges assume legislators did not intend to violate the Constitution. It follows that the burden of proof is on the party that raises the issue of unconstitutionality. In addition, if a court can construe a disputed statute in a manner that allows it to remain intact without tampering with the meaning of the words or if a court can decide a case on nonconstitutional grounds, these courses are to be preferred. Finally, a court will not sit in judgment of the motives or wisdom of legislators, nor will it hold a statute invalid merely because it is deemed to be unwise or undemocratic.

CROSS-REFERENCES

Brown v. Board of Education of Topeka, Kansas; Dred Scott v. Sandford; Due Process of Law; *Gibbons v. Ogden;* Labor Union Sidebar: *National Labor Relations Board v. Jones & Laughlin Steel Corp.; Lochner v. New York; Marbury v. Madison; McCulloch v. Maryland; Pollock v. Farmers' Loan and Trust Co.;* Separation of Powers; Supreme Court of the United States.

JUDICIAL SALE 📖 The transfer of TITLE to and POSSESSION of a debtor's PROPERTY to another in exchange for a price determined in proceedings that are conducted under a JUDGMENT or an order of court by an officer duly appointed and commissioned to do so. 📖

A judicial sale is a method plaintiffs use to enforce a judgment. When a PLAINTIFF wins a judgment against a DEFENDANT in civil court, and the defendant does not pay the judgment, the plaintiff can force the sale of the defendant's property until the judgment is satisfied. The plaintiff forces the sale by filing in court for an EXECUTION on property, which is a seizure of property by the court for the purpose of selling the property.

Judicial sales are regulated by state and federal statute. In Alabama, for example, the judicial sale process begins when a judgment remains unpaid ninety days after it is placed on the record by the court (Ala. Code § 6-9-21 [1995]). The plaintiff must bring an order mandating payment of the judgment and court costs to the county where the defendant's property is located. This order is called a WRIT of execution, and it is issued by the trial court. A writ of execution identifies the amount of the judgment, interest, and court costs that the defendant owes the plaintiff.

Generally, a writ of execution may be levied against any REAL PROPERTY or PERSONAL PROPERTY of the defendant. The plaintiff must file the writ of execution with the PROBATE judge in the county where the defendant's property is located. The plaintiff must also give notice of the execution on the defendant's property to the defendant. Once the writ is filed, the plaintiff has a LIEN on the defendant's property. A lien gives the plaintiff a legally recognized ownership interest in the defendant's property, equal to the amount of the judgment.

Once the plaintiff has obtained a lien on the defendant's property, the judicial sale can begin. The process typically must be carried out within a fixed time period, such as within ninety days after the writ of execution is issued. The sheriff's office in the county where the property is located is responsible for levying, or seizing, the property and for conducting the sale of the property.

The sale of real property may take place at the courthouse. If the property that the plaintiff seeks is perishable and in danger of waste or decay, the sale may occur at some other time and place.

A defendant can avoid a judicial sale after a writ of execution is issued, by paying the judgment, interest, and court costs in full. If the defendant appeals the judgment to a higher court, the defendant may postpone the judicial sale by posting a BOND to secure the DEBT during the appeals process. If the defendant does not plan to APPEAL, and the levying officer is about to seize personal property, the defendant may be able to keep the property until the day of sale if the defendant gives the levying officer a bond made payable to the plaintiff for a certain amount, such as twice the amount in the writ of execution.

Generally, judicial sales are the last resort for a plaintiff trying to collect on a judgment. A defendant who owns or possesses valuable property is usually able to satisfy a judgment in civil court by leveraging the property, or using it to borrow money to pay the judgment.

JUDICIAL WRITS 📖 Orders issued by a judge in the English courts after a lawsuit had begun. 📖

An ORIGINAL WRIT, issued out of the CHANCERY, was the proper document for starting a lawsuit in England for hundreds of years, but courts could issue judicial WRITS during the course of a proceeding or to give effect to their orders after the lawsuit had commenced. Unlike original writs, judicial WRITS were issued under the private SEAL of the courts rather than the king's great seal, and they were sent out in the name of the chief judge of the court hearing the case rather than in the king's name. The CAPIAS was one form of a judicial writ.

JUDICIARY 📖 The branch of government that is endowed with the authority to interpret and apply the law, adjudicate legal disputes, and otherwise administer justice. 📖

The U.S. judiciary comprises a system of state and FEDERAL COURTS, tribunals, and administrative bodies, as well as the judges and other judicial officials who preside over them.

Every society in human history has confronted the question of how to resolve disputes among its members. Many early societies chose a private system of revenge for dispute resolution. As civilization gradually evolved, and the system of revenge became perceived as counterproductive to society, communities began designating individuals to resolve disputes in accordance with established norms and customs. These individuals were usually leaders who were expected to exercise their judgment in an impartial manner.

The origins of JUDICIAL ACTION, judicial power, and judicial process may be traced to the first communities that relied on neutral third parties to resolve legal disputes. Judicial action is any action taken by a court or other judicial body to interpret, apply, or declare what the law is on a particular issue during a legal proceeding. It is also the action taken by a judicial body to settle a legal dispute by issuing an OPINION, order, DECREE, or JUDGMENT. Judicial power is the authority of a court to hear a particular lawsuit or legal dispute, and take judicial action with regard to it. Judicial process is the procedures by which a court takes judicial action or exercises its judicial power.

Ancient Greece, one of the earliest known societies in Western civilization, employed a combination of judicial procedures. Greek rulers, known as *arkhons*, were empowered to hear a variety of disputes, as was the *agora*, a group of respected elders in the community. A court known as the *Areopagus* heard murder cases, and direct retaliation by private citizens was still permitted in many civil disputes. The judicial powers of these institutions were gradually replaced by the *Ekklesia*, an assembly of six thousand jurors that was divided into smaller panels to hear particular cases.

Juries also played an integral role in the development of the English judicial system. As more legal disputes were submitted to juries for resolution, this system became more self-conscious. Concerns were expressed that both judges and juries were rendering biased decisions based on irrelevant and untrustworthy evidence. Litigants complained that trial procedures were haphazard, arbitrary, and unfair. Losing parties sought effective remedies to redress erroneous decisions made at the trial court level. Each of these concerns has manifested itself in the modern judicial system of the United States.

The blueprints for the U.S. judiciary were laid out in 1789. During that year the U.S. Constitution was formally adopted by the states. Article III of the Constitution delineates the general structure of the federal judicial system, including the powers and obligations of federal courts. The JUDICIARY ACT OF 1789 (1 Stat. 73 [codified as amended in 28 U.S.C.A.]) fleshes out many details of federal judicial power that were not addressed by the Constitution. The blueprints for the state judicial

The origins of the jury are in ancient Greece, where the Ekklesia, *an assembly of six thousand jurors, was divided into smaller panels to hear individual cases.*

JOHN NEUBAUER/PHOTOEDIT

systems were created similarly by state constitutional and statutory provisions.

The U.S. judicial system has three principal characteristics: it is part of a federalist system of government, it has a specific role under the federal separation-of-powers doctrine, and it is organized in a hierarchical fashion.

Federalism The judiciary is part of a federalist system in which the state and federal governments share authority over legal matters arising within their geographic boundaries. In some instances both state and federal courts have the power to hear a legal dispute that arises from a single set of circumstances. For example, four Los Angeles police officers who were accused of participating in the 1991 beating of speeding motorist Rodney G. King faced prosecution for excessive use of force in both state and federal court. In other instances a state or federal court has exclusive JURISDICTION over a particular legal matter. For example, state courts typically have exclusive jurisdiction over matrimonial law, and federal courts have exclusive jurisdiction over bankruptcy law.

Separation of Powers Under the separation-of-powers doctrine, the judiciary shares power with the executive and legislative branches of government at both the state and federal levels. The judiciary is delegated the duty of interpreting and applying the laws that are passed by the legislature and enforced by the EXECUTIVE BRANCH.

Article I of the U.S. Constitution grants Congress its lawmaking power, and Article II authorizes the president to sign and VETO legislation and to execute laws that are enacted. Article III grants the federal judiciary the power to adjudicate lawsuits that arise under the Constitution, congressional law, treaties with foreign countries, and certain other instances that are specifically enumerated.

Federal judges are not elected to office. Instead, they are appointed to office by the president of the United States with the advice and consent of the Senate. Once appointed, federal judges hold office for life, unless they resign or are impeached for "Treason, Bribery, or other High Crimes and Misdemeanors" (U.S. Const. art. II, § 4).

The lifetime appointment of federal judges is controversial. On one hand, the federal judiciary runs the risk of growing out of touch with popular sentiment because it is being immunized from the electorate. On the other hand, it is considered necessary for the judiciary to remain independent of popular will so that judges will decide cases according to legal principles, not political considerations.

In many states judges are elected to office. Nonetheless, each state constitution similarly delegates powers among the three branches of government. Accordingly, judges are still expected to decide cases based on the law, not the political considerations that the executive and legislative branches may take into account in executing their duties.

Hierarchy The U.S. judiciary is a hierarchical system of trial and appellate courts at both the state and federal levels. In general, a lawsuit is originally filed with a trial court that hears the suit and determines its merits. Generally, parties have the right to ask an APPELLATE COURT to review the decision of a trial court. Parties aggrieved by a final judgment have the right to appeal the decision. Both state and federal governments provide at least two levels of appellate review, one consisting of intermediate courts of appeal and one consisting of a supreme court. The federal appellate system is divided into eleven numbered circuits, known as the U.S. courts of appeal, plus the Court of Appeals for the District of Columbia. Each

Hierarchy of U.S. Appellate Judiciary

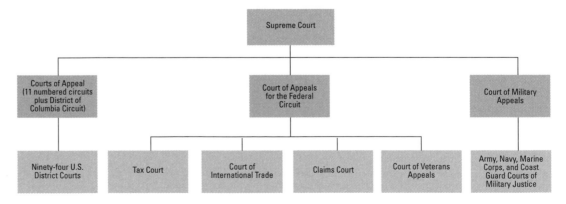

federal appellate court has jurisdiction over a certain geographic area, and may hear appeals only from federal DISTRICT COURTS within that jurisdiction. Specialized courts have been created to hear appeals concerning patents (the U.S. Court of Appeals for the Federal Circuit), international trade (the U.S. Court of International Trade), and military matters (the Court of Military Appeals).

At the state level, a lawsuit may be filed with a court sitting in a particular city, county, or district. At the federal level, Article III, Section 1, of the U.S. Constitution provides that "[t]he judicial Power of the United States, shall be vested in one supreme Court, and in such inferior Courts as the Congress may from time to time ordain and establish." Pursuant to this authority, Congress has established in each state at least one U.S. district court, where lawsuits are commenced regarding federal matters. Congress has also created an intermediate tier of federal appellate courts that sits between the Supreme Court and the federal district courts.

Special Courts   Not all lawsuits begin in an ordinary trial court. Both the state and federal governments have established special courts that are expressly designated to hear specific types of lawsuits. For example, at the federal level, special courts have been created to hear legal claims involving bankruptcy, tax, and military law. At the state level, many governments have established special courts to hear family law and probate matters.

Alternative Dispute Resolution and Administrative Agencies   In certain areas of law, litigants are prohibited from beginning a lawsuit in an ordinary trial court unless they first exhaust other methods of dispute resolution through an administrative body. Since the mid-1930s state and federal governments have created elaborate administrative systems to dispose of certain legal claims before a lawsuit may ever be filed. For example, at the federal level, ADMINISTRATIVE AGENCIES have been created to oversee a number of disputes involving labor law, environmental law, antitrust law, employment discrimination, securities transactions, and national transportation, among others.

Administrative agencies are created by statute, and legislatures may prescribe the qualifications for administrative officials, including administrative law judges, who are appointed by the executive branch, courts of law, and heads of government departments. These agencies are charged with the responsibility of establishing, developing, evaluating, and applying policy over a given area of law. The body of rules, principles, and regulations promulgated by such

agencies and their officials is known as administrative law.

State and federal governments have passed formal rules that set forth the procedures that these administrative bodies must follow. The rules governing federal administrative adjudication are provided in the Administrative Procedure Act (5 U.S.C.A. § 551 et seq. [1988]).

Laws promulgated by state and federal administrative bodies, including adjudicative bodies, are considered no less authoritative than laws enacted by legislatures, decreed by the executive branch, or issued by the judiciary. However, litigants who first exhaust their administrative remedies through the appropriate agency and are dissatisfied with a decision rendered by an administrative law judge, may appeal the decision to an ordinary court of law.

A court's exercise of discretionary power is also influenced by state and federal codes of judicial conduct. These codes require judges to perform their official duties in a fair and impartial manner. In this regard judges must exercise caution to avoid the appearance of impropriety. The violation of requirements set forth in state and federal codes of judicial conduct can result in severe penalties. These mandates impose extra incentive for judges to be evenhanded in the exercise of their discretion.

CROSS-REFERENCES

Administrative Law and Procedure; Alternative Dispute Resolution; Code of Judicial Conduct; Court of Appeal; Court of Claims; Court Opinion; Discretion in Decision Making; Federalism; Judicial Review; Jury; Separation of Powers.

JUDICIARY ACT OF 1789   The Judiciary Act of 1789 established the lower FEDERAL COURTS. Under Article III, Section 1, of the U.S. Constitution, "The judicial Power of the United States, shall be vested in one supreme Court, and in such inferior Courts as the Congress may from time to time ordain and establish." In the Judiciary Act, the first Congress created federal trial courts and federal appeals courts to comply with this provision.

The first Congress engaged in considerable debate over the Judiciary Act. This was not surprising: the Constitutional Convention, which had ended a year and a half earlier, had revealed a deep division between Federalists and Anti-Federalists. Federalists promoted federal powers to protect against local bias and ensure federal supremacy. Anti-Federalists opposed a strong federal government and preferred to leave as much power as possible to the states. Although the debate over the Judiciary Act was not conducted entirely by Federalists and Anti-Federalists, these groups represented the opposing viewpoints.

Many concessions were made to Anti-Federalists in the Constitution. However, the ratification of the Constitution was a victory for Federalists because it created the potential for considerable federal powers. The bill for the Judiciary Act—the first bill to be considered in the first Congress—provided another opportunity for Anti-Federalists to present their arguments against strong federal powers.

On April 7, 1789, the Senate ordered itself to create a committee to draft a bill organizing a federal judiciary. By the end of May, a committee led by OLIVER ELLSWORTH, of Connecticut, WILLIAM PATERSON, of New Jersey, and Caleb Strong, of Massachusetts, had devised a detailed, complex proposal. The committee envisioned a small, unintrusive federal judiciary with exacting jurisdictional requirements. This meant that a case would have to have certain characteristics before it could be heard by a federal court. Remembering criticisms made by the Anti-Federalists at the Constitutional Convention, the committee was careful to avoid giving the federal courts too much authority.

Despite the restrictions on JURISDICTION, Anti-Federalists opposed the bill on the grounds that a federal judiciary in any form would deprive states of the right to exercise their own judicial powers. They argued that state courts were more than capable of deciding federal issues. Furthermore, the provision in Article III, Section 1, of the Constitution did not require Congress to create lower federal courts: it merely suggested that Congress do so.

The Anti-Federalists, led by Richard Henry Lee and William Grayson, both of Virginia, submitted amendments to limit the scope of the act. Samuel Livermore, a congressman from New Hampshire and an Anti-Federalist, moved the House to limit the jurisdiction of inferior federal courts to questions of admiralty. Lee did the same in the Senate. Another proposal consisted of creating no lower federal courts and expanding the jurisdiction of the Supreme Court. All the amendments were voted down. Senator William Maclay, of Pennsylvania, wrote in his diary, "I opposed this bill from the beginning.... The constitution is meant to swallow all the state constitutions, by degrees; and this to swallow, by degrees, all the State judiciaries" (Clinton 1986, 1531).

The Federalists, led by JAMES MADISON, of Virginia, insisted that a reasonable reading of Article III, Section 1, required Congress to establish lower federal courts. According to the Federalists, federal courts were necessary to ensure the supremacy of federal law. The supremacy of federal law over state law had, after all, been established in Article VI of the Constitution, which stated, in part, that "[t]his Constitution, and the Laws of the United States . . . shall be the supreme Law of the Land."

The Federalists argued further that federal courts provided a VENUE that would be less susceptible to BIAS than that of state courts. The Federalists declared that several types of cases were appropriate only in federal court, including cases involving disputes between states; ALIENS, or noncitizens; and crimes against the United States.

Under the proposed act, federal juries would comprise persons from all over the region, decreasing the potential for the jury bias that can exist in closely knit state courts. Also, federal judges would have no allegiance to any particular state because they would have judicial responsibility for several states at once, and thus would be less prone to bias than were state judges.

Eventually, the Federalists won enough support to pass the act. The House approved the bill submitted by the Senate without a recorded vote, and President GEORGE WASHINGTON signed the act into law on September 24, 1789.

The act established two sets of federal courts to operate below the U.S. Supreme Court. On one level, the act created thirteen federal districts. Each of these districts contained a federal trial court that had jurisdiction over minor criminal cases, admiralty and maritime cases, and CIVIL ACTIONS on federal matters.

On another level, the act created three federal CIRCUIT COURTS. The circuit courts were given trial court jurisdiction over serious criminal cases and three categories of civil cases: cases where the United States was a plaintiff; cases where at least one of the parties was alien to the United States; and cases between parties of different states, or "diversity" cases, if the amount at issue exceeded $500. Circuit court jurisdiction over diversity cases was made concurrent with state court jurisdiction. This meant that a federal trial was not mandatory, and a plaintiff could sue in either a state or federal court. Also, if a defendant from another state was being sued in state court for more than $500, she or he could have the case moved to the federal circuit court.

Each of the circuit courts comprised a federal DISTRICT COURT judge and two Supreme Court justices. This composition was a concession to Anti-Federalists. The general idea was that requiring Supreme Court Justices to sit on circuit courts, or "ride circuit," would force them to keep in touch with local concerns. Theoretically, this would prevent the development of the elite judicial aristocracy feared by the Anti-Federalists.

The Judiciary Act also identified the precise jurisdiction of the Supreme Court: The Supreme Court could hear appeals from the federal district and circuit courts. The Supreme Court could also hear appeals from state courts in cases involving federal treaties or statutes, state statutes that were repugnant to the federal Constitution or to federal laws or treaties, and the interpretation of any clause of the Constitution or of federal laws or treaties. In any case, the decision of a state court would be reviewed by the Supreme Court only if it was against federal interests.

The act gave the Supreme Court trial court jurisdiction over controversies between two or more states and between a state and citizens of another state. The Supreme Court was also given trial court jurisdiction to hear cases against ambassadors, public ministers, and consuls or their domestics, with the adjunct that district courts could also hear cases against consuls or vice consuls. (Consuls and vice consuls were government officers living in another country and responsible for the promotion of U.S. business in that country).

The Judiciary Act fixed the number of justices on the U.S. Supreme Court at six. As the nation grew in size, new circuits were added to the original three, and justices were added to the court along with the circuits. By 1863, the number of justices on the Supreme Court had grown to ten. In 1866, Congress reduced the number of justices to seven. In 1869, the figure was set at nine, where it has remained.

In many sections of the act, federal trial court jurisdiction was made concurrent with state court jurisdiction. This meant that federal courts did not have exclusive jurisdiction over many matters involving federal law. One notable exception was that the federal courts were given exclusive jurisdiction to hear cases involving prosecution for the violation of federal criminal laws.

The Judiciary Act did not provide for FEDERAL QUESTION jurisdiction. That is, it did not grant federal courts broad authority to hear all cases that arose under the Constitution or federal law. This may have been because no federal laws were on the books at the time the act was established. Whether intentionally or owing to a lack of foresight, Congress chose to identify in the first Judiciary Act the specific cases that could be heard in federal court. Congress did pass a statute authorizing federal question juris-

diction in 1875. However, to this day, Congress usually grants federal court jurisdiction over new laws in a separate statute or clause.

The creators of the Judiciary Act understood it to be a work-in-progress. On the night before its final passage, Madison, an ardent proponent of the act, wrote that it was "defective both in its general structure, and many of its particular regulations" (Clinton 1986, 1539).

The structure of the federal judiciary has changed dramatically since the passage of the first Judiciary Act. The federal judiciary is now more streamlined. The federal district courts handle all federal trials. The circuit courts are now called U.S. courts of appeals, and they are exclusively appeals courts: they no longer have trial court jurisdiction over any cases. Supreme Court justices no longer have to ride circuit. Despite these changes, the Judiciary Act's idea of creating two levels of federal courts beneath the Supreme Court has remained intact.

The act's concern with establishing limits to federal court jurisdiction now seems quaint. In the more than two centuries since the passage of the act, statutes passed by Congress and decisions issued by the Supreme Court concerning the jurisdiction of federal courts have effectively expanded the reach of federal courts. Federal courts have also increased in number: there are now eleven federal circuits, each containing an appeals court and several federal district courts.

See also DIVERSITY OF CITIZENSHIP; SUPREME COURT OF THE UNITED STATES.

JUDICIARY ACT OF 1801 See MIDNIGHT JUDGES.

JUNIOR 📖 Younger; subsequently born or created; later in rank, tenure, preference, or position. 📖

A junior LIEN is one that is subordinate in rank to another prior lien. This means that the junior lien will be paid off only after the prior lien has been satisfied.

When used in a proper name, junior or its abbreviation, Jr., is merely descriptive and not part of the individual's legal name. The absence of the term at the end of a name has no legal consequence. A signature that omits the description is still valid.

JUNK BOND 📖 A SECURITY issued by a CORPORATION that is considered to offer a high risk to bondholders. 📖

Junk bond is the popular name for high-risk bonds offered by corporations. A bond is a certificate or some other evidence of a DEBT. In the world of corporate finance, a corporation may sell a bond in exchange for cash. The bond contains a promise to repay its purchaser at a

In 1992 Charles Keating, former chairman of American Continental Corporation, was sentenced to ten years in prison for tricking customers of Lincoln Savings and Loan Association into purchasing high-risk junk bonds issued by American Continental. The bailout of the collapsed Lincoln cost taxpayers an estimated $2.6 billion.

certain rate of return, called a yield. A bond is not an equity investment in the corporation; it is debt of the corporation.

A corporate bond is essentially a loan to a corporation. The loan may be secured by a LIEN or MORTGAGE on the corporation's property as security for repayment.

To determine the level of the DEFAULT risk for potential bondholders, financial experts analyze corporations and rate them on a number of factors, including the nature of their business, their financial holdings, their employees, and the length of their existence. The higher the risk for bondholders, the lower the risk rating given the corporation.

Because their ventures are considered risky, low-rated corporations must offer bond yields that are higher than those of high-rated corporations. High-rated corporations have less need for income from bonds, so they do not need to offer high yields. Bonds from these companies are called investment-grade bonds. Low-rated corporations have the need for bond income, so they offer high-yield bonds. These high-yield bonds are junk bonds.

When a corporation fails, bondholders may lose all or part of their investment if the corporation has declared BANKRUPTCY or has no ASSETS. This possibility is more real for junk bonds because they are, by definition, issued by unproven or unhealthy corporations.

For some persons, the high yield of a junk bond can be worth the increased risk of default.

Junk bonds can increase in value if the corporation's rating is upgraded by private bond-rating firms. Junk bonds are also favored by some persons precisely because they contribute capital to young or struggling corporations. Whether to buy a junk bond depends on the investor: conservative investors do not favor them, but speculators and others seeking a quick profit find them attractive.

JURAL The principles of natural and positive rights recognized by law.

Jural pertains to the rights and obligations sanctioned and governed by positive law or that law which is enacted by proper authority. Jural doctrines are founded upon fundamental rules and protect essential rights and duties.

Jural principles are not the same as moral principles. Moral doctrines encompass the entire range of ETHICS or the science of behavior. Jural doctrines include only those areas of moral conduct that are recognized by law.

Jural denotes the state or an organized political society.

JURAT The certificate of an officer that a written instrument was sworn to by the individual who signed it.

Jurat is derived from *jurare*, Latin for "to swear." It is proof that an OATH was taken before an administering officer, such as a notary. In an AFFIDAVIT, a jurat is the clause at the end of the document stating the date, place, and name of the person before whom it was sworn.

JURIDICAL Pertaining to the administration of justice or to the office of a judge.

A *juridical act* is one that conforms to the laws and the rules of court. A *juridical day* is one on which the courts are in session.

JURIMETRICS The study of law and science.

Used primarily in academia to mean a strictly empirical approach to the law, the term *jurimetrics* originated in the 1960s as the use of computers in law practice began to revolutionize the areas of legal research, evidence analysis, and data management. A neologism whose roots suggest JURISPRUDENCE and measurement, it was popularized by the AMERICAN BAR ASSOCIATION (ABA), whose quarterly *Jurimetrics Journal of Law, Science, and Technology* is a widely respected publication with an international focus.

Although the effect of science on law has a long history, modern developments date only to the second half of the twentieth century. Precipitating the rise of the contemporary legal practice—which relies heavily on computers to research relevant law and, in some cases, to analyze evidence—was an emphasis on logical reasoning. Leading the way in this area was the

ABA, which in 1959 began publishing in its journal *Modern Uses of Logic in Law* papers arguing in favor of applying a strict, systematic approach to the law. The advent of more powerful and affordable computers allowed symbolic logic (the use of formulas to express logical problems) to be applied on a more practical scale. As the possibilities inherent in rapid data retrieval caused a burst of research during the mid-1960s, the ABA renamed the journal *Jurimetrics*.

Published by the ABA's Section of Law and Technology, *Jurimetrics* examines a wide range of interrelated scientific and legal topics. The journal's articles cover the influence on law of the so-called hard sciences as well as the social sciences, disciplines such as engineering and communications, methodologies such as symbolic logic and statistics, and the use of technology in law practice, legislation, and adjudication. Thus, article topics range from the state of the art in DNA evidence to experimental research on jury decision making. Also concerned with the regulation of science and technology, *Jurimetrics* examines cutting edge issues such as electronic security and copyright law in the age of the Internet.

See also COMPUTER-ASSISTED LEGAL RESEARCH.

JURIS 📖 [*Latin, Of right; of law.*] A phrase that serves as the root for diverse terms and phrases dealing with the law; for example, jurisdiction, jurisprudence, or jurist. 📖

JURISDICTION 📖 The geographic area over which authority extends; legal authority; the authority to hear and determine CAUSES OF ACTION. 📖

Jurisdiction generally describes any authority over a certain area or certain persons. In the law, jurisdiction sometimes refers to a particular geographic area containing a defined legal authority. For example, the federal government is a jurisdiction unto itself. Its power spans the entire United States. Each state is also a jurisdiction unto itself with power to pass its own laws. Smaller geographic areas, such as counties and cities, are separate jurisdictions to the extent that they have powers independent of the federal and state governments.

Jurisdiction also may refer to the origin of a court's authority. A court may be designated either as a court of GENERAL JURISDICTION or as a court of special jurisdiction. A court of general jurisdiction is a trial court that is empowered to hear all cases that are not specifically reserved for COURTS of special jurisdiction. A court of special jurisdiction is empowered to hear only certain kinds of cases.

Courts of general jurisdiction are often called district courts or superior courts. In New York, however, the court of general jurisdiction is called the Supreme Court of New York. In most jurisdictions other trial courts of special jurisdiction exist apart from the courts of general jurisdiction; examples are probate, tax, traffic, juvenile, and, in some cities, drug courts. On the federal level, the district courts are courts of general jurisdiction. FEDERAL COURTS of special jurisdiction include the TAX COURT and the BANKRUPTCY courts.

Jurisdiction can also be used to define the proper court in which to bring a particular case. In this context a court has either original or APPELLATE jurisdiction over a case. When the court has ORIGINAL JURISDICTION, it is empowered to conduct a trial in the case. When the court has appellate jurisdiction, it may only review the trial court proceedings for error.

Generally, courts of general and special jurisdiction have original jurisdiction over most cases, and appeals courts and the jurisdiction's high court have appellate jurisdiction. But this is not always the case. For example, under Article III, Section 2, Clause 2, of the U.S. Constitution, the U.S. Supreme Court is a court of appellate jurisdiction. However, under the same clause, the Court has original jurisdiction in cases between states. Such cases usually concern disputes over boundaries and waterways.

Finally, jurisdiction refers to the inherent authority of a court to hear a case and declare a judgment. When a plaintiff seeks to initiate suit, he or she must determine where to file the COMPLAINT. The plaintiff must file suit in a court that has jurisdiction over the case. If the court does not have jurisdiction, the defendant may challenge the suit on that ground, and the suit may be dismissed or its result may be overturned in a subsequent ACTION by one of the parties in the case.

A plaintiff may file suit in federal court; however, state courts generally have CONCURRENT JURISDICTION. Concurrent jurisdiction means that both the state and federal court have jurisdiction over the matter.

If a claim can be filed in either state or federal court, and the plaintiff files the claim in state court, the defendant may remove the case to federal court (28 U.S.C.A. § 1441 et seq.). This is a tactical decision. Federal court proceedings are widely considered to be less susceptible to BIAS because the jury pool is drawn from the entire state, not just from the local community.

State courts have concurrent jurisdiction in most cases. Federal courts have exclusive jurisdiction in a limited number of cases, such as federal criminal, antitrust, bankruptcy, patent and copyright, and some admiralty cases, and suits against the U.S. government.

Under federal and state laws and court rules, a court may exercise its inherent authority only if it has two types of jurisdiction: personal and subject matter. PERSONAL JURISDICTION is the authority a court has over the parties in the case. SUBJECT MATTER JURISDICTION is a court's authority over the particular claim or controversy.

State Civil Court Jurisdiction

Personal Jurisdiction Personal jurisdiction is based on territorial concepts. That is, a court can gain personal jurisdiction over a party only if the party has a connection to the geographic area in which the court sits. Traditionally, this connection was satisfied only by the presence of the defendant in the state where the court sat. Since the late nineteenth century, notions of personal jurisdiction have expanded beyond territorial concepts, and courts may gain personal jurisdiction over defendants on a number of grounds. However, the territorial basis remains a reliable route to establishing personal jurisdiction.

A person who has a civil claim may file suit in a court located in her or his home state. If the defendant lives in the same state, the court will have no trouble gaining personal jurisdiction. The plaintiff must simply serve the defendant with a SUMMONS and a copy of the complaint that was filed with the court. Once this is accomplished, the court has personal jurisdiction over both the plaintiff and the defendant. If the defendant lives outside the state, the plaintiff may serve the defendant with the process papers when the defendant appears in the state.

If the defendant lives outside the state and does not plan to reenter the state, the court may gain personal jurisdiction in other ways. Most states have a LONG-ARM STATUTE. This type of statute allows a state court to gain personal jurisdiction over an out-of-state defendant who (1) transacts business within the state, (2) commits a tort within the state, (3) commits a tort outside the state that causes an injury within the state, or (4) owns, uses, or possesses REAL PROPERTY within the state.

If an out-of-state defendant caused an injury while driving inside the state, the court may gain personal jurisdiction over the defendant on the theory that the defendant consented to such jurisdiction by driving on the state's roads. Many states have statutes that create such IMPLIED CONSENT to personal jurisdiction.

When the defendant is a CORPORATION, the corporation is always subject to personal jurisdiction in the courts of the state in which it is incorporated. If the corporation has sufficient contacts in other states, courts in those states may hold that the out-of-state corporation has consented to personal jurisdiction through its contacts with the state. For example, a corporation that solicits business in other states or maintains offices in other states may be subject to suit in those states, even if the corporation is not headquartered or incorporated in those states. A corporation's transaction of business in a foreign state is a sufficient contact to establish personal jurisdiction.

In actions concerning real property located within the state, state courts may use additional means to gain personal jurisdiction over out-of-state defendants. A state court may gain personal jurisdiction over all parties, regardless of their physical location, in a dispute over the title to real property. This type of personal jurisdiction is called IN REM, or "against the thing." Personal jurisdiction over all parties interested in the real property is gained not through the parties but through the presence of the land in the court's jurisdiction.

If a court cannot gain personal jurisdiction over an out-of-state defendant, the plaintiff may be forced to sue the defendant in the state in which the defendant resides or in the state where the injury occurred. For example, a plaintiff who was injured outside his or her home state may have to file suit in the defendant's home state or in the state where the injury occurred if the defendant has no plans to enter the plaintiff's home state.

Subject Matter Jurisdiction Courts of general jurisdiction have subject matter jurisdiction over the majority of civil claims, including actions involving TORTS, CONTRACTS, unpaid DEBT, and CIVIL RIGHTS violations. Courts of general jurisdiction do not have subject matter jurisdiction over claims or controversies that are reserved for courts of special jurisdiction. For example, in a state that has a PROBATE court, all claims involving WILLS and ESTATES must be brought in the probate court, not in a court of general jurisdiction.

In some cases a claim must first be heard by a special ADMINISTRATIVE BOARD before it can be heard by a court. For example, a WORKERS' COMPENSATION claim in most states must be heard by a workers' compensation board before it can be heard in a court of general jurisdiction.

Another consideration in establishing subject matter jurisdiction is the amount in controversy. This is the total of all claims, counterclaims, and cross-claims in the suit. (A COUNTERCLAIM is a CLAIM by a defendant against a plaintiff; a CROSS-CLAIM is a claim by a plaintiff against another plaintiff, or by a defendant against another defendant.) In most jurisdictions, if the amount in controversy does not exceed a certain limit, the case must be heard by a court other than a court of general jurisdiction. This court is usually called a SMALL CLAIMS COURT. The rules in such a court limit the procedures available to the parties so that the court can obtain a simple and speedy resolution to the dispute.

Federal Civil Court Jurisdiction

Personal Jurisdiction To obtain personal jurisdiction over the parties, a federal court follows the procedural rules of the state in which it sits. For example, a federal court in Michigan follows the Michigan state court rules governing personal jurisdiction. The court examines the usual factors in establishing personal jurisdiction, such as the physical location of the parties, the reach of the state's long-arm statute, any consent to personal jurisdiction by the defendant, or the location of real property in a dispute over real property.

Subject Matter Jurisdiction In some cases a plaintiff may file suit in federal court. These cases are limited to (1) claims arising from the U.S. Constitution or federal statutes (FEDERAL QUESTION jurisdiction), (2) claims brought by or against the federal government, and (3) claims in which all opposing parties live in different states and the amount in controversy exceeds $50,000 (diversity jurisdiction). A federal court obtains subject matter jurisdiction over a case if the case meets one or more of these three requirements.

Claims arising from the U.S. Constitution or federal statutes Federal question jurisdiction is covered in 28 U.S.C.A. § 1331. This statute provides that federal district courts have "original jurisdiction of all CIVIL ACTIONS arising under the Constitution, laws, or treaties of the United States." Some claims are expressly identified as federal in the Constitution. These claims include those involving ambassadors and consuls or public ministers, admiralty and maritime claims, and claims made by or against the federal government. Claims that are based on federal law also may be filed in federal court. An action against the federal government based on the NEGLIGENCE of a federal employee, for example, is authorized by the FEDERAL TORT CLAIMS ACT of 1946 (60 Stat. 842 [28 U.S.C.A. § 1346(b), 2674]).

Some cases may combine federal and state issues. In such cases no clear test exists to determine whether a party may file suit in or remove a suit to federal court. Generally, federal courts will decline jurisdiction if a claim is based predominantly on state law. For example, assume that a plaintiff is embroiled in a property dispute with a neighbor. The plaintiff files suit against the neighbor, alleging state-law claims of nuisance, TRESPASS, breach of contract, and ASSAULT. A state official advises the plaintiff that the property belongs to the neighbor (the defendant). If the plaintiff sues the state official in the same suit, alleging a constitutional violation such as the uncompensated taking of property, a federal court may refuse jurisdiction because the case involves predominantly state law.

Federal courts may decline jurisdiction on other grounds if a state court has concurrent jurisdiction. When they do so, they are said to abstain, because they are refraining from exercising their jurisdiction. Federal courts tend to abstain from cases that require the interpretation of state law, if those cases can be decided by state courts. Federal courts abstain to avoid answering unnecessary constitutional questions, to avoid conflict with state courts, and to avoid making errors in determining the meaning of state laws.

Claims brought by or against the federal government Generally, the United States may sue in federal court if its claim is based on federal law. For example, if the federal government seeks to seize the property of a defendant in a drug case, it must base the action on the federal forfeiture statute, not on the FORFEITURE statute of the state in which the property lies.

Generally, state and federal governments have SOVEREIGN IMMUNITY, which means that they may not be sued. However, state and federal governments may consent to suit. On the federal level, Congress has removed the government's IMMUNITY for injuries resulting from the negligent and, in some cases, intentional conduct of federal agencies, federal officers, and other federal employees (60 Stat. 842 [28 U.S.C.A. § 1346(b), 2674, 2680]). Generally, the federal government is liable only for injuries resulting from the performance of official government duties.

If Congress has not waived federal immunity to certain suits, a person may nevertheless file suit against the agents, officers, or employees personally. For example, the U.S. Supreme Court has held that federal agents, officers, and employees who violate constitutional rights may be sued for damages in federal court (*Bivens v. Six Unknown Named Agents of the Federal Bureau of Narcotics*, 403 U.S. 388, 91 S. Ct. 1999, 29 L. Ed. 2d 619 [1971]).

Claims in which all opposing parties live in different states and the amount in controversy exceeds $50,000 Diversity cases provide federal courts with subject matter jurisdiction under 28 U.S.C.A. § 1332. A civil case qualifies as a federal diversity case if all opposing parties live in separate states and the amount in controversy exceeds $50,000. If the opposing parties live in the same state, the case may still qualify for federal subject matter jurisdiction if there is some remaining citizenship diversity between parties. For example, assume that a person is acting as a stakeholder by holding property for a third party. If ownership of the property is in dispute, the stakeholder may join the defendants in the suit to avoid LIABILITY to any of the parties. Such a case may be filed in federal court if a defendant lives in a different state, even if one of the defendants lives in the same state as the stakeholder or in the same state as the other defendants. See also DIVERSITY OF CITIZENSHIP.

State and Federal Criminal Court Jurisdiction

Personal Jurisdiction Personal jurisdiction in a criminal case is established when the defendant is accused of committing a crime in the geographic area in which the court sits. If a crime results in federal charges, the federal court that sits in the state where the offense was committed has personal jurisdiction over the defendant. In a CONSPIRACY case, the defendants may face prosecution in any jurisdiction in which a conspiratorial act took place. This can include a number of states if at least one conspirator crossed state lines or if the conspiracy involved criminal acts in more than one state. KIDNAPPING is another crime that can establish personal jurisdiction in courts in more than one state, if it involves crossing state lines.

Subject Matter Jurisdiction In criminal cases the question of jurisdiction is relatively simple. Subject matter jurisdiction is easily decided because criminal courts or the courts of general jurisdiction have automatic subject matter jurisdiction over criminal cases. In most states minor crimes may be tried in one court, and more serious crimes in another. In Idaho, for example, criminal cases are tried in the district courts. However, MISDEMEANOR cases may be assigned by the district court to a MAGISTRATE (Idaho Code § 1-2208 [1996]). (A magistrate is a judge who is authorized to hear minor civil cases and decide criminal matters without a jury.)

The major question in criminal subject matter jurisdiction is whether the charges are federal or state. If the charges allege a violation of federal criminal law, the defendant will be tried in a federal court located in the state in which the offense was committed. If the charges allege a violation of state law, the defendant will face prosecution in a trial court that has jurisdiction over the area in which the offense was committed. If a crime violates both federal and state law, the defendant may be tried twice: once in state court, and once in federal court.

Venue VENUE is similar to, but separate from, jurisdiction. The venue of a case is the physical location of the courthouse in which the case is tried. If more than one court has both subject matter and personal jurisdiction over a case, the court that first receives the case can send the case, upon request of one of the parties, to a court in another jurisdiction. Unlike jurisdiction, venue does not involve a determination of a court's inherent authority to hear a case.

JURISDICTIONAL DISPUTE 📖 Conflicting claims made by two different LABOR UNIONS to an employer regarding assignment of the work or union representation. 📖

Two basic types of controversies ordinarily arise in such disputes. There can be a disagreement concerning whether certain work should be done by workers in one union or another. For example, there might be a dispute between employees in a carpenters' union and a glaziers' union concerning who should install frames for windows in an apartment building. When this type of dispute arises, there must exist EVIDENCE of a threat of coercive action in order for the National Labor Relations Board (NLRB) to intervene by conducting a hearing and making an assignment of the work.

A jurisdictional dispute might also arise concerning which union should represent employees who are performing a particular type of work.

JURIS DOCTOR 📖 The degree awarded to an individual upon the successful completion of law school. 📖

Juris doctor, or doctor of jurisprudence, commonly abbreviated J.D., is the degree commonly conferred by law schools. It is required in all states except California (which includes an option called law office study) to gain admission to the bar. Gaining admission to the bar means obtaining a LICENSE to practice law in a particular state or in federal court.

Until the 1930s and 1940s, many states did not require a person to have a law school degree in order to obtain a license to practice law. Most lawyers qualified for a license by working as an APPRENTICE for an established attorney for a specified period. By the 1950s most states required a law school degree. State legislatures established this requirement to raise the standards of practicing attorneys and to restrict the number of attorneys. The degree offered by most colleges and universities was called a master of laws (L.L.M.) degree. In the 1960s, as colleges and universities increased the requirements for a law degree, the J.D. replaced the L.L.M. as the primary degree awarded by law schools.

The specific requirements for a J.D. vary from school to school. Generally, the requirements include completing a minimum number of class hours each academic period, and taking certain mandatory courses such as contracts, torts, civil procedure, and criminal law in the first year of law school. All states require that students pass a course on professional responsibility before receiving a J.D. degree.

See also LEGAL EDUCATION.

JURISPRUDENCE 📖 From the Latin term *juris prudentia*, which means "the study, knowledge, or science of law"; in the United States, more broadly associated with the philosophy of law. 📖

Legal philosophy has many aspects, with four types being the most common. The most prevalent form of jurisprudence seeks to analyze, explain, classify, and criticize entire bodies of law, ranging from contract to tort to constitutional law. Legal encyclopedias, law reviews, and law school textbooks frequently contain this type of jurisprudential scholarship.

The second type of jurisprudence compares and contrasts law with other fields of knowledge such as literature, economics, religion, and the social sciences. The purpose of this interdisciplinary study is to enlighten each field of knowledge by sharing insights that have proved important to understanding essential features of the comparative disciplines.

The third type of jurisprudence raises fundamental questions about the law itself. These questions seek to reveal the historical, moral, and cultural underpinnings of a particular legal concept. *The Common Law* (1881), written by OLIVER WENDELL HOLMES, JR., is a well-known example of this type of jurisprudence. It traces the evolution of civil and criminal responsibility from undeveloped societies where liability for

Oliver Wendell Holmes, Jr.'s The Common Law *(1881) traces the evolution of civil and criminal responsibility. His book represents a branch of jurisprudence that seeks to uncover the historical and cultural foundations of law.*

injuries was based on subjective notions of revenge, to modern societies where liability is based on objective notions of reasonableness.

The fourth and fastest-growing body of jurisprudence focuses on even more abstract questions, including, What is law? How does a trial or appellate court judge decide a case? Is a judge similar to a mathematician or a scientist applying autonomous and determinate rules and principles? Or is a judge more like a legislator who simply decides a case in favor of the most politically preferable outcome? Must a judge base a decision only on the written rules and regulations that have been enacted by the government? Or may a judge also be influenced by unwritten principles derived from theology, moral philosophy, and historical practice?

Four schools of jurisprudence have attempted to answer these questions: formalism proposes that law is a science, realism holds that *law* is just another name for politics, POSITIVISM suggests that law must be confined to the written rules and regulations enacted or recognized by the government, and naturalism maintains that the law must reflect eternal principles of justice and morality that exist independent of governmental recognition.

Modern U.S. legal thought began in 1870. In that year, Holmes, the father of the U.S. legal realist movement, wrote his first major essay for the *American Law Review*, and CHRISTOPHER COLUMBUS LANGDELL, the father of U.S. legal formalism, joined the faculty at Harvard Law School.

Legal formalism, also known as conceptualism, treats law like a math or science. Formalists believe that in the same way a mathematician or scientist identifies the relevant axioms, applies them to given data, and systematically reaches a demonstrable theorem, a judge identifies the relevant legal principles, applies them to the facts of a case, and logically deduces a rule that will govern the outcome of a dispute. Judges derive relevant legal principles from various sources of legal authority, including state and federal constitutions, statutes, regulations, and case law.

For example, most states have enacted legislation that prohibits courts from probating a will that was not signed by two witnesses. If a court is presented with a number of wills to probate for the same estate, and only one of those wills has been witnessed by at least two persons, the court can quickly deduce the correct legal conclusion in a formalistic fashion: Each will that has been signed by fewer than two witnesses will have no legal effect, and only the will executed in compliance with the statutory requirements may be probated.

Formalists also apply common-law precedent in a syllogistic fashion. The "mailbox" rule is a common-law doctrine that stands for the proposition that an offer is deemed legally accepted when mailed by the offeree, not when received by the offeror. This bright-line rule enables courts to resolve most disputes in a simple and uncontroversial fashion. So long as the offeree mails the acceptance in a properly addressed envelope bearing the appropriate amount of postage, the acceptance will ordinarily be ruled valid.

Formalists also rely on inductive reasoning to settle legal disputes. Whereas deductive reasoning involves the application of general principles that will yield a specific rule when applied to the facts of a case, inductive reasoning starts with a number of specific rules and infers from them a broader legal principle that may be applied to comparable legal disputes in the future. *Griswold v. Connecticut*, 381 U.S. 479, 85 S. Ct. 1678, 14 L. Ed. 2d 510 (1965), provides an example. In *Griswold*, the Supreme Court ruled that although no express provision of the federal Constitution guarantees the right to PRIVACY, and although no precedent had established such a right, an individual's right to privacy can be inferred from the First, Third, Fourth, Fifth, Ninth, and Fourteenth Amendments and the cases interpreting them. See also GRISWOLD V. CONNECTICUT.

English jurist SIR EDWARD COKE was among the first to popularize the formalistic approach to law in Anglo-American history. Coke believed that the COMMON LAW was "the peculiar science of judges." The common law, Coke said, represented the "artificial perfection of reason" obtained through "long study, observation, and experience." Coke also believed that only lawyers, judges, and others trained in the law could fully comprehend and apply this highest method of reasoning. The rest of society, including the king or queen of England, was not sufficiently learned to do so.

Langdell invigorated Coke's jurisprudence of artificial reason in the United States during the second half of the nineteenth century. Langdell compared the study of law to the study of science, and suggested that law school classrooms were the laboratories of jurisprudence. Judicial reasoning, Langdell believed, parallels the reasoning used in geometric proofs. He urged professors of law to classify and arrange legal principles much as a taxonomist organizes plant and animal life. Langdell articulated what has remained the orthodox school of thought in U.S. jurisprudence throughout the twentieth century.

Since the early 1970s, Professor Ronald M. Dworkin has been the foremost advocate of the formalist approach with some subtle variations. Although Dworkin stops short of explicitly comparing law to science and math, he maintains that law is best explained as a rational and cohesive system of principles that judges must apply with integrity. The principle of integrity requires that judges provide equal treatment to all litigants presenting legal claims that cannot honestly be distinguished. Application of this principle, Dworkin contends, will produce a "right answer" in all cases, even cases presenting knotty and polemical political questions, although every judge may not reach the same conclusion.

The realist movement, which began in the late eighteenth century and gained force during the administration of President FRANKLIN D. ROOSEVELT, was the first to attack formalism. Realists held a skeptical attitude toward Langdellian legal science. "The life of the law has not been logic, it has been experience," Holmes wrote in 1881.

Based on their experience, realists held two beliefs. First, they believed that law is not a scientific enterprise in which deductive reasoning can be applied to reach a determinate outcome in every case. Instead, most litigation presents hard questions that judges must resolve by BALANCING the interests of the parties and ultimately drawing an arbitrary line on one side of the dispute. This line is typically drawn in accordance with the political, economic, and psychological proclivities of the judge.

For example, when a court is asked to decide whether a harmful business activity is a common-law nuisance, the judge must ascertain whether the particular activity is reasonable. The judge does not base this determination on a precise algebraic equation. Instead, the judge balances the competing economic and social interests of the parties, and rules in favor of the litigant with the most persuasive case. Realists would thus contend that judges who are ideologically inclined to foster business growth will authorize the continuation of a harmful activity, whereas judges who are ideologically inclined to protect the environment will not.

Second, realists believed that because judges decide cases based on their political affiliation, the law tends always to lag behind social change. For example, the realists of the late nineteenth century saw a dramatic rise in the disparity between the wealth and working conditions of rich and poor U.S. citizens following the industrial revolution. To protect society's poorest and weakest members, many states began drafting legislation that established a minimum wage and maximum working hours for various classes of exploited workers. This legislation was part of the U.S. Progressive movement, which reflected many of the realists' concerns.

The Supreme Court began striking down such laws as an unconstitutional interference with the freedom of contract guaranteed by the FOURTEENTH AMENDMENT of the U.S. Constitution. U.S. realists claimed that the Supreme Court justices were simply using the freedom-of-contract doctrine to hide the real basis of their decision, which was their personal adherence to free-market principles and laissez-faire economics. The realists argued that the free-market system was not really free at all. They believed that the economic structure of the United States was based on coercive laws such as the EMPLOYMENT-AT-WILL doctrine, which permits an employer to discharge an employee for almost any reason. These laws, the realists asserted, promote the interests of the most powerful U.S. citizens, leaving the rest of society to fend for itself.

Some realists only sought to demonstrate that law is neither autonomous, apolitical, nor determinate. For example, JEROME FRANK, who coined the term *legal realism* and later became a judge on the U.S. Court of Appeals for the Second Circuit, emphasized the psychological foundation of judicial decision making, arguing that a judge's decision may be influenced by mundane things like what she or he ate for breakfast. Frank believed that it is deceptive for the legal profession to perpetuate the myth that the law is clearly knowable or precisely predictable, when it is so plastic and mutable. KARL LLEWELLYN, another founder of the U.S. LEGAL REALISM movement, similarly believed that the law is little more than putty in the hands of a judge who is able to shape the outcome of a case based on personal biases.

Since the mid-1960s, this theme has been echoed by the CRITICAL LEGAL STUDIES movement, which has applied the skeptical insights of the realists to attack courts for rendering decisions based on racial, sexist, and homophobic prejudices. For example, feminist legal scholars have pilloried the Supreme Court's decision in *Craig v. Boren*, 429 U.S. 190, 97 S. Ct. 451, 50 L. Ed. 2d 397 (1976), for offering women less protection against governmental discrimination than is afforded members of other minority groups. Gay legal scholars have similarly assailed the Supreme Court's decision in *Bowers v. Hardwick*, 478 U.S. 186, 106 S. Ct. 2841, 92 L. Ed. 2d 140 (1986), for failing to recognize a fundamental constitutional right to engage in homosexual SODOMY. See also GAY AND LESBIAN RIGHTS.

Other realists, such as ROSCOE POUND, were more interested in using the insights of their movement to reform the law. Pound was one of the original advocates of sociological jurisprudence in the United States. According to Pound, the aim of every law—whether constitutional, statutory, or case—should be to enhance the welfare of society. JEREMY BENTHAM, a legal philosopher in England, planted the seeds of sociological jurisprudence in the eighteenth century when he argued that the law must seek to achieve the greatest good for the greatest number of people in society. Bentham's theory, known as UTILITARIANISM, continues to influence legal thinkers in the United States.

Law and economics is one school of thought that traces its lineage to Benthamite jurisprudence. This school of thought, also known as economic analysis of the law, argues that judges must decide cases in order to maximize the wealth of society. According to law and economics exponents, each person in society is a rational maximizer of his or her own self-interest. Persons who rationally maximize their self-interest are willing to exchange something they value less for something they value more. For example, every day in the United States, people voluntarily give up their time, money, and liberty to acquire food, property, or peace of mind. This school of thought contends that the law must facilitate these voluntary exchanges to maximize the aggregate wealth of society.

Another school of thought Bentham influenced is known as legal pragmatism. Unlike law and economics exponents, legal pragmatists provide no formula for determining the best

Legal realists believe that judicial decision making has a psychological foundation and that it is not predictable or consistent.

STACY PICK/STOCK BOSTON

means to improve the welfare of society. Instead, pragmatists contend that judges must merely set a goal that they hope to achieve in resolving a particular legal dispute, such as the preservation of societal stability, the protection of individual rights, or the delineation of governmental powers and responsibilities. Judges must then draft the best court order to accomplish this goal. Pragmatists maintain that judges must choose the appropriate societal goal by weighing the value of competing interests presented by a lawsuit, and then using a "grab bag" of "anecdote, introspection, imagination, common sense, empathy, metaphor, analogy, precedent, custom, memory, experience, intuition, and induction" to reach the appropriate balance (Posner 1990, 73).

Pragmatism, sometimes called instrumentalism, is best exemplified by Justice Holmes's statement that courts "decide cases first, and determine the principle afterwards." This school of thought is associated with result-oriented jurisprudence, which focuses more on the consequences of a judicial decision than on how the relevant legal principles should be applied.

The realist-formalist dichotomy represents only half of the jurisprudential picture in the United States. The other half comprises a dialog between the positivist and natural-law schools of thought. This dialog revolves around the classic debate over the appropriate sources of law.

Positivists maintain that the only appropriate sources of law are rules and principles that have been expressly enacted or recognized by a governmental entity, like a state or federal legislature, administrative body, or court of law. These rules and principles may be properly considered law, positivists contend, because individuals may be held liable for disobeying them. Positivists believe that other sources for determining right and wrong, such as religion and contemporary morality, are only aspirational, and may not be legitimately consulted by judges when rendering a decision.

Natural-law proponents, or naturalists, agree that governmental rules and regulations are a legitimate source of law, but assert that they are not the only source. Naturalists believe that the law must be informed by eternal principles that existed before the formation of government and are independent of governmental recognition. Depending on the particular strain of NATURAL LAW, these principles may be derived from theology, moral philosophy, human reason, historical practice, and individual conscience.

The dialog between positivists and naturalists has a long history. For many centuries, historians, theologians, and philosophers distinguished positivism from naturalism by distinguishing written law from unwritten law. For example, the Ten Commandments were inscribed on stone tablets, as were many of the laws of the ancient Greeks. Roman Emperor JUSTINIAN I (A.D. 482–565) reduced most of his country's laws to a voluminous written code. At the same time, Christian, Greek, and Roman thinkers all appealed to a higher law that transcended the written law promulgated by human beings.

Prior to the American Revolution, English philosophers continued this debate along the same lines. English political thinkers JOHN AUSTIN and THOMAS HOBBES were strict positivists who believed that the only authority courts should recognize are the commands of the sovereign because only the sovereign is entrusted with the power to back up a command with military and police force. First intimated by Italian philosopher Niccolò Machiavelli, the "sovereign command" theory of law has been equated in the United States with the idea that might makes right.

Contrasted with the writings of Hobbes and Austin were the writings of JOHN LOCKE in England and THOMAS JEFFERSON in America. In his *Second Treatise on Government* (1690), Locke established the idea that all people are born with the inalienable right to life, liberty, and property. Locke's ruminations about individual rights that humans possess in the state of nature prior to the creation of government foreshadowed Jefferson's DECLARATION OF INDEPENDENCE. In 1776, the Declaration announced the self-evident truth that "all men are created equal" and are "endowed by their Creator with certain inalienable Rights," including the right to "Life, Liberty and the pursuit of Happiness."

Both positivism and naturalism have had an enormous influence on how U.S. citizens think about law. The institution of African American SLAVERY, which was recognized by the U.S. Constitution and legalized by legislation passed in the South prior to the Civil War (1861–65), was attacked by abolitionists who relied on higher-law principles of religion and conscience to challenge the moral foundations of human bondage. Following World War II, the Allied powers successfully prosecuted German government officials, industrialists, and military leaders in Nuremberg for committing GENOCIDE against European Jewry, even though the Nazi regime had passed laws authorizing such extermination. The Allies relied in part on the natural-law principle that human dignity is an inviolable right that no government may vitiate by written law. See also NUREMBERG TRIALS.

Positivists and naturalists tend to converge in the area of historical jurisprudence. Historical jurisprudence is marked by judges who consider history, tradition, and custom when deciding a legal dispute. Strictly speaking, history does not completely fall within the definition of either positivism or natural law. Historical events, like the Civil War, are not legislative enactments, although they may be the product of governmental policy. Nor do historical events embody eternal principles of morality, although they may be the product of clashing moral views. Yet, historical events shape both morality and law. Thus, many positivists and naturalists find a place for historical jurisprudence in their legal philosophy.

For example, Justice Holmes was considered a positivist to the extent that he believed that courts should defer to legislative judgment unless a particular statute clearly violates an express provision of the Constitution. But he qualified this stance when a given statute "infringe[s] on fundamental principles as they have been understood by the traditions of our people and our law" (*Lochner v. New York*, 198 U.S. 45, 25 S. Ct. 539, 49 L. Ed. 937 [1905]). In such instances, Holmes felt, courts were justified in striking down a particular written law. See also LOCHNER V. NEW YORK.

BENJAMIN N. CARDOZO, considered an adherent of sociological jurisprudence by some and a realist by others, was another Supreme Court justice who incorporated history into his legal philosophy. When evaluating the merits of a claim brought under the Due Process Clauses of the Fifth and Fourteenth Amendments, Cardozo denied relief to claims that were not "implicit in the concept of ordered liberty" and the "principle[s] of justice [that are] so rooted in the traditions and conscience of our people as to be ranked as fundamental" (*Palko v. Connecticut*, 302 U.S. 319, 58 S. Ct. 149, 82 L. Ed. 288 [1937]).

Each school of jurisprudence is not a self-contained body of thought. The lines separating positivism from realism and natural law from formalism often become blurry. The legal philosophy of Justice Holmes, for example, borrowed from the realist, positivist, pragmatic, and historical strains of thought.

In this regard, some scholars have observed that it is more appropriate to think of jurisprudence as a spectrum of legal thought, where the nuances of one thinker delicately blend with those of the next. Professor Harold Berman, of Harvard Law School, for example, has advocated the development of an integrative jurisprudence, which would assimilate into one philosophy the insights from each school of legal theory. The staying power of any body of legal thought, Berman has suggested, lies not in its name but in its ability to explain the enterprise of law.

CROSS-REFERENCES

Anarchism; Chicago School; Feminist Jurisprudence; Judicial Review; Law; Legal Education; Legal History; Roman Law; Socialism.

JURIST 📖 A JUDGE or legal scholar; an individual who is versed or skilled in law. 📖

The term *jurist* is ordinarily applied to individuals who have gained respect and recognition by their writings on legal topics.

JURISTIC ACT 📖 An action intended and capable of having a legal effect; any conduct by a private individual designed to originate, terminate, or alter a right. 📖

A court performs a juristic act when it makes a decision and hands down a JUDGMENT. An individual who enters into a contractual agreement is also performing a juristic act because of the legal ramifications of his or her agreement.

JURY 📖 In trials, a group of people selected and sworn to inquire into matters of fact and to reach a VERDICT on the basis of the EVIDENCE presented to it. 📖

In U.S. law, decisions in many civil and criminal trials are made by a jury. Considerable power is vested in this traditional body of ordinary men and women, which is charged with deciding matters of fact and delivering a verdict of guilt or innocence based on the evidence in a case. Derived from its historical counterpart in English COMMON LAW, trial by jury has had a central role in U.S. courtrooms since the colonial era, and it is firmly established as a basic guarantee in the U.S. Constitution. Modern juries are the result of a long series of Supreme Court decisions interpreting this constitutional liberty and, in significant ways, extending it.

History The historical roots of the jury date to the eighth century. Long before becoming an impartial body, during the reign of Charlemagne juries interrogated prisoners. In the twelfth century, the Normans brought the jury to England, where its accusatory function remained: citizens acting as jurors were required to come forward as witnesses and give evidence before the monarch's judges. Not until the fourteenth century did jurors cease to be witnesses and begin to assume their modern role as triers of fact. This role was well established in British common law when settlers brought the tradition to America, and after the United States declared its independence, all state constitutions guaranteed the right of jury TRIAL in criminal cases.

Viewing the jury as central to the rights of the new nation, the Founders firmly established its role in the U.S. Constitution. They saw the jury as not only a benefit to the accused but also a check on the judiciary, much as Congress exists as a check on the executive branch. The Constitution establishes and safeguards the right to a trial by jury in four ways: Article III establishes this right in federal criminal cases; the FIFTH AMENDMENT provides for grand juries, or panels that review complaints in criminal cases, hear the evidence of the prosecutor, and decide whether to issue an INDICTMENT that will bring the accused person to trial; the SIXTH AMENDMENT guarantees in serious federal criminal cases the right to trial by a PETIT JURY, the most common form of jury; and the SEVENTH AMENDMENT provides for a jury trial in civil cases where the amount in controversy exceeds $20.

The modern jury is largely a result of decisions of the U.S. Supreme Court, which has shaped and sometimes extended these constitutional rights. One important decision was the Court's 1968 ruling in *Duncan v. Louisiana*, 391 U.S. 145, 88 S. Ct. 1444, 20 L. Ed. 2d 491, which requires states to provide for jury trials in serious criminal cases. Prior to *Duncan*, states had their own rules; Louisiana, for instance, required juries only in cases where the possible punishment was death or hard labor. The Court declared that the right to a jury trial is fundamental. In cases in which the punishment exceeds six months' imprisonment, it ruled, the Due Process Clause of the FOURTEENTH AMENDMENT requires that the protections of the Sixth Amendment apply equally to federal and state criminal prosecutions.

Defendants can, under some circumstances, refuse a jury trial in favor of a trial before a judge. In 1965, the Supreme Court ruled that the constitutional right to a jury trial does not imply a related right to refuse one (*Singer v. United States*, 380 U.S. 24, 85 S. Ct. 783, 13 L. Ed. 2d 630). It observed that juries are important not only to the defendant but also to the government and the public. The government, it said, has an interest in trying cases "before the tribunal which the Constitution regards as most likely to produce a fair result." Thus, in federal cases, rules governing criminal procedure allow a defendant to waive a jury trial only if the government consents and the court gives its approval. States vary in their approach, with some, such as Nebraska and Minnesota, requiring only the court's approval and others, such as Illinois and Louisiana, granting the defendant's wish as long as the decision is informed.

Jury Selection Jury selection is the process of choosing jurors. Not all people are required to serve on the jury: some individuals and members of some occupational groups can be excused if serving would cause them or their family hardship. The Supreme Court has held that the Sixth Amendment merely requires that jurors be selected from a list that does not exclude any identifiable segment of the community (*Taylor v. Louisiana*, 419 U.S. 522, 95 S. Ct. 692, 42 L. Ed. 2d 690 [1975]).

Federal courts select grand and petit juries according to the guidelines in the Jury Selection and Service Act of 1968 (28 U.S.C.A. §§ 1861–78 [1988 & Supp. V 1993]). Generally, most communities use voter registration lists to choose prospective jurors, who are then summoned to appear for jury duty. This group of prospective jurors is called a venire.

Once the venire is assembled, attorneys for both the prosecution and the defense begin a process called voir dire. Literally meaning "to speak the truth," VOIR DIRE is a preliminary examination of the prospective jurors to inquire into their competence and suitability to sit on the jury. Although the judge may ask questions, primarily the attorneys do so. Their goal is to eliminate jurors who may be biased against their side, while choosing the jurors who are most likely to be sympathetic. Attorneys for each side are allowed to reject potential jurors in two ways. They may dismiss anyone for cause, meaning a reason that is relevant to that person's ability and fitness to perform jury duty. And they may issue a limited number of PEREMPTORY CHALLENGES, which are dismissals that do not require a reason.

The process of voir dire—especially in the exercise of peremptory challenges to custom design a jury—has provoked controversy. Defendants can challenge a venire, alleging discrimination, but such complaints are difficult to prove. Thus, critics of the selection process have argued that it skews the composition of juries according to race, class, and gender. In 1990, the Supreme Court held that juries do not have to represent a cross section of a community, but merely must be drawn from a pool that is representative of the community (*Holland v. Illinois*, 493 U.S. 474, 110 S. Ct. 803,

SHOULD THE PEREMPTORY CHALLENGE BE ABOLISHED?

A peremptory challenge permits a party to remove a prospective juror without giving a reason for the removal. This type of challenge has had a long history in U.S. law and has been viewed as a way to ensure an impartial jury. However, use of the peremptory challenge changed as a result of the U.S. Supreme Court decision in *Batson v. Kentucky*, 476 U.S. 79, 106 S. Ct. 1712, 90 L. Ed. 2d 69 (1986), and its progeny, and the changes have led some lawyers and legal commentators to call for its abolition. They argue that these Court decisions have deprived lawyers of their absolute discretion in using the challenges and have turned peremptory challenges into challenges for cause. Defenders of the peremptory challenge believe that the new race and gender requirements initiated by *Batson* simply ensure that jurors will not be excluded on the basis of stereotypes.

Those who favor retention of the peremptory challenge point to its four purposes: The peremptory challenge allows litigants to secure a fair and impartial jury. It gives the parties some control over the jury selection process. It allows an attorney to search for biases during the selection process without fear of alienating a potential juror. If, for example, a juror appears offended by the nature of the questioning, that juror can be excluded even if the answers she gives do not demonstrate bias. Finally, the peremptory challenge serves as an insurance policy when a challenge for cause is denied by the judge and the challenging party still believes that the juror is biased.

Defenders of the peremptory challenge contend that the limitations imposed by the Supreme Court have not substantially impaired the use of the challenge. As a result of *Batson*, a peremptory challenge can be questioned by the opposite side if that side believes that it was based solely on race or gender. The reasoning behind this change

is that striking jurors on the basis of race or gender perpetuates stereotypes that were prejudicial and that were based on historical discrimination. The only way to correct this record is to allow a party to establish a prima facie case of racial or gender discrimination. Defenders believe that to say *Batson* introduced race into the jury selection process is to ignore the part race has already played in the use of peremptory challenges. The other side has the opportunity to offer a nondiscriminatory reason for the challenge. The reason does not have to rise to the level of a "for-cause" challenge. It merely has to be a reasonable concern that can be articulated. Defenders of the challenge argue that this is an acceptable modification of the challenge.

They also point out that other characteristics of jurors are not bound by the *Batson* line of cases. A peremptory challenge based on a juror's religion, age, income, occupation, or political affiliation cannot be questioned as long as it is not a pretext for concealing race or gender bias. Therefore, argue supporters, the peremptory challenge is still a valuable tool in trial proceedings.

Those who argue for the abolition of the peremptory challenge come from two camps. One camp believes that the *Batson* line of cases was a mistake. This group would prefer to return to unrestricted use of the challenge but, knowing that overturning precedent is unlikely, recommends eliminating the challenge. The other camp believes that the racial and gender tests crafted by the Supreme Court in *Batson* and related cases are idealistic creations that are easily subverted in daily courtroom practice. The reality is that allegations of bias using *Batson* rarely are successful.

The group that believes that the changes following *Batson* were a mistake argues that the whole point of the peremptory challenge is that it is made

totally within the discretion of the lawyer. A trial lawyer may have a gut feeling about a juror, a feeling that is difficult to articulate to a judge and does not rise to a for-cause strike. Prior to *Batson* a court would allow this type of peremptory challenge. Since *Batson* the lawyer is required to articulate a reason. The temptation for the lawyer is to invent a "reasonable" explanation rather than risk having the peremptory challenge denied.

These critics argue that the only way for a lawyer to protect a client under this new system is to interrogate prospective jurors concerning intimate, personal matters in order to create defensible grounds for striking them. Lawyers must take more notes during questioning and spend more time evaluating the answers of jurors. The selection of a jury is lengthened if this tactic is chosen, placing more pressure on an overtaxed court system. Therefore, contend these critics, it would be better to abolish peremptory challenges and try other methods of jury selection. One alternative is expanding challenges for cause, allowing lawyers to exclude prospective jurors for legitimate, articulated reasons that do not satisfy the tougher current standards of challenges for cause.

The other group that questions *Batson* points to the difficulty of achieving the racially neutral selection of a jury. Surveys have shown that motions to deny peremptory challenges because of race or gender bias are rarely made, and that when they are judges accept all types of questionable race-neutral explanations to refute them. Other analysis has revealed that the seating of just one person of color or one male or female will defeat a discrimination claim. Faced with this situation, these critics argue that discrimination can easily prevail. Therefore, they conclude, either the peremptory challenge should be abolished or more effective ways of punishing violations should be employed.

See also Peremptory Challenge.

Minnesota's Approach to a More Diverse Jury Pool

Many urban areas have encountered difficulties in providing racially and economically diverse jury pools. Critics of the criminal justice system point out that people of color are overrepresented in the number of individuals arrested, prosecuted, and imprisoned, and underrepresented on criminal juries.

In 1993 the Minnesota Supreme Court Task Force on Racial Bias in the Judicial System issued a report that called for changes in jury management, so as to encourage diversity in juries. The judicial system took several steps to respond to the report.

The Minnesota Supreme Court amended jury management rules to authorize Hennepin and Ramsey Counties, the most populous and racially diverse counties in the state, to adopt new jury selection procedures that guarantee that, by percentage, minority group representation on the grand jury is equal to that in the two counties. Hennepin County implemented a plan that allows grand jurors to be selected randomly unless there are no people of color among the first twenty-one jurors selected, in which case the selection process continues until at least two of the twenty-three grand jurors are people of color.

At the state level, the judicial system secured funds from the legislature to raise the rate of daily juror pay and to pay for drop-in day care for jurors who normally do not use day care. The system also began to reimburse jurors for their mileage to and from the courthouse. These steps were taken to decrease the economic hardship on potential jurors who might otherwise ignore a jury summons or ask to be excused.

107 L. Ed. 2d 905). In 1991, it forbade prosecutors to use their peremptory challenges to exclude potential jurors on the basis of race (*Powers v. Ohio*, 499 U.S. 400, 111 S. Ct. 1364, 113 L. Ed. 2d 411). Along with other complaints—on issues ranging from efficiency to fairness—the decisions provided advocates of jury reform with further ammunition for their efforts to change fundamentally and even eliminate juries.

Jury Size Juries range in size according to their nature. Grand juries are so-called because they are usually larger than petit juries, having from twelve to twenty-three members. Traditionally, petit juries have had twelve members, but the number is not fixed. In 1970, the Supreme Court held that the number twelve was not an essential element of trial by jury (*Williams v. Florida*, 399 U.S. 78, 90 S. Ct. 1893, 26 L. Ed. 2d 446), and it has sanctioned juries of no fewer than six members in criminal cases (*Ballew v. Georgia*, 435 U.S. 223, 98 S. Ct. 1029, 55 L. Ed. 2d 234 [1978]). Parties in federal district courts as well as in many state courts can stipulate that the jury size be any number between six and twelve. Commonly, federal district court juries consist of six persons for civil cases.

Jury Instructions Throughout a trial, the jury receives INSTRUCTIONS from the judge. The judge explains relevant points of law, which the jury is bound to accept and apply. The judge directs the jury to disregard INADMISSIBLE testimony and provides guidelines on how to behave outside of court. During the 1995 trial of O. J. Simpson for the murder of his estranged second wife and a friend of hers, for example, Judge Lance Ito issued daily orders to jurors not to discuss the case with anyone. Some instructions vary across JURISDICTIONS and according to judges, such as whether jurors will be allowed to take notes during the trial; generally, they may not. In certain highly publicized trials, the judge may sequester the jury—that is, isolate its members in private living quarters such as hotel rooms in order to shield them from trial publicity. Violating the judge's orders can result in a juror being dismissed from the trial in favor of an alternate juror.

Jury Verdict Following the closing arguments in a trial, jurors deliberate in private to arrive at a verdict, which is then reported to the court by the jury foreman or forewoman. Defendants in federal jury trials have the right to a unanimous verdict. This is not true in state jury trials, where the size of the jury determines whether unanimity is required: a twelve-member jury may convict without unanimity, a six-member jury cannot.

In some cases, agreement among jurors is very difficult to reach. When jurors fail to reach an agreement, the judge may issue an instruction known as an Allen charge, in which the judge tells the jurors to continue deliberating and to listen carefully to and be deferential toward each other's views. Continued failure to arrive at a verdict results in a HUNG JURY, which necessitates a new trial with a different jury.

In criminal trials in most jurisdictions, the jury's job ends with the delivery of a verdict of guilt or innocence on every count pertaining to the case, and the judge determines SENTENCING. In civil cases, juries generally determine the amount of a DAMAGES award.

See also DUE PROCESS OF LAW; GRAND JURY.

JURY COMMISSION A group of officials charged with the responsibility of choosing the names of prospective JURY members or of selecting the list of jurors for a particular term in court.

The provisions governing these officers vary greatly from one state to another. In certain states, they are elected, and in others, they are appointed by the governor or by judges. Commissioners may be regarded as officers of the state or county or of the court which they serve. In choosing the names to compose the jury list, the commissioners have the power to decide those who are fit to serve as jurors or whether particular individuals possess the qualifications set forth by the statutes. The list, however, must be selected without discrimination from all those qualified to serve as jurors.

JUS [*Latin, right; justice; law; the whole body of law; also a right.*] The term is used in two meanings:

Jus means *law*, considered in the abstract; that is, as distinguished from any specific enactment, which we call, in a general sense, *the law*. Or it means the law taken as a system, an aggregate, a whole. Or it may designate some one particular system or body of particular laws; as in the phrases *jus civile, jus gentium, jus proetorium.*

In a second sense, *jus* signifies a *right*; that is, a power, privilege, faculty, or demand inherent in one person and incident upon another; or a capacity residing in one person of controlling, with the assent and assistance of the state, the actions of another. This is its meaning in the expressions *jus in rem, jus accrescendi, jus possessionis.*

JUS COGENS That body of peremptory principles or norms from which no derogation is permitted; those norms recognized by the international community as a whole as being fundamental to the maintenance of an international legal order.

Elementary rules that concern the safeguarding of peace and notably those that prohibit recourse to force or the threat of force. Norms of a humanitarian nature are included, such as prohibitions against GENOCIDE, SLAVERY, and racial DISCRIMINATION.

Jus cogens may, therefore, operate to invalidate a treaty or agreement between states to the extent of the inconsistency with any such principles or norms.

JUST Legally right; conformity with that which is lawful or fair.

Just cause for an action, for example, is a reason for a course of action that is based upon GOOD FAITH.

JUST CAUSE A reasonable and lawful ground for action.

Appearing in statutes, contracts, and court decisions, the term *just cause* refers to a standard of reasonableness used to evaluate a person's actions in a given set of circumstances. If a person acts with just cause, her or his actions are based on REASONABLE grounds and committed in GOOD FAITH. Whether just cause exists must be determined by the courts through an evaluation of the facts in each case. For example, in *Dubois v. Gentry*, 182 Tenn. 103, 184 S.W. 2d 369 (1945), the Supreme Court of Tennessee faced the question of whether a plaintiff who leased a filling station had acted with just cause in terminating a LEASE contract. The defendant station owner argued that the plaintiff had no right under the terms of the lease to terminate it. The court found that the plaintiff had just cause to terminate the lease because the effort supporting World War II had created an employee shortage and wartime rationing had placed restrictions on gasoline and automobile parts, making it unprofitable to operate the station.

The term *just cause* frequently appears in EMPLOYMENT LAW. Employment disputes often involve the issue of whether an employee's actions constituted just cause for discipline or termination. If the employer was required to have just cause for its action and punished the worker without just cause, a court may order the employer to compensate the worker. LABOR UNIONS typically negotiate for a contract provision stating that an employee cannot be fired absent just cause.

Since the 1980s a just cause standard has developed for employees not protected by an employment or a union contract. This standard is an alternative to the traditional EMPLOYMENT-AT-WILL doctrine. Under the latter, which has been in place since the late 1800s, employees who do not have an employment contract may be terminated at the will of the employer for any reason, or for no reason. Under the new just cause standard, many JURISDICTIONS now hold an employer to its word where the employer has stated it will not fire employees without just cause.

JUST COMPENSATION 📖 Equitable remuneration to the owner of private property that is expropriated for public use through CONDEMNATION, the implementation of the governmental power of EMINENT DOMAIN. 📖

The FIFTH AMENDMENT to the U.S. Constitution proscribes the taking of private property by the government for public use without just compensation. No precise formula exists by which the elements of just compensation can be calculated. Ordinarily, the amount should be based upon the loss to the owner, as opposed to the gain by the taker. The owner should be fairly and fully indemnified for the damage that he or she has sustained. The owner has a right to recover the monetary equivalent of the property taken and is entitled to be put in as good a financial position as he or she would have been in if the property had not been taken. Generally, the measure of DAMAGES for property condemned through eminent domain is its FAIR MARKET VALUE, since the sentimental value to the owner is not an element for consideration. Market value, however, is not an absolute method of valuation but rather a practical standard to aid the courts in their determination of just compensation based upon constitutional requirements.

In 1995 Texas landowners held a rally to protest the limits enforced by the U.S. Fish and Wildlife Service on development of an area west of Austin that is home to some endangered species of songbirds and spiders. The power of eminent domain grants the right to the federal government to take private property in return for just compensation.

When just compensation is assessed, all elements that can appropriately enter into the question of value are regarded. For example, the original cost of the property taken, added to the cost of reproduction or replacement, minus DEPRECIATION, can be considered when the market value of property is determined.

JUS TERTII 📖 The right of a third party. A TENANT or BAILEE or another in possession of property, who pleads that the TITLE is in some person other than that person's LANDLORD or BAILOR, is said to set up a *jus tertii.* 📖

JUSTICE 📖 The proper administration of the law; the fair and equitable treatment of all individuals under the law. A title given to certain judges, such as federal and state supreme court judges. 📖

JUSTICE DEPARTMENT 📖 The Department of Justice (DOJ) is the executive-branch department responsible for handling the legal work of the federal government. 📖

Headquartered in Washington, D.C., the Department of Justice (DOJ) is essentially the largest law firm in the country, with more than one hundred thousand employees nationwide and a budget of approximately $11 billion.

The DOJ comprises many administrative units whose responsibilities involve either representing the United States' interests in court or enforcing federal laws. Many of the department's activities involve traditional legal and investigative functions, such as filing suits on behalf of the United States or apprehending criminals. Other department functions are less lawyerly and more administrative, such as processing citizenship applications, as the Immigration and Naturalization Service does, or planning policy initiatives, as the Office of Policy Development does.

Department Leadership At the top of the department is the ATTORNEY GENERAL, who is appointed by the president and must be confirmed by the Senate. A key member of the president's cabinet, the attorney general supervises the many divisions, bureaus, and offices of the DOJ. Unlike other CABINET members, however, the attorney general also functions as a practicing attorney, serving as the president's legal adviser.

Below the attorney general are the deputy attorney general, the associate attorney general, and the SOLICITOR GENERAL. Although the deputy attorney general is officially the second-highest position in the DOJ, the office of associate attorney general, created in 1977, is often considered to be equally powerful. The deputy attorney general and the associate attorney general divide the department's administrative responsibilities between them, providing direction to the organizational units in the department; they also advise the attorney general in policy matters. The solicitor general is primarily responsible for supervising and conducting government litigation before the federal APPELLATE COURTS, including the Supreme Court.

Department Structure The DOJ is composed of several different units, including divisions, bureaus, and offices. The government's legal business is handled by the department's six litigating divisions: Antitrust, Civil, Civil Rights, Criminal, Environment and Natural Resources, and Tax. Each of these divisions is headed by an assistant attorney general. These divisions handle cases involving the United States that have a broad legal impact.

At the state level, the government is represented by ninety-five U.S. attorneys, who conduct all federal court cases and some federal investigations in their districts. Each state has at least one U.S. attorney, and some of the larger states are divided into districts that each have a U.S. attorney. The U.S. attorneys handle the majority of cases in which the United States is a party. Although the U.S. attorneys report to the DOJ, they traditionally operate with a fair amount of independence and autonomy. Each U.S. attorney is appointed by the president and confirmed by the Senate to a four-year term.

The several bureaus within the DOJ are concerned with various aspects of law enforcement. The U.S. Marshals Service (USMS) is the country's oldest law enforcement agency, having begun as a group of thirteen MARSHALS appointed by GEORGE WASHINGTON; today the USMS has ninety-five marshals and is primarily responsible for providing court security, transporting prisoners, apprehending fugitives, protecting witnesses, and executing federal court orders. The FEDERAL BUREAU OF INVESTIGATION (FBI) is the government's major investigatory agency and the largest unit within the DOJ; the FBI pursues information concerning federal violations, collects evidence in cases involving the United States, and performs other duties assigned by law or by the president. The Immigration and Naturalization Service (INS) enforces U.S. immigration laws, processes applications for naturalization, and represents the government in exclusion and deportation cases. The Drug Enforcement Administration (DEA) combats drug trafficking, investigating major drug dealers, helping to prepare cases against them, and helping foreign governments pursue drug dealers. Also in the DOJ are the Bureau of Prisons (BOP), which oversees the federal prison system, and the Office of Justice Programs (OJP), which administers crime prevention and deterrence programs, including the well-known McGruff the Crime Dog campaign.

The DOJ also houses several offices providing administrative support functions. These include the Office of Legislative Affairs, which coordinates the DOJ's relationship with Congress; the Office of Legal Counsel, which helps the attorney general furnish legal advice to the president; the U.S. Parole Commission, which administers the parole system for federal prisoners; the Executive Office for U.S. Trustees, which administers the handling of BANKRUPTCY cases; and the Foreign Claims Settlement Commission, which handles cases against foreign governments for losses sustained by U.S. citizens.

History of the Department The position of attorney general has its roots in medieval English law. The title *attorney general* can be traced to 1398, when the duke of Norfolk employed attorneys general to witness his banishment. In the years following, the king or queen and other nobles employed attorneys to appear in court on their behalf. In time the office of the king's or queen's attorney became a privileged and powerful position. The attorney general, as the position was called after 1461, became an important political and legal adviser, first to the monarch and later to the House of Commons and the government in general.

When English settlers established colonies in America, they included the office of attorney general in the colonial governments they created. Virginia was the first colony to appoint an attorney general, in 1643, followed by Rhode Island in 1650, and Maryland in 1660; by the end of the seventeenth century, most of the colonies had their own attorneys general. By 1776 a fairly consistent system of courts and law officers had been established in the colonies. With the American Revolution, British officeholders were simply replaced with Americans.

When the Constitution was written in 1789, the Framers did not specifically designate an office of attorney general, instead leaving such administrative details to be determined by statute. The attorney general was created by the JUDICIARY ACT OF 1789, which specified that the office should be filled by "a meet person, learned in the law," who would "prosecute and conduct all suits in the Supreme Court in which the United States shall be concerned, and . . . give his advice and opinion upon questions of law when required by the President of the United States, or when requested by the heads of any of the departments." The act gave the attorney general limited powers and resources, including no provisions for staffing or office expenses; the person filling the office was expected to pay for such items. Because the attorney generalship was designed to be a part-time position, the salary was set at just $1,500 a year and the officeholder was expected to maintain a private legal practice.

The first person to fill the position of attorney general was Edmund Randolph, of Virginia, who was Washington's personal attorney. Though the attorney general initially was not a member of the president's cabinet, Washington valued Randolph's advice so much that he asked Randolph to sit in on his cabinet meetings. Since then the position of the attorney general has been recognized as a cabinet post.

In addition to the office of attorney general, the Judiciary Act of 1789 established the U.S. district attorneys (now called U.S. attorneys)

and the U.S. marshals, who represented the federal government in court and enforced federal laws, respectively, at the state and local levels. Although these officials were statutorily under the supervision of the president, they actually operated with very few checks. To make the government's legal work more controllable and consistent, Attorney General Randolph attempted to bring the U.S. attorneys and marshals under his supervision, arguing that such centralization would help him secure the government's legal interests. However, the legislation that Randolph recommended failed in Congress.

This division of the government's legal work—among the attorney general, the district attorneys and marshals, and also solicitors hired by individual executive departments—resulted in uncoordinated, inconsistent, and inefficient legal service to the federal government. Presidents and attorneys general made several attempts to centralize the government's legal services, but Congress was leery of giving the

Justice Department

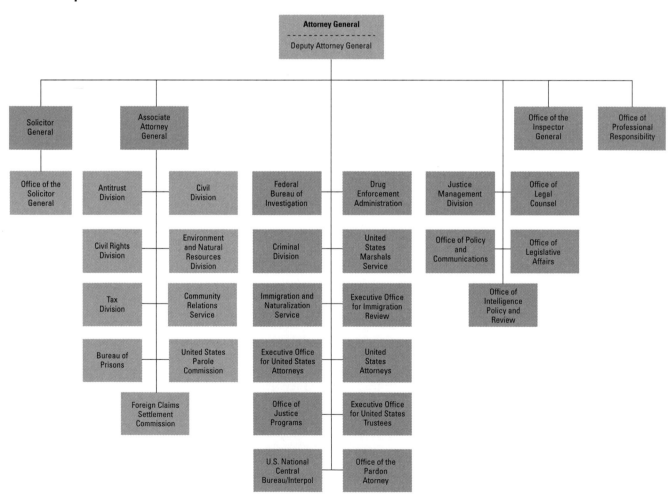

EXECUTIVE BRANCH more power and therefore failed to pass the necessary legislation.

In the early nineteenth century, the office of the attorney general expanded slowly. The workload was light, and until 1814 the attorney general was not required to reside in Washington, D.C., except when the Supreme Court was in session. Significant changes were made, however, when WILLIAM WIRT, attorney general under President JAMES MONROE, took over the office in 1817. Finding that previous attorneys general had kept no records of their work, Wirt established a formal system for recording his official actions and decisions so that future attorneys general would have a record of precedents to follow. Wirt also expanded the duties of the office and created formal operating procedures, greatly increasing his workload. Congress compensated Wirt for his efforts, increasing his salary to $3,500 and providing a clerk and office expenses. These funds, however, were one-time appropriations only; not until 1831 did Congress begin making regular appropriations for office expenses and book purchases.

The next attorney general to make significant changes in the office was CALEB CUSHING, who was appointed attorney general by President FRANKLIN PIERCE in 1853. Unlike his predecessors, Cushing left his own private legal practice and transformed the job of attorney general into a full-time position. Cushing expanded the work performed by the department and was also given additional responsibilities by Congress, including advising treaty commissioners, examining government land titles, administering government patents, and compiling and publishing federal laws. To enable Cushing to complete this work, Congress in 1859 authorized the appointment of an assistant attorney general, who was given control of the U.S. district attorneys. Congress also raised the attorney general's salary to $6,000, finally making it equal to the salaries of other cabinet members.

With the onset of the Civil War, the government's need for legal services and representation increased drastically. All across the country, claimants were filing suits in cases involving issues such as property titles and personal rights. The attorney general's office did not have the resources to handle these cases, nor did it have adequate authority over the district attorneys in the states. The various executive departments were forced to hire outside counsel to represent the government, resulting in enormous costs—nearly $500,000 over four years. These totals came to the attention of Congress, which was trying to curb expenses in the aftermath of the war. To try to economize on the government's legal bills, Congress passed the Judicial Act of 1870, which created the DOJ. The staff was increased by two assistants and a solicitor general, who was to share the attorney general's task of representing the government before the Supreme Court. The act also gave the attorney general positive authority over the U.S. district attorneys and marshals. Although the creation of the DOJ did not materially change the duties of the attorney general, it significantly changed the nature of the job by making it an administrative position responsible for an official bureaucracy.

Even with the creation of the DOJ, the federal government's legal work suffered from a lack of coordination because individual executive departments continued to retain their own solicitors. These solicitors provided legal advice to their departments and claimed the right to represent the departments in court. The conflicts and confusion this created between the departments and the DOJ came to a head during the First World War, when many new government agencies and departments were created, each claiming the right to conduct its own legal work. In response, President WOODROW WILSON issued an EXECUTIVE ORDER (Exec. Order No. 2877 [1918]) requiring all government law officers to operate under the supervision of the DOJ. By the 1920s administrative chaos returned as individual departments again tried to conduct their own legal work. In 1933 President FRANKLIN D. ROOSEVELT issued another executive order (Exec. Order No. 6166 [1933]) consolidating all the government's legal work under the DOJ and the attorney general.

Today many units of the federal government continue to employ their own legal counsel, but those attorneys generally are restricted to rendering legal advice to that department alone and are not permitted to represent the government in court. Tensions do sometimes arise when an executive department and the DOJ take contrary positions on an issue in litigation; when this happens the attorney general and the solicitor general must decide which department's stand will be defended.

JUSTICE OF THE PEACE ▥ A judicial officer with limited power whose duties may include hearing cases that involve civil controversies, conserving the peace, performing judicial acts, hearing minor criminal complaints, and committing offenders. ▥

Justices of the peace are regarded as civil public officers, distinct from peace or police officers. Depending on the region in which they serve, justices of the peace are also known as MAGISTRATES, squires, and police or district judges. In some districts, such as the District of Columbia, justices of the peace are considered officers of the United States. In other regions, their JURISDICTION is limited to a state, city, PRECINCT, COUNTY, or TOWNSHIP.

The position of justice of the peace originated in England in 1361 with the passing of the Justice of the Peace Act. In colonial America the position, with its judicial, executive, and legislative powers, was the community's main political force and therefore the most powerful public office open to colonists. Legal training was not a prerequisite.

Maintaining community order was a priority in the colonial era. The justice of the peace in this period was responsible for arresting and arraigning citizens who violated moral or legal standards. By the early 1800s, the crimes handled by the justice of the peace included drunkenness, adultery, price evasion (selling below a minimum price fixed by law), and public disorder. Justices of the peace also served as county court staff members and heard GRAND JURY and civil cases. The increasing number of criminal, slave, and tax statutes that were passed during the 1800s also broadened the enforcement powers of the justice of the peace.

Today justices of the peace deal with minor criminal matters and preside only in the lowest state courts. Their legal duties encompass standard judicial tasks such as issuing arrest or search warrants, performing marriage ceremonies, handling routine traffic offenses, determining PROBABLE CAUSE, imposing FINES, and conducting INQUESTS.

The duties of a justice of the peace vary by statute, and it is the justice's responsibility to know which actions are within the scope of his or her jurisdiction. For example, a few statutes do not allow justices of the peace to be involved in the operation of another business or profession; however, they can invest in or receive a salary from another business, as long as they are not involved with its operation.

Justices are often considered CONSERVATORS OF THE PEACE. They can arrest criminals or insane people, order the removal of people who behave in a disorderly fashion in a public place, and carry out other duties designed to maintain or restore a peaceful community.

Justices of the peace have limited power in criminal and civil cases. They have jurisdiction over minor criminal matters, including MISDEMEANORS, INFRACTIONS, and petty offenses. Their powers of civil jurisdiction are determined by the respective statutes that govern their posi-

tion. At the highest level, a justice may handle cases that involve CONTRACTS, TORTS, injuries to PERSONAL PROPERTY, and personal injuries such as LIBEL, slander, FALSE IMPRISONMENT, and MALICIOUS PROSECUTION. Justices of the peace do not have jurisdiction over cases that involve real property TITLES, EASEMENTS, or RIGHTS OF WAY.

Depending on the tradition in the area where they serve, justices of the peace are either elected or appointed; the method by which they reach their office has no bearing on how much power they have. Appointments are typically handled by the state's legislative body or governor; however, this task may be delegated to local authorities, such as county supervisors or commissioners.

Once elected or appointed, and before taking office, a justice of the peace is required to take an OATH and post an official BOND. Some statutes also require new justices to sign a sworn statement that they have never been convicted of a misdemeanor or FELONY.

The length of the term of a justice of the peace varies with the constitution or statute that created the position. If a vacancy is created before a term expires, a public official, such as the governor, fills the vacancy; some statutes require that a special election be held. The replacement justice of the peace usually completes only the remainder of the term or serves until the next scheduled election.

Justices of the peace can be removed from their position for a variety of reasons, including official misconduct or conviction for a misdemeanor or felony. They must have knowingly committed the inappropriate act or acts with improper motives. Usually, the statute that defines the position will outline the procedure for removing a justice of the peace from office. Ordinarily, the justice is served with a notice of the charge or charges and is given an opportunity to be heard before she or he is removed.

If a justice of the peace wishes to resign, he or she must present a letter of resignation to the appropriate official; once the resignation is accepted, it cannot be withdrawn.

JUSTICIABLE 📖 Capable of being decided by a court. 📖

Not all cases brought before courts are accepted for their review. The U.S. Constitution limits the FEDERAL COURTS to hearing nine classes of CASES OR CONTROVERSIES, and, in the twentieth century, the Supreme Court has added further restrictions. State courts also have rules requiring matters brought before them to be justiciable.

Before agreeing to hear a case, a court first examines its justiciability. This preliminary review does not address the actual MERITS of the case, but instead applies a number of tests based on judicial doctrines. At their simplest, the tests concern (1) the PLAINTIFF, (2) the adversity between the parties, (3) the substance of the issues in the case, and (4) the timing of the case. For a case to be heard, it must survive this review. In practice, courts have broad power to apply their tests: they commonly emphasize whichever factors they deem important. This irregularity has made the analysis of justiciability a difficult task for lawyers, scholars, and the courts themselves.

Behind the tests for justiciability are a number of legal doctrines. The Supreme Court has declared that the doctrines have both constitutional and prudential components: some parts are required by the Constitution, according to the Court's interpretation of Article III, and some are based on what the Court considers prudent judicial administration. This distinction has important consequences for the limits of judicial power. Congress has the authority to pass laws that override only the prudential limits of JUDICIAL REVIEW; it cannot pass laws that override constitutional limits. Thus, the Supreme Court has insulated the federal courts from congressional influence in some but not all areas of justiciability.

Among the most complex justiciability doctrines is STANDING, which covers the plaintiff. Standing focuses on the party, not on the issues he wishes to have adjudicated (*Flast v. Cohen*, 392 U.S. 83, 88 S. Ct. 1942, 20 L. Ed. 2d 947). A claimant said to have standing has been found by the court to have the right to a trial. To reach such a determination, the court uses several general rules. These rules require that the claimant has suffered an actual or threatened injury; that the case alleges a sufficient connection (or nexus) between the injury and the defendant's action; that the injury can be redressed by a favorable decision; and that the plaintiff neither brings a generalized grievance nor represents a third party. In addition, separate rules govern taxpayers, organizations, legislators, and government entities.

The question of justiciability also involves the legal relationship of the parties in the case, as well as the substance of their dispute. To be found justiciable, the case must involve parties who have an adversary controversy between them. Moreover, the issues in the controversy must be "real and substantial," and therefore more than mere generalized interests common to the public at large. A related rule forbids the federal courts to issue ADVISORY OPINIONS. Dating from the late eighteenth century, it holds

that they must decline to rule on merely hypothetical or abstract questions. In addition, they are restricted from taking cases that address purely POLITICAL QUESTIONS, which are beyond management by the judiciary. Certain state courts do issue advisory opinions on legal questions.

The fourth concern of tests for justiciability, the timing of the case, is evaluated under the concepts of RIPENESS and mootness. The ripeness doctrine holds that a case is justiciable if "the harm asserted has matured sufficiently to warrant judicial intervention" (*Warth v. Seldin*, 422 U.S. 490, 95 S. Ct. 2197, 45 L. Ed. 2d 343 [1975]). The mootness doctrine prevents a court from addressing issues that are hypothetical or dead. A case may become MOOT because of a change in law or in the status of the litigants. Most commonly, it is held to be moot because the court is presented with a fact or event that renders the alleged wrong no longer existent. For example, in 1952 the Supreme Court refused to review a state court decision in a case challenging Bible reading in the public schools. The child behind the suit had already graduated, and the parents and taxpayers who brought the suit could show no financial injury (*Doremus v. Board of Education*, 342 U.S. 429, 72 S. Ct. 394, 96 L. Ed. 475). However, the Court did agree to hear the landmark ABORTION case *Roe v. Wade*, 410 U.S. 113, 93 S. Ct. 705, 35 L. Ed. 2d 147 (1973), even though the plaintiff was no longer pregnant. The Court gave as its reason the length of a woman's gestation period (nine months), which is too short to permit APPELLATE review.

One reason justiciability is complex is that it is replete with numerous arcane rules and exceptions. Another is that courts apply it on an ad hoc basis, inconsistently choosing to emphasize one element of its tests over another. This fact has led legal scholars to despair of ever reaching a unified analysis of justiciability. Some have taken the cynical view that courts will find a case justiciable when they want to hear it, and refuse to find it justiciable when they do not wish to hear it.

JUSTIFICATION A sufficient or acceptable excuse or explanation made in court for an act that is otherwise unlawful; the showing of an adequate reason, in court, why a defendant committed the offense for which he or she is accused that would serve to relieve the defendant of LIABILITY.

A legal EXCUSE for the performance or nonperformance of a particular act that is the basis for exemption from guilt. A classic example is the excuse of SELF-DEFENSE offered as justification for the commission of a murder.

JUSTINIAN I The emperor Justinian I ruled the Eastern Roman, or Byzantine, Empire from 527 until 565. He is significant for his efforts to regain the lost provinces of the Western Roman Empire, his codification of ROMAN LAW, and his architectural achievements.

Justinian was born circa 482 in Pauresium, Illyricum (probably south of modern Niš, Serbia). Justinian came to the throne with the intention of reestablishing the Roman Empire as it had been before the provinces of the Western Roman Empire fell under the control of various Germanic tribes during the fifth century. To this end, he sent his armies against the Vandals in North Africa (roughly, modern Algeria and Tunisia), the Visigoths in Spain, and the Ostrogoths in Italy. The Vandals surrendered in 534, but the Visigoths and Ostrogoths proved more difficult. Justinian's forces never succeeded in capturing more than a small part of Spain and subdued Italy only after a devastating war that ended in 563 with Italy in ruins. Nonetheless, when Justinian died, he could claim with some justice that the Mediterranean Sea was once again a Roman lake.

Justinian's conquests proved ephemeral, however. Within four years of his death, northern Italy had fallen to the Lombards, another Germanic tribe, and by the early eighth century, Muslim armies had conquered North Africa and Spain.

Justinian's achievements in law were more long-lasting. Although several collections of imperial Roman legislation had been compiled in the past, by Justinian's reign even the most recent, the Theodosian Code (*Codex Theodosianus*), which had been issued in 438, was out-of-date. Accordingly in 528 Justinian established a commission of ten experts, including Tribonian, to prepare a new edition, which was completed in 534. The Code (*Codex*), as it was called, contains 4,562 laws from the reign of Hadrian (117-138) to 534.

Roman law, however, encompasses both legislation and JURISPRUDENCE; that is, literature interpreting the law. Despite the importance of jurisprudence, no single collection had ever been made, and some important works were not readily available. Therefore in 530 Justinian

Justinian I

"JUSTICE IS THE CONSTANT AND PERPETUAL WISH TO RENDER TO EVERY ONE HIS DUE."

ordered his commission to collect the most important writings on jurisprudence and to edit and clarify the texts whenever necessary. To complete their task, the commission had to read two thousand books containing over three million lines, but nonetheless they finished the compilation known as the Digest (*Digestum*), or Pandects (*Pandectae*), by December 533.

In the same year, the commissioners issued the Institutes (*Institutiones*), a handbook for law students. Although Justinian had only planned a tripartite compilation of Roman law, imperial legislation did not cease with the completion of the Code in 534. Therefore the edicts issued by Justinian after 534 were collected and came to be known as the Novels (*Novellae*), or New Laws. The Code, Digest, and Institutes had been written in Latin, the traditional language of Rome, but Justinian issued the Novels in Greek in recognition of the fact that Greek was the ordinary language of the Eastern Roman Empire. Together the Code, Digest, Institutes, and Novels came to be known as the CORPUS JURIS CIVILIS ("the corpus of civil law"). The *Corpus juris* not only preserved Roman law for later generations but, after the twelfth century when it came to be known and studied in western Europe, provided inspiration for most European legal systems.

Justinian is also known for the extensive building program that he undertook both in the East and in Italy. The church of Hagia Sophia in Constantinople, which was completed in 562, is considered one of the finest examples of Byzantine architecture. Justinian died November 14, 565, in Constantinople, now Istanbul, Turkey.

JUST WAR The principle of a just war emerged early in the development of scholarly writings on INTERNATIONAL LAW. Under this view, a just war was a means of national self-help whereby a state attempted to enforce rights actually or allegedly based on international law. State practice from the eighteenth to the early part of the twentieth century generally rejected this distinction, however, as WAR became a legally permissible national policy to alter the existing rights of states, irrespective of the actual merits of the controversy.

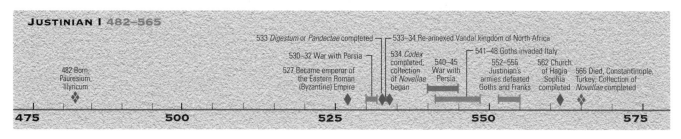

JUSTINIAN I 482–565

482 Born, Pauresium, Illyricum

527 Became emperor of the Eastern Roman (Byzantine) Empire

530–32 War with Persia

533 *Digestum* or *Pandectae* completed

534 *Codex* completed; collection of *Novellae* began

533–34 Re-annexed Vandal kingdom of North Africa

540–45 War with Persia

541–48 Goths invaded Italy

552–555 Justinian's armies defeated Goths and Franks

562 Church of Hagia Sophia completed

565 Died, Constantinople, Turkey; Collection of *Novellae* completed

475   500   525   550   575

Following World War I, diplomatic negotiations resulted in the General Treaty for the Renunciation of War, more commonly known as the KELLOGG-BRIAND PACT, signed in 1928. The signatory nations renounced war as a means to resolve international disputes promising instead to use peaceful methods.

The aims of the Kellogg-Briand Pact were adopted in the Charter of the UNITED NATIONS in 1945. Under the charter, the use or threat of force as an instrument of national policy was condemned, but nations were permitted to use force in individual or collective self-defense against an aggressor. The General Assembly of the United Nations has further defined aggression as armed force by a state against the sovereignty, territorial integrity, or political independence of another state, regardless of the reasons for the use of force. The Security Council is empowered to review the use of force, however, to determine whether the relevant circumstances justify branding one nation as the aggressor and in violation of charter obligations. Under the modern view, a just war is one waged consistent with the Kellogg-Briand Pact and the Charter of the United Nations.

JUVENILE LAW 📖 An area of the law that deals with the actions and well-being of persons who are not yet adults. 📖

In the law a juvenile is defined as a person who is not old enough to be held responsible for criminal acts. In most states and on the federal level, this age threshold is set at eighteen years. In Wyoming a juvenile is a person under the age of nineteen. In some states a juvenile is a person under the age of seventeen, and in Connecticut, New York, and North Carolina, a juvenile is a person under the age of sixteen. These age definitions are significant because they determine whether a young person accused of criminal conduct will be charged with a crime in adult court or will be required to appear in juvenile court.

Juvenile courts generally have authority over three categories of children: juveniles accused of criminal conduct; juveniles neglected or abused by their parents or in need of assistance from the state; and juveniles accused of a STATUS OFFENSE. This last category refers to conduct that is prohibited only to children, such as absence from school (truancy), flight from home, disobedience of reasonable parental controls, and purchase of ALCOHOL, tobacco, or PORNOGRAPHY.

Originally the term *juvenile delinquent* referred to any child found to be within the JURISDICTION of a juvenile court. It included

What Happens to Every 1,000 Juveniles Arrested

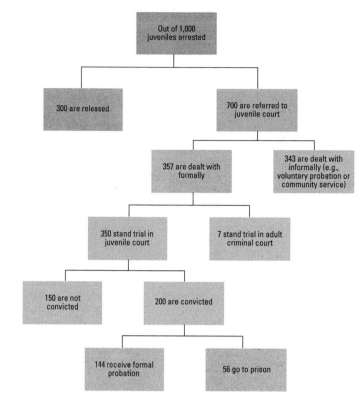

Source: Office of Juvenile Justice and Delinquency.

children accused of status offenses and children in need of state assistance. The term *delinquent* was not intended to be derogatory: its literal meaning suggested a failure of parents and society to raise the child, not a failure of the child.

The modern trend is to separate and label juveniles based on the reason for their juvenile court appearance and the facts of their case. Many states have created three categories for juveniles: delinquents, abused or neglected children, and children in need of services. Delinquents are juveniles who have committed acts that would result in criminal prosecution if committed by an adult. Abused or neglected children are those who are suffering from physical or emotional abuse or who have committed status offenses or petty criminal offenses. Children in need of services are children who are not abused or neglected but are needy in some other way. These children are usually from impoverished homes and require improved nutrition and basic health care.

Generally, the procedures for dealing with abused, neglected, and needy children are less formal than the procedures for dealing with alleged delinquents. The subsequent treatment of nondelinquent juveniles by the courts is also markedly different from the treatment of delinquents. Separation of noncriminal cases from criminal cases removes some of the stigma attached to appearance in juvenile court.

The mission of juvenile courts differs from that of adult courts. Juvenile courts do not have the authority to order punishment. Instead, they respond to juvenile misconduct and misfortune by ordering rehabilitative measures or assistance from government agencies. The juvenile court response to misconduct generally is more lenient than the adult court response.

Juvenile court proceedings are conducted in private, whereas adult proceedings are public. Also, whereas adult criminal courts focus on the offense committed and appropriate punishment, juvenile courts focus on the child and seek to meet the child's needs through rehabilitation, supervision, and treatment. Adult courts may deprive adults of their liberty only for the violation of criminal laws. Juvenile courts, by contrast, are empowered to control and confine juveniles based on a broad range of behavior and circumstances.

History   Before the nineteenth century, children were generally considered to be young adults, and they were expected to behave accordingly. Children over the age of seven years who were accused of crimes were prosecuted in adult court. If convicted they could be confined in an adult prison. By the nineteenth century, most states had created separate work farms and reform schools for convicted children, but some states still sent children to adult prisons. Juveniles were not always rehabilitated in prison. After interacting with adult criminals, they often emerged from prison with increased criminal knowledge and an increased resolve to commit crimes.

In the late nineteenth century, progressive social discourse caused a shift in the general attitude toward children. Social, psychological, and behavioral experts proposed a new understanding of children based on their youth. The progressive theory declared that children should be considered innocent and vulnerable and to lack the mental state required to be held responsible for a criminal offense because they have not acquired the wisdom that comes with age. It followed that juveniles should not be punished for their criminal behavior. Instead, they should be reformed, rehabilitated, and educated.

Juvenile crime was an important element, but not the driving force, behind the creation of the juvenile courts. Juvenile crime rates were quite low in the nineteenth century. Progressives claimed that the biggest problems facing children were neglect and poverty. The industrial revolution caused an increase in the number of urban poor. As poverty increased, so did the incidence of child abandonment, neglect, and abuse. This led to a political push for states to protect those who were in distress.

The perception of the government as a surrogate parent, known as PARENS PATRIAE, also led to the formulation of status offenses. These offenses derived from the idea that the government should help shape the habits and morals of juveniles. Status offenses reflected the notion that state control of juveniles should not be limited to enforcement of the criminal laws. Instead, the state would have additional authority to prohibit a wide variety of acts that were considered precursors to criminal behavior.

The progressive theory won widespread support, and legislatures set to the task of conforming the legal system to the new understanding of children. The Illinois legislature was the first to create a separate court for children. The Juvenile Court Act of 1899 (1899 Ill. Laws 131, 131-37) created the first juvenile court and established a judicial framework that would serve as a model for other states.

The Illinois act raised the age of criminal responsibility to sixteen years. This meant that no person under the age of sixteen could be prosecuted in adult court for a crime. Children accused of a crime would instead be brought to juvenile court.

The Illinois act gave the juvenile court additional authority to control the fate of a variety of troubled youths. These young people included

> any child who for any reason is destitute or homeless or abandoned; or dependent on the public for support; or has not proper parental care or guardianship; or who habitually begs or receives alms; or who is found living in any house of ill fame or with any vicious or disreputable person . . . and any child under the age of 8 years who is found peddling or selling any article or singing or playing any musical instrument upon the street or giving any public entertainment.

The Illinois act also created a new system for the disposition of juveniles. The act specified that all children found to be within the jurisdiction of the court should be given a level of care and discipline similar to "that which should be given by its parents" (§ 3 [1899 Ill. Laws 131, 132]). In all cases the court would attempt to

SHOULD THE JUVENILE JUSTICE SYSTEM BE ABOLISHED?

The juvenile justice system seeks to rehabilitate children, rather than punish them, for their criminal behavior. Since the late 1970s, critics of the juvenile courts have sought to abolish this system, arguing that it has failed in its rehabilitation efforts and in not punishing serious criminal behavior by young people. Defenders of the juvenile justice system contend that for the vast majority of children, the system is a worthwhile means of addressing problems. They maintain that a handful of violent juveniles who have committed horrendous crimes should not lead the public to believe that the system does not provide ways of changing behavior.

Critics of the system allege that the rehabilitation model embraced by juvenile courts is a failed idea. Numerous studies have shown that there is no evidence that any type of rehabilitation program can produce large numbers of reformed children. Therefore, it is both foolish and wasteful to persist in the illusion that government-imposed services will change individual behavior. The primary concern of the legal system, critics argue, should be punishing perpetrators of criminal behavior, regardless of their age.

Critics note that the juvenile courts were set up in the early 1900s to deal with petty crimes and with status offenses, such as truancy and curfew violations. The social and cultural landscape has changed considerably since then. Violent behavior by teenagers has risen steadily since the 1980s. Narcotics trafficking and use, coupled with the growth of criminal gangs and the availability of guns, has led to juveniles committing many murders and robberies. Critics insist that the juvenile courts are no longer relevant when violent, amoral young people terrorize the public.

According to its critics, the juvenile justice system compounds its failure to rehabilitate by sending a message to young people that they can "beat the rap" and avoid any serious consequences for their criminal actions. Too many juveniles are arrested, held, and released time after time, leading to a revolving-door process that sends young people the false message that they will not be held accountable for their behavior. This process ultimately leads to the commission of serious criminal acts that catapult juveniles into the adult criminal court, where, for the first time, they face punishment. Critics believe that it is better to punish a juvenile in the first instance, in order to deter future criminal activity.

Critics also charge that it is wrong to allow juveniles who have been adjudicated delinquent for serious crimes to be released from the jurisdiction of the juvenile court at age eighteen or twenty-one. Serving two or three years in a juvenile corrections facility for a crime that if committed by an adult would result in a ten-year sentence is wrong. The punishment for a crime, argue critics, should be the same, regardless of the age of the perpetrator.

Because of these deficiencies, critics contend, the system should be dismantled. Juveniles should be given full due process rights, including the right to trial by jury, just like adults. This is required because, contrary to what the system's defenders say, juvenile proceedings are not civil actions. Freed from the juvenile justice system's rehabilitative ideology and restrictions on criminal due process rights, juveniles should stand accountable for their criminal actions. Once a juvenile is convicted, a trial court can determine the appropriate sentence. Status offenses, which are rarely enforced anyway, can be treated like any petty misdemeanor. Imposing a small fine is more effective, critics charge, than placing a juvenile under the supervision of the juvenile court.

Defenders of juvenile justice respond that a small minority of violent teenagers have created the misperception that the system is a failure. Though not every child can be rehabilitated, it is unwise to abandon the effort. In every other sphere of society, children are treated differently from adults. This is an acknowledgment that children are not adults and need to be nurtured. For the few juveniles who commit serious crimes and have a poor chance to rehabilitate themselves, current laws provide that they be transferred to adult criminal court. Allowing this alternative is a wiser course, defenders insist, than dismantling the system.

Defenders also contend that many of the alleged defects of the juvenile courts can be traced to inadequate funding and to the environment in which many juveniles are forced to live. They point out that violent subcultures and early childhood traumas caused by abuse, neglect, and exposure to violence make it more difficult to address individual problems. If the system were adequately funded, probation officers and court support personnel could more closely supervise children and rehabilitation efforts. If more energy were put into changing the socioeconomic situation of communities, rehabilitation efforts would improve and crime would decrease.

According to system supporters, placing juveniles in prison will not end the cycle of criminal behavior. The opposite result is more likely, for a teenager may feel stigmatized by a criminal conviction and may believe he is a lost cause, resulting in a return to crime. In addition, the huge amounts expended on incarceration could be better spent on counseling, education, and job training.

The issue of stigmatization concerns defenders of the juvenile justice system. By classifying a juvenile proceeding as a civil action, the system avoids labeling the young person a criminal. If the juvenile stays out of trouble, the juvenile record can be erased when he reaches adulthood. If the system were abolished, a teenager could be convicted and la-

(continued on the next page)

SHOULD THE JUVENILE JUSTICE SYSTEM BE ABOLISHED?
(CONTINUED)

beled a criminal. A criminal conviction can engender difficulties in obtaining employment and in navigating other areas of daily life. It is wrong, defenders contend, to label a person so early in life, for an action that may have been impulsive or motivated by peer pressure. Preserving the juvenile justice system allows many teenagers to learn from their mistakes without prejudicing their adulthood.

Finally, defenders note that many states have changed their laws to deal more severely with violent juvenile offenders. As long as there are ways of diverting these offenders into the adult system, defenders insist, the current juvenile justice system should be maintained.

place the child with a foster family, or a court-approved family responsible for the custody of the child. If foster placement was not accomplished, the child would be placed in a reform school, where he would work and study. Juveniles found to be within the jurisdiction of the court remained under the court's control until the age of twenty-one.

The terminology created for juvenile court was based on the terminology used in civil rather than criminal court. This language helped establish a nonthreatening environment. Juveniles were not charged by an INDICTMENT, as they would have been charged in adult court; rather, they were brought before the juvenile court by way of a PETITION. Juveniles were not arraigned by the court at their first appearance; instead, they were held to appear for an intake hearing. The process was not called a trial but an ADJUDICATION or a HEARING. A juvenile found by the court to have committed a crime was not found guilty but was adjudged delinquent. Finally, instead of fashioning a sentence proportionate to the offense, the juvenile court disposed of the case by focusing on the best interests of the child. This terminology was used in every case, whether the petition concerned a juvenile charged with a crime or a juvenile in need of services or protection.

The Illinois act spawned similar acts in other states, and soon the progressive theory was put into practice across the United States. Juveniles were rehabilitated instead of punished; placed under the control of a juvenile court for a wide range of circumstances, some beyond their own control; and diverted from adult courts and prisons into an informal, relaxed system.

Modern Juvenile Law The basic framework created by the first juvenile court act is largely intact. REHABILITATION, not punishment, remains the aim of the juvenile justice system, and juvenile courts still retain jurisdiction over a wide range of juveniles. The most notable difference between the original model and current juvenile law is that juveniles now have more procedural rights in court. These rights include the right to an attorney and the right to be free from SELF-INCRIMINATION.

All states now maintain a juvenile code, or set of laws relating specifically to juveniles. The state codes regulate a variety of concerns, including the acts and circumstances that bring juveniles within the jurisdiction of the juvenile court, the procedures for juvenile courts, the rights of juveniles, and the range of judicial responses to misconduct or to the need for services.

Juvenile law is largely a matter of state law. On the federal level, Congress maintains in the U.S. Code a chapter on juvenile delinquency (18 U.S.C.A. § 5031 et seq.). The federal juvenile laws are similar to the state juvenile laws, but they deal solely with persons under the age of eighteen who are accused of committing a federal crime, a relatively minor part of the juvenile justice system.

Juvenile courts exist in all states. They may be held in a building or room separate from adult courtrooms. The proceedings are private, and the identity of the juveniles and the records of the proceedings are also private.

Many juveniles come to juvenile court after being arrested by the police for a criminal act. Juveniles accused of crimes may be confined in a secure facility prior to the disposition of their case. Although they should be separated from adults prior to trial, many juveniles accused of crimes find themselves in adult jail populations.

Juveniles charged with a crime do not have the right to a JURY trial in juvenile court. All juvenile cases are heard by a juvenile court judge. At trial a prosecutor representing the state presents EVIDENCE against the juvenile, and the juvenile has an opportunity to respond to the evidence. The juvenile has the right to receive notice of the charges against her, to confront and question WITNESSES, to be free from self-incrimination, and to be represented by an attorney. If the juvenile cannot afford an attorney, the juvenile court will appoint one, at no cost. The juvenile may not be adjudged delinquent unless the prosecution has proved its case BEYOND A REASONABLE DOUBT. This is the same high standard of proof required in adult criminal trials.

The harshest disposition of a juvenile case is commitment to a secure reformatory for rehabilitation. A secure reformatory is usually called a youth development center or something similar suggesting rehabilitation. Secure REFORMATORIES resemble adult prisons in that the inmates are locked inside. The professed goal of reformatories is rehabilitation, but the unspoken goal is often confinement of the juvenile for the protection of the community.

Not all findings of delinquency result in commitment to a secure facility. Juvenile courts usually have the discretion to order any combination of PROBATION, community service, medical treatment, fines, and RESTITUTION. Probation releases the juvenile into the community under the supervision of a youth services officer. As a part of probation, juveniles often must fulfill certain conditions identified by the juvenile court and the youth services officer. These conditions can range from attending school and meeting certain performance requirements, to abstaining from drugs or ALCOHOL. If the juvenile does not fulfill the conditions or commits another offense, she or he may be committed to a secure facility.

For repeated status offenses, a juvenile may be removed from home and placed in a state-approved foster home or some other state facility. Such facilities are usually not secure. However, juveniles ordered to such facilities are required to remain there for the period specified by the juvenile court judge. If they do not, they may be committed to a secure facility.

Juveniles do not have the right to a court-appointed attorney unless they face commitment to a secure facility that is operated by the state or federal government.

Status offenses do not always result in an appearance before juvenile court. Police officers often take intermediate measures before detaining a juvenile and beginning the petition process. These measures range from a simple reprimand to notification of the juvenile's parents. If a juvenile continues to commit status offenses after being excused by the police, he may be detained and eventually declared delinquent.

Abused and neglected juveniles usually come to the attention of juvenile courts through the petitions of state agencies or concerned private parties. In some cases the juvenile may be suffering physical or emotional abuse. In other cases the juvenile may be petitioned because he has committed a number of status offenses or petty offenses. A petition by the state usually seeks to remove the juvenile from the home for placement in foster care or a state facility.

When the state seeks to remove a juvenile from the home, the parents must receive an opportunity to be heard by the juvenile court. The juvenile is also allowed to testify, as are other witnesses. In addition to removing the juvenile from the home, the juvenile court may order that certain parties refrain from contacting the juvenile.

Children in need of services may also be petitioned by third parties. In some cases the juvenile court may simply order counseling for the child or the child's parents. If the parents are financially incapable of supporting the child, the court will usually remove the child from the home until such time as they are financially able to raise the child.

Juveniles have the right to APPEAL juvenile court decisions to adult courts. The number of available appeals varies from jurisdiction to jurisdiction, and can change within a jurisdiction. For example, before 1996 in New Hampshire, juveniles could appeal to the New Hampshire Superior Court and then to the New Hampshire Supreme Court. In 1996 the state legislature changed the law to allow only one appeal

Juvenile Arrests 1970 to 1995

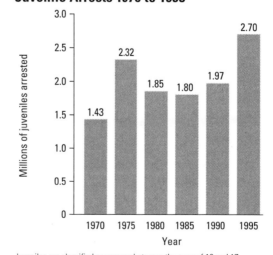

Juveniles are classified as persons between the ages of 10 and 17.

Source: U.S. Federal Bureau of Investigation, *Crime in the United States*, annual.

by a juvenile, to the state supreme court (N.H. Rev. Stat. Ann. § 169-B:29).

The period of time spent in a secure reformatory can vary. In most cases a juvenile committed to a reformatory must remain there until reaching the age of eighteen. However, most states allow juvenile courts to retain jurisdiction over certain juveniles past the age of eighteen at the request of a prosecutor or state agency representative. These holdovers are usually juveniles who have been adjudicated delinquent for a violent crime or have been adjudicated delinquent several times in separate proceedings.

Some states also allow a juvenile court to order incarceration in adult prison for juveniles who are found to be delinquent past a certain age. In New Hampshire, for example, a juvenile found to be delinquent based on a petition filed after the juvenile's sixteenth birthday may be sent to prison. If prison time is ordered, it cannot extend beyond the maximum term allowed for adults or beyond the juvenile's eighteenth birthday (N.H. Rev. Stat. Ann. § 169-B:19).

Some juveniles may be waived, or transferred, into adult court. In this procedure the juvenile court relinquishes its jurisdiction over the juvenile. Waiver is usually reserved for juveniles over a certain age (varying from thirteen to fifteen) who are accused of violent or other serious crimes. On the federal level, for example, a juvenile accused of committing a violent crime that is a FELONY may be tried in adult federal court. Waiver in federal court is also authorized for a juvenile accused of violating federal firearms laws or laws prohibiting the sale of controlled substances (18 U.S.C.A. § 5032 [West 1985 & Supp. Nov. 1994]).

The decision of whether to relinquish jurisdiction is usually made by the juvenile court. However, most jurisdictions have statutes that automatically exclude from juvenile court juveniles charged with violent or other serious crimes. In such cases an adult court prosecutor is required to certify to the adult court that the juvenile should, by law, appear in adult court. This certification takes places in a hearing before the adult trial court. Juveniles have the right to an attorney at this hearing and the right to present any evidence that militates against transfer.

Waiver into adult court has serious consequences for juveniles. In adult court juveniles face nearly all the punishments that may be inflicted on adults, including long-term imprisonment, life in prison, and in some cases death. However, in 1988 the U.S. Supreme Court ruled that no state may execute a juvenile who was under the age of sixteen at the time of the crime (*Thompson v. Oklahoma*, 487 U.S. 815, 108 S. Ct. 2687, 101 L. Ed. 2d 702 [1988]).

CROSS-REFERENCES

Child Abuse; Child Care; Child Labor Laws; Children's Rights; Family Law; *In re Gault*; Infants; Parent and Child; Right to Counsel.

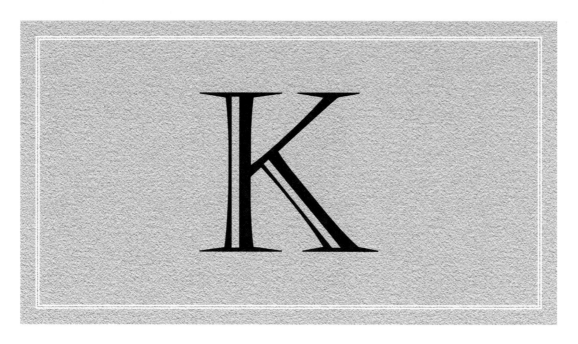

KANGAROO COURT

KANGAROO COURT 📖 [*Slang of U.S. origin.*] An unfair, biased, or hasty judicial proceeding that ends in a harsh punishment; an unauthorized trial conducted by individuals who have taken the law into their own hands, such as those put on by vigilantes or prison inmates; a proceeding and its leaders who are considered sham, corrupt, and without regard for the law. 📖

The concept of kangaroo court dates to the early nineteenth century. Scholars trace its origin to the historical practice of itinerant judges on the U.S. frontier. These roving judges were paid on the basis of how many trials they conducted, and in some instances their salary depended on the fines from the defendants they convicted. The term *kangaroo court* comes from the image of these judges hopping from place to place, guided less by concern for justice than by the desire to wrap up as many trials as the day allowed.

The term is still in common usage by defendants, writers, and scholars critical of a court or a trial. The U.S. Supreme Court has also used it. In *In re Gault*, 387 U.S. 1, 87 S. Ct. 1428, 18 L. Ed. 2d 527 (1967), a case that established that children in juvenile court have the right to DUE PROCESS, the Court reasoned, "Under our Constitution, the condition of being a boy does not justify a kangaroo court." Associate Justice WILLIAM O. DOUGLAS once wrote, "[W]here police take matters in their own hands, seize victims, beat and pound them until they confess, there cannot be the slightest doubt that the police have deprived the victim of a right under the Constitution. It is the right of the accused to be tried by a legally constituted court, not by a kangaroo court" (*Williams v. United States*, 341 U.S. 97, 71 S. Ct. 576, 95 L. Ed. 774 [1951]).

KANSAS-NEBRASKA ACT The Kansas-Nebraska Act of 1854 (10 Stat. 277) was a significant piece of legislation because it dealt with several controversial issues, including SLAVERY, western expansion, and the construction of a transcontinental railroad.

Slavery was a widely debated divisive issue for many years preceding the Civil War and there were several attempts at conciliation. The first of these was the MISSOURI COMPROMISE OF 1820 (3 Stat. 545), which decided the slavery question in regard to the creation of two new states, Missouri and Maine. The compromise declared that Maine was to be admitted as a free state, while Missouri was allowed to enter the Union with no restrictions regarding slavery. Subsequently, however, Missouri entered as a slave state. The compromise also prohibited the extension of slavery north of the 36°30′ latitude which established the southern border of Missouri.

The COMPROMISE OF 1850 (9 Stat. 452) settled another controversy concerning slavery and instituted the doctrine of popular sovereignty, which permitted the residents of the area to decide the question. When Texas and other new territories were acquired as a result of the Mexican War in 1848, and California sought admission to the Union in 1849, the question again arose concerning the slave status of the new areas. The Compromise of 1850 provided that California be admitted as a free state and that the citizens of the new territories of New Mexico and Utah decide whether their states favored or opposed slavery, pursuant to the doctrine of popular sovereignty.

THE PRESIDENTIAL CAMPAIGN OF '56.

The Kansas-Nebraska Act established that whether the states of Kansas and Nebraska would be slave states would be decided by popular vote. This cartoon shows Stephen Douglas as one of three congressmen pulling the slavery monster across the Mason-Dixon line.

In 1854, the Kansas and Nebraska territories were the next areas subjected to a dispute over slavery. Senator STEPHEN A. DOUGLAS of Illinois drafted a bill calling for the creation of two states, Kansas and Nebraska, areas he felt were vital to the construction of a railroad to the Pacific coast. The question of slavery in these states would be decided by popular sovereignty. The reasons for Douglas's excessive concern are speculative but include his support of western expansion and his belief that the popular sovereignty doctrine would cause the least dispute; his hope that his business interests would profit by the construction of a transcontinental railroad with a Chicago terminus and a route through the new territories; and his desire to gain favor in the South to garner support for his future presidential aspirations.

In order for the Kansas-Nebraska Act to be effective, it was necessary to repeal the Missouri Compromise and its boundary restrictions on the territorial extension of slavery. The new act was opposed by antislavery forces and subject to bitter dispute in Congress. President FRANKLIN PIERCE and a faction of Southern congressmen supported the bill and influenced its passage.

The provisions of the Kansas-Nebraska Act did not lead to the peaceful settlement of the issue as intended. In Kansas, the antislavery and proslavery proponents disagreed violently, undermining the effectiveness of the popular sovereignty doctrine. Two opposing governments were established, and acts of destruction and violence ensued, including an assault on the antislavery town of Lawrence. In retaliation, abolitionist John Brown and his followers killed five settlers who advocated slavery. The phrase *Bleeding Kansas* was derived from this violence.

The Lecompton Constitution of 1857 was drafted based upon the results of a Kansas election that offered the voters the choice of limited or unlimited slavery. This angered the abolitionists, who refused to vote. President JAMES BUCHANAN approved the Lecompton Constitution and encouraged its acceptance by Congress, but Douglas and his supporters vehemently opposed the admission of Kansas as a slave state. Another election was held in 1858, and the people of Kansas voted against the Lecompton document; three years later, Kansas entered the Union as a free state.

See also RAILROAD.

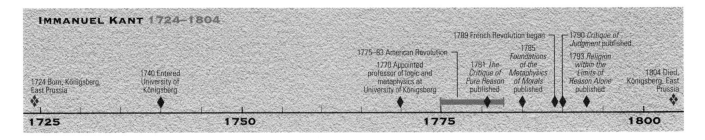

1789 French Revolution began

1790 *Critique of Judgment* published

1775–83 American Revolution

1785 *Foundations of the Metaphysics of Morals* published

1770 Appointed professor of logic and metaphysics at University of Königsberg

1781 *The Critique of Pure Reason* published

1793 *Religion within the Limits of Reason Alone* published

1724 Born, Königsberg, East Prussia

1740 Entered University of Königsberg

1804 Died, Königsberg, East Prussia

1725   1750   1775   1800

KANT, IMMANUEL

Immanuel Kant shook the foundations of Western philosophy in the late eighteenth and early nineteenth centuries. This author and professor did his most important writing between 1781 and 1790 while working at the University of Königsberg, where he spent most of his life. Kant's philosophical model not only swept aside the ideas of the so-called empiricists and rationalists who came before him, it also had a lasting effect outside of philosophy, especially in the areas of ethics and the law. Today, legal scholars still debate his ideas—and their sometimes startling implications—in relation to contemporary issues.

Kant was born into a lower-middle-class family in East Prussia in 1724. A gifted student, he studied in a Latin school from age eight until age sixteen, when he entered the University of Königsberg to take up theology, natural science, and philosophy. The death of his father forced him to abandon his studies in order to work as a private tutor, and he had to wait several years before returning to complete his education. By that time he was already writing serious books. From what is called Kant's precritical period, these early works are primarily scientific. In recognition of his talents, the university made him a lecturer and eventually a professor. He taught logic and metaphysics.

Twenty years later Kant attacked the reigning schools of thought. In this so-called critical period, he wrote his most famous book, *The Critique of Pure Reason* (1781). Kant's work examined the relation of experience and perception: he was concerned with how people know what they know, and just as important, the proper uses of the powers of reasoning. He argued that reality can be perceived only to the extent that it complies with the aptitude of the mind that is doing the perceiving. This places one kind of limitation on what can be known. Kant saw another limitation, too: only phenomena—things that can be experienced—are capable of being understood; everything else is unknown. The human senses, therefore, take supreme precedence in determining what is real.

BIOGRAPHY

Immanuel Kant

"THE GREATEST PROBLEM FOR THE HUMAN SPECIES, THE SOLUTION OF WHICH NATURE COMPELS HIM TO SEEK, IS THAT OF ATTAINING A CIVIL SOCIETY WHICH CAN ADMINISTER JUSTICE UNIVERSALLY."

BIOGRAPHY

APWIDE WORLD PHOTOS

Nicholas deBelleville Katzenbach

These theories have implications for conventional morality. Kant viewed God, freedom, and immortality as incomprehensible: they can only be contemplated; their existence can never be proved. Nonetheless, he argued, all three of them are important as the basis for morality. Kant believed that reason is insufficient to justify moral behavior. The justification for behaving morally has to come from people's sense of duty, which he called the categorical imperative.

Kant continued to develop his philosophy in subsequent books including *Critique of Judgment* (1790) and *Religion within the Limits of Reasons Alone* (1793). The latter enraged the government, resulting in its censorship and an official order to Kant to write no more books about religion.

Philosophers have studied Kant's work for over two centuries, but legal thinkers outside of Europe have only widely treated it in recent years. In the late twentieth century, when many U.S. scholars of law turned to interdisciplinary studies that involved the fields of economics and textual analysis, Kant provided another model for argument. Kant's ideas cover the foundation of law while specifically addressing property, contracts, and criminal punishment. Kant proposed that punishment should be meted out strictly without exception—because of society's duty to seek retribution. "[I]f justice goes," Kant wrote in 1797, "there is no longer any value in men's living on the earth."

See also HEGEL, GEORG WILHELM FRIEDRICH; JURISPRUDENCE.

KATZENBACH, NICHOLAS deBELLEVILLE

Nicholas deBelleville Katzenbach served as U.S. attorney general from 1965 to 1966, during the administration of President LYNDON B. JOHNSON. A distinguished lawyer and law professor before joining the Department of Justice in 1961, Katzenbach played a key role in federal efforts to end racial segregation in the South.

Katzenbach was born January 17, 1922, in Philadelphia and was raised in New Jersey. His father, Edward L. Katzenbach, was a lawyer who served as attorney general of New Jersey

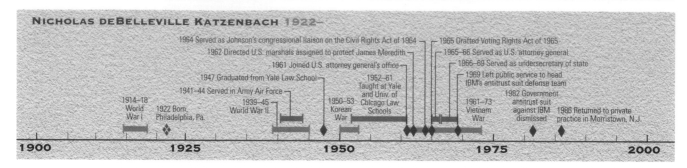

NICHOLAS DeBELLEVILLE KATZENBACH 1922–

1964 Served as Johnson's congressional liaison on the Civil Rights Act of 1964
1962 Directed U.S. marshals assigned to protect James Meredith
1961 Joined U.S. attorney general's office
1947 Graduated from Yale Law School
1941–44 Served in Army Air Force

1965 Drafted Voting Rights Act of 1965
1965–66 Served as U.S. attorney general
1966–69 Served as undersecretary of state
1969 Left public service to head IBM's antitrust suit defense team

1952–61 Taught at Yale and Univ. of Chicago Law Schools

1982 Government antitrust suit against IBM dismissed

1986 Returned to private practice in Morristown, N.J.

1914–18 World War I
1922 Born, Philadelphia, Pa.
1939–45 World War II
1950–53 Korean War
1961–73 Vietnam War

1900 1925 1950 1975 2000

and ran unsuccessfully for governor of New Jersey. Katzenbach graduated from a private high school and in 1941 enlisted in the Army Air Force. During World War II, his bomber was shot down over North Africa and he became a prisoner of war. He read so many books while a prisoner that following his repatriation in 1944, Princeton University allowed him to graduate two years early. After graduating in 1945, he earned a law degree at Yale University Law School. In 1947 Katzenbach was a Rhodes scholar at Oxford University in England.

Katzenbach returned to the United States in 1949 and was admitted to the New Jersey bar in 1950. He was briefly an associate in his father's law firm before becoming in 1950 an attorney-adviser in the Office of General Counsel to the Secretary of the Air Force. During this period Katzenbach first became acquainted with Johnson, then a senator from Texas. In 1952 Katzenbach left Washington, D.C., to teach law at Yale. In 1956 he moved to the University of Chicago Law School as a professor of law.

Attorney General ROBERT F. KENNEDY appointed Katzenbach assistant attorney general of the Office of Legal Counsel in 1961 and promoted him to deputy attorney general in 1962. Katzenbach soon became a national figure, playing a prominent role in federal desegregation efforts in the South. In October 1962 JAMES H. MEREDITH, an African American, attempted to register for classes at the all-white University of Mississippi, in Oxford. Governor Ross Barnett pledged defiance of a federal court order mandating that Meredith be allowed to register. Katzenbach went to Oxford and directed U.S. marshals to protect Meredith as he registered. Riots erupted, and before federal troops arrived to restore order, Katzenbach ordered the marshals to fire tear gas into the unruly crowds.

In 1963 Governor GEORGE WALLACE, of Alabama, pledged to resist the INTEGRATION of the University of Alabama. Wallace confronted Katzenbach at the university and refused to allow him to register James Hood and Vivian Malone. The nationally televised scene was a

"I OBJECT TO SAYING WE ARE AT WAR HERE [IN VIETNAM], ALTHOUGH I REALIZE IN THE POPULAR SENSE THAT MAKES ME PERHAPS LOOK FOOLISH."

symbolic last stand for Wallace and other advocates of racial segregation. Once President JOHN F. KENNEDY ordered that state troops were to come under federal control to enforce the court order, Wallace ended his defiance.

Following the ASSASSINATION of John F. Kennedy, President Johnson announced his determination to pass a strong CIVIL RIGHTS act that would end racial discrimination in employment, education, and other spheres of life. Katzenbach was Johnson's congressional liaison, working with Senator HUBERT H. HUMPHREY (D-Minn.) and Senate minority leader Everett M. Dirksen (R-Ill.) to achieve a compromise that would ensure the act's final passage. The result was the landmark CIVIL RIGHTS ACT of 1964 (42 U.S.C.A. § 2000a et seq.). The following year Katzenbach drafted the Voting Rights Act of 1965 (42 U.S.C.A. § 1973 et seq.), which prohibits states from imposing voting qualifications based on race, color, or membership in a language minority group. This legislation changed the South, as thousands of African Americans were allowed to register to vote for the first time.

President Johnson appointed Katzenbach attorney general in February 1965. Katzenbach continued his work on civil rights legislation and enforcement. In October 1966 Johnson, who was increasingly preoccupied with the growing U.S. involvement in Vietnam, named Katzenbach under secretary of state. In this position Katzenbach became an administration spokesperson for Johnson's Vietnam policies, defending them before Congress on a regular basis.

Katzenbach left government at the end of the Johnson administration, in January 1969, and joined International Business Machines (IBM), a large manufacturer that dominated the U.S. computer market. The Department of Justice had filed an ANTITRUST lawsuit against IBM, and Katzenbach was brought into the corporation to lead the fight against it. For the next thirteen years Katzenbach and a host of attorneys fought the lawsuit, which ultimately was dismissed.

In 1986 Katzenbach left IBM and returned to the practice of law in Morristown, New Jersey. He has remained active in Democratic politics and has served on various national task forces dealing with the justice system.

KEARSE, AMALYA LYLE Amalya Lyle Kearse is a judge with the U.S. Court of Appeals for the Second Circuit.

Kearse was born June 11, 1937, in Vauxhall, New Jersey. Her parents encouraged Kearse to develop her considerable intellectual skills. Her father, the postmaster in her hometown, wanted to become a lawyer, but the Depression prevented him from pursuing his dream. Her mother was a medical doctor who later became an administrator in an antipoverty program. Kearse attended Wellesley College, where she earned her bachelor's degree in philosophy in 1959. "I can trace [the decision to become a litigator] back to a course in international law at Wellesley," she said. "There was a moot court, and I found that very enjoyable." Kearse then enrolled at the University of Michigan Law School, and she graduated cum laude in 1962.

Kearse began her legal career with the Wall Street firm of Hughes, Hubbard, and Reed. After seven years of distinguished and diligent work, she was named a partner, becoming the first black female partner in a major Wall Street firm. Her colleagues have praised her for her incisive analytical skills. When asked about Kearse's qualifications, a senior partner at the Hughes, Hubbard firm said, "She became a partner here not because she is a woman, not because she is a black, but because she is just so damned good—no question about it."

Kearse's outstanding talents eventually came to the attention of President JIMMY CARTER, who named her to the U.S. Court of Appeals for the Second Circuit in 1979. She is the first black woman to serve on that court. During her tenure, she has decided many influential cases. In 1980, she wrote the majority opinion in *U.S. v. Taborda*, 635 F.2d 131 (2d Cir. 1980), a case that concluded that the use of a high-powered telescope to observe drug activity inside an apartment without a WARRANT constituted an unreasonable search and violated the FOURTH AMENDMENT. In other cases, she joined the majority in upholding a New York state ban on SCHOOL PRAYERS (*Brandon v. Board of Education of Guilderland Central School District*, 635 F.2d 971 [2d Cir. 1980]) and helped overturn a lower court's ruling that Vietnam veterans could sue the manufacturers of Agent Orange for alleged damage (*In re "Agent Orange" Product Liability Litigation*, 635 F.2d 987 [2d Cir. 1980]).

Kearse's name has been on the list of potential nominees to fill vacancies on the U.S. Supreme Court. In 1991, she was considered for the vacancy created by the retirement of Justice THURGOOD MARSHALL. After President George Bush's controversial nomination of CLARENCE THOMAS, who was eventually confirmed notwithstanding allegations that he had sexually harassed a former coworker, an opinion article in the *New York Times* urged Bush to nominate Kearse in Thomas's place. The article noted that, because of her years of distinguished service on the court of appeals, Kearse is "among the four or five persons most qualified for the High Court." The article concluded that "what is needed is an appointment that can unify the country in the assurance that the next Supreme Court nominee is a person of unquestioned excellence. Judge Kearse is that person" (*New York Times*, October 10, 1991). Kearse was considered for the Supreme Court again in 1994 when President BILL CLINTON was evaluating possible replacements for retiring justice HARRY A. BLACKMUN. Earlier, in 1992, Clinton had considered her for the post of attorney general.

Kearse is a top-rated bridge player who has written several books about the game. She is a member of the American Law Institute and a fellow in the American College of Trial Lawyers. She has been an adjunct lecturer at New York University Law School, a member of the Executive Committee of the Lawyers' Committee for Civil Rights under Law, and a member of the President's Commission for Selection of Judges. She has also served on the boards of the NATIONAL ASSOCIATION FOR THE ADVANCEMENT OF

BIOGRAPHY

Amalya Lyle Kearse

"THE VERY FACT THAT A PERSON IS IN HIS OWN HOME RAISES A REASONABLE INFERENCE THAT HE INTENDS TO HAVE PRIVACY, AND IF THAT INFERENCE IS BORNE OUT BY HIS ACTIONS, SOCIETY IS PREPARED TO RESPECT HIS PRIVACY."

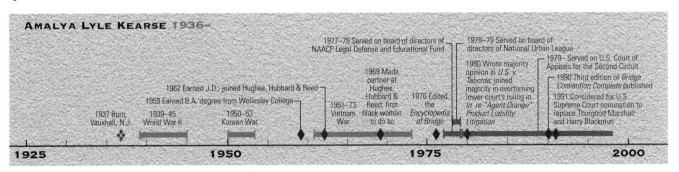

AMALYA LYLE KEARSE 1936–

1937 Born, Vauxhall, N.J.

1939–45 World War II

1950–53 Korean War

1959 Earned B.A. degree from Wellesley College

1961–73 Vietnam War

1962 Earned J.D.; joined Hughes, Hubbard & Reed

1969 Made partner at Hughes, Hubbard & Reed, first black woman to do so

1976 Edited the *Encyclopedia of Bridge*

1977–79 Served on board of directors of NAACP Legal Defense and Educational Fund

1978–79 Served on board of directors of National Urban League

1979 Served on U.S. Court of Appeals for the Second Circuit

1980 Wrote majority opinion in *U.S. v. Taborda*; joined majority in overturning lower court's ruling in *In re "Agent Orange" Product Liability Litigation*

1990 Third edition of *Bridge Convention Complete* published

1991 Considered for U.S. Supreme Court nomination to replace Thurgood Marshall and Harry Blackmun

1925   1950   1975   2000

COLORED PEOPLE's Legal Defense and Education Fund and the National Urban League. Kearse has received many awards and honors, including the ORDER OF THE COIF and the Jason L. Honigman Award for outstanding contribution to a law review editorial board.

KELLOGG, FRANK BILLINGS Frank Billings Kellogg was born December 22, 1856, in Potsdam, New York. He moved to Minnesota at age nine, received an education in law, and was admitted to the bar in 1877. Kellogg subsequently received numerous doctor of laws degrees from various institutions, including McGill University, Montreal, 1913; New York University, 1927; Harvard, 1929; Brown University, 1930; and Occidental University, 1931. He also received two doctor of civil law degrees in 1929, from Trinity College in Connecticut and Oxford University.

After his admission to the bar, Kellogg performed the duties of city and county attorney for St. Paul, Minnesota, and established a legal practice, specializing in corporation law. His expertise earned him the position of special counsel for the United States, and he participated in the case against the General Paper and Standard Oil trusts (*United States v. Standard Oil Co.*, 212 U.S. 579, 29 S.Ct. 689, 53 L.Ed. 259 [1909]). He served as special counsel of the INTERSTATE COMMERCE COMMISSION to probe into the speculative dealings concerning the Harriman railroads.

Kellogg began a phase of government and diplomatic service in 1917, when he became U.S. Senator from Minnesota for a six-year term. He followed this with a one-year appointment as minister to Great Britain. From 1925 to 1929, he performed the duties of secretary of state and negotiated treaties.

In 1928, Kellogg achieved international acclaim for his collaboration with Aristide Briand in the formulation of the Kellogg-Briand Pact, which denounced war as a solution to international disagreements. The pact was subsequently ratified by sixty-three nations. In 1929, the Nobel Peace Prize was bestowed upon Kellogg for his contribution to world peace.

During the latter part of his life, Kellogg acted as judge of the Permanent Court of

Frank Billings Kellogg

"THERE ARE ONLY TWO MEANS OF ENFORCING A TREATY. ONE IS BY WAR, THE OTHER IS BY THE OVERPOWERING STRENGTH OF PUBLIC OPINION."

International Justice. He died December 21, 1937, in St. Paul, Minnesota.

See also KELLOGG-BRIAND PACT.

KELLOGG-BRIAND PACT The Kellogg-Briand Pact, also known as the Pact of Paris, was a TREATY that attempted to outlaw WAR (46 Stat. 2343, T.S. No. 796, 94 L.N.T.S. 57). The treaty was drafted by France and the United States, and on August 27, 1928, was signed by fifteen nations. By 1933 sixty-five nations had pledged to observe its provisions.

Kellogg-Briand contained no sanctions against countries that might breach its provisions. Instead, the treaty was based on the hope that diplomacy and the weight of world opinion would be powerful enough to prevent nations from resorting to the use of force. This soon proved to be a false hope; though Germany, Italy, and Japan were all signatories, the treaty did not prevent them from committing aggressions that led to World War II.

The origin of the Kellogg-Briand Pact was a message that the French foreign minister, Aristide Briand, addressed to the citizens of the United States on April 6, 1927, the tenth anniversary of the United States' entrance into World War I. In this message Briand announced France's willingness to join the United States in an agreement mutually outlawing war. Such an agreement, Briand stated, would "greatly contribute in the eyes of the world to enlarge and fortify the foundation on which the international policy of peace is being erected." Briand's overture to the United States was part of a larger campaign that France was waging to form strategic alliances that would improve its national security. In addition, Briand was influenced by recent conversations with Nicholas Murray Butler and James Thomson Shotwell, U.S. academics who were leaders in the burgeoning U.S. political movement to outlaw war, also known as the outlawry movement.

Initially, Briand's offer generated little reaction in the United States. The U.S. State Department made no response, apparently considering Briand's statement to be simply an expression of friendship. Not until certain leaders in the peace movement, notably Butler, began to generate widespread public support

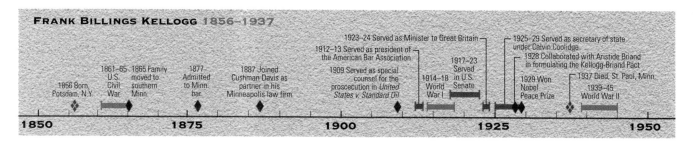

FRANK BILLINGS KELLOGG 1856-1937

for Briand's proposal did the government become involved. But by the middle of June 1927, France and the United States had begun diplomatic conversations aimed at reaching the sort of agreement Briand had proposed in his address.

On June 20 the State Department received the Draft Pact of Perpetual Friendship between France and the United States, written by Briand and transmitted through the U.S. ambassador in Paris. The draft contained just two articles: the first declared that France and the United States renounced war "as an instrument of their national policy towards each other," and the second declared that all conflicts between the two nations would be settled only by "pacific means." Secretary of State FRANK B. KELLOGG and other officials in the U.S. State Department were uncomfortable about entering into such an agreement with France alone, fearing that it would amount to an indirect alliance that would deprive the United States of the freedom to act if France were to go to war with another country. Instead, U.S. officials preferred to expand the agreement into a multilateral treaty involving all the world powers except Russia. On December 28, therefore, Kellogg told Briand that the United States was prepared to enter into negotiations with France to construct a treaty that would condemn war and renounce it as an instrument of national policy; when concluded, the treaty would be open to signature by all nations.

France accepted the United States' offer, and treaty negotiations began in January 1928. By early April the four other Great Powers—Germany, Great Britain, Italy, and Japan—were invited to enter the discussions. Soon after, the invitation was extended to Belgium; Czechoslovakia; Poland; India; and the five British dominions, Australia, Canada, Irish Free State, New Zealand, and South Africa. Several of the parties wanted specific conditions and reservations included in the treaty. These issues were resolved, and on August 27, 1928, diplomats from the fifteen countries met in Paris to sign the treaty. By 1933 fifty additional countries had agreed to observe the treaty's provisions.

The final text of the Kellogg-Briand Pact, like the original draft, was extremely simple and contained just two principal articles. The first stated that the contracting parties "condemn[ed] recourse to war for the solution of international controversies, and renounce[d] it as an instrument of national policy in their relations with one another." In the second the parties agreed that "the settlement or solution of all disputes or conflicts of whatever nature or of whatever origin they may be, which may arise between them, shall never be sought except by pacific means." The treaty therefore outlawed war entirely, providing no exceptions to this general prohibition. The parties, however, generally recognized that war would be permissible in the case of self-defense; several signatories, including the United States, had submitted diplomatic notes prior to the treaty's ratification indicating their understanding that wars entered into in self-defense would be lawful.

When it was signed, the Kellogg-Briand Pact was considered a tremendous milestone in the effort to advance the cause of international peace. In 1929 Kellogg received the Nobel Peace Prize for his work on the treaty. Events soon showed, however, that the pact did not prevent or limit war between the nations. The primary problem was that the treaty provided for no means of enforcement or sanctions against parties who violated its provisions. In addition, it did not address the issues of what constituted self-defense and when self-defense could lawfully be claimed. Because of these large loopholes, the Kellogg-Briand Pact was ultimately an ineffective method for achieving the ambitious and idealistic goal of outlawing war.

KELLY, SHARON PRATT DIXON From 1991 to 1994, the difficult job of running Washington, D.C., belonged to Mayor Sharon Pratt Dixon Kelly. A successful utilities executive with no previous experience in city government, Kelly was voted mayor in the wake of the fall of Marion S. Barry, Jr., from political grace. During her uphill campaign, Kelly portrayed herself as a squeaky-clean political outsider,

BIOGRAPHY

MARKEL/GAMMA-LIAISON

Sharon Pratt Dixon Kelly

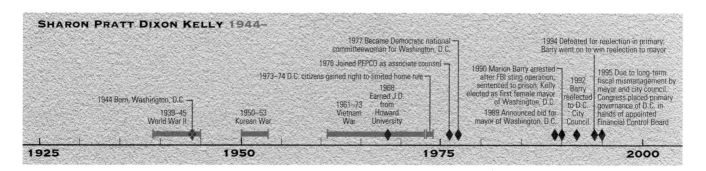

SHARON PRATT DIXON KELLY 1944–

1977 Became Democratic national committeewoman for Washington, D.C.

1976 Joined PEPCO as associate counsel

1973–74 D.C. citizens gained right to limited home rule

1994 Defeated for reelection in primary; Barry went on to win reelection to mayor

1990 Marion Barry arrested after FBI sting operation; sentenced to prison; Kelly elected as first female mayor of Washington, D.C.

1992 Barry reelected to D.C. City Council

1995 Due to long-term fiscal mismanagement by mayor and city council, Congress placed primary governance of D.C. in hands of appointed Financial Control Board

1989 Announced bid for mayor of Washington, D.C.

1944 Born, Washington, D.C.

1968 Earned J.D. from Howard University

1961–73 Vietnam War

1939–45 World War II

1950–53 Korean War

1925   1950   1975   2000

even though she had strong connections to the national Democratic party. A middle-class African American who was born and raised in the District, Kelly promised to reduce crime, cut the city's bloated budget, and clean up corrupt government. Although she was turned out of office after just one term, Kelly earned herself a permanent place in history by becoming the first female mayor of the nation's capital.

Kelly was born January 30, 1944, in Washington, D.C. She was the first child of Mildred Petticord Pratt, who died of cancer when Kelly was just four years old, and Carlisle E. Pratt, who was a lawyer and superior court judge. Family expectations were high for Kelly, whose father gave her a copy of *Black's Law Dictionary* as a birthday gift when she was very young. Kelly did not disappoint her father, graduating from Howard University with a bachelor's degree in political science in 1965 and a law degree in 1968. While in college, Kelly met her first husband, Arrington Dixon, who later became a member of the Washington, D.C., City Council. The couple married in 1967, had two daughters, and divorced in 1982. In 1991, Kelly married business entrepreneur James Kelly III. Although she won the mayoral race as Sharon Pratt Dixon, she changed her last name to Kelly shortly after her 1991 wedding.

Kelly began her legal career as an attorney in her father's firm. She also taught courses at Antioch School of Law, before joining the Potomac Electric Power Company (PEPCO) as associate counsel in 1976. Kelly eventually became the first African American woman to be named vice president at PEPCO. A decisive, hardworking executive, Kelly was involved in lobbying, policy making, and regulatory matters for the utility company. At the same time, she developed a strong interest in local Democratic politics. Kelly became the Democratic national committeewoman from the District of Columbia in 1977 and eventually was the first African American woman to serve as national party treasurer.

Kelly entered politics to try to halt the social and economic deterioration of Washington, D.C. In 1989, she announced her long shot candidacy for mayor. Soon afterward, Barry's career self-destructed with his arrest and subsequent conviction for cocaine possession. After Barry withdrew from the race, Kelly faced three city council members, each of whom had greater name recognition. Kelly was a political unknown whose middle-class background made her suspect to residents in the poorest sections of Washington, D.C. Till then, she had been on the political sidelines, never in the spotlight. To

"DIVISIVENESS HAS NO PLACE IN OUR POLITICS . . . SPITEFULNESS AND HATRED ONLY ERODE THAT WHICH IS TRULY MAGNIFICENT ABOUT OUR COUNTRY."

set herself apart from her opponents, Kelly made a rather rash promise to cut Washington's murder rate, which was the highest in the nation. She also pledged to shrink the city's budget by eliminating two thousand government jobs. On her lapel, Kelly wore a pin shaped like a shovel, to symbolize her campaign promise to "clean house with a shovel, not a broom."

On September 11, 1990, Kelly achieved her first victory at the polls, winning the mayoral primary election by an impressive margin. In November's general election, she handily defeated her Republican opponent, Maurice T. Turner, a former D.C. police chief. Kelly won the mayor's race with 86 percent of the vote, a new district record. Her administration's theme became Yes We Will, a vow to overhaul city government.

During the early days of her administration, Kelly enjoyed success. She coaxed $100 million in emergency aid from the U.S. Congress, helped convince the owners of the Washington Redskins football team to stay in town, and handled riots in the Mount Pleasant neighborhood with considerable aplomb. But problems arose, including political squabbling with city council members and serious budget cuts from Congress. Despite her campaign pledges, Kelly still faced an appalling homicide rate and an overextended city budget. Although her call for deficit reduction was popular, government workers affected by proposed layoffs were openly hostile to her plans.

As her ratings in public opinion polls plummeted, the political fortunes of former mayor Barry rose. In 1992, Barry staged a remarkable political comeback when he was elected to the D.C. City Council, shortly after his release from federal prison. Despite his well-publicized drug problem, Barry remained popular with many voters, particularly those in poor and working-class neighborhoods. Barry was credited with developing the downtown area, attracting new businesses, and focusing national attention on the capital's plight during his twelve years as mayor. He criticized Kelly, focusing on her inability to improve schools, crime rates, and public housing.

In the primary election on September 13, 1994, Kelly was handed a stunning defeat. Barry and D.C. City Council member John Ray finished in a virtual dead heat for first place in the Democratic mayoral primary. A massive voter registration drive brought new supporters into Barry's camp. As a result, many voters turned to candidate Ray as the only realistic alternative to Barry. Kelly received an unmis-

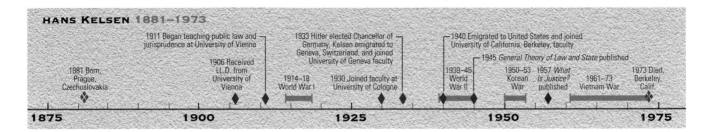

HANS KELSEN 1881–1973

1911 Began teaching public law and jurisprudence at University of Vienna

1933 Hitler elected Chancellor of Germany; Kelsen emigrated to Geneva, Switzerland, and joined University of Geneva faculty

1940 Emigrated to United States and joined University of California, Berkeley, faculty

1906 Received LL.D. from University of Vienna

1945 *General Theory of Law and State* published

1881 Born, Prague, Czechoslovakia

1914–18 World War I

1930 Joined faculty at University of Cologne

1939–45 World War II

1950–53 Korean War

1957 *What Is Justice?* published

1961–73 Vietnam War

1973 Died, Berkeley, Calif.

1875 1900 1925 1950 1975

takable message that her brand of government did not work in the nation's capital. Voters returned Barry to the mayor's office in the November general election.

KELSEN, HANS Hans Kelsen was a European legal philosopher and teacher who emigrated to the United States in 1940 after leaving Nazi Germany. Kelsen is most famous for his studies on law and especially for his idea known as the pure theory of the law.

Kelsen was born in Prague, Czechoslovakia, on October 11, 1881. He studied at several universities, including Berlin, Heidelberg, and Vienna. He received a doctor of laws degree from Vienna in 1906 and began teaching at the school in 1911. He taught public law and JURISPRUDENCE at Vienna until 1930, when he moved to Germany to teach at the University of Cologne. There he taught international law and jurisprudence and served as dean for two years.

With the rise of the Nazi government, he left Germany and emigrated to Switzerland in 1933. He taught at the Graduate Institute of International Studies of the University of Geneva until 1940. He accepted a position as lecturer at the Harvard University Law School the same year, and relocated to the United States. Later in 1940 he accepted a teaching position at the University of California at Berkeley. He remained at Berkeley until his retirement in 1952.

Kelsen's pure theory of the law is fairly abstract. Its objective is knowledge of that which is essential to law; therefore, the theory does not deal with that which is changing and accidental, such as ideals of justice. Kelsen believed that law is a science that deals not with the actual events of the world (what is) but with norms (what ought to be). The legal relation contains the threat of a sanction from an authority in response to a certain act. The legal norm is a relation of condition and consequence: if a certain act is done, a certain consequence ought to follow.

In this theory a legal system is made of a hierarchy of norms. Each norm is derived from its superior norm. The ultimate norm from which every legal norm deduces its validity is

BIOGRAPHY

Hans Kelsen

BIOGRAPHY

Anthony McLeod Kennedy

"THE OBLIGATION TO FOLLOW PRECEDENT BEGINS WITH NECESSITY, AND A CONTRARY NECESSITY MARKS ITS OUTER LIMIT."

the *Grundnorm*, the highest basic norm. The *Grundnorm* is not deduced from anything else but is assumed as an initial hypothesis. A norm is a valid legal norm only because it has been created according to a definite rule.

The theory is independent of morality. It does not matter which particular *Grundnorm* is adopted by a legal order. All that matters is that this basic norm has a minimum effectiveness: it must command a certain amount of obedience, since the effectiveness of the total legal order is necessary for the validity of its norms.

Kelsen received acclaim for authoring many publications, including *General Theory of Law and State* (1945), *The Law of the United Nations* (1950–51), *Principles of International Law* (1952), and *What Is Justice?* (1957).

He died April 20, 1973, in Berkeley, California.

KENNEDY, ANTHONY MCLEOD Anthony McLeod Kennedy was appointed as an associate justice of the U.S. Supreme Court in 1988. Kennedy was the third person nominated by President RONALD REAGAN to fill the vacancy created by the retirement of Justice LEWIS F. POWELL, JR. A judicial conservative, Kennedy has generally voted with the conservative justices on the Court, yet he has split from them in significant rulings on ABORTION rights and gay rights.

Kennedy was born in Sacramento, California, on July 28, 1936. He graduated from Stanford University in 1958 and from Harvard University Law School in 1961. He practiced law in San Francisco and Sacramento, and taught constitutional law at the McGeorge School of Law of the University of the Pacific from 1965 to 1988.

His conservative philosophy and his Republican party affiliation led to Kennedy's first judicial appointment. In 1975 President GERALD R. FORD appointed him to the Ninth Circuit Court of Appeals. Kennedy served on the federal appeals court for thirteen years and wrote over four hundred opinions.

A well-respected jurist, Kennedy entered the national limelight after the Senate rejected President Reagan's first nominee for Powell's

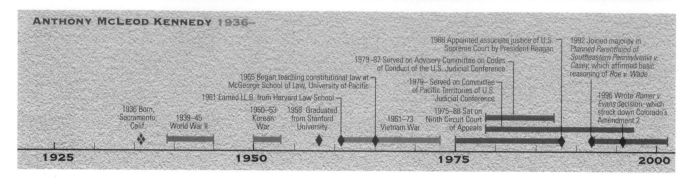

ANTHONY McLEOD KENNEDY 1936–

1936 Born, Sacramento, Calif.

1939–45 World War II

1950–53 Korean War

1958 Graduated from Stanford University

1961 Earned LL.B. from Harvard Law School

1965 Began teaching constitutional law at McGeorge School of Law, University of Pacific

1961–73 Vietnam War

1975–88 Sat on Ninth Circuit Court of Appeals

1979– Served on Committee of Pacific Territories of U.S. Judicial Conference

1979–87 Served on Advisory Committee on Codes of Conduct of the U.S. Judicial Conference

1988 Appointed associate justice of U.S. Supreme Court by President Reagan

1992 Joined majority in *Planned Parenthood of Southeastern Pennsylvania v. Casey,* which affirmed basic reasoning of *Roe v. Wade*

1996 Wrote *Romer v. Evans* decision, which struck down Colorado's Amendment 2

1925   1950   1975   2000

seat on the Court, Judge ROBERT H. BORK, and Reagan's second nominee, Judge DOUGLAS H. GINSBURG, withdrew following his admission that he had smoked marijuana. Kennedy's confirmation hearings were filled with questions that sought to compare his philosophy to Bork's. Bork had embraced the doctrine of ORIGINAL INTENT (the idea that a judge should apply the Constitution only in the exact manner intended by the Constitution's Framers) as the only legitimate means of interpretation. Kennedy testified that original intent was only a starting point in interpreting the Constitution. In his Senate testimony, Kennedy stated his commitment to the principle of STARE DECISIS. This principle refers to the respect for legal precedent created by prior cases and the need to maintain precedent even if the current judges do not agree with the original ruling.

Kennedy was confirmed in February 1988, with many liberal members of Congress feeling he was too conservative, and some conservatives believing he was moderate, a compromise candidate who could survive the confirmation process.

Since taking office as associate justice, Kennedy has proved to be both conservative and moderate, depending on the case. He has usually sided with the conservative members of the Court, but he has gained attention by departing from them in two important cases. In *Planned Parenthood of Southeastern Pennsylvania v. Casey*, 505 U.S. 833, 112 S. Ct. 2791, 120 L. Ed. 2d 674 (1992), watchers had expected the Court to overrule explicitly *Roe v. Wade*, 410 U.S. 113, 93 S. Ct. 705, 35 L. Ed. 2d 147, the 1973 decision that defined the right to choose abortion as a fundamental constitutional right. Kennedy joined with Justices SANDRA DAY O'CONNOR and DAVID H. SOUTER in an opinion that defended the reasoning of *Roe* and the line of cases that followed it.

In 1996 Kennedy wrote a landmark and controversial decision concerning gay rights. In *Romer v. Evans*, __U.S.__, 116 S. Ct. 1620, 134 L. Ed. 2d 855, Kennedy declared unconstitu-

tional an amendment to the Colorado state constitution (West's C.R.S.A. Const. Art. 2, § 30b) that prohibited state and local governments from enacting any law, regulation, or policy that would, in effect, protect the CIVIL RIGHTS of gay men, lesbians, and bisexuals. Kennedy ruled that the amendment violated the Equal Protection Clause of the FOURTEENTH AMENDMENT, noting that the amendment classified gay men and lesbians "not to further a proper legislative end but to make them unequal to everyone else," and adding, "[t]his Colorado cannot do." See also GAY AND LESBIAN RIGHTS.

KENNEDY, EDWARD MOORE Edward Moore ("Ted") Kennedy has served as a U.S. senator from Massachusetts since 1962. The brother of President JOHN F. KENNEDY and Senator ROBERT F. KENNEDY, who were both assassinated, he has championed many liberal social programs, including national health care, and has been a major figure in the Democratic party. His presidential aspirations were damaged because of personal scandal.

Kennedy, the youngest of nine children of Joseph P. Kennedy and Rose Fitzgerald Kennedy, was born February 22, 1932, in Brookline, Massachusetts. He started at Harvard University in 1950, then left in 1951 to serve in the U.S. Army. He returned to college in 1953 and graduated in 1956. He next attended the University of Virginia Law School, where he graduated in 1959. He married Virginia Joan Bennett in 1958. The couple had three children, Kara A., Edward M., Jr., and Patrick J. They were divorced in 1983.

In 1960 Kennedy became an assistant district attorney in Suffolk County, Massachusetts. He soon turned his eye toward politics. After his brother John was elected president in 1960 and had to resign from the U.S. Senate, Kennedy filed in the 1962 election to fill out John's term. His announcement led opponents to criticize him for trading on the Kennedy name. He was only thirty years old, the minimum age for a U.S. senator set by the U.S. Constitution, and

BIOGRAPHY

Edward Moore Kennedy

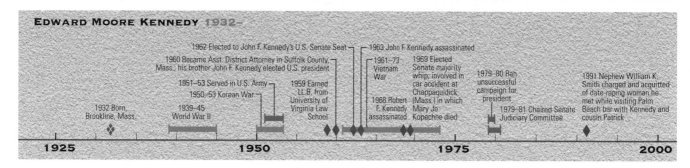

EDWARD MOORE KENNEDY 1932–

1962 Elected to John F. Kennedy's U.S. Senate Seat
1963 John F. Kennedy assassinated
1960 Became Asst. District Attorney in Suffolk County, Mass.; his brother John F. Kennedy elected U.S. president
1961–73 Vietnam War
1969 Elected Senate majority whip; involved in car accident at Chappaquidick (Mass.) in which Mary Jo Kopechne died
1979–80 Ran unsuccessful campaign for president
1991 Nephew William K. Smith charged and acquitted of date-raping woman he met while visiting Palm Beach bar with Kennedy and cousin Patrick
1951–53 Served in U.S. Army
1950–53 Korean War
1959 Earned LL.B. from University of Virginia Law School
1968 Robert F. Kennedy assassinated
1979–81 Chaired Senate Judiciary Committee
1932 Born, Brookline, Mass.
1939–45 World War II

1925   1950   1975   2000

had little experience in politics or the workplace. Nevertheless, Kennedy easily won the election. He won a full six-year term in 1964 and has been reelected five times since.

Despite his youth Kennedy soon emerged as a forceful advocate of social welfare legislation and a respected member of the Senate. He was elected Senate majority whip in 1969, which was highly unusual for a person with little seniority. Kennedy appeared ready to make a presidential bid in 1972. But any hopes in that direction were dashed in the summer of 1969, when his personal conduct became a national scandal.

On July 18, 1969, Kennedy attended a party with friends and staff members on Chappaquiddick Island, Massachusetts. That evening Kennedy drove his car off a narrow bridge on the island. Mary Jo Kopechne, a passenger in the car and former member of his brother Robert's staff, drowned. Kennedy's actions following the accident were disturbing. He did not immediately report what had happened, and he remained in seclusion for days. He pleaded guilty to the MISDEMEANOR charge of leaving the scene of an accident. This plea, coupled with the revelation that he, a married man, had been in the company of a young, unmarried woman, devastated Kennedy's image and political standing. He lost his majority whip position in 1971 and refused to become involved in the 1972 presidential race.

During the 1970s Kennedy concentrated his energies on his senatorial duties. He became the leading advocate of a national health care system that was to be made available to every citizen without regard to income. He also argued for tax reform, arms control, and stronger antitrust laws. From 1979 to 1981, he chaired the Senate Judiciary Committee. He initially supported the administration of Democratic president JIMMY CARTER, but soon criticized Carter's economic policies and leadership style.

His dissatisfaction led him to seek the presidential nomination in 1980. Running against an incumbent of his own party, Kennedy drew the support of liberals and won primaries in ten states. Carter nevertheless won the nomination. However, already weakened by Kennedy's criticisms, Carter lost the general election to RONALD REAGAN.

During the administrations of Reagan and his successor, GEORGE BUSH, Kennedy became the leading liberal critic of Republican policies and politics.

Kennedy's personal life continued to attract attention in the 1990s. In March 1991, Kennedy's nephew, William Kennedy Smith, was charged with rape in Palm Beach, Florida. The alleged assault took place at the Kennedy family compound. Palm Beach police asserted that Kennedy had obstructed justice by misleading police early in their investigation. When police arrived to investigate, they were told Kennedy and Smith had already left the area. Later investigation of travel records indicated Kennedy probably was still in the mansion at the time. Although Smith was acquitted of the charge in December 1991, the nationally televised trial again tarnished Kennedy's reputation. In July 1992 Kennedy married Victoria Reggie, a Washington, D.C., lawyer.

Kennedy has not abandoned his liberal beliefs and has remained a powerful member of the U.S. Senate. He serves on the Labor and Resources Committee, the Judiciary Committee, the Armed Services Committee, and the Joint Economic Committee. In 1996 he sponsored legislation with Republican Senator Nancy Kassebaum of Kansas that makes health insurance portable, so that families do not lose their health insurance coverage if they lose or change jobs.

See also HEALTH CARE LAW.

KENNEDY, JOHN FITZGERALD John Fitzgerald Kennedy was the thirty-fifth president of the United States, serving from 1961 until his ASSASSINATION in 1963. Though his administration had few legislative accomplishments, Kennedy energized the United States by projecting idealism, youth, and vigor.

Kennedy was born May 29, 1917, in Brookline, Massachusetts. His father, Joseph P. Kennedy, was a self-made millionaire and the son of a Boston politician. His mother, Rose

"AMERICA WAS AN IDEA SHAPED IN THE TURBULENCE OF REVOLUTION, THEN GIVEN FORMAL STRUCTURE IN A CONSTITUTION."

BIOGRAPHY

LIBRARY OF CONGRESS

John Fitzgerald Kennedy

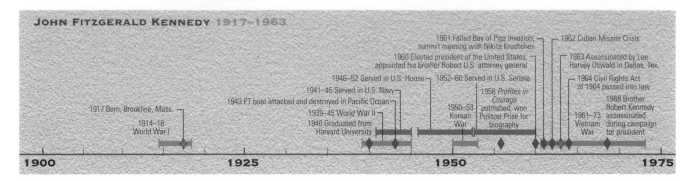

JOHN FITZGERALD KENNEDY 1917–1963

1961 Failed Bay of Pigs invasion; summit meeting with Nikita Krushchev

1962 Cuban Missile Crisis

1960 Elected president of the United States; appointed his brother Robert U.S. attorney general

1963 Assassinated by Lee Harvey Oswald in Dallas, Tex.

1946–52 Served in U.S. House

1952–60 Served in U.S. Senate

1964 Civil Rights Act of 1964 passed into law

1941–45 Served in U.S. Navy

1943 PT boat attacked and destroyed in Pacific Ocean

1956 Profiles in Courage published; won Pulitzer Prize for biography

1968 Brother Robert Kennedy assassinated during campaign for president

1917 Born, Brookline, Mass.

1939–45 World War II

1950–53 Korean War

1961–73 Vietnam War

1914–18 World War I

1940 Graduated from Harvard University

1900   1925   1950   1975

Fitzgerald Kennedy, was the daughter of John F. ("Honey Fitz") Fitzgerald, who served as a Representative and a mayor of Boston. Kennedy, one of nine children, graduated from Harvard University in 1940. His senior thesis, "Why England Slept," which dealt with the reasons Great Britain had been unprepared for World War II, was published in 1940 to great acclaim. His father thought that Kennedy would be a writer or teacher, and that Kennedy's older brother, Joseph P. Kennedy, Jr., would go into politics. World War II changed those plans.

Kennedy joined the Navy in 1941 and commanded a PT boat in the Pacific. In 1943 the boat was attacked and destroyed, and Kennedy emerged a hero owing to his valiant efforts to save his crew. Joseph was killed in action in 1944. Kennedy's father then transferred his political goals to Kennedy.

In 1946 Kennedy was elected to the U.S. House of Representatives from the solidly Democratic Eleventh District of Massachusetts. He was reelected in 1948 and 1950.

In 1952 he was elected to the Senate, defeating the incumbent, Republican Henry Cabot Lodge, Jr. Kennedy kept a low profile at first, working on legislation that benefited Massachusetts. Back problems and other physical maladies bedeviled Kennedy during this period. He underwent two operations on his back to alleviate chronic pain. During his convalescence he wrote *Profiles in Courage* (1956), a series of essays on courageous stands taken by U.S. senators throughout U.S. history. It won the 1957 Pulitzer Prize for biography.

In 1956 Kennedy sought the Democratic vice presidential nomination. He made the presidential nominating speech for ADLAI STEVENSON, of Illinois, who was nominated for a second time to run against DWIGHT D. EISENHOWER. Despite a vigorous effort, Kennedy lost the vice presidential nomination to Senator Estes Kefauver, of Tennessee.

In 1957 Kennedy was appointed to the Senate Foreign Relations Committee, where he

"THE RIGHTS OF EVERY MAN ARE DIMINISHED WHEN THE RIGHTS OF ONE MAN ARE THREATENED."

became a critic of the Eisenhower administration's foreign policy and a champion for increased aid to underdeveloped countries. He also served on the committee that investigated corruption and racketeering in LABOR UNIONS and the head of the Teamsters Union, JAMES R. HOFFA.

In 1960 Kennedy won the Democratic presidential nomination. He selected Senator LYNDON B. JOHNSON, of Texas, as his running mate. After a vigorous campaign that included television debates with Republican RICHARD M. NIXON, Kennedy won the election by fewer than 120,000 popular votes. He was the youngest person ever elected president, and the first Roman Catholic. His impressive inaugural speech contained the popular phrase "Ask not what your country can do for you—ask what you can do for your country."

Once in office Kennedy drafted a series of ambitious measures that were collectively entitled the New Frontier. These policies included expanding the space program, instituting CIVIL RIGHTS legislation, aiding education, improving the tax system, and providing medical care for older citizens through the SOCIAL SECURITY program. Most of the New Frontier programs failed to make it through a Congress dominated by southern Democratic leadership, but many were enacted by President Johnson following Kennedy's assassination.

The Kennedy administration was enmeshed in a series of foreign crises almost immediately. In April 1961 Kennedy was severely criticized for approving an ill-fated invasion of the Bay of Pigs, in Cuba. This clandestine operation, conceived during the Eisenhower administration, was conducted by anti-Communist Cuban exiles trained in the United States and was directed by the Central Intelligence Agency. The invasion achieved public notoriety when it failed and created international tension.

In June 1961 Kennedy and Premier Nikita Khrushchev, of the Soviet Union, met in Vienna to discuss ways of improving Soviet-U.S. relations. Instead of proceeding with those discussions, Khrushchev announced an increased alliance with East Germany. Later the Berlin Wall was constructed to prohibit Western influence and to prevent persons from fleeing East Germany. In response, the United States added to its military forces in Germany.

The most serious crisis occurred in October 1962, when it was learned that Soviet missiles were about to be placed in Cuba. Kennedy issued a forceful statement demanding the dismantling of the missile sites and ordered a BLOCKADE to prevent the delivery of the missiles to Cuba. The world was poised for nuclear war until Khrushchev backed down and agreed to Kennedy's demands. Kennedy's handling of the crisis led to national acclaim.

U.S. involvement in Southeast Asia began to increase during the Kennedy administration. Kennedy agreed to send U.S. advisers to help the South Vietnamese government fight Communist rebels. In 1963 the United States became involved in overthrowing the corrupt and unscrupulous South Vietnamese government of President Ngo Dinh Diem.

On the domestic front, Kennedy dealt with a newly invigorated CIVIL RIGHTS MOVEMENT that was seeking to integrate the South. In 1961 federal marshals were sent to Montgomery, Alabama, to help restore order after race riots erupted. In 1962 Kennedy sent three thousand federal troops into Oxford, Mississippi, to restore order after whites rioted against the University of Mississippi's admission of JAMES MEREDITH, its first African American student. In 1963 Kennedy was forced to federalize the Alabama National Guard in order to integrate the University of Alabama. Later that year he federalized the guard again in order to integrate the public schools in three Alabama cities.

Faced with these problems, Kennedy proposed legislation requiring that hotels, motels, and restaurants admit customers regardless of race. He also asked that the U.S. attorney general be given authority to file court suits demanding the desegregation of public schools. Most of these proposals were passed in the

CIVIL RIGHTS ACT of 1964 (42 U.S.C.A. § 2000a et seq.).

Kennedy's achievements during his brief term as chief executive included an agreement with the Soviet Union to restrict nuclear testing to underground facilities; the creation of the Alliance for Progress to establish economic programs to aid Latin America; and the creation of the Peace Corps program, which provides U.S. volunteers to work in underdeveloped countries.

On November 22, 1963, Kennedy's term was ended by an assassin's bullets in Dallas, and Johnson was sworn in as president. Lee Harvey Oswald was charged with the murder. Oswald was killed two days later by Dallas nightclub owner Jack Ruby, while being moved from the city jail to the county jail. Johnson appointed a commission headed by Chief Justice EARL WARREN to investigate the Kennedy assassination. In its report, issued in September 1964, the commission concluded that Oswald acted alone in murdering Kennedy.

See also CUBAN MISSILE CRISIS; LIMITED TEST BAN TREATY; WARREN COMMISSION.

KENNEDY, ROBERT FRANCIS For more than twenty-five years in public service, Robert Francis Kennedy was at the center of the most important political and legal developments of his time. The younger brother, by five years, of President JOHN F. KENNEDY, in whose cabinet he served, Bobby Kennedy held a number of roles in government: assistant counsel (1953–55) and chief counsel (1955–57) to the Senate Permanent Subcommittee on Investigations, chief counsel of the Senate Rackets Committee (1957–59), U.S. attorney general (1960–63), and finally U.S. senator from New York (1965–68). His major endeavors included probing union corruption in the 1950s and implementing White House policy on the CIVIL RIGHTS MOVEMENT in the early 1960s. He was assassinated in 1968, like his brother before him, while campaigning for the presidency.

Born into one of the United States' most powerful political dynasties, on November 20,

BIOGRAPHY

GAMMA LIAISON

Robert Francis Kennedy

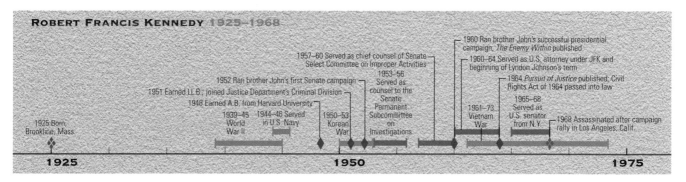

ROBERT FRANCIS KENNEDY 1925–1968

1925 Born, Brookline, Mass.

1939–45 World War II

1944–46 Served in U.S. Navy

1948 Earned A.B. from Harvard University

1950–53 Korean War

1951 Earned LL.B.; joined Justice Department's Criminal Division

1952 Ran brother John's first Senate campaign

1953–56 Served as counsel to the Senate Permanent Subcommittee on Investigations

1957–60 Served as chief counsel of Senate Select Committee on Improper Activities

1960 Ran brother John's successful presidential campaign; *The Enemy Within* published

1960–64 Served as U.S. attorney under JFK and beginning of Lyndon Johnson's term

1961–73 Vietnam War

1964 *Pursuit of Justice* published; Civil Rights Act of 1964 passed into law

1965–68 Served as U.S. senator from N.Y.

1968 Assassinated after campaign rally in Los Angeles, Calif.

1925   1950   1975

1925, in Brookline, Massachusetts, Kennedy was the third son of Joseph P. Kennedy and Rose Fitzgerald Kennedy. Great things were expected of the Kennedy sons, and the means were provided: $1-million trust funds, entrance to the Ivy League, and later, leverage to see that they held government positions. Kennedy's father, a business magnate and former U.S. ambassador to Great Britain, doted on the shy, bookish, and devoutly Catholic young man. His father thought Kennedy was most like himself: tough.

Kennedy was educated at Harvard College, interrupting his studies to serve in World War II as a Navy lieutenant, following the death of his eldest brother, Joseph Patrick Kennedy, Jr., in the war. He served aboard the destroyer *Joseph P. Kennedy* until being discharged in 1946, then returned to Harvard, where he played football and earned his bachelor of arts degree in 1948. He next traveled briefly to Palestine as a war correspondent. Marriage to Ethel Skakel followed in 1950, and a law degree from the University of Virginia in 1951. Kennedy and his wife had eleven children over the next eighteen years.

Kennedy's rapid ascent in national politics began immediately upon his admission to the Massachusetts bar in 1951. He first joined the Criminal Division of the U.S. Justice Department as a prosecutor. The next year, he managed his brother John's senatorial campaign, and in early 1953, he was appointed an assistant counsel to the Senate Permanent Subcommittee on Investigations, which became the bully pulpit for the anti-Communist witch-hunts of its chairman, Senator JOSEPH R. MCCARTHY. Kennedy worked under McCarthy's foremost ally, Chief Counsel Roy Cohn, and investigated international shipping to Communist China, before resigning over disgust with McCarthy in mid-1953. Historians view his role in the Red scare created by the proceedings to have been very limited, although some have argued that Kennedy was initially blind to Senator McCarthy's agenda. Kennedy rejoined the subcommittee in 1954, and became its chief counsel and staff director in 1955.

Under the new leadership of Senator JOHN MCCLELLAN, the subcommittee turned its attention to labor racketeering. Kennedy focused on corruption in the International Brotherhood of Teamsters. Heading a staff of sixty-five investigators, he squared off against the union's presidents, David Beck and JAMES R. HOFFA, in dramatic public hearings at which he often was accompanied by his brother John. Kennedy and the subcommittee believed the union had connections to organized crime; the union viewed

Kennedy as a show-off who was persecuting it for his own political benefit. The union leaders frequently took the FIFTH AMENDMENT, refusing to answer questions under Kennedy's relentless grilling. Beck resigned and was later convicted; Kennedy became a national figure. The hearings began a long-running feud between Kennedy and Hoffa that would continue into the 1960s. Kennedy later devoted considerable resources of the Justice Department to prosecuting Hoffa, ultimately convicted in 1964 for jury tampering, fraud, and conspiracy in the handling of a Teamster benefit fund.

In 1960, Kennedy managed his brother John's presidential campaign. His reward was the position of attorney general, an appointment that brought widespread criticism of the president-elect for nepotism. But Kennedy's brother stood behind his decision, and thus began a relationship unique in presidential history: throughout foreign policy crises in Cuba and Vietnam, domestic unrest over CIVIL RIGHTS, and especially the day-to-day functioning of the White House, Kennedy served as his brother's closest adviser. The two also shared a common problem in the person of Director J. EDGAR HOOVER, of the Federal Bureau of Investigation (FBI), who secretly kept tabs on them while intensifying the FBI's domestic spying during the Kennedy administration.

The greatest crisis facing Attorney General Kennedy was the civil rights movement. The slow pace of change had frustrated civil rights leaders and mounting violence—from beatings to murder—brought pleas to the White House for intercession to protect demonstrators. During the Freedom Rides of 1961, for example, when busloads of black activists sought to integrate bus stations in the South, the movement's leaders appealed for help. Kennedy dispatched Justice Department representatives to Alabama; asked for assurances of protection from Governor John Patterson, of that state; and brought suit to win a court order on behalf of the riders. The administration was reluctant to do more because of concerns about limitations on federal power. Then, in May 1961, after more terrible assaults on the activists in Montgomery, Alabama, the attorney general dispatched five hundred federal marshals to Alabama. Yet the protection rendered did not stop local authorities from arresting, jailing, and beating activists.

The reluctance of the White House to intercede more forcefully had a political rationale as well: the new Kennedy administration had won election by a small margin that included southern support. As critics have noted, concerns about federal authority did not stop the attorney general from later authorizing Director

"SOME MEN SEE THINGS THAT ARE, AND ASK 'WHY?' I SEE THINGS THAT NEVER WERE, AND ASK 'WHY NOT?' "

Hoover to place wiretaps on the Reverend MARTIN LUTHER KING, JR., whom the pro–civil rights White House treated as an ally. Hoover's concerns about King's alleged Communist ties affected the Kennedys. As Kennedy later told an interviewer, "We never wanted to get very close to him just because of these contacts and connections that he had, which we felt were damaging to the civil rights movement." Nor did Kennedy balk at approving the appointment of William Harold Cox, an outspoken racist, as a district judge in Mississippi, for reasons of political expediency, although he later regretted having done so. In time, Kennedy and the president took bolder steps—in 1962, sending five thousand federal marshals to quell rioting in Mississippi, after JAMES H. MEREDITH became the first black man to enter the state's university, and later, securing King's release from jail in Birmingham, Alabama.

The ASSASSINATION of his brother John in 1963 changed the course of Kennedy's life. Besides grieving the loss of his brother, he found he worked uncomfortably under President LYNDON B. JOHNSON, and he soon left the Justice Department. In 1964, he won election in New York to the U.S. Senate, where he served as a liberal voice until announcing his own bid for the presidency in 1968.

Emphasizing a commitment to the concerns of young people, black citizens, and the nation's poor, the Kennedy campaign inspired radicals, the working class, and the dispossessed. Kennedy's opposition to the war in Vietnam was passionate. On a television broadcast, he said,

> Do we have a right here in the United States to say that we're going to kill tens of thousands, make millions of people, as we have . . . refugees, kill women and children? . . . I very seriously question that right. . . . We love our country for what it can be and for the justice it stands for.

Kennedy's candidacy sharply divided the Democratic party between him and his opponent for the nomination, EUGENE MCCARTHY. Kennedy had won primaries in Indiana, Ne-

braska, and finally California, when he was shot at a campaign function on June 4, 1968, by Sirhan Sirhan, a Palestinian immigrant who said his motive was the candidate's support for Israel. The second murder of a Kennedy, following hard on the April 1968 assassination of King, was an immeasurable shock to the nation. It seemed to many to sound the death knell of an era.

Kennedy's contribution to U.S. law is complex. In the 1950s, he helped expose corruption in the nation's unions, but critics have subsequently treated his very personal pursuit of Hoffa as an exercise not only in justice but in vendetta. When he headed the Justice Department in the early 1960s, his advocacy of civil rights had practical limitations imposed by political necessities and legitimate concerns about the balance of state and federal authority; groundbreaking civil rights legislation would, of course, follow in the years after his tenure. It was as a candidate for president that he may have been his most memorable, an ardent and inspirational voice. Through his opposition to the VIETNAM WAR and his support for the disadvantaged, he offered the promise of a new idealism in politics.

BIOGRAPHY

CULVER PICTURES

James Kent

KENT, JAMES James Kent was a U.S. attorney, judge, and scholar who played a central role in adapting the COMMON LAW of England into the common law of the United States. As a justice and later chief justice of the New York Supreme Court and a chancellor of the New York Court of Chancery (then the highest judicial officer in New York), Kent wrote many decisions that became foundations of nineteenth-century law. Kent's great legal treatise *Commentaries on American Law* (1826–30) offered the first comprehensive analysis of U.S. law.

Kent was born July 31, 1763, in Putnam County, New York. In 1777 he entered Yale University. The Revolutionary War periodically disrupted his studies. During one of his forced suspensions, Kent read SIR WILLIAM BLACKSTONE's *Commentaries on the Laws of England* (1765–69), which led him to decide on a legal career. Following college he secured a clerkship

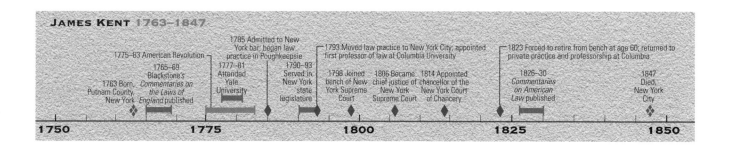

JAMES KENT 1763–1847

1775–83 American Revolution

1765–69 Blackstone's *Commentaries on the Laws of England* published

1763 Born, Putnam County, New York

1777–81 Attended Yale University

1785 Admitted to New York bar; began law practice in Poughkeepsie

1790–93 Served in New York state legislature

1793 Moved law practice to New York City; appointed first professor of law at Columbia University

1798 Joined bench of New York Supreme Court

1806 Became chief justice of New York Supreme Court

1814 Appointed chancellor of the New York Court of Chancery

1823 Forced to retire from bench at age 60; returned to private practice and professorship at Columbia

1826–30 *Commentaries on American Law* published

1847 Died, New York City

1750   1775   1800   1825   1850

with the attorney general of New York, and he was admitted to the New York bar in 1785.

Kent began his law practice in Poughkeepsie, New York. In 1790 he was elected to the New York state legislature, where he served three terms. A steadfast Federalist and supporter of the U.S. Constitution, Kent was committed to a strong national government. After losing a congressional race in 1793, he moved to New York City, where he practiced law and served as a professor of law at Columbia University.

Kent became a member of the New York Supreme Court in 1798, and served as chief justice from 1806 to 1814. He is credited with transforming the court into a professional, respected bench. He introduced the practice of issuing written as well as oral opinions, and was instrumental in appointing an official REPORTER to collect the written opinions into official LAW REPORTS. Kent believed that such reports were necessary so that past PRECEDENTS could be read and cited more easily.

During his time on the court, Kent addressed the then burning issue of whether English precedents could claim the authority of law in the United States. Some members of the New York bar felt that the American Revolution would be unfinished until the United States had a body of law of its own, untainted by the laws of its former imperial master.

Kent disagreed. He argued that the predictability of justice was an indispensable requirement for achieving the commercial progress and stable social order sought by the Federalists. He further suggested that CITATION and the following of precedent were the best means to judicial predictability. Like many Federalists he admired the stability of the English common law and he maintained that it was the best system ever devised to ensure justice and order. Although he did not follow precedent blindly, Kent believed that previous decisions should not be expressly overturned except when absolutely necessary.

Kent was appointed chancellor of the New York Court of Chancery in 1814. This court was a court of EQUITY, which applied rules of fairness, rather than a court of LAW, which applied common and statutory law to the resolution of disputes. Most of the matters before it involved commercial disputes. As chancellor Kent was empowered to do justice based on the particular facts of each case and the equitable principles that had developed in England. He used his equity powers to effect his sense that commercial bargains ought to be subject to some equitable scrutiny to ensure that UNCONSCIONABLE advantage was not taken.

By law Kent was forced to retire from the bench at age sixty, in 1823. He returned to the private practice of law and was reappointed to a professorship at Columbia. He was consulted by lawyers and judges about legal issues, and gave a series of lectures at Columbia that became, in revised form, the core of his *Commentaries*. This treatise, which was published in four volumes, was similar to Blackstone's *Commentaries* in scope but did not follow Blackstone's precisely in form. Kent's *Commentaries* covered INTERNATIONAL LAW, the Constitution and government of the United States, the municipal laws of the states, personal rights, and real and PERSONAL PROPERTY. It quickly became an authoritative and classic example of the U.S. treatise tradition. Five editions were published in Kent's lifetime, and many more followed in the nineteenth century. The twelfth edition (1873) was edited by OLIVER WENDELL HOLMES, JR.

Kent died December 12, 1847, in New York City.

See also BLACKSTONE'S COMMENTARIES.

KENTUCKY RESOLUTIONS 📖 A set of proposals formulated by THOMAS JEFFERSON and approved by the state legislature of Kentucky during 1798 and 1799 in opposition to the enactment of the Alien and Sedition Acts (1 Stat. 566, 570, 577, 596) by Congress. 📖

The Kentucky Resolutions attacked the validity of the Alien and Sedition Acts, the enactment of which were a reaction to the turbulent political climate of France during the late 1700s following the French Revolution. The acts imposed strict residency requirements in order to attain U.S. citizenship, empowered the president to deport or incarcerate ALIENS who were considered "dangerous," and permitted the criminal prosecution of persons who made critical or seditious speeches or writings against the government. The resolutions advocated a strict constructionist view of the federal government which treated the Constitution as an agreement reached among the states as to the particular powers to be exercised by the central government. The federal government could not act in any way unless specifically authorized to do so in the Constitution. The enactment of the Alien and Sedition Acts was considered to be beyond the powers of Congress and, therefore, the acts were void. The resolutions represented the exercise of the right of the state of Kentucky to declare the acts void through nullification (the declaration that such laws were not legally enforceable).

A comparable series of proposals, the Virginia Resolutions, drawn by JAMES MADISON, and approved by the Virginia legislature in 1798, treated the Alien and Sedition Acts in a similar fashion.

"THE DIGNITY OR INDEPENDENCE OF OUR COURTS IS NO MORE AFFECTED BY ADOPTING [ENGLISH JUDICIAL PRECEDENTS], THAN IN ADOPTING THE ENGLISH LANGUAGE."

Both the Kentucky and Virginia Resolutions did not meet with any real success when presented to other states for adoption. They were, however, significant in American legal history because they embodied the clash between two competing principles of government—STATES' RIGHTS versus FEDERALISM.

KEOGH PLAN A retirement account that allows workers who are self-employed to set aside a percentage of their net earnings for retirement income.

Also known as H.R. 10 plans, Keogh plans provide workers who are self-employed with savings opportunities that are similar to those under company PENSION plans or INDIVIDUAL RETIREMENT ACCOUNTS (IRAs). However, Keogh plans allow for a much higher level of contribution, depending on the type of plan selected.

Keogh plans were established in 1962 by the Self-Employed Individuals Tax Retirement Act (26 U.S.C.A. § 1 et seq.) and modified by provisions in the EMPLOYEE RETIREMENT INCOME SECURITY ACT of 1974 (29 U.S.C.A. § 1 et seq.), the Economic Recovery Tax Act of 1981 (26 U.S.C.A. § 1 et seq.), and the Tax Equity and Fiscal Responsibility Act of 1982 (26 U.S.C.A. § 1 et seq.). Keogh plans are considered tax shelters because Keogh contributions, which are deductible from a taxpayer's GROSS INCOME, and the earnings they generate are considered tax free until they are withdrawn when the contributor retires or dies. At the time of withdrawal, the money is taxable as ordinary income.

Self-employed individuals are defined as people who pay their own SOCIAL SECURITY taxes on their net income. This net income cannot include any investment earnings, wages, or salary. The self-employment does not have to be full-time; in fact, workers who are self-employed on the side can have a separate IRA or other retirement account in the pension plan of the company that pays their wages or salary.

Self-employed taxpayers who own a business and set up a Keogh plan for themselves are also required to set up a Keogh plan for each employee who has worked for their company for at least one thousand hours over a period of three or more years. The level of contributions allowed depends on the type of Keogh plan chosen.

Four different types of Keogh plans are available: profit sharing, money-purchase pension, paired, and defined benefit. Profit sharing plans are most often set up by small businesses because they require a minimal contribution by employees. The maximum amount that may be contributed to this type of plan is 13.04 percent of an employee's net income, up to a total of $22,500 a year.

Money-purchase pension plans are often used by high-income earners because the percentage contribution is fixed on an annual basis; the amount can be changed only once a year or through termination of the plan. This plan's contribution limit is 20 percent of net income, up to a total of $30,000 a year.

Paired plans merge the benefit of the high contributions allowed by money-purchase pension plans with the flexibility of profit sharing plans. For example, an employee may make a money-purchase plan contribution of 7 percent and then contribute between 0 and 13 percent of her or his remaining net income to a profit sharing plan. With this plan, an employee can make the maximum 20 percent contribution the money purchase plan allows but still be able to change the contribution amount throughout the year.

Defined-benefit plans require a minimum contribution of $30,000 a year, so are not available to everyone who is self-employed. Generally, contributors to these plans will employ an actuary to determine the amount of money to be contributed.

Payments to Keogh plans in 1992

Number of Returns Filed, by Adjusted Gross Income Level (in thousands)

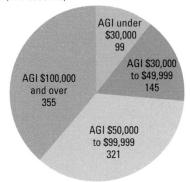

AGI under $30,000 99

AGI $30,000 to $49,999 145

AGI $100,000 and over 355

AGI $50,000 to $99,999 321

Amount Paid into Accounts, by Adjusted Gross Income Level (in millions of dollars)

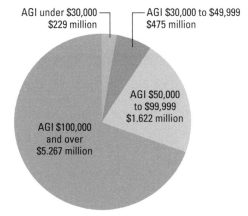

AGI under $30,000 $229 million

AGI $30,000 to $49,999 $475 million

AGI $50,000 to $99,999 $1.622 million

AGI $100,000 and over $5.267 million

Source: U.S. Internal Revenue Service, *Statistics of Income, Individual Income Tax Returns,* annual.

Contributors to all Keogh plans are eligible to begin receiving benefits when they are age 59½. At this point the payments are taxed as income. If any portion of the money in a Keogh plan is withdrawn early (before age 59½), a 10 percent penalty tax is imposed, in addition to the normal INCOME TAX. A 15 percent penalty tax is imposed if the contributor does not start receiving benefits before age 70½.

Money can be collected from a Keogh plan in several different ways. The two most common ways are lump sums and installments. Lump-sum payments are subject to regular income taxes. However, with a tax break called forward averaging, just one tax is paid. This tax is determined by calculating the total amount that would have been paid if the money had been collected in installments. This advantage reduces the amount of total income tax paid on the plan.

Installment distributions can be set up in several different ways and for various lengths. For example, they can be paid annually for ten years or annually for the number of years the recipient is expected to live. Each distribution is taxed as ordinary income.

In the event that the contributor dies before reaching age 59½, the contributor's heirs will receive the money that is in the Keogh plan, minus income taxes. In this case no penalty taxes are imposed for early withdrawal.

As a general rule of thumb, Keogh plan accounts are JUDGMENT PROOF. Their funds can be seized or garnished only in certain situations. For instance, the government can take Keogh funds to pay personal back taxes owed, and a spouse, ex-spouse, or children may be declared entitled to receive a portion of Keogh money by a court order if the contributor owes ALIMONY or CHILD SUPPORT.

KEVORKIAN, JACK Jack Kevorkian has become the most well-known advocate in the United States for the cause of physician-assisted SUICIDE. Having helped over thirty terminally or chronically ill individuals kill themselves since 1990, Kevorkian has sparked a national debate on the ethical issues involved in euthanasia,

often called mercy killing. Though Kevorkian has argued that his actions have prevented needless suffering for patients in pain and allowed them to die with dignity, others see his work as a violation of the medical profession's most cherished ethical principles affirming life over death. Working in an area of vexing ethical issues, Kevorkian has championed himself as a breaker of unnecessary taboos surrounding death.

Kevorkian became a focus of national attention in 1990 after he assisted the suicide of Janet Adkins, a fifty-four-year-old woman suffering from Alzheimer's disease, a degenerative disease of the brain that causes loss of memory and intellectual impairment. Adkins had heard through the media about Kevorkian's invention of a suicide machine that allowed individuals who were ill to administer a lethal dose of poison to themselves. The machine, which Kevorkian assembled out of $45 worth of materials, consisted of three dripping bottles that delivered successive doses of three fluids: a harmless saline solution; a painkiller; and, finally, a poison, potassium chloride. When Adkins contacted Kevorkian about using the machine on her, Kevorkian agreed. Kevorkian diagnosed Adkins as suffering from Alzheimer's and arranged to perform the assisted suicide in a public park, in his rusting 1968 Volkswagen van. After Kevorkian had inserted an intravenous needle into her arm, Adkins pressed a red button that caused the machine to administer the painkiller and then the poison. Within five minutes, Adkins had died of heart failure. Within days, Kevorkian had become a national media celebrity, appearing on such television shows as *Nightline*, *Geraldo*, and *Good Morning, America*.

This first of his assisted suicides illustrated the problems many observers have with Kevorkian's methods. Though she had begun to show early signs of Alzheimer's, Adkins was in good health and was not terminally ill; she committed suicide more out of fear of future suffering than out of current suffering. She had joined the Hemlock Society—an organization

BIOGRAPHY

Jack Kevorkian

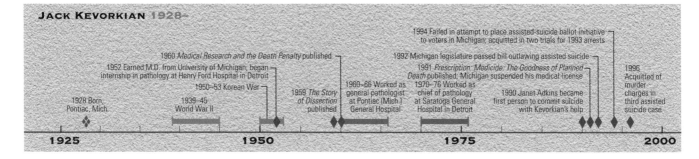

JACK KEVORKIAN 1928–

1928 Born, Pontiac, Mich.

1939–45 World War II

1950–53 Korean War

1952 Earned M.D. from University of Michigan; began internship in pathology at Henry Ford Hospital in Detroit

1959 *The Story of Dissection* published

1960 *Medical Research and the Death Penalty* published

1960–66 Worked as general pathologist at Pontiac (Mich.) General Hospital

1970–76 Worked as chief of pathology at Saratoga General Hospital in Detroit

1990 Janet Adkins became first person to commit suicide with Kevorkian's help

1991 *Prescription: Medicide: The Goodness of Planned Death* published; Michigan suspended his medical license

1992 Michigan legislature passed bill outlawing assisted suicide

1994 Failed in attempt to place assisted-suicide ballot initiative to voters in Michigan; acquitted in two trials for 1993 arrests

1996 Acquitted of murder charges in third assisted suicide case

1925   1950   1975   2000

that advocates voluntary euthanasia for terminally ill patients—before she even became ill. In addition, Adkins's Alzheimer's may have impaired her ability to make decisions. Some observers wondered if she was also suffering from depression, a treatable mental illness. Moreover, in cases in which a terminally ill patient has expressed a desire to die, established rules of medical ethics require that two independent doctors must confirm that the patient's condition is unbearable and irreversible; Kevorkian had ignored this requirement.

Kevorkian was charged with first-degree MURDER in this case, but a district judge ruled that prosecutors failed to show that Kevorkian had planned and carried out Adkins's death. Attempts to prosecute Kevorkian were hampered by Michigan's lack of any law against physician-assisted suicide. Most other states have laws making this act a FELONY.

In early 1991, a Michigan judge issued an INJUNCTION barring Kevorkian's use of the suicide machine, and in the same year, the state of Michigan suspended his medical LICENSE. Kevorkian defied such legal actions and continued to help ailing people end their life. Now that he could no longer prescribe drugs, Kevorkian assisted suicides with a contraption that administered carbon monoxide through a gas mask. As he practiced assisted suicide and published on the subject—describing it in his own terms as "medicide" or "planned death"— he continued to be surrounded by controversy. For example, an autopsy performed on the body of the second person he helped to commit suicide, a patient who had complained of a painful pelvic disease, found no evidence of any disease.

In 1992, the Michigan Legislature passed a bill outlawing assisted suicide, designed specifically to stop Kevorkian's activities (Mich. Comp. Laws § 752.1021). This law was used to charge Kevorkian for assisting in the death of Thomas W. Hyde, Jr., in August 1993. Kevorkian was jailed twice that year, in November and December. During his second jail stay, he went on an eighteen-day fast in which he protested his arrest by drinking only juice. His BAIL was reduced and was paid by Geoffrey Fieger, a flamboyant lawyer who has done a great deal for Kevorkian's cause as his friend and legal counsel. Kevorkian was found not guilty.

Kevorkian then attempted to place before Michigan voters a ballot INITIATIVE, Movement Ensuring the Right to Choose for Yourself (Mercy), which sought to amend the Michigan Constitution to guarantee competent adults the right to request and receive medical assistance in taking their own life. However, he failed to garner enough signatures to put the initiative on the 1994 ballot. In December 1994, the Michigan Supreme Court upheld the law making assisted suicide a crime, and the following year, the U.S. Supreme Court refused to hear Kevorkian's appeal.

Kevorkian continued to assist suicides even as prosecutors in his home county unsuccessfully attempted to convict him on charges of murder or assisted suicide. On May 14, 1996, an Oakland County Circuit Court jury again acquitted Kevorkian of assisted suicide. In this case, the prosecution had argued that assisted suicide was a crime under Michigan common law. After their loss, county prosecutors admitted it was unlikely that they would take Kevorkian to trial again.

In both his actions and his statements, Kevorkian has flouted the ethical standards of the medical profession on the issue of assisted suicide. The American Medical Association, the professional association of physicians, specifically forbids the practice of physician-assisted suicide. Many doctors deplore Kevorkian's techniques and see them as endangering the trust that must exist between physician and patient. Even the Hemlock Society opposes Kevorkian's actions, citing his lack of typical procedural precautions.

Kevorkian's efforts in the cause of assisted suicide are only the latest in a series of his unconventional, even morbid, attempts to make a name for himself in the area of medical research. Kevorkian earned the nickname Dr. Death in 1956, only three years after obtaining his medical degree, when he began making what he called death rounds at the Detroit-area hospital where he was employed. During these rounds, he examined dead bodies in order to collect evidence supporting his contention that the time of a person's death could be determined from the condition of the person's eyes. Kevorkian caused more controversy—and lost his job at the University of Michigan—in 1960 when he published the book *Medical Research and the Death Penalty*, in which he argued for the vivisection (the conduct of medical experiments on live subjects) of prisoners sentenced to death. Claiming it would be "a unique privilege . . . to be able to experiment on a doomed human being," he outlined a plan in which the prisoner-subject would be anesthetized at the time of execution, then used for scientific experiments lasting hours or months, and finally executed using a lethal overdose. According to Kevorkian, this would create both a more pain-

"THE VOLUNTARY SELF-ELIMINATION OF INDIVIDUAL AND MORTALLY DISEASED OR CRIPPLED LIVES TAKEN COLLECTIVELY CAN ONLY *ENHANCE* THE PRESERVATION OF PUBLIC HEALTH AND WELFARE."

less execution and greater advances in medical research. The use of condemned prisoners for medical experimentation and organ donation has remained a consistent theme for Kevorkian. His 1991 book *Prescription: Medicide: The Goodness of Planned Death* rehashes these same arguments while also making a case for assisted suicide. In another unsuccessful venture, Kevorkian re-created experiments conducted by Soviet scientists by taking blood from recently deceased individuals and transfusing it to live patients.

In a later article setting forth his plans for assisted suicide, Kevorkian suggested setting up suicide clinics: "The acceptance of planned death implies the establishment of well-staffed and well-organized medical clinics ('obitoria') where terminally ill patients can opt for death under controlled circumstances of compassion and decorum." As his use of *obitoria* and *medicide* indicate, Kevorkian has a penchant for coining words. He dubbed his first suicide machine alternately a mercitron or a thanatron—the latter from the Greek word for death, *thanatos*—and has used the word *obitiatry* to indicate the medical specialization in death.

Kevorkian was born May 26, 1928, in Pontiac, Michigan. Named Murad Kevorkian at birth by his Armenian immigrant parents, he was the first of his family to attend college. He attended the University of Michigan Medical School and did his internship at Detroit-area hospitals. Acquaintances of Kevorkian testify to his prodigious intellect. The retired physician has demonstrated talent as a writer, painter, and composer. A series of eighteen paintings he did on such grisly topics as genocide, hanging, and cannibalism created a stir in Michigan during the 1960s. Kevorkian has also commented that his unconventional ideas have been influenced by the history of his Armenian ancestors, particularly a GENOCIDE in which 1.5 million Armenians were killed in World War I by the Turks. Kevorkian has never married.

Though many deplore Kevorkian's actions, he has increased public awareness of some of the most difficult ethical issues surrounding DEATH AND DYING. With medical technology's increasing ability to prolong life have come more situations in which the extended life is one of great pain and suffering. Kevorkian's efforts to assist people in their death, though often falling short of accepted professional standards of diagnosis and care, have sparked a needed discussion on these issues.

KEY NUMBERS® The designation devised by West Publishing Company and given to a classification of legal subjects that are organized within their publications according to specific topics and subtopics, with one or more digits preceded by the symbol of a key assigned to each individual classification.

A particular point of law can be traced through different law books by following the cases listed under a Key Number in each series. West Publishing Company developed the Key Number System of Classification during the decade spanning 1897–1906. The system is a valuable research tool because once the topic and Key Number have been located, a researcher has ready access to all American cases that have litigated that issue provided those cases have been reported. There are over 400 Key Numbers arranged by subject matter under seven main headings—persons, property, contracts, torts, crimes, remedies, and government—and thirty-two subdivisions of the system.

KICKBACK The seller's return of part of the purchase price of an item to a buyer or buyer's representative for the purpose of inducing a purchase or improperly influencing future purchases.

Under federal law kickbacks involving government officials or funds provided by the government are illegal. Kickbacks between a contractor and a government official or government employee are prosecuted under the federal BRIBERY statute, 18 U.S.C.A. § 201. Kickbacks between private contractors working under a federal contract are prosecuted under 41 U.S.C.A. §§ 51–58, otherwise known as the Anti-Kickback Enforcement Act of 1986. Kickbacks to employees or officials of foreign governments are prohibited under the Foreign Corrupt Practices Act of 1977 (15 U.S.C.A. § 78dd-1 et seq.). Most states have commercial bribery statutes prohibiting various forms of kickbacks.

One notable public figure accused of profiting from a kickback scheme was Spiro T. Agnew, vice president of the United States under RICHARD M. NIXON. While governor of Maryland, Agnew oversaw a system in which engineering firms working under state construction contracts paid kickbacks that went 25 percent to the state official who arranged the deal, 25 percent to the official who brought the deal to Agnew, and 50 percent directly to Agnew himself. In another arrangement Agnew demanded a kickback of five cents for every pack of cigarettes sold in vending machines located in Maryland state buildings. These kickbacks were secret, illegal, and not reported on Agnew's INCOME TAX returns. Agnew continued to collect them after he became vice president. He resigned the vice presidency in 1973 as part of a plea bargain that allowed him to avoid going to

jail for income TAX EVASION in connection with those kickbacks.

Though many types of kickbacks are prohibited under federal and state law, kickbacks are not illegal per se. If a kickback does not specifically violate federal or state laws and such kickbacks are made to clients throughout the industry, the kickback may be normal, legal, and even tax deductible. According to section 162(a) of the Internal Revenue Code (26 U.S.C.A. § 162), "all the ordinary and necessary expenses" that an individual or business incurs during the taxable year are deductible, including kickbacks as long as the kickbacks are not illegal and are not made to an official or employee of the federal government or to an official or employee of a foreign government.

On several occasions the courts have ruled on the deductibility of specific legal kickbacks. In most cases the courts have found these kickbacks to be not deductible because they are not ordinary in the sense of usual and customary. In *Bertoloni Trucking Co. v. Commissioner of Internal Revenue*, 736 F.2d 1120, 84-2 U.S.T.C. P 9591 (1984), however, the Court of Appeals for the Sixth Circuit interpreted the term *ordinary* quite differently. Reviewing Supreme Court cases dealing with the interpretation of *ordinary* in section 162(a), the court identified two lines of interpretation: one held that the term meant "usual and customary," the other held that the term was intended to distinguish payments of a capital nature from payments of a recurring nature, which were thus deductible currently. In *Bertolini* the court held that this second line of interpretation was more consistent with legislative intent, and thus ruled that kickbacks made by the Bertolini Trucking Company were tax deductible.

In a very similar case, the same court came to a different conclusion. In *Car-Ron Asphalt Pav-*

Spiro Agnew, vice president under Richard Nixon, was accused of taking kickbacks while he was governor of Maryland and later as vice president. He resigned from office rather than face a conviction for tax evasion for the kickbacks.

ing Co. v. Commissioner of Internal Revenue, 758 F.2d 1132 (6th Cir. 1985), Car-Ron Asphalt Paving Company had paid legal kickbacks to Nicholas Festa, the same contractor to whom Bertolini Trucking had paid kickbacks. As in *Bertolini* the Tax Court had ruled that such payments were not tax deductible because they were not necessary and ordinary. As not in *Bertolini*, the appeals court ruled that the payments Car-Ron had made to Festa were not necessary business expenses, since, throughout its thirteen-year history, the company had obtained nearly all of its contracts without making such payments.

Beginning in the 1970s, the health care industry became the particular focus for government efforts to prevent kickbacks. As health care costs escalated in the late 1980s and 1990s, efforts to prevent FRAUD intensified, resulting in 1995 in the passage of the Medicare Fraud Statute (42 U.S.C.A. §§ 1320a–1327b). This statute prohibits kickback schemes such as those in which hospitals pay physicians in private practice for patient referrals, and drug companies and medical device manufacturers pay physicians to prescribe their products to patients. The Medicare Fraud Statute makes it illegal for anyone to pay or receive "any remuneration (including any kickback, bribe or rebate)" to induce the recipient to purchase, order, or recommend purchasing or ordering any service reimbursable under MEDICARE or MEDICAID. Some experts in the area of health care fraud suggest that the Medicare Fraud Statute should be used as a model for constructing a general antikickback statute that would prevent kickback arrangements in all areas of the health care industry, not just Medicare and Medicaid.

KIDNAPPING ◫ The crime of unlawfully seizing and carrying away a person by force or FRAUD, or seizing and detaining a person against his or her will with an intent to carry that person away at a later time. ◫

The law of kidnapping is difficult to define with precision because it varies from JURISDICTION to jurisdiction. Most state and federal kidnapping statutes define the term *kidnapping* vaguely, and courts fill in the details. The federal kidnapping statute, for example, defines kidnapping in part as an offense wherein a person kidnaps another person (18 U.S.C.A. § 1201).

Generally, kidnapping occurs when a person, without lawful authority, physically asports (moves) another person without that other person's consent, with the intent to use the abduction in connection with some other nefarious objective. Under the Model Penal Code (a set of exemplary criminal rules fashioned by the

American Law Institute), kidnapping occurs when any person is unlawfully and nonconsensually asported and held for certain purposes. These purposes include gaining a ransom or reward; facilitating the commission of a FELONY or a flight after the commission of a felony; terrorizing or inflicting bodily injury on the victim or a third person; and interfering with a governmental or political function (Model Penal Code § 212.1).

Kidnapping laws in the United States derive from the COMMON LAW of kidnapping developed by courts in England. Originally, the crime of kidnapping was defined as the unlawful and nonconsensual transportation of a person from one country to another. In the late nineteenth and early twentieth centuries, states began to redefine kidnapping, most notably eliminating the requirement of interstate transport.

On the federal level, Congress passed the LINDBERGH ACT in 1932 to prohibit interstate kidnapping (48 Stat. 781 [codified at 18 U.S.C.A. § 1201 et seq.]). The Lindbergh Act was named for Charles A. Lindbergh, a celebrated aviator and Air Force colonel whose baby was kidnapped and killed in 1932. The act provides that if a victim is not released within twenty-four hours after being abducted, a court may presume that the victim was transported across state lines. This presumption may be rebutted with evidence to the contrary. Other federal kidnapping statutes prohibit kidnapping in U.S. territories, kidnapping on the high seas and in the air, and kidnapping of government officials (18 U.S.C.A. §§ 1201 et seq., 1751 et seq.).

A person convicted of kidnapping is usually sentenced by the court to prison for a certain number of years. In some states, and on the federal level, the term of imprisonment may be the remainder of the offender's natural life. In jurisdictions that authorize the death penalty, a kidnapper is charged with a capital offense if the kidnapping results in death. Kidnapping is severely punished because it is a dreaded offense. It usually occurs in connection with another criminal offense, or underlying crime. It involves violent deprivation of liberty, and it requires a special criminal boldness. Furthermore, the act of moving a crime victim exposes the victim to risks above and beyond those inherent in the underlying crime.

Most kidnapping statutes recognize different types and levels of kidnapping and assign punishment accordingly. New York, for example, bases its definition of first-degree kidnapping on the purpose and length of the abduction. First-degree kidnapping occurs when a person abducts another person to obtain ransom (N.Y. Penal Code § 135.25 [McKinney 1996]). First-degree kidnapping also occurs when the abduction lasts for more than twelve hours and the abductor intends to injure the victim, accomplish or advance the commission of a felony, terrorize the victim or a third person, or interfere with a governmental or political function. An abduction that results in death is also first-degree kidnapping. A first-degree kidnapping in New York is a class A-1 felony, which requires a sentence of at least twenty years in prison (§ 70.00).

New York also has a statute prohibiting kidnapping in the second degree. A person is guilty of second-degree kidnapping if she or he abducts another person (§ 135.20). This crime lacks the aggravating circumstances in first-degree kidnapping, and it is ranked as a class B felony. A person convicted of a class B felony in New York can be sentenced to one to eight years in prison (§ 70.00).

Two key elements are common to all charges of kidnapping. First, the ASPORTATION or DETENTION must be unlawful. Under various state and federal statutes, not all seizures and asportations constitute kidnapping: police officers may arrest and jail a person suspected of a crime, and parents are allowed to reasonably restrict and control the movement of their children.

Second, some aggravating circumstance must accompany the restraint or asportation. This can be a demand for money, a demand for anything of value, an attempt to affect a function of government, an attempt to inflict injury on the abductee, an attempt to terrorize a third party, or an attempt to commit a felony.

In most states, kidnapping statutes specify that any unlawful detention or physical movement of a child, other than that performed by a parent or guardian, constitutes kidnapping. This means that an abduction of a child need not be accompanied by some other circumstance, such as EXTORTION or physical injury, to qualify for the highest level of kidnapping charge. In the absence of an aggravating circumstance, an unlawful, nonconsensual restraint or movement is usually charged as something less than the highest degree or level of kidnapping.

Many states have enacted special laws for car-jacking, a specialized form of kidnapping. Generally, car-jacking occurs when one person forces a driver out of the driver's seat and steals the vehicle. Car-jacking is a felony whether the aggressor keeps the victim in the car or forces the victim from the car. In California, a car-jacking statute is contained within the penal

code's chapter on kidnapping, and it authorizes a sentence of life imprisonment without the possibility of PAROLE for a person found guilty of car-jacking (Cal. Penal Code § 209.5 [West]).

Kidnapping laws are similar to laws on unlawful or felonious restraint, parental kidnapping, and FALSE IMPRISONMENT. These crimes cover the range of unlawful movement and unlawful restraint cases. Felonious or unlawful restraint, also known as simple kidnapping, is the unlawful restraint of a person that exposes the victim to physical harm or places the victim in SLAVERY. It is a lesser form of kidnapping because it does not require restraint for a specified period or specific purpose (such as to secure money or commit a felony). False imprisonment is a relatively inoffensive, harmless restraint of another person. It is usually a misDEMEANOR, punishable by no more than a year in jail. Parental kidnapping is the abduction of a child by a parent. The law on parental kidnapping varies from jurisdiction to jurisdiction: some jurisdictions define it as a felony, others as a misdemeanor. Many states consider parental

Executive Harvey Weinstein was held in a fourteen-foot pit by kidnappers until his family paid a $3 million ransom the kidnappers demanded.

kidnapping less offensive than classic kidnapping because of the strong bond between parents and children.

The chief judicial concern with the charge of kidnapping is DOUBLE JEOPARDY. Double jeopardy is multiple punishment for the same offense, and it is prohibited by the FIFTH AMENDMENT to the U.S. Constitution. Kidnapping often is an act that facilitates another offense, such as RAPE, ROBBERY, or ASSAULT. Rape, robbery, and assault often involve the act of moving a person against her or his will, which is the GRAVAMEN (significant element) of a kidnapping charge. Thus, a persistent problem with kidnapping prosecutions is determining whether a kidnapping conviction would constitute a second punishment for the same act.

Legislatures have passed statutes and courts have fashioned rules to prevent and detect double jeopardy in kidnapping cases. Generally, these laws and rules hold that for kidnapping to be charged as a separate crime, some factor must set the asportation apart from a companion crime. Most courts will sustain multiple convictions if the asportation exposes the victim to increased risk of harm, or results in harm to the victim separate from that caused by the companion offense. In other jurisdictions, the test is whether the asportation involves a change of environment or is designed to conceal a companion offense.

In most states, an asportation of a few feet may constitute the separate offense of kidnapping; in other states, distance is not a factor. In New York, for example, the focus of the kidnapping statute is not distance but purpose. Thus, an asportation of twenty-seven city blocks may not constitute kidnapping if it is merely incidental to a companion crime (*People v. Levy*, 15 N.Y.2d 159, 256 N.Y.S.2d 793, 204 N.E.2d 842 [Ct. App. 1965]). Likewise, an asportation from the borough of Manhattan to the borough of Queens may not constitute kidnapping if it plays no significant role in the commission of another crime (*People v. Lombardi*, 20 N.Y.2d 266, 282 N.Y.S.2d 519, 229 N.E.2d 206 [Ct. App. 1967]).

Some states have eliminated the asportation element from their kidnapping statutes. In Ohio, for example, kidnapping is defined in part as restraining the liberty of another person (Ohio Rev. Code Ann. § 2905.01 [Baldwin 1996]). This creates an increased risk of double jeopardy in kidnapping convictions because, by definition, every robbery, rape, or assault would constitute kidnapping. However, the Ohio state legislature has enacted a statute that prohibits multiple convictions for the same conduct unless the defendant exhibits a separate ANIMUS (separate intent) to commit a separate crime (§ 2941.25). Whether the prosecution proves a separate animus to kidnap is a QUESTION OF FACT based on the circumstances surrounding the crime.

In *State v. Logan*, 60 Ohio St. 2d 126, 397 N.E.2d 1345, 14 Ohio Op. 3d 373 (1979), the Supreme Court of Ohio held that the defendant could not be convicted of both rape and kidnapping when he had moved the victim a mere few feet and had released the victim immediately after the rape. Under the facts of the case, the asportation had no significance apart from the rape offense. According to the court, the defendant had displayed no animus beyond that necessary to commit rape, so punishment for both rape and kidnapping was not warranted.

In contrast, in *State v. Wagner*, 191 Wis. 2d 322, 528 N.W.2d 85 (Ct. App. 1995), the appeals court upheld a separate conviction for kidnapping. In *Wagner*, the defendant approached two women on two separate occasions in a Laundromat. Both times, the defendant tried to force the women into a bathroom to rape them. He was convicted of two counts of attempted first-degree sexual assault, one count of kidnapping while armed, and one count of attempted kidnapping while armed. On appeal, he argued that he should not have been convicted of kidnapping because, under section 940.31(1)(a) of the Wisconsin Statutes, kidnapping is defined in part as the carrying of a person "from one place to another," and he had not taken his victims to another place. The court disagreed, holding that forced movement from one room to another falls within the meaning of the kidnapping statute. Ultimately, the appeals court affirmed the defendant's sentence of seventy-two years in prison.

See also HEARST, PATTY; LINDBERGH KIDNAPPING.

KILBERG DOCTRINE 📖 A principle applied in lawsuits involving conflicts of law that provides that a court in the place where a WRONGFUL DEATH action is brought is not bound by the law of the place where the conduct causing death occurred concerning limitations on DAMAGES. 📖

The rationale behind the Kilberg doctrine is that laws that set limitations on damages are procedural and, therefore, the law of the FORUM should be applied. See also PROCEDURAL LAW.

KIN 📖 Relation by blood or CONSANGUINITY; relatives by birth. 📖

The term *kin* is ordinarily applied to relationships through ties of blood; however, it is sometimes used generally to include family relationships by AFFINITY.

Kindred is a synonym for kin.

Edward King

KING, EDWARD Edward King was a lawyer whose 1844 nomination to the U.S. Supreme Court failed because of political animosity between Congress and the president who proposed him.

King was born January 31, 1794, in Philadelphia. He was well educated and studied law under the prominent Pennsylvania lawyer Charles Chauncey. He was admitted to the Pennsylvania bar in 1816 and soon after entered politics, first as a Federalist and then as a Democrat. Before he was thirty years old, he had established himself as a leader of the Democratic party in Pennsylvania.

King became clerk of the Philadelphia orphans' court in 1824. The following year, he was named president judge of the Philadelphia Court of Common Pleas. He was a highly respected jurist who did more to establish Pennsylvania's EQUITY courts than did all the other judges of the state. Equity courts provided a necessary alternative for petitioners whose claims did not fit into the strictly prescribed rules of the COMMON-LAW or common-pleas courts. Litigants seeking nonmonetary damages, such as an INJUNCTION or SPECIFIC PERFORMANCE of a contract, were without remedy before the establishment of equity jurisdiction.

About the time King was rising to national prominence on the strength of his judicial reputation, the federal government was in flux. Many southern Democrats had become disenchanted with President ANDREW JACKSON and his policies, which they claimed eroded STATES' RIGHTS and led to the economic depression that followed his administration. In 1840, the newly formed Whig party, born of the South's alienation from Jackson, named WILLIAM H. HARRI-

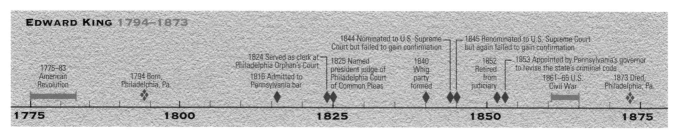

EDWARD KING 1794–1873

1775–83 American Revolution

1794 Born, Philadelphia, Pa.

1824 Served as clerk at Philadelphia Orphan's Court
1816 Admitted to Pennsylvania bar

1825 Named president judge of Philadelphia Court of Common Pleas

1840 Whig party formed

1844 Nominated to U.S. Supreme Court but failed to gain confirmation

1845 Renominated to U.S. Supreme Court but again failed to gain confirmation

1852 Retired from judiciary

1853 Appointed by Pennsylvania's governor to revise the state's criminal code
1861–65 U.S. Civil War

1873 Died, Philadelphia, Pa.

1775   1800   1825   1850   1875

SON and JOHN TYLER as its candidates for president and vice president, respectively. Harrison won the election; one month after his inauguration, he died, and Tyler ascended to the presidency.

Tyler, who had originally been a Democrat, lacked strong congressional support from either the Democrats or the Whigs. When he nominated King to the Supreme Court on June 5, 1844, the Senate voted to postpone consideration of the proposal. Tyler reappointed King on December 4; in January 1845, the Senate again tabled the nomination. Finally, Tyler withdrew King's nomination on February 7.

King continued as president judge in the common-pleas court until his retirement from the judiciary in 1852. Shortly afterward, he was appointed by Pennsylvania's governor to a commission to revise the state's criminal code. The revision, written mainly by King and then reported to the legislature, was adopted almost literally as prepared.

King spent the remaining years of his life traveling and studying. He was a member of the American Philosophical Society and for many years was president of the Board of Directors of Jefferson Medical College. He died in his hometown of Philadelphia on May 8, 1873.

KING, MARTIN LUTHER, JR. For thirteen turbulent years, Martin Luther King, Jr., was the inspirational leader and moral arbiter of the U.S. CIVIL RIGHTS MOVEMENT. An advocate of nonviolence, King helped organize well-publicized BOYCOTTS, marches, and demonstrations to protest segregation and racial injustice. From 1955 to 1968, he was the impassioned voice of African Americans who sought the abolishment of JIM CROW LAWS (a series of regulations enacted to keep the races separate) and the guarantee of equal housing, education, VOTING rights, and employment. Although countless U.S. citizens contributed to the success of the civil rights movement, King is its most enduring symbol. Before his mission was cut short by an assassin's bullet in 1968, he succeeded in permanently raising the social, economic, and political status of all people of color.

BIOGRAPHY

APWIDE WORLD PHOTOS

Martin Luther King, Jr.

King was born January 15, 1929, in Atlanta, Georgia. At an early age, he demonstrated the intellect and drive that would propel him to national prominence. After skipping his senior year of high school, he enrolled in Atlanta's Morehouse College, at the age of fifteen. He earned a degree in sociology from Morehouse in 1948. Since both his father and grandfather were Baptist preachers, it was not surprising when King entered Crozer Theological Seminary, in suburban Philadelphia, at age nineteen. After graduating from Crozer as class valedictorian, King enrolled in Boston University's renowned School of Theology, where he earned a doctor's degree in 1955. While in Boston, he met and married Coretta Scott, a student at the Boston Conservatory.

The young couple moved to Montgomery, Alabama, in 1954, after King accepted a position as minister of the Dexter Avenue Baptist Church. He was only twenty-six years old and had lived in Montgomery for just eighteen months when an African American bus rider changed the course of his life forever.

On December 1, 1955, seamstress ROSA PARKS took a personal stand against the South's Jim Crow laws when she refused to give up her seat to a white person and move to the back of a city bus. In Montgomery, segregated seating on buses was mandated by ordinance. Parks's defiant act galvanized the city's African American community. A bus boycott was organized to support Parks after her arrest and to put an end to segregated public transportation. When the Montgomery Improvement Association was created to direct the protest, a somewhat surprised King was named president. Years later, those involved in the boycott explained that King was selected because of his powerful speaking style, his credibility as a clergyman, and his relatively low profile in Montgomery. Because King was a newcomer, he had not made any enemies within the African American community and had not been corrupted by dishonest white politicians.

With leadership thrust upon him, King took over the boycott. He rose to the challenge,

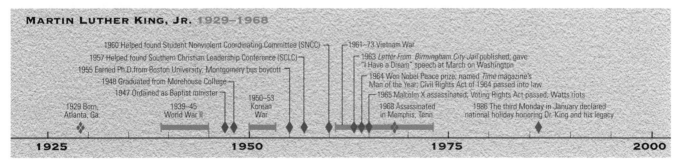

MARTIN LUTHER KING, JR. 1929–1968

1960 Helped found Student Nonviolent Coordinating Committee (SNCC)
1957 Helped found Southern Christian Leadership Conference (SCLC)
1955 Earned Ph.D from Boston University; Montgomery bus boycott
1948 Graduated from Morehouse College
1947 Ordained as Baptist minister

1961–73 Vietnam War
1963 *Letter From Birmingham City Jail* published; gave "I Have a Dream" speech at March on Washington
1964 Won Nobel Peace prize; named *Time* magazine's Man of the Year; Civil Rights Act of 1964 passed into law
1965 Malcolm X assassinated; Voting Rights Act passed; Watts riots

1929 Born, Atlanta, Ga.
1939–45 World War II
1950–53 Korean War
1968 Assassinated in Memphis, Tenn.
1986 The third Monday in January declared national holiday honoring Dr. King and his legacy

1925   1950   1975   2000

creating peaceful strategies that placed the bus company in an economic squeeze and African Americans on the moral high ground. He was greatly influenced by Mohandas K. ("Mahatma") Gandhi's nonviolence movement in India. King denounced violence throughout the citywide boycott, only to encounter death threats, hate mail, physical attacks, mass arrests, and the bombing of his church and home. The possibility of death was constant, but King used his deep religious faith and inner strength to stare down fear. He told his followers, "Love your enemies; bless them that curse you. . . . Remember, if I am stopped, this Movement will not stop, because God is with this Movement."

By November 1956, the boycott had taken the intended financial toll on the transit company. Seventy percent of Montgomery's bus riders were African Americans, and they supported the boycott in droves. The campaign was declared a success when the buses were at last desegregated in December 1956 and Montgomery's ordinance was declared unconstitutional by the U.S. Supreme Court (*Owen v. Browder*, 352 U.S. 903, 77 S. Ct. 145, 1 L. Ed. 2d 114 [1956]). More important, King and his fellow African Americans discovered the power of social protest and the virtue of nonviolence.

After Montgomery, King knew that his true calling was social activism. In 1957, he helped found the SOUTHERN CHRISTIAN LEADERSHIP CONFERENCE, an organization that would guide the growing civil rights movement. During the late 1950s and early 1960s, King took part in dozens of demonstrations throughout the South and was arrested and jailed for his civil disobedience. The national media and the administrations of Presidents DWIGHT D. EISENHOWER and JOHN F. KENNEDY took notice. King became the torchbearer for the nation's CIVIL RIGHTS struggle.

In 1963, King and his fellow activists set out to integrate Birmingham, Alabama, which King called "the most thoroughly segregated city in the country." Unlike Montgomery, where the issue was limited to bus ridership, Birmingham offered a forum for far-reaching objectives. King's goal was to desegregate the entire community—its restaurants, hotels, department stores, rest rooms, and public facilities. As the sit-ins and marches began, the response by some white southerners was ugly. Extremists bombed an African American church, killing four young girls who were attending Sunday School inside. Police commissioner Eugene ("Bull") Connor ordered his officers to use high-pressure water hoses, police dogs, and

clubs against the nonviolent demonstrators. Grade school and high school protesters were jailed alongside adults, and at one point, three thousand African Americans were incarcerated in Birmingham. King himself was jailed and as a result wrote his historic 1963 essay *Letter from Birmingham City Jail*, an eloquent justification of nonviolent resistance to unjust laws. Throughout the saga, television cameras sent searing images of white brutality across the nation. As King hoped, federal intervention was required to handle the situation, and segregation laws were forced off the books.

Perhaps the crowning moment of King's career was the 1963 March on Washington, when 250,000 people from diverse racial and ethnic backgrounds converged in front of the Lincoln Memorial in Washington, D.C. Here, King delivered his famous "I Have a Dream" speech, which described a world of racial equality and harmony. The speech ended with these stirring words:

> When we let freedom ring, when we let it ring from every village and every hamlet, from every state and every city, we will be able to speed up that day when all of God's children, black men and white men, Jews and Gentiles, Protestants and Catholics, will be able at last to join hands and sing in the words of the old Negro spiritual, "Free at last! Free at last! Thank God Almighty, we are free at last!"

King was successful in pressuring the U.S. Congress and President LYNDON B. JOHNSON to support the CIVIL RIGHTS ACT of 1964 (42 U.S.C.A. § 2000a et seq.). The law guaranteed equal access for all U.S. citizens to public accommodations and facilities, employment, and education. In 1965, King's campaign in Selma, Alabama, helped ensure the passage of the Voting Rights Act of 1965 (42 U.S.C.A. § 1973 et seq.), which extended the vote to previously disenfranchised African Americans in the Deep South. The act outlawed the tests, standards, and procedures that were routinely used to disqualify voters on the basis of race.

King received several honors for his work, including the Nobel Peace Prize in 1964. The same year, he was the first African American to be named *Time* magazine's Man of the Year. Since 1986, the third Monday in January has been observed as a federal holiday in honor of King's birthday.

The last years of King's life were difficult, as he struggled with bouts of depression over personal and professional failures. His hold on

"NONVIOLENCE IS THE ANSWER TO THE CRUCIAL POLITICAL AND MORAL QUESTIONS OF OUR TIME; THE NEED FOR MEN TO OVERCOME OPPRESSION AND VIOLENCE WITHOUT RESORTING TO OPPRESSION AND VIOLENCE."

the civil rights movement was clearly weakening. Young African American activists were demanding a more militant approach to achieving social and economic justice. The angrier black power movement appealed to increasing numbers of African Americans who were impatient with the slow pace of King's nonviolent tactics. King's campaigns in northern cities such as Chicago were largely unsuccessful.

On August 11, 1965, just days after the passage of the Voting Rights Act, the African American Watts area of Los Angeles erupted into a riot that lasted six days. Thirty-four people were killed, and $30 million worth of property was damaged. After the upheaval in Watts, King's message and influence were diminished.

In 1967, King publicly criticized the United States' involvement in Vietnam and earned the enmity of his former liberal ally President Johnson. Critics believed that King's entry into the peace movement diluted his efforts to achieve further gains for African Americans.

In the spring of 1968, King planned to participate in the Poor People's Campaign, in Washington, D.C. Before going to the nation's capital, he traveled to Memphis to support striking garbage workers there. On April 4, while standing on the balcony of his room at the Lorraine Motel, in Memphis, he was assassinated by James Earl Ray, a white man.

According to those who knew him, King did not set out to become a martyr for civil rights. As ELLA J. BAKER, a longtime activist, said, "The movement made Martin rather than Martin making the movement." King represents the dignity of the struggle and the sacrifice it required. Despite a tendency to deify King, he should be regarded not as a saint but as an extraordinary individual who used his prodigious talents to change society. When asked to describe his possible legacy, King himself said, "I just want to leave a committed life behind."

CROSS-REFERENCES

Black Panther Party; Carmichael, Stokely; Cleaver, Eldridge; Davis, Angela Yvonne; Evers, Medgar Wiley; Jackson, Jesse; Ku Klux Klan; Liuzzo, Viola; Malcolm X; Marshall, Thurgood; Meredith, James; National Association for the Advancement of Colored People; Randolph, A. Philip; Student Non-Violent Coordinating Committee; Wilkins, Roy.

KING, RODNEY G. The 1991 beating of Rodney G. King by Los Angeles, California, police led to state and federal criminal prosecution of the law enforcement officers involved in the assault, a civil JURY award of $3.8 million to

King for his injuries, and major reforms in the Los Angeles police department. In addition, the April 1992 ACQUITTAL of the white police officers for the beating of King, an African American, touched off RIOTS in Los Angeles that rank as the worst in U.S. history. The controversy surrounding each of these actions raised the issues of race, racism, and police brutality in communities throughout the United States.

On the evening of March 3, 1991, Rodney King was driving his automobile when a highway police officer signaled him to pull over to the side of the road. King, who had been drinking, fled, later testifying that he was afraid he would be returned to prison for violating his PAROLE. A high-speed chase ensued with a number of Los Angeles police officers and vehicles involved. The police eventually pulled King over. After King got out of his car, four officers—Stacey C. Koon, Laurence M. Powell, Timothy E. Wind, and Theodore J. Briseno—kicked King and hit him with their batons more than fifty times while he struggled on the ground.

Unbeknownst to the officers, an amateur photographer, George Holliday, videotaped eighty-one seconds of the beating. The videotape was shown repeatedly on national television and became a symbol of complaints about police brutality.

The four officers were charged with numerous criminal counts, including ASSAULT with a deadly weapon, the use of excessive force, and filing a false police report. Because of the extensive publicity surrounding the case, the trial of the four police officers was conducted in Simi Valley, a predominantly white community located in Ventura County, not far from Los Angeles. During the trial the prosecution used the videotape as its principal source of EVIDENCE and did not have King testify. The defense also used the videotape, examining it frame by frame to bolster its contention that King was resisting arrest and that the violence was necessary to subdue him. The defense also contended that the videotape distorted the events of that night, because it did not capture what happened before and after the eighty-one seconds of tape recording.

On April 29, 1992, the jury, which included ten whites, one Filipino American, and one Hispanic, but no African Americans, found the four police officers not guilty on ten of the eleven counts and could not come to an agreement on the other count. The acquittals stunned many persons who had seen the videotape. Within two hours riots erupted in the predominantly black South Central section of Los Angeles. The riots lasted seventy hours, leaving 60 people dead, more than 2,100 people injured, and between $800 million and $1 billion in damage in Los Angeles. Order was restored through the combined efforts of the police, more than ten thousand NATIONAL GUARD troops, and thirty-five hundred Army and Marine Corps troops.

In the riot's aftermath, criticism of the Los Angeles police, which had escalated after the King beating, grew stronger. Many believed that the longtime police chief, Daryl F. Gates, had not sufficiently prepared for the possibility of civil unrest and had made poor decisions in the first hours of the riots. These criticisms, coupled with the determination by an independent commission headed by Warren G. Christopher (a distinguished attorney who served in the State Department during the administration of President JIMMY CARTER) that Gates should be replaced because of the brutality charges, placed increasing pressure on the police chief. Gates finally resigned in late June 1992.

In August 1992 a federal GRAND JURY indicted the four officers for violating King's CIVIL RIGHTS. Koon was charged with depriving King of DUE PROCESS OF LAW by failing to restrain the other officers. The other three officers were charged with violating King's right against unreasonable SEARCH AND SEIZURE because they had used unreasonable force during the arrest.

At the federal trial, which was held in Los Angeles, the jury was more racially diverse than the one at Simi Valley: two jury members were black, one was Hispanic, and the rest were white. This time King testified about the beating and charged that the officers had used racial epithets. Observers agreed that he was an effective WITNESS. The videotape again was the central piece of evidence for both sides. On April 17, 1993, the jury convicted officers Koon and Powell of violating King's civil rights but acquitted Wind and Briseno. Koon and Powell were sentenced to two and a half years in prison.

King filed a civil lawsuit against the police officers and the city of Los Angeles. After settlement talks broke down, the case went to trial in early 1994. On April 19, 1994, the jury awarded King $3.8 million in COMPENSATORY DAMAGES. However, the jury refused to award King PUNITIVE DAMAGES. In July 1994 the city of Los Angeles struck a deal whereby King agreed to drop any plans to APPEAL the jury's VERDICT on punitive damages. In return, the city of Los Angeles agreed to expedite payment of King's compensatory damages.

KING'S BENCH OR QUEEN'S BENCH

The highest COMMON-LAW court in England until its end as a separate tribunal in 1875.

The Court of the King's Bench or Court of the Queen's Bench derived from the royal court first established by William the Conqueror in the eleventh century. The royal court, called the CURIA REGIS, was not a judicial body in the modern sense. Rather, it was an assembly of English lords and noblemen that resolved matters of special importance to the king. As the king traveled about England, the royal court followed, advising him and deciding cases.

The royal court was reorganized by the Crown in the twelfth and thirteenth centuries, and renamed the Court of the King's Bench or Court of the Queen's Bench. This court existed as an alternative to the Court of Common Pleas, which was comprised of professional judges. At first the two courts heard different types of cases. However, over the course of several centuries, the Court of the King's Bench or Court of the Queen's Bench expanded its jurisdiction to hear virtually any case. This encroached on the power of the Court of Common Pleas, and the two courts competed for cases.

In 1873 Parliament abolished the Court of the King's Bench or Court of the Queen's Bench—then under Queen Victoria—and merged it into the High Court of Justice as the King's Bench Division. The King's Bench Division of the High Court of Justice is empowered to hear appeals of certain cases. The High Court of Justice is akin to a U.S. trial court. It has two other divisions: the Family Division and the Chancery Division.

See also ENGLISH LAW.

KISSINGER, HENRY ALFRED

As a scholar, adviser, and U.S. secretary of state, Henry Alfred Kissinger was an important figure in international affairs in the late twentieth century. The German-born Kissinger became a U.S. citizen in the 1930s, emerged as a leading theorist at Harvard in the 1950s, advised presidents in the 1960s, and defined the course of U.S. foreign policy for much of the 1970s. He won great acclaim for his pragmatic vision of foreign policy as well as his skills as a peace negotiator. In 1973 he shared the Nobel Peace Prize for his efforts in securing a cease-fire in the VIETNAM WAR. However, criticism followed public revelations about his involvement in secret U.S. military and ESPIONAGE operations, and he left public office in 1976 with a controversial record.

BIOGRAPHY

AP/WIDE WORLD PHOTOS

Henry Alfred Kissinger

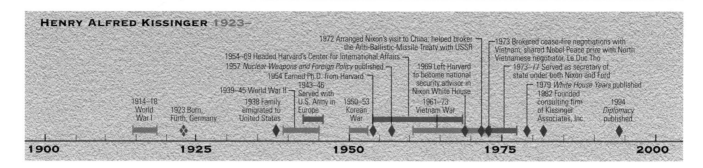

HENRY ALFRED KISSINGER 1923–

1972 Arranged Nixon's visit to China; helped broker the Anti-Ballistic-Missile Treaty with USSR

1973 Brokered cease-fire negotiations with Vietnam; shared Nobel Peace prize with North Vietnamese negotiator, Le Duc Tho

1954–69 Headed Harvard's Center for International Affairs

1957 *Nuclear Weapons and Foreign Policy* published

1954 Earned Ph.D. from Harvard

1969 Left Harvard to become national security advisor in Nixon White House

1973–77 Served as secretary of state under both Nixon and Ford

1979 *White House Years* published

1939–45 World War II

1943–46 Served with U.S. Army in Europe

1982 Founded consulting firm of Kissinger Associates, Inc.

1914–18 World War I

1923 Born, Fürth, Germany

1938 Family emigrated to United States

1950–53 Korean War

1961–73 Vietnam War

1994 *Diplomacy* published

1900   1925   1950   1975   2000

Born May 27, 1923, in Fürth, Germany, and given the first name Heinz, Kissinger was the son of middle-class Jewish parents who fled Nazi persecution while he was a teenager. After the family immigrated to the United States in 1938, he became a U.S. citizen in 1943. Service in the U.S. Army brought Kissinger back to Europe during World War II. Following combat and intelligence duty, he served in the post-war U.S. military government in Germany from 1945 to 1946. Decorated with honors and discharged from the service, he earned a bachelor of arts degree summa cum laude in government studies at Harvard College in 1950, then added a masters and in 1956 a doctorate.

While teaching at Harvard in the 1950s, Kissinger came to national attention with his book *Nuclear Weapons and Foreign Policy* (1957). The book was a bold argument against narrow COLD WAR views of military strategy. It took aim at the reigning defense doctrine of the day, an all-or-nothing approach holding that the United States should retaliate massively with nuclear weapons against any aggressor. Kissinger proposed a different solution based on the approach of *Realpolitik*, the German concept of an intensely pragmatic rather than idealistic vision of international relations. The United States should deploy nuclear weapons strategically around the world as a deterrent, he argued, while relying on conventional, non-nuclear forces in the event of aggression against it. The idea took hold gradually over the next decade.

Rising to the top of his field, Kissinger became a driving force behind Harvard's efforts in the area of foreign policy. Taking increasingly higher positions in its Center for International Affairs and directing its Defense Studies Program, he became much sought after by politicians, diplomats, and government defense specialists in the 1960s. He counseled Presidents JOHN F. KENNEDY and LYNDON B. JOHNSON on foreign policy. In 1968 he advised Governor Nelson A. Rockefeller, of New York, in Rock-

"A CONVENTIONAL ARMY LOSES IF IT DOES NOT WIN. THE GUERILLA ARMY WINS IF IT DOES NOT LOSE."

efeller's unsuccessful campaign for the Republican party nomination for president. After the election, the new president, RICHARD M. NIXON, was quick to hire away his opponent's adviser.

The two terms of Nixon's presidency elevated Kissinger's power. Named first to the position of assistant for national security affairs, a high-level post, he soon eclipsed the president's secretary of state, William P. Rogers, in visibility and influence. Indeed, by the end of Nixon's first term, Kissinger was the acknowledged architect of U.S. foreign policy. His rise to preeminence was complete in 1973 when Nixon made him secretary of state.

Under Nixon, Kissinger had a string of historic successes. He arranged Nixon's breakthrough visit to China in 1972, which ended years of hostile relations between the two nations. Also in 1972, at the STRATEGIC ARMS LIMITATIONS TALKS (SALT 1), he helped broker the ANTI-BALLISTIC-MISSILE TREATY, the landmark agreement to limit nuclear proliferation signed by the United States and the Soviet Union. Traveling widely in what came to be known as shuttle diplomacy, he conducted peace negotiations between the United States and Vietnam en route to the signing of a cease-fire in 1973. In recognition of his efforts, he was awarded the Nobel Peace Prize, with the chief North Vietnamese negotiator, Le Duc Tho. Kissinger also engineered cease-fires between Arab states and Israel after their 1973 war, and persuaded Nixon to ready U.S. forces around the world in order to deter Soviet intervention.

But in 1973 Kissinger also came under harsh attack. Throughout the Vietnam War, antiwar critics had targeted him. Now public revelations about the White House's secret conduct of the war in Southeast Asia led to criticism. It was revealed that in 1969 Kissinger had won Nixon's approval to expand the war into Cambodia, a neutral country, with bombings and subsequent ground incursions by U.S. troops. Eventually critics blamed Kissinger and Nixon for the destruction of Cambodia after the country fell to Khmer Rouge leader Pol Pot, whose forces systematically murdered millions of Cambodians. On the political left, some commentators branded the president and his secretary of state war criminals.

When Nixon's 1974 resignation resulted in the succession of GERALD R. FORD as president, Ford kept Kissinger as both secretary of state and national security adviser. But Kissinger faced mounting criticism in the media and Congress. More revelations came to light: Kissinger had secretly authorized CENTRAL INTELLIGENCE AGENCY operations to overthrow the government of Chile and to support rebels in Angola. He was also attacked for having used wiretaps of federal employees in order to stop security leaks. Whereas Congress had listened attentively to Kissinger during the Nixon administration, the allure of his *Realpolitik* was fading in the more cautious, less interventionist post-Vietnam era. He left office in 1976 with his influence at an all-time low.

In private life Kissinger continued to be active in international affairs. He taught, served as a consultant, and often commented in the media on foreign policy, while also writing two popular memoirs: *White House Years* (1980) and *Years of Upheaval* (1982). President RONALD REAGAN briefly lured Kissinger back into public life in 1983, appointing him to head a commission to make policy recommendations on Latin America.

See also ARMS CONTROL AND DISARMAMENT.

KITING The unlawful practice of drawing CHECKS against a bank account containing insufficient funds to cover them, with the expectation that the necessary funds will be deposited before such checks are presented for payment.

KLEINDIENST, RICHARD GORDON

Richard Gordon Kleindienst served as U.S. attorney general from 1972 to 1973. A prominent Arizona lawyer and Republican party leader, Kleindienst was charged in the WATERGATE scandals and ultimately pleaded guilty to PERJURY in 1974.

Kleindienst was born August 5, 1923, in Winslow, Arizona. He served in the U.S. Army from 1943 to 1946 and then attended college. He graduated from Harvard University in 1947

"IT IS OF UTMOST IMPORTANCE TO THIS ADMINISTRATION IN POWER, AND YOU MEN MUST DO EVERYTHING YOU CAN TO INSURE THAT RESULT."

BIOGRAPHY

Richard Gordon Kleindienst

and received his law degree from Harvard Law School in 1950. He was admitted to the Arizona bar in 1950 and entered practice with a law firm in Phoenix.

Politics soon became a dominant part of Kleindienst's life. He was elected as a Republican to the Arizona House of Representatives in 1953, where he served one term. During the 1950s the western conservative wing of the Republican party started to grow. Senator BARRY M. GOLDWATER, of Arizona, became the standard-bearer of conservatism, and Kleindienst devoted himself to this cause. He led the Young Republicans, and served on the state and national Republican committees. He also took on the role of political mentor to WILLIAM H. REHNQUIST, a young Arizona attorney who would later become chief justice of the U.S. Supreme Court. Kleindienst's political activities climaxed in 1964, when he served as director of field operations for Goldwater's unsuccessful presidential campaign against incumbent LYNDON B. JOHNSON.

Kleindienst then became an ally of RICHARD M. NIXON. He worked on Nixon's successful 1968 presidential campaign and served as general counsel of the Republican National Committee. As a reward for Kleindienst's campaign work, Nixon appointed him deputy attorney general in January 1969. Kleindienst brought to Washington, D.C., his protégé Rehnquist to serve as counsel to Attorney General JOHN N. MITCHELL.

In 1972 Mitchell agreed to resign as attorney general and become head of President Nixon's reelection committee. Kleindienst was appointed attorney general on June 12. At his confirmation hearings, Democratic senators raised questions about an ANTITRUST settlement he had negotiated between the government and International Telephone and Telegraph Corporation (ITT). Rumors suggested that the White House had pressured Kleindienst to drop the antitrust suit. It was also alleged that ITT received a favorable disposition of the lawsuit in return for a large contribution to Nixon's reelection campaign. At his hearings Kleindienst denied he had been pressured by anyone.

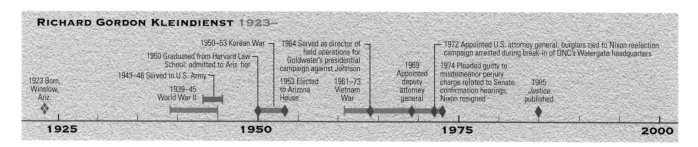

RICHARD GORDON KLEINDIENST 1923–

1923 Born, Winslow, Ariz.

1939–45 World War II

1943–46 Served in U.S. Army

1950 Graduated from Harvard Law School; admitted to Ariz. bar

1950–53 Korean War

1953 Elected to Arizona House

1961–73 Vietnam War

1964 Served as director of field operations for Goldwater's presidential campaign against Johnson

1969 Appointed deputy attorney general

1972 Appointed U.S. attorney general; burglars tied to Nixon reelection campaign arrested during break-in of DNC's Watergate headquarters

1974 Pleaded guilty to misdemeanor perjury charge related to Senate confirmation hearings; Nixon resigned

1985 *Justice* published

1925   1950   1975   2000

On June 17, five days after Kleindienst was sworn in as attorney general, persons working for the Nixon reelection committee broke into Democratic National Committee headquarters at the Watergate office building complex in Washington, D.C. The burglars planted electronic eavesdropping devices in hopes of gaining intelligence on the Democrats' strategy to defeat Nixon. Through their bungling the burglars were arrested.

On January 20, 1973, Kleindienst met with Mitchell and White House advisers to discuss handling the public relations problems that were mounting in the wake of the break-in. As events unfolded prosecutors began to tie the burglars to the White House and the reelection committee leadership. On April 30 Kleindienst and top White House aides H. R. Haldeman, John D. Ehrlichman, and John W. Dean III resigned, amid charges of White House efforts to obstruct justice in the Watergate case.

In 1974 Kleindienst pleaded guilty to a MIS-DEMEANOR perjury charge for failing to testify fully at his Senate confirmation hearings concerning the ITT lawsuit. The charge against him revealed that Nixon had called him in 1971 and told him to drop the case. He later claimed he was innocent of the charge and had not been swayed by Nixon's directive. He was fined $1,000 and sentenced to thirty days in jail, but the judge suspended the sentence. Prosecutors also discovered that ITT had contributed $400,000 to the Nixon campaign following the resolution of the lawsuit, but Kleindienst was never implicated in this matter.

Kleindienst returned to Arizona, where he resumed his law practice. In 1985 he published *Justice*, his account of his time in Washington, D.C.

KNAEBEL, ERNEST Ernest Knaebel was an attorney who became an assistant U.S. attorney for Colorado and later a U.S. Supreme Court reporter of decisions.

Born June 14, 1872, in Manhasset, New York, and raised in New York, Knaebel received his college and legal education at Yale. He received his bachelor of arts degree in 1894, his

bachelor of laws degree summa cum laude in 1896, and his master of laws degree magna cum laude in 1897. After graduating from law school, he was admitted to the New York, New Mexico, and Colorado bars. He practiced law in New York City from 1897 to 1898.

In 1898, Knaebel moved to Colorado and entered private practice with his father in Denver. From 1902 to 1907, he served as assistant U.S. attorney for Colorado. He returned to the East in 1907 to become a special assistant to the attorney general in Washington, D.C., and was named assistant attorney general in 1911. During his tenure with the Justice Department, Knaebel was heavily involved in land-fraud prosecutions, arguing many of the early cases concerning public and Indian land disputes that came before the U.S. Supreme Court. He also organized the Public Lands Division of the Justice Department and directed that division from 1909 to 1916.

In 1916, Knaebel was appointed the REPORTER of decisions for the U.S. Supreme Court. In this capacity, he and his staff were responsible for the slow, painstaking task of editing the Court's decisions and preparing them for publication. The reporter checks all citations in the opinions, corrects typographical and other errors, adds the HEADNOTES summarizing the major points of law, and lists the voting lineup of the justices and the names of counsel. Under Knaebel's tenure, the office of reporter was reorganized by statute and the printing and sale of *U.S. Reports*, the official publication of Supreme Court orders and decisions, was turned over to the U.S. Government Printing Office and the superintendent of documents. Knaebel edited volumes 242 to 321 of *U.S. Reports*.

Knaebel was a member of the American Bar Association, Phi Beta Kappa, and Phi Alpha Delta. He served on the Board of Governors of the Lawyers' Club and was a member of the Cosmos Club and the Yale Club.

Knaebel served as reporter of decisions from 1916 until January 31, 1944, when he retired because of ill health. He died on February 19, 1947, in West Boxford, Massachusetts.

BIOGRAPHY

Ernest Knaebel

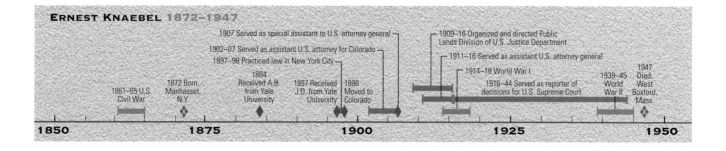

ERNEST KNAEBEL 1872–1947

1850   1875   1900   1925   1950

1861–65 U.S. Civil War

1872 Born, Manhasset, N.Y.

1884 Received A.B. from Yale University

1897 Received J.D. from Yale University

1897–98 Practiced law in New York City

1898 Moved to Colorado

1902–07 Served as assistant U.S. attorney for Colorado

1907 Served as special assistant to U.S. attorney general

1909–16 Organized and directed Public Lands Division of U.S. Justice Department

1911–16 Served as assistant U.S. attorney general

1914–18 World War I

1916–44 Served as reporter of decisions for U.S. Supreme Court

1939–45 World War II

1947 Died, West Boxford, Mass.

KNOWINGLY 📖 Consciously; willfully; subject to complete understanding of the facts or circumstances. 📖

According to provisions contained in the Model Penal Code, an individual is deemed to have acted knowingly in regard to a material element of an offense when: in the event that such element involves the nature of his or her conduct or the circumstances attendant thereto, he or she is aware that the conduct is of such nature or that those circumstances exist; if the element relates to a result of the person's conduct, he or she is conscious of the fact that it is substantially certain that the conduct will precipitate such a result.

When the term *knowingly* is used in an INDICTMENT, it signifies that the defendant knew what he or she was going to do and, subject to such knowledge, engaged in the act for which he or she was charged.

KNOX, PHILANDER CHASE   Philander Chase Knox was a corporate attorney, industrialist, and two-time U.S. senator from Pennsylvania. He served as U.S. attorney general under President WILLIAM MCKINLEY from 1901 to 1904, and as U.S. secretary of state under President WILLIAM HOWARD TAFT from 1909 to 1913.

Knox was born to privilege on May 6, 1853, in Brownsville, Fayette County, Pennsylvania. His banker father, David S. Knox, financed commercial activities in the region around Pittsburgh. His mother, Rebekah Page Knox, was involved in numerous philanthropic and social organizations, and she encouraged her children in community service pursuits.

Knox's early education was in local private schools with the children of other prominent Pennsylvania families. He received a bachelor of arts degree from Mount Union College, in Alliance, Ohio, in 1872. While in college Knox began a lifelong friendship with future president McKinley, who was then district attorney of Stark County, Ohio. McKinley encouraged the young man's interest in the law, and arranged for him to read law in the office of Attorney H. B. Swope, of Pittsburgh.

BIOGRAPHY

Philander Chase Knox

After spending three years with Swope, Knox was admitted to Pennsylvania's Allegheny County bar in 1875. Shortly thereafter he was appointed assistant U.S. district attorney for the Western District of Pennsylvania. Two years later he formed a law partnership with James H. Reed, of Pittsburgh, that would last more than twenty years. In 1880 he formed an equally lasting marital partnership with Lillie Smith, daughter of Pittsburgh businessman Andrew D. Smith.

Knox's professional skills and personal style were well suited to the business climate of his day. He was intimately involved in the industrial development of the Pittsburgh region as well as the organization and direction of the companies forging that development. His efforts made him one of the wealthiest men in Pennsylvania.

Knox, along with many of his business and social peers, was a charter member of the South Fork Fishing and Hunting Club, on Lake Conemaugh, near Johnstown, Pennsylvania. The club erected a dam to create its private lake retreat. When the dam failed on May 31, 1889, an ensuing flood killed more than two thousand people and destroyed countless homes and businesses in its path. Author David McCullough noted in his history *The Johnstown Flood* that no money was ever collected from the club or its members through damage suits. But Knox's family contributed to the relief efforts, and Knox and other businessmen used their resources to help rebuild many of the companies and restore many of the jobs lost in the cataclysm.

By 1897 Knox had sufficiently redeemed himself to be elected president of the Pennsylvania Bar Association. In 1899 his longtime friend President McKinley offered him the position of attorney general of the United States. Knox declined McKinley's initial offer because he was heavily involved in the formation and organization of the Carnegie Steel Company, so the position went to JOHN W. GRIGGS.

When Griggs resigned in 1901, McKinley again offered the position to Knox. This time

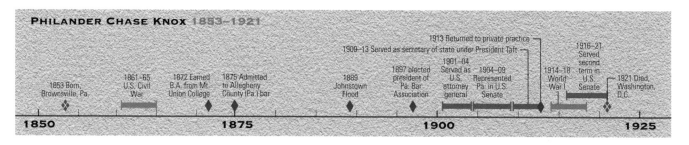

PHILANDER CHASE KNOX 1853–1921

1850 ... 1875 ... 1900 ... 1925

1853 Born, Brownsville, Pa.

1861–65 U.S. Civil War

1872 Earned B.A. from Mt. Union College

1875 Admitted to Allegheny County (Pa.) bar

1889 Johnstown Flood

1897 elected president of Pa. Bar Association

1901–04 Served as U.S. attorney general

1904–09 Represented Pa. in U.S. Senate

1909–13 Served as secretary of state under President Taft

1913 Returned to private practice

1914–18 World War I

1916–21 Served second term in U.S. Senate

1921 Died, Washington, D.C.

Knox accepted. He began his term on April 9, 1901. Within the year he brought an ANTITRUST action against the Northern Securities Company, through which James J. Hill, John Pierpont Morgan, and others had attempted to merge the Great Northern, the Northern Pacific, and the Chicago, Burlington, and Quincy railroads. Knox guided the litigation through several appeals and made the winning argument before the U.S. Supreme Court (*Northern Securities Co. v. United States*, 193 U.S. 197, 24 S. Ct. 436, 48 L. Ed. 679 [1904]).

Later in 1901 he ruled against executive authority—and his own preferences—when he advised that game refuges in the national forests could be established only through legislation. He told President McKinley that he regretted having to make that decision: "I would be glad to find authority for the intervention by the Secretary [of Interior] for the preservation of what is left of the game . . . but it would seem that whatever is done in that direction must be done by Congress, which alone has the power" (Baker 1992, 405).

Knox stayed on as attorney general under President THEODORE ROOSEVELT. In 1902 he traveled to Paris to examine the title to a canal concession across the Isthmus of Panama. Knox validated a French company's questionable title (in a three hundred-page opinion) and opened the way for the United States to purchase the company's interests. The incident is often cited as an example of the law being manipulated by presidential prerogative. Knox reportedly said afterward that Roosevelt's plan to acquire the canal concession was not marred by the slightest taint of legality.

His service as attorney general ended June 10, 1904, when Governor Samuel W. Pennypacker, of Pennsylvania, appointed him to fill the vacancy caused by the death of Senator Matthew S. Quay. Knox took Quay's seat in the U.S. Senate July 1, 1904, and was subsequently elected to a full six-year term. During his term he was active and influential, especially in rail-

"THE CONSCIOUSNESS OF POSSESSING A GIANT'S STRENGTH IS A SUFFICIENT PREVENTIVE AGAINST THE TYRANNY OF USING IT AS A GIANT."

BIOGRAPHY

Charles Everett Koop

road rate legislation. He served on the Judiciary Committee, took a prominent part in a debate over tolls for the Panama Canal, and for a time was chairman of the Senate committee on rules.

He resigned his Senate seat March 4, 1909, to accept President Taft's appointment as secretary of state. Under Taft the focus of foreign policy was the encouragement and protection of U.S. investments abroad. Taft's approach, often called dollar diplomacy, was first applied in 1909, in a failed attempt to help China assume ownership of the Manchurian railways. Tangible proof of Knox's efforts in this attempt can be seen today in Washington, D.C.: the Chinese government gave him two thousand cherry trees that still blossom each spring. More successful attempts at dollar diplomacy were eventually made in Nicaragua and the Caribbean.

In March 1913 Knox returned to the practice of law. He did not last long. Just three years later, he announced his intention to seek a second term in the U.S. Senate. He was elected November 6, 1916. He was an outspoken opponent of the LEAGUE OF NATIONS, and he took a leading role in the successful fight against the ratification of the Treaty of Versailles at the close of World War I because, he said, it imposed "obligations upon the United States which under our Constitution cannot be imposed by the treaty-making power."

On October 12, 1921, Knox collapsed and died outside his Senate chamber in Washington, D.C. He was sixty-eight years old. He was buried near his home at Valley Forge, Pennsylvania.

KOOP, CHARLES EVERETT   Dr. Charles Everett Koop, surgeon general under President RONALD REAGAN, boldly led the United States on controversial health issues such as smoking, ABORTION, infanticide, and AIDS. Koop was a driven, dedicated public servant, committed to doing what he felt was best for the health of the U.S. people. He aggressively confronted pressing health issues while dodging Washington, D.C.'s, political machinery. During his eight-

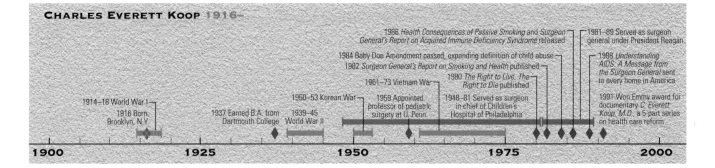

CHARLES EVERETT KOOP 1916–

1986 *Health Consequences of Passive Smoking* and *Surgeon General's Report on Acquired Immune Deficiency Syndrome* released

1984 Baby Doe Amendment passed, expanding definition of child abuse

1982 *Surgeon General's Report on Smoking and Health* published

1980 *The Right to Live, The Right to Die* published

1961–73 Vietnam War

1981–89 Served as surgeon general under President Reagan

1988 *Understanding AIDS: A Message from the Surgeon General* sent to every home in America

1991 Won Emmy award for documentary *C. Everett Koop, M.D.*, a 5-part series on health care reform

1914–18 World War I

1916 Born, Brooklyn, N.Y.

1937 Earned B.A. from Dartmouth College

1939–45 World War II

1950–53 Korean War

1959 Appointed professor of pediatric surgery at U. Penn.

1948–81 Served as surgeon in-chief of Children's Hospital of Philadelphia

1900   1925   1950   1975   2000

year tenure, Koop increased the influence and authority of his post with the Public Health Service. With a passion for medicine and sincere interest in promoting the public's health, Koop was affectionately regarded as "America's family doctor."

Koop was born October 14, 1916, in Brooklyn, the only surviving child of John Everett Koop and Helen Apel Koop. Koop believed from a young age that he was destined to be a doctor—specifically, a surgeon. He spent most of his free time developing the skills he would need for his medical career. As a teenager, he practiced using scissors with both hands, working to become confidently ambidextrous. He labored to improve his manual dexterity by tying tiny knots in threads he sewed through the corners of matchboxes. With the assistance of a family friend and medical student, Koop spent his Saturday mornings watching surgery in the operating room theaters of Manhattan's Columbia Presbyterian Medical Center. Eager to practice on "real" patients, Koop performed surgeries on stray animals while his mother administered anesthesia. He also volunteered and worked at hospitals and clinics across the city.

Koop had a natural tendency to tell the truth, a virtue that, wherever he went, aroused a mixture of contempt and admiration among his peers. One middle school incident of truth telling had a dramatic and positive effect on Koop's future. After he and his classmates caused a disturbance, Koop was the only one to take responsibility for his actions. The teacher responded by slapping him hard enough to raise welts. This convinced Koop's mother that he belonged elsewhere. She promptly enrolled him in the Flatbush School, an excellent college preparatory program that practically guaranteed access to an Ivy League college.

At Flatbush, Koop excelled academically and socially. He participated in football, baseball, basketball, and wrestling. Foreshadowing his future political role, he also successfully campaigned for class president.

One month before his seventeenth birthday, Koop entered Dartmouth College. The Dartmouth coaches quickly recognized Koop's talent at football and awarded him the coveted position of quarterback. However, after a severe concussion damaged his vision and threatened his surgical career, Koop quit the team. He immersed himself in premed studies, majoring in zoology. Having lost his football scholarship, Koop took a series of odd jobs to finance his way through college. To his college friends, the man with the unusual last name became known as Chick Koop.

Koop entered medical school at Cornell University in the fall of 1937. In 1938, he married Elizabeth ("Betty") Flanagan, with whom he eventually raised four children. When the United States entered World War II and many physicians were called to duty, he performed many surgeries that, under normal circumstances, would have been assigned to more senior physicians.

For his next phase of training, Koop and his family moved to Philadelphia. There, he took an internship at Pennsylvania Hospital, followed by a residency at University of Pennsylvania Hospital. After residency, in 1946, Koop became surgeon in chief of Children's Hospital of Philadelphia. He was twenty-nine years old.

During his thirty-two years at Children's Hospital, Koop helped establish pediatric surgery as a medical specialty. At the time he took the job, many surgeons were reluctant to operate on infants and small children because of the risks of sedating them. Koop devised anesthetic techniques for his young patients and worked tirelessly to perfect surgical procedures and postoperative care for children. Along with being a skilled surgeon, he was a compassionate doctor. He was sensitive to the parents of sick and dying children, and helped create support groups to meet their needs.

Koop's work with preterm and malformed babies at Children's Hospital influenced his strong position against abortion, infanticide, and euthanasia. While at Children's Hospital, Koop wrote *The Right to Live, the Right to Die* (1980), a best-seller outlining the relationship between those three practices. He quickly became a spokesman on these issues and committed a great deal of his time to trying to rouse the United States' conscience. Later, after he was nominated surgeon general, Koop was surprised to learn that his Republican supporters valued him more for his stance against abortion than for his impressive medical career.

In 1980, with retirement just one year away, Koop was asked if he would consider the surgeon general's post in Reagan's new administration. The surgeon general is an officer in the United States' Public Health Service Commissioned Corps, a uniformed mobile health unit. Under the leadership of the secretary of the Department of Health and Human Services, the surgeon general administers health policies and supervises personnel in the field. During his time in office, Koop broadened the surgeon general's role from low-profile administrator to high-profile leader.

Koop's surgeon general's reports and frequent testimony influenced the passage of numerous health-related mandates. He became a household name as he gently yet firmly informed the U.S. people about the most preventable threats to their health. Regardless of the political consequences, Koop believed he was obligated to provide accurate information to the public.

Koop launched an antismoking campaign with the 1982 *Surgeon General's Report on Smoking and Health*. In this document, he clearly stated the relationship between cancer deaths and smoking. In the years that followed, Koop produced reports linking smoking to cardiovascular disease and chronic obstructive lung disease.

In an antitobacco campaign, Koop targeted smokeless tobacco products such as chewing tobacco and snuff, citing their connection with various cancers. His actions spurred passage of the Comprehensive Smokeless Tobacco Health Education Act of 1986, 15 U.S.C.A. § 4401 et seq., a mandate to educate the public about this health threat. At Koop's urging, Congress legislated warning labels for smokeless tobacco products.

Koop examined the effects of smoking on nonsmokers in his 1986 report *Health Consequences of Passive Smoking*. Legislators across the nation responded to his report by creating laws to restrict smoking and reduce the risk of passive smoking to nonsmokers. By 1987, smoking was banned in all federal buildings, and regulated in restaurants, hospitals, and other public places in over forty states. In 1988, Koop commissioned studies on smoke in airplanes. Congress reacted to the results of these studies by banning smoking on all flights lasting less than six hours.

Koop publicized the addictive nature of tobacco in his 1988 surgeon general's report. This report forced tobacco officials to agree to more specific surgeon general's labels on cigarettes. However, Koop lost the fight for labels identifying nicotine as an addictive substance.

Though Koop was known for his antiabortion stance, he did little on this issue during his time as surgeon general. He viewed abortion as a moral issue, not a political one, and he strongly disagreed with those who wanted to ban contraceptives and abortion. In response to Koop's position on contraception and sex education, many conservatives who at first supported him turned against him.

Koop faced a dilemma when President Reagan asked him to study the psychological effects of abortion on women. In Koop's opinion, it was a poor strategy to quibble about the effects of abortion on the mother when the effects on the fetus were conclusive. In addition, because both sides of the abortion controversy produced biased studies, the available research was useless. In the end, Koop could not gather evidence to conclusively assert or refute damaging psychological effects of abortion on the mother. He never completed the report.

In 1982, the *Baby Doe* case alarmed the nation. Baby Doe was born with Down's syndrome, which results in mental retardation and other physical problems, and esophageal atresia, an obstruction in the food passageway. The Down's syndrome was not correctable but was compatible with life; the esophageal atresia was incompatible with life but was correctable. On the advice of their obstetrician, the parents chose to forgo treatment, and the baby died. Koop believed that the child was denied treatment because he was retarded, not because the surgery was risky. Koop himself had performed this surgery successfully many times. Judging this to be a case of CHILD ABUSE and infanticide, Koop commented publicly that it is imperative to choose life, even when the quality of that life is not perfect.

In 1983, the nation grappled with similar difficult circumstances surrounding the *Baby Jane Doe* case. Baby Jane was born with spina bifida (a defect in the lower back), an abnormally small head, and hydroencephaly (a condition that causes fluid to collect in the brain). At issue was Baby Jane's right to medical treatment to increase her quality of life despite her physical handicaps. Koop believed that without medical treatment, Baby Jane's spine would become infected, the infection would spread to her brain, and she would become severely retarded. He therefore advocated medical treatment for that condition.

Koop's efforts to educate Congress and the public about the medical injustices affecting handicapped children led to the Baby Doe Amendment (42 U.S.C.A. §§ 5101, 5102, 5103). On October 9, 1984, the amendment extended the laws defining child abuse to include the withholding of fluids, food, and medically indicated treatment from disabled children.

While in office, Koop became embroiled in the politics of educating the public about a growing health threat, AIDS. The Reagan administration prohibited Koop from speaking on the topic for nearly five years. This distressed Koop, who believed it was the surgeon general's duty to inform the public about all health issues. Despite the Reagan administration's purposeful silence on the issue, on October 22, 1986, Koop released *The Surgeon General's Re-*

"I THINK IT IRONIC THAT AT A TIME WHEN SOCIALIST REGIMES ARE COLLAPSING ALL AROUND THE WORLD AND AMERICAN DISENCHANTMENT WITH POLITICS AND GOVERNMENT SEEMS AT AN ALL-TIME HIGH, SO MANY AMERICANS CLAMOR FOR THE GOVERNMENT TO TAKE OVER THE HEALTH-CARE MESS."

port on Acquired Immune Deficiency Syndrome. In it, he clearly stated the facts about the transmission of the disease and identified risk behaviors and preventive measures.

Koop was concerned that all U.S. citizens get the information they needed to stop the spread of AIDS. In May 1988, he sent the mailer *Understanding AIDS: A Message from the Surgeon General* to every household in the United States.

When AIDS first attracted attention, it was labeled a homosexual disease because it was transmitted predominantly through sexual contact among gay males. Koop lost the support of staunch conservatives because he refused to use his position to publicly condemn homosexual behavior. Koop's focus was to educate and save lives. Though he advocated abstinence as the best method for preventing the transmission of AIDS, he also urged the use of condoms by those who continued to engage in risky sexual behavior. Koop spoke against proposals such as mandatory testing and the detention of HIV-positive homosexuals. He challenged those who were against using tax dollars to fund AIDS research. His reasoned approach to the AIDS epidemic helped calm the hysteria of the public.

Shortly after GEORGE BUSH became president, Koop expressed interest in the position of secretary of Health and Human Services. Bush chose Dr. Louis W. Sullivan for that job.

Koop resigned from his position as surgeon general at the end of his second term. He wanted new challenges and looked forward to educating the public without the interference of Washington, D.C., politics. Ironically, Koop's popularity had done a complete flip-flop while he was in office: he had entered his post on the shoulders of conservative Christians, and was leaving it a hero of the liberal press and public.

Even in retirement, Koop continues to fulfill his role as public health educator. He established the Koop Foundation, and The C. Everett Koop Institute at Dartmouth. The Koop Foundation is a private, nonprofit organization dedicated to fitness, education, and research initiatives to promote the health of U.S. citizens. The Koop Institute actively works for reform in medical education and the delivery of medical care. To this end, the institute provides a health information network to help doctors handle challenging medical cases. Still writing, speaking, and consulting on health issues, the diligent Koop perseveres for better and more accessible health care.

See also ACQUIRED IMMUNE DEFICIENCY SYNDROME; HEALTH CARE LAW; SURGEON GENERAL; TOBACCO.

KOREAN WAR The Korean War was a conflict fought on the Korean Peninsula from June 1950 to July 1953. Initially the WAR was between South Korea (Republic of Korea) and North Korea (Democratic People's Republic of Korea) but soon developed into an international war involving the United States and nineteen other nations. The United States sent troops to South Korea as part of a UNITED NATIONS "police action," which sought to repel the Communist aggression of North Korea. Before the war ended in a stalemate, the People's Republic of China had intervened militarily on the side of North Korea, and the Soviet Union had supplied military equipment to the North.

At the end of World War II in 1945, the Soviet Union occupied the Korean Peninsula north of the thirty-eighth degree of latitude, while the U.S. occupied the territory south of it. In 1947, after the United States and the Soviet Union failed to negotiate a reunification of the two separate Korean states, the United States asked the U.N. to solve the problem. The Soviet Union, however, refused a U.N. proposal for a general election in the two Koreas to resolve the issue and encouraged the establishment of a Communist regime under the leadership of Kim Il-sung. South Korea then established a democratic government under the leadership of Syngman Rhee. By 1949 most Soviet and U.S. troops had been withdrawn from the Korean Peninsula.

On June 25, 1950, North Korea, with the tacit approval of the Soviet Union, launched an attack across the thirty-eighth parallel. The U.N. Security Council passed a resolution calling for the assistance of all U.N. members to stop the invasion. Normally, the Soviet Union would have vetoed this resolution, but it was boycotting the Security Council in protest of the U.N.'s decision not to admit the People's Republic of China.

Sixteen nations joined the U.N. forces, with President HARRY S. TRUMAN immediately responding by ordering U.S. forces to assist South Korea. Truman did so without a declaration of war, which until this time had been a prerequisite for U.S. military involvement overseas. Though some Americans criticized Truman for this decision, generally the country supported his action as part of his strategy of "containment," which sought to prevent the spread of COMMUNISM beyond its current borders. Korea became the test case for containment.

The North Korean forces crushed the South Korean army, with the South Koreans holding just the southeastern part of the peninsula. U.N. forces, under the command of General Douglas MacArthur, stabilized the front. On

September 15, 1950, MacArthur made a bold amphibious landing at Inchon, about one hundred miles below the thirty-eighth parallel, cutting off the North Korean forces. The North Korean army was quickly crushed, and more than 125,000 soldiers were captured.

MacArthur then sent U.N. forces into North Korea, proclaiming on November 24 that the troops would be home by Christmas. As U.N. forces neared the Yalu River, which is the border between North Korea and Manchuria, the northeast part of China, the Chinese army attacked them with 180,000 troops. The entrance of China changed the balance of forces. U.S. troops took heavy casualties during the winter of 1950–51 as the Chinese army pushed the U.N. forces back across the thirty-eighth parallel and proceeded south. U.N. forces finally halted the offensive south of Seoul, the capital of South Korea. A U.N. counteroffensive in February 1951 forced the Chinese to withdraw from South Korea. By the end of April, U.N. forces occupied positions slightly north of the thirty-eighth parallel.

It was during this period that President Truman became concerned about the actions of MacArthur. The general publicly expressed his desire to attack Manchuria, BLOCKADE the Chinese coast, and reinforce U.N. forces with troops from Nationalist China, with the goal of achieving victory. Truman, however, favored a limited war, fearing that MacArthur's course would bring the Soviet Union into the war against the United States. When MacArthur continued to make his views known, Truman, as commander in chief, relieved the general of his command on April 11, 1951. The "firing" of MacArthur touched off a firestorm of criticism by Congress and the public against Truman and his apparent unwillingness to win the war. Nevertheless, Truman maintained the limited war strategy, which resulted in a deadlock along the thirty-eighth parallel.

In June 1951 the Soviet Union proposed that cease-fire discussions begin, and in July the representatives of the U.N. and Communist commands began truce negotiations at Kaesong, North Korea. These negotiations were later moved to P'anmunjom.

The Korean War affected U.S. domestic policy. In April 1952 President Truman sparked a constitutional crisis when he seized the U.S. steel industry. With a labor strike by the steelworkers' union imminent, Truman was concerned that the loss of steel production would hurt the Korean War effort. He ordered Secretary of Commerce Charles Sawyer to seize the steel mills and maintain full production. The steel industry challenged the order, bringing it before the Supreme Court. In *Youngstown Sheet and Tube Co. v. Sawyer*, 343 U.S. 579, 72 S. Ct. 863, 96 L. Ed. 1153 (1952), the Court refused to allow the government to seize and operate the steel mills. The majority rejected Truman's claim of inherent executive power in the Constitution to protect the public interest in times of crisis.

Truman's popularity declined because of the war, which contributed to his decision not to run for reelection in 1952. In the presidential race, Republican DWIGHT D. EISENHOWER easily defeated Democrat ADLAI STEVENSON. Eisenhower, a former Army general and World War II hero, pledged to end the war. The truce negotiations, which broke off in October 1952, were resumed in April 1953. After Eisenhower hinted that he was prepared to use nuclear weapons if a settlement was not reached, an ARMISTICE was signed on July 27, 1953.

More than 33,000 U.S. soldiers died in the conflict, and 415,000 South Korean soldiers were killed. It is estimated that 2,000,000 North Koreans and Chinese died. The United States has maintained a military presence in South Korea since the end of the war, because North Korea and South Korea have remained hostile neighbors.

CROSS-REFERENCES

Cold War; Labor Law; Labor Union; Presidential Powers; Stalin, Joseph; Vietnam War; *Youngstown Sheet & Tube Co. v. Sawyer.*

KOREMATSU v. UNITED STATES

Korematsu v. United States, 323 U.S. 214, 65 S. Ct. 193, 89 L. Ed. 194 (1944), was a controversial 6–3 decision of the Supreme Court that affirmed the conviction of a Japanese American citizen who violated an exclusion order that barred all persons of Japanese ancestry from designated military areas during World War II.

Fred Toyosaburo Korematsu, an American citizen of Japanese descent, was convicted in federal court for remaining in a designated military area in California contrary to a Civilian Exclusion Order issued by an army general that required persons of Japanese ancestry to report to assembly centers as a prelude to mass removal from the West Coast. He unsuccessfully appealed his conviction to the circuit court of appeals and was granted *certiorari* by the Supreme Court.

The order that Korematsu was convicted of violating was based upon an EXECUTIVE ORDER, which authorized the military commander to establish military zones and impose restrictions on activities or order exclusion from those areas in order to protect against espionage and sabotage. Federal law made violation of these orders a crime. The entire West Coast and southern

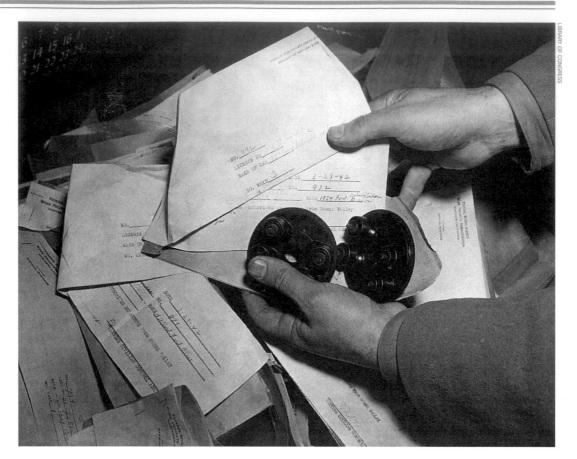

Fred Korematsu was convicted of remaining in a designated military area after the issuance of a Civilian Exclusion Order that required all persons of Japanese descent to evacuate. Once Japanese Americans had arrived at the evacuation camps, U.S. officials removed the distributor caps from their cars so they could not leave. In 1983 a district court vacated Korematsu's conviction and held that racial discrimination should not have been upheld by the Supreme Court.

Arizona were designated as military zones. The restriction and exclusion orders applied to all enemy ALIENS and additionally to American citizens of Japanese ancestry. Pursuant to the executive order, another order imposed an 8 P.M. to 6 A.M. curfew on all persons of Japanese ancestry in designated West Coast military areas. This order and a conviction based on it was challenged in *Hirabayashi v. United States*, 320 U.S. 81, 63 S.Ct. 1375, 87 L.Ed. 1774 (1943), but the Supreme Court upheld the order as " 'protection against espionage and against sabotage' " and sustained the conviction. The Court relied upon that case as support for its refusal to rule that Congress and the president exceeded their war powers in excluding persons of Japanese descent from the West Coast in *Korematsu*. Although it acknowledged that being prohibited from the area where one's home is located is a more severe hardship than a ten-hour curfew, the Court accepted the claims of the government that such drastic measures were necessary to adequately protect the country.

At the start of the majority opinion, the Court stated that any legal restriction that infringes upon the CIVIL RIGHTS of a particular race is "immediately suspect." However, it continued, not all restrictions are unconstitutional. Such limitations are valid when dictated by

public necessity, but they must withstand rigid judicial scrutiny in order to be upheld. The restrictions imposed upon Japanese Americans were deemed by the Court to be necessary for public security during time of war.

Korematsu argued that the rationale of the Court in *Hirabayashi* was erroneous and that when the order in question was promulgated there was no longer any danger of a Japanese invasion of the West Coast. The Court rejected these arguments. Both the curfew and exclusion orders were necessary, since disloyal Americans of Japanese origin could not be easily segregated until subsequent investigations took place. Although the hardship of exclusion fell upon many loyal people, the Court viewed it as one of the harsh results of modern warfare.

The Court affirmed Korematsu's conviction, which has been cited by constitutional scholars as the foundation of the STRICT SCRUTINY test that is applied to suspect classifications made by the government.

In 1983, upon a challenge by Korematsu who was represented by the AMERICAN CIVIL LIBERTIES UNION and the Japanese American Citizens League, U.S. district court judge Marilyn Hall Patel vacated the forty-year-old conviction. Based upon newly discovered evidence—previously withheld government documents—the judge found that the new evidence demonstrated "that the Government knowingly withheld information from the Courts when they were considering the critical question of military necessity in this case." The judge added that "justices of [the Supreme] Court and legal scholars have commented that the [Korematsu] decision is an anachronism in upholding overt racial discrimination as 'compellingly justified,' and that the Korematsu case lies overruled in the court of history."

See also JAPANESE AMERICAN EVACUATION CASES.

KU KLUX KLAN The Ku Klux Klan (KKK) is a white supremacist organization that was founded in 1866. With its characteristic white robes and masks, the secret fraternal organization has used acts of terrorism—including murder, lynching, arson, rape, and bombing—to oppose the granting of CIVIL RIGHTS to African Americans and others. Deriving its membership from native-born, white Protestant U.S. citizens, the KKK has also been anti-Semitic and anti-Catholic and has opposed the immigration of all those it does not view as "racially pure." Other names for the group have been White Brotherhood, Heroes of America, Constitutional Union Guards, and Invisible Empire.

Origins and Initial Growth Ex-Confederate soldiers first established the Ku Klux Klan in Pulaski, Tennessee, in 1866. They developed the first two words of the group's name from the Greek word *kuklos*, meaning "group or band," and took the third as a variant of the word *clan*. Starting as a largely recreational group, the Klan soon turned to intimidating newly freed African Americans. Riding at night, the Klan terrorized and sometimes murdered those it opposed. It adopted its hooded white costume—a guise intended to represent the ghosts of the Confederate dead—to avoid identification and to frighten its victims during its nighttime crimes.

The Klan fed off the post–Civil War resentments of white southerners and attempted to restore that group to political supremacy in the South. The KKK vehemently fought the Reconstruction programs imposed on the South by a Republican Congress. Under Reconstruction, the North sought to restructure southern society on the basis of racial equality. Under this new regime, leading southern whites were disfranchised, while inexperienced African Americans, carpetbaggers (northerners who had migrated to the South following the war), and scalawags (southerners who cooperated with the North) occupied major political offices.

Shortly after the KKK's formation, Nathan Bedford Forrest, a former slave trader and Confederate general, assumed control of the organization and turned it into a militaristic, hierarchical entity. In 1868, Forrest formally disbanded the group after he became appalled by its growing violence. However, the KKK continued to grow, and its atrocities worsened. Drawing the core of its membership from ex-Confederate soldiers, the KKK may have numbered several hundred thousand at its height during Reconstruction.

In 1871, the federal government took a series of steps to counter the KKK and its violence. Congress organized a joint select committee made up of seven senators and fourteen representatives to look into the Klan and its activities. It then passed the Civil Rights Act of 1871, frequently referred to as the KU KLUX KLAN ACT, which made night riding a crime and gave the president the power to suspend HABEAS CORPUS and order the use of federal troops in order to put down conspirators by force. The law also provided criminal and civil penalties for people convicted of private conspiracies—such as those perpetrated by the KKK—intended to deny others their civil rights.

Also in 1871, President ULYSSES S. GRANT relocated troops from the Indian wars on the western plains to South Carolina, in order to put down Klan violence. In October and November of that year, the federal Circuit Court for the District of South Carolina held a series of trials of KKK members suspected of having engaged in criminal conspiracies, but the trials resulted in few convictions.

The Klan declined in influence as the 1870s wore on. Arrests, combined with the return of southern whites to political dominance in the South, diminished its activity and influence.

Resurgence The KKK experienced a resurgence after World War I, reaching a peak of 3 or 4 million members in the 1920s. David W. Griffith's 1915 movie *The Birth of a Nation*, based on Thomas Dixon's 1905 novel *The Clansman*, served as the spark for this revival. The movie depicted the Klan as a heroic force defending the "Aryan birthright" of white southerners against African Americans and Radical Republicans seeking to build a Black Empire in the South. In particular, the movie showed a gallant Klan defending the honor of white women threatened by lecherous African American men.

William J. Simmons renewed the KKK at a Stone Mountain, Georgia, ceremony in 1915. Later, Christian fundamentalist ministers aided recruitment as the Klan portrayed itself as the protector of traditional values during the Jazz Age.

Hugo L. Black and the KKK

Hugo L. Black is remembered as a distinguished U.S. Supreme Court justice, a progressive U.S. Senator, and an able trial attorney. Black also was a member of the Ku Klux Klan (KKK) in the 1920s. Public disclosure of this fact came shortly after his appointment to the Supreme Court was confirmed by the Senate in 1937. The resulting public uproar would probably have doomed his Court appointment if the disclosure had come just a few weeks earlier.

In 1923 Black was a trial attorney in Birmingham, Alabama, which at the time was controlled by members of the Klan. After rebuffing membership several times, he joined the KKK on September 23, 1923. Black later claimed to have left the group after several years, but no clear evidence documented his departure. In 1937 there were allegations he had signed an undated letter resigning from the Klan, which was to have been used to establish a false resignation date if public scandal occurred.

In 1937 Black made a radio address to the nation, in which he admitted his Klan membership but claimed he had resigned and had not had any connection with the group for many years. He also stated he harbored no prejudice against anyone because of their race, religion, or ethnicity.

During his Court career, Black was reluctant to discuss his KKK membership and offered various reasons for why he had joined. To some people he admitted it was a mistake, whereas to others he said the KKK was just another fraternal organization, like the Masons or Elks. It is clear, however, that as an ambitious politician, Black had sought Klan support for his political campaigns. In the 1920s KKK support had been critical to a Democratic politician in Alabama.

Despite his later denial of holding any prejudices, Black was an active member of the KKK for several years. He participated in Klan events throughout Alabama, wearing the organization's characteristic white robes and hood, and initiated new Klan members into the Invisible Empire, reading the Klan oath, which pledged the members to "most zealously and valiantly shield and preserve by any and all justifiable means . . . white supremacy."

See also Black, Hugo Lafayette.

As its membership grew into the millions in the 1920s, the Klan exerted considerable political influence, helping to elect sympathetic candidates to state and national offices. The group was strong not only in southern states such as Georgia, Alabama, Louisiana, and Texas, but also in Oklahoma, California, Oregon, Colorado, Kansas, Missouri, Illinois, Indiana, Ohio, Pennsylvania, New Jersey, and New York. Strongly opposed to non–Anglo-Saxon immigration, the Klan helped secure the passage of strict quotas on IMMIGRATION. In addition to being racist, the group also espoused hatred of Jews, Catholics, socialists, and unions.

By the end of the 1920s, a backlash against the KKK had developed. Reports of its violence turned public sentiment against the group, and its membership declined to about forty thousand. At the same time, Louisiana, Michigan, and Oklahoma passed anti-mask laws intended to frustrate Klan activity. Most of these laws made it a MISDEMEANOR to wear a mask that concealed the identity of the wearer, excluding masks worn for holiday costumes or other legitimate uses. South Carolina, Virginia, and Georgia later passed similar laws.

Anti–Civil Rights Involvement The KKK experienced another, less successful resurgence during the 1960s as African Americans won civil rights gains in the South. Opposed to the CIVIL RIGHTS MOVEMENT and its attempt to end racial segregation and discrimination, the Klan capitalized on the fears of whites, to grow to a membership of about twenty thousand. It portrayed the CIVIL RIGHTS MOVEMENT as a Communist, Jewish conspiracy, and it engaged in terrorist acts designed to frustrate and intimidate the movement's members. KKK adherents were responsible for acts such as the 1963 bombing of the Sixteenth Street Baptist Church in Birmingham, Alabama, in which four young black girls were killed and many others injured, and the 1964 murder of civil rights workers Michael Schwerner, Andrew Goodman, and James Chaney, in Mississippi. The Klan was also responsible for many other beatings, murders, and bombings, including attacks on the Freedom Riders, who sought to integrate interstate buses.

In many instances, the FEDERAL BUREAU OF INVESTIGATION (FBI), then under the control of J. EDGAR HOOVER, had intelligence that would have led to the prevention of Klan violence or conviction of its perpetrators. However, the FBI did little to oppose the Klan during the height of the civil rights movement.

By the 1980s and 1990s, the Klan had shrunk to under ten thousand members and had splintered into several organizations. However, it increasingly cooperated with a proliferating number of other white supremacist groups, including the Order and Aryan Nations. Like these groups, the KKK put new emphasis on whites as an "oppressed majority" victimized by AFFIRMATIVE ACTION and other civil rights measures.

The Klan's campaign of hatred has spurred opposition from many fronts, including Klanwatch, an organization started by lawyer and civil rights activist Morris Dees in 1980. The group is affiliated with Dees's Southern Poverty Law Center, in Montgomery, Alabama. In 1987, Dees won a $7 million civil suit against the Alabama-based United Klans of America for the 1981 murder of a nineteen-year-old man. The suit drove that Klan organization into bankruptcy.

The KKK suffered another setback in 1990, when the Georgia Supreme Court upheld the constitutionality of that state's Anti-Mask Act (Ga. Code Ann. § 16-11-38) by a vote of 6–1 (*State v. Miller*, 260 Ga. 669, 398 S.E.2d 547). The case involved a Klan member who had been arrested for wearing full Klan regalia, including mask, in public and had claimed a FIRST AMENDMENT right to wear such clothing. The court ruled that the law, first passed in 1951, protected a state interest in safeguarding the right of the people to exercise their civil rights and to be free from violence and intimidation. It held that the law did not interfere with the defendant's FREEDOM OF SPEECH.

See also JIM CROW LAWS.

KU KLUX KLAN ACT The Ku Klux Klan Act of 1871 (ch. 22, 17 Stat. 13 [codified as amended at 18 U.S.C.A. § 241, 42 U.S.C.A. §§ 1983, 1985(3), and 1988]), also called the Civil Rights Act of 1871 or the Force Act of 1871, was one of several important CIVIL RIGHTS acts passed by Congress during Reconstruction, the period following the Civil War when the victorious northern states attempted to create a new political order in the South. The act was intended to protect African Americans from violence perpetrated by the KU KLUX KLAN (KKK), a white supremacist group.

In March 1871, President ULYSSES S. GRANT requested from Congress legislation that would address the problem of KKK violence, which

had grown steadily since the group's formation in 1866. Congress responded on April 20, 1871, with the passage of the Ku Klux Klan Act, originally introduced as a bill "to enforce the provisions of the Fourteenth Amendment and for other purposes." Section 1 of the act covered enforcement of the FOURTEENTH AMENDMENT and was later codified, in part, at 42 U.S.C.A. § 1983. Section 2 of the act, codified at 42 U.S.C.A. § 1985(3), provided civil and criminal penalties intended to deal with conspiratorial violence of the kind practiced by the Klan. Both sections of the act were intended to give federal protection to Fourteenth Amendment rights that were regularly being violated by private individuals as opposed to the state.

In addition, the Ku Klux Klan Act gave the president power to suspend the writ of HABEAS CORPUS in order to fight the KKK. President Grant used this power only once, in October 1871, in ten South Carolina counties experiencing high levels of Klan terrorism. The act also banned KKK and other CONSPIRACY members from serving on juries.

The Republicans who framed the Ku Klux Klan Act intended it to provide a federal remedy for private conspiracies of the sort practiced by the KKK against African Americans and others. As had become all too apparent by 1871, local and state courts were ineffective in prosecuting Klan violence. Local and state law enforcement officials, including judges, were often sympathetic to the KKK or were subject to intimidation by the group, as were trial witnesses. The Ku Klux Klan Act would allow victims of Klan violence to take their case to a federal court, where, it was supposed, they would receive a fairer trial.

The act, like other civil rights laws from the Reconstruction era, sparked considerable legal debate. Its detractors claimed that the law improperly expanded federal JURISDICTION to areas of CRIMINAL LAW better left to the states. The Supreme Court took this view in 1883 when it struck down the criminal provisions of the act's second section on the ground that protecting individuals from private conspiracies was a state and not federal function (*United States v. Harris*, 106 U.S. 629, 1 S. Ct. 601, 27 L. Ed. 290). This and other rulings stripped the Ku Klux Klan Act of much of its power. Like many other civil rights laws from its era, it went largely unenforced in succeeding decades.

The remaining civil provisions of the act were later codified under 42 U.S.C.A. § 1985(3), where they have been referred to as the conspiracy statute. These provisions hold, in part, that when two or more persons "conspire or go in disguise on the highway or the premises of another, for the purpose of depriving . . . any person or class of persons of the equal protection of the law," they may be sued by the injured parties. The civil provisions, or § 1985(3), remained generally unused until the 1971 U.S. Supreme Court decision *Griffin v. Breckenridge*, 403 U.S. 88, 91 S. Ct. 1790, 29 L. Ed. 2d 338. In *Griffin*, the Court reaffirmed the original intention of § 1985(3) and ruled that the statute may allow a civil remedy for certain private conspiracies. The *Griffin* case concerned a 1966 incident in Mississippi in which a group of white men stopped a car out of suspicion that one of its three African American occupants was a civil rights worker. The whites proceeded to beat and threaten the African Americans. The Court upheld one victim's claim that, under § 1985(3), the whites had engaged in a conspiracy to deny him the EQUAL PROTECTION of the laws of the United States and Mississippi.

In making its decision, the Court was careful to restrict § 1985 claims to those involving actions motivated by "some racial, or perhaps otherwise class-based, invidiously discriminatory animus." This standard meant that the conspirators in question had to be motivated against a class of persons, not a particular political or social issue. By creating this standard, the Court sought to prevent § 1985(3) from becoming a "general federal tort law" that would cover every type of private conspiracy.

Since *Griffin*, the Court has expressed misgivings about expanding the types of classes protected by the statute. Using the *Griffin* standard, the Court later ruled in *United Brotherhood of Carpenters & Joiners v. Scott*, 463 U.S. 825, 103 S. Ct. 3352, 77 L. Ed. 2d 1049 (1983), that economic or commercial groups could not be considered a class protected by the law. In that case, the Court rejected a claim by nonunion workers who had been attacked by union workers at job sites.

During the 1980s and 1990s, lower FEDERAL COURTS upheld the use of § 1985(3) against antiabortion protesters who blockaded family planning clinics with large demonstrations and disruptions. In one ruling, a federal district court held that an antiabortion group had conspired to violate the right to interstate travel of women seeking to visit family planning clinics (*NOW v. Operation Rescue*, 726 F. Supp. 1483 [E.D. Va. 1989]).

However, in a 1993 case, *Bray v. Alexandria Women's Health Clinic*, 506 U.S. 263, 113 S. Ct. 753, 122 L. Ed. 2d 34, the Supreme Court ruled that § 1985(3) could not be used against antiabortion protesters. The Court held that women seeking abortion cannot be considered a class under the terms of the law.

CROSS-REFERENCES

Civil Rights Acts; *Civil Rights* Cases; Civil Rights Movement; Jim Crow Laws.

BIOGRAPHY

APWIDE WORLD PHOTOS

William Moses Kunstler

KUNSTLER, WILLIAM MOSES

William Moses Kunstler rose to prominence during the CIVIL RIGHTS MOVEMENT in the 1960s. He represented Freedom Riders, MARTIN LUTHER KING, JR., and the CHICAGO EIGHT. Politics and the law are inseparable in his philosophy. He was the author of twelve books, a sometime Hollywood actor, and a cofounder of the CENTER FOR CONSTITUTIONAL RIGHTS (CCR) in Tennessee.

Even as a child, Kunstler liked trouble. He was born July 7, 1919, in New York City, the eldest of three children of Frances Mandelbaum and Monroe B. Kunstler, a physician. Ignoring schoolwork to run with a street gang called the Red Devils, he worried his conservative Jewish family. He read voraciously on his own, and by high school became a straight A student. At Yale, he majored in French and wrote his senior thesis on the satirist Molière. Then he joined the Army and served in World War II as a cryptographer, taking part in General Douglas MacArthur's invasion of the Philippines, earning the Iron Cross, and rising to the rank of major. Afterward, he entered Columbia Law School, mainly to compete with his younger brother, Michael Kunstler.

Kunstler and his brother opened a law practice in 1949. The mundane work bored Kunstler, who wanted more challenge than handling annul-

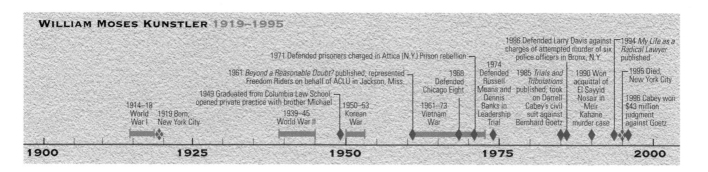

WILLIAM MOSES KUNSTLER 1919–1995

- 1914–18 World War I
- 1919 Born; New York City
- 1939–45 World War II
- 1949 Graduated from Columbia Law School; opened private practice with brother Michael
- 1950–53 Korean War
- 1961 *Beyond a Reasonable Doubt?* published; represented Freedom Riders on behalf of ACLU in Jackson, Miss.
- 1961–73 Vietnam War
- 1968 Defended Chicago Eight
- 1971 Defended prisoners charged in Attica (N.Y.) Prison rebellion
- 1974 Defended Russell Means and Dennis Banks in Leadership Trial
- 1985 *Trials and Tribulations* published; took on Darrell Cabey's civil suit against Bernhard Goetz
- 1986 Defended Larry Davis against charges of attempted murder of six police officers in Bronx, N.Y.
- 1990 Won acquittal of El Sayyid Nosair in Meir Kahane murder case
- 1994 *My Life as a Radical Lawyer* published
- 1995 Died, New York City
- 1996 Cabey won $43 million judgment against Goetz

1900   1925   1950   1975   2000

ments and divorces. He kept busy writing a book on corporate tax law, contributing to the *New York Times Book Review*, teaching at New York Law School, and hosting radio shows whose eclectic guest lists covered personalities ranging from ELEANOR ROOSEVELT to MALCOLM X.

In the mid-1950s, Kunstler successfully represented a local leader of the NATIONAL ASSOCIATION FOR THE ADVANCEMENT OF COLORED PEOPLE who had been denied housing because he was black. In 1956 a black journalist had his PASSPORT confiscated for violating a national ban on travel to China; he was later arrested on return from Cuba for entering the United States without a passport—in violation of an old federal statute. Kunstler persuaded an appellate court to find the statute unconstitutional. The case had been referred to him by the AMERICAN CIVIL LIBERTIES UNION (ACLU), and a bigger assignment would soon be on the way. Meanwhile, he wrote *Beyond a Reasonable Doubt?* (1961) about the 1960 conviction and execution of CARYL CHESSMAN, a case that had provoked international outrage.

In 1961 the ACLU sent Kunstler to Jackson, Mississippi, where civil rights workers were being abused by southern police officers and the courts. Known as the Freedom Riders, these young white and black people tried to force integration by riding interstate buses, flouting segregation laws. Beatings awaited them, followed by arrests and quick convictions for disturbing the peace. Kunstler found only hostility in courtrooms throughout the state. He lost case after case. He asked Mississippi governor Ross Barnett for help, but Barnett only lectured him on the need for segregation. Then Kunstler and a fellow attorney, William Higgs, devised an ingenious strategy: discovering an 1866 law designed to protect ex-slaves, they used it to have the cases of civil rights workers removed from state courts and heard by federal judges. The law also mandated that FEDERAL COURTS grant the defendants BAIL, something Mississippi refused to do.

The civil rights movement lived, prospered, and changed Kunstler's life. He helped found the Center for Constitutional Rights in Nashville, and with its resources, he was so ubiquitous in representing the new leadership that his motto became Have Brief, Will Travel. He defended STOKELY CARMICHAEL, president of the STUDENT NON-VIOLENT COORDINATING COMMITTEE, against sedition charges. He represented leaders of the Black Panthers. But it was his involvement with another prominent black radical, Hubert Geroid Brown—better known as H. Rap Brown—that led him to a new crossroads. Brown's heated speeches around the country struck fear into Congress, which passed in 1968 the so-called Rap Brown statute (18 U.S.C.A. § 2101). The law made it illegal to cross state lines with the intention of inciting a riot. Kunstler saw it as an attempt to crush free speech.

The Rap Brown law created Kunstler's breakthrough case, making him a hero to young people and a virtual outlaw to the legal establishment. In this case, he defended the Chicago Eight, a group of antiwar leaders charged with conspiracy after the Chicago police cracked down on protesters outside the 1968 Democratic National Convention. Among the Eight were Abbie Hoffman and Jerry Rubin, Students for a Democratic Society leader Tom Hayden, and BLACK PANTHER PARTY cofounder Bobbie Seale. The trial drew national attention, divided public opinion, and often thrilled with its circus atmosphere. Kunstler argued ferociously in court with Judge Julius J. Hoffman, especially after the judge ordered Seale to be gagged and bound to a chair.

After the jury's near-total acquittal of the defendants, Judge Hoffman slapped each defendant with a contempt-of-court sentence. He reserved the most serious punishment for Kunstler, giving the attorney four years and thirteen days in prison for twenty-four counts of CONTEMPT. However, this sentence and the sentences of the defendants were all overturned by an appellate court. Kunstler also managed to escape the wrath of the New York bar association, which ultimately dropped its bid to discipline him.

The era of protest that helped create Kunstler's politics came to a close in the early 1970s, but not without a last great upheaval. In 1972 and 1973, leaders of the American Indian Movement (AIM) occupied the historic town of Wounded Knee, South Dakota, in protest of the U.S. government's long practice of ignoring treaties and its hostility toward Native Americans. Kunstler was at the barricades during the seventy-one-day siege, and later he was in court to defend AIM leader Russell Means. He also represented Native American activist Leonard Peltier through fifteen years of litigation.

In the 1980s and 1990s, he represented reputed Mafia bosses, an accused murderer of police officers, one of the so-called Central Park rapists, a youth shot by vigilante Bernhard Goetz, a convicted Atlanta child murderer, and more. He became involved in the cases of defendants accused of plotting to blow up the World Trade Center in New York, as well as the case of Colin Ferguson, a Jamaican immigrant accused of killing six white commuters and wounding nineteen on the Long Island Rail-

"GOVERNMENT-CREATED CRIME HAS BECOME AN ALL TOO FAMILIAR PHENOMENON OF THE PAST DECADE OR SO."

road in 1993. Kunstler's proposed "black rage" defense of Ferguson—in short, that racism could drive a person to murder—provoked a fierce backlash from many critics, including Kunstler's frequent nemesis the attorney ALAN M. DERSHOWITZ.

At the age of seventy-six, Kunstler still reportedly worked fourteen-hour days in his home. Assisted by his partner, attorney Ron Kuby, he took most of his cases for free. He also did a bit of acting, appearing as a fire-breathing judge in director Spike Lee's 1992 film *Malcolm X*. In 1994 he published his twelfth book, *My Life as a Radical Lawyer*, in which he held to his belief that a revolution is still inevitable.

Kunstler died on September 4, 1995, at the age of seventy-six, of heart failure. Ron Kuby, his longtime law partner, vowed to continue doing free legal work in their firm, Kunstler & Kuby, and he established The William Moses Kunstler Fund for Radical Justice as a memorial.

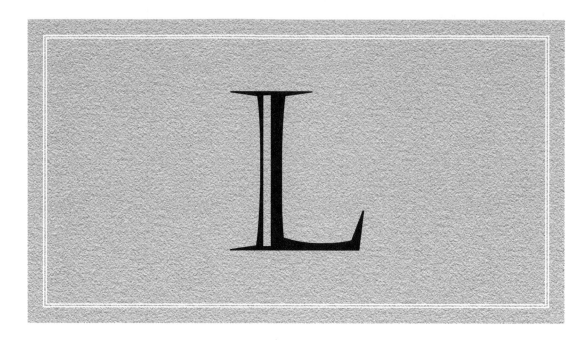

LABOR DEPARTMENT The Department of Labor (DOL) administers federal labor laws for the EXECUTIVE BRANCH of the federal government. Its mission is "to foster, promote, and develop the welfare of the wage earners of the United States, to improve their working conditions, and to advance their opportunities for profitable employment" (29 U.S.C.A. § 551 [1985]). The DOL was created in 1913 out of four bureaus from the Department of Commerce and Labor: the Bureau of Labor Statistics, Bureau of Immigration, Bureau of Naturalization, and Children's Bureau.

The DOL is headed by the secretary of labor, who serves in the president's CABINET. The department's numerous responsibilities include administering and enforcing federal labor laws guaranteeing workers' rights to safe and healthful working conditions, a minimum hourly wage and overtime pay, freedom from employment discrimination, unemployment insurance, and WORKERS' COMPENSATION. The department protects workers' PENSION rights, provides for job training programs, helps workers find jobs, and works to strengthen the COLLECTIVE BARGAINING process. It keeps track of changes in employment, prices, and other economic measurements. The DOL also makes special efforts to address the unique job market problems of minorities, women, children, the elderly, disabled persons, and so on.

Seven major agencies operate within the DOL: the Employment and Training Administration, Pension and Welfare Benefits Administration, Employment Standards Administration, Occupational Safety and Health Administration, Mine Safety and Health Administration,

Bureau of Labor Statistics, and Veterans' Employment and Training Service. Other organizations, including the Women's Bureau, Office of the American Workplace, and Bureau of International Labor Affairs, also function within the department.

Employment and Training Administration The Employment and Training Administration (ETA) administers five major programs that relate to employment services, job training, and unemployment insurance. The ETA also administers a federal-state employment security system, funds and oversees programs to provide work experience and training for groups having difficulty entering or returning to the workforce, and formulates and promotes apprenticeship standards and programs.

The Federal Unemployment Insurance Service (FUIS) oversees the Federal-State Unemployment Compensation Program under provisions of the SOCIAL SECURITY ACT OF 1935 (42 U.S.C.A. § 1305). This program provides income support for unemployed workers. Because unemployment benefits are payable under laws of individual states, the FUIS is primarily an oversight organization providing leadership and policy guidance to the states.

The U.S. Employment Service, under the provisions of the Wagner-Peyser Act (29 U.S.C.A. § 49 et seq.) helps states establish and maintain a system of local public employment offices. The state public employment service is responsible for providing unemployed individuals and other job seekers with job placement, and other employment services.

The Bureau of Apprenticeship and Training formulates and promotes labor standards necessary to safeguard the welfare of APPRENTICES. The Office of Job Training Programs develops and issues federal procedures pertaining to programs targeted at young people and adults who face serious barriers in obtaining employment.

Pension and Welfare Benefits Administration The Pension and Welfare Benefits Administration (PWBA) helps protect the economic future and retirement security of workers, as required under the EMPLOYEE RETIREMENT INCOME SECURITY ACT of 1974 (ERISA) (29 U.S.C.A. § 1001). There are nearly 1 million pension plans and 4.5 million health and welfare plans in the United States. ERISA requires administrators of private pension and welfare plans to provide plan participants with easily understandable summaries of their plans. These summaries are filed with the PWBA, along with annual reports on the financial operations of the plans and on the bonding of persons charged with handling plan funds and assets. Plan administrators must also meet strict FIDUCIARY responsibility standards, which are enforced by the PWBA.

Employment Standards Administration The Employment Standards Administration administers MINIMUM WAGE and overtime standards through its Wage and Hour Division.

This division seeks to protect low-wage incomes as provided by the minimum wage provisions of the FAIR LABOR STANDARDS ACT (29 U.S.C.A. § 201), and to discourage excessively long hours of work through the enforcement of the overtime provisions of the act. The division also determines the prevailing wage rates for federal construction contracts and federally assisted programs for construction, alteration, and repair of public works subject to the DAVIS-BACON ACT (40 U.S.C.A. § 276a) and related acts.

Occupational Safety and Health Administration The Occupational Safety and Health Administration (OSHA) has responsibility for occupational safety and health activities. OSHA was established by the OCCUPATIONAL SAFETY AND HEALTH ACT OF 1970 (29 U.S.C.A. § 651 et seq.). It develops and issues occupational safety and health standards for various industries and occupations. OSHA also formulates and publishes regulations that employers are to follow in maintaining health and safety. It conducts investigations and inspections to determine compliance with these standards and regulations, and if it finds noncompliance, it may issue citations and propose penalties.

Labor Department

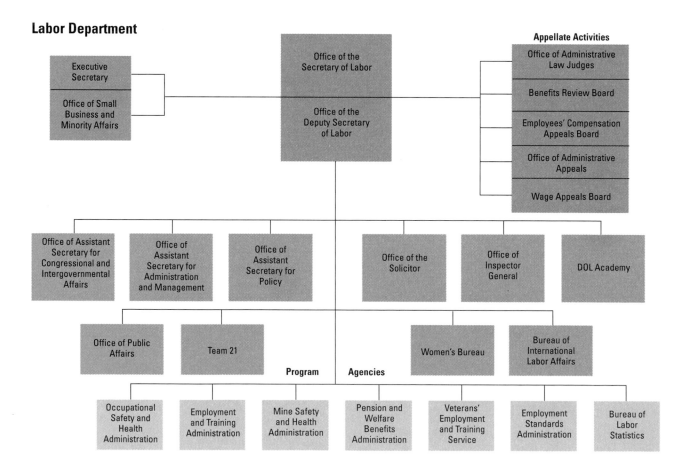

Mine Safety and Health Administration The Mine Safety and Health Administration (MSHA) is responsible for safety and health in coal and other mines in the United States. The Federal Coal Mine Health and Safety Act of 1969 (30 U.S.C.A. § 801 et seq.) gave the MSHA strong enforcement provisions to protect coal miners, and in 1977 the act was amended to protect persons working in the noncoal areas of the mining industry, such as silver mining.

The MSHA develops and promulgates mandatory safety and health standards for the mining industry, inspects mines to ensure compliance, investigates mining accidents, and assesses fines for violations of its regulations. It helps the states develop effective state mine safety and health programs. The MSHA also conducts research on mine safety, in the hope of preventing and reducing mine accidents and occupational diseases.

Bureau of Labor Statistics The Bureau of Labor Statistics is the principal data gathering agency of the federal government in the broad field of labor economics. It has no enforcement or regulatory functions. The bureau collects, processes, analyzes, and disseminates data relating to employment, unemployment, and other characteristics of the labor force. It also analyzes prices and consumer expenditures, economic growth and employment projections, and occupational health and safety. Most of the data are collected by the bureau, the Bureau of the Census, or state agencies.

The basic data are issued in monthly, quarterly, and annual news releases, bulletins, reports, and special publications. Data are also provided electronically, including on the INTERNET.

Veterans' Employment and Training Service The Veterans' Employment and Training Service directs the DOL's veterans' employment and training programs through a nationwide network of support staff. The service's field staff work closely with state employment security agencies to ensure that veterans are provided the priority service required by law. The service provides public information and designs outreach activities that seek to encourage employers to hire veterans. It also administers programs designed to meet the employment and training needs of veterans with service-connected disabilities, Vietnam-era veterans, and veterans recently separated from military service.

Other Agencies The Women's Bureau formulates standards and policies that promote the welfare of wage earning women, improve their working conditions, increase their efficiency, and advance their opportunities for profitable employment.

The Office of the American Workplace was created in 1993 to enhance employer-employee relations and collective bargaining, as well as to ensure that labor unions are run democratically. It works to establish labor-management networks that disseminate information concerning cooperative labor-management relations and high-performance workplace practices. It conducts investigative audits to uncover and remedy criminal and civil violations of federal law. Its Office of Labor-Management Standards conducts criminal and civil investigations to safeguard the financial integrity of unions and to ensure union democracy.

The Bureau of International Labor Affairs carries out the DOL's international responsibilities. It works with other government agencies to formulate international economic, trade, and immigration policies affecting U.S. workers. The bureau represents the United States on delegations to multilateral and bilateral trade negotiations, and in international bodies such as the GENERAL AGREEMENT ON TARIFFS AND TRADE, International Labor Organization, Organization for Economic Cooperation and Development, and other U.N. organizations. It also helps administer the U.S. labor attaché program at embassies abroad and carries out technical assistance projects in other countries.

CROSS-REFERENCES

Employment Law; Labor Law; Labor Union; Mine and Mineral Law.

LABOR LAW 📖 An area of the law that deals with the rights of employers, employees, and labor organizations. 📖

U.S. labor law covers all facets of the legal relationship between employers, employees, and employee LABOR UNIONS. Employers' opposition to recognizing employees' rights to organize and bargain collectively with management has resulted in a system of primarily federal laws and regulations that is adversarial in nature. Modern labor law dates from the passage of the WAGNER ACT of 1935, also known as the National Labor Relations Act (NLRA) (29 U.S.C.A. § 151 et seq.). Congress has passed two major revisions of this act: the TAFT-HARTLEY ACT of 1947, also known as the Labor Management Relations Act (29 U.S.C.A. § 141 et seq.), and the LANDRUM-GRIFFIN ACT of 1959, also known as the Labor Management Reporting and Disclosure Act (29 U.S.C.A. § 401 et seq.).

The railroad and airline industries are governed by the Federal Railway Labor Act (45 U.S.C.A. § 151 et seq.), originally passed in 1926 and substantially amended in 1934. Federal employees are covered by the separate Federal Service Labor Management and Employee Relation Act (5 U.S.C.A. § 7101 et seq. [1978]). Labor law is also made by the National Labor Relations Board (NLRB), an ADMINISTRATIVE AGENCY that enforces federal labor statutes, and by FEDERAL COURTS when they interpret labor legislation and NLRB decisions. In addition, state and municipal employees are covered by state law.

A basic principle of U.S. labor law is that the SUPREMACY CLAUSE of the Constitution authorizes Congress to prohibit states from using their powers to regulate labor relations. The ability of Congress to preempt state labor laws has been defined largely by the U.S. Supreme Court because the NLRA is imprecise about what states can and cannot do. The Court has set out two basic principles concerning preemption: not all state labor laws are preempted by federal statute, and conduct actually protected by the federal statutes is immune from state regulation. For example, vandalism committed by a union organizing campaign may be subject to state criminal and civil sanctions. A STRIKE in an industry subject to the NLRA that is aimed at improving wages cannot be prohibited by the state.

Historical Background Labor law traces its roots to the early 1800s, when employees who banded together to strike for improved working conditions were branded as criminals. By the mid–nineteenth century, the law changed to recognize the right of workers to organize and conduct COLLECTIVE BARGAINING with their employers. Employers, however, were not receptive to unions. Between 1842 and 1932, they routinely used INJUNCTIONS to stop strikes and to frustrate union organizing. The NORRIS-LaGUARDIA ACT (29 U.S.C.A. § 101 et seq.) was passed by Congress in 1932 to curb the use of labor injunctions, preventing employers from going through the federal courts to quash unions. The passage of the Wagner Act three years later signaled the beginning of a new era in labor relations and labor law. The legacy of employer-union conflict shaped the new system of government regulation of labor-management relations.

Modern Labor Law The NLRA is the most important and widely applicable U.S. labor law. Its section 7 (29 U.S.C.A. § 157) guarantees employees "the right to self-

Picketing is a legitimate way of either interfering in the business of an employer or influencing the public against patronizing an employer.

organization, to form, join, or assist labor organizations, to bargain collectively, through representatives of their own choosing, and to engage in other concerted activities for . . . mutual aid or protection." Employees are also entitled to "refrain from any or all such activities." The act prohibits employers and unions from committing "unfair labor practices" that would violate these rights or certain other specified interests of employers and the general public in various circumstances.

Labor law generally addresses one of three different situations: (1) a union attempts to organize the employees of an employer and to get the employer to recognize it as the employees' bargaining representative; (2) a union seeks to negotiate a collective bargaining agreement with an employer; or (3) a union and employer disagree on the interpretation and application of an existing contract between the two. Within these three situations, specific rules have been created to deal with rights of employees and employers.

Organization and Representation of Employees   Under the NLRA neither employers nor unions may physically coerce employees or discriminate against them on the job because they do or do not wish to join a union, engage in a peaceful strike or work stoppage, or exercise other organizational rights. Although an employer is forbidden to discharge peaceful strikers, the employer may hire replacement workers to carry on business.

When the employees of a particular company decide to be represented by a union, they usually contact the union's parent association or local division for aid and guidance. The union may solicit membership by holding meetings to discuss how working conditions can be improved, and by distributing leaflets.

The employees, union, or employer, may file with the NLRB a petition to conduct an election to decide whether the union should be the collective bargaining representative. This petition must meet with the support of at least 30 percent of the employees in the bargaining unit named in the petition. Once the petition has been filed, the NLRB must determine whether any obstacles exist to holding the election. If not, the NLRB will attempt to get the union and employer to agree to an election.

If the union and employer agree to an election, the NLRB conducts a secret ballot election to determine whether the majority of the employees in the bargaining unit desire to be represented by the union. During the election campaign, both employer and union may freely express their views about unionization of employees, but neither may resort to threats or bribes. If the union wins the election, the NLRB will certify it as the exclusive bargaining representative of the employees. The union may then be designated an appropriate bargaining unit of a particular category of workers.

A union is generally entitled to picket or patrol with signs reading "Unfair," for up to thirty days at the place of business of an employer it is trying to organize. To picket longer for organizing purposes, the union must file for an NLRB election. If the union then loses the election, it is forbidden to resume such PICKETING for a year. The U.S. Supreme Court upheld the right to peaceful union picketing in *Thornhill v. Alabama*, 310 U.S. 88, 60 S. Ct. 736, 84 L. Ed. 1093 (1940).

Negotiation of a Collective Bargaining Agreement   Collective bargaining is the process in which an employer and an accredited employee representative negotiate an agreement concerning wages, hours, and other terms and conditions of employment. An employer and a union representing its employees have a mutual obligation under the NLRA to bargain with each other in good faith. The primary goal of collective bargaining is to promote industrial peace between employers and employees. The parties have a duty to try reasonably to accommodate differences and reach common ground, but ultimately they have no obligation to enter into a contract.

The FEDERAL MEDIATION AND CONCILIATION SERVICE or state labor agencies may provide parties with mediators to help them negotiate. Mediators act as neutral facilitators. It is a fundamental part of federal labor policy that unions and management should resolve their disputes through voluntary collective bargaining and not through the imposition of a solution by the government. If a labor dispute becomes serious enough to significantly affect national health or safety, the president has the statutory authority to obtain an eighty-day injunction from the federal courts against any strike or LOCKOUT. This procedure has been used over three dozen times since 1947, but rarely since the 1970s.

Pressure to Resolve a Contract Dispute   When an employer and a union are unable to resolve their differences and negotiate an employment contract, the parties may use different types of pressure to produce an agreement. These types of pressure include boycotts, strikes, the carrying of signs and banners, picketing, and lockouts.

A labor BOYCOTT is any type of union action that seeks to reduce or stop public patronage of a business. It is a refusal to purchase from or to handle the products of a particular employer. Employees may legally exert economic pressure on their employer through a boycott, so long as they act peacefully. But a union is forbidden to engage in a secondary boycott. For example, if a union's primary dispute is with a hardware manufacturer, it may not picket or use other methods to get the employees of a hardware store, who are neutral or secondary parties, to stage a strike at the store in order to force it to cease handling the manufacturer's products.

A strike is a concerted refusal of employees to perform work that they have been assigned, in order to force the employer to grant concessions that the employees have demanded. The right of employees to strike is protected by the courts. A lawful strike must be conducted in an

REINVENTING THE WORKPLACE: IMPROVING QUALITY, OR CREATING COMPANY (SHAM) UNIONS?

Foreign competition, technological change, and concerns about declining productivity have led to significant modifications in the way many U.S. businesses manage their affairs. These changes, which have been championed by a long list of management consultants, have appeared under numerous labels, including *quality circles* and *total quality management (TQM)*. All of these approaches emphasize that the goal of a business is to achieve a high standard of quality in goods manufactured or services provided. To meet this quality goal, businesses have moved away from top-down management, substituting a team approach. Traditional management personnel and line-level workers meet in committees to discuss and resolve issues within the company concerning product, service, and the way work is organized.

The advocates of teamwork and quality circles have hit a legal brick wall in the National Labor Relations Act of 1935 (NLRA) (29 U.S.C.A. § 151 et seq.). Under the NLRA, sections 2(5)

and 8(A)(2), employers are forbidden to create employer-dominated company unions. In *Electromation*, 309 N.L.R.B. 990 (1992), the National Labor Relations Board (NLRB) ruled that Electromation, a nonunion company, could not sponsor an "action committee" because that committee was, under the NLRA provisions, a labor organization. Additional cases have confirmed the NLRB's position on this issue.

IN FOCUS

Proponents of quality circles and teamwork argue that the NLRA is an antiquated set of laws, based on a period of U.S. history when businesses used every tool at their disposal to subvert unions and union organization. The adversarial posture of labor and management may have made sense in the past, this argument goes, but it is counterproductive in an economy that must adapt quickly to world market forces. The most radical proposal by critics of the NLRB's position on this issue is to abolish the NLRA altogether.

More moderate proponents argue instead for changes in the NLRA to permit committees, teams, and more of what they call workplace democracy. They point out that with the steady decline of union membership and blue-collar jobs, traditional labor-management relations have become irrelevant. They note that white-collar workers, who now dominate the U.S. economy, are less likely to join a labor union. Therefore, worker morale and job satisfaction are better when employees are included in the decision-making process of a business.

Proponents of quality circles also believe that a better educated workforce is capable of making informed decisions about its relations with employers. They assert that the days of the employer's being an absolute sovereign are over. It is more productive to allow nonunion employees to organize within the company based on committees and circles. These workers are entitled to the same type of participatory democracy found in labor unions.

Most proponents would give employees the chance to make up their own mind about their work environment. If a union successfully wins over enough

orderly manner and may not be used as a shield for violence or crime. Intimidation and coercion in the course of a strike are unlawful.

The peaceful carrying of signs and banners advertising a labor dispute is ordinarily a lawful means to publicize employees' grievances against an employer.

Picketing consists of posting one or more union members at the site of a strike or boycott, in order to interfere with a particular employer's business or to influence the public against patronizing that employer. It can be reasonably regulated. Lawful picketing is peaceful and honest. The use of force, intimidation, or coercion on a picket line is not constitutionally protected activity. In addition, employees are not acting within their rights when they seize any part of the employer's property.

A lockout is an employer's refusal to admit employees to the workplace, in order to gain a concession from them. In *American Ship Building Co. v. NLRB*, 380 U.S. 300, 85 S. Ct. 955, 13

L. Ed. 2d 855 (1965), the U.S. Supreme Court upheld the right of an employer to lock out employees if the intent is to promote the company's bargaining position and not to destroy the collective bargaining process or the union.

Unfair Labor Practices An UNFAIR LABOR PRACTICE is any action or statement by an employer that interferes with, restrains, or coerces employees in their exercise of the right to organize and conduct collective bargaining. Such interference, restraint, or coercion can arise through threats, promises, or offers to employees.

An unfair labor practice can occur during collective bargaining. In *Auciello Iron Works v. NLRB*,__U.S.__, 116 S. Ct. 1754, 135 L. Ed. 2d 64 (1996), the U.S. Supreme Court upheld an NLRB ruling that the employer had committed an unfair labor practice. After the union accepted one of the employer's collective bargaining proposals, the employer disavowed the agreement because of GOOD FAITH doubts about employees to be certified as the legal bargaining agent, that would indicate dissatisfaction with the employer and would be an acceptable outcome. These proponents would object to unions filing complaints with the NLRB over company committees where the employees have rejected union representation in the past. As long as employees want to participate in a company committee or circle, they should be permitted to do so.

Proponents argue that the bar on these types of workplace organizational innovations hurts workers. These innovations give employees more autonomy to plan work schedules, meet deadlines, operate equipment, make repairs, and handle health and safety issues. In the past an employee could suggest a change to management but then had to stand back and observe whether the change took place. In today's workplace an employee wants to implement as well as suggest improvements.

Finally, proponents note that in union-organized companies unions are free to negotiate the participation of employees in teams and quality circles. They suggest that it is unfair to restrict nonunion employees from electing to participate in similar business management ventures.

The U.S. labor movement has resisted vigorously the introduction of employee involvement programs by management in both union and nonunion environments. Labor union leadership views the introduction of employer-sponsored committees as a return to the past and as a way of undercutting the ability of unions to organize white-collar workers.

Opponents point out the sordid history of U.S. labor relations prior to the passage of the NLRA in 1935. Company-sponsored unions were put forward as a way to resolve disputes over wages, hours, and other conditions of employment. Employees believed that these unions acted in good faith to negotiate a contract with management. In reality, these organizations were sham unions, dominated by the employer. The employers would put company spies in them to monitor what was discussed. Employees were either bought off or fired if they proved too effective in their union duties.

Opponents argue that the NRLA is preserving the independence of labor unions. Without its decisions employers of nonunion employees would use *TQM*, *quality circles*, and other buzzwords to promote a nonunion status that would place employees at a disad-

vantage. Employees will quite likely be intimidated in employer-organized groups, and unable to raise or meaningfully discuss certain issues that management does not want to hear. Without a collective bargaining agreement negotiated by a union, opponents maintain, employees will not have job security or promotion protection.

Opponents also question who makes the decisions in these groups. Though the rhetoric suggests empowerment of employees, employee committees are purely advisory, and the employer retains the authority to decide all issues. In addition, because management creates these committees, management can dissolve them at any time. The inequality of power within a nonunion business dictates that the employer can do whatever management wants, regardless of a recommendation by an employee committee.

The NLRA has placed a barrier to new models of business organization. The distrust of labor unions and their difficulty in making inroads with white-collar workers reconfirms to the unions the need for an adversarial posture with management. Those who seek fundamental change in the way U.S. business operates believe that the NLRA must be amended to accommodate a major shift in economic organization.

---

whether the union still commanded a majority of the employees. The Court reasoned that the employer's doubts arose from facts that the employer had known about before its contract offer had been accepted by the union.

Labor laws are not intended to interfere with an employer's normal exercise of discretion in hiring and firing employees. In general, an employer may hire employees based on their individual merit, with no regard to union affiliation. Refusal to hire an applicant owing to affiliation with a labor union is an unfair labor practice.

The motive of an employer in discharging an employee may be a controlling factor in determining whether the discharge is an unfair labor practice. An employer's history of antiunion bias is an extremely important factor in ascertaining the motive for discharge of an employee. An employer may discharge an employee on various grounds without being guilty of an unfair labor practice. Such grounds include misconduct, unlawful activity, disloyalty, and termination of the business operation. In addition, inefficiency, disobedience, or insubordination are proper grounds for dismissal, provided the discharge is not motivated by the employer's reaction to union activity. Firing an employee based on union activity or membership is an unfair labor practice. Furthermore, the filing of unfair labor practice charges or the giving of testimony in a case based on such charges does not warrant dismissal.

In general, an unfair labor practice exists when an employer contributes financial or any other support to a labor organization. An employer must, therefore, remain neutral between competing unions. It is also an unfair labor practice for an employer to dominate or interfere with the formation or administration of any labor organization.

A union commits an unfair labor practice when it causes, or attempts to cause, an employer to hire, discharge, or discriminate against an employee for the purpose of encouraging or discouraging union activity. The same is true when a union restrains or coerces employees in the exercise of their rights to self-organize; to form, join, or assist labor unions; to bargain collectively; or to refrain from any of these activities. The refusal of a labor organization to bargain collectively or to execute a formal document embodying agreement with an employer is another unfair labor practice.

Contract Enforcement and Contract Disputes Almost every COLLECTIVE BARGAINING AGREEMENT in the United States contains a GRIEVANCE PROCEDURE. In the grievance procedure, the union and the employer try to settle any disputes over the meaning or application of the contract by themselves. If the parties fail, they may invoke ARBITRATION, a procedure that typically calls for referring the issue to an impartial third party for a final and binding determination.

Grievance provisions of a collective bargaining agreement govern the procedure to be followed to settle on-the-job disputes. Typical grievance procedures generally consist of at least three steps: (1) an employee and his or her union steward present their complaint orally to the supervisor, who has the power to settle it; (2) in the event that the matter is not settled at that stage, it is reduced to writing, and the union steward and union officers confer with management; (3) if no agreement is reached, the aggrieved employee may submit the matter to arbitration, which will be binding on all parties.

The arbitration of disputes under a collective bargaining agreement is a matter of contract, and the parties to it may delineate the scope of their arbitration clause. Common grievances settled under arbitration clauses include disputes over SENIORITY rights, employee discipline, PENSION or welfare benefits, rates of pay, and hours of work. Ordinarily, the issue of whether a strike or lockout is a breach of an agreement is a proper subject for arbitration.

The vast majority of union-employer contract disputes are resolved in a grievance procedure, and most of the rest are disposed of routinely through arbitration. Occasionally, a party will resist arbitration or will refuse to comply with an arbitrator's award. In such a case section 301 of the Taft-Hartley Act authorizes a suit in federal court to enforce the agreement to arbitrate or the arbitrator's award.

The federal courts have enforced a pro-arbitration policy in labor contracts. If a union strikes over a grievance it could have arbitrated, the employer may secure an injunction against the strike under section 301 of the Taft-Hartley Act, even though ordinarily the Norris-LaGuardia Act prevents the federal courts from enjoining strikes by labor unions.

Regulation of Unions The Landrum-Griffin Act contains provisions that regulate how labor unions conduct their internal affairs. These provisions seek to prevent union corruption and to guarantee to union members that unions will be run democratically. The act provides a bill of rights for union members, requires certain financial disclosures by unions, prescribes procedures for the election of union officers, and provides civil and criminal remedies for financial abuses by union officers.

Changing Labor-Management Relations For most of the history of U.S. labor-management relations, employers and labor unions have seen each other as adversaries. Federal labor law has been shaped by this adversarial relationship, yet shifts in the structure of the U.S. economy have led to more cooperation. In the 1980s unions agreed to givebacks, in which employees agree to reduced wages and benefits in return for job security, particularly in the manufacturing industries. In response, employers have given unions a larger voice in the allocation of jobs and in the work environment itself.

Since the 1980s, innovations in corporate management that advocate teamwork, quality circles, and total quality management (TQM) have led to legal disputes and questions about the continued vitality of the adversarial model of labor-management relations. Under the NLRA, sections 2(5) and 8(A)(2), employers are prohibited from creating employer-dominated company unions. This prohibition was included in the original NLRA because employers had created sham unions that promised representation for workers but in fact toed the company line.

With the beginning of TQM and quality circles in the late 1980s, some employers have attempted to reinvent the workplace by empowering all levels of workers to help make decisions, instead of delegating this task to a set of managers. The creation of quality circles and employee committees has run afoul of the NLRA provision against employer-created unions. In *Electromation*, 309 N.L.R.B. 990 (1992), the board held that the company's "action committee" was a labor organization involved with and dominated by the company, in violation of sections 2(5) and 8(A)(2). Electromation was a nonunion company. In *E. I. du*

Pont de Nemours & Co., 311 N.L.R.B. 893 (1993), the board considered identical issues in a union-organized company. The board ruled that a series of safety and fitness committees created by du Pont were illegal under the NLRA. These cases illustrate the skepticism of some unions about the true intentions of management, and the difficulty in adjusting to change in some areas of labor law.

See also BARGAINING AGENT; EMPLOYMENT LAW.

LABOR-MANAGEMENT RELATIONS ACT

Federal legislation (29 U.S.C.A. § 141 et seq. [1947]), popularly known as the TAFT-HARTLEY ACT, which governs the conduct of designated union activities, such as by proscribing STRIKES and BOYCOTTS, and establishes the framework for the resolution of labor disputes in times of national emergencies.

See also LABOR LAW; LABOR UNION

LABOR UNION

An association, combination, or organization of employees who band together to secure favorable wages, improved working conditions, and better work hours, and to resolve grievances against employers.

The history of labor unions in the United States has much to do with changes in technology and the development of capitalism. Though labor unions can be compared to European merchant and craft guilds of the Middle Ages, they arose with the factory system and industrial revolution of the nineteenth century.

The first efforts to organize employees were met with fierce resistance by employers. The U.S. legal system played a part in this resistance. In *Commonwealth v. Pullis* (Phila. Mayor's Ct. 1806), generally known as the *Philadelphia Cordwainers'* case, boot makers and shoemakers of Philadelphia were indicted as a combination conspiring to raise their wages. The prosecution argued that the COMMON-LAW doctrine of criminal CONSPIRACY applied. The jury agreed that the union was illegal, and the defendants were fined. From this case came the labor conspiracy doctrine, which held that collective as opposed to individual bargaining would interfere with the natural operation of the marketplace, raise wages to artificially high levels, and destroy competition. This early resistance to unions led to an adversarial relationship between unions and employers.

Between 1806 and 1842, the labor conspiracy doctrine was applied in a handful of cases. Then, during the 1840s, U.S. courts began to question the doctrine. The most important case in this regard was *Commonwealth v. Hunt*, 45 Mass. (4 Met.) 11, 38 Am. Dec. 346 (Mass. 1842), in which Chief Justice LEMUEL

SHAW set aside an INDICTMENT of members of the boot makers union for conspiracy. Shaw agreed with employers that competition was vital to the economy, but concluded that unions were one way of stimulating competition. As long as the methods used by unions were legal, unions were free to seek concessions from employers. By the end of the nineteenth century, courts generally held that STRIKES for higher wages or shorter workdays were legal.

Despite the decline of the labor conspiracy theory, unions faced other legal challenges to their existence. The labor INJUNCTION and prosecution under ANTITRUST LAWS became powerful weapons for employers involved in labor disputes. In an 1896 case, *Vegelahn v. Guntner*, 167 Mass. 92, 44 N.E. 1077, the highest court in Massachusetts upheld an injunction forbidding peaceful PICKETING outside the employer's premises.

The first national labor federation to remain active for more than a few years was the Noble Order of the Knights of Labor. It was established in 1869 and had set as goals the eight-hour workday, equal pay for equal work, and the abolition of child labor. The Knights of Labor grew to 700,000 members by 1886, but went into decline that year with a series of failed strikes. By 1900 it had disappeared.

Labor unions nevertheless gained strength in 1886 with the formation of the American Federation of Labor (AFL). Composed of twenty-five national TRADE UNIONS and numbering over 316,000 members, the AFL was a loose confederation of autonomous unions, each with exclusive rights to deal with the workers and employers in its own field. The AFL concentrated on pursuing achievable goals such as higher wages and shorter hours, renouncing identification with any political party or movement. Members were encouraged to support politicians who were friendly to labor, whatever their party affiliation.

Following the passage of the SHERMAN ANTI-TRUST ACT in 1890 (15 U.S.C.A. § 1 et seq.), prohibiting combinations in restraint of interstate trade, courts used its provisions to punish and ENJOIN labor practices considered wrongful. In the *Danbury Hatters* case (*Loewe v. Lawlor*, 208 U.S. 274, 28 S. Ct. 301, 52 L. Ed. 488 [1908]), the U.S. Supreme Court upheld the application of the act to an appeal in a labor publication for a general BOYCOTT of named nonunion employers. In 1911, in *Gompers v. Buck's Stove & Range Co.*, 221 U.S. 418, 31 S. Ct. 492, 55 L. Ed. 797, the Supreme Court upheld an injunction against a union that had placed the name of the employer on the AFL "We Don't Patronize" list, which was a call for a boycott of the employer.

Opposition to labor unions was particularly intense during the late nineteenth century. Several unsuccessful strikes in the 1890s demonstrated the power of companies to crush unions. In 1892 steelworkers struck against the Carnegie Steel Company's Homestead, Pennsylvania, plant. The company hired private guards to protect the plant, but violence broke out. The strike failed, and most of the workers quit the union and returned to work. In 1894 members of the American Railway Union struck the Pullman Palace Car Company, which made railroad cars. The federal government sent in troops to end the strike.

Despite these setbacks unions gradually increased their political power at the federal level. In 1914 Congress enacted the Clayton Anti-Trust Act, sections 6 (15 U.S.C.A. § 7) and 20 (29 U.S.C.A. § 52), declaring that human labor was not to be considered an article of commerce and that the existence of unions was not to be considered a violation of antitrust laws. In addition, the act prohibited FEDERAL COURTS from issuing injunctions in labor disputes except to prevent irreparable injury to property. This prohibition was absolute when peaceful picketing and boycotts were involved.

Employers had better success fighting unions using the so-called YELLOW-DOG CONTRACT. This agreement required a prospective employee to state that she or he was not a member of a union and would not become one. Though some states enacted laws prohibiting employers from requiring employees to sign this type of contract, the U.S. Supreme Court declared such statutes unconstitutional as an infringement of freedom of contract (*Coppage v. Kansas*, 236 U.S. 1, 35 S. Ct. 240, 59 L. Ed. 441 [1915]).

By 1920 trade unions had over 5 million members. During the 1920s, however, the trade union movement suffered a decline, precipitated in part by a severe economic depression in 1921-22. Unemployment rose, and competition for jobs became intense. By 1929 union membership had dropped to 3.5 million.

The Great Depression of the 1930s caused more unemployment and a further decline in union membership. Unions responded with numerous strikes, but few were successful. Despite these reverses the legal position of unions was enhanced during the 1930s. In 1932 Congress passed the NORRIS-LAGUARDIA ACT (29 U.S.C.A. § 101 et seq.), which declared yellow-dog contracts contrary to PUBLIC POLICY and stringently limited the power of federal courts to issue injunctions in labor disputes. In cases in which an injunction might still be issued, the act imposed strict procedural limitations and safeguards, to prevent past abuses by the courts. The Norris-LaGuardia Act effectively ended "government by injunction" and has remained a basic law in labor disputes.

During the 1930s the AFL itself was in turmoil over the goals and aspirations of the labor movement. The trade unions that dominated the AFL were composed of skilled workers who opposed organizing the unskilled or semiskilled workers on the manufacturing production line. Several unions rebelled at this refusal to organize and formed the Committee for Industrial Organization (CIO). The CIO aggressively organized millions of workers who labored in automobile, steel, and rubber plants. In 1938, unhappy with this effort, the AFL expelled the unions that formed the CIO. The CIO then formed its own organization, changed its name to Congress of Industrial Organizations, and elected John L. Lewis, of the United Mine Workers, as its first president.

The United Mine Workers of America was founded in January 1899. This certificate of membership illustrates the tasks of a mine worker and membership in the union.

THE GRANGER COLLECTION, NEW YORK

NLRB v. Jones & Laughlin Steel Corp.

Labor unions and their members were granted many rights in the National Labor Relations Act (Wagner Act) of 1935 (29 U.S.C.A. § 151 et seq.). At the time the law was passed, it appeared that it might not survive the scrutiny of the Supreme Court. The Court had recently ruled unconstitutional a number of statutes that were part of President Franklin D. Roosevelt's New Deal efforts to strengthen the national economy. However, in a stunning reversal, it upheld the Wagner Act in *NLRB v. Jones & Laughlin Steel Corp.*, 301 U.S. 1, 57 S. Ct. 615, 81 L. Ed. 893 (1937).

In July 1935 thirteen employees of the Jones and Laughlin Steel Corporation plant in Aliquippa, Pennsylvania, were discharged for minor infractions of company rules. Most of these workers had been actively involved in a union. The union filed a charge of unfair labor practices against the steel company with the National Labor Relations Board, claiming that the discharges were because of union membership. At a subsequent NLRB hearing, Jones and Laughlin argued that the Wagner Act was unconstitutional because it regulated labor relations and not interstate commerce. Therefore, Congress had no authority to regulate labor relations. The NLRB rejected the argument, and found that the company was the fourth largest steel producer in the United States and was clearly involved in interstate commerce. It ordered the workers reinstated and directed Jones and Laughlin to cease and desist from these labor practices.

On appeal to the Supreme Court, the NLRB maintained that statistical evidence showed that labor disputes in the steel and other industries greatly affected interstate commerce. In a 5–4 vote, the Supreme Court agreed. Chief Justice Charles E. Hughes, who had previously sided with the conservative bloc in striking down New Deal legislation, cast the decisive vote. Hughes wrote the majority opinion, which held that the Wagner Act was a constitutionally valid application of the Constitution's Commerce Clause to regulate unfair labor practices that burdened interstate commerce.

Jones changed the face of labor relations by requiring employers to treat unions and union workers fairly. It also signaled an end to the Supreme Court's striking down New Deal laws that sought to reshape the national economy. From *Jones* onward the Court permitted the federal government to take a dominant role in matters of commerce.

See also Commerce Clause; Hughes, Charles Evans; New Deal.

U.S. labor relations were dramatically altered in 1935 with the passage by Congress of the National Labor Relations Act, also known as the WAGNER ACT (29 U.S.C.A. § 151 et seq.). For the first time, labor unions were given legal rights and powers under federal law. The act guaranteed the right of COLLECTIVE BARGAINING, free from employer domination or influence. It made it an UNFAIR LABOR PRACTICE for an employer to interfere with employees in the exercise of their right to collectively bargain, to interfere with or influence unions, to discriminate in hiring or firing because of an employee's union membership, to discriminate against an employee who avails herself or himself of legal rights, or to refuse to bargain collectively.

The Wagner Act also established the National Labor Relations Board, with power to investigate employees' complaints and to issue cease and desist orders. If an employer defied such an order, the board could ask a federal court of appeals for an enforcement order, or the employer could ask the court to review the CEASE AND DESIST ORDER. The board could conduct elections to determine which union should represent the employees in a bargaining unit and certify the union as their agent, and it could designate the bargaining unit.

The heart of the Wagner Act was section 7 (29 U.S.C.A. § 157), which stated the public policy that workers have the right to engage in self-organization, in collective bargaining, and in concerted activities in support of self-organization and collective bargaining. Armed with these rights, unions grew in membership and strength during the late 1930s and through World War II.

A number of states reacted negatively to these legal changes by enacting laws that sought to restrict and lessen the power of unions. An antiunion backlash developed after World War II, when strikes against the automobile industry and other large corporations reached record numbers. This reaction culminated in the passage of the Labor-Management Relations Act of 1947, also known as the TAFT-HARTLEY ACT (29 U.S.C.A. § 141 et seq.). The Taft-Hartley Act amended section 7 of the Wagner Act, affirming the rights formulated in 1935 but providing that workers shall have the right to *refrain from* any of the listed activities. Whereas the Wagner Act listed only employer unfair labor practices, Taft-Hartley added union unfair labor practices. The act created the FEDERAL MEDIATION AND CONCILIATION SERVICE, which provides a method for dealing with strikes that create a national emergency. It also banned the CLOSED SHOP, which requires an employer to hire only union members and to discharge any employee who drops union membership. Taft-Hartley effectively replaced the Wagner Act as the basic federal statute regulating labor relations.

In 1955 the AFL and CIO merged into a single organization, the AFL-CIO. The staunchly anti-Communist AFL agreed to the merger only after the CIO had purged its organization of Communists and supporters of Communist ideals. George Meany was appointed the first president of the new organization.

In 1959 Congress enacted the Labor Management Reporting and Disclosure Act, also known as the LANDRUM-GRIFFIN ACT (29 U.S.C.A. § 401 et seq.). Title VII of the act contains many amendments to the Taft-Hartley Act, of which two are especially important. First, Landrum-Griffin made peaceful picketing of organizational or recognitional objectives illegal under certain circumstances. Second, it closed loopholes in the provisions of Taft-Hartley that forbade SECONDARY BOYCOTTS.

Other sections of Landrum-Griffin provided for a bill of rights for union members, financial disclosure requirements for unions and their officers, and safeguards in union elections. All of these matters dealt with internal union practices, strongly suggesting that union corruption had become a problem. In fact, a 1957 congressional investigation of the Teamsters Union had

uncovered widespread corruption and had much to do with these statutory provisions.

Labor unions continued to thrive in the 1960s, as a robust economy relied on a large manufacturing industry to maintain growth. Although no comprehensive union legislation was enacted during the decade, the CIVIL RIGHTS ACT of 1964, as amended by the Equal Employment Opportunity Act of 1972 (42 U.S.C.A. § 2000a et seq.), made an important contribution to national labor policy. The act declared it an unfair labor practice for an employer or union to discriminate against a person by reason of race, religion, color, sex, or national origin. Administration of this provision is vested in the EQUAL EMPLOYMENT OPPORTUNITY COMMISSION (EEOC). Under the Civil Rights Act, if the EEOC is unable to achieve voluntary compliance, the person alleging DISCRIMINATION is authorized to bring a CIVIL ACTION in federal district court. The 1972 amendment gave the EEOC the right to bring such an action. The effect of the law has been to desegregate many trade unions that maintained an all-white membership policy.

The union movement considerably improved working conditions for migrant workers in the late 1960s and the 1970s. The United Farm Workers, under the leadership of CESAR CHAVEZ, led successful boycotts and strikes against California growers, most notably against the wine-grape growers.

Many unions suffered, however, with an economic downturn in the 1970s and 1980s, and with the decline of good-paying manufacturing jobs. Automation of industrial processes reduced the number of workers required on assembly lines. In addition, many U.S. companies moved either to states that did not have a strong union background or to developing countries where labor costs were significantly lower. Union members became more concerned about job security than about higher wages, particularly in the manufacturing industry, agreeing to salary and benefit givebacks. In return, unions sought greater labor-management cooperation and a larger voice in the allocation of jobs and in the work environment.

Union membership has also declined in response to a shift from blue-collar manufacturing jobs to white-collar service and technology jobs. By 1995 just 14.9 percent of the U.S. workforce claimed union membership, compared with a high of 34.7 percent in 1954.

Median Usual Weekly Earnings in 1994

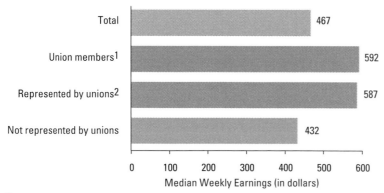

Total — 467
Union members[1] — 592
Represented by unions[2] — 587
Not represented by unions — 432

Median Weekly Earnings (in dollars)

[1]Members of a labor union or an employee association similiar to a labor union.
[2]Members of a labor union or an employee association similar to a union as well as workers who report no union affiliation but whose jobs are covered by a union or an employee association contract.

Source: U.S. Bureau of Labor Statistics, *Employment and Earnings.*

CROSS-REFERENCES

Child Labor Laws; Clayton Act; Craft Union; Employment Law; Hoffa, James Riddle; Labor Law; Right-to-Work Laws.

LACHES 📖 A defense to an equitable action, that bars recovery by the plaintiff because of the plaintiff's undue delay in seeking RELIEF. 📖

Laches is a defense to a proceeding in which a plaintiff seeks equitable relief. Cases in EQUITY are distinguished from cases AT LAW by the type of REMEDY, or judicial relief, sought by the plaintiff. Generally, law cases involve a problem that can be solved by the payment of monetary DAMAGES. Equity cases involve remedies directed by the court against a party.

Types of equitable relief include INJUNCTION, where the court orders a party to do or not to do something; declaratory relief, where the court declares the rights of the two parties to a controversy; and ACCOUNTING, where the court orders a detailed written statement of money owed, paid, and held. Courts have complete discretion in equity, and weigh equitable principles against the facts of the case to determine whether relief is warranted.

The rules of equity are built on a series of legal maxims, which serve as broad statements of principle, the truth and reasonableness of which are self-evident. The basis of equity is contained in the maxim "Equity will not suffer an injustice." Other maxims present reasons for not granting equitable relief. Laches is one such defense.

Laches is based on the legal maxim "Equity aids the vigilant, not those who slumber on their rights." Laches recognizes that a party to an action can lose evidence, witnesses, and a fair chance to defend himself or herself after the passage of time from the date the wrong was committed. If the defendant can show disadvantages because for a long time he or she relied on the fact that no lawsuit would be started, then the case should be dismissed in the interests of justice.

The law encourages a speedy resolution for every dispute. Cases in law are governed by STATUTES OF LIMITATIONS, which are laws that determine how long a person has to file a lawsuit before the right to sue expires. Different types of injuries (e.g., tort and contract) have different time periods in which to file a lawsuit. Laches is the equitable equivalent of statutes of limitations. However, unlike statutes of limita-

tions, laches leaves it up to the court to determine, based on the unique facts of the case, whether a plaintiff has waited too long to seek relief.

REAL ESTATE boundary disputes are resolved in equity and may involve laches. For instance, if a person starts to build a garage that extends beyond the boundary line and into a neighbor's property, and the neighbor immediately files a suit in equity and asks the court to issue an injunction to stop the construction, the neighbor will likely prevail. On the other hand, if the neighbor observes the construction of the garage on her property and does not file suit until the garage is completed, the defendant may plead laches, arguing that the neighbor had ample time to protect her PROPERTY RIGHTS before the construction was completed, and the court may find it unfair to order that the garage be torn down.

The laches defense, like most of equity law, is a general concept containing many variations on the maxim. Phrases used to describe laches include "delay that works to the disadvantage of another," "inexcusable delay coupled with prejudice to the party raising the defense," "failure to assert rights," "lack of diligence," and "neglect or omission to assert a right."

BIOGRAPHY

Robert Marion La Follette

LIBRARY OF CONGRESS

LA FOLLETTE, ROBERT MARION Robert Marion La Follette was an important U.S. political leader during the first part of the twentieth century. He served as governor of and senator from Wisconsin, and was at the forefront of the political reform movement that has been labeled Progressivism.

La Follette was born in Primrose, Wisconsin, on June 14, 1855. He graduated from the University of Wisconsin at Madison in 1879 and then studied law without going to law school. He was admitted to the Wisconsin bar in 1880 and began a legal practice in Madison. He was district attorney for Dane County, Wisconsin, from 1880 to 1884. In 1885 he was elected as a Republican representative to the U.S. Congress. He served three terms and then was defeated in 1890.

Following his loss La Follette resumed his law practice in Madison. During the 1890s he

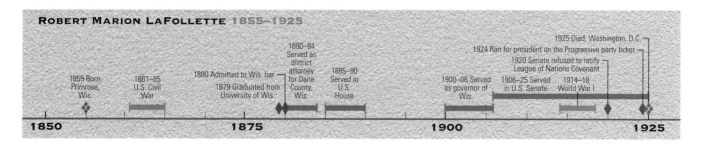

ROBERT MARION LaFOLLETTE 1855–1925

1855 Born, Primrose, Wis.

1861–65 U.S. Civil War

1880 Admitted to Wis. bar
1879 Graduated from University of Wis.

1880–84 Served as district attorney for Dane County, Wis.

1885–90 Served in U.S. House

1900–06 Served as governor of Wis.

1906–25 Served in U.S. Senate

1914–18 World War I

1920 Senate refused to ratify League of Nations Covenant
1924 Ran for president on the Progressive party ticket
1925 Died, Washington, D.C.

1850   1875   1900   1925

became a vocal opponent of state leadership of the Republican party. He rejected its conservatism and its reluctance to allow government a role in correcting social, political, and economic problems that had grown larger during the last two decades of the nineteenth century.

La Follette's reform desires were part of the national Progressive movement. Though not a unified political philosophy, Progressivism was built on the assumption that all levels of government must play an active role in reform. Progressives like La Follette argued that corporate capitalism had given too much power to large economic elites and had created inequities in the social and economic order. In addition, Progressives argued, the political parties, especially at the state and local level, had too much control and were stifling democratic change.

La Follette's ideas proved popular in Wisconsin. He was elected governor in 1900 and immediately began implementing his Progressive agenda. The Wisconsin Legislature passed many of his measures, including those mandating the nomination of candidates by direct vote in primary ELECTIONS, the equalization of taxes, and the regulation of railroad rates.

He returned to the national political arena, serving as U.S. senator from 1906 to 1925. He became a leader of the Progressive wing of the Republican party and frequently voiced opposition to the conservative party leadership. As a senator he advocated tougher regulation of railroads, going so far as to call for public ownership of the rail industry. He believed in progressive income taxes, government control of banking, and conservation of natural resources.

La Follette was an isolationist, holding that the United States should not become entangled in foreign alliances and foreign wars. He voted against the U.S. entry into World War I and later opposed President WOODROW WILSON's plan to have the United States join the LEAGUE OF NATIONS and the WORLD COURT.

The conservative Republican administrations of WARREN G. HARDING and CALVIN COOLIDGE proved too much for La Follette. In 1924, after the Republican National Convention rejected his platform proposals, La Follette left the party. He formed the League for Pro-

"NEITHER THE CLAMOR OF THE MOB NOR THE VOICE OF POWER WILL EVER TURN ME BY THE BREADTH OF A HAIR FROM THE COURSE I MAKE OUT FOR MYSELF."

BIOGRAPHY

ARTIST: JULIAN LAMAR. COLLECTION OF THE SUPREME COURT OF THE UNITED STATES

Joseph Rucker Lamar

gressive Political Action, commonly known as the Progressive party, and accepted its presidential nomination. Drawing support from farm groups, labor unions, and the Socialist party, La Follette waged a spirited third-party campaign. He earned almost 5 million popular votes. But La Follette was not a serious threat to the election of Coolidge; he received only thirteen electoral votes, carrying only his home state of Wisconsin.

Following his defeat La Follette continued as U.S. senator. He died in Washington, D.C., on June 18, 1925. His son, Robert M. La Follette, Jr., succeeded him as senator. The younger La Follette kept the Progressive party alive for another twenty years.

LAMAR, JOSEPH RUCKER Joseph Rucker Lamar served as an associate justice of the U.S. Supreme Court from 1911 to 1916. Unlike many appointees to the Court, Lamar was not selected on the basis of a long political career. As an attorney and Georgia Supreme Court judge, Lamar was recognized for his legal abilities.

Lamar was born in Ruckersville, Georgia, on October 14, 1857. His wealthy family provided generations of leadership in the community, and included LUCIUS Q. C. LAMAR, who served as an associate justice of the U.S. Supreme Court from 1888 to 1893.

Lamar attended the University of Georgia and graduated from Bethany College in West Virginia in 1877. He then attended Washington and Lee Law School and was admitted to the Georgia bar in 1878. From 1880 to 1903, Lamar practiced law in Augusta, Georgia. He often represented corporations, including railroads, and argued several cases before the U.S. Supreme Court.

He served in the Georgia House of Representatives from 1886 to 1889. His legal abilities were used more directly when he was appointed to serve on a commission revising the Georgia code of state laws. Codification is a process of revising and reorganizing legislative laws into a coherent whole. Lamar mastered the highly technical process and revised the civil-law volume himself. The code was approved by the legislature in 1895.

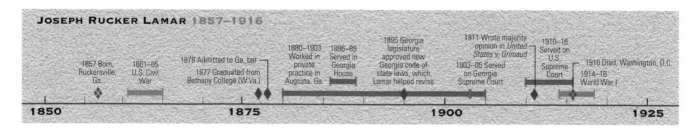

JOSEPH RUCKER LAMAR 1857–1916

1850

1857 Born, Ruckersville, Ga.

1861–65 U.S. Civil War

1878 Admitted to Ga. bar
1877 Graduated from Bethany College (W.Va.)

1875

1880–1903 Worked in private practice in Augusta, Ga.

1886–89 Served in Georgia House

1895 Georgia legislature approved new Georgia code of state laws, which Lamar helped revise

1900

1903–05 Served on Georgia Supreme Court

1911 Wrote majority opinion in *United States v. Grimaud*

1910–16 Served on U.S. Supreme Court

1916 Died, Washington, D.C.
1914–18 World War I

1925

In 1903 he was appointed to the Georgia Supreme Court. He resigned in 1905 to return to his law practice.

Lamar was surprised when President WILLIAM HOWARD TAFT, a Republican, appointed him to the U.S. Supreme Court in 1910. Lamar had met Taft the year before when the president was visiting Augusta, but was not well acquainted with him or his circle. In fact, Democrat WOODROW WILSON, who became president in 1912, was a childhood friend of Lamar's.

During Lamar's brief term on the Court, interstate commerce and the growth of federal regulatory and administrative power were prime topics of legal dispute. Lamar adhered to the majority view in most cases. He wrote the majority opinion in *United States v. Grimaud*, 220 U.S. 506, 31 S. Ct. 480, 55 L. Ed. 563 (1911), which expanded the authority of the EXECUTIVE BRANCH to add details deliberately left open by congressional legislation. Lamar held that it was not an unconstitutional delegation of legislative power to allow administrators to exercise their discretion in filling in the details of laws.

Lamar died January 2, 1916, in Washington, D.C.

LAMAR, LUCIUS QUINTUS CINCINNATUS

Lucius Quintus Cincinnatus Lamar served as an associate justice of the U.S. Supreme Court from 1888 to 1893. Lamar's public service, spanning almost fifty years, included both houses of Congress, the executive branch, and the Confederacy.

Lamar was born September 17, 1825, in Macon, Georgia, the son of a wealthy plantation owner. He graduated from Emory College in 1845 and then apprenticed in the law. He was admitted to the Georgia bar in 1847. In 1849 he moved to Oxford, Mississippi, where he taught mathematics at the University of Mississippi.

He briefly returned to Georgia, where he served in the Georgia House of Representatives in 1853. He relocated to Mississippi in 1855 and began building his political career. He was elected to the U.S. House of Representatives and served from 1857 to 1860, relinquishing his seat with the SECESSION of the southern states in 1861.

BIOGRAPHY

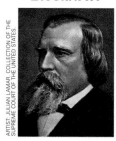

ARTIST: JULIAN LAMAR, COLLECTION OF THE SUPREME COURT OF THE UNITED STATES.

Lucius Quintus Cincinnatus Lamar

Lamar played an important role in the 1861 Mississippi Secession Convention. Although he had doubts about the theory of secession from the Union, he was influenced by his father-in-law, Augustus Longstreet, an avowed separatist. At the convention Lamar drafted the ordinance of secession, which declared Mississippi no longer a part of the Union. He joined the Confederate militia and served as a colonel in the Mississippi regiment. He also acted in various diplomatic capacities for the Confederacy, and from 1864 to 1865, he served as judge advocate of the Army of Virginia.

Following the war Lamar resumed his law practice and teaching career in Oxford. His teaching duties expanded to the University of Mississippi law school. In 1873 Lamar was again elected to the U.S. House of Representatives. In 1877 he was elected to the U.S. Senate. In 1885 President GROVER CLEVELAND appointed Lamar secretary of the interior.

In 1887 President Cleveland nominated Lamar to the U.S. Supreme Court. Republican opponents fought the nomination, arguing that Lamar lacked legal experience and that he was too old. The Senate narrowly approved his nomination, by a vote of 42–38, making Lamar the first southerner to join the Court since JOHN A. CAMPBELL in 1853, and the first Democrat since STEPHEN J. FIELD in 1862. He served on the U.S. Supreme Court from 1888 to 1893.

Lamar's tenure on the Court was spent under the leadership of Chief Justice MELVILLE W. FULLER. The Fuller Court reviewed the efforts of the federal government to regulate interstate commerce and curtail the power of monopolies and trusts. In most cases it agreed with business that the federal government had limited constitutional authority to regulate industry. Lamar concurred, adhering to a belief in the doctrine of FEDERALISM. This doctrine has many facets, including a fundamental assumption that the national government must not intrude on the power of the states to handle their affairs.

Lamar did not author any landmark majority opinions, as he generally received inconsequential cases. He joined in the dissent of Justice JOSEPH P. BRADLEY in *Chicago, Milwaukee & St.*

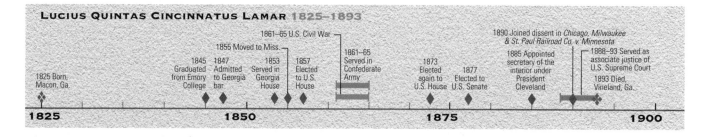

LUCIUS QUINTAS CINCINNATUS LAMAR 1825–1893

1825 Born, Macon, Ga.

1845 Graduated from Emory College

1847 Admitted to Georgia bar

1853 Served in Georgia House

1855 Moved to Miss.

1857 Elected to U.S. House

1861–65 U.S. Civil War

1861–65 Served in Confederate Army

1873 Elected again to U.S. House

1877 Elected to U.S. Senate

1885 Appointed secretary of the interior under President Cleveland

1890 Joined dissent in *Chicago, Milwaukee & St. Paul Railroad Co. v. Minnesota*

1888–93 Served as associate justice of U.S. Supreme Court

1893 Died, Vineland, Ga.

1825   1850   1875   1900

Paul Railroad Co. v. Minnesota, 134 U.S. 418, 10 S. Ct. 462, 33 L. Ed. 970 (1890), which stated that legislatures, not courts, should determine the reasonableness of railroad rates and other PUBLIC POLICY matters.

Lamar died January 23, 1893, in Vineland, Georgia.

LAME DUCK An elected official, who is to be followed by another, during the period of time between the election and the date that the successor will fill the post.

The term *lame duck* generally describes one who holds power when that power is certain to end in the near future. In the United States, when an elected official loses an election, that official is called a lame duck for the remainder of his or her stay in office. The term *lame duck* can apply to any person with decision-making powers, but it is usually refers to presidents, governors, and state and federal legislators.

When a legislature assembles between election day and the day that new legislators assume office, the meeting is called a lame-duck session. On the federal level, under the TWENTIETH AMENDMENT to the U.S. Constitution, the Senate and the House of Representatives must convene on January 3 each year. Incoming legislators assume office that day, and outgoing legislators leave office that day. Thus, from the day after election day in November until late December, retiring and defeated legislators have time to pass more legislation.

Legislatures do not have to conduct lame-duck sessions. In fact, if many of their members will be new in the next legislative session, the idea of their defeated lawmakers voting on legislation may be criticized by the public—especially by those who voted for the incoming legislators. The issue of whether to conduct a session between mid-November and early January is usually decided by a vote of the legislators in office during the last session before the election. The legislature may elect to reconvene on a certain date, to adjourn at the call of the chair of either house or both houses, or to adjourn SINE DIE (without planning a day to reconvene). Also, a lame-duck president or governor has the power to call a lame-duck session.

Lame-duck sessions may be called to pass emergency legislation for the immediate benefit or protection of the public during November or December. They also may be conducted for political purposes. For example, if a certain party stands to lose the presidency or governorship and seats in the new legislature, that party may seek to push through a few last pieces of legislation. Thus, lame-duck sessions can spawn hastily written legislation, and the finished product may be of dubious quality.

The Comprehensive Environmental Response, Compensation, and Liability Act of 1980 (CERCLA), also known as Superfund (42 U.S.C.A. § 9601 et seq.), is a piece of lame-duck legislation. This federal statute, which regulates the cleanup of toxic waste sites, was hurriedly passed by a lame-duck Congress and signed by lame-duck president JIMMY CARTER in December 1980. Congress crafted the statute with virtually no debate and under rules that allowed for no amendments. CERCLA is regarded as problem ridden by persons on all sides of the environmental debate. See also ENVIRONMENTAL LAW.

LAME-DUCK AMENDMENT The popular name given to the TWENTIETH AMENDMENT to the U.S. Constitution.

Senator GEORGE W. NORRIS proposed the amendment on March 2, 1932, as a way to shorten the period of time in election, or even-numbered, years during which members of Congress who had failed to be reelected (the LAME DUCKS) would serve in office until their terms expired.

The handicap of a session of Congress with numerous lame ducks was particularly evident in December 1932. During the thirteen weeks of that session of the Seventy-second Congress, 158 defeated members (out of a total of 431) served until the new Congress convened in March 1933. In the meantime the newly elected members, spurred by their recent electoral victories and the problems of a nationwide economic depression, had to wait inactive and unorganized until the term of the old Congress expired.

The Norris proposal was ratified by the requisite number of state legislatures on January 23, 1933, and took effect on October 15 of that year. The new amendment stipulated that the terms of all members of Congress begin on January 3. It also required Congress to convene on January 3 each year and for the president and vice president to be inaugurated on January 20 rather than in March. Two sections of the amendment also clarified the problem of presidential succession under certain conditions.

LAND GRANT A CONVEYANCE of public property to a subordinate government or corporation; a MUNIMENT OF TITLE issued by a state or government for the donation of some part of the PUBLIC DOMAIN.

A land grant, also known as *land patent*, was made by the U.S. government in 1862, upon its grant to the several states of 30,000 acres of land for each of its senators and representatives serving in Congress. The lands were subsequently sold by the states and, through the proceeds, colleges were established and maintained. Such colleges, which are devoted mainly to teaching agricultural subjects and engineering, are known as *land grant colleges.*

LANDIS, KENESAW MOUNTAIN

Kenesaw Mountain Landis is remembered by some as the trust-busting federal judge who in 1907 imposed a whopping fine against millionaire John D. Rockefeller's Standard Oil. More often, sports fans remember Landis as the first and, arguably, most powerful commissioner of U.S. BASEBALL.

Landis earned a reputation as a stern, highly principled baseball commissioner who ran a tight ship and disapproved of gambling. He antagonized many team owners with his dictatorial style, yet was reelected several times during his twenty-four-year reign.

Although Landis is criticized for maintaining racially segregated major league teams, he is credited with restoring the integrity of the sport after the Black Sox cheating scandal—in which eight members of the Chicago White Sox were accused of throwing the 1919 World Series—nearly ruined baseball. Surprisingly popular with the public, the former judge was elected to the Baseball Hall of Fame in 1944.

Landis was born November 20, 1866, in the small Ohio town of Millville. He was named after the mountaintop near Atlanta where his father, a Union Army surgeon, was wounded in battle during the U.S. Civil War. Although Landis did not finish high school, he attended the University of Cincinnati and the Union College of Law in Chicago. He practiced law in Chicago until 1905 when he was appointed by President THEODORE ROOSEVELT to serve as U.S. district judge for northern Illinois.

Landis made headlines in 1907 when he fined Standard Oil of Indiana a record $29.24 million for illegal freight REBATES. The decision was applauded by the public but thrown out on appeal. Landis remained on the federal bench from 1905 to 1922, also gaining national atten-

BIOGRAPHY

Kenesaw Mountain Landis

"REGARDLESS OF THE VERDICT OF JURIES, NO PLAYER THAT THROWS A BALL GAME, . . . SITS IN CONFERENCE WITH A BUNCH OF CROOKED PLAYERS AND GAMBLERS WHERE THE WAYS AND MEANS OF THROWING A GAME ARE DISCUSSED, AND DOES NOT PROMPTLY TELL HIS CLUB . . . WILL EVER AGAIN PLAY PROFESSIONAL BASEBALL."

tion for his sedition trials of labor leaders and socialists during World War I. After becoming the first baseball commissioner in 1921, Landis retained his judgeship for one year, until members of Congress complained about CONFLICT OF INTEREST in matters pertaining to the sport.

In 1921, Landis replaced the three-person national commission set up in 1903 to oversee the sport of baseball. Although his official title was commissioner for the American and National Leagues of Professional Baseball Clubs and for the National Association of Professional Baseball, Landis was often called simply the czar of baseball.

Landis was asked to do nothing less than save professional baseball. The game suffered a public relations disaster after the White Sox conspiracy and bribery scandal. To cleanse the sport of corruption or the mere appearance of cheating, Landis imposed lifetime bans on the eight White Sox players who had collaborated with gamblers during the 1919 World Series. He also did not hesitate to ban other ballplayers for gambling offenses.

Landis died in Chicago, at age seventy-eight, on November 25, 1944.

LANDLORD

A lessor of REAL PROPERTY; the owner or possessor of an ESTATE in land or a rental property, who, in an exchange for rent, leases it to another individual known as the TENANT.

See also LANDLORD AND TENANT.

LANDLORD AND TENANT

An association between two individuals arising from an agreement by which one individual occupies the other's REAL PROPERTY with permission, subject to a rental fee.

The term *landlord* refers to a person who owns property and allows another person to use it for a fee. The person using the property is called a TENANT. The agreement between a LANDLORD and a tenant is called a LEASE or rental agreement.

The landlord and tenant relationship has its roots in FEUDALISM, a system of land use and ownership that flourished in Europe between the tenth and thirteenth centuries. Under feu-

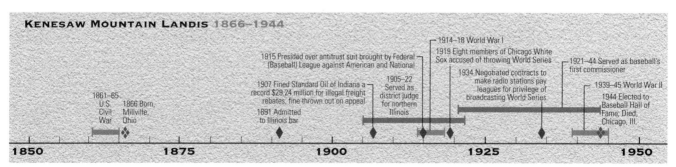

dalism land was owned and controlled by a military or political sovereign ruler. This ruler gave portions of land she or he owned to another person, called a lord. The lord, in turn, could allow another person, called a vassal, to use smaller portions of the lord's land. The vassal pledged allegiance and military or other service to the lord in exchange for the right to live and work on the land.

In 1066 the Normans of France conquered England, and William the Conqueror installed himself as king. King William used the feudal framework of land control to retain political power in faraway lands. Feudalism as a means of political control became obsolete by the fourteenth century, but the hierarchical system of land use and ownership remained.

The contemporary landlord and tenant relationship derives from the relationship between the lord and the vassal. However, today the landlord is the owner of the property—not, like the feudal lord, merely the manager. The tenant is similar to the vassal because the tenant does not own the property but is allowed to use it for a fee.

The landlord and tenant relationship usually refers to a living arrangement. In this respect landlord and tenant law differs from the law regarding leases. In a landlord and tenant relationship, the parties are often referred to as LESSOR (landlord) and LESSEE (tenant). Indeed, a lease is a CONTRACT that creates the same relationship as exists between a landlord and tenant: the lessor owns property and allows the lessee to use it for a fee. However, the law of leases does not necessarily concern itself with living arrangements. A lease agreement may, for example, relate to the use of a good or service. Because living arrangements are vital to human existence, landlord and tenant relationships are treated differently from lease contracts.

Generally, a landlord and tenant relationship exists if (1) the property owner consents to OCCUPANCY of the premises; (2) the tenant acknowledges that the owner has TITLE to the property and a future interest in the property; (3) the owner actually has title to the property; (4) the tenant receives a limited right to use the premises; (5) the owner transfers POSSESSION and control of the premises to the tenant; and (6) a contract to rent exists between the parties.

A rental contract may be implied under the law. That is, landlord and tenant law may apply even in the absence of a written and signed rental agreement between the owner of the property and the person living on the property. Whether a court will imply a relationship depends on the facts of the case. The court will look at a number of factors, including the owner's consent to occupancy of the property, the length of the occupancy, and the exchange of monies, goods, or services. A court's finding that a landlord and tenant relationship exists between two or more persons is significant because the law places duties on both parties in such a relationship.

Traditionally, landlord and tenant law was favorable to landlords. Courts resolved disputes between landlords and tenants according to strict contract and property principles, and tenants often were forced to pick up and move without notice or an opportunity to present an argument to a court. Also, landlords had no obligation to maintain the premises, and many tenants were forced to live in uninhabitable conditions.

In the twentieth century, as urban populations increased and workers became more specialized, landlord and tenant law was forced to change. Typical tenants were no longer as handy at making repairs as were tenants in previous years. They worked long hours, they did not have the time to maintain premises, and building designs and utilities were more complex than before. These developments made maintenance a specialized task that could be carried out only by the landlord.

Before the 1960s landlords were not required to warrant to tenants that a rented property was fit for habitation. Landlords could rent filthy, rat-infested apartments lacking hot water and heat. Although no one was physically forced to live in such an apartment, for many persons it was the only kind they could afford.

In the 1960s and 1970s, states began to enact landlord and tenant laws requiring that domestic rental properties be made fit for their particular purpose. The IMPLIED WARRANTY of HABITABILITY established by statute meant that rental property must have proper plumbing, water, heat, structural integrity, and other basic features necessary for human habitability. These laws required landlords to make domestic rental property habitable even if they did not promise tenants habitable conditions in the rental agreement.

New landlord and tenant statutes further require cities to create housing agencies to enforce the laws governing habitability. These agencies are charged with inspecting domestic rental properties to make sure they meet maintenance standards set forth in statutes and agency regulations. The agencies report to a state agency such as the department of health.

State legislation also governs the financial aspects of the landlord-tenant relationship.

Such statutes regulate security deposits, require plain language in rental contracts, require inventory checklists, set rules on damage to rental units, and establish rights and duties upon termination of the rental agreement. In some states some of these laws are set out in COURT OPINIONS, or CASE LAW. However, most landlord and tenant laws are set out in statutes in an attempt to make information about rights and duties accessible and understandable to both parties.

Contemporary landlord and tenant laws vary from state to state. Local lawmaking bodies may enact additional landlord and tenant laws, provided they do not conflict with state laws.

Generally, landlords must deliver the rented premises to the tenant at the beginning of the TENANCY, and must disclose to the tenant any potential dangers and defects in the premises. The length of the tenancy should be set out in the rental agreement. If no term is written into the agreement, courts will usually deem the tenancy to be month to month. This means that either party must give the other one month's written notice before terminating the tenancy.

One important issue in landlord and tenant law is the implied warranty of habitability. If a landlord breaches the warranty of habitability, the landlord may lose the right to collect rent from the tenant, and the tenant may lose a place to live. *Mannie Joseph, Inc. v. Stewart*, 71 Misc. 2d 160, 335 N.Y.S.2d 709 (1972), illustrates this process. In *Mannie Joseph*, a landlord brought suit against a tenant, seeking back rent. The tenant testified in court that the apartment had no heat, no gas for the stove, no hot water, no running water in the kitchen, low water pressure in the bathroom, "ever-present rats and cockroaches," soggy ceilings and walls, broken windowpanes, no superintendent, and a toilet that did not flush. This TESTIMONY was supported in court by the housing director of the West Harlem Community Organization and verified in a personal visit by Judge Richard S. Lane, who noted that the oral testimony had not been sufficient to prepare him for what he saw.

Judge Lane found that the landlord had breached the implied warranty of habitability, and refused to order the tenant to make back rent payments. In his opinion Lane wondered why the tenant should have to pay for what she was receiving. He abated, or forgave, the rent and ordered the landlord to pay the tenant's court costs.

Lane could have ordered the landlord to make repairs, but there were not enough people still living in the building to warrant such an order. In fact, the department of health had recently ordered the building vacated, and Lane lamented that the tenant would "soon follow her many former co-tenants out into the streets."

Landlords have additional duties and restrictions under landlord and tenant statutes. Under the implied warranty of QUIET ENJOYMENT, a landlord must give notice to the tenant and receive permission from the tenant before entering rented premises. This rule does not apply if there is a bona fide emergency, such as a fire or some other danger to the premises.

A concept related to quiet enjoyment is the tenant's right to REASONABLE use of the premises. Landlords may not substantially interfere with this right. Whether actions by the landlord substantially interfere with a tenant's reasonable use of the premises is determined by the facts of the case. To illustrate, assume that a tenant rents an apartment and works there repairing electronic equipment. The landlord's refusal to allow the tenant to conduct such activity may constitute substantial interference of a reasonable use. If, however, the tenant uses the premises to mix explosive materials, the landlord may have the right to interfere because such a use is unreasonable.

If a landlord is found to have interfered with a tenant's quiet enjoyment or reasonable use of the premises, the tenant may recover DAMAGES. The measure of damages varies by JURISDICTION. Usually, the tenant will not have to pay rent for the period of interference, and the tenant may seek damages for any losses caused by the interference.

There are several reciprocal duties between landlords and tenants. A landlord must keep the premises in good repair, but the tenant must not damage the premises. The tenant must leave the premises in their original condition, accounting for reasonable wear and tear, or risk losing the security deposit. A security deposit is money deposited by the tenant with the landlord to guarantee the tenant's performance under the lease. If the tenant damages the premises, the landlord may keep the security deposit and sue the tenant for damages not covered by the deposit.

A landlord must give a tenant notice to vacate the premises if the landlord wishes to rent the premises to another tenant. The landlord may not do this during a rental period. For example, if a tenant has signed a lease for one year, the landlord may not force the tenant to move until the end of the year. If the lease period expires and the landlord has not found a new tenant and has not issued a new lease to the present tenant, the present tenant may be allowed to stay on the premises on a month-to-month basis.

If the tenant plans to move during a rental period, the tenant must give at least a one-month written notice to the landlord. If the tenant fails to give notice to the landlord and leaves the premises, the tenant may be responsible for future rental payments. However, in this situation, the landlord is under a duty to take reasonable steps to find another tenant. This is called the duty to mitigate damages. Once the landlord finds another tenant, or the original lease expires, the tenant's duty to pay expires. See also MITIGATION OF DAMAGES.

If the lease period expires and the landlord has found a new tenant, but the present tenant refuses to leave the premises, the landlord may sue the present tenant for damages if the landlord could be charging the new tenant more rent. The landlord may also have the tenant evicted by filing suit in court. Such a suit is called a wrongful or UNLAWFUL DETAINER. Unlawful detainers are governed by statute and may be based on damage to the property, nonpayment of rent, or unforeseen changes in the economic conditions of the landlord.

All states provide for unlawful detainer hearings. These proceedings help landlords avoid financial loss. Depending on the statute, a court will schedule an unlawful detainer hearing from one to three weeks after the landlord files suit. In most states the hearing is limited to issues concerning the tenant's and landlord's rights and duties. The majority of states prohibit landlords from removing a tenant's PERSONAL PROPERTY from the premises until after the court orders an EVICTION.

A tenant may avoid eviction for nonpayment of rent by paying the past due rent along with any filing costs incurred by the landlord. If the tenant is unable to pay rent before the court date, the tenant can still present defenses to the eviction in court. For example, the tenant may argue that the rent is not due because the landlord failed to make necessary repairs. If the tenant is unable to defend successfully the failure to pay rent, the court will order the tenant to vacate the premises by a certain date in the near future. In order to collect the unpaid rent, the landlord usually must file a separate action against the tenant.

Sometimes the action or inaction of a landlord may constitute a CONSTRUCTIVE EVICTION. A constructive eviction occurs when the landlord has made living on the premises unbearable or impossible. For example, assume that a landlord has refused to provide heat to rented premises.

This constitutes a constructive eviction, and the tenant is not liable for rent.

The law of eviction differs for tenants in public housing. Public housing is low-cost housing provided by the federal government to impoverished persons. Under the National Public Housing Asset Forfeiture Project (28 U.S.C.A. § 881(a)(7)), the Department of Housing and Urban Development and the Department of Justice may evict persons from public housing without notice and without a hearing, under exigent circumstances—that is, when the eviction is directly necessary to secure an important government or public interest, and there is a special need for prompt action. An eviction from public housing can be initiated only by the proper government authorities. Whether exigent circumstances exist to justify eviction without notice and a hearing depends on the facts of the case. The mere use or possession of illegal narcotics, for example, does not warrant summary eviction. However, if an apartment in a public housing project is being used for constant, high-level drug dealing, such activity may constitute exigent circumstances (*Richmond Tenants Organization v. Kemp*, 956 F.2d 1300 [4th Cir. 1992]). Although public housing tenants have increased eviction risks, the additional eviction procedures that must be followed by governments make eviction of public housing tenants a longer, more complicated process than eviction of private tenants.

A tenant may give his or her rights as a tenant to another person. This is called an ASSIGNMENT, and it is permissible unless the landlord objects or unless it is prohibited in the rental agreement. If a tenant assigns his or her rights, the tenant is still responsible for the payment of rent. In essence the recipient of the rental rights, or assignee, is a tenant of the original tenant, and there is no legal relationship between the assignee and the landlord.

Local laws in some urban areas provide for rent control. Rent control laws limit the amount of rent that a landlord may charge a tenant. In the 1990s most of these laws were repealed.

A landlord may raise rent during a rental period only with sufficient notice to a tenant. The terms of this notice are usually set forth in statutes or ordinances.

Courts often examine lease agreements for unconscionability. UNCONSCIONABLE agreements are ones that unduly favor one party over the other. For example, assume that a rental agreement calls for the payment of damages to the landlord if the tenant leaves the apartment without sufficient notice. If the court considers the amount of damages to be too high, it may reduce the damages owed to the landlord.

Some lease agreements allow either party to break the agreement, and specify an amount of damages that the breaching party must pay to the other in the event of breach. Landlord-tenant relationships governed by such agreements are called tenancies at sufferance. Courts usually examine these agreements to ensure that they are not unconscionable.

In many cities tenant organizations operate to protect the interests of tenants. These organizations offer information and services to tenants. Most tenant groups offer information and services to nonmembers for a fee based on the tenant's ability to pay and the amount of work necessary to resolve the tenant's rental issues. Most states have statutes that prohibit landlords from evicting a tenant based on the tenant's membership or participation in a tenant organization.

Landlords are under no obligation to rent to tenants. However, under the Fair Housing Act of 1968 (42 U.S.C.A. §§ 3601–3619 [1988 & Supp. III 1991]), they may not refuse to rent based on race, color, religion, sex, handicap, familial status, or national origin.

See also RENT STRIKE.

LANDMARK 📖 A structure that has significant historical, architectural, or cultural meaning and that has been given legal protection from alteration and destruction. 📖

Although landmark preservation laws vary by city and state, they have the same basic purpose: to keep landmarks as close to their original condition as possible. A new legal specialty, landmark and preservation law has developed as the number of designated landmarks has grown in the United States.

Landmarks are often buildings such as hotels, homes, skyscrapers, theaters, museums, stores, libraries, churches, and synagogues. Other structures, such as bridges, and even natural points of interest, such as trees, can also be designated as landmarks if they have special historical, architectural, or cultural significance.

New York City divides its landmarks into four categories: individual, interior, scenic, and historic district. Individual landmarks are designated for their exterior. Interior landmarks are noted for the portions of their interior that are open to the public. Scenic landmarks encompass structures that are not buildings, such as bridges, piers, parks, cemeteries, sidewalks, clocks, and trees. Historic district landmarks include entire areas that have architectural unity and quality or that represent a specific architectural period or style. All buildings within a designated historical district are protected from alteration or destruction.

The Chrysler Building in New York City is an example of an individual landmark. At the time of its completion in 1930, it was the tallest building in New York City, at seventy-seven stories and 1,046 feet. Built by Walter P. Chrysler, the founder of the Chrysler Corporation, the building remains a part of the New York City skyline. The building's art deco style is unique. Outside the thirty-first floor, a line of cars made of gray and white bricks encircles the building. The cars have chrome hubcaps, which are embedded in the wall. On each of the four corners of this floor is a buttress, and atop each buttress is a giant steel eagle similar in style to the ornament that used to adorn the Chrysler radiator cap. The floors from the thirty-first to the fifty-ninth make up a tower, and the fifty-ninth floor is marked with eight gargoyles. A spire begins on the fifty-ninth floor, constructed of arches with triangular windows. At night the spire is lit from the inside, highlighting its place in the Manhattan skyline.

Once a landmark has been designated, it is legally protected from alteration or destruction. If the owner of a landmark wishes to change it, the alterations must be approved by the commission or council that governs the landmarks in the city or state in which the landmark is located.

The Landmarks Preservation Commission of New York City is one such body. Since its creation in 1965, the commission has designated more than a thousand landmarks in New York City. The commission creates guidelines for landmark designation, designates landmarks, and reviews applications for the alteration of previously designated landmarks. The group is made up of eleven commissioners, including at least one from each of the five boroughs of New York City.

More than six hundred U.S. cities have ORDINANCES regulating historical preservation of landmarks. Under these ordinances a landmark owner basically has two obligations: first, the owner is responsible for the upkeep of the building or structure, which is a basic requirement for any PROPERTY owner; and second, the owner is required to get advance approval for any exterior improvements or alterations to the landmark. Requests for alterations are made to the appropriate city or state preservation commission.

New York City's Landmarks Preservation Law was passed in 1965, two years after the historic Pennsylvania Station in New York City was demolished to make way for Madison

Square Garden. The demise of this historical structure was one among many that sparked the movement to enact preservation laws to protect landmarks.

Despite their prevalence landmark laws are often challenged by property owners who feel that the laws create undue interference with their use of their property. Typically, a landmark owner argues that a taking has occurred because a city or state preservation council has rejected the owner's application to alter the landmark. A taking is defined as interference with or damage to a private property owner's land-use rights. In ZONING law cases, a taking can occur if a property owner is denied economically viable use of the land or the buildings on the land. In landmark cases the line between taking and a legitimate government-imposed limitation is often blurred.

The 1978 case of *Penn Central Transportation Co. v. New York City*, 438 U.S. 104, 98 S. Ct. 2646, 57 L. Ed. 2d 631, illustrates the strength of New York City's landmark preservation laws over the desires of a landmark owner. Penn Central, the owner of the Grand Central Terminal, leased the building to a company that planned to construct a fifty-story office tower on top of it. However, the New York City Landmarks Preservation Commission had designated the terminal as a historic landmark, and the commission refused to allow the building's exterior to be altered by the planned tower. Penn Central sued the city, and the case went to the U.S. Supreme Court.

Penn Central argued that the construction denial was a taking. New York City argued that "regulating private property for historical, cultural or aesthetic values, if it is done in accord with a comprehensive plan that provides benefit to all, is in the public interest." The city also argued that the meaningful preservation of landmarks meant that any additions should "protect, enhance and perpetuate the original design, rather than overwhelm it."

The Supreme Court ruled that it was constitutional, "as part of a comprehensive program to preserve historic landmarks and historic districts, [to] place restrictions on the development of individual historic landmarks ... without effecting a 'taking.' "

Penn Central established three factors for determining whether a taking has occurred in landmark land-use cases: the economic effect of the regulation on the claimant; how much the regulation affected investment-backed expectations; and the character of the government action—whether there was a legitimate state interest, such as an interest in preserving existing landmarks. New York City's refusal to permit construction did not reduce Penn Central's income or interfere with its original intent of operating the terminal, and because New York City had a legitimate state interest (preserving the landmark in its original state), the Supreme Court ruled that a taking had not occurred and that the landmark law was constitutional.

In the 1980 case of *Agins v. City of Tiburon*, 447 U.S. 255, 100 S. Ct. 2138, 65 L. Ed. 2d 106, the Supreme Court ruled that "regulation is a taking if it doesn't substantially advance legitimate state interests or denies an owner economically viable use of his land." *Agins* established a two-part test to determine whether a taking has occurred. Under *Agins* a regulation is a taking if it does not substantially advance a legitimate state interest and if it denies the landmark owner all economically viable use of the land. The *Agins* ruling clarified the amount of economic effect necessary for a regulation to be considered a taking. If a regulation prevented all economically viable use of the land, it was a taking. However, if a regulation left some economically viable use, it was not considered a taking.

Twelve years later, in *Lucas v. South Carolina Coastal Council*, 505 U.S. 1003, 112 S. Ct. 2886, 120 L. Ed. 2d 798 (1992), the Court clarified its definition of economically viable use, stating that it was any use that was greater than zero.

See also EMINENT DOMAIN; LAND-USE CONTROL.

LANDRUM-GRIFFIN ACT

The Labor-Management Reporting and Disclosure Act of 1959 (29 U.S.C.A. § 401 et seq.), commonly known as the Landrum-Griffin Act, is an important component of federal LABOR LAW. The act was named after its sponsors, Representative Phillip M. Landrum of Georgia and Senator Robert P. Griffin of Michigan. The provisions of Landrum-Griffin seek to prevent union corruption and to guarantee union members that unions will be run democratically.

The act resulted from a highly publicized investigation of union corruption and racketeering chaired by Senator JOHN L. McCLELLAN of Arkansas. The Senate Select Committee on Labor and Management Practices, popularly known as the McClellan Committee, was created in 1957 in large part because of the perception that the Teamsters Union was corrupt and under the influence of organized crime. The McClellan Committee's investigation revealed that officials of the Teamsters Union and other groups had taken union funds for private use and that the union was clearly linked to organized crime. One result of the probe was the expulsion of the Teamsters and two other unions from the American Federation of Labor and Congress of Industrial Organizations (AFL-CIO). The AFL-CIO is the largest U.S. labor organization, a federation of autonomous LABOR UNIONS that is dedicated to enhancing and promoting unionism.

The other result was the passage of the Landrum-Griffin Act. To prevent abuses and acts of oppression, the act attempts to regulate some internal union affairs and provides for reporting to the government on various union transactions and affairs. Senator JOHN F. KENNEDY of Massachusetts was instrumental in inserting title I of the act (29 U.S.C.A. § 411 et seq.), which has been dubbed the union bill of rights. Title I mandates freedom of speech and assembly in the conduct of union meetings, equality of rights regarding voting in elections, the nomination of candidates, and attendance at meetings. A secret ballot is required for voting on increases in dues or assessments. In regard to disciplinary actions, a member must be given written charges, time to prepare a defense, and a fair hearing. The act also guarantees that a member will not be subject to union discipline for attempting to exercise statutory rights. A member must have access to union financial records and has the right to recover misappropriated union assets on behalf of the union when the union fails to do so.

Title II (29 U.S.C.A. § 431 et seq.) deals with the management and reporting of union finances, a particular area of concern for Congress in the wake of the Teamsters Union's misappropriation of funds. The act requires unions to have constitutions and bylaws and to file copies of both with the U.S. secretary of labor. They must file reports that show dues, fees, and assessments; qualifications for membership; financial auditing; and authorization for the disbursement of funds and other types of spending. Unions must also file financial reports that show assets and liabilities at the beginning and end of the fiscal year, receipts, salaries, expense reimbursements, and loans to any officer, employee, member, or business enterprise. Officers and employees of unions may be required to disclose in written reports any personal financial interests that may conflict with duties owed to union members and any transactions or business interests that would present a conflict of interest with union duties.

The act also has provisions that apply when a labor organization suspends the autonomy of a union local and places the local or another unit under a trusteeship. This provision addresses a concern that corrupt national union leaders may take over control of union locals to main-

tain power. The law provides the conditions under which a trusteeship may be imposed and certain restrictions under which it may operate.

Landrum-Griffin also addresses the personal responsibility and integrity of union officers and representatives. Under the act, officers and representatives are held to COMMON-LAW principles of trust relationships through express provisions that they occupy positions of trust in relation to the organization and its members as a group. This means that persons in union leadership positions must act in the best interests of the union. If a union official acts for personal gain, the official can be held accountable for breach of duty. EMBEZZLEMENT of union funds is a federal offense under the act. And persons who have been convicted of certain specified crimes are barred from serving as union officers, agents, or employees for five years after being released from prison.

The Landrum-Griffin Act provides the tools for union democracy, but it also provides greater government control over union affairs previously believed to be the province of the unions themselves.

LAND-USE CONTROL ▣ Activities such as ZONING, the regulation of the development of REAL ESTATE, and city planning. ▣

Land-use controls have been a part of Western civilization since the Roman Empire in 450 B.C. promulgated regulations concerning setback lines of buildings from BOUNDARIES and for distances between trees and boundaries. Regulations on the use of land existed in colonial America, but the demand for public regulation of real estate development did not become significant until the twentieth century. As the United States shifted from a rural to an urban society, city governments sought to gain control over the location of industry, commerce, and

AFL-CIO President Thomas Donahue sat among supporters after being nominated to continue as president of the union; he lost the election in October 1995 to John Sweeney in that union's first contested presidential election. The Landrum-Griffin Act seeks to prevent union corruption and ensure that unions are run democratically.

housing. New York City adopted the first comprehensive zoning ordinance in 1916. By the 1930s zoning laws had been adopted in most urban areas.

The development of master plans and zoning regulations became an accepted part of urban life. Following World War II, housing patterns shifted from the inner city to suburbia. The suburbanization of the United States led to the creation of discrete housing developments. Growing suburban communities began imposing regulations on the amount and type of housing that would be allowed within their municipal boundaries. Beginning in the 1970s, as urban sprawl created problems that crossed municipal borders, attention turned to regional planning. Concerns about the environment and historic preservation led to further regulation of land use.

Federal, state, and local governments, to varying degrees, regulate growth and development through statutory law. Nevertheless, a majority of controls on land stem from actions of private developers and government units. The use of land can be affected by judicial determinations that frequently arise in one of three situations: (1) suits brought by one neighbor against another, (2) suits brought by a public official against a neighboring landowner on behalf of the public at large, and (3) suits involving individuals who share ownership of a particular parcel of land.

Private Land-Use Restrictions   A number of restrictions on land are a result of actions by government units. Many restrictions, however, are created by land developers. Such devices take several forms, and can be either positive or negative in nature. They include defeasible fees, easements, equitable servitudes, and restrictive covenants.

Defeasible Fees   In DEFEASIBLE fee ESTATES, the GRANTOR gives land to the GRANTEE, subject to certain conditions. For example, A might convey a parcel of land to B, provided that it be used for school purposes. The effect of the defeasible fee is that it restricts the use of the property by the possessor. Failure to observe the conditions causes the property to revert to the grantor. Estates of this type are no longer favored in most JURISDICTIONS, because they make the transfer of land cumbersome and do not take into account unforeseen situations. The limited scope of defeasible fees makes them of limited value.

Easements   Easements are rights to use the property of another for particular purposes. A common type of EASEMENT in current use is the affirmative grant to a telephone company to run its line across the property of a private landowner. Easements also are now used for public objectives, such as the preservation of open space and conservation. For example, an easement might preclude someone from building on a parcel of land, which leaves the property open and thereby preserves a park for the public as a whole.

Equitable Servitudes   Equitable servitudes are land-use restrictions enforceable in a court of EQUITY. They are created by the language of the PROMISE in the form of a COVENANT (agreement) between two individuals. For example, suppose A owns a parcel of land on the edge of a city. A subdivides the parcel into ten lots, numbered 1 to 10. A then records a declaration of restrictions, limiting each of the ten lots to use solely for family dwelling, providing that only a single-family house may be built on each lot. A sells the lots to ten people, and each deed contains a reference to the declaration of restrictions by record book and page number, coupled with a provision that the person purchasing the lot and all successive purchasers of the lot are bound by the restrictions.

Restrictive Covenants   Restrictive covenants are provisions in a DEED limiting the use of the property and prohibiting certain uses. They are similar in effect to equitable servitudes, but restrictive covenants RUN with the land because the restrictions are contained in the deed. Restrictive covenants are typically used by land developers to establish minimum house sizes, setback lines, and aesthetic requirements thought to enhance the neighborhood. The legal differences between equitable servitudes and restrictive covenants are less important today, as courts have merged the terms into one general concept.

The Master Plan and Official Map   Municipal land-use regulation begins with a planning process that ultimately results in a comprehensive or master plan followed by ordinances. These ORDINANCES involve the exercise of the municipality's POLICE POWER through zoning, regulation of subdivision developments, street plans, plans for public facilities, and building regulations. Many states provide for the creation of an official map for a municipality. The map shows the location of major streets, existing and projected public facilities, and other such landmarks. Developers must plan their subdivisions in accordance with the official map.

The master plan takes into account the location and type of activities occurring on the land

Dust, Noise, Smells, But Not a Nuisance

Homeowners have a legitimate right to the quiet enjoyment of their property. Nevertheless, when that quiet enjoyment is disturbed by the activities of another property owner, it may be difficult to have those activities declared a private or public nuisance.

In *Karpiak v. Russo,* 450 Pa. Super. 471, 676 A.2d 270 (1996), the Pennsylvania Superior Court ruled that a landscaping supply business that produced dust, loud noises, and unpleasant smells in an area that contained homes as well as businesses was not a private nuisance. The decision illustrates the need for those complaining of a nuisance to prove significant harm.

The landscaping supply company was established in 1984, when the zoning law classified the location as business property. The area was rezoned in 1993, making the area residential. The company sold topsoil, shredded bark, compost, sand, and river rock from spring to late fall. Nearby homeowners complained of dust blowing into their yard and home; noise from trucks, backhoes, and payloaders; and smells from the compost.

The court rejected these claims of nuisance. It first noted that the company had lawfully complied with the zoning ordinance at the time it started the business. There were other businesses on the same street. Just because the neighborhood had been rezoned did not prohibit the continued existence of the landscape business.

More significantly, the court found that none of the complaining parties had suffered any significant harm. Most of the parties worked weekdays and were absent from the neighborhood when the landscape business was in operation. Aside from one person who had to clean his car and outside furniture, no one claimed any damages from the operation of the business. The court concluded that occasional personal discomfort or annoyance did not establish a serious level of harm that could be defined as a private nuisance. People who reside in neighborhoods with businesses close by will sometimes find their comfort subordinated to the commercial needs of business.

and the design and type of physical structures and facilities serving these activities. Long-range projections of population and employment trends are considered. The planning process is designed to enable a locality to plan for the construction of schools, streets, water and sewage facilities, fire and police protection, and other public amenities, and the private use of land is controlled by zoning and subdivision ordinances enacted in compliance with the plan.

Since the 1970s more emphasis has been placed on regional and statewide planning. These planning initiatives have often been based on environmental concerns. Regional planning has become attractive to urban areas that cross state lines. Instead of dealing with two or three competing and conflicting local plans, neighboring municipalities can refer to a regional plan that offers one comprehensive vision and one set of regulations.

Zoning Zoning is the regulation and restriction of REAL PROPERTY by a local government. It is the most common form of land-use regulation, as municipalities rely on it to control and direct the development of property within their borders, according to present and potential uses of the property. Zoning involves the division of territory based on the character of land and structures and their fitness for particular uses. Consideration is given to conserving the value of property and encouraging the most appropriate use of land throughout a particular locality.

A municipality's power to enact zoning regulations is derived from the state in an exercise of its police power. Police power is the inherent power of the government to act for the welfare of those within its jurisdiction. The power to impose zoning restrictions is conferred on a municipality by a state enabling statute.

Zoning laws are intended to promote the health, safety, welfare, convenience, morals, and prosperity of the community at large, and are meant to further the GENERAL WELFARE rather than to improve the economic interests of any particular property owner. They are designed to stabilize neighborhoods and preserve the character of the community by guiding its future growth.

The essential purpose of zoning is to segregate residential, commercial, and industrial districts from one another. Within these three main types of districts there may be additional restrictions as to population density and building height. The use of property within a particular district is for the most part uniform. For

THE WEST WRESTLES WITH WASHINGTON

Beginning in the 1990s, a number of controversial clashes over federal authority have concerned the use of federally owned land. One such struggle, between the Clinton administration and western states, for example, covered a variety of issues: fees for ranchers; water, timber, and mining rights; and environmental restrictions on land use. Each issue was part of a more fundamental question: Who has authority to regulate use of the land—federal or local officials? Challenging the administration in Congress and fighting the federal government in court, a broad coalition of western governors, lawmakers, and business interests sought autonomy and relief from outside regulation. More than sixty western counties asserted legal authority over federal lands within their borders. As political tensions heightened, acts of violence aimed at federal officials raised the stakes in what the media called the county supremacy movement, and the U.S. Department of Justice brought suit to stop it.

The western conflict had been simmering for two decades. A rise of environmental concerns in the 1970s had created a strong lobby that pressed for stricter controls on land use, a demand especially relevant to the millions of acres of federal land in the U.S. West. This development affected western ranchers, who lease federally owned land for their livestock. Early on, environmentalists spurred the passage of the

1971 Wild Horse and Burro Act, 16 U.S.C.A. § 1332 et seq. This law protected wild horses, but at the expense of causing deterioration to land on which livestock graze. Private landowners also chafed under the Endangered Species Act (ESA) (16 U.S.C.A. § 1538(a)(1)(B)). Passed in 1973 to preserve specific vanishing species, the ESA restricted their right to develop their land.

Western quarrels with federal management of the land grew into the so-called Sagebrush Rebellion of the late 1970s and 1980s. This **IN FOCUS** was an attempt by several states to wrest control over land management from the federal government and turn it over to state authorities. The rebels argued that local control would mean less bureaucracy and more responsiveness than could be offered by the federal Bureau of Land Management (BLM), which manages 177 million acres in the western states. Some went further. For instance, in 1979, Nevada declared legislation that the state owned and had control and jurisdiction over all "public lands" within it (Nev. Rev. Stat. §§ 321.596–.599). This claim was largely symbolic in that it excluded federal land such as parks, forests, and wildlife refuges.

Although the rebellion gained slight support from the Reagan administration—whose antiregulatory stance allowed grazing on nearly all public lands—it failed to lead to the transfer of

power that its proponents wanted. Discontent among western political and business leaders remained.

The conflict came to a new crisis in the early 1990s. The election of President Bill Clinton in 1992, and his choice of the environmentally minded Bruce Babbitt as interior secretary, quickly heightened among environmentalists expectations for tougher restrictions. The administration promised broad rangeland reforms. It favored raising the grazing fees charged to cattle ranchers from $1.86 to $4.28 per animal unit month (AUM) (the amount of forage needed to feed one animal for a month) in order to bring the fees closer to the average $8.00 to $15.00 per AUM charged on private land. The proposed reforms also asserted that the federal government would hold title to any water sources developed on federal lands. They imposed more stringent ecological standards, and called for ranchers who abused land to be punished by measures that ranged from reductions in the length of grazing permit terms to outright disqualification from the permit program.

The proposals drew praise from environmentalists. They hailed the administration for trying to bring needed protection to western ecological systems and to cut what they argue is a federal subsidy to ranchers. The National Wildlife Federation called the reforms long overdue. To more radical groups like Rest the West, whose slogan was Cattle-Free by '93, the Clinton admin-

example, if a district is zoned for industrial use, no residential buildings are normally permitted there. However, if a residential building predates the zoning plan, it is permitted to remain. This exception is called a NONCONFORMING USE.

Municipalities exercise wide discretion in fixing the boundaries of commercial and industrial districts. A number of ordinances have been enacted to protect residential zones from encroachment by gasoline stations, public parking facilities, businesses selling intoxicating li-

quors, and factories that produce smoke or odors.

When enacting zoning ordinances, a municipality takes many factors into consideration. The most significant are the density of the population; the site and physical attributes of the land involved; traffic and transportation; the fitness of the land for the permitted use; the character of neighborhoods in the community; the existing uses and zoning of neighboring property; the effect of the permitted use on land istration's efforts were a step toward eliminating ranching on public lands altogether.

But among western business and political interests, the proposals caused an uproar. Opponents called the increase in grazing fees unfair, arguing that it failed to take into account that the more expensive private lands offer ranchers superior grazing as well as improvements such as fences and water sources. Industry representatives claimed the fee hike would crush already struggling ranchers. The American Sheep Industry Association, for example, estimated that a quarter of its members would be driven out of business, at a loss of $1.68 billion in revenues.

In public statements and at meetings throughout the West, ranchers and politicians decried the effort as a giveaway to environmentalists by out-of-touch federal bureaucrats.

The administration tried several times to make the reforms stick. President Clinton originally wanted to make higher grazing fees part of his first budget, but western lawmakers protested. The administration compromised on water issues and the size of the grazing fee, but to no avail. In October 1993, an attempt to pass the reform package was blocked by several filibusters in the U.S. Senate. Although opponents declared victory, Babbitt plowed ahead with a plan to effect the reforms through changes in BLM regulations. Known as Rangeland Reform '94, the revised regulations were put into place in February 1995 after the interior secretary conducted numerous public meetings with ranchers and environ-

mentalists (BLM Grazing Administration Rules and Regulations [60 Fed. Reg. 9894]). The sharp fee hike was shelved in favor of a customary twelve-cent annual increase. Another significant compromise was the establishment of grassroots resource advisory councils, made up of ranchers, environmentalists, and other citizens who would advise the BLM on policy decisions.

The issuance of new regulations, even sweetened by compromise, hardly quelled western opposition. While fighting the rangeland reform battle, western lawmakers had also grappled with the administration over the issue of mining rights. The dispute centered on an 1872 law that allowed mining companies to snap up federal land at $2.50 to $5.00 an acre (the Mining Act of 1872 [30 U.S.C.A. § 22]). The administration said foreign companies were exploiting the law, originally intended to help small prospectors. Nevertheless, western states refused to budge on demands that a higher royalty fee be imposed to compensate the federal government for the incredibly low price for land. Any increase, they said, would cost their states revenue from the mining industry.

Meanwhile, a more radical element in the western conflict had appeared. Between 1991 and 1995, nearly sixty western counties asserted in ordinances that they—not the federal government—had control over federal lands. As this trend grew and became known as the county supremacy movement, the *National Law Journal* noted that it took two legal forms. One was typified by Boundary County, Idaho, whose 1991 ordinance cited local custom and cul-

ture as reasons for requiring all federal and state agencies to comply with its land-use policy plan. The second originated in Nye County, Nevada, where two resolutions in 1993 declared that the county owned all public lands and public roads.

Nye County became a focal point of the new movement. Many of its constituents openly resented federal control of nearly 87 percent of the county's land. In 1994, it became the scene of concern after Dick Carver, a Nevada rancher and Nye County commissioner, used a bulldozer to plow open a forest road over the objections of an armed U.S. Forest Service agent. The incident made Carver a sort of folk hero, and he began delivering lectures in more than twenty states. Hostilities erupted in Nye County, and bombs in New Mexico and Nevada and gunshots in California were aimed at federal employees.

Determined to stop the rebellion and reassert federal authority over federal lands, the U.S. Department of Justice joined one lawsuit and filed another. In March 1996, it won both. In the first, *Boundary Backpackers v. Boundary County*, 913 P.2d 1141, the Idaho Supreme Court invalidated Boundary County's ordinance as unconstitutional. In the second, the U.S. district court in Nevada struck down Nye County's ordinance (*United States v. Nye County*, 920 F.Supp. 1108).

Despite the federal government's victories on some fronts, the West's desire for greater independence and its distrust of federal authority indicate the likelihood of further struggles.

in the surrounding area; any potential decrease in property values; the gain to the public at large weighed against economic hardships imposed on individual property owners; and the amount of time that the property has remained unimproved, reviewed in the context of land development in the area as a whole.

Exclusionary zoning is the practice of using the zoning power to further the parochial interests of a particular municipality at the expense of surrounding regions. Its purpose is to ad-

vance economic and social segregation. Exclusionary zoning involves using zoning to take advantage of the benefits of regional development without being forced to bear the burdens of such development, as well as using zoning to maintain particular municipalities as enclaves of affluence or social homogeneity. Both practices have been strongly condemned in the courts, since they violate the principle that municipal zoning ordinances should advance the general welfare.

Exclusionary zoning takes various forms, such as requirements setting a minimum lot size or house size, the prohibition of multifamily housing, and the prohibition of mobile homes.

A municipality has a legitimate interest in ensuring that residential development proceeds in an orderly and planned manner and that the burdens on municipal services do not increase faster than the services' ability to expand. It must also preserve exceptional environmental and historical features. Increasingly, however, exclusionary techniques have come under fire as unfair ways of preventing the creation of economically, racially, and socially diverse communities.

Nuisance   NUISANCE is an unreasonable, unwarranted, or illegal use by an individual of his or her own property, that in some way injures the rights of others. A nuisance ACTION ordinarily arises between two neighboring landowners or is brought by a government attorney. The person initiating the nuisance action seeks to control or limit the use of the land that is creating the nuisance. Nuisance is based on the principle that no one has the right to use property in a manner such as to injure a neighbor.

A private nuisance arises when there is an interference with the use or QUIET ENJOYMENT of land without an actual TRESPASS or physical invasion. For example, A might sue B, alleging that constant loud noises by B amount to a nuisance to A and A's property, which may or may not adversely affect other property in the area.

A public nuisance extends further than a private nuisance, since it adversely affects the health, morals, safety, welfare, comfort, or convenience of the general public. Statutes in many states precisely define what constitutes a public nuisance. Common examples are water and AIR POLLUTION, the storage of explosives under dangerous conditions, houses of PROSTITUTION, the emission of bad odors or loud noises, and the obstruction of public ways.

A nuisance can be both private and public, since certain activities may be sufficient to constitute a public nuisance while still substantially interfering with the use of the adjoining land to such a degree that a landowner may sue on the ground that a private nuisance is present. Private nuisance refers to the property interest affected, as opposed to the type of conduct.

Nuisances may occur in rural as well as urban areas, but they become more obvious when the area is well established as residential in nature. The fact that an activity of a certain type is permitted in an area under the zoning ordinance does not mean that it may not be stopped if it develops into a nuisance. If an otherwise legitimate activity threatens the health or safety of the community in general, it can be classified as a public nuisance. Usually, however, very little relief is available for someone who intentionally locates in an industrial area.

Waste   WASTE laws prohibit the unreasonable or improper use of land by someone who is in rightful POSSESSION of the land. The most common relationship between waste-law litigants is that of LANDLORD AND TENANT, but waste laws also apply to GRANTORS and GRANTEES, and owners of land for life and their successors.

Waste comes in four forms: voluntary, permissive, ameliorating, and equitable. An intentional act that diminishes the value of land constitutes voluntary waste. Permissive waste is the omission of expected maintenance to land or its property. Ameliorating waste is a land use that is not authorized by the owner but nevertheless improves the value of the property. Finally, if a use is inconsistent with the land's highest use, a person holding a future interest in the land may bring an equitable waste action against the possessor.

A successful action for waste usually results in the awarding of money DAMAGES, but courts sometimes issue an INJUNCTION. This means that the landowner can obtain a court order preventing the possessor from engaging in wasteful acts. If a landowner can show a substantial likelihood of harm if such an order is not issued, and that no other satisfactory legal remedies exist, an injunction may be issued.

Eminent Domain   EMINENT DOMAIN is the right or power of a unit of government or a designated private individual to take private property for public use, following the payment of a fair amount of money to the owner of the property. The FIFTH AMENDMENT to the U.S. Constitution provides, "[N]or shall private property be taken for public use, without just compensation." This is commonly referred to as the Takings Clause. The theory behind eminent domain is that the local government can exercise such power to promote the general welfare in areas of public concern, such as health, safety, or morals.

Eminent domain may be exercised by numerous local government bodies, including drainage, levee, or flood control agencies; HIGHWAY or road authorities; and housing authorities. For example, if a city wishes to build a new bridge, and the land it needs is occupied by

Planned Communities: Read the Fine Print

One in eight people in the United States live in planned communities, which include townhouses, condominiums, co-ops, and entire real estate developments containing single-family homes. A common feature of all planned communities is a homeowner association, which oversees the maintenance and administration of the real estate, especially the common areas shared by all owners. A board of directors of the association, elected by the property owners, enforces the community's rules.

Planned communities often impose a number of restrictions on their members. These are typically contained in the real estate deed, which becomes a contract between the property buyer and the community. Purchasers are bound by these restrictions whether or not they read or understood them. The restrictions may cover a wide range of architectural and aesthetic limitations, and are believed to increase the value of property in the community. Unwary residents may find the limitations extreme.

Residents of planned communities have faced limitations on things such as paint colors, pets, sports and sporting equipment, and outdoor decorations. Under such restrictions homeowners have been threatened with fines for stringing Christmas lights, taken to court because their dog was too heavy, and prohibited from throwing a Frisbee. Association dues can be used to pay for a lawsuit enforcing a restriction, and some bylaws require the defendant homeowner to reimburse the association's legal fees.

---

sixty houses, it may use its eminent domain power to take the sixty houses, remove the buildings, and build the bridge. The government must make JUST COMPENSATION to the affected property owners, who are entitled to the FAIR MARKET VALUE of the property.

The power of eminent domain is exercised through CONDEMNATION proceedings. These proceedings establish the right to take the property by the government or designated private individual (usually PUBLIC UTILITIES) and the amount of compensation to be paid for the property.

The U.S. Supreme Court has examined the relation between land-use regulations and the Takings Clause. In *Lucas v. South Carolina Coastal Council*, 505 U.S. 1003, 112 S. Ct. 2886, 120 L. Ed. 2d 798 (1992), the Court held that a total deprivation of economic use amounts to a taking for which damages may be awarded. *Lucas* involved a developer who had purchased coastal lots to construct two single-family residences. A South Carolina law, which sought to protect the eroding shoreline, prohibited him from building anything except wooden walkways and a wooden deck. The Supreme Court agreed that he was entitled to compensation because this was a regulatory taking.

In *Dolan v. City of Tigard*, 512 U.S. 374, 114 S. Ct. 2309, 129 L. Ed. 2d 304 (1994), the Court limited government power to take private property for the public good. The Court ruled that a city cannot force a store owner to make part of the owner's land a public bike path in exchange for a permit to build a larger store. The decision makes it more difficult for municipalities to require that land developers give up for public purposes part of their property, including sidewalks, access roads, and parks. If the government needs the land, it must compensate the owner.

Historic Districts Since the 1950s more attention has been paid to the preservation of historic districts. Purchase or condemnation by the government for historic preservation purposes is valid. More important, acts establishing historic districts have been upheld as promoting the public welfare. State and local preservation laws have been bolstered by the federal National Historic Preservation Act of 1966 (16 U.S.C.A. § 47 et seq.), which provides a procedure for registering buildings as historic LANDMARKS. Apart from establishing a national register of historic sites, the act provided for the protection and restoration of historic sites and districts.

Environmental Controls ENVIRONMENTAL LAW and regulation have significantly affected land development. With the passage of the NATIONAL ENVIRONMENTAL POLICY ACT of 1969 (NEPA) (42 U.S.C.A. § 4321 et seq.), the public and private sectors were obligated to conform to certain environmental standards. The interrelationship of the objectives of NEPA and more traditional forms of land-use control under police power are illustrated by NEPA's stated objectives, which relate not only to the environment but also to ensuring aesthetically pleasing surroundings, protecting health and safety, preserving historic and cultural heritage, and preserving natural resources.

NEPA requires that every federal agency submit an environmental impact statement (EIS) with every legislative recommendation or program proposing major federal projects that will most likely affect the quality of the surrounding environment. An EIS may be required for projects such as the rerouting of an interstate highway, construction of a new dam, or expansion of a ski resort on federally owned land.

The EIS is a tool to assist in decision making, providing information on the positive and negative environmental effects of the proposed undertaking and alternatives. The EIS must also examine the effect of not implementing the proposed action. This "no-action" alternative may result in the agency's continuing to use existing approaches. Although NEPA requires agencies to consider the environmental consequences of their actions, it does not force them to take the most environmentally sound alternative, nor does it dictate that they pursue the least expensive option.

The effect of environmental policies on land use has been substantial. State governments followed the lead of the federal government and passed statutes that create water and air pollution control agencies. Some states require EISs, and a number have comprehensive legislation.

Land-Use Conflicts Government and judicial bodies usually attempt to make land-use policies responsive to emerging concerns and developing needs. Conflicts result from situations in which localities attempt to block or ignore those needs or from situations in which the response is challenged as an overextension of the police power. The complexity of urban problems and the growth of urban areas place constant tension on the land-use process.

CROSS-REFERENCES

Adjoining Landowners; Endangered Species Act; Environmental Protection Agency; Fish and Fishing; Hunting; Pollution; Solid Wastes, Hazardous Substances, and Toxic Pollutants; Water Rights.

Lanfranc

"YOU CAN OFFER GOD NO GREATER OR MORE PLEASING GIFT THAN YOUR DESIRE TO GOVERN DIVINE AND HUMAN AFFAIRS BY THE APPROPRIATE LAWS."

LANFRANC Lanfranc served as archbishop of Canterbury under William the Conquerer. He reformed the English church, established strong church-state relations, and introduced components of Roman and CANON LAW to England. Under William's reign, he laid the foundation for what succeeding theorists would build into England's secular COMMON-LAW court system. Early U.S. law derived some elements from this system.

Lanfranc was born in about 1005 in Pavia, Italy. He studied law in Pavia and became a respected scholar, principally because of his studies in ROMAN LAW, which was a subject of growing interest in Italy at the time.

Lanfranc established a school at Avranches, Normandy, and taught for three years, until about 1042. After being attacked and almost killed by a highway robber, he went into seclusion at Saint Stephens Abbey at Bec, a newly established monastery. After three years of total seclusion, he returned to teaching, this time at the monastery. He taught there for eighteen years, earning high respect throughout Europe as an instructor of theology. The school became one of the most famous in Europe under his leadership. The future pope Alexander II was among his students.

When William the Conquerer decided to marry Matilda of Flanders, Lanfranc declared that the union would be a violation of canon law. Because of Lanfranc's strong opposition, William threatened to exile him. Lanfranc eventually gave up his stand against the marriage. In about 1051 William married Matilda, despite a papal ban on the union. Lanfranc sought support from the pope and engineered an eventual reconciliation of the papacy with the king. Six years after the wedding, William received the pope's approval to marry Matilda. In 1063 the grateful king appointed Lanfranc the first abbot of Saint Stephens.

Lanfranc also successfully lobbied for papal support for William's subsequent invasion of England. Because of these efforts, Lanfranc became William's closest and most trusted adviser by the time of the invasion in 1066, which resulted in the Norman Conquest.

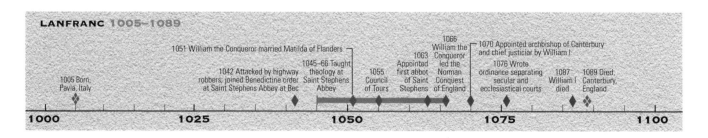

LANFRANC 1005–1089

1005 Born; Pavia, Italy

1042 Attacked by highway robbers; joined Benedictine order at Saint Stephens Abbey at Bec

1045–66 Taught theology at Saint Stephens Abbey

1051 William the Conqueror married Matilda of Flanders

1055 Council of Tours

1063 Appointed first abbot of Saint Stephens

1066 William the Conqueror led the Norman Conquest of England

1070 Appointed archbishop of Canterbury and chief justiciar by William I

1076 Wrote ordinance separating secular and ecclesiastical courts

1087 William I died

1089 Died; Canterbury, England

1000   1025   1050   1075   1100

In 1070 William appointed Lanfranc archbishop of Canterbury and chief justiciar. In the latter capacity, Lanfranc worked as a viceroy, or representative of the king, alongside William and when William was away from court. To reinforce William's dominance as ruler of England, Lanfranc replaced many English bishops with Normans. He also defeated an effort by the archbishop-elect of York to declare independence from Canterbury. He supported absolute veto power for the king and helped lay the precedent for trying bishops before secular courts.

Lanfranc supported papal sovereignty and protected the church from secular influences. He also helped William establish independence for the English church. In 1076 he wrote an important ordinance that separated secular courts from ECCLESIASTICAL COURTS. In addition, he reformed guidelines for the marriage of priests, established ecclesiastical courts, and strengthened monasteries. He died May 28, 1089.

Lanfranc brought to England an understanding of canon and Roman law, which had been more widely embraced in continental Europe. Although he did not replace England's court system with Roman law, he introduced components of that system to England's court system.

Lanfranc's efforts laid the foundation for important writings on ENGLISH LAW in the twelfth and thirteenth centuries. In the twelfth century, the first major text on the common law was written, reputedly by RANULF GLANVILL (his authorship is now disputed). In the thirteenth century, writings by HENRY DE BRACTON built further on the common law with principles from both Roman (or civil) law and canon law. These works were important elements in the establishment of England's eventual common-law system. The scholar FREDERIC W. MAITLAND said that Lanfranc's influence was responsible for "the early precipitation of English law in so coherent a form." The United States borrowed concepts from the English court system that began to develop during the years following the Norman Conquest.

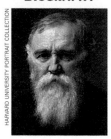

Christopher Columbus Langdell

"LAW, CONSIDERED AS A SCIENCE, CONSISTS OF CERTAIN PRINCIPLES OR DOCTRINES. TO HAVE A MASTERY OF THESE AS TO BE ABLE TO APPLY THEM WITH CONSTANT FACILITY AND CERTAINTY TO THE EVER-TANGLED SKEIN OF HUMAN AFFAIRS, IS WHAT CONSTITUTES A TRUE LAWYER."

LANGDELL, CHRISTOPHER COLUMBUS "Mr. Fox, will you state the facts in the case of *Payne v. Cave?*" That simple question marked the beginning of a revolution in LEGAL EDUCATION. In 1870, Professor Christopher Columbus Langdell, in the first contracts class he taught at Harvard Law School, put the question to a student and forever changed the way lawyers learned their craft. No longer would law students sit passively and take notes while their professor lectured or read out of a legal treatise. Langdell's students read the reports of actual court cases and were required to discuss them in class. Langdell is credited with introducing the case-study method of instruction into U.S. law schools. Although there is evidence that Langdell was not the first to use the CASE METHOD, as dean, he had the opportunity to shape the program of the influential Harvard Law School and in turn the law training programs of schools throughout the United States.

Langdell was born in the small farming town of New Boston, New Hampshire, on May 22, 1826. With the financial assistance of his two sisters, and a later scholarship, Langdell was educated at Exeter Academy. He entered Harvard College in 1848 but left after only one year to begin his legal education by clerking in a law office, a common method of training for lawyers in those days. Within eighteen months, Langdell was back at Harvard, this time in the college's law school, where he remained for three years. Langdell was admitted to the bar in 1854 and practiced law in New York City for sixteen years.

In 1869, Harvard's new president, Charles W. Eliot, an accomplished chemist committed to educational reform, recruited Langdell to be Dane Professor of Law at the law school. It was hoped that Langdell could help revitalize the school, which had been criticized by the legal community as stagnant. In September 1870, Langdell was voted dean of the three-member faculty, a position that allowed him to change the method of legal instruction at Harvard.

Prior to Langdell, the primary teaching method in the nation's law schools was the lecture. Many professors published textbooks

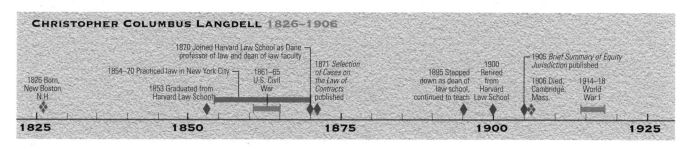

CHRISTOPHER COLUMBUS LANGDELL 1826–1906

1826 Born, New Boston, N.H.

1853 Graduated from Harvard Law School

1854–70 Practiced law in New York City

1861–65 U.S. Civil War

1870 Joined Harvard Law School as Dane professor of law and dean of law faculty

1871 *Selection of Cases on the Law of Contracts* published

1895 Stepped down as dean of law school, continued to teach

1900 Retired from Harvard Law School

1905 *Brief Summary of Equity Jurisdiction* published

1906 Died, Cambridge, Mass.

1914–18 World War I

1825   1850   1875   1900   1925

that were really expanded versions of their lectures. In class, students took notes while professors read lectures, or they were quizzed on specific portions of an assigned textbook reading. Discussion was rare, as it was assumed that the author of the textbook had found and set forth the true rules of law.

Langdell proposed that law students must be given some means of experimentation and research by which they might cut through the excessive verbiage of black-letter rules and discover the fundamental scientific axioms that ought to be used in studying, teaching, and judging the law. CASEBOOKS were to be the students' laboratories. Langdell's case-study method was almost impossible to teach when he first introduced it in 1870 because of a lack of printed case reports. When Langdell introduced the case method at Harvard Law School, he had to write the books he used in his classes. His *Selection of Cases on the Law of Contracts* (1871) was the first modern casebook and became the model for many later such books.

Langdell's new method combined the careful study of the decisions in previous cases, with the Socratic method of teaching. The Socratic method was modeled after that used by the Greek philosopher Socrates. Using this method, Langdell would ask his students a series of questions whose answers were designed to lead to a logical conclusion foreseen by Langdell.

When Langdell first used this method, many of his students were not pleased. In fact, on that first day, many students were unprepared to answer Langdell's questions about the case of *Payne v. Cave.* The majority of students openly condemned this new method, complaining that there was no instruction or imparting of rules and that really nothing had been learned. The newer students who had not studied law before resisted answering questions because they thought it presumptuous of them to offer an opinion on a matter in which they had no formal training. The older students, upset that Langdell imparted no legal rules, thought the answers of their fellow students nothing more than the idle talk of young boys. Students even expressed concern that they could never learn the law in time to graduate if it continued to be taught by such a method. When asked a question by a student, Langdell usually hesitated and then answered by posing a question to the student. This led some to question whether Langdell even knew the law he professed to teach.

Langdell's new method was controversial and not an immediate success. During the first semester he taught with it, his students missed classes regularly, and total enrollment in the course fell to only seven. Dissatisfaction with this educational experiment apparently spawned a new law school, Boston University Law School, and the effects were felt throughout the Harvard Law School, as enrollment fell from 136 in 1870–71 to 113 in 1872–73.

Despite student criticism, Harvard president Eliot remained committed to Langdell and his controversial method. As students began to understand Langdell's method, and in particular his Socratic process involving dialogue between teachers and students, they grew to prefer their active involvement over the relative passivity of the old lecture methods. By 1873–74, Harvard Law School enrollment was again on the rise, and by 1890, the law school was flourishing and the case-study method was firmly established.

Langdell's contributions to legal education go beyond the introduction of the case-study method. As dean of Harvard Law School, he added a third year to what was a two-year curriculum, and required students to pass final exams before they could advance to the next year or graduate. He was also instrumental in hiring professors who were not practicing lawyers or judges, an approach unheard of at the time.

In 1895, Langdell stepped down as dean of Harvard Law School. He continued to teach for five years before retiring in 1900. He died in 1906, at the age of eighty.

LANHAM ACT 📖 A federal statute enacted in 1946 and subsequently amended to revise trademark law. 📖

The Lanham Act of 1946, also known as the Trademark Act (15 U.S.C.A. § 1051 et seq., ch. 540, 60 Stat. 427 [1988 & Supp. V 1993]), is a federal statute that regulates the use of TRADEMARKS in commercial activity. Trademarks are distinctive pictures, words, and other symbols or devices used by businesses to identify their goods and services. The Lanham Act gives trademark users exclusive rights to their marks, thereby protecting the time and money invested in those marks. The act also serves to reduce consumer confusion in the identification of goods and services.

The Lanham Act was not the first federal legislation on trademarks, but it was the first comprehensive federal legislation. Before the Lanham Act, most of trademark law was regulated by a variety of state laws.

The first federal trademark legislation was passed by Congress in 1870 and amended in 1876. In 1879 the U.S. Supreme Court found

The Lanham Act regulates the use of trademarks in commercial activity. Trademarks such as the one for Kentucky Fried Chicken are so well known that even without the letters KFC, most consumers would be able to identify the company.

that legislation unconstitutional. Two subsequent attempts at federal trademark legislation provided little protection for the rights of trademark users. The movement for stronger trademark legislation began in the 1920s, and was championed in the 1930s by Representative Fritz Lanham, of Texas. In 1946 Congress passed the Trademark Act of 1946 and named it the Lanham Act after its chief proponent. Lanham stated in 1946 that the act was designed "to protect legitimate business and the consumers of the country."

The Lanham Act protected trademarks used in commerce and registered with the PATENT AND TRADEMARK OFFICE, in Washington, D.C. It expanded the types of trademarks that deserved legal protection, created legal procedures to help trademark holders enforce their rights, and established an assortment of rights that attached to qualified trademarks.

Congress has amended the act several times since 1946. The most sweeping changes came in 1988. Those changes included an amendment that authorized the protection of trademarks that had not been used in commerce but were created with the intent that they be used in commerce.

LAPSE 📖 The termination or failure of a right or privilege because of a neglect to exercise that right or to perform some DUTY within a time limit, or because a specified contingency did not occur. The expiration of coverage under an INSURANCE policy because of the insured's failure to pay the PREMIUM.

The COMMON-LAW principle that a GIFT in a WILL does not take effect but passes into the ESTATE remaining after the payment of debts and particular gifts, if the BENEFICIARY is alive when the will is executed but subsequently predeceases the TESTATOR. 📖

In its broadest sense, the term *lapse* describes the loss of any right or privilege because of the passage of time or the occurrence or nonoccurrence of a certain event. It is often used by legislatures in reference to governmental con-

cerns. Legislatures may include anti-lapse provisions in statutes to ensure that certain spending programs remain funded from year to year. Lapse also has distinct significance in the law of insurance contracts and wills.

An insurance policy can lapse, or become void, if the insured fails to make payments on it. All states give insureds a GRACE PERIOD, which allows extra time to make a payment owed under a policy. The grace period varies from policy to policy. For example, in Maine the grace period is seven days for health insurance policies with weekly premiums, ten days for such policies with monthly premiums, and thirty-one days for all other such policies (Me. Rev. Stat. Ann. tit. 24-A, § 2707). The grace period in Maine is thirty days for life insurance policies (§ 2505).

Some statutes on insurance policy lapses provide a small measure of protection against lapse. For example, Maine Revised Statutes Annotated, title 24-A, section 2739 (West 1995), states that no insurance company may cancel a health insurance policy within three months of nonpayment unless the insurer provides the insured with a notice of potential lapse within ten to forty-five days after the premium was due. Section 4751 provides that in the event of a STRIKE by insurance agents, no life or noncancellable health, hospital expense, or hospital and surgical expense insurance policy may lapse owing to nonpayment within thirty days of the strike's inception. This law applies only if the agent is responsible for the collection of premiums and is represented in COLLECTIVE BARGAINING by a labor organization that has been recognized by the state.

A will is a document left by a deceased person, who is called a testator or devisor. A will allocates the property of a testator to living persons. If the intended recipient of a gift in a will (called a beneficiary or devisee) dies before the testator, the gift may lapse. This means that the gift is void and is placed back into the estate of the testator. The property becomes part of the RESIDUUM of the estate and may not be disposed of in the manner sought by the testator.

Almost all states have statutes that provide that in the event of a lapse, the gift should go to the ISSUE, or LINEAL descendants, of the deceased devisee. If the beneficiary has no issue, then the gift is left in the estate of the testator.

In some states the anti-lapse statute applies only to grandparents of the testator and lineal descendants of the testator's grandparents. For example, under the Maine Revised Statutes Annotated, title 18-A, section 2-605 (West 1995), the issue of the deceased devisee may receive a gift intended for the deceased devisee, but only if they survived the testator by 120 hours.

LARCENY 📖 The unauthorized taking and removal of the PERSONAL PROPERTY of another by a person who intends to permanently deprive the owner of it; a crime against the right of POSSESSION. 📖

Larceny generally refers to nonviolent THEFT. It is a COMMON-LAW term developed by the royal courts of England in the seventeenth century. In the United States, most JURISDICTIONS have eliminated the crime of larceny from statutory codes, in favor of a general theft statute.

The crime of larceny was developed to punish the taking of property in nonviolent face-to-face encounters, and to set it apart from ROBBERY. Robbery involved some measure of violence in connection with theft, and the courts did not feel that a nonviolent theft should warrant the same punishment as robbery. Larceny was nevertheless punished severely. A person convicted of larceny could receive the death penalty or be sentenced to many years in prison.

The English courts were careful not to encroach on the lawmaking rights of the British Parliament, so they kept the crime of larceny limited and well-defined. A defendant could be convicted of larceny only if he or she had some physical interaction with the victim; the victim relinquished property that was in the victim's possession at the time of the taking; the defendant was not in lawful possession of the stolen goods at the time of the taking; and the defendant actually carried the property away at the time of the interaction.

Over time the English courts recognized the need to expand the concept of larceny. In the absence of legislative action, they created new offenses based on the manner in which the theft was accomplished. EMBEZZLEMENT was created in the eighteenth century to punish the misappropriation of property after lawful possession. This charge would apply, for example, if a store clerk accepted a customer's money in a legal sale, and then took that money for her or his own use. Embezzlement was punished more severely than larceny because it involved a breach of trust.

Larceny by trick was created to punish the taking of property with the owner's consent when that consent was obtained by FRAUD or DECEIT. Before the courts created the offense of larceny by trick, defendants who had swindled their victims were able to argue that they had not committed larceny because the victims had willfully given them the property.

Shortly after the courts created larceny by trick, they created the crime of obtaining property by FALSE PRETENSES. Before, a defendant who induced a person to part with the title to property could escape prosecution because the victim transferred not actual possession of the property but only TITLE to the property. This commercial form of taking was made illegal under the law of false pretenses.

The English courts also began to make distinctions based on the value of the stolen property. GRAND LARCENY was any larceny of property worth more than a certain amount of money. Any larceny of property worth less than that amount was called PETIT LARCENY and was punished less severely.

In time the issue of nonviolent theft became too complex for solution through CASE LAW, and the British Parliament began to enact statutes that more clearly defined it.

The law of larceny and related offenses was adopted in the United States and remained in effect throughout the country's early history. Then, in the twentieth century, many legislatures abolished it in favor of a broad theft statute. In North Dakota, for example, the crime of theft now includes "larceny, stealing, purloining, embezzlement, obtaining money or property by false pretenses, extortion, blackmail, fraudulent conversion, receiving stolen property, misappropriation of public funds, swindling, and the like" (N.D. Cent. Code § 12.1-23-01 [1995]).

The sweeping theft statutes are favored by prosecutors because they make it less likely that a defendant can escape punishment by arguing that one of the discrete elements in a larceny, embezzlement, or related theft was not proved. For example, if a defendant had passed a bad check as down payment on a car and then gained possession of the car, the defendant could defeat the criminal charge of obtaining property by false pretenses, by arguing that the seller kept the title to the car and therefore the defendant could only be guilty of larceny. Under larceny statutes persons who commit theft can escape punishment if the prosecutor does not choose the correct charge. Under broad theft statutes, prosecutors need only be concerned with the intent to steal and the value of the property involved.

In states that have incorporated larceny into a broad theft statute, the punishment for a theft is based largely on the value of the stolen property. In Iowa, for example, theft of property exceeding $10,000 in value, theft directly from another's person, and theft of property in and around certain abandoned buildings is theft in

Larcenies Reported in United States, 1976 to 1996

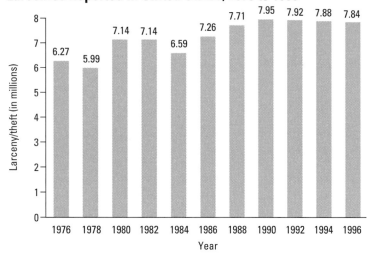

Source: Federal Bureau of Investigation, *Uniform Crime Reports.*

the first degree, a class C FELONY. A class C felony is punishable by a prison term of up to ten years and a fine of at least $500 but no more than $10,000. Theft of property not exceeding $100 in value is theft in the fifth degree, a simple MISDEMEANOR, and it may be punished with a fine of up to $100 and an order to perform some community service specified by the judge (Iowa Code Ann. §§ 714.2, 902.9, 903.1 [West 1995]).

The broad theft statutes do not cover all possible theft offenses. States that have a theft statute also maintain statutes prohibiting such acts as the unauthorized use of an automobile, FORGERY, fraud, deceptive business practices, RECEIVING STOLEN PROPERTY, EXTORTION, theft of services, and theft of property that was lost, mislaid, or delivered by mistake.

Massachusetts is one state that has retained its larceny statutes. The general larceny statute in Massachusetts combines the crime of embezzlement with larceny. Under this statute anyone who

> steals, or with intent to defraud obtains by a false pretense, or whoever unlawfully, and with intent to steal or embezzle, converts, or secretes with intent to convert, the property of another . . . whether such property is or is not in his possession at the time of such conversion or secreting, shall be guilty of larceny. . . . (Mass. Gen. Laws Ann. ch. 266, § 30(1) [West 1996]).

Massachusetts also has several other larceny statutes, some of which identify a certain act as larceny. For example, the crime of false pretenses relating to contracts, banking transactions, or credit is specifically defined as larceny (§ 33). This statute is necessary because the

general larceny statute does not cover such theft.

Larceny and theft are distinct from BURGLARY, which is committed when a person TRESPASSES into a dwelling or other building with the intent to commit a crime therein. Burglary does not necessarily consist of the taking of property, although the intent to steal can upgrade a criminal charge from trespassing to burglary.

Larceny is also different from shoplifting, which involves the theft of property from a place of business. Most states have eliminated the crime of shoplifting along with larceny, embezzlement, false pretenses, and similar offenses, in creating one broad theft statute.

In all states larceny and theft are distinct from robbery. Robbery involves the threat of force or the actual use of force in connection with a theft. The line between robbery, and larceny or theft is unsteady. If a perpetrator plies the victim with alcohol or drugs, most courts consider this a form of force that boosts the crime from larceny or theft to robbery. If a perpetrator simply moves a person who is unconscious through no fault of the perpetrator, the movement may not constitute the kind of force that gives rise to robbery. Most courts refuse to convict a defendant of robbery if the victim was unaware of any use of force, but the defendant may be charged with larceny or theft.

Larceny and theft generally are a matter of state law. Congress maintains a few federal laws regarding thefts that have federal implications. These statutes include theft at lending, credit, and insurance institutions; theft of interstate shipments of goods; theft on waterways and oceans; and theft by court officers.

LASCIVIOUSNESS ▥ LEWDNESS; indecency; obscenity; behavior that tends to deprave the morals in regard to sexual relations. ▥

The statutory offense of lascivious COHABITATION is committed by two individuals who live together as HUSBAND AND WIFE and engage in sexual relations without the sanction of MARRIAGE.

LAST CLEAR CHANCE ▥ In the law of TORTS, the doctrine that excuses or negates the effect of the plaintiff's contributory NEGLIGENCE and permits him or her to recover, in particular instances, DAMAGES regardless of his or her own lack of ordinary CARE. ▥

The rule of last clear chance operates when the PLAINTIFF negligently enters into an area of danger from which the person cannot extricate himself or herself. The DEFENDANT has the final opportunity to prevent the harm that the plaintiff otherwise will suffer. The doctrine was formulated to relieve the severity of the application of the contributory negligence rule against the plaintiff, which completely bars any recovery if the person was at all negligent.

There are as many variations and adaptations of this doctrine as there are JURISDICTIONS that apply it. Four different categories have emerged, which are classified as *helpless plaintiffs, inattentive plaintiffs, observant defendants*, and *inattentive defendants*.

Helpless Plaintiffs Where the plaintiff's previous negligence has placed him or her in a position from which the person is powerless to extricate himself or herself by the exercise of any ordinary care, and the defendant detects the danger while time remains to avoid it but fails to act, the courts have held that the plaintiff can recover.

There must be proof that the defendant discovered the situation, had the time to take action that would have saved the plaintiff, but failed to do what a reasonable person would have done. In the absence of any one of these elements, the courts deny recovery.

If the defendant who has a DUTY to discover the plaintiff's peril does not do so in time to avoid injury to the plaintiff, some courts have permitted recovery under the rationale that the defendant's subsequent negligence is the PROXIMATE CAUSE, or direct cause, of the injury, rather than the contributory negligence of the plaintiff. The defendant must have been able to have discovered the peril through appropriate vigilance so as to avoid its harmful consequences to the plaintiff.

Inattentive Plaintiffs In another group of cases, the plaintiff is not helpless but is in a position to escape injury. The person's negligence consists of failure to pay attention to his or her surroundings and detect his or her own peril. If the defendant discovers the plaintiff's danger and inattentiveness, and is then negligent, a majority of courts allows the plaintiff to recover. Some courts hold that the defendant must actually recognize the plaintiff's danger and inattention. Most courts apply a more objective standard; they require only that the defendant discover the situation and that the plaintiff's peril and inattentiveness be evident to a reasonable person. The discovery can be proved by CIRCUMSTANTIAL EVIDENCE. There is an additional essential qualification that the defendant can frequently, reasonably assume until the last moment that the plaintiff will protect himself or herself, and the defendant has no reason to act until he or she has some notice to the contrary.

If the defendant does not discover the plaintiff's situation—but could do so with appropriate vigilance—neither party can be viewed as possessing the last clear chance. The plaintiff is still in a position to escape, and his or her inattentiveness persists until the juncture of the accident, without the interval of superior opportunity of the defendant. The plaintiff cannot reasonably demand of the defendant greater care for his or her own protection than that which he or she as plaintiff would exercise for himself or herself. Nearly all of the courts have ruled that, in this situation, there can be no recovery.

Observant Defendant The observant defendant is one who actually sees the plaintiff in time to act so as to avoid the harm and assumes that a duty exists to act under the circumstances. The person perceives the plaintiff's helpless or inattentive condition, but thereafter is negligent in failing to act so as to prevent the plaintiff's harm. In most instances, the defendant's conduct is itself the cause of the plaintiff's danger, but this is not a requirement so long as a duty to act exists.

The plaintiff must prove that the defendant actually saw him or her and that a reasonable person would have known that he or she was inattentive or helpless. This is determined by an objective test entailing circumstantial evidence of the defendant's state of mind. The defendant cannot assert unawareness of the plaintiff's powerlessness or inattentiveness when that fact would have been evident to any observer.

Inattentive Defendant The inattentive defendant is one who fails to fulfill the duty to maintain a surveillance in order to see the plaintiff in time to avoid the harm, perceive the person's helpless or inattentive condition, and thereby exercise reasonable care to act in time to avoid the harm. Due to the defendant's negligence, however, he or she fails to see the plaintiff in time, and injury occurs.

Application of Doctrine There are four possible cases in which the rule of last clear chance can be applied.

The typical last clear chance situation involves the *helpless plaintiff* against the *observant defendant*, and all courts that accept the doctrine will apply it. The few courts that do not recognize the rule attain the same result under the doctrine of willful and wanton misconduct.

In the *helpless plaintiff-inattentive defendant* and the *inattentive plaintiff-observant defendant* cases, most jurisdictions that acknowledge the rule apply it.

Where the case entails the *inattentive plaintiff* against the *inattentive defendant*, the justifications for the rule are eliminated, and nearly all jurisdictions refuse to apply it.

The defendant's negligence must occur subsequent to that point in time when the person discovered or should have discovered the plaintiff's peril.

LAST RESORT ◉ A court, such as the U.S. Supreme Court, from which there is no further APPEAL of a JUDGMENT rendered by it in review of a decision in a civil or criminal ACTION by a lower court. ◉

LATENT ◉ Hidden; concealed; that which does not appear upon the face of an item. ◉

For example, a latent defect in the TITLE to a parcel of REAL PROPERTY is one that is not discoverable by an inspection of the title made with ordinary CARE. Similarly, a latent defect in an item of merchandise is one that could not have been discovered by any known or customary inspection or test.

LATERAL SUPPORT ◉ The right of a landowner to have his or her property naturally upheld by the adjoining land or the soil beneath. ◉

The adjoining owner has the duty not to alter the land, such as by lowering it, so as to cause the support to be weakened or removed.

See also ADJOINING LANDOWNERS.

LAW ◉ A body of rules of conduct of binding legal force and effect, prescribed, recognized, and enforced by controlling authority. ◉

In U.S. law, the word *law* refers to any rule that if broken subjects a party to criminal punishment or civil LIABILITY. Laws in the United States are made by federal, state, and local legislatures, judges, the president, state governors, and administrative agencies.

Law in the United States is a mosaic of statutes, treaties, case law, administrative agency regulations, executive orders, and local laws. U.S. law can be bewildering because the laws of the various jurisdictions—federal, state, and local—are sometimes in conflict. Moreover,

The U.S. Supreme Court is the court of last resort for many civil and criminal actions. In 1997 the Court consisted of (back row) Ruth Bader Ginsburg, David Souter, Clarence Thomas, and Stephen Breyer; and (front row) Antonin Scalia, John Paul Stevens, William Rehnquist, Sandra Day O'Connor, and Anthony Kennedy.

U.S. law is not static. New laws are regularly introduced, old laws are repealed, and existing laws are modified, so the precise definition of a particular law may be different in the future from what it is today.

The U.S. Constitution The highest law in the United States is the U.S. Constitution, as amended. No state or federal law may contradict any provision in the Constitution. In a sense the federal Constitution is a collection of inviolable statutes. It can be altered only by AMENDMENT. Amendments pass after they are approved by two-thirds of both houses of Congress or after petition by two-thirds of the state legislatures. Amendments are then ratified by three-fourths of the state legislatures or by conventions in three-fourths of the states. Upon ratification, the amendment becomes part of the Constitution.

Beneath the federal Constitution lies a vast body of other laws, including federal statutes, treaties, court decisions, agency regulations, and executive orders, and state constitutions, statutes, court decisions, agency regulations, and executive orders.

Statutes and Treaties After the federal Constitution, the highest laws are written laws, or STATUTES, passed by elected federal lawmakers. States have their own CONSTITUTION and statutes.

Federal laws generally involve matters that concern the entire country. State laws generally do not reach beyond the borders of the state. Under Article VI, Section 2, of the U.S. Constitution, federal laws have supremacy over state and local laws. This means that when a state or local law conflicts with a federal law, the federal law prevails.

Federal statutes are passed by Congress and signed into law by the president. State statutes are passed by state legislatures and approved by the governor. If a president or governor vetoes, or rejects, a proposed law, the LEGISLATURE may override the VETO if at least two-thirds of the members of each house of the legislature vote for the law.

Statutes are contained in statutory CODES at the federal and state levels. These statutory codes are available in many public libraries, in law libraries, and in some government buildings, such as city halls and courthouses.

On the federal level, the president has the power to enter into treaties, with the advice and consent of Congress. Treaties are agreements with sovereign nations concerning a wide range of topics such as environmental protection and the manufacture of nuclear missiles. A TREATY does not become law until it is approved by

Common-Law Courts

Courts of law are a fundamental part of the U.S. judicial system. The U.S. Constitution and all state constitutions recognize a judicial branch of government that is charged with adjudicating disputes. Beginning in the 1990s, vigilante organizations challenged the judicial system by establishing so-called common-law courts. By 1996 these common-law courts existed in over thirty states. Though they have no legal standing and their actions do not have the force of law, these courts have caused many problems for attorneys, judges, and other government officials.

Traditionally, common-law courts administered the common law, that is, law based on prior decisions rather than statutes. However, these new common-law courts are premised on a mixture of U.S. constitutional law, English common law, and the Bible, all filtered through an often racist and anti-Semitic world view that holds the U.S. legal system to be illegitimate. These common-law courts imitate the formalities of the U.S. justice system, issuing subpoenas, making criminal indictments, and hearing cases. Most of their cases involve divorce decrees and foreclosure actions. Many of the persons on the courts or seeking their assistance are in dire financial circumstances. They wish to prevent the loss of their property by having a common-law court declare them free of the loans they have secured from banks.

Though common-law courts appear to be merely a symbolic attempt by extremists to assert their political legitimacy, the actions of some of them have led to prosecution for criminal conspiracy. Common-law courts have issued arrest warrants for judges and prosecutors in Montana and Idaho, and have threatened sheriffs who refuse to follow their instructions. In 1994 the Garfield County, Montana, prosecutor charged members of a common-law court with criminal syndicalism, for advocating violence against public officials. One court member was sentenced to ten years in prison, and others received shorter sentences.

two-thirds of the U.S. Senate. Most treaties are concerned with the actions of government employees, but treaties also apply to private citizens.

Case Law Statutes are the primary source of law, and the power to enact statutes is reserved to elected lawmakers. However, judicial decisions also have the force of law. Statutes do not cover every conceivable case, and even when a statute does control a case, the COURTS may need to interpret it. Judicial decisions are known collectively as CASE LAW. A judicial decision legally binds the parties in the case, and also may serve as a law in the same prospective sense as does a statute. In other words, a judicial decision determines the outcome of the particular case, and also may regulate future conduct of all persons within the JURISDICTION of the court.

The opinions of courts, taken together, comprise the COMMON LAW. When there is no statute specifically addressing a legal dispute, courts look to prior cases for guidance. The issues, reasoning, and holdings of prior cases guide courts in settling similar disputes. A prior opinion or collection of opinions on a particular legal issue is known as PRECEDENT, and courts generally follow precedent, if any, when deciding cases. Breaking with precedent may be justified when circumstances or attitudes have changed, but following precedent is the norm.

This gives the common law a certain predictability and consistency. The common law often controls civil matters, such as CONTRACT disputes and PERSONAL INJURY cases (TORTS). Almost all criminal laws are statutory, so common law principles are rarely applied in criminal cases.

Sometimes courts hear challenges to statutes or regulations based on constitutional grounds. Courts can make law by striking down part or all of a particular piece of legislation. The Supreme Court has the power to make law binding throughout the country on federal constitutional issues. The highest court in each state has the same power to interpret the state constitution and to issue holdings that have the force of law.

Occasionally courts create new law by departing from existing precedent or by issuing a decision in a case involving novel issues, called a case of FIRST IMPRESSION. If legislators disagree with the decision, they may nullify the holding by passing a new statute. However, if the court believes that the new statute violates a constitutional provision, it may strike down all or part of the new law. If courts and lawmakers are at odds, the precise law on a certain topic can change over and over.

When researching a legal issue, it is helpful to consult relevant case law. The researcher first finds the relevant annotated statutes, and then reads the cases that are listed under the statutes. Reading case law helps the researcher understand how the courts interpret statutes, and also how the courts analyze related issues that are not covered in the statutes. Volumes of case law can be found in some public libraries, in law libraries, in courthouses, and in state government buildings such as statehouses and state libraries.

Agency Regulations and Executive Orders Administrative agencies may also create laws. The federal and state constitutions implicitly give the legislatures the power to create administrative agencies. Administrative agencies are necessary because lawmakers often lack detailed knowledge about important issues, and they need experts to manage the regulation of complex subjects. On the federal level, for example, the Department of the Interior was created by Congress to manage the nation's natural resources. In creating the agency, Congress gave it power to promulgate regulations concerning the use and protection of natural resources.

ADMINISTRATIVE AGENCY regulations have the force of law if they have a binding effect on the rights and duties of persons. For example, Interior Department regulations that prohibit mining or logging in certain areas of the country are considered law, even though they are not formulated by an elected official or judge. Federal administrative agency rules are approved by Congress, so ultimately they are a product of the will of elected officials. Similarly, on the state and local levels, an administrative agency may promulgate rules that have the force of law, but only at the pleasure of the elected lawmakers that created the agency. If an agency seeks to change a regulation, it must, in most cases, inform the public of its intentions and provide the public with an opportunity to voice concerns at a public meeting.

Not all agency regulations have the force of law. Agency rules that merely interpret other rules, state policy, or govern organization, procedure, and practice need not be obeyed by parties outside the agency.

Some administrative agencies have quasi-judicial powers. That is, they have limited authority to hear disputes and make binding decisions on matters relevant to the agency. For example, the Department of Health and Human Services (HHS) has a court with authority to hear cases concerning actions by the HHS, such as the denial of Social Security benefits. An administrative law judge (ALJ) presides over the court, and APPEALS from ALJ decisions can be taken to an HHS appeals council. If an administrative agency has quasi-judicial powers, decisions made by the ALJ and boards of appeals have the force of law.

To find important state agency regulations, contact the state's secretary of state for a list of administrative agencies. Most agencies are named according to their area of concern. For example, a department of gaming is concerned with gambling, and a department of fish, game, and wildlife is concerned with issues related to hunting and wildlife conservation. Agency regulations can be obtained by contacting the agency or the state government libraries generally located in the state capitals.

EXECUTIVE ORDERS are issued to interpret, implement, or administer laws. On the federal level, executive orders are issued by the president or by another EXECUTIVE BRANCH official under the president's direction. Executive orders range from commands for detailed changes in federal administrative agency procedures to commands for military action. To have the force of law, a federal executive order must be published in the *Federal Register*, the official government publication of executive orders and federal administrative agency regulations. On the state level, governors have similar authority to make laws concerning state administrative agencies and state military personnel.

Local Laws Counties, cities, and towns also have the authority to make laws. Local laws are issued by elected lawmakers and local administrative agencies. Local laws cannot conflict with state or federal laws. Decisions by local courts generally operate as law insofar as they apply to the participants in the case. To a lesser extent, local court decisions may have a prospective effect. That is, a local court decision can operate as precedent, but only in cases brought within the same jurisdiction. For example, a decision by a court in Green County may affect future court cases in Green County, but it has no bearing on the law in any other county. Local laws can be found in local courthouses, in local libraries, and in state government libraries.

CROSS-REFERENCES

Administrative Law and Procedure; Civil Law; Congress of the United States; Constitutional Amendment; Constitution of the United States; Court Opinion; Criminal Law; Equity; Federalism; *Federal Register*; Judicial Review; Legislation; Private Law; Procedural Law; Public Law; Stare Decisis.

LAW AND LITERATURE 📖 An interdisciplinary study that examines the relationship between the fields of law and literature, with each field borrowing insights and methods of analysis from the other.

Taught as a comparative studies course in many academic settings, the law and literature curriculum was developed by members of academia and the legal profession who hoped to make law a more humanistic enterprise.

Law and literature is now a burgeoning field of comparative learning. During the 1990s entire scholarly journals were dedicated to the subject. From the mid-1980s to the mid-1990s, state and national BAR ASSOCIATIONS sponsored many theatrical re-creations of legal questions presented in classic works of literature, including those written by William Shakespeare and Charles Dickens.

The Greek philosopher Plato recognized a relationship between law and literature more than two thousand years ago, writing, "A society's law book should, in right and reason, prove, when we open it, far the best and finest work of its whole literature." In the United States, Plato's works were read along with other classic works of literature as part of the general education of most professionals during the eighteenth and nineteenth centuries. Following the U.S. Civil War (1861–65), however, law was seen less as a humanity and more as a science, and the classic works of Western literature played a lesser role in the education of members of the legal profession.

In 1908 the connection between law and literature was reexamined by the preeminent legal scholar JOHN H. WIGMORE, who noted the prevalence of trials and legal themes in many of the world's famous novels (see Wigmore 1908, 574). In 1925 Justice BENJAMIN N. CARDOZO, of the U.S. Supreme Court, published in the *Yale Law Review* a groundbreaking article titled "Law and Literature," which examined the literary styles of judicial opinions.

In the 1960s and 1970s, the ideas of Wigmore and Cardozo formed the foundation of the modern law and literature movement. During this period law was widely perceived as a myopic, rule-oriented vocation that lacked basic human qualities such as sympathy and empathy. A growing number of law students, lawyers, and judges became disenchanted with the limited perspective of their profession, and began exploring other fields of learning for enlightenment. At the same time, high school teachers, college professors, and graduate students began to migrate from the humanities to the legal profession in search of more practical employment opportunities.

Law and literature studies are separated into three areas. The first area involves law *in* literature. This area focuses on the legal themes depicted in novels and other literary works. These fictionalized accounts are used as a prism through which actual proceedings in U.S. courtrooms are scrutinized.

The second area involves law *as* literature. This area studies the educational aspects of actual trials that involve recurring legal disputes over issues such as race relations and the proper role of law enforcement in a free society. This second area of study also analyzes the prose and rhetoric that judges use to explain the legal arguments and conclusions in their judicial opinions.

The third area focuses on law *and* literature. It compares and contrasts the analytical tools each discipline employs when interpreting a particular text, whether it be a CONSTITUTION, a STATUTE, a judicial PRECEDENT, or a work of literature.

See also JURISPRUDENCE; LEGAL EDUCATION.

LAW DAY The date prescribed in a BOND, MORTGAGE, or DEED for payment of the DEBT; the maturity date. May 1st, observed in schools, public assemblies, and courts, in honor of our legal system.

In regard to REAL PROPERTY, the law day is the final date fixed by the court on which the debtor can pay off the mortgage debt, redeem the real estate, and prevent it from being sold after FORECLOSURE proceedings are commenced.

The definition of law day, also known as law date, varies from JURISDICTION to jurisdiction. Some states define law day as the actual due date of the mortgage or any day thereafter until foreclosure, while others view the date of foreclosure and law day as synonymous. In some jurisdictions, the day fixed in the contract for the CLOSING of title is the law day.

LAW FRENCH A corrupt French dialect used by English lawyers from after the Norman Conquest in 1066 until slightly after the end of the Restoration period in 1688.

By the mid–thirteenth century, many of the English gentry and some commoners spoke French, and the language was used in the king's courts and in printed legal materials. After England's wars with France during the reign of Edward III (1327–77), schools no longer taught French. Oral French in the courts was thereafter mostly confined to recitation of formal PLEADINGS, and thus lost grammatical sophistication and suffered a drastic decline in vocabulary.

Law French was primarily a written language and was pronounced as if it were English. It persisted because of tradition and because most of the books in lawyers' libraries were printed in French or in Latin. It also functioned as a form of shorthand for lawyers to use in recording legal propositions. In other words, spoken English was transcribed in French. This use resulted in an artificial technical vocabulary, uncorrupted by the vicissitudes of vernacular English usage. The names of everyday things became increasingly Anglicized, but law French terminology formed the cornerstone of the COMMON-LAW vocabulary. Some of the words still used today are *appeal, arrest, assault, attainder, counsel, covenant, debtor, demand, disclaimer, escrow, heir, indictment, joinder, lessee, larceny, merger, negligence, nuisance, ouster, proof, remainder, tender, suit, tort, trespass,* and *verdict.*

By the mid–Tudor period, in the mid–sixteenth century, the active law French vocabulary consisted of fewer than a thousand words; English was freely substituted for French when the writer's knowledge of French proved inadequate. In 1650 Parliament enacted a statute prohibiting the use of law French in printed books. At the beginning of the Restoration, in 1660, the law was treated as void and there was a widespread, albeit short-lived, reversion to law French. Law French gradually died in the ensuing years. It appears that the last ENGLISH LAW book written in law French was published in 1731. Sir John Comyn, Chief Baron of the Court of Exchequer, wrote his *Digest* in law French but the work was translated into English for its posthumous publication in 1762.

LAWFUL 📖 Licit; legally warranted or authorized. 📖

The terms *lawful* and *legal* differ in that the former contemplates the substance of law, whereas the latter alludes to the form of law. A lawful act is authorized, sanctioned, or not forbidden by law. A legal act is performed in accordance with the forms and usages of law, or in a technical manner. In this sense, *illegal* approaches the meaning of *invalid.* For example, a CONTRACT or WILL, executed without the required formalities, might be regarded as invalid or illegal, but could not be described as unlawful.

The term *lawful* more clearly suggests an ethical content than does the word *legal.* The latter merely denotes compliance with technical or formal rules, whereas the former usually signifies a moral substance or ethical permissibility. An additional distinction is that the word *legal* is used as the synonym of CONSTRUCTIVE, while *lawful* is not. *Legal fraud* is FRAUD implied by law, or made out by construction, but *lawful fraud* would be a contradiction in terms. *Legal* is also used as the antithesis of equitable, just. As a result, *legal estate* is the correct usage, instead of *lawful estate.* Under certain circumstances, however, the two words are used as exact equivalents. A *lawful* WRIT, WARRANT, or PROCESS is the same as a *legal* writ, warrant, or process.

LAW JOURNAL 📖 A magazine or newspaper that contains articles, news items, comments on new laws and case decisions, court calendars, and suggestions for practicing law, for use by attorneys. 📖

LAW MERCHANT 📖 The system of rules and customs and usages generally recognized and adopted by traders as the law for the regulation of their commercial transactions and the resolution of their controversies. 📖

The law merchant is codified in the UNIFORM COMMERCIAL CODE (UCC), a body of law, which has been adopted by the states, that governs mercantile transactions.

LAW OF NATIONS 📖 The body of customary rules that determine the rights and that regulate the intercourse of independent countries in peace and war. 📖

See also INTERNATIONAL LAW.

LAW OF THE CASE 📖 The principle that if the highest APPELLATE COURT has determined a legal question and returned the case to the court below for additional proceedings, the question will not be determined differently on a subsequent APPEAL in the same case where the facts remain the same. 📖

The law of the case expresses the rule that the final judgment of the highest court is the final determination of the rights of the parties. The doctrine of "law of the case" is one of policy only, however, and will be disregarded when compelling circumstances require a redetermination of the point of law decided on the prior appeal. Such circumstances exist when an intervening or contemporaneous change in the law has transpired by the establishment of new PRECEDENT by a controlling authority or the overruling of former decisions.

Courts have ruled that INSTRUCTIONS—directions given by the judge to the jury concerning the law applicable to the case—are the "law of the case" where the appealing defendant, the petitioner, accepted the instructions as correct at the time they were given.

LAW OF THE LAND 📖 The designation of general public laws that are equally binding on all members of the community. 📖

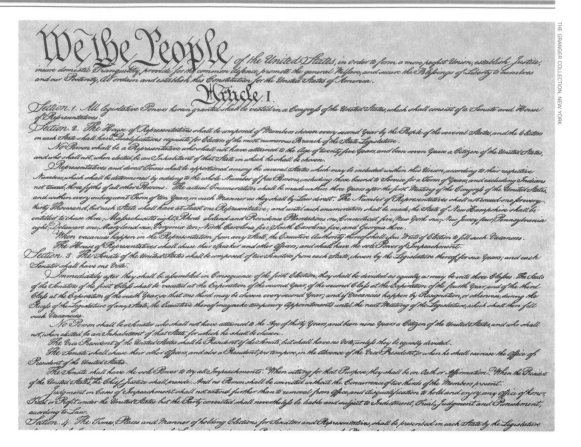

The U.S. Constitution is the law of the land.

The law of the land, embodied in the U.S. Constitution as DUE PROCESS OF LAW, includes all legal and equitable rules defining human rights and duties and providing for their protection and enforcement, both between the state and its citizens and between citizens.

LAW OF THE SEA 📖 The part of public INTERNATIONAL LAW that deals with maritime issues. 📖

The term *law of the sea* appears similar to the term *maritime law*, but it has a significantly different meaning. Maritime law deals with JURISPRUDENCE that governs ships and shipping, and is concerned with CONTRACTS, TORTS, and other issues involving private shipping, whereas the law of the sea refers to matters of public international law.

Many topics are contained within the law-of-the-sea concept. These include the definition of a state's territorial waters, the right of states to fish the oceans and to mine underneath the oceans, and the rights of states to control navigation.

The area outside a state's territorial waters, commonly known as the high seas, was traditionally governed by the principle of freedom of the seas. On the one hand, this meant freedom for fishing, commercial navigation, travel, and migration by both ships and aircraft; freedom for improvement in communication and supply by the laying of submarine cables and pipelines; and freedom for oceanographic research. On the other hand, it meant freedom for naval and aerial warfare, including interference with neutral commerce; freedom for military installations; and freedom to use the oceans as a place to dump wastes. Until World War II, these freedoms continued to be applied to the oceans and airspace outside the states' three-mile territorial limit, with little regulation of abuses other than what could be found in the customary regulations of warfare and neutrality.

Since the 1950s the UNITED NATIONS has attempted to convince the nations of the world to agree to a set of rules that will govern the law of the sea. The First U.N. Conference on the Law of the Sea, which was held in Geneva in 1958, led to the codification of four treaties that dealt with some areas of the law of the sea. In the 1970s the Third U.N. Conference on the Law of the Sea began its work. The conference labored for more than ten years on a comprehensive treaty that would codify international law concerning territorial waters, sea lanes, and ocean resources.

On December 10, 1982, 117 nations signed the U.N. Convention on the Law of the Sea, in Montego Bay, Jamaica. The convention was not signed by the United States, the United Kingdom, and twenty-eight other nations, because of objections to provisions for seabed mining, which they believe would inhibit commercial development.

The convention, which went into effect November 16, 1994, claims the minerals on the ocean floor beneath the high seas as "the common heritage of mankind." The exploitation of minerals is to be governed by global rather than national authority. Production ceilings have been set to prevent economic harm to land-based producers of the same minerals. There have been continuing negotiations with the United States and other nations to resolve this issue, which is the only serious obstacle to universal acceptance of the treaty. A 1994 agreement amended the mining provisions, which led the United States to submit the treaty to the U.S. Senate for ratification. As of mid 1997 the Senate had not ratified the treaty.

A major change under the convention is its extension of a state's territorial waters from 3 to 12 nautical miles. Foreign commercial vessels are granted the right of innocent passage through the 12-mile zone. Beyond the zone all vessels and aircraft may proceed freely. Coastal nations are granted exclusive rights to the fish and marine life in waters extending 200 nautical miles from shore. Every nation that has a continental shelf is granted exclusive rights to the oil, gas, and other resources in the shelf up to 200 miles from shore.

Any legal disputes concerning the treaty and its provisions may be adjudicated by the new Tribunal for the Law of the Sea, by ARBITRATION, or by the INTERNATIONAL COURT OF JUSTICE.

CROSS-REFERENCES

Admiralty and Maritime Law; Environmental Law; Fish and Fishing; Mine and Mineral Law; Navigable Waters; Pollution.

LAW REVIEW 📖 A law school publication containing case summaries written by student members and scholarly articles on current developments in the law, case decisions, and legislation written by law professors, judges, and attorneys. 📖

Law reviews are a source of information on recent developments and current scholarly interpretations of the law. They feature articles written by attorneys, judges, and professors. Students edit them and contribute student notes.

The first law review was established in 1875 as a means for law students to enhance legal scholarship. By 1995 over 450 student-edited law reviews were published in the United States. The majority of law schools in the United States now produce at least one student-

edited law review. Most publish general periodicals, covering any topic of current interest. Many produce publications that focus on a particular area of the law. Harvard, for example, publishes at least eleven special-focus law reviews. Among the most popular topics of special-focus law reviews are international law, comparative law, and ENVIRONMENTAL LAW.

The law review is an offshoot of the TREATISE, which was the principal form of legal writing in the 1800s and was frequently used to teach the law. Legal scholars wrote treatises to discuss legal principles and the cases that illustrated those principles. By the mid-1800s several significant U.S. treatises covered individual topic areas including EVIDENCE, CRIMINAL LAW, DAMAGES, and CONTRACTS. These treatises became the basis of LEGAL EDUCATION.

In the mid-1800s it also became important for lawyers to know more specifically how judges were ruling in their own JURISDICTION. This need led to the growth of regionally specific periodicals produced by attorneys to discuss the legal issues pertinent to their local area. The *American Law Register,* started in Philadelphia in 1852, was the first legal periodical that took a scholarly look at the law, rather than the journalistic slant of earlier periodicals. This publication and the *American Law Review,* from Boston, were the primary inspiration for the student-edited law review.

The first student-edited law review was the *Albany Law School Journal,* which lasted only one year, 1875. This law review contained articles, MOOT COURT arguments, and a calendar of law school events. The first issue included a student commentary that questioned whether after a lecture it was better for a student to read the cases discussed in the lecture or to read treatises on the topic discussed.

The next law review, Columbia Law School's *Columbia Jurist,* did not appear until 1885. This publication lasted only three years but inspired the *Harvard Law Review.*

Established in 1887, the *Harvard Law Review* is still published today and is among the most prestigious, most emulated student-edited law reviews. Before starting their law review, Harvard students approached the faculty to get support for their new venture. Professor JAMES BARR AMES became their adviser and mentor, and other faculty members provided articles for publication. For financial assistance the students approached alumnus LOUIS D. BRANDEIS, who provided money as well as the names of others who would contribute. The students also sold over three hundred subscriptions in the New York City area by the time the first issue was published. The first issue included articles, student news, moot court arguments, case digests, book reviews, and summaries of class lectures. The editors also used the law review to promote the new method of instruction that had recently been introduced at Harvard. This method of instruction combined the use of casebooks and Socratic dialogue—quite a change from the traditional method of textbooks and lectures. The Harvard method of instruction is standard in today's law schools. See also CASE METHOD.

By 1906 law schools at Yale, Pennsylvania, Columbia, Michigan, and Northwestern all had student-edited law reviews. With Harvard these schools were considered the top law schools in the United States. Because they were publishing law reviews, doing so became a status symbol, and many law schools followed suit.

The significance of the law review became evident when judges began citing articles in their decisions. These articles are scholarly studies of the law and frequently offer opinions on how the law can be improved.

Today, the vast number of general and specialty law reviews published around the country cover topics in virtually all areas of practice, from broad areas of law, such as criminal law, INTELLECTUAL PROPERTY, environmental law, and INTERNATIONAL LAW, to more specialized topics, such as women's issues, air and space law, and computer law. Published pieces range from examinations of legal trends in a particular legal area, to analyses of a single case and its implications, to speeches by and about important legal figures. As law reviews have grown in number and variety, they have become important sources for legal research.

LAW REPORTS 📖 Published volumes of the decisions of courts. 📖

Usually, opinions in cases are promptly published in unbound ADVANCE SHEETS just after they are handed down. They are subsequently collected into bound REPORTERS when there are enough to fill a volume. Volumes are numbered in chronological order, and cases are found by referring to volume and page numbers in the CITATION for each case. Many law reports are also offered in CD-ROM format, or provided as part of such online services as WESTLAW and LEXIS.

LAW SCHOOL ADMISSION TEST The Law School Admission Test (LSAT) was first given in 1948 and started to gain prominence in the late 1960s. By the 1980s, when the number of applications to law schools began to rise, it became a standard part of the law school admission process. The test is administered by the Law School Admission Council (LSAC), which is a nonprofit, nonstock corporation with 193 member law schools in the United States and Canada. All members require the LSAT as part of the admission process.

The LSAT is a half-day, six-part test that contains one thirty-minute writing sample and five thirty-five-minute multiple-choice sections. The writing sample is not scored, but is sent to each school to which the student applies. One of the multiple-choice sections (the taker does not know which one) is not scored, but is used to test possible future questions.

The multiple-choice sections are organized into different types of questions: reading comprehension, critical reasoning, and analysis of others' reasoning. These sections are designed to test skills that are important in law school, such as the ability to read complex text with accuracy and draw inferences.

Law schools use applicants' LSAT scores, along with other criteria, to decide who to admit. Some schools require a minimum LSAT score for acceptance. Others use a formula in which the LSAT score is multiplied and then added to the undergraduate grade point average for a total score that helps them decide which students to admit. Still others use the LSAT score to help them make their decision, but have no hard-and-fast rules regarding a minimum score.

Like all standardized tests, the LSAT is intended to be a fair, objective test of the abilities of prospective law students. Most data indicate that the score on the LSAT is a reliable predictor for success during the first year of law school, although it may not be in an individual case.

Since the 1970s the main criticism of the LSAT has come from those who think the test is biased against women and minorities. These critics assert that the information in the test questions, as well as the perspective of the test as a whole, caters to a white male background and viewpoint. A 1995 study by the LSAC showed that women tend to score lower than men on the LSAT and perform slightly below men in their first year of law school. Despite the criticism the LSAT continues to be a primary gatekeeper to law school and the legal profession.

See also LEGAL EDUCATION.

LAWSUIT 📖 A popular designation of a legal proceeding between two parties in the courts, instituted by one party to compel another to do himself or herself justice, regardless of whether the ACTION is based upon LAW or EQUITY. 📖

LAWYER 📖 A person, who through a regular

program of study, is learned in legal matters and has been licensed to practice his or her profession. Any qualified person who prosecutes or defends causes in courts of record or other judicial tribunals of the United States, or of any of the states, or who renders legal advice or assistance in relation to any cause or matter. ▥

See also ATTORNEY.

LAY ▥ Nonprofessional, such as a lay WITNESS who is not a recognized expert in the area that is the subject of the person's TESTIMONY. That which relates to persons or entities not clerical or ecclesiastical; a person not in ecclesiastical orders. To present the formal declarations by the parties of their respective claims and defenses in PLEADINGS. A share of the profits of a fishing or whaling voyage, allotted to the officers and seamen, in the nature of wages. ▥

LAYAWAY ▥ An agreement between a retail seller and a consumer that provides that the seller will retain designated consumer goods for sale to the consumer at a specified price on a future date, if the consumer deposits with the seller an agreed upon sum of money. ▥

LEADING CASE ▥ An important judicial decision that is frequently regarded as having settled or determined the law upon all points involved in such controversies and thereby serves as a guide for subsequent decisions. ▥

Brown v. Board of Education of Topeka, Kansas, 347 U.S. 483, 74 S.Ct. 686, 98 L. Ed. 873 (1954), which declared racial segregation in public schools to be in violation of the EQUAL PROTECTION Clause of the FOURTEENTH AMENDMENT to the U.S. Constitution, is an example of a leading case.

LEADING QUESTION ▥ A query that suggests to the WITNESS how it is to be answered or puts words into the mouth of the witness to be merely repeated in his or her response. ▥

Leading questions should not be used on the DIRECT EXAMINATION of a witness unless necessary to develop the person's TESTIMONY. They are permissible, however, on CROSS-EXAMINATION. When a party calls a HOSTILE WITNESS—the adverse party or a witness identified with the opposing party—leading questions can be employed during the direct examination of such a witness.

LEAGUE OF NATIONS ▥ An international confederation of countries, with headquarters in Geneva, Switzerland, that existed from 1920 to 1946, its creation following World War I and its dissolution following World War II. ▥

Though the League of Nations was a flawed and generally ineffective organization, many of its functions and offices were transferred to the UNITED NATIONS, which has benefited from the hard lessons the league learned.

President WOODROW WILSON, of the United States, was the architect of the League of Nations. When the United States entered World War I on April 6, 1917, Wilson sought to end a war that had raged for three years and to begin constructing a new framework for international cooperation. On January 8, 1918, he delivered an address to Congress that named fourteen points to be used as the guide for a peace settlement. The fourteenth point called for a general association of nations that would guarantee political independence and territorial integrity for all countries.

Following the November 9, 1918, armistice that ended the war, President Wilson led the U.S. delegation to the Paris Peace Conference. Wilson was the only representative of the Great Powers—which included Great Britain, France, and Italy—who truly wanted an international organization. His power and influence were instrumental in establishing the League of Nations.

Although Wilson was the architect of the league, he was unable to secure U.S. Senate ratification of the peace TREATY that included it. He was opposed by isolationists of both major political parties who argued that the United States should not interfere with European affairs, and by Republicans who did not want to commit the United States to supporting the league financially. The treaty was modified several times, but was nevertheless voted down for the last time in March 1920.

Despite the absence of the United States, the League of Nations held its first meeting on November 15, 1920, with forty-two nations represented. The constitution of the league was called a covenant. It contained twenty-six articles that served as operating rules for the league.

The league was organized into three main branches. The council was the main peacekeeping agency, with a membership that varied from eight to fourteen members during its existence. France, Germany, Great Britain, Italy, Japan, and the Soviet Union held permanent seats during the years they were members of the league. The remainder of the seats were held by smaller countries on a rotating basis. Peacekeeping recommendations had to be made by a unanimous vote.

The assembly was composed of all members of the league, and each member country had one vote. The assembly controlled the league's budget, elected the temporary council members, and made amendments to the covenant. A

UPI/CORBIS-BETTMANN

The League of Nations Disarmament Conference met in September 1924 to discuss the reduction of military armaments following World War I. Although President Woodrow Wilson had pushed for the creation of an international organization, Congress blocked U.S. participation and so the United States was never a member of the league.

two-thirds majority vote was required on most matters. When a threat to peace was the issue, a majority vote plus the unanimous consent of the council was needed to recommend action.

The secretariat was the administrative branch of the league. It was headed by a secretary general, who was nominated by the council and approved by the assembly. The secretariat consisted of over six hundred officials, who aided peacekeeping work and served as staff to special study commissions and to numerous international organizations established by the league to improve trade, finance, transportation, communication, health, and science.

President Wilson and others who had sought the establishment of the league had hoped to end the system of interlocking foreign alliances that had drawn the European powers into World War I. The league was to promote collective security, in which the security of each league member was guaranteed by the entire league membership. This goal was undermined by the covenant because the council and the assembly lacked the power to order members to help an attacked nation. It was left up to each country to decide whether a threat to peace warranted its intervention. Because of this voluntary process, the league lacked the authority to quickly and decisively resolve armed conflict.

This defect was revealed in the 1930s. When Japan invaded Manchuria in 1933, the League

of Nations could only issue condemnations. Then, in 1935, Italy, under BENITO MUSSOLINI, invaded Ethiopia. Ethiopia appeared before the assembly and asked for assistance. Britain and France, unwilling to risk war, refused to employ an oil EMBARGO that would have hurt the Italian war effort. In May 1936 Italy conquered the African country.

The league also lost key member states in the 1930s. Japan left in 1933, following the Manchurian invasion. Germany, under the leadership of ADOLF HITLER, also left in 1933, following the league's refusal to end arms limitations imposed on Germany after World War I. Italy withdrew in 1937, and the Soviet Union was expelled in 1939 for invading Finland.

The beginning of World War II, on September 1, 1939, marked the beginning of the end for the League of Nations. Collective security had failed. During the war the secretariat was reduced to a skeleton staff in Geneva, and some functions were transferred to the United States and Canada. With the creation of the United Nations on October 24, 1945, the League of Nations became superfluous. In 1946 the league voted to dissolve and transferred much of its property and organization to the United Nations.

The United Nations followed the general structure of the league, establishing a security council, a general assembly, and a secretariat. It had the benefit of U.S. membership and U.S. financial support, two vital elements denied the League of Nations.

LEASE 📖 A contractual agreement by which one party conveys an ESTATE in PROPERTY to another party, for a limited period, subject to various conditions, in exchange for something of value, but still retains ownership. 📖

A lease contract can involve any property that is not illegal to own. Common lease CONTRACTS include agreements for leasing REAL ESTATE and apartments, manufacturing and farming equipment, and consumer goods such as automobiles, televisions, stereos, and appliances.

Leases are governed by statutes and by COMMON LAW, or precedential cases. Most leases are subject to state laws, but leases involving the U.S. government are subject to federal laws. Generally, federal laws on leases are similar to state laws.

A lease is created when a property owner (the offeror) makes an OFFER to another party (the offeree), and the offeree accepts the offer. The offer must authorize the offeree to possess and use property owned by the offeror for a certain period of time without gaining ownership. A lease must also contain CONSIDERATION, which means that the offeree must give something of value to the offeror. Consideration usually consists of money, but other things of value may be given to the offeror. Finally, the offeror must deliver the property to the offeree or make the property available to the offeree. When a lease is formed, the property owner is called the LESSOR, and the user of the property is called the LESSEE.

Generally, a lease may be written or oral, but a lease for certain types of property must be in writing and signed by both parties. For example, if a lessee seeks to lease REAL PROPERTY (land or buildings) for more than one year, the lease must be in writing. Some leases must be written, signed, and recorded in a registry of deeds. Such leases usually concern real property that will be leased for a period of more than three years.

A lease term begins when the lessee receives a copy of the lease. However, the lease need not be given directly to the lessee; it is enough that the lessee knows that the lease is in the hands of a third person acting on behalf of the lessee. A lease may also take effect when the lessee assumes control over the property.

In all states, leases dealing with commercial goods and services are strictly regulated by statute. Commercial lease laws govern the rights and duties of lessors and lessees in leases that involve commercial goods. Most states have enacted section 2A of the UNIFORM COMMERCIAL CODE, which is a set of exemplary laws formulated by the National Conference of Commissioners on Uniform State Laws and by the American Law Institute. The laws governing commercial leases do not apply to leases of real estate, which are covered by LANDLORD AND TENANT laws.

In all states a court may VOID an UNCONSCIONABLE lease. A lease is unconscionable if it unduly favors one party over the other. For example, assume that a small-business owner leases property for thirty years in order to operate a gas station. The lease contains a clause stating that the lessor may revoke the agreement without cause and without notice. If the lessee performs her obligations under the lease, but the lessor revokes the lease without notice, the clause allowing termination without notice may be found to be unconscionable. A determination of unconscionability must be made by a judge or jury based on the facts of the case. The fact finder may consider factors such as the relative bargaining power of the parties, other terms in the lease, the purpose of the lease, and the potential loss to either party as a result of the terms of the lease.

Commercial leases must contain certain warranties. If they do not, the warranties may be read into them by a court. One such WARRANTY is the warranty of merchantability. Generally, this warranty requires that all leased property be fit for its general purpose. For example, if a passenger vehicle leased for transportation fails to operate, this failure might be a breach of the IMPLIED WARRANTY of merchantability, and the lessee could sue the lessor for damages suffered as a result.

Another warranty implied in commercial leases is the warranty of fitness for a particular purpose. This warranty applies only if the lessor knows how the lessee plans to use the property and that the lessee is relying on the lessor's expertise in choosing the best goods or services.

A lessee may assign a lease to a third party, or assignee. An ASSIGNMENT conveys all rights under the lease to the assignee for the remainder of the lease term, and the assignee assumes a contractual relationship with the original lessor. However, unless the lessor agrees otherwise, the first lessee still retains the original duties under the lease agreement until the lease expires. Generally, an assignment is valid unless it is prohibited by the lessor.

An assignment differs from a sublease. In a sublease the original lessee gives temporary

LEASE
National Housing and Economic Development Law Project Standard Form Lease (California)

1. Parties
The parties to this agreement are _____
_____
_____
_____ , hereinafter called "Landlord,"
and _____
_____
_____
_____
_____ , hereinafter called "Tenant."
If Landlord is the agent of the owner of said property, the owner's name and address is _____
_____

2. Property
Landlord hereby lets the following property to Tenant for the term of this agreement: (a) the property located at
_____
and (b) the following furniture and appliances on said property: _____
_____
_____

3. Term
The term of this agreement shall be for _____ beginning on _____ and ending on
_____

4. Rent
The monthly rental for said property shall be $_____ due and payable on the first day of each month.

5. Utilities
Utilities shall be paid by the party indicated on the following chart:

	Landlord	*Tenant*
Electricity		
Gas		
Water		
Garbage collection		
Trash removal		
Other		

6. Use of Property
Tenant shall use the property only for residential purposes, except for incidental use in his trade or business (such as telephone solicitation of sales orders or arts and craft created for profit), so long as such incidental use does not violate local zoning laws or affect Landlord's ability to obtain fire or liability insurance.

7. Tenant's Duty to Maintain Premises
Tenant shall keep the dwelling unit in a clean and sanitary condition and shall otherwise comply with all state and local laws requiring tenants to maintain rented premises. If damage to the dwelling unit (other than normal wear and tear) is caused by acts or neglect of Tenant or others occupying the premises with his permission, Tenant may repair such damage at his own expense. Upon Tenant's failure to make such repairs, after reasonable notice by Landlord, Landlord may cause such repairs to be made and Tenant shall be liable to Landlord for any reasonable expense thereby incurred by Landlord.

8. Alterations
No substantial alteration, addition, or improvement shall be made by Tenant in or to the dwelling unit without the prior consent of Landlord in writing. Such consent shall not be unreasonably withheld, but may be conditioned upon tenant's agreeing to restore the dwelling unit to its prior condition upon moving out.

9. Noise
Tenant agrees not to allow on his premises any excessive noise or other activity which disturbs the peace and quiet of other tenants in the building. Landlord agrees to prevent other tenants and other persons in the building or common areas from similarly disturbing Tenant's peace and quiet.

A sample lease agreement

Source: Reprinted from E. Rabin, *Fundamentals of Modern Real Property Law* (1974), pp. 157–158.

10. Inspection by Landlord

Landlord or his agent may enter the dwelling unit only for the following purposes: to inspect to see if Tenant is complying with this Agreement, to make repairs, and to exhibit the unit to prospective purchasers, mortgagees, and tenants. Such entries shall not be so frequent as to seriously disturb Tenant's peaceful enjoyment of the premises. Such entries shall take place only with the consent of Tenant, which consent shall not be unreasonably withheld. If, however, Landlord or his agent reasonably believes that an emergency (such as a fire) exists which requires an immediate entry, such entry may be made without Tenant's consent. If such emergency entry occurs, Landlord shall, within two days thereafter, notify Tenant in writing of the date, time, and purpose of such entry.

11. Security Deposit

a) Tenant shall pay Landlord, upon execution of this agreement, a security deposit of $_____ . Said deposit may be applied by Landlord toward reimbursement for any cost incurred because of Tenant's violation of this Agreement, including nonpayment of rent.

b) Landlord shall place this security deposit in a bank savings account or savings and loan institution account bearing the prevailing rate of interest and shall credit such interest to the security deposit. Within 14 days of the date of this Agreement, Landlord shall notify tenant in writing of the location of such account and the account number.

c) Landlord shall inspect the premises within one week prior to termination of this Agreement and, before Tenant vacates, shall give Tenant a written statement of needed repairs and the estimated cost thereof.

d) Within two weeks after Tenant vacates the premises, Landlord shall return to Tenant his security deposit, with accrued interest, less any deductions Landlord is entitled to make under subparagraph (a) of this Paragraph and Paragraph 17. If any deductions are made, Landlord shall also give Tenant a written itemized statement of such deductions and explanations thereof. No deductions shall be made, however, for any repairs not listed in the statement required by subparagraph (c).

12. Landlord's Obligation to Repair and Maintain Premises

a) Landlord shall maintain the building and grounds appurtenant to the dwelling unit in a decent, safe, and sanitary condition, and shall comply with all state and local laws, regulations, and ordinances concerning the condition of dwelling units.

b) Landlord shall take reasonable measures to maintain security on the premises and the building and grounds appurtenant thereto to protect Tenant and other occupants and guests of the premises from burglary, robbery, and other crimes. Tenant agrees to use reasonable care in utilizing such security measures.

c) As repairs are now needed to comply with this paragraph, Landlord specifically agrees to complete the following repairs by the following dates:

Repair	Date

d) If Landlord substantially fails to comply with any duty imposed by this paragraph, Tenant's duty to pay rent shall abate until such failure is remedied. This subparagraph shall apply to defects within Tenant's dwelling unit only if Tenant has notified Landlord or his agent of such defects and has given Landlord a reasonable time to make repairs. The remedy provided by this subparagraph shall not be exclusive of any other remedy provided by law to Tenant for Landlord's violation of this Agreement.

13. Subleasing

Tenant shall not assign this Agreement or sublet the dwelling unit without the written consent of Landlord. Such consent shall not be withheld without good reason relating to the prospective tenant's ability to comply with the provisions of this Agreement. This paragraph shall not prevent Tenant from accommodating guests for reasonable periods.

14. Failure to Pay Rent

If Tenant is unable to pay rent when due, but on or before such due date he gives Landlord or his agent written notice that he is unable to pay said rent on time and the reasons therefore, Landlord shall attempt to work out with Tenant a procedure for paying such rent as soon as possible. If, after 10 days, Landlord and Tenant are unable to

[continued on page 412]

A sample lease agreement (continued)

work out such a procedure, Landlord may serve a notice to pay rent or vacate within 3 days, as provided by California Code of Civil Procedure Section 1161.

15. Destruction of Premises

If the premises become partially or totally destroyed during the term of this Agreement, either party may thereupon terminate this Agreement upon reasonable notice.

16. Tenant's Termination for Good Cause

Upon 30 days written notice, for good cause, Tenant may terminate this Agreement and vacate the premises. Said notice shall state good cause for termination. Good cause shall include, but not be limited to, entry into active duty with U.S. military services, employment in another community, and loss of the main source of income used to pay the rent.

17. Termination

Upon termination of this Agreement, Tenant shall vacate the premises, remove all personal property belonging to him, and leave the premises as clean as he found them (normal wear and tear excepted).

18. Lawsuits

If either party commences a lawsuit against the other to enforce any provision of this Agreement, the successful party shall be awarded court costs from the other. Landlord specifically waives any right to recover treble or other punitive damages pursuant to California Code of Civil Procedure Section 1174.

19. Notices

All notices and rent provided by this Agreement shall be in writing and shall be given to the other party as follows

To the Tenant: at the premises.

To the Landlord: at _____

20. Holdovers

If Tenant holds over upon termination of this Agreement and Landlord accepts Tenant's tender of the monthly rent provided by this Agreement, this Agreement shall continue to be binding on the parties as a month-to-month agreement.

A sample lease agreement (continued)

rights under the lease to a third party, but the third party does not assume a contractual relationship with the lessor. The original lessee retains the same rights and obligations under the lease, and forms a second contractual relationship with the sublessee. Like assignments, subleases generally are valid unless they are prohibited by the lessor.

If a lessor DEFAULTS on his obligations under the lease, the lessee may sue the lessor for DAMAGES. The measure of damages can vary. If a lessor breaches the lease by sending nonconforming goods, or goods that were not ordered by the lessee, the lessee may reject the goods, cancel the lease, and sue the lessor to recover any monies already paid and for damages caused by the shipment of the nonconforming goods. If the lessee defaults on obligations under the lease, the lessor may cancel the lease, withhold or cancel delivery of the goods, or lease the goods to another party and recover from the original lessee any difference between the amount the lessor would have earned under the original lease and the amount the lessor earns on the new lease.

One controversial lease is the rent-to-own lease. Under such a lease, the lessee pays a certain amount of money for a certain period of time, and at the end of the period, the lessee gains full ownership of the leased item. Rent-to-own leases are often associated with consumer goods such as televisions, stereos, appliances, and vehicles. Many rent-to-own leases provide that the lessor may regain possession and ownership of the property if the lessee defaults. Such clauses have been found to be unconscionable if they are exercised after the lessee has paid more than the MARKET VALUE of the leased item.

For example, assume that a party leases a television worth $300. The lease obliges the lessee to make payments of $50 a month for one year. At the end of the lease period, the lessee will have paid $600 for the television. The amount of the total payment may not be unconscionable, because the lessee gains a television without making one large payment. However, if the lessee defaults after making $550 in payments, and the lessor repossesses the television, a court may find that the lessor's actions are unconscionable and order that the television be returned to the lessee.

See also RENT STRIKE; SUBLETTING.

LEASEBACK A transaction whereby land is sold and subsequently rented by the seller from the purchaser who is the new owner.

LEASEHOLD An ESTATE, interest, in REAL PROPERTY held under a rental agreement by which the owner gives another the right to occupy or use land for a period of time.

LEAST RESTRICTIVE MEANS TEST

The "least restrictive means," or "less drastic means," test is a standard imposed by the courts when considering the validity of LEGISLATION that touches upon constitutional interests. If the government enacts a law that restricts a fundamental personal liberty, it must employ the least restrictive measures possible to achieve its goal. This test applies even when the government has a legitimate purpose in adopting the particular law. The least restrictive means test has been applied primarily to the regulation of speech. It can also be applied to other types of regulations, such as legislation affecting interstate commerce.

In *Shelton v. Tucker*, 364 U.S. 479, 81 S. Ct. 247, 5 L. Ed. 2d 231 (1960), the U.S. Supreme Court applied the least restrictive means test to an Arkansas statute that required teachers to file annually an AFFIDAVIT listing all the organizations to which they belonged and the amount of money they had contributed to each organization in the previous five years. B. T. Shelton was one of a group of teachers who refused to file the affidavit and who as a result did not have their teaching contract renewed. Upon reviewing the statute, the Court found that the state had a legitimate interest in investigating the fitness and competence of its teachers, and that the information requested in the affidavit could help the state in that investigation. However, according to the Court, the statute went far beyond its legitimate purpose because it required information that bore no relationship to a teacher's occupational fitness. The Court also found that the information revealed by the affidavits was not kept confidential. The Court struck down the law because its "unlimited and indiscriminate sweep" went well beyond the state's legitimate interest in the qualifications of its teachers.

Two constitutional doctrines that are closely related to the least restrictive means test are the overbreadth and vagueness doctrines. These doctrines are applied to statutes and regulations that restrict constitutional rights. The OVERBREADTH DOCTRINE requires that statutes regulating activities that are not constitutionally pro-

tected must not be written so broadly as to restrict activities that are constitutionally protected.

The vagueness doctrine requires that statutes adequately describe the behavior being regulated. A vague statute may have a chilling effect on constitutionally protected behavior because of fear of violating the statute. Also, law enforcement personnel need clear guidelines as to what constitutes a violation of the law.

The least restrictive means test, the overbreadth doctrine, and the vagueness doctrine all help to preserve constitutionally protected speech and behavior by requiring statutes to be clear and narrowly drawn, and to use the least restrictive means to reach the desired end.

CROSS-REFERENCES
Chilling Effect Doctrine; First Amendment; Freedom of Speech; Void for Vagueness.

LEAVE To give or dispose of by WILL. WILLFUL departure with intent to remain away. See also DESERTION. Permission or authorization to do something.

Leave of court is permission from the judge to take some action in a lawsuit that requires an absence or delay. An attorney might request a leave of court in order to file an amended PLEADING, a formal declaration of a CLAIM, or a DEFENSE.

LEDGER The principal book of accounts of a business enterprise in which all the daily transactions are entered under appropriate headings to reflect the DEBITS and CREDITS of each account.

Information that is contained in a ledger can be admitted into EVIDENCE in a lawsuit pursuant to the BUSINESS RECORD EXCEPTION of the HEARSAY rule.

LEE, CHARLES Charles Lee served as attorney general of the United States from 1795 to 1801 under presidents GEORGE WASHINGTON and JOHN ADAMS.

Lee, born in 1758 in Westmoreland County, Virginia, descended from a prominent English family. His earliest known ancestor, Lionel Lee, received a title and estate from William the Conqueror. The Lee line in the United States traced back to 1649, when Richard Lee, a member of Charles I's Privy Council, emigrated to help settle the Virginia colonies. Prior to the American Revolution, six of Richard Lee's descendants served simultaneously in the governing body known as the Virginia House of Burgesses; one of those descendants was Charles Lee's father, Henry Lee II.

Lee's father was a well-educated farmer with extensive landholdings in Virginia. His mother,

BIOGRAPHY

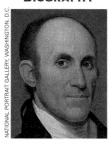

Charles Lee

NATIONAL PORTRAIT GALLERY, WASHINGTON, D.C.

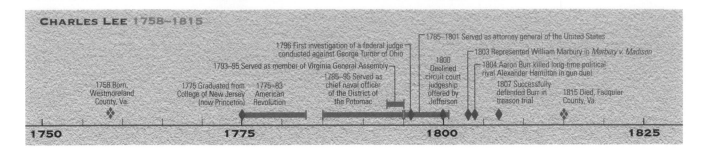

CHARLES LEE 1758–1815

1785–1801 Served as attorney general of the United States

1796 First investigation of a federal judge — conducted against George Turner of Ohio

1803 Represented William Marbury in *Marbury v. Madison*

1793–95 Served as member of Virginia General Assembly

1800 Declined circuit court judgeship offered by Jefferson

1804 Aaron Burr killed long-time political rival Alexander Hamilton in gun duel

1785–95 Served as chief naval officer of the District of the Potomac

1807 Successfully defended Burr in treason trial

1758 Born, Westmoreland County, Va.

1775 Graduated from College of New Jersey (now Princeton)

1775–83 American Revolution

1815 Died, Fauquier County, Va.

1750   1775   1800   1825

Lucy Grymes Lee, had been admired and courted by George Washington prior to her marriage. In fact, Lee's mother continued to cultivate Washington's interest long after her marriage—and it was largely owing to her influence that Lee's brother, Henry Lee III (a future general and statesman, and father of General Robert E. Lee) and Lee himself were able to advance far and fast in their chosen careers.

Lee probably followed his brother to the College of New Jersey (later named Princeton). From the beginning, he was interested in the law. He completed his legal studies in Philadelphia under Attorney Jared Ingersoll, and he was admitted to the bar in about 1780. As a young lawyer, he served as a delegate to the Continental Congress, and he was a member of the Virginia Assembly. But Lee also maintained his family's tradition of military service. He served as chief naval officer of the District of the Potomac for more than a decade. He resigned in December 1795, when he was appointed attorney general of the United States by President Washington.

When Lee's predecessor, Attorney General William Bradford, died suddenly in August 1795, Washington was faced with the difficult task of appointing the nation's third attorney general in just six years. The position had little to recommend it. It was a part-time job with no staff, little power, and many demands. Because Lee felt duty bound to repay Washington for years of family support and patronage, he honored Washington's request to take the job. He served as attorney general for the balance of Washington's term and for the entire Adams administration—from December 10, 1795, to February 18, 1801.

The role of the attorney general in Lee's time was to conduct all the suits in the Supreme Court in which the United States was a party, and to give advice and opinions to the president and Congress when requested. Because few suits had made their way to the High Court through the nation's fledgling court system,

"No act of Congress can extend the original jurisdiction of the Supreme Court beyond the bounds limited by the Constitution."

Lee did not spend much time trying cases. Some of his time was occupied with administrative responsibilities: once in office, his first order of business was to finish a task started by Bradford, the establishment of a fee schedule for compensating federal judicial officers. The vast majority of Lee's time was spent writing opinions that would help to shape the direction of the evolving government.

The nation's first investigation of a federal judge took place in 1796 when the House of Representatives considered a petition to impeach Ohio territorial judge George Turner for criminal misconduct. Given the difficulty of conducting a long-distance IMPEACHMENT proceeding, Lee was asked if there was another way to address the complaint against Turner. Lee's opinion that "a judge may be prosecuted . . . for official misdemeanors or crimes . . . before an ordinary court" cleared the way for the high court in Ohio to settle the matter.

In the 1790s, it was commonly believed that insulting or defaming a representative of a foreign government was punishable by international law. But when Adams asked Lee if the United States could bring a LIBEL action against the editor of *Porcupine's Gazette* for an allegedly defamatory article about a Spanish ambassador, Lee's opinion anticipated the free speech concerns of such a prosecution. Lee conceded that foreign representatives were due the respect of the U.S. citizenry, but he also noted that "the line between freedom and licentiousness of the press [had] not yet been distinctly drawn by judicial decision."

In another international matter, Lee was asked to render an opinion in a volatile EXTRADITION dispute. Jonathan Robbins was charged with murder on board a British ship. British authorities wanted him bound over to face the charges, but he fought extradition, claiming that he was a U.S. citizen who had been imprisoned on the ship. Lee and Secretary of State Timothy Pickering argued that the treaty governing extradition did not apply to crimes committed on the high seas; thus, President Adams was under no obligation to surrender Robbins. The president disagreed with his advisers and delivered Robbins to the British authorities. Adams's decision was extremely unpopular with the public, and his actions may have contributed to the defeat of his party in the subsequent presidential election.

In 1803 Lee represented William Marbury against President Thomas Jefferson's secretary of state, JAMES MADISON (*Marbury v. Madison*, 5 U.S. (1 Cranch) 137, 2 L. Ed. 60 [1803]). Marbury was appointed by Adams, Jefferson's predecessor, as a justice of the peace, but owing to the rush and confusion surrounding the eleventh-hour appointment, Marbury's commission had not been delivered. When Jefferson ordered Madison to withhold delivery of the commission, Marbury filed suit. Lee lost the case when the Supreme Court ruled that the act of Congress under which Marbury had been issued his commission was unconstitutional. Significantly, *Marbury* established the federal judiciary as the supreme authority in determining the constitutionality of law.

Four years later, Lee was more successful in his defense of statesman and former vice president Aaron Burr, who was tried and acquitted on charges of TREASON (a violation of the allegiance one owes to one's sovereign or to the state) (*United States v. Burr*, 25 F. Cas. 2 [1807]). In 1806 Burr had traveled west to promote settlement of land in the Louisiana Territory. His intentions were suspect, and he soon found himself accused of treason for planning to initiate a separation of the western territories from the United States. Lee had been a longtime Burr supporter, and he took the case, winning an acquittal.

Lee died June 24, 1815, in Fauquier County, Virginia.

CROSS-REFERENCES

Electoral College; Judicial Review; *Marbury v. Madison*.

LEGACY 📖 A disposition of PERSONAL PROPERTY by WILL. 📖

In a narrow technical sense, a legacy is distinguishable from a DEVISE, a gift by will of REAL PROPERTY. This distinction, however, will not be permitted to defeat the intent of a TESTATOR—one who makes a will—and these terms can be applied interchangeably to either personal property or real property if the context of the will demonstrates that this was the intention of the testator.

A GENERAL LEGACY, a DEMONSTRATIVE LEGACY, and a SPECIFIC LEGACY represent the three primary types of legacies.

LEGAL 📖 Conforming to the law; required or permitted by law; not forbidden by law. 📖

The term *legal* is often used by the courts in reference to an INFERENCE of the law formulated as a matter of CONSTRUCTION, rather than established by actual proof, such as legal MALICE.

LEGAL ADVERTISING 📖 Any advertising an ATTORNEY purchases or places in publications, outdoor installations, radio, television, or any other written or recorded media. 📖

Legal advertising saw a large increase in the 1990s: $102 million was spent on TV ads in 1991, twenty times more than in 1980. The pros and cons of legal advertising have been widely discussed as the amount of advertising has increased. On the positive side, legal advertising makes the public aware of current legal issues and tells people that there are lawyers willing to assist them. Legal advertising also serves the practical purpose of informing people about the times when it may be necessary to consult a lawyer. Statistics show that two out of three people do not seek the services of a lawyer when they should. On the negative side, legal advertising can be manipulated into something that is more slick than informative. Guidelines and legislation have targeted that type of advertising.

The roots of legal advertising can be traced to England's legal system. However, today's standards are based on canon 27 of the AMERICAN BAR ASSOCIATION's (ABA's) forty-seven canons of professional ETHICS. Originally written in 1908, these guidelines were for both state and local bar associations. Canon 27, which addressed legal advertising, said, "[S]olicitation of business by circulars or advertisements, or by personal communications, or interviews, not warranted by personal relations are unprofessional." In 1937 this rule was modified to allow attorneys to publish listings in legal directories and other publications that were solely for those in the legal community. The next year the ABA ruled that distinctive listings could also be placed in the white pages of public telephone directories. However, this ruling was overturned in 1951.

In 1969 the ABA reclassified the canons and created nine new ones with ethical considerations and disciplinary rules. These were updated to "represent the objectives toward which every member of the profession should strive" (Model Code of Professional Responsibility, Preamble and Preliminary Statement [1969]). The new guidelines, called the ABA Moral Code of Professional Responsibility, operate on the principle that lawyers may advertise to

SHOULD LEGAL ADVERTISING BE RESTRICTED?

Despite a series of rulings by the U.S. Supreme Court that lawyers may advertise their services, the issue of legal advertising remains controversial. Proponents of advertising contend that it provides to consumers information about their legal rights and allows those in need of legal services a way to find an attorney. Opponents charge that advertising demeans the legal profession because promoting legal services through print or electronic media tells the public that lawyers are only out to make money. With the rise of the Internet, legal advertising has moved into a new medium, generating even more questions about the need for restrictions on advertisements.

Opponents of legal advertising are primarily concerned with maintaining the law as a profession. As members of a profession, lawyers have pledged to serve the public interest. For much of U.S. history, lawyers have served as protectors of civil rights and democratic institutions. Those who oppose legal advertising argue that this historic role must be preserved in the face of advertising that is sometimes undignified and demeaning to the profession.

State bar associations and state supreme courts have set standards for the ethical conduct of attorneys. Opponents of advertising believe that the regulation of advertising properly falls within the jurisdiction of these institutions. Though many attorneys may object that regulation restricts their First Amendment right to freedom of expression, the U.S. Supreme Court has never ruled that states are without power to police the legal profession.

Opponents argue that even with the restrictions currently imposed, too many lawyers hurt the profession by producing radio and television advertisements that create the perception that lawyers are ambulance chasers. If restrictions were loosened, this group contends, some lawyers would become even more aggressive in soliciting business. Public dissatisfaction with lawyers and the legal system, which has grown considerably since the 1970s, would continue to increase.

Opponents of advertising believe that purposeful competition between lawyers for clients is a great evil of the profession. The legal profession must concentrate on public service rather than profits. When lawyers advertise they provide the public with a misleading picture of legal services, suggesting that legal issues can be solved as easily as a sink can be fixed. Because the law is complex, the consumer cannot evaluate the quality of the offered services.

Opponents also note that the high cost of advertising must be passed on to the consumer. Also, the financial burden of advertising may encourage a lawyer to pursue nonmeritorious litigation. In addition, if a lawyer works with a high volume of clients generated by advertising, the lawyer may have little opportunity to communicate with a client or fully analyze a legal issue brought to the lawyer.

Those who support fewer restrictions on legal advertising contend that bar associations and bar leaders are out of step with the realities of U.S. society. First, they argue that bar associations were organized in the late nineteenth century to ensure that lawyers were self-regulated. This meant that a bar association could control the behavior of its members and find ways to preserve the monopoly over legal services. These supporters suggest that the public has not been well served by this system.

Though law is a profession, the need to make money has always been acknowledged. Supporters of advertising argue that it is therefore disingenuous for well-heeled lawyers to lament the introduction of competition. They point out that bar leaders have generally come from large corporate law firms, which have no need to advertise for clients but compete for profitable corporate retainers. These firms, they contend, have not provided public service but have concentrated on making profits. If corporate firms had helped with the unmet legal needs of society, perhaps advertising would not be necessary.

Proponents of advertising do not believe that professionalism, public service, and commercialism are mutually exclusive. They contend that lawyers can provide the public with a service by advertising. Much of legal advertising is educational, instructing consumers on what their legal rights are and where they may consult an attorney for free or for a minimal charge. Advertising reaches people who would not otherwise know what to do or where to go with a legal problem.

Proponents of advertising argue that placing the legal profession in the marketplace is not demeaning but democratic. Legal advertising breaks down the elitist notion that lawyers are somehow superior to others in the workforce. Lawyers provide services, many of which are simple. Competition helps to drive down the costs of legal services rather than increase them. Advertising does cost money, but innovative law firms have learned how to use forms, computers, and the services of legal assistants to reduce operating costs. In most cases the quality of legal services has not suffered. As with any business, if consumers are unhappy with the service they receive, they will not return. Proponents contend that the brisk business done by law firms that advertise is evidence of the quality of work they produce.

Those who favor legal advertising generally are convinced that advertisements provide consumers with information about legal services. As long as promotional material is not misleading or false, legal advertising should be subject to minimal restrictions. Proponents note, however, that most lawyers either refrain from advertising or do it in the most conservative way, so as to avoid censure by their bar associations.

IN FOCUS

"Spamming" the Net

L egal advertising has found its way into the phone books and onto radio and television. With the growth of the Internet as an information and communication resource, lawyers and law firms have established home pages on the World Wide Web to provide legal information and advertise their services. This has created new opportunities and new problems.

In April 1993 Laurence Canter and Martha A. Siegel, of the Phoenix, Arizona, law firm of Canter and Siegel, sent an E-mail message to thousands of Internet news groups, advertising their immigration law practice, in the hope of gaining new clients. News groups are electronic bulletin boards where people post messages concerning a very specific topic. They have millions of subscribers.

Canter and Siegel's direct mailing to the news groups cost them virtually nothing compared with the cost of a conventional hard copy mailing. In sending their advertisement, they used a process called spamming, which allows a message to be sent to every news group in existence, regardless of whether a particular group might be interested in the content of the message.

The spamming set off a tidal wave of protests from readers of news groups who were angry that the law firm had violated Internet etiquette. Canter and Siegel's Internet provider received thirty thousand messages, some of which were death threats. The law firm claimed to have received over twenty thousand positive responses and to have gained some new clients.

Though the Internet community and members of the legal community voiced their displeasure at the spamming, Canter and Siegel's advertisement was legal. Their action was analogous to placing an advertisement in a newspaper and hoping a person would read it.

See also E-mail; Internet.

---

educate the public, not just to get publicity or gain monetary rewards. This is not an honor system; the ABA Model Rules of Professional Conduct govern and provide guidelines for legal advertising. The major requirement is that an advertisement must be truthful and not deceptive or misleading. Acceptable content includes the lawyer's and firm's names and their address, phone number, type of services offered, bases of fees, available credit arrangements, foreign language ability, references, and client names (with their prior consent). Acceptable media include newspapers, television, radio, phone and legal directories, outdoor installations, and other written or recorded media. Lawyers are required to keep records listing the use and content of each advertisement, as a tool of enforcement.

A set of specific guidelines set forth by the ABA limits the ability of lawyers to state or imply that they have special knowledge in a particular field of law, such as patent law or admiralty law. Because potential clients do not typically have a way to verify that a lawyer is a qualified specialist, this guideline protects them from deception. However, in *In re R. M. J.*, (455 U.S. 191, 102 S. Ct. 929, 71 L. Ed. 2d 64 (1982), the Supreme Court ruled that lawyers have the right to advertise their area of practice if they use "unsanctioned, non-misleading language." Simply stating that they practice a specific type of law—for example, divorce law—is acceptable; stating that they are specialists in that type of law is not.

Although these guidelines have been helpful in establishing higher standards in legal advertising, several problems have arisen. The major problem is that the guidelines are the ABA's creation, and therefore the legal profession is responsible for enforcing them. As with any type of self-regulation, this has led to enforcement standards that are sometimes lax, and the resulting sometimes inadequate punishment only encourages other lawyers to engage in inappropriate or unethical behavior.

The second main problem is that because state associations can create their own legislation based on the ABA's guidelines, what is acceptable legal advertising in one state may be unacceptable in a neighboring state. This can lead to confusion and violation of ethics codes, as well as image problems for the legal profession.

Current regulations that have developed through the courts provide some constitutional protection for some types of legal advertising. These rulings have stated that blanket prohibition of the following subjects is not allowed: costs of routine services; general areas of practice; advice of people's rights and the attorney's willingness to help them, as in CLASS ACTION suits; direct-mail solicitation of people with a particular legal problem, such as impending foreclosure; and direct-personal solicitation if its purpose is political or ideological, not monetary. States are allowed to have regulations that require disclosures or disclaimers, and they can restrict the publication or broadcast of ads that they find to be deceptive, misleading, or false. The ABA has defined misleading advertisements as those that create unrealistic expectations of the lawyer's ability; compare the lawyer's service to the services of other lawyers; advertise the lawyer's win-loss record, or results the lawyer has obtained for clients; or contain client endorsements.

Several landmark cases have set the standards for today's legal advertisements. In *Bates v. State Bar of Arizona*, 433 U.S. 350, 97 S. Ct. 2691, 53 L. Ed. 2d 810 (1977), the Supreme Court ruled that legal advertising in newspapers is protected by the FIRST AMENDMENT, and that state professional or disciplinary codes cannot prohibit it. However, reasonable restrictions can be placed on deceptive, false, or misleading advertisements.

The Supreme Court dealt with direct-mail solicitation in its next landmark case involving legal advertising, *Shapero v. Kentucky Bar Ass'n*, 486 U.S. 466, 108 S. Ct. 1916, 100 L. Ed. 2d 475 (1988). The Kentucky Bar Association had a statute that prohibited attorneys from using direct-mail solicitation to attract clients. The Supreme Court held that the law violated the First Amendment. The ensuing direct-mail standard was that truthful and nondeceptive ads could be targeted at people with known legal problems.

Continuing on the issue of solicitation, *Ohralik v. Ohio Bar Ass'n*, 436 U.S. 447, 98 S. Ct. 1912, 56 L. Ed. 2d 444 (1978), involved in-person solicitation. An Ohio Bar Association regulation stated, "A lawyer shall not recommend employment, as a private practitioner, of himself, his partner or associate to a non-lawyer who has not sought his advice regarding employment of a lawyer" (Ohio Code of Professional Responsibility, DR 2-103(A) [1979]). The Supreme Court ruled that in-person solicitation has very limited First Amendment protection, and therefore left its regulation up to the individual states.

LEGAL AGE The time of life at which a person acquires full CAPACITY to make his or her own CONTRACTS and DEEDS and to transact business or to enter into some particular contract or relation, such as marriage.

In most states a MINOR attains legal age at eighteen, although for certain acts, such as consuming alcoholic beverages, the age might be higher; for others, such as driving, the age

might be lower. Legal age is synonymous with AGE OF CONSENT or AGE OF MAJORITY.

LEGAL AID A system of nonprofit organizations that provide legal services to people who cannot afford an ATTORNEY.

In the United States, more than sixteen hundred legal aid agencies provide legal representation without cost or for a nominal fee to people who are unable to pay the usual amount for a lawyer's services. These agencies are sponsored by charitable organizations, lawyers' associations, and law schools, and by federal, state, and local governments. In some states legal aid services are partially funded from the interest earned in law firm trust accounts.

The first U.S. legal aid agency was founded in 1876 in New York City by the German Society. The agency assisted German immigrants with legal problems. Beginning in the late nineteenth century, lawyers' associations took the lead in providing low-cost legal services. In 1911 the National Alliance of Legal Aid Societies was established to promote the concept of legal aid to people who were poor. The alliance, now known as the National Legal Aid and Defender Association, publishes information and holds conferences dealing with legal aid issues.

Legal aid agencies handle civil cases, including those concerning ADOPTION, BANKRUPTCY, DIVORCE, employment issues, and LANDLORD AND TENANT disputes. These agencies may not use federal funds to handle criminal cases. The criminal counterpart to the U.S. legal aid system is called the PUBLIC DEFENDER system. Public defenders are funded through state and local agencies and federal grants.

Legal aid agencies are run by attorneys and administrative support staff. They are often supplemented by law students, who participate in legal aid clinics that give students opportunities to work with indigent clients. In addition, many private attorneys volunteer their time to assist these agencies. In some JURISDICTIONS the court may appoint private attorneys to handle legal aid clients. Despite these pro bono (donated) services, legal aid agencies typically have more clients than they can serve. When they do, they may exclude complicated matters, such as divorce, from the legal services they provide.

The scope of legal aid widened dramatically in 1964, when President LYNDON B. JOHNSON established the Office of Legal Services. This agency organized new legal aid programs in many states, then suffered budget cuts in the early 1970s. In 1974 Congress disbanded the office and transferred its functions to the newly created LEGAL SERVICES CORPORATION (Legal Services Corporation Act of 1974, 88 Stat. 378 [42 U.S.C.A. § 2996]). The corporation is a private, nonprofit organization that provides financial support to legal aid agencies through the distribution of grants. It also supports legal aid attorneys and staff through training, research, and technical assistance.

See also PRO BONO PUBLICO; RIGHT TO COUNSEL.

LEGAL ASSISTANT A person, working under the supervision of a LAWYER, qualified through education, training, or work experience to perform substantive legal work that requires knowledge of legal concepts and is customarily, but not exclusively, performed by a lawyer; also known as a PARALEGAL.

Legal assistants, or paralegals, help attorneys deliver legal services. Although they assist attorneys in very technical areas of the law, they are prohibited from practicing law without a LICENSE. Legal assistants cannot represent a client or give legal advice. All work performed by legal assistants must be done under the supervision of an ATTORNEY, who is subject to disciplinary procedures for ethical violations committed by the legal assistant.

The legal assistant profession emerged in the 1960s, as law firms hired persons, usually women, to help lawyers prepare complex or highly detailed cases. These persons typically worked in specialties such as bankruptcy, probate and estate planning, real estate, and civil litigation, where they organized documents, completed forms, and prepared cases for trial.

In 1968 the AMERICAN BAR ASSOCIATION (ABA) created the Special Committee on Lay Assistants for Lawyers. The committee worked to develop the training of nonlawyer assistants, and the utilization of their services to enable lawyers to perform their professional duties more effectively and efficiently. In 1973 the ABA approved the Guidelines for the Approval of Legal Assistant Education Programs, and in 1975 it approved the first eight legal assistant training programs under those guidelines. In 1996 there were 206 ABA-approved education programs in the United States.

A drive for professional standing led to the establishment of two legal assistant organizations. The National Federation of Paralegal Associations (NFPA) was founded in 1974. The NFPA is a federation of sixty member associations that works to improve the educational and professional standing of legal assistants. In 1975 the National Association of Legal Assistants (NALA) was formed.

Both the NFPA and the NALA have worked to increase the educational requirements for becoming a legal assistant. In the 1960s legal assistants learned on the job. In the 1970s a variety of educational options became available: certificate programs, two-year associate of arts degrees in paralegal studies, and four-year bachelor of arts degrees in paralegal studies. In the 1990s postbaccalaureate programs started to appear.

The demand for legal assistants has continued to grow since the 1960s. It is estimated that by the year 2000 there will be one hundred thousand paralegals in the United States, most of them women. A 1995 survey by the NFPA revealed that 94 percent of all legal assistants were women. Besides working for law firms, legal assistants are now employed by corporations, banks, government agencies, and insurance companies. The demand for legal assistants is highest in large cities.

The profession has continued to explore ways to improve its status. For example, the NALA offers a certified legal assistant credential. This credential is based on a two-day examination that includes legal research, legal terminology, ethics, communications, and four areas of substantive law chosen by the candidate. It must be renewed every five years by attending continuing education programs. The NALA also offers specialty examinations to those with advanced knowledge in substantive areas of the law.

The regulation of legal assistants has been addressed by numerous state legislatures, state bar association committees, and state supreme court task forces. None of these entities have implemented regulation, whether it be registration, licensure, or certification.

LEGAL CAP Long stationery with a wide left-hand margin and a narrow right-hand margin, used by attorneys.

The trend of the courts is to move away from permitting a document of this size to be filed. Courts presently recommend or require the use of standard size paper.

LEGAL CAUSE In the law of TORTS, conduct that is a substantial factor in bringing about harm, which is synonymous with PROXIMATE CAUSE.

LEGAL DECISION See COURT OPINION.

LEGAL DETRIMENT A change in position by one to whom a PROMISE has been made, or an assumption of duties or liabilities not previously imposed on the person, due to the person's reliance on the actions of the one who makes the promise.

See also CONSIDERATION; CONTRACTS.

LEGAL EDUCATION Those who sought a legal career in pre-Revolutionary America and for many years thereafter had several options. They could embark on a self-directed course of study; they could serve as an assistant in a clerk of court's office; or they could travel to England to study at the INNS OF COURT. The most common method of obtaining a legal education was through the apprenticeship system.

The apprenticeship system allowed men (it was generally unavailable to women) to acquire education and experience simultaneously by working under an experienced practitioner. Ideally, an APPRENTICE would spend several years learning both the law and the practical aspects of a law practice. However, the quality of ap-

prenticeships varied greatly, depending on the administering attorney's skill and attention. Some apprenticeships were merely a source of cheap labor. THOMAS JEFFERSON once commented that the services he was expected to render as an apprentice were worth more than the instruction he received.

There were no law schools in colonial America. In 1779 Jefferson helped found the first professorship of law, at William and Mary College, installing his apprenticeship mentor, GEORGE WYTHE. Yale, Columbia, the University of Maryland, and Harvard followed suit. The positions they established were part of the general university curriculum and were typically filled by practitioners rather than academicians. This early movement to emphasize the scholarship of law gained little momentum because most lawyers believed that apprenticeships provided sufficient legal training. In 1784, however, proprietary (for-profit) law schools arrived and spurred the transformation of legal education.

Proprietary law schools were essentially specialized and elaborate law offices. The first and most famous was Connecticut's Litchfield School. Its fourteen-month course provided instruction in subjects such as property, contracts, procedure, master-and-servant, and commercial law—similar to the subjects of some of today's first-year law school classes. Litchfield graduated about 1,000 in its forty-nine-year history, including 2 future vice presidents, 101 congressmen, 28 senators, 14 governors, and scores of distinguished state jurists.

The advent of law professorships and proprietary schools notwithstanding, apprenticeships remained the most common way to obtain a legal education until well into the nineteenth century. Until the late 1820s, BAR ASSOCIATIONS exercised significant control over legal education and typically required an apprenticeship of several years. In 1828 ANDREW JACKSON was elected the seventh president of the United States. Jackson, himself a lawyer, styled himself as champion of the common person. State legislatures quickly followed his lead, eschewing anything elitist and reasserting authority long delegated to bar associations. Bar admission standards declined. Nearly anyone who could show "good moral character" was permitted to practice law, regardless of any knowledge of the field. Bar exams, if required at all, were usually perfunctory. By the 1860s only nine of thirty-seven states had retained formal apprenticeship requirements.

Harvard, the first academic law school, had been founded in 1817 by the outright adoption of a proprietary law school. Here, too, stan-

Law Degrees Conferred and Bar Membership, 1960 to 1991

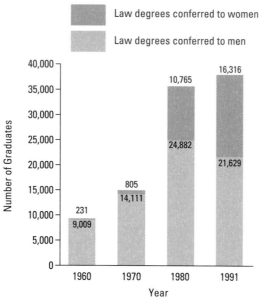

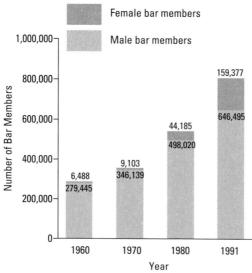

Sources: U.S. National Center for Education Statistics, *Digest of Education Statistics*, annual; American Bar Foundation, Chicago IL, *The Lawyer Statistical Report: The U.S. Legal Professions in the 1990's* and similar reports for 1960 to 1988.

dards dropped. By 1829 students who were denied admission to Harvard College could go directly into the law school, and the school quit giving exams. However, in the same year Justice JOSEPH STORY, of the U.S. Supreme Court, became a Harvard Law professor and augured Harvard's emergence as the first modern law school. In 1850 there were fifteen university law schools. By 1870 the number had barely doubled, but the modern era of legal education was about to begin. That was the year CHRISTOPHER COLUMBUS LANGDELL became dean of Harvard Law School.

Langdell believed that law could be taught as a science. Rather than listening passively to lectures and reading treatises, Langdell's students dissected reported case decisions. Using a technique known as Socratic dialogue, professors bombarded their students with questions, forcing them to analyze the facts, reasoning, and law in each case. In addition, Langdell grouped related cases together, devoting separate books to different topics. This development may seem obvious today, but it was a great innovation at the time. Socratic dialogue and the case-study method are still commonly used, particularly in first-year law classes.

Langdell also instituted tighter admission standards, expanded the program from two to three years, and raised graduation requirements. Other university law schools soon began to adopt some of Harvard's lofty standards. Proprietary schools continued with low admission standards. Part-time evening schools appeared, providing people with a lower income and less general education a way to obtain a legal education.

At the beginning of Langdell's tenure, obtaining one's legal education through law school was still a luxury. The AMERICAN BAR ASSOCIATION (ABA), founded in 1878, along with the Association of American Law Schools (AALS), formed in 1905, worked to consign apprenticeships to the pages of history. In 1917 thirty-six out of forty-nine JURISDICTIONS still required a period of apprenticeship, but future lawyers could substitute law school. In the last half of the nineteenth century, a high school graduate could enter most law schools, but the ABA and the AALS worked to steadily increase admission standards. By 1931 seventeen states required two years of college before admission, and thirty-three had a three-year law curriculum. Just eight years later, forty-one states required at least two years of college. Today there are over 170 accredited law schools and a number of unaccredited programs.

The first woman admitted to the bar was Arabella Mansfield, who became a member of the Illinois bar in 1869. A year later another woman received a law degree. In 1950 the first women—thirteen of them—were admitted to the Harvard Law School. Women still account for only a small portion of the total lawyer population—roughly 20 percent in the mid-1990s. However, their increasing presence in law schools should significantly reduce the imbalance by the early twenty-first century.

Desegregation came no more quickly to the legal profession than to most other professions, despite the pivotal role the profession played in the desegregation process. As recently as 1972, a total 94.1 percent of the United States' ninety-five thousand law students were white. In 1995–96 about 20 percent of all law students were members of minority groups.

Another change for law schools is the growth of clinical programs, which focus on practical skills rather than scholarship. In clinical programs second- and third-year law students work on real cases, learning SUBSTANTIVE LAW and acquiring experience in drafting PLEADINGS, counseling clients, and negotiating settlements under the guidance of a supervising attorney or professor.

Professional legal development continues throughout a lawyer's career. In 1975 Minnesota was the first state to mandate CONTINUING LEGAL EDUCATION for practitioners, requiring forty-five hours of approved legal study every three years. Some states have followed Minnesota's approach, but other states have their own requirements. For example, some states certify specialists, a process that varies greatly. It may require special exams and a certain length of practice, or it may be little more than an identification program.

CROSS-REFERENCES

Bar Examination; Case Method; Law School Admission Test; Litchfield Law School.

LEGALESE 📖 Slang; technical jargon used by attorneys that is often beyond the comprehension of the nonlawyer. 📖

States enact "plain English" laws that require the translation of legalese into everyday language to permit consumers to understand their INSURANCE policies, DEEDS, MORTGAGES, leases, credit card financing agreements, and other legal documents.

LEGAL FICTION 📖 An assumption that something occurred or someone or something exists which, in fact, is not the case, but that is made in the law to enable a court to equitably resolve a matter before it. 📖

In order to do justice, the law will permit or create a legal fiction. For example, if a person undertakes a RENUNCIATION of a LEGACY which is a gift by WILL the person will be deemed to have predeceased the TESTATOR—one who makes a will—for the purpose of distributing the ESTATE.

LEGAL HISTORY 📖 The record of past events that deal with the law. 📖

Legal history is a discipline that examines events of the past that pertain to all facets of the law. It includes analysis of particular laws, legal institutions, individuals who operate in the legal system, and the effect of law on society. U.S. legal history is a relatively new subtopic that began to grow dramatically in the 1960s.

Before the 1960s legal history was confined mostly to biographies of famous lawyers and judges and to technical analysis of particular areas of substantive law. In general it was an afterthought. Political historians made reference to important U.S. Supreme Court cases, but there was little in-depth analysis of topics such as CRIMINAL LAW, the law of SLAVERY, or the development of the state and federal court systems.

The study of U.S. legal history began with the work of James Willard Hurst. In 1950 Hurst published *The Growth of American Law: The Law Makers*, which examined many types of historical sources in order to fashion a history of U.S. law. Hurst went beyond the work of judges and courts to find material about the law in constitutional conventions, legislatures, administrative agencies, and the bar. Among his many other works, Hurst explored the relationship of law and the economy in *Law and Economic Growth: The Legal History of the Lumber Industry in Wisconsin, 1836–1915* (1964).

In his scholarship Hurst tried to integrate PUBLIC LAW (law created by government bodies) with PRIVATE LAW (law implemented through public courts to resolve individual disputes). Legal historians who began researching and writing in the 1960s typically emphasized one of these types of law. Lawrence M. Friedman emphasized the work of private law in *A History of American Law*, first published in 1973. In this book Friedman examined, among many topics, the law of contract, real property, and tort.

Paul L. Murphy focused on public law, writing a series of articles and books relating the U.S. Constitution to the social and cultural pressures of different historical periods. In *World War I and the Origin of Civil Liberties in the United States* (1979), Murphy analyzed the relationship between the United States' experience in war and developing interest in FIRST AMENDMENT civil liberties.

The field of legal history also benefited from the growth of social history in the 1960s. The issues of gender, race, and class became crucial to historians during the Vietnam War period. Legal historians such as Kermit L. Hall have built on these issues, interweaving legal history with social and cultural history to explain how law is both a reactive mechanism, responding to public problems, and an active mechanism, shaping behavior through its rules and structure. Hall's *The Magic Mirror: Law in American History* (1989) was the first major work to synthesize twenty years of social and legal history research into an overview of U.S. law, public and private.

Legal historians have looked at the role of law in U.S. history in several disparate ways. Hurst and many other historians have seen the law as a means of enhancing political and economic consensus. Their view is that law acts as a neutral party through which conflicting interests work to achieve their own ends.

Other, more radical historians see law as a formal device for perpetuating the domination of the ruling economic class. Their viewpoint emphasizes that law is not the expression of neutral rules but a creature of power and politics. Therefore, those who lack power—including women, members of racial minorities, and people who are poor—have been hurt by the law.

The consensus and conflict models of legal historical analysis turn on their positions concerning the principle called the rule of law. This rule, on which all other legal rules are based, has been a basic principle of Western culture since the seventeenth century. It posits that all persons are equal before a neutral and impartial authority, regardless of economic standing, gender, race, family connections, or political connections. Legal historians produce scholarship that goes to the question of whether all persons receive justice.

The field of legal history continues to grow, with historians now exploring every facet of the law. History is no longer defined as just Supreme Court decisions or congressional legislation. Historians examine the inner workings of state courts, frontier law of the nineteenth century, the role of law in slavery, criminal law, legal bias against homosexuality, and more.

CROSS-REFERENCES

Critical Legal Studies; Feminist Jurisprudence; Jurisprudence.

LEGAL LIST STATUTES 📖 State laws that enumerate the investments into which certain institutions and FIDUCIARIES—those who manage money and property for another and who must exercise a standard of CARE in such activity in accordance with law or CONTRACT—can venture. 📖

Legal lists are frequently limited to high caliber SECURITIES that generate a satisfactory yield with a minimum amount of risk to the principal.

LEGAL PROCEEDINGS 📖 All ACTIONS that are authorized or sanctioned by law and instituted in a court or a TRIBUNAL for the acquisition of rights or the enforcement of remedies. 📖

LEGAL PUBLISHING 📖 The production of texts that report laws or discuss the practice of law. 📖

Originally limited to printed materials, legal publishing now encompasses electronic media as well, with most legal publications becoming available on-line or in CD-ROM format.

The first collections of American laws were published in the seventeenth and eighteenth centuries. Printing presses allowed laws to be printed on a regular basis. Colonists relied on English law as COMMON LAW, so local laws were not reported until after the American Revolution. Once the United States gained independence, the number of lawyers grew, along with the need for a printed record of U.S. laws.

The original case REPORTERS were published by individuals without the support of the government. In 1841 Georgia was the first state government to require its judges to write out their decisions. The clerk of the court would send the decisions to the governor, who had the decisions printed and distributed to all the judges in the state.

In the late nineteenth century, John B. West started the National Reporter System. West's *Syllabi* contained the full text of decisions of the Supreme Court of Minnesota. The publication was enlarged to include decisions of Wisconsin and eventually became the *Northwestern Reporter*. West's company soon expanded to cover decisions across the country. The company took responsibility for making sure the REPORTS were accurate. It included HEADNOTES for each case, summarizing the issues of law discussed in the decision. The decisions were published in parts that were later reprinted in hardbound volumes; using these "ADVANCE SHEETS" allowed decisions to be reported more quickly.

Other publishers that began reporting decisions in the 1800s included Matthew Bender and Company, Bancroft-Whitney Company, and The Lawyers Cooperative Publishing Company. Lawyers Cooperative Publishing printed selected decisions; each year it also printed a volume that reported where original decisions were cited in current decisions.

Federal decisions began to be reported in a regular and complete form in the late 1800s. The first volume of *American Law Reports* was printed in 1919 by the Edward Thompson and Lawyers Cooperative Publishing Companies.

With so many decisions being reported, it became difficult to determine the status of a case. Lawyers needed to know whether a case had been overruled or modified; typically they would mark any modifications to a decision in the margins of their reporters. In 1875 Frank S. Shepard published the *Illinois Annotations*. This was a series of sheets that could be cut out and pasted in the margins of the book reporting a case. The sticker format was dropped in 1900, and the CITATOR took on its current table format. Originally covering only cases, Shepard's citator was expanded to include CITATIONS to the Constitution, statutes, and court rules.

The publication of STATUTES followed a history similar to that of cases. Individual states printed their own statutes beginning at the end of the eighteenth century. The first commercial effort to publish federal laws occurred in 1902. In 1924 Congress authorized the publication of the *U.S. Code*. West Publishing Company and the Edward Thompson Company were hired to assist with the publication. Federal law was divided into individual titles. Today statutes are first published as unedited, uncollated statutes called "SLIP LAWS." At the end of each session, the statutes are gathered into the *U.S. Code*.

Little, Brown and Company was the first to publish books specifically for students. In 1871 Little, Brown started publishing CASEBOOKS for students. Casebooks present leading cases in a particular area of law, with accompanying discussion of the law. In 1880 eleven titles were available.

Other common legal publications include practice aids for lawyers, such as form books and practice books. Form books present standard formats for common legal documents. Practice books describe the laws of a particular JURISDICTION or practice area and give guidelines on various aspects of the law.

Legal periodicals make up another segment of the legal publishing market. These include newspapers and newsletters that report on current law. Within law schools student-edited LAW REVIEWS present articles by students, professors, and law school faculty.

Today's legal publishing market includes electronic publishing. Computer-assisted legal research makes it possible to search legal materials on-line. West Publishing's WESTLAW and Reed Elsevier's LEXIS/NEXIS systems give attorneys access to cases, statutes, rules, law reviews and a variety of practice guides. Many jurisdictions are making materials available through the INTERNET. Case law, statutes, and practice guides are available in CD-ROM format for most jurisdictions.

CROSS-REFERENCES

Case Law; Century Digest; Computer-Assisted Legal Research; Court Opinion; Decennial Digest®; Digest; Federal Reporter; Federal Supplement; Hornbook; Law Reports; LEXIS; Shepardizing; Shepard's Citations; Statutes at Large; Treatise; U.S. Code; U.S. Code Annotated; WESTLAW.

LEGAL REALISM 📖 The school of legal philosophy that challenges the orthodox view of U.S. JURISPRUDENCE under which law is characterized as an autonomous system of rules and principles that courts can logically apply in an objective fashion to reach a determinate and apolitical judicial decision. 📖

Legal realists maintain that common-law adjudication is an inherently subjective system that produces inconsistent and sometimes incoherent results that are largely based on the political, social, and moral predilections of state and federal judges.

The U.S. legal realism movement began in 1881 when OLIVER WENDELL HOLMES, JR., published *The Common Law*, an attack on the orthodox view of law. "The life of the law has not been logic," Holmes wrote, "it has been experience" (p. 5). Legal realism flourished during the 1920s and 1930s when ROSCOE POUND, a professor from Harvard Law School, and KARL

Oliver Wendell Holmes, Jr., started the legal realism movement when he published his book The Common Law *in 1881.*

LLEWELLYN, a professor from Yale Law School, published a series of articles debating the nuances of the movement. Although the movement declined after World War II, it continues to influence how judges, lawyers, and laypersons think about the law.

Legal realism is not a unified collection of thought. Many realists, like Pound and Llewellyn, were sharply critical of each other and presented irreconcilable theories. Yet, five strands of thought predominate in the movement. The strands focus on power and economics in society, the persuasion and characteristics of individual judges, society's welfare, a practical approach to a durable result, and a synthesis of legal philosophies.

Power and Economics in Society

The first strand is marked by the nihilistic view that law represents the will of society's most powerful members. This view is articulated by Thrasymachus in Plato's *Republic*, when he tells Socrates that in every government "laws are made by the ruling party in its own interest," and "the ruling element is always the strongest." When courts speak in terms of what is right and just, Thrasymachus said, they are speaking "in the interest of those established in power" (Plato, 18). Justice Holmes echoed these sentiments when he wrote that the law must not be perverted to prevent the natural outcome of dominant public opinion (*Lochner v. New York*, 198 U.S. 45, 25 S. Ct. 539, 49 L. Ed. 937 [1905]).

Realists argued that law frequently equates the dominant power in society with pervasive economic interests. During the incipience of the U.S. legal realism movement in the nineteenth century, the United States was transformed from a static agrarian economy into a dynamic industrial market. Realists asserted that U.S. COMMON LAW facilitated this transformation in a number of ways. When interpreting an insurance contract, one judge remarked in 1802 that courts must not adopt an interpretation that will "embarrass commerce." Instead, the judge said, courts are at liberty to "adopt such a construction as shall most subserve the solid interests of this growing country" (Horowitz 1977, 27).

To help subsidize the growth of a competitive economy in the nineteenth century, realists have argued, U.S. judges commonly frowned on claims brought by litigants seeking monopolistic power. For example, in *Palmer v. Mulligan*, 3 Cai. R. 307, 2 A.D. 270 (1805), a downstream landowner asked the New York Supreme Court to grant him the exclusive right to use river water for commercial activity despite any injuries that might result to upstream owners. The court refused to grant such a right because if it did "the public would be deprived of the benefit which always attends competition and rivalry." In a subsequent case, the New York Supreme Court held that a landowner's right to enjoy his property could be "modified by the exigencies of the social state" (*Losee v. Buchanan*, 51 N.Y. 476 [1873]). The court added, "We must have factories, machinery, dams, canals and railroads."

At the same time the common law was facilitating economic expansion, realists claimed that it was also helping to increase the number of exploited U.S. citizens. Realists were skeptical of the traditional description of the U.S. economy as a free market. They felt that the economy was regulated by common-law principles that safeguarded the interests of society's wealthiest members. In support of this contention, realists pointed to landlord-tenant laws that entitled lessors to evict lessees for technical breaches of their lease, labor laws that allowed management to replace striking workers, and contract laws that permitted employers to terminate their workers without justification.

The realists' economic analysis of law spawned two related movements in U.S. jurisprudence that occupy polar extremes on the political spectrum. One is the conservative law and economics movement, whose adherents believe that common-law principles must be interpreted to maximize the aggregate wealth of society without regard to whether such wealth is distributed equally. The other is the liberal CRITICAL LEGAL STUDIES movement, whose adherents, called crits, believe that the law must be utilized to redistribute wealth, power, and liberty so that every citizen is guaranteed a minimum level of dignity and equality.

Since the mid-1900s, the crits have focused less on what they perceive as economic exploitation in the law, and more on what they see as political exploitation. In this regard they have assailed various U.S. courts for advancing the interests of adult, white, heterosexual males at the expense of women, blacks, and homosexuals. The crits have commonly referenced three cases to corroborate this point: *McCleskey v. Kemp*, 481 U.S. 279, 107 S. Ct. 1756, 95 L. Ed. 2d 262 (1987), in which the Supreme Court rejected a constitutional challenge to CAPITAL PUNISHMENT despite evidence that black defendants are almost three times more likely than whites to receive the death penalty for murdering a white person; *Craig v. Boren*, 429 U.S. 190, 97 S. Ct. 451, 50 L. Ed. 2d 397 (1976), in which the Supreme Court ruled that the EQUAL PROTECTION Clause of the FOURTEENTH AMENDMENT provides less protection against discrimination for women than for members of other minority groups; and *Bowers v. Hardwick*, 478 U.S. 186, 106 S. Ct. 2841, 92 L. Ed. 2d 140 (1986), in which the Supreme Court refused to recognize a constitutional right to engage in homosexual intercourse.

The Persuasion and Characteristics of Individual Judges The second strand of realist thought subscribes to the relativistic view that law is nothing more than what a particular court says it is on a given day, and that the outcome to a legal dispute will vary according to the political, cultural, and religious persuasion of the presiding judge. Some realists, such as JEROME N. FRANK, another prominent thinker in U.S. jurisprudence during the 1920s and 1930s, insisted that a judge's psychological and personality characteristics also sway the judicial decision-making process. Justice BENJAMIN N. CARDOZO, of the Supreme Court, went so far as to characterize judges as legislators in robes.

The notion that judges legislate from the bench was a revolutionary idea that flew in the face of orthodox legal thought in the eighteenth and nineteenth centuries. In *The Federalist*, no. 78, ALEXANDER HAMILTON enunciated the orthodox position when he said the judiciary is the "least dangerous branch" because it has "neither force nor will, but merely judgment." The legislature, Hamilton said, has the power to prescribe the rights and duties by which the country is to be regulated, and the executive has the obligation to enforce these laws through the power of the sword. The role of the judiciary, Hamilton wrote, is simply to interpret and apply the laws passed by the other two branches.

Hamilton's view resonated in the opinions of Chief Justice JOHN MARSHALL, who wrote that "courts are the mere instruments of the law, and can will nothing" (*Osborn v. Bank of United States*, 22 U.S. [9 Wheat.] 738, 6 L. Ed. 204 [1824]). Judicial power, Marshall said, should never be exercised for the purpose of implementing the will of the judge. Instead, courts must exercise their power solely to implement the will of legislators, who, as the elected representatives of the American people, embody the "will of the law."

Hamilton and Marshall both believed that law is an autonomous body of knowledge independent and distinguishable from the personal preferences of the judge applying it, and that it is possible to interpret this body of knowledge in an objective fashion. Adherents to this theory of law are known as formalists. In the nineteenth century, formalists asserted that state and federal law constitute a rational system of rules and principles that judges can apply in a mechanical fashion to reach a clear, certain, and uncontroversial resolution to a legal dispute.

Realists, such as Justice Cardozo, questioned the formalists' assumption that law could be autonomous and objective, or produce demonstrably certain outcomes. In *The Nature of the Judicial Process*, a groundbreaking book first published in 1921, Cardozo argued that law is a malleable instrument that allows judges to mold amorphous words like *reasonable care*, *unreasonable restraint of trade*, and *due process* to justify any outcome they desire.

For example, courts are commonly asked to invalidate CONTRACTS on the ground that one party exercised DURESS and UNDUE INFLUENCE in coercing another party to enter an agreement. Cardozo noted that terms such as *duress* and *undue influence* are subject to interpretation. He argued that judges who are inclined to shape the law in favor of society's weaker members will construe them broadly, invalidating many contracts that stem from predatory behavior. On the other hand, judges who are inclined to shape the law in favor of society's stronger members will construe such words narrowly, allowing particular individuals to benefit from their guile and acumen.

Even when language is clear, Cardozo explained, the law often presents courts with competing and contradictory principles to apply and interpret. For example, in *Riggs v. Palmer*, 115 N.Y. 506, 22 N.E. 188 (1889), the New York Court of Appeals was presented with the question of whether a man could inherit under a WILL that named him as a BENEFICIARY, even though he had murdered the TESTATOR, his grandfather. The lodestar of testamentary interpretation, Cardozo observed, is that courts must interpret a will according to the explicit intentions of the testator. In this case, juxtaposed with this seemingly unequivocal rule was the ancient maxim of EQUITY, "No man shall profit from his own wrong." Depending on the outcome the court of appeals desired to reach in *Riggs*, Cardozo concluded, the panel of three judges could have relied on either legal axiom in support of its decision. In fact, the court was divided on the issue, with two judges voting to disinherit the murderous grandson, and the other voting to enforce the will.

Society's Welfare Convinced that common-law principles can be manipulated by the judiciary, Cardozo was concerned that instability and chaos would result if every judge followed his or her own political convictions when deciding a case. To forestall the onset of such legal disarray, Cardozo and other realists argued that all judges must interpret the law to advance the welfare of society. "Law ought to be guided by consideration of the effects [it will have] on social welfare," Cardozo wrote (Posner 1990, 26). This theory of law is known as sociological jurisprudence, and represents the third major strand of thought in the U.S. legal realism movement. Proponents of sociological jurisprudence encouraged judges to consult communal mores, ethics, and religion, and their own sense of justice when attempting to resolve a lawsuit in accordance with the collective good.

Sociological jurisprudence was foreshadowed by English philosopher JEREMY BENTHAM, who argued that the law must serve the interests of the greatest number of people in society. Bentham, whose legal philosophy is known as utilitarian jurisprudence, defined the collective good in terms of pain and pleasure. Judges should decide cases, Bentham thought, to achieve results that will maximize the pleasure of the majority of the residents in a given community, without much concern for the pain that might be inflicted on the balance of society. See also UTILITARIANISM.

Some realists turned Bentham's philosophy on its head, arguing that the law should serve the interests of the most fragile members in society because they are the least represented in state and federal legislative assemblies. This group of realists was affiliated with the U.S. Progressive movement, which became popular during the first quarter of the twentieth century as it sought to reform society by enacting legislation to protect certain vulnerable classes of employees, particularly women and children, from harsh working conditions. These realists were among the most vocal detractors from the Supreme Court's decision in *Lochner*, which struck down a state law prescribing the maximum number of hours employees could work during a given week in the baking industry.

A Practical Approach to a Durable Result Whereas sociological jurisprudence sought to utilize the common law as an engine of social reform, legal pragmatism, the fourth strand of realist thought, sought to employ common-law principles to resolve legal disputes in the most practical way. Pragmatists argued that a judge should undertake a four-step process when rendering an opinion.

First, the judge must identify the competing interests, values, and policies at stake in the lawsuit. Second, the judge must survey the range of alternative approaches to resolving the legal issues presented by the lawsuit. Third, the judge must weigh the likely consequences of each approach, considering the effect a particular decision may have on not only the parties to the lawsuit but also other individuals faced with similar legal problems. Fourth, the judge must choose a response that will yield the most durable result in the course of the law. This pragmatic legal philosophy is often characterized as result-oriented jurisprudence.

A Synthesis of Legal Philosophies
The fifth strand of realist thought, legal empiricism, attempted to synthesize the other four strands into a single jurisprudence. Made famous by Holmes, legal empiricism claimed that law is best explained as a prediction of what judges will do in a particular case. Empiricists, who were influenced by behaviorists Ivan Pavlov and B. F. Skinner, argued that lawyers can predict the outcome of legal disputes by examining the judicial behavior of a given court.

The empiricists' efforts to integrate the other four schools of legal realism into one coherent philosophy was reflected by their belief that judicial behavior can be influenced by political, economic, sociological, practical, and historical considerations, as well as personal and psychological prejudices and idiosyncracies. Lawyers and laypersons who spend more time studying these elements and less time studying the labyrinth of legal rules and principles that make up the law, the empiricists concluded, will have a better idea of how a judge will rule in a particular case.

ABBREVIATIONS

A.	Atlantic Reporter
A. 2d	Atlantic Reporter, Second Series
AAA	American Arbitration Association; Agricultural Adjustment Act of 1933
AAPRP	All African People's Revolutionary Party
ABA	American Bar Association; Architectural Barriers Act, 1968
ABM Treaty	Anti-Ballistic Missile Treaty of 1972; antiballistic missile
ABVP	Anti-Biased Violence Project
A/C	Account
A.C.	Appeal Cases
ACAA	Air Carrier Access Act
ACF	Administration for Children and Families
ACLU	American Civil Liberties Union
ACS	Agricultural Cooperative Service
Act'g Legal Adv.	Acting Legal Advisor
ACUS	Administrative Conference of the United States
ACYF	Administration on Children, Youth, and Families
A.D. 2d	Appellate Division, Second Series, N.Y.
ADA	Americans with Disabilities Act of 1990
ADAMHA	Alcohol, Drug Abuse, and Mental Health Administration
ADC	Aid to Dependent Children
ADD	Administration on Developmental Disabilities
ADEA	Age Discrimination in Employment Act of 1967
ADR	alternative dispute resolution
AEC	Atomic Energy Commission
AECB	Arms Export Control Board
A.E.R.	All England Law Reports
AFDC	Aid to Families with Dependent Children
aff'd per cur.	affirmed by the court
AFIS	automated fingerprint identification system
AFL	American Federation of Labor
AFL-CIO	American Federation of Labor and Congress of Industrial Organizations
AFRes	Air Force Reserve
AFSCME	American Federation of State, County, and Municipal Employees
AGRICOLA	Agricultural Online Access
AIA	Association of Insurance Attorneys
AID	artificial insemination using a third-party donor's sperm; Agency for International Development

AIDS	acquired immune deficiency syndrome
AIH	artificial insemination using the husband's sperm
AIM	American Indian Movement
AIUSA	Amnesty International, U.S.A. Affiliate
AJS	American Judicature Society
ALEC	American Legislative Exchange Council
ALF	Animal Liberation Front
ALI	American Law Institute
ALJ	administrative law judge
All E.R.	All England Law Reports
ALO	Agency Liaison
A.L.R.	American Law Reports
AMA	American Medical Association
Am. Dec.	American Decisions
amdt.	amendment
Amer. St. Papers, For. Rels.	American State Papers, Legislative and Executive Documents of the Congress of the U.S., Class I, Foreign Relations, 1832–1859
AMVETS	American Veterans (of World War II)
ANA	Administration for Native Americans
Ann. Dig.	Annual Digest of Public International Law Cases
ANZUS	Australia–New Zealand–United States Security Treaty Organization
AOA	Administration on Aging
APA	Administrative Procedure Act of 1946
APHIS	Animal and Plant Health Inspection Service
App. Div.	Appellate Division Reports, N.Y. Supreme Court
Arb. Trib., U.S.-British Convention of 1853	Arbitration Tribunal, Claim Convention of 1853, United States and Great Britain
ARS	Advanced Record System
Art.	article
ASCS	Agriculture Stabilization and Conservation Service
ASM	available seatmile
ASPCA	American Society for the Prevention of Cruelty to Animals
Asst. Att. Gen.	Assistant Attorney General
AT&T	American Telephone and Telegraph
ATFD	Alcohol, Tobacco and Firearms Division
ATLA	Association of Trial Lawyers of America
ATTD	Alcohol and Tobacco Tax Division
ATU	Alcohol Tax Unit
AZT	azidothymidine
BALSA	Black-American Law Student Association
BATF	Bureau of Alcohol, Tobacco and Firearms
BCCI	Bank of Credit and Commerce International
BEA	Bureau of Economic Analysis
Bell's Cr. C.	Bell's English Crown Cases
Bevans	United States Treaties, etc. *Treaties and Other International Agreements of the United States of America, 1776–1949* (compiled under the direction of Charles I. Bevans) (1968–76)
BFOQ	bona fide occupational qualification
BI	Bureau of Investigation
BIA	Bureau of Indian Affairs; Board of Immigration Appeals
BJS	Bureau of Justice Statistics
Black.	Black's United States Supreme Court Reports
Blatchf.	Blatchford's United States Circuit Court Reports
BLM	Bureau of Land Management
BLS	Bureau of Labor Statistics
BMD	ballistic missile defense
BOCA	Building Officials and Code Administrators International
BPP	Black Panther Party for Self-Defense

Brit. and For.	British and Foreign State Papers
Burr.	James Burrows, *Report of Cases Argued and Determined in the Court of King's Bench during the Time of Lord Mansfield* (1766–1780)
BVA	Board of Veterans Appeals
c.	Chapter
C³I	Command, Control, Communications, and Intelligence
C.A.	Court of Appeals
CAA	Clean Air Act
CAB	Civil Aeronautics Board
CAFE	corporate average fuel economy
Cal. 2d	California Reports, Second Series
Cal. 3d	California Reports, Third Series
CALR	computer-assisted legal research
Cal. Rptr.	California Reporter
CAP	Common Agricultural Policy
CATV	community antenna television
CBO	Congressional Budget Office
CCC	Commodity Credit Corporation
CCDBG	Child Care and Development Block Grant of 1990
C.C.D. Pa.	Circuit Court Decisions, Pennsylvania
C.C.D. Va.	Circuit Court Decisions, Virginia
CCEA	Cabinet Council on Economic Affairs
CCR	Center for Constitutional Rights
C.C.R.I.	Circuit Court, Rhode Island
CD	certificate of deposit
CDA	Communications Decency Act
CDBG	Community Development Block Grant Program
CDC	Centers for Disease Control and Prevention; Community Development Corporation
CDF	Children's Defense Fund
CDL	Citizens for Decency through Law
CD-ROM	compact disc read-only memory
CDS	Community Dispute Services
CDW	collision damage waiver
CENTO	Central Treaty Organization
CEQ	Council on Environmental Quality
CERCLA	Comprehensive Environmental Response, Compensation, and Liability Act of 1980
cert.	*certiorari*
CETA	Comprehensive Employment and Training Act
C & F	cost and freight
CFC	chlorofluorocarbon
CFE Treaty	Conventional Forces in Europe Treaty of 1990
C.F. & I.	Cost, freight, and insurance
CFNP	Community Food and Nutrition Program
C.F.R.	Code of Federal Regulations
CFTC	Commodity Futures Trading Commission
Ch.	Chancery Division, English Law Reports
CHAMPVA	Civilian Health and Medical Program at the Veterans Administration
CHEP	Cuban/Haitian Entrant Program
CHINS	children in need of supervision
CHIPS	child in need of protective services
Ch.N.Y.	Chancery Reports, New York
Chr. Rob.	Christopher Robinson, *Reports of Cases Argued and Determined in the High Court of Admiralty* (1801–1808)
CIA	Central Intelligence Agency
CID	Commercial Item Descriptions
C.I.F.	Cost, insurance, and freight
CINCNORAD	Commander in Chief, North American Air Defense Command
C.I.O.	Congress of Industrial Organizations

C.J.	chief justice
CJIS	Criminal Justice Information Services
C.J.S.	Corpus Juris Secundum
Claims Arb. under Spec. Conv., Nielsen's Rept.	Frederick Kenelm Nielsen, *American and British Claims Arbitration under the Special Agreement Concluded between the United States and Great Britain, August 18, 1910* (1926)
CLE	Center for Law and Education
CLEO	Council on Legal Education Opportunity
CLP	Communist Labor Party of America
CLS	Christian Legal Society; critical legal studies (movement), Critical Legal Studies (membership organization)
C.M.A.	Court of Military Appeals
CMEA	Council for Mutual Economic Assistance
CMHS	Center for Mental Health Services
C.M.R.	Court of Military Review
CNN	Cable News Network
CNO	Chief of Naval Operations
C.O.D.	cash on delivery
COGP	Commission on Government Procurement
COINTELPRO	Counterintelligence Program
Coke Rep.	Coke's English King's Bench Reports
COLA	cost-of-living adjustment
COMCEN	Federal Communications Center
Comp.	Compilation
Conn.	Connecticut Reports
CONTU	National Commission on New Technological Uses of Copyrighted Works
Conv.	Convention
Corbin	Arthur L. Corbin, *Corbin on Contracts: A Comprehensive Treatise on the Rules of Contract Law* (1950)
CORE	Congress of Racial Equality
Cox's Crim. Cases	Cox's Criminal Cases (England)
CPA	certified public accountant
CPB	Corporation for Public Broadcasting, the
CPI	Consumer Price Index
CPSC	Consumer Product Safety Commission
Cranch	Cranch's United States Supreme Court Reports
CRF	Constitutional Rights Foundation
CRS	Congressional Research Service; Community Relations Service
CRT	critical race theory
CSA	Community Services Administration
CSAP	Center for Substance Abuse Prevention
CSAT	Center for Substance Abuse Treatment
CSC	Civil Service Commission
CSCE	Conference on Security and Cooperation in Europe
CSG	Council of State Governments
CSO	Community Service Organization
CSP	Center for the Study of the Presidency
C-SPAN	Cable-Satellite Public Affairs Network
CSRS	Cooperative State Research Service
CSWPL	Center on Social Welfare Policy and Law
CTA	*cum testamento annexo* (with the will attached)
Ct. Ap. D.C.	Court of Appeals, District of Columbia
Ct. App. No. Ireland	Court of Appeals, Northern Ireland
Ct. Cl.	Court of Claims, United States
Ct. Crim. Apps.	Court of Criminal Appeals (England)
Ct. of Sess., Scot.	Court of Sessions, Scotland
CU	credit union

CUNY	City University of New York
Cush.	Cushing's Massachusetts Reports
CWA	Civil Works Administration; Clean Water Act
Dall.	Dallas' Pennsylvania and United States Reports
DAR	Daughter of the American Revolution
DARPA	Defense Advanced Research Projects Agency
DAVA	Defense Audiovisual Agency
D.C.	United States District Court
D.C. Del.	United States District Court, Delaware
D.C. Mass.	United States District Court, Massachusetts
D.C. Md.	United States District Court, Maryland
D.C.N.D.Cal.	United States District Court, Northern District, California
D.C.N.Y.	United States District Court, New York
D.C.Pa.	United States District Court, Pennsylvania
DCS	Deputy Chiefs of Staff
DCZ	District of the Canal Zone
DDT	dichlorodiphenyltricloroethane
DEA	Drug Enforcement Administration
Decl. Lond.	Declaration of London, February 26, 1909
Dcv. & B.	Devereux & Battle's North Carolina Reports
Dig. U.S. Practice in Intl. Law	Digest of U.S. Practice in International Law
Dist. Ct. D.C.	United States District Court, District of Columbia
D.L.R.	Dominion Law Reports (Canada)
DNA	deoxyribonucleic acid
DNase	deoxyribonuclease
DNC	Democratic National Committee
DOC	Department of Commerce
DOD	Department of Defense
Dodson	Dodson's Reports, English Admiralty Courts
DOE	Department of Energy
DOER	Department of Employee Relations
DOJ	Department of Justice
DOS	disk operating system
DOT	Department of Transportation
DPT	diphtheria, pertussis, and tetanus
DRI	Defense Research Institute
DSAA	Defense Security Assistance Agency
DUI	driving under the influence; driving under intoxication
DWI	driving while intoxicated
EAHCA	Education for All Handicapped Children Act of 1975
EBT	examination before trial
ECPA	Electronic Communications Privacy Act of 1986
ECSC	Treaty of the European Coal and Steel Community
EDA	Economic Development Administration
EDF	Environmental Defense Fund
E.D.N.Y.	Eastern District, New York
EDP	electronic data processing
E.D. Pa.	Eastern District, Pennsylvania
EDSC	Eastern District, South Carolina
E.D. Va.	Eastern District, Virginia
EEC	European Economic Community; European Economic Community Treaty
EEOC	Equal Employment Opportunity Commission
EFF	Electronic Frontier Foundation
EFT	electronic funds transfer
Eliz.	Queen Elizabeth (Great Britain)
Em. App.	Temporary Emergency Court of Appeals

ENE	early neutral evaluation
Eng. Rep.	English Reports
EOP	Executive Office of the President
EPA	Environmental Protection Agency; Equal Pay Act of 1963
ERA	Equal Rights Amendment
ERISA	Employee Retirement Income Security Act of 1974
ERS	Economic Research Service
ESF	emergency support function; Economic Support Fund
ESRD	End-Stage Renal Disease Program
ETA	Employment and Training Administration
ETS	environmental tobacco smoke
et seq.	*et sequentes* or *et sequentia;* "and the following"
EU	European Union
Euratom	European Atomic Energy Community
Eur. Ct. H.R.	European Court of Human Rights
Ex.	English Exchequer Reports, Welsby, Hurlstone & Gordon
Exch.	Exchequer Reports (Welsby, Hurlstone & Gordon)
Eximbank	Export-Import Bank of the United States
F.	Federal Reporter
F. 2d	Federal Reporter, Second Series
FAA	Federal Aviation Administration; Federal Arbitration Act
FAAA	Federal Alcohol Administration Act
FACE	Freedom of Access to Clinic Entrances Act of 1994
FACT	Feminist Anti-Censorship Task Force
FAO	Food and Agriculture Organization of the United Nations
FAR	Federal Acquisition Regulations
FAS	Foreign Agricultural Service
FBA	Federal Bar Association
FBI	Federal Bureau of Investigation
FCA	Farm Credit Administration
F. Cas.	Federal Cases
FCC	Federal Communications Commission
FCIA	Foreign Credit Insurance Association
FCIC	Federal Crop Insurance Corporation
FCRA	Fair Credit Reporting Act
FCU	Federal credit unions
FDA	Food and Drug Administration
FDIC	Federal Deposit Insurance Corporation
FDPC	Federal Data Processing Center
FEC	Federal Election Commission
Fed. Cas.	Federal Cases
FEMA	Federal Emergency Management Agency
FFB	Federal Financing Bank
FGIS	Federal Grain Inspection Service
FHA	Federal Housing Authority
FHWA	Federal Highway Administration
FIA	Federal Insurance Administration
FIC	Federal Information Centers; Federation of Insurance Counsel
FICA	Federal Insurance Contributions Act
FIFRA	Federal Insecticide, Fungicide, and Rodenticide Act
FIP	Forestry Incentives Program
FIRREA	Financial Institutions Reform, Recovery, and Enforcement Act
FISA	Foreign Intelligence Surveillance Act of 1978
FMCS	Federal Mediation and Conciliation Service
FmHA	Farmers Home Administration
FMLA	Family and Medical Leave Act of 1993
FNMA	Federal National Mortgage Association, "Fannie Mae"
F.O.B.	free on board

FOIA	Freedom of Information Act
FPC	Federal Power Commission
FPMR	Federal Property Management Regulations
FPRS	Federal Property Resources Service
FR	Federal Register
FRA	Federal Railroad Administration
FRB	Federal Reserve Board
FRC	Federal Radio Commission
F.R.D.	Federal Rules Decisions
FSA	Family Support Act
FSLIC	Federal Savings and Loan Insurance Corporation
FSQS	Food Safety and Quality Service
FSS	Federal Supply Service
F. Supp.	Federal Supplement
FTA	U.S.-Canada Free Trade Agreement, 1988
FTC	Federal Trade Commission
FTS	Federal Telecommunications System
FUTA	Federal Unemployment Tax Act
FWPCA	Federal Water Pollution Control Act of 1948
GAO	General Accounting Office; Governmental Affairs Office
GAOR	General Assembly Official Records, United Nations
GA Res.	General Assembly Resolution (United Nations)
GATT	General Agreement on Tariffs and Trade
Gen. Cls. Comm.	General Claims Commission, United States and Panama; General Claims Commission, United States and Mexico
Geo. II	King George II (Great Britain)
Geo. III	King George III (Great Britain)
GM	General Motors
GNMA	Government National Mortgage Association, "Ginnie Mae"
GNP	gross national product
GOP	Grand Old Party (Republican)
GOPAC	Grand Old Party Action Committee
GPA	Office of Governmental and Public Affairs
GPO	Government Printing Office
GRAS	generally recognized as safe
Gr. Br., Crim. Ct. App.	Great Britain, Court of Criminal Appeals
GRNL	Gay Rights National Lobby
GSA	General Services Administration
Hackworth	Green Haywood Hackworth, *Digest of International Law* (1940–44)
Hay and Marriott	Great Britain. High Court of Admiralty, *Decisions in the High Court of Admiralty during the Time of Sir George Hay and of Sir James Marriott, Late Judges of That Court* (1801)
HBO	Home Box Office
HCFA	Health Care Financing Administration
H.Ct.	High Court
HDS	Office of Human Development Services
Hen. & M.	Hening & Munford's Virginia Reports
HEW	Department of Health, Education, and Welfare
HHS	Department of Health and Human Services
Hill	Hill's New York Reports
HIRE	Help through Industry Retraining and Employment
HIV	human immunodeficiency virus
H.L.	House of Lords Cases (England)
H. Lords	House of Lords (England)
HNIS	Human Nutrition Information Service
Hong Kong L.R.	Hong Kong Law Reports
How.	Howard's United States Supreme Court Reports
How. St. Trials	Howell's English State Trials
HUAC	House Un-American Activities Committee

HUD	Department of Housing and Urban Development
Hudson, Internatl. Legis.	Manley O. Hudson, ed., *International Legislation: A Collection of the Texts of Multipartite International Instruments of General Interest Beginning with the Covenant of the League of Nations* (1931)
Hudson, World Court Reps.	Manley Ottmer Hudson, ed., *World Court Reports* (1934–)
Hun	Hun's New York Supreme Court Reports
Hunt's Rept.	Bert L. Hunt, *Report of the American and Panamanian General Claims Arbitration* (1934)
IAEA	International Atomic Energy Agency
IALL	International Association of Law Libraries
IBA	International Bar Association
IBM	International Business Machines
ICBM	intercontinental ballistic missile
ICC	Interstate Commerce Commission
ICJ	International Court of Justice
IDEA	Individuals with Disabilities Education Act, 1975
IEP	individualized educational program
IFC	International Finance Corporation
IGRA	Indian Gaming Regulatory Act, 1988
IJA	Institute of Judicial Administration
IJC	International Joint Commission
ILC	International Law Commission
ILD	International Labor Defense
Ill. Dec.	Illinois Decisions
ILO	International Labor Organization
IMF	International Monetary Fund
INA	Immigration and Nationality Act
IND	investigational new drug
INF Treaty	Intermediate-Range Nuclear Forces Treaty of 1987
INS	Immigration and Naturalization Service
INTELSAT	International Telecommunications Satellite Organization
Interpol	International Criminal Police Organization
Int'l. Law Reps.	International Law Reports
Intl. Legal Mats.	International Legal Materials
IPDC	International Program for the Development of Communication
IPO	Intellectual Property Owners
IPP	independent power producer
IQ	intelligence quotient
I.R.	Irish Reports
IRA	individual retirement account; Irish Republican Army
IRCA	Immigration Reform and Control Act of 1986
IRS	Internal Revenue Service
ISO	independent service organization
ISSN	International Standard Serial Numbers
ITA	International Trade Administration
ITI	Information Technology Integration
ITO	International Trade Organization
ITS	Information Technology Service
ITU	International Telecommunication Union
IUD	intrauterine device
IWC	International Whaling Commission
IWW	Industrial Workers of the World
JCS	Joint Chiefs of Staff
JDL	Jewish Defense League
JOBS	Jobs Opportunity and Basic Skills
John. Ch.	Johnson's New York Chancery Reports
Johns.	Johnson's Reports (New York)
JP	justice of the peace

K.B.	King's Bench Reports (England)
KGB	Komitet Gosudarstvennoi Bezopasnosti (the State Security Committee for countries in the former Soviet Union)
KKK	Ku Klux Klan
KMT	Kuomintang
LAPD	Los Angeles Police Department
LC	Library of Congress
LD50	lethal dose 50
LDEF	Legal Defense and Education Fund (NOW)
LDF	Legal Defense Fund, Legal Defense and Educational Fund of the NAACP
LEAA	Law Enforcement Assistance Administration
L.Ed.	Lawyers' Edition Supreme Court Reports
LMSA	Labor-Management Services Administration
LNTS	League of Nations Treaty Series
Lofft's Rep.	Lofft's English King's Bench Reports
L.R.	Law Reports (English)
LSAS	Law School Admission Service
LSAT	Law School Aptitude Test
LSC	Legal Services Corporation; Legal Services for Children
LSD	lysergic acid diethylamide
LSDAS	Law School Data Assembly Service
LTBT	Limited Test Ban Treaty
LTC	Long Term Care
MAD	mutual assured destruction
MADD	Mothers against Drunk Driving
MALDEF	Mexican American Legal Defense and Educational Fund
Malloy	William M. Malloy, ed., *Treaties, Conventions, International Acts, Protocols, and Agreements between the United States of America and Other Powers* (1910–38)
Martens	Georg Friedrich von Martens, ed., *Noveau recueil général de traités et autres act es relatifs aux rapports de droit international* (Series I, 20 vols. [1843–75]; Series II, 35 vols. [1876–1908]; Series III [1909–])
Mass.	Massachusetts Reports
MCH	Maternal and Child Health Bureau
Md. App.	Maryland, Appeal Cases
M.D. Ga.	Middle District, Georgia
Mercy	Movement Ensuring the Right to Choose for Yourself
Metc.	Metcalf's Massachusetts Reports
MFDP	Mississippi Freedom Democratic party
MGT	Management
MHSS	Military Health Services System
Miller	David Hunter Miller, ed., *Treaties and Other International Acts of the United States of America* (1931–1948)
Minn.	Minnesota Reports
MINS	minors in need of supervision
MIRV	multiple independently targetable reentry vehicle
Misc.	Miscellaneous Reports, New York
Mixed Claims Comm., Report of Decs.	Mixed Claims Commission, United States and Germany, Report of Decisions
M.J.	Military Justice Reporter
MLAP	Migrant Legal Action Program
MLB	major league baseball
MLDP	Mississippi Loyalist Democratic party
Mo.	Missouri Reports
Mod.	Modern Reports, English King's Bench, etc.
Moore, Dig. Intl. Law	John Bassett Moore, *A Digest of International Law*, 8 vols. (1906)
Moore, Intl. Arbs.	John Bassett Moore, *History and Digest of the International Arbitrations to Which the United States Has Been a Party*, 6 vols. (1898)

Morison	William Maxwell Morison, *The Scots Revised Report: Morison's Dictionary of Decisions* (1908–09)
M.P.	member of Parliament
MPAA	Motion Picture Association of America
mpg	miles per gallon
MPRSA	Marine Protection, Research, and Sanctuaries Act of 1972
M.R.	Master of the Rolls
MS-DOS	Microsoft Disk Operating System
MSHA	Mine Safety and Health Administration
NAACP	National Association for the Advancement of Colored People
NAAQS	National Ambient Air Quality Standards
NABSW	National Association of Black Social Workers
NAFTA	North American Free Trade Agreement, 1993
NARAL	National Abortion Rights Action League
NARF	Native American Rights Fund
NARS	National Archives and Record Service
NASA	National Aeronautics and Space Administration
NASD	National Association of Securities Dealers
NATO	North Atlantic Treaty Organization
NAVINFO	Navy Information Offices
NAWSA	National American Woman's Suffrage Association
NBA	National Bar Association
NBC	National Broadcasting Company
NBLSA	National Black Law Student Association
NBS	National Bureau of Standards
NCA	Noise Control Act; National Command Authorities
NCAA	National Collegiate Athletic Association
NCAC	National Coalition against Censorship
NCCB	National Consumer Cooperative Bank
NCE	Northwest Community Exchange
NCJA	National Criminal Justice Association
NCLB	National Civil Liberties Bureau
NCP	national contingency plan
NCSC	National Center for State Courts
NCUA	National Credit Union Administration
NDA	new drug application
N.D. Ill.	Northern District, Illinois
NDU	National Defense University
N.D. Wash.	Northern District, Washington
N.E.	North Eastern Reporter
N.E. 2d	North Eastern Reporter, Second Series
NEA	National Endowment for the Arts
NEH	National Endowment for the Humanities
NEPA	National Environmental Protection Act; National Endowment Policy Act
NFIP	National Flood Insurance Program
NGTF	National Gay Task Force
NHRA	Nursing Home Reform Act, 1987
NHTSA	National Highway Traffic Safety Administration
Nielsen's Rept.	Frederick Kenelm Nielsen, *American and British Claims Arbitration under the Special Agreement Concluded between the United States and Great Britain, August 18, 1910* (1926)
NIEO	New International Economic Order
NIH	National Institutes of Health, the NIH
NIJ	National Institute of Justice
NIRA	National Industrial Recovery Act; National Industrial Recovery Administration
NIST	National Institute of Standards and Technology, the NIST
NTIA	National Telecommunications and Information Administration
N.J.	New Jersey Reports

N.J. Super.	New Jersey Superior Court Reports
NLRA	National Labor Relations Act
NLRB	National Labor Relations Board
No.	Number
NOAA	National Oceanic and Atmospheric Administration
NOW	National Organization for Women
NOW LDEF	National Organization for Women Legal Defense and Education Fund
NOW/PAC	National Organization for Women Political Action Committee
NPDES	National Pollutant Discharge Elimination System
NPL	national priorities list
NPR	National Public Radio
NPT	Non-Proliferation Treaty
NRA	National Rifle Association; National Recovery Act
NRC	Nuclear Regulatory Commission
NSC	National Security Council
NSCLC	National Senior Citizens Law Center
NSF	National Science Foundation
NSFNET	National Science Foundation Network
NTIA	National Telecommunications and Information Administration
NTID	National Technical Institute for the Deaf
NTIS	National Technical Information Service
NTS	Naval Telecommunications System
NTSB	National Transportation Safety Board
N.W.	North Western Reporter
N.W. 2d	North Western Reporter, Second Series
NWSA	National Woman Suffrage Association
N.Y.	New York Court of Appeals Reports
N.Y. 2d	New York Court of Appeals Reports, Second Series
N.Y.S.	New York Supplement Reporter
N.Y.S. 2d	New York Supplement Reporter, Second Series
NYSE	New York Stock Exchange
N.Y. Sup.	New York Supreme Court Reports
NYU	New York University
OAAU	Organization of Afro American Unity
OAP	Office of Administrative Procedure
OAS	Organization of American States
OASDI	Old-age, Survivors, and Disability Insurance Benefits
OASHDS	Office of the Assistant Secretary for Human Development Services
OCED	Office of Comprehensive Employment Development
OCHAMPUS	Office of Civilian Health and Medical Program of the Uniformed Services
OCSE	Office of Child Support Enforcement
OEA	Organización de los Estados Americanos
OFCCP	Office of Federal Contract Compliance Programs
OFPP	Office of Federal Procurement Policy
OICD	Office of International Cooperation and Development
OIG	Office of the Inspector General
OJARS	Office of Justice Assistance, Research, and Statistics
OMB	Office of Management and Budget
OMPC	Office of Management, Planning, and Communications
ONP	Office of National Programs
OPD	Office of Policy Development
OPEC	Organization of Petroleum Exporting Countries
OPIC	Overseas Private Investment Corporation
Ops. Atts. Gen.	Opinions of the Attorneys-General of the United States
Ops. Comms.	Opinions of the Commissioners
OPSP	Office of Product Standards Policy
O.R.	Ontario Reports
OR	Official Records

OSHA	Occupational Safety and Health Administration
OSHRC	Occupational Safety and Health Review Commission
OSM	Office of Surface Mining
OSS	Office of Strategic Services
OST	Office of the Secretary
OT	Office of Transportation
OTA	Office of Technology Assessment
OTC	over-the-counter
OUI	operating under the influence
OWBPA	Older Workers Benefit Protection Act
OWRT	Office of Water Research and Technology
P.	Pacific Reporter
P. 2d	Pacific Reporter, Second Series
PAC	political action committee
Pa. Oyer and Terminer	Pennsylvania Oyer and Terminer Reports
PATCO	Professional Air Traffic Controllers Organization
PBGC	Pension Benefit Guaranty Corporation
PBS	Public Broadcasting Service; Public Buildings Service
P.C.	Privy Council (English Law Reports); personal computer
PCIJ	Permanent Court of International Justice
	Series A—Judgments and Orders (1922–30)
	Series B—Advisory Opinions (1922–30)
	Series A/B—Judgments, Orders, and Advisory Opinions (1931–40)
	Series C—Pleadings, Oral Statements, and Documents relating to Judgments and Advisory Opinions (1923–42)
	Series D—Acts and Documents concerning the Organization of the World Court (1922–47)
	Series E—Annual Reports (1925–45)
PCP	phencyclidine (no need to spell out)
P.D.	Probate Division, English Law Reports (1876–1890)
PDA	Pregnancy Discrimination Act of 1978
PD & R	Policy Development and Research
Perm. Ct. of Arb.	Permanent Court of Arbitration
Pet.	Peters' United States Supreme Court Reports
PETA	People for the Ethical Treatment of Animals
PGM	Program
PHA	Public Housing Agency
Phila. Ct. of Oyer and Terminer	Philadelphia Court of Oyer and Terminer
PHS	Public Health Service
PIC	Private Industry Council
Pick.	Pickering's Massachusetts Reports
PIK	Payment in Kind
PINS	persons in need of supervision
PIRG	Public Interest Research Group
P.L.	Public Laws
PLAN	Pro-Life Action Network
PLI	Practicing Law Institute
PLO	Palestine Liberation Organization
PNET	Peaceful Nuclear Explosions Treaty
POW-MIA	prisoner of war–missing in action
Pratt	Frederic Thomas Pratt, *Law of Contraband of War, with a Selection of Cases from the Papers of the Right Honourable Sir George Lee* (1856)
Proc.	Proceedings
PRP	potentially responsible party
PSRO	Professional Standards Review Organization
PTO	Patents and Trademark Office
PURPA	Public Utilities Regulatory Policies Act

PUSH	People United to Serve Humanity
PWA	Public Works Administration
PWSA	Ports and Waterways Safety Act of 1972
Q.B.	Queen's Bench (England)
Ralston's Rept.	Jackson Harvey Ralston, ed., *Venezuelan Arbitrations of 1903* (1904)
RC	Regional Commissioner
RCRA	Resource Conservation and Recovery Act
RCWP	Rural Clean Water Program
RDA	Rural Development Administration
REA	Rural Electrification Administration
Rec. des Decs. des Trib. Arb. Mixtes	G. Gidel, ed., *Recueil des décisions des tribunaux arbitraux mixtes, institués par les traités de paix* (1922–30)
Redmond	Vol. 3 of Charles I. Bevans, *Treaties and Other International Agreements of the United States of America, 1776–1949* (compiled by C. F. Redmond) (1969)
RESPA	Real Estate Settlement Procedure Act of 1974
RFRA	Religious Freedom Restoration Act
RICO	Racketeer Influenced and Corrupt Organizations
RNC	Republican National Committee
Roscoe	Edward Stanley Roscoe, ed., *Reports of Prize Cases Determined in the High Court of Admiralty before the Lords Commissioners of Appeals in Prize Causes and before the Judicial Committee of the Privy Council from 1745 to 1859* (1905)
ROTC	Reserve Officers' Training Corps
RPP	Representative Payee Program
R.S.	Revised Statutes
RTC	Resolution Trust Company
Ryan White CARE Act	Ryan White Comprehensive AIDS Research Emergency Act of 1990
SAC	Strategic Air Command
SACB	Subversive Activities Control Board
SADD	Students against Drunk Driving
SAF	Student Activities Fund
SAIF	Savings Association Insurance Fund
SALT I	Strategic Arms Limitation Talks of 1969–72
SAMHSA	Substance Abuse and Mental Health Services Administration
Sandf.	Sandford's New York Superior Court Reports
S and L	savings and loan
SARA	Superfund Amendment and Reauthorization Act
Sawy.	Sawyer's United States Circuit Court Reports
SBA	Small Business Administration
SCLC	Southern Christian Leadership Conference
Scott's Repts.	James Brown Scott, ed., *The Hague Court Reports*, 2 vols. (1916–32)
SCS	Soil Conservation Service
SCSEP	Senior Community Service Employment Program
S.Ct.	Supreme Court Reporter
S.D. Cal.	Southern District, California
S.D. Fla.	Southern District, Florida
S.D. Ga.	Southern District, Georgia
SDI	Strategic Defense Initiative
S.D. Me.	Southern District, Maine
S.D.N.Y.	Southern District, New York
SDS	Students for a Democratic Society
S.E.	South Eastern Reporter
S.E. 2d	South Eastern Reporter, Second Series
SEA	Science and Education Administration
SEATO	Southeast Asia Treaty Organization
SEC	Securities and Exchange Commission
Sec.	Section
SEEK	Search for Elevation, Education and Knowledge
SEOO	State Economic Opportunity Office

SEP	simplified employee pension plan
Ser.	Series
Sess.	Session
SGLI	Servicemen's Group Life Insurance
SIP	state implementation plan
SLA	Symbionese Liberation Army
SLBM	submarine-launched ballistic missile
SNCC	Student Nonviolent Coordinating Committee
So.	Southern Reporter
So. 2d	Southern Reporter, Second Series
SPA	Software Publisher's Association
Spec. Sess.	Special Session
SRA	Sentencing Reform Act of 1984
SS	Schutzstaffel (German for Protection Echelon)
SSA	Social Security Administration
SSI	Supplemental Security Income
START I	Strategic Arms Reduction Treaty of 1991
START II	Strategic Arms Reduction Treaty of 1993
Stat.	United States Statutes at Large
STS	Space Transportation Systems
St. Tr.	State Trials, English
STURAA	Surface Transportation and Uniform Relocation Assistance Act of 1987
Sup. Ct. of Justice, Mexico	Supreme Court of Justice, Mexico
Supp.	Supplement
S.W.	South Western Reporter
S.W. 2d	South Western Reporter, Second Series
SWAPO	South-West Africa People's Organization
SWAT	Special Weapons and Tactics
SWP	Socialist Workers party
TDP	Trade and Development Program
Tex. Sup.	Texas Supreme Court Reports
THAAD	Theater High-Altitude Area Defense System
TIA	Trust Indenture Act of 1939
TIAS	Treaties and Other International Acts Series (United States)
TNT	trinitrotoluene
TOP	Targeted Outreach Program
TPUS	Transportation and Public Utilities Service
Tripartite Claims Comm., Decs. and Ops.	Tripartite Claims Commission (United States, Austria, and Hungary), Decisions and Opinions
TRI-TAC	Joint Tactical Communications
TRO	temporary restraining order
TS	Treaty Series, United States
TSCA	Toxic Substance Control Act
TSDs	transporters, storers, and disposers
TTBT	Threshold Test Ban Treaty
TVA	Tennessee Valley Authority
UAW	United Auto Workers; United Automobile, Aerospace, and Agricultural Implements Workers of America
U.C.C.	Uniform Commercial Code; Universal Copyright Convention
U.C.C.C.	Uniform Consumer Credit Code
UCCJA	Uniform Child Custody Jurisdiction Act
UCMJ	Uniform Code of Military Justice
UCPP	Urban Crime Prevention Program
UCS	United Counseling Service
UDC	United Daughters of the Confederacy
UFW	United Farm Workers
UHF	ultrahigh frequency
UIFSA	Uniform Interstate Family Support Act

UIS	Unemployment Insurance Service
UMDA	Uniform Marriage and Divorce Act
UMTA	Urban Mass Transportation Administration
UNCITRAL	United Nations Commission on International Trade Law
UNCTAD	United Nations Conference on Trade and Development
UN Doc.	United Nations Documents
UNDP	United Nations Development Program
UNEF	United Nations Emergency Force
UNESCO	United Nations Educational, Scientific, and Cultural Organization
UNICEF	United Nations Children's Fund
UNIDO	United Nations Industrial and Development Organization
Unif. L. Ann.	Uniform Laws Annotated
UN Repts. Intl. Arb. Awards	United Nations Reports of International Arbitral Awards
UNTS	United Nations Treaty Series
UPI	United Press International
URESA	Uniform Reciprocal Enforcement of Support Act
U.S.	United States Reports
USAF	United States Air Force
U.S. App. D.C.	United States Court of Appeals for the District of Columbia
U.S.C.	United States Code
U.S.C.A.	United States Code Annotated
U.S.C.C.A.N.	United States Code Congressional and Administrative News
USCMA	United States Court of Military Appeals
USDA	U.S. Department of Agriculture
USES	United States Employment Service
USFA	United States Fire Administration
USICA	International Communication Agency, United States
USSC	U.S. Sentencing Commission
U.S.S.R.	Union of Soviet Socialist Republics
UST	United States Treaties
USTS	United States Travel Service
v.	*versus*
VA	Veterans Administration, the VA
VGLI	Veterans Group Life Insurance
Vict.	Queen Victoria (Great Britain)
VIN	vehicle identification number
VISTA	Volunteers in Service to America
VJRA	Veterans Judicial Review Act of 1988
V.L.A.	Volunteer Lawyers for the Arts
VMI	Virginia Military Institute
VMLI	Veterans Mortgage Life Insurance
VOCAL	Victims of Child Abuse Laws
WAC	Women's Army Corps
Wall.	Wallace's United States Supreme Court Reports
Wash. 2d	Washington Reports, Second Series
WAVES	Women Accepted for Volunteer Service
WCTU	Women's Christian Temperance Union
W.D. Wash.	Western District, Washington
W.D. Wis.	Western District, Wisconsin
WEAL	West's Encyclopedia of American Law, Women's Equity Action League
Wend.	Wendell's New York Reports
WFSE	Washington Federation of State Employees
Wheat.	Wheaton's United States Supreme Court Reports
Wheel. Cr. Cases	Wheeler's New York Criminal Cases
Whiteman	Marjorie Millace Whiteman, *Digest of International Law*, 15 vols. (1963–73)
WHO	World Health Organization
WIC	Women, Infants, and Children program
Will. and Mar.	King William and Queen Mary (Great Britain)

WIN	WESTLAW Is Natural; Whip Inflation Now; Work Incentive Program
WIU	Workers' Industrial Union
W.L.R.	Weekly Law Reports, England
WPA	Works Progress Administration
WPPDA	Welfare and Pension Plans Disclosure Act
WWI	World War I
WWII	World War II
Yates Sel. Cas.	Yates' New York Select Cases

BIBLIOGRAPHY

HATE CRIME

Fine, David R. 1994. "Beware That False First Step." *Kentucky Law Journal* 82.

Gaumer, Craig P. 1994. "Punishment for Prejudice: A Commentary on the Constitutionality and Utility of State Statutory Responses to the Problem of Hate Crimes." *South Dakota Law Review* 39.

Jacobs, James B. 1993. "Implementing Hate Crime Legislation Symbolism and Crime Control." In *Annual Survey of American Law, 1992–1993*.

Zwerling, Martin S. 1995. "Legislating against Hate in New York: Bias Crimes and the Lesbian and Gay Community." *Touro Law Review* 11 (winter).

HAYES, RUTHERFORD, BIRCHARD

Barnard, Harry. 1954. *Rutherford B. Hayes and His America*. Indianapolis: Bobbs-Merrill.

Bishop, Arthur. 1969. *Rutherford B. Hayes, 1822–1893*. Dobbs Ferry, N.Y.: Oceana.

Clancy, Herbert J. 1958. *The Presidential Election of 1880*. Chicago: Loyola Univ. Press.

Davison, Kenneth E. 1972. *The Presidency of Rutherford B. Hayes*. Westport, Conn.: Greenwood Press.

Haworth, Paul L. 1927. *The Hayes-Tilden Election*. Indianapolis: Bobbs-Merrill.

Hoogenboom, Ari Arthur. 1988. *The Presidency of Rutherford B. Hayes*. Lawrence, Kan.: Univ. Press of Kansas.

———. 1995. *Rutherford B. Hayes, Warrior and President*. Lawrence, Kan.: Univ. Press of Kansas.

HAYMARKET RIOT

Landsman, Stephan. 1986. "When Justice Fails." Review of *The Haymarket Tragedy*, by Paul Avrich. *Michigan Law Review* 84 (February–April).

Wish, Harvey. 1976. "Haymarket Riot." In *Dictionary of American History*. Edited by Louise B. Ketz. New York: Scribner.

HAYNESWORTH, CLEMENT FURMAN, JR.

Morris, Richard B., ed. 1982. *Encyclopedia of American History*. New York: Harper & Row.

Witt, Elder, ed. 1990. *Guide to the U.S. Supreme Court*. 2d ed. Washington D.C.: Congressional Quarterly.

HAYS, WILLIAM HARRISON

Bergman, Andrew. 1971. *We're in the Money: Depression America and Its Films*. New York: New York Univ. Press.

Christensen, Terry. 1987. *Reel Politics: American Political Movies from Birth of a Nation to Platoon*. New York: Blackwell.

Crisler, B. R. 1984. "Portrait of an Indiana Lawyer." In *The New York Times Encyclopedia of Film: 1937–1940*. Edited by Gene Brown. New York: Times Books.

Maltby, Richard. 1993. " 'Grief in the Limelight': Al Capone, Howard Hughes, the Hays Code, and the Politics of the Unstable Text." In *Movies and Politics: The Dynamic Relationship*. Edited by James Combs. New York: Garland.

Sklar, Robert. 1994. *Movie-Made America: A Cultural History of American Movies*. Rev. and updated ed. New York: Vintage Books.

HEALTH AND HUMAN SERVICES DEPARTMENT

United States Government Manual, 1995–1996. Washington, D.C.: U.S. Government Printing Office.

HEALTH CARE FINANCING ADMINISTRATION

United States Government Manual, 1995–1996. Washington, D.C.: U.S. Government Printing Office.

HEALTH CARE LAW

Coan, L. Frank, Jr. 1996. "You Can't Get There From Here—Questioning the Erosion of ERISA Preemption in Medical Malpractice Actions against HMO's." *Georgia Law Review* 30.

Halvorson, George C. 1993. *Strong Medicine*. New York: Random House.

Pedroza, Kenneth R. 1996. "Cutting Fat or Cutting Corners: Health Care Delivery and Its Respondent Effect on Liability." *Arizona Law Review* 38 (spring).

HEALTH INSURANCE

Ellwood, Paul M., Jr., and George D. Lundberg. 1996. "Managed Care: A Work in Progress." *Journal of the American Medical Association* 276 (October 6).

Freiburg, James P. 1993. "The ABCs of MCOs: An Overview of Managed Care Organizations." *Illinois Bar Journal* 81 (November).

Halvorson, George C. 1993. *Strong Medicine.* New York: Random House.

Harris, Jeffrey R., et al. 1996. "Prevention and Managed Care: Opportunities for Managed Care Organizations, Purchasers of Health Care, and Public Health Agencies." *Journal of the American Medical Association* 275 (January 3).

HEARSAY

Cleary, Edward W., ed. 1984. *McCormick on Evidence.* 3d ed. St. Paul: West.

Darden, Christopher, with Jess Walter. 1996. *In Contempt.* New York: HarperCollins.

Kaplan, John, and Jon R. Waltz. 1987. *Evidence Cases and Materials.* 6th ed. Westbury, N.Y.: Foundation Press.

"O. J. Simpson 1996 Civil Pretrial Motion to Preclude Introduction of Journal." February 12, 1997. Court TV site. World Wide Web.

HEARST, PATTY

Practising Law Institute (PLI). 1985. *Post Traumatic Stress Disorders, and Brainwashing as State of Mind Defenses in Criminal, and Civil Fraud Cases,* by David P. Bancroft. Litigation and Administrative Practice Course Handbook series: Criminal Law and Urban Problems, PLI order no. C4-4174.

HEGEL, GEORG WILHELM FRIEDRICH

Carlson, David G. 1992. "The Hegelian Revival in American Legal Discourse." *University of Miami Law Review* 46 (March).

Hegel, Georg. 1977. *The Difference between Fichte's and Schelling's System of Philosophy.* Translated by H. S. Harris and Walter Cerf. Albany, N.Y.: State Univ. of New York Press.

Hoffheimer, Michael H. 1995. "Hegel's First Philosophy of Law." *Tennessee Law Review* 62 (summer).

HELMS, JESSE ALEXANDER, JR.

Furgurson, Ernest B. 1996. "Hard Right: The Rise of Jesse Helms." New York: Norton.

Snider, William D. 1985. "Helms & Hunt: The North Carolina Senate Race, 1984." Chapel Hill, N.C.: Univ. of North Carolina Press.

HIGH CRIMES AND MISDEMEANORS

Smith, Alexa J. 1995. "Federal Judicial Impeachment: Defining Process Due." *Hastings Law Journal* (January).

Tushner, Mark V. 1995. "Clarence Thomas: The Constitutional Problems." *George Washington Law Review* (March).

Williams, Victor. "Third Branch Independence and Integrity Threatened by Political Branch Irresponsibility." 1995. *Seton Hall Constitutional Law Journal* (summer).

HIGHWAY

Lynch, James. 1986. "The Federal Highway Beautification Act after Metromedia." *Emory Law Journal* 35.

HILL, OLIVER W.

Hill, Oliver. 1994. Telephone interview, November 3.

HIROHITO

Executive Order No. 9066. 1942. *Federal Register* 7:1407.

Hall, Kermit L. 1989. *The Magic Mirror.* New York: Oxford Univ. Press.

Stephens, Otis H., Jr., and John M. Scheb II. 1993. *American Constitutional Law.* St. Paul: West.

HISS, ALGER

Dresser, Rebecca. 1990. "Personal Identity and Punishment." *Boston University Law Review* 70 (May).

Nixon biography. Nixon Library site. World Wide Web. January 1996.

Schrecker, Ellen. 1994. *The Age of McCarthyism: A Brief History with Documents.* Boston: Bedford Books.

HITLER, ADOLF

Hall, Kermit L. 1989. *The Magic Mirror.* New York: Oxford Univ. Press.

HOBBES, THOMAS

Dyzenhaus, David. 1994. "Now the Machine Runs Itself: Carl Schmitt on Hobbes and Kelsen." *Cardozo Law Review* 16 (August).

Hobbes, Thomas. 1651. *Leviathan, or the Matter, Form, and Power of a Commonwealth, Ecclesiastical and Civil.* Reprint, New York: Viking Press, 1982.

Robinson, Reginald Leamon. 1993. "The Impact of Hobbes's Empirical Natural Law on Title VII's Effectiveness: A Hegellian Critique." *Connecticut Law Review* 25 (spring).

HOFFA, JAMES RIDDLE

A&E Home Video. "Hoffa: The True Story." 1992. Video cassette.

Hoffa, James R. 1970. *The Trials of Jimmy Hoffa.*

PBS Frontline. "JFK, Hoffa and the Mob." 1993. Video cassette.

HOFFMAN, WALTER EDWARD

Almanac of the Federal Judiciary.

West. Devitt Award presentation materials provided by the Media Relations Department.

HOMELESS PERSON

Baker, Donald E. 1990–91. "Anti-Homeless Legislation: Unconstitutional Efforts to Punish the Homeless." *University of Miami Law Review* 45 (November 1990–January 1991).

Hanrahan, Patricia M. 1994. "No Home? No Vote. Homeless Are Often Denied That Most Basic Element of Democracy." *Human Rights* 21 (winter).

Jarrett, Beth D., and Wes R. Daniels. 1993. "Law and the Homeless: An Annotated Bibliography." *Law Library Journal* 85 (summer).

Mathews, K. Scott. 1991. "Rights of the Homeless in the 1990s: What Role Will the Courts Play?" *University of Missouri–Kansas City Law Review* 60 (winter).

Siebert, Patricia. 1986. "Homeless People: Establishing Rights to Shelter." *Law and Inequality Journal* 4.

HOMESTEAD ACT OF 1862

Buckley, F. H. "The American Fresh Start." 1995. *Southern California Interdisciplinary Law Journal* (fall).

Chen, Jim. "Of Agriculture's First Disobedience and Its Fruit." 1995. *Vanderbilt Law Review* (October).

Nore, Michael J. " 'Burn This without Fail': The Downfall of Oregon's Sen. John H. Mitchell." 1995. *Oregon State Bar Bulletin* (October).

HOMICIDE

Kadish, Sanfor H., ed. 1983. *Encyclopedia of Crime and Justice*. Vol. 2. New York: Free Press.

Lafave, Wayne R., and Austin W. Scott, Jr. 1986. *Substantive Criminal Law*. Vol. 2. St. Paul: West.

Torcia, Charles E. 1994. *Wharton's Criminal Law*. 15th ed. New York: Clark, Boardman, Callaghan.

HOOKS, BENJAMIN LAWSON

Bigelow, Barbara Carlisle, ed. 1992. *Contemporary Black Biography*. Vol. 2. Detroit: Gale Research.

HOOVER, JOHN EDGAR

Gentry, Curt. 1991. *J. Edgar Hoover: The Man and His Secrets*. New York: Norton.

Powers, Richard G. 1987. *Secrecy and Power: The Life of J. Edgar Hoover*. New York: Free Press.

HOT PURSUIT

Apol, John, and Magistrate Judge Paul J. Komives. 1995. "Criminal Procedure." *Detroit College of Law Review* (summer).

Department of the Army. 1987. "Warrantless Searches and Seizures." *Pamphlet 27-22*.

Search and Seizure Update. 1994. New York: Practising Law Institute.

HOUSE OF REPRESENTATIVES

U.S. House. 1994. Committee on House Administration. *History of the United States House of Representatives, 1789–1994*. 103d Cong. 2d sess. H. Doc. 103-324.

HOUSTON, CHARLES HAMILTON

Elliott, Stephen P., ed. 1986. *A Reference Guide to the United States Supreme Court*. New York: Facts on File.

McNeil, Genna Rae. 1983. *Groundwork: Charles Hamilton Houston and the Struggle for Civil Rights*. Philadelphia: Univ. of Pennsylvania Press.

Witt, Elder, ed. 1990. *Guide to the U.S. Supreme Court*. 2d ed. Washington D.C.: Congressional Quarterly.

HUGHES, CHARLES EVANS

Schwartz, Bernard. 1995. "Supreme Court Superstars: The Ten Greatest Justices." *Tulsa Law Journal* 31 (fall).

HUME, DAVID

Arkin, Marc M. 1995. " 'The Intractable Principle': David Hume, James Madison, Religion, and the Tenth Federalist." *American Journal of Legal History* 39.

HUMPHREY, HUBERT HORATIO

Halberstam, David. 1972. *The Best and the Brightest*. New York: Random House.

O'Neill, William L. 1971. *Coming Apart: An Informal History of America in the 1960s*. New York: Quadrangle Books.

HUNT, WARD

Commission on the Bicentennial of the U.S. Constitution. 1992. "Ward Hunt." In *The Supreme Court of the United States: Its Beginnings and Its Justices, 1790–1991*. Washington, D.C.: Library of Congress.

Friedman, Leon, and Fred L. Israel, eds. 1995. *The Justices of the United States Supreme Court, 1789–1969: Their Lives and Major Opinions*. New York: Chelsea House.

HUNTING

Ugalde, Aileen M. 1991. "The Right to Arm Bears: Activists' Protests against Hunting." *University of Miami Law Review* 45.

HUSBAND AND WIFE

Chriss, Margaret J. 1993. "Troubling Degrees of Authority: The Continuing Pursuit of Unequal Marital Roles." *Law & Inequality Journal* 12 (December).

Keane, Thomas M. 1995. "Aloha, Marriage? Constitutional and Choice of Law Arguments for Recognition of Same-Sex Marriages." *Stanford Law Review* 47 (February).

Nickles, Don. 1996. "Defense of Marriage Act." *Congressional Record* 142.

Waggoner, Lawrence W. 1994. "Marital Property Rights in Transition." *Missouri Law Review* 59 (winter).

Wanamaker, Laura H. 1994. "*Waite v. Waite:* The Florida Supreme Court Abrogates the Doctrine of Interspousal Immunity." *Mercer Law Review* 45 (winter).

ILLEGITIMACY

Hall, Kermit L. 1989. *The Magic Mirror*. New York: Oxford Univ. Press.

IMMUNITY

Sels, John van Loben. 1995. "From Watergate to Whitewater: Congressional Use Immunity and Its Impact on the Independent Counsel." *Georgetown Law Journal* 83.

Stein, Theodore P. 1983. "*Nixon v. Fitzgerald:* Presidential Immunity as a Constitutional Imperative." *Catholic University Law Review* 32 (spring).

IMMUNIZATION PROGRAMS

Hauptly, Denis J., and Mary Mason. 1990. "The National Childhood Vaccine Injury Act." *Federal Bar News and Journal* 37 (October).

King, George H. 1989. "A Prescription for Applying Strict Liability: Not All Drugs Deserve Comment K Immunization." *Arizona State Law Journal* 21 (fall).

Polizzi, Catherine M. 1994–95. "A Proposal for a Federal Aids Immunization Policy." *Journal of Law and Health* 9.

IMPEACHMENT

Baron, Alan I. 1995. "The Curious Case of Alcee Hastings." *Nova Law Review* (spring).

Smith, Alexa J. 1995. "Federal Judicial Impeachment: Defining Process Due." *Hastings Law Journal* 46 (January).

Strasser, Fred. 1989. "Proud, Unrepentant, Judge Hastings Exits." *The National Law Journal* (November 6).

IMPLIED CONSENT

Fuller, M. Elizabeth. 1986. "Implied Consent Statutes: What Is Refusal?" *American Journal of Trial Advocacy* 9 (spring).

IMPLIED WARRANTY

Gonzales, Vincent M. 1987. "The Buyer's Specifications Exception to the Implied Warranty of Fitness for a Particular Purpose: Design or Performance?" *California Law Review* 61 (November).

IMPORT QUOTAS

Benenson, Bob. 1994. "Free Trade Carries the Day As GATT Easily Passes." *Congressional Quarterly Weekly Report* 52 (November 26).

Prepared testimony of Allan I. Mendelowitz. 1995. Federal News Service, congressional hearings testimony (June 14).

"Provisions: GATT Implementing Bill." 1994. *Congressional Quarterly Weekly Report* 52 (November 26).

Reinke, John J. 1985–86. "An Analysis of the Conflicts between Congressional Import Quotas and the General Agreement on Tariffs and Trade." *Fordham International Law Journal* 9.

IMPOSSIBILITY

Bello, Christopher. 1985. "Construction and Application of State Statute Governing Impossibility of Consummation As Defense to Prosecution for Attempt to Commit Crime." *American Law Review* 41.

"Modern Status of the Rules Regarding Impossibility of Performance As Defense in Action for Breach of Contract." 1962. *American Law Reports* 84.

Restatement (Second) of Contracts, §§ 261–265. 1981. St. Paul: American Law Institute Publishers.

IMPOUNDMENT

Collender, Stanley E. 1994. *The Guide to the Federal Budget, Fiscal 1995*. Washington, D.C.: Urban Institute Press.

Pfiffner, James P. 1979. *The President, the Budget, and Congress: Impoundment and the 1974 Budget Act*. Boulder, Colo.: Westview Press.

Schick, Allen. 1995. *The Federal Budget: Politics, Policy, Process*. Washington, D.C.: Brookings.

Shuman, Howard E. 1984. *Politics and the Budget*. Englewood Cliffs, N.J.: Prentice-Hall.

INCARCERATION

Call, Jack E. 1995. "The Supreme Court and Prisoner's Rights." *Federal Probation* 59 (March).

Dlugacz, Henry A. 1993. "*Riggins v. Nevada:* Towards a Unified Standard for a Prisoner's Right to Refuse Medication." *Law and Psychology Review* 17.

Gillmer, Jason A. 1995. "*United States v. Clary:* Equal Protection and the Crack Statute." *American University Law Review* 45.

Kaplan, Wendy J. 1995. "Sentencing Advocacy in the Massachusetts District Courts." *Massachusetts Law Review* 80.

King, Rose E. 1995. "Consent Decree Modification and the Suffolk County Jail: What a Long Strange Trip It's Been." *New England Journal on Criminal and Civil Confinement* 21.

Lilly, J. Robert, and Richard A. Ball. 1993. "Selling Justice: Will Electronic Monitoring Last?" *Northern Kentucky Law Review* 20.

Morris, Norval. 1974. *The Future of Imprisonment*. Chicago: Univ. of Chicago Press.

Ogloff, James R. P., Ronald Roesch, and Stephen D. Hart. 1994. "Mental Health Services in Jails and Prisons: Legal, Clinical, and Policy Issues." *Law and Psychology Review* 18.

Potts, Jeff. 1993. "American Penal Institutions and Two Alternative Proposals for Punishment." *South Texas Law Review* 34.

Robbins, Ira P. 1989. "The Legal Dimensions of Private Incarceration." *American University Law Review* 38.

Sturm, Susan P. 1993. "The Legacy and Future of Corrections Litigation." *University of Pennsylvania Law Review* 142.

Tewksbury, Richard A. 1994. "Improving the Educational Skills of Jail Inmates: Preliminary Program Findings." *Federal Probation* 58 (June).

Tobolowsky, Peggy M., and James F. Quinn. 1993. "Pretrial Release in the 1990s: Texas Takes Another Look at Nonfinancial Release Conditions." *New England Journal on Criminal and Civil Confinement* 19.

INCOME TAX

Posin, Daniel Q. 1983. *Federal Income Taxation*. St. Paul: West.

Willan, Robert M. 1994. *Income Taxes: Concise History and Primer*. Baton Rouge, La.: Claitor's.

INCONTESTABILITY CLAUSE

Schuman, Gary. 1995. "Health and Life Insurance Applications: Their Role in the Claims Review Process." *Defense Counsel Journal* 62.

INDENTURE

Ballam, Deborah A. 1995. "The Traditional View on the Origins of the Employment-At-Will Doctrine: Myth or Reality?" *American Business Law Journal* 33 (fall).

———. 1996. "Exploding the Original Myth Regarding Employment-At-Will: The True Origins of the Doctrine." *Berkeley Journal of Employment and Labor Law* 17.

Riger, Martin. 1991. "The Trust Indenture as Bargained Contract: The Persistence of Myth." *Journal of Corporation Law* 16 (winter).

INDEPENDENT CONTRACTOR

Nunnallee, Walter H. 1992. "Why Congress Needs to Fix the Employee/Independent Contractor Tax Rules." *North Carolina Central Law Journal* 20.

Pacynski, Rick A. 1993. "Legal Challenges in Using Independent Contractors." *Michigan Bar Journal* 72 (July).

"Qualifying as an Independent Contractor." *Nevada Lawyer* 3 (March).

Treasury Department. Internal Revenue Service. 1987. Revenue Ruling 87-41. Washington, D.C.: U.S. Government Printing Office.

INDEPENDENT COUNSEL

Kutler, Stanley I. 1994. "In the Shadow of Watergate: Legal, Political, and Cultural Implications." *Nova Law Review* 18.

O'Sullivan, Julie. 1996. "The Independent Counsel Statute: Bad Law, Bad Policy." *American Criminal Law Review* 33.

Sels, John van Loben. 1995. "From Watergate to Whitewater: Congressional Use Immunity and Its Impact on the Independent Counsel." *Georgetown Law Journal* 83.

Solloway, Robert G. 1988. "The Institutionalized Wolf: An Analysis of the Unconstitutionality of the Independent Counsel Provisions of the Ethics In Government Act of 1978." *Indiana Law Review* 21.

"Workshop: Preliminary Information on Ethics Investigations." 1995. *Journal of Law and Politics* 11.

INDEPENDENT PARTIES

Wilson, James Q. 1992. *American Government: Institutions and Policies.* Lexington, Mass.: Heath.

INDIAN CHILD WELFARE ACT

Bennett, Michele K. 1993. "Native American Children: Caught in the Web of the Indian Child Welfare Act." *Hamline Law Review* 16 (spring).

Gallagher, Brian D. 1994. "Indian Child Welfare Act of 1978: The Congressional Foray into the Adoption Process." *Northern Illinois University Law Review* 15 (fall).

Hemp, Susan J. 1996. "State Court versus Tribal Court Jurisdiction in an Indian Child Custody Case." *Illinois Bar Journal* 84 (April).

Ujke, David M. 1993. "Tribal Court Jurisdiction in Domestic Relations Matters Involving Indian Children: Not Just a Matter of Comity." *Wisconsin Lawyer* 66 (August).

INDIVIDUAL RETIREMENT ACCOUNT

Boes, Richard F., and G. Michael Ransom. 1994. "Untangling the IRA Rules." *Tax Adviser* 25 (August 1).

J. K. Lasser Institute. 1996. *J. K. Lasser's Your Income Tax 1996.* New York: Macmillan.

INFANTS

Davis, Samuel M., and Mortimer D. Schwartz. 1987. *Children's Rights and the Law.* Lexington Books.

Horowitz, Robert M., and Howard A. Davidson. 1984. *Legal Rights of Children.* Blue Ridge Summit, Pa.: McGraw-Hill.

Houlgate, Laurence D. 1980. *The Child and the State.* Baltimore, Md.: Johns Hopkins Univ. Press.

Humm, S. Randall, et al. *Child, Parent, and State.* Philadelphia, Pa.: Temple University Press.

Jackson, Anthony. 1995. "Action for Wrongful Life, Wrongful Pregnancy, and Wrongful Birth in the United States and England." *Loyola of Los Angeles International and Comparative Law Journal* 17 (April).

Jacobs, Thomas A. 1995. *Children and the Law: Rights and Obligations.* New York: Clark Boardman Callaghan.

IN LOCO PARENTIS

Hirshberg, Philip M. "The College's Emerging Duty to Supervise Students: In Loco Parentis." 1994. *Washington University Journal of Urban and Contemporary Law* 46 (summer).

Jackson, Brian. 1991. "The Lingering Legacy of In Loco Parentis: An Historical Survey and Proposal for Reform." *Vanderbilt Law Review* 44 (October).

Walton, Spring, J. 1992. "In Loco Parentis for the 1990s: New Liabilities." *Ohio Northern University Law Review* 19.

INQUISITORIAL SYSTEM

Moskovitz, Myron. 1995. "The O. J. Inquisition: A United States Encounter with Continental Criminal Justice." *Vanderbilt Journal of Transnational Law* 28.

Sward, Ellen E. 1989. "Values, Ideology, and the Evolution of the Adversary System." *Indiana Law Journal* 64.

INSANITY DEFENSE

Bing, Jonathan L. 1996. "Protecting the Mentally Retarded from Capital Punishment: State Efforts Since *Penry* and Recommendations for the Future." *New York University Review of Law and Social Change* 22.

Ellickson, Robert C. 1996. "Controlling Chronic Misconduct in City Spaces: Of Panhandlers, Skid Rows, and Public-Space Zoning." *Yale Law Journal* 105.

Kuby, Ronald L., and William M. Kunstler. 1995. "So Crazy He Thinks He Is Sane: The Colin Ferguson Trial and the Competency Standard." *Cornell Journal of Law and Public Policy* 5.

LaFond, John Q., and Mary L. Durham. 1992. *Back to the Asylum: The Future of Mental Health Law and Policy in the United States.* New York: Oxford Univ. Press.

Morse, Stephen J. 1985. "Excusing the Crazy." *Southern California Law Review* 58.

INSURANCE

Cady, Thomas C., and Christy H. Smith. 1995. "West Virginia's Automobile Insurance Policy Laws: A Practitioner's Guide." *West Virginia Law Review* 97.

Robinson, Eric L. 1992. "The Oregon Basic Health Services Act: A Model for State Reform?" *Vanderbilt Law Review* 45.

INTEGRATION

Brown-Scott, Wendy. 1994. "Justice Thurgood Marshall and the Integrative Ideal." *Arizona State Law Journal* 26.

Carmichael, Stokely, and Charles Hamilton. 1967. *Black Power: The Politics of Liberation in America.* New York: Random House.

Cashmore, Ellis. 1994. *Dictionary of Race and Ethnic Relations.* 3d ed. London: Routledge.

Christian, William. 1994. "Normalization as a Goal: The Americans with Disabilities Act and Individuals with Mental Retardation." *Texas Law Review* 73.

Cruse, Harold. 1987. *Plural but Equal.* New York: Morrow.

Kimerling, Joshua E. 1994. "Black Male Academies: Re-examining the Strategy of Integration." *Buffalo Law Review* 42.

King, Martin Luther, Jr. 1968. *Where Do We Go from Here—Chaos or Community?* Boston: Beacon Press.

Middleton, Michael A. 1995. "*Brown v. Board:* Revisited." *Southern Illinois University Law Journal* 20.

Powell, John A. 1996. "Living and Learning: Linking House and Education." *Minnesota Law Review* 80.

Stewart, Carter M., and S. Felicita Torres. 1996. "Limiting Federal Court Power to Impose School Desegregation Remedies—*Missouri v. Jenkins.*" *Harvard Civil Rights–Civil Liberties Law Review* 31.

Wolters, Raymond. 1996. "Stephen C. Halpern, on the Limits of the Law: The Ironic Legacy of Title VI of the 1964 Civil Rights Act." *American Journal of Legal History* 40.

Young, Andrew. 1995. "Reaffirming Our Faith in Integration." *St. Louis University Law Journal* 39.

INTELLECTUAL PROPERTY

Byrne, John G. 1995. "Changes on the Frontier of Intellectual Property Law: An Overview of the Changes Required by GATT. " *Duquesne Law Review* 34 (fall).

Goldstein, Paul. 1993. *Copyright, Patent, Trademark, and Related State Doctrines: Cases and Materials on the Law of Intellectual Property.* Westbury, N.Y.: Foundation Press.

INTENT

Hall, Kermit L. 1989. *The Magic Mirror.* New York: Oxford Univ. Press.

INTERIOR DEPARTMENT

Friedman, Howard M. 1992. "The Oversupply of Regulatory Reform: From Law to Politics in Administrative Rulemaking." *Nebraska Law Review* 71.

Hines, N. William. 1994. "The Land Ethic and American Agriculture." *Loyola of Los Angeles Law Review* 27.

Pommersheim, Frank, and Shermann Marshall. 1992. "Liberation, Dreams, and Hard Work: An Essay on Tribal Court Jurisprudence." *Wisconsin Law Review* 411.

United States Government Manual, 1995–1996. Washington, D.C.: U.S. Government Printing Office.

Volkman, John M. 1987. "Testing New Forms of River Basin Governance: Implication of the Seattle Master Builders Case." *Environmental Law* 17.

INTERMEDIATE-RANGE NUCLEAR FORCES TREATY

Falkenrath, Richard A. 1995. *Shaping Europe's Military Order: The Origins and Consequences of the CFE Treaty.* Cambridge, Mass.: Massachusetts Institute of Technology Press.

Sheehan, Michael. 1988. *Arms Control: Theory and Practice.* Cambridge, Mass.: Blackwell.

INTERNAL REVENUE SERVICE

Burnham, David. 1989. *A Law unto Itself: Power, Politics, and the IRS.* New York: Random House.

Chommie, John C. 1970. *The Internal Revenue Service.* New York: Praeger.

Richardson, Margaret Milner. 1994. "Reinventing the Internal Revenue Service." *Federal Bar Association Section of Taxation Report* 1 (winter).

Treasury Department. Internal Revenue Service. 1996. *Guide to the Internal Revenue Service.* Washington, D.C.: U.S. Government Printing Office.

Whitman, Donald R., ed. 1983. *Government Agencies.* Westport, Conn.: Greenwood Press.

INTERNATIONAL COURT OF JUSTICE

Kelly, Barbara. 1992. "The International Court of Justice: Its Role in a New World Legal Order." *Touro Journal of Transnational Law* 3.

Lelewer, Joanne K. 1989. "International Commercial Arbitration as a Model for Resolving Treaty Disputes." *New York University Journal of International Law and Policy* 21.

Levarda, Daniela. 1995. "A Comparative Study of U.S. and British Approaches to Discovery Conflicts: Achieving a Uniform System of Extraterritorial Discovery." *Fordham International Law Journal* 18.

INTERNATIONAL LAW

August, Ray. 1995. *Public International Law: Text, Cases, Readings.* Englewood Cliffs, N.J.: Prentice-Hall.

Janis, Mark W. 1988. *An Introduction to International Law.* Boston: Little, Brown.

INTERNET

"ACLU Analysis of the Cox/Wyden Bill (HR 1978)." July 10, 1995. American Civil Liberties Union site. World Wide Web.

"ACLU Cyber-Liberties Alert: Axe the Exon Bill!" April 29, 1995. American Civil Liberties Union site. World Wide Web.

"ACLU Cyber-Liberties Analysis: Revised Exon Amendment." May 25, 1995. American Civil Liberties Union site. World Wide Web.

"A Civil Liberties Ride on the Information Superhighway." 1994. *Civil Liberties: The National Newsletter of the ACLU* 380 (spring).

American Civil Liberties Union site. World Wide Web. Excerpts from Senate floor debate on Exon Bill, taken from the Congressional Record. June 14, 1995. Congressional Quarterly site. America Online.

"Amicus Curiae Brief in r.e. *U.S. v. Jake Baker and Arthur Gonda,* Crim. No. 95-80106, U.S. District Court Eastern District of Michigan Southern Division." April 26, 1995. American Civil Liberties Union site. World Wide Web.

"Can the Use of Cyberspace Be Governed?" 1995. *Congressional Quarterly Researcher* (June 30).

"Constitutional Problems with the Communications Decency Amendment: A Legislative Analysis by the EFF." June 16, 1995. Electronic Frontier Foundation site. World Wide Web.

"Legislative Update: Pending State Legislation to Regulate Online Speech Content." April 17, 1995. American Civil Liberties Union site. World Wide Web.

"Prodigy Stumbles as a Forum Again." Fall 1994. Electronic Frontier Foundation site. World Wide Web.

INTERPRETATION

Hall, Kermit L. 1989. *The Magic Mirror.* New York: Oxford Univ. Press.

Stephens, Otis H., Jr., and John M. Scheb, II. 1993. *American Constitutional Law.* St. Paul: West.

INTERSTATE COMMERCE ACT

Interstate Commerce Commission. 1979. *Interstate Commerce Commission . . . in the Public Interest.*

INTERSTATE COMMERCE COMMISSION

"Commerce: ICC Elimination." 1996. *Congressional Quarterly's News* (January 8).

Interstate Commerce Commission. 1979. *Interstate Commerce Commission . . . in the Public Interest.*
United States Government Manual, 1994–1995. Washington, D.C.: U.S. Government Printing Office.

INTERSTATE COMPACT

Darr, Frank P. 1993. "Electric Holding Company Regulation by Multistate Compact." *Energy Law Journal* 14.

Goble, Dale D. 1986. "The Council and the Constitution: An Article on the Constitutionality of the Northwest Power Planning Council." *Journal of Environmental Law and Litigation* 1.

INVOLUNTARY CONFESSION

Friedman, Lawrence M. 1993. *Crime and Punishment in American History.* New York: Basic Books.

Hall, Kermit L. 1989. *The Magic Mirror.* New York: Oxford Univ. Press.

Stephens, Otis H., Jr., and John M. Scheb II. 1993. *American Constitutional Law.* St. Paul: West.

INVOLUNTARY SERVITUDE

Hall, Kermit L. 1989. *The Magic Mirror.* New York: Oxford Univ. Press.

Stephens, Otis H., Jr., and John M. Scheb II. 1993. *American Constitutional Law.* St. Paul: West.

IRRESISTIBLE IMPULSE

Falk, Patricia J. 1996. "Novel Theories of Criminal Defense Based upon the Toxicity of the Social Environment: Urban Psychosis, Television Intoxication, and Black Rage." *North Carolina Law Review* 74.

Gresham, Anne C. 1993. "The Insanity Plea: A Futile Defense for Serial Killers." *Law and Psychology Review* 17.

Kahan, Dan M. and Martha C. Nussbaum. 1996. "Two Conceptions of Emotion in Criminal Law." *Columbia Law Review* 96.

JACKSON, HOWELL EDMUNDS

Friedman, Leon, and Fred L. Israel, eds. 1969. *The Justices of the United States Supreme Court, 1789– 1969: Their Lives and Major Opinions.* New York: Chelsea House.

JACKSON, ROBERT HOUGHWOUT

Demon, Charles S., et al. 1969. *Mr. Justice Jackson: Four Lectures in His Honor.* New York: William Nelson Crumble Foundation, Columbia Univ. Press.

Gerhart, Eugene C. 1958. *America's Advocate: Robert H. Jackson.* Indianapolis: Bobbs-Merrill.

———. 1961. *Lawyer's Judge.* Albany: Q Corp.

Jackson, Robert H. 1947. *The Nürnberg Case.* New York: Knopf.

———. 1951. *Wartime Security and Liberty under Law.* Buffalo: Univ. of Buffalo School of Law.

Prosaic, Joseph E. 1994. *Nuremberg: Infamy on Trial.* New York: Penguin Books.

Rosenbaum, Alan S. 1993. *Prosecuting Nazi War Criminals.* Boulder, Colo.: Westview Press.

Schubert, Glendon. 1969. *Dispassionate Justice: A Synthesis of the Judicial Opinions of Robert H. Jackson.* Indianapolis: Bobbs-Merrill.

Taylor, Telford. 1992. *The Anatomy of the Nuremberg Trials.* New York: Knopf.

U.S. Supreme Court. 1955. *Proceedings of the Bar and Officers of the Supreme Court of the United States, April 4, 1955, and Proceedings before the Supreme Court of the United States, April 4, 1955, in Memory of Robert Houghwout Jackson.* Washington, D.C.: United States Supreme Court Bar.

JAIL

Call, Jack E. 1995. "The Supreme Court and Prisoner's Rights." *Federal Probation* 59 (March).

Dlugacz, Henry A. 1993. "*Riggins v. Nevada:* Towards a Unified Standard for a Prisoner's Right to Refuse Medication." *Law and Psychology Review* 17.

Kaplan, Wendy J. 1995. "Sentencing Advocacy in the Massachusetts District Courts." *Massachusetts Law Review* 80.

Larowicz, Jamie. 1986. "The Eighth Amendment and State Correctional Overcrowding: The Second Circuit Serves Up an Ounce of Prevention." *Brooklyn Law Review* 52.

Lilly, J. Robert, and Richard A. Ball. 1993. "Selling Justice: Will Electronic Monitoring Last?" *Northern Kentucky Law Review* 20.

Ogloff, James R. P., Ronald Roesch, and Stephen D. Hart. 1994. "Mental Health Services in Jails and Prisons: Legal, Clinical, and Policy Issues." *Law and Psychology Review* 18.

Potts, Jeff. 1993. "American Penal Institutions and Two Alternative Proposals for Punishment." *South Texas Law Review* 34.

Sturm, Susan P. 1993. "The Legacy and Future of Corrections Litigation." *University of Pennsylvania Law Review* 142.

Tewksbury, Richard A. 1994. "Improving the Educational Skills of Jail Inmates: Preliminary Program Findings." *Federal Probation* 58 (June).

Tobolowsky, Peggy M., and James F. Quinn. 1993. "Pretrial Release in the 1990s: Texas Takes Another Look at Nonfinancial Release Conditions." *New England Journal on Criminal and Civil Confinement* 19.

JAMES, WILLIAM

Allen, Gay Wilson. 1967. *William James: A Biography.* New York: Viking Press.

Cloud, Morgan. 1993. "Pragmatism, Positivism, and Principles in Fourth Amendment Theory." *University of California at Los Angeles Law Review* 41 (December).

Hackney, James R., Jr. 1995. "The Intellectual Origins of American Strict Products Liability: A Case Study in American Pragmatic Instrumentalism." *American Journal of Legal History* 39 (October).

Myers, Gerald E. 1986. *William James: His Life and Thought.* New Haven, Conn.: Yale Univ. Press.

Schlegel, John H. 1995. *American Legal Realism and Empirical Social Science.* Chapel Hill, N.C.: Univ. of North Carolina Press.

JAPANESE AMERICAN EVACUATION CASES

Executive Order No. 9066. 1942. *Federal Register* (February 19).

Irons, Peter. 1983. *Justice at War.* Berkeley, Cal.: Univ. of California Press.

Morris, Arval A. 1984. "Justice, War, and the Japanese American Evacuation and Internment." *Washington Law Review* 59 (September).

Nash, Philip T. 1985. "Moving for Redress and Justice for All." *Yale Law Journal* 94 (January).

Tateishi, John. 1984. *And Justice for All.* New York: Random House.

Weglyn, Michi. 1976. *Years of Infamy.* New York: Morrow.

War Department. 1942. *Final Report: Japanese Evacuation from the West Coast.* Washington, D.C.: U.S. Government Printing Office.

JAWORSKI, LEON

Jaworski, Leon. 1976. *The Right and the Power.* New York: Reader's Digest Press.

———. 1979. *Confession and Avoidance.* Garden City, N.Y.: Anchor Press.

———. 1981. *Crossroads.* Elgin, Ill.: Cook.

Woodward, Bob, and Carl Bernstein. 1976. *The Final Days.* New York: Simon & Schuster.

JAY, JOHN

Jay, William. 1833. *The Life of John Jay.* New York: Harper.

Monaghan, Frank. 1935. *John Jay: Defender of Liberty.* New York: Bobbs-Merrill.

Morris, Richard B., ed. 1975. *John Jay: The Making of a Revolutionary.* New York: Harper & Row.

———. 1985. *Witnesses at the Creation: Hamilton, Madison, Jay, and the Constitution.* New York: Holt, Rinehart & Winston.

Rossiter, Clinton Lawrence. 1964. *Alexander Hamilton and the Constitution.* New York: Harcourt, Brace & World.

JEFFERSON, THOMAS

Hall, Kermit L. 1989. *The Magic Mirror.* New York: Oxford Univ. Press.

Stephens, Otis H., Jr., and John M. Scheb II. 1993. *American Constitutional Law.* St. Paul: West.

JIM CROW LAWS

Quarles, Benjamin. 1987. "The Negro in the Making of America." Collier Books.

JOHNSON, ANDREW

Castel, Albert. 1979. *The Presidency of Andrew Johnson.* Lawrence, Kans.: Regents Press of Kansas.

Foner, Eric, and Olivia Mahoney. 1995. *America's Reconstruction: People and Politics after the Civil War.* New York: Harper Perennial.

Horowitz, Robert F. 1979. *The Great Impeacher: A Political Biography of James M. Ashley.* New York: Brooklyn College Press.

Jones, James S. 1901. *Life of Andrew Johnson, Seventeenth President of the United States.* Greeneville, Tenn.: East Tennessee.

Lomask, Milton. 1960. *Andrew Johnson: President on Trial.* New York: Farrar, Straus, & Cudahy.

Rehnquist, William H. 1992. *Grand Inquests: The Historic Impeachments of Justice Samuel Chase and President Andrew Johnson.* New York: Morrow.

Simpson, Brooks D. 1987. *Advice after Appomattox: Letters to Andrew Johnson, 1865–1866.* Edited by Leroy P. Graf and John Muldowney. Knoxville, Tenn.: Univ. of Tennessee Press.

Stalcup, Brenda, ed. 1995. *Reconstruction: Opposing Viewpoints.* San Diego: Greenhaven Press.

JOHNSON, JAMES WELDON

Fleming, Robert E. 1987. *James Weldon Johnson.* Boston: Twayne.

Johnson, James Weldon. 1933. *Along This Way: The Autobiography of James Weldon Johnson.* New York: Viking Press.

Levy, Eugene. 1982. "James Weldon Johnson and the Development of the NAACP." *Black Leaders of the Twentieth Century.* Edited by John H. Franklin. Urbana, Ill.: Univ. of Illinois Press.

JOHNSON, REVERDY

Foner, Eric. 1988. *Reconstruction: America's Unfinished Revolution.* New York: Harper & Row.

Hall, Kermit L. 1989. *The Magic Mirror.* New York: Oxford Univ. Press.

Stephens, Otis H., Jr., and John M. Scheb II. 1993. *American Constitutional Law.* St. Paul: West.

JOHNSON, THOMAS

Witt, Elder, ed. 1990. *Guide to the U.S. Supreme Court.* 2d ed. Washington, D.C.: Congressional Quarterly.

JOHNSON, WILLIAM

Witt, Elder, ed. 1990. *Guide to the U.S. Supreme Court.* 2d ed. Washington, D.C.: Congressional Quarterly.

JOINT ESTATE

Berger, Michael J. *Estate Planning.* Vol. 18. Warren Gorham Lamont.

Ritchie, Alford, and Effland. 1977. *Decedents' Estates and Trusts.* University Casebook series.

JOINT OPERATING AGREEMENT

Fink, Mark H. 1990. "The Newspaper Preservation Act of 1970: Help for the Needy or the Greedy?" *Detroit College of Law Review* 1990 (spring).

Painter, William S. 1993. "Recent Legislation, Cases, and Other Developments Affecting Healthcare Providers and Integrated Delivery Systems." *American Law Institute–American Bar Association* SB51 (February).

Steel, Robbie. 1989. "Joint Operating Agreements in the Newspaper Industry: A Threat to First Amendment Freedoms." *University of Pennsylvania Law Review* 138 (November).

Wall, Guy E. 1992. "Joint Oil and Gas Operations in Louisiana." *Louisiana Law Review* 53 (September).

JOINT RESOLUTION

Bacon, Donald C., Roger H. Davidson, and Morton Keller, eds. 1995. *The Encyclopedia of the United States Congress.* New York: Simon & Schuster.

Congressional Quarterly. 1983. *Congress A to Z.* 2d ed. Washington, D.C.: Congressional Quarterly.

———. 1991. *Congressional Quarterly's Guide to Congress.* 4th ed. Washington, D.C.: Congressional Quarterly.

Dickson, Paul, and Paul Clancy, eds. 1993. *The Congress Dictionary: The Ways and Meanings of Capitol Hill.* New York: Wiley.

"Only Bills and Joint Resolutions Can Become Law." 1994. *Congressional Quarterly News* (December 19).

JOINT VENTURE

Harrigan, Kathryn Rudie. 1986. *Managing for Joint Venture Success*. Lexington, Mass.: Lexington Books.

Levins, Cary, and James S. Lawlor. 1988. "Legal Considerations of Joint Ventures." In *The Handbook of Joint Venturing*. Edited by John D. Carter, Robert F. Cushman, and C. Scott Hartz. Homewood, Ill.: Dow Jones–Irwin.

Practising Law Institute (PLI). 1996. *Joint Ventures: Practices in Search of Principles*, by Stephen V. Bomse. January–February. Corporate Law and Practice Course Handbook series, PLI order no. B4-7134.

———. 1996. *Monopolies and Joint Ventures*, by William T. Lifland. Corporate Law and Practice Course Handbook series, PLI order no. B4-7128, May–July.

JONES, ELAINE RUTH

Blannon, Nancy. 1995. "Affirmative Action in Action: Its Past and Its Future." *Human Rights* 22 (fall).

Jones, Elaine R., et al. 1994. "The Death of Fairness?" Panel discussion. *Houston Law Review* 31 (winter).

JONES ACT

Beer, Peter. 1986. "Keeping Up with the Jones Act." *Tulane Law Review* 61 (December).

Buckley, William F. 1995. "The Jones Act: Its Applicability Clarified." *Rhode Island Bar Journal* 44 (October).

Kelly, Wendy A. 1995. "*Chandris, Inc. v. Latsis:* The Supreme Court Addresses the Vessel Connection Requirement for Seaman Status under The Jones Act." *Tulane Law Review* 70 (December).

Robertson, David W. 1985. "A New Approach to Determining Seaman Status." *Texas Law Review* 64 (August).

JORDAN, BARBARA C.

Jordan, Barbara, and Shelby Hearon. 1979. *Barbara Jordan: A Self-Portrait*. New York: Doubleday.

JUDGMENT CREDITOR

Lippman, Steven N. 1996. "Proceedings Supplementary and Uniform Fraudulent Transfer Act Dual Remedies to Execute against a Judgment Debtor's Transferred Assets." *Florida Bar Journal* 70 (January).

JUDICIAL CONFERENCE OF THE UNITED STATES

Easton, Eric B. 1995. "Closing the Barn Door after the Genie Is Out of the Bag: Recognizing a 'Futility Principle' in First Amendment Jurisprudence." *DePaul Law Review* 45.

Hall, Robert H. 1994. "Federal Circuit Judicial Councils: A Legislative History and Revisions Needed Today." *Georgia State University Law Review* 11.

Heaney, Gerald W. 1991. "The Reality of Guidelines Sentencing: No End to Disparity." *American Criminal Law Review* 28.

Marder, Nancy S. 1995. "Beyond Gender: Peremptory Challenges and the Roles of the Jury." *Texas Law Review* 73.

Metz, Stephen A. 1996. "Justice Through the Eye of a Camera: Cameras in the Courtrooms in the United States, Canada, England, and Scotland." *Dickinson Journal of International Law* 14 (spring).

Reinhardt, Stephen. 1995. "Judicial Speech and the Open Judiciary." *Loyola of Los Angeles Law Review* 28.

Weber, Mark C. 1994. "The Federal Civil Rules Amendment of 1993 and Complex Litigation: A Comment on Transsubstantivity and Special Rules for Large and Small Federal Cases." *Review of Litigation* 14.

Wood, Harlington, Jr. 1995. "Judiciary Reform: Recent Improvements in Federal Judicial Administration." *American University Law Review* 44.

JUDICIAL IMMUNITY

Morgan, Thomas D., and Ronald D. Rotunda. 1993. *Professional Responsibility: Problems and Materials*. 5th ed. Westbury, N.Y.: Foundation Press.

Stephens, Otis H., Jr., and John M. Scheb II. 1993. *American Constitutional Law*. St. Paul: West.

JUDICIAL REVIEW

Hall, Kermit L. 1989. *The Magic Mirror*. New York: Oxford Univ. Press.

Stephens, Otis H., Jr., and John M. Scheb II. 1993. *American Constitutional Law*. St. Paul: West.

JUDICIARY

MacDowell, Douglas M. 1978. *The Law in Classical Athens*. Ithaca, N.Y.: Cornell Univ. Press.

JUDICIARY ACT OF 1789

Bourguignon, Henry J. 1995. "The Federal Key to the Judiciary Act of 1789." *South Carolina Law Review* 46.

Clinton, Robert N. 1986. "A Mandatory View of Federal Court Jurisdiction: Early Implementation of and Departures from the Constitutional Plan." *Columbia Law Review* 86.

Low, Peter W., and John C. Jeffries, Jr. 1994. *Federal Courts and the Law of Federal-State Relations*. 3d ed. Westbury, N.Y.: Foundation Press.

Wells, Michael L., and Edward J. Larson. 1995. "Original Intent and Article III." *Tulane Law Review* 70.

JUNK BOND

Boyer, Allen. 1989. "For the Love of Money." *Georgia Law Review* 23.

JURIMETRICS

American Bar Association. "Information for Authors." 1995. *Jurimetrics Journal* 35 (Spring). World Wide Web.

"Computer Power and Legal Reasoning." 1986. *American Bar Association Law Practice Management* (September).

Jacob, Bernard E. "Ancient Rhetoric, Modern Legal Thought, and Politics: A Review Essay on the Translation of Viehweg's 'Topics and Law.'" 1995. *Northwestern University Law Review* 89 (summer).

"Scientific Evidence Symposium: Jurisprudence or 'Juriscience'?" 1984. *William and Mary Law Review* (summer).

JURISDICTION

Meslar, Roger W., ed. 1990. *Legalines Civil Procedure*. 3d ed. Chicago, Ill.: Harcourt Brace Jovanovich Legal and Professional Publications.

JURIS DOCTOR

Morgan, Thomas D., and Ronald D. Rotunda. 1993. *Professional Responsibility: Problems and Materials.* 5th ed. Westbury, N.Y.: Foundation Press.

Wilson, Debbie, reference librarian, University of New Hampshire, Durham. 1996. Telephone interview, July 5.

JURISPRUDENCE

Dworkin, Ronald M. 1977. *Taking Rights Seriously.* Cambridge: Harvard Univ. Press.

Grey, Thomas C. 1983. "Langdell's Orthodoxy." *University of Pittsburgh Law Review* 45.

Holmes, Oliver Wendell, Jr. 1963. *The Common Law.* Boston: Little, Brown.

Horwitz, Morton J. 1992. *The Transformation of American Law: 1870–1960.* New York: Oxford Univ. Press.

Michael, Helen. 1991. "The Role of Natural Law in Early American Constitutionalism: Did the Founders Contemplate Judicial Enforcement of 'Unwritten' Individual Rights?" *North Carolina Law Review* 69.

Posner, Richard A. 1990. *Problems of Jurisprudence.* Cambridge: Harvard Univ. Press.

Stoner, James. 1992. *Common Law and Liberal Theory.* Lawrence, Kan.: Univ. Press of Kansas.

JURY

Amar, Akhil Reed. 1995. "Reinventing Juries: Ten Suggested Reforms." *University of California at Davis Law Review* 28 (summer).

Leach, Brian E. 1995. "Extending *Batson v. Kentucky* to Gender and Beyond: The Death Knell for the Peremptory Challenge?" *Southern Illinois University Law Journal* 19.

Minnesota State Court Administration. Office of Research and Planning. 1993. *Minnesota Supreme Court Task Force on Racial Bias in the Judicial System: Final Report.* St. Paul.

Minnesota State Court Administration. Office of Research and Planning. Implementation Committee on Multicultural Diversity and Fairness in the Courts. 1994. *Progress Report.* St. Paul.

———. 1995. *Progress Report.* St. Paul.

Montoya, Jean. 1996. "The Future of the Post-*Batson* Peremptory Challenge." *University of Michigan Journal of Law Reform* 29.

Sklansky, Joseph J. 1996. "Right to Jury Trial." *Georgetown Law Journal* 84 (April).

Stephens, Otis H., Jr., and John M. Scheb II. 1993. *American Constitutional Law.* St. Paul: West.

JUST CAUSE

Delmendo, Wendi J. 1991. "Determining Just Cause: An Equitable Solution for the Workplace." *Washington Law Review* 66 (July).

JUSTICE DEPARTMENT

Clayton, Cornell. 1992. *The Politics of Justice.* New York: M. E. Sharpe.

Huston, Luther A. 1967. *The Department of Justice.* New York: Praeger.

Justice Department. 1994. *The Department of Justice.* Washington, D.C.: U.S. Government Printing Office.

———. 1994. *United States Department of Justice.* Washington, D.C.: U.S. Government Printing Office.

Langeluttig, Albert G. 1927. *The Department of Justice of the United States.* Baltimore: Johns Hopkins Press.

Levy, Leonard W., and Louis Fisher, eds. 1994. *Encyclopedia of the American Presidency.* Vol. 3. New York: Simon & Schuster.

Meador, Daniel J. 1980. *The President, the Attorney General, and the Department of Justice.* Charlottesville, Va.: White Burkett Miller Center of Public Affairs.

JUSTICE OF THE PEACE

Forte, David F. 1996. "Marbury's Travail: Federalist Politics and William Marbury's Appointment as Justice of the Peace." *Catholic University Law Review* 45 (winter).

JUSTICIABLE

Chemerinsky, Erwin. 1990. "A Unified Approach to Justiciability." *Connecticut Law Review* 22 (summer).

Galloway, Russell, W., Jr. 1990. "Basic Justiciability Analysis." *Santa Clara Law Review* 1990 (winter).

Tsen Lee, Evan. 1992. "Deconstitutionalizing Justiciability: The Example of Mootness." *Harvard Law Review* 105 (January).

JUVENILE LAW

Bernard, Thomas J. 1992. *The Cycle of Juvenile Justice.* New York: Oxford Univ. Press.

Burke, Michael K. 1995. "This Old Court: Abolitionists Once Again Line Up the Wrecking Ball on the Juvenile Court When All It Needs Is a Few Alterations." *University of Toledo Law Review* 26.

Clark, J. David. 1990. "Juveniles and the Death Penalty: A Square Peg in a Round Hole." *Mississippi College Law Review* 10.

Feld, Barry C. 1991. "The Transformation of the Juvenile Court." *Minnesota Law Review* 75.

Knauerhase, Evelyn C. 1990. "The Federal Circle Game: The Precarious Constitutional Status of Status Offenders." *Cooley Law Review* 7.

Martin, D. Ross. 1994. "Conspiratorial Children? The Intersection of the Federal Juvenile Delinquency Act and Federal Conspiracy Law." *Boston University Law Review* 74.

Mills, Deborah L. 1996. "*United States v. Johnson:* Acknowledging the Shift in the Juvenile Court System from Rehabilitation to Punishment." *DePaul Law Review* 45.

Stetzer, William T. 1996. "The Worst of Both Worlds." *Washburn Law Journal* 35.

KANT, IMMANUEL

Fletcher, George P. 1987. "Why Kant." *Columbia Law Review* 87 (April).

Kant, Immanuel. 1991. "Metaphysical First Principles of the Doctrine of Right." In *The Metaphysics of Morals.* Translated by Mary Gregor. Quoted in Jeremy Waldron, "Kant's Legal Positivism," *Harvard Law Review* 109 (May 1996).

Waldron, Jeremy. 1996. "Kant's Legal Positivism." *Harvard Law Review* 109 (May).

KATZENBACH, NICHOLAS deBELLEVILLE

Branch, Taylor. 1988. *Parting the Waters.* New York: Simon & Schuster.

O'Neill, William L. 1971. *Coming Apart: An Informal History of America in the 1960s.* New York: Quadrangle Books.

KELLOGG-BRIAND PACT

Arend, Anthony C., and Robert J. Beck. 1993. *International Law and the Use of Force*. London: Routledge.

Ferrell, Robert H. 1952. *Peace in Their Time*. New Haven, Conn.: Yale Univ. Press.

Lunardini, Christine A. 1994. *The American Peace Movement in the Twentieth Century*. Santa Barbara, Cal.: ABC-CLIO.

Miller, David H. 1928. *The Peace Pact of Paris*. New York: Putnam.

Pauling, Linus, ed. 1986. *World Encyclopedia of Peace*. Oxford: Pergamon Press.

KENNEDY, EDWARD MOORE

Senator Edward Kennedy site. November 17, 1996. World Wide Web.

KENNEDY, ROBERT FRANCIS

Guthman, Edwin O., and Jeffrey Shulman, eds. 1988. *Robert Kennedy in His Own Words: The Unpublished Recollections of the Kennedy Years*. New York: Bantam Books.

"Remembering the Kennedys." 1984. *Journal of American Studies* 18 (December).

Schlesinger, Arthur M., Jr. 1978. *Robert Kennedy and His Times*. Boston: Houghton Mifflin.

KEOGH PLAN

Cheeks, James E. 1989. *The Dow Jones–Irwin Guide to Keoghs*. Homewood, Ill.: Dow Jones–Irwin.

Tyson, Eric. 1995. *Personal Finance for Dummies*. Chicago: IDG Books Worldwide.

KEVORKIAN, JACK

Betzold, Michael. 1993. *Appointment with Dr. Death*. Troy, Mich.: Momentum.

Goldsworthy, Joan. 1991. "Jack Kevorkian." In *Newsmakers: 1991 Cumulation*.

KICKBACK

Chemerinsky, Erwin. 1983. "Controlling Fraud against the Government." *Notre Dame Law Review* 58.

Szarwark, Ernest J. 1986. "Bribes, Kickbacks, and Rebates: How New Developments Affect the Tax Results." *The Journal of Taxation* 64.

Williams, Charles J. 1995. "Toward a Comprehensive Health Care Anti-Kickback Statute." *University of Missouri—Kansas City Law Review* 64.

KIDNAPPING

Blinka, Daniel D., and Thomas J. Hammer. 1995. "Court of Appeals Digest." *Wisconsin Lawyer* 68 (April).

Diamond, John L. 1985. "Kidnapping: A Modern Definition." *American Journal of Criminal Law* 13.

Hillebrand, Joseph R. 1991. "Parental Kidnapping and the Tort of Custodial Interference: Not in a Child's Best Interests." *Indiana Law Review* 25.

Kaplan, John, and Robert Weisberg. 1991. *Criminal Law: Cases and Materials*. 2d ed. Boston: Little, Brown.

Onion, John F. 1995. "Mass Media's Impact on Litigation: A Judge's Perspective." *Review of Litigation* 14.

KING, MARTIN LUTHER, JR.

DeBenedetti, Charles. 1986. *Peace Heroes in Twentieth-Century America*. Bloomington, Ind.: Indiana Univ. Press.

Garrow, David J. 1986. *Bearing the Cross: Martin Luther King, Jr., and the Southern Christian Leadership Conference*. New York: Morrow.

Miroff, Bruce. 1993. *Icons of Democracy: American Leaders as Heroes, Aristocrats, Dissenters, and Democrats*. New York: HarperCollins.

Oates, Stephen B. 1982. *Let the Trumpet Sound: The Life of Martin Luther King, Jr*. New York: Harper & Row.

KING'S BENCH OR QUEEN'S BENCH

Kambour, Sarah Obaditch. 1994. "Symposium on the U.S. Pharmaceutical Industry in the 1990s: Facing Health Care Reform, Regulation, and Judicial Controls." *Seton Hall Law Review* 24.

KLEINDIENST, RICHARD GORDON

Kutler, Stanley I. 1990. *The Wars of Watergate*. New York: Knopf.

KNOX, PHILANDER CHASE

Baker, Nancy V. 1992. *Conflicting Loyalties: Law and Politics in the Attorney General's Office, 1789–1990*. Lawrence, Kans.: Univ. Press of Kansas.

Dictionary of American Biography. Twenty Volumes and Supplements. New York: Charles Scribner's Sons, 1928–1936. (Volume V, Hibben-Larkin edited by Dumas Malone, Pages 479–480.)

Reisman, W. Michael. 1983. "The Struggle for the Falklands." *Yale Law Journal* (December).

KOOP, CHARLES EVERETT

C. Everett Koop Foundation, Inc., site. World Wide Web.

Koop, C. Everett. 1991. *Koop: The Memoirs of America's Family Doctor*. Random House, New York.

The Koop Institute site. World Wide Web.

KOREAN WAR

Stephens, Otis H., Jr., and John M. Scheb II. 1993. *American Constitutional Law*. St. Paul: West.

KU KLUX KLAN

Allen, Wayne R. 1991. "Klan, Cloth, and Constitution: Anti-Mask Laws and the First Amendment." *Georgia Law Review* 25 (spring).

Grossman, Mark. 1993. "Ku Klux Klan." *Civil Rights Movement*. Santa Barbara, Cal.: ABC-CLIO.

Newman, Roger K. 1994. *Hugo Black: A Biography*. New York: Pantheon Books.

KU KLUX KLAN ACT

Brown, Bruce. 1991. "Injunctive Relief and Section 1985(3): Anti-Abortion Blockaders Meet the 'Ku Klux Klan Act.'" *Buffalo Law Review* 39 (fall).

Gormley, Ken. 1985. "Private Conspiracies and the Constitution: A Modern Vision of 42 U.S.C. Section 1985(3)." *Texas Law Review* 64 (November).

Hall, Kermit L. 1984. "Political Power and Constitutional Legitimacy: The South Carolina Ku Klux Klan Trials, 1871–1872." *Emory Law Journal* 33 (fall).

Mcmurtry, Joy Hollingsworth, and Patti S. Pennock. 1995. "Ending the Violence: Applying the Ku Klux Klan Act, RICO, and FACE to the Abortion Controversy." *Land and Water Law Review* 30.

KUNSTLER, WILLIAM MOSES

Kunstler, William. 1962. *The Case for Courage.* New York: Morrow.

———. 1994. *My Life as a Radical Lawyer.* Birch Lane Press.

LABOR DEPARTMENT

United States Government Manual, 1996–1997. Washington, D.C.: U.S. Government Printing Office.

LABOR LAW

Hall, Kermit L. 1989. *The Magic Mirror.* New York: Oxford Univ. Press.

Squire, Madelyn C. 1993. "Reality or Myth: Participatory Programs and Workplace Democracy—A Proposal for a Different Role for Unions." *Stetson Law Review* 23.

Wade, David R. 1994. "When Two Worlds Collide: Company Unions and Employee Empowerment in the Aftermath of *NLRB v. Electromation* and *NLRB v. DuPont.*" *Ohio Northern University Law Review* 21.

LABOR UNION

Hall, Kermit L. 1989. *The Magic Mirror.* New York: Oxford Univ. Press.

Stephens, Otis H., Jr., and John M. Scheb II. 1993. *American Constitutional Law.* St. Paul: West.

LA FOLLETTE, ROBERT MARION

Hall, Kermit L. 1989. *The Magic Mirror.* New York: Oxford Univ. Press.

LAMAR, JOSEPH RUCKER

Hall, Kermit L. 1989. *The Magic Mirror.* New York: Oxford Univ. Press.

Stephens, Otis H., Jr., and John M. Scheb II. 1993. *American Constitutional Law.* St. Paul: West.

LAMAR, LUCIUS QUINTUS CINCINNATUS

Hall, Kermit L. 1989. *The Magic Mirror.* New York: Oxford Univ. Press.

Stephens, Otis H., Jr., and John M. Scheb II. 1993. *American Constitutional Law.* St. Paul: West.

LAME DUCK

Clerk's office, New Hampshire state legislature. 1996. Telephone interview, September 25.

Kuhnle, Tom. 1996. "The Rebirth of Common Law Action for Addressing Hazardous Waste Contamination." *Stanford Environmental Law Journal* 15.

Thurmond, William M. 1996. "CERCLA's 'All Appropriate Inquiry': When Is Enough, Enough?" *Florida Bar Journal* 70 (March).

LANDLORD AND TENANT

Federlein, Walter J. 1996. "1995 PA 79: An Affirmative Act for Senior Citizen Tenants." *Michigan Bar Journal* 75.

Gerchick, Randy G. 1994. "No Easy Way Out: Making the Summary Eviction Process a Fairer and More Efficient Alternative to Landlord Self-Help." *University of California at Los Angeles Law Review* 41.

Kelley, Robert H. 1995. "Any Reports of the Death of the Property Law Paradigm for Leases Have Been Greatly Exaggerated." *Wayne Law Review* 41.

LANDMARK

Diamonstein, Barbaralee. 1992. *Landmarks: Eighteen Wonders of the New York World.* New York: Abrams.

Kayden, Jerold S. 1995. "Historic Preservation and the New Takings Cases: Landmarks Preserved." *Fordham Environmental Law Journal* 6.

———. 1996. "Hunting for Quarks: Constitutional Takings, Property Rights, and Government Regulation." *Washington University Journal of Urban and Contemporary Law* 50 (fall).

Nivala, John. 1996. "The Future for Our Past: Preserving Landmark Preservation." *New York University Environmental Law Journal* 5.

LANDRUM-GRIFFIN ACT

Hall, Kermit L. 1989. *The Magic Mirror.* New York: Oxford Univ. Press.

Stephens, Otis H., Jr., and John M. Scheb II. 1993. *American Constitutional Law.* St. Paul: West.

LAND-USE CONTROL

Chapman, Stephen B., and Robert L. Glicksman. 1996. "Regulatory Reform and (Breach of) the Contract with America: Improving Environmental Policy or Destroying Environmental Protection?" *Kansas Journal of Law Public Policy* 5 (winter).

Feller, Joseph M. 1995. " 'Til the Cows Come Home: The Fatal Flaw in the Clinton Administration's Public Lands Grazing Policy." *Environmental Law* 25 (summer).

"Sagebrush Rebellion Dealt Setback." 1996. *National Law Journal* (April 1).

LANFRANC

Butler, Denis. 1966. *1066: The Story of a Year.* New York: Putnam.

Lloyd, Alan. 1966. *The Making of the King, 1066.* New York: Holt, Rinehart & Winston.

Macdonald, Allan J. 1926. *Lanfranc: A Study of His Life, Work, and Writing.* New York: Oxford Univ. Press.

LANGDELL, CHRISTOPHER COLUMBUS

Grey, Thomas C. 1983. "Langdell's Orthodoxy." *University of Pittsburgh Law Review* 45.

Speziale, Marcia. 1980."Langdell's Concept of Law as Science: The Beginning of Anti-Formalism in American Legal Theory." *Vermont Law Review* 5.

Weaver, Russell L. 1991. "Langdell's Legacy: Living with the Case Method." *Villanova Law Review* 36.

LANHAM ACT

Curtis, Ted, and Joel H. Stempler. 1995. "So What Do We Name the Team? Trademark Infringement, the Lanham Act, and Sports Franchises." *Columbia-VLA Journal of Law and the Arts* 19.

Kearney, Brian J. 1986. "The Trademark Counterfeiting Act of 1984: A Sensible Legislative Response to the Ills of Commercial Counterfeiting." *Fordham Urban Law Journal* 14.

Pierce, Kenneth R. 1990. "Origins of the Use Requirement and an Overview of the New Federal Trademark Law." *Florida Bar Journal* 64 (May).

Thill, Russell George. 1994. "The 1988 Trademark Law Revision Act: Damage Awards for False Advertising and Consumer Standing under Section 43(A)—Congress Drops the Ball Twice." *DePaul Business Law Journal* 6.

LARCENY

Genco, Courtney C. 1992. "What Happened to *Durland?* Mail Fraud, RICO, and Justifiable Reliance." *Notre Dame Law Review* 68.

Kaplan, John, and Robert Weisberg. 1991. *Criminal Law: Cases and Materials.* 2d ed. Boston: Little, Brown.

LAW AND LITERATURE

Cardozo, Benjamin N. 1925. "Law and Literature." *Yale Law Review* 14.

Fischer, John. 1993. "Reading Literature/Reading Law: Is There a Literary Jurisprudence?" *Texas Law Review* 72.

Freedman, James O. 1985. "The Law as Educator." *Iowa Law Review* 70.

Koffler, Judith. 1989. Review of *Forged Alliance: Law and Literature* and *Law and Literature: A Misunderstood Relation*, by Richard A. Posner, and *Interpreting Law and Literature: A Hermeneutic Reader*, edited by Sanford Levinson and Steven Mailloux. *Columbia Law Review* 89.

Posner, Richard A. 1988. *Law and Literature: A Misunderstood Relation.* Boston: Harvard Univ. Press.

———. 1995. "Judges' Writing Styles: Do They Matter?" *University of Chicago Law Review* 62.

Wigmore, John L. 1908. "A List of Legal Novels." *Illinois Law Review* 2.

LAW FRENCH

Baker, J. H. 1989. *Manual of Law French.* 2d ed. Brookfield, Vt.: Gower.

Hartnick, Alan J. 1994. "The Use of Latin in Law Today." *New York State Bar Journal* 39 (February).

LAW OF THE SEA

Buck, Eugene H. November 1996. *United Nations Convention on the Law of the Sea: Living Resources Provisions.* Congressional Research Service (CRS) report for Congress. CRS site. World Wide Web.

LAW REVIEW

Colella, Ugo A. 1995. "Foreword: The Law Review Is Better than Spinach." *Tulane Law Review* (November).

Skilton, John S. 1995. "Seventy-five Years of the *Wisconsin Law Review:* Turning the Pages." *Wisconsin Law Review* 1995.

Swygert, Michael I., and Jon W. Bruce. 1985. "The Historical Origins, Founding, and Early Development of Student-edited Law Reviews." *Hastings Law Journal* 36 (May).

LEAST RESTRICTIVE MEANS TEST

Rotunda, Ronald D., and John E. Nowak. 1992. *Treatise on Constitutional Law: Substance and Procedure.* St. Paul: West.

LEE, CHARLES

Baker, Nancy V. 1983. *Conflicting Loyalties: Law and Politics in the Attorney General's Office, 1789–1990.* Lawrence, Kan.: Univ. Press of Kansas.

Elkins, Stanley, and Eric McKitrick. 1993. *The Age of Federalism.* New York: Oxford Univ. Press.

Nagel, Paul C. 1990. *The Lees of Virginia: Seven Generations of an American Family.* New York: Oxford Univ. Press.

Wilson, James Grant, and John Fiske, eds. 1887. *Appleton's Cyclopaedia of American Biography.* Vol. 3. New York: Appleton.

LEGAL ADVERTISING

Dobrowalski, Lauren. 1994. "Maintaining the Dignity of the Profession: An International Perspective on Legal Advertising and Solicitation." *Dickinson Journal of International Law* 12 (winter).

Hansen, Mark. 1994. "Lawyers' Internet Ad Angers Users." *American Bar Association Journal* (July).

Peltz, Robert D. 1989. "Legal Advertising—Opening Pandora's Box?" *Stetson Law Review* 19 (fall).

Siegel, Martha A. 1994. Letter. *American Bar Association Journal* (September).

Thier, Whitney. 1991. "In a Dignified Manner: The Bar, the Court, and Lawyer Advertising." *Tulane Law Review* 66.

LEGAL AID

Hall, Kermit L. 1989. *The Magic Mirror.* New York: Oxford Univ. Press.

LEGAL ASSISTANT

Kligerman, Susan D. 1996. "Perspectives on the Paralegal Tradition." National Federation of Paralegal Associations site. World Wide Web. September.

National Association of Legal Assistants site. September 1996. World Wide Web.

LEGAL EDUCATION

Gee, E. Gordon, and Donald W. Jackson. 1977. "Bridging the Gap: Legal Education and Lawyer Competency." *Brigham Young University Law Review* 1977.

Rose, Jonathan. 1994. "The MacCrate Report's Restatement of Legal Education: The Need for Reflection and Horse Sense." *Journal of Legal Education* 44 (December).

Schwartz, Bernard. 1974. *The American Heritage History of the Law in America.* New York: American Heritage.

Van Tuyl, Ian. 1996. *The Best Law Schools.* 1997 ed. New York: Random House.

LEGAL HISTORY

Hall, Kermit L. 1989. *The Magic Mirror.* New York: Oxford Univ. Press.

Stephens, Otis H., Jr., and John M. Scheb II. 1993. *American Constitutional Law.* St. Paul: West.

LEGAL PUBLISHING

Berring, Robert C. 1994. "Collapse of the Structure of the Legal Research Universe: The Imperative of Digital Information." *Washington Law Review* 69 (January).

Ogden, Patti J. 1983. " 'Mastering the Lawless Science of Our Law': A Story of Legal Citation." *Law Library Journal* 85 (winter).

Surrency, Erwin C. 1990. *A History of American Law Publishing.* Dobbs Ferry, N.Y.: Oceana.

Swygert, Michael I., and Jon W. Bruce. 1985. "The Historical Origins, Founding, and Early Development of Student-edited Law Reviews." *Hastings Law Journal* 36 (May).

LEGAL REALISM

Hamilton, Alexander. 1787–88. *The Federalist Papers* no. 78.

Holmes, Oliver Wendell, Jr. 1963. *The Common Law.* Boston: Little, Brown.

Horwitz, Morton J. 1977. *The Transformation of American Law, 1780–1860.* Boston: Harvard Univ. Press.

Plato. 1941. *The Republic of Plato.* Translated by Francis MacDonald Cornford. New York: Oxford Univ. Press.

Posner, Richard A. 1990. *Cardozo: A Study in Reputation.* Chicago: Univ. of Chicago Press.

TABLE OF
CASES CITED

INDEX

BY NAME

References that include photos or exhibits are printed in *italic* type.

INDEX

BY SUBJECT

References that include photos or exhibits are printed in *italic* type.

A

Abandonment
of highway, 39–40
in medical treatment, 17
Abortion, 93
Abuse
child, 146
domestic, 94
Accidental injury, 152–153
Achille Lauro (cruise ship), 42
Action, joinder of, 261–262
Act to Promote the Welfare of American Seamen in the Merchant Marine of the United States, 269
Administrative agency regulations, 401
Administrative board, 294
Administrative hearings, 23–24
Administrative law judges (ALJs), 24–25
Administrative Procedure Act (APA), 24, 25
Adultery, 30, 93
Advanced Research Projects Agency Network (ARPANET), 202–203, 204
Advertising, legal, 415–418
Affection, alienation of, 30, 93
Affidavit, 148
AFL-CIO, 53, 374, 385
African Charter on Human and Peoples' Rights, 82
Age
discrimination in, 13, 132
legal, 418
Age Discrimination in Employment Act (1975), 13, 132
Agency for Health Care Policy and Research, 15

Agency for Toxic Substances and Disease Registry, 15
Agency regulations, 401
Agreed judgment, 274
AIDS, 353–354
Aid to Families with Dependent Children (AFDC), 15, 146–147
Aircraft Piracy Act, 42
Airplane hijacking, 42
Air travel insurance, 169
Alabama claims, 51
Alien and Seditions Acts, 334
Alienation of affection, 30, 93
Aliens, illegal, 97
Allen charge, 304–305
Alliance for Progress, 331
Alteration of highway, 40
Alternative dispute resolution and administrative agencies, 289
Amateur Action BBS, 203
American Bar Association (ABA), 421
Moral Code of Professional Responsibility, 415–416
American Civil Liberties Union (ACLU), 203
American Convention on Human Rights, 82
American Federation of Labor (AFL), 371
American Federation of Labor and Congress of Industrial Organizations (AFL-CIO), 53, 374, 385
American Independent party, 138
American-Indian Movement (AIM), 361
American Japanese Evacuation Claims Act (1948), 243
American Law Institute, 409
American Law Reports, 423

471